THE
HARPER
ANTHOLOGY
OF POETRY

THE
HARPER
ANTHOLOGY
OF POETRY

JOHN FREDERICK NIMS

1817

HARPER & ROW, PUBLISHERS, New York
Cambridge, Hagerstown, Philadelphia, San Francisco,
London, Mexico City, São Paulo, Sydney

PR
1175
H298
1981

Acknowledgments

CONRAD AIKEN: "The Things" and "Doctors' Row" from *Collected Poems,* by Conrad Aiken. Copyright © 1953, 1970 by Conrad Aiken. Reprinted by permission of Oxford University Press, Inc.
A. R. AMMONS: "The Constant," "Cut the Grass," "Life in the Boondocks," and "Mechanism." Reprinted from *Collected Poems, 1951–1971,* by A. R. Ammons, by permission of W. W. Norton & Company, Inc. Copyright © 1972 by A. R. Ammons.
ANON.: "Theh Thet Hi Can Wittes Fule-Wis" from *English Lyrics of the XIII Century,* by Carleton Brown (Oxford University Press).
ANON.: "Another Year" from *The Early English Carols,* by Richard Greene (Oxford University Press).
ANON.: "A God and Yet a Man?" from *Religious Lyrics of the XV Century,* ed. by Carleton Brown (Oxford University Press).
ANON.: "I Heard a Noise and Wishèd for a Sight," from *Elizabethan Lyrics,* ed. by Norman Ault, p. 233. Longmans, Green. Reprinted by permission of Oona Ault.
JOHN ASHBERY: "The Instruction Manual." Copyright © 1956 John Ashbery. Reprinted by permission of Georges Borchardt, Inc. "Mixed Feelings" and "As One Put Drunk into the Packet-Boat" from *Self-Portrait in a Convex Mirror,* by John Ashbery. Copyright © 1975 by John Ashbery. Reprinted by permission of Viking Penguin Inc.
MARGARET ATWOOD: "You Take My Hand And" and "At First I Was Given Centuries" from *Power Politics,* by Margaret Atwood. Copyright © 1971 by Margaret Atwood. "Siren Song" from *You Are Happy,* by Margaret Atwood. Copyright © 1974 by Margaret Atwood. Reprinted by permission of Harper & Row, Publishers, Inc. and the author. All poems are included in *Selected Poems* (Simon & Schuster, Inc.).
W. H. AUDEN: "Ode to Terminus." Copyright © 1968 by W. H. Auden. "In Praise of Limestone." Copyright 1951 by W. H. Auden. "The Shield of Achilles." Copyright 1952 by W. H. Auden. Reprinted from *W. H. Auden: Collected Poems,* by W. H. Auden, edited by Edward Mendelson, by permission of Random House, Inc. "In Memory of W. B. Yeats," "Lullaby," "In Memory of Sigmund Freud," and "Musée des Beaux Arts." Copyright 1940 and renewed 1968 by W. H. Auden. Reprinted from *W. H. Auden: Collected Poems,* by W. H. Auden, edited by Edward Mendelson, by permission of Random House, Inc. and Faber and Faber Ltd.
MARGARET AVISON: "Hiatus" from *Winter Sun* and "Water and Worship" and "A Lament" from *sunblue.* Reprinted by permission of the author.

(Acknowledgments are continued on page 822.)

Sponsoring Editor: Phillip Leininger
Project Editor: Claudia Kohner
Designer: Robert Sugar
Production Manager: Marion Palen
Compositor: TriStar Graphics
Printer and Binder: Halliday Lithograph Corporation
Art Studio: Vantage Art Inc.
Cover/jacket illustration: *Pegasus Triumphant,* by Odilon Redon, from the collection of State Museum Kröller-Müller, Otterlo, The Netherlands
Galaxy photograph (following p. 763):
Lick Observatory, University of California, Santa Cruz

The Harper Anthology of Poetry
Copyright © 1981 by John Frederick Nims.

Library of Congress Cataloging in Publication Data
Main entry under title:

The Harper anthology of poetry.

Includes bibliographical references and index.
1. English poetry. 2. American poetry.
I. Nims, John Frederick, 1913–
PR1175.H298   1981   821'.008   80-27259
ISBN 0-06-044847-4
ISBN 0-06-044846-6 (pbk.)

CONTENTS

ON MAKING AN ANTHOLOGY

Why do so at all?

Because why not? An anthology is a collection of poems. Collecting things needs little defense; we recognize it as something childish but very natural. Like the pack-rat and the crow, people, from childhood on, are by nature collectors. Of almost everything, in a world so largely made up of collectibles: pieces of rock, old bottle-glass, cast-iron toys, dead butterflies. As a boy, I collected cigar-bands, scuffing the Chicago curbs, head down, an eye out for those crinkled bits of gold and crimson, with their foreign mottoes and tiny portraits of exotic señoritas. Sometimes crouching, almost underfoot, on a busy sidewalk in the December winds to chip a rare specimen out of the frozen gutter, its ice marbled with the ocher veinings of those who preferred to chaw and spurt their tobacco rather than light up.

Even earlier, almost without knowing it, I had begun to collect poems. I must have been only 4 or so when I heard my father, in melancholy surf-booming voice, intone: "Break, break, break, On thy cold gray stones, O sea. . . ." Probably my first poem. Others came too in the same offhand fashion. They were not neatly classified and coddled in notebooks, as the colorful *La Violeta* and *Belle of Monterey* were; mostly they were left to shift for themselves in any old corner of the memory, turning up at intervals when I was looking for something else. Some are in this book.

There are anthologists, I am told, content to ply the shears and slather paste. I found it urgent to establish something like physical contact with the poems; to know them as they first came into the world. Easy enough with contemporary poems—those of Eliot, or Stevens, or Auden—which I saw in the pages of magazines or in books come freshly off the press in smart new jackets. But making contact with books that came out in 1855 or 1798 or 1633 or 1557 took more doing. Even so, not satisfied with what some editor told me the poem was, I felt I had to make sure of it before I could count it as a catch. It mattered to handle the books, to turn their pages, to see and *feel* them as the poet's contemporaries had done. This compulsion took me to the rare-book rooms of famous libraries, especially of the Houghton and Widener at Harvard and the Newberry in Chicago. For years this was a pleasant pastime—cleaner too than chipping at the mottled ice.

With the earliest poems here, done a century or more before the invention of printing in Europe, there was little to get back to. For the early ballads we have no manuscripts to speak of; the poems survived orally for centuries before finding their way into print in such collections as *The Tea-Table Miscellany* of 1729 or *The Scots Musical Museum* half a century later. For a few scarce early poems—Dunbar, some of Skelton—I had to rely on photographic facsimiles. But beginning with a poem of Skelton's published in *Pithy pleasaunt and profitable workes of maister Skelton, Poete Laureate* (1568), I have seen nearly all of these poems in the books they originally appeared in. *Seen* means more than *looked at*; it means I have taken a printed text into the rare-book room and compared it literally—letter by letter—with the original. Since the first printed texts were not always the soundest, it meant looking too at later printings and checking with what the standard editions had concluded.

This dusty industry had its pleasures. It is a satisfaction to be able to say: "I have known this poem from its birth" and not merely "I have taken this poem on faith from an accredited editor." How different the poems look, there on their old stamping grounds, from the computerized uniformity they assume in the columns of modern reprints.

Can anyone pick up John Donne's packed and huddled little *Poems* of 1633 without feeling something like an electrical tingle? Or George Herbert's *The Temple*, of the same year—a humble three by five inches in small type, a book hardly larger than the palm you hold it in? Very different, half a century later, the generous volume of Andrew Marvell's *Miscellaneous Poems*, complete with portrait—but then Marvell was a "Late Member of the Honorable House of Commons." (Not one of these great names had a single book—not even the slimmest of chapbooks—published during the writer's lifetime.)

Skipping to a later century, what a luxury to open the 1819 edition of Cantos I and II of Byron's *Don Juan* and to find, on a page larger than this one, two leisurely stanzas, instead of the four to seven per page we are likely to get in a busy modern edition. Or to pick up a copy of the *Lyrical Ballads* of 1798, in which Wordsworth and Coleridge redirected the course of poetry, and to find written in it the name of an early owner: "A. Tennyson. Christmas day, 1838." Or to leaf through the copy of Herman Melville's *Battle-Pieces* that belonged to Mrs. Melville and to find a handwritten revision that gives a better reading than the printed one.

Literary trivia, some of this, but trivia high in human interest. What would have been mere literary texts, had I been willing to snip and paste, had now become Memorable Experiences.

With a few poets I had the richer excitement of handling their very manuscripts. At Yale, the little handwritten book of poems that Edward Taylor left in 1729 with instructions to his heirs that it was not to be printed, its 400 pages of cramped and thorny script denser and smaller than single-spaced typing. Almost without readers for 200 years. At Harvard, the manuscripts of Jones Very's poems, some scrawled off in pencil, apparently as they came to him, with abbreviations and without punctuation, some written with deliberate care for the printer's eye. At Harvard also, the manuscript book in which Frederick Goddard Tuckerman wrote out, on lined paper, his grief-stricken sonnets, with afterthoughts and revisions written between the lines. Most moving of all, at Harvard and Amherst the very packets that Emily Dickinson left threaded together in her bureau drawer: hard to believe those were my fingers on the page where hers had lingered. I went through all these papers as much out of devotion as scholarship. Not just as a bibliographer, surely. And yet in just a few cases, with just a few words, these amateur browsings turned up truer readings than the scholars had given us.

This turning over of faded pages was done for my own reassurance and pleasure; I had no thought of passing on to today's readers the spellings of yesterday, in which the words seem to come not from the poet's living throat but from Ye Olde Antique Shoppe.

All poets were modern poets when they wrote; their readers were contemporary readers. They would have seen, in 1609, nothing unusual in the look of Shakespeare's Sonnet 73, which begins:

> That time of yeeare thou maift in me behold,
> When yellow leaues, or none, or few doe hange
> Vpon thofe boughes which fhake againft the could,
> Bare rn'wd quiers, where late the fweet birds fang . . .

For most of us, this presentation impedes the passionate immediacy of the poem; no matter how fweetly the birds fing, they will never quite be real. All easy enough for scholars, but one should not have to become a scholar to read, without these inky tics and twitches, great poems of the past. We can give our readers Elizabethan spelling; we cannot give them Elizabethan eyes.

What came from the poet's pen was clear and fresh and *modern*; I would like it, as far as possible, to look that way today. Having once made sure what the poet wrote, I felt free to update spelling and punctuation (which the poet, or the printer, did not use consistently) toward what the poet might have used if writing now. A wish to present the poems in their immediacy has led me also to reduce the capital letters of which writers and printers made profuse but inconsistent use during the seventeenth century and later, as in Marvell's "On a Drop of Dew":

> See how the Orient Dew
> Shed from the Bosom of the Morn,
> Into the blowing Roses . . .

This begins to look too much like a swanky ad, perhaps for a perfume labelled Orient Dew.

The dozen or so anonymous lyrics written before 1400—before the invention of printing in their part of the world—are harder to deal with. As written down so long ago, they look even stranger than the script of around 1500 in which the words of "Western Wind" (p. 30) are written. To set them in type at all is to be false to the way the anonymous authors would have seen them; they were composed, in any case, for the ear and not the eye. With these poems I have taken the risk of providing modern versions facing the originals, in the hope of giving in today's English some notion of what the medieval verse was like as verse. One hopes the new versions will encourage the reader's eye to move across the page to the real poems. This is the only updating I have done that changes wording. To modernize Chaucer is a cruelty; much of the charm of his work is to be found not only in the narrative but in the music and the rhythm—change his words, and the charm (from *carmen*: poetry and magic) is quite gone. Half a dozen fifteenth-century lyrics also require much of their early spelling. The old ballads are given in the Scottish spellings in which we are used to seeing them.

And by what authority, no doubt some readers wonder, are *you* telling *us* what the best poems are? Not *telling*, quite. What I am doing is offering. Anthology: Ἀνθολογία—a gathering of flowers. An anthology is a bouquet. One may of course quarrel with a bouquet, find it in good taste or in bad. But I have not made these choices wholly on my own. Though this is an anthology of poetry in English, my taste and expectations have been formed on a broader base: on human nature as it expressed itself also in other languages and over centuries more remote than any covered here. I have had my long-time advisers; let me introduce them.

For many years I have been hearing voices. Mostly they came to me in English, sometimes as fresh and crisp as today's headlines, sometimes broad or drawled or in a brogue, as if from a far country across the sea, or from a century long gone, when shadowy figures danced around the Maypole. They came in other languages too; sometimes in ancient Greek or its island dialects, or in the resonant Latin that echoed off the marble of the Colosseum or the pillars of a Sabine farm. Sometimes they came, with music, in the language of the troubadours near Fonqualquier or Ventadorn, or of those who wandered south across the Pyrenees, or on into Andalucía. At times they came in indignant Tuscan with its dusky aspirates. Or they came in French, the *bon bec* Villon loved. They came from tough Castile or soft Galicia. Some later came from Weimar.

The voices I heard were those of poems talking. Telling me the human secrets we all share. Telling me about themselves, and what they were. These voices have been my advisers over many years. I still turn to them with a question when I hear a new voice and wonder if it is genuine or only one of the many phantoms that come like mayflies with the season. From whatever century, in whatever language, what they said was much the same. They told me it is not true that humanity evolved from some lower form toward the end of the 1950s. Proofs of humanity, they told me, go back many centuries before that time; voices vibrantly human can be heard from the time of Sappho, of Catullus, of the Archpriest, of the Anglo-Saxon minstrels who wrote "The Seafarer" and "The Wanderer," of the anonymous medieval poets who in the "Harley Lyrics" sang the joy and pain of lovers in the spring.

The voices told me that humankind changes little as the centuries pass and that the same scenes are played over and over again. They told me that we have eyes that make the empty air prismatic; that we have ears that make the dumbest sound-waves speak. That we have other sensors too—for warmth, for smell, for texture and the contours of the world. Through these, part by part, the universe takes shape within our heads. So consciousness awakes and with it passion, enough to singe or freeze the very flesh. Such abundance of conscious life that skull and breast cannot contain it, any more than a volcano can its lava.

They said that with a poet all this inner seething converts to words—to shapes of breath that leave the body to report on the glowing gulfs within. It is breath not blown away, as most breath is; it is breath trying to create for itself, out of words that have color and weight and reek and gusto, a body like the body it just left. We are none of us, the poems mocked, mere disembodied spirits. We must have, as your English poet said, a local habitation and a name. Must have imagery, as you yourselves have retina and eardrum and fine fingertips for feeling. Must speak in throat- and lip-shaped phrases, must move in rhythms as your heart does, on tides for which your breathing sets the tempo. Must have a skeleton of healthy sense, a skin in touch with textures of the world. We are made, they told me, in *your* image; we have no other archetype but you.

They taught me that poems are good to the degree that—while existing as voice alone—they can beam the intensities of our nature into the world of words. When I ask them what quality they think essential, they answer: *life!* They repeat *vitality, intensity.* Inertness, dullness, they warn, are the qualities most alien to their nature. Poems have the kind of life we have when most alive, the kind that sets the eye aglow and cheek aflush, that makes the fists clench or the fingertips caress. The poet's knack is to transfuse that vitality into words, to make words so resonant, so vibrant with the *poet's* feeling that they take on a life and behavior of their own, begin to interact in strange ways— loving and cantankerous—with one another, doing with their shape and heft and sound and rhythm what our bodies do with changing pressure in the arteries, electric currents through the galaxies of nerve. A poem is a success to the degree that it transfuses the passionate complexity of our being—our body-and-soul being, not dry mind alone—into a body-and-soul made all of words as palpable as things are. Men and women must have written such poems almost from the dawn of consciousness on earth, though none remain to us as old as their ice-age animals in caves are. Of those that do, the many myriads, this anthology can give only a selection from poems written in one language over a small part of human history.

For me, then, poetry has been defined by poems themselves, and not by a passel of critics waving butterfly nets with labels like *provenance* and *genre.* What poems have told me has to do with the essence of poetry and not with its changing shapes. I have not bothered them merely with frivolous questions like "Is this a proper sonnet?" or "Is this an accepted form of heroic couplet?" The breath of poetry, like everything else in the universe, does indeed come forth in shape and rhythm, but in no prescribed ones. Often it finds its own, as nature does. In this it is far freer than the heart, that fuddy-duddies on in old iambic, far freer than the breath, still timed to pulses metered in pentameter.

We like to collect things. And we like to show our collections to others— that too is childish but very natural. But we show them only if we feel there is something special about them—one unique piece of rock, one bottle of oddly vivid green. I have become fond of my collection of poems, even take pride in it. This seems an allowable pride; none of these poems is of my writing; the pride I take is in the work of others. When I read them I feel like the old woman in William Carlos Williams's poem, munching the plums from her paper bag:

> They taste good to her
> They taste good
> to her. They taste
> good to her

These poems taste good to me—I have included nothing only because urged by someone else to do so, least of all because urged by a computerization of modern preferences or by the constituency of some currently influential poet.

Many anthologies have a solemn air; we might go so far as to say, a prune-faced look. As if the garden of poetry, which should be a Garden of Earthly Delights, had a sign over the gate proclaiming ENJOYMENT STRICTLY FORBIDDEN. As great a poet as Robert Frost often used the word *fun* in speaking of poetry. Too many anthologies do not see it that way. NO LAUGHTER ON THE PREMISES. Though poetry expresses the full range of our human nature, it is not so with them: our sense of humor and our sense of nonsense have been exiled from this garden. And yet it was the sensible Horace who said, "Dulce est desipere in loco," which we might English as "There are times when it's fun to act silly." This too is a well-authenticated part of our nature, and quite possibly a safety valve against our darker energies.

A second fault is that too many anthologies favor the star system. To shift our figure to a more relevant field, they favor great corporations over small businesses; they like Big Names, prefer cartels, monopolies, conglomerates to the friendly corner wordsmith. If we look over the whole range of poetry in English, we find that many of the most charming, poignant, and memorable poems have come from bit-part poets who never achieved superstar status, from poets like Dyer, Tichborne, Greene, Southwell, Greville, Dekker, Godolphin, Cartwright, Cowley, Rochester, Barnes, Beddoes, Emily Brontë, Clough. Not one of these is given a cameo role, or even the time of day, in too many anthologies.

Is it really better to have 15 poems by Herrick than 12 by Herrick and one by, say, Tichborne, Davenant, Godolphin? Or one by Waller? Is it really better to have 24 poems by Tennyson than 18 by Tennyson and one by Barnes, Peacock, Beddoes, Emily Brontë, Clough, Meredith? Poems 19–24 add little to our sense of the genuine greatness of Tennyson, whereas a spicing of poems by the lesser names would appreciably expand our sense of the range, verve, and originality of poetry in English.

A good poem is always in some way surprising; so is an anthology that is really alive. Too many anthologies have few surprises; they tend to stay in well-worn ruts and take no chances. If we stick to the middle of the road, however, we will know very little about the countryside, especially about its dewiest and greenest coverts. Why not fling over the reins now and then and do something simply for the wild fun of it, as poets themselves have been known to do?

In chipping out poems for my collection, I came on a number of finds I take pleasure in passing on. Long-shot poets like Jordan and Flatman. Or, to mention half a dozen of the poems that most surprised me, there are these:

Cleveland's "Upon the Death of Mr. King Drowned in the Irish Seas." We all know Milton's "Lycidas"; why not see how the same lamentable loss was treated by another who—judging by sales—was the most popular poet of the time? The difference between the two poems is a brilliant demonstration of the difference between a great poem and a clever one, and has much to show us about the ways of poetry.

Swift's "Rhapsody" on poetry, as humorously true today of the tacky world of literary scramblers as it ever was.

Elizabeth Barrett Browning's poem on "male chauvinism" and women as sex objects—a poem her magazine editor, a famous novelist, rejected "for indecency." Who would have expected so frank a poem from a Victorian lady with three names?

Clough's "Natura Naturans," with its cosmic and lyrical physicality. Who would have expected anything so outspoken, so almost "confessional," from a well-brought-up young Victorian?

Ambassador James Russell Lowell's poem about political corruption and the public's indifference to it, a poem written in 1872 but prophetic of the world of Watergate a century later.

John Davidson's "A Runnable Stag," whose athletic vitality, said T.S. Eliot, "has run in my head for a good many years now."

Too many anthologies will surprise us, though not pleasantly, in their downgrading of American poets. Possibly we could do without Freneau—possibly. Much more puzzling is the omission of Jones Very and Frederick Goddard Tuckerman, who wrote some of the best poems of their century. Sometimes not even such important American pioneers as Masters, Sandburg, Lindsay are to be found. It is embarrassing to mention what vogue poets of a later decade are there in place of them, possibly because, with contemporary poets, too many anthologies jettison their exclusivist policy for the use of the scattergun. Unable to make up their mind which ones belong, they include a little of everybody whose name has flashed, however wanly and fitfully, across the contemporary skies.

When included, Americans often suffer in comparative statistics. Is it odious to notice that in an anthology much used in American colleges there are 24 poems of Tennyson to 6 of Whitman, with Tennyson outscoring the American in line totals by 3 to 2? Or to notice later that there are only 6 poems of Wallace Stevens, one of the great poets of the century, directly after the same number by the wistful but hardly major Edward Thomas? A bad Stevens selection at that, with 4 poems from his first book and only 2 from the half dozen books that followed. As if Stevens had been given a quick glance but not read through. We get the same impression of shabby treatment in the Cummings selections (nothing from his last four books), the Auden selections (his prolific last two decades disregarded), and the Wilbur selections (his last four books, covering 25 years, ignored). We think again of those 6 Edward Thomas poems when we notice that there are only 3 by Edwin Arlington Robinson, a far more significant poet.

Of the way anthologists fumble when dealing with their contemporaries we have no lack of horrible examples from the past. One might think that Sir Arthur Quiller-Couch, after weighing the best poems of many centuries for *The Oxford Book of English Verse*, could have dealt judiciously with the poets of his own time. And yet he puts, ranked with the mighty dead, such names as Henry Cust, the Honorable Emily Lawless, Norman Gale, John Swinnerton Phillimore, and Wilfred Thorley. In an authoritative anthology of *The Younger American Poets* published in 1904, we find such names as Frederick Lawrence Knowles, Alice Brown, Arthur Upson; the editor regrets the absence of Holman F. Day, Virginia Cloud, Josephine Dodge Daskam. And who are among the missing? Robinson, then age 35. Robert Frost, then age 30.

Such examples should be a warning, but they never are. Whenever we pick up an anthology with such a title as *The Hundred Best Contemporary Poets,* we can be sure it will contain a very high proportion of Thorleys, Phillimores, and Daskams. And quite possibly no Robinsons or Frosts. It is stirring to think that somewhere there is a brilliant young poet, belaurelled with Guggenheims and darling of many an arts council, o'er whose shoulders even now the benevolent Muse inclines and, beaming on that brow that might be the young Apollo's, vows with maternal pride, "He will be the Holman F. Day of his era!"

Our nearsightedness with our contemporaries tends to magnify mediocrities. On the other hand, as the biographies in this anthology show, many of the best poets throughout the centuries have been invisible in their own time. Many have written their letter to the world only to have it lie in the dead-letter offices of posterity for decades, or even centuries. The odds are not impossible that the young man or woman who will one day be recognized as the greatest poet of our time has made no effort to push into the limelight; perhaps, like Donne, Herbert, and Marvell, this poet will not publish so much as a single chapbook all life long.

Explanations: Notes and Format

The first date given beneath a poem is the date of composition, when known. After this is given the title of the book (in a few cases the journal) in which the poem was first published, followed by the date of publication. Later editions that have a bearing on the text are generally mentioned. Later readings are sometimes introduced silently; an anthology such as this is not the place to detail the textual history of variants. Bibliographers will know where to find that kind of information.

The notes that accompany the poems sometimes sketch in the historical background necessary for their appreciation, as with Dryden's "Absalom and Achitophel," or the circumstances that gave rise to the poem, as with Pope's "The Rape of the Lock." Allusions—for instance, to mythology or the Bible— are generally explained. Some notes simply remark on what seems to the editor a matter of more than usual human or linguistic interest. Most archaic or uncommon words are defined. A case can be made for glossing no words that can be found in the dictionary. My own feeling is that the poems here should be primarily sources of pleasure and not tools for vocabulary building. I would like to think of readers enjoying the poems in pleasant spots in which it is not always handy to bring along a dictionary.

All the poems by living writers, and the notes on those poems, have been sent to the poets for their approval. Often these poets have added explanatory comments or corrected the original notes. What they have added seems to me of interest; it is not always possible to find artists willing to admit us into their workshops.

The footnotes mean to be informative rather than interpretive, but with some poems, such as Donne's "The Ecstasy," the line between information and interpretation is a fine one, which enthusiasm may have led the editor to transgress. Originally, a good deal of interpretation accompanied the poems, especially those that seemed to require a shift in our reading habits, or that were structured on a special system of thought, a special body of allusion, or a technique that broke sharply with the familiar. Most of the writers so explicated were twentieth-century ones. This interpretation has now been relegated to the back of the book (p. 764), where it can be ignored by those not in need of it. Signposts in the footnotes direct readers to such further elucidation. T. S. Eliot's "The Waste Land" comes in for the most detailed annotation and explanation, as an unusually concentrated and allusive example of what poets in our century may be up to. Other poets considered in some detail are Yeats, Stevens, and Roethke. Cummings and Ashbery too are poets some readers might like a little guidance with at first.

A section on prosody ("Tools of the Trade"), also at the back of the book (p. 785), goes into the nature of versification in English more fully than is possible in the footnotes, and also presents some of the forms that poets have chosen to work in. The footnotes refer us to the prosody section when that seems desirable.

The biographies of the poets are of necessity miniatures. With the poets of our own time much colorful personal detail has been omitted. So has the listing of such honors as Guggenheim, Bollingen, and National Book Awards, which have been given to nearly all the recent poets included.

Acknowledgments

I am grateful to many people for their help with this anthology. For the use of rare books and manuscripts, I am grateful for the courteous assistance of the directors and staffs of the Houghton and Widener Libraries at Harvard, the Robert Frost Library at Amherst, the Beinecke Library at Yale, and the Newberry Library in Chicago.

I am under obligation also to the many poets and critics kind enough to examine the contents and make their own suggestions about poets, poems, and procedures. I wish I could have accommodated all the selections they desired to see; to have done so would have given us an Ideal Anthology beyond the possibilities of any real world of publishing. Particularly I want to thank Paul Breslin, Robert Fitzgerald, Brewster Ghiselin, John E. Grant, Mary Lynn Grant, H. T. Kirby-Smith, Joseph Langland, Harry Levin, Helen Marlborough, Jerome Mazzaro, William Meredith, James E. Miller, Julian Moynahan, Alicia Ostriker, Robert Pack, Robert Pinsky, Karl Shapiro, William Stafford, Peter Stitt, Hollis Summers, Michael True, Helen Vendler, Jeanne Murray Walker, Aubrey Williams, John Williams, Miller Williams.

For handling the arduous correspondence about permissions, I am indebted to Helen Klaviter of the staff of *Poetry*.

J.F.N

THE
HARPER
ANTHOLOGY
OF POETRY

Anonymous Poems of Before 1400

About the year 1200, the first poem on page 2 was jotted down by an unhappy lover on the margin of a manuscript not even his own. Writing materials were scarce. English—it was the reign of Richard the Lionhearted—was very different from the English we are at ease with. The king himself did not speak it; Provençal and French were his languages.

Beneath the poem is a literal translation into the kind of English we speak today—nearly 800 years later. The trouble with such a translation is that it gives only the thought of the poem. The thought is no more the poem than the mind is the whole human being, with senses and emotions and the rhythms of breath and heartbeat. The poet cared about the way his poem sounded; he cared about its rhythms and its elaborate little dance of rhymes; he cared about its songlike qualities. What he cared about most is lost in literal translation.

The first dozen or so poems in our book are accompanied, on facing pages, by reconstructions—reconstitutions—in modern English. They are not, and are not meant to be, literal (word-for-word) translations. On page 5, for example, "your cheek's pale rose" is not the literal translation of "thi faire rode" (though it is not false to the poet's feeling). It is added to preserve the rhyme, which the poet thought so important he would not have omitted it for any urgency of his thought. Our modern versions are meant to sound like poems, meant to give some idea of how the poems might have sounded to the people of the age they were written in. But the modernizations are only substitutes: the genuine poetry will be found on the left-hand pages. It is worth a little effort to find it there.

How our language itself sounded so many centuries ago we can only guess. There are no survivors to instruct us; no tapes or recordings. In England itself there were regional dialects that differed; these changed with the years. The sturdy consonants were no doubt much like ours. No nonsense in the spelling: if written, they were pronounced, like the *k* in *knight* and *knife*, a mere ghost-letter now. Many vowels tended to be purer and broader than they now are, almost Italian in sonority, so that early English—at least through Chaucer—had a richer, more operatic flow than speech today. Many unaccented *e*'s, now silent or omitted, were then heard; in our first poem we have *wittès, blissè, allè* (sounding like *wít-tes, blíss-uh, áll-uh*) for our *wits, bliss, all*. If these *e*'s are not pronounced, syllables are omitted, the rhythm falters and is lost. Such *e*'s are dotted (*è*) in this book to remind us of their presence. The dots are only a convenience; some are tentative, suggestive. Only those the rhythm calls for are so marked; we may if we choose enrich some lines by sounding others.

Theh Thet Hi Can Wittes Fule-Wis

Theh thet hi can wittès fule-wis
of worldles blissè nabbe ic nout
for a lafdi thet is pris
of allè thet in burè goth
sethen furst the heo was his   5
iloken in castel wal of ston
nes ic hol ne blithe iwis
ne thrimindè mon
lifth mon non bildeth me
abiden & blithè for to boe   10
ned efter mi death me longgeth
I mai siggen wel by me
herdè thet wo hongeth

Soon after 1200. C. Brown, *English Lyrics of the XIII Century*, 1932.

Though I am very wise, / of joy in this world I have none / because of a lady who is the prize / of all those that go in the rooms. / Since first she was his, / locked in a castle wall of stone, / I was not whole nor happy indeed / nor a thriving man. / There lives no man who encourages me / to stay and be happy. / I am longing for my death. / I may well say that in my case / woe hangs hard.

Mirie It Is While Sumer Ilast

Mirie it is while sumer ilast
with fughelès song.
Oc nu necheth windès blast
and weder strong.
Ei, ei, what this nicht is long.
And ich wid wel michel wrong
soregh and murne and fast.

c. 1225. Sir John Stainer, *Early Bodleian Music*, II, 1901.

1 **Ilast:** lasts   2 **fugheles:** birds'   3 **oc nu necheth:** but now approaches   5 **what this nicht is long:** how long this night is!   6 **ich wid wel michel wrong:** I, because of very great wrong

Sumer Is Icumen In

Sumer is icumen in.
Lhudè sing cuccu.
Groweth sed and bloweth med
and springth the wdè nu.
Sing cuccu.   5

Awè bleteth after lomb.
Lhouth after calvè cu.
Bulluc sterteth, buckè verteth.
Murie sing cuccu.
Cuccu, cuccu,   10
Wel singès thu cuccu.
Ne swik thu naver nu.

Sing cuccu nu. Sing cuccu.
Sing cuccu. Sing cuccu nu.

c. 1230–1240? c. 1310? J. Ritson, *Ancient Songs*, 1790 (published 1792).

1 **sumer:** warm spring weather   **is icumen:** has come   3 **sed:** seed   **bloweth med:** the meadow blossoms   4 **wde nu:** wood now   6 **awe:** ewe   7 **lhouth:** loweth   **cu:** cow   8 **sterteth:** starts, leaps   **verteth:** turns, twists, cavorts (*or perhaps:* breaks wind)   12 **ne . . . nu:** Don't you ever stop now!

Though I've a Clever Head

Though I've a clever head, I know,
  Joy in this world have I none,
And all for a lady—of those who go
  In hall and chamber, the fairest one!
When first she became another's, though,   5
  Locked in a castle wall of stone,
I was a ruined man, struck low:
  All skin and bone.
    No one now can encourage me
    To live, be happy. I'd rather be   10
      Down with the dead tomorrow.
    I can well say this of me:
      Heavy hangs my sorrow.

Merry It Is

Merry it is, while the summer last,
  With birds in song.
But now it's on us, the wintry blast
  And weather strong.
  Oh! how the night is long!
  And I, being done so great a wrong,
Sorrow and mourn and fast.

6 The **wrong** the speaker is done is at the hands of an unresponsive lover.

Now the Summer's Come

Now the summer's come again!
Loud sing, cuckoo!
Seed a-growing! Mead a-blowing!
Green grow the woods too.
Sing, cuckoo!   5

Sheep are bleating for their lambs,
Cows for their calves moo.
Bull, he snorts! Buck cavorts!
Merry sing, cuckoo!
Cuckoo, cuckoo,   10
Good singing, cuckoo!
Don't ever stop now!

Sing, cuckoo, now. Sing, cuckoo.
Sing, cuckoo. Sing, cuckoo, now.

Like most of these early poems, this is a *song*, very lovely with its music. Recited—as it was never meant to be—it sounds silly, as words for music often do without their music. This is no mere barnyard ditty—elaborate instructions are given in Latin for the proper performance (in several voices) of the music, which is very sophisticated.

Nou Goth Sonne Under Wode

Nou goth sonne under wode;
me reweth, Marye, thi fairė rode.
Nou goth sonne under tre;
me reweth, Marye, thi sonne and the.

c. 1240. H. W. Robbins, *Merure de Seinte Eglise* . . . , 1924.

1 **Nou goth sonne:** now goes the sun/Son   2 **me reweth:** I am sorry for   **rode:** face, complexion (not *rood*, in the sense of *cross*)   3 **tre:** tree/cross

Foweles in the Frith

Fowelės in the frith,
the fisses in the flod,
And i mon waxė wod.
Mulch sorw I walkė with
for beste of bon and blod.

c. 1270. J. Stafford Smith, *Musica Antiqua*, I, 1812.

1 **foweles:** birds   **frith:** wood   3 **mon waxe wod:** must become crazy   4 **mulch sorw:** much sorrow   5 **bon and blod:** bone and blood (the modern idiom would be *flesh and blood*)

Ubi Sunt Qui Ante Nos Fuerunt?

Where beth they biforen us weren,
Houndės ladden and havekės beren,
And hadden feld and wode?
The richė levedies in hoere bour,
That wereden gold in hoere tressour,   5
With hoere brightė rode?

Eten and drounken and maden hem glad;
Hoere lif was al with gamen ilad;
Men keneleden hem biforen;
They beren hem wel swithe heye.   10
And in a twincling of an eye
Hoere soulės weren forloren.

Where is that lawing and that song,
That trayling and that proude yong,
Tho havekės and tho houndės?   15
Al that joye is went away,
That wele is comen to *weylaway*,
To manie hardė stoundes.

Hoere paradis hy nomen here,
And now they lien in helle ifere: 20

Before 1275. F. J. Furnivall, *Minor Poems of the Vernon MS.*, part II, 1901.

The Latin title is translated by the first line: "Where are they who were before us?"

2 **houndes . . . beren:** led hounds and carried hawks   4 **levedies:** ladies   **hoere bour:** their chamber   5 **tressour:** headband, hair ribbons   6 **rode:** face, complexion   8 **with gamen ilad:** spent in pleasure   10 **wel swithe heye:** very proudly indeed   12 **forloren:** lost   13 **lawing:** laughing   14 **trayling:** trailing (of skirts, etc.)   **yong:** going, way of walking   15 **tho:** those   17 **wele:** well-being, welfare   **weylaway:** a lament, *alas!*   18 **stoundes:** times   19 **hy nomen:** they took   20 **ifere:** together

Under the Wood

Under the wood the sun now goes;
Mary, I'm sad for your cheek's pale rose.
Under the tree the Son goes too;
Mary, I'm sad for your Son and you.

Birds in the Wood

Birds in the wood,
　The fishes in the flood. .
Surely I go mad—
All the grief I've had
　For best of flesh and blood!

Where Are the Ones Who Lived Before?

Where are the ones who lived before,
With hound at stirrup and hawk to soar,
　The field and the wood their own?
The ladies rich in their castle room,
With gold in their hair, and flesh a-bloom,　　　　　　　　　　5
　Whose radiant faces shone?

Ate a while, drank a while, mingled in mirth,
Made people kneel to them, down to the earth,
　Nothing but fun—so clever.
Full of themselves they were, head held high　　　　　　　　10
—Then, in the twinkling of an eye,
　Their souls were lost forever.

Where is that laughing and that song,
The long skirt trailing, the knee so strong?
　The hound and the hawk—no more?　　　　　　　　　　15
All that joy is gone away;
All turned to a wailing "Wellaway!"
　They've many a grief in store.

Tried to make earth their heaven as well.
Where are they now? Down deep in hell.　　　　　　　　20

These poignant stanzas, with their grisly warning, are followed by six stanzas that end on a joyful note. In them we are exhorted to live a life of energetic virtue, fighting the devil and his temptations, and thereby winning for ourselves heaven, "that merry land."

The fuir hit brennès evere;
Long is *ay* and long is *ho*,
Long is *wy* and long is *wo*;
Thennes ne cometh they nevere. . . .

21 **fuir hit brennes:** fire, it burns   22–23 **ay, ho, wy, wo:** exclamations of grief

Of One That Is So Fair and Bright

Of one that is so fair and bright
velud maris stella,
brighter than the dayès light,
parens et puella,
ic crye to thee, thou see to me;   5
levedy, pray thy sone for me,
tam pia,
that ic motè comè to thee,
Maria.

Levedy, flowr of allè thing,   10
rosa sine spina,
thou berè Jesu, hevenè king,
gratia divina.
Of allè thou berst the pris,
levedy, quene of Paraÿs,   15
electa,
maidè mildè, moder *es*
effecta.

Al this world was forlore
Eva peccatrice,   20
til our lord was y-bore
de te genetrice.
With *Avé* it went away,
thuster night, and comth the day
salutis.   25
The wel springeth out of thee
virtutis.

Wel he wot he is thy sone,
ventre quem portasti;
he wil nought wernè thee thy bone,   30
parvum quem lactasti.
So hendè and so good he is,
he haveth brought us to blis
superni;
that haveth y-dut the foulè put   35
inferni.

Thirteenth century. T. Wright and J. C. Halliwell, *Reliquiae Antiquae*, I, 1841–1843 (stanzas in different order).

2 like the star of the sea   4 mother and maiden   5 **ic:** I   6 **levedy:** lady   7 so good   8 **mote:** may   11 rose without a thorn   12 **hevene king:** king of heaven   13 by divine grace   14 **berst the pris:** win the prize   15 **Paraÿs:** Paradise   16 chosen   17–18 **es effecta:** art made   19 **forlore:** utterly lost   20 because of Eve, the sinner   22 of you, the mother   23 **Avé:** Hail! (Hail, Mary!)   24 **thuster:** dark   25 of salvation   27 [well] of virtue   28 **wot:** knows   29 Whom you carried in your womb   30 **nought . . . bone:** not refuse you your request   31 Whom you nursed when He was small   32 **hende:** gracious   34 of heaven above   35 **y-dut . . . put:** shut the . . . pit   36 of hell

In fire that burns forever.
Long they cry "Ay!" and long cry "Oh!"
Long they cry "Why!" and long cry "Woe!"
　　And when do they leave there? Never....

Of One That Is So Fair and Bright

Of one that is so fair and bright
　　Velut maris stella,
Brighter than the day is light,
　　Parens et puella,
I cry to thee, O look to me,
Lady, pray thy Son for me,
　　Tam pia,
Pray that I may come to thee,
　　Maria.

Lady, flower of every thing,
　　Rosa sine spina,
Who bore Jesus, Heaven's king,
　　Gratia divina.
Among women, thou art prize,
Lady, queen of Paradise
　　Electa.
Maid—yet mother (none denies)
　　Effecta.

All this world lay lost, forlorn,
　　Eva peccatrice,
Till the day our Lord was born
　　De te genetrice.
"Ave" drove the night away;
After darkness came the day
　　Salutis;
Thou art source and spring, I say,
　　Virtutis.

Well He knows He is thy Son,
　　Ventre quem portasti;
All you wish, He wishes done,
　　Parvum quem lactasti.
So gracious and so good He is,
He leads us on the way to bliss
　　Superni.
And now has blocked the ugly pit
　　Inferni.

Latin lines are translated in the footnotes on the facing page.

20, 23 Significance was seen in the fact that *Ave* is *Eva* reversed.

Of care, conseil thou ert best,
felix fecundata;
of allè wery thou ert rest,
mater honorata.   40
Bisek him with mildè mod,
that for us allè shad his blod
in cruce,
that we moten comen til him
in luce.   45

38 fortunate(ly) fruitful   40 honored mother   41 **bisek:** beseech   **milde mod:** gracious heart
43 on the cross   44 **moten comen til:** may come to   45 in the light

Erthe Toc of Erthe

Erthè toc of erthe erthè wyth woh,
erthe other erthè to the earthè droh,
erthè leyde erthe in erthenè throh,
tho hevede erthe of erthe erthe ynoh.

Probably thirteenth century. *Earth upon Earth,* ed. H. Murray, 1911.

1 **toc:** took   **woh:** evil, wrong   2 **droh:** drew   3 **erthene throh:** earthen coffin   4 **tho hevede:** then
had   **ynoh:** enough

Alysoun

Bytwenè Mersh and Averil
when spray biginneth to springe,
the lutel fowl hath hirè wyl
on hyrè lud to singe.
Ich libbe in love-longinge   5
for semlokest of allè thinge;
he may me blissè bringe;
icham in hirè baundoun.

> An hendy hap ichabbe ihent,
> ichot from hevene it is me sent,   10
> from allè wymmen my love is lent,
> and lyght on Alysoun.

On hew hire her is fayr ynoh,
hirè browè broune, hire eyè blake;
with lossom chere he on me loh,   15
with middel smal and wel imake.
Bote he me wollè to hirè take
for to ben hire owen make,
longè to lyven ichullè forsake
and feyè fallen adoun.   20

Probably thirteenth century. Ritson, op. cit.

3 **lutel fowl:** little bird   4 **on hyre lud:** in her language   5 **ich libbe:** I live   6 **semlokest:** seem-
liest, fairest   7 **he:** she   8 **icham:** I am   **baundoun:** power   9 **hendy hap:** lucky chance, gracious
fortune   **ichabbe ihent:** I have received   10 **ichot:** I know   11 **lent:** turned away   13 **on hew hire
her:** in color her hair   **ynoh:** enough   15 **lossom:** lovely, lovable   **chere,** face, expression   **loh:**
laughed   17 **bote he:** unless she   18 **make:** mate   19 **ichulle:** I will   20 **feye:** fated to die

To the careworn, kindliest,
　　Felix fecundata;
To the weary, giving rest,
　　Mater honorata.　　　　　　　　　　　　　40
Beg Him—gently, gently, thus—
Him Who gave His blood for us
　　In cruce,
We may come to where He is
　　In luce.　　　　　　　　　　　　　　　45

Earth Took of Earth

Earth took of earth earth with ill;
Earth other earth gave earth with a will.
Earth laid earth in the earth stock-still:
Then earth in earth had of earth its fill.

This riddling little poem plays on the several meanings of *earth*—the world, dust, the body of man, earthly possessions, the grave.

Alison

In March and April, thereabout,
　　When leaf and petal spring,
Their little lingos ringing out,
　　The birds begin to sing.
　　I live in love-longing　　　　　　　　5
　　For the world's fairest thing.
　　The joy that she could bring!
　　　　I'm in her power alone.

　　　　What luck! I'm luckiest lad alive!
　　　　With help of heaven I hope to thrive.　　10
　　　　All other women?—forgotten! I've
　　　　Discovered Alison!

Her eyes are black, her lashes brown,
　　Her long hair glossy, fair as fair.
She, laughing, looks me up and down　　　　15
　　—Such looks of love!—slim-waisted there
　　And graceful. Oh I couldn't bear
　　To live without her long, I swear.
　　Without, I'd stumble in despair
　　　　And, doomed, be stricken down.　　　　20

An hendy hap ichabbe ihent,
ichot from hevene it is me sent,
from allè wymmen my love is lent,
and lyght on Alysoun.

Nightès when I wende and wake,   25
forthi mine wongès waxeth won;
levedi, all for thinè sake
longinge is ilent me on.
In world nis non so wyter mon
that all hirè bounté tellè con;   30
hirè swyre is whittorè then the swon,
and feyrest may in toune.

An hendy hap ichabbe ihent,
ichot from hevene it is me sent,
from allè wymmen my love is lent,   35
and lyght on Alysoun.

Icham for wowyng all forwake,
wery so water in wore,
lest eny revè me my make
ichabbe iyirned yore.   40
Betere is tholien whylè sore
then mournen evermore.
Geynest under gore,
herknè to my roun.

An hendy hap ichabbe ihent,   45
ichot from hevene it is me sent,
from allè wymmen my love is lent,
and lyght on Alysoun.

---

25 **wende:** twist, turn   26 **forthi:** therefore   **wonges waxeth won:** cheeks become pale   27 **levedi:** lady   28 **ilent me on:** come on me   29 **nis...mon:** is no man so wise   30 **bounté:** excellence   31 **swyre:** neck   32 **may:** maiden   **in toune:** in town, in the world   37 **wowyng:** wooing   **forwake:** worn out from loss of sleep   38 **wore:** weir, turbulent pool   39 **reve:** take away   40 **iyirned:** yearned for   **yore:** for a long time   41 **tholien:** suffer, endure   **whyle:** for a while   43 **geynest:** kindest   **under gore:** in gown, among women   44 **roun:** song

What luck! I'm luckiest lad alive!
With help of heaven I hope to thrive.
All other women?—forgotten! I've
Discovered Alison!

At midnight when I toss and turn   25
    (No wonder if my cheeks are pale),
O lady! it's for you I yearn;
    It's love come on me tooth and nail.
    The canniest scholar's bound to fail
    Appraising her beauty in detail.   30
    Throat snowy as yon swan a-sail—
            O far the fairest one!

What luck! I'm luckiest lad alive!
With help of heaven I hope to thrive.
All other women?—forgotten! I've   35
Discovered Alison!

I've wooed her till I'm faint for rest,
    Weary as water in weir,
In fear the one I love the best
    Another should find dear.   40
    Better endure a while my fear
    Than fail, and mourn for many a year.
    O best of any in women's gear,
            Take notice what I've sung.

What luck! I'm luckiest lad alive!   45
With help of heaven I hope to thrive.
All other women?—forgotten! I've
Discovered Alison!

Lenten Ys Come with Love to Toune

Lenten ys come with love to toune,
with blosmen & with briddès roune,
that al this blissè bryngeth;
dayès-eyès in this dales,
notès suete of nyhtegales,   5
uch foul song singeth.
The threstelcoc him threteth oo;
away is huere wynter woo,
when wodèrovè springeth.
This foulès singeth ferly fele,   10
ant wlyteth on huere wynne wele,
that al the wodè ryngeth.

The rosè rayleth hire rode,
the levès on the lyhtè wode
waxen al with wille.   15
The monè mandeth hire bleo,
the lilie is lossom to seo,
the fenyl & the fille;
wowès this wildè drakes,
milès murgeth huere makes,   20
ase strem that striketh stille;
mody meneth so doth mo,
ichot ycham on of tho,
for love that likes ille.

The monè mandeth hire lyht,   25
so doth the semly sonnè bryht,
when briddès singeth breme;
deawès donketh the dounes,
deorès with huere dernè rounes,
domès fortè deme;   30
wormès woweth under cloude,
wymmen waxeth wounder proude,
so wel hit wol hem seme.
Yef me shal wontè wille of on,
this wunnè weole y wole forgon,   35
ant wyht in wodè be fleme.

Probably thirteenth century. Ibid.

1 **lenten:** spring 2 **briddes roune:** birds' song 4 **dayes-eyes:** daisies 6 **uch foul:** each bird
7 **threstelcoc:** thrush **him threteth oo:** bickers always 8 **huere . . . woo:** their . . . woe 9 **wode-rove:** woodruff (a flowering plant) 10 **ferly fele:** wonderfully many 11 **ant wlyteth:** and warbles
wynne wele: wealth of bliss 13 **rayleth hire rode:** puts on her color 16 **mandeth hire bleo:** sends
forth her brightness 17 **lossom to seo:** lovely to see 18 **fenyl:** fennel (the herb) **fille:** wild
thyme 19 **wowes:** woo 20 **miles murgeth:** animals cheer **makes:** mates 21 **striketh stille:**
flows gently 22 **mody:** the passionate or moody [man] **meneth:** complains **mo:** more, others
23 **ichot ycham:** I know I am **on of tho:** one of those 24 **likes ille:** is unhappy 26 **semly:** seemly,
handsome 27 **breme:** loudly, gloriously 28 **deawes donketh the dounes:** dews dampen the downs
(high rolling country) 29 **deores:** wild animals **derne rounes:** secret voices 30 **domes forte
deme:** for to deem dooms, make decisions (animals have mysterious means of communication by
which they live in agreement) 31 **cloude:** clod, earth 33 **hem seme:** suit them 34 **yef:** if **wonte
wille:** not have my desire 35 **wunne weole:** wealth of bliss **y wole forgon:** I will forgo, abandon
36 **whyt:** quickly **fleme:** a fugitive, exile

It's Spring Returning, It's Spring and Love

It's spring returning, it's spring and love!
The buds, the birds, are about, above.
    Spring, and the joy it's bringing!
There's many a daisy down the dale,
Many a gala nightingale,   5
    Many a songbird singing.
The thrush is spunky and says his say,
Now woes of the winter wear away;
    And sprigs of the mint are springing.
The birds are flocking—afield, afar—   10
To tell high heaven how glad they are
    And set the woodland ringing.

The rose is swank in her rosy hood;
The leaves are a-sparkle in the wood
    And grow out green with a will.   15
The moon is sending us word she's bright;
The lily-flower is the day's delight.
    There's fennel and thyme and dill.
It's wooing time for the duck and drake;
Four-footed things, for their favorite's sake,   20
    Purr soft as a brook half-still.
The lover's moody—and others too;
I grant I'm a grumbler with that crew
    Who grieve for love grown chill.

The moon up there—she's a shining one!   25
By day there's the ever-splendid sun,
    And birds stir perkily.
There's dew a-dowsing the upland runs;
The wild things, gifted with mystic tongues,
    Speak forest policy.   30
Worms cuddle close in their clammy haunt;
Women, proud of their beauty, flaunt
    That pride—fine sight to see!
I'll have my way with a certain one,
Or all my joy in the world is done.   35
    It's off in the woods for me.

Winter Wakeneth All My Care

Winter wakeneth all my care,
now these leavès waxeth bare;
ofte I sike and mournè sare
    when hit cometh in my thought
    of this worldes joy, how hit goth all to nought.   5

Now hit is and now hit nis,
also hit ne'er nere, ywis.
That mony mon saith, soth hit is:
    all goth but Godès wille;
    all we shulè deyè though us like ille.   10

All that grain men graveth green,
now hit falloweth all by-dene;
Jesu, help that hit be seen
    and shield us from helle,
    for I not whider I shall ne how longe here dwelle.   15

Probably thirteenth century. Ibid.

2 **waxeth**: become 3 **sike**: sigh **sare**: sore(ly) 4 **hit**: it 6 **nis**: is not 7 **also**: just as if **ne'er nere**: never had been **ywis**: indeed 8 **that mony mon**: what many a man **soth**: truth 10 **though us like ille**: though we do not like it 11 **graveth**: plant 12 **falloweth**: withers **by-dene**: quickly 15 **not**: do not know **shall**: shall go **ne**: nor

Icham of Irlaunde

Icham of Irlaunde
ant of the holy londe
    of Irlande.
Godè sirè pray ich thee
for of sayntè charité
come ant daunce wyt me
    in Irlaunde.

Earlier fourteenth century. H. Heuser, *Anglia,* XXX, 1907.

1 **icham**: I am 2 **ant**: and 4 **ich**: I

Winter Wakens All My Care

Winter wakens all my care:
Trees—the leafy trees!—are bare.
I go mournful everywhere,
  When sunk in the one thought:
  All the world's joy so soon amounts to nought.   5

Now it's here and now it's—where?
Vanished. As if never there.
Here's a notion many share:
  All but God's will goes by.
  Like it or like it not, we're born to die.   10

Sweet and green the grain we grow.
Sour and brown it withers, though.
Make me mindful, Lord—and so
  Shun hell. I'm soon away
  —Don't know the place I'm for. Don't know the day.   15

I Am from Ireland

I am from Ireland,
And from the holy land
  Of Ireland.
Good sir, I pray thee,
Of holy charity,
Come and dance with me
  In Ireland.

This fragment, sometimes called "The Irish Dancer," is probably part of a *carol*; see the prosody section.

Richard Rolle
(c. 1300–1349)

As a young man, Rolle ran away to become a hermit. He studied theology briefly in Paris, and wandered about in times of political upheaval and military disorder. His religious and mystical works survive in more manuscripts than those of any other medieval writer.

Ghostly Gladness

Ghostly gladness in Jesu and joy in heart,
With sweetness in soul of the savor of heaven in hope,
Is health until hele.
And my life lends in love, and lightsomeness unlappes my thought.
I dread nought that me may work woe, so mickel I wot of wele.   5
It were no wonder if death were dear,
That I might see him that I seek.
But now it is lengthèd from me,
And me behooves live here, till he will me loose.
List and lere of this lore, and thee shall nought mislike.   10
Love makes me to mell, and joy gars me jangle.
Look thou lead thy life in lightsomeness,
And heaviness, hold it away.
Sorriness, let it not sit with thee,
But in gladness of God evermore make thou thy glee.   15

---

c. 1343. *Richard Rolle of Hampole*, ed. C. Horstmann, 1895.

Found in manuscript collections of Rolle's poems of spiritual joy, this is what today we would call a *prose poem*; see the prosody section. The line arrangement as *free verse* (see the prosody section) is the editor's.

1 **ghostly:** spiritual   3 **hele:** salvation   4 **lends:** dwells   **lightsomeness:** cheerfulness   **unlappes:** enfolds   5 **mickel I wot:** much I know   **wele:** welfare   10 **list and lere:** listen and learn   11 **mell:** talk   **gars me jangle:** makes me talk merrily on

Geoffrey Chaucer
(c. 1343–1400)

Captured and ransomed as a young soldier in France, Chaucer later served on diplomatic missions for Edward III and held important political posts. His life suggests that he was a shrewd, amused, sophisticated, substantial man of affairs, on familiar terms with the great men of his time.

Now Welcom, Somer

Now welcom, somer, with thy sonnè softe,
That hast this wintres wedres overshake,
And driven away the longè nyghtès blake.

Seynt Valentyn, that art ful hy on-lofte,
Thus singen smalè foulès for thy sake: 5
    Now welcom, somer, with thy sonnè softe,
    That hast this wintres wedres overshake,

Early 1380s in *The Parliament of Fowles*. First printed by William Caxton, 1477–1478. *Works*, ed. W. W. Skeat, 1894–1897.

For the form of this poem, a *roundel*, see the prosody section.

1 **somer:** the season of warmer weather, spring   2 **overshake:** shaken off   4 **hy on-lofte:** high aloft   5 **foules:** birds

Wel han they causè for to gladen ofte,
Sith ech of hem recovered hath his make;
Ful blisful mowe they singen whan they wake:　　　　10
　　Now welcom, somer, with thy sonnè softe,
　　That hast this wintres wedres overshake,
　　And driven away the longè nyghtès blake.

8 **han:** have　**to gladen:** to be glad　9 **sith ech of hem:** since each of them　**make:** mate　10 **mowe:** may

Hyd, Absolon, Thy Gilte Tresses Clere

Hyd, Absolon, thy giltè tresses clere;
Ester, ley thou thy mekenesse all adoun;
Hyd, Jonathas, all thy frendly manere;
Penelope and Marcia Catoun,
Mak of youre wifhod no comparisoun;　　　　5
Hyde ye youre beautés, Isoude and Eleyne:
My lady cometh, that all this may disteyne.

Thy fairè body, lat it nat appere,
Lavine, and thou, Lucresse of Romè toun,
And Polixene, that boghten love so dere,　　　　10
And Cleopatre, with all thy passioun,
Hyde ye your trouthe of love and your renoun;
And thou, Tisbé, that hast for love swich peyne:
My lady cometh, that all this may disteyne.

Hero, Dido, Laudomia, alle yfere,　　　　15
And Phyllis, hanging for thy Demophoun,
And Canacé, espièd by thy chere,
Ysiphilé, betrayèd with Jasoun,
Maketh of your trouthè neyther boost ne soun,
Nor Ypermystre or Adriane, ye tweyne:　　　　20
My lady cometh, that all this may disteyne.

c. 1385 in *The Legend of Good Women*. First printed by W. Thynne, 1532. Ibid.

The form is *rhyme royal;* see the prosody section. The names in the poem, mostly feminine, are those of individuals celebrated for their beauty. Some are biblical, others from classical or medieval legend or history.

4 **Marcia Catoun:** Cato's Marcia　5 **wifhod:** womanhood　7 **disteyne:** bedim, overshadow　10 **boghten:** paid for　13 **swich:** such　15 **yfere:** together　16 **hanging for:** hanging herself for love of　17 **espièd . . . chere:** recognized by your appearance　19 **soun:** sound

Merciles Beautée

I

Your yën two wol slee me sodenly;
I may the beautée of hem not sustene,
So woundeth hit throughout my hertè kene.

And but your word wol helen hastily
My hertès woundè, while that hit is grene,　　　　5

c. 1390? T. Percy, *Reliques of Ancient English Poetry,* I, 1765.

1 **yën:** eyes　2 **hem:** them　3 **hit:** it　4 **but:** unless　5 **grene:** green, fresh

Your yën two wol slee me sodenly;
I may the beautée of hem not sustene.

Upon my trouthe, I sey you feithfully
That ye ben of my lyf and deth the quene;
For with my deth the trouthe shal be sene.   10
     Your yën two wol slee me sodenly;
     I may the beautée of hem not sustene,
     So woundeth hit throughout my hertè kene.

II

So hath your beautée fro your hertè chacèd
Pitée, that me ne availeth not to pleyne;   15
For Daunger halt your mercy in his cheyne.

Giltless, my deth thus han ye me purchacèd;
I sey you sooth, me nedeth not to feyne;
     So hath your beautée fro your hertè chacèd
     Pitée, that me ne availeth not to pleyne.   20

Allas! that nature hath in you compassèd
So greet beautée, that no man may atteyne
To mercy, though he stervè for the peyne.
     So hath your beautée fro your hertè chacèd
     Pitée, that me ne availeth not to pleyne,   25
     For Daunger halt your mercy in his cheyne.

III

Sin I fro Love escapèd am so fat,
I never thenk to ben in his prison lene;
Sin I am free, I count him not a bene.

He may answere, and seyè this and that;   30
I do no fors, I speke right as I mene.
     Sin I fro Love escapèd am so fat,
     I never thenk to ben in his prison lene.

Love hath my name ystrike out of his sclat,
And he is strike out of my bokès clene   35
For evermo; ther is non other mene.
     Sin I fro Love escapèd am so fat,
     I never thenk to ben in his prison lene;
     Sin I am free, I count him not a bene.

15 **pleyne:** complain   16 **Daunger:** disdain, aloofness   **halt:** holds   17 **purchaced:** procured, provided   18 **sooth:** truth   23 **sterve:** die   27 **sin:** since   29 **bene:** bean   31 **do no fors:** do not care   34 **ystrike ... sclat:** struck ... list (slate)   36 **mene:** means, way

The Pardoner's Tale

In Flaundres whilom was a compaignye
Of yongė folk that haunteden folye,
As riot, hasard, stywės, and tavernes,
Where as with harpės, lutės, and gyternes,
They daunce and pleyen at dees bothe day and nyght,   5
And eten also and drynken over hir myght,
Thurgh which they doon the devel sacrifise
Withinne that develes temple, in cursėd wise,
By superfluytée abhomynable.
Hir othės been so grete and so dampnable   10
That it is grisly for to heere hem swere.
Oure blissed Lordės body they totere,—
Hem thoughte that Jewės rente hym noght ynough;
And ech of hem at otheres synnė lough.
And right anon thanne comen tombesteres   15
Fetys and smale, and yongė frutesteres,
Syngeres with harpės, baudės, wafereres,
Whiche been the verray develes officeres
To kyndle and blowe the fyr of lecherye,
That is annexėd unto glotonye.   20
The hooly writ take I to my witnesse
That luxurie is in wyn and dronkenesse.
Lo, how that dronken Looth, unkyndely,
Lay by his doghtres two, unwityngly;
So dronke he was, he nystė what he wroghte.   25
Herodės, whoso wel the stories soghte,
Whan he of wyn was repleet at his feeste,
Right at his owene table he yaf his heeste
To sleen the Baptist John, ful giltėlees. . . .
Thise riotourės thre of whiche I telle,   30
Longe erst er primė rong of any belle,
Were set hem in a taverne for to drynke,
And as they sat, they herde a bellė clynke
Biforn a cors, was cariėd to his grave.
That oon of hem gan callen to his knave: 35
"Go bet," quod he "and axė redily
What cors is this that passeth heer forby;
And looke that thou reporte his namė weel."

1390s. First printed by Caxton, 1478?, 1484. Text from *Works*, 2nd ed., ed. F. N. Robinson, 1957.

Pardoners, sellers of pardons or papal indulgences, were sometimes churchmen and sometimes confidence men in ecclesiastical robes. Chaucer's pardoner, who seems to have been in minor orders (below the priesthood), dealt also in fraudulent relics. His moral tale, on the evils of avarice, is followed by suggestions that his listeners give generously for his pardons and other merchandise.

The *e*'s (though probably to be pronounced) are not dotted when hypermetric; i.e., when they constitute an extra (eleventh) syllable not necessary to the structure of *iambic pentameter* (see prosody section). Examples in the first three lines: compaignye, folye, tavernes.

1 **whilom:** once upon a time   3 **hasard, stywes:** gambling and stews (houses of prostitution)   4 **gyternes:** citterns (guitars)   5 **dees:** dice   6 **over:** beyond (their capacity)   7 **doon:** do   11 **hem:** them ('em)   12 **totere:** tear to pieces   14 **lough:** laughed   15 **tombesteres:** dancing girls   16 **fetys and smale:** pretty and slim   **frutesteres:** girls who sold fruit (like cigarette-girls)   17 **baudes:** bawds, pimps   **wafereres:** sellers of cakes and so forth   22 **luxurie:** lust, lechery   23 **Looth:** Lot (cf. Gen. 19:31 ff.)   **unkyndely:** unnaturally   25 **he...wroghte:** he didn't know what he was doing   26 **whoso...soghte:** whoever looks up the accounts (cf. Matt. 14, Mark 6)   28 **yaf his heeste:** gave his command   29 **sleen:** slay   After 29, about 70 lines of sermonizing on the evils of gluttony, drunkenness, and gambling are omitted.   30 **riotoures:** riotous livers   31 **erst er:** before   **prime:** prime, the first part of the day (6 A.M. till 9)   34 **cors:** corpse   35 **knave:** boy, servant, page   36 **go bet:** go fast, get going   **axe:** ask

"Sire," quod this boy, "it nedeth never-a-deel;
It was me toold er ye cam heer two houres.   40
He was, pardée, an old felawe of youres;
And sodeynly he was yslayn to-nyght,
Fordronke, as he sat on his bench upright.
Ther cam a privée theef men clepeth Deeth,
That in this contrée al the peple sleeth,   45
And with his spere he smoot his herte atwo,
And wente his wey withouten wordès mo.
He hath a thousand slayn this pestilence.
And, maister, er ye come in his presence,
Me thynketh that it werè necessárie   50
For to be war of swich an adversárie.
Beth redy for to meete hym everemoore;
Thus taughtè me my dame; I sey namoore."
"By seintè Marie!" seyde this taverner,
"The child seith sooth, for he hath slayn this yeer,   55
Henne over a mile, withinne a greet village,
Bothe man and womman, child, and hyne, and page;
I trowe his habitacioun be there.
To been avysèd greet wysdom it were,
Er that he dide a man a dishonour."   60
        "Ye, Goddès armès!" quod this riotour,
"Is it swich peril with hym for to meete?
I shall hym seke by wey and eek by strete,
I make avow to Goddès dignè bones!
Herkneth, felawès, we thre been al ones;   65
Lat ech of us holde up his hand til oother,
And ech of us bicomen otheres brother,
And we wol sleen this falsè traytour Deeth.
He shal be slayn, he that so manye sleeth,
By Goddès dignitée, er it be nyght!"   70
        Togidres han thise thre hir trouthès plight
To lyve and dyen ech of hem for oother,
As though he were his owene yborè brother.
And up they stirte, al dronken in this rage,
And forth they goon towardès that village   75
Of which the taverner hadde spoke biforn.
And many a grisly ooth thanne han they sworn,
And Cristès blessed body al torente—
Deeth shal be deed, if that they may hym hente!
        Whan they han goon nat fully half a mile,   80
Right as they wolde han troden over a stile,
An oold man and a povre with hem mette.
This oldè man ful mekely hem grette,
And seydè thus, "Now, lordès, God yow see!"
        The proudeste of thise riotourès three   85
Answerde agayn, "What, carl, with sory grace!
Why artow al forwrappèd save thy face?

---

39 **quod:** said   **nedeth . . . deel:** is not at all necessary   41 **pardée:** indeed, certainly   42 **to-nyght:** last night   43 **fordronke:** dead drunk   44 **privée:** secret   **clepeth:** call   48 **this pestilence:** during this attack of the plague   51 **swich:** such   53 **dame:** mother   55 **seith sooth:** tells the truth   56 **henne over a mile:** a mile away from here   57 **hyne:** servant, farm laborer   58 **trowe:** think   59 **avysèd:** forewarned   64 **digne:** worthy   65 **al ones:** all one, of one mind   71 **hir trouthes plight:** made their promises   73 **ybore:** born   74 **stirte:** started, jumped   **rage:** passion, madness   78 **torente:** torn to pieces (cf. "armes" and "bones" in 61 and 64)   79 **hente:** catch, seize   81 **stile:** steps to climb over fence   83 **grette:** greeted   84 **God yow see:** God protect you   86 **carl:** churl, peasant   **with sory grace:** a curse, like "Go to hell!"   87 **artow:** art thou (*thou* was more informal or ruder than *you*)   **forwrappèd:** wrapped up

Why lyvestow so longe in so greet age?"
   This oldè man gan looke in his visage,
And seydè thus: "For I ne kan nat fynde   90
A man, though that I walkèd into Ynde,
Neither in citée ne in no village,
That woldè chaunge his youthè for myn age;
And therfore moot I han myn agè stille,
As longè tyme as it is Goddès wille.   95
Ne Deeth, allas! ne wol nat han my lyf.
Thus walke I, lyk a restèlees kaityf,
And on the ground, which is my moodres gate,
I knokkè with my staf, bothe erly and late,
And seyè 'Leevè mooder, leet me in!   100
Lo how I vanysshe, flessh, and blood, and skyn!
Allas! whan shul my bonès been at reste?
Mooder, with yow wolde I chaungè my cheste
That in my chambre longè tyme hath be,
Ye, for an heyrè clowt to wrappe in me!'   105
But yet to me she wol nat do that grace,
For which ful pale and welkèd is my face.
   But, sires, to yow it is no curteisye
To speken to an old man vileynye,
But he trespasse in word, or elles in dede.   110
In Hooly Writ ye may yourself wel rede:
'Agayns an oold man, hoor upon his heed,
Ye sholde arise;' wherfore I yeve yow reed,
Ne dooth unto an oold man noon harm now,
Namoore than that ye wolde men did to yow   115
In agè, if that ye so longe abyde.
And God be with yow, where ye go or ryde!
I moot go thider as I have to go."
   "Nay, oldè cherl, by God, thou shalt nat so,"
Seydè this oother hasardour anon;   120
"Thou partest nat so lightly, by Seint John!
Thou spak right now of thilkè traytour Deeth,
That in this contrée alle oure freendès sleeth.
Have heer my trouthe, as thou art his espye,
Telle where he is, or thou shalt it abye,   125
By God, and by the hooly sacrement!
For soothly thou art oon of his assent
To sleen us yongè folk, thou falsè theef!"
   "Now, sires," quod he, "if that yow be so leef
To fyndè Deeth, turne up this crokèd wey,   130
For in that grove I lafte hym, by my fey,
Under a tree, and there he wole abyde;
Noght for youre boost he wole him no thyng hyde.
Se ye that ook? Right there ye shal hym fynde.
God savè yow, that boghte agayn mankynde,   135
And yow amende!" Thus seyde this oldè man;

---

88 lyvestow: livest thou **89 looke ... visage:** look him in the face **91 Ynde:** India (considered the end of the world) **94 moot:** must **97 kaityf:** wretch **100 leeve:** dear **101 vanysshe:** waste away **103 cheste:** clothes chest **105 heyre clowt:** haircloth rag **in me:** me in **107 welkèd:** withered **110 but:** unless **112 hoor:** white **113 yeve yow reed:** give you (this) advice **114 ne dooth:** don't do **116 so longe abyde:** live so long **117 where:** wherever **go:** walk **120 hasardour:** gambler **122 thilke:** that same **124 trouthe:** promise **espye:** spy **125 abye:** pay for **127 soothly:** truly **oon of his assent:** in agreement with him **129 yow ... leef:** you'd so much like **131 fey:** faith **132 abyde:** stay **135 boghte agayn:** redeemed **136 yow amende:** make you better

And everich of thise riotourès ran
Til he cam to that tree, and ther they founde
Of floryns fyne of gold ycoynèd rounde
Wel ny an eightè busshels, as hem thoughte.   140
No lenger thanne after Deeth they soughte,
But ech of hem so glad was of that sighte,
For that the floryns been so faire and brighte,
That doun they sette hem by this precious hoord.
The worste of hem, he spak the firstè word.   145
      "Bretheren," quod he, "taak kep what that I seye;
My wit is greet, though that I bourde and pleye.
This tresor hath Fortune unto us yiven,
In myrthe and joliftée oure lyf to lyven,
And lightly as it comth, so wol we spende.   150
Ey! Goddès precious dignitée! who wende
To-day that we sholde han so fair a grace?
But myghte this gold be carièd fro this place
Hoom to myn hous, or ellès unto youres—
For wel ye woot that al this gold is oures—   155
Thanne were we in heigh felicitée.
But trewely, by daye it may nat bee.
Men woldè seyn that we were thevès stronge,
And for oure owene tresor doon us honge.
This tresor moste ycarièd be by nyghte   160
As wisely and as slyly as it myghte.
Wherfore I rede that cut among us alle
Be drawe, and lat se wher the cut wol falle;
And he that hath the cut with hertè blithe
Shal rennè to the town, and that ful swithe,   165
And brynge us breed and wyn ful prively.
And two of us shul kepen subtilly
This tresor wel; and if he wol nat tarie,
Whan it is nyght, we wol this tresor carie,
By oon assent, where as us thynketh best."   170
That oon of hem the cut broghte in his fest,
And bad hem drawe, and looke where it wol falle;
And it fil on the yongeste of hem alle,
And forth toward the toun he wente anon.
And also soonè as that he was gon,   175
That oon of hem spak thus unto that oother:
"Thow knowest wel thou art my sworen brother;
Thy profit wol I tellè thee anon.
Thou woost wel that oure felawe is agon.
And heere is gold, and that ful greet plentée,   180
That shal departed been among us thre.
But nathelees, if I kan shape it so
That it departed were among us two,
Hadde I nat doon a freendès torn to thee?"
      That oother answerde, "I noot hou that may be.   185
He woot wel that the gold is with us tweye;
What shal we doon? What shal we to hym seye?"
      "Shall it be conseil?" seyde that firstè shrewe,

137 **everich:** every one   139 **floryns:** florins, Florentine gold coins   140 **ny:** nigh   146 **taak kep:** pay attention to   147 **bourde:** jest   148 **yiven:** given   150 **lightly:** easily (like "easy come, easy go")   151 **wende:** would have thought   155 **woot:** know   158 **stronge:** violent   159 **doon us honge:** have us hanged   162 **rede:** advise   162-163 **cut ... Be drawe:** lots be drawn   165 **swithe:** swiftly   175 **also soone:** just as soon   179 **woost:** knowest   181 **departed:** divided   182 **nathelees:** nevertheless   **shape:** arrange, plan   185 **noot:** don't know   188 **Shal it be conseil?:** You want my advice?   **shrewe:** scoundrel

"And I shal tellen in a wordès fewe
What we shal doon, and brynge it wel aboute."   190
    "I grauntè," quod that oother, "out of doute,
That, by my trouthe, I wol thee nat biwreye."
    "Now," quod the firste, "thou woost wel we be tweye,
And two of us shul strenger be than oon.
Looke whan that he is set, that right anoon   195
Arys as though thou woldest with hym pleye,
And I shal ryve hym thurgh the sydès tweye
Whil that thou strogelest with hym as in game,
And with thy daggere looke thou do the same;
And thanne shal al this gold departed be,   200
My deerè freend, bitwixen me and thee.
Thanne may we bothe oure lustès all fulfille,
And pleye at dees right at oure owene wille."
And thus acorded been thise shrewès tweye
To sleen the thridde, as ye han herd me seye.   205
    This yongeste, which that wentè to the toun,
Ful ofte in herte he rolleth up and doun
The beautée of thise floryns newe and brighte.
"O Lord!" quod he, "if so were that I myghte
Have al this tresor to myself allone,   210
Ther is no man that lyveth under the trone
Of God that sholdè lyve so murye as I!"
And attè laste the feend, oure enemy,
Putte in his thought that he sholde poyson beye,
With which he myghtè sleen his felawes tweye;   215
For-why the feend foond hym in swich lyvynge
That he hadde levè, him to sorwe brynge.
For this was outrely his fulle entente,
To sleen hem bothe, and nevere to repente.
And forth he gooth, no lenger wolde he tarie,   220
Into the toun, unto a pothecarie,
And preydè hym that he hym woldè selle
Som poyson, that he myghte his rattes quelle;
And eek ther was a polcat in his hawe,
That, as he seyde, his capouns hadde yslawe,   225
And fayn he woldè wreke hym, if he myghte,
On vermyn that destroyèd hym by nyghte.
    The pothecarie answerde, "And thou shalt have
A thyng that, also God my soulè save,
In al this world ther is no creature,   230
That eten or dronken hath of this confiture
Noght but the montance of a corn of whete,
That he ne shal his lif anon forlete;
Ye, sterve he shal, and that in lassè while
Than thou wolt goon a paas nat but a mile,   235
This poysoun is so strong and violent."
    This cursed man hath in his hond yhent
This poysoun in a box, and sith he ran
Into the nextè strete unto a man,
And borwed of hym largè botelles thre;   240

---

192 **biwreye:** betray   195 **set:** seated   **right anoon:** right away   197 **ryve:** pierce   213 **feend:** fiend, the devil   216 **for-why:** because   221 **pothecarie:** apothecary   223 **quelle:** kill   224 **hawe:** hedge, yard   225 **his capouns hadde yslawe:** had killed his capons (chickens)   226 **fayn he wolde wreke hym:** he would like to avenge himself   229 **also:** so   231 **confiture:** mixture   232 **montance:** amount   **corn:** grain   233 **forlete:** lose   234 **sterve:** die   235 **goon a paas:** walk at a footpace   237 **yhent:** taken   238 **sith:** then

And in the two his poyson pourèd he;
The thridde he keptè clenè for his drynke.
For al the nyght he shoop hym for to swynke
In cariynge of the gold out of that place.
And whan this riotour, with sory grace,   245
Hadde filled with wyn his gretè botels thre,
To his felawes agayn repaireth he.
What nedeth it to sermone of it moore?
For right as they hadde cast his deeth bifoore,
Right so they han hym slayn, and that anon.   250
And whan that this was doon, thus spak that oon:
"Now lat us sitte and drynke, and make us merie,
And afterward we wol his body berie."
And with that word it happèd hym, par cas,
To take the botel ther the poyson was,   255
And drank, and yaf his felawe drynke also,
For which anon they storven bothè two.

243 **shoop hym:** prepared himself **swynke:** labor 245 **with sory grace:** evilly, fatefully 249 **cast:** planned 254 **it happèd hym:** he happened

Anonymous Poems of the Fifteenth Century

I Sing of a Mayden

I sing of a mayden
    That is makèles;
King of allè kingès
    To her son she ches.

He cam also stillè   5
    Ther his moder was,
As dew in Aprillè
    That falleth on the gras.

He cam also stillè
    To his moderes bowr,   10
As dew in Aprillè
    That falleth on the flowr.

He cam also stillè
    Ther his moder lay,
As dew in Aprillè   15
    That falleth on the spray.

Moder and maiden
    Was never none but she;
Wel may swich a lady
    Godès moder be.   20

Earlier fifteenth century. T. Wright, *Songs and Carols* . . . , IV, 1856.

2 **makeles:** (1) without an equal; (2) without a mate 4 **to her son:** for her son **ches:** chose 5 **also stille:** just as quietly 6 **ther:** where 7 **Aprille:** pronounced to rhyme with *stillè* 10 **bowr:** room 19 **swich:** such

Adam Lay Ibounden

Adam lay ibounden,
    Bounden in a bond,
Foure thousand winter
    Thoght he not too long;
And al was for an appil,   5
    An appil that he tok,
As clerkès finden
    Wreten in here bok.

Ne hadde the appil takè ben,
    The appil taken ben,   10
Ne hadde never our lady
    A ben hevenè quene;
Blessed be the timè
    That appil takè was!
Therfore we moun singen   15
    "Deo gracias."

Earlier fifteenth century. Ibid.

1 **ibounden:** bound 3 Some thought the story of Adam and Eve dated back to 4000 B.C. 7 **clerkes:** learned men 8 **here:** their 9 **ne hadde:** had not 12 **a ben:** have been **hevene quene:** queen of heaven 15 **moun:** may 16 Thanks be to God!

I Have a Gentil Cock

I have a gentil cock
    Croweth me day;
He doth me risen erly
    My matins for to say.

I have a gentil cock,   5
    Comen he is of gret;
His comb is of red coral,
    His tayl is of jet.

I have a gentil cock,
    Comen he is of kinde;   10
His comb is of red coral,
    His tayl is of inde.

His leggès ben of azure,
    So gentil and so smale;
His sporès arn of silver white   15
    Into the wortèwale.

His eynen arn of cristal,
    Loken all in aumber;
And every night he percheth him
    In mine ladyes chaumber.   20

Earlier fifteenth century. Ibid.

1 **gentil:** noble, fine 3 **doth me risen:** makes me get up 4 **matins:** morning prayers 6 **of gret:** of a great family 10 **of kinde:** of good stock 12 **inde:** indigo 16 **wortewale:** root 18 **loken:** set

Swarte-Smeked Smithes

Swarte-smeked smithes, smatered with smoke,
Drive me to deth with din of her dintes;
Swich nois on nightes ne herd men never!
What knavene cry and clatering of knockes;
The cammede kongons cryen after "Coal! coal!"   5
And blowen here bellowes that al here brain brestes.
"Huf! puf!" saith that one; "Haf! paf!" that other.
They spitten and sprawlen and spellen many spelles;
They gnawen and gnachen, they grones togedere,
And holden hem hote with here hard hamers.   10
Of a bulle-hide ben here barm-felles;
Here schankes been schackeled for the fire-flinderes.
Hevy hameres they han that hard ben handled;
Stark strokes they striken on a steled stokke;
"Lus, bus! Las, das!" rowten by rowe.   15
Swich dolful a dreme the devil it to-drive!
The maister longeth a litel and lasheth a lesse;
Twineth hem twain and toucheth a treble.
"Tik, tak! hic, hak! tiket, taket! tik, tak!
Lus, bus! lus, das!" Swich lyf they leden,   20
Alle clothe-mares, Christ hem give sorwe!
May no man for bren-wateres on night han his rest!

First half of fifteenth century. Wright and Halliwell, op. cit., I.

This complaint about boisterous blacksmiths that keep the neighborhood awake by working at night may be the noisiest poem in English. For the *strong-stress rhythm*, and for the reason words like *smithès* do not have the *e*'s dotted, see the prosody section.

1 **swarte-smeked:** smoked black **smatered:** smutty 2 **her dintes:** their blows 3 **swich:** such 4 **knavene cry:** cry of assistants 5 **cammede kongons:** pug-nosed bastards 6 **here:** their **brestes:** bursts 8 **spellen many spelles:** tell many stories 9 **gnawen and gnachen:** make gnawing and gnashing noises 10 **holden hem hote:** keep themselves hot, work up a sweat 11 **barm-felles:** leather aprons 12 **fire-flinderes:** sparks of fire 14 **steled stokke:** steel anvil 15 **rowten by rowe:** crash in turn 16 **dreme:** noise **to-drive:** drive away 17–18 The master beats a small piece longer, hammers a smaller one, twists the two together, makes a shrill noise. 21 **clothe-mares:** horse-armorers 22 **bren-wateres:** blacksmiths, who "burn water" by dipping hot iron in it

I Wende to Dede

I wende to dede, knight stithe in stoure,
Thurghe fight in felde I won the flowr.
No fightes me taught the dede to quell:
I wende to dede; sooth I yow tell.

I wende to dede, a king iwisse;   5
What helpes honor or worldès blisse?
Dede is to man the kindè way.
I wendè to be clad in clay.

I wende to dede, clerk ful of skill,
That couth with worde men mar and dill.   10

Fifteenth century. J. Strutt, *Horda Angel-Cynnan . . .*, III, 1775–1776.

1 **wende to dede:** go to death **stithe in stoure:** tough in battle 2 **the flowr:** distinction, acclaim 3 **the dede to quell:** to kill death 4 **sooth:** the truth 5 **iwisse:** indeed 7 **kinde way:** way of nature 9 **clerk:** scholar, learned man 10 **couth:** knew how to, could **mar:** ruin **dill:** dull, stupefy

Soon has me made the dede an ende.
Bes ware with me! to dede I wende.

11 **soon . . . ende:** Death soon made an end of me.   12 **bes ware with me:** beware, with me [as your example]

Another Year

> *Who wot now that is here*
> *Where he shall be another year?*

Another year it may betide
This company to be full wide,
And never another here to abide: 5
    Christ may send now such a year.

> *Who wot now,* etc.

Another year it may befall
The least that is within this hall
To be more master than we all;   10
    Christ may send now such a year.

> *Who wot now,* etc.

These lords that been wonder-great,
They threaten poor men for to beat;
It lendeth little in their threat;   15
    Christ may send such a year.

> *Who wot now,* etc.

Mid-fifteenth century. R. Greene, *The Early English Carols*, 1935.

This poem is a *carol*; see the prosody section.

1 **wot:** knows   4 **wide:** widely scattered   9 **least:** least important one   15 **it lendeth little:** little is contained

Charles d'Orléans
(1394–1465)

One of the finest of early French poets, Charles (nephew of the king of France) was captured at the battle of Agincourt (1415). During his 25 years as prisoner in England, he came to speak our language better than his own and wrote parallel poems in English and French—the English, it seems, often the earlier version.

The Smiling Mouth and Laughing Eyen Grey

The smiling mouth and laughing eyen grey,
The breastès round, and long small armès twain,
The handès smooth, and sidès straight and plain,
Your feetès lite—what should I further say?
It is my craft when ye are far away   5
To muse thereon in stinting of my pain.

1430–1440. *Poems, Written in English, by Charles Duke of Orléans*, ed. G. W. Taylor, 1827.

See *roundel* in the prosody section.

2 **small:** slender   3 **plain:** smooth   4 **lite:** little   5 **craft:** scheme, occupation

The smiling mouth and laughing eyen grey,
The breastès round, and long small armès twain.

So would I pray you, if I durst or may,
The sight to see as I have seen,   10
Forwhy that craft me is most fain
'And will be to the hour in which I deye:
        The smiling mouth and laughing eyen grey,
        The breastès round, and long small armès twain.

11 **forwhy:** because   **me is most fain:** pleases me the most   12 **deye:** die

Well, Wanton Eye

Well, wanton eye, but must ye needès play?
Your lookès nice ye let them run too wide.
I dread me sore if that ye be espied,
And then we must it both right dear aby.
Take some and leave some to another day,   5
And for our ease, swift from your theftès glide.
        Well, wanton eye, but must ye needès play?
        Your lookès nice ye let them run too wide.

For might once slander get you under key,
Ye should be then from all such theftès tied.   10
So fie for shame! let reason be your guide,
And steal—spare not!—when ye see time, and may.
        Well, wanton eye, but must ye needès play?
        Your lookès nice ye let them run too wide.

_____

1430–1440. Ibid.

2 **lookes nice:** foolish glances (because they are indiscreet in staring at his love where others might notice and spread scandal)   4 **aby:** pay the penalty for

Anonymous Poems of the Earlier Sixteenth Century

A God and Yet a Man?

A god and yet a man?
        A maid and yet a mother?
Wit wonders what wit can
        Conceive, this or the other?

A god, and can he die?   5
        A dead man, can he live?
What wit can well reply?
        What reason reason give?

God, truth itself, doth teach it;
        Man's wit sinks too far under   10
By reason's power to reach it.
        Believe and leave to wonder.

_____

c. 1500. C. Brown, *Religious Lyrics of the XVth Century*, 1939.

A Lyke-Wake Dirge

This ae nighte, this ae nighte,
    Every nighte and alle;
Fire and sleete, and candle lighte,
    And Christe receive thye saule.

When thou from hence away are past,   5
    Every nighte and alle;
To Whinny-muir thou comest at laste;
    And Christe receive thye saule.

If ever thou gavest hosen and shoon,
    Every nighte and alle;   10
Sit thee down, and put them on;
    And Christe receive thye saule.

If hosen and shoon thou ne'er gavest nane,
    Every nighte and alle;
The whinnes shall pricke thee to the bare bane   15
    And Christe receive thye saule.

From Whinny-muir when thou mayst passe,
    Every nighte and alle;
To Brigg o' Dread thou comest at laste;
    And Christ receive thye saule.   20

From Brigg o' Dread when thou mayst passe,
    Every nighte and alle;
To purgatory fire thou comest at laste,
    And Christe receive thye saule.

If ever thou gavest meate or drinke,   25
    Every nighte and alle;
The fire shall never make thee shrinke,
    And Christe receive thye saule.

If meate or drinke thou never gavest nane,
    Every nighte and alle;   30
The fire will burn thee to the bare bane;
    And Christe receive thye saule.

This ae nighte, this ae nighte,
    Every nighte and alle;
Fire and sleete, and candle lighte,   35
    And Christe receive thye saule.

Sir Walter Scott, *Minstrelsy of the Scottish Border*, I, 1802.

This dirge was sung over the corpse at a wake, as the soul was thought to be starting its journey into the afterlife, first across a plain of thorns and thistles, and then over a Bridge of Dread into the fires of Purgatory. If the dead person had been charitable in life and given shoes to the poor, shoes would be returned to him now and he would be safe from the thorns and thistles. If he had given food and drink to the poor, he would be safe from the flames. There is evidence that the dirge was sung during the reign of Queen Elizabeth (1558–1603); it is thought to be much older than that.

lyke-wake: wake for a corpse   1 **ae:** one   3 **sleete:** probably for *salt*, a plate of which was placed on the breast of the corpse as a symbol of enduring life (salt preserves) and to keep away the devil 4 **saule:** soul   7 **Whinny-muir:** a moor of furze, prickly plants   9 **hosen and shoon:** stockings and shoes   15 **bane:** bone   19 **Brigg:** Bridge

Western Wind

Western wind, when will thou blow,
    The small rain down can rain?
Christ, if my love were in my arms
    And I in my bed again!

That is the way we are likely to come on this famous quatrain today. Scholars working with the poetry of the time when it was written—about 1500—would prefer to see it like this:

Westron wynde when wyll thow blow
the smalle rayne downe can rayne
Chryst yf my love were in my armys
and I yn my bed agayne

But the poem was never printed that way. It seems it was never printed at all in its own time—nor for nearly 300 years thereafter. In 1792 Joseph Ritson published it in a collection called Ancient Songs. *The words, as first written down with their music in a book of songs thought to date back to almost 1500, looked like this:*

The British Library, The British Museum

It is easy to forget, in looking at poems in a book such as this one, that the neat, quiet, even lines may have behind them a troubled manuscript history which scholars are still trying to unriddle.

---

c. 1500. Ritson, op. cit.

Lully, Lulley, Lully, Lulley

Lully, lulley, lully, lulley,
The fawcon hath born my mak away.

He bare hym up, he bare hym down;
He bare hym in to an orchard browne.

In that orchard ther was an halle,   5
That was hangid with purpill and pall.

And in that hall ther was a bedde;
Hit was hangid with gold so redde.

Early sixteenth century. E. Flügel, *Anglia*, XXVI, 1903.

2 **fawcon:** falcon **mak:** mate 3 **bare:** bore 6 **pall:** rich cloth

And yn that bed ther lieth a knyght,
His wowndės bledyng day and nyght.   10

By that bedes side kneleth a may,
And she wepeth both nyght and day.

And by that beddes side ther stondeth a ston,
Corpus Christi wretyn ther on.

11 **may:** maiden   14 **Corpus Christi:** Body of Christ

Benedicite, What Dreamèd I This Night?

Benedicite, what dreamèd I this night?
Methought the world was turnèd up-so-down,
The sun, the moon, had lost their force and light,
The sea also drownèd both tower and town.
Yet more marvel, how that I heard the sound
Of onė's voice saying, "Bear in thy mind,
Thy lady hath forgotten to be kind."

c. 1500. Sir John Hawkins, *A General History of the Science and Practice of Music*, III, 1776.

1 **benedicite:** bless me! for heaven's sake!

William Dunbar
(1460?–1520?)

Dunbar (*dun-bår*), apparently ordained a priest, was associated with the Scottish court while James IV (1488–1513) was king. Little is known of his life.

Done Is a Battell on the Dragon Blak

Done is a battell on the dragon blak,
Our campioun Christ confoundit hes his force;
The yettis of hell ar brokin with a crak,
The signe triumphall rasit is of the Croce,
The divillis trimmillis with hiddouss voce,   5
The saulis ar borrowit and to the bliss can go,
Chryst with his blud our ransonis dois indoce:
Surrexit Dominus de sepulchro.

Dungin is the deidly dragon Lucifer,
The crewall serpent with the mortall stang;   10
The auld kene tegir with his teith on char,
Whilk in a wait hes lyne for us so lang,
Thinking to grip us in his clowis strang;
The mercifull Lord wald nocht that it wer so,
He maid him for to felye of that fang: 15
Surrexit Dominus de sepulchro.

Early sixteenth century? Hailes, *Ancient Scottish Poems*, 1770.

Dunbar is probably the greatest of the Scottish poets. It is worth a little effort, then, to follow his rich Scots dialect in spite of its odd-looking spelling.

2 **campioun:** champion   **confoundit:** confounded (*-it* = our *-ed* in past participles)   3 **yettis:** gates   4 **rasit:** raised   5 **divillis trimmillis:** devils tremble   6 **saulis . . . borrowit:** souls . . . ransomed   7 **indoce:** endorse   8 The Lord has risen from the tomb.   9 **dungin:** struck, overcome   10 **stang:** sting   11 **on char:** ajar, open   12 **whilk:** which   13 **clowis strang:** strong claws   14 **wald nocht:** did not wish   15 **felye:** fail   **fang:** thing seized, prize

He for our saik that sufferit to be slane,
And lyk a lamb in sacrifice wes dicht,
Is lyk a lyone rissin up agane,
And as a gyane raxit him on hicht;   20
Sprungin is Aurora radius and bricht,
On loft is gone the glorius Appollo,
The blisfull day departit fro the nicht:
Surrexit Dominus de sepulchro.

The grit victour agane is rissin on hicht,   25
That for our querrell to the deth wes woundit;
The sone that wox all paill now schynis bricht,
And dirknes clerit, our fayth is now refoundit;
The knell of mercy fra the hevin is soundit,
The Christin ar deliverit of thair wo,   30
The Jowis and thair errour ar confoundit:
Surrexit Dominus de sepulchro.

The fo is chasit, the battell is done ceiss,
The presone brokin, the jevellouris fleit and flemit;
The weir is gon, confermit is the peiss,   35
The fetteris lowsit and the dungeoun temit,
The ransoun maid, the presoneris redemit;
The feild is win, ourcumin is the fo,
Dispulit of the tresur that he yemit:
Surrexit Dominus de sepulchro.   40

18 **dicht:** treated   20 **gyane:** giant   **raxit:** reached, stretched   **hicht:** high   21 **Aurora:** the dawn **radius:** radiant   22 **on loft:** aloft   25 **grit:** great   27 **wox:** grew   28 **refoundit:** refounded, reestablished   33 **done ceiss:** made to cease   34 **jevellouris:** jailers   **fleit:** frightened   **flemit:** banished 35 **weir:** war   36 **temit:** emptied   39 **dispulit:** despoiled   **yemit:** kept, guarded

I That in Heill Wes and Glaidnes

I that in heill wes and glaidnes
Am trublit now with gret seiknes
And feblit with infermité;
    Timor mortis conturbat me.

Our plesance heir is all vane glory,   5
This fals warld is bot transitory,
The flesche is brukle, the Fend is sle;
    Timor mortis conturbat me.

The stait of man dois change and vary,
Now sound, now seik, now blyth, now sary,   10
Now dansand mirry, now like to dee.
    Timor mortis conturbat me.

No stait in erd heir standis sickir.
As with the wynd wavis the wickir,
Wavis this warldis vanité.   15
    Timor mortis conturbat me.

c. 1505. *The Chepman and Myllar Prints*, no. 10, c. 1508.

1 **heill wes:** health was   2 **trublit:** troubled [-it = -ed]   4 The fear of death deeply disturbs me. 5 **plesance:** pleasure   7 **brukle:** brittle, frail   **Fend is sle:** Fiend is sly   10 **sary:** sorry   11 **dansand:** dancing [-and=-ing]   13 **erd:** earth   **sickir:** sure, secure   14 **wickir:** branch

Onto the ded gois all estatis,
Princis, prelotis, and potestatis,
Baith riche and pur of all degré.
　Timor mortis conturbat me.　　　　　　　　　　20

He takis the kynchtis in to feild,
Anarmit under helme and scheild;
Victour he is at all mellé.
　Timor mortis conturbat me.

That strang unmercifull tyrand　　　　　　　　　25
Takis on the moderis breist sowkand
The bab, full of benignité.
　Timor mortis conturbat me.

He takis the campion in the stour,
The capitane closit in the tour,　　　　　　　　30
The lady in bour full of bewté;
　Timor mortis conturbat me.

He sparis no lord for his piscence,
Na clerk for his intelligence.
His awfull strak may no man fle;　　　　　　　35
　Timor mortis conturbat me.

Art magicianis and astrologgis,
Rethoris, logicianis, and theologgis,
Thame helpis no conclusionis sle.
　Timor mortis conturbat me.　　　　　　　　40

In medicyne the most practicianis,
Lechis, surrigianis, and physicianis,
Thame self fra ded may not supplé;
　Timor mortis conturbat me.

I se that makaris amang the laif　　　　　　　45
Playis heir ther pageant, syne gois to graif;
Sparit is nocht ther faculté;
　Timor mortis conturbat me.

He has done petuously devour
The noble Chaucer, of makaris flouir,　　　　　50
The Monk of Bery, and Gower, all thre;
　Timor mortis conturbat me.

The gude Syr Hew of Eglintoun,
And eik Heryot, and Wyntoun,
He hes tane out of this cuntré;　　　　　　　55
　Timor mortis conturbat me.

---

17 **ded:** death　18 **potestatis:** powers, rulers　22 **anarmit:** armed　23 **mellé:** melee　29 **campion:** champion　**stour:** conflict　33 **piscence:** puissance, power　35 **strak:** stroke　37 **art magicianis:** practitioners of the art of magic　39 **thame:** them　41 **most:** greatest　42 **lechis:** doctors　**surrigianis:** surgeons　43 **supplé:** help, save　45 **makaris:** makers, poets　**laif:** rest　46 **syne:** then　**graif:** grave　47 **faculté:** art, profession　51 **the Monk of Bery:** John Lydgate [Poets mentioned in the following stanzas need not be identified; the names are impressive for their number and sonority. Many are quite unknown.]　54 **eik:** also　55 **hes:** has (both spellings occur in the poem; words did not then have a single correct spelling)

That scorpioun fell hes done infek
Maister Johne Clerk and James Afflek
Fra balat making and trigidé;
  Timor mortis conturbat me.   60

Holland and Barbour he has berevit;
Allace, that he nought with us levit
Schir Mungo Lockert of the Le;
  Timor mortis conturbat me.

Clerk of Tranent eik he has tane,   65
That maid the anteris of Gawane;
Schir Gilbert Hay endit has he;
  Timor mortis conturbat me.

He has Blind Hary and Sandy Traill
Slaine with his schour of mortall haill,   70
Whilk Patrik Johnestoun mycht nought fle;
  Timor mortis conturbat me.

He hes reft Merseir his endite,
That did in luf so lifly write,
So schort, so quyk, of sentence hie;   75
  Timor mortis conturbat me.

He hes tane Roull of Aberdene,
And gentill Roull of Corstorphine;
Two bettir fallowis did no man se;
  Timor mortis conturbat me.   80

In Dunfermeline he has done roune
With Maister Robert Henrisoun;
Schir Johne the Ros enbrast hes he.
  Timor mortis conturbat me.

And he has now tane, last of aw,   85
Gud gentil Stobo and Quintyne Schaw,
Of wham all wichtis hes peté;
  Timor mortis conturbat me.

Gud Maister Walter Kennedy
In point of dede lyis veraly.   90
Gret reuth it were that so suld be;
  Timor mortis conturbat me.

Sen he has all my brether tane,
He will nought lat me lif alane.
On forse I man his nyxt pray be;   95
  Timor mortis conturbat me.

Sen for the deid remeid is non,
Best is that we for dede dispone.
Eftir our deid that lif may we;
  Timor mortis conturbat me.   100

57–59 **done infek . . . fra:** made . . . incapable of   59 **balat:** poem, song   **trigidé:** tragic narrative
62 **allace:** alas   66 **anteris:** adventures   71 **whilk:** which   73 **endite:** writing   74 **luf so lifly:** love
so lively   75 **sentence hie:** high sentiment   81 **done roune:** talked with   85 **aw:** all   87 **wichtis:**
people   91 **reuth:** pity   **suld:** should   93 **sen:** since   95 **on forse:** necessarily   **man:** must   97 **re-
meid:** remedy   98 **dispone:** prepare

John Skelton
(1460–1529)

Skelton, honored as "laureate" by both universities and ordained a priest when nearly 40, was tutor to the future King Henry VIII and—after a few years as high-spirited country pastor—recalled to court as the king's royal orator. Much of his writing was a bold attack on corruption in church and state.

Upon a Dead Man's Head

Skelton Laureate, upon a dead man's head that was sent to him from an honorable gentlewoman for a token, devised this ghostly meditation in English, convenable in sentence, commendable, lamentable, lachrymable, profitable for the soul.

> Your ugly token
> My mind hath broken
> From worldly lust.
> For I have discusst
> We are but dust,   5
> And die we must.
>   It is general
> To be mortal.
> I have well espied
> No man may him hide   10
> From death hollow-eyed,
> With sinews widerèd,
> With bonès shiderèd,
> With his worm-eaten maw,
> And his ghastly jaw   15
> Gasping aside,
> Naked of hide,
> Neither flesh nor fell.
>   Then by my counsel
> Look that ye spell   20
> Well this gospel.
> For wherso we dwell,
> Death will us quell,
> And with us mell.
>   For all our pampered paunches   25
> There may no fraunchis,
> Nor worldly bliss
> Redeem us from this;
> Our days be dated
> To be checkmated   30
> With draughtès of death,
> Stopping our breath,
> Our eyen sinking,
> Our bodies stinking,
> Our gummès grinning,   35
> Our soulès brinning.
> To whom then shall we sue

c. 1495. *Skelton Laureate agaynste a comely coystrowne that curyowsly chawntyd and curryshly cowntred* ..., c. 1500.

convenable in sentence: befitting in meaning   **12 widerèd:** withered   **13 shiderèd:** shattered   **18 fell:** skin, pelt   **20 spell:** read carefully letter by letter   **23 quell:** kill   **24 mell:** meddle, mingle   **26 fraunchis:** franchise, special privilege   **31 draughtes:** move in chess   **36 brinning:** burning

For to have rescue
But to sweet Jesu,
On us then for to rue?   40
  O goodly child
Of Mary mild,
Then be our shield
That we be not exíled
To the dun dale   45
Of bootless bale,
Nor to the lake
Of fiendès black.
But grant us grace
To see Thy face,   50
And to purcháse
Thine heavenly place,
And thy palace
Full of solace,
Above the sky   55
That is so high.
Eternally
To behold and see
The Trinity.

    Amen.   60

Mirez–vous–y.

46 **bootless bale:** helpless sorrow   61 Look at yourself there (in the skull).

My Darling Dear, My Daisy Flower

     With lullay, lullay, *like a child,*
     Thou sleepest too long, thou art beguiled.

"My darling dear, my daisy flower,
Let me," quod he, "lie in your lap."
"Lie still," quod she, "my paramour.
Lie still hardèly, and take a nap."   5
His head was heavy, such was his hap,
All drowsy dreaming, drowned in sleep,
That of his love he took no keep.

     With Hey lullay, *etc.*   10

With *ba! ba! ba!* and *bas! bas! bas!*
She cherished him both cheek and chin,
That he wist never where he was.
He had forgotten all deadly sin.
He wanted wit her love to win: 15
He trusted her payment and lost all his prey.
She left him sleeping and stole away.

     With Hey lullay, *etc.*

c. 1500. *Dyvers Ballettys and dyties solacyous* . . . , c. 1500.

6 **hardely:** boldly   7 **hap:** luck, fortune   9 **took no keep:** paid no attention   13 **wist:** knew

The rivers rough, the waters wan,
She sparèd not to wet her feet;   20
She waded over; she found a man
That halsed her heartily and kissed her sweet.
Thus after her cold she caught a heat.
"My love," she said, "routeth in his bed;
Ywis he hath an heavy head."   25

> *With* Hey lullay, *etc.*

What, dreamest thou, drunkard, drowsy pate?
Thy lust and liking is from thee gone.
Thou blinkard blowbowl, thou wakest too late.
Behold thou liest, luggard, alone.   30
Well may thou sigh, well may thou groan
To deal with her so cowardly.
Ywis, pole-hatchet, she bleared thine eye!

> *With* Hey lullay, *etc.*

19 **wan:** dark, gloomy   22 **halsed:** embraced   24 **routeth:** snores   25 **ywis:** certainly   29 **blinkard:** bleary-eyed, blinking   **blowbowl:** sot   30 **luggard:** sluggard   33 **pole-hatchet:** blockhead   **bleared thine eye:** pulled the wool over your eyes, hoodwinked you

Anonymous Ballads

The early ballads are notoriously hard to date. They may have been in circulation for centuries before seeing any kind of publication. Since we know that by the late sixteenth century a large body of ballads had been in existence for generations, it seems not unreasonable to place our ballads here, even though many of them—no doubt altered by modernization, by local speech habits, or even by deliberate antiquing—surfaced only in later centuries.

Sir Patrick Spens

The king sits in Dumferling toune,
    Drinking the blude-reid wine:
"O whar will I get guid sailor,
    To sail this schip of mine?"

Up and spak an eldern knicht,   5
    Sat at the kings richt kne:
"Sir Patrick Spens is the best sailor,
    That sails upon the se."

The king has written a braid letter,
    And signd it wi' his hand;   10
And sent it to Sir Patrick Spens,
    Was walking on the sand.

The first line that Sir Patrick red,
    A loud lauch lauchèd he:
The next line that Sir Patrick red,   15
    The teir blinded his ee.

T. Percy, op. cit., I.

1 **Dumferling:** Dunfermline, a town above the north shore of the Firth of Forth in Scotland
9 **braid:** broad, long, important-looking   14 **lauch:** laugh   16 **ee:** eye

"O wha is this has don this deid,
   This ill deid don to me;
To send me out this time o' the yeir,
   To sail upon the se?   20

"Mak haste, mak haste, my mirry men all,
   Our guid schip sails the morne."
"O say na sae, my master deir,
   For I feir a deadlie storme.

"Late, late yestreen I saw the new moone   25
   Wi' the auld moone in hir arme;
And I feir, I feir, my deir master,
   That we will cum to harme."

O our Scots nobles wer richt laith
   To weet their cork-heild shoone;   30
Bot lang owre a' the play wer playd,
   Thair hats they swam aboone.

O lang, lang, may thair ladies sit
   Wi' thair fans into their hand,
Or eir they se Sir Patrick Spens   35
   Cum sailing to the land.

O lang, lang, may the ladies stand,
   Wi' thair gold kems in their hair,
Waiting for thair ain deir lords,
   For they'll se thame na mair.   40

Haf owre, haf owre to Aberdour,
   It's fiftie fadom deip,
And thair lies guid Sir Patrick Spens,
   Wi' the Scots lords at his feit.

17 **wha:** who   23 **na sae:** not so   25 **yestreen:** yesterday evening   26 **auld:** old   29 **richt laith:** right loath   30 **weet...shoone:** wet...shoes   31 **bot lang owre a':** but long before all   32 **swam aboone:** floated above   35 **or eir:** before ever   38 **kems:** combs   40 **na mair:** no more   41 **haf owre:** half way over   **Aberdour:** a town on the Firth about ten miles east of Dunfermline

The Twa Corbies

As I was walking all alane,
I heard twa corbies making a mane;
The tane unto the t'other say,
"Where sall we gang and dine to-day?"

"In behint yon auld fail dyke,   5
I wot there lies a new slain knight;
And nae body kens that he lies there,
But his hawk, his hound, and lady fair.

Scott, op. cit., III, 1803 (as "second edition").

twa corbies: two crows   1 **alane:** alone   2 **mane:** moan   3 **the tane:** the one   4 **sall we gang:** shall we go   5 **auld fail dyke:** old turf wall   6 **wot:** know   7 **nae body kens:** nobody knows

"His hound is to the hunting gane,
His hawk to fetch the wild-fowl hame,
His lady's ta'en another mate,
So we may mak our dinner sweet.

"Ye'll sit on his white hausebane,
And I'll pike out his bonny blue een:
Wi' ae lock o his gowden hair
We'll theek our nest when it grows bare.

"Mony a one for him makes mane,
But nane sall ken where he is gane:
O'er his white banes, when they are bare,
The wind sall blaw for evermair."

9 **gane:** gone 10 **hame:** home 13 **hausebane:** neck bone 14 **een:** eyes 15 **ae:** one **gowden:**
golden 16 **theek:** thatch 17 **mony:** many

Thomas Rymer

True Thomas lay on Huntlie bank;
   A ferlie he spièd wi' his e'e;
And there he saw a ladye bright,
   Come riding down by the Eildon Tree.

Her shirt was o' the grass-green silk,
   Her mantle o' the velvet fyne;
At ilka tett of her horse's mane,
   Hang fifty silver bells and nine.

True Thomas, he pull'd aff his cap,
   And louted low down to his knee,
"All hail, thou mighty queen of heav'n!
   For thy peer on earth I never did see."

"O no, O no, Thomas," she said,
   "That name does not belang to me;
I am but the queen of fair Elfland,
   That am hither come to visit thee.

"Harp and carp, Thomas," she said,
   "That name does not belang to me;
I am but the queen of fair Elfland,
   That am hither come to visit thee.

"Harp and carp, Thomas," she said;
   "Harp and carp along wi' me;
And if ye dare to kiss my lips,
   Sure of your bodie I will be."

Ibid., II.

1 **Huntlie:** a small river in southern Scotland. The Eildon Hills (line 4) are in the vicinity. 2 **ferlie:**
marvel **e'e:** eye 7 **ilka tett:** each tuft 10 **louted:** bowed 17 **carp:** sing, recite (to the harp)

"Betide me weal, betide me woe,   25
    That weird shall never daunton me."
Syne he has kissed her rosy lips,
    All underneath the Eildon Tree.

"Now, ye maun go wi' me," she said;
    "True Thomas, ye maun go wi' me;   30
And ye maun serve me seven years,
    Thro' weal or woe as may chance to be."

She mounted on her milk-white steed;
    She's taen True Thomas up behind;
And aye, whene'er her bridle rung,   35
    The steed flew swifter than the wind.

O they rade on, and farther on;
    The steed gaed swifter than the wind;
Until they reached a desart wide,
    And living land was left behind.   40

"Light down, light down, now, True Thomas,
    And lean your head upon my knee:
Abide and rest a little space,
    And I will shew you ferlies three.

"O see ye not yon narrow road,   45
    So thick beset with thorns and briers?
That is the path of righteousness,
    Though after it but few enquires.

"And see not ye that braid braid road,
    That lies across that lily leven?   50
That is the path of wickedness,
    Though some call it the road to heaven.

"And see not ye that bonny road,
    That winds about the fernie brae?
That is the road to fair Elfland,   55
    Where thou and I this night maun gae.

"But, Thomas, ye maun hold your tongue,
    Whatever ye may hear or see,
For, if you speak word in Elflyn land,
    Ye'll ne'er get back to your ain countrie."   60

O they rade on, and farther on,
    And they waded thro rivers aboon the knee,
And they saw neither sun nor moon,
    But they heard the roaring of the sea.

It was mirk mirk night, and there was nae stern light,   65
    And they waded through red blude to the knee;

26 **weird:** fate **daunton:** daunt 27 **syne:** then 29 **maun:** must 35 **aye:** always 38 **gaed:**
went 49 **braid:** broad 50 **lily leven:** lovely lea (?) 54 **brae:** hillside 56 **maun gae:** must go
60 **ain:** own 62 **aboon:** above 65 **mirk:** dark **nae stern:** no star

For a' the blude, that's shed on earth,
    Rins through the springs o' that countrie.

Syne they came on to a garden green,
    And she pu'd an apple frae a tree—   70
"Take this for thy wages, True Thomas,
    It will give thee the tongue that can never lie."

"My tongue is mine ain," True Thomas said;
    "A gudely gift ye wad gie to me!
I neither dought to buy nor sell,   75
    At fair or tryst where I may be.

"I dought neither speak to prince or peer,
    Nor ask of grace from fair ladye."
"Now hold thy peace!" the lady said,
    "For as I say, so must it be."   80

He has gotten a coat of the even cloth,
    And a pair of shoes of velvet green;
And, till seven years were gane and past,
    True Thomas on earth was never seen.

70 **pu'd:** pulled **frae:** from 74 **wad gie:** would give 75 **dought:** would dare 76 **tryst:** meeting, market 81 **even:** smooth

Lord Randal

"O where hae ye been, Lord Randal, my son?
O where hae ye been, my handsome young man?"
"I hae been to the wild wood; mother, make my bed soon,
For I'm weary wi' hunting, and fain wald lie down."

"Where gat ye your dinner, Lord Randal, my son?   5
Where gat ye your dinner, my handsome young man?"
"I din'd wi' my true-love; mother, make my bed soon,
For I'm weary wi' hunting, and fain wald lie down."

"What gat ye to your dinner, Lord Randal, my son?
What gat ye to your dinner, my handsome young man?"   10
"I gat eels boil'd in broo; mother, make my bed soon,
For I'm weary wi' hunting, and fain wald lie down."

"What became of your bloodhounds, Lord Randal, my son?
What became of your bloodhounds, my handsome young man?"
"O they swell'd and they died; mother, make my bed soon,   15
For I'm weary wi' hunting, and fain wald lie down."

"O I fear ye are poison'd, Lord Randal, my son!
I fear ye are poison'd, my handsome young man!"
"O yes! I am poison'd; mother, make my bed soon,
For I'm sick at the heart, and I fain wald lie down."   20

Ibid., III.

1 **hae:** have 4 **fain wald:** would like to 5 **gat:** got 11 **broo:** broth, juice

Edward, Edward

"Why dois your brand sae drap wi' bluid,
          Edward, Edward?
Why dois your brand sae drap wi' bluid,
    And why sae sad gang yee, O?"
"O, I hae killed my hauke sae guid,   5
          Mither, mither:
O, I hae killed my hauke sae guid,
    And I had nae mair bot hee, O."

"Your haukis bluid was nevir sae reid;
          Edward, Edward.   10
Your haukis bluid was nevir sae reid,
    My deir son I tell thee, O."
"O, I hae killed my reid-roan steid,
          Mither, mither:
O, I hae killed my reid-roan steid,   15
    That erst was sae fair and frie, O."

"Your steid was auld, and ye hae gat mair,
          Edward, Edward:
Your steid was auld, and ye hae gat mair,
    Sum other dule ye drie, O."   20
"O, I hae killed my fadir deir,
          Mither, mither:
O, I hae killed my fadir deir,
    Alas, and wae is mee, O."

"And whatten penance wul ye drie for that,   25
          Edward, Edward?
And whatten penance wul ye drie for that,
    My deir son, now tell me, O."
"Ile set my feit in yonder boat,
          Mither, mither: 30
Ile set my feit in yonder boat,
    And Ile fare ovir the sea, O."

"And what wul ye doe wi' your towirs and your ha',
          Edward, Edward?
And what wul ye doe wi' your towirs and your ha',   35
    That were sae fair to see, O?"
"Ile let thame stand til they doun fa',
          Mither, mither:
I'le let thame stand til they doun fa',
    For here nevir mair maun I bee, O."   40

"And what wul ye leive to your bairns and your wife,
          Edward, Edward?
And what wul ye leive to your bairns and your wife,
    Whan ye gang ovir the sea, O?"

Percy, op. cit., I.

1 Why does your sword so drip with blood?   4 **gang yee:** do you go   7 **hae:** have   **guid:** good
8 **nae mair bot:** no more but   9 **reid:** red   16 **erst:** before   17 **auld:** old   **mair:** more   20 **dule ye
drie:** sorrow you suffer   24 **wae:** woe   25 **wul ye drie:** will you suffer   33 **ha':** hall   37 **fa':** fall
40 **maun:** must   41 **bairns:** children

"The warldis room, late tham beg thrae life,
      Mither, mither:
The warldis room, late tham beg thrae life,
    For thame nevir mair wul I see, O."   45

"And what wul ye leive to your ain mither deir,
      Edward, Edward?   50
And what wul ye leive to your ain mither deir?
    My deir son, now tell me, O."
"The curse of hell frae me sall ye beir,
      Mither, mither:
The curse of hell frae me sall ye beir,   55
    Sic conseils ye gave to me, O."

45 warldis: world's **late tham beg thrae:** let them beg through **49 ain:** own **53 frae:** from **sall ye beir:** shall you bear **56 sic:** such

Waly, Waly

O waly, waly up the bank,
    And waly, waly, down the brae,
And waly, by yon river side
    Where I and my love wont to gae!

O waly, waly, but love be bonny,   5
    A little while when it is new,
But when it is auld, it waxeth cauld,
    And fades away like morning dew.

I leant my back unto an aik,
    I thought it was a trusty tree;   10
But first it bow'd, and syne it brak,
    ·And sae did my fause love to me.

When cockle-shells turn siller bells,
    And mussles grow on ev'ry tree,
When frost and snaw shall warm us a'   15
    Then shall my love prove true to me.

Now Arthur's-seat shall be my bed,
    The sheets shall ne'er be fyl'd by me;
Saint Anton's well shall be my drink,
    Since my truelove's forsaken me.   20

O Mart'mas wind, when wilt thou blow,
    And shake the green leaves off the tree?
O gentle death, when wilt thou come
    And tak a life that wearies me?

'Tis not the frost that freezes fell,   25
    Nor blawing snaw's inclemency;

A. Ramsay, *The Tea-Table Miscellany,* II, 1729.

waly: exclamation of grief **2 brae:** hillside **4 wont to gae:** used to go **7 auld...cauld:** old ...cold **9 aik:** oak **11 syne:** then **12 sae:** so **fause:** false **13 siller:** silver **15 snaw:** snow **a':** all **17 Arthur's-seat:** hill in Edinburgh **19 Saint Anton's well:** a well beneath Arthur's-seat **21 Mart'mas:** November (Martinmas is November 11) **25 fell:** skin **26 blawing snaw:** blowing snow

'Tis not sic cauld that makes me cry,
    But my love's heart grown cauld to me.

When we came in by Glasgow town,
    We were a comely sight to see;   30
My love was cled in velvet black,
    And I mysel in cramasie.

But had I wist before I kiss'd,
    That love had been sae ill to win,
I'd lock'd my heart in a case of gold,   35
    And pinn'd it with a silver pin.

Oh, oh, if my young babe were born,
    And set upon the nurse's knee,
And I mysel were dead and gane!
    For a maid again I'll never be.   40

27 **sic cauld:** such cold   31 **cled:** clad   32 **cramasie:** crimson   33 **wist:** known   39 **gane:** gone

The Gypsy Laddie

The gypsies came to our good lord's gate,
    And wow but they sang sweetly!
They sang sae sweet and sae very compleat
    That down came the fair lady.

And she came tripping down the stair,
    And a' her maids before her;   5
As soon as they saw her well-far'd face,
    They coost the glamer o'er her.

"Gae tak frae me this gay mantile,
    And bring to me a plaidie;   10
For if kith and kin and a' had sworn,
    I'll follow the gypsie laddie.

"Yestreen I lay in a well-made bed,
    And my good lord beside me;
This night I'll ly in a tenant's barn,   15
    Whatever shall betide me."

"Come to your bed," says Johnny Faa,
    "Oh come to your bed, my deary;
For I vow and I swear, by the hilt of my sword,
    That your lord shall nae mair come near ye."   20

"I'll go to bed to my Johnny Faa,
    I'll go to bed to my deary;
For I vow and I swear, by what past yestreen,
    That my lord shall nae mair come near me.

Ibid., IV, 1740.

3 **sae . . . compleat:** so . . . perfectly   6 **a':** all   7 **well-far'd:** well-favored, pretty   8 **coost the glamer:** cast a spell   9 **gae tak frae:** go take from   10 **plaidie:** ordinary plaid garment   13 **yestreen:** yesterday evening   17 **Johnny Faa:** a well-known gypsy name   20 **nae mair:** no more

"I'll mak a hap to my Johnny Faa,   25
 And I'll mak a hap to my deary;
And he's get a' the coat gaes round,
 And my lord shall nae mair come near me."

And when our lord came hame at een,
 And speir'd for his fair lady,   30
The tane she cry'd, and the other reply'd,
 "She's away with the gypsie laddie."

"Gae saddle to me the black, black steed,
 Gae saddle and make him ready;
Before that I either eat or sleep,   35
 I'll gae seek my fair lady."

And we were fifteen well-made men,
 Altho' we were nae bonny;
And we were a' put down for ane,
 A fair young wanton lady.   40

25 **hap:** covering (quilt, coat, etc.)   29 **hame at een:** home at evening   30 **speir'd:** asked   31 **the tane:** the one   38 **bonny:** handsome   39 **ane:** one

The Demon Lover

"O where have you been, my long, long love,
 This long seven years and more?"
"O I'm come to seek my former vows
 Ye granted me before."

"O hold your tongue of your former vows, 5
 For they will breed sad strife;
O hold your tongue of your former vows
 For I am become a wife."

He turn'd him right and round about,
 And the tear blinded his ee;   10
"I wad never hae trodden on Irish ground,
 If it had not been for thee.

"I might have had a king's daughter,
 Far, far beyond the sea;
I might have had a king's daughter,   15
 Had it not been for love o' thee."

"If ye might have had a king's daughter,
 Yersell ye had to blame;
Ye might have taken the king's daughter,
 For ye kend that I was nane.   20

"If I was to leave my husband dear,
 And my two babes also,
O what have you to take me to,
 If with you I should go?"

Scott, op. cit., II, 1812.

10 **ee:** eye   11 **wad...hae:** would...have   20 **kend:** knew   **nane:** none

"I hae seven ships upon the sea,   25
    The eighth brought me to land;
With four-and-twenty bold mariners,
    And music on every hand."

She has taken up her two little babes,
    Kiss'd them baith cheek and chin;   30
"O fair ye weel, my ain two babes,
    For I'll never see you again."

She set her foot upon the ship,
    No mariners could she behold;
But the sails were o' the taffetie,   35
    And the masts o' the beaten gold.

She had not sail'd a league, a league,
    A league but barely three,
When dismal grew his countenance,
    And drumlie grew his ee.   40

They had not sailed a league, a league,
    A league but barely three,
Until she espied his cloven foot,
    And she wept right bitterlie.

"O hold your tongue of your weeping," says he,   45
    "Of your weeping now let me be;
I will show you how the lilies grow
    On the banks of Italy."

"O what hills are yon, yon pleasant hills,
    That the sun shines sweetly on?"   50
"O yon are the hills of heaven," he said,
    "Where you will never win."

"O whaten a mountain is yon," she said,
    "All so dreary wi' frost and snow?"
"O yon is the mountain of hell," he cried,   55
    "Where you and I will go."

He struck the tapmast wi' his hand,
    The foremast wi' his knee;
And he brak that gallant ship in twain,
    And sank her in the sea.   60

30 **baith:** both   31 **weel:** well   **ain:** own   40 **drumlie:** gloomy   57 **tapmast:** topmast

The Unquiet Grave

"The wind doth blow today, my love,
    And a few small drops of rain;
I never had but one true love,
    In cold grave she was lain.

"I'll do as much for my true love   5
    As any young man may;

Charlotte Latham, "Some West Sussex Superstitions Lingering in 1868," *The Folk Lore Record*, I, 1878.

I'll sit and mourn all at her grave
    For a twelvemonth, and a day."

The twelvemonth and a day being up,
    The dead began to speak,   10
"Oh who sits weeping on my grave,
    And will not let me sleep?"

" 'Tis I, my love, sits on your grave
    And will not let you sleep,
For I crave one kiss of your clay-cold lips   15
    And that is all I seek."

"You crave one kiss of clay-cold lips,
    But my breath smells earthy strong;
If you have one kiss of my clay-cold lips
    You time will not be long: 20

" 'Tis down in yonder garden green,
    Love, where we used to walk,
The finest flower that ere was seen
    Is withered to a stalk.

"The stalk is withered dry, my love,   25
    So will our hearts decay;
So make yourself content, my love,
    Till God calls you away."

Sir Thomas Wyatt
(1503–1542)

A distinguished courtier and diplomat under Henry VIII, Wyatt was sent on missions to France and Italy and named ambassador to Spain. Twice threatened with execution, he put up a witty defense against false charges of treason and was restored to the royal favor.

Forget Not Yet

Forget not yet the tried intent
Of such a truth as I have meant;
My great travail so gladly spent
        Forget not yet.

Forget not yet when first began   5
The weary life ye know, since whan
The suit, the service, none tell can,
        Forget not yet.

Forget not yet the great assays,
The cruel wrongs, the scornful ways,   10
The painful patience in denays
        Forget not yet.

Devonshire MS. In G. F. Nott, *The Works of . . . Sir Thomas Wyatt . . .* , 1816, and K. Muir and P. Thomson, *The Collected Works . . .* , 1969.

9 assays: trials, efforts   **11 denays:** denials

Forget not yet, forget not this,
How long ago hath been, and is,
The mind that never means amiss;
        Forget not yet.   15

Forget not then thine own approved,
The which so long hath thee so loved,
Whose steadfast faith yet never moved,
        Forget not this.   20

Whoso List to Hunt

sonnet

Whoso list to hunt, I know where is an hind,
But as for me, alas, I may no more.
The vain travail hath wearied me so sore,
I am of them, that furthest come behind.
Yet may I by no means my wearied mind   5
Draw from the deer: but as she fleeth afore,
Fainting I follow. I leave off therefore,
Since in a net I seek to hold the wind.   *nice line – metaphor*
Who list her hunt, I put him out of doubt,
As well as I may spend his time in vain;   10
And, graven with diamonds, in letters plain
There is written, her fair neck round about:
"Noli me tangere, for Caesar's I am,
And wild for to hold, though I seem tame."

---

c. 1527. Egerton MS. In Nott, op. cit., and Muir and Thomson, op. cit.

For the *sonnet* form, see the prosody section. The poem is thought to refer to an interest Wyatt had in Anne Boleyn before the king fell in love with her.

1 **whoso list:** whoever wants   **hind:** female deer   13 **Noli me tangere:** Touch me not (John 20:17)
Caesar: for Wyatt, probably Henry VIII

They Flee from Me

They flee from me that sometime did me seek,
With naked foot stalking in my chamber.
I have seen them gentle, tame, and meek
That now are wild and do not remember
That sometime they put themself in danger   5
To take bread at my hand, and now they range
Busily seeking with a continual change.

Thankèd be fortune, it hath been otherwise
Twenty times better, but once in special:
In thin array, after a pleasant guise,   10
When her loose gown from her shoulders did fall
And she me caught in her arms long and small;
Therewith all sweetly did me kiss,
And softly said, "Dear heart, how like you this?"

It was no dream; I lay broad waking.   15
But all is turnèd through my gentleness

1533–1536. Richard Tottel, *Songs and Sonnets* ("Tottel's Miscellany"), 1557, as "The Lover Showeth How He Is Forsaken of Such as He Sometime Enjoyed."

2 **stalking:** walking softly, stealthily   5 **danger:** subjection, [my] power—but also the modern meaning   10 **guise:** (1) manner, way; (2) a masked entertainment   12 **small:** slender

Into a strange fashion of forsaking;
And I have leave to go, of her goodness,
And she also to use newfangleness.
But since that I so kindèly am servèd,   20
I would fain know what she hath deservèd.

19 **newfangleness:** inconstancy, love of novelty   20 **kindely:** according to [her and my] nature, but also—with irony—the modern meaning

My Galley Chargèd with Forgetfulness

My galley chargèd with forgetfulness
Through sharp seas in winter nights doth pass
'Twene rock and rock; and eke mine enemy, alas,
That is my lord, steereth with cruelness.
And every oar a thought in readiness   5
As though that death were light in such a case;
An endless wind doth tear the sail apace
Of forcèd sighs and trusty fearfulness.
A rain of tears, a cloud of dark disdain
Hath done the wearied cords great hinderance,   10
Wreathèd with error and eke with ignorance.
The stars be hid that led me to this pain,
Drownèd is reason that should me comfort,
And I remain despairing of the port.

1528–1532. Ibid., as "The Lover Compareth His State to a Ship in Perilous Storm Tossed on the Sea."

1 **chargèd:** cargoed

My Lute, Awake

My lute, awake! perform the last
Labor that thou and I shall waste
And end that I have now begun,
For when this song is sung and past,
My lute, be still, for I have done.   5

As to be heard where ear is none,
As lead to grave in marble stone,
My song may pierce her heart as soon.
Should we then sigh or sing or moan?
No, no, my lute, for I have done.   10

The rocks do not so cruelly
Repulse the waves continually
As she my suit and affection,
So that I am past remedy,
Whereby my lute and I have done.   15

Proud of the spoil that thou hast got
Of simple hearts through love's shot,
By whom, unkind, thou hast them won,
Think not he hath his bow forgot,
Although my lute and I have done.   20

1533–1536. Ibid., as "The Lover Complaineth the Unkindness of His Love" [*sic*].

3 **that:** that which   7 **grave:** engrave

Vengeance shall fall on thy disdain
That makest but game on earnest pain;
Think not alone under the sun
Unquit to cause thy lovers plain
Although my lute and I have done.   25

Perchance thee lie withered and old
The winter nights that are so cold,
Plaining in vain unto the moon;
Thy wishes then dare not be told.
Care then who list, for I have done.   30

And then may chance thee to repent
The time that thou hast lost and spent
To cause thy lovers sigh and swoon;
Then shalt thou know beauty but lent,
And wish and want as I have done.   35

Now cease, my lute; this is the last
Labor that thou and I shall waste
And ended is that we begun.
Now is this song both sung and past;
My lute, be still, for I have done.   40

22 **makest but game on:** only make fun of   24 **unquit:** unpunished   **plain:** complaint, lament
30 **who list:** whoever wants to

Henry Howard, Earl of Surrey
(1517–1547)

High-spirited and dissatisfied, devoted to knightly adventures then out of fashion, and with a claim to the throne of England itself, Surrey did little to endear himself to those in power at Henry's court. Rashly attempting an escape after being arrested for treason and conspiracy, he was beheaded at the age of 29.

Set Me Whereas the Sun Doth Parch the Green

Set me whereas the sun doth parch the green,
Or where his beams do not dissolve the ice;
In temperate heat where he is felt and seen;
With proud people, in presence sad and wise.
Set me in high, or yet in low degree;   5
In the long night, or in the shortest day;
In clearest sky, or where clouds thickest be;
In lusty youth, or when my hairs are gray.
Set me in heaven, in earth, or else in hell,
In hill, or dale, or in the foaming flood;   10
Thrall or at large, alive whereso I dwell;
Sick or in health, in evil fame or good—
Hers will I be, and only with this thought
Comfort myself, although my chance be nought.

Ibid., as "Vow to Love Faithfully Howsoever He Be Rewarded."

So Cruel Prison

So cruel prison how could betide, alas,
As proud Windsor? where I in lust and joy
With a king's son my childish years did pass
In greater feasts than Priam's sons of Troy;

Where each sweet place returns a taste full sour: 5
The large green courts, where we were wont to hove
With eyes cast up unto the maidens' tower,
And easy sighs, such as folk draw in love;

The stately sales, the ladies bright of hew,
The dances short, long tales of great delight,   10
With words and looks that tigers could but rue
Where each of us did plead the other's right;

The palm play where, despoilèd for the game,
With dazèd eyes oft we by gleams of love
Have missed the ball, and got sight of our dame,   15
To bait her eyes, which kept the leads above;

The gravelled ground, with sleeves tied on the helm,
On foaming horse, with swords and friendly hearts,
With cheer as though one should another whelm,
Where we have fought, and chasèd oft with darts;   20

With silver drops the mead yet spread for ruth,
In active games of nimbleness and strength,
Where we did strain, trailèd by swarms of youth,
Our tender limbs that yet shot up in length;

The secret groves, which oft we made resound   25
Of pleasant plaint and of our ladies' praise,
Recording oft what grace each one had found,
What hope of speed, what dread of long delays;

The wild forest, the clothèd holts with green,
With reins avaled, and swift ybreathèd horse,   30
With cry of hounds and merry blasts between
Where we did chase the fearful hart of force;

The void walls eke, that harbored us each night,
Wherewith, alas, reviveth in my breast

1537. Ibid., as "Prisoned in Windsor, He Recounteth His Pleasure There Passed."

In 1537 Surrey was confined in Windsor Castle (the royal residence on the south bank of the Thames west of London) for striking a courtier. Probably, recalling the happy years he had spent there as a boy, he wrote the poem then.

1 **betide:** happen   2 **lust:** pleasure   3 **king's son:** Henry Fitzroy, Duke of Richmond, illegitimate son of Henry VIII   4 **Priam:** King of Troy during the Trojan War, Priam had fifty sons—enough for large parties.   6 **hove:** hover, linger   9 **sales:** salons, halls   13 **palm play:** a game like handball   **despoilèd:** with outer clothes removed   16 **bait:** attract   **leads:** leaded roof or gallery   17 **sleeves:** love tokens given by their ladies   21 **ruth:** pity   26 **plaint:** complaint, lament   28 **speed:** success   29 **holts:** woods, wooded hills   30 **avaled:** slackened   32 **of force:** in the open, with hounds in full cry   33 **void:** empty, deserted   **eke:** also

The sweet accord, such sleeps as yet delight,   35
The pleasant dreams, the quiet bed of rest;

The secret thoughts imparted with such trust,
The wanton talk, the diverse change of play,
The friendship sworn, each promise kept so just,
Wherewith we passed the winter nights away.   40

And, with this thought, the blood forsakes my face,
The tears berain my cheeks of deadly hue,
The which as soon as sobbing sighs, alas,
Upsupped have, thus I my plaint renew:

"O place of bliss, renewer of my woes,   45
Give me accompt, where is my noble fere,
Whom in thy walls thou didst each night enclose,
To other lief, but unto me most dear?"

Echo, alas, that doth my sorrow rue,
Returns thereto a hollow sound of plaint.   50
Thus I alone, where all my freedom grew,
In prison pine with bondage and restraint,

And with remembrance of the greater grief
To banish the less, I find my chief relief.

42 berain: wet, rain down   **44 upsupped:** drunk up   **46 accompt:** account **fere:** companion
48 lief: dear

George Gascoigne
(c. 1539–1577)

Gascoigne (from the evidence of his meters, the name was pronounced *gáscon*) was a law student and Member of Parliament, often involved in litigation, once imprisoned for debt. A soldier for two years in the Netherlands, he was captured and released; thereafter he resumed his busy life as man of letters.

The Lullaby of a Lover

Sing lullaby, as women do,
    Wherewith they bring their babes to rest;
And lullaby can I sing too,
    As womanly as can the best.
With lullaby they still the child;   5
And, if I be not much beguiled,
Full many wanton babes have I
Which must be stilled with lullaby.

First lullaby my youthful years;
    It is now time to go to bed,   10
For crooked age and hoary hairs
    Have won the haven within my head.
With lullaby then, youth, be still,
With lullaby content thy will;

A Hundreth Sundry Flowers, 1573.

Since courage quails and comes behind,   15
Go sleep, and so beguile thy mind.

Next lullaby my gazing eyes
    Which wonted were to glance apace;
For every glass may now suffice
    To show the furrows in my face.   20
With lullaby then, wink awhile,
With lullaby your looks beguile;
Let no fair face nor beauty bright
Entice you eft with vain delight.

And lullaby my wanton will;   25
    Let reason's rule now reign thy thought,
Since all too late I find by skill
    How dear I have thy fancies bought.
With lullaby now take thine ease,
With lullaby thy doubts appease;   30
For trust to this, if thou be still,
My body shall obey thy will.

Eke lullaby my loving boy;
    My little Robin, take thy rest
Since age is cold and nothing coy,   35
    Keep close thy coin, for so is best.
With lullaby be thou content,
With lullaby thy lusts relent;
Let others pay which have mo pence;
Thou art too poor for such expense.   40

Thus, lullaby my youth, mine eyes,
    My will, my ware, and all that was:
I can no mo delays devise;
    But welcome pain, let pleasure pass.
With lullaby now take your leave,   45
With lullaby your dreams deceive;
And when you rise with waking eye,
Remember then this lullaby.

24 **eft:** again, after   33 **eke:** also   35 **coy:** amorous   39 **mo:** more

And if I Did, What Then?

"And if I did, what then?
Are you aggrieved therefore?
The sea hath fish for every man,
And what would you have more?"

Thus did my mistress once   5
Amaze my mind with doubt;
And popped a question for the nonce
To beat my brains about.

Ibid.

For the form, see *Short Meter* in the prosody section.

Whereto I thus replied:
"Each fisherman can wish   10
That all the seas at every tide
Were his alone to fish;

"And so did I, in vain;
But since it may not be,
Let such fish there as find the gain,   15
And leave the loss for me.

"And with such luck and loss
I will content myself,
Till tides of turning time may toss
Such fishers on the shelf.   20

"And when they stick on sands,
That every man may see,
Then will I laugh and clap my hands,
As they do now at me."

Sir Edward Dyer
(1543–1607)

Dyer, a typical Renaissance man, was (off and on) a favorite of Queen Elizabeth, a court-
ier and diplomat, a backer of naval expeditions and explorations, one of the leading ama-
teur alchemists of his time, and a poet and patron of poets.

The Lowest Trees Have Tops

The lowest trees have tops, the ant her gall,
The fly her spleen, the little sparks their heat;
The slender hairs cast shadows, though but small,
And bees have stings, although they be not great.
    Seas have their source, and so have shallow springs;   5
    And love is love, in beggars as in kings.

Where rivers smoothest run, deep are the fords;
The dial stirs, yet none perceives it move;
The firmest faith is in the fewest words;
The turtles cannot sing, and yet they love.   10
    True hearts have eyes and ears, no tongues to speak:
    They hear and see and sigh, and then they break.

By 1599. *A Poetical Rhapsody*, 1602.

8 **dial:** sundial   10 **turtles:** turtledoves

Edmund Spenser
(1552?–1599)

A member of the literary circle around Sir Philip Sidney and author of *The Faerie Queene*,
Spenser spent most of his adult life in government service in Ireland, first as secretary to
the lord deputy, later as justice and sheriff. He died in London the year after his Irish cas-
tle was attacked and looted by insurgents.

From **Amoretti**

LXVIII

Most glorious Lord of life, that on this day
    Didst make thy triumph over death and sin,
    And having harrowed hell didst bring away
    Captivity thence captive, us to win:
This joyous day, dear Lord, with joy begin,   5
    And grant that we for whom thou didest die,
    Being with thy dear blood clean washed from sin,
    May live for ever in felicity,
And that thy love we weighing worthily,
    May likewise love thee for the same again;   10
    And for thy sake, that all like dear didst buy,
    With love may one another entertain:
So let us love, dear love, like as we ought;
    Love is the lesson which the Lord us taught.

LXX

Fresh spring, the herald of love's mighty king,
    In whose coat-armour richly are displayed
    All sorts of flowers, the which on earth do spring,
    In goodly colours gloriously arrayed,
Go to my love, where she is careless laid   5
    Yet in her winter's bower not well awake;
    Tell her the joyous time will not be stayed
    Unless she do him by the forelock take.
Bid her, therefore, herself soon ready make
    To wait on love amongst his lovely crew,   10
    Where every one that misseth then her make
    Shall be by him amerced with penance due.
Make haste therefore, sweet love, whilst it is prime,
    For none can call again the passèd time.

LXXV

One day I wrote her name upon the strand,
    But came the waves and washèd it away.
    Again I wrote it with a second hand,
    But came the tide and made my pains his prey.
"Vain man," said she, "that dost in vain essay   5
    A mortal thing so to immortalize;
    For I myself shall like to this decay,
    And eke my name be wipèd out likewise."
"Not so," quod I, "let baser things devise
    To die in dust, but you shall live by fame;   10
    My verse your virtues rare shall eternize,
    And in the heavens write your glorious name:
Where, whereas death shall all the world subdue,
    Our love shall live, and later life renew."

1594–1595. *Amoretti and Epithalamion,* 1595.

LXVIII: 3 **harrowed:** robbed (of the souls of the virtuous)   11 **like dear:** equally dear, with equal
cost   LXX: 2 **coat-armour:** coat of arms, especially when embroidered on a garment   11 **make:**
mate   12 **amerced:** punished, fined   13 **prime:** early morning   LXXV: 8 **eke:** also   9 **quod:** said

Prothalamion   *marriage poem*

Calm was the day, and through the trembling air
Sweet-breathing Zephyrus did softly play,
A gentle spirit, that lightly did delay
Hot Titan's beams, which then did glister fair;
When I (whom sullen care,   5
Through discontent of my long fruitless stay
In princes' court, and expectation vain
Of idle hopes, which still do fly away
Like empty shadows, did afflict my brain)
Walked forth to ease my pain   10
Along the shore of silver-streaming Thames;
Whose rutty bank, the which his river hems,
Was painted all with variable flowers,
And all the meads adorned with dainty gems   *far away*
Fit to deck maidens' bowers,   15
And crown their paramours
Against the bridal day, which is not long:
    Sweet Thames run softly, till I end my song.

There in a meadow by the river's side
A flock of nymphs I chancèd to espy,   20
All lovely daughters of the flood thereby,
With goodly greenish locks all loose untied
As each had been a bride;
And each one had a little wicker basket
Made of fine twigs entrailèd curiously,   25
In which they gathered flowers to fill their flasket,
And, with fine fingers, cropped full feateously
The tender stalks on high.
Of every sort which in that meadow grew
They gathered some; the violet, pallid blue,   30
The little daisy that at evening closes,
The virgin lily and the primrose true,
With store of vermeil roses,
To deck their bridegrooms' posies
Against the bridal day, which was not long: 35
    Sweet Thames run softly, till I end my song.

With that I saw two swans of goodly hue
Come softly swimming down along the Lee;

1596. *Prothalamion*, 1596.

Spenser coined the word *prothalamion*, a song before a wedding, for his "spousal verse" by analogy with the word *epithalamion*, which means "[song] before the bridal chamber," and which he had used as title the year before for a poem about his own marriage. "Prothalamion" was written in celebration of the double marriage of Elizabeth and Katherine Somerset, daughters of the Earl of Worcester, a favorite of Queen Elizabeth and a close friend of the Earl of Essex, then at the height of his prestige and influence. In the poem the two young women—imagined in the form of beautiful swans—are seen as they go by river to Essex House in London, perhaps for the engagement ceremony.

2 **Zephyrus:** the west wind   4 **Titan:** the sun-god Helios, whose father was Hyperion, one of the Titans or first generation of Greek gods   5–9 Spenser had been disappointed in his hopes that his literary achievements would be rewarded by a political appointment.   11 **Thames:** the river that runs through London   12 **rutty:** rutted, sculptured by the currents   14 **meads:** meadows   16 **paramours:** lovers—without the disparaging sense the word now has   17 **against:** in preparation for **long:** a long ways away   22 **greenish:** sea-goddesses, mermaids, etc., commonly have green hair   25 **entrailèd:** interlaced   26 **flasket:** a long shallow basket   27 **feateously:** deftly, gracefully   33 **vermeil:** vermilion   38 **the Lee:** The river Lea once flowed into the Thames near the eastern edge of London. Man-made improvements have cut off the Lea; nowadays the swans would have come by a navigation canal, the Limehouse Cut.

Two fairer birds I yet did never see;
The snow which doth the top of Pindus strew   40
Did never whiter shew,
Nor Jove himself, when he a swan would be
For love of Leda, whiter did appear;
Yet Leda was, they say, as white as he,
Yet not so white as these, nor nothing near;   45
So purely white they were
That even the gentle stream, the which them bare,
Seemed foul to them, and bade his billows spare
To wet their silken feathers, lest they might
Soil their fair plumes with water not so fair,   50
And mar their beauties bright,
That shone as heaven's light,
Against their bridal day, which was not long:
    Sweet Thames run softly, till I end my song.

Eftsoons the nymphs, which now had flowers their fill,   55
Ran all in haste to see that silver brood
As they came floating on the crystal flood;
Whom when they saw, they stood amazèd still
Their wondering eyes to fill;
Them seemed they never saw a sight so fair,   60
Of fowls so lovely that they sure did deem
Them heavenly born, or to be that same pair
Which through the sky draw Venus' silver team;
For sure they did not seem
To be begot of any earthly seed,   65
But rather angels, or of angels' breed;
Yet were they bred of summer's-heat, they say,
In sweetest season, when each flower and weed
The earth did fresh array;
So fresh they seemed as day,   70
Even as their bridal day, which was not long:
    Sweet Thames run softly, till I end my song.

Then forth they all out of their baskets drew
Great store of flowers, the honour of the field,
That to the sense did fragrant odours yield,   75
All which upon those goodly birds they threw,
And all the waves did strew,
That like old Peneus' waters they did seem
When down along by pleasant Tempe's shore,
Scattered with flowers, through Thessaly they stream,   80
That they appear, through lilies' plenteous store,
Like a bride's chamber-floor.
Two of those nymphs meanwhile two garlands bound
Of freshest flowers which in that mead they found,
The which presenting all in trim array,   85
Their snowy foreheads therewithal they crowned,
Whilst one did sing this lay

---

39 birds: Here and elsewhere in the poem a *bird/bride* pun is probably intended. **40 Pindus:** a mountain range in Greece. Snow on classical mountains is presumably whiter than other snow. **41 shew:** show **42–43 Jove ... Leda:** cf. W. B. Yeats, "Leda and the Swan" (p. 467) **48 to them:** compared to them **55 eftsoons:** soon after **60 them seemed:** it seemed to them **62 that same pair:** In classical poetry, the chariot of Venus, goddess of love, was often drawn by swans (or doves or sparrows). **67 summer's-heat:** a pun on their family name: Somerset **78 Peneus:** name of a river (and its river-god) that flowed through the vale of Tempe in Thessaly in northern Greece

Prepared against that day,
Against their bridal day, which was not long:
    Sweet Thames run softly, till I end my song.   90

"Ye gentle birds! the world's fair ornament,
And heaven's glory, whom this happy hour
Doth lead unto your lovers' blissful bower,
Joy may you have, and gentle heart's content
Of your love's couplement;   95
And let fair Venus, that is queen of love,
With her heart-quelling son upon you smile,
Whose smile, they say, hath virtue to remove
All love's dislike, and friendship's faulty guile
For ever to assoil.   100
Let endless peace your steadfast hearts accord,
And blessed plenty wait upon your board,
And let your bed with pleasures chaste abound,
That fruitful issue may to you afford,
Which may your foes confound,   105
And make your joys redound
Upon your bridal day, which is not long:
    Sweet Thames run softly, till I end my song."

So ended she; and all the rest around
To her redoubled that her undersong,   110
Which said their bridal day should not be long:
And gentle Echo from the neighbour ground
Their accents did resound.
So forth those joyous birds did pass along,
Adown the Lee that to them murmured low,   115
As he would speak but that he lacked a tongue,
Yet did by signs his glad affection show,
Making his stream run slow.
And all the fowl which in his flood did dwell
Gan flock about these twain, that did excel   120
The rest, so far as Cynthia doth shend
The lesser stars. So they, enrangèd well,
Did on those two attend,
And their best service lend
Against their wedding day, which was not long: 125
    Sweet Thames run softly, till I end my song.

At length they all to merry London came,
To merry London, my most kindly nurse,
That to me gave this life's first native source,
Though from another place I take my name,   130
An house of ancient fame:
There when they came whereas those bricky towers
The which on Thames' broad aged back do ride,
Where now the studious lawyers have their bowers,

95 **couplement:** coupling, union   97 **heart-quelling son:** Cupid, that subdues and conquers hearts
100 **assoil:** pardon, absolve   101 **accord:** bring to agreement or harmony   110 **redoubled . . . under-
song:** reechoed that refrain of hers   112 **Echo:** cf. Sidney, "Ye Goatherd Gods," line 12   121 **Cyn-
thia:** moon and moon-goddess   **shend:** put to shame   122 **enrangèd:** arranged   129–131 Sidney
means that he was born in London, but is related to the family of the rich Sir John Spencer [*sic*] of
Althorpe in Northampton.   134 **studious lawyers:** law students at the Inner Temple and Middle
Temple, two of the four "inns of court," which were like colleges for the study of law

There whilom wont the Templar knights to bide,   135
Till they decayed through pride:
Next whereunto there stands a stately place,
Where oft I gainèd gifts and goodly grace
Of that great lord, which therein wont to dwell,
Whose want too well now feels my friendless case;   140
But ah! here fits not well
Old woes, but joys to tell
Against the bridal day, which is not long:
    Sweet Thames run softly, till I end my song.

Yet therein now doth lodge a noble peer,   145
Great England's glory and the world's wide wonder,
Whose dreadful name late through all Spain did thunder,
And Hercules' two pillars standing near
Did make to quake and fear:
Fair branch of honour, flower of chivalry!   150
That fillest England with thy triumphs' fame,
Joy have thou of thy noble victory,
And endless happiness of thine own name
That promiseth the same;
That through thy prowess and victorious arms   155
Thy country may be freed from foreign harms,
And great Eliza's glorious name may ring
Through all the world, filled with thy wide alarms,
Which some brave Muse may sing
To ages following,   160
Upon the bridal day, which is not long:
    Sweet Thames run softly, till I end my song.

From those high towers this noble lord issuing,
Like radiant Hesper when his golden hair
In the ocean billows he hath bathèd fair,   165
Descended to the river's open viewing,
With a great train ensuing.
Above the rest were goodly to be seen
Two gentle knights of lovely face and feature,
Beseeming well the bower of any queen,   170
With gifts of wit and ornaments of nature
Fit for so goodly stature,

135 **whilom wont:** formerly were accustomed   **the Templar knights:** the Knights Templar, a religious and military order founded by Crusaders in Jerusalem early in the twelfth century to protect the Holy Sepulchre and pilgrims visiting it. The great wealth and power they acquired over the next two centuries led to rumors about secret evils in the order; these in turn led to persecution in many countries. The order was suppressed early in the fourteenth century; the London Temple was leased to law students.   137 **a stately place:** Essex House, formerly called Leicester House, had been the London residence of Robert Dudley, Earl of Leicester, a favorite of Queen Elizabeth (cf. T. S. Eliot, "The Waste Land," note to line 279). Leicester, one of the most powerful men in England, had been a patron of Spenser until his death in 1588.   140 **whose want ... case:** In my situation—without powerful friends—I feel his absence very deeply.   145 **a noble peer:** The Earl of Essex, stepson of Leicester, now lodged there. He had returned to England a celebrity after leading a successful and profitable attack on the Spanish city of Cadiz in August of 1596, three months before the double wedding the poem is celebrating. Himself a favorite of Elizabeth, Essex seemed to have a brilliant future before him; Spenser may well have hoped for his patronage. (Five years later Essex was beheaded for attempting to seize control of the government.)   148 **Hercules' two pillars:** the rocky tips of Spain and Africa at the Straits of Gibraltar   153–154 The family name of Essex was Devereux, which seemed a short form of the French *devenir heureux* (become happy).   157 **Eliza:** Queen Elizabeth   158 **alarms:** calls to arms   164 **Hesper:** the evening star—but apparently as it would arise the next morning (no longer Hesperus)   167 **ensuing:** following   169 **two ... knights:** the bridegrooms-to-be   170 **beseeming:** befitting

That like the twins of Jove they seemed in sight
Which deck the baldric of the heavens bright;
They two, forth pacing to the river's side,   175
Received those two fair brides, their love's delight;
Which, at the appointed tide,
Each one did make his bride
Against their bridal day, which is not long:
    Sweet Thames run softly, till I end my song.   180

173 **the twins of Jove:** Castor and Pollux, who after death became the Gemini (Twins) of the zodiac   174 **baldric:** a belt worn transversely from shoulder to hip; here, the zodiac   177 **tide:** time

Christopher Marlowe
(1564–1593)

Thanks to his "mighty line" and the aspiring heroes who delivered it, Marlowe became the most famous dramatist before Shakespeare. His life was nearly as lurid as his plays: he did secret service work for Queen Elizabeth; had a reputation for violence and unorthodox religious opinions; and was killed in his late twenties in a tavern brawl that had overtones of political intrigue.

The Passionate Shepherd to His Love

Come live with me and be my love,
And we will all the pleasures prove
That valleys, groves, hills, and fields,
Woods, or steepy mountain yields.

And we will sit upon the rocks,   5
Seeing the shepherds feed their flocks,
By shallow rivers, to whose falls
Melodious birds sing madrigals.

And I will make thee beds of roses
And a thousand fragrant posies,   10
A cap of flowers, and a kirtle
Embroidered all with leaves of myrtle;

A gown made of the finest wool,
Which from our pretty lambs we pull;
Fair linèd slippers for the cold,   15
With buckles of the purest gold;

A belt of straw and ivy buds
With coral clasps and amber studs:
And if these pleasures may thee move,
Come live with me and be my love.   20

The shepherd swains shall dance and sing
For thy delight each May morning:
If these delights thy mind may move,
Then live with me and be my love.

c. 1589. *England's Helicon*, 1600.

Marlowe's poem is placed here (a decade ahead of where Marlowe belongs) so that his poem can be seen with Ralegh's reply to it, which follows this poem.

11 **kirtle:** gown

Sir Walter Ralegh
(1552?–1618)

Ralegh's life seemed to follow the script of a sensational adventure movie: son of a poor gentleman, he was a soldier in France and Ireland, found himself the favorite of Queen Elizabeth and the most envied figure at her court, angered her by a rash marriage, regained her favor by explorations in South America and by capturing Spanish treasure ships, was sentenced to death in 1603 by King James, pardoned at the last moment, spent 13 years as prisoner (during which he wrote his *History of the World*), was released to lead an expedition to "El Dorado" in Guiana, got into skirmishes with the Spaniards in which his son was killed, and on his return to England was beheaded.

The Nymph's Reply to the Shepherd

If all the world and love were young,
And truth in every shepherd's tongue,
These pretty pleasures might me move
To live with thee and be thy love.

Time drives the flocks from field to fold,   5
When rivers rage and rocks grow cold;
And Philomel becometh dumb;
The rest complains of cares to come.

The flowers do fade, and wanton fields
To wayward winter reckoning yields: 10
A honey tongue, a heart of gall,
Is fancy's spring, but sorrow's fall.

Thy gowns, thy shoes, thy beds of roses,
Thy cap, thy kirtle, and thy posies
Soon break, soon wither, soon forgotten,   15
In folly ripe, in reason rotten.

Thy belt of straw and ivy buds,
Thy coral clasps and amber studs,
All these in me no means can move
To come to thee and be thy love.   20

But could youth last, and love still breed,
Had joys no date, nor age no need,
Then these delights my mind might move
To live with thee and be thy love.

---

c. 1589. Ibid., 1600.

7 **Philomel:** the nightingale

As You Came from the Holy Land

As you came from the holy land
    Of Walsingham,

Before 1600. Thomas Deloney, *The Garland of Good Will*, 1631, 1678. Reprinted in *Early English Poetry*, Percy Society, XXX, 1852.

This poem, perhaps based on an earlier ballad, is probably Ralegh's.

2 **Walsingham:** the shrine of Our Lady at Little Walsingham in Norfolk was famous throughout Europe

Met you not with my true love
   By the way as you came?

     How should I know your true love,   5
       That have met many a one
     As I went to the holy land,
       That have come, that have gone?

She is neither white nor brown
   But as the heavens fair;   10
There is none hath a form so divine
   In the earth, in the air.

     Such a one did I meet, good sir,
       Such an angelic face,
     Who like a queen, like a nymph did appear   15
       By her gait, by her grace.

She hath left me here all alone,
   All alone as unknown,
Who sometimes did me lead with herself,
   And me loved as her own.   20

     What's the cause that she leaves you alone,
       And a new way doth take,
     Who loved you once as her own
       And her joy did you make?

I have loved her all my youth,   25
   But now old, as you see—
Love likes not the falling fruit
   From the withered tree.

Know that love is a careless child
   And forgets promise past;   30
He is blind, he is deaf when he list
   And in faith never fast.

His desire is a dureless content
   And a trustless joy;
He is won with a world of despair   35
   And is lost with a toy.

Of womankind such indeed is the love
   Or the word *love* abused,
Under which many childish desires
   And conceits are excused.   40

But true love is a durable fire
   In the mind ever burning;
Never sick, never old, never dead,
   From itself never turning.

31 **list**: wants to be   33 **dureless**: not lasting   36 **toy**: trifle

The Lie

Go, soul, the body's guest,
Upon a thankless arrant.
Fear not to touch the best;
The truth shall be thy warrant.
Go, since I needs must die,   5
And give the world the lie.

Say to the court, it glows
And shines like rotten wood;
Say to the church, it shows
What's good, and doth no good.   10
If church and court reply,
Then give them both the lie.

Tell potentates, they live
Acting by others' action.
Not loved unless they give,   15
Not strong but by affection.
If potentates reply,
Give potentates the lie.

Tell men of high condition
That manage the estate,   20
Their purpose is ambition,
Their practice only hate.
And if they once reply,
Then give them all the lie.

Tell them that brave it most,   25
They beg for more by spending,
Who, in their greatest cost,
Seek nothing but commending.
And if they make reply,
Then give them all the lie.   30

Tell zeal it wants devotion;
Tell love it is but lust;
Tell time it metes but motion;
Tell flesh it is but dust.
And wish them not reply,   35
For thou must give the lie.

Tell age it daily wasteth;
Tell honor how it alters;
Tell beauty how she blasteth;
Tell favor how it falters.   40
And as they shall reply,
Give every one the lie.

1593–1596. *A Poetical Rhapsody,* 1608 (2nd ed.).

2 **arrant:** errand   6 **give . . . the lie:** tell the world it lies   33 **metes:** measures   39 **blasteth:** withers, is blighted

Tell wit how much it wrangles
In tickle points of niceness;
Tell wisdom she entangles   45
Herself in over-wiseness.
And when they do reply,
Straight give them both the lie.

Tell physic of her boldness;
Tell skill it is prevention;   50
Tell charity of coldness;
Tell law it is contention.
And as they do reply,
So give them still the lie.

Tell fortune of her blindness;   55
Tell nature of decay;
Tell friendship of unkindness;
Tell justice of delay.
And if they will reply,
Then give them all the lie.   60

Tell arts they have no soundness,
But vary by esteeming;
Tell schools they want profoundness,
And stand too much on seeming.
If arts and schools reply,   65
Give arts and schools the lie.

Tell faith it's fled the city;
Tell how the country erreth;
Tell manhood shakes off pity;
Tell virtue least preferrèd.   70
And if they do reply,
Spare not to give the lie.

So when thou hast, as I
Commanded thee, done blabbing,
Although to give the lie   75
Deserves no less than stabbing,
Stab at thee he that will,
No stab thy soul can kill.

44 **tickle:** ticklish, difficult, uncertain   **niceness:** oversubtlety

Even Such Is Time

Even such is time that takes in trust
Our youth, our joys, our all we have,
And pays us but with age and dust,
Who in the dark and silent grave,
When we have wandered all our ways,   5
Shuts up the story of our days.
But from this earth, this grave, this dust,
My God shall raise me up, I trust.

1618? R. Brathwayte, *Remains After Death*, 1618. Text from *Reliquiae Wottonianae*, 1651.

Said to have been written the night before Ralegh's execution.

Fulke Greville, Lord Brooke
(1554–1628)

Greville shared the interests of his closest friend, Sir Philip Sidney: diplomacy, government, war, religion, poetry. Noted for his business ability, he became Secretary of the Navy and Chancellor of the Exchequer. None of his poetry was published in his lifetime.

From **Caelica**

XXII

I, with whose colors Myra dressed her head;
I, that ware posies of her own hand-making;
I, that mine own name in the chimneys read
By Myra finely wrought ere I was waking;
  Must I look on in hope time coming may   5
  With change bring back my turn again to play?

I, that on Sunday at the church-stile found
A garland sweet, with true-love knots in flowers,
Which I to wear about mine arm was bound
That each of us might know that all was ours;   10
  Must I now lead an idle life in wishes?
  And follow Cupid for his loaves and fishes?

I, that did wear the ring her mother left;
I, for whose love she gloried to be blamed;
I, with whose eyes her eyes committed theft;   15
I, who did make her blush when I was named;
  Must I lose ring, flowers, blush, theft and go naked,
  Watching with sighs, till dead love be awakèd?

I, that when drowsy Argus fell asleep,
Like jealousy o'rewatchèd with desire,   20
Was even warnèd modesty to keep,
While her breath, speaking, kindled nature's fire;
  Must I look on a-cold, while others warm them?
  Do Vulcan's brothers in such fine nets arm them?

Was it for this that I might Myra see   25
Washing the water with her beauties, white?
Yet would she never write her love to me;
Thinks wit of change while thoughts are in delight?
  Mad girls must safely love as they may leave;
  No man can print a kiss; lines may deceive.   30

By 1586. *Caelica*. In *Certain Learned and Elegant Works...*, 1633.

In the first three stanzas the speaker recalls the various ways in which Myra had indicated she loved him: she had worn ribbons he gave her, made bouquets for him, written his name in the soot of the chimney, and so forth.

2 **ware:** wore   7 **church-stile:** steps over the fence or wall enclosing the churchyard   12 **Cupid ... fishes:** be one of the multitude her love favors, not her favorite   15 **committed theft:** stole glances [at the speaker]   19 **Argus:** the sleepless, hundred-eyed watchman of Greek mythology; here, probably a chaperone   24 **Vulcan's brothers:** Vulcan, the husband of Venus, once trapped her and her lover Mars in a fine net. Here, a way of frustrating such lovers as the speaker?   28 **thinks ... delight:** Does the mind think of another lover when happy with one?   29 **mad ... leave:** Wild girls must take precautions in love if they plan to change lovers—they should not write love letters.

C

In night, when colors all to black are cast,
Distinction lost or gone down with the light,
The eye, a watch to inward senses placed,
Not seeing, yet still having power of sight,

Gives vain alarums to the inward sense,   5
Where fear, stirred up with witty tyranny,
Confounds all powers, and through self-offense
Doth forge and raise impossibility,

Such as in thick depriving darknesses
Proper reflections of the error be,   10
And images of self-confusednesses,
Which hurt imaginations only see;
    And from this nothing seen, tells news of devils,
    Which but expressions be of inward evils.

Before 1600. Ibid.

6 **witty:** ingenious, imaginative   8 **impossibility:** things that could not possibly exist   9-14 Things
we imagine we see in the darkness are projections of disorders in our own psyche.

O Wearisome Condition of Humanity

O wearisome condition of humanity!
Born under one law, to another bound;
Vainly begot, and yet forbidden vanity,
Created sick, commanded to be sound.
What meaneth nature by these diverse laws?   5
Passion and reason self-division cause.
Is it the mark or majesty of power
To make offences that it may forgive?
Nature herself doth her own self deflower,
To hate those errors she herself doth give.   10
For how should man think that he may not do,
If nature did not fail, and punish too?
Tyrant to others, to herself unjust,
Only commands things difficult and hard;
Forbids us all things which it knows is lust,   15
Makes easy pains, unpossible reward.
If nature did not take delight in blood,
She would have made more easy ways to good.
We that are bound by vows and by promotion,
With pomp of holy sacrifice and rites,   20
To teach belief in good and still devotion,
To preach of heaven's wonders and delights—
Yet, when each of us in his own heart looks,
He finds the God there far unlike his books.

Before 1600? *Mustapha*, 1609.

11 **that:** that which   16 **easy ... reward:** pain easy, reward impossible   17 **blood:** our physical na-
ture   19 **promotion:** advancement, self-improvement

Sir Philip Sidney
(1554–1586)

Probably the most admired young man of his time, Sidney was a diplomat, at home in several languages; an accomplished athlete, horseman, and tournament superstar; and a gallant soldier who was fatally wounded leading an attack on the Spaniards at a town in the Netherlands to which he had been sent as governor. His early death was the occasion for national mourning.

Ye Goatherd Gods

Strephon:	Ye goatherd gods, that love the grassy mountains,
	Ye nymphs which haunt the springs in pleasant valleys,
	Ye satyrs joyed with free and quiet forests,
	Vouchsafe your silent ears to plaining music,
	Which to my woes gives still an early morning, 5
	And draws the dolour on till weary evening.

Klaius: O Mercury, foregoer to the evening,
O heavenly huntress of the savage mountains,
O lovely star, entitled of the morning,
While that my voice doth fill these woeful valleys,   10
Vouchsafe your silent ears to plaining music,
Which oft hath Echo tired in secret forests.

Strephon: I that was once free-burgess of the forests,
Where shade from sun, and sport I sought in evening,
I that was once esteemed for pleasant music,   15
Am banished now among the monstrous mountains
Of huge despair, and foul affliction's valleys,
Am grown a screech-owl to myself each morning.

Klaius: I that was once delighted every morning,
Hunting the wild inhabiters of forests,   20
I that was once the music of these valleys,
So darkened am, that all my day is evening,
Heart-broken so that molehills seem high mountains,
And fill the vales with cries instead of music.

Strephon: Long since, alas, my deadly swannish music   25
Hath made itself a crier of the morning,
And hath with wailing strength climbed highest mountains;
Long since my thoughts more desert be than forests;
Long since I see my joys come to their evening,
And state thrown down to overtrodden valleys.   30

By 1580. *The Countess of Pembroke's Arcadia*, 1590.

In *The Countess of Pembroke's Arcadia*, Strephon and Klaius (whose names, from the Greek, mean "the writher" and "the weeper") are two gentlemen who have become shepherds and retired to the country because of their love for a beautiful shepherdess (a high-born lady in disguise). She has rejected their love and gone away; the poem laments her absence. In form it is a double *sestina* (see the prosody section); Sidney was the first to use the sestina form in English.

4 plaining: complaining, lamenting   **7 Mercury:** the planet nearest the sun, seen only just before sunrise, or just after sunset—on which occasion it is foregoer to the evening   **8 heavenly huntress:** Artemis (Diana), the moon-goddess of mythology   **9 star:** Venus as morning star; its Greek name meant "of the morning."   **12 Echo:** in mythology, a nymph who, in punishment for her chattering, was allowed only to repeat what was said to her; in love with Narcissus, she pined away until only her voice was left.   **13 free-burgess:** citizen with full rights   **25 swannish:** Swans were thought to sing (their swan song) only when dying.   **28 desert:** deserted, desolate   **30 state:** eminence, position of dignity or power

<table>
<tr><td>*Klaius:*</td><td>Long since the happy dwellers of these valleys
Have prayed me leave my strange exclaiming music,
Which troubles their day's work, and joys of evening;
Long since I hate the night, more hate the morning;
Long since my thoughts chase me like beasts in forests,
And make me wish myself laid under mountains.</td><td>35</td></tr>
</table>

Strephon: Meseems I see the high and stately mountains
           Transform themselves to low dejected valleys;
           Meseems I hear in these ill-changèd forests
           The nightingales do learn of owls their music;   40
           Meseems I feel the comfort of the morning.
           Turned to the mortal serein of an evening.

Klaius: Meseems I see a filthy cloudy evening,
           As soon as sun begins to climb the mountains;
           Meseems I feel a noisome scent, the morning,   45
           When I do smell the flowers of these valleys;
           Meseems I hear, when I do hear sweet music,
           The dreadful cries of murdered men in forests.

Strephon: I wish to fire the trees of all these forests;
           I give the sun a last farewell each evening;   50
           I curse the fiddling finders-out of music;
           With envy I do hate the lofty mountains;
           And with despite despise the humble valleys;
           I do detest night, evening, day, and morning.

Klaius: Curse to myself my prayer is, the morning;   55
           My fire is more than can be made with forests;
           My state more base than are the basest valleys;
           I wish no evenings more to see, each evening;
           Shamèd, I hate myself in sight of mountains,
           And stop my ears, lest I grow mad with music.   60

Strephon: For she, whose parts maintained a perfect music,
           Whose beauties shined more than the blushing morning,
           Who much did pass in state the stately mountains,
           In straightness passed the cedars of the forests,
           Hath cast me, wretch, into eternal evening,   65
           By taking her two suns from these dark valleys.

Klaius: For she, with whom compared the Alps are valleys,
           She, whose least word brings from the spheres their music,
           At whose approach the sun rose in the evening,
           Who, where she went, bore in her forehead morning,   70
           Is gone, is gone from these our spoilèd forests,
           Turning to deserts our best pastured mountains.

Strephon: These mountains witness shall, so shall these valleys,
Klaius: These forests eke, made wretched by our music;
           Our morning hymn this is, and song at evening.   75

---

37 **meseems:** it seems to me   42 **mortal:** deadly   **serein:** a fine moisture from cloudless skies after sunset, thought insalubrious   61 **she:** the absent love whom the two are lamenting   63 **pass:** surpass   66 **her two suns:** her eyes   68 **music:** In the old astronomy, it was thought that the "spheres" of the heavens made celestial music as they moved together.   71 **spoilèd:** despoiled (by her absence)   74 **eke:** also

From **Astrophil and Stella**

1

Loving in truth, and fain in verse my love to show,
    That she, dear she, might take some pleasure of my pain,
    Pleasure might cause her read, reading might make her know,
    Knowledge might pity win, and pity grace obtain,
I sought fit words to paint the blackest face of woe,   5
    Studying inventions fine, her wits to entertain,
    Oft turning others' leaves to see if thence would flow
    Some fresh and fruitful showers upon my sun-burned brain.
But words came halting forth, wanting invention's stay;
    Invention, nature's child, fled step-dame study's blows,   10
    And other's feet still seemed but strangers in my way.
Thus, great with child to speak, and helpless in my throes,
    Biting my truant pen, beating myself for spite,
    Fool, said my Muse to me, look in thy heart and write.

31

With how sad steps, O moon, thou climb'st the skies,
    How silently, and with how wan a face.
    What, may it be that even in heavenly place
    That busy archer his sharp arrows tries?
Sure, if that long-with-love-acquainted eyes   5
    Can judge of love, thou feel'st a lover's case;
    I read it in thy looks; thy languished grace
    To me, that feel the like, thy state descries.
Then, even of fellowship, O moon, tell me,
    Is constant love deemed there but want of wit?   10
    Are beauties there as proud as here they be?
Do they above love to be loved, and yet
    Those lovers scorn whom that love doth possess?
    Do they call virtue there ungratefulness?

41

Having this day my horse, my hand, my lance
    Guided so well, that I obtained the prize,

c. 1582. *The Countess of Pembroke's Arcadia* . . . , 3rd ed., 1598. (A corrupt text, unlicensed and unauthorized, had been published in 1591 as *Syr P.S. His Astrophel and Stella*.)

Sidney's series of 108 sonnets and 11 interspersed songs traces the emotional history of a young nobleman called Astrophil (Greek: star-lover) who, at times happy in his passion, suffers from his growing love for a beautiful lady called Stella (Latin: star) he might once have had but who is now married—it seems unhappily—to another man. After the ups and downs of a conflict between love and duty, the sequence ends in the sadness of separation. The young man is in many ways like Sidney himself; the young woman was taken by Sidney's contemporaries (with "rich" evidence in the sonnets) to be Penelope Devereux, married to Lord Rich. The emotions of the young man seem to be based on experience, but how closely the story of the sonnets follows the real lives of Sidney and Penelope Rich we can never be sure.

1:1 **fain:** desirous   6 **inventions:** things to write about, and ways to write about them, as discovered by the imagination   8 **sun-burned:** dried up by the fire of love   9 **stay:** support   14 **look in thy heart:** what he will see there is the image of Stella, his love, the natural inspiration of his poetry.

31:9 **of fellowship:** out of friendship (because we're in the same situation)   14 **virtue . . . ungratefulness:** ungratefulness a virtue

Both by the judgment of the English eyes,
    And of some sent from that sweet enemy France:
Horsemen my skill in horsemanship advance;   5
    Town-folks my strength; a daintier judge applies
    His praise to sleight, which from good use doth rise;
    Some lucky wits impute it but to chance;
Others, because of both sides I do take
    My blood from them who did excel in this,   10
    Think Nature me a man of arms did make.
How far they shoot awry! the true cause is,
    Stella looked on, and from her heavenly face
    Sent forth the beams, which made so fair my race.

41:5 **advance:** call attention to, praise   6 **daintier:** more discriminating   7 **sleight:** skill, strategy
use: practice   8 **lucky:** attributing things to luck

Only Joy, Now Here You Are

Only joy, now here you are,
Fit to hear and ease my care;
Let my whispering voice obtain
Sweet reward for sharpest pain:
Take me to thee, and thee to me!   5
"No, no, no, no, my dear—let be."

Night hath closed all in her cloak;
Twinkling stars love-thoughts provoke;
Danger hence good care doth keep;
Jealousy itself doth sleep.   10
Take me to thee, and thee to me!
"No, no, no, no, my dear—let be."

Better place no wit can find,
Cupid's yoke to loose or bind.
These sweet flowers on fine bed too   15
Us in their best language woo:
Take me to thee, and thee to me!
"No, no, no, no, my dear—let be."

This small light the moon bestows
Serves thy beams but to disclose,   20
So to raise my hap more high.
Fear not else; none can us spy:
Take me to thee, and thee to me!
"No, no, no, no, my dear—let be."

That you heard was but a mouse;   25
Dumb sleep holdeth all the house.
Yet asleep, methinks they say:
Young folks, take time while you may.
Take me to thee, and thee to me!
"No, no, no, no, my dear—let be."   30

Niggard time threats, if we miss
This large offer of our bliss,

c. 1582. Ibid.

21 **hap:** luck   31 **niggard:** miserly

Long stay ere he grant the same.
Sweet, then, while each thing doth frame,
Take me to thee, and thee to me!   35
"No, no, no, no, my dear—let be."

Your fair mother is abed,
Candles out and curtains spread;
She thinks you do letters write—
Write, but first let me endite: 40
Take me to thee, and thee to me!
"No, no, no, no, my dear—let be."

Sweet, alas! why strive you thus?
Concord better fitteth us.
Leave to Mars the force of hands;   45
Your power in your beauty stands.
Take me to thee, and thee to me!
"No, no, no, no, my dear—let be."

Woe to me, and do you swear
Me to hate but I forebear?   50
Cursèd be my destines all
That brought me so high to fall.
Soon with my death I will please thee!
"No, no, no, no, my dear—let be."

34 **frame:** be favorable, shape up well   50 **but:** unless   51 **destines:** destinies

Robert Southwell
(1561–1595)

Southwell (*sŭth'll*, not *south well*), brought up as a Catholic, was ordained as a Jesuit in Rome. Well aware that his life would be in danger in Protestant England, he chose to return there as a "missionary." After many narrow escapes he was captured, tortured repeatedly, kept in solitary for three years, then put to death in his thirties.

The Burning Babe

As I in hoary winter's night
    stood shivering in the snow,
Surprised I was with sudden heat
    which made my heart to glow,

And lifting up a fearful eye   5
    to view what fire was near,
A pretty babe all burning bright
    did in the air appear,

Who, scorchèd with excessive heat,
    such floods of tears did shed   10
As though his floods should quench his flames
    which with his fears were fed.

St. Peter's Complaint, 1602.

1 **hoary:** white, frosty

"Alas," quoth he, "but newly born,
    in fiery heats I fry,
Yet none approach to warm their hearts   15
    or feel my fire but I.

"My faultless breast the furnace is;
    the fuel wounding thorns;
Love is the fire, and sighs the smoke,
    the ashes, shame and scorns.   20

"The fuel justice layeth on
    and mercy blows the coals;
The metal in the furnace wrought
    are men's defilèd souls,

"For which, as now on fire I am   25
    to work them to their good,
So will I melt into a bath
    To wash them in my blood."

With this he vanished out of sight,
    and swiftly shrunk away,   30
And straight I callèd unto mind
    that it was Christmas day.

Chidiock Tichborne
(1558?–1586)

Nothing is known of Tichborne's life except that he was executed—hanged, drawn, and quartered—at the age of 18, when implicated in the Babington Conspiracy, which aimed at the assassination of Elizabeth, the release of Mary, Queen of Scots, and a Catholic uprising in England.

Tichborne's Elegy

> *Written with his own hand in the Tower
> before his execution.*

My prime of youth is but a frost of cares;
    My feast of joy is but a dish of pain;
My crop of corn is but a field of tares;
    And all my good is but vain hope of gain:
The day is past, and yet I saw no sun;   5
And now I live, and now my life is done.

My tale was heard, and yet it was not told;
    My fruit is fallen, and yet my leaves are green;
My youth is spent, and yet I am not old;
    I saw the world, and yet I was not seen: 10
My thread is cut, and yet it is not spun;
And now I live, and now my life is done.

I sought my death, and found it in my womb;
    I looked for life, and saw it was a shade;

Verses of Praise and Joy, 1586.

3 tares: a kind of weed

I trod the earth, and knew it was my tomb;   15
   And now I die, and now I was but made:
My glass is full, and now my glass is run;
And now I live, and now my life is done.

17 **glass:** hourglass

Robert Greene
(1558–1592)

Greene, with degrees from Oxford and Cambridge, made himself known in his twenties in the wilder bohemian circles of London. When he died there a few years later, he had over 35 literary works to his credit: plays, prose tales, exposés of London low life, moralistic tracts—and, scattered among them, many charming poems.

The Shepherd's Wife's Song

Ah, what is love? It is a pretty thing,
As sweet unto a shepherd as a king;
    And sweeter too,
For kings have cares that wait upon a crown,
And cares can make the sweetest love to frown: 5
    Ah then, ah then,
If country loves such sweet desires do gain,
What lady would not love a shepherd swain?

His flocks are folded, he comes home at night
As merry as a king in his delight;   10
    And merrier too,
For kings bethink them what the state require,
Where shepherds careless carol by the fire:
    Ah then, ah then,
If country loves such sweet desires do gain,   15
What lady would not love a shepherd swain?

He kisseth first, then sits as blithe to eat
His cream and curds as doth the king his meat;
    And blither too,
For kings have often fears when they do sup,   20
Where shepherds dread no poison in their cup:
    Ah then, ah then,
If country loves such sweet desires do gain,
What lady would not love a shepherd swain?

To bed he goes, as wanton then, I ween,   25
As is a king in dalliance with a queen;
    More wanton too,
For kings have many griefs affects to move,
Where shepherds have no greater grief than love: 30
    Ah then, ah then,
If country loves such sweet desires do gain,
What lady would not love a shepherd swain?

Greene's Mourning Garment, 1590.

18 **curds:** a thickened milk product (like cottage cheese)   25 **wanton:** lusty   **ween:** think   28 **affects to move:** to influence their emotions

Upon his couch of straw he sleeps as sound
As doth the king upon his beds of down;
        More sounder too,   35
For cares cause kings full oft their sleep to spill,
Where weary shepherds lie and snort their fill:
        Ah then, ah then,
If country loves such sweet desires do gain,
What lady would not love a shepherd swain?   40

Thus with his wife he spends the year, as blithe
As doth the king at every tide or sithe;
        And blither too,
For kings have wars and broils to take in hand,
Where shepherds laugh and love upon the land: 45
        Ah then, ah then,
If country loves such sweet desires do gain,
What lady would not love a shepherd swain?

36 **spill:** spoil   42 **sithe:** time   44 **broils:** brawls, disturbances

Anthony Munday (?)
(1560–1633)

While still in his teens, Munday worked as a actor and secret agent (or spy) in France and
Italy. He was a prolific writer of poetry and prose, and a popular dramatist.

I Serve a Mistress Whiter Than the Snow

I serve a mistress whiter than the snow,
Straighter than cedar, brighter than the glass,
Finer in trip and swifter than the roe,
More pleasant than the field of flowering grass,
        More gladsome to my withering joys that fade   5
        Than winter's sun or summer's cooling shade;

Sweeter than swelling grape of ripest wine,
Softer than feathers of the fairest swan,
Smoother than jet, more stately than the pine,
Fresher than poplar, smaller than my span,   10
        Clearer than beauty's fiery-pointed beam,
        Or icy crust of crystal's frozen stream.

Yet is she curster than the bear by kind,
And harder-hearted than the agèd oak,
More glib than oil, more fickle than the wind,   15
Stiffer than steel, no sooner bent but broke.
        Lo, thus my service is a lasting sore,
        Yet will I serve although I die therefore.

Two Italian Gentlemen, 1584.

3 **trip:** light, graceful way of walking   10 **smaller . . . span:** more slender than the circle my fingers
can make   13 **curster:** more cross, harder to get along with   **kind:** nature   15 **glib:** slippery

Samuel Daniel
(1562–1619)

After working on the staff of the English ambassador in Paris, Daniel served as tutor to noble families and as attendant on the queen. He wrote dramas, masques, and a prose "Defense of Ryme" in addition to his poetry.

Ulysses and the Siren

Siren: Come, worthy Greek, Ulysses, come,
        Possess these shores with me;
    The winds and seas are troublesome,
        And here we may be free.
    Here may we sit and view their toil   5
        That travail in the deep,
    And joy the day in mirth the while,
        And spend the night in sleep.

Ulysses: Fair nymph, if fame or honour were
        To be attained with ease,   10
    Then would I come and rest me there,
        And leave such toils as these.
    But here it dwells, and here must I
        With danger seek it forth;
    To spend the time luxuriously   15
        Becomes not men of worth.

Siren: Ulysses, oh be not deceived
        With that unreal name.
    This honour is a thing conceived,
        And rests on others' fame;   20
    Begotten only to molest
        Our peace, and to beguile
    The best thing of our life, our rest,
        And give us up to toil.

Ulysses: Delicious nymph, suppose there were   25
        Nor honour nor report,
    Yet manliness would scorn to wear
        The time in idle sport;
    For toil doth give a better touch
        To make us feel our joy,   30
    And ease finds tediousness as much
        As labour yields annoy.

Certain Small Poems, 1605.

In Book XII of the *Odyssey* Homer describes how the attractive Sirens on their island sing to lure passing sailors ashore. Once ashore, the sailors are killed. Ulysses, forewarned, escapes their spell. Daniel makes this incident the occasion for a debate between Ulysses, who advocates a life of strenuous endeavor for what is right and honorable, and one of the Sirens, who advocates a life of pleasure-loving idleness.

19 conceived: only imagined   **22 beguile:** deceive, steal by deception   **29 touch:** touchstone, test

Siren:	Then pleasure likewise seems the shore,
	Whereto tends all your toil,
	Which you forego, to make it more,
	And perish oft the while.
	Who may disport them diversely
	Find never tedious day,
	And ease may have variety
	As well as action may.

Siren: Then pleasure likewise seems the shore,
     Whereto tends all your toil,
Which you forego, to make it more,
     And perish oft the while.   35
Who may disport them diversely
     Find never tedious day,
And ease may have variety
     As well as action may.   40

Ulysses: But natures of the noblest frame
     These toils and dangers please,
And they take comfort in the same
     As much as you in ease;
And with the thought of actions past   45
     Are recreated still;
When pleasure leaves a touch, at last,
     To show that it was ill.

Siren: That doth opinion only cause
     That 's out of custom bred,   50
Which makes us many other laws
     Than ever nature did.
No widows wail for our delights,
     Our sports are without blood;
The world, we see, by warlike wights   55
     Receives more hurt than good.

Ulysses: But yet the state of things require
     These motions of unrest;
And these great spirits of high desire
     Seem born to turn them best;   60
To purge the mischiefs that increase
     And all good order mar;
For oft we see a wicked peace
     To be well changed for war.

Siren: Well, well, Ulysses, then I see   65
     I shall not have thee here;
And therefore I will come to thee,
     And take my fortunes there.
I must be won, that cannot win,
     Yet lost were I not won;   70
For beauty hath created been
     To undo, or be undone.

55 **wights:** men

Mark Alexander Boyd
(1563–1601)

A Scottish scholar and law student who wrote poetry in Latin and could converse in ancient Greek, Boyd led a life of adventurous wandering throughout much of Europe, enlisting now in this army, now in that one.

Venus and Cupid

Fra bank to bank, fra wood to wood I rin,
  Ourhailit with my feeble fantasie;
  Like til a leaf that fallis from a tree,
Or til a reed ourblawin with the win.
Twa gods guides me: the ane of tham is blin,   5
  Yea and a bairn brocht up in vanitie;
  The next a wife ingenrit of the sea,
And lichter nor a dauphin with her fin.

Unhappy is the man for evermair
  That tills the sand and sawis in the air;   10
  But twice unhappier is he, I lairn,
That feidis in his hairt a mad desire,
And follows on a woman thro' the fire,
  Led by a blind and teachit by a bairn.

The Oxford Book of Verse, 1900.

In the opinion of Ezra Pound, this sonnet in Scots (which derives its Cupid imagery, at the end, from the French poet Ronsard) is "the most beautiful sonnet in the [English] language."

1 **fra:** from **rin:** run 2 **ourhailit:** overwhelmed 3 **til:** to 4 **ourblawin:** blown over **win:** wind
5 **twa:** two **ane:** one **blin:** blind 6 **bairn:** child 7 **ingenrit:** born 8 **lichter nor:** lighter than
dauphin: dolphin 10 **sawis:** sows 14 **teachit:** taught

Michael Drayton
(1563–1631)

Drayton's life, unlike that of most of our early poets, seems to have been uneventful, devoted to the production of a large and varied body of poetry, much of it a patriotic celebration of England and English ways.

From Idea

6

How many paltry, foolish, painted things,
That now in coaches trouble every street,
Shall be forgotten, whom no poet sings,
Ere they be well wrapped in their winding-sheet.
Where I to thee eternity shall give,   5
When nothing else remaineth of these days,
And queens hereafter shall be glad to live
Upon the alms of thy superfluous praise.
Virgins and matrons, reading these my rhymes,
Shall be so much delighted with thy story   10
That they shall grieve they lived not in these times,
To have seen thee, their sex's only glory:
  So shalt thou fly above the vulgar throng,
  Still to survive in my immortal song.

61

Since there's no help, come let us kiss and part—
Nay, I have done: you get no more of me;

Poems, 1619.

And I am glad, yea, glad with all my heart,
That thus so cleanly I myself can free.
Shake hands for ever, cancel all our vows,   5
And when we meet at any time again,
Be it not seen in either of our brows
That we one jot of former love retain.
Now at the last gasp of love's latest breath,
When, his pulse failing, Passion speechless lies,   10
When Faith is kneeling by his bed of death,
And Innocence is closing up his eyes,
    Now, if thou wouldst, when all have given him over,
    From death to life thou might'st him yet recover.

To the Virginian Voyage

You brave heroic minds,
Worthy your country's name,
    That honor still pursue,
    Go, and subdue,
Whilst loitering hinds   5
Lurk here at home with shame.

Britons, you stay too long;
Quickly aboard bestow you,
    And with a merry gale
    Swell your stretched sail,   10
With vows as strong
As the winds that blow you.

Your course securely steer,
West and by south forth keep.
    Rocks, lee-shores, nor shoals,   15
    When Aeolus scowls,
You need not fear:
So absolute the deep.

And cheerfully at sea
Success you still entice,   20
    To get the pearl and gold,
    And, ours to hold,
Virginia,
Earth's only paradise.

Where nature hath in store   25
Fowl, venison, and fish,
    And the fruitfullest soil,
    Without your toil,
Three harvests more
All greater than your wish.   30

1606. *Poems Lyric and Pastoral,* 1606.

Preparations for an expedition to Virginia continued through much of 1606. Three ships, with 140 people on board, sailed in December.

5 hinds: peasants   **16 Aeolus:** god of the winds

And the ambitious vine
Crowns with his purple mass
    The cedar reaching high
    To kiss the sky,
The cypress, pine   35
And useful sassafras.

To those, the golden age
Still nature's laws doth give,
    No other cares that tend,
    But them to defend   40
From winter's age,
That long there doth not live.

When as the luscious smell
Of that delicious land
    Above the seas that flows   45
    The clear wind throws,
Your hearts to swell
Approaching the dear strand.

In kenning of the shore
(Thanks to God first given)   50
    O you the happiest men
    Be frolic then;
Let cannons roar,
Frighting the wide heaven.

And in regions far   55
Such heroes bring ye forth
    As those from whom we came,
    And plant our name
Under that star
Not known unto our north.   60

And as there plenty grows
Of laurel everywhere,
    Apollo's sacred tree,
    You may it see
A poet's brows   65
To crown, that may sing there.

Thy voyages attend,
Industrious Hakluyt,
    Whose reading shall inflame
    Men to seek fame,   70
And much commend
To after-times thy wit.

---

31 ambitious: climbing—the Latin root meant "to go around" (to get votes) **36 useful sassafras:** This North American plant had, among other medical properties, "power to comfort the liver." **52 frolic:** happy **68 Hakluyt:** Richard Hakluyt (1552?–1616), the geographer and editor of explorers' narratives, was a backer of the Virginia enterprise of 1606. Drayton got some details about Virginia from Hakluyt's accounts of earlier voyages.

William Shakespeare
(1564–1616)

Shakespeare's life, vivid and tumultuous as it must have been within, seems to have been unremarkable. His father was a small business man in a country town; the son's education seems not to have gone beyond the local grammar school. At 18 he married a woman in her mid-twenties; a daughter was born soon after, twins two years later. Then for nearly a decade Shakespeare drops out of sight—perhaps he was a schoolmaster in the country. In 1592 he surfaces as an actor in London and a playwright already of some note—able, within five years, to buy one of the largest houses in his home town. Liked and admired, he lived a quiet and industrious life in London until, at the age of 46, he chose an early retirement to the country, where he died five years later.

From **Sonnets**

18

Shall I compare thee to a summer's day?
Thou art more lovely and more temperate.
Rough winds do shake the darling buds of May,
And summer's lease hath all too short a date.
Sometime too hot the eye of heaven shines,   5
And often is his gold complexion dimmed;
And every fair from fair sometime declines,
By chance, or nature's changing course, untrimmed;
But thy eternal summer shall not fade,
Nor lose possession of that fair thou owest,   10
Nor shall death brag thou wanderest in his shade,
When in eternal lines to time thou growest.
   So long as men can breathe or eyes can see,
   So long lives this, and this gives life to thee.

29

When, in disgrace with fortune and men's eyes,
I all alone beweep my outcast state,
And trouble deaf heaven with my bootless cries,
And look upon myself and curse my fate,
Wishing me like to one more rich in hope,   5
Featured like him, like him with friends possessed,
Desiring this man's art, and that man's scope,
With what I most enjoy contented least;
Yet in these thoughts myself almost despising,
Haply I think on thee, and then my state,   10
Like to the lark at break of day arising
From sullen earth, sings hymns at heaven's gate;
   For thy sweet love remembered such wealth brings,
   That then I scorn to change my state with kings.

1592–1599; some perhaps later. *Shake-Speares Sonnets . . .* , 1609.

Luminous as the poetry of most of the sonnets is, with its meditations on time and change, beauty and mortality, loyalty and betrayal, friendship, true love and degrading lust, their exact relationship with the events of Shakespeare's own life remains clouded in obscurity. Of the 154 sonnets, the first 17 urge a young nobleman to marry so as not to deprive posterity of offspring as handsome and worthy as he. Numbers 18 to 126 are about the passionate friendship the poet comes to feel for the young man—a friendship troubled by estrangements, separations, and (it seems) an affair between the young man and the mysterious "dark lady" of sonnets 127 to 154, with whom the poet had become violently and miserably involved.

18: 8 **untrimmed:** stripped of its trim or ornament   10 **owest:** ownest   14 **this:** this poem
29: 3 **bootless:** useless, unavailing   10 **haply:** perhaps

30

When to the sessions of sweet silent thought
I summon up remembrance of things past,
I sigh the lack of many a thing I sought.
And with old woes new wail my dear time's waste.
Then can I drown an eye, unused to flow,   5
For precious friends hid in death's dateless night,
And weep afresh love's long since canceled woe,
And moan the expense of many a vanished sight;
Then can I grieve at grievances foregone,
And heavily from woe to woe tell o'er   10
The sad account of fore-bemoanèd moan,
Which I new pay as if not paid before.
    But if the while I think on thee, dear friend,
    All losses are restored and sorrows end.

33

Full many a glorious morning have I seen
Flatter the mountain tops with sovereign eye,
Kissing with golden face the meadows green,
Gilding pale streams with heavenly alchemy;
Anon permit the basest clouds to ride   5
With ugly rack on his celestial face,
And from the forlorn world his visage hide,
Stealing unseen to west with this disgrace.
Even so my sun one early morn did shine
With all-triumphant splendor on my brow;   10
But out alack, he was but one hour mine,
The region cloud hath masked him from me now.
    Yet him for this my love no whit disdaineth;
    Suns of the world may stain when heaven's sun staineth.

57

Being your slave, what should I do but tend
Upon the hours and times of your desire?
I have no precious time at all to spend,
Nor services to do till you require.
Nor dare I chide the world-without-end hour   5
Whilst I, my sovereign, watch the clock for you,
Nor think the bitterness of absence sour
When you have bid your servant once adieu.
Nor dare I question with my jealous thought
Where you may be, or your affairs suppose,   10
But, like a sad slave, stay and think of naught
Save where you are how happy you make those.
    So true a fool is love that in your will,
    Though you do anything, he thinks no ill.

30: 1–2 **sessions ... summon up:** imagery and language are legal   9 **foregone:** bygone   11 **fore-be-moanèd moan:** sorrows already sorrowed over   33: 11 **out alack:** alas!   12 **region cloud:** cloud over the region, local cloudiness

64

When I have seen by time's fell hand defaced
The rich proud cost of outworn buried age,
When sometime lofty towers I see down-razed,
And brass eternal slave to mortal rage;
When I have seen the hungry ocean gain   5
Advantage on the kingdom of the shore,
And the firm soil win of the watery main,
Increasing store with loss and loss with store;
When I have seen such interchange of state,
Or state itself confounded to decay,   10
Ruin hath taught me thus to ruminate,
That time will come and take my love away.
    This thought is as a death, which cannot choose
    But weep to have that which it fears to lose.

65

Since brass, nor stone, nor earth, nor boundless sea,
But sad mortality o'ersways their power,
How with this rage shall beauty hold a plea,
Whose action is no stronger than a flower?
O, how shall summer's honey breath hold out   5
Against the wrackful siege of battering days,
When rocks impregnable are not so stout,
Nor gates of steel so strong but time decays?
O, fearful meditation, where, alack,
Shall time's best jewel from time's chest lie hid?   10
Or what strong hand can hold his swift foot back,
Or who his spoil of beauty can forbid?
    O, none, unless this miracle have might,
    That in black ink my love may still shine bright.

66

Tired with all these, for restful death I cry,
As, to behold desert a beggar born,
And needy nothing trimmed in jollity,
And purest faith unhappily forsworn,
And gilded honor shamefully misplaced,   5
And maiden virtue rudely strumpeted,
And right perfection wrongfully disgraced,
And strength by limping sway disabled,
And art made tongue-tied by authority,
And folly (doctorlike) controlling skill,   10
And simple truth miscalled simplicity,
And captive good attending captain ill.
    Tired with all these, from these would I be gone,
    Save that to die, I leave my love alone.

64: 1 **fell:** cruel 3 **sometime:** formerly 9 **state:** (1) condition; (2) land, territory; (3) grandeur, stateliness; (4) political power. (The poet may well have had all in mind.) 65: 1 **Since brass:** Since (there is neither) brass 10 **time's best jewel:** the poet's love **time's chest:** the chest (or perhaps coffin) in which time, the real owner, would store what he takes back from us 66: 2 **desert:** merit 3 **needy nothing:** a nonentity without talent or qualification **jollity:** finery 4 **forsworn:** renounced, abandoned 6 **strumpeted:** treated as, or called, a prostitute 8 **sway:** authority, power 10 **doctorlike:** posing as an expert 11 **simplicity:** simple-mindedness, stupidity

71

No longer mourn for me when I am dead
Than you shall hear the surly sullen bell
Give warning to the world that I am fled
From this vile world with vilest worms to dwell.
Nay, if you read this line, remember not   5
The hand that writ it, for I love you so
That I in your sweet thoughts would be forgot,
If thinking on me then should make you woe.
O, if, I say, you look upon this verse,
When I, perhaps, compounded am with clay,   10
Do not so much as my poor name rehearse,
But let your love even with my life decay,
      Lest the wise world should look into your moan,
      And mock you with me after I am gone.

73

That time of year thou mayst in me behold
When yellow leaves, or none, or few, do hang
Upon those boughs which shake against the cold,
Bare ruined choirs where late the sweet birds sang.
In me thou seest the twilight of such day   5
As after sunset fadeth in the west,
Which by and by black night doth take away,
Death's second self, that seals up all in rest.
In me thou seest the glowing of such fire
That on the ashes of his youth doth lie,   10
As the deathbed whereon it must expire,
Consumed with that which it was nourished by.
      This thou perceivest, which makes thy love more strong,
      To love that well which thou must leave ere long.

107

Not mine own fears nor the prophetic soul
Of the wide world dreaming on things to come
Can yet the lease of my true love control,
Supposed as forfeit to a confined doom.
The mortal moon hath her eclipse endured,   5
And the sad augurs mock their own presage,
Incertainties now crown themselves assured,
And peace proclaims olives of endless age.
Now with the drops of this most balmy time
My love looks fresh, and death to me subscribes,   10
Since, spite of him, I'll live in this poor rhyme,
While he insults o'er dull and speechless tribes:
      And thou in this shalt find thy monument,
      When tyrants' crests and tombs of brass are spent.

107: Because it is not certain to what events of his time Shakespeare is here referring, this has been
called the most difficult of the sonnets. 1 **prophetic soul:** a general premonition (of things to
come) 3 **lease:** duration 4 **forfeit...doom:** due to expire in a limited time 5 **mortal moon...
endured:** Most authorities take this to refer to the death of Queen Elizabeth in 1603, though half a
dozen other "eclipses" have been suggested (for example, that of the Spanish Armada in 1588).
6 **sad augurs...presage:** Prophets or predicters of doom (civil war?) now see they were wrong.
8 **olives...age:** eternal peace (The olive branch is a symbol of peace.) 10 **subscribes:** submits
12 **insults:** triumphs, exults

116

Let me not to the marriage of true minds
Admit impediments; love is not love
Which alters when it alteration finds,
Or bends with the remover to remove.
Oh no, it is an ever-fixèd mark   5
That looks on tempests and is never shaken;
It is the star to every wandering bark,
Whose worth's unknown, although his height be taken.
Love's not time's fool, though rosy lips and cheeks
Within his bending sickle's compass come;   10
Love alters not with his brief hours and weeks,
But bears it out even to the edge of doom.
    If this be error and upon me proved,
    I never writ, nor no man ever loved.

129

The expense of spirit in a waste of shame
Is lust in action; and, till action, lust
Is perjured, murderous, bloody, full of blame,
Savage, extreme, rude, cruel, not to trust;
Enjoyed no sooner but despisèd straight;   5
Past reason hunted, and no sooner had,
Past reason hated as a swallowed bait
On purpose laid to make the taker mad;
Mad in pursuit, and in possession so;
Had, having, and in quest to have, extreme;   10
A bliss in proof, and proved, a very woe,
Before, a joy proposed; behind, a dream.
    All this the world well knows, yet none knows well
    To shun the heaven that leads men to this hell.

130

My mistress' eyes are nothing like the sun;
Coral is far more red than her lips' red;
If snow be white, why then her breasts are dun;
If hairs be wires, black wires grow on her head.
I have seen roses damasked, red and white,   5
But no such roses see I in her cheeks,
And in some perfumes is there more delight
Than in the breath that from my mistress reeks.
I love to hear her speak, yet well I know
That music hath a far more pleasing sound.   10

116: 8 **worth's ... taken:** power remains inestimable or mysterious, though his altitude can be measured by navigators   129:   1–2 lust is the subject: *lust ... is ... expense ...*   **expense of spirit:** expenditure of vital energy or spiritual force   **waste:** a pun: *waste/waist*   11 **in proof:** while being experienced   12 **before:** when anticipated   **behind:** when over   **a dream:** only an illusion   130: Shakespeare is not saying that the woman he loves is ugly or even plain; he is simply deriding the exaggerated clichés of sentimental love poets, who keep saying that the eyes of the lady they idolize are bright as the sun (or like stars), her lips red as coral, her skin white as snow, her hair like golden filigree, her cheeks like roses, her breath like perfume, and so on. The woman he loves, Shakespeare tells us, is real flesh and blood, not a piece of confectionery.   3 **dun:** a dull off-white   4 **wires:** for Elizabethans, fine filigree wire   5 **damasked:** of two or more colors mingled   8 **reeks:** breathes, is exhaled (*Reek* did not refer to an unpleasant smell in Shakespeare's day, or for a hundred years thereafter.)

I grant I never saw a goddess go;
My mistress when she walks treads on the ground.
    And yet, by heaven, I think my love as rare
    As any she, belied with false compare.

146

Poor soul, the center of my sinful earth,
[Feeding] these rebel powers that thee array,
Why dost thou pine within and suffer dearth,
Painting thy outward walls so costly gay?
Why so large cost, having so short a lease,   5
Dost thou upon thy fading mansion spend?
Shall worms, inheritors of this excess,
Eat up thy charge? Is this thy body's end?
Then, soul, live thou upon thy servant's loss,
And let that pine to aggravate thy store;   10
Buy terms divine in selling hours of dross;
Within be fed, without be rich no more:
    So shalt thou feed on death, that feeds on men,
    And death once dead, there's no more dying then.

130: 13 **rare:** fine, marvellous 14 **any she:** any woman **belied:** falsified 146: 2 Shakespeare's printer made a mistake in setting up this line. Apparently repeating words from line 1, he gives "My sinful earth these rebel powers that thee array." It seems that the first three words should be omitted, and their place taken by a two-syllable word (accent on either syllable) that makes sense here and that Shakespeare might have used. One scholar made a list of 400 possible words—all used by Shakespeare. "Feeding," as in our text, is one possibility. Among many other learned guesses are: *Fooled by, Foiled by, Filed* (defiled) *by, Gulled by, Tricked by, Starved by, Bearing, Thrall to, Prince of, Seat of, Sport of, Leagued with, Amid.*

Spring

When daisies pied and violets blue,
    And lady-smocks all silver-white,
And cuckoo-buds of yellow hue
    Do paint the meadows with delight,
The cuckoo then, on every tree,   5
Mocks married men, for thus sings he,
      Cuckoo, cuckoo! O word of fear,
      Unpleasing to a married ear.

When shepherds pipe on oaten straws,
    And merry larks are ploughmen's clocks,   10
When turtles tread, and rooks, and daws,
    And maidens bleach their summer smocks,
The cuckoo then, on every tree,
Mocks married men, for thus sings he,
      Cuckoo, cuckoo! O word of fear,   15
      Unpleasing to a married ear.

c. 1594. *Love's Labors Lost,* 1598.

1 **pied:** many-colored 2, 3 **lady-smocks, cuckoo-buds:** spring flowers, associated with the return of the cuckoo in spring. The second may be our buttercups. 6 **mocks married men:** because the cuckoo's call suggests *cuckold,* the derisive term for a man whose wife is unfaithful. *Cuckold* derives from *cuckoo*—a bird that lays its eggs in other birds' nests. 9 **oaten straws:** rustic musical instruments 11 **turtles tread:** turtledoves mate **rooks:** European crows **daws:** jackdaws, European birds rather like small crows or grackles

Winter

When icicles hang by the wall,
   And Dick the shepherd blows his nail,
And Tom bears logs into the hall,
   And milk comes frozen home in pail,
When blood is nipped, and ways be foul,   5
Then nightly sings the staring owl,
      Tu-whit, tu-who! A merry note,
      While greasy Joan doth keel the pot.

When all around the wind doth blow,
   And coughing drowns the parson's saw,   10
And birds sit brooding in the snow,
   And Marian's nose looks red and raw,
When roasted crabs hiss in the bowl,
Then nightly sings the staring owl,
      Tu-whit, tu-who! A merry note,   15
      While greasy Joan doth keel the pot.

---

c. 1594. Ibid.

A companion piece to the song preceding.

8 **keel:** cool, keep from boiling over, by stirring, skimming, etc.   10 **saw:** wise old saying, platitude   13 **crabs:** crabapples

O Mistress Mine, Where Are You Roaming?

O mistress mine, where are you roaming?
Oh, stay and hear! your true love's coming,
   That can sing both high and low:
Trip no further, pretty sweeting;
Journeys end in lovers' meeting,   5
   Every wise man's son doth know.

What is love? 'tis not hereafter;
Present mirth hath present laughter;
   What's to come is still unsure:
In delay there lies no plenty: 10
Then come kiss me, sweet-and-twenty,
   Youth's a stuff will not endure.

---

c. 1601. *Twelfth Night*, in *Mr. William Shakespeare's Comedies, Histories, and Tragedies*, 1623.

Fear No More the Heat o' the Sun

Fear no more the heat o' the sun,
   Nor the furious winter's rages;
Thou thy worldly task hast done,
   Home art gone, and ta'en thy wages:
Golden lads and girls all must,   5
As chimney-sweepers, come to dust.

Fear no more the frown o' the great;
   Thou art past the tyrant's stroke:
Care no more to clothe and eat;
   To thee the reed is as the oak: 10

---

c. 1609. *Cymbeline*, ibid.

The sceptre, learning, physic, must
All follow this, and come to dust.

Fear no more the lightning-flash,
 Nor the all-dreaded thunder-stone;
Fear not slander, censure rash;   15
 Thou hast finished joy and moan:
All lovers young, all lovers must
Consign to thee, and come to dust.

No exorciser harm thee!
Nor no witchcraft charm thee!   20
Ghost unlaid forbear thee!
Nothing ill come near thee!
Quiet consummation have;
And renownèd be thy grave!

11 **physic:** medicine, physical science 14 **thunder-stone:** thunderbolt 18 **consign to:** make a contract with

Full Fathom Five Thy Father Lies

Full fathom five thy father lies;
 Of his bones are coral made;
Those are pearls that were his eyes:
 Nothing of him that doth fade
But doth suffer a sea-change
Into something rich and strange.
Sea-nymphs hourly ring his knell:
       Ding-dong.
Hark! now I hear them, *ding-dong, bell.*

---

c. 1611. *The Tempest*, ibid.

Thomas Campion
(1567–1620)

One of the best songwriters of his age, Campion was the most musically talented of English authors—distinguished both as composer and poet. He had studied law, but by 1606 was supporting himself as a physician.

My Sweetest Lesbia, Let Us Live and Love

My sweetest Lesbia, let us live and love,
And though the sager sort our deeds reprove,
Let us not weigh them. Heaven's great lamps do dive
Into their west, and straight again revive;
But, soon as once set is our little light,   5
Then must we sleep one ever-during night.

P. Rosseter, *A Book of Airs*, 1601.

The first stanza translates the first six lines of a well-known poem by Catullus, beginning "Vivamus, mea Lesbia, atque amemus. . . ." Lesbia is the name the Roman poet used for the lady to whom he wrote love poems.

If all would lead their lives in love like me,
Then bloody swords and armour should not be;
No drum nor trumpet peaceful sleeps should move,
Unless alarm came from the camp of love. 10
But fools do live and waste their little light,
And seek with pain their ever-during night.

When timely death my life and fortune ends,
Let not my hearse be vexed with mourning friends;
But let all lovers, rich in triumph, come 15
And with sweet pastimes grace my happy tomb:
And, Lesbia, close up thou my little light,
And crown with love my ever-during night.

13 **timely:** in good time

I Care Not for These Ladies

I care not for these ladies
That must be wooed and prayed;
Give me kind Amaryllis,
The wanton country maid.
Nature art disdaineth; 5
Her beauty is her own.
    Her when we court and kiss,
    She cries, "Forsooth, let go!"
    But when we come where comfort is,
    She never will say no. 10

If I love Amaryllis,
She gives me fruit and flowers,
But if we love these ladies,
We must give golden showers.
Give them gold that sell love, 15
Give me the nutbrown lass,
    Who, when we court and kiss,
    She cries, "Forsooth, let go!"
    But when we come where comfort is,
    She never will say no. 20

These ladies must have pillows
And beds by strangers wrought,
Give me a bower of willows,
Of moss and leaves unbought,
And fresh Amaryllis 25
With milk and honey fed,
    Who, when we court and kiss,
    She cries, "Forsooth, let go!"
    But when we come where comfort is,
    She never will say no. 30

Ibid.

3 **Amaryllis:** Ever since Vergil used the name for a beautiful shepherdess in one of his poems of country life, poets have used it for attractive girls in pastoral settings. 4 **wanton:** sportive, fun-loving 8 **forsooth:** please! really!

It Fell on a Summer's Day

It fell on a summer's day
While sweet Bessie sleeping lay
In her bower, on her bed,
Light with curtains shadowèd,
Jamey came; she him spies,   5
Opening half her heavy eyes.

Jamey stole in through the door;
She lay slumbering as before.
Softly to her he drew near;
She heard him, yet would not hear.   10
Bessie vowed not to speak;
He resolved that dump to break.

First a soft kiss he doth take;
She lay still, and would not wake.
Then his hands learned to woo;   15
She dreamt not what he would do,
But still slept, while he smiled
To see love by sleep beguiled.

Jamey then began to play;
Bessie as one buried lay,   20
Gladly still through this sleight
Deceived in her own deceit.
And since this trance begun
She sleeps every afternoon.

Ibid.

3 **bower:** room   10 **would not:** pretended not to   12 **dump:** reverie   21 **sleight:** trick

When Thou Must Home to Shades of Underground

When thou must home to shades of underground,
And there arrived, a new admirèd guest,
The beauteous spirits do ingirt thee round,
White Iopé, blithe Helen and the rest,
To hear the stories of thy finished love   5
From that smooth tongue whose music hell can move;

Then wilt thou speak of banqueting delights,
Of masks and revels which sweet youth did make,
Of tourneys and great challenges of knights,
And all these triumphs for thy beauty's sake.   10
When thou hast told these honours done to thee,
Then tell, oh tell, how thou didst murder me!

Ibid.

4 **Iopé:** a beautiful girl the Roman poet Tibullus (II, xxviii B, 51) mentions as being in the under-
world. Scholars are not sure who she is—Cassiope? Antiope?—or even if the Latin text is sound. Iopé
may indeed be a ghost.   **Helen:** as usual, Helen of Troy   8 **masks:** masked balls or *(masques)* dramatic
entertainments in costume   12 **murder:** cause me to die of love for you

Follow Your Saint, Follow with Accents Sweet

Follow your saint, follow with accents sweet,
Haste you, sad notes, fall at her flying feet.
There, wrapped in cloud of sorrow, pity move,
And tell the ravisher of my soul I perish for her love:
But, if she scorns my never-ceasing pain,   5
Then burst with sighing in her sight and ne'er return again.

All that I sung still to her praise did tend,
Still she was first, still she my songs did end;
Yet she my love and music both doth fly,
The music that her echo is and beauty's sympathy.   10
Then let my notes pursue her scornful flight:
It shall suffice that they were breathed and died for her delight.

Ibid.

1 **saint:** the one you worship, the person you love

Shall I Come, Sweet Love, to Thee

Shall I come, sweet love, to thee
      When the evening beams are set?
Shall I not excluded be,
      Will you find no feignèd let?
            Let me not, for pity, more   5
            Tell the long hours at your door.

Who can tell what thief or foe,
      In the covert of the night,
For his prey will work my woe,
      Or through wicked foul despite?   10
            Do not mock me in thy bed,
            While these cold nights freeze me dead.

But to let such dangers pass,
      Which a lover's thoughts disdain,
'Tis enough in such a place   15
      To attend love's joys in vain:
            So may I die unredressed
            Ere my long love be possessed.

The Third and Fourth Book of Airs, 1617.

4 **feignèd let:** pretended impediment   6 **tell:** count

Thrice Toss These Oaken Ashes in the Air

Thrice toss these oaken ashes in the air,
Thrice sit thou mute in this enchanted chair;
Then thrice three times tie up this true love's knot,
And murmur soft, "She will, or she will not."

Go burn these poisonous weeds in yon blue fire,   5
These screech-owl's feathers and this prickling brier,

Ibid.

1–10 Magic spells and rituals to win the love of his lady.

This cypress gathered at a dead man's grave,
That all thy fears and cares an end may have.

Then come, you fairies, dance with me a round,
Melt her hard heart with your melodious sound.   10
In vain are all the charms I can devise;
She hath an art to break them with her eyes.

Thomas Nashe
(1567–1601)

Nashe, as pamphleteer, took an active part in the literary life of London, with its quarrels
and controversies. He wrote one celebrated adventure novel, *The Unfortunate Traveller*,
and the masque (dramatic entertainment) from which his most famous poem comes.

Adieu, Farewell Earth's Bliss

Adieu, farewell earth's bliss!
This world uncertain is:
Fond are life's lustful joys;
Death proves them all but toys.
None from his darts can fly;   5
I am sick, I must die.
    Lord, have mercy on us.

Rich men, trust not in wealth:
Gold cannot buy you health;
Physic himself must fade.   10
All things to end are made;
The plague full swift goes by.
I am sick, I must die.
    Lord, have mercy on us.

Beauty is but a flower   15
Which wrinkles will devour;
Brightness falls from the air;
Queens have died young and fair;
Dust hath closed Helen's eye.
I am sick, I must die.   20
    Lord, have mercy on us.

Strength stoops unto the grave;
Worms feed on Hector brave.
Swords may not fight with fate;
Earth still holds ope her gate.   25
Come, come, the bells do cry.
I am sick, I must die.
    Lord, have mercy on us.

Wit with his wantonness
Tasteth death's bitterness;   30

---

c. 1592. *Summer's Last Will and Testament*, 1600.

This "doleful ditty," as it is called in Nashe's play, is thought to express the apprehension felt in London during a visitation of the plague.

3 **fond:** foolish   4 **toys:** trifles   19 **Helen:** Helen of Troy, who stands for physical beauty   23 **Hector:** the Trojan hero, who stands for strength and courage   29 **wantonness:** playfulness

Hell's executioner
Hath no ears for to hear
What vain art can reply.
I am sick, I must die.
    Lord, have mercy on us.   35

Haste therefore, each degree,
To welcome destiny:
Heaven is our heritage;
Earth but a player's stage.
Mount we unto the sky!   40
I am sick, I must die.
    Lord, have mercy on us.

36 **degree:** social level

Sir Henry Wotton
(1568–1639)

Wotton, who spoke German and Italian well enough to pass for a native, spent most of his life in diplomatic posts. An expert in art and architecture, he was a Member of Parliament in between his several appointments as ambassador to Venice.

On His Mistress, the Queen of Bohemia

You meaner beauties of the night
    That poorly satisfy our eyes
More by your number than your light,
    You common people of the skies,
    What are you when the moon doth rise?   5

You wandering chanters of the wood
    That warble forth Dame Nature's lays,
Thinking your passions understood
    By weaker accents, what's your praise
    When Philomel her voice doth raise?   10

You violets that first appear,
    By your pure purple mantles known,
Like the proud virgins of the year,
    As if the spring were all your own,
    What are you when the rose is blown?   15

So, when my mistress shall be seen
    In form and beauty of her mind,
By virtue first, then choice, a queen,
    Oh tell if she were not designed
    The eclipse and glory of her kind?   20

1619. M. East, *Sixth Set of Books*, 1624. Text from *Reliquiae Wottonianae . . .*, 1651.

The queen of Bohemia was Elizabeth, daughter of King James of England. She married the German Prince Frederick, who in 1619 became (briefly) king of Bohemia. The queen was then in her early twenties.

10 **Philomel:** the nightingale   15 **blown:** blossomed

Thomas Dekker (?)
(c. 1572–1632)

Not much is known about Dekker's life, except that he was more than once imprisoned for debt. In prose pamphlets sometimes about low life, and in the many jolly plays in which he had a hand, he wrote with gusto about his native London.

Art Thou Poor, yet Hast Thou Golden Slumbers?

Art thou poor, yet hast thou golden slumbers?
    O sweet content!
Art thou rich, yet is thy mind perplexed?
    O punishment!
Dost thou laugh to see how fools are vexed   5
To add to golden numbers, golden numbers?
O sweet content! O sweet content!

    Work apace, apace, apace, apace;
    Honest labour bears a lovely face;
    Then hey nonny nonny, hey nonny nonny!   10

Canst drink the waters of the crispèd spring?
    O sweet content!
Swimm'st thou in wealth, yet sink'st in thine own tears?
    O punishment!
Then he that patiently want's burden bears   15
No burden bears, but is a king, a king!
O sweet content! O sweet content!

    Work apace, *etc.*

---

c. 1600. H. Chettle, W. Haughton, and T. Dekker, *The Pleasant Comedy of Patient Grissill*, 1603.

11 **crispèd:** rippling

Anonymous Lyrics from Songbooks

I Heard a Noise and Wishèd for a Sight

I heard a noise and wishèd for a sight,
I looked for life and did a shadow see
Whose substance was the sum of my delight,
Which came unseen, and so did go from me.
    Yet hath conceit persuaded my content   5
    There was a substance where the shadow went.

I did not play Narcissus in conceit,
I did not see my shadow in a spring:
I know mine eyes were dimmed with no deceit,

---

c. 1597. Oxford, Bodleian MS. Rawl. Poet. 148. Shorter version in T. Bateson, *Second Set of Madrigals*, 1618. N. Ault, *Elizabethan Lyrics*, 1925.

5 **conceit:** imagination, fancy   **content:** happiness   7 **Narcissus:** in Greek mythology, the young man who fell in love with his own reflection in a pool

I saw the shadow of some worthy thing;   10
    For, as I saw the shadow glancing by,
    I had a glimpse of something in mine eye.

But what it was, alas, I cannot tell,
Because of it I had no perfect view;
But as it was, by guess, I wish it well   15
And will until I see the same anew.
    Shadow, or she, or both, or choose you whither:
    Blest be the thing that brought the shadow hither.

17 **whither:** whether

Weep You No More, Sad Fountains

Weep you no more, sad fountains;
    What need you flow so fast?
Look how the snowy mountains
    Heaven's sun doth gently waste.
      But my sun's heavenly eyes   5
      View not your weeping,
      That now lies sleeping
    Softly, now softly lies
      Sleeping.

Sleep is a reconciling,   10
    A rest that peace begets:
Doth not the sun rise smiling
    When fair at even he sets?
      Rest you then, rest, sad eyes,
      Melt not in weeping,   15
      While she lies sleeping
    Softly, now softly lies
      Sleeping.

    John Dowland, *The Third and Last Book of Songs or Airs*, 1603.

Thule, the Period of Cosmography

Thule, the period of cosmography,
    Doth vaunt of Hecla, whose sulphureous fire
Doth melt the frozen clime and thaw the sky;
    Trinacrian Etna's flames ascend not higher:
These things seem wondrous, yet more wondrous I,   5
Whose heart with fear doth freeze, with love doth fry.

The Andalusian merchant, that returns
    Laden with cochineal and china dishes,
Reports in Spain how strangely Fogo burns
    Amidst an ocean full of flying fishes: 10
These things seem wondrous, yet more wondrous I,
Whose heart with fear doth freeze, with love doth fry.

    Thomas Weelkes, *Madrigals of Six Parts . . .* , 1600.

1 **Thule:** for the ancients, the most northerly point of the known world, probably Iceland   **period:** final point   2 **Hecla:** Hekla, a volcano in Iceland, famous for its spectacular eruptions   4 **Trinacrian Etna:** Mt. Etna in Sicily   7 **Andalusian:** from Andalusia, a region in southern Spain   8 **cochineal:** a scarlet dye   9 **Fogo:** a volcano on Fogo Island (Cape Verde Islands)

Fine Knacks for Ladies

Fine knacks for ladies, cheap, choice, brave and new.
    Good pennyworths, but money cannot move:
I keep a fair but for the fair to view;
    A beggar may be liberal of love.
Though all my wares be trash, the heart is true.   5

Great gifts are guiles and look for gifts again;
    My trifles come as treasures from my mind:
It is a precious jewel to be plain;
    Sometimes in shell the orient'st pearls we find.
Of others take a sheaf, of me a grain.   10

Within this pack, pins, points, laces, and gloves,
    And divers toys fitting a country fair;
But in my heart, where duty serves and loves,
    Turtles and twins, court's brood, a heavenly pair.
Happy the heart that thinks of no removes.   15

John Dowland, *Second Book of Songs or Airs*, 1600.

A peddler's song.

2 **money cannot move:** "Money alone cannot influence me to sell."   9 **orient'st:** brightest, like (1) oriental pearls; (2) the rising sun   11 **points:** laces, ties   14 **turtles:** turtledoves, symbols of fidelity in love   15 **removes:** separations, partings

The Silver Swan

The silver swan, who living had no note,
When death approached, unlocked her silent throat.
Leaning her breast against the reedy shore,
Thus sung her first and last, and sung no more:
Farewell all joys! O death, come close mine eyes;
More geese than swans now live, more fools than wise.

Orlando Gibbons, *The First Set of Madrigals and Motets . . .* , 1612.

John Donne
(1572–1631)

As a young law student, Donne was already speculating about religion and writing much passionate, sharp-witted poetry. After taking part in naval expeditions against the Spaniards, he became secretary to Sir Thomas Edgerton and seemed on his way to a promising diplomatic career. In 1601 he ruined his chances by secretly marrying Ann More, the under-age niece of Edgerton's wife. After years of poverty, during which 12 children were born, Donne gave up his hopes of a political career and was ordained an Anglican priest—a decisive step in the change from "Jack Donne" of the sensuous love poems and angry satires into "Dr. Donne," the greatest preacher of his time. Though few of his poems were printed during his lifetime, many were circulated in manuscript. Neglected as a poet after his own century, he became a favorite of such twentieth-century masters as Yeats and Eliot.

The Anniversary

        All kings, and all their favorites,
        All glory of honors, beauties, wits,

---

c. 1603? *Poems*, 1633.

The sun itself, which makes times, as they pass,
Is elder by a year, now, than it was
When thou and I first one another saw: 5
All other things, to their destruction draw,
    Only our love hath no decay;
This, no tomorrow hath, nor yesterday;
Running, it never runs from us away,
But truly keeps his first, last, everlasting day.   10

    Two graves must hide thine and my corse,
      If one might, death were no divorce;
Alas, as well as other princes, we
(Who prince enough in one another be)
Must leave at last in death, these eyes, and ears,   15
Oft fed with true oaths, and with sweet salt tears;
    But souls where nothing dwells but love
(All other thoughts being inmates) then shall prove
This, or a love increasèd there above,
When bodies to their graves, souls from their graves remove.   20

    And then we shall be thoroughly blest,
      But we no more, than all the rest;
Here upon earth, we are kings, and none but we
Can be such kings, nor of such subjects be;
Who is so safe as we? where none can do   25
Treason to us, except one of us two.
    True and false fears let us refrain,
Let us love nobly, and live, and add again
Years and years unto years, till we attain
To write threescore: this is the second of our reign.   30

11 **corse:** corpse   18 **inmates:** lodgers, temporary residents   **prove:** experience

Song

Go, and catch a falling star,
    Get with child a mandrake root,
Tell me, where all past years are,
    Or who cleft the devil's foot,
Teach me to hear mermaids singing,   5
Or to keep off envy's stinging,
    And find
    What wind
Serves to advance an honest mind.

If thou beest born to strange sights,   10
    Things invisible to see,
Ride ten thousand days and nights
    Till age snow white hairs on thee;
Thou, when thou return'st, wilt tell me

Probably before 1600. Ibid.

2 **mandrake root:** The bifurcated root of the mandrake looked like a grotesque human shape, and suggested many superstitious fancies. It was considered an aphrodisiac, promoter of fertility, and so forth.

All strange wonders that befell thee, 15
    And swear
    Nowhere
Lives a woman true and fair.

If thou find'st one, let me know;
    Such a pilgrimage were sweet. 20
Yet do not; I would not go,
    Though at next door we might meet,
Though she were true, when you met her,
And last till you write your letter,
    Yet she 25
    Will be
False, ere I come, to two or three.

The Sun Rising

    Busy old fool, unruly sun,
    Why dost thou thus
Through windows, and through curtains call on us?
Must to thy motions lovers' seasons run?
    Saucy pedantic wretch, go chide 5
    Late school boys, and sour prentices,
  Go tell court-huntsmen that the King will ride,
  Call country ants to harvest offices;
Love, all alike, no season knows, nor clime,
Nor hours, days, months, which are the rags of time. 10

    Thy beams, so reverend and strong
    Why shouldst thou think?
I could eclipse and cloud them with a wink,
But that I would not lose her sight so long:
    If her eyes have not blinded thine, 15
    Look, and tomorrow late, tell me
  Whether both the Indias of spice and mine
  Be where thou left'st them, or lie here with me.
Ask for those Kings whom thou saw'st yesterday,
And thou shalt hear: all here in one bed lay. 20

    She's all states, and all princes, I,
    Nothing else is.
Princes do but play us; compared to this,
All honor's mimic; all wealth alchemy.
    Thou, sun, art half as happy as we, 25
    In that the world's contracted thus;
  Thine age asks ease, and since thy duties be
  To warm the world, that's done in warming us.
Shine here to us, and thou art everywhere;
This bed thy center is, these walls, thy sphere. 30

---

c. 1603? Ibid.

7 **Go tell ...**: King James liked to get up early to go hunting—an annoyance to the "court hunts-men." 8 **country ants**: farm laborers 17 **both the Indias**: the East Indies, noted for spices, and the West Indies, noted for gold (*mine*) 24 **alchemy**: a hoax, a false show of splendor

The Canonization

For God's sake hold your tongue, and let me love,
  Or chide my palsy, or my gout,
My five gray hairs or ruined fortune flout,
    With wealth your state, your mind with arts improve,
      Take you a course, get you a place,   5
      Observe his honor, or his grace,
Or the King's real, or his stampèd face
  Contemplate, what you will, approve,
  So you will let me love.

Alas, alas, who's injured by my love?   10
  What merchant's ships have my sighs drowned?
Who says my tears have overflowed his ground?
    When did my colds a forward spring remove?
      When did the heats which my veins fill
      Add one more to the plaguy bill?   15
Soldiers find wars, and lawyers find out still
  Litigious men, which quarrels move,
  Though she and I do love.

Call us what you will, we are made such by love;
  Call her one, me another fly,   20
We are tapers too, and at our own cost die,
    And we in us find the eagle and the dove.
      The Phoenix riddle hath more wit
      By us: we two being one, are it;
So to one neutral thing both sexes fit.   25
  We die and rise the same, and prove
  Mysterious by this love.

We can die by it, if not live by love,
  And if unfit for tombs and hearse
Our legend be, it will be fit for verse;   30
    And if no piece of chronicle we prove,
      We'll build in sonnets pretty rooms;
      As well a well-wrought urn becomes
The greatest ashes, as half-acre tombs,
  And by these hymns, all shall approve   35
  Us canonized for love:

And thus invoke us: You whom reverend love
  Made one another's hermitage;
You, to whom love was peace, that now is rage;
    Who did the whole world's soul contract, and drove   40
      Into the glasses of your eyes
      (So made such mirrors, and such spies,

---

c. 1603? Ibid.

canonization: process of being declared a saint   **1 love:** rhymes on *love* run through all five stanzas   **5 course:** career   **6 his honor:** a judge   **his grace:** a duke or archbishop   **7 stampèd face:** on a coin   **13 forward:** early   **15 plaguy bill:** weekly list of plague victims   **20 fly:** moth, insect attracted by flame   **21 die:** experience sexual climax [colloquial]   **22 eagle ... dove:** masculine and feminine qualities   **23 Phoenix riddle:** The Phoenix was a mythological bird which, consumed in flames, rose again from its own ashes.   **31 chronicle:** history   **39 rage:** madness, violence

That they did all to you epitomize)
    Countries, towns, courts: beg from above
    A pattern of your love.   45

A Valediction: Of Weeping

        Let me pour forth
My tears before thy face, whilst I stay here,
For thy face coins them, and thy stamp they bear,
And by this mintage they are something worth,
        For thus they be   5
        Pregnant of thee;
Fruits of much grief they are, emblems of more,
When a tear falls, that thou falls which it bore,
So thou and I are nothing then, when on a diverse shore.

        On a round ball   10
A workman that hath copies by, can lay
An Europe, Afric, and an Asia,
And quickly make that, which was nothing, all;
        So doth each tear,
        Which thee doth wear,   15
A globe, yea world, by that impression grow,
Till thy tears mixed with mine do overflow
This world, by waters sent from thee, my heaven dissolvèd so.

        O more than moon,
Draw not up seas to drown me in thy sphere,   20
Weep me not dead, in thine arms, but forbear
To teach the sea, what it may do too soon;
        Let not the wind
        Example find,
To do me more harm, than it purposeth;   25
Since thou and I sigh one another's breath,
Whoe'er sighs most, is cruellest, and hastes the other's death.

After 1600. Ibid.

valediction: leave-taking, farewell 2 **whilst I stay here:** before I leave 3 **coins them:** each tear reflects your face, like that on a coin 8 **that thou:** that image of you, destroyed when the tear falls 11 **workman:** maker of terrestrial globes 15 **which thee doth wear:** which shows your image 18 **heaven:** She, his "heaven," is now dissolved in tears. 19 **more than moon:** The moon can raise only the tides; she raises *seas* of tears in him. 22 **what it may do:** drown him—he is about to make an actual sea voyage.

The Relic

        When my grave is broke up again
        Some second guest to entertain,
        (For graves have learned that woman-head
        To be to more than one a bed)
        And he that digs it spies   5
A bracelet of bright hair about the bone,

After 1600. Ibid.

1 **broke up again:** Cemeteries were sometimes reused. 3 **woman-head:** womanhood, womanly trait

Will he not let us alone,
And think that there a loving couple lies,
Who thought that this device might be some way
To make their souls, at the last busy day,   10
Meet at this grave, and make a little stay?

If this fall in a time, or land,
Where mis-devotion doth command,
Then, he that digs us up will bring
Us to the bishop, and the king,   15
        To make us relics; then
Thou shalt be a Mary Magdalen, and I
        A something else thereby;
All women shall adore us, and some men;
And, since at such time miracles are sought,   20
I would have that age by this paper taught
What miracles we harmless lovers wrought.

First, we loved well and faithfully,
Yet knew not what we loved, nor why;
Difference of sex no more we knew,   25
Than our guardian angels do;
        Coming and going, we
Perchance might kiss, but not between those meals;
        Our hands ne'er touched the seals,
Which nature, injured by late law, sets free: 30
These miracles we did; but now, alas,
All measure, and all language, I should pass,
Should I tell what a miracle she was.

10 **the last busy day:** the day of judgment   13 **mis-devotion:** a superstitious form of religion
17 **Mary Magdalen:** because of the "bright hair"—Mary Magdalen was depicted with long golden
hair   18 **a something else:** probably one of her lovers   27 **coming and going:** Kisses of salutation
and parting were thought innocent and even sanctioned by the Bible.   30 **late law:** restrictions, im-
posed later in man's history, on the innocent freedom nature seemed to allow

The Ecstasy

Where, like a pillow on a bed,
    A pregnant bank swelled up, to rest
The violet's reclining head,
    Sat we two, one another's best.
Our hands were firmly cémented   5
    With a fast balm, which thence did spring,
Our eye-beams twisted, and did thread
    Our eyes, upon one double string;
So t'intergraft our hands, as yet
    Was all the means to make us one,   10
And pictures in our eyes to get
    Was all our propagation.

After 1600. Ibid.

Ecstasy means the state of being outside oneself, free from the limitations of the body. Donne imag-
ines the souls of the two lovers as leaving their bodies and fusing in a new unity, in which they
achieve a vision of the nature of their love and of the interdependence of body and soul.

6 **fast balm:** warm moisture bonding their palms together   7–8 **eyebeams . . . :** as if their eyeballs
were beads strung on the steady back-and-forth gaze between them   9–12 **So t'intergraft . . . :** They
are only holding hands and looking at their reflection in each other's eyes.

As 'twixt two equal armies, fate
  Suspends uncertain victory,
Our souls (which to advance their state   15
  Were gone out) hung 'twixt her, and me.
And whilst our souls negotiate there,
  We like sepulchral statues lay;
All day, the same our postures were,
  And we said nothing, all the day.   20
If any, so by love refined,
  That he soul's language understood,
And by good love were grown all mind,
  Within convenient distance stood,
He (though he knew not which soul spake,   25
  Because both meant, both spake the same)
Might thence a new concoction take,
  And part far purer than he came.
"This ecstasy doth unperplex"
  (We said) "and tell us what we love;   30
We see by this, it was not sex;
  We see, we saw not what did move:
But as all several souls contain
  Mixture of things, they know not what,
Love, these mixed souls doth mix again,   35
  And makes both one, each this and that.
A single violet transplant,
  The strength, the color, and the size,
(All which before was poor, and scant)
  Redoubles still, and multiplies.   40
When love, with one another so
  Interinanimates two souls,
That abler soul, which thence doth flow,
  Defects of loneliness controls.
We then, who are this new soul, know   45
  Of what we are composed, and made,
For, the atomies of which we grow,
  Are souls, whom no change can invade.
But oh alas, so long, so far
  Our bodies why do we forbear?   50
They are ours, though they are not we; we are
  The intelligences, they the sphere.
We owe them thanks, because they thus,
  Did us, to us, at first convey,
Yielded their forces, sense, to us,   55
  Nor are dross to us, but allay.
On man heaven's influence works not so,
  But that it first imprints the air,
So soul into the soul may flow,
  Though it to body first repair.   60

---

18 sepulchral statues: statues on a tomb   **21-26 If any . . . :** if anyone could have read our minds—or our mind, since they were one   **27 concoction:** a process of refining by heat   **29 unperplex:** clarify   **31 sex:** According to the Oxford English Dictionary, Donne was the first writer to use this word with its modern meaning.   **42 interinanimates:** animates each through the other   **43 that abler soul:** the joint soul, a blend of both, which results   **44 defects of loneliness:** defects of each in isolation   **47 atomies:** elements, components   **50 forbear:** shun, ignore   **52 intelligences:** Angelic intelligences were thought to control the "spheres," the clear, whirling, concentric bubbles, one within the other, that made up the heavens in the old cosmology.   **55 sense:** sense-perception, sensation   **56 dross:** scum or foreign matter thrown off by melting metals   **allay:** alloy, metal added to another, often (as here) to improve it in some way   **57-58 not so, / But that:** only if (Even astral influences need the physical air to travel through or manifest themselves in.)

As our blood labors to beget
   Spirits, as like souls as it can,
Because such fingers need to knit
   That subtle knot, which makes us man:
So must pure lovers' souls descend   65
   To affections, and to faculties,
Which sense may reach and apprehend,
   Else a great prince in prison lies.
To our bodies turn we then, that so
   Weak men on love revealed may look;   70
Love's mysteries in souls do grow,
   But yet the body is his book.
And if some lover, such as we,
   Have heard this dialogue of one,
Let him still mark us, he shall see   75
   Small change, when we're to bodies gone."

62 **spirits:** subtle fluids or vapors produced by the blood to serve as tie between body and soul
63 **need:** are needed 65–68 **so must . . . :** so the souls need emotion and physical faculties to commu-
nicate with one another—otherwise the soul is like a prince imprisoned 71–72 **Love's mysteries . . . :**
Though love is spiritual in origin, its operation can be seen—or "read"—only in the body.

A Valediction: Forbidding Mourning

As virtuous men pass mildly away,
   And whisper to their souls, to go,
Whilst some of their sad friends do say,
   The breath goes now, and some say, no:

So let us melt, and make no noise,   5
   No tear-floods, nor sigh-tempests move;
'Twere profanation of our joys
   To tell the laity our love.

Moving of the earth brings harms and fears,
   Men reckon what it did and meant,   10
But trepidation of the spheres,
   Though greater far, is innocent.

Dull sublunary lovers' love
   (Whose soul is sense) cannot admit
Absence, because it doth remove
   Those things which elemented it.   15

But we by a love, so much refined,
   That ourselves know not what it is,
Inter-assured of the mind,
   Care less, eyes, lips, and hands to miss.   20

Our two souls therefore, which are one,
   Though I must go, endure not yet

1611? Ibid.

8 **laity:** the ordinary people, unsubtle in the ways of love 9 **moving of the earth:** earthquakes
11 **trepidation of the spheres:** the precession of the equinoxes (whose complete revolution takes
26,000 years) 13 **sublunary:** earthly (beneath the moon) 14 **whose soul is sense:** whose soul is
limited to physical sensations 16 **elemented it:** were its elements

A breach, but an expansion,
    Like gold to airy thinness beat.

If they be two, they are two so   25
    As stiff twin compasses are two:
Thy soul, the fixed foot, makes no show
    To move, but doth, if the other do.

And though it in the center sit,
    Yet when the other far doth roam,   30
It leans, and hearkens after it,
    And grows erect, as that comes home.

Such wilt thou be to me, who must
    Like the other foot, obliquely run;
Thy firmness makes my circle just,   35
    And makes me end, where I begun.

24 **gold . . . beat:** Gold can be hammered so thin that it would take 2000 sheets to make up the thickness of this page. 26 **stiff twin compasses:** the kind used for drawing circles—two legs with a pivot at the top

From Holy Sonnets

At the Round Earth's Imagined Corners

At the round earth's imagined corners, blow
Your trumpets, angels, and arise, arise
From death, you numberless infinities
Of souls, and to your scattered bodies go,
All whom the flood did, and fire shall o'erthrow,   5
All whom war, dearth, age, agues, tyrannies,
Despair, law, chance, hath slain, and you whose eyes
Shall behold God, and never taste death's woe.
But let them sleep, Lord, and me mourn a space,
For, if above all these, my sins abound,   10
'Tis late to ask abundance of Thy grace,
When we are there; here on this lowly ground,
Teach me how to repent; for that's as good
As if Thou hadst sealed my pardon with Thy blood.

1 **round earth's imagined corners:** as shown on flat maps

Death Be Not Proud

Death be not proud, though some have callèd thee
Mighty and dreadful, for thou art not so;
For those whom thou think'st thou dost overthrow
Die not, poor death, nor yet canst thou kill me.
From rest and sleep, which but thy pictures be,   5
Much pleasure, then from thee much more must flow,
And soonest our best men with thee do go,
Rest of their bones, and soul's delivery.
Thou art slave to fate, chance, kings, and desperate men,
And dost with poison, war, and sickness dwell,   10
And poppy, or charms can make us sleep as well,

And better than thy stroke; why swell'st thou then?
One short sleep past, we wake eternally,
And death shall be no more; death, thou shalt die.

12 **swell'st:** swell up with pride

Batter My Heart, Three-Personed God

Batter my heart, three-personed God; for You
As yet but knock, breathe, shine, and seek to mend;
That I may rise, and stand, o'erthrow me, and bend
Your force, to break, blow, burn and make me new.
I, like an usurped town, to another due,   5
Labor to admit You, but oh, to no end!
Reason, Your viceroy in me, me should defend,
But is captived, and proves weak or untrue.
Yet dearly I love You, and would be lovèd fain,
But am betrothed unto Your enemy: 10
Divorce me, untie, or break that knot again,
Take me to You, imprison me, for I
Except You enthrall me, never shall be free,
Nor ever chaste, except You ravish me.

———————————

Probably 1607–1610. Ibid.

9 **would be lovèd fain:** would gladly be loved

A Hymn to God the Father

I
Wilt Thou forgive that sin where I begun,
　　Which was my sin, though it were done before?
Wilt Thou forgive that sin through which I run,
　　And do run still: though still I do deplore?
　　　　When Thou hast done, Thou hast not done,   5
　　　　　　For I have more.

II
Wilt Thou forgive that sin which I have won
　　Others to sin? and, made my sin their door?
Wilt Thou forgive that sin which I did shun
　　A year or two: but wallowed in a score?   10
　　　　When Thou hast done, Thou hast not done,
　　　　　　For I have more.

III
I have a sin of fear, that when I have spun
　　My last thread, I shall perish on the shore;
But swear by Thyself that at my death Thy Son   15
　　Shall shine as He shines now, and heretofore;
　　　　And, having done that, Thou hast done,
　　　　　　I fear no more.

———————————

1623. Ibid.

5 Such puns as: "When thou hast done, thou hast not Donne . . ." are no doubt intended.

Ben Jonson
(1573?–1637)

Jonson's schooling was cut short so that he could be apprenticed as a bricklayer. Before he was 20 he had fought in the Netherlands. He was imprisoned when a play he was in was closed for being seditious, and again the following year for killing a fellow actor in a duel. Meanwhile he had begun the series of realistic comedies that made him famous. Though Jonson rubbed many important people the wrong way, his reputation for learning, the solidity of his talent, and the skill with which he wrote court entertainments kept him for the most part in favor. His last dozen years were plagued by quarrels with other artists and his own crippling illnesses.

Hymn to Diana

Queen and huntress, chaste and fair,
Now the sun is laid to sleep,
Seated in thy silver chair,
State in wonted manner keep:
    Hesperus entreats thy light,   5
    Goddess excellently bright.

Earth, let not thy envious shade
Dare itself to interpose;
Cynthia's shining orb was made
Heaven to clear when day did close: 10
    Bless us then with wishèd sight,
    Goddess excellently bright.

Lay thy bow of pearl apart,
And thy crystal-shining quiver;
Give unto the flying hart   15
Space to breathe, how short soever:
    Thou that mak'st a day of night,
    Goddess excellently bright.

By 1600. *Cynthia's Revels*, 1601.

Diana, also called Cynthia (line 9), was the goddess of the moon, of virginity, and of hunting.

5 **Hesperus:** the evening star

On My First Son

Farewell, thou child of my right hand, and joy.
    My sin was too much hope of thee, loved boy;
Seven years thou wert lent to me, and I thee pay,
    Exacted by thy fate, on the just day.
Oh, could I lose all father now. For why   5
    Will man lament the state he should envý?—
To have so soon 'scaped world's and flesh's rage,
    And, if no other misery, yet age.

1603. *Epigrams.* In *Works*, 1616.

Jonson's son Benjamin died in 1603 on his seventh birthday.

1 **child of my right hand:** the meaning of *Benjamin* (Hebrew)   5 **all father:** all quality of being a father

Rest in soft peace, and, asked, say here doth lie
   Ben Jonson his best piece of poetry.   10
For whose sake, henceforth, all his vows be such
   As what he loves may never like too much.

11 **Ben Jonson his:** Ben Jonson's

Still to Be Neat, Still to Be Dressed

Still to be neat, still to be dressed,
As you were going to a feast;
Still to be powdered, still perfumed:
Lady, it is to be presumed,
Though art's hid causes are not found,   5
All is not sweet, all is not sound.

Give me a look, give me a face,
That makes simplicity a grace;
Robes loosely flowing, hair as free:
Such sweet neglect more taketh me   10
Than all the adulteries of art;
They strike mine eyes, but not my heart.

By 1609. *Epicoene, or The Silent Woman.* Ibid.

11 **adulteries:** adulterations, falsifications

Epitaph on Elizabeth, L.H.

Wouldst thou hear what man can say
   In a little? Reader, stay.
Underneath this stone doth lie
   As much beauty as could die;
Which in life did harbour give   5
   To more virtue than doth live.
If at all she had a fault,
   Leave it buried in this vault.
One name was Elizabeth,
   The other, let it sleep with death: 10
Fitter, where it died, to tell
   Than that it lived at all. Farewell.

By 1612. *Epigrams.* Ibid.

The subject's name has slept with death, as Jonson wished: she is still unidentified.

To Heaven

Good and great God, can I not think of thee
   But it must, straight, my melancholy be?
Is it interpreted in me disease
   That, laden with my sins, I seek for ease?
Oh be thou witness, that the reins dost know   5
   And hearts of all, if I be sad for show,

By 1612. *The Forest.* In *Works,* 1616.

2 **must . . . be:** must . . . be interpreted as a fit of depression   5 **reins:** kidneys (once thought the organs of emotion)

And judge me after, if I dare pretend
   To ought but grace, or aim at other end.
As thou art all, so be thou all to me,
   First, midst, and last, converted one and three;   10
My faith, my hope, my love, and in this state
   My judge, my witness, and my advocate.
Where have I been this while exiled from thee?
   And whither rapt, now thou but stoopest to me?
Dwell, dwell here still; oh being everywhere   15
   How can I doubt to find thee ever here?
I know my state, both full of shame and scorn,
   Conceived in sin, and unto labor born,
Standing with fear, and must with horror fall,
   And destined unto judgment, after all.   20
I feel my griefs too, and there scarce is ground
   Upon my flesh to inflict another wound.
Yet dare I not complain, or wish for death
   With holy Paul, lest it be thought the breath
Of discontent, or that these prayers be   25
   For weariness of life, not love of thee.

10 **converted one and three:** convertibly one and three—a reference to the Trinity   14 **rapt:** carried away (in spirit), enraptured   24 **Paul:** Rom. 7:24: "who shall deliver me from the body of this death?"

To the Memory of My Beloved the Author
Mr. William Shakespeare, and What He Hath Left Us

To draw no envy, Shakespeare, on thy name
   Am I thus ample to thy book and fame,
While I confess thy writings to be such
   As neither man nor muse can praise too much.
'Tis true, and all men's suffrage. But these ways   5
   Were not the paths I meant unto thy praise,
For seeliest ignorance on these may light
   Which, when it sounds at best, but echoes right;
Or blind affection, which doth ne'er advance
   The truth, but gropes and urgeth all by chance;   10
Or crafty malice might pretend this praise
   And think to ruin where it seemed to raise.
These are as some infamous baud or whore
   Should praise a matron. What could hurt her more?
But thou art proof against them, and indeed   15
   Above the ill fortune of them, or the need.
I therefore will begin. Soul of the age!
   The applause, delight, and wonder of our stage!
My Shakespeare, rise; I will not lodge thee by
   Chaucer, or Spenser, or bid Beaumont lie   20
A little further, to make thee a room.
   Thou art a monument without a tomb,
And art alive still, while thy book doth live
   And we have wits to read, and praise to give.

1623. *Mr. William Shakespeare's Comedies, Histories, and Tragedies,* 1623.

2 **ample:** in writing at some length   5 **suffrage:** allowance, consent   7 **seeliest:** most simple, silliest   13 **as:** as if   20 The three poets named were buried in Westminster Abbey.

That I not mix thee so, my brain excuses—   25
   I mean with great, but disproportioned muses,
For, if I thought my judgement were of years,
   I should commit thee surely with thy peers,
And tell how far thou didst our Lyly outshine,
   Or sporting Kyd, or Marlowe's mighty line.   30
And though thou hadst small Latin and less Greek,
   From thence to honor thee, I would not seek
For names, but call forth thundering Aeschylus,
   Euripides and Sophocles to us,
Pacuvius, Accius, him of Cordova dead,   35
   To life again, to hear thy buskin tread
And shake a stage; or, when thy socks were on
   Leave thee alone, for the comparison
Of all that insolent Greece or haughty Rome
   Sent forth, or since did from their ashes come.   40
Triumph, my Britain, thou hast one to show
   To whom all scenes of Europe homage owe.
He was not of an age, but for all time!
   And all the muses still were in their prime
When like Apollo he came forth to warm   45
   Our ears, or like a Mercury to charm.
Nature herself was proud of his designs,
   And joyed to wear the dressing of his lines,
Which were so richly spun, and woven so fit
   As, since, she will vouchsafe no other wit.   50
The merry Greek, tart Aristophanes,
   Neat Terence, witty Plautus, now not please;
But antiquated and deserted lie,
   As they were not of nature's family.
Yet must I not give nature all; thy art,   55
   My gentle Shakespeare, must enjoy a part.
For though the poet's matter nature be,
   His art doth give the fashion. And that he
Who casts to write a living line, must sweat
   (Such as thine are) and strike the second heat   60
Upon the muses' anvil; turn the same
   (And himself with it) that he thinks to frame;
Or, for the laurel, he may gain a scorn:
   For a good poet's made, as well as born.
And such wert thou. Look how the father's face   65
   Lives in his issue; even so, the race
Of Shakespeare's mind and manners brightly shines
   In his well turnèd and true-filèd lines,
In each of which, he seems to shake a lance
   As brandished at the eyes of ignorance.   70

---

26 **disproportioned:** not in your class   29–30 Three Elizabethan dramatists are named; *sporting* makes the name *Kyd/kid* a pun; Marlowe's *mighty line* refers to the vigor and sonority of the *iambic pentameter* used in his plays (see the prosody section).   33–34 three Greek tragedians of the great period (fifth century B.C.)   35 The first two are obscure Roman tragedians (second century B.C.); "him of Cordova" is the Roman tragedian Seneca (then "dead" over 1500 years).   36 **buskin:** the high boot worn by ancient tragic actors   37 **socks:** the light shoes worn by ancient comic actors   45 **Apollo:** This handsome young god had diversified interests: primarily a sun-god, he interested himself also in music, archery, prophecy, medicine, and—what here concerns Jonson—poetry.   46 **Mercury:** Trickster, magician, herald, orator, inventor of the lyre, patron of thieves—we can assume this god had a certain charisma.   51–52 three ancient writers of comedy, the first Greek, the other two Roman   59 **casts:** intends, tries   62 **frame:** shape   63 **laurel:** symbol of poetry—here, the reward given a good poet   68 **true-filèd:** polished, filed, to accuracy   69 **shake a lance:** cf. shake-spear

Sweet swan of Avon! what a sight it were
  To see thee in our waters yet appear,
And make those flights upon the banks of Thames
  That so did take Eliza and our James.
But stay, I see thee in the hemisphere   75
  Advanced, and made a constellation there.
Shine forth, thou star of poets, and with rage
  Or influence chide or cheer the drooping stage,
Which, since thy flight from hence, hath mourned like night
  And despairs day, but for thy volume's light.   80

71 **swan of Avon:** Sacred to Apollo, the swan was a symbol of beauty, dignity, immortality; wild swans (unlike the mute ones we see in parks) have a musical call. The Avon is the river of Shakespeare's birthplace, Stratford-on-Avon. 73 **Thames:** river through London 74 **Eliza . . . James:** Queen Elizabeth and King James, who succeeded her in 1603 78 **influence:** as stars are thought to "influence" earthly events 80 **despairs:** casts into despair **volume:** the 1623 volume of plays

An Ode: To Himself

     Where dost thou careless lie
       Buried in ease and sloth?
     Knowledge that sleeps doth die;
     And this security,
       It is the common moth   5
That eats on wits and arts, and oft destroys them both.

     Are all the Aonian springs
       Dried up? lies Thespia waste?
     Doth Clarius' harp want strings
       That not a nymph now sings?   10
     Or droop they as disgraced
To see their seats and bowers by chattering pies defaced?

     If hence thy silence be,
       As 'tis too just a cause,
     Let this thought quicken thee: 15
     Minds that are great and free
       Should not on fortune pause;
'Tis crown enough to virtue still: her own applause.

     What though the greedy fry
       Be taken with false baits   20
     Of worded balladry,
     And think it poesy?
       They die with their conceits,
And only piteous scorn upon their folly waits.

     Then take in hand thy lyre,   25
       Strike in thy proper strain,
     With Japhet's line, aspire
       Sol's chariot for new fire,

1629. *The Underwood.* In *Works,* 1640.

4 **security:** smugness, carelessness 7 **Aonian:** Mt. Helicon, sacred to the Muses, was in Aonia; Thespiae (so spelled) was a town at its foot. 9 **Clarius:** Apollo 12 **pies:** magpies, noisy birds 19 **fry:** young people ("small fry") 27 **Japhet:** Prometheus (son of Japhet) stole fire from heaven to benefit man. **aspire:** aspire to, rise to 28 **Sol:** Apollo, the sun

          To give the world again:
Who aided him, will thee—the issue of Jove's brain.   30

         And since our dainty age
            Cannot endure reproof,
         Make not thyself a page
         To that strumpet the stage,
            But sing high and aloof, ·   35
Safe from the wolf's black jaw, and the dull ass's hoof.

30 Minerva, born directly from Jove's brain, goddess of skilled craftsmen

Anonymous

Loving Mad Tom

From the hag and hungry goblin
That into rags would rend ye
The spirit that stands by the naked man
In the Book of Moons defend ye!
That of your five sound senses   5
You never be forsaken,
Nor wander from yourselves with Tom
Abroad to beg your bacon.

    While I do sing "Any food, any feeding,
    Feeding, drink, or clothing,"   10
    Come dame or maid, be not afraid,
    Poor Tom will injure nothing.

Of thirty bare years have I
Twice twenty been enragèd,
And of forty been three times fifteen   15
In durance soundly cagèd,
On the lordly lofts of Bedlam,
With stubble soft and dainty,
Brave bracelets strong, sweet whip's ding-dong,
With wholesome hunger plenty.   20

    And now I sing, etc.

With a thought I took for Maudlin
And a cruse of cockle pottage,
With a thing thus tall, sky bless you all,
I befell into this dotage.

By 1615. *Le Prince d'Amour . . .* , 1660. (*Giles Earle his book 1615*, edited P. Warlock, 1932.)

If this poem does not always make easy sense, it must be remembered that the speaker is a wandering madman, given to delusions and interested in magic. He blames his insanity on his love for a certain Maudlin. Now released from the London lunatic asylum, where he was bound, beaten, and starved (the standard treatment for the insane), he wanders about, getting food and money by theft and threat. Generally harmless, he is dangerous when mistreated.

4 **Book of Moons:** book of astrology? 14 **enragèd:** out of my mind 17 **Bedlam:** the Hospital of St. Mary of Bethlehem, a London madhouse 18 **stubble:** rough straw 19 **bracelets:** hand-cuffs 21 **Maudlin:** Magdalen (girl's name), perhaps a prostitute 22 **cruse:** pot, bowl **cockle pottage:** shellfish chowder (thought an aphrodisiac) 23 **sky:** heaven, God

I slept not since the Conquest,   25
Till then I never wakèd,
Till the roguish boy of love where I lay
Me found and stripped me naked.

 And now I sing, etc.

When I short have shorn my sow's face
And swigged my horny barrel,   30
In an oaken inn I pound my skin
As a suit of gilt apparel.
The moon's my constant mistress,
And the lowly owl my morrow;
The flaming drake and the nightcrow make   35
Me music to my sorrow.

 While I do sing, etc.

The palsy plagues my pulses
When I prig your pigs or pullen,
Your culvers take, or matchless make
Your chanticleer, or sullen;   40
When I want provant, with Humphrey
I sup; and when benighted
I repose in Paul's with waking souls,
Yet never am affrighted.

 But I do sing, etc.

I know more than Apollo,   45
For oft when he lies sleeping
I see the stars at bloody wars
In the wounded welkin weeping;
The moon embrace her shepherd
And the queen of love her warrior,   50
While the first doth horn the star of morn
And the next the heavenly farrier.

 While I do sing, etc.

The Gipsy Snap and Pedro
Are none of Tom's comradoes.
The punk I scorn and the cutpurse sworn   55
And the roaring boy's bravadoes.
The meek, the white, the gentle
Me handle, touch, and spare not,
But those that cross Tom Rhinoceros
Do what the panther dare not.   60

25 the Conquest: the Norman Conquest (1066)   **27 boy of love:** Cupid   **30 swigged my horny barrel:** drunk my rough barrelful (?)   **31 in an oaken inn:** under an oak tree (?); in the stocks (?) **pound:** impound, enclose   **35 drake:** dragon   **38 prig:** steal **pullen:** poultry   **39 culvers:** doves **matchless:** without a mate   **40 chanticleer:** rooster **sullen:** goose (?) (solan: a seafowl resembling a goose)   **41 provant:** food   **Humphrey:** To "dine with Duke Humphrey" meant "to go dinnerless." **43 Paul's:** the churchyard of St. Paul's Cathedral in London   **48 welkin:** heaven   **49 shepherd:** Endymion, with whom the moon was in love   **50 queen of love:** Venus, who was in love with Mars **51 horn:** betray by infidelity   **star of morn:** Phosphorus, thought of here as the husband of the moon   **52 farrier:** blacksmith (Venus was the wife of Vulcan, god of metalworking.)   **55 punk:** prostitute   **56 roaring boy:** boisterous bully   **57 white:** innocent, honest

Although I sing, etc.

With an host of furious fancies
Whereof I am commander,
With a burning spear, and a horse of air,
To the wilderness I wander.
By a knight of ghosts and shadows   65
I summoned am to tourney,
Ten leagues beyond the wide world's end.
Methinks it is no journey.

Yet will I sing, etc.

John Webster
(1580?–1625?)

Nothing is known about Webster's life. We are not even sure which of several John Web-
sters it was who wrote the two greatest tragedies of the period next to Shakespeare's, *The
White Devil* and *The Duchess of Malfi.*

Call for the Robin-Redbreast and the Wren

Call for the robin-redbreast and the wren,
Since o'er shady groves they hover
And with leaves and flowers do cover
The friendless bodies of unburied men.
Call unto his funeral dole   5
The ant, the field-mouse, and the mole,
To rear him hillocks that shall keep him warm
And, when gay tombs are robbed, sustain no harm;
But keep the wolf far thence, that 's foe to men,
For with his nails he'll dig them up again.   10

---

c. 1610. *The White Devil,* 1612.

In Webster's play, a mother sings this dirge over the body of her son, murdered by his brother.

1 It was thought that robins covered the bodies of the abandoned dead. Wrens were thought to be
their mates.   5 **dole:** something given in charity   9 **wolf:** Superstition had it that wolves would dig
up the bodies of murdered men and eat all but the face, which they would leave as evidence against
the murderer.

Hark, Now Everything Is Still

Hark, now everything is still—
The screech-owl and the whistler shrill
Call upon our dame aloud,
And bid her quickly don her shroud.
Much you had of land and rent;   5
Your length in clay's now competent.
A long war disturbed your mind;

1613–1614. *The Duchess of Malfi,* 1623.

In Webster's play, this song is sung to the duchess just before she is murdered.

2 **whistler:** an unidentified bird whose mysterious cry was thought to be a warning of death
6 **competent:** sufficient

Here your perfect peace is signed.
Of what is't fools make such vain keeping?
Sin their conception, their birth weeping;   10
Their life, a general mist of error;
Their death, a hideous storm of terror.
Strew your hair with powders sweet,
Don clean linen, bathe your feet,
And, the foul fiend more to check,   15
A crucifix let bless your neck.
'Tis now full tide 'tween night and day;
End your groan, and come away.

17 **full tide:** exactly the time

Francis Beaumont (?)
(1584–1616)

Beaumont is best known as half of the famous writing team of Beaumont and Fletcher, responsible for most of the *Fifty Comedies and Tragedies* (1679).

Aspatia's Song

Lay a garland on my hearse of the dismal yew;
Maidens, willow branches bear; say I dièd true.
My love was false, but I was firm from my hour of birth;
Upon my buried body lay lightly, gentle earth.

By 1611. *The Maid's Tragedy*, 2nd ed., 1622 (not in 1st ed.).

This song occurs in *The Maid's Tragedy* (about 1610), by Francis Beaumont and John Fletcher. Beaumont is supposed to have written the part in which the song occurs. It is sung by the jilted maid, Aspatia, who three acts later procures her own death by disguising herself as a man and provoking her former lover (who of course repents) into a duel.

William Basse (?)
(c. 1583–1653?)

Little is known about Basse, who published only a few poems while still young and left much verse in manuscript.

A Memento for Mortality

> *Taken from the view of sepulchres of so many kings*
> *and nobles, as lie interred in the Abbey of Westminster.*

Mortality, behold, and fear,
What a change of flesh is here.
Think how many royal bones
Sleep within this heap of stones,
Hence removed from beds of ease,   5
Dainty fare, and what might please,

W.B. and E.P., *A Help to Discourse, or, a Miscellany of Merriment* . . . , 1619.

This poem, of uncertain authorship, is sometimes attributed to Francis Beaumont.

1 **mortality:** humanity

Fretted roofs, and costly shows
To a roof that flats the nose:
Which proclaims all flesh is grass;
How the world's fair glories pass;   10
That there is no trust in health,
In youth, in age, in greatness, wealth,
For if such could have reprieved
Those had been immortal-lived.
Know from this the world's a snare,   15
How that greatness is but care,
How all pleasures are but pain,
And how short they do remain:
For here they lie had realms and lands,
That now want strength to stir their hands,   20
Where from their pulpits sealed with dust
They preach: *In greatness is no trust.*
Here's an acre sown indeed
With the richest royalest seed
That the earth did e'er suck in   25
Since the first man died for sin.
Here the bones of birth have cried,
Though Gods they were, as men they died.
Here are sands, ignoble things,
Dropped from the ruined sides of kings;   30
With whom the poor man's earth being shown,
The difference is not easily known.
Here's a world of pomp and state
Forgotten, dead, disconsolate;
Think, then, this scythe that mows down kings   35
Exempts no meaner mortal things.
Then bid the wanton lady tread
Amid these mazes of the dead;
And these, truly understood,
More shall cool and quench the blood   40
Than her many sports a-day
And her nightly wanton play.
Bid her paint till day of doom,
To this favour she must come.
Bid the merchant gather wealth,   45
The usurer exact by stealth,
The proud man beat it from his thought,
Yet to this shape all must be brought.

7 **fretted:** ornamented in relief   19 **had:** who had   44 **favour:** appearance

Sir Francis Kynaston
(1587–1642)

A Member of Parliament whose interests were chiefly literary, Kynaston founded an academy and wrote a masque, a long heroic poem, and shorter poems to a certain Cynthia he admitted he was "scarcely acquainted" with.

To Cynthia

On her being an incendiary

Say, sweetest, whether thou didst use me well
If when in my heart's house I let thee dwell
A welcome inmate, and did not require
More than a kiss a day for rent or hire,
Thou wert not only pleased to stop the rent,   5
But, most ungrateful, burnt the tenement.
Henceforth it will ensue that thou didst carry
The branded name of an incendiary:
No heart will harbor thee, and thou, like poor
As I, mayest lodging beg from door to door.   10
If it be so, my ready course will be
To get a license and re-edify
My wasted heart. If Cupid shall inquire
By what mishap my heart was set on fire,
I'll say, my happy fortune was to get   15
Thy beauty's crop, which being green and wet
With showers of tears, I did too hasty in,
Before that thoroughly withered it had been,
So, heating in the mow, it soon became
At first a smoke and afterwards a flame.   20
At this love's little king will much admire
How cold and wet conjoined can cause a fire,
Having no heat themselves, but I do know
What he will say, for he will bid me go
And build my heart of stone: so shall I be   25
Safe from the lightning of thine eyes and thee,
The cold and hardness of stone hearts best serving
For coy green beauties and them best preserving.
Yet here is danger, for if thou be in't,
My heart to stone, and thine harder than flint   30
Knocking together may strike fire, and set
Much more on fire than hath been burnèd yet.
If so it hap, then let those flames calcine
My heart to cinders, so it soften thine:
A heart which until then doth serve the turn   35
To enflame others, but itself not burn.

Leoline and Sydanis, 1642.

incendiary: arsonist   9 **like poor:** as poor   12 **re-edify:** rebuild   16 **green and wet:** As any farmer knows, hay stored with a high moisture content is dangerously subject to spontaneous combustion. 17 **did:** brought   21 **little king:** Cupid   29 **in't:** in it   33 **hap:** happen   **calcine:** burn to ashes 34 **so:** provided that

William Browne
(1591?–1643?)

Browne studied law, lived for a time in France, was tutor to a young lord, and specialized in pastoral poetry, most of it written in his twenties.

On the Countess Dowager of Pembroke

Underneath this sable hearse
Lies the subject of all verse:
Sidney's sister, Pembroke's mother.
Death, ere thou hast slain another
Fair and learn'd and good as she,
Time shall throw a dart at thee.

1621? William Camden, *Remains Concerning Britain* . . . , 1623 (with an inferior second stanza). Other versions in Francis Osborne's *Traditionall Memoyres on the Raigne of King James*, 1658, and *Poems of William, Earl of Pembroke and Sir Benjamin Rudyard*, 1660.

Probably the most admired of Elizabethan ladies after the queen, Mary Sidney (1561–1621), Sir Philip Sidney's sister, married Henry Herbert, the Earl of Pembroke. After his death in 1601 she became the Countess Dowager (widowed countess). Patroness of poets and editor of her brother's works, she was a poet herself. Her son William Herbert (1580–1630), the "Pembroke" of the poem (and some believe the "Mr. W. H." to whom Shakespeare's sonnets are dedicated as their "only begetter"), was also one of the most attractive figures of his age, admired as much for his integrity as for his charm and learning. He also wrote poetry.

1 **hearse:** here, probably the rich black cloth draped over coffin or tomb, though the word basically meant the iron rack that supported it   6 **Time . . . thee:** The world itself will end.

Robert Herrick
(1591–1674)

A priest in the Church of England, and briefly an army chaplain, Herrick was one of the "sons of Ben" who gathered around Jonson in various London taverns. In 1629 he became a country pastor. Loyal to the king in the Civil War, he was ejected from his post by the Puritans in 1647 and did not return until the restoration of the monarchy in 1660. *Hesperides*, his only book published during his lifetime, came out in 1648, when he was approaching 60. It did not do well; up-to-date readers of the 1640s thought of it as belonging to the old-fashioned twenties.

The Argument of His Book

I sing of brooks, of blossoms, birds and bowers;
Of April, May, of June and July-flowers.
I sing of maypoles, hock-carts, wassails, wakes,
Of bridegrooms, brides, and of their bridal cakes.
I write of youth, of love, and have access   5
By these to sing of cleanly wantonness.
I sing of dews, of rains, and piece by piece
Of balm, of oil, of spice, and ambergris.
I sing of times trans-shifting; and I write
How roses first came red and lilies white.   10

Hesperides, 1648.

Argument: summary of subjects   3 **hock-carts:** the decorated carts that brought home the final load of the harvest   **wassails:** A *wassail* was originally a toast or salutation: "Be in good health!" Hence it came to mean a drink, a festive celebration, a party (especially around Christmas) with drinks and carols.   6 **cleanly wantonness:** wholesome lovemaking, healthy fun   8 **ambergris:** a waxy substance found floating in tropical seas, used especially in perfumery (literally, *grey amber*)

I write of groves, of twilights, and I sing
The court of Mab, and of the fairy king.
I write of hell; I sing, and ever shall,
Of heaven, and hope to have it after all.

12 **Mab:** the mischievous fairy queen thought to inspire our dreams

Why Flowers Change Color

These fresh beauties, we can prove,
Once were virgins sick of love,
Turned to flowers. Still in some
Colors go and colors come.

Ibid.

Dreams

Here we are, all, by day; by night we're hurled
By dreams, each one, into a several world.

Ibid.

2 **several:** separate, individual

The Scare-Fire

Water, water I desire,
Here's a house of flesh on fire:
Ope the fountains and the springs,
And come all to bucketings;
What ye cannot quench, pull down;
Spoil a house, to save a town.
Better 'tis that one should fall,
Than by one to hazard all.

Ibid.

The Scare-Fire: scare-fire: a sudden conflagration

Delight in Disorder

A sweet disorder in the dress
Kindles in clothes a wantonness:
A lawn about the shoulders thrown
Into a fine distraction;
An erring lace, which here and there   5
Enthralls the crimson stomacher;
A cuff neglectful, and thereby
Ribbons to flow confusedly;
A winning wave, deserving note,

Ibid.

2 **wantonness:** *Wanton,* as Herrick uses it, is close to the modern *sexy.* 3 **lawn:** sheer linen
4 **distraction:** It is pulled a little aside or apart, revealingly. (Latin *distractus,* pulled aside, separated.
Herrick is fond of using words in their original Latin sense.) The modern meaning is also present: it
distracts (pleasantly) the beholder. 5 **erring:** astray, loose 6 **stomacher:** an ornamental dickey,
sometimes jeweled, worn beneath the laces (ties) of the bodice

In the tempestuous petticoat;   10
A careless shoe-string, in whose tie
I see a wild civility,
Do more bewitch me, than when art
Is too precise in every part.

11 **careless shoestring:** more like a casually tied ribbon than a modern shoestring trailing messily

Corinna's Going A-Maying

Get up, get up for shame, the blooming morn
Upon her wings presents the god unshorn.
   See how Aurora throws her fair
   Fresh-quilted colours through the air:
   Get up, sweet slug-a-bed, and see   5
   The dew bespangling herb and tree.
Each flower has wept, and bowèd toward the east,
Above an hour since; yet you not drest,
   Nay! not so much as out of bed?
   When all the birds have matins said,   10
   And sung their thankful hymns, 'tis sin,
   Nay, profanation to keep in,
Whenas a thousand virgins on this day
Spring sooner than the lark to fetch in May.

Rise and put on your foliage, and be seen   15
To come forth, like the spring-time, fresh and green,
   And sweet as Flora. Take no care
   For jewels for your gown or hair:
   Fear not; the leaves will strew
   Gems in abundance upon you: 20
Besides, the childhood of the day has kept,
Against you come, some orient pearls unwept.
   Come, and receive them while the light
   Hangs on the dew-locks of the night,
   And Titan on the eastern hill   25
   Retires himself, or else stands still
Till you come forth. Wash, dress, be brief in praying:
Few beads are best when once we go a-Maying.

Come, my Corinna, come; and coming, mark
How each field turns a street, each street a park   30
   Made green and trimmed with trees: see how
   Devotion gives each house a bough
   Or branch; each porch, each door, ere this,
   An ark, a tabernacle is,
Made up of white-thorn neatly interwove,   35
As if here were those cooler shades of love.   .

Ibid.

a-maying: May Day was the occasion for festivity in the England of Herrick's time. Young and old, rich and poor would be up by dawn to go "a-maying" into the woods, from which they would bring back flowering branches, especially of the "may" or hawthorn, to decorate streets and houses. The mass excursion would be diversified by singing, picnics, romance—all the pleasures which the poet refers to.   2 **the god:** the sun-god, the sun (*Titan* in line 25)   **unshorn:** with rich golden locks, in full strength (like Samson unshorn)   3 **Aurora:** the goddess of dawn   4 **fresh-quilted colours:** a patchwork or crazy-quilt of rich color   10 **matins:** morning prayers   17 **Flora:** the goddess of flowers   22 **against:** in preparation for when   **orient:** bright   28 **beads:** rosary beads, prayers   35 **white-thorn:** hawthorn

Can such delights be in the street
And open fields, and we not see't?
   Come, we'll abroad: and let's obey
   The proclamation made for May,   40
And sin no more, as we have done, by staying;
But, my Corinna, come, let's go a-Maying.

There's not a budding boy or girl this day
But is got up and gone to bring in May.
   A deal of youth, ere this, is come   45
   Back and with white-thorn laden home.
   Some have dispatched their cakes and cream,
   Before that we have left to dream:
And some have wept and wooed, and plighted troth,
And chose their priest, ere we can cast off sloth: 50
   Many a green-gown has been given;
   Many a kiss, both odd and even;
   Many a glance too has been sent
   From out the eye, love's firmament:
Many a jest told of the keys betraying   55
This night, and locks picked: yet we're not a-Maying.

Come, let us go, while we are in our prime,
And take the harmless folly of the time.
   We shall grow old apace, and die
   Before we know our liberty.   60
   Our life is short, and our days run
   As fast away as does the sun.
And as a vapour or a drop of rain,
Once lost, can ne'er be found again:
   So when or you or I are made   65
   A fable, song, or fleeting shade,
   All love, all liking, all delight
   Lies drowned with us in endless night.
Then, while time serves, and we are but decaying,
Come, my Corinna, come, let's go a-Maying.   70

51 **green-gown:** grass-stained dress

To the Virgins, to Make Much of Time

Gather ye rose-buds while ye may,
   Old time is still a-flying;
And this same flower that smiles today,
   Tomorrow will be dying.

The glorious lamp of heaven, the sun,   5
   The higher he's a-getting,
The sooner will his race be run,
   And nearer he's to setting.

That age is best, which is the first,
   When youth and blood are warmer;   10
But being spent, the worse and worst
   Times still succeed the former.

Ibid.

Then be not coy, but use your time,
    And while ye may, go marry;
For having lost but once your prime,   15
    You may forever tarry.

Upon Julia's Clothes

Whenas in silks my Julia goes,
Then, then, methinks, how sweetly flows
That liquefaction of her clothes.

Next, when I cast mine eyes and see
That brave vibration each way free,
Oh how that glittering taketh me!

Ibid.

5 **brave:** fine, splendid

A Thanksgiving to God, for His House

Lord, Thou hast given me a cell
    Wherein to dwell;
And little house, whose humble roof
    Is weather-proof;
Under the spars of which I lie   5
    Both soft and dry;
Where Thou my chamber for to ward
    Hast set a guard
Of harmless thoughts, to watch and keep
    Me, while I sleep.   10
Low is my porch, as is my fate,
    Both void of state;
And yet the threshold of my door
    Is worn by the poor,
Who thither come, and freely get   15
    Good words, or meat.
Like as my parlor, so my hall
    And kitchen's small:
A little buttery, and therein
    A little bin,   20
Which keeps my little loaf of bread
    Unchipped, unflayed;
Some brittle sticks of thorn or briar
    Make me a fire,
Close by whose living coal I sit   25
    And glow like it.
Lord, I confess too, when I dine
    The pulse is Thine,
And all those other bits, that be
    There placed by Thee;   30
The worts, the purslain, and the mess
    Of watercress,

Noble Numbers, 1647. (Published with *Hesperides*, 1648.)

5 **spars:** beams   19 **buttery:** pantry (originally for bottles: "bottlery")   22 **unflayed:** not skinned or decrusted (as by mice)   28 **pulse:** peas, beans, etc.   31 **worts:** herbs or vegetables   **purslain:** a salad- or pot-herb   **mess:** a serving of food (cf. mess-hall)

Which of Thy kindness Thou hast sent;
  And my content
Makes those, and my beloved beet,   35
  To be more sweet.
'Tis Thou that crownest my glittering hearth
  With guiltless mirth;
And givest me wassail-bowls to drink,
  Spiced to the brink.   40
Lord, 'tis Thy plenty-dropping hand
  That soils my land;
And givest me, for my bushel sown,
  Twice ten for one;
Thou makest my teeming hen to lay   45
  Her egg each day;
Besides my healthful ewes to bear
  Me twins each year;
The while the conduits of my kine
  Run cream (for wine).   50
All these, and better Thou dost send
  Me, to this end,
That I should render, for my part,
  A thankful heart;
Which, fired with incense, I resign,   55
  As wholly Thine;
But the acceptance, that must be,
  My Christ, by Thee.

39 **wassail-bowls:** cf. Herrick's "The Argument of His Book," line 3 42 **soils:** enriches

Henry King
(1592–1669)

King, like Herrick a churchman, married Anne Berkeley when she was 16; her death eight years later moved him to write one of the great elegies in English. Named Bishop of Chichester in 1642, he was expelled by the Puritans the following year, not to return until the Restoration. King was a close friend of Donne's and the executor of his will.

An Exequy

 To his matchless never to be forgotten friend

Accept, thou shrine of my dead saint,
Instead of dirges this complaint;
And for sweet flowers to crown thy hearse,
Receive a strew of weeping verse
From thy grieved friend, whom thou might'st see 5
Quite melted into tears for thee.

 Dear loss! since thy untimely fate
My task hath been to meditate
On thee, on thee: thou art the book,
The library whereon I look,   10

c. 1624. *Poems, Elegies, Paradoxes, and Sonnets,* 1657.

Exequy means "funeral rites"; here it seems to take on the meaning "funeral ode."

2 **complaint:** lament 4 **strew:** a scattering (like a scattering of flowers)

Though almost blind. For thee, loved clay,
I languish out, not live, the day,
Using no other exercise
But what I practise with mine eyes:
By which wet glasses I find out   15
How lazily time creeps about
To one that mourns; this, only this
My exercise and business is:
So I compute the weary hours
With sighs dissolvèd into showers.   20

    Nor wonder if my time go thus
Backward and most preposterous;
Thou hast benighted me, thy set
This eve of blackness did beget,
Who wast my day (though overcast   25
Before thou hadst thy noontide past),
And I remember must in tears
Thou scarce hadst seen so many years
As day tells hours. By thy clear sun
My love and fortune first did run;   30
But thou wilt never more appear
Folded within my hemisphere,
Since both thy light and motion,
Like a fled star, is fallen and gone,
And 'twixt me and my soul's dear wish   35
The earth now interposèd is,
Which such a strange eclipse doth make
As ne'er was read in almanac.

    I could allow thee for a time
To darken me and my sad clime;   40
Were it a month, a year, or ten,
I would thy exile live till then;
And all that space my mirth adjourn,
So thou wouldst promise to return;
And putting off thy ashy shroud   45
At length disperse this sorrow's cloud.

    But woe is me! the longest date
Too narrow is to calculate
These empty hopes: never shall I
Be so much blessed as to descry   50
A glimpse of thee, till that day come
Which shall the earth to cinders doom,
And a fierce fever must calcine
The body of this world like thine,
My little world! That fit of fire   55
Once off, our bodies shall aspire
To our souls' bliss: then we shall rise,
And view ourselves with clearer eyes
In that calm region, where no night
Can hide us from each other's sight.   60

---

22 **preposterous:** backward, contrary to reason (the Latin root meant "with hindside in front")
53 **calcine:** burn to ashes

Meantime, thou hast her, earth: much good
May my harm do thee. Since it stood
With heaven's will I might not call
Her longer mine, I give thee all
My short-lived right and interest   65
In her, whom living I loved best:
With a most free and bounteous grief,
I give thee what I could not keep.
Be kind to her, and prithee look
Thou write into thy Doomsday book   70
Each parcel of this rarity
Which in thy casket shrined doth lie:
See that thou make thy reckoning straight,
And yield her back again by weight;
For thou must audit on thy trust   75
Each grain and atom of this dust,
As thou wilt answer him that lent,
Not gave thee, my dear monument.

    So close the ground, and 'bout her shade
Black curtains draw; my bride is laid.   80

    Sleep on, my love, in thy cold bed
Never to be disquieted.
My last good night! Thou wilt not wake
Till I thy fate shall overtake:
Till age, or grief, or sickness must   85
Marry my body to that dust
It so much loves; and fill the room
My heart keeps empty in thy tomb.
Stay for me there; I will not fail
To meet thee in that hollow vale.   90
And think not much of my delay;
I am already on the way,
And follow thee with all the speed
Desire can make, or sorrows breed.
Each minute is a short degree   95
And every hour a step towards thee.
At night when I betake to rest,
Next morn I rise nearer my west
Of life, almost by eight hours' sail,
Than when sleep breathed his drowsy gale.   100

    Thus from the sun my bottom steers,
And my day's compass downward bears:
Nor labour I to stem the tide
Through which to thee I swiftly glide.

    'Tis true, with shame and grief I yield,   105
Thou, like the van, first took'st the field,
And gotten hast the victory
In thus adventuring to die
Before me, whose more years might crave

---

69 prithee: [I] pray thee   **100 gale:** a gentle breeze (a poetic usage)   **101 bottom:** hull, ship
106 van: vanguard, advance troops

A just precedence in the grave.   110
But hark! my pulse like a soft drum
Beats my approach, tells thee I come;
And slow howe'er my marches be,
I shall at last sit down by thee.

    The thought of this bids me go on,   115
And wait my dissolution
With hope and comfort. Dear (forgive
The crime) I am content to live
Divided, with but half a heart,
Till we shall meet and never part.   120

Francis Quarles
(1592–1644)

Quarles spent several years in Ireland as secretary to an archbishop. His *Emblems*, religious poems to accompany woodcuts, was the most popular book of verse of his century. In his last years he took to prose to support himself; when he died, his wife and nine children (out of 18 born) were left in poverty.

On the World

The world's an inn; and I her guest.
I eat; I drink; I take my rest.
My hostess, nature, does deny me
Nothing, wherewith she can supply me;
Where, having stayed a while, I pay
Her lavish bills, and go my way.

Divine Fancies, 1632.

On Zacchaeus

Methinks I see, with what a busy haste
Zacchaeus climbed the tree. But oh how fast,
How full of speed, canst thou imagine, when
Our Savior called, he powdered down again!
He ne'er made trial if the boughs were sound   5
Or rotten, nor how far 'twas to the ground.
There was no danger feared: at such a call,
He'll venture nothing, that dare fear a fall.
Needs must he down, by such a spirit driven;
Nor could he fall, unless he fell to heaven.   10
Down came Zacchaeus ravished from the tree:
Bird that was shot ne'er dropped so quick as he.

Ibid.

Cf. Luke, 19:2–6. "And, behold, there was a man named Zacchæus . . . and he was rich. And he sought to see Jesus who he was; and could not for the press, because he was little of stature. And he ran before, and climbed up into a sycomore tree to see him. . . . And when Jesus came to the place, he looked up, and saw him, and said unto him, Zacchæus, make haste, and come down; for to-day I must abide at thy house. And he made haste, and came down, and received him joyfully. . . ."

4 powdered: rushed

George Herbert
(1593–1633)

The son of Donne's friend, Lady Magdalen Herbert, George Herbert was chosen "public orator" at Cambridge, a position from which his two predecessors had gone on to become secretary of state. Herbert gave up prospects of worldly advancement to become a priest of the Church of England. He spent his last three years as country pastor of the little church at Bemerton, working also on the poems which were published after his death.

Easter-Wings

Lord, who createdst man in wealth and store,
  Though foolishly he lost the same,
    Decaying more and more
      Till he became
        Most poor: 5

        With thee
      Oh let me rise
    As larks, harmoniously,
  And sing this day thy victories:
Then shall the fall further the flight in me.   10

My tender age in sorrow did begin:
  And still with sicknesses and shame
    Thou didst so punish sin,
      That I became
        Most thin.   15

        With thee
      Let me combine.
    And feel thy victory:
  For, if I imp my wing on thine,
Affliction shall advance the flight in me.   20

1630?–1633. *The Temple*, 1633.

Some poets, as far back as ancient Greece, have enjoyed playing with the shape of the poem on the page. So we have poems that look like hourglasses, altars, eggs, crosses, trees, decanters, swans, etc. Herbert has not merely made a design, but has made an effort to fit the thought to the line-length: "thin" and "poor," for example, occur in the thinnest, poorest lines.

1 **store:** abundance of goods   10 The Fall of man (which necessitated Christ's death and resurrection) shall help us rise higher.   18 The metrically erroneous "this day," not in the MS. but in most printed editions, is here omitted.   19 **imp:** in falconry, to graft feathers on an injured wing to improve flight

Redemption

Having been tenant long to a rich Lord,
  Not thriving, I resolvèd to be bold,
  And make a suit unto him, to afford

1630?–1633. Ibid.

Relations between man and God are seen in terms of real estate, with God the landlord, man the tenant. Before redemption by Christ, the lease was hard.

A new small-rented lease, and cancel the old.
In heaven at his manor I him sought: 5
   They told me there, that he was lately gone
   About some land, which he had dearly bought
Long since on earth, to take possession.
I straight returned, and knowing his great birth,
   Sought him accordingly in great resorts;   10
   In cities, theatres, gardens, parks, and courts:
At length I heard a ragged noise and mirth
   Of thieves and murderers: there I him espied,
   Who straight, *Your suit is granted*, said, and died.

Jordan (I)

Who says that fictions only and false hair
Become a verse? Is there in truth no beauty?
Is all good structure in a winding stair?
May no lines pass, except they do their duty
    Not to a true, but painted chair?   5

Is it no verse, except enchanted groves
And sudden arbours shadow coarse-spun lines?
Must purling streams refresh a lover's loves?
Must all be veiled, while he that reads, divines,
    Catching the sense at two removes?   10

Shepherds are honest people; let them sing:
Riddle who list, for me, and pull for prime:
I envy no man's nightingale or spring;
Nor let them punish me with loss of rhyme,
    Who plainly say, *My God, My King*.   15

1630?–1633. Ibid.

By his title Herbert probably means that the source of his inspiration is the Old Testament river rather than any of the Grecian springs or streams of the classical Muses. His poem is a protest against the "false hair" of worldly love poetry, the artificiality of pastoral poetry, and the obscurity of much "metaphysical" poetry.

2 **become:** are becoming to, belong in   6–8 *Enchanted* and *purling* (murmuring) make fun of the clichés of pastoral poetry.   7 **sudden:** Landscape architects planned gardens so that turns in the path would bring about surprising vistas, etc.   12 **who list:** whoever wants to   **for me:** as far as I'm concerned   **pull for prime:** draw for a winning hand (as in the game of primero); strive to excel   15 Herbert's religious poetry is as true as any other—just as his final rhyme *(sing-spring-King)* is a true rhyme.

Church-Monuments

While that my soul repairs to her devotion,
Here I intomb my flesh, that it betimes
May take acquaintance of this heap of dust;
To which the blast of death's incessant motion,
Fed with the exhalation of our crimes,   5
Drives all at last. Therefore I gladly trust

My body to this school, that it may learn
To spell his elements, and find his birth

1630?–1633. Ibid.

1 **repairs:** takes herself, goes   2 **betimes:** in good time

Written in dusty heraldry and lines;
Which dissolution sure doth best discern,   10
Comparing dust with dust, and earth with earth.
These laugh at jet and marble put for signs,

To sever the good fellowship of dust,
And spoil the meeting. What shall point out them,
When they shall bow, and kneel, and fall down flat   15
To kiss those heaps, which now they have in trust?
Dear flesh, while I do pray, learn here thy stem
And true descent: that when thou shalt grow fat

And wanton in thy cravings, thou mayst know,
That flesh is but the glass, which holds the dust   20
That measures all our time; which also shall
Be crumbled into dust. Mark here below
How tame these ashes are, how free from lust,
That thou mayst fit thy self against thy fall.

Virtue

Sweet day, so cool, so calm, so bright,
The bridal of the earth and sky:
The dew shall weep thy fall tonight;
     For thou must die.

Sweet rose, whose hue angry and brave   5
Bids the rash gazer wipe his eye:
Thy root is ever in its grave,
     And thou must die.

Sweet spring, full of sweet days and roses,
A box where sweets compacted lie: 10
My music shows ye have your closes,
     And all must die.

Only a sweet and virtuous soul,
Like seasoned timber, never gives;
But though the whole world turn to coal,   15
     Then chiefly lives.

1630?–1633. Ibid.

10 **sweets:** perfumes (not candies)   11 **closes:** (1) cadences (music); (2) conclusions   15 **turn to coal:** a reference to the conflagration of Doomsday—not to the geology of fossil fuel

The Pearl

Matthew, 13

I know the ways of learning; both the head
And pipes that feed the press, and make it run;
What reason hath from nature borrowèd,
Or of itself, like a good housewife, spun

1630?–1633. Ibid.

Matthew, 13 [45]: " . . . the kingdom of heaven is like unto a merchant man . . . Who, when he had found one pearl of great price, went and sold all that he had, and bought it."   2 **press:** olive or wine press (as metaphors for the productivity of knowledge); or the printing press

In laws and policy; what the stars conspire,   5
What willing nature speaks, what forced by fire;
Both the old discoveries, and the new-found seas,
The stock and surplus, cause and history.
All these stand open, or I have the keys:
                    Yet I love thee.   10

I know the ways of honour, what maintains
The quick returns of courtesy and wit:
In vies of favours whether party gains,
When glory swells the heart, and moldeth it
To all expressions both of hand and eye,   15
Which on the world a true-love-knot may tie,
And bear the bundle, wheresoe'er it goes;
How many drams of spirit there must be
To sell my life unto my friends or foes:
                    Yet I love thee.   20

I know the ways of pleasure, the sweet strains,
The lullings and the relishes of it;
The propositions of hot blood and brains;
What mirth and music mean; what love and wit
Have done these twenty hundred years, and more;   25
I know the projects of unbridled store:
My stuff is flesh, not brass; my senses live,
And grumble oft, that they have more in me
Than he that curbs them, being but one to five:
                    Yet I love thee.   30

I know all these, and have them in my hand:
Therefore not seelèd, but with open eyes
I fly to thee, and fully understand
Both the main sale, and the commodities;
And at what rate and price I have thy love;   35
With all the circumstances that may move;
Yet through these labyrinths, not my groveling wit,
But thy silk twist let down from heaven to me,
Did both conduct and teach me, how by it
                    To climb to thee.   40

6 **fire:** in the furnace of scientist or alchemist   11–20 about *savoir faire,* worldly wisdom: The poet is saying that he knows about diplomatic conduct and how to get on in the world.   13 **vies:** competition   **whether:** which   17 **bear the bundle:** act as a servant   18 **drams of spirit:** (1) amount of courage; (2) amount of liquor   26 **unbridled store:** uncontrolled wealth   32 **seelèd:** sewn shut (like the eyes of a falcon during training)   34 **commodities:** advantages, profits   36 **move:** have a bearing, influence   38 **silk twist:** thread or cord of twisted silk (here, divine guidance)

The Collar

> I struck the board, and cried, "No more.
>   I will abroad.

1630?–1633. Ibid.

The theme of rebellion carries over into the form of the poem, which, with its irregular line-lengths and unpredictable far-apart rhymes, is almost like free verse.

1 **struck the board:** pounded the table in rebellion   2 **I will abroad:** I will travel, break away from here.

What? shall I ever sigh and pine?
My lines and life are free; free as the road,
   Loose as the wind, as large as store.   5
      Shall I be still in suit?
      Have I no harvest but a thorn
      To let me blood, and not restore
What I have lost with cordial fruit?
           Sure there was wine   10
          Before my sighs did dry it: there was corn
          Before my tears did drown it.
      Is the year only lost to me?
      Have I no bays to crown it?
No flowers, no garlands gay? all blasted?   15
      All wasted?
      Not so, my heart: but there is fruit,
          And thou hast hands.
      Recover all thy sigh-blown age
On double pleasures: leave thy cold dispute   20
Of what is fit, and not. Forsake thy cage,
        Thy rope of sands,
Which petty thoughts have made, and made to thee
      Good cable, to enforce and draw,
          And be thy law,   25
While thou didst wink and wouldst not see.
         Away; take heed:
         I will abroad.
Call in thy death's-head there: tie up thy fears.
         He that forbears   30
      To suit and serve his need,
        Deserves his load."
But as I raved and grew more fierce and wild
        At every word,
      Me thoughts I heard one calling, *Child!*   35
      And I replied, *My Lord.*

4 lines: directions in life, lines of work, fate **5 store:** abundant means **6 in suit:** in service (to someone else) **8 let me blood:** make me bleed **9 cordial:** nourishing, life-giving **13 only lost:** lost only **14 bays:** laurels, honors **19 sigh-blown:** blown away in sighs, wasted **22 rope of sands:** an image of futility **23 made to thee:** made seem to thee **26 wink:** kept your eyes closed **29 death's-head:** skull, reminder of death **31 to suit:** to follow, conform to **35 me thoughts:** it seemed to me

The Pulley

     When God at first made man,
Having a glass of blessings standing by;
"Let us" (said he) "pour on him all we can:
Let the world's riches, which dispersèd lie,
     Contract into a span."   5

     So strength first made a way;
Then beauty flowed; then wisdom, honour, pleasure:
When almost all was out, God made a stay,

1630?–1633. Ibid.

5 span: distance from thumb-tip to tip of little finger of outspread hand—small space

Perceiving that alone of all his treasure
    Rest in the bottom lay.   ·   10

    "For if I should" (said he)
"Bestow this jewel also on my creature,
He would adore my gifts instead of me,
And rest in nature, not the God of nature:
    So both should losers be.   15

    "Yet let him keep the rest,
But keep them with repining restlessness:
Let him be rich and weary, that at least,
If goodness lead him not, yet weariness
    May toss him to my breast."   20

Thomas Carew
(1594?–1640)

After working with English diplomats in Venice, The Hague, and Paris, Carew was given an appointment at court. Years of pleasure-loving laxity, it is said, were followed by a death bed repentance. His poems, amorous and graceful, were published a few weeks after his death.

Ask Me No More

Ask me no more where Jove bestows,
When June is past, the fading rose;
For in your beauty's orient deep,
These flowers, as in their causes, sleep.

Ask me no more whither do stray   5
The golden atoms of the day;
For in pure love heaven did prepare
Those powders to enrich your hair.

Ask me no more whither doth haste
The nightingale, when May is past;   10
For in your sweet dividing throat
She winters, and keeps warm her note.

Ask me no more where those stars light,
That downwards fall in dead of night;
For in your eyes they sit, and there   15
Fixèd become, as in their sphere.

Ask me no more if east or west
The phoenix builds her spicy nest;
For unto you at last she flies,
And in your fragrant bosom dies.   20

Before 1639. *Poems,* 1640.

3 **orient:** brilliant, beautiful   11 **dividing:** singing "divisions" (melodic ornamentations of a tune) 18 **phoenix:** This mythical bird was thought to feed on incense and fragrant gums and to die in a fire made of aromatic materials.

James Shirley
(1596–1666)

When the London theaters were closed in 1636 because of the plague, Shirley went to Dublin for four years to work with the Irish theater. Considered a leading dramatist of the time, he is now chiefly remembered for the one poem in this anthology.

The Glories of Our Blood and State

The glories of our blood and state
  Are shadows, not substantial things;
There is no armour against fate;
  Death lays his icy hand on kings:
      Sceptre and crown   5
      Must tumble down,
And in the dust be equal made
With the poor crooked scythe and spade.

Some men with swords may reap the field,
  And plant fresh laurels where they kill;   10
But their strong nerves at last must yield;
  They tame but one another still:
      Early or late,
      They stoop to fate,
And must give up their murmuring breath,   15
When they, pale captives, creep to death.

The garlands wither on your brow;
  Then boast no more your mighty deeds;
Upon death's purple altar now,
  See where the victor-victim bleeds: 20
      Your heads must come
      To the cold tomb;
Only the actions of the just
Smell sweet and blossom in their dust.

The Contention of Ajax and Ulysses, 1659. (Published with *Honoria and Mammon.*)

Edmund Waller
(1606–1687)

Waller, a Member of Parliament while still in his teens, sympathized with its side during the Civil War but was arrested for conspiring to restore the king to power. Released, he lived abroad for some years; he returned to serve in Parliament for the last 25 years of his life.

Go, Lovely Rose

    Go, lovely rose,
Tell her that wastes her time and me
    That now she knows,
When I resemble her to thee,
How sweet and fair she seems to be.   5

Poems . . . , 1645.

Tell her that's young
And shuns to have her graces spied,
    That hadst thou sprung
In deserts where no men abide,
Thou must have uncommended died.   10

    Small is the worth
Of beauty from the light retired:
    Bid her come forth,
Suffer herself to be desired,
And not blush so to be admired.   15

    Then die, that she
The common fate of all things rare
    May read in thee,
How small a part of time they share
That are so wondrous sweet and fair.   20

Of My Lady Isabella Playing on the Lute

Such moving sounds from such a careless touch,
So unconcerned herself, and we so much!
What art is this, that with so little pains
Transports us thus, and o'er the spirit reigns?
The trembling strings about her fingers crowd   5
And tell their joy for every kiss aloud.
Small force there needs to make them tremble so;
Touched by that hand, who would not tremble too?
Here love takes stand, and while she charms the ear,
Empties his quiver on the listening deer: 10
Music so softens and disarms the mind
That not an arrow does resistance find.
Thus the fair tyrant celebrates the prize,
And acts herself the triumph of her eyes.
    So Nero once with harp in hand surveyed   15
    His flaming Rome, and as it burned he played.

Poems . . . , 1645. As revised in *Collected Poems . . . ,* 1682.

6 **kiss:** touch of her fingers as they "kiss" the strings   10 **empties . . . deer:** Love, as Cupid, shoots his arrows at the listening audience, so that all fall in love with the musician.   15 **Nero:** It was said (it seems falsely) that Nero himself started the fire that destroyed two-thirds of Rome, and that while watching it he diverted himself by reciting verses on the burning of Troy, accompanying himself on the lyre (not the "fiddle").

Of the Last Verses in the Book

When we for age could neither read nor write,
The subject made us able to indite.
The soul with nobler resolutions decked,
The body stooping, does herself erect:
No mortal parts are requisite to raise   5
Her that unbodied can her Maker praise.

The seas are quiet, when the winds give o'er;
So calm are we, when passions are no more:
For then we know how vain it was to boast

Collected Poems . . . , 1686.

Of fleeting things, so certain to be lost.   10
Clouds of affection from our younger eyes
Conceal that emptiness, which age descries.

The soul's dark cottage, battered and decayed,
Lets in new light through chinks that time has made.
Stronger by weakness, wiser men become   15
As they draw near to their eternal home:
Leaving the old, both worlds at once they view
That stand upon the threshold of the new.

Sir William Davenant
(1606–1668)

Davenant began to write plays while a page in the household of Fulke Greville. Later a favorite at court, he sided with the king during the Civil War and was knighted for his services. In 1656 he presented *The Siege of Rhodes* at his house in London; it was the first opera staged in England, the first entertainment to use painted sets, and the first to bring a woman on the stage as actress.

Wake All the Dead!

Wake all the dead! what ho! what ho!
How soundly they sleep whose pillows lie low!
They mind not poor lovers who walk above
On the decks of the world in storms of love.
   No whisper now nor glance can pass   5
   Through wickets or through panes of glass;
For our windows and doors are shut and barred.
Lie close in the church, and in the churchyard.
   In every grave make room, make room!
   The world's at an end, and we come, we come.   10

The state is now love's foe, love's foe;
Has seized on his arms, his quiver and bow;
Has pinioned his wings, and fettered his feet,
Because he made way for lovers to meet.
   But, O sad chance, his judge was old;   15
   Hearts cruel grow when blood grows cold.
No man being young his process would draw.
O heavens, that love should be subject to law!
   Lovers go woo the dead, the dead!
   Lie two in a grave, and to bed, to bed!   20

The Law Against Lovers, acted 1662. In *The Works . . .* , 1673.

6 **wickets:** small openings; loopholes, grilles, etc.   11 **the state:** the government, as making laws that interfere with lovers and love affairs   **love:** here personified as Cupid, with wings, arrows, etc.   17 **his process would draw:** would draw up a summons (legal)

John Milton
(1608–1674)

Until about 30, Milton worked hard—generally till midnight—at his studies and on his poetry, which he sometimes wrote in Latin or Italian. After a year in Italy, he began to devote himself to prose works in defense of civil and religious liberty. (Long as his poems are, the bulk of his prose is four times as great.) During the strife between king and Parliament, he worked as Cromwell's secretary, handling correspondence in Latin and writing Puritan propaganda. His eyesight, long under strain, failed completely when he was 43; but he continued working as hard as ever. Arrested when the monarchy was restored in 1660, he was soon released. In 1663 he married the young wife—his third—who survived him. Though troubled by illness and poverty, he continued to dictate his poems. The greatest, *Paradise Lost,* was first published in 1667, and again (revised) in the year of his death.

L'Allegro

Hence loathèd Melancholy,
   Of Cerberus and blackest midnight born,
In Stygian cave forlorn
   'Mongst horrid shapes, and shrieks, and sights unholy.
Find out some uncouth cell   5
   Where brooding darkness spreads his jealous wings,
And the night-raven sings;
   There under ebon shades and low-browed rocks,
As ragged as thy locks,
   In dark Cimmerian desert ever dwell.   10
But come, thou goddess fair and free,
In heaven ycleped Euphrosyne,
And by men heart-easing Mirth,
Whom lovely Venus at a birth
With two sister Graces more   15
To ivy-crownèd Bacchus bore;
Or whether (as some sager sing)
The frolic wind that breathes the spring,
Zephyr, with Aurora playing
As he met her once a-Maying,   20
There on beds of violets blue
And fresh-blown roses washed in dew,
Filled her with thee, a daughter fair,
So buxom, blithe, and debonair.
Haste thee, nymph, and bring with thee   25
Jest and youthful jollity,
Quips and cranks, and wanton wiles,
Nods, and becks, and wreathèd smiles,
Such as hang on Hebe's cheek
And love to live in dimple sleek;   30
Sport that wrinkled Care derides,

1631–1632(?). *Poems . . . ,* 1645.

Milton's companion poems, "L'Allegro" and "Il Penseroso," contrast two kinds of personality, two ways of life, the first light-hearted and cheerful, the second serious and thoughtful.

2 **Cerberus:** the three-headed dog that guarded the entrance to the underworld   3 **Stygian:** pertaining to the river Styx in the underworld; pitch-dark   5 **uncouth:** unknown, weird   10 **Cimmerian:** perpetually dark, like the land of the Cimmerians in Homer's *Odyssey*   12 **ycleped:** named   **Euphrosyne:** one of the three Graces; her name means "mirth" in Greek (The English pronunciation is *you-frôze-a-knee.*)   14–16 According to the traditional view, Mirth is the child of love (Venus) and wine (Bacchus).   17 By "some sager" Milton seems to have meant himself; he made up this more respectable genealogy: Mirth is the child of the west wind (Zephyr) and the dawn (Aurora).   24 **buxom:** agreeable, merry (The word has since changed meaning.)   27 **cranks:** jokes, puns   28 **becks:** beckoning gestures   **wreathèd:** *To wreathe* (in this sense) meant only "to twist, to writhe, to change" (expression). *Wreathed smiles* may have been influenced by the notion of smiles hung like circling wreathes on the face.   29 **Hebe:** (*hē-be*) goddess of youth and spring, cupbearer to the gods

And Laughter holding both his sides.
Come, and trip it as you go
On the light fantastic toe,
And in thy right hand lead with thee   35
The mountain nymph, sweet Liberty;
And if I give thee honor due,
Mirth, admit me of thy crew
To live with her, and live with thee,
In unreprovèd pleasures free;   40
To hear the lark begin his flight,
And singing startle the dull night
From his watch-tower in the skies,
Till the dappled dawn doth rise;
Then to come in spite of sorrow,   45
And at my window bid good morrow
Through the sweet-briar, or the vine,
Or the twisted eglantine,
While the cock with lively din
Scatters the rear of darkness thin,   50
And to the stack, or the barn door,
Stoutly struts his dames before;
Oft listening how the hounds and horn
Cheerly rouse the slumbering morn,
From the side of some hoar hill,   55
Through the high wood echoing shrill.
Sometime walking not unseen
By hedgerow elms, on hillocks green,
Right against the eastern gate
Where the great sun begins his state,   60
Robed in flames, and amber light,
The clouds in thousand liveries dight,
While the plowman near at hand
Whistles o'er the furrowed land,
And the milkmaid singeth blithe,   65
And the mower whets his scythe,
And every shepherd tells his tale
Under the hawthorn in the dale.
Straight mine eye hath caught new pleasures
Whilst the landscape round it measures: 70
Russet lawns and fallows gray
Where the nibbling flocks do stray,
Mountains on whose barren breast
The laboring clouds do often rest;
Meadows trim with daisies pied,   75
Shallow brooks, and rivers wide.
Towers and battlements it sees
Bosomed high in tufted trees,
Where perhaps some beauty lies,
The cynosure of neighboring eyes.   80
Hard by, a cottage chimney smokes
From betwixt two agèd oaks,
Where Corydon and Thyrsis met

33 **trip it:** come dancing   50 **scatters the rear:** routs the last traces   51 **stack:** stack of hay etc.
55 **hoar:** white with dew and early-morning mist   62 **liveries:** colorful costumes   **dight:** dressed
67 **tells his tale:** counts his sheep (and perhaps also the modern meaning)   71 **fallows:** plowed land
(sometimes left fallow, or unused)   75 **pied:** of mixed colors   78 **bosomed:** nestled, hidden   80 **cy-
nosure:** anything brilliant enough to attract wide attention (The Cynosure is the Little Dipper or its
pole star.)   83 **Corydon, Thyrsis:** conventional names for country people in pastoral poetry—as are
Phyllis and Thestylis, below

Are at their savory dinner set
Of herbs, and other country messes,   85
Which the neat-handed Phyllis dresses;
And then in haste her bower she leaves,
With Thestylis to bind the sheaves,
Or, if the earlier season lead,
To the tanned haycock in the mead.   90
Sometimes with secure delight
The upland hamlets will invite,
When the merry bells ring round
And the jocund rebecs sound
To many a youth, and many a maid,   95
Dancing in the checkered shade;
And young and old come forth to play
On a sunshine holiday,
Till the livelong daylight fail;
Then to the spicy nut-brown ale,   100
With stories told of many a feat:
How Faery Mab the junkets eat;
She was pinched and pulled, she said;
And he by friar's lantern led
Tells how the drudging goblin sweat   105
To earn his cream-bowl duly set,
When in one night, ere glimpse of morn,
His shadowy flail hath threshed the corn
That ten day-laborers could not end;
Then lies him down the lubber fiend,   110
And stretched out all the chimney's length
Basks at the fire his hairy strength;
And crop-full out of doors he flings
Ere the first cock his matin rings.
Thus done the tales, to bed they creep,   115
By whispering winds soon lulled asleep.
Towered cities please us then,
And the busy hum of men,
Where throngs of knights and barons bold
In weeds of peace high triumphs hold,   120
With store of ladies, whose bright eyes
Rain influence and judge the prize
Of wit, or arms, while both contend
To win her grace, whom all commend.
There let Hymen oft appear   125
In saffron robe with taper clear,
And pomp, and feast, and revelry,
With mask, and antique pageantry—
Such sights as youthful poets dream
On summer eves by haunted stream.   130
Then to the well-trod stage anon,
If Jonson's learned sock be on,
Or sweetest Shakespeare, fancy's child,

---

91 **secure:** carefree   94 **rebecs:** fiddles   102 **Faery Mab:** mischievous fairy queen in folklore   **junkets:** custards   **eat:** ate   103 **she:** one of the storytellers—as is *he* in the next line   104 **friar's lantern:** will-o'-the-wisp   105 **drudging goblin:** Robin Goodfellow, a mischievous hairy goblin of folklore, who would do fantastic amounts of work for food   **sweat:** sweated   110 **lubber:** apparently from Lobbin, which he was sometimes called   113 **crop-full:** with full stomach   114 **matin:** morning prayer (spirits, goblins, etc. disappeared at cockcrow)   117 **then:** on other occasions—not after they fall asleep   120 **weeds of peace:** clothes for a holiday in peacetime   122 **rain influence:** as stars were thought to do, to affect our fate   125 **Hymen:** god of marriage   128 **mask:** masque, masked ball or dramatic entertainment   132 **sock:** light shoe worn by ancient comic actors

Warble his native wood-notes wild.
And ever against eating cares   135
Lap me in soft Lydian airs,
Married to immortal verse
Such as the meeting soul may pierce
In notes, with many a winding bout
Of linkèd sweetness long drawn out,   140
With wanton heed, and giddy cunning, ⟵ *paradoxes, oxymoron*
The melting voice through mazes running;
Untwisting all the chains that tie
The hidden soul of harmony,
That Orpheus' self may heave his head   145
From golden slumber on a bed
Of heaped Elysian flowers, and hear
Such strains as would have won the ear
Of Pluto to have quite set free
His half-regained Eurydice.   150
These delights, if thou canst give,
Mirth, with thee I mean to live.

136 **Lydian:** one of the modes of ancient Greek music: sweet and languorous   141 **wanton heed:** playful care   145 **Orpheus:** the legendary poet and musician whose wife Eurydice (*you-ríd-a-see*) was held by Pluto, lord of the underworld. She was "half-regained" because Pluto agreed to free her if Orpheus would lead her up to earth without looking back at her—but he did look back and so lost her. 147 **Elysian:** belonging to Elysium, the paradise of Greek mythology

Il Penseroso

Hence, vain deluding joys,
    The brood of folly without father bred;
How little you bestead,
    Or fill the fixèd mind with all your toys;
Dwell in some idle brain,   5
    And fancies fond with gaudy shapes possess,
As thick and numberless
    As the gay motes that people the sunbeams,
Or likest hovering dreams,
    The fickle pensioners of Morpheus' train.   10
But hail, thou goddess sage and holy,
Hail, divinest Melancholy,
Whose saintly visage is too bright
To hit the sense of human sight;
And therefore to our weaker view   15
O'erlaid with black, staid wisdom's hue—
Black, but such as in esteem
Prince Memnon's sister might beseem,
Or that starred Ethiop queen that strove
To set her beauty's praise above   20
The sea nymphs, and their powers offended.

1631–1632 (?). Ibid.

Penseroso: The correct Italian word for "the thoughtful man" would be *pensieroso*.   3 **bestead:** avail, help   4 **fixèd:** stable, steady   **toys:** trifles   6 **fond:** foolish   10 **pensioners:** retainers, attendants **Morpheus:** god of sleep   12 **Melancholy:** clearly not the "loathèd Melancholy" of line 1 of "L'Allegro." Here *melancholy*—though it implies a touch of pleasurable sadness—means "the thoughtful seriousness of a mind concerned with the higher interests, not with amusement and worldly 'toys.'" 18 **Memnon:** an Ethiopian prince praised for his appearance in the *Odyssey*. Milton assumes his sister was beautiful.   **beseem:** become, befit   19 **Ethiop queen:** Cassiopeia, who was turned into the constellation of that name for boasting that her daughter was more beautiful than the sea nymphs

Yet thou art higher far descended:
Thee bright-haired Vesta long of yore
To solitary Saturn bore,
His daughter she (in Saturn's reign,   25
Such mixture was not held a stain);
Oft in glimmering bowers, and glades
He met her, and in secret shades
Of woody Ida's inmost grove,
While yet there was no fear of Jove.   30
Come, pensive nun, devout and pure,
Sober, steadfast, and demure,
All in a robe of darkest grain
Flowing with majestic train,
And sable stole of cypress lawn   35
Over thy decent shoulders drawn.
Come, but keep thy wonted state,
With even step, and musing gait,
And looks commercing with the skies,
Thy rapt soul sitting in thine eyes: 40
There held in holy passion still
Forget thyself to marble, till
With a sad leaden downward cast,
Thou fix them on the earth as fast.
And join with thee calm peace, and quiet,   45
Spare fast, that oft with gods doth diet,
And hears the Muses in a ring
Aye round about Jove's altar sing.
And add to these retirèd leisure
That in trim gardens takes his pleasure;   50
But first, and chiefest, with thee bring,
Him that yon soars on golden wing,
Guiding the fiery-wheelèd throne,
The cherub Contemplation;
And the mute silence hist along,   55
'Less Philomel will deign a song
In her sweetest, saddest plight,
Smoothing the rugged brow of night,
While Cynthia checks her dragon yoke
Gently o'er the accustomed oak,   60
Sweet bird that shunn'st the noise of folly,
Most musical, most melancholy!
Thee, chantress, oft the woods among
I woo to hear thy even-song;
And missing thee, I walk unseen   65
On the dry smooth-shaven green,
To behold the wandering moon
Riding near her highest noon,

---

22 **descended:** Milton makes up this genealogy.   23 **Vesta:** Roman goddess of hearth and home
24 **Saturn:** the god who ruled during the Golden Age before Jove, his usurping son, came to power.
His throne was on Mount Ida in Crete. Those born under his sign are thought to have a tendency
toward melancholy (cf. the word *saturnine*).   33 **grain:** color   35 **cypress lawn:** sheer linen or cot-
ton   39 **commercing:** dealing, communicating   42 **forget thyself to marble:** become so oblivious to
yourself that you seem to be a marble statue   43 **sad:** serious   46 **spare fast:** moderate diet   48 **aye:**
forever   53 **fiery-wheelèd throne:** Cherubs and fiery wheels are associated with the throne of God
in Ezekiel's vision (Ezek. 10).   54 **cherub Contemplation:** Cherubs (far from being cute and "cheru-
bic") were the second highest order of angels, capable of contemplating the divine mysteries. 55 **hist:**
to summon quietly, with a "hist!"   56 **'less:** unless   **Philomel:** the nightingale   57 **plight:** mood
59 **Cynthia:** the goddess of the moon, whose chariot was drawn by dragons   63 **chauntress:** female
singer (with suggestions of *enchantress*)   64 **even-song:** evening song

Like one that had been led astray
Through the heaven's wide pathless way;   70
And oft, as if her head she bowed,
Stooping through a fleecy cloud.
Oft on a plat of rising ground
I hear the far-off curfew sound
Over some wide-watered shore,   75
Swinging slow with sullen roar;
Or, if the air will not permit,
Some still removèd place will fit,
Where glowing embers through the room
Teach light to counterfeit a gloom,   80
Far from all resort of mirth,
Save the cricket on the hearth,
Or the bellman's drowsy charm,
To bless the doors from nightly harm.
Or let my lamp at midnight hour   85
Be seen in some high lonely tower,
Where I may oft outwatch the Bear
With thrice great Hermes, or unsphere
The spirit of Plato to unfold
What worlds, or what vast regions hold   90
The immortal mind that hath forsook
Her mansion in this fleshly nook;
And of those daemons that are found
In fire, air, flood, or under ground,
Whose power hath a true consent   95
With planet, or with element.
Sometime let gorgeous tragedy
In sceptered pall come sweeping by,
Presenting Thebes, or Pelops' line,
Or the tale of Troy divine.   100
Or what (though rare) of later age
Ennobled hath the buskined stage.
But, O sad virgin, that thy power
Might raise Musaeus from his bower,
Or bid the soul of Orpheus sing   105
Such notes as warbled to the string
Drew iron tears down Pluto's cheek,
And made Hell grant what love did seek!
Or call up him that left half told
The story of Cambuscan bold,   110
Of Camball and of Algarsife,
And who had Canacé to wife
That owned the virtuous ring and glass,

---

73 **plat:** small plot, small area   83 **bellman:** man with bell who went about making public announcements; he also served as night watchman and called the hours.   87 **the Bear:** The Great Bear (our Big Dipper), as a circumpolar constellation, never dips below the horizon—to "outwatch" it is to stay up all night.   88 **Hermes:** Hermes Trismegístus [thrice-great] was a legendary Egyptian magician and occult philosopher. **unsphere:** call down from his sphere   89 **Plato:** the Greek philosopher, who might be expected to have interesting things to say about the afterlife, now that he was a part of it   93 **daemons:** spirits ruling the "four elements" (earth, water, air, fire)   98 **sceptered pall:** royal robes   99 **Thebes:** Oedipus, probably the greatest of Greek tragic heroes, was King of Thebes. **Pelops:** His "line" included Agamemnon, Orestes, Electra, all prominent in Greek tragedy.   102 **buskined stage:** tragic drama (The buskin was a high boot worn by ancient tragic actors.) Milton is saying that good tragedy has been "rare" since the time of the ancient Greeks.   104 **Musaeus:** a mythical early poet associated with Orpheus   105–107 **Orpheus:** cf. "L'Allegro," lines 145–150 and notes there.   109 **him:** Chaucer, whose unfinished "Squire's Tale" dealt with magic. The following half dozen lines refer to characters and events in it.   113 **virtuous:** having magical power

And of the wondrous horse of brass
On which the Tartar king did ride;   115
And if ought else great bards beside
In sage and solemn tunes have sung,
Of tourneys and of trophies hung,
Of forests, and enchantments drear
Where more is meant than meets the ear.   120
Thus, night, oft see me in thy pale career
Till civil-suited morn appear,
Not tricked and frounced as she was wont
With the Attic boy to hunt,
But kerchiefed in a comely cloud   125
While rocking winds are piping loud,
Or ushered with a shower still,
When the gust hath blown his fill,
Ending on the rustling leaves
With minute drops from off the eaves.   130
And when the sun begins to fling
His flaring beams, me, goddess, bring
To archèd walks of twilight groves
And shadows brown that Sylvan loves
Of pine, or monumental oak,   135
Where the rude ax with heavèd stroke
Was never heard the nymphs to daunt,
Or fright them from their hallowed haunt.
There in close covert by some brook
Where no profaner eye may look,   140
Hide me from day's garish eye,
While the bee with honeyed thigh
That at her flowery work doth sing,
And the waters murmuring
With such consort as they keep,   145
Entice the dewy-feathered sleep;
And let some strange mysterious dream
Wave at his wings in airy stream,
Of lively portraiture displayed,
Softly on my eyelids laid;   150
And as I wake, sweet music breathe
Above, about, or underneath,
Sent by some spirit to mortals good,
Or the unseen Genius of the wood.
But let my due feet never fail   155
To walk the studious cloister's pale,
And love the high embowèd roof
With antic pillars massy-proof,
And storied windows richly dight
Casting a dim religious light.   160
There let the pealing organ blow
To the full-voiced choir below,

---

120 **more is meant** . . . : Poems of romance and chivalry by such poets as the Italian Ariosto and Edmund Spenser often had allegorical meanings beyond what the readers saw at first glance.   122 **civil-suited**: quietly dressed   123 **tricked**: decked out   **frounced**: with hair curled   **wont**: accustomed   124 **the Attic boy**: Céphalus, the Greek boy that Aurora (the dawn) was in love with   130 **minute drops**: drops that fall every minute   134 **Sylvan**: god of forests   145 **consort**: harmony   148 **wave**: undulate (?)   **his**: sleep's (?)   149 **portraiture**: imagery   154 **Genius**: guardian spirit   156 **pale**: enclosure   157 **embowèd**: arched   158 **antic**: (1) fantastically decorated; (2) antique   **massy-proof**: strong enough to resist the weight they support   159 **storied**: with Biblical stories depicted in stained glass   **dight**: adorned

In service high and anthems clear,
As may with sweetness, through mine ear,
Dissolve me into ecstasies   165
And bring all heaven before mine eyes.
And may at last my weary age
Find out the peaceful hermitage,
The hairy gown and mossy cell,
Where I may sit and rightly spell   170
Of every star that heaven doth show,
And every herb that sips the dew;
Till old experience do attain
To something like prophetic strain.
These pleasures, Melancholy, give,   175
And I with thee will choose to live.

169 **hairy:** of rough cloth   170 **spell:** study, consider

Lycidas

*In this monody the author bewails a learned friend,
unfortunately drowned in his passage from Chester
on the Irish Seas, 1637, and by occasion foretells the
ruin of our corrupted clergy, then in their height.*

Yet once more, O ye laurels, and once more,
Ye myrtles brown, with ivy never sere,
I come to pluck your berries harsh and crude,
And with forced fingers rude
Shatter your leaves before the mellowing year.   5
Bitter constraint and sad occasion dear
Compels me to disturb your season due:
For Lycidas is dead, dead ere his prime,
Young Lycidas, and hath not left his peer.
Who would not sing for Lycidas? he knew   10
Himself to sing, and build the lofty rhyme.
He must not float upon his watery bier
Unwept, and welter on the parching wind,
Without the meed of some melodious tear.
    Begin then, sisters of the sacred well,   15
That from beneath the seat of Jove doth spring,
Begin, and somewhat loudly sweep the string.
Hence with denial vain, and coy excuse;
So may some gentle muse

1637. *Justa Edovardo King Naufrago* . . . , 1638. Text from *Poems* . . . , 1645.

monody: an ode sung by a single voice; a lament   **learned friend:** The friend was Edward King, a Cambridge acquaintance of Milton's. He had planned to become a clergyman, hence Milton's reflections on the state of the church. Milton is not only bewailing the young man's death; that sad occasion enabled him to express himself on a number of other things that were on his mind at the time—his own mission in life, for example, and the vanity of worldly fame. In his elegy Milton chooses to use the conventions of pastoral poetry, much employed by Greek, Latin, and Renaissance poets; it imagines life as taking place in a let's-pretend countryside of shepherds and shepherdesses who seem to have few real duties but much time for amateur music and romance. In this imaginary world Milton and King are not fellow students at college, they are fellow shepherds who "fed the same flock." Milton calls his friend not "Edward" but "Lycidas," a name that Vergil had used for a young shepherd. For a very different poem on King's death—published in the same memorial volume as Milton's—see John Cleveland's "Upon the Death of Mr. King Drowned in the Irish Seas" (p. 157).
1-2 **laurels ... myrtles ... ivy:** These three evergreens symbolize poetry.   2 **sere:** dry, withered
3 **crude:** not yet matured [Milton, not yet 30, did not feel ready for so ambitious a poem.]   6 **dear:** heartfelt   14 **meed:** gift   15 **sisters:** the Muses   19 **some ... muse:** some other poet

With lucky words favor my destined urn,   20
And as he passes turn,
And bid fair peace be to my sable shroud.
For we were nursed upon the self-same hill,
Fed the same flock, by fountain, shade, and rill.
   Together both, ere the high lawns appeared   25
Under the opening eyelids of the morn,
We drove afield, and both together heard
What time the gray-fly winds her sultry horn,
Battening our flocks with the fresh dews of night,
Oft till the star that rose at evening, bright,   30
Toward heaven's descent had sloped his westering wheel.
Meanwhile the rural ditties were not mute,
Tempered to the oaten flute,
Rough satyrs danced, and fauns with cloven heel
From the glad sound would not be absent long,   35
And old Damoetas loved to hear our song.
   But O the heavy change, now thou art gone,
Now thou art gone, and never must return!
Thee, shepherd, thee the woods and desert caves,
With wild thyme and the gadding vine o'ergrown,   40
And all their echoes mourn.
The willows and the hazel copses green
Shall now no more be seen,
Fanning their joyous leaves to thy soft lays.
As killing as the canker to the rose,   45
Or taint-worm to the weanling herds that graze,
Or frost to flowers, that their gay wardrobe wear
When first the white thorn blows;
Such, Lycidas, thy loss to shepherd's ear.
   Where were ye, nymphs, when the remorseless deep   50
Closed o'er the head of your loved Lycidas?
For neither were ye playing on the steep
Where your old bards, the famous Druids, lie,
Nor on the shaggy top of Mona high,
Nor yet where Deva spreads her wizard stream.   55
Ay me, I fondly dream!
Had ye been there—for what could that have done?
What could the Muse herself that Orpheus bore,
The Muse herself for her enchanting son
Whom universal nature did lament,   60
When by the rout that made the hideous roar
His gory visage down the stream was sent,
Down the swift Hebrus to the Lesbian shore.
   Alas! What boots it was uncessant care
To tend the homely, slighted shepherd's trade,   65
And strictly meditate the thankless muse?
Were it not better done, as others use,

---

28 **gray-fly:** beetlelike insect **winds:** blows   29 **battening:** feeding   33 **oaten:** made of an oat straw   36 **Damoetas:** unidentified; perhaps an elderly tutor at the university   45 **canker:** destructive bug   46 **taint-worm:** intestinal worm that infests young cattle   **weanling:** newly weaned   53 **Druids:** an order of ancient Celtic poet-priest-magicians   54 **Mona:** the island of Anglesey, off the northern coast of Wales   55 **Deva:** the river Dee, which empties into the Irish Sea—thought to have prophetic powers   56 **fondly:** foolishly   58 **the Muse:** Calliope, chief of the Muses, mother of Orpheus   58 **Orpheus:** legendary Greek poet and musician [referred to in "L'Allegro" and "Il Penseroso"], torn to pieces by angered Thracian women. His head—still singing—was swept down the river Hebrus (in Thrace) and across the Aegean to the island of Lesbos.   64 **what boots it:** what good does it do   65 **shepherd's trade:** poetry—in this pastoral world   66 **muse:** here, poetry itself   67 **use:** habitually do

To sport with Amaryllis in the shade,
Or with the tangles of Neaera's hair?
Fame is the spur that the clear spirit doth raise   70
(That last infirmity of noble mind)
To scorn delights, and live laborious days;
But the fair guerdon when we hope to find,
And think to burst out into sudden blaze,
Comes the blind Fury with the abhorrèd shears,   75
And slits the thin-spun life. "But not the praise,"
Phoebus replied, and touched my trembling ears;
"Fame is no plant that grows on mortal soil,
Nor in the glistering foil
Set off to the world, nor in broad rumor lies,   80
But lives and spreads aloft by those pure eyes
And perfect witness of all-judging Jove;
As he pronounces lastly on each deed,
Of so much fame in Heaven expect thy meed."
   O fountain Arethuse, and thou honored flood,   85
Smooth-sliding Mincius, crowned with vocal reeds,
That strain I heard was of a higher mood:
But now my oat proceeds,
And listens to the herald of the sea
That came in Neptune's plea;   90
He asked the waves, and asked the felon winds,
What hard mishap hath doomed this gentle swain?
And questioned every gust of rugged wings
That blows from off each beakèd promontory;
They knew not of his story,   95
And sage Hippotades their answer brings,
That not a blast was from his dungeon strayed,
The air was calm, and on the level brine
Sleek Panope with all her sisters played.
It was that fatal and perfidious bark,   100
Built in the eclipse, and rigged with curses dark,
That sunk so low that sacred head of thine.
   Next Camus, reverend sire, went footing slow,
His mantle hairy, and his bonnet sedge,
Inwrought with figures dim, and on the edge   105
Like to that sanguine flower inscribed with woe.
"Ah! who hath reft," quoth he, "my dearest pledge?"
Last came, and last did go,
The pilot of the Galilean lake;
Two massy keys he bore of metals twain   110
(The golden opes, the iron shuts amain).
He shook his mitered locks, and stern bespake,
"How well could I have spared for thee, young swain,
Enow of such as, for their bellies' sake,

68–69 **Amaryllis . . . Neæra:** girls' names, borrowed from classical poetry   73 **guerdon:** reward
75 **Fury:** death—of the three Fates, the one that cuts the thread of our life   77 **Phoebus:** Apollo, god
of beauty, poetry, etc. His touching the ear is a gesture of reproof.   79 **foil:** gold or silver plate placed
to increase the brightness of precious stones   85 **Arethuse:** a spring in Sicily, symbolic here of Sicil-
ian pastoral poetry   86 **Mincius:** an Italian river near Vergil's birthplace—recalling Latin pastoral
poetry   88 **oat:** see line 33   89 **herald of the sea:** the sea-god Triton   92 **swain:** young shepherd
(Lycidas)   96 **Hippotades:** Aeolus, god of the winds   99 **Panope:** a sea nymph   103 **Camus:** a per-
sonification of the river Cam, representing Cambridge   104 **hairy:** with the fur trimming of aca-
demic robes (?)   **sedge:** a water plant with a flaglike flower   106 **flower:** the hyacinth, the markings
on whose petals were thought to spell the Greek word for *Alas!*   109 **pilot:** St. Peter, with the keys of
heaven and a bishop's cap (miter)   111 **amain:** with force   114 **enow:** enough

Creep and intrude, and climb into the fold!   115
Of other care they little reckoning make
Than how to scramble at the shearers' feast,
And shove away the worthy bidden guest.
Blind mouths! that scarce themselves know how to hold
A sheep-hook, or have learned ought else the least   120
That to the faithful herdman's art belongs!
What recks it them? What need they? They are sped;
And when they list, their lean and flashy songs
Grate on their scrannel pipes of wretched straw;
The hungry sheep look up, and are not fed,   125
But, swollen with wind and the rank mist they draw,
Rot inwardly, and foul contagion spread;
Besides what the grim wolf with privy paw
Daily devours apace, and nothing said.
But that two-handed engine at the door   130
Stands ready to smite once, and smite no more."
   Return, Alpheus, the dread voice is past
That shrunk thy streams; return, Sicilian Muse,
And call the vales, and bid them hither cast
Their bells, and flowrets of a thousand hues.   135
Ye valleys low where the mild whispers use
Of shades and wanton winds and gushing brooks,
On whose fresh lap the swart star sparely looks,
Throw hither all your quaint enameled eyes,
That on the green turf suck the honeyed showers,   140
And purple all the ground with vernal flowers.
Bring the rathe primrose that forsaken dies,
The tufted crow-toe, and pale jessamine,
The white pink, and the pansy freaked with jet,
The glowing violet,   145
The musk-rose, and the well-attired woodbine,
With cowslips wan that hang the pensive head,
And every flower that sad embroidery wears:
Bid amaranthus all his beauty shed,
And daffodillies fill their cups with tears,   150
To strew the laureate hearse where Lycid lies.
For so to interpose a little ease,
Let our frail thoughts dally with false surmise.
Ay me! Whilst thee the shores and sounding seas
Wash far away, where'er thy bones are hurled,   155
Whether beyond the stormy Hebrides,
Where thou perhaps under the whelming tide
Visit'st the bottom of the monstrous world;

---

119 **blind mouths:** Bad clergymen are all mouth (greedy) and blind to the truth.   120 **a sheep-hook:** symbolic of the pastor's life   121 **herdman:** pastor, clergyman   122 **What recks it them?:** What do they care?   **they are sped:** have made their way in life, have prospered   123 **list:** want to   124 **scrannel:** thin, scratchy straw: see line 33   128 **wolf:** apparently those against what Milton considered the true religion. Their group "devours" because it makes converts.   130 **two-handed engine:** It is not clear what Milton means this ominous engine to represent. Many guesses have been made: the two houses of Parliament, the combined forces of England and Scotland, a two-handed sword belonging to God, or to St. Michael, etc.   132 **Alpheus:** the Greek river (or its god) whose waters were thought to flow unmixed through the sea to rise in the "fountain Arethuse" of line 85   136 **use:** are accustomed to be   138 **swart star:** Sirius, the Dog Star, associated with the hot weather that burns, tans, makes swart (black)   142 **rathe:** early   143 **crow-toe:** wild hyacinth   144 **freaked:** streaked whimsically, freakishly [Milton made up the word.]   146 **woodbine:** honeysuckle   149 **amaranthus:** an imaginary flower thought never to fade   151 **laureate:** crowned with laurel   153 **false surmise:** the notion that the body of Lycidas (not recovered from the water) is available, and that the flowers feel any real concern for him   156 **Hebrides:** islands off the western coast of Scotland

Or whether thou, to our moist vows denied,
Sleep'st by the fable of Bellerus old,   160
Where the great vision of the guarded mount
Looks toward Namancos and Bayona's hold;
Look homeward, angel, now, and melt with ruth;
And, O ye dolphins, waft the hapless youth.
  Weep no more, woeful shepherds, weep no more,   165
For Lycidas, your sorrow, is not dead,
Sunk though he be beneath the watery floor;
So sinks the day-star in the ocean bed,
And yet anon repairs his drooping head,
And tricks his beams, and with new-spangled ore   170
Flames in the forehead of the morning sky:
So Lycidas sunk low, but mounted high,
Through the dear might of him that walked the waves
Where, other groves and other streams along,
With nectar pure his oozy locks he laves,   175
And hears the unexpressive nuptial song,
In the blest kingdoms meek of joy and love.
There entertain him all the saints above,
In solemn troops and sweet societies
That sing, and singing in their glory move,   180
And wipe the tears forever from his eyes.
Now, Lycidas, the shepherds weep no more;
Henceforth thou art the genius of the shore,
In thy large recompense, and shalt be good
To all that wander in that perilous flood.   185
  Thus sang the uncouth swain to the oaks and rills,
While the still morn went out with sandals gray;
He touched the tender stops of various quills,
With eager thought warbling his Doric lay:
And now the sun had stretched out all the hills,   190
And now was dropped into the western bay.
At last he rose, and twitched his mantle blue:
Tomorrow to fresh woods and pastures new.

160 **Bellerus:** a fabulous figure, apparently invented by Milton, named for Bellerium (Land's End) in Cornwall   161 **great vision:** the vision of St. Michael, who was said to appear on the mountain in Cornwall named for him   162 **Namáncos and Bayona:** place-names of an old region and a city in northwest Spain, about 500 miles south of the guarded mount, across the Atlantic   163 **angel:** St. Michael   **ruth:** pity   164 **dolphins:** probably an allusion to the early Greek poet Arion, saved from drowning by a dolphin. There are other legends of dolphin rescues.   168 **day-star:** sun   170 **tricks:** trims   173 **him:** Christ   176 **unexpressive:** inexpressible   183 **genius:** protective local deity   186 **uncouth:** unknown, obscure [Milton himself]   188 **stops ... quills:** finger-holes ... pipes   189 **Doric:** Much Greek pastoral poetry was in the Doric dialect.

On the Late Massacre in Piedmont

Avenge, O Lord, thy slaughtered saints, whose bones
    Lie scattered on the Alpine mountains cold,
    Even them who kept thy truth so pure of old
    When all our fathers worshiped stocks and stones,
Forget not: in thy book record their groans   5
    Who were thy sheep and in their ancient fold

1655. *Poems,* 1673.

1 **saints:** The Vaudois, thought of as the first Protestants (twelfth century), lived in Alpine villages near the French-Italian border. In 1655 they were pursued and massacred by soldiers of the Duke of Savoy (Piedmont).

Slain by the bloody Piedmontese that rolled
    Mother with infant down the rocks. Their moans
The vales redoubled to the hills, and they
    To heaven. Their martyred blood and ashes sow   10
    O'er all the Italian fields where still doth sway
The triple tyrant: that from these may grow
    A hundredfold, who having learnt thy way
    Early may fly the Babylonian woe.

12 **triple tyrant:** The papal crown had three tiers.   14 **Babylonian:** The papal court was identified with Babylon of the Apocalypse by its enemies.

On His Blindness

When I consider how my light is spent,
    Ere half my days, in this dark world and wide,
    And that one talent which is death to hide
    Lodged with me useless, though my soul more bent
To serve therewith my Maker, and present   5
    My true account, lest he returning chide.
    "Doth God exact day-labor, light denied?"
    I fondly ask; but patience to prevent
That murmur, soon replies, "God doth not need
    Either man's work or his own gifts; who best   10
    Bear his mild yoke, they serve him best, his state
Is kingly. Thousands at his bidding speed
    And post o'er land and ocean without rest:
    They also serve who only stand and wait."

1655? Ibid.

1 **light is spent:** vision is extinguished   2 **half my days:** Milton's weak eyesight failed gradually from overwork; he was totally blind by the age of 43.   3 **talent:** See Matt. 25:14–30 for the parable of the "wicked and slothful servant" who hid his one talent in the earth instead of using it productively. [The *talent* was an ancient unit of weight and coinage, but the modern meaning is also relevant.] 8 **fondly:** foolishly   12 **thousands:** The angels are the messengers of God.   13 **post:** travel rapidly

On His Dead Wife

Methought I saw my late espousèd saint
    Brought to me like Alcestis from the grave,
    Whom Jove's great son to her glad husband gave,
    Rescued from death by force, though pale and faint.
Mine, as whom washed from spot of childbed taint   5
    Purification in the old Law did save,
    And such as yet once more I trust to have
    Full sight of her in heaven without restraint,
Came vested all in white, pure as her mind.
    Her face was veiled, yet to my fancied sight   10
    Love, sweetness, goodness, in her person shined

1658. Ibid.

Milton's second and best beloved wife died in her late twenties, three weeks after childbirth, in 1658. They had been married for less than two years.

2 **Alcestis,** in Euripides' play of that name, gives her life to save that of her husband. Hercules, "Jove's great son," rescues her after wrestling with Death; he brings her back, veiled, to her husband.   6 **purification...:** Mosaic law required the purification of women after childbirth (Lev. 12).   9 **vested:** dressed   10 **veiled:** as that of Alcestis was on her return from death. Milton, blind when he married his wife, had never seen her face.   **fancied:** imagined

So clear as in no face with more delight.
    But O as to embrace me she inclined,
    I waked, she fled, and day brought back my night.

Sir John Suckling
(1609–1642)

Suckling, who inherited large estates, cut quite a figure at court as "the greatest gallant of his time and the greatest gamester both for bowling and cards." He is said to have invented cribbage. After some military adventures and political intrigue, he fled to France and is thought to have died by suicide. He wrote four plays; his reputation rests on a handful of lyrics.

Why So Pale and Wan, Fond Lover?

Why so pale and wan, fond lover?
    Prithee, why so pale?
Will, when looking well can't move her,
    Looking ill prevail?
    Prithee, why so pale?   5

Why so dull and mute, young sinner?
    Prithee, why so mute?
Will, when speaking well can't win her,
    Saying nothing do 't?
    Prithee, why so mute?   10

Quit, quit, for shame; this will not move,
    This cannot take her;
If of herself she will not love,
    Nothing can make her:
    The devil take her!   15

Aglaura, 1638.

2 prithee: [I] pray thee; please

Sidney Godolphin
(1610–1643)

"Little Sid" Godolphin became a Member of Parliament at the age of 18. A staunch royalist, he joined the king's army at the beginning of the Civil War in 1642, was killed in battle the following February. Most of his poems remained in manuscript until the twentieth century.

Lord, When the Wise Men Came from Far

Lord, when the wise men came from far,
Led to thy cradle by a star,
Then did the shepherds too rejoice,
Instructed by thy angel's voice.
Blest were the wise men in their skill,   5
And shepherds in their harmless will.

G. Saintsbury, *Minor Poets of the Caroline Period,* II, 1906 (3 vols., 1905–1921).

Wise men, in tracing nature's laws,
Ascend unto the highest cause;
Shepherds with humble fearfulness
Walk safely, though their light be less.   10
Though wise men better know the way,
It seems no honest heart can stray.

There is no merit in the wise
But love, the shepherds' sacrifice.
Wise men, all ways of knowledge passed,   15
To the shepherds' wonder come at last.
To know can only wonder breed,
And not to know is wonder's seed.

A wise man at the altar bows,
And offers up his studied vows,   20
And is received. May not the tears,
Which spring too from a shepherd's fears,
And sighs upon his frailty spent,
Though not distinct, be eloquent?

'Tis true, the object sanctifies   25
All passions which within us rise,
But since no creature comprehends
The cause of causes, end of ends,
He who himself vouchsafes to know
Best pleases his creator so.   30

When then our sorrows we apply
To our own wants and poverty,
When we look up in all distress,
And our own misery confess,
Sending both thanks and prayers above,   35
Then, though we do not know, we love.

29 **himself . . . to know:** is content to know himself   31 **apply:** ascribe

---

William Cartwright
(1611–1643)

Cartwright was known at Oxford, where he became instructor in metaphysics, as a "florid and seraphical" preacher whose style impressed even King Charles. He died of the "camp disease," a wartime epidemic; it is said the king himself wore black the day of his funeral.

On a Virtuous Young Gentlewoman That Died Suddenly

When the old flaming prophet climbed the sky,
Who, at one glimpse, did vanish, and not die,
He made more preface to a death, than this:
So far from sick, she did not breathe amiss.
She who to heaven more heaven doth annex,   5
Whose lowest thought was above all our sex,

Comedies, Tragicomedies, with Other Poems, 1651.

1 **prophet:** Elijah (2 Kings 2:11)   3 **preface:** preliminaries, preparations

Accounted nothing death, but to be reprieved,
And died as free from sickness as she lived.
Others are dragged away or must be driven,
She, only, saw her time and stepped to heaven,   10
Where Seraphims view all her glories o'er
As one returned, that had been there before.
For while she did this lower world adorn,
Her body seemed rather assumed than born;
So rarefied, advanced, so pure and whole,   15
That body might have been another's soul;
And equally a miracle it were
That she could die, or that she could live here.

Anne Bradstreet
(1612–1672)

Anne's father, Thomas Dudley, had fought for Queen Elizabeth against the Spaniards. As Puritan religious dissenters, the Dudleys, with Anne's husband, Simon Bradstreet (later governor of Massachusetts), sailed for America in 1630. The first years, near Boston and later at Andover, were difficult; Anne, though often ill, had eight children, all but one alive when she died at the age of 60. With little formal schooling, she was well read; some 800 books were destroyed when the Bradstreet house burned down in 1666.

To My Dear and Loving Husband

If ever two were one, then surely we.
If ever man were loved by wife, then thee;
If ever wife was happy in a man,
Compare with me, ye women, if you can.
I prize thy love more than whole mines of gold,   5
Or all the riches that the East doth hold.
My love is such that rivers cannot quench,
Nor aught but love from thee give recompense.
Thy love is such I can no way repay,
The heavens reward thee manifold, I pray.   10
Then while we live, in love let's so perséver
That when we live no more, we may live ever.

The two poems of Anne Bradstreet given here, "which she never meant should come to public view," were found among her papers after her death. Not in her book *The Tenth Muse Lately Sprung Up in America* (London, 1650), they were published, "at the desire of some friends who knew her well," in *Several Poems . . .* , Boston, 1678.

A Letter to Her Husband, Absent upon Public Employment

My head, my heart, mine eyes, my life—nay, more,
My joy, my magazine of earthly store,
If two be one, as surely thou and I,
How stayest thou there, whilst I at Ipswich lie?
So many steps, head from the heart to sever;   5
If but a neck, soon should we be together.

Ibid.

2 **magazine:** storehouse   4 **Ipswich:** about 25 miles north of Boston; the Bradstreets lived there briefly, before moving to their permanent home at Andover.

I, like the earth this season, mourn in black,
My sun is gone so far in his zodiac,
Whom whilst I 'joyed, nor storms nor frosts I felt;
His warmth such frigid colds did cause to melt.   10
My chillèd limbs now numbèd lie forlorn;
Return, return, sweet Sol, from Capricorn!
In this dead time, alas, what can I more
Than view those fruits which through thy heat I bore?
Which sweet contentment yield me for a space,   15
True living pictures of their father's face.
O strange effect! now thou art southward gone,
I weary grow, the tedious day so long;
But when thou northward to me shalt return,
I wish my sun may never set, but burn   20
Within the Cancer of my glowing breast,
The welcome house of him, my dearest guest.
Where ever, ever stay, and go not thence,
Till nature's sad decree shall call thee hence;
     Flesh of thy flesh, bone of thy bone,   25
    I here, thou there, yet both but one.

7 **this season:** winter, or toward winter, when plant life is in mourning   8 **my sun . . . :** Her husband's travel southward is compared to the southward path of the sun toward the winter solstice. 9 **'joyed:** enjoyed   12 **Sol:** the sun   **Capricorn:** the constellation and sign of the zodiac that accompany the winter solstice   14 **those fruits:** their children. Anne, married at about 16 and now in her early twenties, had four at the time; she was later to have four more.   17 **strange effect:** strange, because in her husband's absence the shortest days of the year (in winter) seem longest   21 **Cancer:** the constellation and sign of the zodiac that attends the summer solstice

Thomas Jordan
(1612?–1685)

Jordan was actor, poet, playwright, royalist pamphleteer, and, from 1671, laureate to the city of London, responsible for the poetry and pageantry of the lord mayor's annual shows.

The Careless Gallant

Let us drink and be merry, dance, joke and rejoice,
With claret and sherry, theorbo and voice;
The changeable world to our joy is unjust,
All treasure uncertain, then down with your dust;
     In frolics dispose your pounds, shillings, and pence,   5
     For we shall be nothing a hundred years hence.

We'll sport and be free with Frank, Betty, and Dolly,
Have lobsters and oysters to cure melancholy;
Fish dinners will make a man spring like a flea,
Dame Venus, love's lady, was born of the sea;   10
     With her and with Bacchus we'll tickle the sense,
     For we shall be past it a hundred years hence.

Your beautiful bit who hath all eyes upon her,
That her honesty sells for a hogo of honor,

The Triumphs of London, 1675.

2 **theorbo:** bass lute   14 **honesty:** chastity, good name   **hogo:** spicy taste, tidbit (French: *haut goût*)

Whose lightness and brightness doth shine in such splendor   15
That none but the stars are thought fit to attend her,
    Though now she be pleasant and sweet to the sense,
    Will be damnable mouldy a hundred years hence.

Then why should we turmoil in cares and in fears,
Turn all our tranquillity to sighs and tears?   20
Let's eat, drink and play till the worms do corrupt us,
For I say that *Post mortem nulla voluptas;*
    Let's deal with our damsels, that we may from thence
    Have broods to succeed us a hundred years hence.

Your usurer that in the hundred takes twenty,   25
Who wants in his wealth and pines in his plenty,
Lays up for a season which he shall ne'er see,
The year of one thousand eight hundred and three
    Shall have changed all his bags, his houses and rents
    For a worm-eaten coffin a hundred years hence.   30

Your Chancery lawyer, who by "conscience" thrives
In spinning a suit to the length of three lives,
A suit which the client doth wear out in slavery,
Whilst pleader makes "conscience" a cloak for his knavery,
    May boast of his subtlety i' th' present tense,   35
    But *non est inventus* a hundred years hence.

Your most Christian monsieur who rants it in riot,
Not suffering his more Christian neighbors live quiet,
Whose numberless legions that to him belongs
Consists of more nations than Babel had tongues,   40
    Though numerous as dust, in despite of defence,
    Shall all lie in ashes a hundred years hence.

We mind not the councils of such bloody elves;
Let us set foot to foot, and be true to ourselves;
Our honesty from our good-fellowship springs;   45
We aim at no selfish preposterous things.
    We'll seek no preferment by subtle pretence,
    Since all shall be nothing a hundred years hence.

22 *Post mortem nulla voluptas:* after death no pleasure   31–32 **Chancery lawyer:** lawyer in a court case who, insisting he is doing the right thing, drags out the case over three generations for his own profit   36 *non est inventus:* he is not [to be] found   43 **elves:** here, mischievous, spiteful creatures   47 **preferment:** advancement, getting ahead

Richard Crashaw
(1612?–1649)

Son of a Puritan preacher and anti-Catholic controversialist, young Crashaw was High Anglican in his sympathies. When the struggle between king and Parliament broke out, he was deprived of his post at Cambridge and went to Holland, to Paris, and then to Rome, where (having become a Roman Catholic) he was given a post in the household of the cardinal who was governor of the city. Crashaw died two years later at Loreto (in Italy).

On the Blessed Virgin's Bashfulness

That on her lap she casts her humble eye,
'Tis the sweet pride of her humility.
The fair star is well fixed, for where oh where
Could she have fixed it on a fairer sphere?
'Tis heaven, 'tis heaven she sees; heaven's God there lies;
She can see heaven, and ne'er lift up her eyes.
This new guest to her eyes new laws hath given:
'Twas once *look up*, 'tis now *look down* to heaven.

Steps to the Temple, 1646.

Two Went Up into the Temple to Pray

Two went to pray? oh rather say
One went to brag, th'other to pray;

One stands up close and treads on high,
Where th'other dares not send his eye.

One nearer to God's altar trod;
The other to the altar's God.

Ibid.

The title is from Luke 18, the parable of the Pharisee and the publican.

Hymn of the Nativity

Sung as by the Shepherds

Chorus: Come, we shepherds whose blest sight
            Hath met love's noon in nature's night.
            Come, lift we up our loftier song
            And wake the sun that lies too long.

            To all our world of well-stolen joy   5
                He slept, and dreamed of no such thing.
            While we found out heaven's fairer eye
                And kissed the cradle of our king.
                    Tell him he rises now, too late
                    To show us aught worth looking at.   10

            Tell him we now can show him more
                Than he e'er showed to mortal sight;
            Than he himself e'er saw before,
                Which to be seen needs not his light.
                    Tell him, Tityrus, where th'hast been;   15
                    Tell him, Thyrsis, what th'hast seen.

The Hymn

Tityrus: Gloomy night embraced the place
            Where the noble infant lay.

Carmen Deo Nostro . . . , Paris, 1652 (lines 83–88 from *Steps to the Temple*, 1646).

5 **well-stolen joy:** in seeing the Christ child before the sun itself did ("*Well*-stolen" refers to
the sometimes illicit joys of earthly lovers.) The *he*'s and *him*'s of the next two stanzas refer to the
sun.   15–16 **Tityrus, Thyrsis:** in pastoral poetry, conventional names of shepherds (like Lycidas)

　　　The babe looked up and showed his face;
　　　　　In spite of darkness, it was day. 　　　　20
　　　　　　　It was thy day, sweet, and did rise
　　　　　　　Not from the east, but from thine eyes.

Thyrsis: 　Winter chid aloud, and sent
　　　　　The angry north to wage his wars;
　　　The north forgot his fierce intent, 　　　　25
　　　　　And left perfumes instead of scars.
　　　　　　　By those sweet eyes' persuasive powers,
　　　　　　　Where he meant frost, he scattered flowers.

Both: 　　We saw thee in thy balmy nest,
　　　　　Young dawn of our eternal day! 　　　　30
　　　We saw thine eyes break from their east
　　　　　And chase the trembling shades away.
　　　　　　　We saw thee, and we blessed the sight;
　　　　　　　We saw thee by thine own sweet light.

Tityrus: 　Poor world, said I, what wilt thou do 　　35
　　　　　To entertain this starry stranger?
　　　Is this the best thou canst bestow,
　　　　　A cold and not too cleanly manger?
　　　　　　　Contend, ye powers of heaven and earth,
　　　　　　　To fit a bed for this huge birth. 　　　　40

Thyrsis: 　Proud world, said I, cease your contest,
　　　　　And let the mighty babe alone.
　　　The phoenix builds the phoenix' nest;
　　　　　Love's architecture is his own.
　　　　　　　The babe whose birth embraves this morn 　45
　　　　　　　Made his own bed e'er he was born.

Tityrus: 　I saw the curled drops, soft and slow,
　　　　　Come hovering o'er the place's head,
　　　Offering their whitest sheets of snow
　　　　　To furnish the fair infant's bed. 　　　　50
　　　　　　　Forbear, said I, be not too bold;
　　　　　　　Your fleece is white, but 'tis too cold.

Thyrsis: 　I saw the obsequious seraphims
　　　　　Their rosy fleece of fire bestow,
　　　For well they now can spare their wings, 　　55
　　　　　Since heaven itself lies here below.
　　　　　　　Well done, said I, but are you sure
　　　　　　　Your down, so warm, will pass for pure?

Tityrus: 　No, no, your king's not yet to seek
　　　　　Where to repose his royal head. 　　　　60
　　　See, see, how soon his new-bloomed cheek
　　　　　'Twixt mother's breasts is gone to bed.
　　　　　　　Sweet choice, said we, no way but so,
　　　　　　　Not to lie cold, yet sleep in snow.

---

43 **phoenix:** mythical bird of great beauty; any uniquely marvellous being [Other qualities of the phoenix have been referred to in earlier poems.]　45 **embrave:** make brave or splendid　59 **'s not yet to:** does not yet have to

Both: We saw thee in thy balmy nest,   65
   Bright dawn of our eternal day!
We saw thine eyes break from their east
   And chase the trembling shades away.
    We saw thee and we blessed the sight;
    We saw thee by thine own sweet light.   70

Full Chorus: Welcome, all wonders in one sight!
   Eternity shut in a span.
Summer in winter. Day in night.
   Heaven in earth, and God in man.
    Great little one! whose all-embracing birth   75
    Lifts earth to heaven, stoops heaven to earth.

Welcome! though nor to gold nor silk,
   To more than Caesar's birthright is:
Two sister-seas of virgin milk,
   With many a rarely tempered kiss   80
    That breathes at once both maid and mother,
    Warms in the one, cools in the other.

She sings thy tears asleep, and dips
   Her kisses in thy weeping eye;
She spreads the red leaves of thy lips   85
   That in their buds yet blushing lie,
    She 'gainst those mother diamonds tries
    The points of her young eagle's eyes.

Welcome! though not to those gay flies
   Gilded i'the beams of earthly kings,   90
Slippery souls in smiling eyes;
   But to poor shepherds, home-spun things,
    Whose wealth's their flock; whose wit, to be
    Well read in their simplicity.

Yet when young April's husband showers   95
   Shall bless the fruitful Maia's bed,
We'll bring the first-born of her flowers
   To kiss thy feet and crown thy head.
    To thee, dread lamb, whose love must keep
    The shepherds more than they the sheep.   100

To thee, meek majesty, soft king
   Of simple graces and sweet loves,
Each of us his lamb will bring,
   Each his pair of silver doves;
    Till burnt at last in fire of thy fair eyes,   105
    Ourselves become our own best sacrifice.

72 **span:** a small space, the distance from thumb-tip to little finger in the outspread hand   87–88 The lines mean that mother and child gaze into each other's eyes. (Eagles were thought to have eyes so strong they could gaze into the sun.)   89 **gay flies:** courtiers in fancy clothes   95 **husband:** here an adjective with *showers*   96 **Maia:** May

From A Hymn to the Name and Honor of the Admirable St. Teresa

Love, thou art absolute sole lord
Of life and death. To prove the word
We'll now appeal to none of all
Those thy old soldiers, great and tall,
Ripe men of martyrdom, that could reach down   5
With strong arms their triumphant crown;
Such as could with lusty breath
Speak loud into the face of death
Their great Lord's glorious name, to none
Of those whose spacious bosoms spread a throne   10
For love at large to fill. Spare blood and sweat
And see him take a private seat,
Making his mansion in the mild
And milky soul of a soft child.
    Scarce has she learnt to lisp the name   15
Of martyr, yet she thinks it shame
Life should so long play with that breath
Which, spent, can buy so brave a death.
She never undertook to know
What death with love should have to do;   20
Nor has she e'er yet understood
Why to show love, she should shed blood,
Yet though she cannot tell you why,
She can love, and she can die.
    Scarce has she blood enough to make   25
A guilty sword blush for her sake;
Yet has she a heart dares hope to prove
How much less strong is death than love.
    Be love but there, let poor six years
Be posed with the maturest fears   30
Man trembles at, you straight shall find
Love knows no nonage, nor the mind.
'Tis love, not years or limbs, that can
Make the martyr, or the man.
    Love touched her heart, and lo, it beats   35
High, and burns with such brave heats,
Such thirsts to die, as dares drink up
A thousand cold deaths in one cup.
Good reason; for she breathes all fire;
Her weak breast heaves with strong desire   40
Of what she may, with fruitless wishes,
Seek for amongst her mother's kisses.
    Since 'tis not to be had at home
She'll travel to a martyrdom.

Steps to the Temple, 1646; revised, 1648.

St. Teresa of Ávila (1515–1582), Spanish Carmelite nun whose life combined profound mystical experience of the love of God with shrewd practical sense; most of her life was spent founding and administering—against much opposition in a man's world—"reformed" convents throughout Spain. The first chapter of her autobiography describes, not without humor, her childhood interest in martyrs and martyrdom.

29 six years: "...I was, I suppose, about six or seven years old...." (*Life*, chap. I)   **30 posed with:** placed with, balanced against   **32 nonage:** period of being underage

No home for her, confesses she,   45
But where she may a martyr be.
   She'll to the Moors; and trade with them
For this unvalued diadem:
She'll offer them her dearest breath,
With Christ's name in it, in change for death: 50
She'll bargain with them, and will give
Them God; and teach them how to live
In him: or, if they this deny,
For him she'll teach them how to die.
So shall she leave amongst them sown   55
Her Lord's blood; or at least her own.
   Farewell then, all the world, adieu!
Teresa is no more for you.
Farewell, all pleasures, sports, and joys,
Never till now esteemèd toys: 60
Farewell, whatever dear may be,
Mother's arms, or father's knee:
Farewell house, and farewell home!
She's for the Moors, and martyrdom.
   Sweet, not so fast! lo, thy fair Spouse,   65
Whom thou seek'st with so swift vows,
Calls thee back, and bids thee come
To embrace a milder martyrdom.
   Blest powers forbid, thy tender life
Should bleed upon a barbarous knife: 70
Or some base hand have power to rase
Thy breast's soft cabinet, and uncase
A soul kept there so sweet: Oh no,
Wise heaven will never have it so.
Thou art love's victim, and must die   75
A death more mystical and high:
Into love's arms thou shalt let fall
A still surviving funeral . . .

48 **unvalued:** invaluable   59-60 **pleasures . . . toys:** For a while, St. Teresa admits, she had the usual teenage interests: "I began to deck myself out and try to attract others by my appearance, taking great trouble with my hands and hair, using perfumes and all the vanities I could get—and there were a good many of them, for I was very fastidious" (*Life,* chap. II). They were "never till now esteemèd toys" because she had not previously realized they were "toys" (trifles).   71 **rase:** (1) cut; (2) raze, destroy   78 **still surviving funeral:** living death—her life will be her martyrdom.
   The entire poem has 182 lines.

From **The Flaming Heart**

> *Upon the Book and Picture of the*
> *Seraphical Saint Teresa*

O thou undaunted daughter of desires!
By all thy dower of lights and fires,
By all the eagle in thee, all the dove;
By all thy lives and deaths of love;
By thy large draughts of intellectual day,   5

Carmen Deo Nostro . . . , Paris, 1652.

See the notes on the preceding poem. This excerpt consists of the last 16 lines of a 108-line poem.

2 **dower:** (1) dowry; (2) endowment   3 **eagle . . . dove:** Cf. John Donne, "The Canonization," line 22.

And by thy thirsts of love more large than they,
By all thy brim-filled bowls of fierce desire,
By thy last morning's draught of liquid fire,
By the full kingdom of that final kiss
That seized thy parting soul, and sealed thee His,   10
By all the heavens thou hast in Him
(Fair sister of the seraphim!)
By all of Him we have in thee,
Leave nothing of my self in me.
Let me so read thy life that I   15
Unto all life of mine may die!

John Cleveland
(1613–1658)

Cleveland, son of a country clergyman, sided with the king when the Civil War broke
out and was deprived of his post at Cambridge. After the king's surrender in 1646, Cleve-
land seems to have gone into hiding (probably with friends) for about ten years. Four-
teen separate editions of his poems make him the most popular poet of his age. He is at
his best in political satires, which greatly irritated the Puritans.

Upon the Death of Mr. King Drowned in the Irish Seas

    I like not tears in tune, nor will I prize
His artificial grief, that scans his eyes;
Mine weep down pious beads, but why should I
Confine them to the muses' rosary?
I am no poet here; my pen's the spout   5
Where the rain-water of my eyes runs out
In pity of that name, whose fate we see
Thus copied out in grief's hydrography.
The muses are not mermaids; though upon
His death the ocean might turn Helicon.   10
The sea's too rough for verse; who rhymes upon't,
With Xerxes strives to fetter the Hellespont.
My tears will keep no channels, know no laws
To guide their streams; but like the waves, their cause,
Run with disturbance, till they swallow me   15
As a description of his misery.
But can his spacious virtue find a grave
Within the impostumed bubble of a wave?
Whose learning if we sound, we must confess
The sea but shallow, and him bottomless.   20
Could not the winds to countermand thy death
With their whole card of lungs redeem thy breath?
Or some new island in thy rescue peep

1637. *Justa Edovardo King Naufrago . . .* , 1638. *The Character of a London diurnal . . .* , 5th ed., 1647.

Cleveland's elegy is about the same death that moved Milton to write "Lycidas."

1 tears in tune: cf. Milton's "melodious tear" (line 14)   **2 scans his eyes:** imposes an artificial
rhythm, or "scansion," on their tears   **4 the muses' rosary:** conventional or routine expression
8 hydrography: writing about water (about seas, lakes, etc.); but here, by a sort of pun, writing *in* wa-
ter (in tears)   **10 Helicon:** the Greek mountain sacred to the Muses   **12 Xerxes . . . :** Xerxes the Great,
King of Persia, on his expedition against Greece in 480 B.C., bridged the Hellespont, the narrow strait
between Europe and Asia.   **18 the impostumed bubble:** An *impostume* is a festered swelling, like a
boil or infected pimple.   **19–20 learning . . . bottomless:** King's learning was deeper than the sea.
22 card of lungs: a map with pictures of puffing winds at the corners   **23 peep:** appear above the
surface

To heave thy resurrection from the deep?
That so the world might see thy safety wrought   25
With no less miracle than thyself was thought.
The famous Stagirite, who in his life
Had nature as familiar as his wife,
Bequeathed his widow to survive with thee,
Queen dowager of all philosophy,   30
An ominous legacy, that did portend
Thy fate, and predecessor's second end.
Some have affirmed that what on earth we find
The sea can parallel for shape and kind:
Books, arts, and tongues were wanting; but in thee   35
Neptune hath got an university.
     We'll dive no more for pearls. The hope to see
Thy sacred relics of mortality
Shall welcome storms, and make the seaman prize
His shipwreck now more than his merchandise.   40
He shall embrace the waves, and to thy tomb,
As to a Royaller Exchange, shall come.
What can we now expect? Water and fire,
Both elements our ruin do conspire;
And that dissolves us, which doth us compound: 45
One Vatican was burnt, another drowned.
We of the gown our libraries must toss
To understand the greatness of our loss,
Be pupils to our grief, and so much grow
In learning, as our sorrows overflow.   50
When we have filled the rundlets of our eyes,
We'll issue forth, and vent such elegies
As that our tears shall seem the Irish seas,
We floating islands, living Hebrides.

26 **thought:** thought to be   27 **Stágirite:** Aristotle, born at Stagira in Macedonia. Cleveland is saying that King was as learned as Aristotle in the ways of nature.   31–32 **portend/Thy fate:** According to one (unsubstantiated) story, Aristotle drowned himself, in frustration, in a river whose tidal changes he was unable to explain.   32 **second end:** because in King's death Aristotle died again   37–40 Cleveland is saying that the remains of the dead young man are of more value than pearls, and hence pearl divers will give up their work. Sailors would now rather be shipwrecked than make a profitable voyage, since, if shipwrecked, they might get to see King at the bottom of the ocean.   42 **Royaller Exchange:** the Royal Exchange, an official commercial establishment in London (cf. our "stock exchange"). The bottom of the sea, where King lies, is now more "royal" than any place of business. 45 **dissolves . . . compound:** Our bodies are made up of water and fire (warmth); both can destroy us.   46 **one Vatican:** The Vatican, the Pope's residence, has a famous library; there is no record of its being burnt. Cleveland may be thinking of the library at Alexandria, destroyed by fire. **another:** King had so much learning that his loss is like the loss of a great library.   47 **We of the gown:** scholars **toss:** ruffle the pages of (in search of material)   49 **pupils:** a pun on pupils of the eye   51 **rundlets:** casks   54 **Hebrides:** cf. "Lycidas," line 156

Abraham Cowley
(1618–1667)

Expelled from his post at Cambridge by the parliamentarians in 1643, Cowley followed the queen to France, where he served as her "cipher secretary" (dealing with messages in code) and acted as a royalist agent. Arrested on his return to England ten years later, he was soon released, to spend the rest of his life quietly in the country, recognized as a leading literary figure and devoting himself to science and literature.

The Spring

1

Though you be absent here, I needs must say
The trees as beauteous are, and flowers as gay
    As ever they were wont to be;
    Nay, the birds' rural music too
    Is as melodious and free   5
    As if they sung to pleasure you:
I saw a rosebud ope this morn; I'll swear
The blushing morning opened not more fair.

2

How could it be so fair, and you away?
How could the trees be beauteous, flowers so gay?   10
    Could they remember but last year
    How you did them, they you delight,
    The sprouting leaves which saw you here
    And called their fellows to the sight
Would, looking round for the same sight in vain,   15
Creep back into their silent barks again.

3

Where'er you walked, trees were as reverend made
As when of old gods dwelt in every shade.
    Is't possible they should not know
    What loss of honor they sustain   20
    That thus they smile and flourish now
    And still their former pride retain?
Dull creatures! 'tis not without cause that she
Who fled the god of wit was made a tree.

4

In ancient times, sure they much wiser were   25
When they rejoiced the Thracian verse to hear.
    In vain did nature bid them stay
    When Orpheus had his song begun;
    They called their wondering roots away
    And bade them silent to him run.   30
How would those learned trees have followed you?
You would have drawn them, and their poet too.

5

But who can blame them now? For, since you're gone,
They're here the only fair, and shine alone.
    You did their natural rights invade: 35
    Wherever you did walk or sit,
    The thickest boughs could make no shade,
    Although the sun had granted it;

The Mistress . . . , 1647.

23–24 she . . . tree: Daphne, fleeing from Apollo, "the god of wit," escaped him by turning into a laurel tree.   **28 Orpheus:** This legendary Greek singer [met several times in earlier poems] was from Thrace in the Balkan peninsula. His music was said to be so irresistible that the very trees and rocks would follow him.   **34 fair:** fair creatures

The fairest flowers could please no more, near you,
Than painted flowers, set next to them, could do.   40

6

Whene'er then you come hither, that shall be
The time, which this to others is, to me.
    The little joys which here are now
    The name of punishment do bear,
    When by their sight they let us know   45
    How we deprived of greater are.
'Tis you the best of seasons with you bring;
This is for beasts, and that for men the spring.

42 **the time:** the real springtime   48 **this:** spring by the calendar   **that:** the springtime of your presence

Richard Lovelace
(1618–1657)

Lovelace left Oxford early to live at court, where he was admired as "one of the handsomest men in England." He engaged in two military expeditions against the Scots. In 1642 he was imprisoned for several weeks for presenting an anti-Puritan petition to the House of Commons. Active for the royalist cause, he was captured and again imprisoned in 1648. Though inheriting large estates, he is reported to have died in poverty in London.

To Lucasta, Going to the Wars

Tell me not, sweet, I am unkind,
    That from the nunnery
Of thy chaste breast and quiet mind
    To war and arms I fly.

True, a new mistress now I chase,   5
    The first foe in the field;
And with a stronger faith embrace
    A sword, a horse, a shield.

Yet this inconstancy is such
    As you too shall adore;   10
I could not love thee, dear, so much,
    Loved I not honour more.

Lucasta, 1649.

Lovelace took part in the 1639–1640 English expedition against Scotland.

To Althea, from Prison

When love with unconfinèd wings
    Hovers within my gates,
And my divine Althea brings
    To whisper at the grates;
When I lie tangled in her hair   5
    And fettered to her eye,

1642? Ibid.

The gods that wanton in the air
    Know no such liberty.

When flowing cups run swiftly round
    With no allaying Thames,   10
Our careless heads with roses bound,
    Our hearts with loyal flames;
When thirsty grief in wine we steep,
    When healths and draughts go free,
Fishes that tipple in the deep   15
    Know no such liberty.

When, like committed linnets, I
    With shriller throat shall sing
The sweetness, mercy, majesty
    And glories of my king;   20
When I shall voice aloud, how good
    He is, how great should be,
Enlargèd winds that curl the flood
    Know no such liberty.

Stone walls do not a prison make,   25
    Nor iron bars a cage;
Minds innocent and quiet take
    That for an hermitage:
If I have freedom in my love,
    And in my soul am free,   30
Angels alone that soar above
    Enjoy such liberty.

7 **wanton:** sport   10 **with no allaying Thames:** with no water to dilute them   14 **healths:** drinks ("To your health!")   17 **committed:** caged   **linnets:** European finches, songbirds   23 **enlargèd:** freed, unconfined

Andrew Marvell
(1621–1678)

During the Civil War, Marvell's sympathies were divided: he admired both King Charles and Cromwell. For about a dozen years, up to the Restoration, he worked for the secretary of state as assistant to Milton. Except for two years on a diplomatic mission to Russia, from 1659 on he was a Member of Parliament. Few of his poems were published during his lifetime.

On a Drop of Dew

See how the orient dew,
Shed from the bosom of the morn
    Into the blowing roses,
Yet careless of its mansion new,
For the clear region where 'twas born,   5
    Round in itself incloses;
    And in its little globe's extent,

1650–1652? *Miscellaneous Poems*, 1681.

1 **orient:** (1) shining; (2) born at sunrise   3 **blowing:** blooming   5 **for:** because of   6 **round . . . incloses:** roundly encloses itself in

Frames as it can its native element.
    How it the purple flower does slight,
        Scarce touching where it lies,
        But gazing back upon the skies,
          Shines with a mournful light;
            Like its own tear,
Because so long divided from the sphere.
        Restless it rolls and unsecure,
          Trembling lest it grow impure:
    Till the warm sun pity its pain,
And to the skies exhale it back again.
          So the soul, that drop, that ray
Of the clear fountain of eternal day,
Could it within the human flower be seen,
         Remembering still its former height,
         Shuns the sweet leaves and blossoms green;
         And, recollecting its own light,
Does, in its pure and circling thoughts, express
The greater heaven in an heaven less.
         In how coy a figure wound,
         Every way it turns away:
        So the world excluding round,
         Yet receiving in the day.
        Dark beneath, but bright above:
         Here disdaining, there in love,
    How loose and easy hence to go:
    How girt and ready to ascend.
      Moving but on a point below,
      It all about does upwards bend.
Such did the manna's sacred dew distill;
White, and entire, though congealed and chill.
Congealed on earth: but does, dissolving, run
Into the glories of the almighty sun.

10

15

20

25

30

35

40

8 **frames:** makes [and the modern meaning]   **native element:** heaven [Dew was thought to fall from
there.] 14 **sphere:** heaven 21 **human flower:** human body 24 **recollecting:** gathering again [also
the modern meaning] 27 **coy:** reserved 34 **girt:** prepared 37 **manna:** the food miraculously giv-
en the Israelites on their journey through the wilderness. "And when the dew that lay was gone up,
behold, upon the face of the wilderness there lay a small round thing . . . and when the sun waxed
hot, it melted . . ." (Exod. 16).

A Dialogue Between the Soul and Body

Soul

    O who shall from this dungeon raise
A soul enslaved so many ways?
With bolts of bones, that fettered stands
In feet; and manacled in hands:
Here blinded with an eye; and there
Deaf with the drumming of an ear;
A soul hung up, as 'twere, in chains
Of nerves, and arteries, and veins;

5

Later 1640s? Ibid.

1 **dungeon:** the body 5 **blinded with an eye:** Our physical vision blinds us to spiritual reality

Tortured, besides each other part,
In a vain head and double heart.   10

        Body

    O who shall me deliver whole
From bonds of this tyrannic soul?
Which, stretched upright, impales me so
That mine own precipice I go;
And warms and moves this needless frame   15
(A fever could but do the same);
And, wanting where its spite to try,
Has made me live to let me die;
A body that could never rest,
Since this ill spirit it possessed.   20

        Soul

    What magic could me thus confine
Within another's grief to pine?
Where whatsoever it complain,
I feel, that cannot feel, the pain.
And all my care itself employs   25
That to preserve, which me destroys;
Constrained not only to endure
Diseases, but, what's worse, the cure;
And ready oft the port to gain,
Am shipwrecked into health again.   30

        Body

    But physic yet could never reach
The maladies thou me dost teach:
Whom first the cramp of hope does tear;
And then the palsy shakes of fear;
The pestilence of love does heat;   35
Or hatred's hidden ulcer eat;
Joy's cheerful madness does perplex,
Or sorrow's other madness vex;
Which knowledge forces me to know,
And memory will not forgo.   40
What but a soul could have the wit
To build me up for sin so fit?
So architects do square and hew
Green trees that in the forest grew.

10 **double:** faithless, deceiving [cf. *double*-cross, *two*-time, etc.]   15 **needless:** needing nothing: happy enough without the bothersome soul   17 **wanting where:** lacking a place   20 **it possessed:** possessed it   28 **worse, the cure:** worse, because it keeps the soul in the body [also a possible gibe at the medicine of the time]   29 **port:** heaven   31 **physic:** medicine.   43 **square and hew:** distort what is natural

To His Coy Mistress

    Had we but world enough and time,   *time words*
This coyness, lady, were no crime.

1646–1653? Ibid.

coy: reserved, stand-offish

We would sit down, and think which way
To walk, and pass our long love's day.
Thou by the Indian Ganges' side 5
Shouldst rubies find; I by the tide
Of Humber would complain. I would
Love you ten years before the Flood;
And you should, if you please, refuse
Till the conversion of the Jews. 10
My vegetable love should grow
Vaster than empires, and more slow.
An hundred years should go to praise
Thine eyes, and on thy forehead gaze;
Two hundred to adore each breast; 15
But thirty thousand to the rest;
An age at least to every part,
And the last age should show your heart.
For, lady, you deserve this state;
Nor would I love at lower rate. 20
      But at my back I always hear
Time's wingèd chariot hurrying near;
And yonder all before us lie
Deserts of vast eternity.
Thy beauty shall no more be found, 25
Nor, in thy marble vault, shall sound
My echoing song. Then worms shall try
That long preserved virginity:
And your quaint honour turn to dust;
And into ashes all my lust. 30
The grave's a fine and private place,
But none, I think, do there embrace.
      Now, therefore, while the youthful hue
Sits on thy skin like morning dew,
And while thy willing soul transpires 35
At every pore with instant fires,
Now let us sport us while we may;
And now, like amorous birds of prey,
Rather at once our time devour
Than languish in his slow-chapped power. 40
Let us roll all our strength and all
Our sweetness up into one ball;

6 **rubies:** The fieriness of the ruby naturally associated it with Venus and love; it was also thought to "remove evil thoughts and control amorous desires." 7 **Humber:** an English estuary flowing into the North Sea. Marvell grew up near it (his father was drowned in it). 8 **Flood:** Noah's Old Testament flood 10 **conversion of the Jews:** not supposed to take place until the end of time 11 **vegetable:** vegetating slowly, gradually 18 **heart:** qualities of mind and soul, ranked above her physical charms 19 **state:** royal treatment 22 **Time's wingèd chariot:** The personified sun (Apollo) had a chariot drawn by wingèd horses (one of which was named Chronos, or Time). Or Marvell may have invented this bit of mythology. 29 **quaint:** The O.E.D. gives many meanings for this adjective: *dainty, elegant, elaborate, strange, odd, proud, prim, disdainful.* A sexual meaning is also possible. 34 **dew:** The original printing of the poem reads "morning glew"—a famous crux (textual puzzle). Some think the *glew* is a spelling of *glow* (as *shew* is used for *show*). Some think *glew* means *glue* (like Donne's *fast balm* in "The Ecstasy"), the sticky gum given off by some trees. Many editors think *glew* is a misprint for *dew.* All we are sure of is that Marvell wrote a one-syllable word rhyming with *hue.* 35 **transpires:** passes through, as vapor, moisture, perfume—a delicate way of saying her skin is warm and moist, alive. Her soul is "willing," though the girl is "coy." 40 **slow-chapped:** slow-jawed, slowly devouring 42 **one ball:** The image would seem to be that of a pomander (or sachet), a compressed mixture of aromatic substances, carried as a charm against infection. Some think it's a cannon ball, shot through the iron gates. Marvell is saying: let us pack together, as one, my masculine strength and your feminine sweetness.

And tear our pleasures with rough strife
Through the iron gates of life.
Thus, though we cannot make our sun   45
Stand still, yet we will make him run.

44 **iron gates:** Some see this as a reference to the Iron Gates, a narrow gorge in the valley of the Dan-
ube, but the gates can be taken simply as any barrier (of convention, prohibition, etc.) which lovers
have to force to enjoy their love.   45–46 **sun/Stand still:** The words seem an echo of the Biblical "So
the sun stood still in the midst of heaven, and hasted not to go down about a whole day" (Josh. 10),
when the Lord stopped the sun so that Joshua could finish a battle against the enemies of the Israe-
lites. Marvell may have remembered too that Zeus delayed the sun for the space of three nights when
making love to Alcmene, who became as a result the mother of Hercules.   46 **run:** race with excite-
ment

The Garden

I

How vainly men themselves amaze
To win the palm, the oak, or bays;
And their uncessant labours see
Crowned from some single herb or tree,
Whose short and narrow-vergèd shade   5
Does prudently their toils upbraid;
While all flowers and all trees do close
To weave the garlands of repose

II

Fair Quiet, have I found thee here,
And Innocence, thy sister dear!   10
Mistaken long, I sought you then
In busy companies of men.
Your sacred plants, if here below,
Only among the plants will grow.
Society is all but rude   15
To this delicious solitude.

III

No white nor red was ever seen
So amorous as this lovely green.
Fond lovers, cruel as their flame,
Cut in these trees their mistress' name: 20
Little, alas, they know or heed
How far these beauties hers exceed!
Fair trees! wheres'e'er your barks I wound,
No name shall but your own be found.

IV

When we have run our passion's heat,   25
Love hither makes his best retreat.
The gods, that mortal beauty chase,
Still in a tree did end their race.

Probably 1650–1652. Ibid.

1 **amaze:** bewilder   2 **the palm . . . :** Wreathes or branches of these single plants were rewards for, or
emblems of, various kinds of triumph—military, civic, poetic, etc.   5 **narrow-vergèd:** limited, con-
fined   7 **close:** join together   15 **all but rude:** all of it is nothing but savage   16 **to:** compared
with   23 **wheres'e'er:** wheresoever   25 **heat:** course (as in a race)

Apollo hunted Daphne so,
Only that she might laurel grow;
And Pan did after Syrinx speed,   30
Not as a nymph, but for a reed.

V

What wondrous life in this I lead!
Ripe apples drop about my head;
The luscious clusters of the vine   35
Upon my mouth do crush their wine;
The nectarine and curious peach
Into my hands themselves do reach;
Stumbling on melons as I pass,
Ensnared with flowers, I fall on grass.   40

VI

Meanwhile the mind, from pleasure less,
Withdraws into its happiness:
The mind, that ocean where each kind
Does straight its own resemblance find;
Yet it creates, transcending these,   45
Far other worlds, and other seas;
Annihilating all that's made
To a green thought in a green shade.

VII

Here at the fountain's sliding foot,
Or at some fruit-tree's mossy root,   50
Casting the body's vest aside,
My soul into the boughs does glide:
There like a bird it sits and sings,
Then whets and combs its silver wings;
And, till prepared for longer flight,   55
Waves in its plumes the various light.

VIII

Such was that happy garden-state
While man there walked without a mate:
After a place so pure and sweet,
What other help could yet be meet?   60
But 'twas beyond a mortal's share
To wander solitary there:
Two Paradises 'twere in one,
To live in Paradise alone.

IX

How well the skilful gardener drew   65
Of flowers and herbs this dial new,

29–31 **Apollo ... Syrinx:** Daphne became a tree to escape Apollo, and Syrinx became a reed to escape
Pan. Marvell changes the myths to fit his argument.   37 **curious:** choice, exquisite   41 **pleasure less:**
inferior pleasure [the merely physical pleasures of the preceding stanza]   43–44 **ocean ... find:** It
was thought there was a sea-creature corresponding to each sort of land-creature.   47–48 **annihilat-
ing ... shade:** reducing the thought of everything else to a pure (and restful) garden-thought
51 **vest:** vesture, garment   54 **whets:** Birds preening their feathers seem to be whetting (sharpening)
their bills.   56 **various light:** play of changing light   57 **garden-state:** state of man in the Garden of
Eden   60 **help ... meet:** "And the Lord God said, It is not good that the man should be alone; I will
make him an help meet for him" (Gen. 2).   **meet:** fitting, appropriate   66 **dial:** flowers and herbs ar-
ranged as, or around, a sundial

Where, from above, the milder sun
Does through a fragrant zodiac run;
And, as it works, the industrious bee
Computes its time as well as we.   70
How could such sweet and wholesome hours
Be reckoned but with herbs and flowers?

70 **time:** a *time/thyme* pun

An Horatian Ode upon Cromwell's Return from Ireland

The forward youth that would appear
Must now forsake his muses dear,
    Nor in the shadows sing
    His numbers languishing.
'Tis time to leave the books in dust   5
And oil the unusèd armor's rust:
    Removing from the wall
    The corslet of the hall.
So restless Cromwell could not cease
In the inglorious arts of peace,   10
    But through adventurous war
    Urgèd his active star:
And, like the three-forked lightning, first
Breaking the clouds where it was nursed,
    Did thorough his own side   15
    His fiery way divide.
For 'tis all one to courage high,
The emulous or enemy;
    And with such, to inclose
    Is more than to oppose.   20
Then burning through the air he went
And palaces and temples rent;
    And Caesar's head at last
    Did through his laurels blast.
'Tis madness to resist or blame   25
The force of angry heaven's flame;
    And, if we would speak true,
    Much to the man is due,
Who from his private gardens where

1650. *Miscellaneous Poems*, 1681; cancelled from all but two known copies. *The Works of Andrew Marvell*, ed. E. Thompson, 1776.

The background of the poem is the English Civil War (1642–1651) between the royalists, who supported King Charles I, and the parliamentarians, who resisted the king for political and religious reasons. After the king's execution in 1649, support in Ireland and Scotland for the royalist cause was still a danger to the newly proclaimed republic; Cromwell, the parliamentary general, went to Ireland that year with an army to subdue the royalists and the Irish allied with them. This he did efficiently and ruthlessly, returning to England in triumph in May 1650 because of a fresh threat from Scotland. Marvell must have written his poem about this time, just before Cromwell left for Scotland in July.

Horatian Ode: for the form, see the prosody section.   1 **forward:** spirited, ardent   2 **muses:** literary interests   8 **corslet:** body armor   12 **Urgèd . . . star:** directed his destiny   15 **his own side:** Cromwell had to overcome opposition from members of his own party, as lightning has to break through its own cloud before striking.   17–20 **'tis all one . . . :** A high-spirited man resists envious rivals of his own party just as he resists the enemy.   22 **palaces and temples:** Cromwell's men destroyed many royalist strongholds—the royalists tended to be "high church" rather than Puritan, hence their "temples."   23 **Caesar:** here, Charles I, beheaded in spite of his "laurels" or emblems of honor. Laurels were thought to be safe from lightning.   29 **private gardens:** Before called into political and military action, Cromwell had been a farmer.

He lived reservèd and austere,   30
    As if his highest plot
    To plant the bergamot,
Could by industrious valor climb
To ruin the great work of time,
    And cast the kingdom old   35
    Into another mold;
Though justice against fate complain
And plead the ancient rights in vain;
    But those do hold or break
    As men are strong or weak.   40
Nature that hateth emptiness
Allows of penetration less;
    And therefore must make room
    Where greater spirits come.
What field of all the Civil Wars,   45
Where his were not the deepest scars?
    And Hampton shows what part
    He had of wiser art—
Where, twining subtle fears with hope,
He wove a net of such a scope,   50
    That Charles himself might chase
    To Carisbrooke's narrow case;
That thence the Royal Actor borne
The tragic scaffold might adorn,
    While round the armèd bands   55
    Did clap their bloody hands.
He nothing common did or mean
Upon that memorable scene;
    But with his keener eye
    The ax's edge did try;   60
Nor called the gods with vulgar spite
To vindicate his helpless right,
    But bowed his comely head
    Down as upon a bed.
This was that memorable hour   65
Which first assured the forcèd power.
    So when they did design
    The Capitol's first line,
A bleeding head where they begun
Did fright the architects to run;   70
    And yet in that the state
    Foresaw its happy fate.
And now the Irish are ashamed
To see themselves in one year tamed:
    So much one man can do   75
    That does both act and know.

---

32 **bergamot:** an elegant sort of pear   36 **another mold:** Cromwell was instrumental in changing the long-established monarchy into a commonwealth or republic.   41–42 **Nature . . . penetration:** Nature abhors a vacuum, but is even more opposed to having two things in the very same place; and so with leaders.   47–52: **Hampton . . . case:** Charles, captured by enemy soldiers, had been confined to his palace at Hampton Court. A few months later, though he had given his word not to escape, he did so and fled to Carisbrooke Castle on the Isle of Wight—a political mistake that contributed to his downfall. Cromwell—it seems wrongly—was thought to have induced the king to escape by a subtle use of suggestion.   **case:** confinement, restricted opportunities 53-64 Charles died bravely, without appeals for mercy.   66 **assured:** made sure, confirmed   **forcèd power:** Cromwell and the parliamentarians had taken over by force.   68 **Capitol:** the temple of Jupiter in Rome. A human head (*caput*) discovered as the foundations were being dug was taken as a favorable omen—as the severed head of the king now was.

They can affirm his praises best,
And have, though overcome, confessed
    How good he is, how just,
    And fit for highest trust;   80
Nor yet grown stiffer with command
But still in the Republic's hand;
    How fit he is to sway
    That can so well obey.
He to the Commons' feet presents   85
A kingdom, for his first year's rents;
    And, what he may, forbears
    His fame, to make it theirs;
And has his sword and spoils ungirt,
To lay them at the public's skirt.   90
    So when the falcon high
    Falls heavy from the sky,
She, having killed, no more does search
But on the next green bough to perch;
    Where, when he first does lure,   95
    The falconer has her sure.
What may not then our isle presume
While victory his crest does plume!
    What may not others fear
    If thus he crown each year!   100
A Caesar he ere long to Gaul,
To Italy an Hannibal,
    And to all states not free
    Shall climacteric be.
The Pict no shelter now shall find   105
Within his party-colored mind;
    But from this valor sad
    Shrink underneath the plaid:
Happy if in the tufted brake
The English hunter him mistake,   110
    Nor lay his hounds in near
    The Caledonian deer.
But thou, the wars' and fortune's son,
March indefatigably on,
    And for the last effect   115
    Still keep thy sword erect:
Besides the force it has to fright
The spirits of the shady night,
    The same arts that did gain
    A power must it maintain.   120

77 **his praises:** Scholars, and common sense, suggest that it is very unlikely the Irish would have praised Cromwell at this time!   83-84 **How fit . . . :** Having been a good soldier, he is now fit to be a ruler.   85 **Commons:** After the execution of the king, the House of Lords was abolished with the monarchy; the House of Commons was the controlling body.   87-88 **what he may . . . :** as far as he can, passes on the credit for his victories to the Commons   89 **ungirt:** taken off   95 **lure:** the technical word in falconry for recalling the falcon. (The victorious Cromwell has now settled quietly down for the moment, like a falcon that has done its work.)   101 **Caesar:** the conquerer of Gaul   102 **Hannibal:** the Carthaginian commander who, toward the close of the third century B.C., campaigned in Italy and won several important victories over the Roman armies   104 **climacteric:** epoch-making, climactic   105 **Pict:** Celtic tribe in Scotland. Here it means the Scots in general.   106 **party-colored:** of more than one color, changeable, unreliable (It was thought that the word *Pict* was from the Latin *pictus*, "painted, colored," because the Picts tattooed themselves.)   107 **sad:** earnest, steadfast   108 **plaid:** also "party-colored," and hence appropriate to the Scots   109 **brake:** bushes, in which plaid would serve as camouflage   112 **Caledonian:** Scottish   116 **keep . . . erect:** remain prepared for further campaigns   117-118 **Besides . . . night:** in addition to the fact that the hilt of the sword, shaped like a cross, is a protection against evil spirits

Henry Vaughan
(1621?–1695)

Vaughan studied law, but by his mid-thirties had published translations of medical trea-
tises and begun to practice as a country doctor in his native Wales. His poetry, under the
influence of George Herbert, became prevailingly religious; it was generally neglected
until the nineteenth century.

The Retreat

    Happy those early days! when I
Shined in my angel-infancy.
Before I understood this place
Appointed for my second race,
Or taught my soul to fancy aught   5
But a white celestial thought;
When yet I had not walked above
A mile or two from my first love,
And looking back, at that short space,
Could see a glimpse of His bright face;   10
When on some gilded cloud, or flower
My gazing soul would dwell an hour,
And in those weaker glories spy
Some shadows of eternity;
Before I taught my tongue to wound   15
My conscience with a sinful sound,
Or had the black art to dispense
A several sin to every sense,
But felt through all this fleshly dress
Bright shoots of everlastingness.   20
    Oh how I long to travel back
And tread again that ancient track!
That I might once more reach that plain
Where first I left my glorious train,
From whence the enlightened spirit sees   25
That shady city of palm trees.
But, ah! my soul with too much stay
Is drunk, and staggers in the way.
Some men a forward motion love,
But I by backward steps would move,   30
And when this dust falls to the urn,
In that state I came return.

Probably 1648–1650. *Silex Scintillans,* 1650.

This poem is based on a belief in the happy preexistence of the soul in a spiritual realm before our
birth in this world, and in the innocence and holiness of early childhood because closer to that bliss-
ful preexistence.

18 **several:** separate, particular   24 **train:** (1) way of life; (2) angelic companionship   26 **city:** Jeri-
cho (the promised land)

Peace

My soul, there is a country
    Far beyond the stars,
Where stands a wingèd sentry

Probably 1648–1650. Ibid.

3 **sentry:** the Archangel Michael

All skillful in the wars;
There, above noise and danger,   5
   Sweet peace sits crowned with smiles,
And one born in a manger
   Commands the beauteous files.
He is thy gracious friend,
   And (O my soul, awake!)   10
Did in pure love descend
   To die here for thy sake.
If thou canst get but thither,
   There grows the flower of peace,
The rose that cannot wither,   15
   Thy fortress, and thy ease.
Leave then thy foolish ranges;
   For none can thee secure,
But one who never changes,
   Thy God, thy life, thy cure.   20

The World

I saw Eternity the other night
Like a great ring of pure and endless light,
   All calm as it was bright;
And round beneath it, Time, in hours, days, years,
   Driven by the spheres,   5
Like a vast shadow moved, in which the world
   And all her train were hurled.
The doting lover in his quaintest strain
   Did there complain;
Near him, his lute, his fancy, and his flights,   10
   Wit's sour delights;
With gloves and knots, the silly snares of pleasure;
   Yet his dear treasure
All scattered lay, while he his eyes did pour
   Upon a flower.   15

The darksome statesman hung with weights and woe,
Like a thick midnight fog, moved there so slow
   He did nor stay nor go;
Condemning thoughts, like sad eclipses, scowl
   Upon his soul,   20
And clouds of crying witnesses without
   Pursued him with one shout.
Yet digged the mole, and, lest his ways be found,
   Worked under ground,
Where he did clutch his prey; but One did see   25
   That policy.
Churches and altars fed him, perjuries
   Were gnats and flies;
It rained about him blood and tears, but he
   Drank them as free.   30

The fearful miser on a heap of rust
Sat pining all his life there, did scarce trust

Probably 1648–1650. Ibid.

8 quaintest: most affected, most far-fetched **23 the mole:** the statesman, working in secret
28 gnats and flies: insignificant trifles

His own hands with the dust;
Yet would not place one piece above, but lives
   In fear of thieves.   35
Thousands there were as frantic as himself,
   And hugged each one his pelf.
The downright epicure placed heaven in sense
   And scorned pretense;
While others, slipped into a wide excess,   40
   Said little less;
The weaker sort, slight, trivial wares enslave,
   Who think them brave;
And poor despisèd truth sat counting by
   Their victory.   45

Yet some, who all this while did weep and sing,
And sing and weep, soared up into the ring;
   But most would use no wing.
"O fools," said I, "thus to prefer dark night
   Before true light,   50
To live in grots, and caves, and hate the day
   Because it shows the way,
The way which from this dead and dark abode
   Leads up to God,
A way where you might tread the sun, and be   55
   More bright than he."
But as I did their madness so discuss,
   One whispered thus:
This ring the Bridegroom did for none provide
   But for his bride.   60

37 **pelf:** riches   38 **sense:** sensual pleasure   43 **brave:** splendid

John Dryden
(1631–1700)

The leading man of letters during the second half of the century, Dryden supported himself, during the 1660s and 1670s, by writing some 20 plays, often accompanied by critical essays. In the 1680s he began his series of satiric and doctrinal poems. When the Catholic King James II came to the throne in 1685, Dryden became a Catholic. When the "Glorious Revolution" of 1688 brought in the Protestant King William, Dryden refused to change back—with the result that he lost his laureateship and a government stipend. During his last years he busied himself with translations and adaptations of the classics.

From Mac Flecknoe
OR, A SATIRE UPON THE TRUE-BLUE PROTESTANT POET, T.S.

All human things are subject to decay,
And when fate summons, monarchs must obey.

1678. *Mac Flecknoe. Printed for D. Green,* 1682 (not authorized). Text from *Miscellany Poems,* Vol. I, 1684.

In this poem, written in 1678, Dryden is making fun of the dramatist Thomas Shadwell, whom he shows, with some exaggeration, as a stupid and tedious writer. We are not sure what exactly provoked the poem, though there were political, literary, and personal differences between the two men. Since the satire is not political or religious, the subtitle with its "True-Blue Protestant" seems to have been added by the publisher to make the poem seem more involved in controversy. A number of lines (many of them, in their references to long-forgotten plays, their characters, and their authors, almost as tedious as Shadwell himself) have been omitted here. The line numbering is that of the complete version.

This Flecknoe found, who, like Augustus, young
Was called to empire, and had governed long;
In prose and verse, was owned, without dispute,   5
Through all the realms of *Nonsense*, absolute.
This aged Prince, now flourishing in peace,
And blest with issue of a large increase,
Worn out with business, did at length debate
To settle the succession of the State;   10
And, pondering which of all his sons was fit
To reign, and wage immortal war with wit,
Cried: " 'T is resolved; for nature pleads, that he
Should only rule, who most resembles me.
Sh—— alone my perfect image bears,   15
Mature in dulness from his tender years.
Sh—— alone, of all my sons, is he
Who stands confirmed in full stupidity.
The rest to some faint meaning make pretense,
But Sh—— never deviates into sense.   20
Some beams of wit on other souls may fall,
Strike through, and make a lucid interval;
But Sh——'s genuine night admits no ray,
His rising fogs prevail upon the day.
Besides, his goodly fabric fills the eye,   25
And seems designed for thoughtless majesty;
Thoughtless as monarch oaks that shade the plain,
And, spread in solemn state, supinely reign.
Heywood and Shirley were but types of thee,
Thou last great prophet of tautology."   30

· · ·

Here stopped the good old sire, and wept for joy   60
In silent raptures of the hopeful boy.
All arguments, but most his plays, persuade,
That for anointed dulness he was made.
   Close to the walls which fair Augusta bind
(The fair Augusta much to fears inclined,)   65
An ancient fabric raised t' inform the sight,
There stood of yore, and Barbican it hight:
A watchtower once; but now, so fate ordains,
Of all the pile an empty name remains.
From its old ruins brothel-houses rise,   70
Scenes of lewd loves, and of polluted joys;
Where their vast courts the mother-strumpets keep,
And, undisturbed by watch, in silence sleep.

3 **Flecknoe:** Richard Flecknoe, an Irish poetaster (bad poet) who, according to the poem, must have died recently. In Dryden's poem he is the very King of Dullness, now about to choose his successor. His son Mac Flecknoe (*Mac* means *son of*) is even better qualified than he, since even duller, and is therefore chosen to succeed him. Flecknoe and Shadwell were of course not really related; their only bond was their stupidity.   **Augustus:** Augustus Caesar (63 B.C.–A.D. 14) was only 18 when Julius Caesar was killed. Proclaimed emperor when he was 35, he ruled for four decades.   12 **wit:** quick intelligence and what it produces (good poetry, for example)   15 **Sh ———:** Shadwell, a tongue-in-cheek way of seeming to conceal the name; but it also suggests, as in line 103, a vulgar word.   25 **goodly fabric:** impressive build, corpulence   28 **supinely:** passively, lazily   29 **Heywood and Shirley:** earlier dramatists, out of fashion in Dryden's time, but not badly regarded today   **types:** in Biblical terminology, someone or something in the Old Testament supposed to foreshadow someone or something in the New Testament   30 **tautology:** pointless repetition   61 **boy:** Shadwell, immensely fat and approaching 40   64 ff. Shadwell was to be crowned as King of Dullness in a disreputable part of town.   64 **Augusta:** ("majestic, revered") an ancient name for London   65 **fears:** of Catholic plots against the state, more imaginary [Dryden implies] than real   66 **fabric:** structure   67 **Barbican:** a defensive tower, part of the old fortifications, become a center of vice and vulgar amusements   69 **pile:** large or imposing building

Near these a Nursery erects its head,
Where queens are formed, and future heroes bred;
Where unfledged actors learn to laugh and cry,
Where infant punks their tender voices try.

· · ·

    Now Empress Fame had published the renown
Of Sh——'s coronation through the town.
Roused by report of Fame, the nations meet,
From near Bunhill, and distant Watling Street.
No Persian carpets spread th' imperial way,
But scattered limbs of mangled poets lay;
From dusty shops neglected authors come,
Martyrs of pies and relics of the bum.
Much Heywood, Shirley, Ogleby there lay,
But loads of Sh—— almost choked the way.

· · ·

The sire then shook the honors of his head,
And from his brows damps of oblivion shed,
Full on the filial dullness: long he stood,
Repelling from his breast the raging god;
At length burst out in this prophetic mood:
    "Heavens bless my son! From Ireland let him reign
To far Barbadoes on the western main;
Of his dominion may no end be known,
And greater than his father's be his throne.
Beyond love's kingdom let him stretch his pen!"
He paused, and all the people cried, "Amen!"
Then thus continued he: "My son, advance
Still in new impudence, new ignorance.
Success let others teach, learn thou from me
Pangs without birth, and fruitless industry.

· · ·

And when false flowers of rhetoric thou wouldst cull,
Trust Nature, do not labor to be dull.

· · ·

Like mine, thy gentle numbers feebly creep;
Thy tragic Muse gives smiles, thy comic sleep.
With whate'er gall thou settest thyself to write,
Thy inoffensive satires never bite.
In thy felonious heart though venom lies,
It does but touch thy Irish pen, and dies.
Thy genius calls thee not to purchase fame

75

95

100

135

140

145

165

197

200

74 **Nursery:** place for the training of young actors (with suggestions of a house of prostitution)
77 **punks:** prostitutes   97 **Bunhill...Watling Street:** a not very extensive middle-class merchant
area   101 The unsold books of dull writers might end up as wrapping paper in bakeries, or in pri-
vies. **bum:** backside   102 **Ogleby:** a versatile Scotsman, translator of the classics   137–138 Like pro-
phetic Sibyls in classical poetry, Flecknoe at first resists the god that would inspire him. Here and
elsewhere Dryden is writing parodies of classical passages.   139–140 **from Ireland ... to far Barba-
does:** The kingdom sounds impressive, but is nearly all water.   143 **love's kingdom:** Flecknoe wrote
a play called *Love's Kingdom.*   148 **pangs without birth:** labor pains (efforts to write) that come to
nothing   199 **gall:** bitterness   202 **Irish:** In Dryden's England, "Irish" was disparaging. The line
may mean that one poison counteracts another; or that there is no bite in an Irish pen, as there are no
snakes in Ireland.

In keen iambics, but mild anagram.
Leave writing plays and choose for thy command 205
Some peaceful province in acrostic land.
There thou mayest wings display and altars raise,
And torture one poor word ten thousand ways.
Or, if thou wouldst thy different talents suit,
Set thy own songs, and sing them to thy lute." 210
    He said: but his last words were scarcely heard; ⎫
For Bruce and Longvil had a trap prepared,   ⎬
And down they sent the yet declaiming bard.   ⎭
Sinking he left his drugget robe behind,
Borne upwards by a subterranean wind. 215
The mantle fell to the young prophet's part,
With double portion of his father's art.

204 **iambics:** The iambic rhythm (with units of two syllables, the second stressed or weightier than the first, as in *desire, adore,* etc.) was the usual rhythm for satire in Greek poetry. **anagram:** a kind of word game in which letters of a word or phrase are rearranged to form new words 206 **acrostic:** another kind of word play in which the first letters (e.g.) of each line of a poem are made to spell out words, phrases, and such. Both *anagram* and *acrostic* are used here to refer to kinds of poetry more remarkable for ingenuity and novelty of technique than for the good sense of intelligence and passion. 207 **wings ... and altars:** the kind of pattern poetry illustrated by Herbert's "Easter-Wings" (p. 125). 211–213 The bracket at the end of the lines indicates that there are three rhyming lines instead of the usual couplet (two lines). 212 **Bruce and Longvil:** characters in Shadwell's play *The Virtuoso,* who spring a trap door on a foolish and talky courtier in mid-oration 214 **drugget:** coarse woolen 214–217 The lines parody the Old Testament passage about Elijah's rising to heaven in a chariot of fire. Whereas Elijah goes up, Flecknoe goes down. "And Elisha said, 'I pray thee, let a double portion of thy spirit be upon me' ... and ... behold, there appeared a chariot of fire ... and Elijah went up by a whirlwind into heaven. ... And Elisha saw it, and he cried, 'My father! My father!' ... He took up the mantle of Elijah that fell from him, and went back" (2 Kings 2:9–13).

From **Absalom and Achitophel**

In pious times, ere priestcraft did begin,
Before polygamy was made a sin;
When man on many multiplied his kind,

1681. *Absalom and Achitophel,* 1681. Text from *Miscellany Poems,* Vol. I, 1684.

"Absalom and Achitophel" was a weapon in the political skirmishing between the Whigs and Tories in 1681. The name Whig, from Whiggamore, had originally been applied to the Presbyterians who in 1648 resisted the royalist cause in Scotland; in 1681 it was used of those who were against the king, Charles II, in the matter of the succession to the throne. Derisively they labelled their opponents Tories, a name originally given to the Irish outlaws who harried and plundered the English settlers; it came to be used of any Irish who were Catholic and royalist. Now, in 1681, it was used of all those on the king's side in the current struggle over the succession.

Charles, who had spent many years in exile and poverty after the execution of his father in 1649, had a number of illegitimate children—some 14 were acknowledged. But none of these could be heir to the throne. Next in line was the brother of the king, James, Duke of York. But James was a Catholic—hence the violent Whig opposition to his ever becoming king. Led by Anthony Ashley Cooper, Earl of Shaftesbury, the Whigs several times proposed in Parliament that James be barred and that the handsome and popular (but not very bright) James Scott, Duke of Monmouth, an illegitimate son of the king, be declared heir. Though fond of his son, Charles was totally opposed to the exclusion of his brother. Parliament was dissolved, and Shaftesbury arrested on a charge of treason.

It is said that the king asked Dryden to write his poem in the hope of strengthening the case against Shaftesbury and influencing the forthcoming trial. The poem itself is a political allegory: Dryden tells the story of Charles, his son Monmouth, and the Whig leader Shaftesbury in terms of the Old Testament story of King David, his beloved but rebellious son Absalom, and the son's evil adviser Achitophel (Ahithophel), as related in 2 Sam. 15–18. Current events in England are ingeniously transferred to the world of the Old Testament—the English are called "the Jews," London is called "Sion," and so forth. Everything means something else—though the real meanings would have been quite clear to Dryden's readers. Dryden was not original in noting the Old Testament parallel; a number of other writers had referred to Charles as a David figure.

We have here only the beginning of Dryden's long poem: he describes, with humorous verve, the Old Testament precedent for the king's "polygamy," the character of the beloved but rebellious son, and the political instability and restlessness of the English.

Ere one to one was cursedly confined;
When nature prompted, and no law denied   5
Promiscuous use of concubine and bride;
Then Israel's monarch, after Heaven's own heart,
His vigorous warmth did variously impart
To wives and slaves; and, wide as his command,
Scattered his Maker's image through the land.   10
Michal, of royal blood, the crown did wear,
A soil ungrateful to the tiller's care:
Not so the rest; for several mothers bore
To godlike David several sons before.
But since like slaves his bed they did ascend,   15
No true succession could their seed attend.
Of all this numerous progeny was none
So beautiful, so brave, as Absalom:
Whether, inspired by some diviner lust,
His father got him with a greater gust;   20
Or that his conscious destiny made way,
By manly beauty, to imperial sway.
Early in foreign fields he won renown,
With kings and states allied to Israel's crown:
In peace the thoughts of war he could remove,   25
And seemed as he were only born for love.
Whate'er he did, was done with so much ease,
In him alone 't was natural to please.
His motions all accompanied with grace;
And paradise was opened in his face.   30
With secret joy indulgent David viewed
His youthful image in his son renewed:
To all his wishes nothing he denied;
And made the charming Annabel his bride.
What faults he had (for who from faults is free?)   35
His father could not, or he would not see.
Some warm excesses which the law forbore,
Were construed youth that purged by boiling o'er,
And Amnon's murther, by a specious name,
Was called a just revenge for injured fame.   40
Thus praised and loved the noble youth remained,
While David, undisturbed, in Sion reigned.
But life can never be sincerely blest;
Heaven punishes the bad, and proves the best.
The Jews, a headstrong, moody, murmuring race,   45
As ever tried th' extent and stretch of grace;
God's pampered people, whom, debauched with ease,

11 **Michal**: the daughter of Saul and the first of David's many wives; they had no children. She stands for Catherine of Braganza, Princess of Portugal, whom Charles married in 1662. She was childless. 18 **Absalom**: James Scott, Duke of Monmouth, was born in 1649. His mother was "a Welsh woman of no good fame." He seems to have been as charming and impressive as the Absalom Dryden portrays. A contemporary writer describes him as having every personal advantage except that he was "greatly deficient in mental accomplishments." 20 **gust**: gusto, pleasure 23 **foreign fields**: Monmouth served with distinction with the French forces in Holland, and as commander of the king's army against the Scots. 24 **Israel**: England 26 **born for love**: "All the . . . beautiful of the fair sex were at his devotion . . . [he was] the universal terror of husbands and lovers. . . ." 34 **Annabel**: Anne, Countess of Buccleuch, whom Monmouth married in 1663 37 **forebore**: kept hands off, refused to punish 38 **construed**: interpreted as 39 **Amnon's murther**: In the Old Testament story, Absalom ordered the murder of Amnon because he had violated Absalom's (and his own) sister. In the allegory, Monmouth's "warm excess" was probably the savage but not fatal attack on Sir John Coventry, who had referred to the king's amours in Parliament. 40 **fame**: reputation 42 **Sion**: London 45 **the Jews**: the English

No King could govern, nor no God could please;
(Gods they had tried of every shape and size,
That god-smiths could produce, or priests devise):   50
These Adam-wits, too fortunately free,
Began to dream they wanted liberty;
And when no rule, no precedent was found,
Of men by laws less circumscribed and bound;
They led their wild desires to woods and caves,   55
And thought that all but savages were slaves.
They who, when Saul was dead, without a blow,
Made foolish Ishbosheth the crown forego;
Who banished David did from Hebron bring,
And with a general shout proclaimed him King: 60
Those very Jews, who, at their very best,
Their humor more than loyalty expressed,
Now wondered why so long they had obeyed
An idol-monarch, which their hands had made;
Thought they might ruin him they could create,   65
Or melt him to that golden calf, a State.

• • •

Of these the false Achitophel was first,   150
A name to all succeeding ages curst:
For close designs and crooked counsels fit;
Sagacious, bold, and turbulent of wit;
Restless, unfixed in principles and place;
In power unpleased, impatient of disgrace: 155
A fiery soul, which, working out its way, ⎤
Fretted the pigmy body to decay,   ⎬
And o'er-informed the tenement of clay. ⎦
A daring pilot in extremity,
Pleased with the danger, when the waves went high,   160
He sought the storms, but, for a calm unfit,
Would steer too nigh the sands, to boast his wit.
Great wits are sure to madness near allied,
And thin partitions do their bounds divide;
Else why should he, with wealth and honor blest,   165
Refuse his age the needful hours of rest?
Punish a body which he could not please;
Bankrupt of life, yet prodigal of ease?
And all to leave what with his toil he won,
To that unfeathered two-legged thing, a son;   170
Got, while his soul did huddled notions try;
And born a shapeless lump, like anarchy.

---

51 Adam-wits: men minded like Adam, who, before the Fall, thought he needed more freedom than he had   **52 wanted:** lacked   **55 they led ... caves:** They tried to return, as "noble savages," to a primitive state in which no rule was necessary.   **57 Saul:** Oliver Cromwell, who died in 1658   **58 Ishbosheth:** Saul's son; here, Oliver's son Richard, who briefly succeeded him as Lord Protector   **59 Hebron:** Scotland   **62 humor:** caprice, momentary mood   **66 State:** a republic, which (Dryden believed) gave only the illusion of greater freedom   **150 these:** opponents of the king and his policies   **Achitophel:** Shaftesbury. See introductory note to this poem. Born in 1621, he fought on the king's side in the Civil Wars, yet became a member of Cromwell's council of state, yet was one of those in favor of inviting King Charles to return in 1660. In politics he changed sides several times, and was proud of his skillful timing in doing so.   **157 pigmy body:** Shaftesbury suffered from a poor constitution and bad health.   **158 o'er-informed:** overloaded, was too lively for   **162 boast his wit:** show off his skill   **166 his age:** He turned 60 the year the poem was written, and died two years later.   **168** Though at the end of his life, he was wasteful of the rest he needed.   **170 unfeathered ...:** The definition of man as "a two-legged unfeathered animal" is ascribed to Plato. Shaftesbury's son was of little worth.   **171 huddled:** confused, hurried

In friendship false, implacable in hate;
Resolved to ruin or to rule the State.
To compass this the triple bond he broke;   175
The pillars of the public safety shook;
And fitted Israel for a foreign yoke.
Then seized with fear, yet still affecting fame,
Usurped a patriot's all-atoning name.
So easy still it proves in factious times   180
With public zeal to cancel private crimes.
How safe is treason, and how sacred ill,
Where none can sin against the people's will!
Where crowds can wink, and no offense be known,
Since in another's guilt they find their own!   185
Yet fame deserved no enemy can grudge;
The statesman we abhor, but praise the judge.
In Israel's courts ne'er sat an Abbethdin
With more discerning eyes, or hands more clean;
Unbribed, unsought, the wretched to redress;   190
Swift of dispatch, and easy of access.
O, had he been content to serve the crown,
With virtues only proper to the gown;
Or had the rankness of the soil been freed
From cockle, that oppressed the noble seed;   195
David for him his tuneful harp had strung,
And Heaven had wanted one immortal song.
But wild Ambition loves to slide, not stand,
And Fortune's ice prefers to Virtue's land.

• • •

In the first rank of these did Zimri stand,
A man so various, that he seemed to be   545
Not one, but all mankind's epitome:
Stiff in opinions, always in the wrong;
Was everything by starts, and nothing long;
But, in the course of one revolving moon,
Was chymist, fiddler, statesman, and buffoon: 550
Then all for women, painting, rhyming, drinking,
Besides ten thousand freaks that died in thinking.
Blest madman, who could every hour employ,
With something new to wish, or to enjoy!
Railing and praising were his usual themes;   555
And both (to show his judgment) in extremes:

---

175 **triple bond:** the alliance between England, Sweden, and Holland, broken when Charles joined with France against the Dutch   177 **foreign yoke:** The secret agreement with France constituted a foreign entanglement (for which Shaftesbury was not really responsible).   178 **affecting fame:** caring about his reputation   179 **patriot:** Whigs in favor of exclusion called themselves "Patriots" in 1680.   180–191 These lines were added in an "Augmented and Revised" edition soon after the first printing.   184 **wink:** connive in, close their eyes to (offenses)   188 **Abbethdin:** among the Jews, a presiding judge of the civil court. Shaftesbury, as Lord Chancellor, had a good record.   193 **the gown:** of a judge   195 **cockle:** weeds   197 **wanted:** lacked (David would not have written one of the immortal psalms in which he complains about his enemies: Psalm 3? 109?)   199 **ice prefers:** likes to take chances   544 **Zimri:** George Villiers, Duke of Buckingham (1628–1687). A boyhood friend of Charles and his chief adviser after 1667, he later turned against the king and sided with his opponents. A man of scattered talents, he had ridiculed Dryden in *The Rehearsal*, a play he had written ten years before. There are two Biblical Zimris Dryden may have had in mind (neither in the story of David). Zimri in Num. 25 is killed for an illicit love affair; Buckingham, the lover of the Countess of Shrewsbury, had killed her husband in 1668. Zimri in 1 Kings 16 is an unfaithful commander of chariots who conspires against and kills his master Elah. Dryden thought his portrait of Zimri was "worth the whole poem."   550 **chymist:** alchemist. For years Buckingham thought he was about to discover the philosopher's stone, which would turn base metals into gold.

So over-violent, or over-civil,
That every man, with him, was God or Devil.
In squandering wealth was his peculiar art:
Nothing went unrewarded but desert.   560
Beggared by fools, whom still he found too late,
He had his jest, and they had his estate.
He laughed himself from court, then sought relief
By forming parties, but could ne'er be chief;
For, spite of him, the weight of business fell   565
On Absalom and wise Achitophel:
Thus, wicked but in will, of means bereft,
He left not faction, but of that was left. . . .

560 **desert:** merit 561 **found:** found out, saw through 568 **faction:** political party, political intrigue

Farewell, Ungrateful Traitor

Farewell, ungrateful traitor,
    Farewell, my perjured swain;
Let never injured creature
    Believe a man again.
The pleasure of possessing   5
Surpasses all expressing,
But 'tis too short a blessing,
    And love too long a pain.

'Tis easy to deceive us
    In pity of your pain;   10
But when we love you leave us
    To rail at you in vain.
Before we have descried it
There is no bliss beside it,
But she that once has tried it   15
    Will never love again.

The passion you pretended
    Was only to obtain,
But when the charm is ended
    The charmer you disdain.   20
Your love by ours we measure
Till we have lost our treasure,
But dying is a pleasure
    When living is a pain.

The Spanish Friar, 1681.

To the Memory of Mr. Oldham

Farewell, too little and too lately known,
Whom I began to think and call my own;
For sure our souls were near allied, and thine
Cast in the same poetic mould with mine.

1683–1684. *The Works of Mr. John Oldham, Together with His Remains*, 1684.

Mr. Oldham: John Oldham (1653–1683). Dryden was particularly impressed by the rugged satires of the younger poet.

One common note on either lyre did strike,   5
And knaves and fools we both abhorred alike:
To the same goal did both our studies drive,
The last set out the soonest did arrive.
Thus Nisus fell upon the slippery place,
While his young friend performed and won the race.   10
O early ripe! to thy abundant store
What could advancing age have added more?
It might (what nature never gives the young)
Have taught the numbers of thy native tongue.
But satire needs not those, and wit will shine   15
Through the harsh cadence of a rugged line.
A noble error, and but seldom made,
When poets are by too much force betrayed.
Thy generous fruits, though gathered ere their prime   ⎫
Still showed a quickness; and maturing time   ⎬   20
But mellows what we write to the dull sweets of rhyme. ⎭
Once more, hail and farewell; farewell, thou young,
But ah too short, Marcellus of our tongue;
Thy brows with ivy, and with laurels bound;
But fate and gloomy night encompass thee around.   25

7 **studies:** studious efforts   8 **last ... arrive:** Though 22 years younger than Dryden, Oldham became known as a satirist a year or two earlier.   9–10 Vergil (*Aeneid*, V, 315–339) describes the footrace in which Nisus, the older of two friends, is about to win but slips and falls. He deliberately interferes with the runner in second place, so that his young friend Eurylus, running third, is the winner. 14 **numbers:** harmonious rhythms   20 **quickness:** vigor, pungency   22 **hail and farewell:** *Ave atque vale!*—the Latin formula for saluting the dead. (Note the several Roman references in the poem.) 23 **Marcellus:** The promising son and heir of Augustus, born in 42 B.C., died at the age of 20. His death was mourned by Vergil (*Aeneid*, VI, 854–886).

A Song for St. Cecilia's Day

1

From harmony, from heavenly harmony
   This universal frame began:
  When Nature underneath a heap
    Of jarring atoms lay,
  And could not heave her head,   5
The tuneful voice was heard from high
   "Arise, ye more than dead!"
Then cold, and hot, and moist, and dry
In order to their stations leap,
  And Music's power obey.   10
From harmony, from heavenly harmony
   This universal frame began:
   From harmony to harmony

   Published as a single half-sheet, 1687; then in *Examen Poeticum* (the third part of *Miscellany Poems*), 1693.

St. Cecilia, the Roman martyr, is thought of as the patron saint of sacred music; she is often represented as playing the organ. Her day is November 22. Dryden's poem, set to music by the Italian composer and organist Giovanni Baptista Draghi, was performed on that day in 1687 with orchestra and chorus, as one of a series of annual concerts.

1-2 **from harmony:** It was a Platonic doctrine that music organized the cosmos from the state of primeval chaos.   8 **cold ... dry:** earth, fire, water, air—the four "elements" out of which, according to ancient belief, the universe is made

Through all the compass of the notes it ran,
The diapason closing full in man.   15

2

What passion cannot Music raise and quell!
    When Jubal struck the corded shell
    His listening brethren stood around,
      And, wondering, on their faces fell
    To worship that celestial sound.   20
Less than a god they thought there could not dwell
    Within the hollow of that shell
    That spoke so sweetly and so well.
What passion cannot Music raise and quell?

3

    The trumpet's loud clangor   25
      Excites us to arms,
    With shrill notes of anger
      And mortal alarms.
    The double double double beat
      Of the thundering drum   30
      Cries "Hark! the foes come;
Charge, charge, 'tis too late to retreat!"

4

The soft complaining flute
    In dying notes discovers
    The woes of hopeless lovers,   35
Whose dirge is whispered by the warbling lute.

5

    Sharp violins proclaim
Their jealous pangs and desperation,
Fury, frantic indignation,
Depth of pains, and height of passion   40
    For the fair disdainful dame.

6

But oh, what art can teach,
What human voice can reach
    The sacred organ's praise?
Notes inspiring holy love,   45
    Notes that wing their heavenly ways
To mend the choirs above.

7

Orpheus could lead the savage race,
And trees unrooted left their place
    Sequacious of the lyre: 50
But bright Cecilia raised the wonder higher:

15 **diapason:** the entire range of musical notes   17 **Jubal:** "the father of all such as handle the harp and organ" (Gen. 4:21)   **corded shell:** The first lyre was imagined as a tortoise shell strung with gut.   26 ff. Each of the following stanzas tries to imitate, in sound and rhythm, the instruments it mentions and to describe the emotions these arouse.   33 **complaining:** plaintive, lamenting   34 **discovers:** reveals   47 **mend:** amend, improve   48 **Orpheus:** Cf. A. Cowley, "The Spring," 25 ff. (p. 159, gloss).   50 **sequacious of:** following

When to her organ vocal breath was given,
An angel heard, and straight appeared,
   Mistaking earth for heaven.

      Grand Chorus

   As from the power of sacred lays   55
     The spheres began to move,
   And sung the great Creator's praise
     To all the blest above;
   So when the last and dreadful hour
   This crumbling pageant shall devour,   60
   The trumpet shall be heard on high,
   The dead shall live, the living die,
   And Music shall untune the sky.

61 **trumpet:** of the day of judgment   63 **untune the sky:** bring to a close the mortal music of time

Song *from* **The Secular Masque**

All, all of a piece throughout:
Thy chase had a beast in view;
Thy wars brought nothing about;
Thy lovers were all untrue.
'Tis well an old age is out,
And time to begin a new.

   1700. *The Pilgrim . . . Written Originally by Mr. Fletcher . . . Likewise a Prologue, Epilogue, Dialogue and Masque, Written by the Late Great Poet Mr. Dryden, just before his Death, being the Last of his Works,* 1700.

In "The Secular Masque," written in the year of his death, Dryden looks back at the whole seventeenth century. He sees it as frivolous, futile, dissolute. "The poet alludes to the sylvan sports of James the First, the bloody wars of his son [Charles I], and the licentious gallantry which reigned in the courts of Charles II and James" (Sir Walter Scott).

Katherine Philips
(1631–1664)

Daughter of a London merchant, Katherine Philips (known as "the matchless Orinda") married a Welsh Puritan who was a Member of Parliament. Her home in Wales became the meeting place of a romantic literary group; her works, circulating in manuscript, brought her such a wide reputation that a pirated edition was published. Her translation of Corneille's tragedy *Pompey* was successfully produced in Dublin.

An Answer to Another Persuading a Lady to Marriage

Forbear, bold youth; all's heaven here,
   And what you do aver
To others courtship may appear,
   'Tis sacrilege to her.

She is a public deity;   5
   And were't not very odd
She should depose herself to be
   A petty household god?

   Poems, 1667, as numbered quatrains. (Pirated edition, 1664.)

First make the sun in private shine
    And bid the world adieu,   10
That so he may his beams confine
    In compliment to you:

But if of that you do despair,
    Think how you did amiss
To strive to fix her beams which are   15
    More bright and large than this.

15 fix: confine to one place

Thomas Traherne
(1637–1674)

Traherne, who was unmarried, was rector of a small parish near his home town in western England and later a chaplain in London. He was so little concerned with publication that none of his poetry appeared in his lifetime; the manuscripts he left, not even signed, were discovered by mere luck and published only in our century.

Wonder

How like an angel came I down!
    How bright are all things here!
When first among his works I did appear
    Oh how their glory me did crown!
The world resembled his eternity,   5
    In which my soul did walk;
    And every thing that I did see
        Did with me talk.

The skies in their magnificence,
    The lively, lovely air,   10
Oh how divine, how soft, how sweet, how fair!
    The stars did entertain my sense;
And all the works of God so bright and pure,
    So rich and great, did seem,
    As if they ever must endure   15
        In my esteem.

A native health and innocence
    Within my bones did grow,
And while my God did all his glories show,
    I felt a vigour in my sense   20
That was all spirit: I within did flow
    With seas of life like wine;
    I nothing in the world did know
        But 'twas divine.

Harsh ragged objects were concealed,   25
    Oppressions, tears and cries,

1669–1674. *Poetical Works*, ed. B. Dobell, 1903. *Centuries, Poems, and Thanksgivings*, ed. H. M. Margoliouth, 1958.

16 esteem: valuation

Sins, griefs, complaints, dissensions, weeping eyes
   Were hid, and only things revealed
Which heavenly spirits and the angels prize.
    The state of innocence   30
    And bliss, not trades and poverties,
       Did fill my sense.

    The streets were paved with golden stones;
      The boys and girls were mine.
Oh how did all their lovely faces shine!   35
    The sons of men were holy ones.
Joy, beauty, welfare did appear to me.
     And every thing which here I found,
    While like an angel I did see,
       Adorned the ground.   40

    Rich diamond and pearl and gold
      In every place was seen;
Rare splendors, yellow, blue, red, white and green
    Mine eyes did everywhere behold;
Great wonders clothed with glory did appear;   45
     Amazement was my bliss;
    That and my wealth was everywhere:
       No joy to this!

    Cursed and devised proprieties,
      With envy, avarice   50
And fraud (those fiends that spoil even Paradise)
    Fled from the splendor of mine eyes,
And so did hedges, ditches, limits, bounds:
     I dreamed not aught of those,
    But wandered over all men's grounds   55
       And found repose.

    Proprieties themselves were mine
      And hedges, ornaments;
Walls, boxes, coffers, and their rich contents
    Did not divide my joys, but shine.   60
Clothes, ribbons, jewels, laces, I esteemed
     My joys by others worn;
    For me they all to wear them seemed
      When I was born.

48 **to:** compared with   49 **proprieties:** properties, possessions

Shadows in the Water

In unexperienced infancy
Many a sweet mistake doth lie:
Mistake though false, intending true;
A seeming somewhat more than view,
    That doth instruct the mind   5
    In things that lie behind,

1669–1674. *Poems of Felicity,* ed. H. I. Bell, 1910. Margoliouth, op. cit.

3 **intending true:** with a true meaning

And many secrets to us show
Which afterwards we come to know.

Thus did I by the water's brink
Another world beneath me think;   10
And, while the lofty spacious skies
Reversèd there abused mine eyes,
 I fancied other feet
 Came mine to touch and meet;
As by some puddle I did play   15
Another world within it lay.

Beneath the water, people drowned
Yet with another heaven crowned
In spacious regions seemed to go
Freely moving to and fro: 20
 In bright and open space
 I saw their very face;
Eyes, hands, and feet they had like mine;
Another sun did with them shine.

'Twas strange that people there should walk   25
And yet I could not hear them talk:
That through a little watery chink,
Which one dry ox or horse might drink,
 We other worlds should see
 Yet not admitted be;   30
And other confines there behold
Of light and darkness, heat and cold.

I called them oft, but called in vain;
No speeches we could entertain;
Yet did I there expect to find   35
Some other world, to please my mind.
 I plainly saw by these
 A new Antipodes,
Whom, though they were so plainly seen,
A film kept off that stood between.   40

By walking men's reversèd feet
I chanced another world to meet;
Though it did not to view exceed
A phantasm, 'tis a world indeed,
 Where skies beneath us shine,   45
 And earth by art divine
Another face presents below,
Where people's feet against ours go.

Within the regions of the air,
Compassed about with heavens fair,   50
Great tracts of land there may be found
Enriched with fields and fertile ground;
 Where many numerous hosts
 In those far distant coasts,

12 **abused:** deceived   38 **Antipodes:** a world directly opposite our own (the Greek word means the *feet against* of line 48)

For other great and glorious ends,   55
Inhabit, my yet unknown friends.

O ye that stand upon the brink,
Whom I so near me, through the chink,
With wonder see, what faces there,
Whose feet, whose bodies, do ye wear?   60
    I my companions see
    In you, another me.
They seemèd others, but are we;
Our second selves those shadows be.

Look how far off those lower skies   65
Extend themselves! scarce with mine eyes
I can them reach. O ye my friends,
What secret borders on those ends?
    Are lofty heavens hurled
    'Bout your inferior world?   70
Are ye the representatives
Of other people's distant lives?

Of all the playmates which I knew
That here I do the image view
In other selves, what can it mean   75
But that below the purling stream
    Some unknown joys there be
    Laid up in store for me?—
To which I shall, when that thin skin
Is broken, be admitted in.   80

76 **purling:** softly murmuring

Thomas Flatman
(1637–1688)

A lawyer by profession, Flatman was poet and painter, especially esteemed for his minia-
tures. His *Poems* (1674) were republished, with additions, four times before his death.

An Appeal to Cats in the Business of Love

Ye cats that at midnight spit love at each other,
Who best feel the pangs of a passionate lover,
I appeal to your scratches and your tattered fur,
If the business of love be no more than to purr.
Old Lady Grimalkin with her gooseberry eyes,   5
Knew something when a kitten, for why she is wise;
You find by experience, the love-fit's soon o'er,
Puss! Puss! lasts not long, but turns to *Cat-whore!*
    Men ride many miles,
    Cats tread many tiles,   10
  Both hazard their necks in the fray;
    Only cats, when they fall
    From a house or a wall,
Keep their feet, mount their tails, and away!

Poems and Songs, the Fourth Edition, with Many Additions and Amendments, 1686.

5 **Grimalkin:** a name given a cat, especially an old female cat   6 **for why:** wherefore   14 **mount:**
raise

Edward Taylor
(c. 1642–1729)

Taylor, the best poet of colonial America, was born in England; he sailed for our shores in 1668. Upon his graduation from Harvard (founded about 30 years before) he became minister in the frontier village of Westfield, Massachusetts, which was more than once exposed to the threat of Indian attacks. There he spent his remaining 58 years as pastor and physician. Fourteen children were born of his two marriages. Since he did not publish his poems—and told his heirs not to—his manuscript volume was almost unknown until the 1930s.

From God's Determinations

The Preface

Infinity, when all things it beheld
In nothing, and of nothing all did build,
Upon what base was fixed the lathe, wherein
He turned this globe, and riggaled it so trim?
Who blew the bellows of his furnace vast?   5
Or held the mould wherein the world was cast?
Who laid its corner-stone? Or whose command?
Where stand the pillars upon which it stands?
Who laced and filleted the earth so fine,
With rivers like green ribbons smaragdine?   10
Who made the seas its selvage, and it locks
Like a quilt ball within a silver box?
Who spread its canopy? Or curtains spun?
Who in this bowling alley bowled the sun?
Who made it always when it rises set   15
To go at once both down, and up to get?
Who the curtain rods made for this tapestry?
Who hung the twinkling lanterns in the sky?
Who? Who did this? Or who is He? Why, know
It's only Might Almighty this did do.   20
His hand hath made this noble work which stands
His glorious handiwork not made by hands.
Who spake all things from nothing; and with ease
Can speak all things to nothing, if He please.
Whose little finger at His pleasure can   25
Outmete ten thousand worlds with half a span.
Whose Might Almighty can by half a looks
Root up the rocks and rock the hills by the roots.
Can take this mighty world up in His hand
And shake it like a squitchen or a wand.   30
Whose single frown will make the heavens shake
Like as an aspen leaf the wind makes quake.
Oh, what a might is this whose single frown
Doth shake the world as it would shake it down?
Which all from nothing fet, from nothing all;   35
Hath all on nothing set, lets nothing fall.

---

c. 1685? *The Poetical Works of Edward Taylor*, ed. T. H. Johnson, 1939. *The Poems of Edward Taylor*, ed. D. E. Stanford, 1960. Taylor's 400-page MS. volume of "Poetical Works" (1671–1725) is in the Beinecke Library at Yale.

3 **lathe:** potter's lathe, potter's wheel   4 **riggaled:** grooved   9 **filleted:** ribboned, bound with fillets   10 **smaragdine:** emerald   11 **selvage:** edge, border   26 **outmete:** outmeasure   **span:** distance from tip of outstretched thumb to little finger   30 **squitchen:** switch (?)   35 **fet:** fetched

Gave all to nothing man indeed, whereby
Through nothing man all might Him glorify.
In nothing then embossed the brightest gem
More precious than all preciousness in them.   40
But nothing man did throw down all by sin,
And darkenèd that lightsome gem in him,
    That now his brightest diamond is grown
    Darker by far than any coalpit stone.

From **Preparatory Meditations**

      II, 29. *While the Ark Was Building.* **1 Peter 3:20**

What shall I say, my Lord? With what begin?
    Immense profaneness wormholes ery part.
The world is saddlebacked with loads of sin.
    Sin cracks the axletree of this great cart.
    Floodgates of fiery vengeance open fly   5
    And smoky clouds of wrath darken the sky.

The fountains of the deep up broken are.
    The cataracts of heaven do boil o'er
With wallowing seas. Thunder and lightnings tear
    Spouts out of heaven; floods out from hell do roar   10
    To overflow and drownd the world, all drowned
    And overflown with sin, that doth abound.

Oh for an ark, an ark of gopher wood!
    This flood's too stately to be rode upon
By other boats, which are base swilling tubs.   15
    It gulps them up as gudgeons. And they're gone.
    But Thou, my Lord, dost antitype this ark,
    And rodest upon these waves that toss and bark.

Thy human nature (oh, choice timber rich!)
    Bituminated o'er within, and out   20
With dressing of the Holy Spirit's pitch,
    Propitiatory grace, parged round about.
    This ark will ride upon the flood, and live
    Nor passage to a drop through chink-holes give.

This ark will swim upon the fiery flood: 25
    All showers of fire the heavens rain on it will
Slide off; though hell's and heaven's spouts out stood
    And meet upon't to crush't to shivers, still
    It neither sinks, breaks, fires, nor leaky proves,
    But lives upon them all and upward moves.   30

1699. *Poems by Edward Taylor,* ed. B. D. Simison (*Yale University Library Gazette,* 28, 29, 1954). Stanford, op. cit.

1 **Peter 3:20:** "... when once the longsuffering of God waited in the days of Noah, while the ark was a-preparing, wherein few, that is, eight souls were saved by water."   2 **ery:** every   3 **saddle-backed:** swaybacked, with sagging back   13 **gopher wood:** the wood of which Noah's ark was built   14 **stately:** majestic, powerful   15 **swilling:** sloshing, slurping [A "swill-tub" is a tub for swill or hogwash.]   16 **gudgeons:** small fish, often used for bait   17 **antitype:** are the very thing symbolized by   20 **bituminated:** covered with pitch   22 **parged:** plastered

All that would not be drownded must be in't,
    Be arked in Christ, or else the cursed rout
Or crimson sins, their cargo, will them sink
    And suffocate in hell, because without.
      Then ark me, Lord, thus in Thyself that I   35
      May dance upon these drownding waves with joy.

Sweet ark, with concord sweetened, in thee feed
    The calf, and bear, lamb, lion at one crib;
Here rattlesnake and squirrel jar not, breed.
    The hawk and dove, the leopard, and the kid   40
      Do live in peace, the child and cockatrice.
      As if red sin tantara'd in no vice.

Take me, my Lord, into thy golden ark.
    Then when Thy flood of fire shall come, I shall,
Though hell spews streams of flames, and th' heavens spark   45
    Out storms of burning coals, swim safe o'er all.
      I'll make Thy curlèd flames my cittern's wire
      To toss my songs of praise, rung on them, higher.

34 **because without:** because they are outside 39 **jar:** jangle, quarrel 41 **cockatrice:** legendary monster; serpent 42 **tantara'd:** summoned with a tantara (flourish of trumpets) 47 **cittern:** ancient musical instrument like a guitar

     II, 68 [A]. *The Sun of Righteousness, etc.* **Mal. 4:2**

Methinks I spy Almighty holding in
    His hand the crystal sky and sun in't bright:
As candle and bright lantern lightening
    The world with this bright lantern's flaming light,
      Endungeoning all darkness underground,   5
      Making all sunshine day heavenward abound.

The spiritual world this world doth, Lord, outvie;
    Its sky this crystal lantern doth o'ermatch.
Its sun Thou art, that in'ts bright canopy
    Outshines that candle darkness doth dispatch.   10
      Thy crystal globe of glorious sunshine furled,
      Light, life and heat in't Sundayeth the world.

The world without the sun's as dungeon dark.
    The sun without its light would dungeons spring.
The moon and stars are but as chilly sparks   15
    Of dying fire. The sun cheers ery thing.
      But oh Thy light, lightsome, delightsome, falls
      Upon the soul above all cordials.

All light delights. Yet dozed wood-light is cold.
    Some light hath heat yet darkness doth it bound,   20
As lamp and glowworm light. The stars do hold
    A twinkling lifeless light. The sun is found

1705. Stanford, op. cit.

Mal. 4:2: "But unto you that fear my name shall the Sun of righteousness arise with healing in his wings. . . ." 12 **Sundayeth:** makes a holy day, a holiday of 16 **ery:** every 18 **cordials:** comforting or exhilarating medicines or drinks 19 **dozed:** soft with rot, luminescent

A ball of light, of life, warmth to nature's race.
But Thou'rt that sun that shines out saving grace.

Dozed wood-light is but glimmer, with no smoke.   25
    And candle light's a smoky lifeless thing.
The light lodged in the glowworm's petticoat
    Is but a show. Starlight's night's twinkling.
    Moonlight is nightish; sun makes day; these all
    Without our visive organs lightless fall.   30

But Thou, my Lord, no dozèd wood-shine art.
    No smoky candle light rose from Thy wick.
Thy light ne'er lined the glowworm's velvet part.
    Thy shine makes stars, moons, sunlight darkness thick.
    Thou art the sun of heaven's bright light rose in   35
    The heavenly orbs. And heaven's blest glories' spring.

Were all the trees on earth fired torches made,
    And all her grass, wax candles set on flame,
This light could not make day, this lightsome trade
    Would be a darksome smoke when sun shines plain.   40
    But Thy shine, Lord, darkens this sunshine bright,
    And makes the seeing organ, and its light.

Within the horizontal hemisphere
    Of this blest sun, Lord, let me mansion have.
Make day, Thou shining sun, unto me clear,   45
    Thy sorry servant earnestly doth crave.
    Let not the moon e'er intervene or fix
    Between me and this sun to make eclipse.

O bright, bright day! Lord, let this sunshine flow.
    Drive hence my sin and darkness, great, profound,   50
And up them coffin in earth's shade below
    In darkness gross, on th'other side the ground.
    Ne'er let the soil spew fogs to foil the light
    Of this sweet air pregnant with sunbeams bright.

How shall my soul (such thoughts enravish me)   55
    Under the canopy of this bright day
Imparadised, lightened and livened be,
    Bathed in this sunshine 'mong bright angels play,
    And with them strive in sweetest tunes expressed
    Which can Thy glorious praises sing out best.   60

30 **visive:** optic

John Wilmot, Earl of Rochester
(1647–1680)

One of the wittiest and most charming young men at court, Rochester was also one of the wildest. Imprisoned for kidnapping the beautiful heiress he married two years later, he made amends, while still under 20, by serving with distinction in several naval battles. In and out of trouble, banished and recalled, he yet worked hard enough on his writing to be known as one of the best poets of his time. During his last years he turned more and more to philosophy and religion; experiencing some kind of deathbed repentance, he ordered his "profane and lewd" writings to be burned. To no avail: there were some 50 editions by 1800.

The Disabled Debauchee

As some brave admiral, in former war
    Deprived of force, but pressed with courage still,
Two rival fleets appearing from afar,
    Crawls to the top of an adjacent hill,

From whence (with thoughts full of concern) he views   5
    The wise and daring conduct of the fight,
And each bold action to his mind renews
    His present glory and his past delight;

From his fierce eyes flashes of fire he throws
    As from black clouds when lightning breaks a way;   10
Transported, thinks himself amidst the foes,
    And, absent, yet enjoys the bloody day;

So, when my days of impotence approach,
    And I'm by pox or wine's unlucky chance
Forced from the pleasing billows of debauch,   15
    On the dull shore of lazy temperance,

My pains at least some respite shall afford,
    While I behold the battles you maintain,
When fleets of glasses sail about the board,
    From whose broadsides volleys of wit shall rain.   20

Nor let the sight of honorable scars
    Which my too forward valor did procure
Frighten new 'listed soldiers from the wars;
    Past joys have more than paid what I endure.

Should any youth, worth being drunk, prove nice,   25
    And from his fair inviter meanly shrink,
'Twould please the ghost of my departed vice
    If, at my counsel, he repent and drink.

Or should some cold-complexioned sot forbid,
    With his dull morals, our bold night-alarms,   30
I'll fire his blood by telling what I did,
    When I was strong and able to bear arms.

I'll tell of whores attacked, their lords at home,
    Bawds' quarters beaten up, and fortress won;
Windows demolished, watches overcome,   35
    And handsome ills by my contrivance done . . .

With tales like these I will such thoughts inspire,
    As to important mischief shall incline;
I'll make him long some ancient church to fire,
    And fear no lewdness he's called to by wine.   40

1675? *Poems on Several Occasions . . .* , 1680 (with a few readings from other editions).

14 **pox:** venereal disease 25 **nice:** scrupulous, prim 29 **cold-complexioned:** cold by disposition or temperament 36–37 Following the London edition of 1691 (and the preference of such modern anthologists as W. H. Auden and R. P. Warren), I omit here a stanza whose sudden explicit coarseness seems at odds with the tone of mock-heroic majesty Rochester intends.

Thus, statesmanlike, I'll saucily impose,
   And, safe from action, valiantly advise;
Sheltered in impotence, urge you to blows,
   And, being good for nothing else, be wise.

Love and Life

All my past life is mine no more,
   The flying hours are gone,
Like transitory dreams given o'er,
Whose images are kept in store
   By memory alone.   5

Whatever is to come, is not;
   How can it then be mine?
The present moment's all my lot,
And that, as fast as it is got,
   Phyllis, is wholly thine.   10

Then talk not of inconstancy,
   False hearts, and broken vows;
If I, by miracle, can be
This live-long minute true to thee,
   'Tis all that heaven allows.   15

Songs for 1, 2, and 3 Voices Composed by Henry Bowman, 1677. Text from *Poems on Several Occasions . . . ,* 1680.

Jonathan Swift
(1667–1745)

Swift, born posthumously of English parents in Dublin, attended Trinity College there. For about ten years he was secretary to a man of letters in England, where he was ordained an Anglican priest. When he returned to his parish in Ireland, the power of his writing had won him influential English admirers; in 1710 the Tories made him their chief political writer. His reward was not the English bishopric he had hoped for, but the deanship of St. Patrick's Cathedral in Dublin. From there he became the voice of Ireland, lashing out against the injustices his country was suffering. He was buried in his own cathedral under the Latin epitaph he had written—he lies "where savage indignation can no longer lacerate the heart."

A Description of the Morning

Now hardly here and there an hackney-coach,
Appearing, showed the ruddy morn's approach.
Now Betty from her master's bed had flown,
And softly stole to discompose her own.
The slipshod prentice from his master's door   5
Had pared the dirt, and sprinkled round the floor.
Now Moll had whirled her mop with dextrous airs,
Prepared to scrub the entry and the stairs.
The youth with broomy stumps began to trace

1709. *The Tatler,* no. 9, 1709. *Miscellanies in Prose and Verse,* 1711.

1 **hackney-coach:** a coach for hire   9 **broomy stumps:** worn-down brooms—he is looking for old nails etc.

The kennel-edge, where wheels had worn the place.   10
The small-coal man was heard with cadence deep,
Till drowned in shriller notes of chimney-sweep,
Duns at his lordship's gate began to meet,
And Brickdust Moll had screamed through half the street.
The turnkey now his flock returning sees,   15
Duly let out a-nights to steal for fees;
The watchful bailiffs take their silent stands;
And schoolboys lag with satchels in their hands.

10 **kennel:** gutter, open sewer   11 **small-coal man:** seller of charcoal or small pieces of coal
13 **duns:** creditors, bill collectors   14 **brickdust:** an abrasive used for cleaning   15 **turnkey:** jailer
16 **fees:** The jailer gets his cut.   17 **bailiffs:** police officers who serve writs, make arrests, and so on

From On Poetry: A Rhapsody

All human race would fain be wits,
And millions miss, for one that hits.
Young's universal passion, pride,
Was never known to spread so wide.
Say, Britain, could you ever boast   5
Three poets in an age at most?
Our chilling climate hardly bears
A sprig of bays in fifty years,
While every fool his claim alleges,
As if it grew in common hedges.   10
What reason can there be assigned
For this perverseness in the mind?
Brutes find out where their talents lie:
A bear will not attempt to fly:
A foundered horse will oft debate   15
Before he tries a five-barred gate;
A dog by instinct turns aside,
Who sees the ditch too deep and wide.
But man we find the only creature
Who, led by folly, combats nature;   20
Who, when she loudly cries "Forbear!"
With obstinacy fixes there,
And, where his genius least inclines,
Absurdly bends his whole designs.

Not empire to the rising sun,   25
By valor, conduct, fortune won,
Nor highest wisdom in debates
For framing laws to govern states;
Nor skill in sciences profound
So large to grasp the circle round,   30
Such heavenly influence require
As how to strike the Muses' lyre.

1733. *On Poetry: A Rapsody* [sic] . . . , 1733. *Poems,* 1735.

1 **would fain be:** would gladly be, wants to be   3 **Young's universal passion:** Edward Young (1683–
1765) published a series of satires (1725–1728) on "The Universal Passion" (the love of fame).
8 **bays:** laurel or laurellike plant symbolizing true poetic inspiration or achievement.   15 **foun-
dered:** crippled   25 **to the rising sun:** stretching far to the east

Not beggar's brat, on bulk begot;
Not bastard of a pedlar Scot,
Not boy brought up to cleaning shoes,   35
The spawn of Bridewell, or the stews,
Not infants dropped, the spurious pledges
Of gypsies littering under hedges,
Are so disqualified by fate
To rise in church, or law, or state,   40
As he, whom Phoebus in his ire
Hath blasted with poetic fire.

What hope of custom in the fair,
While not a soul demands your ware?
Where you have nothing to produce   45
For private life, or public use?
Court, city, country want you not;
You cannot bribe, betray, or plot.
For poets, law makes no provision:
The wealthy have you in derision.   50
Of state affairs you cannot smatter,
Are awkward when you try to flatter. . . .
Poor starveling bard, how small thy gains!
How unproportioned to thy pains!   60

And here a simile comes pat in:
Though chickens take a month to fatten,
The guests in less than half an hour
Will more than half a score devour.
So, after toiling twenty days   65
To earn a stock of pence and praise,
Thy labors, grown the critic's prey,
Are swallowed o'er a dish of tea—
Gone, to be never heard of more,
Gone, where the chickens went before.   70

How shall a new attempter learn
Of differing spirits to discern,
And how distinguish which is which,
The poet's vein, or scribbling itch?
Then hear an old experienced sinner   75
Instructing thus a young beginner.

Consult yourself, and if you find
A powerful impulse urge your mind,
Impartial, judge within your breast
What subject you can manage best;   80
Whether your genius most inclines
To satire, praise, or humorous lines,
To elegies in mournful tone,
Or prologue sent from hand unknown.
Then, rising with Aurora's light,   85
The Muse invoked, sit down to write;

---

33 **bulk:** a projection or ledge outside of shop windows. Homeless prostitutes who might avail them-
selves of bulks were called "bulkers."   36 **Bridewell:** a London jail   **stews:** houses of prostitution,
red-light district   38 **littering:** having their offspring   41 **Phoebus:** Apollo, god of poetry   43 **cus-
tom:** finding customers   51 **smatter:** talk glibly of things you know little about   68 **tea:** then pro-
nounced *tay*   84 **from hand unknown:** anonymously, unsigned   85 **Aurora:** goddess of dawn

Blot out, correct, insert, refine,
Enlarge, diminish, interline;
Be mindful, when invention fails,
To scratch your head, and bite your nails.   90

    Your poem finished, next your care
Is needful, to transcribe it fair.
In modern wit all printed trash is
Set off with numerous breaks—
                and dashes—

    To statesman would you give a wipe,   95
You print it in *italic type*.
When letters are in vulgar shapes,
'Tis ten to one the wit escapes;
But when in CAPITALS expressed,
The dullest reader smokes a jest;   100
Or else perhaps he may invent
A better than the poet meant,
As learned commentators view
In Homer more than Homer knew.

    Your poem in its modish dress,   105
Correctly fitted for the press,
Convey by penny-post to Lintot,
But let no friend alive look into't.
If Lintot thinks 'twill quit the cost,
You need not fear your labor lost;   110
And how agreeably surprised
Are you to see it advertised!
The hawker shows you one in print,
As fresh as farthings from the mint:
The product of your toil and sweating,   115
A bastard of your own begetting!

    Be sure at Will's the following day;
Lie snug, to hear what critics say.
And if you find the general vogue
Pronounces you a stupid rogue,   120
Damns all your thoughts as low and little,
Be still, and swallow down your spittle.
Be silent as a politician,
For talking may beget suspicion;
Or praise the judgment of the town,   125
And help yourself to run it down.
Give up your fond paternal pride,
Nor argue on the weaker side;
For poems read without a name
We justly praise, or justly blame;   130
And critics have no partial views,
Except they know whom they abuse.
But since you ne'er provoked their spite,

95 **give a wipe:** take a swipe at   100 **smokes:** suspects, scents   107 **penny-post:** a mail service set up in London and its vicinity around 1680 to deliver mail for a penny   **Lintot:** Barnaby Bernard Lintot (1676–1736), a London publisher and bookseller   109 **quit:** make up for   113 **hawker:** peddler, salesman   117 **be sure at:** be sure you are at   **Will's:** one of the many London coffeehouses where men would meet to discuss politics, literature, personalities, and so on   118 **lie snug:** lie low

Depend upon't, their judgment's right.
But if you blab, you are undone;   135
Consider what a risk you run.
You lose your credit all at once;
The town will mark you for a dunce;
The vilest doggerel Grubstreet sends
Will pass for yours with foes and friends.   140
And you must bear the whole disgrace,
Till some fresh blockhead takes your place.

    Your secret kept, your poem sunk,
And sent in quires to line a trunk,
If still you be disposed to rhyme,   145
Go try your hand a second time.
Again you fail, yet safe's the word,
Take courage, and attempt a third.
But first with care employ your thoughts,
Where critics marked your former faults.   150
The trivial turns, the borrowed wit,
The similes that nothing fit;
The cant which every fool repeats,
Town-jests, and coffee-house conceits;
Descriptions tedious, flat and dry,   155
And introduced the Lord knows why;
Or where we find your fury set
Against the harmless alphabet;
On A——'s and B——'s your malice vent,
While readers wonder whom you meant.   160
A public or a private robber,
A statesman or a South-Sea jobber,
A prelate who no God believes,
A Parliament, or den of thieves,
A pick-purse, at the bar, or bench,   165
A duchess or a suburb wench.
Or oft when epithets you link,
In gaping lines to fill a chink,
Like stepping stones to save a stride,
In streets where kennels are too wide,   170
Or like a heel-piece to support
A cripple with one foot too short,
Or like a bridge that joins a marish
To moorlands of a different parish.
So have I seen ill-coupled hounds   175
Drag different ways in miry grounds.
So geographers in Afric maps
With savage pictures fill their gaps,
And o'er unhabitable downs
Place elephants for want of towns.   180

    • • •

139 **Grubstreet:** a London street much inhabited by literary "hacks" who scribbled for a living
144 **inquires:** unbound (A quire is 24 sheets of paper.)   150 **fault:** pronounced "fought" in earlier
centuries   153 **cant:** conventional, trite, or insincere opinions or sentiments that are common proper-
ty 162 **South-Sea:** The "South Sea Bubble" in the 1720s was a fever of speculation in trade possibili-
ties with Spanish America; when the bubble burst, widespread financial ruin resulted.   **jobber:**
broker (often with suggestions of corruption), "operator"   165 **... bar, or bench:** as lawyer or judge
166 **suburb:** Houses of prostitution were often in outlying areas.   170 **kennels:** gutters   173 **mar-
ish:** marsh   179 **downs:** undulating treeless plains

Hobbes clearly proves that every creature
Lives in a state of war by nature.   320
The greater for the smaller watch,
But meddle seldom with their match.
A whale of moderate size will draw
A shoal of herrings down his maw.
A fox with geese his belly crams;   325
A wolf destroys a thousand lambs.
But search among the rhyming race,
The brave are worried by the base.
If on Parnassus' top you sit,
You rarely bite, are always bit: 330
Each poet of inferior size
On you shall rail and criticize,
And strive to tear you limb from limb
While others do as much for him.
The vermin only tease and pinch   335
Their foes superior by an inch.
So, naturalists observe, a flea
Hath smaller fleas that on him prey,
And these have smaller yet to bite'em,
And so proceed *ad infinitum*.   340
Thus every poet in his kind
Is bit by him that comes behind,
Who, though too little to be seen,
Can tease and gall and give the spleen;
Call "Dunces!" "Fools!" and "Sons of Whores!"   345
Lay Grubstreet at each others' doors;
Extol the Greek and Roman masters
And curse our modern poetasters.
Complain, as many an ancient bard did,
How genius is no more rewarded;   350
How wrong a taste prevails among us;
How much our ancestors outsung us;
Can personate an awkward scorn
For those who are not poets born;
And all their brother dunces lash,   355
Who crowd the press with hourly trash. . . .

319 **Hobbes:** Thomas Hobbes (1588–1679), English philosopher who wrote in his *Leviathan* (1656) that "The condition of man . . . is a condition of war of everyone against everyone."   329 **Parnassus:** a mountain in Greece sacred to Apollo and the Muses   340 **ad infinitum:** without end or limit   344 **give the spleen:** irritate, anger, put in a bad humor   348 **poetasters:** inferior poets

Isaac Watts
(1674–1748)

A London pastor from 1699 until his health failed in 1712, Watts went to spend a restful week with friends in the country—and stayed on for the next 36 years, only occasionally visiting his church. During that time he wrote much on religion, philosophy, and science, but is most celebrated as one of the first and greatest of English hymn writers.

The Sluggard

'Tis the voice of the sluggard; I heard him complain,
"You have waked me too soon; I must slumber again."

Divine Songs Attempted in Easy Language for the Use of Children, 1715 (with stanzas numbered). Oxford University Press facsimile, 1971.

As the door on its hinges, so he on his bed,
Turns his sides, and his shoulders, and his heavy head.

"A little more sleep, and a little more slumber,"   5
Thus he wastes half his days, and his hours without number,
And when he gets up, he sits folding his hands,
Or walks about sauntering, or trifling he stands.

I passed by his garden, and saw the wild brier,
The thorn and the thistle grow broader and higher;   10
The clothes that hang on him are turning to rags;
And his money still wastes, till he starves, or he begs.

I made him a visit, still hoping to find
He had took better care for improving his mind:
He told me his dreams, talked of eating and drinking;   15
But he scarce reads his Bible, and never loves thinking.

Said I then to my heart, "Here's a lesson for me:
That man's but a picture of what I might be.
But thanks to my friends for their care in my breeding,
Who taught me betimes to love working and reading."   20

20 **betimes:** in good time, early

The Day of Judgement

AN ODE ATTEMPTED IN ENGLISH SAPPHICS

When the fierce north wind with his airy forces
Rears up the Baltic to a foaming fury,
And the red lightning with a storm of hail comes
           Rushing amain down,

How the poor sailors stand amazed and tremble!   5
While the hoarse thunder like a bloody trumpet
Roars a loud onset to the gaping waters
           Quick to devour them.

Such shall the noise be and the wild disorder
(If things eternal may be like these earthly)   10
Such the dire terror when the great archangel
           Shakes the creation,

Tears the strong pillars of the vault of heaven,
Breaks up old marble, the repose of princes,
Sees the graves open, and the bones arising,   15
           Flames all around 'em.

Hark, the shrill outcries of the guilty wretches!
Lively bright horror and amazing anguish
Stare through their eyelids, while the living worm lies
           Gnawing within them.   20

Horae Lyricae . . . , 1706.

For the form, see *Sapphic stanza* in tne prosody section.

4 **amain:** with full force

Thoughts like old vultures prey upon their heart-strings,
And the smart twinges, when their eye beholds the
Lofty judge frowning, and a flood of vengeance
      Rolling afore him.

Hopeless immortals! how they scream and shiver   25
While devils push them to the pit, wide yawning
Hideous and gloomy, to receive them headlong
      Down to the center.

Stop here, my fancy! All away, ye horrid
Doleful ideas! Come arise to Jesus,   30
How he sits Godlike! And the saints around him
      Throned and adoring.

Oh may I sit there when he comes triumphant
Dooming the nations, then arise to glory,
While our *Hosannahs* all along the passage   35
      Shout the Redeemer.

John Gay
(1685–1732)

Educated at a country grammar school and apprenticed to a London silk dealer, Gay began, with the encouragement of friends and patrons, to write his good-humored poems of city and country life. Among his works is *The Beggar's Opera*, the most popular play of the century and the source of Brecht's *The Threepenny Opera* (1928).

'Twas When the Seas Were Roaring

'Twas when the seas were roaring
    With hollow blasts of wind;
A damsel lay deploring,
    All on a rock reclined.
Wide o'er the rolling billows   5
    She cast a wistful look;
Her head was crowned with willows
    That tremble o'er the brook.

"Twelve months are gone and over,
    And nine long tedious days.   10
Why didst thou, venturous lover,
    Why didst thou trust the seas?
Cease, cease, thou cruel ocean,
    And let my lover rest;
Ah! what's thy troubled motion   15
    To that within my breast?

"The merchant, robbed of pleasure,
    Sees tempests in despair;
But what's the loss of treasure
    To losing of my dear?   20
Should you some coast be laid on
    Where gold and diamonds grow,

The What D'Ye Call It: A Tragi-Comi-Pastoral Farce, 1715. (With stanzas numbered.)

You'd find a richer maiden,
    But none that loves you so.

"How can they say that nature   25
    Has nothing made in vain?
Why then beneath the water
    Should hideous rocks remain?
No eyes the rocks discover,
    That lurk beneath the deep,   30
To wreck the wandering lover,
    And leave the maid to weep."

All melancholy lying,
    Thus wailed she for her dear;
Repayed each blast with sighing,   35
    Each billow with a tear;
When, o'er the white wave stooping,
    His floating corpse she spied;
Then like a lily drooping
    She bowed her head, and died.   40

Alexander Pope
(1688–1744)

The dominant figure in English poetry in the first half of the eighteenth century suffered from curvature of the spine and a tubercular infection that left him only 4 feet 6 inches tall. Because of his health and his Catholic religion, he did not go to one of the universities, but from childhood on read Latin, Greek, French, and Italian. By the time he was 17, his poetry was known to the best critics. In retaliation against those who disliked his translation of Homer and his edition of Shakespeare, he wrote his *Dunciad*, or epic of the duces (1628), with updated versions over the next 15 years. From 1718 on, he lived at a country villa on the Thames at Twickenham (*twit-nam*), entertaining distinguished friends and working at his philosophical and moral epistles in verse.

From **An Essay on Criticism**

'Tis hard to say, if greater want of skill
Appear in writing or in judging ill;
But, of the two, less dangerous is the offense
To tire our patience, than mislead our sense:
Some few in that, but numbers err in this,   5
Ten censure wrong for one who writes amiss;
A fool might once himself alone expose,
Now one in verse makes many more in prose.
    'Tis with our judgments as our watches; none
Go just alike, yet each believes his own.   10
In poets as true genius is but rare,
True taste as seldom is the critic's share;
Both must alike from Heaven derive their light,
These born to judge, as well as those to write.
Let such teach others who themselves excel,   15
And censure freely who have written well.

1706?–1711. *An Essay on Criticism*, 1711. With some later readings.

13 **from Heaven:** Inborn talent or genius is necessary.

Authors are partial to their wit, 'tis true,
But are not critics to their judgment too?

· · ·

First follow Nature, and your judgment frame
By her just standard, which is still the same:
Unerring Nature, still divinely bright,   70
One clear, unchanged, and universal light,
Life, force, and beauty, must to all impart,
At once the source, and end, and test of art.
Art from that fund each just supply provides,
Works without show, and without pomp presides: 75
In some fair body thus the informing soul
With spirits feeds, with vigor fills the whole,
Each motion guides, and every nerve sustains,
Itself unseen, but in the effects, remains.
Some to whom Heaven in wit has been profuse,   80
Want as much more, to turn it to its use;
For wit and judgment often are at strife,
Though meant each other's aid, like man and wife.
'Tis more to guide than spur the Muse's steed;
Restrain his fury, than provoke his speed;   85
The wingèd courser, like a generous horse,
Shows most true mettle when you check his course.
    Those rules of old discovered, not devised,
And Nature still, but Nature methodized.

· · ·

    Some beauties yet no precepts can declare,
For there's a happiness as well as care.
Music resembles poetry, in each   ⎫
Are nameless graces which no methods teach,   ⎬
And which a master hand alone can reach.   ⎭   145
If, where the rules not far enough extend,
(Since rules were made but to promote their end)
Some lucky licence answers to the full
The intent proposed, that licence is a rule.
Thus Pegasus, a nearer way to take,   150
May boldly deviate from the common track.
Great wits sometimes may gloriously offend,
And rise to faults true critics dare not mend;
From vulgar bounds with brave disorder part,   155
And snatch a grace beyond the reach of art,
Which, without passing through the judgment, gains
The heart, and all its end at once attains.

· · ·

17 **wit:** the ability to invent or conceive; imagination   68 **Nature:** for Pope and others of his time, the created universe as reflecting the mind of God, which is orderly, harmonious, reasonable   76 **informing:** giving form or essential character, as the soul is said to inform the body   77 **spirits:** cf. John Donne, "The Ecstasy," line 62   81 **want:** are lacking, need   84 **the Muse's steed:** Pegasus, the winged horse, symbol of poetic inspiration   86 **generous:** spirited   88 **rules:** The rules of art, for Pope, are not arbitrary, but are derived from "Nature" itself—just as the "law" of gravitation is not arbitrary.   142 **happiness:** felicity, luck, serendipity   148 **licence:** liberty, apparent breaking of the rules

A little learning is a dangerous thing; 215
Drink deep, or taste not the Pierian spring:
There shallow draughts intoxicate the brain,
And drinking largely sobers us again.
Fired at first sight with what the Muse imparts,
In fearless youth we tempt the heights of arts, 220
While from the bounded level of our mind,
Short views we take, nor see the lengths behind,
But more advanced, behold with strange surprise
New, distant scenes of endless science rise!
So pleased at first, the towering Alps we try, 225
Mount o'er the vales, and seem to tread the sky;
The eternal snows appear already past,
And the first clouds and mountains seem the last:
But those attained, we tremble to survey
The growing labors of the lengthened way, 230
The increasing prospect tires our wandering eyes,
Hills peep o'er hills, and Alps on Alps arise!

• • •

In wit, as nature, what affects our hearts
Is not the exactness of peculiar parts;
'Tis not a lip, or eye, we beauty call, 245
But the joint force and full result of all.

• • •

True wit is Nature to advantage dressed,
What oft was thought, but ne'er so well expressed,
Something, whose truth convinced at sight we find,
That gives us back the image of our mind: 300
As shades more sweetly recommend the light,
So modest plainness sets off sprightly wit:
For works may have more wit than does 'em good,
As bodies perish through excess of blood.
Others for language all their care express, 305
And value books, as women men, for dress:
Their praise is still—the style is excellent:
The sense, they humbly take upon content.
Words are like leaves; and where they most abound,
Much fruit of sense beneath is rarely found. 310
False eloquence, like the prismatic glass,
Its gaudy colors spreads on every place;
The face of nature we no more survey,
All glares alike, without distinction gay.

• • •

But most by numbers judge a poet's song,
And smooth or rough, with them, is right or wrong;
In the bright Muse though thousand charms conspire,
Her voice is all these tuneful fools admire, 340
Who haunt Parnassus but to please their ear,

216 **Pierian spring:** a spring sacred to the Muses in Pieria (Macedonia)   224 **science:** knowledge in general   244 **peculiar:** individual   297 **True wit:** here not just imagination, but also the right diction to express (or "dress") what one conceives or imagines   304 **excess of blood:** which might, it was thought, burst a blood vessel   308 **upon content:** without question, on trust   311 **prismatic glass:** a prism, which breaks up white light into the colors of the spectrum   337 **numbers:** versification, meter, melodious verse

Not mend their minds; as some to church repair,
Not for the doctrine but the music there.
These, equal syllables alone require,
Though oft the ear the open vowels tire,　　345
While expletives their feeble aid do join,
And ten low words oft creep in one dull line,
While they ring round the same unvaried chimes,
With sure returns of still expected rhymes.
Where'er you find *the cooling western breeze*,　　350
In the next line, it *whispers through the trees;*
If crystal streams *with pleasing murmurs creep*,
The reader's threatened (not in vain) with *sleep.*
Then, at the last and only couplet fraught
With some unmeaning thing they call a thought,　　355
A needless Alexandrine ends the song,
That, like a wounded snake, drags its slow length along.

• • •

True ease in writing comes from art, not chance,
As those move easiest who have learned to dance.
'Tis not enough no harshness gives offense,
The sound must seem an echo to the sense.　　365
Soft is the strain when Zephyr gentle blows,
And the smooth stream in smoother numbers flows;
But when loud surges lash the sounding shore,
The hoarse, rough verse should like the torrent roar.
When Ajax strives some rock's vast weight to throw,　　370
The line too labors, and the words move slow;
Not so, when swift Camilla scours the plain,
Flies o'er the unbending corn, and skims along the main. . . .

344 equal: evenly flowing　**345 open vowels:** two vowel sounds coming together, as *tho' oft, the ear,* and *the open,* which Pope uses to illustrate what he means. Called *hiatus* ("gaping"), such a combination is unpleasant to pronounce.　**346 expletives:** a word that simply fills in (e.g., for the sake of the meter) without adding to the meaning; for example, *do* in *do join* in this line　347 A series of monosyllables can be dull and heavy, as in this line, but need not be.　**356 Alexandrine:** a line of six feet (twelve syllables), as contrasted with the five feet of *iambic pentameter* (see prosody section). Pope gives an example of a dragging Alexandrine in the line that follows, and an example of a fast-moving one in line 373.　**365 sound . . . an echo to the sense:** Examples of sound echoing sense are given in the next few lines.　**366 strain:** tune　**Zephyr:** the west wind　**370 Ajax:** brawny Greek hero at the siege of Troy. To mimic his muscular effort in throwing the boulder, Pope makes the two lines about him hard to pronounce.　**372 Camilla:** speedy Italian female warrior who fought against Aeneas. Vergil (*Aeneid*, VII, 803 ff.) says she could have run across fields of grain without hurting the tender tips and across water without getting her feet wet.

The Rape of the Lock

AN HEROI-COMICAL POEM

Canto I

What dire offense from amorous causes springs,
What mighty contests rise from trivial things,
I sing—This verse to Caryll, muse! is due;
This, even Belinda may vouchsafe to view:
Slight is the subject, but not so the praise,   5
If she inspire, and he approve my lays.
   Say what strange motive, goddess! could compel
A well-bred lord to assault a gentle belle?
O say what stranger cause, yet unexplored,
Could make a gentle belle reject a lord?   10
In tasks so bold, can little men engage,
And in soft bosoms dwells such mighty rage?
   Sol through white curtains shot a timorous ray,
And oped those eyes that must eclipse the day:
Now lapdogs give themselves the rousing shake,   15
And sleepless lovers, just at twelve, awake:
Thrice rung the bell, the slipper knocked the ground,
And the pressed watch returned a silver sound.
Belinda still her downy pillow pressed,
Her guardian Sylph prolonged the balmy rest.   20
'Twas he had summoned to her silent bed
The morning dream that hovered o'er her head.
A youth more glittering than a birth-night beau,
(That even in slumber caused her cheek to glow)

1712–1714. (See introductory note.) *The Rape of the Lock*, 1714.

When a young nobleman, Robert, Lord Petre, snipped off a lock of hair from the pretty head of Arabella Fermor, "Belle" and her family reacted with anger, so that a chill fell upon relationships that had been warm before. John Caryll, a good friend of all concerned, suggested to Pope that he write a poem to show how silly the quarrel really was—"to make a jest of it," as Pope wrote, "and laugh them together again." This he did by writing a mock-heroic (or "heroi-comical") poem about it: a poem that counterfeited the truly heroic by using, for a trivial subject, diction and techniques associated with such poets as Homer, Vergil, and Milton and such grand subjects as the fall of Troy, the founding of Rome, the story of Adam and Eve—a poem that poked fun both at its own subject and at heroic grandiloquence.

In great epics, the gods and goddesses play a part. When first printed in 1712 as a poem in two cantos, "The Rape of the Lock" was without this supernatural intervention. Two years later, in the five-canto version we have here, the supernatural "machinery" has been borrowed from the mythology of the Rosicrucians (a mystic society claiming ancient roots), which enjoyed enough of a vogue in Pope's time to be quite familiar to his readers—perhaps as Tolkien would be to us today. According to this mythology, the four elements—earth, air, fire, water—were inhabited by sylphs, gnomes, and other fairyland creatures who had once been human but who in their new life assigned to the element they were best qualified for by temperament. Though invisible, they took part in human affairs, either as guardian spirits (if sylphs) or as mischief-makers (if gnomes). Ariel, the chief sylph and guardian of Belinda in the poem, describes their nature in I, 41–104, and their duties and the penalties for failure in II, 73–136.

rape: taking by force   **1** We might in passing notice the six s-sounds. Tennyson thought their hissing was "horrible."   **3 is due**: Pope apparently owed Caryll a favor.   **4 Belinda**: a fashionable name at the time, related by its sound to *belle* (an attractive girl) and "Belle" Fermor, whom it stands for   **7 goddess**: The collaboration of the Muse is commonly solicited at the beginning of an epic.   **10 reject**: Although Lord Petre had married another lady, we are not sure the belle of the poem did in fact reject him.   **12 And . . . rage**: This line playfully echoes a question from Vergil's *Aeneid* (I, II): "Tantaene animis caelestibus irae?" ("Are there in heavenly minds such great rages?") The fun of Pope's poem is greatly increased for a reader who knows his Homer and Vergil—as many would have known them in Pope's day. There are well over a hundred such echoes in the poem, few of which we will have space to point out here.   **13 Sol**: the sun   **14 those eyes**: the eyes of beautiful women. Belinda herself is not yet awake.   **17** Two ways of summoning the maid   **18 pressed watch**: "Repeater" watches would chime the hour and quarter hour when a pin was pressed.   **20 Sylph**: In the speech that follows, the Sylph describes what a Sylph is.   **23 birth-night beau**: The Sylph appears to Belinda, in a dream, in the form of a handsome young man dressed for a birthday celebration at court.

Seemed to her ear his winning lips to lay,   25
And thus in whispers said, or seemed to say:
 "Fairest of mortals, thou distinguished care
Of thousand bright inhabitants of air!
If e'er one vision touched thy infant thought,
Of all the nurse and all the priest have taught, 30
Of airy elves by moonlight shadows seen,
The silver token, and the circled green,
Or virgins visited by angel powers,
With golden crowns and wreaths of heavenly flowers,
Hear and believe! thy own importance know, 35
Nor bound thy narrow views to things below.
Some secret truths, from learnèd pride concealed,
To maids alone and children are revealed:
What though no credit doubting wits may give?
The fair and innocent shall still believe. 40
Know, then, unnumbered spirits round thee fly,
The light militia of the lower sky;
These, though unseen, are ever on the wing,
Hang o'er the box, and hover round the Ring.
Think what an equipage thou hast in air, 45
And view with scorn two pages and a chair.
As now your own, our beings were of old,
And once enclosed in woman's beauteous mold;
Thence, by a soft transition, we repair
From earthly vehicles to these of air. 50
Think not, when woman's transient breath is fled,
That all her vanities at once are dead:
Succeeding vanities she still regards,
And though she plays no more, o'erlooks the cards.
Her joy in gilded chariots, when alive, 55
And love of ombre, after death survive.
For when the fair in all their pride expire,
To their first elements their souls retire:
The sprites of fiery termagants in flame
Mount up, and take a Salamander's name. 60
Soft yielding minds to water glide away,
And sip, with nymphs, their elemental tea.
The graver prude sinks downward to a Gnome,
In search of mischief still on earth to roam.
The light coquettes in Sylphs aloft repair, 65
And sport and flutter in the fields of air.
 "Know farther yet; whoever fair and chaste
Rejects mankind, is by some Sylph embraced:
For spirits, freed from mortal laws, with ease
Assume what sexes and what shapes they please. 70

---

30 all . . . taught: Nurse and priest were thought to teach folklore and superstition.   **32 silver token:** coins left as reward (cf. the "tooth fairy" today)   **circled green:** Rings of bright grass were thought left by fairy dancers.   **42 militia:** Supernatural beings are often imagined in military formation—cf. the angels as "the hosts of heaven."   **44 box:** at the theater   **Ring:** a circular drive where fashionable people could be seen in their coaches   **45 equipage:** a coach with all the extras—horses, footmen, and the rest   **46 chair:** sedan chair (cf. Swift, "A Description of a City Shower," line 43)   **50 vehicles:** our bodies, "vehicles" for the soul [also a pun: equipage]   **55 chariots:** carriages   **56 ombre:** a popular card game; cf. Canto III   **59 sprights:** spirits   **termagant:** "a scold; a bawling turbulent woman" (Johnson's *Dictionary*). Fiery women end up as fire-spirits.   **60 Salamander:** a fairylike creature thought to live in fire (not salamander: a lizardlike amphibian)   **62 tea:** pronounced *tay* in Pope's time, to rhyme with *away*. Tea seemed an appropriate drink for watery spirits.   **63 Gnome:** an earth-spirit; an elflike creature that lives in the earth, guards mines, treasures, etc. Pope's Gnomes are gloomy troublemakers.   **65 Sylphs:** The air is their element.

What guards the purity of melting maids,
In courtly balls and midnight masquerades,
Safe from the treacherous friend, the daring spark,
The glance by day, the whisper in the dark;
When kind occasion prompts their warm desires,   75
When music softens, and when dancing fires?
'Tis but their Sylph, the wise celestials know,
Though *honor* is the word with men below.
    "Some nymphs there are, too conscious of their face,
For life predestined to the Gnomes' embrace.   80
These swell their prospects and exalt their pride,
When offers are disdained, and love denied.
Then gay ideas crowd the vacant brain,
While peers and dukes, and all their sweeping train,
And garters, stars, and coronets appear,   85
And in soft sounds, "Your Grace" salutes their ear.
'Tis these that early taint the female soul,
Instruct the eyes of young coquettes to roll,
Teach infant cheeks a bidden blush to know,
And little hearts to flutter at a beau.   90
    "Oft when the world imagine women stray,
The Sylphs through mystic mazes guide their way
Through all the giddy circle they pursue,
And old impertinence expel by new.
What tender maid but must a victim fall   95
To one man's treat, but for another's ball?
When Florio speaks what virgin could withstand,
If gentle Damon did not squeeze her hand?
With varying vanities, from every part,
They shift the moving toyshop of their heart;   100
Where wigs with wigs, with sword-knots sword-knots strive,
Beaux banish beaux, and coaches coaches drive.
This erring mortals levity may call,
Oh blind to truth! the Sylphs contrive it all.
    "Of these am I, who thy protection claim,   105
A watchful sprite, and Ariel is my name.
Late, as I ranged the crystal wilds of air,
In the clear mirror of thy ruling star
I saw, alas! some dread event impend,
Ere to the main this morning sun descend.   110
But heaven reveals not what, or how, or where:
Warned by the Sylph, O pious maid, beware!
This to disclose is all thy guardian can:
Beware of all, but most beware of man!"
    He said; when Shock, who thought she slept too long,   115
Leaped up, and waked his mistress with his tongue.
'Twas then, Belinda, if report say true,
Thy eyes first opened on a billet-doux;

---

73 **spark:** fashionable gallant   77 **celestials:** heavenly beings   79–80 **Some . . . embrace:** Instead of having Sylphs to watch over them, vain young ladies are attended by mischievous Gnomes, who get them in trouble.   81 **swell their prospects:** inflate their hopes   85 **garters, stars, and coronets:** emblems of knighthood, rank, etc.   86 **"Your Grace":** way of addressing a duke or duchess   94 **impertinence:** what is unsuitable, not pertinent; silliness, trifle, etc.   96 **treat:** entertainment, with food, drink, etc.   97–98 **Florio . . . Damon:** fancy names for men making advances to ladies   101 **sword-knot:** decorative ribbon on sword-hilt   102 **drive:** drive off, chase away [also a pun]   106 **Ariel:** a Hebrew name, much used for a spirit in magical writings. Cf. Shakespeare's Ariel in *The Tempest*.   110 **main:** ocean   115 **Shock:** her dog. The "shock" was a kind of small poodle with long shaggy hair.   118 **billet-doux:** love letter

"Wounds," "charms" and "ardors" were no sooner read,
But all the vision vanished from thy head.   120
     And now, unveiled, the toilet stands displayed,
Each silver vase in mystic order laid.
First, robed in white, the nymph intent adores,
With head uncovered, the cosmetic powers.
A heavenly image in the glass appears,   125
To that she bends, to that her eyes she rears;
The inferior priestess, at her altar's side,
Trembling, begins the sacred rites of pride.
Unnumbered treasures ope at once, and here
The various offerings of the world appear;   130
From each she nicely culls with curious toil,
And decks the goddess with the glittering spoil.
This casket India's glowing gems unlocks,
And all Arabia breathes from yonder box.
The tortoise here and elephant unite,   135
Transformed to combs, the speckled and the white.
Here files of pins extend their shining rows,
Puffs, powders, patches, bibles, billet-doux.
Now awful beauty puts on all its arms;
The fair each moment rises in her charms,   140
Repairs her smiles, awakens every grace,
And calls forth all the wonders of her face;
Sees by degrees a purer blush arise,
And keener lightnings quicken in her eyes.
The busy Sylphs surround their darling care;   145
These set the head, and those divide the hair,
Some fold the sleeve, whilst others plait the gown;
And Betty's praised for labors not her own.

119 **"wounds"** ... **"ardors"**: terminology used in typical love letters   121 **toilet:** dressing-table
125 **image:** her own   127 **inferior priestess:** her maid   131 **nicely:** fastidiously   **curious:** careful
134 **all Arabia:** Many scents and perfumes came from there.   135 **tortoise ... elephant:** tortoise-
shell and ivory   138 **patches:** beauty patches, tiny pieces of black silk used to cover blemishes or
bring out the whiteness of the skin   **bibles:** not big family bibles, but little ones in de luxe bindings,
prayer-book size   139 **awful:** awesome   143 **purer blush:** thanks of course to rouge   144 **keener
lightnings:** She used belladonna to dilate the pupils, or perhaps used mascara around the eyes.
147 **plait:** arrange in folds   148 **Betty:** her maid—a name used to refer to maids in general

Canto II

Not with more glories, in the ethereal plain,
The sun first rises o'er the purpled main,
Than issuing forth, the rival of his beams
Launched on the bosom of the silver Thames.
Fair nymphs, and well-dressed youths around her shone,   5
But every eye was fixed on her alone.
On her white breast a sparkling cross she wore,
Which Jews might kiss, and infidels adore.
Her lively looks a sprightly mind disclose,
Quick as her eyes, and as unfixed as those: 10
Favors to none, to all she smiles extends,
Oft she rejects, but never once offends.
Bright as the sun, her eyes the gazers strike,

3 **rival:** Belinda. She is about to make her epic voyage (cf. Odysseus) a dozen miles upstream from
London to Hampton Court Palace.   8 **Jews ... infidels:** Even non-Christians would adore a cross—if
Belinda wore it.

And, like the sun, they shine on all alike.
Yet graceful ease, and sweetness void of pride,   15
Might hide her faults, if belles had faults to hide:
If to her share some female errors fall,
Look on her face, and you'll forget 'em all.
  This nymph, to the destruction of mankind,
Nourished two locks, which graceful hung behind   20
In equal curls, and well conspired to deck
With shining ringlets the smooth ivory neck.
Love in these labyrinths his slaves detains,
And mighty hearts are held in slender chains.
With hairy springes we the birds betray,   25
Slight lines of hair surprise the finny prey,
Fair tresses man's imperial race ensnare,
And beauty draws us with a single hair.
  The adventurous Baron the bright locks admired,
He saw, he wished, and to the prize aspired: 30
Resolved to win, he meditates the way,
By force to ravish, or by fraud betray;
For when success a lover's toil attends,
Few ask, if fraud or force attained his ends.
  For this, ere Phoebus rose, he had implored   35
Propitious heaven, and every power adored,
But chiefly Love—to Love an altar built,
Of twelve vast French romances, neatly gilt.
There lay three garters, half a pair of gloves;
And all the trophies of his former loves.   40
With tender billets-doux he lights the pyre,
And breathes three amorous sighs to raise the fire;
Then prostrate falls, and begs with ardent eyes
Soon to obtain, and long possess, the prize:
The powers gave ear, and granted half his prayer;   45
The rest, the winds dispersed in empty air.
  But now secure the painted vessel glides,
The sunbeams trembling on the floating tides,
While melting music steals upon the sky,
And softened sounds along the waters die.   50
Smooth flow the waves, the zephyrs gently play,
Belinda smiled, and all the world was gay.
All but the Sylph—with careful thoughts opprest,
The impending woe sat heavy on his breast.
He summons straight his denizens of air;   55
The lucid squadrons round the sails repair:
Soft o'er the shrouds aërial whispers breathe,
That seemed but zephyrs to the train beneath.
Some to the sun their insect wings unfold,
Waft on the breeze, or sink in clouds of gold;   60
Transparent forms, too fine for mortal sight,
Their fluid bodies half dissolved in light.
Loose to the wind their airy garments flew,
Thin glittering textures of the filmy dew;
Dipped in the richest tincture of the skies,   65
Where light disports in ever-mingling dyes,

---

25 **hairy springes:** traps, nooses of fine cord   35 **Phoebus:** the sun   45 **half:** Fate permits him to
steal one of the two ringlets.   47 **secure:** carefree   51 **zephyrs:** soft (western) breezes   56 **repair:**
gather   57 **shrouds:** supporting ropes   64 **textures . . . dew:** gossamer, fine floating spider filaments

While every beam new transient colors flings,
Colors that change whene'er they wave their wings.
Amid the circle, on the gilded mast,
Superior by the head, was Ariel placed;   70
His purple pinions opening to the sun,
He raised his azure wand, and thus begun.
    "Ye Sylphs and Sylphids, to your chief give ear,
Fays, Fairies, Genii, Elves, and Daemons, hear!
Ye know the spheres and various tasks assigned   75
By laws eternal to the aërial kind.
Some in the fields of purest aether play,
And bask and whiten in the blaze of day.
Some guide the course of wandering orbs on high,
Or roll the planets through the boundless sky.   80
Some less refined, beneath the moon's pale light
Pursue the stars that shoot athwart the night,
Or suck the mists in grosser air below,
Or dip their pinions in the painted bow,
Or brew fierce tempests on the wintry main,   85
Or o'er the glebe distil the kindly rain.
Others on earth o'er human race preside,
Watch all their ways, and all their actions guide:
Of these the chief the care of nations own,
And guard with arms divine the British throne.   90
    "Our humbler province is to tend the fair,
Not a less pleasing, though less glorious care.
To save the powder from too rude a gale,
Nor let the imprisoned essences exhale,
To draw fresh colors from the vernal flowers,   95
To steal from rainbows e'er they drop in showers
A brighter wash; to curl their waving hairs,
Assist their blushes, and inspire their airs;
Nay oft, in dreams, invention we bestow,
To change a flounce, or add a furbelow.   100
    "This day, black omens threat the brightest fair
That e'er deserved a watchful spirit's care;
Some dire disaster, or by force, or sleight,
But what, or where, the fates have wrapped in night.
Whether the nymph shall break Diana's law,   105
Or some frail China jar receive a flaw,
Or stain her honor, or her new brocade,
Forget her prayers, or miss a masquerade,
Or lose her heart, or necklace, at a ball;
Or whether Heaven has doomed that Shock must fall.   110
Haste then, ye spirits! to your charge repair:
The fluttering fan be Zephyretta's care;
The drops to thee, Brillante, we consign;
And, Momentilla, let the watch be thine;
Do thou, Crispissa, tend her favorite lock;   115

70 **superior ... head:** taller by a head, as epic leaders are   73 **Sylphids:** young or female Sylphs
74 **Fays:** fairies **Genii ... Daemons:** protective spirits   77 **aether:** pure upper air, above the
moon   84 **painted bow:** rainbow   86 **glebe:** cultivated ground   94 **essences:** perfumes   98 **inspire
their airs:** suggest ways they can put on airs   100 **furbelow:** gathered or puckered piece of cloth to
ornament a dress   105 **Diana's law:** Diana was goddess of virginity.   105–110 Pope mingles the se-
rious and the trivial to suggest (always playfully) that his "nymphs" can't tell the difference.
112–115 **Zephyretta ... Crispissa:** the made-up names suggest bright, gentle little beings. To *crisp*
meant to "curl." (Pope associates the quick little letter *i* with his Sylphs.)   113 **drops:** diamond ear-
rings

Ariel himself shall be the guard of Shock.
   "To fifty chosen Sylphs, of special note,
We trust the important charge, the petticoat:
Oft have we known that sevenfold fence to fail,
Though stiff with hoops, and armed with ribs of whale.   120
Form a strong line about the silver bound,
And guard the wide circumference around.
   "Whatever spirit, careless of his charge,
His post neglects, or leaves the fair at large,
Shall feel sharp vengeance soon o'ertake his sins,   125
Be stopped in vials, or transfixed with pins;
Or plunged in lakes of bitter washes lie,
Or wedged whole ages in a bodkin's eye:
Gums and pomatums shall his flight restrain,
While clogged he beats his silken wings in vain;   130
Or alum styptics with contracting power
Shrink his thin essence like a rivelled flower.
Or as Ixion fixed, the wretch shall feel
The giddy motion of the whirling mill,
In fumes of burning chocolate shall glow,   135
And tremble at the sea that froths below!"
   He spoke; the spirits from the sails descend;
Some, orb in orb, around the nymph extend,
Some thrid the mazy ringlets of her hair,
Some hang upon the pendants of her ear;   140
With beating hearts the dire event they wait,
Anxious, and trembling for the birth of fate.

119–120 **sevenfold fence:** the hoopskirt (or hoop petticoat) stiffened with whalebone. *Seven* often has
magical potency.   128 **bodkin:** large needle   129 **gums and pomatums:** perfumed gummy sub-
stances or ointments   131 **alum styptics:** astringent medications for the skin   132 **rivelled:** wrin-
kled, withered   133 **Ixion:** in Greek mythology, a king punished by being bound forever to a revolv-
ing wheel in the underworld   139 **thrid:** thread, make their way through

Canto III

Close by those meads, for ever crowned with flowers,
Where Thames with pride surveys his rising towers,
There stands a structure of majestic frame,
Which from the neighboring Hampton takes its name.
Here Britain's statesmen oft the fall foredoom   5
Of foreign tyrants, and of nymphs at home;
Here thou, great Anna! whom three realms obey,
Dost sometimes counsel take—and sometimes tea.
   Hither the heroes and the nymphs resort,
To taste awhile the pleasures of a court;   10
In various talk the instructive hours they past,
Who gave the ball, or paid the visit last;
One speaks the glory of the British queen,

3 **structure:** Hampton Court Palace.   5–6 In these lines, we have a figure of speech Pope is fond of,
because it juxtaposes incongruous objects. Called *zeugma* (yoking), it employs a word that governs or
has a bearing on two other words, but on each in a different way. Examples: "He drives her to work
and me crazy." "He was full of happiness and good bourbon." In Pope, the statesmen plan the *fall* of
foreign tyrants and the *fall* of girls they seduce. So in lines 7 and 8, in which Queen Anne is said to
take counsel—and sometimes [*take*] tea. The let-down we feel in such uses of zeugma can be comic or
ironic.   7 **great Anna:** Queen Anne, who reigned from 1702 to 1714. By her three realms Pope may
mean England, Ireland, and Scotland. His "obey" would be funnier, though, if by the third realm he
meant France, to the throne of which English monarchs still made a preposterous claim.   11 **instruc-
tive:** We see how "instructive" in the next few lines.   12 **the visit:** Ladies of fashion paid visits to
one another on the evening of appointed days, accompanied by servants with lights.

And one describes a charming Indian screen;
A third interprets motions, looks, and eyes;   15
At every word a reputation dies.
Snuff, or the fan, supply each pause of chat,
With singing, laughing, ogling, *and all that.*
    Meanwhile, declining from the noon of day,
The sun obliquely shoots his burning ray;   20
The hungry judges soon the sentence sign,
And wretches hang that jurymen may dine;
The merchant from the Exchange returns in peace,
And the long labors of the toilet cease—
Belinda now, whom thirst of fame invites,   25
Burns to encounter two adventurous knights,
At ombre singly to decide their doom;
And swells her breast with conquests yet to come.
Straight the three bands prepare in arms to join,
Each band the number of the sacred nine.   30
Soon as she spread her hand, the aërial guard
Descend, and sit on each important card:
First Ariel perched upon a Matador,
Then each, according to the rank they bore;
For Sylphs, yet mindful of their ancient race,   35
Are, as when women, wondrous fond of place.
    Behold, four Kings in majesty revered,
With hoary whiskers and a forky beard;
And four fair Queens whose hands sustain a flower,
The expressive emblem of their softer power;   40
Four Knaves in garbs succinct, a trusty band,
Caps on their heads, and halberts in their hand;
And particolored troops, a shining train,
Draw forth to combat on the velvet plain.
    The skilful nymph reviews her force with care;   45
"Let spades be trumps!" she said, and trumps they were.
    Now move to war her sable Matadors,

17 **snuff, or the fan:** The taking of snuff was in vogue at the time. And the ladies could flutter their fans in between remarks.   21–22 Judge and jury hurry up their work—even if it means hanging people without cause—to get home to dinner.   23 **Exchange:** the Royal Exchange, a commercial center, like our stock market   26–27 **two . . . ombre:** Ombre (pronounced *omber*) was a fashionable card game of the time, rather like three-handed bridge, in which one player (the *ombre* or *hombre*) tried to win more tricks than either of the two opponents—here the "two adventurous knights."   29–30 **three . . . nine:** The cards were dealt in three batches of threes to the players, so that each had nine cards. The rest of the cards in the 40-card deck (8s, 9s, and 10s were removed) were put in a stock or pool, from which players would draw cards to replace those they chose to discard after trumps were decided on.   33 **Matador:** The three highest-ranking cards were called Matadors: first was always the ace of spades, third always the ace of clubs. In second place was the 7 if trumps were a red suit, the 2 if a black suit.   36 **place:** rank.   37–42 The face cards described here are from the deck of Pope's time, not the same in appearance as our modern deck. Our double-headed cards show only the upper part of the body; his cards showed the full figures, head to toe. His knaves (jacks) are in "garb succinct"—girded up short garments, ending above the knee, instead of in trailing robes. Their halberts were combined battle-axes and pikes on long shafts; the modern jack of hearts has something similar to his left. The "particolored troops" are the other cards of the red and black suits. The "velvet plain" (or "verdant field" of line 52) is the green-topped card table.   46 **"Let spades be trumps!":** As player to the right of the dealer, Belinda got first chance to be *ombre*, the one who took on the other two. She liked what she saw in her hand, chose to be *ombre*, and as such could name trumps. Her declaration recalls the grandeur of Gen. 1:3: "And God said, Let there be light: and there was light."   47–100 There is no point in our trying to master the complicated rules of a card game fashionable in 1712. Pope worked out his strategy carefully: he made up a real game with real cards on the table before him. We can follow the general course of the game easily enough. Though there are three players, Pope almost ignored the anonymous third (whose cards are too weak to take a single trick anyway). The game becomes an epic duel between Belinda and the Baron. Since each has nine cards, there will be nine tricks, of which Belinda will have to win five. She holds the four top cards in the deck, and proceeds to play them, easily winning the first four tricks. Here is how the play develops, trick by trick:

And four fair queens whose hands sustain a
flower
The expressive emblem of their softer power; . . .

Four Knaves in garbs succinct, a trusty band,
Caps on their heads, and halberts in their
hand; . . .

With his broad sabre next, a chief in years,
The hoary Majesty of Spades appears,
Puts forth one manly leg, to sight revealed;
The rest, his many-colored robe concealed. . . .

The club's black tyrant first her victim died,
Spite of his haughty mien, and barbarous pride:
What boots the regal circle on his head,
His giant limbs in state unwieldy spread?
That long behind he trails his pompous robe,
And of all monarchs only grasps the globe?

In show like leaders of the swarthy Moors.

The Tricks **[1]** Spadillio first, unconquerable lord!

Led off two captive trumps, and swept the board.   50

[2] As many more Manillio forced to yield,

And marched a victor from the verdant field.

[3] Him Basto followed, but his fate more hard

Gained but one trump and one plebeian card.

[4] With his broad sabre next, a chief in years,   55

The hoary Majesty of Spades appears,

Puts forth one manly leg, to sight revealed;

The rest, his many-colored robe concealed.

The rebel Knave, who dares his prince engage,

Proves the just victim of his royal rage.   60

Even mighty Pam, that kings and queens o'erthrew,

And mowed down armies in the fights of Lu,

Sad chance of war! now, destitute of aid,

Falls undistinguished by the victor spade!

Thus far both armies to Belinda yield;   65

Now to the Baron fate inclines the field.

[5] His warlike Amazon her host invades,

The imperial consort of the crown of spades.

The club's black tyrant first her victim died,

Spite of his haughty mien, and barbarous pride: 70

What boots the regal circle on his head,

His giant limbs in state unwieldy spread?

That long behind he trails his pompous robe,

And of all monarchs only grasps the globe?

[6]   The Baron now his diamonds pours apace;   75

The embroidered King who shows but half his face,

[7] And his refulgent Queen, with powers combined,

Of broken troops an easy conquest find.

Clubs, diamonds, hearts, in wild disorder seen,

With throngs promiscuous strew the level green.   80

Thus when dispersed a routed army runs,

Of Asia's troops, and Afric's sable sons,

With like confusion different nations fly,

[1] Belinda leads with the ace of spades, called *Spadille,* which Pope turns into the more swashbuckling "Spadillio."

[2] She then plays her second Matador (the 2 of spades), called *Manille*—for Pope, "Manillio."

[3] She plays the third highest card, the ace of clubs, called *Basto.* Since the trumps were unevenly divided among her opponents, it takes only one trump. The Baron has two left.

[4] She takes her fourth trick with the king of spades. With her trumps used up, she is now in trouble.

57 one manly leg: as shown on cards of the time   **59 rebel Knave:** the jack of spades   **61 mighty Pam:** The jack of clubs (played by the third player) is the most powerful card in a different card game called Loo or Lu.

SCORE: Belinda, 4; Baron, 0

[5] Belinda leads with the king of clubs, which is trumped by the Baron's queen of spades, his "warlike Amazon"—the Amazons were female warriors of antiquity.

69 club's black tyrant: The king of clubs, whose appearance on the cards Pope knew, is described in the next five lines. His "globe" is the golden ball he carried as symbol of authority (he still has it on modern cards).   **71 boots:** avails

[6] With Belinda's trumps gone, the Baron can now play his high diamonds. He takes this trick with the king (still in profile, "one-eyed," on modern cards).

[7] Now he takes a trick with the queen of diamonds.

81–86: an "epic simile," like those of Homer, developed at some length   **84 habit:** dress, uniform   **dye:** color

Of various habit and of various dye,
The pierced battalions disunited fall,   85
In heaps on heaps; one fate o'erwhelms them all.
[8]   The Knave of Diamonds tries his wily arts,
And wins (oh shameful chance!) the Queen of Hearts.
At this, the blood the virgin's cheek forsook,
A livid paleness spreads o'er all her look;   90
She sees, and trembles at the approaching ill,
Just in the jaws of ruin, and Codille.
And now (as oft in some distempered state)
On one nice trick depends the general fate,
[9]   An Ace of Hearts steps forth: the King unseen   95
Lurked in her hand, and mourned his captive Queen.
He springs to vengeance with an eager pace,
And falls like thunder on the prostrate Ace.
The nymph exulting fills with shouts the sky,
The walls, the woods, and long canals reply.   100
    Oh thoughtless mortals! ever blind to fate,
Too soon dejected, and too soon elate!
Sudden these honors shall be snatched away,
And cursed for ever this victorious day.
    For lo! the board with cups and spoons is crowned,   105
The berries crackle, and the mill turns round.
On shining altars of Japan they raise
The silver lamp; the fiery spirits blaze.
From silver spouts the grateful liquors glide,
While China's earth receives the smoking tide.   110
At once they gratify their scent and taste,
And frequent cups prolong the rich repast.
Straight hover round the fair her airy band;
Some, as she sipped, the fuming liquor fanned,
Some o'er her lap their careful plumes displayed,   115
Trembling, and conscious of the rich brocade.
Coffee (which makes the politician wise,
And see through all things with his half-shut eyes)
Sent up in vapors to the Baron's brain
New stratagems, the radiant lock to gain.   120
Ah cease, rash youth! desist ere 'tis too late,
Fear the just gods, and think of Scylla's fate!
Changed to a bird, and sent to flit in air,

[8] His jack of diamonds takes her queen of hearts, since she cannot follow suit.

SCORE: Belinda, 4; Baron, 4

Belinda now has reason to be worried. Everything depends on the last trick—on what card the Baron has in his hand. If he has another diamond, she loses and will be given "Codille," the term used when the *ombre* does not make the number of tricks he ought to. If he holds a heart, she wins, because her last card is the highest-ranking heart.

93 **distempered:** disordered   94 **nice:** exactly right

[9] The Baron plays his ace of hearts; but the ace (when hearts are *not* trumps) is outranked by the face-cards of that suit. Belinda wins!

FINAL SCORE: Belinda, 5; Baron, 4

106 **berries** . . . : coffeebeans are ground and roasted   107 **altars of Japan:** lacquered (japanned) tables   109 **grateful:** pleasant   110 **China's earth:** chinaware, teacups   113 **airy band:** the Sylphs   115 **o'er her lap** . . . : so she won't get coffee stains on her dress   122–124 **Scylla . . . Nisus:** not *the* Scylla, paired with Charybdis. This Scylla, in love with her father's enemy Minos, cuts from her father's head the magic purple hair on which the safety of his kingdom depends so that she can give it to Minos. When he spurns the dishonorable gift and sails away, she clings to his ship, but is turned into a bird. (Ovid, *Metamorphoses*, VIII, 1 ff.)

She dearly pays for Nisus' injured hair!
But when to mischief mortals bend their will,   125
How soon they find fit instruments of ill!
Just then, Clarissa drew with tempting grace
A two-edged weapon from her shining case;
So ladies in romance assist their knight,
Present the spear, and arm him for the fight.   130
He takes the gift with reverence, and extends
The little engine on his fingers' ends;
This just behind Belinda's neck he spread,
As o'er the fragrant steams she bends her head.
Swift to the lock a thousand sprites repair,   135
A thousand wings, by turns, blow back the hair,
And thrice they twitched the diamond in her ear;
Thrice she looked back, and thrice the foe drew near.
Just in that instant, anxious Ariel sought
The close recesses of the virgin's thought;   140
As, on the nosegay in her breast reclined,
He watched the ideas rising in her mind,
Sudden he viewed, in spite of all her art,
An earthly lover lurking at her heart.
Amazed, confused, he found his power expired,   145
Resigned to fate, and with a sigh retired.
    The peer now spreads the glittering forfex wide,
To enclose the lock; now joins it, to divide.
Even then, before the fatal engine closed,
A wretched Sylph too fondly interposed;   150
Fate urged the shears, and cut the Sylph in twain
(But airy substance soon unites again),
The meeting points the sacred hair dissever
From the fair head, for ever and for ever!
    Then flashed the living lightning from her eyes,   155
And screams of horror rend the affrighted skies.
Not louder shrieks to pitying heaven are cast,
When husbands or when lapdogs breathe their last,
Or when rich China vessels, fallen from high,
In glittering dust and painted fragments lie!   160
    "Let wreaths of triumph now my temples twine,"
(The victor cried) "the glorious prize is mine!
While fish in streams, or birds delight in air,
Or in a coach and six the British fair,
As long as Atalantis shall be read,   165
Or the small pillow grace a lady's bed,
While visits shall be paid on solemn days,
When numerous wax-lights in bright order blaze,
While nymphs take treats, or assignations give,
So long my honor, name, and praise shall live!"   170
    What time would spare, from steel receives its date,
And monuments, like men, submit to fate!
Steel could the labor of the gods destroy,
And strike to dust the imperial towers of Troy;

---

127 **Clarissa:** an unidentified friend of the Baron   143–146 Ariel loses his power because Belinda's thoughts are now possessed by an earthly lover. Cf. I, 67–68.   147 **forfex:** scissors (Latin)   164 **coach and six:** coach with six horses   165 **Atalantis:** a scandalous account of *Secret Memoirs and Manners of Several Persons of Quality, of Both Sexes. From the New Atlantis* . . . (written by Mrs. Manley, who was arrested for libel), published a few years before.   167 Cf. III, 12   171 **date:** final day   173–174 **labor . . . Troy:** Troy was thought to have been built by Apollo and Poseidon.

Steel could the works of mortal pride confound,   175
And hew triumphal arches to the ground.
What wonder then, fair nymph! thy hairs should feel
The conquering force of unresisted steel?

Canto IV

But anxious cares the pensive nymph oppressed,
And secret passions labored in her breast.
Not youthful kings in battle seized alive,
Not scornful virgins who their charms survive,
Not ardent lovers robbed of all their bliss,   5
Not ancient ladies when refused a kiss,
Not tyrants fierce that unrepenting die,
Not Cynthia when her manteau's pinned awry,
E'er felt such rage, resentment, and despair,
As thou, sad virgin! for thy ravished hair.   10
   For, that sad moment, when the Sylphs withdrew,
And Ariel weeping from Belinda flew,
Umbriel, a dusky melancholy sprite
As ever sullied the fair face of light,
Down to the central earth, his proper scene,   15
Repaired to search the gloomy Cave of Spleen.
   Swift on his sooty pinions flits the Gnome,
And in a vapor reached the dismal dome.
No cheerful breeze this sullen region knows,
The dreaded East is all the wind that blows.   20
Here, in a grotto, sheltered close from air,
And screened in shades from day's detested glare,
She sighs for ever on her pensive bed,
Pain at her side, and Megrim at her head.
   Two handmaids wait the throne: alike in place,   25
But differing far in figure and in face.
Here stood Ill Nature like an ancient maid,
Her wrinkled form in black and white arrayed;
With store of prayers, for mornings, nights, and noons,
Her hand is filled; her bosom with lampoons.   30
   There Affectation, with a sickly mien
Shows in her cheek the roses of eighteen,
Practiced to lisp, and hang the head aside,
Faints into airs, and languishes with pride;
On the rich quilt sinks with becoming woe,   35
Wrapped in a gown, for sickness, and for show.
The fair ones feel such maladies as these,
When each new nightdress gives a new disease.

---

8 **Cynthia:** any clothes-conscious lady   **manteau:** loose robe or cloak   13 **Umbriel:** a gnome whose
name *(umbra:* shadow) suggests gloominess **sprite:** spirit 16 **Cave of Spleen:** The spleen is an or-
gan on our left side once thought to be the seat of the emotions, and especially of melancholy. By
Pope's time it had become the fashionable name for melancholia, depression, ill humor, hypochon-
dria, oversensitivity—a self-pitying state of mind which could lead to real or imaginary physical ail-
ments and even insanity. Here Spleen is personified as a doleful figure in the underworld. The
Gnome's mission corresponds to such journeys to the underworld as those of Odysseus in Homer and
Aeneas in Vergil.   18 **vapor:** Since mistiness and dampness were thought to cause spleen, "the va-
pors" became a name for it.   20 **East:** The east wind was thought to bring on the spleen.   24 **side:**
Recall the location of the spleen.   **Megrim:** migraine, sick headache   25 **wait:** wait on   29 **prayers:**
of gloomy, self-righteous religiosity   30 **lampoons:** cruel personal satire   31 **Affectation:** false be-
havior, a pretending to be what one is not—here, a sickliness and languor put on for show   34 **airs:**
pretended moods, attitudes

A constant vapor o'er the palace flies;
Strange phantoms rising as the mists arise;   40
Dreadful, as hermit's dreams in haunted shades,
Or bright as visions of expiring maids.
Now glaring fiends, and snakes on rolling spires,
Pale spectres, gaping tombs, and purple fires:
Now lakes of liquid gold, Elysian scenes,   45
And crystal domes, and angels in machines.
    Unnumbered throngs on every side are seen
Of bodies changed to various forms by Spleen.
Here living teapots stand, one arm held out,
One bent; the handle this, and that the spout: 50
A pipkin there like Homer's tripod walks;
Here sighs a jar, and there a goose-pie talks;
Men prove with child, as powerful fancy works,
And maids turned bottles, call aloud for corks.
    Safe passed the Gnome through this fantastic band,   55
A branch of healing spleenwort in his hand.
Then thus addressed the power: "Hail, wayward Queen!
Who rule the sex to fifty from fifteen,
Parent of vapors and of female wit,
Who give the hysteric, or poetic fit,   60
On various tempers act by various ways,
Make some take physic, others scribble plays;
Who cause the proud their visits to delay,
And send the godly in a pet to pray,
A nymph there is, that all thy power disdains,   65
And thousands more in equal mirth maintains.
But oh! if e'er thy Gnome could spoil a grace,
Or raise a pimple on a beauteous face,
Like citron-waters matrons' cheeks inflame,
Or change complexions at a losing game;   70
If e'er with airy horns I planted heads,
Or rumpled petticoats, or tumbled beds,
Or caused suspicion when no soul was rude,
Or discomposed the headdress of a prude,
Or e'er to costive lapdog gave disease,   75
Which not the tears of brightest eyes could ease:
Hear me, and touch Belinda with chagrin;
That single act gives half the world the spleen."
    The goddess with a discontented air
Seems to reject him, though she grants his prayer.   80
A wondrous bag with both her hands she binds,
Like that where once Ulysses held the winds;
There she collects the force of female lungs,
Sighs, sobs, and passions, and the war of tongues.

42 **visions:** Pope sees these as hectic or hysterical.   43–46 **fiends . . . :** The phantoms of the next four
lines are suggested by spectacular effects in the theater of Pope's day. The "machines" are stage ma-
chinery by which these are produced.   43 **spires:** coils   45 **Elysian:** heavenly (In classical myth the
souls of the just went to Elysium.)   47–54 examples of delusion and insanity brought on by spleen
51 **pipkin:** small footed pot   **Homer's tripod:** In *Iliad,* XVIII (439 ff.), there are stools that walk.
53 **fancy:** imagination   56 **spleenwort:** a fern thought effective against disorders of the spleen. As
Aeneas carries the golden bough to the underworld (*Aeneid,* VI), Umbriel carries this rather silly-
sounding plant.   62 **physic:** medicine   63 **visits:** Cf. III, 12, 167   64 **in a pet:** in a sulk, huff
69 **citron-waters:** lemon-flavored brandy   71 **airy horns:** groundless suspicion of a wife's infidelity
(A husband whose wife was unfaithful was said to have horns.)   74 A prude's headdress would have
been prim, puritanical.   75 **costive:** constipated   78 **gives . . . the spleen:** in sympathy with Belin-
da's grief   82 **Like that . . . :** Aeolus, the god of the winds, gave Odysseus the storm winds shut up in
a leather bag so they would not interfere with his voyage (*Odyssey,* X, 19 ff.).

A vial next she fills with fainting fears,   85
Soft sorrows, melting griefs, and flowing tears.
The Gnome rejoicing bears her gifts away,
Spreads his black wings, and slowly mounts to day.
   Sunk in Thalestris' arms the nymph he found,
Her eyes dejected and her hair unbound.   90
Full o'er their heads the swelling bag he rent,
And all the furies issued at the vent.
Belinda burns with more than mortal ire,
And fierce Thalestris fans the rising fire.
"O wretched maid!" she spread her hands, and cried,   95
(While Hampton's echoes, "Wretched maid!" replied)
"Was it for this you took such constant care
The bodkin, comb, and essence to prepare;
For this your locks in paper durance bound,
For this with torturing irons wreathed around?   100
For this with fillets strained your tender head,
And bravely bore the double loads of lead?
Gods! shall the ravisher display your hair,
While the fops envy, and the ladies stare!
Honor forbid! at whose unrivalled shrine   105
Ease, pleasure, virtue, all, our sex resign.
Methinks already I your tears survey,
Already hear the horrid things they say,
Already see you a degraded toast,
And all your honor in a whisper lost!   110
How shall I, then, your helpless fame defend?
'Twill then be infamy to seem your friend!
And shall this prize, the inestimable prize,
Exposed through crystal to the gazing eyes,
And heightened by the diamond's circling rays,   115
On that rapacious hand for ever blaze?
Sooner shall grass in Hyde Park Circus grow,
And wits take lodgings in the sound of Bow;
Sooner let earth, air, sea, to chaos fall,
Men, monkeys, lapdogs, parrots, perish all!"   120
   She said; then raging to Sir Plume repairs,
And bids her beau demand the precious hairs:
(Sir Plume, of amber snuffbox justly vain,
And the nice conduct of a clouded cane)
With earnest eyes, and round unthinking face,   125
He first the snuffbox opened, then the case,
And thus broke out—"My Lord, why, what the devil?
Zounds! damn the lock! 'fore Gad, you must be civil!
Plague on't! 'tis past a jest—nay prithee, pox!
Give her the hair"—he spoke, and rapped his box.   130
   "It grieves me much" (replied the peer again)
"Who speaks so well should ever speak in vain.
But by this lock, this sacred lock I swear,

89 **Thalestris:** in mythology, queen of the Amazons. In reality, it seems she was Mrs. Gertrude Mor-
ley, wife of Sir George Browne (cf. line 121). 98 **bodkin:** long hairpin **essence:** perfume 99 **pa-
per durance:** confinement in paper curlers 101 **fillets:** headbands 102 **lead:** The curlers were fas-
tened with strips of soft lead. 109 **toast:** a lady frequently toasted by drinks in her honor
117 **Hyde Park Circus:** the driving Ring mentioned in I, 44. It was dusty from continual use.
118 **Bow:** Bowchurch, whose bells could be heard in a mercantile section of London that wits would
have considered vulgar. 121 **Sir Plume:** Sir George Browne, the cousin of Arabella Fermor's mother.
He was greatly angered by Pope's showing him as a silly irascible blurter. 124 **nice conduct:** precise
way of handling **clouded:** with its head, perhaps amber, mottled or variegated 128 **Zounds!:** an
oath (God's wounds)

(Which never more shall join its parted hair,
Which never more its honors shall renew,   135
Clipped from the lovely head where late it grew)
That while my nostrils draw the vital air,
This hand, which won it, shall for ever wear."
He spoke, and speaking, in proud triumph spread
The long-contended honors of her head.   140
   But Umbriel, hateful Gnome! forbears not so;
He breaks the vial whence the sorrows flow.
Then see! the nymph in beauteous grief appears,
Her eyes half languishing, half drowned in tears;
On her heaved bosom hung her drooping head,   145
Which, with a sigh, she raised; and thus she said:
   "For ever cursed be this detested day,
Which snatched my best, my favorite curl away!
Happy! ah ten times happy had I been,
If Hampton Court these eyes had never seen!   150
Yet am not I the first mistaken maid,
By love of courts to numerous ills betrayed.
Oh had I rather unadmired remained
In some lone isle, or distant northern land;
Where the gilt chariot never marks the way,   155
Where none learn ombre; none e'er taste bohea!
There kept my charms concealed from mortal eye,
Like roses that in deserts bloom and die.
What moved my mind with youthful lords to roam?
O had I stayed, and said my prayers at home!   160
'Twas this, the morning omens seemed to tell;
Thrice from my trembling hand the patch box fell;
The tottering china shook without a wind,
Nay, Poll sat mute, and Shock was most unkind!
A Sylph too warned me of the threats of fate,   165
In mystic visions, now believed too late!
See the poor remnants of these slighted hairs!
My hands shall rend what even thy rapine spares:
These, in two sable ringlets taught to break,
Once gave new beauties to the snowy neck;   170
The sister lock now sits uncouth, alone,
And in its fellow's fate foresees its own;
Uncurled it hangs, the fatal shears demands;
And tempts once more thy sacrilegious hands.
Oh hadst thou, cruel! been content to seize   175
Hairs less in sight, or any hairs but these!"

140 **long-contended honors . . . :** long-fought-over locks that honored her head   156 **bohea:** a kind
of tea (rhymes with *way*)   162 **patch box:** case for beauty patches (cf. I, 138)

Canto V

She said: the pitying audience melt in tears,
But fate and Jove had stopped the Baron's ears.
In vain Thalestris with reproach assails,
For who can move when fair Belinda fails?
Not half so fixed the Trojan could remain,   5

5 **the Trojan:** Aeneas, when Dido and her sister Anna were pleading with him not to leave (*Aeneid*,
IV, *passim*)

While Anna begged and Dido raged in vain.
Then grave Clarissa graceful waved her fan;
Silence ensued, and thus the nymph began:
   "Say why are beauties praised and honored most,
The wise man's passion, and the vain man's toast?   10
Why decked with all that land and sea afford,
Why angels called, and angel-like adored?
Why round our coaches crowd the white-gloved beaux,
Why bows the side-box from its inmost rows?
How vain are all these glories, all our pains,   15
Unless good sense preserve what beauty gains:
That men may say, when we the front-box grace,
'Behold the first in virtue, as in face!'
Oh! if to dance all night, and dress all day,
Charmed the smallpox, or chased old age away,   20
Who would not scorn what housewife's cares produce,
Or who would learn one earthly thing of use?
To patch, nay ogle, might become a saint,
Nor could it sure be such a sin to paint.
But since, alas! frail beauty must decay,   25
Curled or uncurled, since locks will turn to gray;
Since painted or not painted, all shall fade,
And she who scorns a man, must die a maid;
What then remains, but well our power to use,
And keep good humor still what'er we lose?   30
And trust me, dear! good humor can prevail,
When airs, and flights, and screams, and scolding fail.
Beauties in vain their pretty eyes may roll;
Charms strike the sight, but merit wins the soul."
   So spoke the dame, but no applause ensued;   35
Belinda frowned, Thalestris called her prude.
"To arms, to arms!" the fierce virago cries,
And swift as lightning to the combat flies.
All side in parties, and begin the attack;
Fans clap, silks rustle, and tough whalebones crack;   40
Heroes' and heroines' shouts confus'dly rise,
And bass and treble voices strike the skies.
No common weapons in their hands are found,
Like gods they fight, nor dread a mortal wound.
   So when bold Homer makes the gods engage,   45
And heavenly breasts with human passions rage;
'Gainst Pallas, Mars; Latona, Hermes arms;
And all Olympus rings with loud alarms.
Jove's thunder roars, heaven trembles all around;
Blue Neptune storms, the bellowing deeps resound;   50
Earth shakes her nodding towers, the ground gives way;

---

7 **Clarissa:** not so "grave" that she didn't offer the scissors to the Baron in the first place (III, 127). She is the voice of common sense and good humor in the poem; but her voice goes unheard.   14 **side-box:** in the theater (as in "front-box," line 17)   20 **smallpox:** Later in the century, 18 members of the Petre family were to die of the smallpox within 27 years. The young Lord Petre who had stolen the lock of hair—the Baron of the poem—had himself died of it in 1713, a year before the poem was published. For contemporary readers, this fact would give poignancy to the line. Many readers have felt an undercurrent of melancholy in this apparently light-hearted poem.   35 After such a speech in a true epic, there is generally great applause.   37 **virago:** a female warrior, a mannish woman   39 The ensuing battle, fought with such weapons as fans, hairpins, flashing eyes, frowns, and pinches of snuff, is the mock-heroic counterpart of the mighty battles of the *Iliad,* the *Odyssey,* and the *Aeneid.* 47 In the *Iliad* (Book XX, *passim*) Pallas (Athena) and Hermes fight with the Greeks; Mars and Latona (mother of Apollo and Diana) with the Trojans. The jumble of names suggests the confusion of battle (cf. I, 101–102).

And the pale ghosts start at the flash of day!
  Triumphant Umbriel on a sconce's height
Clapped his glad wings, and sat to view the fight:
Propped on their bodkin spears, the sprites survey   55
The growing combat, or assist the fray.
  While through the press enraged Thalestris flies,
And scatters death around from both her eyes,
A beau and witling perished in the throng,
One died in metaphor, and one in song.   60
"O cruel nymph! a living death I bear,"
Cried Dapperwit, and sunk beside his chair.
A mournful glance Sir Fopling upwards cast,
"Those eyes are made so killing"—was his last.
Thus on Maeander's flowery margin lies   65
The expiring swan, and as he sings he dies.
  When bold Sir Plume had drawn Clarissa down,
Chloe stepped in, and killed him with a frown;
She smiled to see the doughty hero slain,
But at her smile, the beau revived again.   70
  Now Jove suspends his golden scales in air,
Weighs the men's wits against the lady's hair;
The doubtful beam long nods from side to side;
At length the wits mount up, the hairs subside.
  See, fierce Belinda on the Baron flies,   75
With more than usual lightning in her eyes;
Nor feared the Chief the unequal fight to try,
Who sought no more than on his foe to die.
But this bold lord, with manly strength endued,
She with one finger and a thumb subdued: 80
Just where the breath of life his nostrils drew,
A charge of snuff the wily virgin threw;
The Gnomes direct, to every atom just,
The pungent grains of titillating dust.
Sudden, with starting tears each eye o'erflows,   85
And the high dome re-echoes to his nose.
  "Now meet thy fate," incensed Belinda cried,
And drew a deadly bodkin from her side.
(The same, his ancient personage to deck,
Her great great grandsire wore about his neck   90
In three seal rings; which after, melted down,
Formed a vast buckle for his widow's gown:
Her infant grandame's whistle next it grew,
The bells she jingled, and the whistle blew;
Then in a bodkin graced her mother's hairs,   95
Which long she wore, and now Belinda wears.)
  "Boast not my fall" (he cried) "insulting foe!
Thou by some other shalt be laid as low.
Nor think, to die dejects my lofty mind;

---

53 **sconce:** candle on a wall bracket   59-64 **beau and witling . . . :** The beau, Dapperwit, who dies in his metaphor of "a living death," stands for all those sentimental lovers who, while in good health, say they are "dying" of love; the witling, Sir Fopling, dies with a line from a popular opera about "killing" eyes. Their names, taken from plays of the period, suggest foolish dandies.   65 **Maeander:** a river that "meandered" in Phrygia—a haunt of swans   66 **swan:** Dying swans were thought to have a beautiful "swan-song."   71 **scales:** Gods in the epics commonly weigh causes in their scales to see which is the weightier and deserves to win.   78 **die:** a *double entendre*, as in John Donne's "The Canonization," line 21   81 Cf. IV, 137   88 **bodkin:** The word can mean *dagger*, as well as *blunt needle* and *ornamental hairpin*. Belinda draws it as if it were a dagger, but line 96 seems to say it's a hairpin. 89-96 The history of Belinda's hairpin is a burlesque of the history of such illustrious objects as scepters and helmets in Homer.

All that I dread is leaving you behind! 100
Rather than so, ah let me still survive,
And burn in Cupid's flames—but burn alive."
    "Restore the lock!" she cries; and all around
"Restore the lock!" the vaulted roofs rebound.
Not fierce Othello in so loud a strain 105
Roared for the handkerchief that caused his pain.
But see how oft ambitious aims are crossed,
And chiefs contend till all the prize is lost!
The lock, obtained with guilt, and kept with pain,
In every place is sought, but sought in vain: 110
With such a prize no mortal must be blest,
So heaven decrees! with heaven who can contest?
    Some thought it mounted to the lunar sphere,
Since all things lost on earth are treasured there.
There heroes' wits are kept in ponderous vases, 115
And beaux' in snuffboxes and tweezer cases.
There broken vows, and deathbed alms are found,
And lovers' hearts with ends of riband bound;
The courtier's promises, and sick man's prayers,
The smiles of harlots, and the tears of heirs, 120
Cages for gnats, and chains to yoke a flea,
Dried butterflies, and tomes of casuistry.
    But trust the Muse—she saw it upward rise,
Though marked by none but quick, poetic eyes:
(So Rome's great founder to the heavens withdrew, 125
To Proculus alone confessed in view).
A sudden star, it shot through liquid air,
And drew behind a radiant trail of hair.
Not Berenice's locks first rose so bright,
The heavens bespangling with dishevelled light. 130
The Sylphs behold it kindling as it flies,
And pleased pursue its progress through the skies.
    This the beau monde shall from the Mall survey,
And hail with music its propitious ray.
This, the blest lover shall for Venus take, 135
And send up vows from Rosamonda's lake.
This Partridge soon shall view in cloudless skies,
When next he looks through Galileo's eyes;
And hence the egregious wizard shall foredoom

---

105 **Othello:** One of the most painful "proofs" of Desdemona's unfaithfulness was a handkerchief Othello had given her and which Iago, who found it, asserted she had given to a lover.   114 **all things lost:** In *Orlando Furioso*, by the Italian poet Ariosto, Orlando's missing wits are found on the moon (canto 34, stanzas 68 ff.)   117–122 There is something insincere or futile in all the objects named. "Dried butterflies" would be collected by dabblers in natural science. By "tomes of casuistry" Pope meant large books about small ethical disputes and distinctions.   123 ff. Pope solves the quarrel over the lock of hair by having it elude both parties and soar off into the heavens, where it finds a place among the heavenly bodies.   125 **Rome's great founder:** Romulus, mythical founder of Rome, disappeared in a storm. Proculus, a senator, reported that Romulus had appeared to him to confirm the story of his ascent to heaven.   127 **liquid:** clear   128 **trail of hair:** like a comet (from the Greek *cometes*, "long-haired")   129 **Berenice's locks:** Berenice, the wife of Ptolemy III of Egypt, promised a lock of hair to the gods if her husband would return safely from a military campaign. On his return the lock was left in a temple—but disappeared overnight. A court astronomer pacified the angry king by telling him he had discovered the lock of hair among the stars, where it had become the constellation we still call Coma Berenices, or Berenice's Hair. A Greek poem on the subject was translated by Catullus.   133 **beau monde:** the world of high society   **the Mall:** an enclosed walk in St. James Park much frequented by people of society   136 **Rosamonda's lake:** a pond near the corner of the park associated with unhappy lovers   137–140 **Partridge:** John Partridge, whom Pope called "a ridiculous stargazer, who in his almanack every year never failed to predict the downfall of the Pope, and the King of France, then at war with the English."   138 **Galileo's eyes:** the telescope, which Galileo had improved

The fate of Louis, and the fall of Rome.   140
   Then cease, bright nymph! to mourn thy ravished hair
Which adds new glory to the shining sphere!
Not all the tresses that fair head can boast
Shall draw such envy as the lock you lost.
For, after all the murders of your eye,   145
When, after millions slain, yourself shall die;
When those fair suns shall set, as set they must,
And all those tresses shall be laid in dust;
This lock, the Muse shall consecrate to fame,
And midst the stars inscribe Belinda's name!   150

140 **Louis:** Louis XIV, king of France   142 **sphere:** the heaven [It rhymed with *hair*.]   147 **suns:** Belinda's eyes

Samuel Johnson
(1709–1784)

Johnson, the most frequently quoted English author next to Shakespeare, dropped out of college probably for financial reasons, briefly taught school, married a woman 20 years older than he, and went to London, where for many years he lived by doing journalistic hack work—meanwhile writing poems and prose pieces that caught the attention of discriminating readers. In 1749 he published his best poem, "The Vanity of Human Wishes." The last 20 years of his life were eased by a government pension, which enabled him to enjoy what he loved the most—the pleasures of friendship, society, and conversation.

A Short Song of Congratulation

Long expected one and twenty,
Lingering year, at length is flown;
Pride and pleasure, pomp and plenty,
Great Sir John, are all your own.

Loosened from the minor's tether,   5
Free to mortgage or to sell,
Wild as wind, and light as feather,
Bid the sons of thrift farewell.

Call the Betseys, Kates, and Jennys,
All the names that banish care,   10
Lavish of your grandsire's guineas,
Show the spirit of an heir.

All that prey on vice and folly
Joy to see their quarry fly,
Here the gamester light and jolly,   15
There the lender grave and sly.

Wealth, my lad, was made to wander,
Let it wander as it will;

1780. H. L. Piozzi, *British Synonymy*, 1794 (some variants from later printings).

Sir John Lade, a young man of Johnson's acquaintance, came of age and into a large estate (zeugma) in 1780. Sir John was the young man who once suddenly asked, "Mr. Johnson, would you advise me to marry?" and was told "I would advise no man to marry, sir, who is not likely to propagate understanding." Johnson's ironic poem was prophetic: Sir John squandered his large estate and died childless.

11 **guineas:** money (A guinea was a gold coin worth just over a pound.)

Call the jockey, call the pander,
Bid them come, and take their fill.   20

When the bonny blade carouses,
Pockets full, and spirits high,
What are acres? What are houses?
Only dirt, or wet or dry.

Should the guardian, friend, or mother   25
Tell the woes of wilful waste,
Scorn their counsel, scorn their pother,
You can hang or drown at last.

21 **blade:** a lively, dashing young man

Thomas Gray
(1716–1771)

Gray, a quiet scholar at Cambridge, may have worked for as long as ten years on his *Elegy*, which was to become the most celebrated poem of the century and perhaps the most familiar of all English poems. Not entirely pleased with its popular success, he gave himself more and more to historical and scientific studies; in 1768 he was made Professor of Modern History at Cambridge.

Elegy Written in a Country Churchyard

The curfew tolls the knell of parting day,
The lowing herd wind slowly o'er the lea,
The ploughman homeward plods his weary way,
And leaves the world to darkness and to me.

Now fades the glimmering landscape on the sight,   5
And all the air a solemn stillness holds,
Save where the beetle wheels his droning flight,
And drowsy tinklings lull the distant folds;

Save that from yonder ivy-mantled tower
The moping owl does to the moon complain   10
Of such, as wandering near her secret bower,
Molest her ancient solitary reign.

Beneath those rugged elms, that yew-tree's shade,
Where heaves the turf in many a moldering heap,
Each in his narrow cell forever laid,   15
The rude forefathers of the hamlet sleep.

The breezy call of incense-breathing morn,
The swallow twittering from the straw-built shed,
The cock's shrill clarion, or the echoing horn,
No more shall rouse them from their lowly bed.   20

1746–1750. An Elegy Wrote in a Country Church Yard, 1751. Text from Designs by Mr. R. Bentley for Six Poems by Mr. T. Gray, 1753. Some readings from Poems, 1768.

4 me: the person imagined meditating in the poem, perhaps Gray, perhaps a made-up persona, like Gray in many ways   **16 rude:** plain, simple, unsophisticated   **19 clarion:** a shrill trumpet, or the sound it makes

For them no more the blazing hearth shall burn,
Or busy housewife ply her evening care;
No children run to lisp their sire's return,
Or climb his knees the envied kiss to share.

Oft did the harvest to their sickle yield;   25
Their furrow oft the stubborn glebe has broke;
How jocund did they drive their team afield!
How bowed the woods beneath their sturdy stroke!

Let not Ambition mock their useful toil,
Their homely joys, and destiny obscure;   30
Nor Grandeur hear with a disdainful smile
The short and simple annals of the poor.

The boast of heraldry, the pomp of power,
And all that beauty, all that wealth e'er gave,
Awaits alike the inevitable hour: 35
The paths of glory lead but to the grave.

Nor you, ye proud, impute to these the fault,
If Memory o'er their tomb no trophies raise,
Where through the long-drawn aisle and fretted vault
The pealing anthem swells the note of praise.   40

Can storied urn or animated bust
Back to its mansion call the fleeting breath?
Can Honour's voice provoke the silent dust,
Or Flattery soothe the dull cold ear of Death?

Perhaps in this neglected spot is laid   45
Some heart once pregnant with celestial fire;
Hands that the rod of empire might have swayed,
Or waked to ecstasy the living lyre.

But Knowledge to their eyes her ample page,
Rich with the spoils of time, did ne'er unroll;   50
Chill Penury repressed their noble rage,
And froze the genial current of the soul.

Full many a gem of purest ray serene,
The dark unfathomed caves of ocean bear;
Full many a flower is born to blush unseen,   55
And waste its sweetness on the desert air.

Some village Hampden, that with dauntless breast
The little tyrant of his fields withstood;
Some mute inglorious Milton here may rest,
Some Cromwell, guiltless of his country's blood.   60

---

26 glebe: soil   **33** The blustery *b*s and *p*s of the line are expressive; there are many such effects in this poem.   **heraldry:** nobility; those entitled to a coat of arms   **35** *Hour* is the subject of the sentence.   **39 fretted:** ornately carved   **41 storied urn:** funeral urn with biographical detail   **animated:** realistic, lifelike   **42 its mansion:** the body   **43 provoke:** call forth (Latin)   **57 Hampden:** John Hampden (1594–1643) was a Member of Parliament who in 1637 refused to pay an illegal tax levied by Charles I. He died in the Civil Wars.   **60 Cromwell:** cf. Marvell's "Horatian Ode ..." (p. 167). Right or wrong, Cromwell was responsible for what many thought needless bloodshed.

The applause of listening senates to command,
The threats of pain and ruin to despise,
To scatter plenty o'er a smiling land,
And read their history in a nation's eyes

Their lot forbade; nor circumscribed alone   65
Their growing virtues, but their crimes confined;
Forbade to wade through slaughter to a throne,
And shut the gates of mercy on mankind;

The struggling pangs of conscious truth to hide,
To quench the blushes of ingenuous shame,   70
Or heap the shrine of Luxury and Pride
With incense kindled at the Muse's flame.

Far from the madding crowd's ignoble strife,
Their sober wishes never learned to stray;
Along the cool sequestered vale of life   75
They kept the noiseless tenor of their way.

Yet even these bones from insult to protect,
Some frail memorial still erected nigh,
With uncouth rhymes and shapeless sculpture decked,
Implores the passing tribute of a sigh.   80

Their name, their years, spelt by the unlettered Muse,
The place of fame and elegy supply;
And many a holy text around she strews,
That teach the rustic moralist to die.

For who, to dumb Forgetfulness a prey,   85
This pleasing anxious being e'er resigned,
Left the warm precincts of the cheerful day,
Nor cast one longing lingering look behind?

On some fond breast the parting soul relies,
Some pious drops the closing eye requires;   90
Even from the tomb the voice of Nature cries,
Even in our ashes live their wonted fires.

For thee, who mindful of the unhonoured dead
Dost in these lines their artless tale relate,
If chance, by lonely contemplation led,   95
Some kindred spirit shall inquire thy fate,

Haply some hoary-headed swain may say,
"Oft have we seen him at the peep of dawn

---

65 **circumscribed:** limited   70 **ingenuous shame:** the shame an honest person should naturally feel when not living up to his ideals   71–72 The lines refer to those who write poetry that flatters the vices of the rich and powerful.   73 **madding:** acting like madmen   76 **tenor:** habitual course   79 **uncouth:** unlearned, rough   81 **the unlettered Muse:** primitive, naive poetry   88 The line lingers on *l* sounds.   92 **wonted:** usual, accustomed   93 **thee:** This *thee* has perplexed a number of scholars. Who is he? Some think the "stonecutter" of four stanzas above, who is not, however, particularly mindful of the dead, but only doing his job. The one really mindful of the dead and relating their tale in these lines is the person through whose mind these thoughts are passing, the "me" of line 4. He is addressing himself here; and in the stanzas that follow imagines the death of such a dreamy, introverted, rather sentimental person as he sees himself to be.   95 **if chance:** if it happens that   97 **haply:** perhaps   **hoary-headed swain:** white-haired countryman

Brushing with hasty steps the dews away
To meet the sun upon the upland lawn.   100

"There at the foot of yonder nodding beech
That wreathes its old fantastic roots so high,
His listless length at noontide would he stretch,
And pore upon the brook that babbles by.

"Hard by yon wood, now smiling as in scorn,   105
Muttering his wayward fancies he would rove;
Now drooping, woeful-wan, like one forlorn,
Or crazed with care, or crossed in hopeless love.

"One morn I missed him on the customed hill,
Along the heath, and near his favorite tree;   110
Another came; nor yet beside the rill,
Nor up the lawn, nor at the wood was he;

"The next, with dirges due, in sad array,
Slow through the church-way path we saw him borne.
Approach and read (for thou canst read) the lay,   115
Graved on the stone beneath yon agèd thorn."

The Epitaph

Here rests his head upon the lap of earth
A youth to Fortune and to Fame unknown;
Fair Science frowned not on his humble birth,
And Melancholy marked him for her own.   120

Large was his bounty, and his soul sincere;
Heaven did a recompense as largely send:
He gave to Misery all he had, a tear;
He gained from Heaven ('twas all he wished) a friend.

No farther seek his merits to disclose,   125
Or draw his frailties from their dread abode,
(There they alike in trembling hope repose)
The bosom of his Father and his God.

100 **lawn:** as in "Lycidas," line 25   105 **hard by:** close to   110 **heath:** waste land, open land general-
ly too poor for cultivation   111 **rill:** brook   115 **thou canst read:** The "kindred spirit" of line 96 can
of course read, since "kindred" to the person whose meditations these are. The old countryman,
though he speaks so well, apparently cannot.   **lay:** poem   **The Epitaph:** Gray composes here an
imaginary epitaph for the speaker of the poem, a person in many ways like the poet himself. Gray's
birth was humble, he was poor most of his life, he had a deep knowledge not only of poetry but of
history, "fair Science," philosophy, art; he was given to melancholy, capable of warm friendships for
a few, fond of seclusion. After he wrote the "Elegy . . ." he was not unknown to fame, but was indif-
ferent to it and suspicious of it.   121 **bounty:** kindness, generosity

William Collins
(1721–1759)

Son of a wealthy hatter who was mayor of Chichester, Collins was writing poetry by the
time he was 12. After Oxford he went to London as man about town and literary aspirant.
In 1751 he fell ill, tried to cure himself by travel, and in 1754 was confined for a time in a
lunatic asylum.

Ode, Written in the Beginning of the Year 1746

How sleep the brave, who sink to rest
By all their country's wishes blest!
When Spring, with dewy fingers cold,
Returns to deck their hallowed mould,
She there shall dress a sweeter sod   5
Than Fancy's feet have ever trod.

By fairy hands their knell is rung,
By forms unseen their dirge is sung;
There Honour comes, a pilgrim grey,
To bless the turf that wraps their clay,   10
And Freedom shall awhile repair
To dwell a weeping hermit there!

Odes on Several Descriptive and Allegoric Subjects, 1747. Text from R. Dodsley, *A Collection of Poems by Several Hands*, I, 1748.

The date suggests that Collins is honoring the English dead who fell at the battle of Falkirk, January 17, 1746, while resisting the Scottish army raised by Charles Edward, the "Bonnie Prince Charlie" of romance, who, as grandson of King James II, claimed the throne of England. Victor at Falkirk, Charles Edward was decisively defeated at Culloden in April.

6 than Fancy's feet . . . : than one could imagine   **11 repair:** go (Latin: *re-patria:* return to one's country)

Ode to Evening

If aught of oaten stop or pastoral song
May hope, chaste Eve, to soothe thy modest ear,
     Like thy own solemn springs,
     Thy springs and dying gales,
O nymph reserved, while now the bright-haired sun   5
Sits in yon western tent, whose cloudy skirts,
     With brede ethereal wove,
     O'erhang his wavy bed;
Now air is hushed, save where the weak-eyed bat
With short shrill shriek flits by on leathern wing,   10
     Or where the beetle winds
     His small but sullen horn,
As oft he rises midst the twilight path,
Against the pilgrim borne in heedless hum:
     Now teach me, maid composed,   15
     To breathe some softened strain,
Whose numbers stealing through thy darkening vale
May not unseemly with its stillness suit;
     As musing slow, I hail
     Thy genial loved return!   20
For when thy folding star arising shows
His paly circlet, at his warning lamp
     The fragrant Hours, and elves
     Who slept in flowers the day,

1746. *Odes on Several Descriptive and Allegoric Subjects*, 1747. Text from R. Dodsley, *Collection*, I, 1748.

A poem in stanzaic form (two pentameters; two tetrameters) that has no rhyme, the first such we have seen. Milton had used this very same form in his translation of Horace's Pyrrha ode (I, v).

1 oaten stop: a musical pipe, with fingerholes to *stop*, made out of an oaten straw   **3 springs:** here, brooks   **4 gales:** gentle winds   **7 brede:** braid, embroidery   **11 winds:** blows   **14 pilgrim:** walker, traveller   **17 numbers:** rhythms, verses   **21 folding:** indicating it's sheepfold time

And many a nymph who wreathes her brows with sedge,   25
And sheds the freshening dew, and, lovelier still,
    The Pensive Pleasures sweet,
    Prepare thy shadowy car.
Then lead, calm votaress, where some sheety lake
Cheers the lone heath, or some time-hallowed pile,   30
    Or upland fallows grey,
    Reflect its last cool gleam.
But when chill blustering winds or driving rain
Forbid my willing feet, be mine the hut
    That from the mountain's side   35
    Views wilds and swelling floods,
And hamlets brown, and dim-discovered spires,
And hears their simple bell, and marks o'er all
    Thy dewy fingers draw
    The gradual dusky veil.   40
While Spring shall pour his showers, as oft he wont,
And bathe thy breathing tresses, meekest Eve!
    While Summer loves to sport
    Beneath thy lingering light;
While sallow Autumn fills thy lap with leaves,   45
Or Winter, yelling through the troublous air,
    Affrights thy shrinking train,
    And rudely rends thy robes;
So long, sure-found beneath the sylvan shed,
Shall Fancy, Friendship, Science, rose-lipped Health,   50
    Thy gentlest influence own,
    And hymn thy favourite name!

29 **votaress:** woman devoted to religion   30 **pile:** impressive structure   31 **fallows:** unused farmland   37 **dim-discovered:** seen with difficulty   41 **wont:** is accustomed to   42 **breathing:** emitting fragrance   47 **train:** attendants, retinue   49 **sylvan shed:** shelter in the woods

Christopher Smart
(1722–1771)

After Cambridge, Smart supported himself in London by prolific hack writing. The strain of years of overwork, financial struggle, and excessive drinking led in 1756 to a breakdown and his confinement—for the next seven years he was either in a private home or a public institution for the insane. Deeply religious as he was, and meditating on himself and on the nature of poetry while so confined, he began to write with vigor and originality. After his release he did some of his best work; his life was quiet and industrious. He could not, however, earn a living; in 1770 he was arrested for debt and committed to prison, where he died the following year.

From **Jubilate Agno**

For I will consider my Cat Jeoffry.
For he is the servant of the Living God duly and daily serving him.

This section, 1759–1760. *Rejoice in the Lamb*, W. F. Stead, 1939. *Jubilate Agno*, ed. W. H. Bond, 1954. Fragment B2, 697–770.

For the form, see *free verse* in the prosody section. "Jubilate Agno" means "Rejoice in the Lamb"; the Lamb is Christ. The poem was written during the four years Smart spent in a private home for the insane, confined there because of excesses brought on by his drinking and his unconventional religious practices. Protected, in the madhouse, from alcohol and the distractions of life in the world, and reasonably happy with his gardening and his cat Jeoffry, Smart wrote "Jubilate Agno" as a kind of spiritual journal: a hymn of praise to God for His works and an invitation to all of us to join in that praise.

For at the first glance of the glory of God in the East he worships in
his way.
For is this done by wreathing his body seven times round
with elegant quickness.
For then he leaps up to catch the musk, which is the blessing of God
upon his prayer.   5
For he rolls upon prank to work it in.
For having done duty and received blessing he begins to consider
himself.
For this he performs in ten degrees.
For first he looks upon his fore-paws to see if they are clean.
For secondly he kicks up behind to clear away there.   10
For thirdly he works it upon stretch with the fore-paws extended.
For fourthly he sharpens his paws by wood.
For fifthly he washes himself.
For Sixthly he rolls upon wash.
For Seventhly he fleas himself, that he may not be interrupted upon the
beat.   15
For Eighthly he rubs himself against a post.
For Ninthly he looks up for his instructions.
For Tenthly he goes in quest of food.
For having considered God and himself he will consider his neighbour.
For if he meets another cat he will kiss her in kindness.   20
For when he takes his prey he plays with it to give it a chance.
For one mouse in seven escapes by his dallying.
For when his day's work is done his business more properly begins.
For he keeps the Lord's watch in the night against the adversary.
For he counteracts the powers of darkness by his electrical skin and
glaring eyes.   25
For he counteracts the Devil, who is death, by brisking about the life.
For in his morning orisons he loves the sun and the sun loves him.
For he is of the tribe of Tiger.
For the Cherub Cat is a term of the Angel Tiger.
For he has the subtlety and hissing of a serpent, which in goodness he
suppresses.   30
For he will not do destruction if he is well-fed, neither will he spit
without provocation.
For he purrs in thankfulness, when God tells him he's a good Cat.
For he is an instrument for the children to learn benevolence upon.
For every house is incomplete without him and a blessing is lacking
in the spirit.
For the Lord commanded Moses concerning the cats at the departure of
the Children of Israel from Egypt.   35
For every family had one cat at least in the bag.
For the English Cats are the best in Europe.
For he is the cleanest in the use of his fore-paws of any quadruped.
For the dexterity of his defence is an instance of the love of God to him
exceedingly.
For he is the quickest to his mark of any creature.   40
For he is tenacious of his point.

5 **musk:** perhaps a ball of some musky substance attractive to cats (catnip?), which Jeoffry would
jump for, catch, and roll around with   6 **upon prank:** prankishly, playfully   11 **works it upon
stretch:** stretches energetically   14 **upon wash:** upon having washed   15 **upon the beat:** on his dai-
ly round   24 **the adversary:** the devil   26 **brisking about the life:** living briskly, positively
27 **orisons:** prayers   29 The cherubic little cat is a form of the great angelic tiger.   35 **The Lord
commanded Moses . . . :** He commanded him to "take your flocks and your herds . . . and be gone"
(Exod. 12:32). Smart assumes this naturally included the family cats. [No cats are mentioned in the Bi-
ble.]   37 Smart's ardent patriotism extended even to cats.

For he is a mixture of gravity and waggery.
For he knows that God is his Saviour.
For there is nothing sweeter than his peace when at rest.
For there is nothing brisker than his life when in motion.   45
For he is of the Lord's poor and so indeed is he called by benevolence
    perpetually—Poor Jeoffry! poor Jeoffry! the rat has bit thy throat.
For I bless the name of the Lord Jesus that Jeoffry is better.
For the divine spirit comes about his body to sustain it in complete cat.
For his tongue is exceeding pure so that it has in purity what it wants in
    music.
For he is docile and can learn certain things.   50
For he can set up with gravity which is patience upon approbation.
For he can fetch and carry, which is patience in employment.
For he can jump over a stick which is patience upon proof positive.
For he can spraggle upon waggle at the word of command.
For he can jump from an eminence into his master's bosom.   55
For he can catch the cork and toss it again.
For he is hated by the hypocrite and miser.
For the former is afraid of detection.
For the latter refuses the charge.
For he camels his back to bear the first notion of business.   60
For he is good to think on, if a man would express himself neatly.
For he made a great figure in Egypt for his signal services.
For he killed the Ichneumon-rat very pernicious by land.
For his ears are so acute that they sting again.
For from this proceeds the passing quickness of his attention.   65
For by stroking of him I have found out electricity.
For I perceived God's light about him both wax and fire.
For the Electrical fire is the spiritual substance, which God sends from
    heaven to sustain the bodies both of man and beast.
For God has blessed him in the variety of his movements.
For, tho' he cannot fly, he is an excellent clamberer.   70
For his motions upon the face of the earth are more than any other
    quadruped.
For he can tread to all the measures upon the music.
For he can swim for life.
For he can creep.

42 **waggery:** mischief, playfulness 49 **wants:** lacks 51 **set up:** sit up 54 **spraggle upon waggle:**
This may mean the cat can sprawl and roll when his master waggles a stick, or it may just be Smart's
way of saying the cat likes to twist and frolic. 60 **camels:** arches it till it looks like a camel's
62 **Egypt:** where cats were worshipped 63 **Ichneumon-rat:** The ichneumon is the mongoose,
thought of as beneficial since it destroys rats and mice. Smart misunderstood its nature. Or he may
have confused its name with that of the ichneumon fly, a parasite. 64 **sting:** tingle (?) 67 **wax and
fire:** increase and blaze out (?) Or perhaps *wax* and *fire* are nouns—a candle image. 72 **tread:**
dance 74 This may not have been the concluding line of this section; pages are missing after it.

The Nativity of Our Lord

Where is this stupendous stranger,
    Swains of Solyma, advise,
Lead me to my Master's manger,
    Show me where my Saviour lies?

O Most Mighty! O Most Holy!   5
    Far beyond the seraph's thought,

c. 1763. *A Translation of the Psalms of David*, 1765.

2 **swains of Solyma:** shepherds of Jerusalem

Art thou then so mean and lowly
    As unheeded prophets taught?

O the magnitude of meekness!
    Worth from worth immortal sprung;   10
O the strength of infant weakness,
    If eternal is so young!

If so young and thus eternal,
    Michael tune the shepherd's reed,
Where the scenes are ever vernal,   15
    And the loves be love indeed!

See the God blasphemed and doubted
    In the schools of Greece and Rome;
See the powers of darkness routed,
    Taken at their utmost gloom.   20

Nature's decorations glisten
    Far above their usual trim;
Birds on box and laurel listen,
    As so near the cherubs hymn.

Boreas now no longer winters   25
    On the desolated coast;
Oaks no more are riven in splinters
    By the whirlwind and his host.

Spinks and ouzels sing sublimely,
    "We too have a Saviour born;"   30
Whiter blossoms burst untimely
    On the blest Mosaic thorn.

God all-bounteous, all-creative,
    Whom no ills from good dissuade,
Is incarnate, and a native   35
    Of the very world he made.

23 **box:** an evergreen shrub   25 **Boreas:** the north wind   27 **riven:** split, shattered   29 **spinks:** finches   **ouzels:** blackbirds   32 **Mosaic thorn:** Christ's mother was seen as a branch of the tree of Jesse (David's father) of which Jesus was the flowering. "Mosaic" in that the prophecy which said "there shall come forth a rod out of the stem of Jesse, and a Branch shall grow out of his roots . . ." (Isa. 11:1) is in the Old Testament, in which Moses is the dominant figure. [Perhaps with reminiscences of Aaron's rod, which burst into flower, and of the burning blackberry bush in which Jehovah appeared to Moses.]

From A Song to David

Strong is the lion—like a coal   451
His eyeball—like a bastion's mole
    His chest against the foes:
Strong, the gier-eagle on his sail,

1762–1763. *A Song to David*, 1763.

These are the last eleven stanzas of the 500-line "A Song to David" (the psalmist-king of the Old Testament), which like "Jubilate Agno" is a song of praise to God and his creation. One critic has called it "that skyscraper among eighteenth-century lyrics."

452 **bastion's mole:** a projecting rampart's massive structure   454 **gier-eagle:** a bird mentioned in the Bible, perhaps the Egyptian vulture

Strong against tide, the enormous whale   455
  Emerges as he goes.

But stronger still, in earth and air,
And in the sea, the man of prayer,
  And far beneath the tide;
And in the seat to faith assigned,   460
Where ask is have, where seek is find
  Where knock is open wide.

Beauteous the fleet before the gale;
Beauteous the multitudes in mail,
  Ranked arms and crested heads: 465
Beauteous the garden's umbrage mild,
Walk, water, meditated wild,
  And all the bloomy beds.

Beauteous the moon full on the lawn;
And beauteous, when the veil's withdrawn,   470
  The virgin to her spouse:
Beauteous the temple decked and filled,
When to the heaven of heavens they build
  Their heart-directed vows.

Beauteous, yea beauteous more than these,   475
The shepherd king upon his knees,
  For his momentous trust;
With wish of infinite conceit,
For man, beast, mute, the small and great,
  And prostrate dust to dust.   480

Precious the bounteous widow's mite;
And precious, for extreme delight,
  The largess from the churl:
Precious the ruby's blushing blaze,
And alba's blest imperial rays,   485
  And pure cerulean pearl.

Precious the penitential tear;
And precious is the sigh sincere,
  Acceptable to God:
And precious are the winning flowers,   490
In gladsome Israel's feast of bowers,
  Bound on the hallowed sod.

More precious that diviner part
Of David, even the Lord's own heart,
  Great, beautiful, and new: 495
In all things where it was intent,
In all extremes, in each event,
  Proof—answering true to true.

Glorious the sun in mid career;
Glorious the assembled fires appear;   500

---

466 umbrage: shade   **467 meditated wild:** carefully planned "wild" part of garden   **478 conceit:** conception, meaning   **483 largess:** gift, especially a generous one   **churl:** farmhand, poor country man   **485 alba:** a (white) pearl   **486 cerulean:** sky-blue

Glorious the comet's train:
Glorious the trumpet and alarm;
Glorious the almighty stretched-out arm;
  Glorious the enraptured main:

Glorious the northern lights a-stream;   505
Glorious the song, when God's the theme;
  Glorious the thunder's roar;
Glorious hosannah from the den;
Glorious the catholic amen;
  Glorious the martyr's gore: 510

Glorious—more glorious, is the crown
Of Him that brought salvation down
  By meekness, called thy Son;
Thou that stupendous truth believed,
And now the matchless deed's achieved,   515
  DETERMINED, DARED, *and* DONE.

509 **catholic:** universal

Oliver Goldsmith
(1730?–1774)

Goldsmith, born in Ireland, drifted about and worked at various jobs before settling down to journalism and literary hack work in London, where his charming essays soon brought him to the attention of men prominent in literature and society. His best-known poem, "The Deserted Village," has to do with the displacement of poor people in the country; his play *She Stoops to Conquer* is one of the most successful comedies of the century.

When Lovely Woman Stoops to Folly

When lovely woman stoops to folly,
  And finds too late that men betray,
What charm can soothe her melancholy,
  What art can wash her guilt away?

The only art her guilt to cover,   5
  To hide her shame from every eye,
To give repentance to her lover,
  And wring his bosom—is to die.

1760–1762. *The Vicar of Wakefield,* 1766.

William Cowper
(1731–1800)

Cowper (who pronounced his name *cooper*) suffered from attacks of depression, the second of which saw him confined to an asylum for 18 months, troubled by religious doubts and despair. Afterwards he was given a home with the kindly Unwin family and cared for by their pastor John Newton (the author of "Amazing Grace"). Thereafter he seemed a different man, fond of gardening and visiting and, with his friend Newton, writing the *Olney Hymns.* His long poem *The Task* (1785) was a sensation; people of the highest ranks now wanted to meet the man who had seemed so sad a failure.

Lines Written During a Period of Insanity

Hatred and vengeance, my eternal portion,
Scarce can endure delay of execution,
Wait, with impatient readiness, to seize my
               Soul in a moment.

Damned below Judas: more abhorred than he was,   5
Who for a few pence sold his holy Master.
Twice-betrayed Jesus me, the last delinquent,
               Deems the profanest.

Man disavows, and Deity disowns me:
Hell might afford my miseries a shelter;   10
Therefore hell keeps her ever-hungry mouths all
               Bolted against me.

Hard lot! encompassed with a thousand dangers;
Weary, faint, trembling with a thousand terrors;
I'm called, if vanquished, to receive a sentence   15
               Worse than Abiram's.

Him the vindictive rod of angry justice
Sent quick and howling to the center headlong;
I, fed with judgment, in a fleshly tomb, am
               Buried above ground.   20

---

c. 1774. *Memoirs of . . . the Life of William Cowper* (Cox edition), 1816.

The meter is Sapphic, as in Watts, "The Day of Judgement." In periods of insanity, Cowper was convinced that he was damned forever: too deeply damned for even hell to receive him.

16 **Abiram:** One of the three leaders of a rebellion against Moses: "And the earth opened her mouth, and swallowed them up . . . They, and all that appertained to them, went down alive into the pit, and the earth closed upon them . . ." (Num. 16:32–33).   19 **fed with judgment:** In Ezek. 34:16, the Lord says of bad shepherds who have not fed their flocks, "I will destroy the fat and the strong; I will feed them with judgment."

Epitaph on a Hare

Here lies, whom hound did ne'er pursue,
    Nor swifter greyhound follow,
Whose foot ne'er tainted morning dew,
    Nor ear heard huntsman's halloo;

Old Tiny, surliest of his kind,   5
    Who, nursed with tender care,
And to domestic bounds confined,
    Was still a wild jack-hare.

Though duly from my hand he took
    His pittance every night,   10
He did it with a jealous look,
    And, when he could, would bite.

1783. *Poems*, 1800.

Cowper also wrote a little essay on the three hares he kept as diversion at a time when he was "much indisposed both in mind and body." Tiny, the subject of the epitaph, lived to be nine years old, dying "of some hurt in his loins by a fall." Though surly and inclined to bite, Tiny was "very entertaining in his way; even his surliness was matter for mirth."

His diet was of wheaten bread,
    And milk, and oats, and straw;
Thistles, or lettuces instead,   15
    With sand to scour his maw.

On twigs of hawthorn he regaled,
    On pippins' russet peel,
And, when his juicy salads failed,
    Sliced carrot pleased him well.   20

A Turkey carpet was his lawn,
    Whereon he loved to bound,
To skip and gambol like a fawn,
    And swing his rump around.

His frisking was at evening hours,   25
    For then he lost his fear,
But most before approaching showers,
    Or when a storm drew near.

Eight years and five round-rolling moons
    He thus saw steal away,   30
Dozing out all his idle noons,
    And every night at play.

I kept him for his humour's sake,
    For he would oft beguile
My heart of thoughts that made it ache,   35
    And force me to a smile.

But now beneath his walnut shade
    He finds his long last home,
And waits, in snug concealment laid,
    Till gentler Puss shall come.   40

He, still more aged, feels the shocks
    From which no care can save,
And, partner once of Tiny's box,
    Must soon partake his grave.

17 **regaled:** feasted   18 **pippins:** a kind of apple   21 **Turkey:** turkey-red. Cowper tells how he "always admitted them into the parlor after supper, where, the carpet affording their feet a firm hold, they would frisk, bound, and play...."   40 **Puss:** in spite of the name, another male hare, who outlived Tiny by two years

The Poplar Field

The poplars are felled, farewell to the shade
And the whispering sound of the cool colonnade,
The winds play no longer, and sing in the leaves,
Nor Ouse on his bosom their image receives.

Twelve years have elapsed since I last took a view   5
Of my favourite field and the bank where they grew,

1784. Ibid.

4 **Ouse:** a river [same vowel sound as the first syllable of "bosom"]

And now in the grass behold they are laid,
And the tree is my seat that once lent me a shade.

The blackbird has fled to another retreat
Where the hazels afford him a screen from the heat,   10
And the scene where his melody charmed me before,
Resounds with his sweet-flowing ditty no more.

My fugitive years are all hasting away,
And I must ere long lie as lowly as they,
With a turf on my breast, and a stone at my head,   15
Ere another such grove shall arise in its stead.

'Tis a sight to engage me, if any thing can,
To muse on the perishing pleasures of man;
Though his life be a dream, his enjoyments, I see,
Have a being less durable even than he.   20

Philip Freneau
(1752–1832)

Freneau, born in New York City and a Princeton graduate, has been called the father of American poetry. He served in the Revolutionary War with the New Jersey militia and on a privateer. Until 1790 he was a sea captain; then for a decade or more he was an ardent political journalist whom Thomas Jefferson once credited with saving the country when it seemed to be falling back into monarchy.

The Indian Burying Ground

In spite of all the learned have said,
I still my old opinion keep;
The *posture*, that *we* give the dead,
Points out the soul's eternal sleep.

Not so the ancients of these lands—   5
The Indian, when from life released,
Again is seated with his friends,
And shares again the joyous feast.

His imaged birds, and painted bowl,
And venison, for a journey dressed,   10
Bespeak the nature of the soul,
ACTIVITY, that knows no rest.

His bow, for action ready bent,
And arrows, with a head of stone,
Can only mean that life is spent,   15
And not the old ideas gone.

Thou, stranger, that shalt come this way,
No fraud upon the dead commit—

1787. *Miscellaneous Works*, 1788. With later revisions.

Freneau's later note to the second stanza reads, "The North American Indians bury their dead in a sitting posture; decorating the corpse with wampum, the images of birds, quadrupeds, &c: And (if that of a warrior) with bows, arrows, tomhawks and other military weapons."

Observe the swelling turf, and say
They do not *lie*, but here they *sit*.   20

Here still a lofty rock remains,
On which the curious eye may trace
(Now wasted, half, by wearing rains)
The fancies of a ruder race.

Here still an aged elm aspires,   25
Beneath whose far-projecting shade
(And which the shepherd still admires)
The children of the forest played!

There oft a restless Indian queen
(Pale *Shebah*, with her braided hair)   30
And many a barbarous form is seen
To chide the man that lingers there.

By midnight moons, o'er moistening dews,
In habit for the chase arrayed,
The hunter still the deer pursues,   35
The hunter and the deer, a shade!

And long shall timorous fancy see
The painted chief, and pointed spear,
And Reason's self shall bow the knee
To shadows and delusions here.   40

Thomas Chatterton
(1752–1770)

As a child Chatterton lived in the past, teaching himself to read from old manuscripts.
When 11 or 12, he began to write poems in what he—and most of his readers—took to be
the language of the fifteenth century. Though the poems were forgeries, the poetic skill
was genuine. At 17 "the marvellous boy," as Wordsworth called him, went off to London
for a literary career; when his immediate hopes were disappointed, he took arsenic in a
rented garret.

Minstrel's Song *from* Ælla

O! synge untoe mie roundelaie,
O! droppe the brynie teare wythe mee,
Daunce ne moe atte hallie daie,

1768. *Ælla; A Tragical Interlude*, in *Poems, Supposed to Have Been Written at Bristol by Thomas Rowley
and Others in the Fifteenth Century*, 1777.

Scholars would know Chatterton's language was far from accurate, but it looked very old and fooled
many. Instead of writing

> O, sing unto my roundelay,
> O, drop the briny tear with me,
> Dance no more at holy day,
> Like a running river be;
> > My love is dead,
> > Gone to his death-bed,
> > All under the willow tree.

he wrote his first stanza as above, deliberately archaizing the language by changing words and their
spelling and sprinkling it all liberally with extra *e*'s. A strange music in the eighteenth century, his
poetry anticipated that of the romantic poets who so much admired him.

Lycke a reynynge ryver bee;
     Mie love ys dedde,   5
     Gon to hys death-bedde,
     Al under the wyllowe tree.

Blacke hys cryne as the wyntere nyghte,
Whyte hys rode as the sommer snowe,
Rodde hys face as the mornynge lyghte,   10
Cale he lyes ynne the grave belowe;
     Mie love ys dedde,
     Gon to hys deathe-bedde,
     Al under the wyllowe tree.

Swote hys tyngue as the throstles note,   15
Quycke ynn daunce as thoughte canne bee,
Defte hys taboure, codgelle stote,
O! hee lyes bie the wyllowe tree;
     Mie love ys dedde,
     Gonne to hys deathe-bedde,   20
     Alle underre the wyllowe tree.

Harke! the ravenne flappes hys wynge,
In the briered delle belowe;
Harke! the dethe-owle loude dothe synge,
To the nyghte-mares as heie goe;   25
     Mie love ys dedde,
     Gonne to hys deathe-bedde,
     Al under the wyllowe tree.

See! the whyte moone sheenes onne hie;
Whyterre ys mie true loves shroude;   30
Whyterre yanne the mornynge skie,
Whyterre yanne the evenynge cloude;
     Mie love ys dedde,
     Gon to hys deathe-bedde,
     Al under the wyllowe tree.   35

Heere, uponne mie true loves grave,
Schalle the baren fleurs be layde,
Nee one hallie Seyncte to save
Al the celness of a mayde.
     Mie love ys dedde,   40
     Gonne to hys death-bedde,
     Alle under the wyllowe tree.

Wythe mie hondes I'lle dente the brieres
Rounde his hallie corse to gre,
Ouphante fairie, lyghte youre fyres,   45
Heere mie boddie stylle schalle bee.
     Mie love ys dedde,
     Gon to hys death-bedde,
     Al under the wyllowe tree.

---

8 **cryne:** hair 9 **rode:** complexion 10 **rodde:** ruddy 11 **cale:** cold 15 **swote hys tyngue:** sweet his tongue **throstle:** thrush 17 **taboure:** small drum **codgelle stote:** cudgel stout 25 **heie:** they 30 **whyterre:** whiter 31 **yanne:** than 38 **nee:** nor 39 **celness:** coolness 43 **dente:** fasten 44 **corse:** corpse **gre:** grow 45 **ouphante:** elfin

Comme, wythe acorne-coppe & thorne,   50
Drayne mie hartys blodde awaie;
Lyfe and all yttes goode I scorne,
Daunce bie nete, or feaste by daie.
     Mie love ys dedde,
     Gon to hys death-bedde,   55
     Al under the wyllowe tree.

Waterre wytches, crownede wythe reytes,
Bere mee to yer leathalle tyde.
I die; I comme; mie true love waytes.
Thos the damselle spake, and dyed.   60

52 **yttes:** its   53 **nete:** night   57 **reytes:** water-flags, sedge   60 **thos:** thus

William Blake
(1757–1828)

Blake, an art student at the age of 10 and at 15 apprenticed to an engraver, became equally great as artist and poet. Besides completing a dozen or more elaborately produced little volumes of his own work (see note), Blake, assisted by his wife, illustrated the books of others, did paintings in tempera and water color, and made many engravings. Though he was one of the best poets and artists of his time, his life was, from a worldly point of view, a failure. He had perceptive admirers, but was ignored by the general public; for a century there was not even a stone to mark his grave.

To the Muses

Whether on Ida's shady brow,
    Or in the chambers of the East,
The chambers of the sun, that now
    From ancient melody have ceased;

Whether in Heaven ye wander fair,   5
    Or the green corners of the earth,
Or the blue regions of the air,
    Where the melodious winds have birth;

Whether on crystal rocks ye rove,
    Beneath the bosom of the sea   10
Wandering in many a coral grove,
    Fair Nine, forsaking poetry!

By 1777. *Poetical Sketches,* 1783.

The poem above is the only one in our selection that appeared in a printed book: *Poetical Sketches,* paid for by the poet's friends, was a little edition of 50 copies that included poems he wrote from the time he was 12 until he was 20. All of his other works were offered to a limited public in a way that showed his skill as artist. Technically trained as an engraver through seven difficult years as apprentice, he cut the text of his poems, in reverse, on copper plates and provided them with illustrations. They were then printed in colored inks and tinted by hand with water colors. The process, invented by Blake, was so time consuming that there were never many copies of his illuminated books, and no two were exactly alike.

the Muses: The nine Muses were the mythological divinities that for the Greeks and Romans sponsored the arts and sciences—in particular poetry. **1 Ida:** The two Mt. Idas, one in Crete, one near Troy, were sometimes confused. Neither is particularly associated with the Muses, whose favorite mountains were Helicon and Parnassus in Greece. Blake means Ida to stand for classical poetry. **2 the chambers of the East:** where the sacred bards of the Old Testament wrote their poems, which Blake thought more truly inspired than the works of Homer, Vergil, and the other classical poets

How have you left the ancient love
    That bards of old enjoyed in you!
The languid strings do scarcely move!   15
    The sound is forced, the notes are few!

Introduction *to* Songs of Experience

Hear the voice of the Bard!
Who Present, Past, and Future sees;
Whose ears have heard
The holy word
That walked among the ancient trees,   5

Calling the lapsèd Soul,
And weeping in the evening dew;
That might control
The starry pole
And fallen, fallen light renew!   10

"O Earth, O Earth, return!
Arise from out the dewy grass;
Night is worn,
And the morn
Rises from the slumberous mass.   15

"Turn away no more;
Why wilt thou turn away?
The starry floor,
The watery shore,
Is given thee till the break of day."   20

1789–1790. *Songs of Experience*, 1794. The Houghton Library copy (Harvard). The original engravings of the Blake poems given here can be seen in such modern reproductions as those in David Bindman, *The Complete Graphic Works of William Blake*, 1978. Punctuation—unclear, inconsistent, or missing in the engraved plates and Note-Book—is supplied in the texts we give.

1 **Bard:** For Blake, the true poet is inspired, as the holy prophets were; he brings us truths not limited to the here and now.　4　**the holy word:** Cf. Gen. 3:8: "And they heard the voice of the LORD God walking in the garden in the cool of the day: and . . . hid themselves . . . amongst the trees of the garden."　6 **lapsèd Soul:** man after his Fall　8 **that:** probably parallel with the *that* of line 5; the antecedent then is *holy word*. Others take it differently.　9 **starry pole:** the world of science, of materialism—inferior, for Blake, to the world of imaginative vision　10 **fallen light:** man's original innocence, liberty, imaginative vision　11 **Earth:** earth too degenerated with the Fall of man　15 **slumberous mass:** mere dull matter　18 **starry floor:** In Blake's thought, stars stand for science, reason, the Newtonian universe—a machine of mere circling wheels.　19 **watery shore:** For Blake, the Biblical flood stood for mankind submerged in matter.　20 **break of day:** the Apocalypse, the dawn of Eternity, our rebirth into original innocence

The Tyger

Tyger, Tyger, burning bright
In the forests of the night,
What immortal hand or eye
Could frame thy fearful symmetry?

1789–1794. Ibid.

See Additional Notes, p. 764. "The Tyger" is one of several paired poems in *Songs of Innocence* and *Songs of Experience*; it is the answer of experience to the innocence of Blake's well-known "nursery poem" that begins, "Little lamb, who made thee?"

In what distant deeps or skies   5
Burnt the fire of thine eyes?
On what wings dare he aspire?
What the hand, dare seize the fire?

And what shoulder, and what art,
Could twist the sinews of thy heart?   10
And when thy heart began to beat,
What dread hand? and what dread feet?

What the hammer? what the chain?
In what furnace was thy brain?
What the anvil? what dread grasp   15
Dare its deadly terrors clasp?

When the stars threw down their spears,
And watered heaven with their tears,
Did he smile his work to see?
Did he who made the Lamb make thee?   20

Tyger, Tyger, burning bright
In the forests of the night,
What immortal hand or eye
Dare frame thy fearful symmetry?

7 **he:** the one whose "hand or eye" made the tiger   12 **dread hand ... feet:** that would stay to complete the making of the tiger as it came to life   17–18 **stars ... tears:** the surrender of the rebellious angels before the creation of man, or perhaps [Grant] the angelic wars of *Paradise Lost* or *Revelation*.

Ah, Sun-Flower!

Ah, Sun-flower! weary of time,
Who countest the steps of the Sun,
Seeking after that sweet golden clime
Where the traveller's journey is done;

Where the Youth pined away with desire,
And the pale Virgin shrouded in snow,
Arise from their graves, and aspire
Where my Sun-flower wishes to go.

1789–1794. Ibid.

See Additional Notes, p. 764.

The Garden of Love

I went to the Garden of Love,
And saw what I never had seen:
A Chapel was built in the midst,
Where I used to play on the green.

And the gates of this Chapel were shut,   5
And "Thou shalt not" writ over the door;

1789–1794. Ibid.

So I turned to the Garden of Love,
That so many sweet flowers bore;

And I saw it was filled with graves,
And tomb-stones where flowers should be;   10
And Priests in black gowns were walking their rounds,
And binding with briars my joys and desires.

The Sick Rose

O Rose, thou art sick.
The invisible worm
That flies in the night,
In the howling storm,

Has found out thy bed
Of crimson joy:
And his dark secret love
Does thy life destroy.

1789–1794. Ibid.

See Additional Notes, p. 764.

London

I wander through each chartered street,
Near where the chartered Thames does flow,
And mark in every face I meet
Marks of weakness, marks of woe.

In every cry of every Man,   5
In every Infant's cry of fear,
In every voice, in every ban,
The mind-forged manacles I hear.

How the Chimney-sweeper's cry
Every blackening Church appals;   10
And the hapless Soldier's sigh
Runs in blood down Palace walls.

But most through midnight streets I hear
How the youthful Harlot's curse
Blasts the new born Infant's tear,   15
And blights with plagues the Marriage hearse.

1789–1794. Ibid.

The imagery of this poem concentrates many of the things Blake thought wrong with the society of his time: rampant commercialism, man's own self-defeating dogmas and prejudices, child labor, war, ecclesiastical and political tyranny, and the bondage of matrimony and the evils of prostitution.

1–2 **chartered:** Originally a *charter* (as in the Great Charter or Magna Carta) granted liberties or privileges to the people, but by Blake's time the word also meant "hired out." He means that everything in London, even the river, is for hire or already belongs to a specially privileged group. 7 **ban:** (1) a summoning to arms; (2) a proclamation of marriage; (3) an ecclesiastical denunciation or curse; (4) a prohibition   8 **mind-forged manacles:** restraints on liberty imposed by man's own mistaken ways of thinking   9 **Chimney-sweeper:** Very young boys were used in the sooty work of cleaning chimneys.   13–16 Blake was against marriage as a form of restraint that he thought led to prostitution and the social evils that resulted from it.

A Poison Tree

I was angry with my friend:
I told my wrath, my wrath did end.
I was angry with my foe:
I told it not, my wrath did grow.

And I watered it in fears,   5
Night and morning with my tears;
And I sunnèd it with smiles,
And with soft deceitful wiles.

And it grew both day and night,
Till it bore an apple bright;   10
And my foe beheld it shine,
And he knew that it was mine,

And into my garden stole,
When the night had veiled the pole:
In the morning glad I see   15
My foe outstretched beneath the tree.

1789–1794 Ibid.

And Did Those Feet in Ancient Time

And did those feet in ancient time
Walk upon England's mountains green?
And was the holy Lamb of God
On England's pleasant pastures seen?

And did the Countenance Divine   5
Shine forth upon our clouded hills?
And was Jerusalem builded here
Among these dark Satanic Mills?

Bring me my Bow of burning gold:
Bring me my Arrows of desire: 10
Bring me my Spear: O clouds, unfold!
Bring me my Chariot of fire.

I will not cease from Mental Fight,
Nor shall my Sword sleep in my hand,
Till we have built Jerusalem   15
In England's green and pleasant Land.

c. 1804. *Milton,* dated 1804 (but produced c. 1807–1809?). Only four copies exist.

1 **those feet:** those of Christ, present in England in the days of its original innocence, which Blake, as an inspired bard, is working to restore   8 **Mills:** A later reference in "Milton" to the "Starry Mills of Satan" beneath the earth shows that Blake has more in mind than the growth of industrialism. 9–12 **Bow ... fire:** accouterments of the inspired poet, the chariot perhaps suggested by the one seen by the prophet in Ezek. 1.

Mock On, Mock On, Voltaire, Rousseau

Mock on, mock on, Voltaire, Rousseau:
Mock on, mock on: 'tis all in vain!
You throw the sand against the wind,
And the wind blows it back again.

And every sand becomes a Gem 5
Reflected in the beams divine;
Blown back they blind the mocking Eye,
But still in Israel's paths they shine.

The Atoms of Democritus
And Newton's particles of light 10
Are sands upon the Red Sea shore,
Where Israel's tents do shine so bright.

c. 1803. Note-Book (c. 1800–1803). Unpunctuated. Called the "Rossetti MS." because owned by D. G. Rossetti, it was published in facsimile by D. V. Erdman and D. K. Moore (1973; 1977).

1 **Voltaire, Rousseau:** Though admired by Blake from their revolutionary ardor, they are derided here as irreligious.   9 **Democritus:** the Greek philosopher who held that matter was made up of particles or atoms   10 **Newton:** In Newton's theory, light consisted of particles—hence, he too is seen as a materialist.   11 **Red Sea shore:** The children of Israel were encamped by there when the pursuing Egyptians caught up with them.

Epilogue *to* The Gates of Paradise

To the Accuser Who is the God of this World

Truly, My Satan, thou art but a Dunce,
And dost not know the Garment from the Man.
Every Harlot was a Virgin once,
Nor canst thou ever change Kate into Nan.

Though thou art Worshipped by the Names Divine
Of Jesus and Jehovah, thou art still
The Son of Morn in weary Night's decline,
The lost Traveller's Dream under the Hill.

c. 1818. *For the Sexes: The Gates of Paradise*, 1793–1818. Unpunctuated.

The Accuser: a false view of God as jealous tyrant who accuses man for his failings and demands atonement; Blake's name for this distortion is "Satan."   1 The line is suggested by Edward Young, *Night Thoughts*, VIII, 1417: "Satan, thy master, I dare call a dunce. . . ." Blake did engravings for Young's poem.   3 Cf. Blake's "Jerusalem," chap. 3, plate 61, line 52: "Every Harlot was once a Virgin: every Criminal an Infant Love. . . ."   8 **the lost Traveller:** man, whose dream, or delusion, is Satan **the Hill:** True spiritual revelations are often made on high places (cf. Moses on Sinai).

Robert Burns
(1759–1796)

Burns was the son of a Scottish farmer whose struggle against poverty made the poet sensitive to social injustice. No mere plowboy poet, he knew some French and Latin and had read the poets from Shakespeare on with careful attention to technique. His first book made him a celebrity at 27; a few years later he was relieved from the hardships of farming by being given a post with the excise service (like our internal revenue department). He busied himself too as collector, retoucher, and composer of Scottish songs. The strain of his early years probably led to the heart disease of which he died in his thirties.

To a Mouse

On Turning Her Up in Her Nest, With the Plough,
November, 1785

Wee, sleeket, cowran, timorous beastie,
Oh what a panic's in thy breastie!
Thou need na start awa sae hasty,
      Wi' bickering brattle!
I wad be laith to rin an' chase thee,   5
      Wi' murdering pattle!

I'm truly sorry Man's dominion
Has broken Nature's social union,
An' justifies that ill opinion,
      Which makes thee startle,   10
At me, thy poor, earth-born companion,
      An' fellow-mortal!

I doubt na, whyles, but thou may thieve;
What then? poor beastie, thou maun live!
A daimen-icker in a thrave   15
      'S a sma' request:
I'll get a blessin wi' the lave,
      And never miss't!

Thy wee-bit housie, too, in ruin!
It's silly wa's the win's are strewin!   20
An' naething, now, to big a new ane,
      O' foggage green!
An' bleak December's winds ensuin,
      Baith snell an' keen!

Thou saw the fields laid bare an' wast,   25
An' weary winter comin fast,
An' cozie here, beneath the blast,
      Thou thought to dwell,
Till crash! the cruel coulter passed
      Out thro' thy cell.   30

That wee-bit heap o' leaves an' stibble,
Has cost thee monie a weary nibble!
Now thou's turned out, for a' thy trouble,
      But house or hald,
To thole the winter's sleety dribble,   35
      And cranreuch cauld!

But, mousie, thou art no thy-lane,
In proving foresight may be vain:

1785. *Poems, Chiefly in the Scottish Dialect*, 1786 (Kilmarnock).

For the *Burns stanza*, see the section on prosody.

1 **sleeket:** smooth, glossy **cowran:** cowering 3 **na...awa sae:** not...away so 4 **bickering brattle:** scurrying hurry 5 **wad be laith:** would be loath **rin:** run 6 **pattle:** spade 13 **whyles:** sometimes 14 **maun:** must 15 **daimen-icker:** occasional ear of corn **thrave:** two piles of corn 16 **sma':** small 17 **lave:** rest 20 **wa's:** walls **win's:** winds 21 **big:** build **ane:** one 22 **foggage:** rank grass 24 **baith snell:** both bitter 29 **coulter:** plowshare 31 **stibble:** stubble 32 **monie:** many 34 **but:** without **hald:** home 35 **thole:** endure 36 **cranreuch:** frost 37 **thy-lane:** alone, by yourself

The best laid schemes o' mice an' men,
  Gang aft agley,   40
An' lea'e us nought but grief an' pain,
  For promised joy!

Still, thou art blest, compared wi' me!
The present only toucheth thee:
But och! I backward cast my e'e,   45
  On prospects drear!
And forward, tho' I canna see,
  I guess and fear!

---

40 **gang aft agley:** go often awry 41 **lea'e:** leave 45 **e'e:** eye

A Red, Red Rose

Oh my love's like a red, red rose
  That's newly sprung in June;
Oh my love's like the melody
  That's sweetly played in tune.

As fair art thou, my bonnie lass,   5
  So deep in love am I;
And I will love thee still, my dear,
  Till a' the seas gang dry.

Till a' the seas gang dry, my dear,
  And the rocks melt wi' the sun: 10
I will love thee still, my dear,
  While the sands o' life shall run.

And fare thee weel, my only love!
  And fare thee weel, a while!
And I will come again, my love,   15
  Tho' it were ten thousand mile!

By 1794. *The Scots Musical Museum*, V, 1796.

8 **a':** all **gang:** go 13 **weel:** well

Oh Wert Thou in the Cauld Blast

Oh wert thou in the cauld blast,
  On yonder lea, on yonder lea,
My plaidie to the angry airt,
  I'd shelter thee, I'd shelter thee;
Or did misfortune's bitter storms   5
  Around thee blaw, around thee blaw,
Thy bield should be my bosom,
  To share it a', to share it a'.

Or were I in the wildest waste,
  Sae black and bare, sae black and bare, 10

1796. *Collected Works*, 2nd ed., ed. J. Currie, 1801.

1 **cauld:** cold 2 **lea:** meadow 3 **plaidie:** long piece of woollen cloth used as cloak **airt:** direction 6 **blaw:** blow 7 **bield:** shelter, cover

The desert were a paradise,
    If thou wert there, if thou wert there.
Or were I monarch o' the globe,
    Wi' thee to reign, wi' thee to reign,
The brightest jewel in my crown,   15
    Wad be my queen, wad be my queen.

William Wordsworth
(1770–1850)

Wordsworth's mother died when he was 8, his father when he was 13; much alone in youth, he turned to Nature, and also to poetry, for comfort. Finding life at Cambridge restrictive, he was an indifferent student. Sympathy with the revolutionary changes in France took him there in 1791; he fell in love with a French girl; their daughter was born in 1792. Events separated the parents: out of money, Wordsworth had to return to England; a few weeks later a 20-years war broke out between the two countries. In 1895 Wordsworth and his devoted sister Dorothy met Coleridge; for some years the three were close, with the two men collaborating on the *Lyrical Ballads* of 1798. In 1802 Wordsworth married an old school friend; they had three children. Most of the poet's best work was done by 1806; for his last 37 years he lived quietly at Rydal Mount, near his birthplace in northwestern England.

Lines Written a Few Miles Above Tintern Abbey

*On Revisiting the Banks of the Wye During a Tour,
July 13, 1798*

Five years have passed; five summers, with the length
Of five long winters! and again I hear
These waters, rolling from their mountain-springs
With a sweet inland murmur.—Once again
Do I behold these steep and lofty cliffs,   5
Which on a wild secluded scene impress
Thoughts of more deep seclusion; and connect
The landscape with the quiet of the sky.
The day is come when I again repose
Here, under this dark sycamore, and view   10
These plots of cottage-ground, these orchard-tufts,
Which, at this season, with their unripe fruits,
Among the woods and copses lose themselves,
Nor, with their green and simple hue, disturb
The wild green landscape. Once again I see   15
These hedge-rows, hardly hedge-rows, little lines
Of sportive wood run wild; these pastoral farms
Green to the very door; and wreathes of smoke
Sent up, in silence, from among the trees,
With some uncertain notice, as might seem,   20
Of vagrant dwellers in the houseless woods,
Or of some hermit's cave, where by his fire
The hermit sits alone.

                     Those beauteous forms,
Through a long absence, have not been to me
As is a landscape to a blind man's eye: 25
But oft, in lonely rooms, and mid the din

1798. *Lyrical Ballads*, 1798.

Tintern Abbey: a picturesque ruined medieval abbey on the river Wye near the southern border of Wales   13 **copses:** coppices, thickets of small trees

Of towns and cities, I have owed to them,
In hours of weariness, sensations sweet,
Felt in the blood, and felt along the heart,
And passing even into my purer mind   30
With tranquil restoration:—feelings too
Of unremembered pleasure; such, perhaps,
As may have had no trivial influence
On that best portion of a good man's life;
His little, nameless, unremembered acts   35
Of kindness and of love. Nor less, I trust,
To them I may have owed another gift,
Of aspect more sublime; that blessed mood,
In which the burthen of the mystery,
In which the heavy and the weary weight   40
Of all this unintelligible world
Is lightened:—that serene and blessed mood,
In which the affections gently lead us on,
Until, the breath of this corporeal frame,
And even the motion of our human blood   45
Almost suspended, we are laid asleep
In body, and become a living soul:
While with an eye made quiet by the power
Of harmony, and the deep power of joy,
We see into the life of things.

                              If this   50
Be but a vain belief, yet, oh! how oft,
In darkness, and amid the many shapes
Of joyless day-light; when the fretful stir
Unprofitable, and the fever of the world,
Have hung upon the beatings of my heart,   55
How oft, in spirit, have I turned to thee
O sylvan Wye! Thou wanderer through the woods,
How often has my spirit turned to thee!

And now, with gleams of half-extinguished thought,
With many recognitions dim and faint,   60
And somewhat of a sad perplexity,
The picture of the mind revives again:
While here I stand, not only with the sense
Of present pleasure, but with pleasing thoughts
That in this moment there is life and food   65
For future years. And so I dare to hope
Though changed, no doubt, from what I was, when first
I came among these hills; when like a roe
I bounded o'er the mountains, by the sides
Of the deep rivers, and the lonely streams,   70
Wherever nature led; more like a man
Flying from something that he dreads, than one
Who sought the thing he loved. For nature then
(The coarser pleasures of my boyish days,
And their glad animal movements all gone by,)   75
To me was all in all.—I cannot paint
What then I was. The sounding cataract
Haunted me like a passion: the tall rock,
The mountain, and the deep and gloomy wood,

68 **roe:** kind of deer

Their colours and their forms, were then to me   80
An appetite: a feeling and a love,
That had no need of a remoter charm,
By thought supplied, or any interest
Unborrowed from the eye.—That time is past,
And all its aching joys are now no more,   85
And all its dizzy raptures. Not for this
Faint I, nor mourn nor murmur: other gifts
Have followed, for such loss, I would believe,
Abundant recompence. For I have learned
To look on nature, not as in the hour   90
Of thoughtless youth, but hearing oftentimes
The still, sad music of humanity,
Not harsh nor grating, though of ample power
To chasten and subdue. And I have felt
A presence that disturbs me with the joy   95
Of elevated thoughts; a sense sublime
Of something far more deeply interfused,
Whose dwelling is the light of setting suns,
And the round ocean, and the living air,
And the blue sky, and in the mind of man,   100
A motion and a spirit, that impels
All thinking things, all objects of all thought,
And rolls through all things. Therefore am I still
A lover of the meadows and the woods,
And mountains; and of all that we behold   105
From this green earth; of all the mighty world
Of eye and ear, both what they half-create,
And what perceive; well pleased to recognize
In nature and the language of the sense,
The anchor of my purest thoughts, the nurse,   110
The guide, the guardian of my heart, and soul
Of all my moral being.
                         Nor, perchance,
If I were not thus taught, should I the more
Suffer my genial spirits to decay:
For thou art with me, here, upon the banks   115
Of this fair river; thou, my dearest friend,
My dear, dear friend, and in thy voice I catch
The language of my former heart, and read
My former pleasures in the shooting lights
Of thy wild eyes. Oh! yet a little while   120
May I behold in thee what I was once,
My dear, dear sister! And this prayer I make,
Knowing that Nature never did betray
The heart that loved her, 'tis her privilege,
Through all the years of this our life, to lead   125
From joy to joy: for she can so inform
The mind that is within us, so impress
With quietness and beauty, and so feed
With lofty thoughts, that neither evil tongues,
Rash judgments, nor the sneers of selfish men,   130
Nor greetings where no kindness is, nor all

---

87 **faint:** weaken 109 **sense:** senses 114 **genial spirits:** natural energies, cheerful nature (Milton's Samson feels his "genial spirits droop") 116 **friend:** His sister Dorothy, a year or two younger, a close and sympathetic companion, had been with Wordsworth on his earlier visit. He feels she has retained a freshness he has lost in the five intervening years. 126 **inform:** form

The dreary intercourse of daily life,
Shall e'er prevail against us, or disturb
Our cheerful faith that all which we behold
Is full of blessings. Therefore let the moon   135
Shine on thee in thy solitary walk;
And let the misty mountain winds be free
To blow against thee: and in after years,
When these wild ecstasies shall be matured
Into a sober pleasure, when thy mind   140
Shall be a mansion for all lovely forms,
Thy memory be as a dwelling-place
For all sweet sounds and harmonies; Oh! then,
If solitude, or fear, or pain, or grief,
Should be thy portion, with what healing thoughts   145
Of tender joy wilt thou remember me,
And these my exhortations! Nor, perchance,
If I should be, where I no more can hear
Thy voice, nor catch from thy wild eyes these gleams
Of past existence, wilt thou then forget   150
That on the banks of this delightful stream
We stood together; and that I, so long
A worshipper of Nature, hither came,
Unwearied in that service: rather say
With warmer love, oh! with far deeper zeal   155
Of holier love. Nor wilt thou then forget,
That after many wanderings, many years
Of absence, these steep woods and lofty cliffs,
And this green pastoral landscape, were to me
More dear, both for themselves, and for thy sake.   160

She Dwelt Among the Untrodden Ways

She dwelt among the untrodden ways
    Beside the springs of Dove,
A maid whom there were none to praise
    And very few to love:

A violet by a mossy stone   5
    Half hidden from the eye!
Fair as a star, when only one
    Is shining in the sky.

She lived unknown, and few could know
    When Lucy ceased to be;   10
But she is in her grave, and oh,
    The difference to me!

1799. *Lyrical Ballads,* 1800.

2 **Dove:** There are several streams of that name in England; it is not certain which (if any) Wordsworth had in mind.   10 **Lucy:** unidentified

A Slumber Did My Spirit Seal

A slumber did my spirit seal;
    I had no human fears:

1799. Ibid.

She seemed a thing that could not feel
    The touch of earthly years.

No motion has she now, no force;
    She neither hears nor sees;
Rolled round in earth's diurnal course,
    With rocks, and stones, and trees.

Three Years She Grew in Sun and Shower

Three years she grew in sun and shower;
Then Nature said, "A lovelier flower
    On earth was never sown;
This child I to myself will take;
She shall be mine, and I will make   5
    A lady of my own.

"Myself will to my darling be
Both law and impulse: and with me
    The girl, in rock and plain,
In earth and heaven, in glade and bower,   10
Shall feel an overseeing power
    To kindle or restrain.

"She shall be sportive as the fawn
That wild with glee across the lawn
    Or up the mountain springs;   15
And hers shall be the breathing balm,
And hers the silence and the calm
    Of mute insensate things.

"The floating clouds their state shall lend
To her; for her the willow bend;   20
    Nor shall she fail to see
Even in the motions of the storm
Grace that shall mould the maiden's form
    By silent sympathy.

"The stars of midnight shall be dear   25
To her; and she shall lean her ear
    In many a secret place
Where rivulets dance their wayward round,
And beauty born of murmuring sound
    Shall pass into her face.   30

"And vital feelings of delight
Shall rear her form to stately height,
    Her virgin bosom swell;
Such thoughts to Lucy I will give
While she and I together live   35
    Here in this happy dell."

Thus Nature spake—The work was done—
How soon my Lucy's race was run!

1799. Ibid.

She died, and left to me
This heath, this calm and quiet scene;   40
The memory of what has been,
    And never more will be.

The World Is Too Much with Us

The world is too much with us; late and soon,
Getting and spending, we lay waste our powers:
Little we see in Nature that is ours;
We have given our hearts away, a sordid boon!
This sea that bares her bosom to the moon;   5
The winds that will be howling at all hours,
And are up-gathered now like sleeping flowers;
For this, for everything, we are out of tune;
It moves us not.—Great God! I'd rather be
A pagan suckled in a creed outworn;   10
So might I, standing on this pleasant lea,
Have glimpses that would make me less forlorn;
Have sight of Proteus rising from the sea;
Or hear old Triton blow his wreathèd horn.

---

c. 1802. *Poems in Two Volumes*, 1807.

4 boon: gift   **13 Proteus:** in Greek mythology, a sea-god   **14 Triton:** another Greek sea-god, often represented as using a large seashell as trumpet

Resolution and Independence

There was a roaring in the wind all night;
The rain came heavily and fell in floods;
But now the sun is rising calm and bright;
The birds are singing in the distant woods;
Over his own sweet voice the stock-dove broods;   5
The jay makes answer as the magpie chatters;
And all the air is filled with pleasant noise of waters.

All things that love the sun are out of doors;
The sky rejoices in the morning's birth;
The grass is bright with rain-drops;—on the moors   10
The hare is running races in her mirth;
And with her feet she from the plashy earth
Raises a mist; that, glittering in the sun,
Runs with her all the way, wherever she doth run.

I was a traveller then upon the moor;   15
I saw the hare that raced about with joy;
I heard the woods and distant waters roar;

1802. Ibid. (with later revisions).

See Additional Notes, p. 764. In October 1800 William Wordsworth and his sister met an old man who had been a leech-gatherer (the blood-sucking wormlike leeches were much used by physicians; it was thought beneficial to reduce the blood supply in the sick). The two were impressed by the courage and dignity of one who had seen so much adversity. The old man was in Wordsworth's mind for a year and a half before he wrote the poem. Wordsworth said that poetry is "the spontaneous overflow of powerful feelings," but he added that the emotion had to be "contemplated" and "recollected in tranquillity."

5 stock-dove: wild pigeon   **6 magpie:** a noisy bird like a jay   **12 plashy:** drenched, puddly

Or heard them not, as happy as a boy:
The pleasant season did my heart employ:
My old remembrances went from me wholly;   20
And all the ways of men, so vain and melancholy.

But, as it sometimes chanceth, from the might
Of joy in minds that can no further go,
As high as we have mounted in delight
In our dejection do we sink as low;   25
To me that morning did it happen so;
And fears and fancies thick upon me came;
Dim sadness—and blind thoughts, I knew not, nor could name.

I heard the sky-lark warbling in the sky;
And I bethought me of the playful hare: 30
Even such a happy child of earth am I;
Even as these blissful creatures do I fare;
Far from the world I walk, and from all care;
But there may come another day to me—
Solitude, pain of heart, distress, and poverty.   35

My whole life I have lived in pleasant thought,
As if life's business were a summer mood;
As if all needful things would come unsought
To genial faith, still rich in genial good;
But how can he expect that others should   40
Build for him, sow for him, and at his call
Love him, who for himself will take no heed at all?

I thought of Chatterton, the marvellous boy,
The sleepless soul that perished in his pride;
Of him who walked in glory and in joy   45
Following his plough, along the mountainside:
By our own spirits are we deified:
We poets in our youth begin in gladness;
But thereof come in the end despondency and madness.

Now, whether it were by peculiar grace,   50
A leading from above, a something given,
Yet it befell that, in this lonely place,
When I with these untoward thoughts had striven,
Beside a pool bare to the eye of heaven
I saw a man before me unawares: 55
The oldest man he seemed that ever wore grey hairs.

As a huge stone is sometimes seen to lie
Couched on the bald top of an eminence,
Wonder to all who do the same espy,
By what means it could thither come, and whence;   60
So that it seems a thing endued with sense:
Like a sea-beast crawled forth, that on a shelf
Of rock or sand reposeth, there to sun itself;

22–28 Wordsworth was subject to sudden alternations of exultation and depression.   39 **genial:** inborn (with suggestions of *pleasant, cheerful,* etc.)   43 **Chatterton:** cf. p. 238   45 **him:** Robert Burns (p. 245), whose last years were unhappy

Such seemed this man, not all alive nor dead,
Nor all asleep—in his extreme old age: 65
His body was bent double, feet and head
Coming together in life's pilgrimage;
As if some dire constraint of pain, or rage
Of sickness felt by him in times long past,
A more than human weight upon his frame had cast.   70

Himself he propped, limbs, body, and pale face,
Upon a long grey staff of shaven wood:
And, still as I drew near with gentle pace,
Upon the margin of that moorish flood
Motionless as a cloud the old man stood,   75
That heareth not the loud winds when they call;
And moveth all together, if it move at all.

At length, himself unsettling, he the pond
Stirred with his staff, and fixedly did look
Upon the muddy water, which he conned,   80
As if he had been reading in a book:
And now a stranger's privilege I took;
And, drawing to his side, to him did say,
"This morning gives us promise of a glorious day."

A gentle answer did the old man make,   85
In courteous speech which forth he slowly drew:
And him with further words I thus bespake,
"What occupation do you there pursue?
This is a lonesome place for one like you."
Ere he replied, a flash of mild surprise   90
Broke from the sable orbs of his yet-vivid eyes,

His words came feebly, from a feeble chest,
But each in solemn order followed each,
With something of a lofty utterance dressed—
Choice word and measured phrase, above the reach   95
Of ordinary men; a stately speech;
Such as grave livers do in Scotland use,
Religious men, who give to God and man their dues.

He told, that to these waters he had come
To gather leeches, being old and poor: 100
Employment hazardous and wearisome!
And he had many hardships to endure:
From pond to pond he roamed, from moor to moor;
Housing, with God's good help, by choice or chance;
And in this way he gained an honest maintenance.   105

The old man still stood talking by my side;
But now his voice to me was like a stream
Scarce heard; nor word from word could I divide;
And the whole body of the man did seem
Like one whom I had met with in a dream;   110

---

74 **moorish:** boggy   80 **conned:** studied   97 **grave livers:** men who live seriously, earnestly

Or like a man from some far region sent,
To give me human strength, by apt admonishment.

My former thoughts returned: the fear that kills;
And hope that is unwilling to be fed;
Cold, pain, and labour, and all fleshly ills;   115
And mighty poets in their misery dead.
—Perplexed, and longing to be comforted,
My question eagerly did I renew,
"How is it that you live, and what is it you do?"

He with a smile did then his words repeat;   120
And said that, gathering leeches, far and wide
He travelled; stirring thus about his feet
The waters of the pools where they abide.
"Once I could meet with them on every side;
But they have dwindled long by slow decay;   125
Yet still I persevere, and find them where I may."

While he was talking thus, the lonely place,
The old man's shape, and speech—all troubled me:
In my mind's eye I seemed to see him pace
About the weary moors continually,   130
Wandering about alone and silently.
While I these thoughts within myself pursued,
He, having made a pause, the same discourse renewed.

And soon with this he other matter blended,
Cheerfully uttered, with demeanour kind,   135
But stately in the main; and when he ended,
I could have laughed myself to scorn to find
In that decrepit man so firm a mind.
"God," said I, "be my help and stay secure;
I'll think of the leech-gatherer on the lonely moor!"   140

119 The poet repeats the question because, lost in his meditations, he has not heard the answer
(though he has summarized it for us two stanzas above). Lewis Carroll makes fun of this repetition in
his parody "The White Knight's Ballad" (p. 428)   122 **about:** One much-used anthology of Words-
worth selections prints "above his feet." Wading barefoot would be a good way of attracting
leeches—but the old man is not that desperate. A manuscript of Wordsworth gives "He gather'd
Leeches, stirring at his feet," but "about" is the word the poet decided on.   125 **decay:** decrease
139 **stay:** support

Composed upon Westminster Bridge

Earth has not anything to show more fair:
Dull would he be of soul who could pass by
A sight so touching in its majesty:
This city now doth, like a garment, wear
The beauty of the morning; silent, bare,   5
Ships, towers, domes, theatres, and temples lie
Open unto the fields, and to the sky;

1802. Ibid.

Wordsworth and his sister crossed this London bridge early one July morning in 1802 on their way to
Calais. Some readers have felt a kind of irony in the fact that the poet describes a city scene with the
kind of rapture generally reserved for rural landscapes.

All bright and glittering in the smokeless air.
Never did sun more beautifully steep
In his first splendour, valley, rock, or hill;   10
Ne'er saw I, never felt, a calm so deep!
The river glideth at his own sweet will:
Dear God! the very houses seem asleep;
And all that mighty heart is lying still!

London, 1802

Milton! thou shouldst be living at this hour:
England hath need of thee: she is a fen
Of stagnant waters: altar, sword, and pen,
Fireside, the heroic wealth of hall and bower,
Have forfeited their ancient English dower   5
Of inward happiness. We are selfish men;
Oh! raise us up, return to us again;
And give us manners, virtue, freedom, power.
Thy soul was like a Star, and dwelt apart;
Thou hadst a voice whose sound was like the sea: 10
Pure as the naked heavens, majestic, free,
So didst thou travel on life's common way,
In cheerful godliness; and yet thy heart
The lowliest duties on herself did lay.

1802. Ibid.

Wordsworth, who himself favored a plain and simple life, was worried in 1802 about the state of England's soul. Land owners and the middle class were prospering as corn prices went up and war profits were being made. His country, he felt, was becoming more and more devoted to materialistic values; it was too rich and living too richly—especially when contrasted with a France impoverished by the Revolution. "Plain living and high thinking are no more," he wrote in another sonnet of 1802.

2 **fen:** swamp

Ode: Intimations of Immortality from Recollections of Early Childhood

> *The child is father of the man;*
> *And I could wish my days to be*
> *Bound each to each by natural piety.*

I

There was a time when meadow, grove, and stream,
The earth, and every common sight,
        To me did seem
    Apparelled in celestial light,
The glory and the freshness of a dream.   5
It is not now as it hath been of yore;—
        Turn whereso'er I may,
            By night or day,
The things which I have seen I now can see no more.

1802–1804. Ibid. (with later revisions).

See Additional Notes (p. 764). Wordsworth likes to use capital letters with nouns he especially respects: Rose, Moon, Beast, Child, Pansy, Boy, Bird, and so forth. These have been demoted as distracting and overly solemn to the modern eye. The three-line epigraph is from the little poem "My Heart Leaps Up," which Wordsworth wrote the day before beginning the *Ode*.

II

The rainbow comes and goes,　　　　　　　　　　　10
　And lovely is the rose;
　The moon doth with delight
Look round her when the heavens are bare;
　Waters on a starry night
　Are beautiful and fair;　　　　　　　　　　　15
The sunshine is a glorious birth;
But yet I know, where'er I go,
That there hath passed away a glory from the earth.

III

Now, while the birds thus sing a joyous song,
　And while the young lambs bound　　　　　　　20
　　As to the tabor's sound,
To me alone there came a thought of grief:
A timely utterance gave that thought relief,
　And I again am strong:
The cataracts blow their trumpets from the steep;　　25
No more shall grief of mine the season wrong;
I hear the echoes through the mountains throng,
The winds come to me from the fields of sleep,
　And all the earth is gay;
　　　Land and sea　　　　　　　　　　　30
　Give themselves up to jollity,
　　And with the heart of May
Doth every beast keep holiday;—
　　Thou child of joy,
Shout round me, let me hear thy shouts, thou happy shepherd-boy!　35

IV

Ye blessed creatures, I have heard the call
　Ye to each other make; I see
The heavens laugh with you in your jubilee;
　My heart is at your festival,
　My head hath its coronal,　　　　　　　　40
The fullness of your bliss, I feel—I feel it all.
　O evil day! if I were sullen
　While earth herself is adorning,
　　This sweet May-morning,
　And the children are culling　　　　　　　45
　　On every side,
　In a thousand valleys far and wide,
　Fresh flowers; while the sun shines warm,
And the babe leaps up on his mother's arm:—
　I hear, I hear, with joy I hear!　　　　　　50
　—But there's a tree, of many, one,
A single field which I have looked upon,
Both of them speak of something that is gone:
　The pansy at my feet
　Doth the same tale repeat:　　　　　　　55
Whither is fled the visionary gleam?
Where is it now, the glory and the dream?

---

21 **tabor:** small drum　23 **timely utterance:** probably the writing of "My Heart Leaps Up"　40 **coronal:** a festive wreath—probably just figurative　57 For a long time Wordsworth found himself unable to answer these questions. Two years went by before he resumed work on the poem. When he did, he invoked the theory of the preexistence of the soul: the belief, held by Plato and others, that we

V

Our birth is but a sleep and a forgetting:
The soul that rises with us, our life's star,
      Hath had elsewhere its setting,   60
      And cometh from afar:
    Not in entire forgetfulness,
    And not in utter nakedness,
But trailing clouds of glory do we come
      From God, who is our home: 65
Heaven lies about us in our infancy!
Shades of the prison-house begin to close
      Upon the growing boy,
        But he
Beholds the light, and whence it flows,   70
      He sees it in his joy;
The youth, who daily farther from the east
    Must travel, still is Nature's priest,
      And by the vision splendid
      Is on his way attended;   75
At length the man perceives it die away,
And fade into the light of common day.

VI

Earth fills her lap with pleasures of her own;
    Yearnings she hath in her own natural kind;
And, even with something of a mother's mind,   80
      And no unworthy aim,
    The homely nurse doth all she can
To make her foster-child, her inmate man,
    Forget the glories he hath known,
And that imperial palace whence he came.   85

VII

Behold the child among his new-born blisses,
A six years' darling of a pigmy size!
See, where 'mid work of his own hand he lies,
Fretted by sallies of his mother's kisses,
With light upon him from his father's eyes!   90
See, at his feet, some little plan or chart,
Some fragment from his dream of human life,
Shaped by himself with newly-learnèd art;
    A wedding or a festival,
    A mourning or a funeral;   95
      And this hath now his heart,
    And unto this he frames his song:
      Then will he fit his tongue
To dialogues of business, love, or strife;
      But it will not be long   100
      Ere this be thrown aside,
      And with new joy and pride
The little actor cons another part;

---

are born into this world after a glorious existence in a spiritual realm of which we have inklings in childhood but forget as this world closes in around us. Wordsworth admitted he was not really a proponent of such a belief, but only "took hold of the notion of pre-existence as having sufficient foundation in humanity for authorizing me to make for my purpose the best use of it I could as a Poet."
69 But he: printing this as a separate line is a MS. correction Wordsworth made; it gives the missing rhyme for *infancy* three lines above.   **82 homely:** plain, simple, kind

Filling from time to time his "humorous stage"
With all the persons, down to palsied age,   105
That life brings with her in her equipage;
      As if his whole vocation
      Were endless imitation.

VIII

Thou, whose exterior semblance doth belie
      Thy soul's immensity;   110
Thou best philosopher, who yet dost keep
Thy heritage, thou eye among the blind,
That, deaf and silent, read'st the eternal deep,
Haunted for ever by the eternal mind,—
      Mighty prophet! Seer blest!   115
      On whom those truths do rest,
Which we are toiling all our lives to find,
In darkness lost, the darkness of the grave;
Thou, over whom thy immortality
Broods like the day, a master o'er a slave,   120
A presence which is not to be put by;
Thou little child, yet glorious in the might
Of heaven-born freedom on thy being's height,
Why with such earnest pains dost thou provoke
The years to bring the inevitable yoke,   125
Thus blindly with thy blessedness at strife?
Full soon thy soul shall have her earthly freight,
And custom lie upon thee with a weight,
Heavy as frost, and deep almost as life!

IX

      O joy! that in our embers   130
      Is something that doth live,
      That nature yet remembers
      What was so fugitive!
The thought of our past years in me doth breed
Perpetual benediction: not indeed   135
For that which is most worthy to be blest—
Delight and liberty, the simple creed
Of childhood, whether busy or at rest,
With new-fledged hope still fluttering in his breast:—
      Not for these I raise   140
      The song of thanks and praise;
    But for those obstinate questionings
    Of sense and outward things,
    Fallings from us, vanishings;
    Blank misgivings of a creature   145
Moving about in worlds not realized,

104 **"humorous stage"**: from Samuel Daniel's dedicatory sonnet to Fulke Greville in *Musophilus*. "Humorous" plays were those in which the characters were shown possessed by a dominant "humor": disposition, temperament, eccentricity, etc. 109 **Thou**: the child 109-121 Wordsworth's friend Coleridge objected to this exaltation of the child ("best philosopher," "Mighty prophet! Seer blest!") as an example of "thoughts and images too great for the subject." If Wordsworth means that the child shares in divinity, said Coleridge, the words would make as much sense "of a *bee*, or a *dog*, or a *field of corn* . . ." (*Biog. Lit.*, XXII). 142-144 **questionings . . . vanishings:** Wordsworth at some periods would be so "rapt into an unreal transcendental world of ideas that the external world seemed no longer to exist . . ." and he would have to grasp some object, a tree or fence perhaps, to convince himself that the physical world was there.

High instincts before which our mortal Nature
Did tremble like a guilty thing surprised:
  But for those first affections,
  Those shadowy recollections,   150
 Which, be they what they may,
Are yet the fountain-light of all our day,
Are yet a master-light of all our seeing;
 Uphold us, cherish, and have power to make
Our noisy years seem moments in the being   155
Of the eternal silence: truths that wake,
  To perish never:
Which neither listlessness, nor mad endeavour,
  Nor man nor boy,
Nor all that is at enmity with joy,   160
Can utterly abolish or destroy!
  Hence in a season of calm weather
  Though inland far we be,
Our souls have sight of that immortal sea
  Which brought us hither,   165
  Can in a moment travel thither,
And see the children sport upon the shore,
And hear the mighty waters rolling evermore.

     X
Then sing, ye birds, sing, sing a joyous song!
  And let the young lambs bound   170
  As to the tabor's sound!
We in thought will join your throng,
 Ye that pipe and ye that play,
 Ye that through your hearts today
 Feel the gladness of the May!   175
What though the radiance which was once so bright
Be now for ever taken from my sight,
  Though nothing can bring back the hour
Of splendour in the grass, of glory in the flower;
  We will grieve not, rather find   180
  Strength in what remains behind;
  In the primal sympathy
  Which having been must ever be;
  In the soothing thoughts that spring
  Out of human suffering;   185
  In the faith that looks through death,
In years that bring the philosophic mind.

     XI
And O ye fountains, meadows, hills, and groves,
Forbode not any severing of our loves!
Yet in my heart of hearts I feel your might; 190
I only have relinquished one delight
To live beneath your more habitual sway.
I love the brooks which down their channels fret,
Even more than when I tripped lightly as they;
The innocent brightness of a new-born day 195
  Is lovely yet;
The clouds that gather round the setting sun
Do take a sober colouring from an eye

That hath kept watch o'er man's mortality;
Another race hath been, and other palms are won.   200
Thanks to the human heart by which we live,
Thanks to its tenderness, its joys, and fears,
To me the meanest flower that blows can give
Thoughts that do often lie too deep for tears.

200 **palms:** palm leaves, symbols of victory   203 **meanest:** plainest, most ordinary

Surprised by Joy — Impatient as the Wind

Surprised by joy—impatient as the wind
I turned to share the transport—Oh, with whom
But thee, deep buried in the silent tomb,
That spot which no vicissitude can find?
Love, faithful love, recalled thee to my mind—   5
But how could I forget thee? Through what power,
Even for the least division of an hour,
Have I been so beguiled as to be blind
To my most grievous loss!—That thought's return
Was the worst pang that sorrow ever bore,   10
Save one, one only, when I stood forlorn,
Knowing my heart's best treasure was no more;
That neither present time, nor years unborn
Could to my sight that heavenly face restore.

1812–1815. *Poems,* 2 vols., 1815 (with two words changed in later versions).

3 **thee:** Wordsworth's second daughter, Catherine, born September 6, 1808, died June 5, 1812.

The Solitary Reaper

Behold her, single in the field,
Yon solitary Highland lass!
Reaping and singing by herself;
Stop here, or gently pass!
Alone she cuts and binds the grain,   5
And sings a melancholy strain;
O listen! for the vale profound
Is overflowing with the sound.

No nightingale did ever chaunt
More welcome notes to weary bands   10
Of travellers in some shady haunt,
Among Arabian sands:
A voice so thrilling ne'er was heard
In spring-time from the cuckoo-bird,
Breaking the silence of the seas   15
Among the farthest Hebrides.

1805. *Poems in Two Volumes,* 1807.

Wordsworth had travelled in Scotland a couple of years before he wrote this poem, and no doubt saw solitary reapers, but the poem was suggested, as he acknowledged, by a sentence in Thomas Wilkinson's *Tour in Scotland,* which he read in manuscript: "Passed by a female who was reaping alone, she sung in Erse as she bended over her sickle, the sweetest human voice I ever heard. Her strains were tenderly melancholy, and felt delicious long after they were heard no more."

16 **Hebrides:** islands off the western coast of Scotland

Will no one tell me what she sings?—
Perhaps the plaintive numbers flow
For old, unhappy, far-off things,
And battles long ago: 20
Or is it some more humble lay,
Familiar matter of to-day?
Some natural sorrow, loss, or pain,
That has been, and may be again?

Whate'er the theme, the maiden sang   25
As if her song could have no ending;
I saw her singing at her work,
And o'er the sickle bending;—
I listened, motionless and still;
And, as I mounted up the hill,   30
The music in my heart I bore,
Long after it was heard no more.

From **The River Duddon**

Return

A dark plume fetch me from yon blasted yew,
Perched on whose top the Danish Raven croaks;
Aloft, the imperial Bird of Rome invokes
Departed ages, shedding where he flew
Loose fragments of wild wailing, that bestrew   5
The clouds and thrill the chambers of the rocks;
And into silence hush the timorous flocks,
That, calmly couching while the nightly dew
Moistened each fleece, beneath the twinkling stars
Slept amid that lone Camp on Hardknot's height,   10
Whose guardians bent the knee to Jove and Mars:
Or near that mystic round of Druid frame
Tardily sinking by its proper weight
Deep into patient earth, from whose smooth breast it came!

1818–1819. *Miscellaneous Poems*, III, 1820.

The Duddon was a river in the Lake District of western England which Wordsworth had known from his childhood on. "Return" is from a series of 34 sonnets, most of them written in 1818–1819.

2 the Danish Raven: The raven was an emblem of the Danes who, beginning about the year 800, invaded and colonized parts of Britain.   **3 the imperial Bird of Rome:** The eagle, a symbol of power, majesty, military might, and empire among many people, was an emblem of the Roman Empire, and particularly of their legions. The Romans ruled over much of Britain for about 400 years, leaving in the first half of the fifth century. Wordsworth is referring to actual eagles living in the vicinity of the Duddon.   **10 Camp on Hardknot's height:** remains of a Roman *castrum* (fort) over Hardknot Pass in the Duddon Valley   **11 Jove and Mars:** the chief Roman god and his son, the god of war   **12 mystic round:** Many circles of huge upright stones are to be found in Britain and elsewhere. They date from about the time of Stonehenge (the most famous of the stone circles), which was begun about 1800 B.C. Though it has been thought their purpose was astronomical, it seems likelier they served as holy places for the celebration of birth and death rituals.   **Druid:** The Druids were a mysterious order of priest-magicians among the Celts in Gaul and Britain. First mentioned by Caesar, they came into existence centuries after the stone circles were built.

From **The Prelude**

From Book I

Fair seed-time had my soul, and I grew up
Fostered alike by beauty and by fear:
Much favoured in my birthplace, and no less
In that belovèd Vale to which erelong
We were transplanted—there were we let loose   305
For sports of wider range. Ere I had told
Ten birth-days, when among the mountain-slopes
Frost, and the breath of frosty wind, had snapped
The last autumnal crocus, 'twas my joy
With store of springes o'er my shoulder hung   310
To range the open heights where woodcocks run
Among the smooth green turf. Through half the night,
Scudding away from snare to snare, I plied
That anxious visitation;—moon and stars
Were shining o'er my head. I was alone,   315
And seemed to be a trouble to the peace
That dwelt among them. Sometimes it befell
In these night wanderings, that a strong desire
O'erpowered my better reason, and the bird
Which was the captive of another's toil   320
Became my prey; and when the deed was done
I heard among the solitary hills
Low breathings coming after me, and sounds
Of undistinguishable motion, steps
Almost as silent as the turf they trod.   325

Nor less when spring had warmed the cultured Vale,
Moved we as plunderers where the mother-bird
Had in high places built her lodge; though mean
Our object and inglorious, yet the end
Was not ignoble. Oh! when I have hung   330
Above the raven's nest, by knots of grass
And half-inch fissures in the slippery rock
But ill sustained, and almost (so it seemed)
Suspended by the blast that blew amain,
Shouldering the naked crag, oh, at that time   335
While on the perilous ridge I hung alone,
With what strange utterance did the loud dry wind

1798–1800.

Wordsworth stated that he wrote "The Prelude"—which was subtitled "Growth of a Poet's Mind"—
between 1799 and 1805. In the poem, which he thought of as written for Coleridge, he reflects on the
important experiences of his life: his childhood and the effect of nature on his spirit; his years at
school; his vacations and walking tour in France and Switzerland; his life in London; his year of resi-
dence in France; his hopes for the French Revolution and his disappointment in its outcome. Think-
ing the poem fell short of what he aspired to, he decided not to publish it in his lifetime. Over 30
years later he was reported working on it six or seven hours a day. The version published in 1850
shows for the most part a stylistic improvement but is often less outspoken in its views than the ver-
sion read to Coleridge over 40 years before. The difference does not greatly affect the selections given
here, which are from the published version.

303 **birthplace:** Cockermouth, in the Lake District in northwestern England   304 **Vale:** the valley of
Esthwaite Water (about 25 miles southeast of Wordsworth's birthplace) where he spent his school-
days   **erelong:** before long   310 **springes:** traps, snares for birds or small game   311 **woodcock:** a
gamebird like the snipe   320 **toil:** perhaps work, effort, though *toil* can also mean "a net to catch
game"   326 **cultured:** cultivated   334 **amain:** with full force

Blow through my ear! the sky seemed not a sky
Of earth—and with what motion moved the clouds!

Dust as we are, the immortal spirit grows   340
Like harmony in music; there is a dark
Inscrutable workmanship that reconciles
Discordant elements, makes them cling together
In one society. How strange that all
The terrors, pains, and early miseries,   345
Regrets, vexations, lassitudes interfused
Within my mind, should e'er have borne a part,
And that a needful part, in making up
The calm existence that is mine when I
Am worthy of myself! Praise to the end!   350
Thanks to the means which Nature deigned to employ;
Whether her fearless visitings, or those
That came with soft alarm, like hurtless light
Opening the peaceful clouds; or she may use
Severer interventions, ministry   355
More palpable, as best might suit her aim.

One summer evening (led by her) I found
A little boat tied to a willow tree
Within a rocky cave, its usual home.
Straight I unloosed her chain, and stepping in   360
Pushed from the shore. It was an act of stealth
And troubled pleasure, nor without the voice
Of mountain-echoes did my boat move on;
Leaving behind her still, on either side,
Small circles glittering idly in the moon,   365
Until they melted all into one track
Of sparkling light. But now, like one who rows,
Proud of his skill, to reach a chosen point
With an unswerving line, I fixed my view
Upon the summit of a craggy ridge,   370
The horizon's utmost boundary; far above
Was nothing but the stars and the grey sky.
She was an elfin pinnace; lustily
I dipped my oars into the silent lake,
And, as I rose upon the stroke, my boat   375
Went heaving through the water like a swan;
When, from behind that craggy steep till then
The horizon's bound, a huge peak, black and huge,
As if with voluntary power instinct
Upreared its head. I struck and struck again,   380
And growing still in stature the grim shape
Towered up between me and the stars, and still,
For so it seemed, with purpose of its own
And measured motion like a living thing,
Strode after me. With trembling oars I turned,   385
And through the silent water stole my way
Back to the covert of the willow tree;
There in her mooring-place I left my bark,—
And through the meadows homeward went, in grave

---

373 **elfin pinnace:** magical little boat—as if made by or for elves   379 **instínct:** (adjective) impelled, infused   388 **bark:** small boat [poetic]

And serious mood; but after I had seen   390
That spectacle, for many days, my brain
Worked with a dim and undetermined sense
Of unknown modes of being; o'er my thoughts
There hung a darkness, call it solitude
Or blank desertion. No familiar shapes   395
Remained, no pleasant images of trees,
Of sea or sky, no colours of green fields;
But huge and mighty forms, that do not live
Like living men, moved slowly through the mind
By day, and were a trouble to my dreams.   400

    Wisdom and Spirit of the universe!
Thou Soul that art the eternity of thought,
That givest to forms and images a breath
And everlasting motion, not in vain
By day or star-light thus from my first dawn   405
Of childhood didst thou interwine for me
The passions that build up our human soul;
Not with the mean and vulgar works of man,
But with high objects, with enduring things—
With life and nature—purifying thus   410
The elements of feeling and of thought,
And sanctifying, by such discipline,
Both pain and fear, until we recognise
A grandeur in the beatings of the heart.
Nor was this fellowship vouchsafed for me   415
With stinted kindness. In November days,
When vapours rolling down the valley made
A lonely scene more lonesome, among woods,
At noon and 'mid the calm of summer nights,
When, by the margin of the trembling lake,   420
Beneath the gloomy hills homeward I went
In solitude, such intercourse was mine;
Mine was it in the fields both day and night,
And by the waters, all the summer long.

    And in the frosty season, when the sun   425
Was set, and visible for many a mile
The cottage windows blazed through twilight gloom,
I heeded not their summons: happy time
It was indeed for all of us—for me
It was a time of rapture! Clear and loud   430
The village clock tolled six,—I wheeled about,
Proud and exulting like an untired horse
That cares not for his home. All shod with steel,
We hissed along the polished ice in games
Confederate, imitative of the chase   435
And woodland pleasures,—the resounding horn,
The pack loud chiming, and the hunted hare.
So through the darkness and the cold we flew,
And not a voice was idle; with the din
Smitten, the precipices rang aloud;   440
The leafless trees and every icy crag
Tinkled like iron; while far distant hills
Into the tumult sent an alien sound

---

435 **confederate:** united, in a band

Of melancholy not unnoticed, while the stars
Eastward were sparkling clear, and in the west   445
The orange sky of evening died away.
Not seldom from the uproar I retired
Into a silent bay, or sportively
Glanced sideway, leaving the tumultuous throng,
To cut across the reflex of a star   450
That fled, and, flying still before me, gleamed
Upon the glassy plain; and oftentimes,
When we had given our bodies to the wind,
And all the shadowy banks on either side
Came sweeping through the darkness, spinning still   455
The rapid line of motion, then at once
Have I, reclining back upon my heels,
Stopped short; yet still the solitary cliffs
Wheeled by me—even as if the earth had rolled
With visible motion her diurnal round!   460
Behind me did they stretch in solemn train,
Feebler and feebler, and I stood and watched
Till all was tranquil as a dreamless sleep.

   Ye Presences of Nature in the sky
And on the earth! Ye Visions of the hills!   465
And Souls of lonely places! can I think
A vulgar hope was yours when ye employed
Such ministry, when ye through many a year
Haunting me thus among my boyish sports,
On caves and trees, upon the woods and hills,   470
Impressed upon all forms the characters
Of danger or desire; and thus did make
The surface of the universal earth
With triumph and delight, with hope and fear,
Work like a sea? . . .   475

449 glanced: slid off, veered   **450 reflex:** reflection

From Book III

The Evangelist St. John my patron was:
Three Gothic courts are his, and in the first
Was my abiding-place, a nook obscure;
Right underneath, the College kitchens made
A humming sound, less tuneable than bees,   50
But hardly less industrious; with shrill notes
Of sharp command and scolding intermixed.
Near me hung Trinity's loquacious clock,
Who never let the quarters, night or day,
Slip by him unproclaimed, and told the hours   55
Twice over with a male and female voice.
Her pealing organ was my neighbor too;
And from my pillow, looking forth by light
Of moon or favoring stars, I could behold

By 1804.

46 Wordsworth attended St. John's College, Cambridge. 50 **tuneable:** tuneful, musical   53 **Trinity:**
Wordsworth's window looked out on Trinity College Chapel.

The antechapel where the statue stood   60
Of Newton with his prism and silent face,
The marble index of a mind for ever
Voyaging through strange seas of Thought, alone. . . .

61 **Newton:** Sir Isaac Newton was a fellow of Trinity College. His experiments with prisms showed
that white light is made up of the colors of the spectrum.

From Book VII

Rise up, thou monstrous ant-hill on the plain
Of a too busy world! Before me flow,   150
Thou endless stream of men and moving things!
Thy everyday appearance, as it strikes—
With wonder heightened, or sublimed by awe—
On strangers, of all ages; the quick dance
Of colors, lights, and forms; the deafening din;   155
The comers and the goers face to face,
Face after face; the string of dazzling wares,
Shop after shop, with symbols, blazoned names,
And all the tradesman's honors overhead:
Here, fronts of houses, like a title-page,   160
With letters huge inscribed from top to toe,
Stationed above the door, like guardian saints;
There, allegoric shapes, female or male,
Or physiognomies of real men,
Land-warriors, kings, or admirals of the sea,   165
Boyle, Shakespeare, Newton, or the attractive head
Of some quack-doctor, famous in his day.

● ● ●

As the black storm upon the mountain top
Sets off the sunbeam in the valley, so   620
That huge fermenting mass of humankind
Serves as a solemn background, or relief,
To single forms and objects, whence they draw,
For feeling and contemplative regard,
More than inherent liveliness and power.   625
How oft, amid those overflowing streets,
Have I gone forward with the crowd, and said
Unto myself, "The face of every one
That passes by me is a mystery!"
Thus have I looked, nor ceased to look, oppressed   630
By thoughts of what and whither, when and how,
Until the shapes before my eyes became
A second-sight procession, such as glides
Over still mountains, or appears in dreams;
And once, far-travelled in such mood, beyond   635
The reach of common indication, lost
Amid the moving pageant, I was smitten
Abruptly, with a view (a sight not rare)

1804.

149 **monstrous ant-hill:** London, where Wordsworth lived for four months after leaving Cambridge
in January 1791   164 **physiognomies:** faces, especially as revealing character   166 **Boyle:** Robert
Boyle (1627–1691), Anglo-Irish physicist and chemist   633 **second-sight:** visionary, hallucinatory, as
if seen by ESP

Of a blind beggar, who, with upright face,
Stood, propped against a wall, upon his chest   640
Wearing a written paper, to explain
His story, whence he came, and who he was.
Caught by the spectacle my mind turned round
As with the might of waters; an apt type
This label seemed of the utmost we can know,   645
Both of ourselves and of the universe;
And, on the shape of that unmoving man,
His steadfast face and sightless eyes, I gazed,
As if admonished from another world.

•   •   •

         . . . From these sights   675
Take one,—that ancient festival, the Fair,
Holden where martyrs suffered in past time,
And named of St. Bartholomew; there, see
A work completed to our hands, that lays,
If any spectacle on earth can do,   680
The whole creative powers of man asleep!—
For once, the Muse's help will we implore,
And she shall lodge us, wafted on her wings,
Above the press and danger of the crowd,
Upon some showman's platform. What a shock   685
For eyes and ears! what anarchy and din,
Barbarian and infernal,—a phantasma,
Monstrous in colour, motion, shape, sight, sound!
Below, the open space, through every nook
Of the wide area, twinkles, is alive   690
With heads; the midway region, and above,
Is thronged with staring pictures and huge scrolls,
Dumb proclamations of the Prodigies;
With chattering monkeys dangling from their poles,
And children whirling in their roundabouts;   695
With those that stretch the neck and strain the eyes,
And crack the voice in rivalship, the crowd
Inviting; with buffoons against buffoons
Grimacing, writhing, screaming,—him who grinds
The hurdy-gurdy, at the fiddle weaves,   700
Rattles the salt-box, thumps the kettle-drum,
And him who at the trumpet puffs his cheeks,
The silver-collared Negro with his timbrel,
Equestrians, tumblers, women, girls, and boys,
Blue-breeched, pink-vested, with high-towering plumes. 705
All moveables of wonder, from all parts,
Are here—Albinos, painted Indians, Dwarfs,
The Horse of knowledge, and the learned Pig,
The Stone-eater, the man that swallows fire,
Giants, Ventriloquists, the Invisible Girl,   710
The Bust that speaks and moves its goggling eyes,
The Wax-work, Clock-work, all the marvellous craft
Of modern Merlins, Wild Beasts, Puppet-shows,

676 **the Fair:** St. Bartholomew's Fair, "Bartlemy Fair," was held in September. Charles Lamb took
Wordsworth and his sister Dorothy there in 1802.   677 **holden:** held   687 **phantasma:** phantom, il-
lusion, hallucination   695 **roundabouts:** merry-go-rounds   701 **salt-box:** a sort of rough rattle
703 **timbrel:** tambourine   713 **Merlins:** Merlin was a magician in the Arthurian legends.

All out-o'-the-way, far-fetched, perverted things,
All freaks of nature, all Promethean thoughts   715
Of man, his dullness, madness, and their feats
All jumbled up together, to compose
A Parliament of Monsters. Tents and Booths
Meanwhile, as if the whole were one vast mill,
Are vomiting, receiving on all sides,   720
Men, women, three-years children, babes in arms.

O blank confusion! true epitome
Of what the mighty city is herself
To thousands upon thousands of her sons,
Living amid the same perpetual whirl   725
Of trivial objects, melted and reduced
To one identity, by differences
That have no law, no meaning, and no end—
Oppression, under which even highest minds
Must labor, whence the strongest are not free. . . .   730

715 **Promethean:** wildly or madly inventive (Prometheus, in Greek mythology, was both trickster
and master craftsman.)

From Book XI

O pleasant exercise of hope and joy!   105
For mighty were the auxiliars which then stood
Upon our side, us who were strong in love!
Bliss was it in that dawn to be alive,
But to be young was very Heaven! O times,
In which the meagre, stale, forbidding ways   110
Of custom, law, and statute, took at once
The attraction of a country in romance!
When Reason seemed the most to assert her rights,
When most intent on making of herself
A prime enchantress—to assist the work,   115
Which then was going forward in her name!
Not favoured spots alone, but the whole Earth,
The beauty wore of promise—that which sets
(As at some moments might not be unfelt
Among the bowers of Paradise itself)   120
The budding rose above the rose full blown.
What temper at the prospect did not wake
To happiness unthought of? The inert
Were roused, and lively natures rapt away!
They who had fed their childhood upon dreams,   125
The play-fellows of fancy, who had made
All powers of swiftness, subtilty, and strength
Their ministers,—who in lordly wise had stirred
Among the grandest objects of the sense,
And dealt with whatsoever they found there   130
As if they had within some lurking right

1804? *The Prelude, or Growth of a Poet's Mind,* 1850.

This passage expresses the exultation and hopeful idealism that Wordsworth shared with many others
toward the beginning of the French Revolution, which seemed to augur a new golden age in which
man, set free from tyranny and oppression, could live in accordance with nature and reason. He was
later disillusioned by the bloody excesses of those who had begun as liberators and reformers.

106 **auxiliars:** helpers   122 **temper:** temperament

To wield it;—they, too, who of gentle mood
Had watched all gentle motions, and to these
Had fitted their own thoughts, schemers more mild,
And in the region of their peaceful selves;—   135
Now was it that *both* found, the meek and lofty
Did both find helpers to their hearts' desire,
And stuff at hand, plastic as they could wish,—
Were called upon to exercise their skill,
Not in Utopia,—subterranean fields,—   140
Or some secreted island, Heaven knows where!
But in the very world, which is the world
Of all of us,—the place where, in the end,
We find our happiness, or not at all. . . .

138 **plastic:** capable of being shaped or molded

Sir Walter Scott
(1771–1832)

Scott, a native of Edinburgh, published a collection of old ballads (from which several in this anthology are derived) and three narrative poems before turning to the series of historical novels that made his reputation.

Madge Wildfire's Death Song

Proud Maisie is in the wood,
    Walking so early;
Sweet Robin sits on the bush,
    Singing so rarely.

"Tell me, thou bonny bird,   5
    When shall I marry me?"
—"When six braw gentlemen
    Kirkward shall carry ye."

"Who makes the bridal bed,
    Birdie, say truly?"   10
—"The grey-headed sexton
    That delves the grave duly.

"The glow-worm o'er grave and stone
    Shall light thee steady;
The owl from the steeple sing   15
    Welcome, proud lady!"

The Heart of Midlothian, 1818.

The song is sung by the "poor maniac" Madge Wildfire on her deathbed (chap. 40).

7 **braw:** brave, good-looking   8 **kirkward:** churchward   12 **delves:** digs

Samuel Taylor Coleridge
(1772–1834)

For all of his brilliance, Coleridge was unlucky in life and had trouble coping with its daily demands. He made plans for a commune in America for married couples, and, apparently to qualify, made an unhappy marriage. He later fell deeply in love, but did not believe in divorce. He suffered from bad health, but the opiate prescribed led him into an addiction he long struggled against. He conceived plans and projects in abundance, but could carry out few of them. Association with Wordsworth (1797–1801) stimulated him to his best poetry, but alongside his friend he felt a sense of failure. Between depressions there were courageous bursts of activity in which he lectured and wrote brilliantly on literature, philosophy, politics, religion. The last 18 years of his life he spent quietly in a London suburb, cared for by a doctor friend and cheered by the admiration of younger writers.

The Rime of the Ancient Mariner

Argument

How a Ship having passed the Line was driven by storms to the cold Country towards the South Pole; and how from thence she made her course to the tropical Latitude of the Great Pacific Ocean; and of the strange things that befell; and in what manner the Ancyent Marinere came back to his own Country.

Part I

An ancient Mariner meeteth three Gallants bidden to a wedding-feast, and detaineth one.	It is an ancient Mariner, And he stoppeth one of three. "By thy long grey beard and glittering eye, Now wherefore stopp'st thou me?

"The Bridegroom's doors are opened wide,   5
And I am next of kin;
The guests are met, the feast is set:
May'st hear the merry din."

He holds him with his skinny hand,
"There was a ship," quoth he.   10
"Hold off! unhand me, grey-beard loon!"
Eftsoons his hand dropt he.

The Wedding-Guest is spellbound by the eye of the old seafaring man, and constrained to hear his tale.	He holds him with his glittering eye— The Wedding-Guest stood still, And listens like a three years' child: 15 The Mariner hath his will.

The Wedding-Guest sat on a stone:
He cannot choose but hear;

1797–1798. *Lyrical Ballads,* 1798; As revised in *Sibylline Leaves,* 1817, and later.

In his *Biographia Literaria* (chap. XIV) Coleridge describes how he and Wordsworth decided to try two different approaches for the volume of *Lyrical Ballads* they published in 1798. Wordsworth was to take subjects from ordinary life and attempt to bring home to readers their novelty, their loveliness and wonder. Coleridge was to take subjects that were supernatural ("or at least romantic") and make them believable by giving the characters the emotions we would expect them to feel if the events were indeed real. In that way Coleridge hoped to procure for imaginary happenings "that willing suspension of disbelief for the moment, which constitutes poetic faith." He was successful with such readers as Charles Lamb, who wrote Wordsworth that he disliked "all the miraculous part of ["The Ancient Mariner"]; but the feelings of the man under the operation of such scenery, dragged me along like [the Pied Piper]." The text we have here is as Coleridge revised it after its original publication in 1798; the marginal comments too were added later. So was a Latin quotation from Thomas Burnet, a seventeenth-century theologian, to the effect that there are more invisible beings in the universe than visible, and that although they are mysterious to us it is good to imagine their "greater and better world," to keep in perspective the narrowness and triviality of our daily life. For years Coleridge had been an avid reader of travel narratives; many of the apparently fantastic details of his poem are remembered from his reading.

argument, 1: the *Line* is the equator   **12 eftsoons:** at once

And thus spake on that ancient man,
The bright-eyed Mariner.   20

"The ship was cheered, the harbour cleared,
Merrily did we drop

The Mariner tells how the ship sailed southward with a good wind and fair weather, till it reached the line.

Below the kirk, below the hill,
Below the lighthouse top.

The Sun came up upon the left,   25
Out of the sea came he!
And he shone bright, and on the right
Went down into the sea.

Higher and higher every day,
Till over the mast at noon—"   30
The Wedding-Guest here beat his breast,
For he heard the loud bassoon.

The Wedding-Guest heareth the bridal music; but the Mariner continueth his tale.

The bride hath paced into the hall,
Red as a rose is she;
Nodding their heads before her goes   35
The merry minstrelsy.

The Wedding-Guest he beat his breast,
Yet he cannot choose but hear;
And thus spake on that ancient man,
The bright-eyed Mariner.   40

The ship driven by a storm toward the south pole.

"And now the STORM-BLAST came, and he
Was tyrannous and strong:
He struck with his o'ertaking wings,
And chased us south along.

With sloping masts and dipping prow,   45
As who pursued with yell and blow
Still treads the shadow of his foe,
And forward bends his head,
The ship drove fast, loud roared the blast,
And southward aye we fled.   50

And now there came both mist and snow,
And it grew wondrous cold:
And ice, mast-high, came floating by,
As green as emerald.

The land of ice, and of fearful sounds where no living thing was to be seen.

And through the drifts the snowy clifts   55
Did send a dismal sheen:
Nor shapes of men nor beasts we ken—
The ice was all between.

The ice was here, the ice was there,
The ice was all around: 60
It cracked and growled, and roared and howled,
Like noises in a swound!

23 **kirk:** church   36 **minstrelsy:** group of musicians   50 **aye:** (pronounced $\bar{a}$) always   55 **drifts:** ice floes   **clifts:** either *cliffs* or *clefts* (crevasses or fissures)   57 **ken:** see   62 **swound:** swoon

Till a great sea-bird, called the Albatross, came through the snow-fog, and was received with great joy and hospitality.	At length did cross an Albatross, Through the fog it came; As if it had been a Christian soul, We hailed it in God's name. 65

It ate the food it ne'er had eat,
And round and round it flew.
The ice did split with a thunder-fit;
The helmsman steered us through!   70

And lo! the Albatross proveth a bird of good omen, and followeth the ship as it returned northward through fog and floating ice.

And a good south wind sprung up behind;
The Albatross did follow,
And every day, for food or play,
Came to the mariners' hollo!

In mist or cloud, on mast or shroud,   75
It perched for vespers nine;
Whiles all the night, through fog-smoke white,
Glimmered the white Moon-shine."

The ancient Mariner inhospitably killeth the pious bird of good omen.

"God save thee, ancient Mariner!
From the fiends, that plague thee thus!—   80
Why look'st thou so?"—"With my cross-bow
I shot the ALBATROSS."

Part II

"The Sun now rose upon the right:
Out of the sea came he,
Still hid in mist, and on the left   85
Went down into the sea.

And the good south wind still blew behind,
But no sweet bird did follow,
Nor any day for food or play
Came to the mariners' hollo!   90

His shipmates cry out against the ancient Mariner, for killing the bird of good luck.

And I had done a hellish thing,
And it would work 'em woe:
For all averred, I had killed the bird
That made the breeze to blow.
Ah wretch! said they, the bird to slay,   95
That made the breeze to blow!

But when the fog cleared off, they justify the same, and thus make themselves accomplices in the crime.

Nor dim nor red, like God's own head,
The glorious Sun uprist:
Then all averred, I had killed the bird
That brought the fog and mist.   100
'Twas right, said they, such birds to slay,
That bring the fog and mist.

The fair breeze continues; the ship enters the Pacific Ocean, and sails northward, even till it reaches the Line.

The fair breeze blew, the white foam flew,
The furrow followed free;
We were the first that ever burst   105
Into that silent sea.

75 **shroud:** rope bracing the mast

Down dropt the breeze, the sails dropt down,
'Twas sad as sad could be;
And we did speak only to break
The silence of the sea!   110

All in a hot and copper sky,
The bloody Sun, at noon,
Right up above the mast did stand,
No bigger than the Moon.

Day after day, day after day,   115
We stuck, nor breath nor motion;
As idle as a painted ship
Upon a painted ocean.

Water, water, everywhere,
And all the boards did shrink;   120
Water, water, everywhere,
Nor any drop to drink.

The very deep did rot: O Christ!
That ever this should be!
Yea, slimy things did crawl with legs   125
Upon the slimy sea.

About, about, in reel and rout
The death-fires danced at night;
The water, like a witch's oils,
Burnt green, and blue and white.   130

And some in dreams assurèd were
Of the Spirit that plagued us so;
Nine fathom deep he had followed us
From the land of mist and snow.

And every tongue, through utter drought,   135
Was withered at the root;
We could not speak, no more than if
We had been choked with soot.

Ah! well-a-day! what evil looks
Had I from old and young!   140
Instead of the cross, the Albatross
About my neck was hung."

Part III

"There passed a weary time. Each throat
Was parched, and glazed each eye.
A weary time! a weary time!   145
How glazed each weary eye,
When looking westward, I beheld
A something in the sky.

The ship hath been suddenly becalmed.

And the Albatross begins to be avenged.

A Spirit had followed them; one of the invisible inhabitants of this planet, neither departed souls nor angels; concerning whom the learned Jew, Josephus, and the Platonic Constantinopolitan, Michael Psellus, may be consulted. They are very numerous, and there is no climate or element without one or more.

The shipmates, in their sore distress, would fain throw the whole guilt on the ancient Mariner: in sign whereof they hang the dead sea-bird round his neck.

The ancient Mariner beholdeth a sign in the element afar off.

128 **death-fires:** eerie lights reported seen in cemeteries and elsewhere. (Some decaying things—flesh included—have a luminous glow.)   129–130 **the water . . . :** Some of the details that seem eeriest in the poem are scientifically sound: certain kinds of sea life are luminous and make the water seem to glow, at times in color.

At first it seemed a little speck,
And then it seemed a mist;   150
It moved and moved, and took at last
A certain shape, I wist.

A speck, a mist, a shape, I wist!
And still it neared and neared:
As if it dodged a water-sprite,   155
It plunged and tacked and veered.

At its nearer approach, it seemeth him to be a ship; and at a dear ransom he freeth his speech from the bonds of thirst.

With throats unslaked, with black lips baked,
We could nor laugh nor wail;
Through utter drought all dumb we stood!
I bit my arm, I sucked the blood,   160
And cried, A sail! a sail!

With throats unslaked, with black lips baked,
Agape they heard me call:

A flash of joy;

Gramercy! they for joy did grin,
And all at once their breath drew in,   165
As they were drinking all.

And horror follows. For can it be a ship that comes onward without wind or tide?

See! see! (I cried) she tacks no more!
Hither to work us weal;
Without a breeze, without a tide,
She steadies with upright keel!   170

The western wave was all a-flame.
The day was well nigh done!
Almost upon the western wave
Rested the broad bright Sun;
When that strange shape drove suddenly   175
Betwixt us and the Sun.

It seemeth him but the skeleton of a ship.

And straight the Sun was flecked with bars,
(Heaven's Mother send us grace!)
As if through a dungeon-grate he peered
With broad and burning face.   180

And its ribs are seen as bars on the face of the setting Sun.

Alas! (thought I, and my heart beat loud)
How fast she nears and nears!
Are those *her* sails that glance in the Sun,
Like restless gossameres?

The Spectre-Woman and her Death-mate, and no other on board the skeleton ship.

Are those *her* ribs through which the Sun   185
Did peer, as through a grate?
And is that Woman all her crew?
Is that a DEATH? and are there two?
Is DEATH that woman's mate?

Like vessel, like crew! Death and Life-in-Death have diced for the ship's crew, and she (the latter) winneth the ancient Mariner.

Her lips were red, *her* looks were free,   190
Her locks were yellow as gold:
Her skin was as white as leprosy,

---

152 **wist:** knew   155 **water-sprite:** a spirit believed to haunt the waters   164 **gramercy:** an exclamation of surprise, like "For heaven's sake!"   168 **weal:** good   184 **gossameres:** *gossamer* is filmy floating cobweb

The Night-mare LIFE-IN-DEATH was she,
Who thicks man's blood with cold.

The naked hulk alongside came,   195
And the twain were casting dice;
'The game is done! I've won! I've won!'
Quoth she, and whistles thrice.

No twilight within the
courts of the Sun.

The Sun's rim dips; the stars rush out:
At one stride comes the dark;   200
With far-heard whisper, o'er the sea,
Off shot the spectre-bark.

At the rising of the
Moon,

We listened and looked sideways up!
Fear at my heart, as at a cup,
My life-blood seemed to sip!   205
The stars were dim, and thick the night,
The steersman's face by his lamp gleamed white;
From the sails the dew did drip—
Till clomb above the eastern bar
The hornèd Moon, with one bright star   210
Within the nether tip.

One after another,

One after one, by the star-dogged Moon,
Too quick for groan or sigh,
Each turned his face with a ghastly pang,
And cursed me with his eye.   215

His shipmates drop
down dead.

Four times fifty living men,
(And I heard nor sigh nor groan)
With heavy thump, a lifeless lump,
They dropped down one by one.

But Life-in-Death begins
her work on the ancient
Mariner.

The souls did from their bodies fly,—   220
They fled to bliss or woe!
And every soul, it passed me by,
Like the whizz of my cross-bow!"

Part IV

The Wedding-Guest
feareth that a Spirit is
talking to him;

"I fear thee, ancient Mariner!
I fear thy skinny hand!   225
And thou art long, and lank, and brown,
As is the ribbed sea-sand.

"I fear thee and thy glittering eye,
And the skinny hand, so brown."—

But the ancient Mariner
assureth him of his
bodily life, and
proceedeth to relate his
horrible penance.

"Fear not, fear not, thou Wedding-Guest!   230
This body dropt not down.

Alone, alone, all, all alone,
Alone on a wide wide sea!
And never a saint took pity on
My soul in agony.   235

---

197 **won:** She has won the lives of the crew—except for the mariner, who lives on to suffer.
211 **within . . . :** A star could not be *within* the tip of the moon; it would be eclipsed by the moon's
dark bulk. But, a scientific commentator has pointed out, in Coleridge's time there were many refer-
ences to strange lights, like stars, seen on the dark area of the moon.

**He despiseth the
creatures of the calm,**

The many men, so beautiful!
And they all dead did lie:
And a thousand thousand slimy things
Lived on; and so did I.

**And envieth that *they*
should live, and so many
lie dead.**

I looked upon the rotting sea,   240
And drew my eyes away;
I looked upon the rotting deck,
And there the dead men lay.

I looked to heaven, and tried to pray;
But or ever a prayer had gushed,   245
A wicked whisper came, and made
My heart as dry as dust.

I closed my lids, and kept them close,
And the balls like pulses beat;
For the sky and the sea, and the sea and the sky   250
Lay like a load on my weary eye,
And the dead were at my feet.

**But the curse liveth for
him in the eye of the
dead men.**

The cold sweat melted from their limbs,
Nor rot nor reek did they:
The look with which they looked on me   255
Had never passed away.

An orphan's curse would drag to hell
A spirit from on high;
But oh! more horrible than that
Is the curse in a dead man's eye!   260
Seven days, seven nights, I saw that curse,
And yet I could not die.

**In his loneliness and
fixedness he yearneth
towards the journeying
Moon, and the stars that
still sojourn, yet still
move onward; and every
where the blue sky
belongs to them, and is
their appointed rest, and
their native country and
their own natural homes,
which they enter
unannounced, as lords
that are certainly
expected and yet there is
a silent joy at their
arrival.**

The moving Moon went up the sky,
And nowhere did abide:
Softly she was going up,   265
And a star or two beside—

Her beams bemocked the sultry main,
Like April hoar-frost spread;
But where the ship's huge shadow lay,
The charmèd water burnt alway   270
A still and awful red.

**By the light of the Moon
he beholdeth God's
creatures of the great
calm.**

Beyond the shadow of the ship,
I watched the water-snakes:
They moved in tracks of shining white,
And when they reared, the elfish light   275
Fell off in hoary flakes.

Within the shadow of the ship
I watched their rich attire:
Blue, glossy green, and velvet black,

---

245 or: ere, before   271 red: not necessarily fantastic; the bioluminescence of some sea life is red.
272, 277 **Beyond . . . Within . . . :** In the moonlight they seem white; in the shadow their luminescent
colors show.

They coiled and swam; and every track   280
Was a flash of golden fire.

Their beauty and their
happiness.

O happy living things! no tongue
Their beauty might declare:
A spring of love gushed from my heart,
And I blessed them unaware: 285

He blesseth them in his
heart.

Sure my kind saint took pity on me,
And I blessed them unaware.

The spell begins to
break.

The self-same moment I could pray;
And from my neck so free
The Albatross fell off, and sank   290
Like lead into the sea."

Part V

"Oh sleep! it is a gentle thing,
Beloved from pole to pole!
To Mary Queen the praise be given!
She sent the gentle sleep from Heaven,   295
That slid into my soul.

By grace of the holy
Mother, the ancient
Mariner is refreshed
with rain.

The silly buckets on the deck,
That had so long remained,
I dreamt that they were filled with dew;
And when I awoke, it rained.   300

My lips were wet, my throat was cold,
My garments all were dank;
Sure I had drunken in my dreams,
And still my body drank.

I moved, and could not feel my limbs: 305
I was so light—almost
I thought that I had died in sleep,
And was a blessèd ghost.

He heareth sounds and
seeth strange sights and
commotions in the sky
and the element.

And soon I heard a roaring wind:
It did not come anear;   310
But with its sound it shook the sails,
That were so thin and sere.

The upper air burst into life!
And a hundred fire-flags sheen.
To and fro they were hurried about!   315
And to and fro, and in and out,
The wan stars danced between.

And the coming wind did roar more loud,
And the sails did sigh like sedge;
And the rain poured down from one black cloud;   320
The Moon was at its edge.

The thick black cloud was cleft, and still
The Moon was at its side:

297 **silly:** simple, innocent   312 **sere:** thin, worn   314 **sheen:** bright, shining

Like waters shot from some high crag,
The lightning fell with never a jag,   325
A river steep and wide.

The loud wind never reached the ship,
Yet now the ship moved on!
Beneath the lightning and the Moon
The dead men gave a groan.   330

They groaned, they stirred, they all uprose,
Nor spake, nor moved their eyes;
It had been strange, even in a dream,
To have seen those dead men rise.

The helmsman steered, the ship moved on;   335
Yet never a breeze up-blew;
The mariners all 'gan work the ropes,
Where they were wont to do;
They raised their limbs like lifeless tools—
We were a ghastly crew.   340

The body of my brother's son
Stood by me, knee to knee:
The body and I pulled at one rope,
But he said nought to me."

"I fear thee, ancient Mariner!"   345
"Be calm, thou Wedding-Guest!
'Twas not those souls that fled in pain,
Which to their corses came again,
But a troop of spirits blest:

For when it dawned—they dropped their arms,   350
And clustered round the mast;
Sweet sounds rose slowly through their mouths,
And from their bodies passed.

Around, around, flew each sweet sound,
Then darted to the Sun;   355
Slowly the sounds came back again,
Now mixed, now one by one.

Sometimes a-dropping from the sky
I heard the sky-lark sing;
Sometimes all little birds that are,   360
How they seemed to fill the sea and air
With their sweet jargoning!

And now 'twas like all instruments,
Now like a lonely flute;
And now it is an angel's song,   365
That makes the heavens be mute.

It ceased; yet still the sails made on
A pleasant noise till noon,
A noise like of a hidden brook

338 **wont:** accustomed 362 **jargoning:** warbling, twittering

In the leafy month of June,   370
That to the sleeping woods all night
Singeth a quiet tune.

Till noon we quietly sailed on,
Yet never a breeze did breathe:
Slowly and smoothly went the ship,   375
Moved onward from beneath.

The lonesome Spirit from the south-pole carries on the ship as far as the Line, in obedience to the angelic troop, but still requireth vengeance.

Under the keel nine fathom deep,
From the land of mist and snow,
The spirit slid: and it was he
That made the ship to go.   380
The sails at noon left off their tune,
And the ship stood still also.

The Sun, right up above the mast,
Had fixed her to the ocean:
But in a minute she 'gan stir,   385
With a short uneasy motion—
Backwards and forwards half her length
With a short uneasy motion.

Then like a pawing horse let go,
She made a sudden bound: 390
It flung the blood into my head,
And I fell down in a swound.

The Polar Spirit's fellow-dæmons, the invisible inhabitants of the element, take part in his wrong; and two of them relate, one to the other, that penance long and heavy for the ancient Mariner hath been accorded to the Polar Spirit, who returneth southward.

How long in that same fit I lay,
I have not to declare;
But ere my living life returned,   395
I heard and in my soul discerned
Two voices in the air.

'Is it he?' quoth one, 'Is this the man?
By him who died on cross,
With his cruel bow he laid full low   400
The harmless Albatross.

The spirit who bideth by himself
In the land of mist and snow,
He loved the bird that loved the man
Who shot him with his bow.'   405

The other was a softer voice,
As soft as honey-dew:
Quoth he, 'The man hath penance done,
And penance more will do.'"

Part VI

First Voice

"'But tell me, tell me! speak again,   410
Thy soft response renewing—
What makes that ship drive on so fast?
What is the ocean doing?'

---

394 **have not:** am unable   407 **honey-dew:** a sweetish secretion on the leaves of plants

Second Voice

'Still as a slave before his lord,
The ocean hath no blast;   415
His great bright eye most silently
Up to the Moon is cast—

If he may know which way to go;
For she guides him smooth or grim.
See, brother, see! how graciously   420
She looketh down on him.'

First Voice

The Mariner hath been
cast into a trance; for the
angelic power causeth
the vessel to drive
northward faster than
human life could
endure.

'But why drives on that ship so fast,
Without or wave or wind?'

Second Voice

'The air is cut away before,
And closes from behind.   425

'Fly, brother, fly! more high, more high!
Or we shall be belated:
For slow and slow that ship will go,
When the Mariner's trance is abated.'

The supernatural motion
is retarded; the Mariner
awakes, and his penance
begins anew.

I woke, and we were sailing on   430
As in a gentle weather:
'Twas night, calm night, the moon was high;
The dead men stood together.

All stood together on the deck,
For a charnel-dungeon fitter: 435
All fixed on me their stony eyes,
That in the Moon did glitter.

The pang, the curse, with which they died,
Had never passed away:
I could not draw my eyes from theirs,   440
Nor turn them up to pray.

The curse is finally
expiated.

And now this spell was snapt: once more
I viewed the ocean green,
And looked far forth, yet little saw
Of what had else been seen—   445

Like one, that on a lonesome road
Doth walk in fear and dread,
And having once turned round walks on,
And turns no more his head;
Because he knows, a frightful fiend   450
Doth close behind him tread.

But soon there breathed a wind on me,
Nor sound nor motion made:
Its path was not upon the sea,
In ripple or in shade.   455

435 **charnel-dungeon:** dungeon where the bodies of the dead are thrown

It raised my hair, it fanned my cheek
Like a meadow-gale of spring—
It mingled strangely with my fears,
Yet it felt like a welcoming.

Swiftly, swiftly flew the ship,   460
Yet she sailed softly too:
Sweetly, sweetly blew the breeze—
On me alone it blew.

And the ancient Mariner
beholdeth his native
country.

Oh! dream of joy! is this indeed
The light-house top I see?   465
Is this the hill? is this the kirk?
Is this mine own countree?

We drifted o'er the harbour-bar,
And I with sobs did pray—
O let me be awake, my God!   470
Or let me sleep alway.

The harbour-bay was clear as glass,
So smoothly it was strewn!
And on the bay the moonlight lay,
And the shadow of the Moon.   475

The rock shone bright, the kirk no less,
That stands above the rock:
The moonlight steeped in silentness
The steady weathercock.

And the bay was white with silent light,   480
Till rising from the same,

The angelic spirits leave
the dead bodies,

Full many shapes, that shadows were,
In crimson colours came.

A little distance from the prow

And appear in their own
forms of light.

Those crimson shadows were: 485
I turned my eyes upon the deck—
Oh, Christ, what saw I there!

Each corse lay flat, lifeless and flat,
And, by the holy rood!
A man all light, a seraph-man,   490
On every corse there stood.

This seraph-band, each waved his hand:
It was a heavenly sight!
They stood as signals to the land,
Each one a lovely light;   495

This seraph-band, each waved his hand,
No voice did they impart—
No voice; but oh! the silence sank
Like music on my heart.

---

473 **strewn:** spread level, calmed   488 **corse:** corpse   489 **rood:** cross   490 **seraph-man:** Seraphs, the highest order of angels, are often depicted as fiery, reddish.

But soon I heard the dash of oars,   500
I heard the Pilot's cheer;
My head was turned perforce away
And I saw a boat appear.

The Pilot and the Pilot's boy,
I heard them coming fast: 505
Dear Lord in Heaven! it was a joy
The dead men could not blast.

I saw a third—I heard his voice:
It is the Hermit good!
He singeth loud his godly hymns   510
That he makes in the wood.
He'll shrieve my soul, he'll wash away
The Albatross's blood."

Part VII

The Hermit of the
Wood,
"This Hermit good lives in that wood
Which slopes down to the sea.   515
How loudly his sweet voice he rears!
He loves to talk with marineres
That come from a far countree.

He kneels at morn, and noon, and eve—
He hath a cushion plump: 520
It is the moss that wholly hides
The rotted old oak-stump.

The skiff-boat neared: I heard them talk,
'Why, this is strange, I trow!
Where are those lights so many and fair,   525
That signal made but now?'

Approacheth the ship
with wonder.
'Strange, by my faith!' the Hermit said—
'And they answered not our cheer!
The planks looked warped! and see those sails,
How thin they are and sere!   530
I never saw aught like to them,
Unless perchance it were

Brown skeletons of leaves that lag
My forest-brook along;
When the ivy-tod is heavy with snow,   535
And the owlet whoops to the wolf below,
That eats the she-wolf's young.'

'Dear Lord! it hath a fiendish look—'
(The Pilot made reply)
'I am a-feared'—'Push on, push on!'   540
Said the Hermit cheerily.

The boat came closer to the ship,
But I nor spake nor stirred;

---

501 **cheer:** cry, halloo 502 **perforce:** by force, irresistibly 512 **shrieve:** absolve 524 **trow:** think,
do believe 535 **tod:** clump 537 **That eats . . . :** Hungry male wolves were thought to eat their cubs.

The boat came close beneath the ship,
And straight a sound was heard.   545

The ship suddenly sinketh.

Under the water it rumbled on,
Still louder and more dread:
It reached the ship, it split the bay;
The ship went down like lead.

The ancient Mariner is saved in the Pilot's boat.

Stunned by that loud and dreadful sound,   550
Which sky and ocean smote,
Like one that hath been seven days drowned
My body lay afloat;
But swift as dreams, myself I found
Within the Pilot's boat.   555

Upon the whirl, where sank the ship,
The boat spun round and round;
And all was still, save that the hill
Was telling of the sound.

I moved my lips—the Pilot shrieked   560
And fell down in a fit;
The holy Hermit raised his eyes,
And prayed where he did sit.

I took the oars: the Pilot's boy,
Who now doth crazy go,   565
Laughed loud and long, and all the while
His eyes went to and fro.
'Ha! ha!' quoth he, 'full plain I see,
The Devil knows how to row.'

And now, all in my own countree,   570
I stood on the firm land!
The Hermit stepped forth from the boat,
And scarcely he could stand.

The ancient Mariner earnestly entreateth the Hermit to shrieve him; and the penance of life falls on him.

'O shrieve me, shrieve me, holy man.'
The Hermit crossed his brow.   575
'Say quick,' quoth he. 'I bid thee say—
What manner of man art thou?'

Forthwith this frame of mine was wrenched
With a woful agony,
Which forced me to begin my tale;   580
And then it left me free.

And ever and anon throughout his future life an agony constraineth him to travel from land to land;

Since then, at an uncertain hour,
That agony returns:
And till my ghastly tale is told,
This heart within me burns.   585

I pass, like night, from land to land;
I have strange power of speech;

---

552 **seven days drowned:** The bodies of the drowned rise to the surface after about a week.
560 **shrieked:** Apparently the Pilot had thought the Mariner was dead.

That moment that his face I see,
I know the man that must hear me:
To him my tale I teach.   590

What loud uproar bursts from that door!
The wedding-guests are there:
But in the garden-bower the bride
And bride-maids singing are:
And hark the little vesper bell,   595
Which biddeth me to prayer!

O Wedding-Guest! this soul hath been
Alone on a wide wide sea:
So lonely 'twas, that God himself
Scarce seemèd there to be.   600

O sweeter than the marriage-feast,
'Tis sweeter far to me,
To walk together to the kirk
With a goodly company!—

To walk together to the kirk,   605
And all together pray,
While each to his great Father bends,
Old men, and babes, and loving friends
And youths and maidens gay!

And to teach, by his own example, love and reverence to all things that God made and loveth.

Farewell, farewell! but this I tell   610
To thee, thou Wedding-Guest!
He prayeth well, who loveth well
Both man and bird and beast.

He prayeth best, who loveth best
All things both great and small;   615
For the dear God who loveth us,
He made and loveth all."

The Mariner, whose eye is bright,
Whose beard with age is hoar,
Is gone: and now the Wedding-Guest   620
Turned from the bridegroom's door.

He went like one that hath been stunned,
And is of sense forlorn:
A sadder and a wiser man,
He rose the morrow morn.   625

623 **forlorn**: bereft

Frost at Midnight

The frost performs its secret ministry,
Unhelped by any wind. The owlet's cry

1798. *Fears in Solitude, . . . France, an Ode; and Frost at Midnight . . .* , 1798 (a pamphlet). Text as in *Sibylline Leaves*, 1817, with later revisions.

This is probably the best of what Coleridge called his "conversation poems." Though he addresses his sleeping child, he is really talking to himself about his past and future life.

Came loud—and hark, again! loud as before.
The inmates of my cottage, all at rest,
Have left me to that solitude, which suits   5
Abstruser musings: save that at my side
My cradled infant slumbers peacefully.
'Tis calm indeed! so calm, that it disturbs
And vexes meditation with its strange
And extreme silentness. Sea, hill, and wood,   10
This populous village! Sea, and hill, and wood,
With all the numberless goings-on of life,
Inaudible as dreams! the thin blue flame
Lies on my low-burnt fire, and quivers not;
Only that film, which fluttered on the grate,   15
Still flutters there, the sole unquiet thing.
Methinks, its motion in this hush of nature
Gives it dim sympathies with me who live,
Making it a companionable form,
Whose puny flaps and freaks the idling spirit   20
By its own moods, interprets, everywhere
Echo or mirror seeking of itself,
And makes a toy of thought.

                                  But O! how oft,
How oft, at school, with most believing mind,
Presageful, have I gazed upon the bars,   25
To watch that fluttering *stranger!* and as oft
With unclosed lids, already had I dreamt
Of my sweet birth-place, and the old church-tower,
Whose bells, the poor man's only music, rang
From morn to evening, all the hot Fair-day,   30
So sweetly, that they stirred and haunted me
With a wild pleasure, falling on mine ear
Most like articulate sounds of things to come!
So gazed I, till the soothing things, I dreamt,
Lulled me to sleep, and sleep prolonged my dreams!   35
And so I brooded all the following morn,
Awed by the stern preceptor's face, mine eye
Fixed with mock study on my swimming book:
Save if the door half opened, and I snatched
A hasty glance, and still my heart leaped up,   40
For still I hoped to see the *stranger's* face,
Townsman, or aunt, or sister more beloved,
My play-mate when we both were clothed alike!

    Dear babe, that sleepest cradled by my side,
Whose gentle breathings, heard in this deep calm,   45
Fill up the interspersèd vacancies
And momentary pauses of the thought!
My babe so beautiful! it thrills my heart
With tender gladness, thus to look at thee,
And think that thou shalt learn far other lore,   50

---

7 **infant:** his son Hartley, born a year and a half before the poem was written   15 **film:** soot on the grate, "supposed to portend the arrival of some absent friend" (Coleridge) and referred to as the *stranger* in lines 26 and 41   24 **school:** at Christ's Hospital, in London   28 **birth-place:** Ottery St. Mary, in the country. His father was rector at the church there.   30 **Fair-day:** market day, often an occasion for pleasure as well as business   37 **preceptor:** James Boyer, of whom Coleridge wrote: "At school I enjoyed the inestimable advantage of a very sensible, though at the same time a very severe master" (*Biog. Lit*, I).   38 **swimming:** seen through blurred vision   43 **play-mate:** his sister Ann **clothed alike:** so young there was no distinction between boy's and girl's clothes

And in far other scenes! For I was reared
In the great city, pent 'mid cloisters dim,
And saw nought lovely but the sky and stars.
But *thou*, my babe! shalt wander like a breeze
By lakes and sandy shores, beneath the crags   55
Of ancient mountain, and beneath the clouds.
Which image in their bulk both lakes and shores
And mountain crags: so shalt thou see and hear
The lovely shapes and sounds intelligible
Of that eternal language, which thy God   60
Utters, who from eternity doth teach
Himself in all, and all things in himself.
Great universal teacher! he shall mould
Thy spirit, and by giving make it ask.

    Therefore all seasons shall be sweet to thee,   65
Whether the summer clothe the general earth
With greenness, or the redbreast sit and sing
Betwixt the tufts of snow on the bare branch
Of mossy apple-tree, while the nigh thatch
Smokes in the sun-thaw; whether the eave-drops fall   70
Heard only in the trances of the blast,
Or if the secret ministry of frost
Shall hang them up in silent icicles,
Quietly shining to the quiet moon.

53 **sky and stars:** At school in London, Coleridge used to lie on the roof to observe the heavens (cf. Wordsworth, *The Prelude*, VI, 267 ff.).   54 **but *thou . . . :*** He plans a country upbringing for his son.
71 **trances of the blast:** times when the wind is quiet

Kubla Khan

In Xanadu did Kubla Khan
A stately pleasure-dome decree:
Where Alph, the sacred river, ran

    1797 or 1798. *Christabel: Kubla Khan . . .* , 1816.

"Kubla Khan," according to Coleridge's account, was given to him in a dream. He was led to publish it, at the request of Lord Byron, "rather as a psychological curiosity, than on the ground of any supposed *poetic* merits." As Coleridge tells the story, he had taken two grains of opium because he was unwell, and had fallen asleep reading a sentence from *Purchas His Pilgrimage,* a compilation of geography, travel, and history first published in 1613. The sentence Coleridge fell asleep over was: "In Xamdu did Cublai Can build a stately Palace, encompassing sixteen miles of plain ground with a wall, wherein are fertile meadows, pleasant springs, delightful streams, and all sorts of beasts of chase and game, and in the middest thereof a sumptuous house of pleasure." He "continued for about three hours in a profound sleep, at least of the external senses, during which time he has the most vivid confidence, that he could not have composed less than from two to three hundred lines; if that indeed can be called composition in which all the images rose up before him as *things,* with a parallel production of the correspondent expressions, without any sensation or consciousness of effort. On awaking he appeared to himself to have a distinct recollection of the whole, and taking his pen, ink, and paper, instantly and eagerly wrote down the lines that are here preserved. At this moment he was unfortunately called out by a person on business from Porlock, and detained by him above an hour, and on his return to his room, found, to his no small surprise and mortification, that though he still retained some vague and dim recollection of the general purport of the vision, yet, with the exception of some eight or ten scattered lines and images, all the rest had passed away like the images on the surface of a stream into which a stone has been cast, but, alas! without the after restoration of the latter!" Besides the sentence from Purchas (pronounced *purkas*), other details from Coleridge's wide reading found their way into the dream-poem and have been identified.

1 **Xanadu:** a more euphonious form of *Xamdu* (or *Xaindu, Xandu*) of Purchas. Kublai Khan, the first Mongol emperor of China (thirteenth century), had his summer capitol there (modern Shang-tu).
3 **Alph:** a name probably suggested by that of the river Alpheus of antiquity, which not only ran unmixed through the sea, but also ran underground at times. Cf. "Lycidas," line 132.

Through caverns measureless to man
   Down to a sunless sea.   5
So twice five miles of fertile ground
With walls and towers were girdled round:
And there were gardens bright with sinuous rills,
Where blossomed many an incense-bearing tree;
And here were forests ancient as the hills,   10
Enfolding sunny spots of greenery.

But oh! that deep romantic chasm which slanted
Down the green hill athwart a cedarn cover!
A savage place! as holy and enchanted
As e'er beneath a waning moon was haunted   15
By woman wailing for her demon-lover!
And from this chasm, with ceaseless turmoil seething,
As if this earth in fast thick pants were breathing,
A mighty fountain momently was forced:
Amid whose swift half-intermitted burst   20
Huge fragments vaulted like rebounding hail,
Or chaffy grain beneath the thresher's flail:
And 'mid these dancing rocks at once and ever
It flung up momently the sacred river.
Five miles meandering with a mazy motion   25
Through wood and dale the sacred river ran,
Then reached the caverns measureless to man,
And sank in tumult to a lifeless ocean:
And 'mid this tumult Kubla heard from far
Ancestral voices prophesying war!   30
   The shadow of the dome of pleasure
   Floated midway on the waves;
   Where was heard the mingled measure
   From the fountain and the caves.
It was a miracle of rare device,   35
A sunny pleasure-dome with caves of ice!

   A damsel with a dulcimer
   In a vision once I saw:
   It was an Abyssinian maid,
   And on her dulcimer she played,   40
   Singing of Mount Abora.
   Could I revive within me
   Her symphony and song,
   To such a deep delight 'twould win me,
That with music loud and long,   45
I would build that dome in air,
That sunny dome! those caves of ice!
And all who heard should see them there,
And all should cry, Beware! Beware!
His flashing eyes, his floating hair!   50
Weave a circle round him thrice,
And close your eyes with holy dread,
For he on honey-dew hath fed,
And drunk the milk of Paradise.

---

8 **rills:** small brooks 13 **athwart:** across 19 **momently:** from moment to moment, every moment
41 **Mount Abora:** probably the Mount Amara in Abyssinia which Milton mentions in *Paradise Lost*,
IV, 281

Walter Savage Landor
(1775–1864)

Landor, who left Oxford after a dispute with the authorities, fought against Napoleon in Spain with troops whose salary he paid himself. In 1814, after a quarrel with neighbors, he left England to spend 20 years in Italy. In 1858, after being convicted of libel, he again left England for Italy, where he spent his last years. Impetuous and hot tempered, Landor was generous, honorable, and devoted to liberty.

Rose Aylmer

Ah what avails the sceptred race!
    Ah what the form divine!
What every virtue, every grace!
    Rose Aylmer, all were thine.

Rose Aylmer, whom these wakeful eyes
    May weep, but never see,
A night of memories and sighs
    I consecrate to thee.

1800. *Simonidea*, 1806. Revised, *Gebir, Count Julian, and Other Poems*, 1831, and in *Works*, 1846.

Landor met Rose Aylmer when she was 18 or 19, he in his early twenties. She died in India two years later. When he died, 64 years after her, a lock of her hair was found in his desk.

1 **the sceptred race:** royalty, nobility. She was the daughter of Lord Aylmer.

On Seeing a Hair of Lucretia Borgia

Borgia, thou once wert almost too august
And high for adoration; now thou'rt dust.
All that remains of thee these plaits unfold—
Calm hair, meandering in pellucid gold.

1823–1825. *Works*, 1846.

Lucretia Borgia: Born in 1480, the daughter of the Spanish cardinal who became Pope Alexander VI, she was a glamorous figure in the political world of her time. By her third marriage she became Duchess of Ferrara, a city that became a center for art and poetry. A lock of her hair was preserved in the Ambrosian Library in Milan. Lord Byron admired it as "the prettiest and fairest imaginable—I never saw fairer...." He is reported to have stolen a single hair—with Pope's line in mind ("The Rape of the Lock," II, 28)—which later inspired Landor's poem.

3 **plaits:** braids (though there was only a single hair)

Past Ruined Ilion Helen Lives

Past ruined Ilion Helen lives,
    Alcestis rises from the shades;
Verse calls them forth; 'tis verse that gives
    Immortal youth to mortal maids.

Gebir, Count Julian, and Other Poems, 1831; *Works*, 1846.

1 **Ilion:** Troy   **Helen:** Helen of Troy   2 **Alcestis:** Cf. Milton, "On His Dead Wife," line 2, p. 146. An inferior third stanza, dropped after the 1831 publication, indicates that the poem was addressed to "Ianthe," Landor's name for Sophia Jane Swift, an Irish girl for whom many of his best poems were written. When Landor met her, she was engaged to another man, whom she married. Later in life, after she had been twice married and twice widowed, they met again.

Soon shall Oblivion's deepening veil
    Hide all the peopled hills you see,
The gay, the proud, while lovers hail
    These many summers you and me.

Dirce

Stand close around, ye Stygian set,
    With Dirce in one boat conveyed!
Or Charon, seeing, may forget
    That he is old and she a shade.

Ibid.

Charon, in Greek mythology, is the aged ferryman who takes the souls of the dead (the "Stygian set")
over the river Styx in the underworld. Dirce is Landor's name for a girl so beautiful that even as a
shade (or ghost) she could arouse an amorous passion in Charon, old as he is.

Remain, Ah Not in Youth Alone

Remain, ah not in youth alone,
    Though youth, where you are, long will stay,
But when my summer days are gone,
    And my autumnal haste away.
"Can I be always by your side?"
    No; but the hours you can, you must,
Nor rise at Death's approaching stride,
    Nor go when dust is gone to dust.

Works, 1846.

Well I Remember How You Smiled

Well I remember how you smiled
    To see me write your name upon
The soft sea-sand . . . "Oh! what a child!
    You think you're writing upon stone!"
I have since written what no tide
    Shall ever wash away, what men
Unborn shall read o'er ocean wide
    And find Ianthe's name again.

Heroic Idylls, with Additional Poems, 1863.

8 **Ianthe:** Cf. note on "Past Ruined Ilion Helen Lives."

Leigh Hunt
(1784–1859)

Hunt worked as a journalist in London, where he and his brother once spent two years in
prison for criticizing the prince regent. As journalist and editor, he favored progressive
causes. Besides his poetry, he wrote essays and novels. He was a friend of many writers
and a shrewd critic of their work.

The Fish, the Man, and the Spirit

To a Fish

You strange, astonished-looking, angle-faced,
   Dreary-mouthed, gaping wretches of the sea,
   Gulping salt-water everlastingly,
Cold-blooded, though with red your blood be graced,
And mute, though dwellers in the roaring waste;   5
   And you, all shapes beside, that fishy be,—
   Some round, some flat, some long, all devilry,
Legless, unloving, infamously chaste:—

O scaly, slippery, wet, swift, staring wights,
   What is't ye do? What life lead? eh, dull goggles?   10
How do ye vary your vile days and nights?
   How pass your Sundays? Are ye still but joggles
In ceaseless wash? Still nought but gapes, and bites,
   And drinks, and stares, diversified with boggles?

A Fish Answers

Amazing monster! that, for aught I know,   15
   With the first sight of thee didst make our race
   For ever stare! O flat and shocking face,
Grimly divided from the breast below!
Thou that on dry land horribly dost go
   With a split body and most ridiculous pace,   20
   Prong after prong, disgracer of all grace,
Long-useless-finned, haired, upright, unwet, slow!

O breather of unbreathable, sword-sharp air,
   How canst exist? How bear thyself, thou dry
And dreary sloth? What particle canst share   25
   Of the only blessed life, the watery?
I sometimes see of ye an actual *pair*
   Go by! linked fin by fin! most odiously.

The Fish Turns into a Man, and Then into a Spirit, and Again Speaks

Indulge thy smiling scorn, if smiling still,
   O man! and loathe, but with a sort of love;   30
   For difference must its use by difference prove,
And, in sweet clang, the spheres with music fill.
One of the spirits am I, that at his will
   Live in whate'er has life—fish, eagle, dove—
   No hate, no pride, beneath nought, nor above,   35
A visitor of the rounds of God's sweet skill.

Man's life is warm, glad, sad, 'twixt loves and graves,
   Boundless in hope, honoured with pangs austere,
Heaven-gazing; and his angel-wings he craves:—
   The fish is swift, small-needing, vague yet clear.   40
A cold, sweet, silver life, wrapped in round waves,
   Quickened with touches of transporting fear.

By 1836. *Poetical Works*, 1844.

9 **wights:** creatures   10 **goggles:** things that squint, gape, roll their eyes, etc.   14 **boggles:** fusses, bothers, bungles

Thomas Love Peacock
(1785–1866)

Largely self-educated, a writer of verse by the time he was 10, Peacock passed nearly all of his working life as an administrator with the East India Company and, after 1836, as its chief examiner. A friend of Shelley and other poets, he wrote mostly novels, in which many of his poems occur as songs.

The War-Song of Dinas Vawr

The mountain sheep are sweeter,
But the valley sheep are fatter;
We therefore deemed it meeter
To carry off the latter.
We made an expedition;   5
We met a host, and quelled it;
We forced a strong position,
And killed the men who held it.

On Dyfed's richest valley,
Where herds of kine were browsing,   10
We made a mighty sally,
To furnish our carousing.
Fierce warriors rushed to meet us;
We met them, and o'erthrew them:
They struggled hard to beat us;   15
But we conquered them, and slew them.

As we drove our prize at leisure,
The king marched forth to catch us:
His rage surpassed all measure,
But his people could not match us.   20
He fled to his hall-pillars;
And, ere our force we led off,
Some sacked his house and cellars,
While others cut his head off.

We there, in strife bewildering,   25
Spilt blood enough to swim in:
We orphaned many children,
And widowed many women.
The eagles and the ravens
We glutted with our foemen;   30
The heroes and the cravens,
The spearmen and the bowmen.

We brought away from battle,
And much their land bemoaned them,
Two thousand head of cattle,   35
And the head of him who owned them:

The Misfortunes of Elphin, 1829.

This ironic exaltation of the glories of war is described in Peacock's novel of medieval Wales as "the quintessence of all the war-songs that ever were written, and the sum and substance of all the appetencies, tendencies, and consequences of military glory." After the song the victorious soldiers, "having sung themselves hoarse with their own praises, subsided one by one into drunken sleep...." Dynas Vawr was a petty king in the time of King Arthur. Dyfed is the old name for a region in Wales.

Ednyfed, king of Dyfed,
His head was borne before us;
His wine and beasts supplied our feasts,
And his overthrow, our chorus.   40

George Gordon, Lord Byron
(1788–1824)

The son of Captain ("Mad Jack") Byron and a Scottish heiress, Byron, though handsome and athletic, was born with a club foot. At 10, he inherited the title and estates of an English great uncle. In college he lived recklessly, but also published, at 18, his first book of poetry. Soon after, he set out for two years of travel in Greece, Albania, and Turkey. His experiences enlivened parts of "Childe Harold's Pilgrimage" (1812), which enjoyed a success as sensational as the author's own personality and his life with its several love affairs—one with his half-sister. A series of romantic "oriental tales" followed; one sold 10,000 copies the day it was published. In 1815 he married a lady who proved too serious for him; a separation was arranged; Byron left England never to return. In Italy he fell in love with the young Countess Guiccioli, with whom he spent the next four years. Her relatives introduced him to secret revolutionary groups; he was watched by the Italian police as a dangerous subversive. In 1823, concerned about the Greek fight for independence from Turkey, he sailed off to give what help he could. He died of a fever the following year in Greece, where he is remembered as a national hero.

The Destruction of Sennacherib

The Assyrian came down like the wolf on the fold,
And his cohorts were gleaming in purple and gold;
And the sheen of their spears was like stars on the sea,
When the blue wave rolls nightly on deep Galilee.

Like the leaves of the forest when summer is green,   5
That host with their banners at sunset were seen:
Like the leaves of the forest when autumn hath blown,
That host on the morrow lay withered and strown.

For the Angel of Death spread his wings on the blast,
And breathed in the face of the foe as he passed;   10
And the eyes of the sleepers waxed deadly and chill,
And their hearts but once heaved—and for ever grew still!

And there lay the steed with his nostril all wide,
But through it there rolled not the breath of his pride;
And the foam of his gasping lay white on the turf,   15
And cold as the spray of the rock-beating surf.

And there lay the rider distorted and pale,
With the dew on his brow, and the rust on his mail;
And the tents were all silent, the banners alone,
The lances unlifted, the trumpet unblown.   20

1815. *Hebrew Melodies*, 1815.

Byron's poem is suggested by 2 Kings 19, which tells how Sennacherib, King of Assyria, is about to attack the people of Israel. "And it came to pass that night, that the angel of the LORD went out, and smote in the camp of the Assyrians an hundred fourscore and five thousand: and when they arose early in the morning, behold, they all were dead corpses. So Sennacherib king of Assyria departed. . . ."

And the widows of Ashur are loud in their wail,
And the idols are broke in the temple of Baal;
And the might of the Gentile, unsmote by the sword,
Hath melted like snow in the glance of the Lord!

21 Ashur: Asshur (so spelled) was the national god of the Assyrians, but Byron may be using the word to mean Assyria.   **22 Baal:** The god generally referred to in the Old Testament by that name is Phoenician, not Assyrian. Byron probably used the name to stand for any anti-Israel deity.

Stanzas for Music

There's not a joy the world can give like that it takes away,
When the glow of early thought declines in feeling's dull decay;
'Tis not on youth's smooth cheek the blush alone, which fades so fast,
But the tender bloom of heart is gone, ere youth itself be past.

Then the few whose spirits float above the wreck of happiness   5
Are driven o'er the shoals of guilt or ocean of excess:
The magnet of their course is gone, or only points in vain
The shore to which their shivered sail shall never stretch again.

Then the mortal coldness of the soul like death itself comes down;
It cannot feel for others' woes, it dare not dream its own;   10
That heavy chill has frozen o'er the fountain of our tears,
And though the eye may sparkle still, 'tis where the ice appears.

Though wit may flash from fluent lips, and mirth distract the breast,
Through midnight hours that yield no more their former hope of rest;
'Tis but as ivy-leaves around the ruined turret wreath,   15
All green and wildly fresh without, but worn and grey beneath.

Oh could I feel as I have felt,—or be what I have been,
Or weep as I could once have wept, o'er many a vanished scene:
As springs in deserts found seem sweet, all brackish though they be,
So, midst the withered waste of life, those tears would flow to me.   20

1815. *Poems,* 1816.

About a year after he wrote these lines, Byron called them "the *truest,* though the most melancholy" he had yet written.

So We'll Go No More A-Roving

So we'll go no more a-roving
    So late into the night,
Though the heart be still as loving,
    And the moon be still as bright.

For the sword outwears its sheath,   5
    And the soul wears out the breast,
And the heart must pause to breathe,
    And love itself have rest.

1817. *Letters and Journals of Lord Byron,* 1830.

Byron sent this poem from Venice in a letter to Thomas Moore in February, 1817, telling Moore that the Carnival had just ended and that he was exhausted from the late nights, etc. He added that he found "the sword wearing out the scabbard," though he had just turned 29.

Though the night was made for loving,
    And the day returns too soon,
Yet we'll go no more a-roving
    By the light of the moon.   10

From **Don Juan**

From Canto the Second

CIV

The shore looked wild, without a trace of man,
    And girt by formidable waves; but they
Were mad for land, and thus their course they ran,
    Though right ahead the roaring breakers lay: 835
A reef between them also now began
    To show its boiling surf and bounding spray,
But finding no place for their landing better,
They ran the boat for shore—and overset her.

CV

But in his native stream, the Guadalquivir,   840
    Juan to lave his youthful limbs was wont;
And having learnt to swim in that sweet river,
    Had often turned the art to some account:
A better swimmer you could scarce see ever,
    He could, perhaps, have passed the Hellespont,   845
As once (a feat on which ourselves we prided)
Leander, Mr. Ekenhead, and I did.

CVI

So here, though faint, emaciated, and stark,
    He buoyed his boyish limbs, and strove to ply
With the quick wave, and gain, ere it was dark,   850
    The beach which lay before him, high and dry:
The greatest danger here was from a shark,
    That carried off his neighbour by the thigh;

1818–1819. *Don Juan* (cantos I and II), 1819. With MS. readings from E. H. Coleridge's edition of the *Works* (1898–1904).

The narrative in Byron's masterpiece follows, through 16 cantos, the travels and adventures in love and war of young Don Juan (a name Byron pronounced not in the Spanish way but as *jôo-un*, as his rhymes on it make clear). Byron uses his narrative to make fun of the pretensions and hypocrisies of society by his irreverent comments on the manners and customs of different nations and classes. In "Canto the First" we are told that Don Juan has been educated (under the supervision of his culture-loving mother) in several sciences and, with the help of expurgated classics, in several languages. At the age of 16 he is introduced to the pains and pleasures of first love by a beautiful lady in her early twenties. Discovered by her husband in the lady's chamber, he is sent abroad on his travels. In "Canto the Second" his ship is sunk in a storm and most of the crew lost; a few survive (with recourse to cannibalism) in an open boat. We join the last four as land is sighted.

840 **Guadalquivir:** the river that flows through Seville, where Don Juan was born. The accent is properly on the last syllable, but Byron pronounces it to rhyme with *river*.   845 **the Hellespont:** the strait between the Sea of Marmara and the Aegean Sea, now called the Dardanelles. In May of 1810 Byron and Marine Lieutenant Ekenhead swam from Sestos on the European side to Abydos on the Asian side. The distance was only about a mile, but, in cold water and against a dangerous current, they swam some four miles during the hour and ten minutes they were in the water. Leander, as Ovid tells the story in his *Heroides*, was the young Greek who swam the Hellespont nightly to visit Hero, whom he loved; he drowned one stormy night when the torch with which she guided him was blown out.

As for the other two, they could not swim,
So nobody arrived on shore but him. . . .   855

CVIII

There, breathless, with his digging nails he clung
    Fast to the sand, lest the returning wave,   865
From whose reluctant roar his life he wrung,
    Should suck him back to her insatiate grave:
And there he lay, full length, where he was flung,
    Before the entrance of a cliff-worn cave,
With just enough of life to feel its pain,   870
And deem that it was saved, perhaps, in vain. . . .

CXII

His eyes he opened, shut, again unclosed,
    For all was doubt and dizziness; he thought
He still was in the boat, and had but dozed,
    And felt again with his despair o'erwrought,
And wished it death in which he had reposed,   900
    And then once more his feelings back were brought,
And slowly by his swimming eyes was seen
A lovely female face of seventeen.

CXIII

'Twas bending close o'er his, and the small mouth
    Seemed almost prying into his for breath;   905
And chafing him, the soft warm hand of youth
    Recalled his answering spirits back from death:
And, bathing his chill temples, tried to soothe
    Each pulse to animation, till beneath
Its gentle touch and trembling care, a sigh   910
To these kind efforts made a low reply. . . .

CXV

And lifting him with care into the cave,   920
    The gentle girl, and her attendant—one
Young, yet her elder, and of brow less grave,
    And more robust of figure—then begun
To kindle fire, and as the new flames gave
    Light to the rocks that roofed them, which the sun   925
Had never seen, the maid, or whatsoe'er
She was, appeared, distinct, and tall, and fair.

CXVI

Her brow was overhung with coins of gold,
    That sparkled o'er the auburn of her hair—
Her clustering hair, whose longer locks were rolled   930
    In braids behind; and though her stature were
Even of the highest for a female mould,
    They nearly reached her heel; and in her air
There was a something which bespoke command,
As one who was a Lady in the land. . . .   935

CXVIII

Her brow was white and low, her cheek's pure dye
    Like twilight rosy still with the set sun;   945
Short upper lip—sweet lips! that make us sigh

Ever to have seen such; for she was one
Fit for the model of a statuary
    (A race of mere impostors, when all's done—
I've seen much finer women, ripe and real,   950
Than all the nonsense of their stone ideal). . . .

CXX

And such was she, the lady of the cave: 960
    Her dress was very different from the Spanish,
Simpler, and yet of colours not so grave;
    For, as you know, the Spanish women banish
Bright hues when out of doors, and yet, while wave
    Around them (what I hope will never vanish)   965
The basquiña and the mantilla, they
Seem at the same time mystical and gay.

CXXI

But with our damsel this was not the case:
    Her dress was many-coloured, finely spun;
Her locks curled negligently round her face,   970
    But through them gold and gems profusely shone:
Her girdle sparkled, and the richest lace
    Flowed in her veil, and many a precious stone
Flashed on her little hand; but, what was shocking,
Her small snow feet had slippers, but no stocking. . . .   975

CXXIII

And these two tended him, and cheered him both
    With food and raiment, and those soft attentions,   985
Which are—as I must own—of female growth,
    And have ten thousand delicate inventions:
They made a most superior mess of broth,
    A thing which poesy but seldom mentions,
But the best dish that e'er was cooked since Homer's   990
Achilles ordered dinner for new comers.

CXXIV

I'll tell you who they were, this female pair,
    Lest they should seem Princesses in disguise;
Besides, I hate all mystery, and that air
    Of clap-trap, which your recent poets prize;   995
And so, in short, the girls they really were
    They shall appear before your curious eyes,
Mistress and maid; the first was only daughter
Of an old man, who lived upon the water.

CXXV

A fisherman he had been in his youth,   1000
    And still a sort of fisherman was he;
But other speculations were, in sooth,
    Added to his connection with the sea,
Perhaps not so respectable, in truth:
    A little smuggling, and some piracy,   1005

---

966 **basquiña:** a skirt, generally black, for street wear   **mantilla:** a light scarf worn over the head and shoulders   991 **Achilles ordered dinner:** When Ajax, Odysseus, and a couple of others came to Achilles to try to reconcile him with Agamemnon, Achilles served mutton, goat, and pork roasted over an open fire, baskets of good bread, and cups of wine (*Iliad*, IX, 202 ff.).   1002 **sooth:** truth

Left him, at last, the sole of many masters
Of an ill-gotten million of piastres. . . .   1007

CXXVIII

He had an only daughter, called Haidee,
    The greatest heiress of the Eastern Isles;   1025
Besides, so very beautiful was she,
    Her dowry was as nothing to her smiles:
Still in her teens, and like a lovely tree
    She grew to womanhood, and between whiles
Rejected several suitors, just to learn   1030
How to accept a better in his turn.

CXXIX

And walking out upon the beach, below
    The cliff, towards sunset, on that day she found,
Insensible—not dead, but nearly so—
    Don Juan, almost famished, and half drowned;   1035
But being naked, she was shocked, you know,
    Yet deemed herself in common pity bound,
As far as in her lay, "to take him in,
A stranger" dying—with so white a skin. . . .

CXXXVI

And pensive to her father's house she went,
    Enjoining silence strict to Zoe, who
Better than her knew what, in fact, she meant,   1090
    She being wiser by a year or two:
A year or two's an age when rightly spent,
    And Zoe spent hers, as most women do,
In gaining all that useful sort of knowledge
Which is acquired in nature's good old college.   1095

CXXXVII

The morn broke, and found Juan slumbering still
    Fast in his cave, and nothing clashed upon
His rest; the rushing of the neighbouring rill,
    And the young beams of the excluded sun,
Troubled him not, and he might sleep his fill;   1100
    And need he had of slumber yet, for none
Had suffered more—his hardships were comparative
To those related in my grand-dad's "Narrative."

CXXXVIII

Not so Haidee; she sadly tossed and tumbled,
    And started from her sleep, and, turning o'er,   1105
Dreamed of a thousand wrecks, o'er which she stumbled,
    And handsome corpses strewed upon the shore;

1007 **piastres:** units of Turkish currency—Turkey then controlled Greece.   1024 **Haidee:** The name
(rhyming with *she* and *tree* and written without an accent mark over the first *e* in the first edition) oc-
curs in a popular Greek song which Byron heard often in the winter of 1810-1811 in Athens. His
poem "Translation of the Romaic Song" is an English version of it.   1038-1039 **"to take him in . . .":**
Cf. Matt. 25:35: "I was a stranger, and ye took me in."   1088 **pensive . . . :** An irreverent echo of the
last line of Milton's *Paradise Regained?*—"Home to his mother's house private returned" [our Savior].
1089 **Zoe:** (pronounced *Zô-ay*) the attendant of line 921   1102 **comparative:** comparable
1103 **grand-dad's "Narrative":** Admiral John Byron, 1723-1786, known as "Foulweather Jack," was
shipwrecked when 18 on the coast of Patagonia, near the southern tip of South America. In 1768 he
published the "Narrative" of his "great distresses," which included starvation and imprisonment.

And woke her maid so early that she grumbled,
　　And called her father's old slaves up, who swore
In several oaths—Armenian, Turk, and Greek—　　　　　　　　　　1110
They knew not what to think of such a freak. . . .

CXLII

And down the cliff the island virgin came,
　　And near the cave her quick light footsteps drew,
While the sun smiled on her with his first flame,
　　And young Aurora kissed her lips with dew,
Taking her for a sister; just the same　　　　　　　　　　　　1140
　　Mistake you would have made on seeing the two,
Although the mortal, quite as fresh and fair,
Had all the advantage, too, of not being air.

CXLIII

And when into the cavern Haidee stepped
　　All timidly, yet rapidly, she saw　　　　　　　　　　　　　1145
That like an infant Juan sweetly slept;
　　And then she stopped, and stood as if in awe
(For sleep is awful), and on tiptoe crept
　　And wrapped him closer, lest the air, too raw,
Should reach his blood, then o'er him still as death　　　　　1150
Bent, with hushed lips, that drank his scarce-drawn breath.

CXLIV

And thus like to an angel o'er the dying
　　Who die in righteousness, she leaned; and there
All tranquilly the shipwrecked boy was lying,
　　As o'er him lay the calm and stirless air:　　　　　　　　　1155
But Zoe the meantime some eggs was frying,
　　Since, after all, no doubt the youthful pair
Must breakfast—and, betimes, lest they should ask it,
She drew out her provision from the basket.

CXLV

She knew that the best feelings must have victual,　　　　　　1160
　　And that a shipwrecked youth would hungry be;
Besides, being less in love, she yawned a little,
　　And felt her veins chilled by the neighbouring sea;
And so, she cooked their breakfast to a tittle;
　　I can't say that she gave them any tea,　　　　　　　　　　1165
But there were eggs, fruit, coffee, bread, fish, honey,
With Scio wine—and all for love, not money. . . .

CLVIII

He ate, and he was well supplied; and she,
　　Who watched him like a mother, would have fed　　　　　　1265
Him past all bounds, because she smiled to see
　　Such appetite in one she had deemed dead:
But Zoe, being older than Haidee,
　　Knew (by tradition, for she ne'er had read)
That famished people must be slowly nurst,　　　　　　　　　1270
And fed by spoonfuls, else they always burst.

1111 **freak:** odd, unusual behavior   1139 **Aurora:** goddess of the dawn   1148 **awful:** inspiring
awe   1158 **betimes:** in good time   1164 **to a tittle:** to a T; to perfection   1167 **Scio:** the Italian form
of Chios, name of a Greek island famous for its wine

CLIX

And so she took the liberty to state,
　　Rather by deeds than words, because the case
Was urgent, that the gentleman, whose fate
　　Had made her mistress quit her bed to trace　　　　1275
The sea-shore at this hour, must leave his plate,
　　Unless he wished to die upon the place—
She snatched it, and refused another morsel,
Saying, he had gorged enough to make a horse ill.

CLX

Next they—he being naked, save a tattered　　　　1280
　　Pair of scarce decent trousers—went to work,
And in the fire his recent rags they scattered,
　　And dressed him, for the present, like a Turk,
Or Greek—that is, although it not much mattered,
　　Omitting turban, slippers, pistol, dirk—　　　　1285
They furnished him, entire, except some stitches,
With a clean shirt, and very spacious breeches.

CLXI

And then fair Haidee tried her tongue at speaking,
　　But not a word could Juan comprehend,
Although he listened so that the young Greek in　　　　1290
　　Her earnestness would ne'er have made an end;
And, as he interrupted not, went eking
　　Her speech out to her protégé and friend,
Till pausing at the last her breath to take,
She saw he did not understand Romaic.　　　　1295

CLXII

And then she had recourse to nods, and signs,
　　And smiles, and sparkles of the speaking eye,
And read (the only book she could) the lines
　　Of his fair face, and found, by sympathy,
The answer eloquent, where the soul shines　　　　1300
　　And darts in one quick glance a long reply;
And thus in every look she saw expressed
A world of words, and things at which she guessed.

CLXIII

And now, by dint of fingers and of eyes,
　　And words repeated after her, he took　　　　1305
A lesson in her tongue; but by surmise,
　　No doubt, less of her language than her look:
As he who studies fervently the skies
　　Turns oftener to the stars than to his book,
Thus Juan learned his *alpha beta* better　　　　1310
From Haidee's glance than any graven letter.

CLXIV

'Tis pleasing to be schooled in a strange tongue
　　By female lips and eyes—that is, I mean,
When both the teacher and the taught are young,

1285 **dirk:** dagger   1292–1293 **eking . . . out:** adding to, prolonging   1293 **protégé:** literally, someone under the care and protection of another   1295 **Romaic:** the kind of Greek commonly spoken at the time   1310 **alpha beta:** the first two letters of the Greek alphabet; ABC's

As was the case, at least, where I have been;   1315
They smile so when one's right, and when one's wrong
        They smile still more, and then there intervene
Pressure of hands, perhaps even a chaste kiss;—
I learned the little that I know by this:

CLXV

That is, some words of Spanish, Turk, and Greek,   1320
        Italian not at all, having no teachers;
Much English I cannot pretend to speak,
        Learning that language chiefly from its preachers,
Barrow, South, Tillotson, whom every week
        I study, also Blair—the highest reachers   1325
Of eloquence in piety and prose—
I hate your poets, so read none of those....

CLXVII

Return we to Don Juan. He begun
        To hear new words, and to repeat them; but
Some feelings, universal as the sun,
        Were such as could not in his breast be shut
More than within the bosom of a nun: 1340
        He was in love—as you would be, no doubt,
With a young benefactress—so was she,
Just in the way we very often see.

CLXVIII

And every day by daybreak—rather early
        For Juan, who was somewhat fond of rest—   1345
She came into the cave, but it was merely
        To see her bird reposing in his nest;
And she would softly stir his locks so curly,
        Without disturbing her yet slumbering guest,
Breathing all gently o'er his cheek and mouth,   1350
As o'er a bed of roses the sweet south.

CLXIX

And every morn his colour freshlier came,
        And every day helped on his convalescence;
'Twas well, because health in the human frame
        Is pleasant, besides being true love's essence,   1355
For health and idleness to passion's flame
        Are oil and gunpowder; and some good lessons
Are also learnt from Ceres and from Bacchus,
Without whom Venus will not long attack us....

1321 Byron originally wrote, "Italian rather more, having more teachers." He may have erased it to spare the feelings of the Italian countess he was in love with—or out of tongue-in-cheek drollery. 1324 **Barrow:** Isaac Barrow (1630–1677), professor of Greek and mathematics at Cambridge, whose sermons have been regarded as among the best in English—but extremely long   **South:** Robert South (1634–1716), a witty preacher at the court of Charles II   **Tillotson:** John Tillotson (1630–1694), a very popular preacher who became archbishop of Canterbury   1325 **Blair:** Hugh Blair (1718–1800), a Scottish preacher who wrote five volumes of sermons and lectured on rhetoric   1327 Byron disliked many of the poets of his time, among them Wordsworth and Coleridge.   1358–1359 **Ceres . . . Bacchus . . . Venus:** the goddess of agriculture and particularly of grains (cf. *cereal*); the god of wine; the goddess of love. The personifications mean that food and drink are prerequisites to lovemaking.

CLXXI

When Juan woke he found some good things ready,
    A bath, a breakfast, and the finest eyes
That ever made a youthful heart less steady,   1370
    Besides her maid's, as pretty for their size;
But I have spoken of all this already—
    And repetition's tiresome and unwise—
Well—Juan, after bathing in the sea,
Came always back to coffee and Haidee.   1375

CLXXII

Both were so young, and one so innocent,
    That bathing passed for nothing; Juan seemed
To her, as 'twere, the kind of being sent,
    Of whom these two years she had nightly dreamed,
A something to be loved, a creature meant   1380
    To be her happiness, and whom she deemed
To render happy; all who joy would win
Must share it—happiness was born a twin.

CLXXIII

It was such pleasure to behold him, such
    Enlargement of existence to partake   1385
Nature with him, to thrill beneath his touch,
    To watch him slumbering, and to see him wake:
To live with him for ever were too much;
    But then the thought of parting made her quake;
He was her own, her ocean-treasure, cast   1390
Like a rich wreck—her first love, and her last. . . .

CLXXVI

Now she prolonged her visits and her talk
    (For they must talk), and he had learned to say
So much as to propose to take a walk—   1410
    For little had he wandered since the day
On which, like a young flower snapped from the stalk,
    Drooping and dewy on the beach he lay—
And thus they walked out in the afternoon,
And saw the sun set opposite the moon.   1415

CLXXVII

It was a wild and breaker-beaten coast,
    With cliffs above, and a broad sandy shore,
Guarded by shoals and rocks as by an host,
    With here and there a creek, whose aspect wore
A better welcome to the tempest-tost;   1420
    And rarely ceased the haughty billow's roar,
Save on the dead long summer days, which make
The outstretched ocean glitter like a lake.

CLXXVIII

And the small ripple spilt upon the beach
    Scarcely o'erpassed the cream of your champagne,   1425

1418 **host**: army

When o'er the brim the sparkling bumpers reach,
 That spring-dew of the spirit! the heart's rain!
Few things surpass old wine; and they may preach
  Who please—the more because they preach in vain—
Let us have wine and woman, mirth and laughter,   1430
Sermons and soda-water the day after.

CLXXIX

Man, being reasonable, must get drunk;
 The best of life is but intoxication:
Glory, the grape, love, gold, in these are sunk
  The hopes of all men, and of every nation;   1435
Without their sap, how branchless were the trunk
  Of life's strange tree, so fruitful on occasion!
But to return—Get very drunk, and when
You wake with headache—you shall see what then! . . . .

CLXXXI

The coast—I think it was the coast that I
 Was just describing—Yes, it *was* the coast—
Lay at this period quiet as the sky,   1450
  The sands untumbled, the blue waves untossed,
And all was stillness, save the sea-bird's cry,
  And dolphin's leap, and little billow crossed
By some low rock or shelve, that made it fret
Against the boundary it scarcely wet. . . .   1455

CLXXXIII

It was the cooling hour, just when the rounded
 Red sun sinks down behind the azure hill,   1465
Which then seems as if the whole earth it bounded,
  Circling all nature, hushed, and dim, and still,
With the far mountain-crescent half surrounded
  On one side, and the deep sea calm and chill
Upon the other, and the rosy sky   1470
With one star sparkling through it like an eye. . . .

CLXXXV

They looked up to the sky, whose floating glow   1480
 Spread like a rosy ocean, vast and bright;
They gazed upon the glittering sea below,
  Whence the broad moon rose circling into sight;
They heard the waves' splash, and the wind so low,
  And saw each other's dark eyes darting light   1485
Into each other—and, beholding this,
Their lips drew near, and clung into a kiss;

CLXXXVI

A long, long kiss, a kiss of youth, and love,
 And beauty, all concentrating like rays
Into one focus, kindled from above;   1490
  Such kisses as belong to early days,
Where heart, and soul, and sense, in concert move,
  And the blood's lava, and the pulse a blaze,

1426 **bumpers:** cups or glasses filled to the brim 1489 **concentrating:** formerly pronounced *concên-trating,* as here 1492 **in concert:** together, concertedly

Each kiss a heart-quake—for a kiss's strength,
I think, it must be reckoned by its length.   1495

CLXXXVII

By length I mean duration; theirs endured
    Heaven knows how long—no doubt they never reckoned;
And if they had, they could not have secured
    The sum of their sensations to a second:
They had not spoken, but they felt allured,   1500
    As if their souls and lips each other beckoned,
Which, being joined, like swarming bees they clung—
Their hearts the flowers from whence the honey sprung.

CLXXXVIII

They were alone, but not alone as they
    Who shut in chambers think it loneliness;   1505
The silent ocean, and the starlight bay,
    The twilight glow, which momently grew less,
The voiceless sands, and dropping caves, that lay
    Around them, made them to each other press,
As if there were no life beneath the sky   1510
Save theirs, and that their life could never die.

CLXXXIX

They feared no eyes nor ears on that lone beach;
    They felt no terrors from the night; they were
All in all to each other: though their speech
    Was broken words, they *thought* a language there—   1515
And all the burning tongues the passions teach
    Found in one sigh the best interpreter
Of nature's oracle—first love—that all
Which Eve has left her daughters since her fall.

CXC

Haidee spoke not of scruples, asked no vows,   1520
    Nor offered any; she had never heard
Of plight and promises to be a spouse,
    Or perils by a loving maid incurred;
She was all which pure ignorance allows,
    And flew to her young mate like a young bird;   1525
And, never having dreamt of falsehood, she
Had not one word to say of constancy.

CXCI

She loved, and was belovèd—she adored,
    And she was worshipped after nature's fashion—
Their intense souls, into each other poured,   1530
    If souls could die, had perished in that passion—
But by degrees their senses were restored,
    Again to be o'ercome, again to dash on;
And, beating 'gainst *his* bosom, Haidee's heart
Felt as if never more to beat apart.   1535

CXCII

Alas! they were so young, so beautiful,
    So lonely, loving, helpless, and the hour

1522 **plight:** a solemn promise, engagement

Was that in which the heart is always full,
　　And, having o'er itself no further power,
Prompts deeds eternity can not annul,   1540
　　But pays off moments in an endless shower
Of hell-fire—all prepared for people giving
Pleasure or pain to one another living.

CXCIII

Alas! for Juan and Haidee! they were
　　So loving and so lovely—till then never,   1545
Excepting our first parents, such a pair
　　Had run the risk of being damned for ever:
And Haidee, being devout as well as fair,
　　Had, doubtless, heard about the Stygian river,
And hell and purgatory—but forgot   1550
Just in the very crisis she should not.

CXCIV

They look upon each other, and their eyes
　　Gleam in the moonlight; and her white arm clasps
Round Juan's head, and his around her lies
　　Half buried in the tresses which it grasps;   1555
She sits upon his knee, and drinks his sighs,
　　He hers, until they end in broken gasps;
And thus they form a group that's quite antique,
Half naked, loving, natural, and Greek.

CXCV

And when those deep and burning moments passed,   1560
　　And Juan sunk to sleep within her arms,
She slept not, but all tenderly, though fast,
　　Sustained his head upon her bosom's charms;
And now and then her eye to Heaven is cast,
　　And then on the pale cheek her breast now warms,   1565
Pillowed on her o'erflowing heart, which pants
With all it granted, and with all it grants.

CXCVI

An infant when it gazes on a light,
　　A child the moment when it drains the breast,
A devotee when soars the Host in sight,   1570
　　An Arab with a stranger for a guest,
A sailor when the prize has struck in fight,
　　A miser filling his most hoarded chest,
Feel rapture; but not such true joy are reaping
As they who watch o'er what they love while sleeping.   1575

CXCVII

For there it lies so tranquil, so beloved,
　　All that it hath of life with us is living;
So gentle, stirless, helpless, and unmoved,
　　And all unconscious of the joy 'tis giving;
All it hath felt, inflicted, passed, and proved,   1580
　　Hushed into depths beyond the watcher's diving:

1549 **the Stygian river**: the river Styx, which (in classical mythology) the souls of the dead were ferried over on their way to the underworld   1570 **the Host**: the eucharistic wafer or bread 1572 **prize has struck**: ship he hopes to capture has struck its colors (lowered its flag in sign of surrender)

There lies the thing we love with all its errors
And all its charms, like death without its terrors.

CXCVIII

The lady watched her lover—and that hour
    Of love's, and night's, and ocean's solitude,   1585
O'erflowed her soul with their united power;
    Amidst the barren sand and rocks so rude
She and her wave-worn love had made their bower,
    Where nought upon their passion could intrude,
And all the stars that crowded the blue space   1590
Saw nothing happier than her glowing face.

CXCIX

Alas! the love of women! it is known
    To be a lovely and a fearful thing;
For all of theirs upon that die is thrown,
    And if 'tis lost, life hath no more to bring   1595
To them but mockeries of the past alone,
    And their revenge is as the tiger's spring,
Deadly, and quick, and crushing; yet, as real
Torture is theirs—what they inflict they feel.

CC

They are right; for man, to man so oft unjust,   1600
    Is always so to women: one sole bond
Awaits them—treachery is all their trust;
    Taught to conceal, their bursting hearts despond
Over their idol, till some wealthier lust
    Buys them in marriage—and what rests beyond?   1605
A thankless husband—next, a faithless lover—
Then dressing, nursing, praying—and all's over.

CCI

Some take a lover, some take drams or prayers,
    Some mind their household, others dissipation,
Some run away, and but exchange their cares,   1610
    Losing the advantage of a virtuous station;
Few changes e'er can better their affairs,
    Theirs being an unnatural situation,
From the dull palace to the dirty hovel:
Some play the devil, and then write a novel.   1615

CCII

Haidee was nature's bride, and knew not this;
    Haidee was passion's child, born where the sun
Showers triple light, and scorches even the kiss
    Of his gazelle-eyed daughters; she was one
Made but to love, to feel that she was his   1620
    Who was her chosen: what was said or done
Elsewhere was nothing. She had nought to fear,
Hope, care, nor love, beyond—her heart beat *here.* . . .

1594 **upon that die . . .:** All is risked on that one throw of the dice. 1608 **drams:** drinks
1615 **write a novel:** Lady Caroline Lamb, after her love affair with Byron, published in 1816 her novel *Glenarvon*, in which the main character, meant to represent Byron, is guilty of seduction, kidnapping, and murder.

CCIV

And now 'twas done—on the lone shore were plighted
    Their hearts; the stars, their nuptial torches, shed
Beauty upon the beautiful they lighted:
    Ocean their witness, and the cave their bed,   1635
By their own feelings hallowed and united,
    Their priest was solitude, and they were wed:
And they were happy—for to their young eyes
Each was an angel, and earth Paradise. . . .

1632 **plighted:** promised (to each other)

Percy Bysshe Shelley
(1792–1822)

Son of a conservative country squire and Member of Parliament, Shelley was expelled from Oxford (where he had studied chemistry and physics as well as philosophy) for writing a pamphlet taken as antireligious. Soon afterwards he eloped with the 16-year-old Harriet Westbrook, by whom he had two children. Three years later he left Harriet to go off to Europe with a more intellectual 17-year-old, Mary Godwin, who, when only 19, wrote the famous *Frankenstein*. Harriet was later found drowned, an apparent suicide. Shelley then married Mary, by whom he had three children, two of whom died about a year after the family had left England for Italy. There Shelley worked hard at his writing. He and a friend were drowned when a sudden storm overwhelmed their little sailboat in the Gulf of Spezia, near Pisa.

Hymn to Intellectual Beauty

The awful shadow of some unseen Power
    Floats though unseen among us, visiting
    This various world with as inconstant wing
As summer winds that creep from flower to flower;
Like moonbeams that behind some piny mountain shower,   5
        It visits with inconstant glance
        Each human heart and countenance:
Like hues and harmonies of evening,
        Like clouds in starlight widely spread,
        Like memory of music fled,   10
        Like aught that for its grace may be
Dear, and yet dearer for its mystery.

Spirit of Beauty, that dost consecrate
    With thine own hues all thou dost shine upon
    Of human thought or form, where art thou gone?   15
Why dost thou pass away and leave our state,
This dim vast vale of tears, vacant and desolate?
        Ask why the sunlight not forever
        Weaves rainbows o'er yon mountain river,
Why aught should fail and fade that once is shown,   20
        Why fear and dream and death and birth
        Cast on the daylight of this earth
        Such gloom, why man has such a scope
For love and hate, despondency and hope?

1816. *Rosalind and Helen*, 1819.

1 **awful:** awe-inspiring, awesome **Power:** This Power (Intellectual Beauty) is a reality beyond what the senses can normally perceive.

No voice from some sublimer world hath ever   25
  To sage or poet these responses given:
  Therefore the names of daemon, ghost, and Heaven,
Remain the records of their vain endeavor,
Frail spells, whose uttered charm might not avail to sever,
      From all we hear and all we see,   30
      Doubt, chance, and mutability.
Thy light alone, like mist o'er mountains driven,
    Or music by the night wind sent
    Through strings of some still instrument,
    Or moonlight on a midnight stream,   35
Gives grace and truth to life's unquiet dream.

Love, hope, and self-esteem, like clouds depart
  And come, for some uncertain moments lent.
  Man were immortal, and omnipotent,
Didst thou, unknown and awful as thou art,   40
Keep with thy glorious train firm state within his heart.
      Thou messenger of sympathies
      That wax and wane in lovers' eyes;
Thou, that to human thought art nourishment,
      Like darkness to a dying flame!   45
      Depart not as thy shadow came,
      Depart not—lest the grave should be,
Like life and fear, a dark reality.

While yet a boy I sought for ghosts, and sped
  Through many a listening chamber, cave and ruin,   50
  And starlight wood, with fearful steps pursuing
Hopes of high talk with the departed dead.
I called on poisonous names with which our youth is fed:
      I was not heard, I saw them not;
      When musing deeply on the lot   55
Of life, at that sweet time when winds are wooing
      All vital things that wake to bring
      News of birds and blossoming,
      Sudden, thy shadow fell on me;
I shrieked, and clasped my hands in ecstasy!   60

I vowed that I would dedicate my powers
  To thee and thine: have I not kept the vow?
  With beating heart and streaming eyes, even now
I call the phantoms of a thousand hours
Each from his voiceless grave: they have in visioned bowers   65
      Of studious zeal or love's delight
      Outwatched with me the envious night:
They know that never joy illumed my brow,
      Unlinked with hope that thou wouldst free
      This world from its dark slavery,   70
      That thou—O awful Loveliness,
Wouldst give whate'er these words cannot express.

The day becomes more solemn and serene
  When noon is past: there is a harmony

---

27 **daemon:** in Greek mythology, a subordinate deity, between god and man   34 **instrument:** an Aeolian harp   69–70 **free/This world:** not just in a spiritual sense—Shelley was passionately concerned with political and religious liberty.

In autumn, and a lustre in its sky,   75
Which through the summer is not heard nor seen,
As if it could not be, as if it had not been!
　　　　Thus let thy power, which like the truth
　　　　Of nature on thy passive youth
Descended, to my onward life supply   80
　　　　Its calm, to one who worships thee,
　　　　And every form containing thee,
　　　　Whom, Spirit fair, thy spells did bind
To fear himself, and love all human kind.

Ozymandias

I met a traveller from an antique land
Who said: Two vast and trunkless legs of stone
Stand in the desert. Near them, on the sand,
Half sunk, a shattered visage lies, whose frown,
And wrinkled lip, and sneer of cold command,   5
Tell that its sculptor well those passions read
Which yet survive, stamped on these lifeless things,
The hand that mocked them and the heart that fed;
And on the pedestal these words appear:
"My name is Ozymandias, king of kings: 10
Look on my works, ye Mighty, and despair!"
Nothing beside remains. Round the decay
Of that colossal wreck, boundless and bare,
The lone and level sands stretch far away.

1817. Ibid.

"Ozymandias" is the Greek form of Usermare-setepenre, a name of Ramses II (Ramses the Great) who, beginning in 1304 B.C., reigned for 67 chiefly triumphant years, during which he produced not only 100 sons but also countless colossal statues of himself and ostentatious monuments to his victories all over the kingdom. Many of the statues, some over 60 feet high, are still standing, with their boastful inscriptions. In Ramses' mortuary temple at Thebes there is such a fallen statue as Shelley describes. In the year Shelley wrote the poem, Egyptian antiquities were being shown at the British Museum, which Shelley visited, and there was much comment on them in the press. In lines 4–6, Shelley is crediting the ancient sculptors with his own hatred of tyranny; the faces of Ramses which have survived are composed and pleasant enough—no "wrinkled lip." It would have been dangerous to do satiric portraits on so gigantic a scale.

Ode to the West Wind

I

O wild west wind, thou breath of autumn's being,
Thou from whose unseen presence the leaves dead
Are driven like ghosts from an enchanter fleeing,

Yellow, and black, and pale, and hectic red,
Pestilence-stricken multitudes! O thou   5
Who chariotest to their dark wintry bed

The wingèd seeds, where they lie cold and low,
Each like a corpse within its grave, until
Thine azure sister of the spring shall blow

1819. *Prometheus Unbound,* 1820.

See Additional Notes (p. 764).

Her clarion o'er the dreaming earth, and fill   10
(Driving sweet buds like flocks to feed in air)
With living hues and odours plain and hill:

Wild spirit, which art moving everywhere;
Destroyer and preserver; hear, O hear!

II
Thou on whose stream, 'mid the steep sky's commotion,   15
Loose clouds like earth's decaying leaves are shed,
Shook from the tangled boughs of heaven and ocean,

Angels of rain and lightning: there are spread
On the blue surface of thine airy surge,
Like the bright hair uplifted from the head   20

Of some fierce Maenad, even from the dim verge
Of the horizon to the zenith's height,
The locks of the approaching storm. Thou dirge

Of the dying year, to which this closing night
Will be the dome of a vast sepulchre,   25
Vaulted with all thy congregated might

Of vapours, from whose solid atmosphere
Black rain, and fire, and hail will burst: O hear!

III
Thou who didst waken from his summer dreams
The blue Mediterranean, where he lay.   30
Lulled by the coil of his crystalline streams,

Beside a pumice isle in Baiae's bay,
And saw in sleep old palaces and towers
Quivering within the wave's intenser day,

All overgrown with azure moss and flowers   35
So sweet, the sense faints picturing them! Thou
For whose path the Atlantic's level powers

Cleave themselves into chasms, while far below
The sea-blooms and the oozy woods which wear
The sapless foliage of the ocean, know   40

Thy voice, and suddenly grow gray with fear,
And tremble and despoil themselves: O hear!

IV
If I were a dead leaf thou mightest bear;
If I were a swift cloud to fly with thee;
A wave to pant beneath thy power, and share   45

---

10 **clarion:** a trumpet with a clear high tone   18 **Angels:** in the original Greek sense of messengers
21 **Maenad:** in Greek mythology, a woman inspired to ecstatic frenzy, often destructive, by Diony-
sius, god of drunkenness and uninhibited behavior   32 **Baiae:** a fashionable seaside resort of the an-
cient Romans on the Bay of Naples to the west of Naples itself. Some ruins, submerged when the wa-
ter level of the Mediterranean rose, are visible underwater.   41 **grow gray:** Shelley's own note states
that underwater vegetation undergoes the same seasonal changes as vegetation on land.

The impulse of thy strength, only less free
Than thou, O uncontrollable! if even
I were as in my boyhood, and could be

The comrade of thy wanderings over heaven,
As then, when to outstrip thy skiey speed   50
Scarce seemed a vision; I would ne'er have striven

As thus with thee in prayer in my sore need.
O! lift me as a wave, a leaf, a cloud!
I fall upon the thorns of life! I bleed!

A heavy weight of hours has chained and bowed   55
One too like thee: tameless, and swift, and proud.

V

Make me thy lyre, even as the forest is:
What if my leaves are falling like its own?
The tumult of thy mighty harmonies

Will take from both a deep autumnal tone,   60
Sweet though in sadness. Be thou, spirit fierce,
My spirit! Be thou me, impetuous one!

Drive my dead thoughts over the universe,
Like withered leaves, to quicken a new birth;
And, by the incantation of this verse,   65

Scatter, as from an unextinguished hearth
Ashes and sparks, my words among mankind!
Be through my lips to unawakened earth

The trumpet of a prophecy! O wind,
If winter comes, can spring be far behind?   70

54–56 Admirers of Shelley have to come to terms with his occasional expressions of sentimental self-pity and humorless self-commendation.

To a Skylark

    Hail to thee, blithe spirit!
      Bird thou never wert,
   That from heaven or near it
      Pourest thy full heart
In profuse strains of unpremeditated art.   5

    Higher still and higher
      From the earth thou springest
   Like a cloud of fire;
      The blue deep thou wingest,
And singing still dost soar, and soaring ever singest.   10

    In the golden lightning
      Of the sunken sun,

1820. Ibid.

See Additional Notes (p. 765).

O'er which clouds are brightening,
　　Thou dost float and run;
Like an unbodied joy whose race is just begun.　　　　　　15

　　The pale purple even
　　　Melts around thy flight;
　　Like a star of heaven,
　　　In the broad daylight
Thou art unseen, but yet I hear thy shrill delight,　　　20

　　Keen as are the arrows
　　　Of that silver sphere
　　Whose intense lamp narrows
　　　In the white dawn clear,
Until we hardly see, we feel that it is there.　　　　　25

　　All the earth and air
　　　With thy voice is loud,
　　As, when night is bare,
　　　From one lonely cloud
The moon rains out her beams, and heaven is overflowed.　　30

　　What thou art we know not;
　　　What is most like thee?
　　From rainbow clouds there flow not
　　　Drops so bright to see,
As from thy presence showers a rain of melody:　　　35

　　Like a poet hidden
　　　In the light of thought,
　　Singing hymns unbidden,
　　　Till the world is wrought
To sympathy with hopes and fears it heeded not;　　　40

　　Like a high-born maiden
　　　In a palace tower,
　　Soothing her love-laden
　　　Soul in secret hour
With music sweet as love, which overflows her bower;　　45

　　Like a glow-worm golden
　　　In a dell of dew,
　　Scattering unbeholden
　　　Its aërial hue
Among the flowers and grass which screen it from the view;　　50

　　Like a rose embowered
　　　In its own green leaves,
　　By warm winds deflowered,
　　　Till the scent it gives
Makes faint with too much sweet those heavy-wingèd thieves.　　55

　　Sound of vernal showers
　　　On the twinkling grass,

16 **even:** evening   22 **silver sphere:** the moon, which loses its brightness at sunrise   48 **unbehol-
den:** (1) unbeheld, unseen; (2) under no obligation

Rain-awakened flowers,
    All that ever was
Joyous and clear and fresh, thy music doth surpass.   60

    Teach us, sprite or bird,
        What sweet thoughts are thine:
    I have never heard
        Praise of love or wine
That panted forth a flood of rapture so divine.   65

    Chorus hymeneal,
        Or triumphal chaunt,
    Matched with thine would be all
        But an empty vaunt,
A thing wherein we feel there is some hidden want.   70

    What objects are the fountains
        Of thy happy strain?
    What fields, or waves, or mountains?
        What shapes of sky or plain?
What love of thine own kind? what ignorance of pain?   75

    With thy clear keen joyance
        Languor cannot be;
    Shadow of annoyance
        Never came near thee;
Thou lovest, but ne'er knew love's sad satiety.   80

    Waking or asleep,
        Thou of death must deem
    Things more true and deep
        Than we mortals dream,
Or how could thy notes flow in such a crystal stream?   85

    We look before and after,
        And pine for what is not;
    Our sincerest laughter
        With some pain is fraught;
Our sweetest songs are those that tell of saddest thought.   90

    Yet if we could scorn
        Hate and pride and fear,
    If we were things born
        Not to shed a tear,
I know not how thy joy we ever should come near.   95

    Better than all measures
        Of delightful sound,
    Better than all treasures
        That in books are found,
Thy skill to poet were, thou scorner of the ground!   100

    Teach me half the gladness
        That thy brain must know;

61 **sprite:** spirit

Such harmonious madness
    From my lips would flow,
The world should listen then, as I am listening now.   105

The world would listen to me as I'm listening to you.

Chorus *from* Hellas

The world's great age begins anew,
    The golden years return,
The earth doth like a snake renew
    Her winter weeds outworn:
Heaven smiles, and faiths and empires gleam,   5
Like wrecks of a dissolving dream.

A brighter Hellas rears its mountains
    From waves serener far;
A new Peneus rolls his fountains
    Against the morning star.   10
Where fairer Tempes bloom, there sleep
Young Cyclads on a sunnier deep.

A loftier Argo cleaves the main,
    Fraught with a later prize;
Another Orpheus sings again,   15
    And loves, and weeps, and dies.
A new Ulysses leaves once more
Calypso for his native shore.

Oh, write no more the tale of Troy,
    If earth Death's scroll must be!   20
Nor mix with Laian rage the joy
    Which dawns upon the free:
Although a subtler Sphinx renew
Riddles of death Thebes never knew.

Another Athens shall arise,   25
    And to remoter time

1821. *Hellas*, 1822.

In 1821 the Greek War of Independence broke out, with battles between the Greeks and the Turks. To show his sympathy with the Greek cause, Shelley wrote his "lyrical drama" *Hellas* in the fall of that year. ("Hellas" is the ancient name for Greece.) The final chorus expresses Shelley's hopes for a new Golden Age of freedom and happiness. The first line is a translation of line 5 of Vergil's "Eclogue IV": "Magnus ab integro saeclorum nascitur ordo"; Shelley owes other details to Vergil's prophetic vision of a new Golden Age after a period of warfare: the return of Saturn, the serpent (which in Vergil dies), the second Argo, Orpheus. Vergil foresees another Trojan War; Shelley (line 19) hopes we will not.

4 weeds: garments; here, the old skin the snake sloughs off   **9 Peneus:** a beautiful river in Greece   **11 Tempes:** Tempe was the valley through which the Peneus flowed.   **12 Cyclads:** the Greek islands around Delos   **13 Argo:** In Greek legend, the Argo was the first sea-going ship ever built. In it Jason and the Argonauts sailed for the golden fleece.   **15 Orpheus:** the legendary Greek poet and musician. Cf. Milton's "L'Allegro," line 145, and "Lycidas," line 58.   **17 Ulysses:** the Roman name for Odysseus, who, on his 10-year adventurous voyage home from Troy, was entertained for seven years—increasingly against his will—by the lovely sea-nymph Calypso   **21 Laian:** Laius, the father of Oedipus, was unknowingly killed by his son in a roadside quarrel about right-of-way.   **23 Sphinx:** a female monster with beautiful human face and body of a lion. Sent to Thebes as a punishment, she devoured human victims when the riddle she asked was not properly answered. [Her riddle: "Which animal goes on four feet in the morning, two at midday, and three in the evening?" Answer: "Man, who as a baby crawls on all fours, when mature walks upright, and in old age walks with a cane."] When Oedipus gave the right answer, the Sphinx killed herself.

Bequeath, like sunset to the skies,
  The splendour of its prime;
And leave, if nought so bright may live,
All earth can take or Heaven can give.   30

Saturn and Love their long repose
  Shall burst, more bright and good
Than all who fell, than One who rose,
  Than many unsubdued:
Not gold, not blood, their altar dowers,   35
But votive tears and symbol flowers.

Oh, cease! must hate and death return?
  Cease! must men kill and die?
Cease! drain not to its dregs the urn
  Of bitter prophecy.   40
The world is weary of the past,
Oh, might it die or rest at last!

31 **Saturn and Love:** "among the deities of a real or imaginary state of innocence and happiness"
[Shelley's note] 32–34 **more bright ... unsubdued:** These lines, perhaps as irreligious, were re-
placed by asterisks in the 1822 edition. 33 **all who fell:** "the Gods of Greece, Asia, and Egypt" [Shel-
ley] **One:** Christ 34 **the many unsubdued:** "the monstrous objects of the idolatry of China, India,
the Antarctic islands, and the native tribes of America" [Shelley] 35 **their altar:** that of Saturn and
Love

John Clare
(1793–1864)

Clare, son of a poor farmworker, had little education—only about 3 months a year until
he was 12, an age at which he was already working hard at "correcting" his poems. At 26
he was married; he had eight children. His first book, published in London in 1820,
made him the literary sensation of the year. His next two, though better, failed to sell. By
1837 the physical and mental strain of rural drudgery proved too much: Clare was taken
into a benevolent private asylum. When he left four years later he walked home—80
miles in less than 4 days—still confused about his identity (sometimes thinking he was
Byron, sometimes a prize-fighter). He spent the rest of his life in a new and enlightened
asylum—well treated, allowed some liberty, and encouraged to write. Many poems he
wrote remained unpublished until the 1950s.

Badger

When midnight comes a host of dogs and men
Go out and track the badger to his den,
And put a sack within the hole, and lie
Till the old grunting badger passes by.
He comes and hears—they let the strongest loose.   5
The old fox hears the noise and drops the goose.
The poacher shoots and hurries from the cry,
And the old hare half wounded buzzes by.
They get a forkèd stick to bear him down

1835–1837. *John Clare: Poems Chiefly from Manuscript*, ed. by E. Blunden and A. Porter, 1920.

Clare's poem is given in the familiar short form in which it has generally appeared since its first pub-
lication in 1920. In a version published in 1967, there are two additional 14-line sections: a prelimi-
nary one that describes how the badger looks and walks and how the badger hunt begins, and a final
one that tells how he can sometimes be tamed and kept to fight dogs. The shorter, starker version, as
given here, is dramatically more effective.

And clap the dogs and take him to the town,   10
And bait him all the day with many dogs,
And laugh and shout and fright the scampering hogs.
He runs along and bites at all he meets:
They shout and hollo down the noisy streets.

He turns about to face the loud uproar   15
And drives the rebels to their very door.
The frequent stone is hurled where'er they go;
When badgers fight, then everyone's a foe.
The dogs are clapped and urged to join the fray;
The badger turns and drives them all away.   20
Though scarcely half as big, demure and small,
He fights with dogs for hours and beats them all.
The heavy mastiff, savage in the fray,
Lies down and licks his feet and turns away.
The bulldog knows his match and waxes cold,   25
The badger grins and never leaves his hold.
He drives the crowd and follows at their heels
And bites them through—the drunkard swears and reels.

The frighted women take the boys away,
The blackguard laughs and hurries on the fray.   30
He tries to reach the woods, an awkward race,
But sticks and cudgels quickly stop the chase.
He turns again and drives the noisy crowd
And beats the many dogs in noises loud.
He drives away and beats them every one,   35
And then they loose them all and set them on.
He falls as dead and kicked by boys and men,
Then starts and grins and drives the crowd again;
Till kicked and torn and beaten out he lies
And leaves his hold and cackles, groans, and dies.   40

10 **clap:** urge on by clapping [The 1967 edition prints this line as: "And clapt the dogs and bore him to the town."]   11 **bait:** harass, torment by tying him up and setting the dogs on him (cf. the verb *to badger*)   21 **demure:** Clare seems to mean that the animal looks deceptively harmless. The 1967 edition gives the unlikely *dimute* ("diminute, diminished").   25 **waxes:** grows

First Love

I ne'er was struck before that hour
    With love so sudden and so sweet.
Her face it bloomed like a sweet flower
    And stole my heart away complete.
My face turned pale as deadly pale,   5
    My legs refused to walk away,
And when she looked "What could I ail?"
    My life and all seemed turned to clay.

And then my blood rushed to my face
    And took my eyesight quite away.   10
The trees and bushes round the place
    Seemed midnight at noonday.
I could not see a single thing,
    Words from my eyes did start;

1844–1850. Ibid.

They spoke as chords do from the string   15
    And blood burnt round my heart.

Are flowers the winter's choice?
    Is love's bed always snow?
She seemed to hear my silent voice
    Not love's appeals to know.   20
I never saw so sweet a face
    As that I stood before:
My heart has left its dwelling-place
    And can return no more.

Autumn

The thistledown's flying, though the winds are all still,
On the green grass now lying, now mounting the hill,
The spring from the fountain now boils like a pot;
Through stones past the counting it bubbles red-hot.

The ground parched and cracked is like overbaked bread,   5
The greensward all wracked is, bents dried up and dead.
The fallow fields glitter like water indeed,
And gossamers twitter, flung from weed unto weed.

Hill-tops like hot iron glitter bright in the sun,
And the rivers we're eying burn to gold as they run;   10
Burning hot is the ground, liquid gold is the air;
Whoever looks round sees Eternity there.

1842–1864. Ibid.

1 **thistledown:** the downy or feathery threads on which seeds of thistle, dandelion, and so on are airborne 6 **greensward:** green turf **bents:** stalky grasses 7 **fallow:** plowed land left idle 8 **gossamers:** fine floating cobwebs **twitter:** tremble, quiver

I Am

I am—yet what I am, none cares or knows;
    My friends forsake me like a memory lost;
I am the self-consumer of my woes—
    They rise and vanish in oblivion's host,
Like shadows in love, frenzied stifled throes—   5
    And yet I am, and live—like vapours tossed

Into the nothingness of scorn and noise,
    Into the living sea of waking dreams,
Where there is neither sense of life or joys,
    But the vast shipwreck of my life's esteems;   10
Even the dearest that I love the best
    Are strange—nay, rather stranger than the rest.

I long for scenes where man hath never trod,
    A place where woman never smiled or wept—

---

c. 1844. *The Life of John Clare,* by Frederick Martin, 1865 (some readings from later editions).

There to abide with my Creator God,　　　　　　　　　15
　　And sleep as I in childhood sweetly slept,
Untroubling and untroubled where I lie,
　　The grass below—above, the vaulted sky.

She Tied Up Her Few Things

She tied up her few things
And laced up her shoe strings
And put on her bonnet worn through at the crown;
Her apron tied tighter—
Than snow her cap's whiter—　　　　　　　　　5
She lapped up her earnings and left our old town.

The dog barked again
All the length o' his chain,
And licked her hand kindly and huffed her good-bye;
Old hens prated loudly,　　　　　　　　　10
The cock strutted proudly,
And the horse at the gate turned to let her go by.

The thrasher-man stopping
The old barn floor whopping
Wished o'er the door-cloth her luck and no harm;　　15
Bees hummed round the thistle
While the red robins whistle;
And she, just one look on the old mossy farm.

'Twas Michaelmas season
They'd got corn and peas in　　　　　　　　　20
And all the fields cleared save some rakings and tithes;
Cote-pigeon flocks muster
Round bean-shelling cluster
And done are the whettings o' reap hooks and scythes.

Next year's flowers a-springing　　　　　　　　　25
Will miss Jinney's singing—
She opened her Bible and turned a leaf down.
In her bosom's forewarnings
She lapped up her earnings
And ere the sun's set'll be in her own town.　　　30

1845–1850. *Madrigals and Chronicles* . . . , ed. by Edmund Blunden, 1924.

6 **lapped:** wrapped　14 **whopping:** pounding　19 **Michaelmas:** September 29　21 **tithes:** literally, the one-tenth of produce supposed to be donated to the church; here, small amounts

John Keats
(1795–1821)

Keats's father, a livery-stable keeper, died when his son was 8; his mother, when he was 14. Apprenticed to a surgeon, Keats passed the medical examination that would have allowed him to practice as pharmacist. His interest, however, was poetry; though his first two books (1817 and 1818) were ignored or attacked, he continued to work at it. In the fall of 1818 he watched over his brother Tom, then dying of tuberculosis. About then he fell in love with the lively and sympathetic Fanny Brawne, to whom he became engaged a year later. In 1819, from March through June, Keats wrote nearly all of his greatest poetry. Only a few months later it was clear that he was seriously ill. In September 1820, he and the artist Joseph Severn sailed for Italy and its milder climate; he died there of tuberculosis the following January. Feeling that his talent had come to nothing, he asked that his tombstone, in Rome, bear the inscription "Here lies one whose name was writ in water."

On First Looking into Chapman's Homer

Much have I travelled in the realms of gold
    And many goodly states and kingdoms seen;
    Round many western islands have I been
Which bards in fealty to Apollo hold.
Oft of one wide expanse had I been told   5
    That deep-browed Homer ruled as his demesne;
    Yet never did I breathe its pure serene
Till I heard Chapman speak out loud and bold:
Then felt I like some watcher of the skies
    When a new planet swims into his ken;   10
Or like stout Cortez when with eagle eyes
    He stared at the Pacific—and all his men
Looked at each other with a wild surmise—
    Silent, upon a peak in Darien.

1816. *Poems,* 1817.

Keats wrote this poem early one morning after he and a friend had spent the whole night reading George Chapman's translation of Homer, published in 1616. The Elizabethan vigor of Chapman's version came as a revelation to Keats, who was then 20 years old.

1 **realms of gold:** regions of poetry   4 **fealty:** fidelity   **Apollo:** god of poetry   6 **demesne:** domain   7 **serene:** clear atmosphere   11 **Cortez:** Hernán Cortés was the conquerer of Mexico (1519–1521). It was not Cortés but Vasco Núñez de Balboa who in 1513 crossed the Isthmus of Panama from the settlement at Darién and sighted the Pacific from a hill near the Gulf of St. Miguel.

When I Have Fears That I May Cease to Be

When I have fears that I may cease to be
    Before my pen has gleaned my teeming brain,
Before high-pilèd books, in charactery,
    Hold like rich garners the full-ripened grain;
When I behold, upon the night's starred face,   5
    Huge cloudy symbols of a high romance,
And think that I may never live to trace
    Their shadows, with the magic hand of chance;
And when I feel, fair creature of an hour,
    That I shall never look upon thee more,   10
Never have relish in the fairy power
    Of unreflecting love—then on the shore
Of the wide world I stand alone, and think
Till love and fame to nothingness do sink.

1818. *Life, Letters and Literary Remains of John Keats . . . ,* 1848.

2 **gleaned:** harvested completely   3 **charactery:** written letters   11 **fairy:** working as by enchantment—as in a fairy tale   12 **unreflecting:** untroubled by the necessity of thinking

La Belle Dame sans Merci

A Ballad

O what can ail thee, knight-at-arms,
    Alone and palely loitering?
The sedge has withered from the lake,
    And no birds sing.

O what can ail thee, knight-at-arms,   5
    So haggard and so woe-begone?
The squirrel's granary is full,
    And the harvest's done.

I see a lily on thy brow
    With anguish moist and fever dew;   10
And on thy cheek a fading rose
    Fast withereth too.

"I met a lady in the meads,
    Full beautiful—a faery's child,
Her hair was long, her foot was light,   15
    And her eyes were wild.

"I made a garland for her head,
    And bracelets too, and fragrant zone;
She looked at me as she did love,
    And made sweet moan.   20

"I set her on my pacing steed,
    And nothing else saw all day long,
For sideways would she lean, and sing
    A faery's song.

"She found me roots of relish sweet,   25
    And honey wild, and manna dew;
And sure in language strange she said—
    'I love thee true!'

"She took me to her elfin grot,
    And there she wept and sighed full sore,   30
And there I shut her wild wild eyes
    With kisses four.

"And there she lullèd me asleep,
    And there I dreamed—ah! woe betide!
The latest dream I ever dreamed   35
    On the cold hill side.

"I saw pale kings, and princes too,
    Pale warriors, death-pale were they all;

1819. Ibid. (With some readings from *The Indicator*, May 10, 1820.)

The title ("The Beautiful Lady Without Pity") is that of a poem by the fifteenth-century French poet, Alain Chartier, an English translation of which had at one time been ascribed to Chaucer. Cf. "The Eve of St. Agnes," lines 291–292.

13 **meads:** meadows   18 **zone:** belt

Who cried—'La Belle Dame sans merci
    Hath thee in thrall!'   40

"I saw their starved lips in the gloam,
    With horrid warning gapèd wide,
And I awoke, and found me here,
    On the cold hill side.

"And this is why I sojourn here,   45
    Alone and palely loitering,
Though the sedge has withered from the lake,
    And no birds sing."

40 **in thrall:** under her spell   41 **gloam:** gloom, darkness

Bright Star! Would I Were Steadfast as Thou Art

Bright star, would I were steadfast as thou art—
    Not in lone splendour hung aloft the night
And watching, with eternal lids apart,
    Like nature's patient, sleepless eremite,
The moving waters at their priestlike task   5
    Of pure ablution round earth's human shores,
Or gazing on the new soft-fallen mask
    Of snow upon the mountains and the moors—
No—yet still steadfast, still unchangeable,
    Pillowed upon my fair love's ripening breast,   10
To feel forever its soft fall and swell,
    Awake forever in a sweet unrest,
Still, still to hear her tender-taken breath,
And so live ever—or else swoon to death.

1819–1820. Ibid.

4 **eremite:** hermit   11 **soft fall and swell:** Keats's earlier version. His later "soft swell and fall," with its clustering of sibilants, is less pleasant.

Ode to a Nightingale

My heart aches, and a drowsy numbness pains
    My sense, as though of hemlock I had drunk,
Or emptied some dull opiate to the drains
    One minute past, and Lethe-wards had sunk:
'Tis not through envy of thy happy lot,   5
    But being too happy in thy happiness—
        That thou, light-wingèd dryad of the trees,
            In some melodious plot

1819. *Lamia, Isabella, The Eve of St. Agnes, and Other Poems,* 1820.

According to Charles Brown, a friend of Keats, "In the spring of 1819 a nightingale had built her nest near my house. Keats felt a tranquil and continual joy in her song; and one morning he took his chair from the breakfast-table to the grass-plot under a plum-tree, where he sat for two or three hours. When he came into the house, I perceived he had some scraps of paper in hand, and these he was quietly thrusting behind some books. On inquiry, I found those scraps, four or five in number, contained his poetic feeling on the song of our nightingale."

2 **hemlock:** a poisonous plant; medically used as a powerful sedative   3 **drains:** dregs   4 **Lethe-wards:** toward Lethe, in classical mythology the underworld river whose waters caused forgetfulness of the past in the drinker   7 **dryad:** a tree-nymph

Of beechen green, and shadows numberless,
   Singest of summer in full-throated ease.   10

O for a draught of vintage! that hath been
   Cooled a long age in the deep-delvèd earth,
Tasting of Flora and the country green,
   Dance, and Provençal song, and sun-burnt mirth!
O for a beaker full of the warm South,   15
   Full of the true, the blushful Hippocrene,
      With beaded bubbles winking at the brim,
        And purple-stainèd mouth;
That I might drink, and leave the world unseen,
   And with thee fade away into the forest dim: 20

Fade far away, dissolve, and quite forget
   What thou among the leaves hast never known,
The weariness, the fever, and the fret
   Here, where men sit and hear each other groan;
Where palsy shakes a few, sad, last gray hairs,   25
   Where youth grows pale, and spectre-thin, and dies;
      Where but to think is to be full of sorrow
        And leaden-eyed despairs;
Where beauty cannot keep her lustrous eyes,
   Or new love pine at them beyond to-morrow.   30

Away! away! for I will fly to thee,
   Not charioted by Bacchus and his pards,
But on the viewless wings of poesy,
   Though the dull brain perplexes and retards:
Already with thee! tender is the night,   35
   And haply the Queen-Moon is on her throne,
      Clustered around by all her starry fays;
        But here there is no light,
Save what from heaven is with the breezes blown
      Through verdurous glooms and winding mossy ways.   40

I cannot see what flowers are at my feet,
   Nor what soft incense hangs upon the boughs,
But, in embalmèd darkness, guess each sweet
   Wherewith the seasonable month endows
The grass, the thicket, and the fruit-tree wild;   45
   White hawthorn, and the pastoral eglantine;
      Fast-fading violets covered up in leaves;
        And mid-May's eldest child,
The coming musk-rose, full of dewy wine,
      The murmurous haunt of flies on summer eves.   50

---

12 **deep-delvèd:** dug deep   13 **Flora:** the Roman goddess of flowering plants (flora)   14 **Provençal song:** Provence was the region in southern France where the poetry of the troubadours flourished in the late Middle Ages.   15 **the warm South:** the Mediterranean world   16 **Hippocrene:** the spring on Mt. Helicon in Greece (sacred to the Muses) whose waters were thought to inspire poetry. "The true, the blushful Hippocrene" is not water but red wine.   26 **youth . . . dies:** Keats's brother Tom had died of tuberculosis a few months before, at the age of 19. Keats, his constant companion during his last weeks, had watched him grow pale, and specter-thin, and die. Within two years of writing this poem, Keats himself was to be dead of the same disease at the age of 25.   32 **Bacchus:** the god of wine, sometimes represented in a chariot drawn by leopards ("pards")   33 **viewless:** invisible   35 **the night:** If Brown's account is reliable, the night and its details are all imagined.   37 **fays:** fairy-tale creatures   43 **embalmèd:** perfumed   46 **eglantine:** sweetbriar, a kind of wild rose

Darkling I listen; and for many a time
  I have been half in love with easeful death,
Called him soft names in many a musèd rhyme,
  To take into the air my quiet breath;
Now more than ever seems it rich to die,   55
  To cease upon the midnight with no pain,
    While thou art pouring forth thy soul abroad
      In such an ecstasy!
Still wouldst thou sing, and I have ears in vain→
  To thy high requiem become a sod.   60

Thou wast not born for death, immortal bird!
  No hungry generations tread thee down;
The voice I hear this passing night was heard
  In ancient days by emperor and clown:
Perhaps the self-same song that found a path   65
  Through the sad heart of Ruth, when, sick for home,
    She stood in tears amid the alien corn;
      The same that oft-times hath
Charmed magic casements, opening on the foam
  Of perilous seas, in faery lands forlorn.   70

Forlorn! the very word is like a bell
  To toll me back from thee to my sole self!
Adieu! the fancy cannot cheat so well
  As she is famed to do, deceiving elf.
Adieu! adieu! thy plaintive anthem fades   75
  Past the near meadows, over the still stream,
    Up the hill-side; and now 'tis buried deep
      In the next valley-glades:
Was it a vision, or a waking dream?
  Fled is that music:—Do I wake or sleep?   80

---

51 **darkling:** in the dark   60 **a sod:** a mere piece of earth   66 **Ruth:** After the death of her husband, Ruth left her native land to accompany her mother-in-law Naomi back to Bethlehem, where Naomi was from. There Ruth at first supported both, by gleaning in the fields of "alien corn," though the Old Testament account (the Book of Ruth) does not mention that she was sad or homesick.   73 **fancy:** the poet's imagination

Ode on a Grecian Urn

Thou still unravished bride of quietness!
  Thou foster-child of silence and slow time,
Sylvan historian, who canst thus express
  A flowery tale more sweetly than our rhyme:
What leaf-fringed legend haunts about thy shape   5
  Of deities or mortals, or of both,
    In Tempe or the dales of Arcady?

1819. Ibid.

No specific urn has been identified as the one Keats was contemplating. He was interested in ancient art and frequently went to the British Museum to admire the Elgin Marbles—sculptures from the Parthenon which Lord Elgin had brought from Greece and which were installed in the Museum in 1816. Details from these—or at least their spirit—would have influenced his poem. He also made a tracing of an engraving of an amphora, a two-handled vase with decorative figures and foliage, that was in the Louvre.

1 **unravished:** virginal, not subjected to the constraints and disillusion of actuality   3 **sylvan historian:** because it implies a course of events in a wooded setting   5 **legend:** (1) explanatory inscription; (2) myth or tale   7 **Tempe:** lovely valley in Greece (cf. Shelley, *Chorus* from *Hellas*, line 11)   **Arcady:** Arcadia, a region of rural areas and small villages in Greece

What men or gods are these? What maidens loath?
What mad pursuit? What struggle to escape?
      What pipes and timbrels? What wild ecstasy?   10

Heard melodies are sweet, but those unheard
    Are sweeter; therefore, ye soft pipes, play on;
Not to the sensual ear, but, more endeared,
    Pipe to the spirit ditties of no tone:
Fair youth, beneath the trees, thou canst not leave   15
    Thy song, nor ever can those trees be bare;
      Bold lover, never, never canst thou kiss,
    Though winning near the goal—yet, do not grieve;
She cannot fade, though thou hast not thy bliss,
    Forever wilt thou love, and she be fair!   20

Ah, happy, happy boughs! that cannot shed
    Your leaves, nor ever bid the spring adieu;
And, happy melodist, unwearièd,
    Forever piping songs forever new;
More happy love! more happy, happy love!   25
    Forever warm and still to be enjoyed,
      Forever panting and forever young;
    All breathing human passion far above,
That leaves a heart high-sorrowful and cloyed,
    A burning forehead, and a parching tongue.   30

Who are these coming to the sacrifice?
    To what green altar, O mysterious priest,
Lead'st thou that heifer lowing at the skies,
    And all her silken flanks with garlands dressed?
What little town by river or sea-shore,   35
    Or mountain-built with peaceful citadel,
      Is emptied of its folk, this pious morn?
    And, little town, thy streets for evermore
Will silent be; and not a soul to tell
    Why thou art desolate, can e'er return.   40

O Attic shape! Fair attitude! with brede
    Of marble men and maidens overwrought,
With forest branches and the trodden weed;
    Thou, silent form! dost tease us out of thought
As doth eternity: cold pastoral!   45
    When old age shall this generation waste,
      Thou shalt remain, in midst of other woe
    Than ours, a friend to man, to whom thou say'st,
"Beauty is truth, truth beauty,"—that is all
    Ye know on earth, and all ye need to know.   50

---

10 **timbrels:** tambourines 11 **those unheard:** music we imagine 29 **high-sorrowful:** sad because
of lofty hopes or contemplations 41 **Attic:** Athenian—Attica was the region around Athens **brede:**
braid, interwoven design 42 **marble:** like Greek sculpture. The vase, unless purely decorative or ar-
chitectural, would not have been of marble **overwrought:** decorated over its surface 49–50 As
printed in 1820, only the first five words are in quotation marks, as if the rest expressed the poet's
own sponsorship of what will seem to some readers mere simplistic double-talk. But early MSS. sug-
gest that the two lines belong together and are the imagined message of the urn: the voice of art, of
imaginative vision, telling us of its own faith (whatever scientists, philosophers, etc. may think) in
the transcendental unity of beauty and truth, and of the sufficiency of that faith as a consolation for
life on earth.

Ode on Melancholy

No, no, go not to Lethe, neither twist
    Wolf's-bane, tight-rooted, for its poisonous wine;
Nor suffer thy pale forehead to be kissed
    By nightshade, ruby grape of Proserpine;
Make not your rosary of yew-berries,   5
    Nor let the beetle, nor the death-moth be
      Your mournful Psyche, nor the downy owl
A partner in your sorrow's mysteries;
    For shade to shade will come too drowsily,
      And drown the wakeful anguish of the soul.   10

But when the melancholy fit shall fall
    Sudden from heaven like a weeping cloud,
That fosters the droop-headed flowers all,
    And hides the green hill in an April shroud;
Then glut thy sorrow on a morning rose,   15
    Or on the rainbow of the salt sand-wave,
      Or on the wealth of globèd peonies;
Or if thy mistress some rich anger shows,
    Emprison her soft hand, and let her rave,
      And feed deep, deep upon her peerless eyes.   20

She dwells with beauty—beauty that must die;
    And joy, whose hand is ever at his lips
Bidding adieu; and aching pleasure nigh,
    Turning to poison while the bee-mouth sips:
Ay, in the very temple of delight   25
    Veiled Melancholy has her sovran shrine,
      Though seen of none save him whose strenuous tongue
Can burst joy's grape against his palate fine;
    His soul shall taste the sadness of her might,
      And be among her cloudy trophies hung.   30

1819. Ibid.

1 **Lethe:** Cf. "Ode to a Nightingale," line 4.   2 **Wolf's-bane:** aconite, a poisonous herb used as a seda-
tive (Keats, as a medical student, had a knowledge of the pharmaceutical properties of plants.)
4 **nightshade:** called "deadly nightshade," a poisonous plant which, as belladonna, has sedative prop-
erties. It has shiny black berries. **Proserpine:** queen of the underworld, the realm of the dead
5 **yew-berries:** the yew, often planted in cemeteries (cf. Gray's "Elegy," line 13), was a symbol of sor-
row. The berries are poisonous.   6–7 **beetle ... death-moth ... owl:** All had associations with death
and cemeteries. Cf. Gray's "moping owl" (line 10). The "Death's-head moth" is a large moth with
skull-like markings.   7 **Psyche:** the Greek word means soul (cf. *psychology*, etc.), often symbolized,
in Greek art, as a butterfly. In mythology, Psyche is also a beautiful girl, "mournful" because cruelly
tormented by Venus, whose jealousy she aroused.   9 **shade to shade:** darkness on darkness, gloom
on gloom—though Keats may be playing on such meanings as *ghost, spirit, death,* etc.   21 **she:** Melan-
choly

To Autumn

Season of mists and mellow fruitfulness,
    Close bosom-friend of the maturing sun;
Conspiring with him how to load and bless
    With fruit the vines that round the thatch-eaves run;

1819. Ibid.

This autumnal ode, Keats's "last great lyric," was written on September 19.

3 **conspiring:** The word is enriched by its etymology: to "breathe with."

To bend with apples the mossed cottage-trees,   5
    And fill all fruit with ripeness to the core;
        To swell the gourd, and plump the hazel shells
    With a sweet kernel; to set budding more,
And still more, later flowers for the bees,
Until they think warm days will never cease,   10
        For summer has o'er-brimmed their clammy cells.

Who hath not seen thee oft amid thy store?
    Sometimes whoever seeks abroad may find
Thee sitting careless on a granary floor,
    Thy hair soft-lifted by the winnowing wind;   15
Or on a half-reaped furrow sound asleep,
    Drowsed with the fumes of poppies, while thy hook
        Spares the next swath and all its twinèd flowers:
And sometime like a gleaner thou dost keep
    Steady thy laden head across a brook;   20
    Or by a cider-press, with patient look,
        Thou watchest the last oozings hours by hours.

Where are the songs of spring? Ay, where are they?
    Think not of them, thou hast thy music too,—
While barrèd clouds bloom the soft-dying day,   25
    And touch the stubble-plains with rosy hue;
Then in a wailful choir the small gnats mourn
    Among the river sallows, borne aloft
        Or sinking as the light wind lives or dies;
And full-grown lambs loud bleat from hilly bourn;   30
    Hedge-crickets sing; and now with treble soft
    The red-breast whistles from a garden-croft;
        And gathering swallows twitter in the skies.

11 **clammy:** heavily liquid—without the suggestions of *chill* and *eerie* the word sometimes has to-day   12 **thee:** Autumn is personified as a somewhat dreamy lady, her work now almost done.   **store:** abundance   15 **winnowing:** To *winnow* is to toss grain into the air so that the useless chaff (light seed coverings) is blown away.   17 **fumes of poppies:** here thought of as an opiate   **hook:** hooked knife, sickle   18 **swath:** width covered by the sweep of a scythe or sickle   28 **sallows:** willows   30 **bourn:** (1) burn, small brook; (2) limit, boundary (enclosure)   32 **garden-croft:** small garden next to house

The Eve of St. Agnes

    St. Agnes' Eve—Ah, bitter chill it was!
    The owl, for all his feathers, was a-cold;
    The hare limped trembling through the frozen grass,
    And silent was the flock in woolly fold:
    Numb were the beadsman's fingers, while he told   5
    His rosary, and while his frosted breath,
    Like pious incense from a censer old,
    Seemed taking flight for heaven, without a death,
Past the sweet Virgin's picture, while his prayer he saith.

1819. Ibid.

St. Agnes' Eve is January 20—supposedly the coldest night of the year. Keats wrote the poem in the week or so after that date in 1819. St. Agnes was the patroness of unmarried girls; the folk belief was that those who went to bed supperless on the night of her feast-day would see their future husband in their dreams.

5 **beadsman:** one given a small pension on condition he pray for his benefactor

His prayer he saith, this patient, holy man;   10
Then takes his lamp, and riseth from his knees,
And back returneth, meagre, barefoot, wan,
Along the chapel aisle by slow degrees:
The sculptured dead, on each side, seem to freeze,
Emprisoned in black, purgatorial rails: 15
Knights, ladies, praying in dumb orat'ries,
He passeth by; and his weak spirit fails
To think how they may ache in icy hoods and mails.

Northward he turneth through a little door,
And scarce three steps, ere music's golden tongue   20
Flattered to tears this aged man and poor;
But no—already had his deathbell rung:
The joys of all his life were said and sung:
His was harsh penance on St. Agnes' Eve:
Another way he went, and soon among   25
Rough ashes sat he for his soul's reprieve,
And all night kept awake, for sinners' sake to grieve.

That ancient beadsman heard the prelude soft;
And so it chanced, for many a door was wide,
From hurry to and fro. Soon, up aloft,   30
The silver, snarling trumpets 'gan to chide:
The level chambers, ready with their pride,
Were glowing to receive a thousand guests:
The carvèd angels, ever eager-eyed,
Stared, where upon their heads the cornice rests,   35
With hair blown back, and wings put cross-wise on their breasts.

At length burst in the argent revelry,
With plume, tiara, and all rich array,
Numerous as shadows haunting faerily
The brain, new-stuffed, in youth, with triumphs gay   40
Of old romance. These let us wish away,
And turn, sole-thoughted, to one lady there,
Whose heart had brooded, all that wintry day,
On love, and winged St. Agnes' saintly care,
As she had heard old dames full many times declare.   45

They told her how, upon St. Agnes' Eve,
Young virgins might have visions of delight,
And soft adorings from their loves receive
Upon the honeyed middle of the night,
If ceremonies due they did aright;   50
As, supperless to bed they must retire,
And couch supine their beauties, lily-white;
Nor look behind, nor sideways, but require
Of heaven with upward eyes for all that they desire.

Full of this whim was thoughtful Madeline: 55
The music, yearning like a god in pain,
She scarcely heard: her maiden eyes divine,
Fixed on the floor, saw many a sweeping train
Pass by—she heeded not at all: in vain

---

16 **orat'ries:** oratories, places to pray, chapels or side-chapels 18 **mails:** suits of armor 37 **argent:**
silver; here, bright as silver, splendid **revelry:** throng of revellers 58 **train:** long skirt

Came many a tiptoe, amorous cavalier,   60
And back retired; not cooled by high disdain,
But she saw not: her heart was otherwhere:
She sighed for Agnes' dreams, the sweetest of the year.

She danced along with vague, regardless eyes,
Anxious her lips, her breathing quick and short: 65
The hallowed hour was near at hand: she sighs
Amid the timbrels, and the thronged resort
Of whisperers in anger, or in sport;
'Mid looks of love, defiance, hate, and scorn,
Hoodwinked with faery fancy; all amort,   70
Save to St. Agnes and her lambs unshorn,
And all the bliss to be before to-morrow morn.

So, purposing each moment to retire,
She lingered still. Meantime, across the moors,
Had come young Porphyro, with heart on fire   75
For Madeline. Beside the portal doors,
Buttressed from moonlight, stands he, and implores
All saints to give him sight of Madeline,
But for one moment in the tedious hours,
That he might gaze and worship all unseen;   80
Perchance speak, kneel, touch, kiss—in sooth such things have been.

He ventures in: let no buzzed whisper tell:
All eyes be muffled, or a hundred swords
Will storm his heart, love's feverous citadel:
For him, those chambers held barbarian hordes,   85
Hyena foemen, and hot-blooded lords,
Whose very dogs would execrations howl
Against his lineage: not one breast affords
Him any mercy, in that mansion foul,
Save one old beldame, weak in body and in soul.   90

Ah, happy chance! the aged creature came,
Shuffling along with ivory-headed wand,
To where he stood, hid from the torch's flame,
Behind a broad hall-pillar, far beyond
The sound of merriment and chorus bland: 95
He startled her; but soon she knew his face,
And grasped his fingers in her palsied hand,
Saying, "Mercy, Porphyro! hie thee from this place:
They are all here to-night, the whole blood-thirsty race!

"Get hence! get hence! there's dwarfish Hildebrand;   100
He had a fever late, and in the fit
He cursèd thee and thine, both house and land:
Then there's that old Lord Maurice, not a whit
More tame for his gray hairs—Alas me! flit!
Flit like a ghost away."—"Ah, gossip dear,   105
We're safe enough; here in this arm-chair sit,

---

67 **timbrels:** tambourines (cf. "Ode on a Grecian Urn," line 10)   70 **Hoodwinked with faery fancy:**
deceived by a kind of fairy tale   **all amort:** (French, *à la mort*) like one dead (to the world around
her)   71 **her lambs:** Lambs were associated with St. Agnes (*agnus* is Latin for *lamb*); two lambs
were blessed at the mass on her feast-day and their wool later woven by the nuns.
77 **buttressed:** in the shadow of a buttress   81 **sooth:** truth   90 **beldame:** old woman, old nurse
98 **hie thee:** get yourself away   105 **gossip:** godparent, close (woman) friend

And tell me how"—"Good saints! not here, not here;
Follow me, child, or else these stones will be thy bier."

He followed through a lowly archèd way,
Brushing the cobwebs with his lofty plume;   110
And as she muttered "Well-a—well-a-day!"
He found him in a little moonlight room,
Pale, latticed, chill, and silent as a tomb.
"Now tell me where is Madeline," said he,
"O tell me, Angela, by the holy loom   115
Which none but secret sisterhood may see,
When they St. Agnes' wool are weaving piously."

"St. Agnes! Ah! it is St. Agnes' Eve—
Yet men will murder upon holy days:
Thou must hold water in a witch's sieve,   120
And be liege-lord of all the elves and fays,
To venture so: it fills me with amaze
To see thee, Porphyro!—St. Agnes' Eve!
God's help! my lady fair the conjuror plays
This very night: good angels her deceive!   125
But let me laugh awhile, I've mickle time to grieve."

Feebly she laugheth in the languid moon,
While Porphyro upon her face doth look,
Like puzzled urchin on an aged crone
Who keepeth closed a wonderous riddle-book,   130
As spectacled she sits in chimney nook.
But soon his eyes grew brilliant, when she told
His lady's purpose; and he scarce could brook
Tears, at the thought of those enchantments cold,
And Madeline asleep in lap of legends old.   135

Sudden a thought came like a full-blown rose,
Flushing his brow, and in his painèd heart
Made purple riot: then doth he propose
A stratagem, that makes the beldame start:
"A cruel man and impious thou art: 140
Sweet lady, let her pray, and sleep, and dream
Alone with her good angels, far apart
From wicked men like thee. Go, go!—I deem
Thou canst not surely be the same that thou didst seem."

"I will not harm her, by all saints I swear,"   145
Quoth Porphyro: "O may I ne'er find grace
When my weak voice shall whisper its last prayer,
If one of her soft ringlets I displace,
Or look with ruffian passion in her face:
Good Angela, believe me by these tears;   150
Or I will, even in a moment's space,
Awake, with horrid shout, my foemen's ears,
And beard them, though they be more fanged than wolves and bears."

120 **hold water**...: have magical powers   121 **fays**: fairies   124 **the conjurer plays**: is practicing
magic   126 **mickle**: much   133 **brook**: hold back

"Ah! why wilt thou affright a feeble soul?
A poor, weak, palsy-stricken, churchyard thing,   155
Whose passing-bell may ere the midnight toll;
Whose prayers for thee, each morn and evening,
Were never missed,"—Thus plaining, doth she bring
A gentler speech from burning Porphyro;
So woeful, and of such deep sorrowing,   160
That Angela gives promise she will do
Whatever he shall wish, betide her weal or woe.

Which was, to lead him, in close secrecy,
Even to Madeline's chamber, and there hide
Him in a closet, of such privacy   165
That he might see her beauty unespied,
And win perhaps that night a peerless bride,
While legioned faeries paced the coverlet,
And pale enchantment held her sleepy-eyed.
Never on such a night have lovers met,   170
Since Merlin paid his demon all the monstrous debt.

"It shall be as thou wishest," said the dame:
"All cates and dainties shall be storèd there
Quickly on this feast-night: by the tambour frame
Her own lute thou wilt see: no time to spare,   175
For I am slow and feeble, and scarce dare
On such a catering trust my dizzy head.
Wait here, my child, with patience, kneel in prayer
The while: Ah! thou must needs the lady wed,
Or may I never leave my grave among the dead."   180

So saying, she hobbled off with busy fear.
The lover's endless minutes slowly passed;
The dame returned, and whispered in his ear
To follow her; with aged eyes aghast
From fright of dim espial. Safe at last,   185
Through many a dusky gallery, they gain
The maiden's chamber, silken, hushed, and chaste;
Where Porphyro took covert, pleased amain.
His poor guide hurried back with agues in her brain.

Her faltering hand upon the balustrade,   190
Old Angela was feeling for the stair,
When Madeline, St. Agnes' charmèd maid,
Rose, like a missioned spirit, unaware:
With silver taper's light, and pious care,
She turned, and down the aged gossip led   195
To a safe level matting. Now prepare,

155 churchyard thing: person almost ready for burial   **156 passing-bell:** bell rung as one "passes on"   **158 plaining:** complaining, grieving   **168 legioned faeries:** legions of fairies. Cf. the Sylphs in Pope's "The Rape of the Lock."   **171 Merlin . . . :** Merlin is the magician in the stories of King Arthur. Since Keats is speaking of how "lovers met," Merlin's "debt" could be the promise he made to his mistress, Viviane, to join her ("for so I have covenanted and promised") even though he knew it meant he would be imprisoned forever through the spells he had taught her. Viviane might be called "his demon" in that she "knew so many enchantments that never other woman knew so much." The story is told in an edition of Sir Thomas Malory published in 1817.   **173 cates:** delicacies   **174 tambour:** frame to hold embroidery   **188 amain:** greatly

Young Porphyro, for gazing on that bed;
She comes, she comes again, like ring-dove frayed and fled.

Out went the taper as she hurried in;
Its little smoke, in pallid moonshine, died: 200
She closed the door, she panted, all akin
To spirits of the air, and visions wide:
No uttered syllable, or, woe betide!
But to her heart, her heart was voluble,
Paining with eloquence her balmy side;   205
As though a tongueless nightingale should swell
Her throat in vain, and die, heart-stifled, in her dell.

A casement high and triple-arched there was,
All garlanded with carven imageries,
Of fruits, and flowers, and bunches of knot-grass,   210
And diamonded with panes of quaint device,
Innumerable of stains and splendid dyes,
As are the tiger-moth's deep-damasked wings;
And in the midst, 'mong thousand heraldries,
And twilight saints, and dim emblazonings,   215
A shielded scutcheon blushed with blood of queens and kings.

Full on this casement shone the wintry moon,
And threw warm gules on Madeline's fair breast,
As down she knelt for Heaven's grace and boon;
Rose-bloom fell on her hands, together pressed,   220
And on her silver cross soft amethyst,
And on her hair a glory, like a saint:
She seemed a splendid angel, newly dressed,
Save wings, for heaven:—Porphyro grew faint:
She knelt, so pure a thing, so free from mortal taint.   225

Anon his heart revives: her vespers done,
Of all its wreathèd pearls her hair she frees;
Unclasps her warmèd jewels one by one;
Loosens her fragrant bodice; by degrees
Her rich attire creeps rustling to her knees: 230
Half-hidden, like a mermaid in sea-weed,
Pensive awhile she dreams awake, and sees,
In fancy, fair St. Agnes in her bed,
But dares not look behind, or all the charm is fled.

Soon, trembling in her soft and chilly nest,   235
In sort of wakeful swoon, perplexed she lay,
Until the poppied warmth of sleep oppressed
Her soothèd limbs, and soul fatigued away;
Flown, like a thought, until the morrow-day;
Blissfully havened both from joy and pain;   240
Clasped like a missal where swart paynims pray;

---

198 **frayed:** frightened   205 **balmy:** like balm, fragrant   210 **knot-grass:** grass with jointed stems
213 **tiger-moth:** a large scarlet and brown moth   **deep-damasked:** richly colored (especially with the
red of the "damask rose")   216 **shielded scutcheon:** a coat of arms shaped (as usual) like a shield
blushed with blood: was crimson with indications of royal blood   218 **gules:** red (in heraldry)
219 **boon:** favor   222 **a glory:** a gloriole, halo   237 **poppied:** like an opiate   241 **swart paynims:**
swarthy pagans

Blinded alike from sunshine and from rain,
As though a rose should shut, and be a bud again.

Stolen to this paradise, and so entranced,
Porphyro gazed upon her empty dress,   245
And listened to her breathing, if it chanced
To wake into a slumberous tenderness;
Which when he heard, that minute did he bless,
And breathed himself: then from the closet crept,
Noiseless as fear in a wide wilderness,   250
And over the hushed carpet, silent, stepped,
And 'tween the curtains peeped where, lo!—how fast she slept.

Then by the bed-side, where the faded moon
Made a dim, silver twilight, soft he set
A table, and, half anguished, threw thereon   255
A cloth of woven crimson, gold, and jet:—
O for some drowsy Morphean amulet!
The boisterous, midnight, festive clarion,
The kettle-drum, and far-heard clarionet,
Affray his ears, though but in dying tone:—   260
The hall door shuts again, and all the noise is gone.

And still she slept an azure-lidded sleep,
In blanchèd linen, smooth, and lavendered,
While he from forth the closet brought a heap
Of candied apple, quince, and plum, and gourd;   265
With jellies soother than the creamy curd,
And lucent syrups, tinct with cinnamon;
Manna and dates, in argosy transferred
From Fez; and spiced dainties, every one,
From silken Samarcand to cedared Lebanon.   270

These delicates he heaped with glowing hand
On golden dishes and in baskets bright
Of wreathèd silver: sumptuous they stand
In the retirèd quiet of the night,
Filling the chilly room with perfume light.—   275
"And now, my love, my seraph fair, awake!
Thou art my heaven, and I thine eremite:
Open thine eyes, for meek St. Agnes' sake,
Or I shall drowse beside thee, so my soul doth ache."

Thus whispering, his warm, unnervèd arm   280
Sank in her pillow. Shaded was her dream
By the dusk curtains:—'twas a midnight charm
Impossible to melt as icèd stream;

---

252 **curtains:** bed-curtains 257 **Morphean amulet:** a charm employing the power of Morpheus, god
of dreams 260 **affray:** startle, frighten 263 **blanchèd:** bleached 264–270 The gourmet spread
(apparently never eaten) has been much criticized as improbable—even though Porphyro knows
Madeline has not eaten, and even though such exotic food might be available on the night of a big
party in the palace. Apropos or not, the savory "heap" does contribute to the atmosphere of sensuous
opulence Keats is creating. 266 **soother:** smoother, sweeter 267 **lucent:** clear, bright **tinct:** fla-
vored 268 **argosy:** large merchant ship, or fleet of such ships 269 **Fez:** city in Morocco. Like the
names in the next line, it suggests exotic glamor. 270 **Samarcand:** an ancient city of central Asia,
north of Afghanistan 277 **eremite:** hermit; here, worshipper

The lustrous salvers in the moonlight gleam;
Broad golden fringe upon the carpet lies: 285
It seemed he never, never could redeem
From such a stedfast spell his lady's eyes;
So mused, awhile, entoiled in woofèd phantasies.

Awakening up, he took her hollow lute,—
Tumultuous,—and, in chords that tenderest be,   290
He played an ancient ditty, long since mute,
In Provence called, "La belle dame sans merci":
Close to her ear touching the melody;—
Wherewith disturbed, she uttered a soft moan:
He ceased—she panted quick—and suddenly   295
Her blue affrayèd eyes wide open shone:
Upon his knees he sank, pale as smooth-sculptured stone.

Her eyes were open, but she still beheld,
Now wide awake, the vision of her sleep:
There was a painful change, that nigh expelled   300
The blisses of her dream so pure and deep
At which fair Madeline began to weep,
And moan forth witless words with many a sigh;
While still her gaze on Porphyro would keep;
Who knelt, with joinèd hands and piteous eye,   305
Fearing to move or speak, she looked so dreamingly.

"Ah, Porphyro!" said she, "but even now
Thy voice was at sweet tremble in mine ear,
Made tunable with every sweetest vow;
And those sad eyes were spiritual and clear: 310
How changed thou art! how pallid, chill, and drear!
Give me that voice again, my Porphyro,
Those looks immortal, those complainings dear!
Oh leave me not in this eternal woe,
For if thou diest, my love, I know not where to go."   315

Beyond a mortal man impassioned far
At these voluptuous accents, he arose,
Ethereal, flushed, and like a throbbing star
Seen 'mid the sapphire heaven's deep repose;
Into her dream he melted, as the rose   320
Blendeth its odour with the violet,—
Solution sweet: meantime the frost-wind blows
Like love's alarum, pattering the sharp sleet
Against the window-panes; St. Agnes' moon hath set.

'Tis dark: quick pattereth the flaw-blown sleet.   325
"This is no dream, my bride, my Madeline!"
'Tis dark: the icèd gusts still rave and beat:
"No dream, alas! alas! and woe is mine!
Porphyro will leave me here to fade and pine.—
Cruel! what traitor could thee hither bring?   330
I curse not, for my heart is lost in thine,

---

288 **entoiled:** involved, absorbed   **woofèd:** woven   292 **Provence:** Cf. "Ode to a Nightingale,"
line 14. For the song, cf. Keats's poem of the same title.   323 **love's alarum:** a warning for lovers
325 **flaw-blown:** blown by gusts of wind

Though thou forsakest a deceivèd thing:—
A dove forlorn and lost with sick unprunèd wing."

"My Madeline! sweet dreamer! lovely bride!
Say, may I be for aye thy vassal blest?   335
Thy beauty's shield, heart-shaped and vermeil-dyed?
Ah, silver shrine, here will I take my rest
After so many hours of toil and quest,
A famished pilgrim,—saved by miracle.
Though I have found, I will not rob thy nest   340
Saving of thy sweet self; if thou think'st well
To trust, fair Madeline, to no rude infidel.

"Hark! 'tis an elfin-storm from faery land,
Of haggard seeming, but a boon indeed:
Arise—arise! the morning is at hand;—   345
The bloated wassaillers will never heed:—
Let us away, my love, with happy speed;
There are no ears to hear, or eyes to see,—
Drowned all in Rhenish and the sleepy mead:
Awake! arise! my love, and fearless be,   350
For o'er the southern moors I have a home for thee."

She hurried at his words, beset with fears,
For there were sleeping dragons all around,
At glaring watch, perhaps, with ready spears—
Down the wide stairs a darkling way they found.—   355
In all the house was heard no human sound.
A chain-drooped lamp was flickering by each door;
The arras, rich with horseman, hawk, and hound,
Fluttered in the besieging wind's uproar;
And the long carpets rose along the gusty floor.   360

They glide, like phantoms, into the wide hall;
Like phantoms, to the iron porch, they glide;
Where lay the porter, in uneasy sprawl,
With a huge empty flagon by his side:
The wakeful bloodhound rose, and shook his hide,   365
But his sagacious eye an inmate owns:
By one, and one, the bolts full easy slide:—
The chains lie silent on the footworn stones:—
The key turns, and the door upon its hinges groans.

And they are gone: aye, ages long ago   370
These lovers fled away into the storm.
That night the Baron dreamt of many a woe,
And all his warrior-guests, with shade and form
Of witch, and demon, and large coffin-worm,
Were long be-nightmared. Angela the old   375
Died palsy-twitched, with meagre face deform;
The beadsman, after thousand *Ave*'s told,
For aye unsought for slept among his ashes cold.

333 **unprunèd:** unpreened, uncared for   335 **for aye:** forever   336 **vermeil-dyed:** vermilion   337 **here . . . rest:** This poem often recalls *Romeo and Juliet*. There is a particularly ominous echo here: Romeo, in his final speech, just before killing himself, says, "here / Will I set up my everlasting rest. . . ."   344 **haggard:** wild   **boon:** piece of luck, blessing   349 **Rhenish:** Rhine wine   **mead:** drink made of fermented honey   355 **darkling:** in the dark   366 **owns:** knows, acknowledges   376 **deform:** deformed   377 *Ave's*: Hail, Mary's

This Living Hand

This living hand, now warm and capable
Of earnest grasping, would, if it were cold
And in the icy silence of the tomb,
So haunt thy days and chill thy dreaming nights
That thou would wish thine own heart dry of blood
So in my veins red life might stream again,
And thou be conscience-calmed—see here it is—
I hold it toward you.

1819. *The Poetical Works of John Keats,* 6th ed., H. Buxton Forman, 1898.

William Barnes
(1801–1886)

Though Barnes, who wrote much of his poetry in the rural dialect of his native Dorset (near Wales), might seem a "peasant poet," he was a sophisticated scholar whose *Philological Grammar* (1854) was based on comparisons of more than 60 languages. He spent most of his life as a simple country schoolmaster, in middle age ordained an Anglican priest. Though a defender of Anglo-Saxon English, he imported into his poetry elaborate techniques from the many literatures he knew. Gerard Manley Hopkins thought Barnes's dialect poems had "more true poetry than Burns"; Thomas Hardy edited a volume of his work in 1908.

Musings

Before the falling summer sun
    The boughs are shining all as gold,
And down below them waters run,
    As there in former years they rolled;
The poolside wall is glowing hot,   5
    The pool is in a dazzling glare,
And makes it seem as, ah! 'tis not,
    A summer when my life was fair.

The evening, gliding slowly by,
    Seems one of those that long have fled;   10
The night comes on to star the sky
    As then it darkened round my head.
A girl is standing by yon door,
    As one in happy times was there,
And this day seems, but is no more,   15
    A day when all my life was fair.

We hear from yonder feast the hum
    Of voices, as in summers past;
And hear the beatings of the drum
    Again come throbbing on the blast.   20
There neighs a horse in yonder plot,
    As once there neighed our petted mare,
And summer seems, but ah! is not
    The summer when our life was fair.

A Selection from Unpublished Poems . . . , 1870.

The Wife A-Lost

Since I noo mwore do zee your feäce,
    Up steäirs or down below,
I'll zit me in the lwonesome pleäce,
    Where flat-boughed beech do grow:
Below the beeches' bough, my love,   5
    Where you did never come,
An' I don't look to meet ye now,
    As I do look at hwome.

Since you noo mwore be at my zide,
    In walks in zummer het,   10
I'll goo alwone where mist do ride,
    Drough trees a-drippèn wet:
Below the raïn-wet bough, my love,
    Where you did never come,
An' I don't grieve to miss ye now,   15
    As I do grieve at hwome.

Since now bezide my dinner-bwoard
    Your vaïce do never sound,
I'll eat the bit I can avword,
    A-vield upon the ground;   20
Below the darksome bough, my love,
    Where you did never dine,
An' I don't grieve to miss ye now,
    As I at hwome do pine.

Since I do miss your vaïce an' feäce   25
    In praÿer at eventide,
I'll praÿ wi' woone sad vaïce vor greäce
    To goo where you do bide;
Above the tree an' bough, my love,
    Where you be gone avore,   30
An' be a-waïtèn vor me now,
    To come vor evermwore.

1852–1859. *Hwomely Rhymes: A Second Collection of Poems in the Dorset Dialect*, 1859.

Barnes chose to write most of his poems in his native Dorset dialect. In it, z stands for our s (*zee, zit* for *see, sit,* etc.); *v* for our *f* (*a-vield, avore* for *a-field, afore,* etc.); the ending *-ing* is written *-èn* (*a-drippèn* for *a-dripping,* etc.). Among the vowels, *wo* stands for the long *o* sound (*mwore, hwome, wold* for *more, home, old,* etc.); *oo* is sometimes our *o* (*noo, goo* for *no, go*); other vowel sounds are drawled into diphthongs (*feäce, steäirs* for *face, stairs; vaïce* for *voice,* etc.).

10 **het:** heat   12 **drough:** through   19 **avword:** afford

Ralph Waldo Emerson
(1803–1882)

Emerson, whose family was poor, worked his way through Harvard, taught for a few years, then returned to the Harvard Divinity School. Independent, uncomfortable with traditional doctrines and duties, he resigned soon after his ordination and went to Europe for a year, where he met Wordsworth and Coleridge, among others. In 1834 a legacy from his first wife, who had died three years before, enabled him to settle down in Concord in scholarly leisure; he remarried in 1834. During the rest of his life he lectured, edited *The Dial*, published his influential *Essays*, and became known for his poems.

Concord Hymn

Sung at the Completion of the Battle Monument,
July 4, 1837

By the rude bridge that arched the flood,
    Their flag to April's breeze unfurled,
Here once the embattled farmers stood
    And fired the shot heard round the world.

The foe long since in silence slept;   5
    Alike the conqueror silent sleeps;
And Time the ruined bridge has swept
    Down the dark stream which seaward creeps.

On this green bank, by this soft stream,
    We set to-day a votive stone;   10
That memory may their deed redeem,
    When, like our sires, our sons are gone.

Spirit, that made those heroes dare
    To die, and leave their children free,
Bid Time and Nature gently spare   15
    The shaft we raise to them and thee.

1837. *Poems,* 1847 (as "Hymn").

The monument commemorated the battles of Lexington and Concord, April 19, 1775, when a detachment of British soldiers sent to destroy munitions at Concord met with resistance at both towns. Though compelled to retreat, they left dead a number of the "embattled farmers" and gave the Americans a tremendous propaganda victory, news of which (to the discredit of the British party then in power) might be said to have gone "round the world."

10 **votive:** pertaining to a vow; offered in gratitude or devotion

Ode

Inscribed to W. H. Channing

Though loath to grieve
The evil time's sole patriot,
I cannot leave
My honied thought
For the priest's cant,   5
Or statesman's rant.

If I refuse
My study for their politique,
Which at the best is trick,
The angry Muse   10
Puts confusion in my brain.

But who is he that prates
Of the culture of mankind,
Of better arts and life?

1846. Ibid.

The Rev. William Henry Channing (1810–1884) was a humanitarian who apparently had been urging Emerson to be more of an activist in the fight against slavery. He was a nephew of the famous William Ellery Channing (1780–1842), who also spoke out for social reform. Emerson is saying that a poet and thinker should not leave his "chosen work" to take an active part in the "cant" and "rant" of politics, even though his sympathies are all for reform. The poem itself is strongly partisan.

Go, blindworm, go,   15
Behold the famous States
Harrying Mexico
With rifle and with knife!

Or who, with accent bolder,
Dare praise the freedom-loving mountaineer?   20
I found by thee, O rushing Contoocook!
And in thy valleys, Agiochook!
The jackals of the negro-holder.

The God who made New Hampshire
Taunted the lofty land   25
With little men;—
Small bat and wren
House in the oak:—
If earth-fire cleave
The upheaved land, and bury the folk,   30
The southern crocodile would grieve.
Virtue palters; Right is hence;
Freedom praised, but hid;
Funeral eloquence
Rattles the coffin-lid.   35

What boots thy zeal,
O glowing friend,
That would indignant rend
The northland from the south?
Wherefore? to what good end?   40
Boston Bay and Bunker Hill
Would serve things still;—
Things are of the snake.

The horseman serves the horse,
The neatherd serves the neat,   45
The merchant serves the purse,
The eater serves his meat;
'Tis the day of the chattel,
Web to weave, and corn to grind;
Things are in the saddle,   50
And ride mankind.

There are two laws discrete,
Not reconciled,—
Law for man, and law for thing;
That last builds town and fleet,   55
But it runs wild,
And doth the man unking.

15 **blindworm:** a burrowing lizard with tiny eyes   16–18 The war with Mexico (1846–1848) was seen by Emerson and others, especially in New England, as an unprovoked war of expansionism aimed at securing more slave territory.   21 **Contoocook:** a river in New Hampshire   22 **Agiochook:** Indian name for the White Mountains (New Hampshire)   23 **jackals...:** sympathizers with the institution of slavery   31 **southern crocodile:** the institution of slavery and its defenders   32 **palters:** mumbles, deals crookedly or evasively, equivocates   **hence:** gone away   36 **what boots...:** what good does it do   37 **glowing:** ardent   **friend:** Channing—or others who believe in splitting north and south   41 The Boston-area place-names stand for New England.   42 **serve:** be in servitude to (also in lines 44–47)   43 **the snake:** evil   45 **neatherd ... neat:** cattle-herder ... cattle   48 **chattel:** material possessions

'Tis fit the forest fall,
The steep be graded,
The mountain tunnelled,   60
The sand shaded,
The orchard planted,
The glebe tilled,
The prairie granted,
The steamer built.   65

Let man serve law for man;
Live for friendship, live for love,
For truth's and harmony's behoof;
The state may follow how it can,
As Olympus follows Jove.   70

   Yet do not I implore
The wrinkled shopman to my sounding woods,
Nor bid the unwilling senator
Ask votes of thrushes in the solitudes.
Every one to his chosen work;—   75
Foolish hands may mix and mar;
Wise and sure the issues are.
Round they roll till dark is light,
Sex to sex, and even to odd;—
The over-god   80
Who marries Right to Might,
Who peoples, unpeoples,—
He who exterminates
Races by stronger races,
Black by white faces,—   85
Knows to bring honey
Out of the lion;
Grafts gentlest scion
On pirate and Turk.

The Cossack eats Poland,   90
Like stolen fruit;
Her last noble is ruined,
Her last poet mute:
Straight, into double band
The victors divide;   95
Half for freedom strike and stand;—
The astonished Muse finds thousands at her side.

---

63 **glebe:** soil   66–70 Human values should come first; political values second.   68 **behoof:** bene-
fit   70 **Olympus . . . Jove:** Mount Olympus, the home of the gods in classical mythology, was under
the command of Jove.   86–87 In the Old Testament, Judg. 14 tells how Samson killed a young lion
with his bare hands. When he returned after a time to look at the carcass, he found that a swarm of
bees had settled in it and filled it with honey, which he ate. Later he made up a riddle about how
"Out of the eater came forth meat, and out of the strong came forth sweetness." The incident stands
for the way in which good can come out of evil.   90 **Cossack . . . Poland:** Much of Poland had been
under Russian domination for over half a century. Uprisings in 1830 and again in 1846 (the year of
Emerson's poem) were harshly repressed, sometimes with the help of the Cossacks, proverbially sav-
age Russian cavalrymen.   93 **her last poet:** perhaps a reference to Adam Mickiewicz (1798–1855), the
great Polish romantic poet, who wrote little poetry during the last 20 years of his life, much of which
was given over to patriotic activities

Days

Daughters of Time, the hypocritic Days,
Muffled and dumb like barefoot dervishes,
And marching single in an endless file,
Bring diadems and faggots in their hands.
To each they offer gifts after his will,   5
Bread, kingdoms, stars, and sky that holds them all.
I, in my pleachèd garden, watched the pomp,
Forgot my morning wishes, hastily
Took a few herbs and apples, and the Day
Turned and departed silent. I, too late,   10
Under her solemn fillet saw the scorn.

1851. *May-Day and Other Pieces*, 1867.

7 **pleachèd:** with interwoven branches (for decorative effect)

Brahma

If the red slayer think he slays,
    Or if the slain think he is slain,
They know not well the subtle ways
    I keep, and pass, and turn again.

Far or forgot to me is near;   5
    Shadow and sunlight are the same;
The vanished gods to me appear;
    And one to me are shame and fame.

They reckon ill who leave me out;
    When me they fly, I am the wings;   10
I am the doubter and the doubt,
    And I the hymn the Brahmin sings.

The strong gods pine for my abode,
    And pine in vain the sacred Seven;
But thou, meek lover of the good!   15
    Find me, and turn thy back on heaven.

1856? Ibid.

See Additional Notes (p. 765).

Thomas Lovell Beddoes
(1803–1849)

Son of a well-known scientist and writer, Beddoes published verse and drama while still at Oxford. In Germany, where he went to study medicine, he became interested in revolutionary movements. Obsessed with the thought of death, he worked for years on his poetic tragedy *Death's Jest Book*, which was published after his suicide in Switzerland.

Dream-Pedlary

I

If there were dreams to sell,
  What would you buy?
Some cost a passing-bell;
  Some a light sigh,
That shakes from life's fresh crown   5
Only a roseleaf down.
    If there were dreams to sell,
    Merry and sad to tell,
    And the crier rung the bell,
        What would you buy?   10

II

A cottage lone and still,
  With bowers nigh,
Shadowy, my woes to still,
  Until I die.
Such pearl from life's fresh crown   15
Fain would I shake me down.
    Were dreams to have at will,
    This would best heal my ill,
        This would I buy.

III

But there were dreams to sell,   20
  Ill didst thou buy;
Life is a dream, they tell,
  Waking, to die.
Dreaming a dream to prize,
Is wishing ghosts to rise;   25
    And, if I had the spell
    To call the buried, well,
        Which one would I?

IV

If there are ghosts to raise,
  What shall I call,   30
Out of hell's murky haze,
  Heaven's blue hall?
Raise my loved long-lost boy
To lead me to his joy.
    There are no ghosts to raise;   35
    Out of death lead no ways;
        Vain is the call.

V

Know'st thou not ghosts to sue?
  No love thou hast.
Else lie, as I will do,   40
  And breathe thy last.

1829–1837. *The Poems Posthumous and Collected*, 1851.

Dream-Pedlary: the business of dealing in dreams   3 **passing-bell:** bell tolled when one passes on (cf. "The Eve of St. Agnes," line 156)   9 **crier:** one who "cries" or announces goods for sale   12 **bowers:** pleasant woody recesses, arbors   16 **fain:** gladly   38 **sue:** implore

So out of life's fresh crown
Fall like a rose-leaf down.
    Thus are the ghosts to woo;
    Thus are all dreams made true,   45
        Ever to last!

Elizabeth Barrett Browning
(1806–1861)

When about 15, Elizabeth Barrett, whose girlhood was spent pleasantly in a country house near Wales, fell ill, probably from a spinal injury, which left her an invalid for much of her life. When she was about 30, her family moved to Wimpole Street in London; the contributions she sent to magazines from her bedside made her well known in the literary world. A fan letter from Robert Browning, six years younger than she, led to their meeting, to their falling in love, and—though her high-handed father had forbidden his children to marry—to their marriage. As her health improved, the Brownings established a house in Florence, where a son was born two years later and where Mrs. Browning interested herself in such liberal causes as Italian independence and the abolition of slavery in America.

From Sonnets from the Portuguese

XVIII

I never gave a lock of hair away
To a man, dearest, except this to thee,
Which now upon my fingers thoughtfully,
I ring out to the full brown length and say
"Take it." My day of youth went yesterday;   5
My hair no longer bounds to my foot's glee,
Nor plant I it from rose or myrtle-tree,
As girls do, any more: it only may
Now shade on two pale cheeks the mark of tears,
Taught drooping from the head that hangs aside   10
Through sorrow's trick. I thought the funeral-shears
Would take this first, but love is justified:
Take it thou—finding pure, from all those years,
The kiss my mother left there when she died.

XXVIII

My letters! all dead paper, mute and white!
And yet they seem alive and quivering
Against my tremulous hands which loose the string
And let them drop down on my knee tonight.
This said, he wished to have me in his sight   5
Once, as a friend: this fixed a day in spring
To come and touch my hand . . . a simple thing,
Yet I wept for it!—this, . . . the paper's light . . .
Said, *Dear, I love thee*; and I sank and quailed
As if God's future thundered on my past.   10

1846. *Poems*, 1850.

Elizabeth Barrett Browning wrote her series of 44 sonnets to Robert Browning before their marriage in 1846, but did not show them to him for three years. Her husband suggested the "ambiguous" title to conceal their autobiographical nature. She was an admirer of the love poems of the Portuguese poet Camoens (1524–1580); in her "Catarina to Camoens" she assumes the persona of a woman he loved. Browning affectionately called her "my little Portuguese." The two sonnets given here are simpler, more direct and personal than the famous "How do I love thee? Let me count the ways. . . ."

This said, *I am thine*—and so its ink has paled
With lying at my heart that beat too fast,
And this . . . O love, thy words have ill availed
If, what this said, I dared repeat at last!

Lord Walter's Wife

"But why do you go?" said the lady, while both sate under the yew,
And her eyes were alive in their depth, as the kraken beneath the sea-blue.

"Because I fear you," he answered;—"because you are far too fair,
And able to strangle my soul in a mesh of your gold-coloured hair."

"Oh, that," she said, "is no reason! Such knots are quickly undone,   5
And too much beauty, I reckon, is nothing but too much sun."

"Yet farewell so," he answered;—"the sunstroke's fatal at times.
I value your husband, Lord Walter, whose gallop rings still from the limes."

"Oh, that," she said, "is no reason. You smell a rose through a fence:
If two should smell it, what matter? who grumbles, and where's
    the pretence?"   10

"But I," he replied, "have promised another, when love was free,
To love her alone, alone, who alone and afar loves me."

"Why, that," she said, "is no reason. Love's always free, I am told.
Will you vow to be safe from the headache on Tuesday, and think it will hold?"

"But you," he replied, "have a daughter, a young little child, who was laid
In your lap to be pure; so I leave you: the angels would make me afraid."

"Oh, that," she said, "is no reason. The angels keep out of the way;
And Dora, the child, observes nothing, although you should please me and
    stay."

At which he rose up in his anger,—"Why, now, you no longer are fair!
Why, now, you no longer are fatal, but ugly and hateful, I swear."   20

At which she laughed out in her scorn,—"These men! Oh, these men over-nice,
Who are shocked if a colour not virtuous, is frankly put on by a vice."

Her eyes blazed upon him—"And *you!* You bring us your vices so near
That we smell them! You think in our presence a thought 'twould defame us to
    hear!

"What reason had you, and what right,—I appeal to your soul from my life,—
To find me too fair as a woman? Why, sir, I am pure, and a wife.

1860. *Last Poems,* 1862.

This treatment of relations between the sexes was rejected "for indecency" (as Mrs. Browning wrote a
friend) by Thackeray, then editor of the *Cornhill Magazine,* because of what was considered the risqué
character of its theme. Thackeray described it as about "unlawful passion, felt by a man for a woman."
But what may have shocked the famous novelist even more was the frankness with which the woman
put the "unlawful passion" in its place.

2 **kraken:** a sea-monster of Scandinavian mythology   8 **limes:** linden trees, here probably lining the
drive   11 **when love was free:** when I had no ties, was free to choose

"Is the day-star too fair up above you? It burns you not. Dare you imply
I brushed you more close than the star does, when Walter had set me as high?

"If a man finds a woman too fair, he means simply adapted too much
To uses unlawful and fatal. The praise!—shall I thank you for such?   30

"Too fair?—not unless you misuse us! and surely if, once in a while,
You attain to it, straightway you call us no longer too fair, but too vile.

"A moment,—I pray your attention!—I have a poor word in my head
I must utter, though womanly custom would set it down better unsaid.

"You grew, sir, pale to impertinence, once when I showed you a ring.   35
You kissed my fan when I dropped it. No matter!—I've broken the thing. ,

"You did me the honour, perhaps, to be moved at my side now and then
In the senses—a vice, I have heard, which is common to beasts and some men.

"Love's a virtue for heroes!—as white as the snow on high hills,
And immortal as every great soul is that struggles, endures, and fulfils.   40

"I love my Walter profoundly,—you, Maude, though you faltered a week,
For the sake of . . . what was it? an eyebrow? or, less still, a mole on a cheek?

"And since, when all's said, you're too noble to stoop to the frivolous cant
About crimes irresistible, virtues that swindle, betray, and supplant,

"I determined to prove to yourself that, whate'er you might dream or avow
By illusion, you wanted precisely no more of me than you have now.

"There! Look me full in the face!—in the face. Understand, if you can,
That the eyes of such women as I am, are clean as the palm of a man.

"Drop his hand, you insult him. Avoid us for fear we should cost you a scar—
You take us for harlots, I tell you, and not for the women we are.   50

"You wronged me: but then I considered . . . there's Walter! And so at the end,
I vowed that he should not be mulcted, by me, in the hand of a friend.

"Have I hurt you indeed? We are quits then. Nay, friend of my Walter, be
    mine!
Come Dora, my darling, my angel, and help me to ask him to dine."

41 **Maude:** here, the man's (probably last) name   52 **mulcted:** punished (by the loss of his friend)

Henry Wadsworth Longfellow
(1807–1882)

Longfellow, the most popular American poet of his century (though his reputation has
not held up), was born in Portland, Maine. After studying Romance languages in Europe,
he returned to teach at Bowdoin; a second trip, to study Germanic languages, was fol-
lowed by his appointment as professor of modern languages at Harvard. After two dec-
ades of domestic happiness, his wife died tragically in 1861 when a candle flame set her
gown afire. Thereafter Longfellow began his translation of Dante's *Divine Comedy*. His
seventy-fifth birthday was the occasion of national celebration in America.

The Jewish Cemetery at Newport

How strange it seems! These Hebrews in their graves,
    Close by the street of this fair seaport town,
Silent beside the never-silent waves,
    At rest in all this moving up and down!

The trees are white with dust, that o'er their sleep   5
    Wave their broad curtains in the south wind's breath,
While underneath these leafy tents they keep
    The long, mysterious Exodus of Death.

And these sepulchral stones, so old and brown,
    That pave with level flags their burial-place,   10
Seem like the tablets of the Law, thrown down
    And broken by Moses at the mountain's base.

The very names recorded here are strange,
    Of foreign accent, and of different climes;
Alvares and Rivera interchange   15
    With Abraham and Jacob of old times.

"Blessed be God! for he created Death!"
    The mourners said, "and Death is rest and peace;"
Then added, in the certainty of faith,
    "And giveth Life that nevermore shall cease."   20

Closed are the portals of their Synagogue,
    No Psalms of David now the silence break,
No Rabbi reads the ancient Decalogue
    In the grand dialect the Prophets spake.

Gone are the living, but the dead remain,   25
    And not neglected; for a hand unseen,
Scattering its bounty, like a summer rain,
    Still keeps their graves and their remembrance green.

How came they here? What burst of Christian hate,
    What persecution, merciless and blind,   30
Drove o'er the sea—that desert desolate—
    These Ishmaels and Hagars of mankind?

They lived in narrow streets and lanes obscure,
    Ghetto and Judenstrass, in mirk and mire;

1852. *The Courtship of Miles Standish*, 1858.

Newport, Rhode Island, has the oldest synagogue in America (1763); it is now a national historic site.

8 **Exodus:** The Greek word *exodus* means a going out or a departure; as title of the second book of the Bible it refers to the departure of the Israelites from Egypt.   10 **flags:** flagstones   11–12 **the tablets ... broken:** In Exod. 32 we are told how Moses, angry at seeing the Israelites worshipping the golden calf, threw down the "tables of testimony" God had given him on Mount Sinai "and brake them beneath the mount."   15 **Alvares and Rivera:** Many of the early Jewish settlers were Portuguese or Spanish.   16 **Abraham and Jacob:** Biblical patriarchs (founders of the ancient Hebrew families). Jacob was Abraham's grandson.   23 **Decalogue:** the ten commandments   32 **Ishmaels and Hagars:** Hagar was an Egyptian slave-girl of Sarah, the wife of Abraham. Sarah, childless then herself, gave Hagar to Abraham as his wife; Ishmael was the son born of their union. When Isaac was later born to Sarah and Abraham, Hagar and Ishmael were sent off to wander in the desert. Protected by Jehovah, Ishmael became the father of the race of desert Arabs. Cf. Gen. 16 and 21.   34 **Judenstrass[e]:** Street of Jews (German)

Taught in the school of patience to endure   35
    The life of anguish and the death of fire.

All their lives long, with the unleavened bread
    And bitter herbs of exile and its fears,
The wasting famine of the heart they fed,
    And slaked its thirst with marah of their tears.   40

Anathema maranatha! was the cry
    That rang from town to town, from street to street;
At every gate the accursed Mordecai
    Was mocked and jeered, and spurned by Christian feet.

Pride and humiliation hand in hand   45
    Walked with them through the world where'er they went;
Trampled and beaten were they as the sand,
    And yet unshaken as the continent.

For in the background figures vague and vast
    Of patriarchs and of prophets rose sublime,   50
And all the great traditions of the Past
    They saw reflected in the coming time.

And thus forever with reverted look
    The mystic volume of the world they read,
Spelling it backward, like a Hebrew book,   55
    Till life became a Legend of the Dead.

But ah! what once has been shall be no more!
    The groaning earth in travail and in pain
Brings forth its races, but does not restore,
    And the dead nations never rise again.   60

37 **unleavened bread:** Cf. Exod. 12. The feast of unleavened bread (bread made without yeast) was established by Jehovah as the Israelites left Egypt—possibly because they left in such haste that they did not have time to leaven the bread dough they had.   40 **marah:** bitterness (Hebrew)   41 **Anathema maranatha:** Taken as a curse when used by St. Paul in 1 Cor. 16:22: "If any man love not the Lord Jesus Christ, let him be Anathema Maranatha." The first word is Greek, the second Aramaic.   43 **Mordecai:** the foster father of Esther, whose beauty won her the love of and marriage with Ahasuerus, King of Persia. When Haman, the favorite of the king, plotted the death of Mordecai and other Jewish captives of the Persians, Mordecai, grieving, pleaded against the persecution. Saved by Esther, he was triumphant against his enemies. Longfellow sees him as a type of the persecuted Jew in the Christian era.   53 **reverted:** turned backwards

Divina Commedia, I

Oft have I seen at some cathedral door
    A laborer, pausing in the dust and heat,
    Lay down his burden, and with reverent feet
    Enter, and cross himself, and on the floor
Kneel to repeat his paternoster o'er;   5
    Far off the noises of the world retreat;
    The loud vociferations of the street
    Become an undistinguishable roar.

1864. *The Divine Comedy*, I, 1865.

Longfellow's translation of Dante's *Divine Comedy* was published in three volumes, 1865–1867. This sonnet accompanied volume one (*The Inferno*).

5 **paternoster:** the Our Father

So, as I enter here from day to day,
    And leave my burden at this minster gate,   10
    Kneeling in prayer, and not ashamed to pray,
The tumult of the time disconsolate
    To inarticulate murmurs dies away,
    While the eternal ages watch and wait.

10 **minster:** an important church, often a cathedral

Edgar Allan Poe
(1809–1849)

Poe's mother was an English actress—not then a respectable profession—who died when her son was two; his father was an alcoholic actor who disappeared soon afterwards. After five years in England, Poe attended the University of Virginia. At 18, he published his first book of poetry and enlisted in the army. In 1835 he married his 13-year-old cousin, thereafter moving from Baltimore to Philadelphia to New York, working hard at stories, poems, and reviews, but—though he had much personal charm—losing job after job because of his drinking. In 1845 the success of "The Raven" made him a celebrity in New York.

To Helen

Helen, thy beauty is to me
    Like those Nicean barks of yore,
That gently, o'er a perfumed sea,
    The weary, way-worn wanderer bore
    To his own native shore.   5

On desperate seas long wont to roam,
    Thy hyacinth hair, thy classic face,
Thy Naiad airs have brought me home
    To the glory that was Greece,
And the grandeur that was Rome.   10

Lo! in yon brilliant window-niche
    How statue-like I see thee stand,
    The agate lamp within thy hand!
Ah, Psyche, from the regions which
    Are Holy-Land!   15

1831–1843. *Poems*, 1831. This text from *The Raven and Other Poems*, 1845.

2 **Nicean:** of any of the ancient cities named Nicea, or perhaps of the island of Nysa, associated with Bacchus. Some think it means "victorious," from the Greek word for victory (Niké).   4 perhaps just any wanderer in life, though specific wanderers have been suggested—Bacchus, Menelaus, Ulysses, Catullus   7 **hyacinth:** crisply curled, like hyacinth petals   8 **Naiad:** a water nymph   14 **Psyche:** the soul personified as a goddess

Edward FitzGerald
(1809–1883)

FitzGerald spent his life as a country gentleman, translating from Greek and Spanish as well as from Persian, writing admirable letters to his many friends, and sailing for several months a year in the North Sea. His *Rubáiyát*, which was to become one of the best-known poems in English, was ignored on its publication, until the poet Rossetti came on a copy by chance and brought it to the attention of literary friends.

From The Rubáiyát of Omar Khayyám

I

Awake! for Morning in the Bowl of Night
Has flung the Stone that puts the Stars to Flight:
　　And Lo! the Hunter of the East has caught
The Sultán's Turret in a Noose of Light.

IIa

Before the phantom of False morning died,　　　　　　　　　5
Methought a Voice within the Tavern cried,
　　"When all the Temple is prepared within,
Why lags the drowsy Worshipper outside?"

III

And, as the Cock crew, those who stood before
The Tavern shouted—"Open then the Door!　　　　　　　　10
　　You know how little while we have to stay,
And, once departed, may return no more."

IV

Now the New Year reviving old Desires,
The thoughtful Soul to Solitude retires,
　　Where the WHITE HAND OF MOSES on the Bough　　　　　15
Puts out, and Jesus from the Ground suspires.

V

Irám indeed is gone with all its Rose,
And Jamshýd's Seven-ringed Cup where no one knows;
　　But still the Vine her ancient Ruby yields,
And still a Garden by the Water blows.　　　　　　　　　　20

VI

And David's Lips are lockt; but in divine
High piping Pehleví, with "Wine! Wine! Wine!
　　Red Wine!"—the Nightingale cries to the Rose
That yellow Cheek of hers to incarnadine.

1856–1879. *The Rubáiyát of Omar Khayyám,* 1859; 2nd ed., 1868; 5th ed., 1889.

During his lifetime, the Persian Omar Khayyám, who died around 1130, was more celebrated as mathematician than as poet. A favorite poetic form of his was the *rubá'i* or quatrain *(rubáiyát* is the plural); some think he may have written as many as a thousand of these unconnected little poems; stricter scholars doubt the authenticity of all but about a hundred. FitzGerald gave his selection of separate quatrains the continuity of a single sustained elegy, set against the changing background of a single day, from morning to night. Some quatrains he translated as units; some, as he said, he "mashed together" to make new units; a very few he drew from his reading of other Persian poets. Whether faithful or not as translation (and scholars of Persian feel that on the whole he was faithful), he has given us one of the best-known and most popular of all English poems. First published anonymously in 1859, it was brought out in enlarged and revised editions in 1868, 1872, 1879, and (posthumously) 1889. Since some of FitzGerald's revisions are improvements and some are not, it seemed desirable here to pick out a selection that would incorporate the best readings of several editions. Stanzas with simple numbers are from the first edition; those with *a* numbers from the second; those with *b* numbers from the fifth.

5 **False morning:** the brightening of the horizon about an hour before dawn   13 **New Year:** For Omar it began with the vernal equinox, which for us is the first day of spring.   15 **WHITE HAND** ...: in Exod. 4:6 the hand of Moses is, briefly and by miracle, "leprous as snow." But in the version Omar knew it is white, as many spring blossoms are.   16 **Jesus ... suspires:** The fragrance of spring is like the healing breath of Jesus.   17 **Irám:** a garden "planted by King Shaddád . . . now sunk somewhere in the sands of Arabia" [FitzGerald's note]   18 **Jamshýd:** a mythical Persian hero whose cup, symbolic of the seven planets, the seven seas, etc., was used in prophecy   21 **David:** the psalmist   22 **Pehleví:** FitzGerald thought this language, commonly called Pahlevi, "the old heroic Sanskrit of Persia."

VII

Come, fill the Cup, and in the Fire of Spring   25
The Winter Garment of Repentance fling:
　　The Bird of Time has but a little way
To fly—and Lo! the Bird is on the Wing.

XIa

With me along the Strip of Herbage strown
That just divides the desert from the sown,   30
　　Where name of Slave and Sultán is forgot—
And Peace to Máhmúd on his golden Throne?

XIIb

A Book of Verses underneath the Bough,
A Jug of Wine, a Loaf of Bread—and Thou
　　Beside me singing in the Wilderness—   35
Oh, Wilderness were Paradise enow!

XIIIb

Some for the Glories of This World; and some
Sigh for the Prophet's Paradise to come;
　　Ah, take the Cash, and let the Credit go,
Nor heed the rumble of a distant Drum!   40

XVa

Look to the blowing Rose about us—"Lo,
Laughing," she says, "into the world I blow:
　　At once the silken tassel of my Purse
Tear, and its Treasure on the Garden throw."

XIV

The Worldly Hope men set their Hearts upon   45
Turns Ashes—or it prospers; and anon,
　　Like Snow upon the Desert's dusty Face
Lighting a little Hour or two—is gone.

XV

And those who husbanded the Golden Grain,
And those who flung it to the Winds like Rain,   50
　　Alike to no such aureate Earth are turned
As, buried once, Men want dug up again.

XVIIIa

Think, in this battered Caravanserai
Whose Portals are alternate Night and Day,
　　How Sultán after Sultán with his Pomp   55
Abode his destined Hour, and went his way.

XIXa

They say the Lion and the Lizard keep
The Courts where Jamshýd gloried and drank deep:
　　And Bahrám, that great Hunter—the Wild Ass
Stamps o'er his Head, but cannot break his Sleep.   60

32 **Máhmúd:** Islamic Sultan and conqueror (971–1030) whose court was a center of Perso-Islamic literature 36 **enow:** enough 38 **Prophet:** Mohammed 49 **Golden Grain:** money 51 **aureate:** golden 53 **Caravanserai:** an inn for caravans 59 **Bahrám:** a Persian king who was swallowed up in a swamp while hunting the wild ass

XXIVa

I sometimes think that never blows so red
The Rose as where some buried Cæsar bled;
    That every Hyacinth the Garden wears
Dropt in her Lap from some once lovely Head.

XIX

And this delightful Herb whose tender Green   65
Fledges the River's Lip on which we lean—
    Ah, lean upon it lightly! for who knows
From what once lovely Lip it springs unseen!

XX

Ah, my Belovèd, fill the Cup that clears
To-day of past Regrets and future Fears—   70
    To-morrow?—Why, To-morrow I may be
Myself with Yesterday's Seven Thousand Years.

XXIIa

For some we loved, the loveliest and the best
That from his Vintage rolling Time has prest,
    Have drunk their Cup a Round or two before,   75
And one by one crept silently to rest.

XXIIIa

And we, that now make merry in the Room
They left, and Summer dresses in new bloom,
    Ourselves must we beneath the Couch of Earth
Descend—ourselves to make a Couch—for whom?   80

XXIII

Ah, make the most of what we yet may spend,
Before we too into the Dust descend;
    Dust into Dust, and under Dust, to lie,
Sans Wine, sans Song, sans Singer, and—sans End.

XXVIIa

Alike for those who for To-day prepare,   85
And those that after some To-morrow stare,
    A Muezzín from the Tower of Darkness cries,
"Fools! your Reward is neither Here nor There."

XXVI

Oh, come with old Khayyám, and leave the Wise
To talk; one thing is certain, that Life flies;   90
    One thing is certain, and the Rest is Lies;
The Flower that once has blown for ever dies.

XXVIIb

Myself when young did eagerly frequent
Doctor and Saint, and heard great argument
    About it and about: but evermore   95
Came out by the same door where in I went.

63 **Hyacinth:** The flower was said to have sprung from the blood of a Greek youth of that name, accidently killed by Apollo. 66 **fledges:** is like feathers on 72 **Seven Thousand Years:** The literal meaning of the Persian is that when we die we are as dead as those who died seven thousand years ago. 84 **sans:** without 87 **Muezzín:** Mohammedan crier who calls the faithful to prayer

XXVIII

With them the Seed of Wisdom did I sow,
And with my own hand laboured it to grow:
    And this was all the Harvest that I reaped—
"I came like Water, and like Wind I go."   100

XXIX

Into this Universe, and *why* not knowing,
Nor *whence*, like Water willy-nilly flowing;
    And out of it, as Wind along the Waste,
I know not *whither*, willy-nilly blowing.

XXXIb

Up from Earth's Centre through the Seventh Gate   105
I rose, and on the Throne of Saturn sate;
    And many a Knot unraveled by the Road;
But not the Master-knot of Human Fate.

XXXII

There was a Door to which I found no Key:
There was a Veil past which I could not see: 110
    Some little Talk awhile of ME and THEE
There seemed—and then no more of THEE and ME.

XXXVIa

Earth could not answer: nor the Seas that mourn
In flowing Purple, of their Lord forlorn;
    Nor Heaven, with those eternal Signs revealed   115
And hidden by the sleeve of Night and Morn.

LVa

Oh, plagued no more with Human or Divine,
To-morrow's tangle to itself resign,
    And lose your fingers in the tresses of
The Cypress-slender Minister of Wine.   120

LXIXa

Why, if the Soul can fling the Dust aside,
And naked on the Air of Heaven ride,
    Is't not a Shame—is't not a Shame for him
So long in this Clay suburb to abide!

XXXVb

Then to the lip of this poor earthen Urn   125
I leaned, the Secret of my Life to learn:
    And Lip to Lip it murmured—"While you live
Drink!—for, once dead, you never shall return."

XXXIXa

I think the Vessel, that with fugitive
Articulation answered, once did live,   130
    And drink; and that impassive Lip I kissed,
How many Kisses might it take—and give!

106 **Saturn:** "Lord of the Seventh Heaven" [FitzGerald]. It was then the farthest known planet. Omar—a famous astronomer—may mean he has gone as far as astronomy can take him.   111 **Talk ...of ME and THEE:** "of some dividual [individual] Existence or Existence or Personality distinct from the Whole" [FitzGerald]   120 **Minister...:** the tavern-girl who serves the wine [supposedly forbidden to Mohammedans]   124 **Clay suburb:** the body

XXXVI

For in the Market-place, one Dusk of Day,
I watched the Potter thumping his wet Clay:
    And with its all obliterated Tongue   135
It murmured—"Gently, Brother, gently, pray!"

XXXVII

Ah, fill the Cup:—what boots it to repeat
How Time is slipping underneath our Feet:
    Unborn TO-MORROW, and dead YESTERDAY,
Why fret about them if TO-DAY be sweet!   140

XLVIIIb

A Moment's Halt—a momentary taste
Of BEING from the Well amid the Waste—
    And Lo!—the phantom Caravan has reached
The NOTHING it set out from—Oh, make haste!

LVIIa

You know, my Friends, how bravely in my House   145
For a new Marriage I did make Carouse;
    Divorced old barren Reason from my Bed,
And took the Daughter of the Vine to Spouse.

XLII

And lately, by the Tavern Door agape,
Came stealing through the Dusk an Angel Shape   150
    Bearing a Vessel on his Shoulder; and
He bid me taste of it; and 'twas—the Grape!

XLIII

The Grape that can with Logic absolute
The Two-and-Seventy jarring Sects confute:
    The subtle Alchemist that in a Trice   155
Life's leaden Metal into Gold transmute.

XLVI

For in and out, above, about, below,
'Tis nothing but a Magic Shadow-show
    Played in a Box whose Candle is the Sun,
Round which we Phantom Figures come and go.   160

LXXIVa

Impotent Pieces of the Game He plays
Upon this Chequer-board of Nights and Days;
    Hither and thither moves, and checks, and slays,
And one by one back in the Closet lays.

L

The Ball no Question makes of Ayes and Noes,   165
But Right or Left as strikes the Player goes;
    And He that tossed Thee down into the Field,
He knows about it all—HE knows—HE knows!

---

136 **"Gently, Brother . . ."**: the clay that speaks was once a man   137 **what boots it . . .**: what good does it do! . . .   154 **Two-and-Seventy . . .**: "the Seventy-two Religions supposed to divide the world" or "the Seventy-two Sects into which Islamism so soon split" [FitzGerald]   165 The imagery refers to the game of polo.

LXXVIa

The Moving Finger writes; and, having writ,
Moves on: nor all your Piety nor Wit   170
    Shall lure it back to cancel half a Line,
Nor all your Tears wash out a Word of it.

LII

And that inverted Bowl we call The Sky,
Whereunder crawling cooped we live and die,   175
    Lift not thy hands to *It* for help—for It
Rolls impotently on as Thou or I.

LIX

Listen again. One evening at the Close
Of Ramazán, ere the better Moon arose,
    In that old Potter's Shop I stood alone
With the clay Population round in Rows.   180

LX

And, strange to tell, among the Earthen Lot
Some could articulate, while others not:
    And suddenly one more impatient cried—
"Who *is* the Potter, pray, and who the Pot?"

LXI

Then said another—"Surely not in vain   185
My Substance from the common Earth was ta'en,
    That He who subtly wrought me into Shape
Should stamp me back to common Earth again."

LXXXVb

Another said—"Why, ne'er a peevish Boy,
Would break the Bowl from which he drank in joy,   190
    And He that with his hand the Vessel made
Will surely not in after Wrath destroy."

LXIII

None answered this; but after Silence spake
A Vessel of a more ungainly Make:
    "They sneer at me for leaning all awry;   195
What! did the Hand then of the Potter shake?"

LXV

Then said another with a long-drawn Sigh,
"My Clay with long oblivion is gone dry:
    But, fill me with the old familiar Juice,
Methinks I might recover by-and-by!"   200

LXVI

So while the Vessels one by one were speaking,
One spied the little Crescent all were seeking:

---

178 **Ramazán:** the sacred month of fasting, during which one may not eat from dawn to sunset   **better Moon:** the new moon that marks the end of this difficult month   186 **ta'en:** taken   189 **Another:** This reading, found in earlier editions, replaces here the "A Second" of *b*.   202 **the little Crescent:** the new moon

And then they jogged each other, "Brother, Brother!
Hark to the Porter's Shoulder-knot a-creaking!"

LXIX

Indeed the Idols I have loved so long   205
Have done my Credit in Men's Eye much wrong:
    Have drowned my Honour in a shallow Cup,
And sold my Reputation for a Song.

LXX

Indeed, indeed, Repentance oft before
I swore—but was I sober when I swore?   210
    And then and then came Spring, and Rose-in-hand
My thread-bare Penitence apieces tore.

LXXI

And much as Wine has played the Infidel,
And robbed me of my Robe of Honour—well,
    I often wonder what the Vintners buy   215
One half so precious as the Goods they sell.

LXXII

Alas, that Spring should vanish with the Rose!
That Youth's sweet-scented Manuscript should close!
    The Nightingale that in the Branches sang,
Ah, whence, and whither flown again, who knows!   220

CVIIIa

Ah, Love! could you and I with Fate conspire
To grasp this sorry Scheme of Things entire,
    Would not we shatter it to bits—and then
Re-mould it nearer to the Heart's Desire!

LXXIV

Ah, Moon of my Delight, who knowest no wane,   225
The Moon of Heaven is rising once again:
    How oft hereafter rising shall she look
Through this same Garden after me—in vain!

LXXV

And when Thyself with shining Foot shall pass
Among the Guests Star-scattered on the Grass,   230
    And in thy joyous Errand reach the Spot
Where I made one—turn down an empty Glass!

204 **Shoulder-knot:** on the strap that supports the wine jars he carries

Alfred, Lord Tennyson
(1809–1892)

Tennyson, who was not "Lord Tennyson" until he was 75, was the fourth of 12 children
of a country clergyman who took to drink. Growing up in a turbulent rectory amid mel-
ancholy vistas, he and his brother became proficient at verse-writing. At Cambridge,
which he left without taking a degree, he made friends with Arthur Hallam, later en-
gaged to his sister; Hallam's sudden death in 1833 was a blow from which he was long in

recovering. Three years later he fell in love, but the lady's father objected to his bohemianism: he smoked, drank, had liberal views on religion—and was very poor. Fourteen years dragged on, until in 1850 the success of "In Memoriam," the poet's friendship with Queen Victoria, and his appointment as poet laureate combined to make him an accepted suitor. The rest of his life was on the whole quiet; though he abhorred publicity, he was popularly recognized as the greatest poet of his time. Rangy and powerful, a rough-looking loner with the manners of a countryman, he seemed more at home striding across the moors than in a Victorian drawing room.

Ulysses

It little profits that an idle king,
By this still hearth, among these barren crags,
Matched with an aged wife, I mete and dole
Unequal laws unto a savage race,
That hoard, and sleep, and feed, and know not me.   5
I cannot rest from travel; I will drink
Life to the lees. All times I have enjoyed
Greatly, have suffered greatly, both with those
That loved me, and alone; on shore, and when
Thro' scudding drifts the rainy Hyades   10
Vext the dim sea. I am become a name;
For always roaming with a hungry heart
Much have I seen and known,—cities of men
And manners, climates, councils, governments,
Myself not least, but honored of them all,—   15
And drunk delight of battle with my peers,
Far on the ringing plains of windy Troy.
I am a part of all that I have met;
Yet all experience is an arch wherethro'
Gleams that untravelled world whose margin fades   20
For ever and for ever when I move.
How dull it is to pause, to make an end,
To rust unburnished, not to shine in use!
As tho' to breathe were life! Life piled on life
Were all too little, and of one to me   25
Little remains; but every hour is saved
From that eternal silence, something more,
A bringer of new things; and vile it were
For some three suns to store and hoard myself,
And this gray spirit yearning in desire   30
To follow knowledge like a sinking star,
Beyond the utmost bound of human thought.
    This is my son, mine own Telemachus,
To whom I leave the sceptre and the isle,—
Well-loved of me, discerning to fulfil   35

1833. *Poems*, 1842.

There is a hint in Homer's *Odyssey* as to the restlessness of Ulysses after his return to Ithaca. But Tennyson owes more to the account in Canto XXVI of Dante's *Inferno*, in which Ulysses, convinced that man is made "to pursue virtue and knowledge," and eager, even in old age, to adventure further, embarks with a few companions on a last "mad voyage." For five months he sails southwest in the unknown Atlantic until, as he comes in sight of a mysterious mountain, his ship is destroyed by a whirlwind. Tennyson wrote the poem in 1833, a few weeks after he was told of the sudden death of his best friend, the brilliantly talented Arthur Henry Hallam, at the age of 22—Hallam was the fiancé of Tennyson's sister. Almost overcome by grief, Tennyson wrote "Ulysses" to show that "life must be fought out to the end."

3 **mete and dole:** measure carefully and deal out   4 **unequal:** because they depend on (possibly trivial) circumstances   7 **lees:** sediment at the very bottom of a bottle of wine   10 **Hyades:** a group of stars in the constellation Taurus thought to indicate rain when they rose with the sun

This labor, by slow prudence to make mild
A rugged people, and thro' soft degrees
Subdue them to the useful and the good.
Most blameless is he, centred in the sphere
Of common duties, decent not to fail   40
In offices of tenderness, and pay
Meet adoration to my household gods,
When I am gone. He works his work, I mine.
  There lies the port; the vessel puffs her sail;
There gloom the dark broad seas. My mariners, 45
Souls that have toiled, and wrought, and thought with me,—
That ever with a frolic welcome took
The thunder and the sunshine, and opposed
Free hearts, free foreheads,—you and I are old;
Old age hath yet his honor and his toil. 50
Death closes all; but something ere the end,
Some work of noble note, may yet be done,
Not unbecoming men that strove with Gods.
The lights begin to twinkle from the rocks;
The long day wanes; the slow moon climbs; the deep 55
Moans round with many voices. Come, my friends.
'Tis not too late to seek a newer world.
Push off, and sitting well in order smite
The sounding furrows; for my purpose holds
To sail beyond the sunset, and the baths 60
Of all the western stars, until I die.
It may be that the gulfs will wash us down;
It may be we shall touch the Happy Isles,
And see the great Achilles, whom we knew.
Tho' much is taken, much abides; and tho' 65
We are not now that strength which in old days
Moved earth and heaven, that which we are, we are,—
One equal temper of heroic hearts,
Made weak by time and fate, but strong in will
To strive, to seek, to find, and not to yield. 70

42 **meet:** appropriate 48 **opposed:** countered with 58 **smite:** strike (with the oars) 63 **the Happy Isles:** In classical mythology, the souls of the virtuous dead might be met on these islands, thought of as west of Gibraltar.

Tithonus

The woods decay, the woods decay and fall,
The vapors weep their burthen to the ground,
Man comes and tills the field and lies beneath,
And after many a summer dies the swan.
Me only cruel immortality 5
Consumes; I wither slowly in thine arms,
Here at the quiet limit of the world,

1833–1859. *Enoch Arden*, 1864.

A companion piece to "Ulysses," begun about the same time, "Tithonus"—with its meditation on youth, age, and immortality—was also influenced by the shock of Hallam's death. According to the myth, Tithonus was a handsome mortal with whom Aurora, goddess of the dawn, fell in love. She asked Zeus to make her young man immortal; her request was granted. She had forgotten, however, to ask that he remain youthful.

2 **burthen:** burden (The line means that clouds etc. condense as rain.) 4 **swan:** Swans are proverbially long-lived; their whiteness makes them a symbol of old age.

A white-haired shadow roaming like a dream
The ever-silent spaces of the East,
Far-folded mists, and gleaming halls of morn.   10
        Alas! for this gray shadow, once a man—
So glorious in his beauty and thy choice,
Who madest him thy chosen, that he seemed
To his great heart none other than a God!
I asked thee, "Give me immortality."   15
Then didst thou grant mine asking with a smile,
Like wealthy men who care not how they give.
Buy thy strong Hours indignant worked their wills,
And beat me down and marred and wasted me,
And tho' they could not end me, left me maimed   20
To dwell in presence of immortal youth,
Immortal age beside immortal youth,
And all I was in ashes. Can thy love,
Thy beauty, make amends, tho' even now,
Close over us, the silver star, thy guide,   25
Shines in those tremulous eyes that fill with tears
To hear me? Let me go; take back thy gift.
Why should a man desire in any way
To vary from the kindly race of men,
Or pass beyond the goal of ordinance   30
Where all should pause, as is most meet for all?
        A soft air fans the cloud apart; there comes
A glimpse of that dark world where I was born.
Once more the old mysterious glimmer steals
From thy pure brows, and from thy shoulders pure,   35
And bosom beating with a heart renewed.
Thy cheek begins to redden thro' the gloom,
Thy sweet eyes brighten slowly close to mine,
Ere yet they blind the stars, and the wild team
Which love thee, yearning for thy yoke, arise,   40
And shake the darkness from their loosened manes,
And beat the twilight into flakes of fire.
        Lo! ever thus thou growest beautiful
In silence, then before thine answer given
Departest, and thy tears are on my cheek.   45
        Why wilt thou ever scare me with thy tears,
And make me tremble lest a saying learnt,
In days far-off, on that dark earth, be true?
"The Gods themselves cannot recall their gifts."
        Ay me! ay me! with what another heart   50
In days far-off, and with what other eyes
I used to watch—if I be he that watched—
The lucid outline forming round thee; saw
The dim curls kindle into sunny rings;
Changed with thy mystic change, and felt my blood   55
Glow with the glow that slowly crimsoned all
Thy presence and thy portals, while I lay,
Mouth, forehead, eyelids, growing dewy-warm
With kisses balmier than half-opening buds
Of April, and could hear the lips that kissed   60
Whispering I knew not what of wild and sweet,

---

25 **silver star:** Venus, which, as morning star, precedes the dawn   30 **goal of ordinance:** the appoint-
ed limit—probably the Biblical three score and ten years   59 **balmier:** more fragrant

Like that strange song I heard Apollo sing,
While Ilion like a mist rose into towers.
    Yet hold me not for ever in thine East;
How can my nature longer mix with thine?   65
Coldly thy rosy shadows bathe me, cold
Are all thy lights, and cold my wrinkled feet
Upon thy glimmering thresholds, when the steam
Floats up from those dim fields about the homes
Of happy men that have the power to die,   70
And grassy barrows of the happier dead.
Release me, and restore me to the ground.
Thou seest all things, thou wilt see my grave;
Thou wilt renew thy beauty morn by morn,
I earth in earth forget these empty courts,   75
And thee returning on thy silver wheels.

62–63 **Apollo ... Ilion ...:** According to legend, Troy (Ilion) was built by the music of Apollo.
71 **barrows:** large mounds of earth over the bodies of the dead

Break, Break, Break

Break, break, break,
    On thy cold gray stones, O sea!
And I would that my tongue could utter
    The thoughts that arise in me.

O, well for the fisherman's boy,   5
    That he shouts with his sister at play!
O, well for the sailor lad,
    That he sings in his boat on the bay!

And the stately ships go on
    To their haven under the hill;   10
But O for the touch of a vanished hand,
    And the sound of a voice that is still!

Break, break, break,
    At the foot of thy crags, O sea!
But the tender grace of a day that is dead   15
    Will never come back to me.

Probably 1834. *Poems*, 1842.

Tears, Idle Tears

    Tears, idle tears, I know not what they mean,
Tears from the depth of some divine despair
Rise in the heart, and gather to the eyes,
In looking on the happy autumn-fields,
And thinking of the days that are no more.   5

1839–1847. *The Princess*, 1847.

A friend of Tennyson reports that "He told me that he was moved to write *Tears, Idle Tears* at Tintern Abbey [Hallam is buried nearby]; and that it was not real woe, as some people might suppose; 'it was rather the yearning that young people occasionally experience for that which seems to have passed away from them for ever'" (Hallam Lord Tennyson, *Alfred Lord Tennyson: A Memoir* (2 vols.), 1897, II, 73).

Fresh as the first beam glittering on a sail,
That brings our friends up from the underworld,
Sad as the last which reddens over one
That sinks with all we love below the verge;
So sad, so fresh, the days that are no more.   10

    Ah, sad and strange as in dark summer dawns
The earliest pipe of half-awakened birds
To dying ears, when unto dying eyes
The casement slowly grows a glimmering square;
So sad, so strange, the days that are no more.   15

    Dear as remembered kisses after death,
And sweet as those by hopeless fancy feigned
On lips that are for others; deep as love,
Deep as first love, and wild with all regret;
O Death in Life, the days that are no more!   20

From **In Memoriam**

Prologue

Strong Son of God, immortal Love,
    Whom we, that have not seen thy face,
    By faith, and faith alone, embrace,
Believing where we cannot prove;

Thine are these orbs of light and shade;   5
    Thou madest Life in man and brute;
    Thou madest Death; and lo, thy foot
Is on the skull which thou hast made.

Thou wilt not leave us in the dust:
    Thou madest man, he knows not why,   10
    He thinks he was not made to die;
And thou hast made him: thou are just.

Thou seemest human and divine,
    The highest, holiest manhood, thou.
    Our wills are ours, we know not how;   15
Our wills are ours, to make them thine.

Our little systems have their day;
    They have their day and cease to be;
    They are but broken lights of thee,
And thou, O Lord, art more than they.   20

We have but faith: we cannot know,
    For knowledge is of things we see;

1833–1850. *In Memoriam*, 1850.

No other event of Tennyson's life seems to have had such an emotional effect on him as the death of Arthur Henry Hallam, his own close friend and his sister's fiancé. "In Memoriam," his memorial poems to Hallam, written at many times and places over many years, were not published until 1850. Tennyson said that he did not write them "with any view of weaving them into a whole, or for publication, until I found that I had written so many." He did not intend the poems to speak only for himself, but to be "the voice of the human race" meditating on its "fear, doubts, and suffering," which Tennyson believed could find "answer and relief only through Faith in a God of Love."

5 **orbs:** "sun and moon" [Tennyson]

And yet we trust it comes from thee,
A beam in darkness: let it grow.

Let knowledge grow from more to more,　　　　　　25
　　But more of reverence in us dwell;
　　That mind and soul, according well,
May make one music as before,

But vaster. We are fools and slight;
　· We mock thee when we do not fear:　　　　　　30
　　But help thy foolish ones to bear;
Help thy vain worlds to bear thy light.

Forgive what seemed my sin in me,
　　What seemed my worth since I began;
　　For merit lives from man to man,　　　　　　35
And not from man, O Lord, to thee.

Forgive my grief for one removed,
　　Thy creature, whom I found so fair.
　　I trust he lives in thee, and there
I find him worthier to be loved.　　　　　　40

Forgive these wild and wandering cries,
　　Confusions of a wasted youth;
　　Forgive them where they fail in truth,
And in thy wisdom make me wise.

III

O sorrow, cruel fellowship!
　　O Priestess in the vaults of Death!
　　O sweet and bitter in a breath,
What whispers from thy lying lip?

"The stars," she whispers, "blindly run;　　　　　　5
　　A web is woven across the sky;
　　From out waste places comes a cry,
And murmurs from the dying sun:

"And all the phantom, Nature, stands—
　　With all her music in her tone,　　　　　　10
　　A hollow echo of my own,—
A hollow form with empty hands."

And shall I take a thing so blind,
　　Embrace her as my natural good;
　　Or crush her, like a vice of blood,　　　　　　15
Upon the threshold of the mind?

VII

Dark house, by which once more I stand
　　Here in the long unlovely street,

Prologue 27 **according:** harmonizing　VII: 1 **house:** Hallam's house on Wimpole St. in London

Doors, where my heart was used to beat
So quickly, waiting for a hand,

A hand that can be clasped no more—   5
   Behold me, for I cannot sleep,
   And like a guilty thing I creep
At earliest morning to the door.

He is not here; but far away
   The noise of life begins again,   10
   And ghastly thro' the drizzling rain
On the bald street breaks the blank day.

L

Be near me when my light is low,
   When the blood creeps, and the nerves prick
   And tingle; and the heart is sick,
And all the wheels of Being slow.

Be near me when the sensuous frame   5
   Is racked with pangs that conquer trust;
   And Time, a maniac scattering dust,
And Life, a Fury slinging flame.

Be near me when my faith is dry,
   And men the flies of latter spring,   10
   That lay their eggs, and sting and sing
And weave their petty cells and die.

Be near me when I fade away,
   To point the term of human strife,
   And on the low dark verge of life   15
The twilight of eternal day.

LV

The wish, that of the living whole
   No life may fail beyond the grave,
   Derives it not from what we have
The likest God within the soul?

Are God and Nature then at strife,   5
   That Nature lends such evil dreams?
   So careful of the type she seems,
So careless of the single life,

That I, considering everywhere
   Her secret meaning in her deeds,
   And finding that of myriad seeds   10
She often brings but one to bear,

L: 8 **Fury:** The avenging Furies of Greek mythology carried torches. **14 term:** termination
LV: **4 the likest God:** most like God **7 type:** species **11 myriad:** a large number; the original
Greek word meant 10,000. Tennyson originally wrote "fifty" but authorized the change, presumably
in the interests of scientific accuracy.

I falter where I firmly trod,
  And falling with my weight of cares
  Upon the great world's altar-stairs
That slope thro' darkness up to God,

I stretch lame hands of faith, and grope,
  And gather dust and chaff, and call
  To what I feel is Lord of all,
And faintly trust the larger hope.

15

20

LVI

"So careful of the type?" but no.
  From scarpèd cliff and quarried stone
  She cries, "A thousand types are gone;
I care for nothing, all shall go.

"Thou makest thine appeal to me.
  I bring to life, I bring to death;
  The spirit does but mean the breath:
I know no more." And he, shall he,

Man, her last work, who seemed so fair,
  Such splendid purpose in his eyes,
  Who rolled the psalm to wintry skies,
Who built him fanes of fruitless prayer,

Who trusted God was love indeed
  And love Creation's final law—
  Tho' Nature, red in tooth and claw
With ravin, shrieked against his creed—

Who loved, who suffered countless ills,
  Who battled for the True, the Just,
  Be blown about the desert dust,
Or sealed within the iron hills?

No more? A monster then, a dream,
  A discord. Dragons of the prime,
  That tare each other in their slime,
Were mellow music matched with him.

O life as futile, then, as frail!
  O for thy voice to soothe and bless!
  What hope of answer, or redress?
Behind the veil, behind the veil.

5

10

15

20

25

XCV

By night we lingered on the lawn,
  For underfoot the herb was dry;

LVI: 2 **scarpèd:** steep, rugged   **cliff . . . stone . . . :** a reference to fossil evidence   3 **she:** Nature, as in LV   7 **spirit:** The primary meaning of *spiritus* (Latin) is *breath*. Nature, physical science, can only know spirit in a physical sense, not a spiritual or religious one.   12 **fanes:** shrines   16 **ravin:** preying on and devouring others   22 **Dragons:** dinosaurs etc.   **prime:** earliest age   23 **tare:** tore   28 **behind the veil:** veiled in mystery. Some think a reference to a statue of Truth in ancient Egypt which it was fatal to unveil.

And genial warmth; and o'er the sky
The silvery haze of summer drawn;

And calm that let the tapers burn   5
　　Unwavering: not a cricket chirred;
　　The brook alone far off was heard,
And on the board the fluttering urn.

And bats went round in fragrant skies,
　　And wheeled or lit the filmy shapes   10
　　That haunt the dusk, with ermine capes
And woolly breasts and beaded eyes;

While now we sang old songs that pealed
　　From knoll to knoll, where, couched at ease,
　　The white kine glimmered, and the trees   15
Laid their dark arms about the field.

But when those others, one by one,
　　Withdrew themselves from me and night,
　　And in the house light after light
Went out, and I was all alone,   20

A hunger seized my heart; I read
　　Of that glad year which once had been,
　　In those fallen leaves which kept their green,
The noble letters of the dead.

And strangely on the silence broke   25
　　The silent-speaking words, and strange
　　Was love's dumb cry defying change
To test his worth; and strangely spoke

The faith, the vigor, bold to dwell
　　On doubts that drive the coward back,   30
　　And keen thro' wordy snares to track
Suggestion to her inmost cell.

So word by word, and line by line,
　　The dead man touched me from the past,
　　And all at once it seemed at last   35
The living soul was flashed on mine,

And mine in this was wound, and whirled
　　About empyreal heights of thought,
　　And came on that which is, and caught
The deep pulsations of the world,   40

Æonian music measuring out
　　The steps of Time—the shocks of Chance—
　　The blows of Death. At length my trance
Was cancelled, stricken thro' with doubt.

XCV: 6 **chirred:** made a trilled insect-sound   8 **fluttering urn:** the tea-urn, with the flame fluttering under it   10 **lit:** alighted [The subject is *shapes,* which Tennyson said referred to moths.]   23 **fallen leaves:** letters from Hallam   **green:** freshness   36 **the living soul:** "The Deity, maybe" [Tennyson] 38 **empyreal:** celestial, sublime   39 **that which is:** ultimate reality ("I have often had the feeling of being whirled up and rapt into the Great Soul" [Tennyson].   41 **Æonian:** lasting for eons (long ages). In geology an eon is a billion years.

Vague words! but ah, how hard to frame   45
   In matter-moulded forms of speech,
   Or even for intellect to reach
Thro' memory that which I became;

Till now the doubtful dusk revealed
   The knolls once more where, couched at ease,   50
   The white kine glimmered, and the trees
Laid their dark arms about the field;

And sucked from out the distant gloom
   A breeze began to tremble o'er
   The large leaves of the sycamore,   55
And fluctuate all the still perfume,

And gathering freshlier overhead,
   Rocked the full-foliaged elms, and swung
   The heavy-folded rose, and flung
The lilies to and fro, and said,   60

"The dawn, the dawn," and died away;
   The East and West, without a breath,
   Mixed their dim lights, like life and death,
To broaden into boundless day.

CXXIII

There rolls the deep where grew the tree.
   O earth, what changes hast thou seen!
   There where the long street roars, hath been
The stillness of the central sea.

The hills are shadows, and they flow   5
   From form to form, and nothing stands;
   They melt like mist, the solid lands,
Like clouds they shape themselves and go.

But in my spirit will I dwell,
   And dream my dream, and hold it true;   10
   For though my lips may breathe adieu,
I cannot think the thing farewell.

XCV: 4 **matter-moulded:** physical material
CXXIII: 3–4 Areas where city streets are now busy were once deep under the primeval seas.

"Frater Ave Atque Vale"

Row us out from Desenzano, to your Sirmione row!
So they rowed, and there we landed—"O venusta Sirmio!"

1880. *Tiresias and Other Poems,* 1885.

The Latin title, which means "Brother, hail and farewell," is the closing phrase of poem 101 of Catullus, the Roman poet whose dates are about 84–54 B.C. "Ave atque vale" was a regular formula of farewell to the dead. Tennyson has more than Latin poetry on his mind; his own brother Charles had died the year before the poem was written.

1 **Desenzano:** a little town on the southwest shore of the Lake of Garda in northern Italy, near Verona. It is a few miles from the fishing village of Sirmione (the ancient Sirmio), which is near the end of a narrow peninsula extending into the lake. Catullus had a villa there.   2 **"O venusta Sirmio":** "O lovely Sirmio," a quotation from Catullus, 31

There to me thro' all the groves of olive in the summer glow,
There beneath the Roman ruin where the purple flowers grow,
Came that "Ave atque Vale" of the poet's hopeless woe,   5
Tenderest of Roman poets nineteen hundred years ago,
"Frater ave atque vale"—as we wandered to and fro
Gazing at the Lydian laughter of the Garda Lake below
Sweet Catullus's all-but-island, olive-silvery Sirmio!

8 **Lydian laughter:** The phrase derives from the same poem of Catullus, lines 13–14. "Lydian" be-
cause the ancient Etruscans, who had settled in the region, were thought to have come from Lydia in
Asia Minor.   9 **all-but-island:** Catullus (31, 1) had classified Sirmio as a "paene insula" or "almost is-
land"—our *peninsula*.   **olive-silvery:** In the region there are many olive trees, with their silvery-
green leaves.

Robert Browning
(1812–1889)

Except for trips to Russia and Italy, Browning lived with his prosperous parents until, at
the age of 34, he married Elizabeth Barrett. He was largely self-educated in his father's li-
brary; his literary work, which included a number of plays, had been subsidized by his
parents. During his 15 years of marriage in Italy, he wrote comparatively little, but that
little included some of his best poems, though they were not well received at the time by
either critics or book buyers. After his wife's death in 1861, Browning returned to Eng-
land. *The Ring and the Book* (1868–1869), based on a seventeenth-century murder trial, was
an immediate success; it made Browning one of the most sought-after literary figures of
his day.

Porphyria's Lover

The rain set early in to-night,
  The sullen wind was soon awake,
It tore the elm-tops down for spite,
  And did its worst to vex the lake:
  I listened with heart fit to break.   5
When glided in Porphyria; straight
  She shut the cold out and the storm,
And kneeled and made the cheerless grate
  Blaze up, and all the cottage warm;
  Which done, she rose, and from her form   10
Withdrew the dripping cloak and shawl,
  And laid her soiled gloves by, untied
Her hat and let the damp hair fall,
  And, last, she sat down by my side
  And called me. When no voice replied,   15
She put my arm about her waist,
  And made her smooth white shoulder bare,
And all her yellow hair displaced,
  And, stooping, made my cheek lie there,
  And spread, o'er all, her yellow hair,   20
Murmuring how she loved me—she
  Too weak, for all her heart's endeavour,

1834? *Dramatic Lyrics (Bells and Pomegranates,* III), 1842.

Originally printed as one of two "Madhouse Cells"; Browning was interested in studies of abnormal
behavior.

To set its struggling passion free
  From pride, and vainer ties dissever,
  And give herself to me for ever.   25
But passion sometimes would prevail,
  Nor could to-night's gay feast restrain
A sudden thought of one so pale
  For love of her, and all in vain:
  So, she was come through wind and rain.   30
Be sure I looked up at her eyes
  Happy and proud; at last I knew
Porphyria worshipped me; surprise
  Made my heart swell, and still it grew
  While I debated what to do.   35
That moment she was mine, mine, fair,
  Perfectly pure and good: I found
A thing to do, and all her hair
  In one long yellow string I wound
  Three times her little throat around,   40
And strangled her. No pain felt she;
  I am quite sure she felt no pain.
As a shut bud that holds a bee,
  I warily oped her lids: again
  Laughed the blue eyes without a stain.   45
And I untightened next the tress
  About her neck; her cheek once more
Blushed bright beneath my burning kiss:
  I propped her head up as before,
  Only, this time my shoulder bore   50
Her head, which droops upon it still:
  The smiling rosy little head,
So glad it has its utmost will,
  That all it scorned at once is fled,
  And I, its love, am gained instead!   55
Porphyria's love: she guessed not how
  Her darling one wish would be heard.
And thus we sit together now,
  And all night long we have not stirred,
  And yet God has not said a word!   60

My Last Duchess

Ferrara

That's my last Duchess painted on the wall,
Looking as if she were alive. I call
That piece a wonder, now: Frà Pandolf's hands
Worked busily a day, and there she stands.

1842. Ibid.

Under the rule of the Este family, Ferrara, in northern Italy, was a center of art and culture during the Renaissance. The figure of the coolly murderous Duke, who reveals more of his character than he means to in this dramatic monologue, may have been suggested to Browning by Alfonso II (sixteenth century), whose first wife died suspiciously, after three years of marriage, at the age of 17. Before long the Duke was working to arrange a marriage with the relative of a nobleman whose castle was at Innsbruck. The Duchess of the poem is his "last" only in the sense of "most recent."

3 **Frà Pandolf:** an imaginary artist. *Frà* is short for *Frate* (Brother), used with the name of a monk or friar.

Will't please you sit and look at her? I said   5
"Frà Pandolf" by design, for never read
Strangers like you that pictured countenance,
The depth and passion of its earnest glance,
But to myself they turned (since none puts by
The curtain I have drawn for you, but I)   10
And seemed as they would ask me, if they durst,
How such a glance came there; so, not the first
Are you to turn and ask thus. Sir, 'twas not
Her husband's presence only, called that spot
Of joy into the Duchess' cheek: perhaps   15
Frà Pandolf chanced to say "Her mantle laps
Over my lady's wrist too much," or "Paint
Must never hope to reproduce the faint
Half-flush that dies along her throat": such stuff
Was courtesy, she thought, and cause enough   20
For calling up that spot of joy. She had
A heart—how shall I say?—too soon made glad,
Too easily impressed; she liked whate'er
She looked on, and her looks went everywhere.
Sir, 'twas all one! My favour at her breast,   25
The dropping of the daylight in the West,
The bough of cherries some officious fool
Broke in the orchard for her, the white mule
She rode with round the terrace—all and each
Would draw from her alike the approving speech,   30
Or blush, at least. She thanked men,—good! but thanked
Somehow—I know now how—as if she ranked
My gift of a nine-hundred-years-old name
With anybody's gift. Who'd stoop to blame
This sort of trifling? Even had you skill   35
In speech—(which I have not)—to make your will
Quite clear to such an one, and say, "Just this
Or that in you disgusts me; here you miss,
Or there exceed the mark"—and if she let
Herself be lessoned so, nor plainly set   40
Her wits to yours, forsooth, and made excuse,
—E'en then would be some stooping; and I choose
Never to stoop. Oh sir, she smiled, no doubt,
Whene'er I passed her; but who passed without
Much the same smile? This grew; I gave commands;   45
Then all smiles stopped together. There she stands
As if alive. Will't please you rise? We'll meet
The company below, then. I repeat,
The Count your master's known munificence
Is ample warrant that no just pretence   50
Of mine for dowry will be disallowed;
Though his fair daughter's self, as I avowed
At starting, is my object. Nay, we'll go
Together down, sir. Notice Neptune, though,
Taming a sea-horse, thought a rarity,   55
Which Claus of Innsbruck cast in bronze for me!

---

41 **forsooth:** indeed   45 When asked what commands the Duke had given, Browning said he had or-
dered her put to death—then he added, after a pause, "Or he might have had her shut up in a con-
vent." The *as if* of line 47 suggests she is dead.   56 **Claus of Innsbruck:** an imaginary artist

The Bishop Orders His Tomb at St. Praxed's Church

Rome, 15—

Vanity, saith the preacher, vanity!
Draw round my bed: is Anselm keeping back?
Nephews—sons mine . . . ah God, I know not! Well—
She, men would have to be your mother once,
Old Gandolf envied me, so fair she was!   5
What's done is done, and she is dead beside,
Dead long ago, and I am Bishop since,
And as she died so must we die ourselves,
And thence ye may perceive the world's a dream.
Life, how and what is it? As here I lie   10
In this state-chamber, dying by degrees,
Hours and long hours in the dead night, I ask
"Do I live, am I dead?" Peace, peace seems all.
Saint Praxed's ever was the church for peace;
And so, about this tomb of mine. I fought   15
With tooth and nail to save my niche, ye know:
—Old Gandolf cozened me, despite my care;
Shrewd was that snatch from out the corner South
He graced his carrion with, God curse the same!
Yet still my niche is not so cramped but thence   20
One sees the pulpit o' the epistle-side,
And somewhat of the choir, those silent seats,
And up into the aery dome where live
The angels, and a sunbeam's sure to lurk:
And I shall fill my slab of basalt there,   25
And 'neath my tabernacle take my rest,
With those nine columns round me, two and two,
The odd one at my feet where Anselm stands:
Peach-blossom marble all, the rare, the ripe
As fresh-poured red wine of a mighty pulse.   30
—Old Gandolf with his paltry onion-stone,
Put me where I may look at him! True peach,
Rosy and flawless: how I earned the prize!
Draw close: that conflagration of my church
—What then? So much was saved if aught were missed!   35
My sons, ye would not be my death? Go dig
The white-grape vineyard where the oil-press stood,

1844. *Dramatic Romances and Lyrics (Bells and Pomegranates*, VII), 1845.

Santa Prassede (St. Praxedes) was a Roman virgin. The church named for her, in Rome, goes back to at least the fifth century. It contains some remarkable early mosaics and other works of art, though it is not as grand as the Bishop makes it sound, and has no dome (line 23)—nor any such tomb as the Bishop hoped for. The Bishop himself is fictional; he is in Browning's view a typical art-loving worldly churchman of the Renaissance. Ruskin said of the poem, "I know no other piece of modern English, prose or poetry, in which there is so much told . . . of the Renaissance spirit,—its worldliness, inconsistency, pride, hypocrisy, ignorance of itself, love of art, of luxury, of good Latin" (*Modern Painters,* IV, chap. XX).

1 Cf. the opening of Eccles.: ". . . Vanity of vanities, saith the Preacher, vanity of vanities; all is vanity." 3 **nephews:** his illegitimate sons; Anselm, mentioned in the line above, seems to be the favorite 4 **have:** believe, assert 5 **Gandolf:** a rival churchman, now dead 17 **cozened:** tricked, cheated 21 **epistle-side:** the right side, to one facing the altar 25 **basalt:** a hard dark-grey or black igneous rock, inferior to the antique black marble the Bishop later asks for (line 54) 26 **tabernacle:** an ornate canopied structure 31 **onion-stone:** an inferior marble that flakes easily 34 The Bishop, sometime in his past, seems to have used arson to cover robbery.

Drop water gently till the surface sink,
And if ye find . . . Ah God, I know not, I! . . .
Bedded in store of rotten fig-leaves soft,   40
And corded up in a tight olive-frail,
Some lump, ah God, of *lapis lazuli,*
Big as a Jew's head cut off at the nape,
Blue as a vein o'er the Madonna's breast . . .
Sons, all have I bequeathed you, villas, all,   45
That brave Frascati villa with its bath,
So, let the blue lump poise between my knees,
Like God the Father's globe on both his hands
Ye worship in the Jesu Church so gay,
For Gandolf shall not choose but see and burst!   50
Swift as a weaver's shuttle fleet our years:
Man goeth to the grave, and where is he?
Did I say basalt for my slab, sons? Black—
'Twas ever antique-black I meant! How else
Shall ye contrast my frieze to come beneath?   55
The bas-relief in bronze ye promised me,
Those Pans and Nymphs ye wot of, and perchance
Some tripod, thyrsus, with a vase or so,
The Saviour at his sermon on the mount,
Saint Praxed in a glory, and one Pan   60
Ready to twitch the Nymph's last garment off,
And Moses with the tables . . . but I know
Ye mark me not! What do they whisper thee,
Child of my bowels, Anselm? Ah, ye hope
To revel down my villas while I gasp   65
Bricked o'er with beggar's mouldy travertine
Which Gandolf from his tomb-top chuckles at!
Nay, boys, ye love me—all of jasper, then!
'Tis jasper ye stand pledged to, lest I grieve.
My bath must needs be left behind, alas!   70
One block, pure green as a pistachio-nut,
There's plenty jasper somewhere in the world—
And have I not Saint Praxed's ear to pray
Horses for ye, and brown Greek manuscripts,
And mistresses with great smooth marbly limbs?   75
—That's if ye carve my epitaph aright,
Choice Latin, picked phrase, Tully's every word,
No gaudy ware like Gandolf's second line—
Tully, my masters? Ulpian serves his need!
And then how I shall lie through centuries,   80
And hear the blessed mutter of the mass,
And see God made and eaten all day long,

41 **frail:** basket   42 *lapis lazuli:* a semiprecious rich blue stone   46 **Frascati:** a resort city in the hills
15 miles southeast of Rome   49 **Jesu Church:** Il Jesù is a baroque Jesuit church in Rome built in 1568.
Among its elaborate works of art is a sculptured Trinity with a globe of the world made out of the
largest known block of lapis lazuli.   51 **weaver's shuttle:** Cf. Job 7:6: "My days are swifter than a
weaver's shuttle, and are spent without hope."   57 **Pans:** pagan rural gods   **wot:** know   58 **thyr-
sus:** a florally decorated staff carried by Dionysius (god of wine, revelry, etc.) and his attendants   60
glory: gloriole, halo, rays of light   62 **tables:** stone tablets or slabs. Cf. Exod. 24:11: "And the Lord
said unto Moses . . . I will give thee tables of stone, and a law, and commandments. . . ."   66 **traver-
tine:** ordinary limestone used for building   75 The Bishop will pray for mistresses to a saint celebrat-
ed for her chastity!   77 **Tully:** Marcus Tullius Cicero (106–43 B.C.), the purity of whose Latin became
the standard of excellence   79 **Ulpian:** late Latin writer on law (170–228 A.D.). By his time Latin had
lost its classical purity.

And feel the steady candle-flame, and taste
Good strong thick stupefying incense-smoke!
For as I lie here, hours of the dead night,   85
Dying in state and by such slow degrees,
I fold my arms as if they clasped a crook,
And stretch my feet forth straight as stone can point,
And let the bedclothes, for a mortcloth, drop
Into great laps and folds of sculptor's-work: 90
And as yon tapers dwindle, and strange thoughts
Grow, with a certain humming in my ears,
About the life before I lived this life,
And this life too, popes, cardinals and priests,
Saint Praxed at his sermon on the mount,   95
Your tall pale mother with her talking eyes,
And new-found agate urns as fresh as day,
And marble's language, Latin pure, discreet,
—Aha, ELUCESCEBAT quoth our friend:
No Tully, said I, Ulpian at the best!   100
Evil and brief hath been my pilgrimage.
All *lapis*, all, sons! Else I give the Pope
My villas! Will ye ever eat my heart?
Ever your eyes were as a lizard's quick,
They glitter like your mother's for my soul,   105
Or ye would heighten my impoverished frieze,
Piece out its starved design, and fill my vase
With grapes, and add a vizor and a Term,
And to the tripod ye would tie a lynx
That in his struggle throws the thyrsus down,   110
To comfort me on my entablature
Whereon I am to lie till I must ask
"Do I live, am I dead?" There, leave me, there!
For ye have stabbed me with ingratitude
To death—ye wish it—God, ye wish it! Stone—   115
Gritstone, a-crumble! Clammy squares which sweat
As if the corpse they keep were oozing through—
And no more *lapis* to delight the world!
Well go! I bless ye. Fewer tapers there,
But in a row: and, going, turn your backs   120
—Ay, like departing altar-ministrants,
And leave me in my church, the church for peace,
That I may watch at leisure if he leers—
Old Gandolf, at me, from his onion-stone,
As still he envied me, so fair she was!   125

87 **crook:** the Bishop's ceremonial crozier, emblematic of a shepherd's crook   89 **mortcloth:** funeral pall, draped over the coffin   95 The Bishop is momentarily delirious, confusing St. Praxedes with Christ.   99 **Elucescebat:** a late-Latin word for *came into prominence* or *was illustrious*. Cicero used the word *elucebat*. The capitals indicate that the word was engraved on Gandolf's tomb.   108 **vizor:** decorative mask   **Term:** a bust on a pedestal; originally an image of Terminus, the ancient god of boundaries. Cf. W. H. Auden, "Ode to Terminus," p. 635   111 **entablature:** stonework (frieze, cornice, etc.) above the pillars   116 **gritstone:** a cheap kind of sandstone

A Toccata of Galuppi's

I

Oh Galuppi, Baldassaro, this is very sad to find!
I can hardly misconceive you; it would prove me deaf and blind;
But although I take your meaning, 'tis with such a heavy mind!

II

Here you come with your old music, and here's all the good it brings.
What, they lived once thus at Venice where the merchants were the kings,   5
Where Saint Mark's is, where the Doges used to wed the sea with rings?

III

Ay, because the sea's the street there; and 'tis arched by . . . what you call
. . . Shylock's bridge with houses on it, where they kept the carnival:
I was never out of England—it's as if I saw it all.

IV

Did young people take their pleasure when the sea was warm in May?   10
Balls and masks begun at midnight, burning ever to mid-day,
When they made up fresh adventures for the morrow, do you say?

V

Was a lady such a lady, cheeks so round and lips so red,—
On her neck the small face buoyant, like a bell-flower on its bed,
O'er the breast's superb abundance where a man might base his head?   15

VI

Well, and it was graceful of them—they'd break talk off and afford
—She, to bite her mask's black velvet—he, to finger on his sword,
While you sat and played Toccatas, stately at the clavichord?

VII

What? Those lesser thirds so plaintive, sixths diminished, sigh on sigh,
Told them something? Those suspensions, those solutions—"Must we die?"
Those commiserating sevenths—"Life might last! we can but try!"

1847? *Men and Women*, 1855.

A toccata is a musical composition, in the style of an improvisation, for a keyboard instrument, which gives the performer an opportunity to display his or her technical ability (the Italian *toccare* means "to touch"). Baldassare Galuppi (1706–1785) was a Venetian composer known chiefly for his comic operas; his music has been found vivacious and attractive. "The delight that poured from his music, the unhesitating spontaneity of one phrase galloping after another as if doubt had never existed in the world, the brilliant clarity, the lightness that seems to be a defiance . . . made him famous everywhere. . . . That was what Venice loved; that was why he was perhaps her most adored servant in music . . ." (Maurice Rowdon, *The Silver Age of Venice*, p. 145). If his music seems "cold" to the speaker of the poem, a nineteenth-century Englishman interested in reason and science, it is probably not because of its technical proficiency but because it is a reminder of mortality.

6 **St. Mark's:** the cathedral in Venice   **Doges . . . :** the Doge, the chief magistrate of Venice, would symbolically wed the city to the sea every year by tossing a ring into the Adriatic.   8 **Shylock's bridge:** the Rialto bridge, in the commercial section of Venice, which is mentioned in Shakespeare's *Merchant of Venice*   14 **bell-flower:** a plant with showy bell-shaped flowers   18 **clavichord:** an early keyboard instrument, a predecessor of the piano   19–21 **lesser thirds . . . sixths . . . :** Several technical terms for harmonic relationships are used in these lines. Browning had a good knowledge of music, to which he was devoted; he himself composed, and he loved to improvise on the piano. He even thought, for a time, of writing an opera.   20–27 The quotations are imagined as coming from people of Galuppi's own time.

VIII

"Were you happy?"—"Yes."—"And are you still as happy?"—"Yes. And you?"
—"Then, more kisses!"—"Did *I* stop them, when a million seemed so few?"
Hark, the dominant's persistence till it must be answered to!

IX

So, an octave struck the answer. Oh, they praised you, I dare say!   25
"Brave Galuppi! that was music! good alike at grave and gay!
I can always leave off talking when I hear a master play!"

X

Then they left you for their pleasure: till in due time, one by one,
Some with lives that came to nothing, some with deeds as well undone,
Death stepped tacitly and took them where they never see the sun.   30

XI

But when I sit down to reason, think to take my stand nor swerve,
While I triumph o'er a secret wrung from nature's close reserve,
In you come with your cold music till I creep thro' every nerve.

XII

Yes, you, like a ghostly cricket, creaking where a house was burned:
"Dust and ashes, dead and done with, Venice spent what Venice earned.   35
The soul, doubtless, is immortal—where a soul can be discerned.

XIII

"Yours for instance: you know physics, something of geology,
Mathematics are your pastime; souls shall rise in their degree;
Butterflies may dread extinction,—you'll not die, it cannot be!

XIV

"As for Venice and her people, merely born to bloom and drop,   40
Here on earth they bore their fruitage, mirth and folly were the crop:
What of soul was left, I wonder, when the kissing had to stop?

XV

"Dust and ashes!" So you creak it, and I want the heart to scold.
Dear dead women, with such hair, too—what's become of all the gold
Used to hang and brush their bosoms? I feel chilly and grown old.   45

24 **dominant:** the fifth note of the scale   35–43 Galuppi, or the spirit of his music, is imagined as addressing the speaker.   43 **want:** lack

Love Among the Ruins

I

Where the quiet-coloured end of evening smiles
      Miles and miles
On the solitary pastures where our sheep
      Half-asleep

1852. Ibid.

Browning seems to have had no one ruined city in mind. He was probably influenced by archaeological reports about Babylon, Nineveh, Thebes (in Egypt), Tarquinia (in Italy), and others. The scenery is that of the Campagna, or plain around Rome, which has many ruins.

Tinkle homeward thro' the twilight, stray or stop   5
            As they crop—
Was the site once of a city great and gay,
            (So they say)
Of our country's very capital, its prince
            Ages since   10
Held his court in, gathered councils, wielding far
            Peace or war.

II

Now,—the country does not even boast a tree,
            As you see,
To distinguish slopes of verdure, certain rills   15
            From the hills
Intersect and give a name to, (else they run
            Into one)
Where the domed and daring palace shot its spires
            Up like fires   20
O'er the hundred-gated circuit of a wall
            Bounding all,
Made of marble, men might march on nor be pressed,
            Twelve abreast.

III

And such plenty and perfection, see, of grass   25
            Never was!
Such a carpet as, this summer-time, o'er-spreads
            And embeds
Every vestige of the city, guessed alone,
            Stock or stone—   30
Where a multitude of men breathed joy and woe
            Long ago;
Lust of glory pricked their hearts up, dread of shame
            Struck them tame;
And that glory and that shame alike, the gold   35
            Bought and sold.

IV

Now,—the single little turret that remains
            On the plains,
By the caper overrooted, by the gourd
            Overscored,   40
While the patching houseleek's head of blossom winks
            Through the chinks—
Marks the basement whence a tower in ancient time
            Sprang sublime,
And a burning ring, all round, the chariots traced   45
            As they raced,
And the monarch and his minions and his dames
            Viewed the games.

---

15 **rills**: small brooks   39 **caper**: a low prickly Mediterranean shrub. The buds are used as a relish.
40 **overscored**: marked, roughened, scratched all over   41 **houseleek**: a kind of blossoming sedum
that grows on old roofs or walls   47 **minions**: favorites

V

And I know, while thus the quiet-coloured eve
  Smiles to leave   50
To their folding, all our many-tinkling fleece
  In such peace,
And the slopes and rills in undistinguished grey
  Melt away—
That a girl with eager eyes and yellow hair   55
  Waits me there
In the turret whence the charioteers caught soul
  For the goal,
When the king looked, where she looks now, breathless, dumb
  Till I come.   60

VI

But he looked upon the city, every side,
  Far and wide,
All the mountains topped with temples, all the glades'
  Colonnades,
All the causeys, bridges, aqueducts,—and then, 65
  All the men!
When I do come, she will speak not, she will stand,
  Either hand
On my shoulder, give her eyes the first embrace
  Of my face,   70
Ere we rush, ere we extinguish sight and speech
  Each on each.

VII

In one year they sent a million fighters forth
  South and North,
And they built their gods a brazen pillar high 75
  As the sky,
Yet reserved a thousand chariots in full force—
  Gold, of course.
Oh heart! oh blood that freezes, blood that burns!
  Earth's returns   80
For whole centuries of folly, noise and sin!
  Shut them in,
With their triumphs and their glories and the rest!
  Love is best.

51 **folding:** return to the sheepfolds   65 **causeys:** causeways, raised paths or roads

Edward Lear
(1812–1888)

Lear, who was of Danish descent and the youngest of 21 children, supported himself by his drawing from the age of 15—he did artwork for the British Museum and bird illustrations and gave lessons to Queen Victoria. Though an epileptic, he travelled widely and daringly to such places as Albania, Egypt, and Ceylon. He is remembered not only for his drawings but as the first great writer of nonsense poems and an early master of the limerick.

How Pleasant to Know Mr. Lear!

How pleasant to know Mr. Lear!
    Who has written such volumes of stuff!
Some think him ill-tempered and queer,
    But a few think him pleasant enough.

His mind is concrete and fastidious,   5
    His nose is remarkably big;
His visage is more or less hideous,
    His beard it resembles a wig.

He has ears, and two eyes, and ten fingers,
    Leastways if you reckon two thumbs;   10
Long ago he was one of the singers,
    But now he is one of the dumbs.

He sits in a beautiful parlour,
    With hundreds of books on the wall;
He drinks a great deal of Marsala,   15
    But never gets tipsy at all.

He has many friends, laymen and clerical,
    Old Foss is the name of his cat;
His body is perfectly spherical.
    He weareth a runcible hat.   20

When he walks in a waterproof white,
    The children run after him so!
Calling out, "He's come out in his night-
    Gown, that crazy old Englishman, oh!"

He weeps by the side of the ocean,   25
    He weeps on the top of the hill;
He purchases pancakes and lotion,
    And chocolate shrimps from the mill.

He reads but he cannot speak Spanish,
    He cannot abide ginger-beer: 30
Ere the days of his pilgrimage vanish,
    How pleasant to know Mr. Lear!

1879. *The Complete Nonsense of Edward Lear*, ed. H. Jackson, 1947.

Lear wrote the poem when a young lady he knew reported to him that another young lady had said, "How pleasant to know Mr. Lear!"

15 **Marsala:** a dessert wine from Sicily   20 **runcible:** a nonsense word Lear made up   30 **ginger-beer:** a carbonated soft drink flavored with ginger.

Jones Very
(1813–1880)

Very was born in Salem, Massachusetts, the son of a sea captain. After graduating from Harvard, he stayed on briefly as tutor of Greek while going to the divinity school. An access of religious enthusiasm in 1838 resulted in his withdrawal for a month of rest in a nearby asylum. He spent the rest of his life at Salem as a Unitarian preacher. Most of his best poems were written during a period of religious intensity between 1836 and 1841.

Enoch

I looked to find a man who walked with God,
Like the translated patriarch of old;—
Though gladdened millions on His footstool trod,
Yet none with Him did such sweet converse hold;
I heard the wind in low complaint go by   5
That none its melodies like him could hear;
Day unto day spoke wisdom from on high,
Yet none like David turned a willing ear;
God walked alone unhonored through the earth;
For Him no heart-built temple open stood,   10
The soul forgetful of her nobler birth
Had hewn Him lofty shrines of stone and wood,
And left unfinished and in ruins still
The only temple He delights to fill.

1838. Harvard MS. Am 1405 (Houghton). *Essays and Poems*, 1839.

Enoch, of the sixth generation after Adam, lived to be 365 years old. Cf. Gen. 5:24: "And Enoch walked with God: and he was not; for God took him."

2 **translated:** taken to heaven without dying   **patriarch:** one of the early scriptural fathers   3 **footstool:** Cf. Isa. 66:1: "Thus saith the LORD, The heaven is my throne, and the earth is my footstool. . . ."
8 **David:** King David, the psalmist

The Spirit Land

Father! Thy wonders do not singly stand,
Nor far removed where feet have seldom strayed;
Around us ever lies the enchanted land
In marvels rich to Thine own sons displayed;
In finding Thee are all things round us found;   5
In losing Thee are all things lost beside;
Ears have we but in vain strange voices sound,
And to our eyes the vision is denied;
We wonder in the country far remote,
Mid tombs and ruined piles in death to dwell;   10
Or on the records of past greatness dote,
And for a buried soul the living sell;
While on our path bewildered falls the night
That ne'er returns us to the fields of light.

1838. Ibid.

9 **wonder:** Though the printed texts read *wander*, the *o* is quite distinct in Very's MS., carefully written for the printer. The poem is about "wonders."   10 **piles:** structures

The Presence

I sit within my room and joy to find
That Thou who always loves art with me here,
That I am never left by Thee behind,
But by Thyself Thou keep'st me ever near;
The fire burns brighter when with Thee I look,   5
And seems a kinder servant sent to me;

1838. Ibid.

5 **burns:** generally printed as *turns*, though the *b* is distinct in the two MS. versions

With gladder heart I read Thy holy book,
Because Thou art the eyes by which I see;
This aged chair, that table, watch, and door
Around in ready service ever wait;   10
Nor can I ask of Thee a menial more
To fill the measure of my large estate,
For Thou Thyself, with all a father's care,
Where'er I turn, art ever with me there.

11 **a menial more:** one more servant

The Dead

I see them, crowd on crowd they walk the earth
Dry leafless trees no autumn wind laid bare;
And in their nakedness find cause for mirth,
And all unclad would winter's rudeness dare;
No sap doth through their clattering branches flow,   5
Whence springing leaves and blossoms bright appear;
Their hearts the living God have ceased to know,
Who gives the springtime to th'expectant year;
They mimic life, as if from him to steal
His glow of health to paint the livid cheek;   10
They borrow words for thoughts they cannot feel,
That with a seeming heart their tongue may speak;
And in their show of life more dead they live
Than those that to the earth with many tears they give.

1838. Ibid.

"The dead" are those who, while physically alive, have no true spiritual life, and are therefore more dead than the dead they bury.

Henry David Thoreau
(1817–1862)

Thoreau (best pronounced *thôr-oh*) was born in Concord, Massachusetts, where his mother (like Emerson's) kept a boarding house and his father owned a small pencil factory. Most of his life Thoreau lived in the one, worked in the other. At Harvard he came under the influence of Very and especially of Emerson, who suggested he keep a journal (which finally grew to 39 volumes) and for whom he worked as handyman. Most of his verse— in which there is less poetry than in his prose—was written within a few years of his leaving Harvard in 1837. More interested in living than in earning a living, he was never well off. He tried teaching, and at times worked as a surveyor. In opposition to the Mexican War he wrote his essay "Civil Disobedience"; he was active too in the antislavery movement. From 1845 to 1847 he lived alone at Walden Pond.

Though All the Fates Should Prove Unkind

Though all the fates should prove unkind,
Leave not your native land behind.
The ship, becalmed, at length stands still;
The steed must rest beneath the hill;
But swiftly still our fortunes pace   5
To find us out in every place.

A Week on the Concord and Merrimack Rivers, 1849.

The vessel, though her masts be firm,
Beneath her copper bears a worm;
Around the cape, across the line,
Till fields of ice her course confine;   10
It matters not how smooth the breeze,
How shallow or how deep the seas,
Whether she bears Manila twine,
Or in her hold Madeira wine,
Or China teas, or Spanish hides,   15
In port or quarantine she rides;
Far from New England's blustering shore,
New England's worm her hulk shall bore,
And sink her in the Indian seas,
Twine, wine, and hides, and China teas.   20

9 **line:** the equator 14 **Madeira:** islands off the coast of Portugal, famous for their dessert wine
16 **quarantine:** period during which a newly arrived ship is kept in isolation from the port

Emily Brontë
(1818–1848)

Emily's father, Patrick Brunty, was an Irishman who changed the spelling of his name
when he came to England as a Methodist minister. His three daughters—Charlotte, Emi-
ly, and Anne, who grew up in a lonely rectory on the moors—all became famous in liter-
ature. They worked at times as teachers and governesses; the two elder ones went to
Brussels to study French and German. In 1846 poems of the three were published, under
assumed masculine names, as *Poems by Currer, Ellis, and Acton Bell.* Two copies were sold.
But within a year three of their novels—including *Wuthering Heights* and *Jane Eyre*—had
been published. What fame they won was not long to enjoy: within two years Emily and
Anne had succumbed to illness; Charlotte lived till 1855.

Song

The linnet in the rocky dells,
    The moor-lark in the air,
The bee among the heather bells,
    That hide my lady fair:

The wild deer browse above her breast;   5
    The wild birds raise their brood;
And they her smiles of love caressed,
    Have left her—solitude!

I ween, that when the grave's dark wall
    Did first her form retain,   10

1844. *Poems by Currer, Ellis, and Acton Bell,* 1846.

When Emily Brontë was 13 or 14 years old, she, with her younger sister Anne, made up an imaginary
island kingdom in the North Pacific called Gondal. Over the years they evolved and wrote out—with
attention to its geography, history, involved personal relationships, and the rest—an epic of their pas-
sionate and eventful race: its wars, its conquests, its politics, its romances, its tragedies. Nearly all of
the poems Emily wrote are lyric expressions of high points in that visionary history—her impas-
sioned reactions to events and characters that existed in her imagination. In "Song," the captain of the
Queen's Guards is lamenting the death of the lady he served.

1 **linnet:** a kind of European finch 3 **bells:** bell-shaped flowers 5 The sentence structure of lines
1–4 is abandoned here, left incomplete, and a new structure begins. This kind of sentence irregularity
is called *anacoluthon* (not following, not on track). 9 **ween:** imagine, think

They thought their hearts could ne'er recall
    The light of joy again.

They thought the tide of grief would flow
    Unchecked through future years;
But where is all their anguish now,   15
    And where are all their tears?

Well, let them fight for honor's breath,
    Or pleasure's shade pursue—
The dweller in the land of death
    Is changed and careless too.   20

And if their eyes should watch and weep
    Till sorrow's source were dry,
She would not, in her tranquil sleep,
    Return a single sigh!

Blow, west-wind, by the lonely mound,   25
    And murmur, summer-streams—
There is no need of other sound
    To soothe my lady's dreams.

21 **watch:** stay awake—keep a vigil, as at a *wake*

Remembrance

Cold in the earth—and the deep snow piled above thee,
Far, far removed, cold in the dreary grave!
Have I forgot, my only love, to love thee,
Severed at last by time's all-severing wave?

Now, when alone, do my thoughts no longer hover   5
Over the mountains, on that northern shore;
Resting their wings where heath and fern-leaves cover
Thy noble heart for ever, ever more?

Cold in the earth—and fifteen wild Decembers,
From those brown hills, have melted into spring: 10
Faithful, indeed, is the spirit that remembers
After such years of change and suffering!

Sweet love of youth, forgive, if I forgot thee
While the world's tide is bearing me along;
Other desires and other hopes beset me,   15
Hopes which obscure, but cannot do thee wrong.

No later light has lightened up my heaven,
No second morn has ever shone for me;
All my life's bliss from thy dear life was given,
All my life's bliss is in the grave with thee.   20

1845. Ibid.

The heroine of the Gondal epic, Rosina of Alcona (she has other names too), is lamenting the death, by assassination, of her husband, the Emperor Julius Brenzaida.

But when the days of golden dreams had perished,
And even despair was powerless to destroy,
Then did I learn how existence could be cherished,
Strengthened, and fed without the aid of joy.

Then did I check the tears of useless passion—   25
Weaned my young soul from yearning after thine;
Sternly denied its burning wish to hasten
Down to that tomb already more than mine.

And, even yet, I dare not let it languish,
Dare not indulge in memory's rapturous pain;   30
Once drinking deep of that divinest anguish,
How could I seek the empty world again?

Arthur Hugh Clough
(1819–1861)

Clough (pronounced to rhyme with *tough*) was the son of a cotton merchant who, when the boy was 13, moved to Charleston, South Carolina, for 13 years. Clough, after graduating from Oxford, stayed on for some years as a fellow. When he became engaged in 1852 he sailed for America in the hope of bettering his fortune, but returned the next year to take a minor post in the education office. Married in 1854, he died in Florence seven years later. Though Clough's worldly career was disappointing, his brilliance was admired by many of the leading literary men of the time, among them Matthew Arnold. Most of his work was still in manuscript when he died; once published, it made him a favorite of late Victorian readers.

Natura Naturans

Beside me,—in the car,—she sat,
    She spake not, no, nor looked to me:
From her to me, from me to her,
    What passed so subtly stealthily?
As rose to rose that by it blows   5
    Its interchanged aroma flings;
Or wake to sound of one sweet note
    The virtues of disparted strings.

Beside me, nought but this!—but this,
    That influent as within me dwelt   10
Her life, mine too within her breast,
    Her brain, her every limb she felt:
We sat; while o'er and in us, more
    And more, a power unknown prevailed,

1846–1847. *Ambarvalia, Poems by Thomas Burbidge and Arthur H. Clough,* 1849.

Natura naturans is nature as a creative force, as distinct from *natura naturata,* which is nature as already created. In this poem the creative force of nature that the poet is interested in is sexual attraction, without which our world would not exist. The "me" of the poem becomes aware of this force when he finds himself sitting next to a young lady in a railway carriage. Though he hardly looks at the girl—doesn't know whether she's blond or brunette—he is overwhelmingly aware of the attraction, which he relates to gravitation among "stones and earths," and so on up through lichens, flowers, insects, birds, other animals—and finally back to the happy human lovers of the Garden of Eden and to "the mystic name of Love." In Victorian times such a theme was considered improper by many.

8 **virtues:** powers, ability to respond   **disparted:** separated—Clough is referring to the sympathetic vibrations on stringed instruments.   10 **influent:** having influence

Inhaling, and inhaled,—and still   15
    'Twas one, inhaling or inhaled.

Beside me, nought but this;—and passed;
    I passed; and know not to this day
If gold or jet her girlish hair,
    If black, or brown, or lucid-grey   20
Her eye's young glance: the fickle chance
    That joined us, yet may join again;
But I no face again could greet
    As hers, whose life was in me then.

As unsuspecting mere a maid   25
    As, fresh in maidhood's bloomiest bloom,
In casual second-class did e'er
    By casual youth her seat assume;
Or vestal, say, of saintliest clay,
    For once by balmiest airs betrayed   30
Unto emotions too too sweet
    To be unlingeringly gainsaid:

Unowning then, confusing soon
    With dreamier dreams that o'er the glass
Of shyly ripening woman-sense   35
    Reflected, scarce reflected, pass,
A wife may-be, a mother she
    In Hymen's shrine recalls not now,
She first in hour, ah, not profane,
    With me to Hymen learnt to bow.   40

Ah no!—Yet owned we, fused in one,
    The Power which e'en in stones and earths
By blind elections felt, in forms
    Organic breeds to myriad births;
By lichen small on granite wall   45
    Approved, its faintest feeblest stir
Slow-spreading, strengthening long, at last
    Vibrated full in me and her.

In me and her—sensation strange!
    The lily grew to pendent head,   50
To vernal airs the mossy bank
    Its sheeny primrose spangles spread,
In roof o'er roof of shade sun-proof
    Did cedar strong itself outclimb,
And altitude of aloe proud   55
    Aspire in floreal crown sublime;

Flashed flickering forth fantastic flies,
    Big bees their burly bodies swung,
Rooks roused with civic din the elms,
    And lark its wild reveillez rung;   60

---

29 **vestal:** virgin   32 **unlingeringly gainsaid:** denied without hesitation   38 **Hymen:** ancient god of marriage   55 **aloe:** an East Indian tree   59 **rooks:** European birds rather like crows   60 **reveillez:** reveille, signal to get up

In Libyan dell the light gazelle,
    The leopard lithe in Indian glade,
And dolphin, brightening tropic seas,
    In us were living, leapt and played:

Their shells did slow crustacea build,   65
    Their gilded skins did snakes renew,
While mightier spines for loftier kind
    Their types in amplest limbs outgrew;
Yea, close compressed in human breast,
    What moss, and tree, and livelier thing,   70
What earth, sun, star of force possessed,
    Lay budding, burgeoning forth for spring.

Such sweet preluding sense of old
    Led on in Eden's sinless place
The hour when bodies human first   75
    Combined the primal prime embrace,
Such genial heat the blissful seat
    In man and woman owned unblamed,
When, naked both, its garden paths
    They walked unconscious, unashamed: 80

Ere, clouded yet in mistiest dawn,
    Above the horizon dusk and dun,
One mountain crest with light had tipped
    That orb that is the spirit's sun;
Ere dreamed young flowers in vernal showers   85
    Of fruit to rise the flower above,
Or ever yet to young desire
    Was told the mystic name of Love.

82 **dusk and dun:** dusky and dark

The Latest Decalogue

Thou shalt have one God only; who
Would be at the expense of two?
No graven images may be
Worshipped, except the currency;
Swear not at all; for, for thy curse,   5
Thine enemy is none the worse;
At church on Sunday to attend
Will serve to keep the world thy friend;
Honour thy parents; that is, all
From whom advancement may befall;   10
Thou shalt not kill; but needst not strive
Officiously to keep alive;
Do not adultery commit;
Advantage rarely comes of it;
Thou shalt not steal; an empty feat,   15
When it's so lucrative to cheat;

1850? *Poems*, 1862. The last four lines were first printed in the 1951 Oxford edition.

Decalogue: the Ten Commandments

Bear not false witness; let the lie
Have time on its own wings to fly;
Thou shalt not covet; but tradition
Approves all forms of competition.   20

The sum of all is, thou shalt love,
If anybody, God above;
At any rate shall never labour
More than thyself to love thy neighbour.

Come Home, Come Home!

Come home, come home! and where an home hath he
Whose ship is driving o'er the driving sea?
To the frail bark here plunging on its way
To the wild waters shall I turn and say
      Ye are my home?   5

Fields once I walked in, faces once I knew,
Familiar things my heart had grown unto,
Far away hence behind me lie; before
The dark clouds mutter and the deep seas roar
      Not words of home.   10

Beyond the clouds, beyond the waves that roar
There may indeed, or may not be, a shore,
Where fields as green and friendly hearts as true
The old foregone appearance may renew
      As of an home.   15

But toil and care must add day on to day,
And weeks bear months and months bear years away,
Ere, if at all, the way-worn traveller hear
A voice he dare believe say in his ear
      Come to thy home.   20

Come home, come home! and where an home hath he
Whose ship is driving o'er the driving sea?
Through clouds that mutter and o'er seas that roar
Is there indeed, or is there not a shore
      That is our home?   25

1852. *Poems*, 1862. This version is from a probably later MS. printed in the Oxford edition.

This poem was printed with a group which the 1869 edition of the poems said "were composed either during the writer's voyage across the Atlantic in 1852, or during his residence in America."

3 **bark:** ship

James Russell Lowell
(1819–1891)

Lowell, born in Cambridge, studied law at Harvard, though he never practiced. After college he wrote not only poetry but also articles against slavery and the Mexican War. For 20 years he taught at Harvard as Longfellow's successor; he was an influential magazine editor. From 1877 to 1880 he was minister to Spain; from 1880 to 1885, the socially popular ambassador to England.

Tempora Mutantur

The world turns mild; democracy, they say,
Rounds the sharp knobs of character away,
And no great harm, unless at grave expense
Of what needs edge of proof, the moral sense;
For man or race is on the downward path   5
Whose fibre grows too soft for honest wrath,
And there's a subtle influence that springs
From words to modify our sense of things.
A plain distinction grows obscure of late:
Man, if he will, may pardon; but the state   10
Forgets its function if not fixed as fate.
So thought our sires: a hundred years ago,
If men were knaves, why, people called them so,
And crime could see the prison-portal bend
Its brow severe at no long vista's end.   15
In those days for plain things plain words would serve;
Men had not learned to admire the graceful swerve
Wherewith the Æsthetic Nature's genial mood
Makes public duty slope to private good;
No muddled conscience raised the saving doubt;   20
A soldier proved unworthy was drummed out,
An officer cashiered, a civil servant
(No matter though his piety were fervent)
Disgracefully dismissed, and through the land
Each bore for life a stigma from the brand   25
Whose far-heard hiss made others more averse
To take the facile step from bad to worse.
The Ten Commandments had a meaning then,
Felt in their bones by least considerate men,
Because behind them Public Conscience stood,   30
And without wincing made their mandates good.
But now that "Statesmanship" is just a way
To dodge the primal curse and make it pay,
Since office means a kind of patent drill
To force an entrance to the nation's till,   35
And peculation something rather less
Risky than if you spelt it with an *s*;
Now that to steal by law is grown an art,
Whom rogues the sires, their milder sons call smart,
And "slightly irregular" dilutes the shame   40
Of what had once a somewhat blunter name.
With generous curve we draw the moral line:
Our swindlers are permitted to resign;
Their guilt is wrapped in deferential names,
And twenty sympathize for one that blames.   45
Add national disgrace to private crime,
Confront mankind with brazen front sublime,
Steal but enough, the world is unsevere,—
Tweed is a statesman, Fisk a financier;

1872. *Heartsease and Rue*, 1888.

Tempora Mutantur: *Tempora mutantur, et nos mutamur in illis: Times change, and we change with them.* The Latin line is of uncertain origin.   **4 edge of proof:** a strong, sharp edge   **21 drummed out:** dishonorably discharged   **22 cashiered:** dismissed   **49 Tweed:** W. M. "Boss" Tweed (1823–1878), New York politician   **Fisk:** Jim Fisk (1834–1872), securities promoter and Broadway character, whose large-scale maneuvers led to a financial crash in 1869. He was shot by an associate.

Invent a mine, and be—the Lord knows what; 50
Secure, at any rate, with what you've got.
The public servant who has stolen or lied,
If called on, may resign with honest pride:
As unjust favor put him in, why doubt
Disfavor as unjust has turned him out? 55
Even if indicted, what is that but fudge
To him who counted-in the elective judge?
Whitewashed, he quits the politician's strife
At ease in mind, with pockets filled for life:
His "lady" glares with gems whose vulgar blaze 60
The poor man through his heightened taxes pays,
Himself content if one huge Kohinoor
Bulge from a shirt-front ampler than before,
But not too candid, lest it haply tend
To rouse suspicion of the People's Friend. 65
A public meeting, treated at his cost,
Resolves him back more virtue than he lost;
With character regilt he counts his gains;
What's gone was air, the solid good remains;
For what is good, except what friend and foe 70
Seem quite unanimous in thinking so,
The stocks and bonds which, in our age of loans,
Replace the stupid pagan's stocks and stones?
With choker white, wherein no cynic eye
Dares see idealized a hempen tie, 75
At parish-meetings he conducts in prayer,
And pays for missions to be sent elsewhere;
On 'Change respected, to his friends endeared,
Add but a Sunday-school-class, he's revered,
And his too early tomb will not be dumb 80
To point a moral for our youth to come.

62 **Kohinoor:** (Persian: "mountain of light") a famous Indian diamond weighing 106 carats
74 **choker:** something worn around the neck, neckerchief, stiff collar   75 **hempen tie:** hangman's
noose   78 **'Change:** Exchange, stock exchange

Walt Whitman
(1819–1892)

Walter Whitman, as he was known until he was 35, was born on Long Island, of English, Dutch, and Welsh descent; his father was a struggling farmer and carpenter. When Whitman was 4, the family moved to Brooklyn. When 12, he learned the printer's trade, which he worked at in his teens, as well as teaching country school and contributing poems to newspapers. In his twenties and early thirties he had several jobs as editor or carpenter, all the while reading extensively, and still finding time to loaf, stroll, and contemplate. In 1855 he published *Leaves of Grass* at his own expense, probably setting some of the type himself. Emerson was one of the very few to recognize its greatness. Throughout the rest of his life, Whitman revised and added; the final "deathbed edition" of 1891–1892 was the ninth. He returned to editorial work until the Civil War, during which he devoted much of his time to visiting soldiers, as a wound-dresser, friend, and consoler, in the Washington hospitals. To support himself he found clerical jobs—once he was fired when a higher official looked into *Leaves of Grass* and found it scandalous. An English edition in 1868 edited by William Rossetti (brother of Dante Gabriel and Christina) won him many admirers, among them Alfred Tennyson—a fact which impressed such American literary figures as Longfellow and Lowell, who had looked down on Whitman. In 1873 he suffered a paralytic stroke and moved to Camden, New Jersey, where, except for train trips to Denver and Ontario, he spent the rest of his life, working, often in loneliness, at new editions of his poetry and occasional newspaper pieces. By the time of his death, the Camden invalid enjoyed a reputation that was worldwide: selections of his poetry had been translated into nearly all of the civilized languages.

From **Leaves of Grass (1855)**

11

Twenty-eight young men bathe by the shore,
Twenty-eight young men, and all so friendly,
Twenty-eight years of womanly life, and all so lonesome.

She owns the fine house by the rise of the bank,
She hides handsome and richly drest aft the blinds of the window.   5

Which of the young men does she like the best?
Ah the homeliest of them is beautiful to her.

Where are you off to, lady? for I see you,
You splash in the water there, yet stay stock still in your room.

Dancing and laughing along the beach came the twenty-ninth bather,   10
The rest did not see her, but she saw them and loved them.

The beards of the young men glistened with wet, it ran from their
    long hair,
Little streams passed all over their bodies.

An unseen hand also passed over their bodies,
It descended tremblingly from their temples and ribs.   15

The young men float on their backs, their white bellies swell to the
    sun. . . . they do not ask who seizes fast to them,
They do not know who puffs and declines with pendant and
    bending arch,
They do not think whom they souse with spray.

32

I think I could turn and live awhile with the animals . . . . they are so
    placid and self-contained,
I stand and look at them sometimes half the day long.

They do not sweat and whine about their condition,
They do not lie awake in the dark and weep for their sins,
They do not make me sick discussing their duty to God,   5
Not one is dissatisfied. . . . not one is demented with the mania of own-
    ing things,
Not one kneels to another nor to his kind that lived thousands of years
    ago,
Not one is respectable or industrious over the whole earth.

Leaves of Grass, 1855.

When *Leaves of Grass* was first published in 1855, the sections were untitled and unnumbered. These became sections 11 and 32 of what he later called "Song of Myself" (the self is not only Whitman's; he is speaking for humanity). These verses remain pretty much as Whitman first published them. But— since he seems to write freely and spontaneously—it is surprising to discover that he subjected his work to "almost incessant revision," as his editors say, in matters of diction, rhythm, and arrangement.

32: 8 **industrious:** later changed to *unhappy*

So they show their relations to me and I accept them;
They bring me tokens of myself.... they evince them plainly in their
　　possession.　　　　　　　　　　　　　　　　　　　　　　　　　10

I do not know where they got those tokens,
I must have passed that way untold times ago and negligently dropt
　　them,
Myself moving forward then and now and forever,
Gathering and showing more always and with velocity,
Infinite and omnigenous and the like of these among them;　　　　15
Not too exclusive toward the reachers of my remembrancers,
Picking out here one that shall be my amie,
Choosing to go with him on brotherly terms.

A gigantic beauty of a stallion, fresh and responsive to my caresses,
Head high in the forehead and wide between the ears,　　　　　　20
Limbs glossy and supple, tail dusting the ground,
Eyes well apart and full of sparkling wickedness.... ears finely cut and
　　flexibly moving.

His nostrils dilate.... my heels embrace him.... his well built limbs
　　tremble with pleasure.... we speed around and return.

I but use you a moment and then I resign you stallion.... and do not
　　need your paces, and outgallop them,
And myself as I stand or sit pass faster than you.　　　　　　　25

15 **omnigenous:** of all kinds 16 **remembrancer:** one who reminds 17 **amie:** the French word
means friend (female); later changed to *one that I love*

Out of the Cradle Endlessly Rocking

Out of the cradle endlessly rocking,
Out of the mocking-bird's throat, the musical shuttle,
Out of the Ninth-month midnight,
Over the sterile sands and the fields beyond, where the child
　　leaving his bed wander'd alone, bareheaded, barefoot,
Down from the shower'd halo,　　　　　　　　　　　　　　　5
Up from the mystic play of shadows twining and twisting as if
　　they were alive,
Out from the patches of briers and blackberries,
From the memories of the bird that chanted to me,
From your memories sad brother, from the fitful risings and fallings
　　I heard,
From under that yellow half-moon late-risen and swollen as if with tears,　10
From those beginning notes of yearning and love there in the mist,
From the thousand responses of my heart never to cease,
From the myriad thence-arous'd words,
From the word stronger and more delicious than any,
From such as now they start the scene revisiting,　　　　　　　15
As a flock, twittering, rising, or overhead passing,
Borne hither, ere all eludes me, hurriedly,
A man, yet by these tears a little boy again,
Throwing myself on the sand, confronting the waves,

Probably 1858. *Leaves of Grass*, 1860. This text from *Leaves of Grass*, 1881.

3 **Ninth-month:** the Quaker term for September

I, chanter of pains and joys, uniter of here and hereafter,   20
Taking all hints to use them, but swiftly leaping beyond them,
A reminiscence sing.

Once Paumanok,
When the lilac-scent was in the air and Fifth-month grass was growing,
Up this seashore in some briers,   25
Two feather'd guests from Alabama, two together,
And their nest, and four light-green eggs spotted with brown,
And every day the he-bird to and fro near at hand,
And every day the she-bird crouch'd on her nest, silent, with bright eyes,
And every day I, a curious boy, never too close, never disturbing them,   30
Cautiously peering, absorbing, translating.

Shine! shine! shine!
Pour down your warmth, great sun!
While we bask, we two together.

Two together!   35
Winds blow south, or winds blow north,
Day come white, or night come black,
Home, or rivers and mountains from home,
Singing all time, minding no time,
While we two keep together.   40

. Till of a sudden,
May-be kill'd, unknown to her mate,
One forenoon the she-bird crouch'd not on the nest,
Nor return'd that afternoon, nor the next,
Nor ever appear'd again.   45

And thenceforward all summer in the sound of the sea,
And at night under the full of the moon in calmer weather,
Over the hoarse surging of the sea,
Or flitting from brier to brier by day,
I saw, I heard at intervals the remaining one, the he-bird,   50
The solitary guest from Alabama.

Blow! blow! blow!
Blow up sea-winds along Paumanok's shore;
I wait and I wait till you blow my mate to me.

Yes, when the stars glisten'd,   55
All night long on the prong of a moss-scallop'd stake,
Down almost amid the slapping waves,
Sat the lone singer wonderful causing tears.

He call'd on his mate,
He pour'd forth the meanings which I of all men know.   60

Yes my brother I know,
The rest might not, but I have treasur'd every note,
For more than once dimly down to the beach gliding,
Silent, avoiding the moonbeams, blending myself with the shadows,

---

23 **Paumanok:** the Indian name for Long Island   32 ff. Sections in italics represent the song of the mocking-bird—as "translated" by the listening boy.

Recalling now the obscure shapes, the echoes, the sounds and sights
    after their sorts,   65
The white arms out in the breakers tirelessly tossing,
I, with bare feet, a child, the wind wafting my hair,
Listen'd long and long.

Listen'd to keep, to sing, now translating the notes,
Following you my brother.   70

Soothe! soothe! soothe!
Close on its wave soothes the wave behind,
And again another behind embracing and lapping, every one close,
But my love soothes not me, not me.

Low hangs the moon, it rose late,   75
It is lagging—O I think it is heavy with love, with love.

O madly the sea pushes upon the land,
With love, with love.

O night! do I not see my love fluttering out among the breakers?
What is that little black thing I see there in the white?   80

Loud! loud! loud!
Loud I call to you, my love!

High and clear I shoot my voice over the waves,
Surely you must know who is here, is here,
You must know who I am, my love.   85

Low-hanging moon!
What is that dusky spot in your brown yellow?
O it is the shape, the shape of my mate!
O moon do not keep her from me any longer.

Land! land! O land!   90
Whichever way I turn, O I think you could give me my mate back again
    if you only would,
For I am almost sure I see her dimly whichever way I look.

O rising stars!
Perhaps the one I want so much will rise, will rise with some of you.

O throat! O trembling throat!   95
Sound clearer through the atmosphere!
Pierce the woods, the earth,
Somewhere listening to catch you must be the one I want.

Shake out carols!
Solitary here, the night's carols!   100
Carols of lonesome love! death's carols!
Carols under that lagging, yellow, waning moon!
O under that moon where she droops almost down into the sea!
O reckless despairing carols.

But soft! sink low!
Soft! let me just murmur,   105
And do you wait a moment you husky-nois'd sea,
For somewhere I believe I heard my mate responding to me,

So faint, I must be still, be still to listen,
But not altogether still, for then she might not come immediately to me. 110

Hither my love!
Here I am! here!
With this just-sustain'd note I announce myself to you,
This gentle call is for you my love, for you.

Do not be decoy'd elsewhere, 115
That is the whistle of the wind, it is not my voice,
That is the fluttering, the fluttering of the spray,
Those are the shadows of leaves.

O darkness! O in vain!
O I am very sick and sorrowful. 120

O brown halo in the sky near the moon, drooping upon the sea!
O troubled reflection in the sea!
O throat! O throbbing heart!
And I singing uselessly, uselessly all the night.

O past! O happy life! O songs of joy! 125
In the air, in the woods, over fields,
Loved! loved! loved! loved! loved!
But my mate no more, no more with me!
We two together no more.

The aria sinking, 130
All else continuing, the stars shining,
The winds blowing, the notes of the bird continuous echoing,
With angry moans the fierce old mother incessantly moaning,
On the sands of Paumanok's shore gray and rustling,
The yellow half-moon enlarged, sagging down, drooping, the face
    of the sea almost touching, 135
The boy ecstatic, with his bare feet the waves, with his hair the
    atmosphere dallying,
The love in the heart long pent, now loose, now at last tumultuously
    bursting,
The aria's meaning, the ears, the soul, swiftly depositing,
The strange tears down the cheeks coursing,
The colloquy there, the trio, each uttering, 140
The undertone, the savage old mother incessantly crying,
To the boy's soul's questions sullenly timing, some drown'd secret
    hissing,
To the outsetting bard.

Demon or bird! (said the boy's soul,)
Is it indeed toward your mate you sing? or is it really to me? 145
For I, that was a child, my tongue's use sleeping, now I have heard you,
Now in a moment I know what I am for, I awake,
And already a thousand singers, a thousand songs, clearer, louder
    and more sorrowful than yours,
A thousand warbling echoes have started to life within me, never to die.

---

130 **aria:** an air or melody; especially—in opera—an accompanied elaborate melody sung by a single voice. Whitman attended the Italian opera as often as he could while in New York; many readers have noticed something like an operatic use of voice in such poems as this one. "But for the opera," said Whitman, "I could never have written *Leaves of Grass*." 144 **Demon:** attendant divinity or spirit (in this sense generally spelled *daimon* or *dæmon*)

O you singer solitary, singing by yourself, projecting me,   150
O solitary me listening, never more shall I cease perpetuating you,
Never more shall I escape, never more the reverberations,
Never more the cries of unsatisfied love be absent from me,
Never again leave me to be the peaceful child I was before what
    there in the night,
By the sea under the yellow and sagging moon,   155
The messenger there arous'd, the fire, the sweet hell within,
The unknown want, the destiny of me.

O give me the clew! (it lurks in the night here somewhere,)
O if I am to have so much, let me have more!

A word then, (for I will conquer it,)   160
The word final, superior to all,
Subtle, sent up—what is it?—I listen;
Are you whispering it, and have been all the time, you sea-waves?
Is that it from your liquid rims and wet sands?

Whereto answering, the sea,   165
Delaying not, hurrying not,
Whisper'd me through the night, and very plainly before daybreak,
Lisp'd to me the low and delicious word death,
And again death, death, death, death,
Hissing melodious, neither like the bird nor like my arous'd child's
    heart,   170
But edging near as privately for me rustling at my feet,
Creeping thence steadily up to my ears and laving me softly all over,
Death, death, death, death, death.

Which I do not forget,
But fuse the song of my dusky demon and brother,   175
That he sang to me in the moonlight on Paumanok's gray beach,
With the thousand responsive songs at random,
My own songs awaked from that hour,
And with them the key, the word up from the waves,
The word of the sweetest song and all songs,   180
That strong and delicious word which, creeping to my feet,
(Or like some old crone rocking the cradle, swathed in sweet
    garments, bending aside,)
The sea whisper'd me.

168 **low and delicious word:** not because Whitman regarded death as an escape or as peaceful oblivion, but because he felt the "joyful certainty of an immortal happiness after death" (R. Asselineau, *The Evolution of Walt Whitman*, I, 190)

I Hear America Singing

I hear America singing, the varied carols I hear,
Those of mechanics, each one singing his as it should be blithe
    and strong,
The carpenter singing his as he measures his plank or beam,
The mason singing his as he makes ready for work, or leaves off
    work,
The boatman singing what belongs to him in his boat, the deckhand
    singing on the steamboat deck,   5

Leaves of Grass, 1860.

The shoemaker singing as he sits on his bench, the hatter singing
    as he stands,
The wood-cutter's song, the ploughboy's on his way in the morning,
    or at noon intermission or at sundown,
The delicious singing of the mother, or of the young wife at work,
    or of the girl sewing or washing,
Each singing what belongs to him or her and to none else,
The day what belongs to the day—at night the party of young fellows,
    robust, friendly,   10
Singing with open mouths their strong melodious songs.

When I Heard the Learn'd Astronomer

When I heard the learn'd astronomer,
When the proofs, the figures, were ranged in columns before me,
When I was shown the charts and diagrams, to add, divide, and
    measure them,
When I sitting heard the astronomer where he lectured with much
    applause in the lecture-room,
How soon unaccountable I became tired and sick,   5
Till rising and gliding out I wander'd off by myself,
In the mystical moist night-air, and from time to time,
Look'd up in perfect silence at the stars.

Drum-Taps, 1865.

Give Me the Splendid Silent Sun

1

Give me the splendid silent sun with all his beams full-dazzling,
Give me juicy autumnal fruit ripe and red from the orchard,
Give me a field where the unmow'd grass grows,
Give me an arbor, give me the trellis'd grape,
Give me fresh corn and wheat, give me serene-moving animals
    teaching content,   5
Give me nights perfectly quiet as on high plateaus west of the
    Mississippi, and I looking up at the stars,
Give me odorous at sunrise a garden of beautiful flowers where I
    can walk undisturb'd,
Give me for marriage a sweet-breath'd woman of whom I should
    never tire,
Give me a perfect child, give me away aside from the noise of the
    world a rural domestic life,
Give me to warble spontaneous songs recluse by myself, for my
    own ears only,   10
Give me solitude, give me Nature, give me again O Nature your
    primal sanities!

These demanding to have them, (tired with ceaseless excitement,
    and rack'd by the war-strife,)
These to procure incessantly asking, rising in cries from my heart,
While yet incessantly asking still I adhere to my city,
Day upon day and year upon year O city, walking your streets,   15
Where you hold me enchain'd a certain time refusing to give me up,

Drum-Taps, 1865. Text from *Leaves of Grass,* 1881.

Yet giving to make me glutted, enrich'd of soul, you give me
      forever faces;
(O I see what I sought to escape, confronting, reversing my cries,
I see my own soul trampling down what it ask'd for.)

2

Keep your splendid silent sun,   20
Keep your woods O Nature, and the quiet places by the woods,
Keep your fields of clover and timothy, and your corn-fields and
      orchards,
Keep the blossoming buckwheat fields where the Ninth-month bees hum;
Give me faces and streets—give me these phantoms incessant
      and endless along the trottoirs!
Give me interminable eyes—give me women—give me comrades
      and lovers by the thousand!   25
Let me see new ones every day—let me hold new ones by the
      hand every day!
Give me such shows—give me the streets of Manhattan!
Give me Broadway, with the soldiers marching—give me the
      sound of the trumpets and drums!
(The soldiers in companies or regiments—some starting away,
      flush'd and reckless,
Some, their time up, returning with thinn'd ranks, young, yet very
      old, worn, marching, noticing nothing;)   30
Give me the shores and wharves heavy-fringed with black ships!
O such for me! O an intense life, full to repletion and varied!
The life of the theatre, bar-room, huge hotel, for me!
The saloon of the steamer! the crowded excursion for me! the
      torchlight procession!
The dense brigade bound for the war, with high piled military
      wagons following;   35
People, endless, streaming, with strong voices, passions, pageants,
Manhattan streets with their powerful throbs, with beating drums
      as now,
The endless and noisy chorus, the rustle and clank of muskets,
      (even the sight of the wounded,)
Manhattan crowds, with their turbulent musical chorus!
Manhattan faces and eyes forever for me.   40

24 **trottoirs:** (French) sidewalks   28 **soldiers:** The poem was written near the end of the Civil War.
34 **saloon:** salon—lounge, hall

When Lilacs Last in the Dooryard Bloom'd

1

When lilacs last in the dooryard bloom'd,
And the great star early droop'd in the western sky in the night,
I mourn'd, and yet shall mourn with ever-returning spring.

1865. Sequel to *Drum-Taps*, 1865–1866. Text from *Leaves of Grass*, 1881.

Abraham Lincoln was shot on April 14, 1865; he died the following day. A week later the funeral
train left Washington; after stops in many cities, it reached Springfield, Illinois, where Lincoln was
buried on May 4. Whitman wrote his threnody (lamentation) in the weeks after the assassination.

1 **lilacs:** The sight or fragrance of lilacs, in full bloom at the time, continued to remind Whitman of
Lincoln's death. They were also blooming around the house where the president died; the surgeon
who attended him found that throughout his life the scent of lilacs brought back the horror of that
night. But here the "perennial" lilacs are also a symbol of enduring life.   2 **great star:** Venus, the
evening star, associated with the fallen leader

Ever-returning spring, trinity sure to me you bring,
Lilac blooming perennial and drooping star in the west,   5
And thought of him I love.

2

O powerful western fallen star!
O shades of night—O moody, tearful night!
O great star disappear'd—O the black murk that hides the star!
O cruel hands that hold me powerless—O helpless soul of me!   10
O harsh surrounding cloud that will not free my soul.

3

In the dooryard fronting an old farm-house near the white-wash'd
    palings,
Stands the lilac-bush tall-growing with heart-shaped leaves of rich
    green,
With many a pointed blossom rising delicate, with the perfume
    strong I love,
With every leaf a miracle—and from this bush in the dooryard,   15
With delicate-color'd blossoms and heart-shaped leaves of rich
    green,
A sprig with its flower I break.

4

In the swamp in secluded recesses,
A shy and hidden bird is warbling a song.

Solitary the thrush,   20
The hermit withdrawn to himself, avoiding the settlements,
Sings by himself a song.

Song of the bleeding throat,
Death's outlet song of life, (for well dear brother I know,
If thou wast not granted to sing thou would'st surely die.)   25

5

Over the breast of the spring, the land, amid cities,
Amid lanes and through old woods, where lately the violets peep'd
    from the ground, spotting the gray debris,
Amid the grass in the fields each side of the lanes, passing the
    endless grass,
Passing the yellow-spear'd wheat, every grain from its shroud in
    the dark-brown fields uprisen,
Passing the apple-tree blows of white and pink in the orchards,   30
Carrying a corpse to where it shall rest in the grave,
Night and day journeys a coffin.

6

Coffin that passes through lanes and streets,
Through day and night with the great cloud darkening the land,
With the pomp of the inloop'd flags with the cities draped in black,   35
With the show of the States themselves as of crape-veil'd women
    standing,
With processions long and winding and the flambeaus of the night,

19 **shy . . . bird**: the hermit thrush, which some think has the most beautiful song of any American
bird   30 **blows**: blossoms   37 **flambeaus**: torches

With the countless torches lit, with the silent sea of faces and the
    unbared heads,
With the waiting depot, the arriving coffin, and the sombre faces,
With dirges through the night, with the thousand voices rising
    strong and solemn,   40
With all the mournful voices of the dirges pour'd around the coffin,
The dim-lit churches and the shuddering organs—where amid
    these you journey,
With the tolling tolling bells' perpetual clang,
Here, coffin that slowly passes,
I give you my sprig of lilac.   45

                            7
(Nor for you, for one alone,
Blossoms and branches green to coffins all I bring,
For fresh as the morning, thus would I chant a song for you O
    sane and sacred death.

All over bouquets of roses,
O death, I cover you over with roses and early lilies,   50
But mostly and now the lilac that blooms the first,
Copious I break, I break the sprigs from the bushes,
With loaded arms I come, pouring for you,
For you and the coffins all of you O death.)

                            8
O western orb sailing the heaven,   55
Now I know what you must have meant as a month since I
    walk'd,
As I walk'd in silence the transparent shadowy night,
As I saw you had something to tell as you bent to me night after
    night,
As you droop'd from the sky low down as if to my side, (while
    the other stars all look'd on,)
As we wander'd together the solemn night, (for something I know
    not what kept me from sleep,)   60
As the night advanced, and I saw on the rim of the west how full
    you were of woe,
As I stood on the rising ground in the breeze in the cool transparent
    night,
As I watch'd where you pass'd and was lost in the netherward
    black of the night,
As my soul in its trouble dissatisfied sank, as where you sad orb,
Concluded, dropt in the night, and was gone.   65

                            9
Sing on there in the swamp,
O singer bashful and tender, I hear your notes, I hear your call,
I hear, I come presently, I understand you,
But a moment I linger, for the lustrous star has detain'd me,
The star my departing comrade holds and detains me.   70

                            10
O how shall I warble myself for the dead one there I loved?
And how shall I deck my song for the large sweet soul that has
    gone?

---

63 **netherward:** downward (as light fades in the west)

And what shall my perfume be for the grave of him I love?

Sea-winds blown from east and west,
Blown from the Eastern sea and blown from the Western sea, till
    there on the prairies meeting, 75
These and with these and the breath of my chant,
I'll perfume the grave of him I love.

11

O what shall I hang on the chamber walls?
And what shall the pictures be that I hang on the walls,
To adorn the burial-house of him I love? 80

Pictures of growing spring and farms and homes,
With the Fourth-month eve at sundown, and the gray smoke lucid
    and bright,
With floods of the yellow gold of the gorgeous, indolent, sinking sun,
    burning, expanding the air,
With the fresh sweet herbage under foot, and the pale green leaves
    of the trees prolific,
In the distance the flowing glaze, the breast of the river, with a
    wind-dapple here and there, 85
With ranging hills on the banks, with many a line against the sky,
    and shadows,
And the city at hand with dwellings so dense, and stacks of
    chimneys,
And all the scenes of life and the workshops, and the workmen
    homeward returning.

12

Lo, body and soul—this land,
My own Manhattan with spires, and the sparkling and hurrying
    tides, and the ships, 90
The varied and ample land, the South and the North in the light,
    Ohio's shores and flashing Missouri,
And ever the far-spreading prairies cover'd with grass and corn.

Lo, the most excellent sun so calm and haughty,
The violet and purple morn with just-felt breezes,
The gentle soft-born measureless light, 95
The miracle spreading bathing all, the fulfill'd noon,
The coming eve delicious, the welcome night and the stars,
Over my cities shining all, enveloping man and land.

13

Sing on, sing on you gray-brown bird,
Sing from the swamps, the recesses, pour your chant from the
    bushes, 100
Limitless out of the dusk, out of the cedars and pines.

Sing on dearest brother, warble your reedy song,
Loud human song, with voice of uttermost woe.

O liquid and free and tender!
O wild and loose to my soul—O wondrous singer! 105
You only I hear—yet the star holds me, (but will soon depart,)
Yet the lilac with mastering odor holds me.

14

Now while I sat in the day and look'd forth,
In the close of the day with its light and the fields of spring, and
    the farmers preparing their crops,
In the large unconscious scenery of my land with its lakes and
    forests,   110
In the heavenly aerial beauty, (after the perturb'd winds and the
    storms,)
Under the arching heavens of the afternoon swift passing, and the
    voices of children and women,
The many-moving sea-tides, and I saw the ships how they
    sail'd,
And the summer approaching with richness, and the fields all busy
    with labor,
And the infinite separate houses, how they all went on, each with
    its meals and minutia of daily usages,   115
And the streets how their throbbings throbb'd, and the cities pent
    —lo, then and there,
Falling upon them all and among them all, enveloping me with the
    rest,
Appear'd the cloud, appear'd the long black trail,
And I knew death, its thought, and the sacred knowledge of
    death.

Then with the knowledge of death as walking one side of me,   120
And the thought of death close-walking the other side of me,
And I in the middle as with companions, and as holding the
    hands of companions,
I fled forth to the hiding receiving night that talks not,
Down to the shores of the water, the path by the swamp in the
    dimness,
To the solemn shadowy cedars and ghostly pines so still.   125

And the singer so shy to the rest receiv'd me,
The gray-brown bird I know receiv'd us comrades three,
And he sang the carol of death, and a verse for him I love.

From deep secluded recesses,
From the fragrant cedars and the ghostly pines so still,   130
Came the carol of the bird.

And the charm of the carol rapt me,
As I held as if by their hands my comrades in the night,
And the voice of my spirit tallied the song of the bird.

Come lovely and soothing death,   135
Undulate round the world, serenely arriving, arriving,
In the day, in the night, to all, to each,
Sooner or later delicate death.

Prais'd be the fathomless universe,
For life and joy, and for objects and knowledge curious,   140
And for love, sweet love—but praise! praise! praise!
For the sure-enwinding arms of cool-enfolding death.

115 **minutia:** for *minutiae,* small details   134 **tallied:** matched, corresponded with

Dark mother always gliding near with soft feet,
Have none chanted for thee a chant of fullest welcome?
Then I chant it for thee, I glorify thee above all,   145
I bring thee a song that when thou must indeed come, come
    unfalteringly.

Approach strong deliveress,
When it is so, when thou hast taken them I joyously sing the dead,
Lost in the loving floating ocean of thee,
Laved in the flood of thy bliss O death.   150

From me to thee glad serenades,
Dances for thee I propose saluting thee, adornments and feastings
    for thee,
And the sights of the open landscape and the high-spread sky are
    fitting,
And life and the fields, and the huge and thoughtful night.

The night in silence under many a star,   155
The ocean shore and the husky whispering wave whose voice I
    know,
And the soul turning to thee O vast and well-veil'd death,
And the body gratefully nestling close to thee.

Over the tree-tops I float thee a song,
Over the rising and sinking waves, over the myriad fields and the
    prairies wide,   160
Over the dense-pack'd cities all and the teeming wharves and ways,
I float this carol with joy, with joy to thee O death.

15

To the tally of my soul,
Loud and strong kept up the gray-brown bird,
With pure deliberate notes spreading filling the night.   165

Loud in the pines and cedars dim,
Clear in the freshness moist and the swamp-perfume,
And I with my comrades there in the night.

While my sight that was bound in my eyes unclosed,
As to long panoramas of visions.   170

And I saw askant the armies,
I saw as in noiseless dreams hundreds of battle-flags,
Borne through the smoke of the battles and pierc'd with missiles
    I saw them,
And carried hither and yon through the smoke, and torn and
    bloody,
And at last but a few shreds left on the staffs, (and all in silence,)   175
And the staffs all splinter'd and broken.

I saw battle-corpses, myriads of them,
And the white skeletons of young men, I saw them,
I saw the debris and debris of all the slain soldiers of the war,

---

150 **laved:** bathed   171 **askant:** askance, with a sidelong glance

But I saw they were not as was thought,   180
They themselves were fully at rest, they suffer'd not,
The living remain'd and suffer'd, the mother suffer'd,
And the wife and the child and the musing comrade suffer'd,
And the armies that remain'd suffer'd.

16

Passing the visions, passing the night,   185
Passing, unloosing the hold of my comrades' hands,
Passing the song of the hermit bird and the tallying song of my
      soul,
Victorious song, death's outlet song, yet varying ever-altering song,
As low and wailing, yet clear the notes, rising and falling, flooding
      the night,
Sadly sinking and fainting, as warning and warning, and yet again
      bursting with joy,   190
Covering the earth and filling the spread of the heaven,
As that powerful psalm in the night I heard from recesses,
Passing, I leave thee lilac with heart-shaped leaves,
I leave thee there in the door-yard, blooming, returning with
      spring.

I cease from my song for thee,   195
From my gaze on thee in the west, fronting the west, communing
      with thee,
O comrade lustrous with silver face in the night.

Yet each to keep and all, retrievements out of the night,
The song, the wondrous chant of the gray-brown bird,
And the tallying chant, the echo arous'd in my soul,   200
With the lustrous and drooping star with the countenance full
      of woe,
With the holders holding my hand nearing the call of the bird,
Comrades mine and I in the midst, and their memory ever to
      keep, for the dead I loved so well,
For the sweetest, wisest soul of all my days and lands—and this
      for his dear sake,
Lilac and star and bird twined with the chant of my soul,   205
There in the fragrant pines and the cedars dusk and dim.

The Dalliance of the Eagles

Skirting the river road, (my forenoon walk, my rest,)
Skyward in air a sudden muffled sound, the dalliance of the eagles,
The rushing amorous contact high in space together,
The clinching interlocking claws, a living, fierce, gyrating wheel,
Four beating wings, two beaks, a swirling mass tight grappling,   5
In tumbling turning clustering loops, straight downward falling,
Till o'er the river pois'd, the twain yet one, a moment's lull,
A motionless still balance in the air, then parting, talons loosing,
Upward again on slow-firm pinions slanting, their separate diverse flight,
She hers, he his, pursuing.   10

Leaves of Grass, 1881.

Whitman himself had never seen the mating of eagles but wrote the poem—with much reworking—
from a description given him by the naturalist John Burroughs.

Reconciliation

Word over all, beautiful as the sky,
Beautiful that war and all its deeds of carnage must in time be
    utterly lost,
That the hands of the sisters Death and Night incessantly softly
    wash again, and ever again, this soil'd world;
For my enemy is dead, a man divine as myself is dead,
I look where he lies white-faced and still in the coffin—I draw near,
Bend down and touch lightly with my lips the white face in the coffin.

Sequel to Drum-Taps, 1865–1866.

A Noiseless Patient Spider

A noiseless patient spider,
I mark'd where on a little promontory it stood isolated,
Mark'd how to explore the vacant vast surrounding,
It launch'd forth filament, filament, filament, out of itself,
Ever unreeling them, ever tirelessly speeding them.   5

And you O my soul where you stand,
Surrounded, detached, in measureless oceans of space,
Ceaselessly musing, venturing, throwing, seeking the spheres to
    connect them,
Till the bridge you will need be form'd, till the ductile anchor hold,
Till the gossamer thread you fling catch somewhere, O my soul.   10

1868. *Leaves of Grass*, 5th ed., with "Passage to India," 1871; revised, *Leaves of Grass*, 1881.

9 **ductile:** capable of being drawn out (as metal made into wire)

A Clear Midnight

This is thy hour O Soul, thy free flight into the wordless,
Away from books, away from art, the day erased, the lesson done,
Thee fully forth emerging, silent, gazing, pondering the themes
    thou lovest best,
Night, sleep, death and the stars.

1880. *Leaves of Grass*, 1881.

Herman Melville
(1819–1891)

Melville, forced to drop out of school when his merchant father went bankrupt, worked at various jobs before signing on as a sailor. When 21, he went to the South Seas on a whaler, jumped ship, was captured and lived among cannibals, was imprisoned and escaped, and drifted from island to island. Out of these experiences came his first five tales of adventure and then *Moby-Dick* (1851)—which was not a popular success. Neither were the four books that followed; Melville, still in his thirties, turned to verse for most of the rest of his life. For 20 years he was a customs inspector in New York. In 1876 he published *Clarel*, a two-volume philosophical poem based on memories of the Holy Land; few read it. For some 30 years after his death, Melville was almost ignored; his importance has been rediscovered only in recent decades.

The March into Virginia

Ending in the First Manassas
(July, 1861)

Did all the lets and bars appear
    To every just or larger end,
Whence should come the trust and cheer?
    Youth must its ignorant impulse lend—
Age finds place in the rear.   5
    All wars are boyish, and are fought by boys,
The champions and enthusiasts of the state:
    Turbid ardors and vain joys
      Not barrenly abate—
    Stimulants to the power mature,   10
      Preparatives of fate.

Who here forecasteth the event?
What heart but spurns at precedent
And warnings of the wise,
Contemned foreclosures of surprise?   15
The banners play, the bugles call,
The air is blue and prodigal.
    No berrying party, pleasure-wooed,
No picnic party in the May,
Ever went less loth than they   20
    Into that leafy neighborhood.
In Bacchic glee they file toward Fate,
Moloch's uninitiate:
Expectancy, and glad surmise
Of battle's unknown mysteries.   25
All they feel is this: 'tis glory,
A rapture sharp, though transitory,
Yet lasting in belaureled story.
So they gayly go to fight,
Chatting left and laughing right.   30

But some who this blithe mood present,
    As on in lightsome files they fare,
Shall die experienced ere three days are spent—
    Perish, enlightened by the vollied glare;
Or shame survive, and, like to adamant,   35
    The throe of Second Manassas share.

1862–1866. Battle-Pieces and Aspects of the War, 1866.

In July 1861, the Union Army under General McDowell moved confidently into Virginia; "the march resembled a picnic more than a military operation" (R. P. Warren), with politicians, sightseers, and their ladies in carriages ready with food and champagne to celebrate the victory, but before long the army, defeated at the little stream called Bull Run near Manassas, was fleeing back to Washington, spectators and all.

1 **let:** hindrance   15 **contemned:** scorned, disdained   18 **berrying:** a grim pun on *burying*   22 **Bacchic:** wildly celebrating; Bacchus is the Latin name of Dionysius, god of wine and revelry.   23 **Moloch:** pagan deity to whom parents burned their own children in sacrifice (2 Kings 23:10)   35 **shame:** In the copy of *Battle-Pieces* owned by Mrs. Melville (now in the Houghton Library at Harvard), *shame* is crossed out and *some* written in—possibly a better reading, since parallel with the *some* four lines above.   36 **Second Manassas:** The Northern forces were again defeated at Bull Run the following year.

Commemorative of a Naval Victory

Sailors there are of gentlest breed,
    Yet strong, like every goodly thing;
The discipline of arms refines,
    And the wave gives tempering.
    The damasked blade its beam can fling;   5
It lends the last grave grace:
The hawk, the hound, and sworded nobleman
    In Titian's picture for a king,
Are of hunter or warrior race.

In social halls a favored guest   10
    In years that follow victory won,
How sweet to feel your festal fame
    In woman's glance instinctive thrown:
    Repose is yours—your deed is known,
It musks the amber wine;   15
It lives, and sheds a light from storied days
    Rich as October sunsets brown,
Which make the barren place to shine.

But seldom the laurel wreath is seen
    Unmixed with pensive pansies dark;   20
There's a light and a shadow on every man
    Who at last attains his lifted mark—
    Nursing through night the ethereal spark.
Elate he never can be;
He feels that spirits which glad had hailed his worth,   25
    Sleep in oblivion.—The shark
Glides white through the phosphorus sea.

1865? Ibid.

4–5 the wave . . . : Water tempers (strengthens) the sailor by his experience at sea, and also tempers steel, which is "damasked" (as at Damascus), given wavy lines which ornament a sword blade. **8 Titian's picture:** thought to be "The Man with a Falcon," by the Italian painter (1477–1576) **15 musks:** gives a bouquet or tang to **19 laurel wreath:** emblematic of victory **20 pensive pansies:** *pansy* is from the French *pensée* (thought) **26–27 The shark . . . :** an image of menace, danger, death, and, paradoxically, of power and beauty

Billy in the Darbies

Good of the Chaplain to enter Lone Bay
And down on his marrow-bones here and pray

1891? *Billy Budd and Other Prose Pieces,* ed. by R. M. Weaver, 1924.

When Melville died in 1891 he left an unfinished novel, first published in 1924 as *Billy Budd, Foretopman,* about an innocent and virtuous young sailor hanged for an unintended murder. The poem above, supposed to be the "rude utterance" composed by the "tarry hands" of a fellow sailor, imagines Billy's thoughts as he waits in the darbies (handcuffs, fetters) in Lone Bay (solitude) the night before the execution. Sacramental meanings have been found in the poem: the ray of moonlight (heaven's blessing?), the going "aloft from alow" (death and resurrection?), the "parting cup" (the sacrament? Christ's chalice?), and so on. It seems that the novel itself developed from Melville's preliminary note to this poem.

2 marrow-bones: knees

For the likes just o' me, Billy Budd.—But, look:
Through the port comes the moon-shine astray!
It tips the guard's cutlass and silvers this nook;   5
But 'twill die in the dawning of Billy's last day.
A jewel-block they'll make of me tomorrow,
Pendant pearl from the yard-arm-end
Like the ear-drop I gave to Bristol Molly—
O, 'tis me, not the sentence they'll suspend.   10
Ay, Ay, all is up; and I must up too
Early in the morning, aloft from alow.
On an empty stomach, now, never it would do.
They'll give me a nibble—bit o' biscuit ere I go.
Sure, a messmate will reach me the last parting cup;   15
But, turning heads away from the hoist and the belay,
Heaven knows who will have the running of me up!
No pipe to those halyards.—But aren't it all sham?
A blur's in my eyes; it is dreaming that I am.
A hatchet to my hawser? All adrift to go?   20
The drum roll to grog, and Billy never know?
But Donald he has promised to stand by the plank;
So I'll shake a friendly hand ere I sink.
But—no! It is dead then I'll be, come to think.—
I remember Taff the Welshman when he sank.   25
And his cheek it was like the budding pink.
But me they'll lash me in hammock, drop me deep
Fathoms down, fathoms down, how I'll dream fast asleep.
I feel it stealing now. Sentry, are you there?
Just ease these darbies at the wrist,   30
And roll me over fair,
I am sleepy, and the oozy weeds about me twist.

---

7 **jewel-block:** the block (pulley) at the end of a yard-arm   8 **pendant:** hanging—like a jewel, and like Billy himself   9 **ear-drop:** earring—but "drop" was also a slang term for gallows   10 **suspend:** another grim pun   12 **aloft from alow:** Cf. "Lycidas," 172: "So Lycidas sunk low, but mounted high...." It is thought that Melville had Milton's poem in mind.   16 **belay:** To belay is to make a rope fast by figure-eighting it around a cleat.   18 **halyards:** ropes, whose hauling up for the hanging will not be signalled by the usual pipe   **sham:** delusion, illusion   21 **drum roll to grog:** signal for the crew to have its tot of grog (rum—generally—and water)   27–32 R. P. Warren, in his edition of Melville's selected poems, points out the "audio-symbolic" effect of the prevailing vowel-run on words in ē: *me-deep-dream-asleep-feel-stealing-ease-these-me-sleepy-weeds-me*.   32 **oozy weeds:** weeds as darbies? Cf. "Lycidas," 175: "With nectar pure his oozy locks he laves...."

Frederick Goddard Tuckerman
(1821–1873)

Born of a prosperous Boston family, Tuckerman went to Harvard, where Jones Very was his tutor. Though he studied law and was admitted to the bar, he never practiced. In 1847 he married and settled in Greenfield, Massachusetts, giving his time to poetry and his other interests, which included the sciences. His poetry, much of it about the death of his wife ten years after their marriage, was privately printed in 1860, reissued four years later. Though praised by Tennyson and other literary men, it was, like Melville's, largely ignored until recent decades.

From **Sonnets**

II, iii

Yes: though the brine may from the desert deep
Run itself sweet before it finds the foam,
Oh what to him—the deep heart once a home
For love and light—is left?—to walk and weep;
Still, with astonished sorrow, watch to keep   5
On his dead day: he weeps and knows his doom
Yet standeth stunned—as one who climbs a steep
And dreaming softly of the cottage room,
The faces round the porch, the rose in showers,
Gains the last height between his heart and it;   10
And from the windows where his children sleep
Sees the red fire fork, or later come
Finds, where he left his home, a smouldering pit—
Blackness, and scalding stench, for love and flowers.

II, xv

Gertrude and Gulielma, sister-twins,
Dwelt in the valley at the farmhouse old;
Nor grief had touched their locks of dark and gold
Nor dimmed the fragrant whiteness of their skins:
Both beautiful, and one in height and mould;   5
Yet one had loveliness which the spirit wins
To other worlds: eyes, forehead, smile, and all
More softly serious than the twilight's fall.
The other—can I e'er forget the day
When, stealing from a laughing group away   10
To muse with absent eye and motion slow,
Her beauty fell upon me like a blow?
Gertrude! with red flowerlip, and silk black hair.
Yet Gulielma was by far more fair.

II, xvi

Under the mountain, as when first I knew
Its low dark roof, and chimney creeper-twined,
The red house stands; and yet my footsteps find
Vague in the walks, waste balm and feverfew.
But they are gone: no soft-eyed sisters trip   5
Across the porch, or lintels, where, behind,
The mother sat,—sat knitting with pursed lip.
The house stands vacant in its green recess,
Absent of beauty as a broken heart;
The wild rain enters, and the sunset wind   10
Sighs in the chambers of their loveliness,

1857–1860. *Poems*, 1860.

II, iii: There are slight differences, chiefly of punctuation, between the text of the poem as printed in *Poems*, 1860, and as written out by Tuckerman in his own MS. book, now at the Houghton Library at Harvard [MS. Am 1349 (2)]. The present text, where there is a choice, is based on what seem to be sense and clarity. A few changes in punctuation have been made on the same grounds. The poem is probably about the death of the poet's wife in 1857—the subject of many of his poems.   3 **to:** such is the MS. reading. *Poems*, 1860, has *for*. **the:** *Poems.* MS. has *whose*. 5 **watch:** vigil. II, xvi: 4 **waste balm and feverfew:** aromatic plants (or weeds) of field and roadside

Or shakes the pane: and in the silent noons
The glass falls from the window, part by part,
And ringeth faintly in the grassy stones.

II, xviii

And Change with hurried hand has swept these scenes:
The woods have fallen, across the meadow-lot
The hunter's trail and trap-path is forgot,
And fire has drunk the swamps of evergreens;
Yet for a moment let my fancy plant   5
These autumn hills again: the wild dove's haunt,
The wild deer's walk: in golden umbrage shut,
The Indian river runs, Quonecktacut!
Here, but a lifetime back, where falls tonight
Behind the curtained pane a sheltered light   10
On buds of rose or vase of violet
Aloft upon the marble mantel set,
Here in the forest-heart hung blackening
The wolf-bait on the bush beside the spring.

14 **ringeth**: MS. *tinkles*. II, xviii: 7 **umbrage**: shade 8 **Quonecktacut**: Greenfield, Massachusetts,
where Tuckerman spent most of his life, is on the Connecticut River. 14 **wolf-bait**: wolf poison—
probably poisoned meat

Matthew Arnold
(1822–1888)

The son of Thomas Arnold, clergyman and headmaster of the Rugby School for boys, Ar-
nold was for a few years private secretary to a government official. When 29 he was ap-
pointed inspector of schools, with routine duties to which he devoted himself conscien-
tiously for 35 years. In 1857 he was elected to the professorship of poetry at Oxford,
which he held, part-time, for ten years. His first book of poetry appeared when he was
29, his last when he was 45; thereafter he produced little verse. In the time his official
duties left him, he wrote extensively on literature, religion, education, culture. In 1883–
1884 and again two years later he made lecture tours of America.

Dover Beach

The sea is calm to-night.
The tide is full, the moon lies fair
Upon the straits; on the French coast the light
Gleams and is gone; the cliffs of England stand,
Glimmering and vast, out in the tranquil bay.   5
Come to the window, sweet is the night-air!
Only, from the long line of spray
Where the sea meets the moon-blanched land,
Listen! you hear the grating roar
Of pebbles which the waves draw back, and fling,   10
At their return, up the high strand,
Begin, and cease, and then again begin,

Probably 1851. *New Poems,* 1867.

Dover is a port and seaside resort on the English Channel opposite Calais in France. Arnold spent two
or three days there not long after his marriage in June 1851, and may have written the poem then.

4 **cliffs**: The famous "white cliffs of Dover" rise on each side of the small bay in which the town
is situated.

With tremulous cadence slow, and bring
The eternal note of sadness in.

Sophocles long ago   15
Heard it on the Ægæan, and it brought
Into his mind the turbid ebb and flow
Of human misery; we
Find also in the sound a thought,
Hearing it by this distant northern sea.   20

The Sea of Faith
Was once, too, at the full, and round earth's shore
Lay like the folds of a bright girdle furled.
But now I only hear
Its melancholy, long, withdrawing roar,   25
Retreating, to the breath
Of the night-wind, down the vast edges drear
And naked shingles of the world.

Ah, love, let us be true
To one another! for the world, which seems   30
To lie before us like a land of dreams,
So various, so beautiful, so new,
Hath really neither joy, nor love, nor light,
Nor certitude, nor peace, nor help for pain;
And we are here as on a darkling plain   35
Swept with confused alarms of struggle and flight,
Where ignorant armies clash by night.

15-18 **Sophocles:** the Greek tragedian (496?-406 B.C.), as such concerned with human misery. Arnold seems to have had no particular passage in mind. Some think he is referring to *Antigone*, lines 583–591, but that is about a catastrophic storm, not a "turbid ebb and flow." 16 **Ægæan:** the arm of the Mediterranean between Greece and modern Yugoslavia 23 **girdle:** the image is one of a kind of sash, not an undergarment 28 **shingles:** gravelly beaches (Beds of rounded stones along the seashore, generally larger than pebbles, are called *shingle*.) 35 **darkling:** dark, in the dark 35-37 Arnold, a classical scholar, is probably recalling Thucydides, (471?-400? B.C.), the Greek historian whom Arnold's father had translated. In his *History of the Peloponnesian War*, VII, chapter 44, there is a famous description of a battle by night in which the Athenians were thrown into confusion and panic.

The Scholar-Gypsy

Go, for they call you, shepherd, from the hill;
    Go, shepherd, and untie the wattled cotes!
        No longer leave thy wistful flock unfed,
    Nor let thy bawling fellows rack their throats,
        Nor the cropped herbage shoot another head.   5
            But when the fields are still,
        And the tired men and dogs all gone to rest,

Probably 1852-1853. *Poems*, 1853.

The story of the scholar-gypsy is from Joseph Glanvill's *The Vanity of Dogmatizing* (1661), an attack on scholastic philosophy, which tells how a young Oxford student, forced to drop his studies because of poverty, joined a band of wandering gypsies. When later discovered among them by old college friends, he said that the gypsies had a kind of occult wisdom he was learning, which he meant to reveal to the world once he had mastered it. Arnold himself once said the poem was inspired by the carefree jauntings of his college days. It is, in effect, a lament for the gypsy energies and attitudes of youth as opposed to Victorian propriety.

2 **wattled cotes:** sheds made of "wattles," woven poles, branches, etc.

And only the white sheep are sometimes seen
  Cross and recross the strips of moon-blanched green,
Come, shepherd, and again begin the quest!   10

Here, where the reaper was at work of late—
  In this high field's dark corner, where he leaves
    His coat, his basket, and his earthen cruse,
  And in the sun all morning binds the sheaves,
    Then here, at noon, comes back his stores to use—   15
      Here will I sit and wait,
  While to my ear from uplands far away
    The bleating of the folded flocks is borne,
    With distant cries of reapers in the corn—
All the live murmur of a summer's day.   20

Screened is this nook o'er the high, half-reaped field,
  And here till sun-down, shepherd! will I be.
    Through the thick corn the scarlet poppies peep,
  And round green roots and yellowing stalks I see
    Pale pink convolvulus in tendrils creep;   25
      And air-swept lindens yield
  Their scent, and rustle down their perfumed showers
    Of bloom on the bent grass where I am laid,
    And bower me from the August sun with shade;
And the eye travels down to Oxford's towers.   30

And near me on the grass lies Glanvill's book—
  Come, let me read the oft-read tale again!
    The story of the Oxford scholar poor,
  Of pregnant parts and quick inventive brain,
    Who, tired of knocking at preferment's door,   35
      One summer-morn forsook
  His friends, and went to learn the gypsy-lore,
    And roamed the world with that wild brotherhood,
    And came, as most men deemed, to little good,
But came to Oxford and his friends no more.   40

But once, years after, in the country-lanes,
  Two scholars, whom at college erst he knew,
    Met him, and of his way of life enquired;
  Whereat he answered, that the gypsy-crew,
    His mates, had arts to rule as they desired   45
      The workings of men's brains,
  And they can bind them to what thoughts they will.
    "And I," he said, "the secret of their art,
    When fully learned, will to the world impart;
But it needs heaven-sent moments for this skill."   50

This said, he left them, and returned no more.
  But rumours hung about the country-side,
    That the lost Scholar long was seen to stray,
  Seen by rare glimpses, pensive and tongue-tied,
    In hat of antique shape, and cloak of grey,   55
      The same the gypsies wore.

---

13 **cruse:** jar   25 **convolvulus:** plants of the morning-glory family   34 **pregnant parts:** creative gifts
or abilities   35 **preferment:** advancement, promotion   39 **deemed:** thought   42 **erst:** formerly

Shepherds had met him on the Hurst in spring;
  At some lone alehouse in the Berkshire moors,
    On the warm ingle-bench, the smock-frocked boors
Had found him seated at their entering,   60

But, 'mid their drink and clatter, he would fly.
  And I myself seem half to know thy looks,
    And put the shepherds, wanderer! on thy trace;
And boys who in lone wheatfields scare the rooks
    I ask if thou hast passed their quiet place;   65
      Or in my boat I lie
Moored to the cool bank in the summer-heats,
    'Mid wide grass meadows which the sunshine fills,
    And watch the warm, green-muffled Cumner hills,
And wonder if thou haunt'st their shy retreats.   70

For most, I know, thou lov'st retirèd ground!
  Thee at the ferry Oxford riders blithe,
    Returning home on summer-nights, have met
Crossing the stripling Thames at Bab-lock-hithe,
    Trailing in the cool stream thy fingers wet,   75
      As the punt's rope chops round;
And leaning backward in a pensive dream,
    And fostering in thy lap a heap of flowers
    Plucked in shy fields and distant Wychwood bowers,
And thine eyes resting on the moonlit stream.   80

And then they land, and thou art seen no more!
  Maidens, who from the distant hamlets come
    To dance around the Fyfield elm in May,
Oft through the darkening fields have seen thee roam,
    Or cross a stile into the public way.   85
      Oft thou hast given them store
Of flowers—the frail-leafed, white anemone,
    Dark bluebells drenched with dews of summer eves,
    And purple orchises with spotted leaves—
But none hath words she can report of thee.   90

And, above Godstow Bridge, when hay-time's here
  In June, and many a scythe in sunshine flames,
    Men who through those wide fields of breezy grass
Where black-winged swallows haunt the glittering Thames,
    To bathe in the abandoned lasher pass,   95
      Have often passed thee near
Sitting upon the river bank o'ergrown;
    Marked thine outlandish garb, thy figure spare,
    Thy dark vague eyes, and soft abstracted air—
But, when they came from bathing, thou wast gone!   100

At some lone homestead in the Cumner hills,
  Where at her open door the housewife darns,

---

57 Hurst: a hill south of Oxford. All of the place-names in the following stanzas refer to localities not many miles from Oxford; "distant Wychwood" (line 79) is only about 12 miles away. **59 ingle-bench:** a bench by the fireplace **boors:** country people **64 rooks:** birds like the crow **74 stripling Thames:** the Thames where still narrow **76 punt:** a flat-bottomed boat with square ends, propelled by a pole **chops:** swings suddenly **85 stile:** steps over a fence or wall **95 lasher:** pool below a weir (dam)

Thou hast been seen, or hanging on a gate
To watch the threshers in the mossy barns.
 Children, who early range these slopes and late   105
  For cresses from the rills,
Have known thee eying, all an April-day,
 The springing pastures and the feeding kine;
 And marked thee, when the stars come out and shine,
Through the long dewy grass move slow away.   110

In autumn, on the skirts of Bagley Wood—
 Where most the gypsies by the turf-edged way
  Pitch their smoked tents, and every bush you see
With scarlet patches tagged and shreds of grey,
  Above the forest-ground called Thessaly—   115
   The blackbird, picking food,
Sees thee, nor stops his meal, nor fears at all;
 So often has he known thee past him stray,
 Rapt, twirling in thy hand a withered spray,
And waiting for the spark from heaven to fall.   120

And once, in winter, on the causeway chill
 Where home through flooded fields foot-travellers go,
  Have I not passed thee on the wooden bridge,
Wrapped in thy cloak and battling with the snow,
  Thy face tow'rd Hinksey and its wintry ridge?   125
   And thou hast climbed the hill,
And gained the white brow of the Cumner range;
 Turned once to watch, while thick the snowflakes fall,
 The line of festal light in Christ-Church hall—
Then sought thy straw in some sequestered grange.   130

But what—I dream! Two hundred years are flown
 Since first thy story ran through Oxford halls,
  And the grave Glanvill did the tale inscribe
That thou wert wandered from the studious walls
  To learn strange arts, and join a gypsy-tribe;   135
   And thou from earth art gone
Long since, and in some quiet churchyard laid—
 Some country-nook, where o'er thy unknown grave
 Tall grasses and white flowering nettles wave,
Under a dark, red-fruited yew-tree's shade.   140

—No, no, thou hast not felt the lapse of hours!
 For what wears out the life of mortal men?
  'Tis that from change to change their being rolls;
'Tis that repeated shocks, again, again,
  Exhaust the energy of strongest souls   145
   And numb the elastic powers.
Till having used our nerves with bliss and teen,
 And tired upon a thousand schemes our wit,
 To the just-pausing Genius we remit
Our worn-out life, and are—what we have been.   150

---

106 **rills:** small brooks 121 **causeway:** raised path or road 129 **Christ-Church hall:** the dining hall
of Christ Church College 130 **grange:** farm, especially one with outbuildings 147 **teen:** sorrow,
woe 149 **Genius:** the guardian spirit that accompanies us through life

Thou hast not lived, why should'st thou perish, so?
  Thou hadst *one* aim, *one* business, *one* desire;
    Else wert thou long since numbered with the dead!
  Else hadst thou spent, like other men, thy fire!
    The generations of thy peers are fled,   155
      And we ourselves shall go;
  But thou possessest an immortal lot,
      And we imagine thee exempt from age
      And living as thou liv'st on Glanvill's page,
  Because thou hadst—what we, alas! have not.   160

For early didst thou leave the world, with powers
  Fresh, undiverted to the world without,
    Firm to their mark, not spent on other things;
  Free from the sick fatigue, the languid doubt,
    Which much to have tried, in much been baffled, brings.   165
      O life unlike to ours!
  Who fluctuate idly without term or scope,
      Of whom each strives, nor knows for what he strives,
      And each half-lives a hundred different lives;
  Who wait like thee, but not, like thee, in hope.   170

Thou waitest for the spark from heaven! and we,
  Light half-believers of our casual creeds,
    Who never deeply felt, nor clearly willed,
  Whose insight never has borne fruit in deeds,
    Whose vague resolves never have been fulfilled;   175
      For whom each year we see
  Breeds new beginnings, disappointments new;
      Who hesitate and falter life away,
      And lose to-morrow the ground won to-day—
  Ah! do not we, wanderer! await it too?   180

Yes, we await it!—but it still delays,
  And then we suffer! and amongst us one,
    Who most has suffered, takes dejectedly
  His seat upon the intellectual throne;
    And all his store of sad experience he   185
      Lays bare of wretched days;
  Tells us his misery's birth and growth and signs,
      And how the dying spark of hope was fed,
      And how the breast was soothed, and how the head,
  And all his hourly varied anodynes.   190

This for our wisest! and we others pine,
  And wish the long unhappy dream would end,
    And waive all claim to bliss, and try to bear;
  With close-lipped patience for our only friend,
    Sad patience, too near neighbour to despair—   195
      But none has hope like thine!
  Thou through the fields and through the woods dost stray,

---

182 **one:** Goethe? Coleridge? Carlyle? Tennyson? All have been suggested, with Tennyson seeming the likeliest. The phrase "intellectual throne" is from his "The Palace of Art" (line 216); he had been made poet laureate about two years before Arnold wrote his lines; and the last part of the stanza could serve as a description of his "In Memoriam." 190 **anodynes:** drugs that alleviate pain

Roaming the country-side, a truant boy,
Nursing thy project in unclouded joy,
And every doubt long blown by time away.   200

O born in days when wits were fresh and clear,
And life ran gaily as the sparkling Thames;
Before this strange disease of modern life,
With its sick hurry, its divided aims,
Its heads o'ertaxed, its palsied hearts, was rife—   205
Fly hence, our contact fear!
Still fly, plunge deeper in the bowering wood!
Averse, as Dido did with gesture stern
From her false friend's approach in Hades turn,
Wave us away, and keep thy solitude!   210

Still nursing the unconquerable hope,
Still clutching the inviolable shade,
With a free, onward impulse brushing through,
By night, the silvered branches of the glade—
Far on the forest-skirts, where none pursue,   215
On some mild pastoral slope
Emerge, and resting on the moonlit pales
Freshen thy flowers as in former years
With dew, or listen with enchanted ears,
From the dark dingles, to the nightingales!   220

But fly our paths, our feverish contact fly!
For strong the infection of our mental strife,
Which, though it gives no bliss, yet spoils for rest;
And we should win thee from thy own fair life,
Like us distracted, and like us unblest.   225
Soon, soon thy cheer would die,
Thy hopes grow timorous, and unfixed thy powers,
And thy clear aims be cross and shifting made;
And then thy glad perennial youth would fade,
Fade, and grow old at last, and die like ours.   230

Then fly our greetings, fly our speech and smiles!
—As some grave Tyrian trader, from the sea,
Descried at sunrise an emerging prow
Lifting the cool-haired creepers stealthily,
The fringes of a southward-facing brow   235
Among the Ægean isles;
And saw the merry Grecian coaster come,
Freighted with amber grapes, and Chian wine,
Green, bursting figs, and tunnies steeped in brine—
And knew the intruders on his ancient home,   240

208–209 **Dido . . . :** Dido, Queen of Carthage, had killed herself when forsaken by Aeneas, whom she loved and had aided. When he saw her during his visit to the underworld, she refused to greet him (*Aeneid*, VI, 469–473). 217 **pales:** stakes of a fence 220 **dingles:** wooded dells 232 **Tyrian:** Tyre, one of the great cities of the ancient Phoenicians, was on the coast of Syria. The Tyrians were famous traders; cf. Isa. 23:8: "Tyre . . . whose traffickers are the honourable of the earth." The point of the long comparison between the scholar-gypsy and the grave Tyrian is that both fled from a light-hearted, busy, and boisterous civilization whose interests were good food and wine, to a people remote and shy—the gypsies, the dark Iberians. 237 **coaster:** a ship chiefly for coastal trade 238 **Chian wine:** The Greek island of Chios was famous for its wine. 239 **tunnies:** tuna

The young light-hearted masters of the waves—
    And snatched his rudder, and shook out more sail;
    And day and night held on indignantly
O'er the blue Midland waters with the gale,
    Betwixt the Syrtes and soft Sicily,   245
        To where the Atlantic raves
    Outside the western straits; and unbent sails
      There, where down cloudy cliffs, through sheets of foam,
      Shy traffickers, the dark Iberians come;
    And on the beach undid his corded bales.   250

244 Midland: *Medi-terranean* means "mid-land." **245 Syrtes:** regions of coastal North Africa across from Sicily, called "soft" here because warm, luxuriant, wealthy **247 outside . . . straits:** beyond Gibraltar **unbent:** unloosened, untied **249 Iberians:** ancient inhabitants of the Spanish peninsula. Herodotus (the Greek historian of the fifth century B.C.) describes (iv, 196) how very shy and polite they are in their manner of trading.

Coventry Patmore
(1823–1896)

Patmore, who went to college in France, supported himself for many years by working in the library of the British Museum. Twice widowed, each time after 15 happy years, Patmore married for the third time when close to 60. The central theme of his poetry is the happiness and holiness of married love, often seen as symbolic of divine love. In his last two decades he wrote essays on literature, art, architecture, and politics.

A London Fête

All night fell hammers, shock on shock;
With echoes Newgate's granite clanged:
The scaffold built, at eight o'clock
They brought the man out to be hanged.
Then came from all the people there   5
A single cry, that shook the air;
Mothers held up their babes to see,
Who spread their hands, and crowed for glee;
Here a girl from her vesture tore
A rag to wave with, and joined the roar;   10
There's a man, with yelling tired,
Stopped, and the culprit's crime inquired;
A sot, below the doomed man dumb,
Bawled his health in the world to come;
These blasphemed and fought for places;   15
These, half-crushed, cast frantic faces,
To windows, where, in freedom sweet,
Others enjoyed the wicked treat.
At last, the show's black crisis pended;
Struggles for better standings ended;   20
The rabble's lips no longer cursed,
But stood agape with horrid thirst;
Thousands of breasts beat horrid hope;

Tamerton Church-Tower and Other Poems, 1853, with later revisions.

Patmore called this "A Sketch in the Manner of Hogarth"—the great eighteenth-century artist especially known for his satiric engravings on social and political themes.

2 Newgate: the London prison

Thousands of eyeballs, lit with hell,
Burnt one way all, to see the rope   25
Unslacken as the platform fell.
The rope flew tight; and then the roar
Burst forth afresh; less loud, but more
Confused and affrighting than before.
A few harsh tongues for ever led   30
The common din, the chaos of noises,
But ear could not catch what they said.
As when the realm of the damned rejoices
At winning a soul to its will,
That clatter and clangour of hateful voices   35
Sickened and stunned the air, until
The dangling corpse hung straight and still.
The show complete, the pleasure past,
The solid masses loosened fast:
A thief slunk off, with ample spoil,   40
To ply elsewhere his daily toil;
A baby strung its doll to a stick;
A mother praised the pretty trick;
Two children caught and hanged a cat;
Two friends walked on, in lively chat;   45
And two, who had disputed places,
Went forth to fight, with murderous faces.

The Revelation

An idle poet, here and there,
    Looks round him; but, for all the rest,
The world, unfathomably fair,
    Is duller than a witling's jest.
Love wakes men, once a lifetime each;   5
    They lift their heavy lids, and look;
And, lo, what one sweet page can teach,
    They read with joy, then shut the book.
And some give thanks, and some blaspheme,
    And most forget; but, either way,   10
That and the child's unheeded dream
    Is all the light of all their day.

The Betrothal, 1854.

4 **witling:** a man of little wit who tries to be witty

Magna Est Veritas

   Here, in this little Bay,
Full of tumultuous life and great repose,
Where, twice a day,
The purposeless, glad ocean comes and goes,

The Unknown Eros, 1877.

In 1875 Patmore, having resigned from his post in the British Museum some years before, settled in the old town of Hastings on the Channel; his "little Bay" was probably in the vicinity. The "huge town" would be London. (This little poem was a favorite of Robert Frost.)

***Magna est veritas et praevalebit*:** The Latin quotation, a variant of 3 Esd. 4:41 of the Apocrypha, is translated in line 9.

Under high cliffs, and far from the huge town,   5
I sit me down.
For want of me the world's course will not fail:
When all its work is done, the lie shall rot;
The truth is great, and shall prevail,
When none cares whether it prevail or not.   10

George Meredith
(1828–1909)

Meredith's father was a naval outfitter who went bankrupt. The boy attended college in
Germany for two years; later he began the study of law but dropped it in favor of litera-
ture. At 21 he married the widowed daughter of Peacock, a woman several years older
than he, with a five-year-old daughter. The marriage was, he said, "a blunder"; after nine
years his wife ran off to Capri with an artist; she died three years later. The troubles of
the marriage are the subject of his sequence *Modern Love*, today thought his most impres-
sive work, though its frankness was found in bad taste in his own time. After living with
Rossetti and Swinburne for a year, Meredith married again, this time happily. He wrote
many novels, but not until the 1880s did he achieve fame and popularity.

From **Modern Love**

XXX

What are we first? First, animals; and next
Intelligences at a leap; on whom
Pale lies the distant shadow of the tomb,
And all that draweth on the tomb for text.
Into which state comes Love, the crowning sun: 5
Beneath whose light the shadow loses form.
We are the lords of life, and life is warm.
Intelligence and instinct now are one.
But nature says: "My children most they seem
When they least know me: therefore I decree   10
That they shall suffer." Swift doth young Love flee,
And we stand wakened, shivering from our dream.
Then if we study Nature we are wise.
Thus do the few who live but with the day:
The scientific animals are they.—   15
Lady, this is my sonnet to your eyes.

L

Thus piteously Love closed what he begat:
The union of this ever-diverse pair!
These two were rapid falcons in a snare,
Condemned to do the flitting of the bat.
Lovers beneath the singing sky of May,   5
They wandered once; clear as the dew on flowers:
But they fed not on the advancing hours:
Their hearts held cravings for the buried day.
Then each applied to each that fatal knife,
Deep questioning, which probes to endless dole.   10

1861. *Modern Love*, 1862.

L: 10 **dole**: sorrow

Ah, what a dusty answer gets the soul
When hot for certainties in this our life!—
In tragic hints here see what evermore
Moves dark as yonder midnight ocean's force,
Thundering like ramping hosts of warrior horse,   15
To throw that faint thin line upon the shore!

15 **ramping:** rearing, raging

Lucifer in Starlight

On a starred night Prince Lucifer uprose.
Tired of his dark dominion swung the fiend
Above the rolling ball in cloud part screened,
Where sinners hugged their spectre of repose.
Poor prey to his hot fit of pride were those.   5
And now upon his western wing he leaned,
Now his huge bulk o'er Afric's sands careened,
Now the black planet shadowed Arctic snows.
Soaring through wider zones that pricked his scars
With memory of the old revolt from Awe,   10
He reached a middle height, and at the stars,
Which are the brain of heaven, he looked, and sank.
Around the ancient track marched, rank on rank,
The army of unalterable law.

Poems and Lyrics of the Joy of Earth, 1883.

Dante Gabriel Rossetti
(1828–1882)

Rossetti was born in London, the son of an Italian political exile, professor, and poet. In boyhood the son had decided to become a painter; when about 20 he and others founded the Pre-Raphaelite Brotherhood, with the intention of breaking free from academic conventions and of getting back to a more personal kind of expression, like that (they thought) in earlier Italian art. Rossetti had also been translating early Italian poetry and writing poetry of his own, some of it published in the four issues of *The Germ* the brotherhood put out in 1850. About that time they also discovered 17-year-old Elizabeth Siddal, whose spectacular red-gold hair and sea-green eyes are to be seen in many paintings by Rossetti and his friends. She and Rossetti were understood to be engaged, but the wedding was delayed until 1860 through years of misunderstandings (cf. "The Woodspurge") and of illness. Two years later she died of an overdose of sleeping potion; with her he buried the poems he had written for her. When they were somewhat eerily exhumed (cf. "Life-in-Love") and published ten years later, they were attacked for their sensuality, as belonging to "the fleshly school of poetry." Though for some time successful as a painter, Rossetti began to suffer from depression and paranoia perhaps brought on by a sedative he had been taking, often with whiskey; in his last decade he lived very much a recluse.

The Woodspurge

The wind flapped loose, the wind was still,
Shaken out dead from tree and hill:
I had walked on at the wind's will,—
I sat now, for the wind was still.

1856. *Poems*, 1870.

The woodspurge is an English variety of the common spurge; it has small greenish-yellow flowers.

Between my knees my forehead was,—   5
My lips, drawn in, said not Alas!
My hair was over in the grass,
My naked ears heard the day pass.

My eyes, wide open, had the run
Of some ten weeds to fix upon;   10
Among those few, out of the sun,
The woodspurge flowered, three cups in one.

From perfect grief there need not be
Wisdom or even memory:
One thing then learnt remains to me,—   15
The woodspurge has a cup of three.

From **The House of Life**

XIX. Silent Noon

Your hands lie open in the long fresh grass,—
    The finger-points look through like rosy blooms:
    Your eyes smile peace. The pasture gleams and glooms
'Neath billowing skies that scatter and amass.
All round our nest, far as the eye can pass,   5
    Are golden kingcup-fields with silver edge
    Where the cow-parsley skirts the hawthorn-hedge.
'Tis visible silence, still as the hour-glass.

Deep in the sun-searched growths the dragon-fly
Hangs like a blue thread loosened from the sky:—   10
    So this winged hour is dropt to us from above.
Oh! clasp we to our hearts, for deathless dower,
This close-companioned inarticulate hour
    When twofold silence was the song of love.

1871. *Ballads and Sonnets*, 1881.

XXXVI. Life-in-Love

Not in thy body is thy life at all
    But in this lady's lips and hands and eyes;
    Through these she yields thee life that vivifies
What else were sorrow's servant and death's thrall.
Look on thyself without her, and recall   5
    The waste remembrance and forlorn surmise
    That lived but in a dead-drawn breath of sighs
O'er vanished hours and hours eventual.

1869–1870. *Poems*, 1870.

The House of Life, Rossetti's sequence of 101 sonnets, is named for one of the twelve sections, or "houses," into which astrologers divide the heavens. The poems, written over three decades, are loosely connected, though most are about love. About half were written during the poet's ten or more years of troubled passion for Elizabeth Siddal; when she died he left the only manuscript in her coffin, under her golden hair. In 1869 friends persuaded Rossetti to retrieve the manuscript for publication, together with the sonnets he had written since.

XIX: 6 **kingcup:** buttercup   7 **cow-parsley:** a tall English wildflower, more beautiful than its name   12 **dower:** dowry XXXVI: 2 **this lady's lips** . . . : This sonnet was written not to Elizabeth but to a living lady whose love consoled him for past sorrows.

Even so much life hath the poor tress of hair
    Which, stored apart, is all love hath to show 10
    For heart-beats and for fire-heats long ago;
Even so much life endures unknown, even where,
    'Mid change the changeless night environeth,
    Lies all that golden hair undimmed in death.

9 **poor tress of hair:** Soon after falling in love with Elizabeth, Rossetti wrote his sister Christina (below) that he was treasuring a lock of hair "radiant as the tresses of Aurora."   14 **golden hair:** When the coffin was opened, witnesses reported that the tresses were as radiant as in life.

Christina Rossetti
(1830–1894)

The sister of Dante Gabriel, Christina was devoted to her widowed mother, to her high Anglican religion (which led her to reject at least two suitors), and to her poetry, which won her a following during her lifetime. She also wrote several volumes of devotional prose.

Dream-Love

Young Love lies sleeping
    In May-time of the year,
Among the lilies,
    Lapped in the tender light:
White lambs come grazing, 5
    White doves come building there;
And round about him
    The May-bushes are white.

Soft moss the pillow
    For oh, a softer cheek; 10
Broad leaves cast shadow
    Upon the heavy eyes:
There winds and waters
    Grow lulled and scarcely speak;
There twilight lingers 15
    The longest in the skies.

Young Love lies dreaming;
    But who shall tell the dream?
A perfect sunlight
    On rustling forest tips; 20
Or perfect moonlight
    Upon a rippling stream;
Or perfect silence,
    Or a song of cherished lips.

Burn odors round him 25
    To fill the drowsy air;
Weave silent dances
    Around him to and fro;
For oh, in waking,
    The sights are not so fair, 30

1854. *The Prince's Progress,* 1866.

8 **May-bushes:** hawthorn   25 **odors:** incenses

And song and silence
    Are not like these below.

Young Love lies dreaming
    Till summer days are gone,—
Dreaming and drowsing   35
    Away to perfect sleep:
He sees the beauty
    Sun hath not looked upon,
And tastes the fountain
    Unutterably deep.   40

Him perfect music
    Doth hush unto his rest,
And through the pauses
    The perfect silence calms:
Oh, poor the voices   45
    Of earth from east to west,
And poor earth's stillness
    Between her stately palms.

Young Love lies drowsing
    Away to poppied death;   50
Cool shadows deepen
    Across the sleeping face:
So fails the summer
    With warm, delicious breath;
And what hath autumn   55
    To give us in its place?

Draw close the curtains
    Of branchèd evergreen;
Change cannot touch them
    With fading fingers sere: 60
Here the first violets
    Perhaps will bud unseen,
And a dove, may be,
    Return to nestle here.

60 **sere:** withered

Up-Hill

Does the road wind up-hill all the way?
    Yes, to the very end.
Will the day's journey take the whole long day?
    From morn to night, my friend.

But is there for the night a resting-place?   5
    A roof for when the slow dark hours begin.
May not the darkness hide it from my face?
    You cannot miss that inn.

Shall I meet other wayfarers at night?
    Those who have gone before.   10

1858. *Goblin Market,* 1862.

Then must I knock, or call when just in sight?
   They will not keep you standing at that door.

Shall I find comfort, travel-sore and weak?
   Of labour you shall find the sum.
Will there be beds for me and all who seek?   15
   Yea, beds for all who come.

Emily Dickinson
(1830–1886)

Emily Dickinson was born in Amherst, Massachusetts, where her father was a lawyer, a congressman, and treasurer of the college. She died 56 years later in the house she was born in. She left Massachusetts only once; during the last 15 years of her life she rarely left the house. Admitted as a vivacious and fun-loving 16-year-old to what was later Mount Holyoke College, she stayed only a year. Passing through Philadelphia in 1854 she heard a brilliant preacher; though she saw him only twice afterwards, she was desolated when he moved to California in 1861. During the year that followed she wrote a poem a day; she took to dressing only in white from then on; the experience of love and renunciation, as a sort of spiritual wife, became her "Calvary." Some years before, she had begun to collect her poems in manuscript packets of a few sheets of stationery folded over book-fashion and secured by a loop of thread at the fold. During her lifetime only seven of her poems were published, all anonymously and most without her knowledge. After her death nearly 1800 poems were found in a small box in her bureau. A small selection, doctored to make them more acceptable, was published in 1890. Other volumes followed, and by 1945 most of the poems had been published.

Went Up a Year This Evening!

Went up a year this evening!
I recollect it well!
Amid no bells nor bravoes
The bystanders will tell!
Cheerful—as to the village—   5
Tranquil—as to repose—
Chastened—as to the Chapel
This humble Tourist rose!
Did not talk of returning!
Alluded to no time   10
When, were the gales propitious—
We might look for him!
Was grateful for the Roses
In life's diverse bouquet—
Talked softly of new species   15
To pick another day;
Beguiling thus the wonder
The *wondrous* nearer drew—
Hands bustled at the moorings—
The crowd respectful grew—   20

---

c. 1859. Harvard, Packet 1 (H If). *Poems,* 1881. The authoritative text for this and the following poems is *The Poems of Emily Dickinson,* edited by T. H. Johnson, Harvard University Press, 1955.

In this poem, a death of the year before is seen in terms of a balloon ascension.

11 **gales:** breezes

Ascended from our vision
To Countenances new!
A Difference—A Daisy—
Is all the rest I knew!

24 **knew:** *Knew* is the accepted reading, but in Emily Dickinson's handwriting, *know* and *knew* look alike; this seems to be *know* in her MS. *Know* avoids the monotony of four pure rhymes in a row after *drew-grew-new*, and the identical rhyme with *new*. Even at this early date she likes off-rhymes (*new-know*). *Know* also makes better sense: one notices a difference—and certainly daisies—not at the time of death but afterwards.

How Many Times These Low Feet Staggered

How many times these low feet staggered—
Only the soldered mouth can tell—
Try—can you stir the awful rivet—
Try—can you lift the hasps of steel!

Stroke the cool forehead—hot so often—   5
Lift—if you care—the listless hair—
Handle the adamantine fingers
Never a thimble—more—shall wear—

Buzz the dull flies—on the chamber window—
Brave—shines the sun through the freckled pane—   10
Fearless—the cobweb swings from the ceiling—
Indolent Housewife—in Daisies—lain!

c. 1860. Harvard, Packet 15 (H 78b). *Poems*, 1890.

6 **care:** *care* or *can* (as in *Poems*, 1890)? Not clear from her handwriting. *Care* gives a rhyme with *hair* that some may like and some may think an unpleasant jingle.   7 **adamantine:** rigid, unyielding

There's a Certain Slant of Light

There's a Certain Slant of light—
Winter afternoons—
That oppresses, like the Heft
Of Cathedral Tunes—

Heavenly Hurt, it gives us—   5
We can find no scar,
But internal difference
Where the Meanings, are—

None may teach it—Any—
'Tis the Seal Despair—   10
An imperial affliction
Sent us of the Air—

When it comes, the Landscape listens—
Shadows—hold their breath—
When it goes, 'tis like the Distance   15
On the look of Death—

c. 1861. Harvard, Packet 23 (H 74d). Ibid.

I Dreaded That First Robin, So

I dreaded that first Robin, so,
But He is mastered, now,
I'm some accustomed to Him grown,
He hurts a little, though—

I thought if I could only live   5
Till that first Shout got by—
Not all Pianos in the Woods
Had power to mangle me—

I dared not meet the Daffodils—
For fear their Yellow Gown   10
Would pierce me with a fashion
So foreign to my own—

I wished the Grass would hurry—
So when 'twas time to see—
He'd be too tall, the tallest one   15
Could stretch to look at me—

I could not bear the Bees should come,
I wished they'd stay away
In those dim countries where they go,
What word had they, for me?   20

They're here, though; not a creature failed—
No Blossom stayed away
In gentle deference to me—
The Queen of Calvary—

Each one salutes me, as he goes,   25
And I, my childish Plumes,
Lift, in bereaved acknowledgment
Of their unthinking Drums—

c. 1862. Amherst, Packet 85 (Bingham 28a). *Poems,* 1891.

She Dealt Her Pretty Words Like Blades

She dealt her pretty words like Blades—
How glittering they shone—
And every One unbared a Nerve
Or wantoned with a Bone—

She never deemed—she hurt—   5
That—is not Steel's Affair—
A vulgar grimace in the Flesh—
How ill the Creatures bear—

To Ache is human—not polite—
The Film upon the eye   10
Mortality's old Custom—
Just locking up—to Die.

c. 1862. Harvard, Packet 19 (H 104a). *Further Poems,* 1929.

4 wantoned: played carelessly   **5 deemed:** thought

What Soft—Cherubic Creatures

What Soft—Cherubic Creatures—
These Gentlewomen are—
One would as soon assault a Plush—
Or violate a Star—

Such Dimity Convictions—   5
A Horror so refined
Of freckled Human Nature—
Of Deity—ashamed—

It's such a common—Glory—
A Fisherman's—Degree—   10
Redemption—Brittle Lady—
Be so—ashamed of Thee—

---

c. 1862. Amherst, Packet 91 (Bingham 74c). *Poems*, 1896.

5 **Dimity:** a "nice" kind of light and dainty cotton   10 **Fisherman's — Degree:** like that of the apostles   12 **ashamed:** Cf. "Whosoever shall be ashamed of me . . . , of him shall the Son of man be ashamed, when he shall come in his own glory, and in his Father's" (Luke 9:26).

I Heard a Fly Buzz—When I Died

I heard a Fly buzz—when I died—
The Stillness in the Room
Was like the Stillness in the Air—
Between the Heaves of Storm—

The Eyes around—had wrung them dry—   5
And Breaths were gathering firm
For that last Onset—when the King
Be witnessed—in the Room—

I willed my Keepsakes—Signed away
What portion of me be   10
Assignable—and then it was
There interposed a Fly—

With Blue—uncertain—stumbling Buzz—
Between the light—and me—
And then the Windows failed—and then   15
I could not see to see—

---

c. 1862. Amherst, Packet 84 (Bingham 20c). Ibid.

See Additional Notes (p. 765).

After Great Pain, a Formal Feeling Comes

After great pain, a formal feeling comes—
The Nerves sit ceremonious, like Tombs—
The stiff Heart questions was it He, that bore,
And Yesterday, or Centuries before?

---

c. 1862. Harvard, Packet 6 (H 26c). *Further Poems*, 1929.

A psychiatrist-critic has found this poem to be an accurate description of the catatonic state that can be brought on by shock or suffering.

The Feet, mechanical, go round—   5
Of Ground, or Air, or Ought—
A Wooden way
Regardless grown,
A Quartz contentment, like a stone—   10

This is the Hour of Lead—
Remembered, if outlived,
As Freezing persons, recollect the Snow—
First—Chill—then Stupor—then the letting go—

5-8 Numerals written in the margin of the MS. (1/3/2/4) suggest that the poet intended to change
the order of lines 6 and 7.   7 **ought**: aught, anything (or just possibly *nought, nothing*?)

I Started Early—Took My Dog

I started Early—Took my Dog—
And visited the Sea—
The Mermaids in the Basement
Came out to look at me—

And Frigates—in the Upper Floor   5
Extended Hempen Hands—
Presuming Me to be a Mouse—
Aground—upon the Sands—

But no Man moved Me—till the Tide
Went past my simple Shoe—   10
And past my Apron—and my Belt
And past my Bodice—too—

And made as He would eat me up
As wholly as a Dew
Upon a Dandelion's Sleeve—   15
And then—I started—too—

And He—He followed—close behind—
I felt His Silver Heel
Upon my Ankle—Then my Shoes
Would overflow with Pearl—   20

Until We met the Solid Town—
No One He seemed to know—
And bowing—with a Mighty look—
At me—The Sea withdrew—

c. 1862. Harvard, Packet 5 (H 382a). *Poems,* 1891.

See Additional Notes (p. 765).

Because I Could Not Stop for Death

Because I could not stop for Death—
He kindly stopped for me—
The Carriage held but just Ourselves—
And Immortality.

c. 1863. Harvard, Packet 31 (H 165a). *Poems,* 1890.

We slowly drove—He knew no haste   5
And I had put away
My labor and my leisure too,
For His Civility—

We passed the School, where Children strove
At Recess—in the Ring—   10
We passed the Fields of Gazing Grain—
We passed the Setting Sun—

Or rather—He passed Us—
The Dews drew quivering and chill—
For only Gossamer, my Gown—   15
My Tippet—only Tulle—

We paused before a House that seemed
A Swelling of the Ground—
The Roof was scarcely visible—
The Cornice—in the Ground—   20

Since then—'tis Centuries—and yet
Feels shorter than the Day
I first surmised the Horses' Heads
Were toward Eternity—

15 **Gossamer:** very light material, like spider webs that float on the breeze   16 **Tippet:** long scarf or shoulder cape   **Tulle:** sheer silk

It Dropped So Low — in My Regard

It dropped so low—in my Regard—
I heard it hit the Ground—
And go to pieces on the Stones
At bottom of my Mind—

Yet blamed the Fate that flung it—*less*
Than I denounced Myself,
For entertaining Plated Wares
Upon my Silver Shelf—

c. 1863. Harvard, Packet 12 (H 58c). *Poems,* 1896.

8 **Silver Shelf:** not silver *shelf*, but *silver* shelf—shelf to keep silver on

My Life Had Stood — a Loaded Gun

My Life had stood—a Loaded Gun—
In Corners—till a Day
The Owner passed—identified—
And carried Me away—

And now We roam in Sovereign Woods—   5
And now We hunt the Doe—

c. 1863. Harvard, Packet 24 (H 131a). *Further Poems,* 1929.

See Additional Notes (p. 765).

5 **in:** *The,* one of four alternate words in the manuscript, will seem preferable to some.   **Sovereign:** royal, supreme, excellent

And every time I speak for Him
The Mountains straight reply—

And do I smile, such cordial light
Upon the Valley glow—   10
It is as a Vesuvian face
Had let its pleasure through—

And when at Night—Our good Day done—
I guard My Master's Head—
'Tis better than the Eider-Duck's   15
Deep Pillow—to have shared—

To foe of His—I'm deadly foe—
None stir the second time—
On whom I lay a Yellow Eye—
Or an emphatic Thumb—   20

Though I than He—may longer live
He longer must—than I—
For I have but the power to kill,
Without—the power to die—

8 **reply**: echo   11 **Vesuvian**: aglow like Vesuvius, the volcano near Naples   15 **Eider-Duck**: a large northern sea-duck having especially soft down (eiderdown) used to fill pillows, comforters, etc.

A Narrow Fellow in the Grass ✓

A narrow Fellow in the Grass
Occasionally rides—
You may have met Him—did you not
His notice sudden is—

The Grass divides as with a Comb—   5
A spotted shaft is seen—
And then it closes at your feet
And opens further on—

He likes a Boggy Acre
A Floor too cool for Corn—   10
Yet when a Boy, and Barefoot—
I more than once at Noon
Have passed, I thought, a Whip lash
Unbraiding in the Sun
When stooping to secure it   15
It wrinkled, and was gone—

Several of Nature's People
I know, and they know me—

c. 1865. Amherst, Packet 88 (Bingham 53a). *Poems*, 1891.

This is one of the seven poems (out of nearly 1800) published during Emily Dickinson's lifetime. It was in the *Springfield Daily Republican* (a liberal Republican newspaper, one of the most influential in the country) on February 14, 1866. The editor, a close friend of the Dickinson family, admired the poem, but wondered "How did that girl ever know that a boggy field wasn't good for corn?" (line 10). The poem, apparently submitted without the writer's knowledge ("It was robbed of me," she later wrote), was printed anonymously as "The Snake."

I feel for them a transport
Of cordiality—

But never met this Fellow
Attended, or alone
Without a tighter breathing
And Zero at the Bone—

The Wind Begun to Knead the Grass

The Wind begun to knead the Grass—
As Women do a Dough—
He flung a Hand full at the Plain—
A Hand full at the Sky—
The Leaves unhooked themselves from Trees—
And started all abroad—
The Dust did scoop itself like Hands—
And throw away the Road—
The Wagons quickened on the Street—
The Thunders gossiped low—
The Lightning showed a yellow Head—
And then a livid Toe—
The Birds put up the Bars to Nests—
The Cattle flung to Barns—
Then came one drop of Giant Rain—
And then, as if the Hands
That held the Dams—had parted hold—
The Waters Wrecked the Sky—
But overlooked my Father's House—
Just Quartering a Tree—

5

10

15

20

c. 1864. *Poems . . .*, Johnson, 1955. Three manuscript copies exist. Two others exist of the slightly different versions in *Poems*, 1891.

The Bustle in a House ✓

The Bustle in a House
The Morning after Death
Is solemnest of industries
Enacted upon Earth—

The Sweeping up the Heart
And putting Love away
We shall not want to use again
Until Eternity.

c. 1866. Harvard, Packet 35 (H 189c). *Poems*, 1890.

Lewis Carroll
(Charles L. Dodgson)
(1832–1898)

Though best known as a writer of fantasy, humor, and sophisticated nonsense, Carroll was an Oxford professor, a brilliant mathematician, and a logician with several scholarly volumes to his credit. He was happiest in the company of children, especially of little girls, of whom he took lovely early photographs.

The White Knight's Ballad

I'll tell thee everything I can:
    There's little to relate.
I saw an aged aged man,
    A-sitting on a gate.
"Who are you, aged man?" I said.   5
    "And how is it you live?"
And his answer trickled through my head,
    Like water through a sieve.

He said "I look for butterflies
    That sleep among the wheat: 10
I make them into mutton-pies,
    And sell them in the street.
I sell them unto men," he said,
    "Who sail on stormy seas;
And that's the way I get my bread—   15
    A trifle, if you please."

But I was thinking of a plan
    To dye one's whiskers green,
And always use so large a fan
    That they could not be seen.   20
So, having no reply to give
    To what the old man said,
I cried "Come, tell me how you live!"
    And thumped him on the head.

His accents mild took up the tale: 25
    He said "I go my ways,
And when I find a mountain-rill
    I set it in a blaze;
And thence they make a stuff they call
    Rowland's Macassar-Oil—   30
Yet twopence-halfpenny is all
    They give me for my toil."

But I was thinking of a way
    To feed oneself on batter,
And so go on from day to day   35
    Getting a little fatter.

1856–1872. *Through the Looking-Glass*, 1872.

Alice (of *Alice in Wonderland*) meets the White Knight, a bumbling, gentle, melancholy old fellow thought to be a caricature of Carroll himself, in chapter VIII of *Through the Looking-Glass* (1872). He sings his ballad about an old man rather like himself (and like Carroll) to comfort her as they part. "The aged aged man" recalls the old leech-gatherer of Wordsworth's "Resolution and Independence" (p. 253); Carroll is amusing himself at the expense of that poem. The burlesque was more direct in an earlier version that began:

    I met an aged, aged man
        Upon the lonely moor:
    I knew I was a gentleman,
        And he was but a boor.

16 **a trifle**: the aged man is begging   27 **rill**: small stream   30 **Rowland's Macassar-Oil**: a much publicized hair-oil, made by Rowland and Son, the ingredients of which were supposed to come from Macassar on the Indonesian island of Celebes

I shook him well from side to side,
    Until his face was blue:
"Come, tell me how you live," I cried,
    "And what it is you do!"   40

He said "I hunt for haddocks' eyes
    Among the heather bright,
And work them into waistcoat-buttons
    In the silent night.
And these I do not sell for gold   45
    Or coin of silvery shine,
But for a copper halfpenny,
    And that will purchase nine.

"I sometimes dig for buttered rolls,
    Or set limed twigs for crabs: 50
I sometimes search the grassy knolls
    For wheels of Hansom-cabs.
And that's the way " (he gave a wink)
    "By which I get my wealth—
And very gladly will I drink   55
    Your Honor's noble health."

I heard him then, for I had just
    Completed my design
To keep the Menai bridge from rust
    By boiling it in wine.   60
I thanked him much for telling me
    The way he got his wealth,
But chiefly for his wish that he
    Might drink my noble health.

And now, if e'er by chance I put   65
    My fingers into glue,
Or madly squeeze a right-hand foot
    Into a left-hand shoe,
Or if I drop upon my toe
    A very heavy weight,   70
I weep, for it reminds me so
Of that old man I used to know—
Whose look was mild, whose speech was slow,
Whose hair was whiter than the snow,
Whose face was very like a crow,   75
With eyes, like cinders, all aglow,
Who seemed distracted with his woe,
Who rocked his body to and fro,
And muttered mumblingly and low,
As if his mouth were full of dough,   80
Who snorted like a buffalo—
That summer evening long ago,
    A-sitting on a gate.

50 **limed:** smeared with a sticky substance to catch birds   52 **Hansom-cabs:** two-wheeled carriages
or "cabriolets" (whence our word *cab*) designed by Joseph Hansom in 1834   59 **Menai bridge:** a sus-
pension bridge in North Wales

William Morris
(1834–1896)

Interested at Oxford in medieval history, architecture, art, and literature, Morris had the most varied career of any of the Victorians. Painter and architect as well as the author of poems and prose romances, he became interested in problems of home design after his 1859 marriage to Jane Burden, a favorite model of Rossetti's. With his friends he produced furniture, carpets, and tapestries that went against the current of Victorian taste and helped to change it. Among his designs—the Morris chair. Meanwhile he wrote; his collected works consist of 24 large volumes. All the while he was politically active in support of liberal (or "Socialist") causes; he was twice arrested at demonstrations broken up by the police. Near the end of his life he established the Kelmscott Press, which did handsome editions in types and motifs he designed.

The Haystack in the Floods

Had she come all the way for this,
To part at last without a kiss?
Yea, had she borne the dirt and rain
That her own eyes might see him slain
Beside the haystack in the floods?   5

Along the dripping leafless woods,
The stirrup touching either shoe,
She rode astride as troopers do;
With kirtle kilted to her knee,
To which the mud splashed wretchedly;   10
And the wet dripped from every tree
Upon her head and heavy hair,
And on her eyelids broad and fair;
The tears and rain ran down her face.
By fits and starts they rode apace,   15
And very often was his place
Far off from her; he had to ride
Ahead, to see what might betide
When the roads crossed; and sometimes, when
There rose a murmuring from his men,   20
Had to turn back with promises;
Ah me! she had but little ease;
And often for pure doubt and dread
She sobbed, made giddy in the head
By the swift riding; while, for cold,   25
Her slender fingers scarce could hold
The wet reins; yea, and scarcely, too,
She felt the foot within her shoe
Against the stirrup: all for this,

The Defense of Guenevere and Other Poems, 1858.

Morris, probably assisted by his reading of the *Chronicles* of Froissart, has made up a story set in France soon after the battle of Poitiers (1356) in which the English defeated a larger French force. Though much of the story is left to our imagination, we see an English knight, Robert of Marny, trying to reach the safety of the English-held territory of Gascony, in the southwest of France. He has rescued his French mistress Jehane (Jeanne) from the hands of the French, who are demanding her life in Paris—we are not sure why, though her association with an Englishman may have something to do with it. Before reaching Gascony, the pair, with their few unreliable soldiers, are intercepted by Godmar, described as a "Judas," or traitor, who also wants Jehane. Morris may have picked up a few details from the story of Joan of Arc (the trial in Paris, for example), though she was not born until the following century.

9 **kirtle:** dress   15 **apace:** rapidly

To part at last without a kiss 30
Beside the haystack in the floods.

For when they neared that old soaked hay,
They saw across the only way
That Judas, Godmar, and the three
Red running lions dismally 35
Grinned from his pennon, under which
In one straight line along the ditch,
They counted thirty heads.

          So then,
While Robert turned round to his men,
She saw at once the wretched end, 40
And, stooping down, tried hard to rend
Her coif the wrong way from her head,
And hid her eyes; while Robert said:
"Nay, love, 'tis scarcely two to one,
At Poictiers where we made them run 45
So fast—why, sweet my love, good cheer,
The Gascon frontier is so near,
Nought after this."

          But, "O!" she said,
"My God! my God! I have to tread
The long way back without you; then 50
The court at Paris; those six men;
The gratings of the Chatelet;
The swift Seine on some rainy day
Like this, and people standing by
And laughing, while my weak hands try 55
To recollect how strong men swim.
All this, or else a life with him,
For which I should be damned at last.
Would God that this next hour were past!"

He answered not, but cried his cry, 60
"St. George for Marny!" cheerily;
And laid his hand upon her rein.
Alas! no man of all his train
Gave back that cheery cry again;
And, while for rage his thumb beat fast 65
Upon his sword-hilts, some one cast
About his neck a kerchief long,
And bound him.

          Then they went along
To Godmar; who said: "Now, Jehane,
Your lover's life is on the wane 70
So fast, that, if this very hour
You yield not as my paramour,
He will not see the rain leave off—

34-35 **three . . . lions:** Since the time of Richard I (who died in 1199) three running lions had been associated with English arms, not French. Hence Godmar is a "Judas"? 42 **coif:** a tight cap 51 **six men:** the six judges 52 **the Chatelet:** the prison in Paris 53-56 **Seine:** the river that runs through Paris. Jehane is referring to a trial by ordeal: she will be thrown into the river and, if she survives, it will be assumed she is protected by evil powers and is guilty. If she drowns it will prove that she is—or was—innocent. 61 **St. George:** the patron of England

Nay, keep your tongue from gibe and scoff,
Sir Robert, or I slay you now."   75

She laid her hand upon her brow,
Then gazed upon the palm, as though
She thought her forehead bled, and—"No!"
She said, and turned her head away,
As there were nothing else to say,   80
And everything were settled: red
Grew Godmar's face from chin to head:
"Jehane, on yonder hill there stands
My castle, guarding well my lands:
What hinders me from taking you,   85
And doing that I list to do
To your fair wilful body, while
Your knight lies dead?"

                        A wicked smile
Wrinkled her face, her lips grew thin,
A long way out she thrust her chin: 90
"You know that I should strangle you
While you were sleeping; or bite through
Your throat, by God's help—ah!" she said,
"Lord Jesus, pity your poor maid!
For in such wise they hem me in,   95
I cannot choose but sin and sin,
Whatever happens: yet I think
They could not make me eat or drink,
And so should I just reach my rest."
"Nay, if you do not my behest,   100
O Jehane! though I love you well,"
Said Godmar, "would I fail to tell
All that I know?" "Foul lies," she said.
"Eh? lies, my Jehane? by God's head,
At Paris folks would deem them true!   105
Do you know, Jehane, they cry for you:
'Jehane the brown! Jehane the brown!
Give us Jehane to burn or drown!'—
Eh—gag me Robert!—sweet my friend,
This were indeed a piteous end   110
For those long fingers, and long feet,
And long neck, and smooth shoulders sweet;
An end that few men would forget
That saw it—So, an hour yet:
Consider, Jehane, which to take   115
Of life or death!"

                        So, scarce awake,
Dismounting, did she leave that place,
And totter some yards: with her face
Turned upward to the sky she lay,
Her head on a wet heap of hay,   120
And fell asleep: and while she slept,
And did not dream, the minutes crept
Round to the twelve again; but she,

---

86 **list:** please   100 **behest:** command   105 **deem:** believe   109 **me:** for me

Being waked at last, sighed quietly,
And strangely childlike came, and said: 125
"I will not." Straightway Godmar's head,
As though it hung on strong wires, turned
Most sharply round, and his face burned.

For Robert—both his eyes were dry,
He could not weep, but gloomily   130
He seemed to watch the rain; yea, too,
His lips were firm; he tried once more
To touch her lips; she reached out, sore
And vain desire so tortured them,
The poor grey lips, and now the hem   135
Of his sleeve brushed them.

                  With a start
Up Godmar rose, thrust them apart;
From Robert's throat he loosed the bands
Of silk and mail; with empty hands
Held out, she stood and gazed, and saw   140
The long bright blade without a flaw
Glide out from Godmar's sheath, his hand
In Robert's hair; she saw him bend
Back Robert's head; she saw him send
The thin steel down; the blow told well,   145
Right backward the knight Robert fell,
And moaned as dogs do, being half dead,
Unwitting, as I deem: so then
Godmar turned grinning to his men,
Who ran, some five or six, and beat   150
His head to pieces at their feet.

Then Godmar turned again and said:
"So, Jehane, the first fitte is read!
Take note, my lady, that your way
Lies backward to the Chatelet!"   155
She shook her head and gazed awhile
At her cold hands with a rueful smile,
As though this thing had made her mad.

This was the parting that they had
Beside the haystack in the floods.   160

153 **fitte:** section of a song or story

Algernon Charles Swinburne
(1837–1909)

The son of an admiral, Swinburne spent much of his childhood near the sea. At Oxford
he made the acquaintance of the Pre-Raphaelites and took up drinking. His early poetry
brought him much notoriety: the music was intoxicating to the young, but the themes—
often deviant forms of eroticism—were found perverse and scandalous. After several lat-
er volumes, more subdued and shifting from the amatory to the political, the excesses of
his life led to a breakdown with epileptic seizures. He was rescued by a friend, a literary
lawyer, who kept him sober and safe for the next 30 years in a quiet suburban villa. Dur-
ing that time he produced over 20 books of poetry, drama, and criticism.

Chorus *from* Atalanta in Calydon

When the hounds of spring are on winter's traces,
    The mother of months in meadow or plain
Fills the shadows and windy places
    With lisp of leaves and ripple of rain;
And the brown bright nightingale amorous   5
Is half assuaged for Itylus,
For the Thracian ships and the foreign faces,
    The tongueless vigil, and all the pain.

Come with bows bent and with emptying of quivers,
    Maiden most perfect, lady of light,   10
With a noise of winds and many rivers,
    With a clamour of waters, and with might;
Bind on thy sandals, O thou most fleet,
Over the splendour and speed of thy feet;
For the faint east quickens, the wan west shivers,   15
    Round the feet of the day and the feet of the night.

Where shall we find her, how shall we sing to her,
    Fold our hands round her knees, and cling?
O that man's heart were as fire and could spring to her,
    Fire, or the strength of the streams that spring!   20
For the stars and the winds are unto her
As raiment, as songs of the harp-player;
For the risen stars and the fallen cling to her,
    And the southwest-wind and the west-wind sing.

For winter's rains and ruins are over,   25
    And all the season of snows and sins;
The days dividing lover and lover,
    The light that loses, the night that wins;
And time remembered is grief forgotten,
And frosts are slain and flowers begotten,   30
And in green underwood and cover
    Blossom by blossom the spring begins.

The full streams feed on flower of rushes,
    Ripe grasses trammel a travelling foot,
The faint fresh flame of the young year flushes   35
    From leaf to flower and flower to fruit;
And fruit and leaf are as gold and fire,
And the oat is heard above the lyre,

1863. *Atlanta in Calydon*, 1865.

In "Atalanta in Calydon" Swinburne wanted to "in some degree reproduce for English readers the likeness of a Greek tragedy. . . ." The first chorus from his verse-play, given here, is a hymn to Artemis, goddess of the moon (line 2) and of hunting (line 9).

5–8 The version of the nightingale myth which Swinburne is following has Tereus, king of Thrace, cut out the tongue of his wife Procne and hide her away, as if dead, so she will not interfere with his love for her sister Philomela. The sisters, however, get revenge by killing Itylus, the son of Tereus and Procne, and serving flesh from his cooked body to the father at dinner. The pursued ladies escape his rage by divine help: Procne is turned into a nightingale, Philomela into a swallow. (A more familiar version of the myth is Ovid's: Philomela is raped and mutilated (to silence her); she becomes the nightingale, often referred to as "Philomela" by the poets.) The sisters were from Greece, hence the "foreign faces" in Thrace. 28 **light that loses . . .**: days get shorter in winter, nights longer 34 **trammel:** catch, impede   38 **the oat:** the shepherd's pipe (or *panpipe*) of oaten straw [as in several earlier poems]

And the hoofèd heel of a satyr crushes
    The chestnut-husk at the chestnut-root.   40

And Pan by noon and Bacchus by night,
    Fleeter of foot than the fleet-foot kid,
Follows with dancing and fills with delight
    The Mænad and the Bassarid;
And soft as lips that laugh and hide   45
The laughing leaves of the trees divide,
And screen from seeing and leave in sight
    The god pursuing, the maiden hid.

The ivy falls with the Bacchanal's hair
    Over her eyebrows hiding her eyes;   50
The wild vine slipping down leaves bare
    Her bright breast shortening into sighs;
The wild vine slips with the weight of its leaves,
But the berried ivy catches and cleaves
To the limbs that glitter, the feet that scare   55
    The wolf that follows, the fawn that flies.

39 **satyr:** a goat-footed country deity or half-god, depicted as lustful and fun-loving   41 **Pan:** the goat-footed god of nature, the countryside, the shepherds   **Bacchus:** god of wine   44 **Mænad:** female devotee of Bacchus, given to orgies   **Bassarid:** a Thracian maenad   47–48 The leaves hide the fleeing maiden, but let her peek out at the pursuing god.   49 **Bacchanal:** follower of Bacchus, with whom ivy is associated   52 **shortening:** as she exhales

The Garden of Proserpine

Here, where the world is quiet;
    Here, where all trouble seems
Dead winds' and spent waves' riot
    In doubtful dreams of dreams;
I watch the green field growing   5
For reaping folk and sowing,
For harvest-time and mowing,
    A sleepy world of streams.

I am tired of tears and laughter,
    And men that laugh and weep;   10
Of what may come hereafter
    For men that sow to reap:
I am weary of days and hours,
Blown buds of barren flowers,
Desires and dreams and powers   15
    And everything but sleep.

Poems and Ballads, 1866.

Proserpine (Proserpina) was the daughter of Zeus and Demeter who, as earth-mother, was goddess of grains and fruits, sowing and reaping (line 59). The daughter, while gathering flowers, was seized by Pluto, god of the underworld, and taken down to his dark kingdom, where she became queen of the dead (as in this poem). Later she was permitted to spend half the year in the world above ground, so that she stands for birth and death, the cyclical processes of nature. Swinburne said his poem was "expressive . . . of that brief total pause of passion and of thought, when the spirit, without fear or hope of good things or evil, hungers and thirsts only after the perfect sleep." World-weary after the wear and tear of our passionate active life, the soul drifts away from the real world of trouble, of sowing and reaping, into a dreamy state of feeling beyond it all, where it feels itself drifting even further into oblivion. But Swinburne did say "*brief* . . . pause"; the poem seems more the musical expression of a languorous mood than of a philosophical position.

Here life has death for neighbour,
    And far from eye or ear
Wan waves and wet winds labour,
    Weak ships and spirits steer;   20
They drive adrift, and whither
They wot not who make thither;
But no such winds blow hither,
    And no such things grow here.

No growth of moor or coppice,   25
    No heather-flower or vine,
But bloomless buds of poppies,
    Green grapes of Proserpine,
Pale beds of blowing rushes
Where no leaf blooms or blushes   30
Save this whereout she crushes
    For dead men deadly wine.

Pale, without name or number,
    In fruitless fields of corn,
They bow themselves and slumber   35
    All night till light is born;
And like a soul belated,
In hell and heaven unmated,
By cloud and mist abated
    Comes out of darkness morn.   40

Though one were strong as seven,
    He too with death shall dwell,
Nor wake with wings in heaven,
    Nor weep for pains in hell;
Though one were fair as roses,   45
His beauty clouds and closes;
And well though love reposes,
    In the end it is not well.

Pale, beyond porch and portal,
    Crowned with calm leaves, she stands   50
Who gathers all things mortal
    With cold immortal hands;
Her languid lips are sweeter
Than love's who fears to greet her
To men that mix and meet her   55
    From many times and lands.

She waits for each and other,
    She waits for all men born;
Forgets the earth her mother,
    The life of fruits and corn;   60
And spring and seed and swallow
Take wing for her and follow

21–22: Those who drift into this dreamy state—Proserpine's garden (which is also death itself)—do not know (or care) where they are bound for.   **25 coppice**: thicket of small trees   **27 poppies**: as a source of opium, associated with sleep and death; in mythology, sacred to Proserpine, who is sometimes depicted wearing a garland of them   **34 corn**: wheat

Where summer song rings hollow
    And flowers are put to scorn.

There go the loves that wither,   65
    The old loves with wearier wings;
And all dead years draw thither,
    And all disastrous things;
Dead dreams of days forsaken,
Blind buds that snows have shaken,   70
Wild leaves that winds have taken,
    Red strays of ruined springs.

We are not sure of sorrow,
    And joy was never sure;
To-day will die to-morrow;   75
    Time stoops to no man's lure;
And love, grown faint and fretful,
With lips but half regretful
Sighs, and with eyes forgetful
    Weeps that no loves endure.   80

From too much love of living,
    From hope and fear set free,
We thank with brief thanksgiving
    Whatever gods may be
That no life lives for ever;   85
That dead men rise up never;
That even the weariest river
    Winds somewhere safe to sea.

Then star nor sun shall waken,
    Nor any change of light: 90
Nor sound of waters shaken,
    Nor any sound or sight:
Nor wintry leaves nor vernal,
Nor days nor things diurnal;
Only the sleep eternal   95
    In an eternal night.

76 **lure:** technically, a bunch of feathers used by the falconer to recall the falcon, who was said to *stoop* when he flew down to it

Thomas Hardy
(1840–1928)

At 16, Hardy was apprenticed to an architect with an office next to the school kept by William Barnes, who encouraged his love for literature. For five years Hardy worked as architect in London, but more and more his interests were turning to literature. He published his first novel when about 30; it was followed by 15 others in the next 25 years. In 1896 the hostile reception accorded *Jude the Obscure,* with its frank consideration of sexual themes, induced Hardy to turn to poetry, which he had been writing over the years. When he was 58, his first book of poetry came out. Seven others followed, concluding with *Winter Words,* which appeared posthumously in the year of his death at the age of 87. On the basis of these books Hardy ranks as one of the greatest of twentieth-century poets, though he was 60 when the century began and over 70 when his best poems began to appear.

Neutral Tones

We stood by a pond that winter day,
And the sun was white, as though chidden of God,
And a few leaves lay on the starving sod;
   —They had fallen from an ash, and were gray.

Your eyes on me were as eyes that rove   5
Over tedious riddles of years ago;
And some words played between us to and fro
   On which lost the more by our love.

The smile on your mouth was the deadest thing
Alive enough to have strength to die;   10
And a grin of bitterness swept thereby
   Like an ominous bird a-wing. . . .

Since then, keen lessons that love deceives,
And wrings with wrong, have shaped to me
Your face, and the God-curst sun, and a tree,   15
   And a pond edged with grayish leaves.

1867. *Wessex Poems*, 1898.

2 **chidden of:** rebuked by

"I Look into My Glass"

I look into my glass,
And view my wasting skin,
And say, "Would God it came to pass
My heart had shrunk as thin!"

For then, I, undistrest   5
By hearts grown cold to me,
Could lonely wait my endless rest
With equanimity.

But Time, to make me grieve,
Part steals, lets part abide;   10
And shakes this fragile frame at eve
With throbbings of noontide.

Ibid.

Drummer Hodge

I

They throw in Drummer Hodge, to rest
   Uncoffined—just as found:
His landmark is a kopje-crest
   That breaks the veldt around;

1899. *Poems of the Past and the Present*, 1901 (dated 1902). As "The Dead Drummer."

The background is the South African (or Boer) War of 1899–1902 between the British and the Dutch settlers of South Africa.

1 **Hodge:** a generally derisive nickname for a country bumpkin. Hardy uses the word sympathetically—the farmboy is not just a "Hodge."   3 **kopje:** (pronounced and sometimes spelled *koppie*) a small hill   4 **veldt:** the South African grassland, with scattered brush

And foreign constellations west   5
    Each night above his mound.

II

Young Hodge the Drummer never knew—
    Fresh from his Wessex home—
The meaning of the broad Karoo,
    The Bush, the dusty loam,   10
And why uprose to nightly view
    Strange stars amid the gloam.

III

Yet portion of that unknown plain
    Will Hodge for ever be;
His homely Northern breast and brain   15
    Grow to some Southern tree,
And strange-eyed constellations reign
    His stars eternally.

5 **west:** move westward   8 **Wessex:** the ancient kingdom of the West Saxons. Hardy uses the old name for the southwest counties of England, especially Dorset, the scene of his novels and many of his poems.   9 **Karoo:** the plateau region of South Africa   10 **the Bush:** uncleared bushy or forested land   12 **gloam:** twilight

The Darkling Thrush

I leant upon a coppice gate
    When Frost was spectre-gray,
And Winter's dregs made desolate
    The weakening eye of day.
The tangled bine-stems scored the sky   5
    Like strings of broken lyres,
And all mankind that haunted nigh
    Had sought their household fires.

The land's sharp features seemed to be
    The Century's corpse outleant,   10
His crypt the cloudy canopy,
    The wind his death-lament.
The ancient pulse of germ and birth
    Was shrunken hard and dry,
And every spirit upon earth   15
    Seemed fervourless as I.

At once a voice arose among
    The bleak twigs overhead
In a full-hearted evensong
    Of joy illimited;   20

1900. Ibid.

Originally published on December 29, 1900, as "By the Century's Deathbed," the poem is a lament for the dying century, in which science and reason seemed to have overwhelmed spiritual reality. Bird-lovers tell us this bird is a missel-thrush, which feeds on mistletoe berries and sings merrily in even the worst winter weather. For "darkling" (in the dark, shrouded in darkness), cf. Keats, "Ode to a Nightingale," line 51, and Arnold, "Dover Beach," line 35. Hardy would probably like us to have these passages in mind.

1 **coppice gate:** gate to a small grove   5 **scored:** marked, as if with scratches   6 **strings of broken lyres:** sometimes shown on tombstones to symbolize life's ended music   19 **evensong:** vespers, song or prayers at evening [the associations are religious]

An aged thrush, frail, gaunt, and small,
    In blast-beruffled plume,
Had chosen thus to fling his soul
    Upon the growing gloom.

So little cause for carolings   25
    Of such ecstatic sound
Was written on terrestrial things
    Afar or nigh around,
That I could think there trembled through
    His happy good-night air   30
Some blessed Hope, whereof he knew
    And I was unaware.

The Self-Unseeing

Here is the ancient floor,
Footworn and hollowed and thin,
Here was the former door
Where the dead feet walked in.

She sat here in her chair,   5
Smiling into the fire;
He who played stood there,
Bowing it higher and higher.

Childlike, I danced in a dream;
Blessings emblazoned that day;   10
Everything glowed with a gleam;
Yet we were looking away!

1892–1901. Ibid.

About a visit Hardy made in the 1890s to his childhood home, with memories of an evening of music
and dancing with his parents long ago.

3 **former door:** When the house was remodelled, what had been a door was made a window.   4 **the
dead feet:** Hardy's father died in 1892.   5 **she:** his mother   7 **he:** his father, playing the violin

After the Fair

The singers are gone from the Cornmarket-place
    With their broadsheets of rhymes,
The street rings no longer in treble and bass
    With their skits on the times,
And the Cross, lately thronged, is a dim naked space   5
    That but echoes the stammering chimes.

From Clock-corner steps, as each quarter ding-dongs,
    Away the folk roam

1902. *Time's Laughingstocks*, 1909.

From a series of poems called "At Casterbridge Fair." Casterbridge is Hardy's name for Dorchester (in
Dorset), near the place he was born. Until the mid-1930s, when automobile traffic led to its abandon-
ment, a fair was held there annually in February. The place-names in the poem are local: Cornmarket-
place is at the "Cross" where the main streets cross; the "chimes" are from St. Peter's church there,
which until World War I played not only hymns but also popular music.

4 **skits on the times:** comic or political ballads

By the "Hart" and Grey's Bridge into byways and "drongs,"   10
    Or across the ridged loam:
The younger ones shrilling the lately heard songs,
    The old saying, "Would we were home."

The shy-seeming maiden so mute in the fair
    Now rattles and talks,
And that one who looked the most swaggering there   15
    Grows sad as she walks,
And she who seemed eaten by cankering care
    In statuesque sturdiness stalks.

And midnight clears High Street of all but the ghosts
    Of its buried burghees,   20
From the latest far back to those old Roman hosts
    Whose remains one yet sees,
Who loved, laughed, and fought, hailed their friends, drank their toasts
    At their meeting-times here, just as these!

9 the "**Hart**": the White Hart Tavern "**drongs**": lanes between hedgerows   14 **rattles**: talks in a quick, lively way   17 **cankering**: nagging, like a canker sore   20 **burghees**: inhabitants of a burgh (town)   21 **Roman hosts**: It is typical of Hardy to take the scene centuries back into Roman times when Dorchester was the Roman settlement of Durnovaria.

The Man He Killed

"Had he and I but met
    By some old ancient inn,
We should have sat us down to wet
    Right many a nipperkin!

"But ranged as infantry,   5
    And staring face to face,
I shot at him as he at me,
    And killed him in his place.

"I shot him dead because—
    Because he was my foe,   10
Just so: my foe of course he was;
    That's clear enough; although

"He thought he'd 'list, perhaps,
    Off-hand like—just as I—
Was out of work—had sold his traps—   15
    No other reason why.

"Yes; quaint and curious war is!
    You shoot a fellow down
You'd treat if met where any bar is,
    Or help to half-a-crown."   20

1902. Ibid.

The magazine publication gave the scene as the Fox Inn, near Dorchester. The speaker is a soldier returned from the South African War. Like "Drummer Hodge," the poem is a protest against imperialistic war, which the soldiers themselves do not understand.

4 **nipperkin**: a measure of beer or wine—half a pint or so   13 **'list**: enlist   15 **traps**: belongings
20 **half-a-crown**: about half a dollar

The Voice

Woman much missed, how you call to me, call to me,
Saying that now you are not as you were
When you had changed from the one who was all to me,
But as at first, when our day was fair.

Can it be you that I hear? Let me view you, then,   5
Standing as when I drew near to the town
Where you would wait for me: yes, as I knew you then,
Even to the original air-blue gown!

Or is it only the breeze, in its listlessness
Travelling across the wet mead to me here,   10
You being ever dissolved to wan wistlessness,
Heard no more again far or near?

    Thus I; faltering forward,
    Leaves around me falling,
Wind oozing thin through the thorn from norward,   15
    And the woman calling.

1912. *Satires of Circumstance*, 1914.

After nearly 40 years of marriage, Hardy's wife died in 1912. For about half of their life together, the marriage had been happy, and then misunderstandings and estrangements had developed. After her death, Hardy remembered with grief their early happiness.

11 **wistlessness:** inattentiveness, vagueness   15 **norward:** northward

During Wind and Rain

    They sing their dearest songs—
    He, she, all of them—yea,
    Treble and tenor and bass,
      And one to play;
    With the candles mooning each face. . . .   5
      Ah, no; the years O!
How the sick leaves reel down in throngs!

    They clear the creeping moss—
    Elders and juniors—aye,
    Making the pathway neat   10
      And the garden gay;
    And they build a shady seat. . . .
      Ah, no; the years, the years;
See, the white storm-birds wing across!

    They are blithely breakfasting all—   15
    Men and maidens—yea,
    Under the summer tree,
      With a glimpse of the bay,
    While pet fowl come to the knee. . . .
      Ah, no; the years O!   20
And the rotten rose is ript from the wall.

1913? *Moments of Vision*, 1917.

Based on scenes Hardy's first wife remembered from her childhood. Each pleasant memory is followed by an image of mutability: of menace or decline.

They change to a high new house,
He, she, all of them—aye,
Clocks and carpets, and chairs
    On the lawn all day,   25
And brightest things that are theirs. . . .
    Ah, no; the years, the years;
Down their carved names the rain-drop ploughs.

Channel Firing

That night your great guns, unawares,
Shook all our coffins as we lay,
And broke the chancel window-squares,
We thought it was the Judgment-day

And sat upright.   While drearisome   5
Arose the howl of wakened hounds:
The mouse let fall the altar-crumb,
The worms drew back into the mounds,

The glebe cow drooled.   Till God called, "No;
It's gunnery practice out at sea   10
Just as before you went below;
The world is as it used to be:

"All nations striving strong to make
Red war yet redder.   Mad as hatters
They do no more for Christés sake   15
Than you who are helpless in such matters.

"That this is not the judgment-hour
For some of them's a blessed thing,
For if it were they'd have to scour
Hell's floor for so much threatening. . . .   20

"Ha, ha.   It will be warmer when
I blow the trumpet (if indeed
I ever do; for you are men,
And rest eternal sorely need)."

So down we lay again.   "I wonder,   25
Will the world ever saner be,"
Said one, "than when He sent us under
In our indifferent century!"

And many a skeleton shook his head.
"Instead of preaching forty year,"   30
My neighbour Parson Thirdly said,
"I wish I had stuck to pipes and beer."

1914. *Satires of Circumstance*, 1914.

The "channel firing" is gunnery practice in the English Channel off Portland Harbor (near Dorchester) three months before the outbreak of World War I. Hardy imagines it as awakening the dead.

3 **chancel:** the part of a church containing the altar and seats for clergy and choir   9 **glebe cow:** cow pastured on land belonging to the clergyman

Again the guns disturbed the hour,
Roaring their readiness to avenge,
As far inland as Stourton Tower,   35
And Camelot, and starlit Stonehenge.

35 **Stourton Tower:** a monument built on the channel north of Portland Harbor to commemorate the victory of King Alfred over the Danes (A.D. 879)   36 **Camelot:** the legendary seat of King Arthur, apparently near Glastonbury, northwest of Portland Harbor   **Stonehenge:** the site of an ancient British civilization preceding the Celts and Romans. All three of these places, within about 50 miles of Portland Harbor, represent military powers that have come to nothing.

The Oxen

Christmas Eve, and twelve of the clock.
    "Now they are all on their knees,"
An elder said as we sat in a flock
    By the embers in hearthside ease.

We pictured the meek mild creatures where   5
    They dwelt in their strawy pen,
Nor did it occur to one of us there
    To doubt they were kneeling then.

So fair a fancy few would weave
    In these years! Yet, I feel,   10
If someone said on Christmas Eve,
    "Come; see the oxen kneel,

"In the lonely barton by yonder coomb
    Our childhood used to know,"
I should go with him in the gloom,   15
    Hoping it might be so.

1915. *Moments of Vision,* 1917.

According to an old folk legend, oxen kneel on Christmas Eve in honor of Christ's birth, as they did in the stable at Bethlehem. Hardy heard the legend as a child; he later finds it hard to believe, in "these years" of World War I.

13 **barton:** farmyard   **coomb:** valley

In Time of "The Breaking of Nations"

I

Only a man harrowing clods
    In a slow silent walk
With an old horse that stumbles and nods
    Half asleep as they stalk.

II

Only thin smoke without flame   5
    From the heaps of couch-grass;

1915. Ibid.

Hardy said that the poem expressed a feeling that had moved him first in 1870, during the Franco-Prussian War: the feeling that our human life of work and love goes on in spite of the destruction of war. But he wrote the poem 40 years later, during the war with Germany. In a footnote he refers to the Biblical passage from Jer. 51:20—God's judgment against Babylon: "Thou art my battle axe and weapons of war: for with thee will I break in pieces the nations...."

6 **couch-grass:** a rough grass that spreads like a weed, quack grass

Yet this will go onward the same
  Though Dynasties pass.

III

Yonder a maid and her wight
  Come whispering by: 10
War's annals will fade into night
  Ere their story die.

9 **wight:** man [archaic]

The Garden Seat

Its former green is blue and thin,
And its once firm legs sink in and in;
Soon it will break down unaware,
Soon it will break down unaware.

At night when reddest flowers are black   5
Those who once sat thereon come back;
Quite a row of them sitting there,
Quite a row of them sitting there.

With them the seat does not break down,
Nor winter freeze them, nor floods drown,   10
For they are as light as upper air,
They are as light as upper air!

1914–1922. *Late Lyrics and Earlier*, 1922.

Suggested by the decaying garden seats at Hardy's house in Dorchester, which further evoked the image of those now dead who had once been seen sitting there.

Gerard Manley Hopkins
(1844–1889)

As a boy Hopkins showed talent in both writing and drawing; in later life he composed music that might be called experimental. At Oxford, after a struggle, he was received into the Roman Catholic Church by Cardinal Newman. In 1868 he decided to become a Jesuit priest; sent to Wales to study theology, he also looked into the music of classical Welsh poetry and learned Greek. After being ordained in 1877, he served as parish priest and professor of classics in London, Liverpool, Glasgow, and elsewhere; he was much disturbed by the poverty and squalor he found in the great industrial centers. English to the bone, he found Ireland uncongenial when appointed Professor of Greek in Dublin; he died of typhoid there at the age of 44. During his life he published even less than Emily Dickinson—only three pieces of light verse in a college magazine. Thirty years after his death Robert Bridges, one of the few friends who had seen his poetry, published an edition which won Hopkins a host of admirers and imitators among the younger poets.

God's Grandeur

The world is charged with the grandeur of God.
  It will flame out, like shining from shook foil;

1877. *Lyra Sacra*, ed. H. C. Beeching, 1895. *Poems*, 1918.

2 **shook foil:** gold foil, gold leaf, which when shaken gives off a dazzle of light. Hopkins compared it to different kinds of lightning.

It gathers to a greatness, like the ooze of oil
Crushed. Why do men then now not reck his rod?
Generations have trod, have trod, have trod;   5
    And all is seared with trade; bleared, smeared with toil;
    And wears man's smudge and shares man's smell: the soil
Is bare now, nor can foot feel, being shod.

And for all this, nature is never spent;
    There lives the dearest freshness deep down things;   10
And though the last lights off the black West went
    Oh, morning, at the brown brink eastward, springs—
Because the Holy Ghost over the bent
    World broods with warm breast and with ah! bright wings.

3-4 **ooze of oil/Crushed:** olive oil, for example, or various aromatic oils extracted by crushing
4 **reck his rod:** pay attention to his command   13 **Holy Ghost** ...: Cf. Gen. 1:2: "And the Spirit of
God moved upon the face of the waters"; and Milton, *Paradise Lost*, I, 17 ff.:

    ... Thou O Spirit ...
Wast present, and with mighty wings outspread
Dove-like satst brooding on the vast Abyss. ...

Spring

Nothing is so beautiful as Spring—
    When weeds, in wheels, shoot long and lovely and lush;
    Thrush's eggs look little low heavens, and thrush
Through the echoing timber does so rinse and wring
The ear, it strikes like lightnings to hear him sing;   5
    The glassy peartree leaves and blooms, they brush
    The descending blue; that blue is all in a rush
With richness; the racing lambs too have fair their fling.

What is all this juice and all this joy?
    A strain of the earth's sweet being in the beginning   10
In Eden garden.—Have, get, before it cloy,

    Before it cloud, Christ, lord, and sour with sinning,
Innocent mind and Mayday in girl and boy,
    Most, O maid's child, thy choice and worthy the winning.

1877. *Robert Bridges and Contemporary Poets* (vol. vii of *Poets and Poetry of the Nineteenth Century*), ed.
A. H. Miles, 1893; 2nd ed., 1906. *Poems,* 1918.

The Windhover

To Christ Our Lord

I caught this morning morning's minion, king-
    dom of daylight's dauphin, dapple-dawn-drawn Falcon, in his riding
Of the rolling level underneath him steady air, and striding

1877. *Poems,* 1918.

The windhover (pronounced *wíndev'r*) is a kestrel or small hawk that likes to hang or hover with its
head into the wind. For the rhythm of this and the three following poems, see *sprung rhythm* in the
prosody section.

1 **minion:** darling   2 **dauphin:** prince   **dapple-dawn-drawn:** outlined against (or attracted by) the
dappled dawn   3 **rolling ... air:** The usual word order would be: the steady air rolling level under-
neath him. The dislocation may be because the windhover (like a hang-glider) would feel the motion
of the air before it registered on the brain as air.

High there, how he rung upon the rein of a wimpling wing
In his ecstasy! then off, off forth on swing,   5
   As a skate's heel sweeps smooth on a bow-bend: the hurl and gliding
   Rebuffed the big wind. My heart in hiding
Stirred for a bird,—the achieve of, the mastery of the thing!

Brute beauty and valour and act, oh, air, pride, plume, here
   Buckle! AND the fire that breaks from thee then, a billion   10
Times told lovelier, more dangerous, O my chevalier!

   No wonder of it: shéer plód makes plough down sillion
Shine, and blue-bleak embers, ah my dear,
   Fall, gall themselves, and gash gold-vermilion.

4 rung upon the rein: pivots on a wingtip (probably). A horse being trained is said to "ring on the rein" when it goes in a circle at the end of a long rein. **wimpling:** pleated, rippling   **6 bow-bend:** a curve like that of a bow   **7 in hiding:** perhaps because the poet is only an observer, or because, like Christ at Nazareth, he is living the "hidden life" of a religious   **9–14** See Additional Notes (p. 765).   **12 sillion:** furrow (French, *sillon*). Many words of French origin in the poem associate it with a world of chivalry and chevaliers.

Pied Beauty

Glory be to God for dappled things—
   For skies of couple-colour as a brinded cow;
      For rose-moles all in stipple upon trout that swim;
Fresh-firecoal chestnut-falls; finches' wings;
   Landscape plotted and pieced—fold, fallow, and plough;   5
      And áll trádes, their gear and tackle and trim.

All things counter, original, spare, strange;
   Whatever is fickle, freckled (who knows how?)
      With swift, slow; sweet, sour; adazzle, dim;
He fathers-forth whose beauty is past change: 10
             Praise him.

1877. Ibid.

Hopkins called this a "Curtal Sonnet"—see *sonnet* in the prosody section.

2 couple-color: two colors together   **brinded:** brindled, streaked   **4 ...chestnut...:** chestnuts as bright as burning coals   **6 áll trádes:** Hopkins put accents, like musical notations, over words he wanted stressed, dwelt on, in reading.   **7 counter:** going counter, opposite [as in the pairings two lines below]

Felix Randal

Felix Randal the farrier, O is he dead then? my duty all ended,
Who have watched his mould of man, big-boned and hardy-handsome
Pining, pining, till time when reason rambled in it and some
Fatal four disorders, fleshed there, all contended?

Sickness broke him. Impatient, he cursed at first, but mended   5
Being anointed and all; though a heavenlier heart began some

1880. Ibid.

Hopkins knew and took care of the blacksmith of the poem when he was doing parish work in the small industrial town of Bedford Leigh in 1879.

1 farrier: blacksmith   **6 anointed:** given the sacrament for those thought dying

Months earlier, since I had our sweet reprieve and ransom
Tendered to him. Ah well, God rest him all road ever he offended!

This seeing the sick endears them to us, us too it endears.
My tongue had taught thee comfort, touch had quenched thy tears,   10
Thy tears that touched my heart, child, Felix, poor Felix Randal;

How far from then forethought of, all thy more boisterous years,
When thou at the random grim forge, powerful amidst peers,
Didst fettle for the great grey drayhorse his bright and battering sandal!

7 **reprieve and ransom:** confession and communion   8 **all road ever:** in whatever ways [the expression sounds literary, but is heard in dialect]   13 **random:** roughly built of stones of irregular shapes and sizes   14 **fettle:** prepare

Spring and Fall

To a Young Child

Márgarét, áre you grieving
Over Goldengrove unleaving?
Leáves, líke the things of man, you
With your fresh thoughts care for, can you?
Áh! ás the heart grows older   5
It will come to such sights colder
By and by, nor spare a sigh
Though worlds of wanwood leafmeal lie;
And yet you *will* weep and know why.
Now no matter, child, the name: 10
Sórrow's spríngs áre the same.
Nor mouth had, no nor mind, expressed
What heart heard of, ghost guessed:
It ís the blight man was born for,
It is Margaret you mourn for.   15

1880. *Robert Bridges and Contemporary Poets, etc.* . . . , 1893. *Poems*, 1918.

Hopkins, who thought of the rhythm of his poems almost as a musician thinks of rhythm, here puts written accents on words or syllables he would like us to stress more strongly than we normally might. He wrote the poem while out walking—this may have had some effect on its physical rhythm. The incident is imaginary.

2 **Goldengrove:** a pretty name, like one a child would make up, for a grove in autumn   **unleaving:** losing its leaves   8 **wanwood:** a coined word for woods that have gone wan in fall   **leafmeal:** (1) in leafy pieces (cf. *piecemeal*); (2) ground to leafy meal   13 **ghost:** spirit

I Wake and Feel the Fell of Dark, Not Day

I wake and feel the fell of dark, not day.
What hours, O what black hoùrs we have spent

Probably 1885. *Poems*, 1918.

This poem is one of what are called the "terrible sonnets," which Hopkins wrote near the end of his life, when he found himself in a state of spiritual trial and desolation, like that "dark night of the soul," as St. John of the Cross called it, by which even saints have been tested. He was unwell, suffered from insomnia (see line 1); he was unhappy too in his work and surroundings and felt that he was "time's eunuch" (as he says in the poem that follows)—one who was producing nothing of value.

1 **fell:** (1) the hairy skin of an animal, as if the darkness were a threatening creature; (2) rancor or bitterness (from the Latin word *fel*, which means *gall* or *bile*, and which Hopkins would have known); (3) the adjective *fell*, meaning *cruel* or *fierce*, used as a noun. Of these, the first seems most likely after the verb *feel*.

This night! what sights you, heart, saw; ways you went!
And more must, in yet longer light's delay.

With witness I speak this. But where I say   5
Hours I mean years, mean life. And my lament
Is cries countless, cries like dead letters sent
To dearest him that lives alas! away.

I am gall, I am heartburn. God's most deep decree
Bitter would have me taste: my taste was me;   10
Bones built in me, flesh filled, blood brimmed the curse.

Selfyeast of spirit a dull dough sours. I see
The lost are like this, and their scourge to be
As I am mine, their sweating selves; but worse.

5 with witness: I know by experience what I am saying.   **8 him:** God   **10 me:** because when one
feels abandoned by God he has only his *me* or godless self left

Thou Art Indeed Just, Lord

> *Justus quidem tu es, Domine, si disputem tecum;*
> *verumtamen justa loquar ad te: Quare via impiorum*
> *prosperatur? &c.*

Thou art indeed just, Lord, if I contend
With thee; but, sir, so what I plead is just.
Why do sinners' ways prosper? and why must
Disappointment all I endeavour end?
Wert thou my enemy, O thou my friend,   5
How wouldst thou worse, I wonder than thou dost
Defeat, thwart me? Oh, the sots and thralls of lust
Do in spare hours more thrive than I that spend,

Sir, life upon thy cause. See, banks and brakes
Now, leavèd how thick! lacèd they are again   10
With fretty chervil, look, and fresh wind shakes

Them; birds build—but not I build; no, but strain,
Time's eunuch, and not breed one work that wakes.
Mine, O thou lord of life, send my roots rain.

1889. *Robert Bridges and Contemporary Poetry* . . . , 1893 (only in part). *Poems,* 1918.

The quotation is from Jer. 12:1: "Righteous art thou, O LORD, when I plead with thee: yet let me talk
with thee of thy judgments: Wherefore doth the way of the wicked prosper?" The second half of Hop-
kins's second line is closer to the sense of the Latin.

7 thralls: slaves   **9 brakes:** beds of fern   **11 fretty chervil:** cow-parsley, which has elaborate, orna-
mental ("fretted") leaves   **13 Time's eunuch:** See Matt. 19:12 ". . . there be eunuchs, which have
made themselves eunuchs for the kingdom of heaven's sake."

Robert Bridges
(1844–1930)

A physician in London for over 10 years, Bridges gave up his practice, retired to the
country, and devoted himself to poetry. Though not well known to the public, he was
named poet laureate in 1913.

The Evening Darkens Over

The evening darkens over
After a day so bright,
The windcapt waves discover
That wild will be the night.
There's sound of distant thunder.   5

The latest sea-birds hover
Along the cliff's sheer height;
As in the memory wander
Last flutterings of delight,
White wings lost on the white.   10

There's not a ship in sight;
And as the sun goes under,
Thick clouds conspire to cover
The moon that should rise yonder.
Thou art alone, fond lover.   15

Shorter Poems, 1890.

John Davidson
(1857–1909)

Davidson, a Scotsman, worked mostly as a teacher until his early thirties, when he went
to London to make a living as a writer. After years of courageous struggle against pover-
ty, illness, and indifference, he was found drowned in the English Channel. His work
has been admired by readers as discriminating as T. S. Eliot.

A Runnable Stag

When the pods went pop on the broom, green broom,
    And apples began to be golden-skinned,
We harboured a stag in the Priory coomb,
    And we feathered his trail up-wind, up-wind,
    We feathered his trail up-wind—   5
        A stag of warrant, a stag, a stag,
        A runnable stag, a kingly crop,
        Brow, bay and tray and three on top,
        A stag, a runnable stag.

Then the huntsman's horn rang yap, yap, yap,   10
    And 'Forwards' we heard the harbourer shout;
But 'twas only a brocket that broke a gap
    In the beechen underwood, driven out,
    From the underwood antlered out
        By warrant and might of the stag, the stag,   15
        The runnable stag, whose lordly mind
        Was bent on sleep, though beamed and tined
        He stood, a runnable stag.

By 1905. *Holiday and Other Poems,* 1906.

runnable: old enough (about five years) to be "run" (hunted)   1 **broom:** a wild shrub   3 **harboured:**
traced to its lair   **coomb:** valley   4 **feathered:** set the hounds on   6 **of warrant:** warrantable, old
enough to kill   7 **crop:** head, pair of antlers   8 **bay:** second branch of a stag's head   **tray:** third
branch   11 **harbourer:** tracker   12 **brocket:** two-year-old stag   17 **beamed and tined:** fully ant-
lered (The *beam* is the main trunk of the stag's horn; the *tine* is a branch.)

So we tufted the covert till afternoon
    With Tinkerman's Pup and Bell-of-the-North;   20
And hunters were sulky and hounds out of tune
    Before we tufted the right stag forth,
    Before we tufted him forth,
        The stag of warrant, the wily stag,
        The runnable stag with his kingly crop,   25
        Brow, bay and tray and three on top,
        The royal and runnable stag.

It was Bell-of-the-North and Tinkerman's Pup
    That stuck to the scent till the copse was drawn.
'Tally ho! tally ho!' and the hunt was up,   30
    The tufters whipped and the pack laid on,
    The resolute pack laid on,
        And the stag of warrant away at last,
        The runnable stag, the same, the same,
        His hoofs on fire, his horns like flame,   35
        A stag, a runnable stag.

'Let your gelding be: if you check or chide
    He stumbles at once and you're out of the hunt;
For three hundred gentlemen, able to ride,
    On hunters accustomed to bear the brunt,   40
    Accustomed to bear the brunt,
        Are after the runnable stag, the stag,
        The runnable stag with his kingly crop,
        Brow, bay and tray and three on top,
        The right, the runnable stag.'   45

By perilous paths in coomb and dell,
    The heather, the rocks, and the river-bed,
The pace grew hot, for the scent lay well,
    And a runnable stag goes right ahead,
    The quarry went right ahead—   50
        Ahead, ahead, and fast and far;
        His antlered crest, his cloven hoof,
        Brow, bay and tray and three aloof,
        The stag, the runnable stag.

For a matter of twenty miles and more,   55
    By the densest hedge and the highest wall,
Through herds of bullocks he baffled the lore
    Of harbourer, huntsman, hounds and all,
    Of harbourer, hounds and all—
        The stag of warrant, the wily stag,   60
        For twenty miles, and five and five,
        He ran, and he never was caught alive,
        This stag, this runnable stag.

When he turned at bay in the leafy gloom,
    In the emerald gloom where the brook ran deep,   65
He heard in the distance the rollers boom,
    And he saw in a vision of peaceful sleep,
    In a wonderful vision of sleep,

19, 22 **tufted:** beat, dislodged 20 names of dogs 29 **copse:** grove **drawn:** searched 30 "Tally ho!": cry when the stag is sighted 37 **gelding:** gelded horse

A stag of warrant, a stag, a stag,
A runnable stag in a jewelled bed,
Under the sheltering ocean dead,   70
A stag, a runnable stag.

So a fateful hope lit up his eye,
And he opened his nostrils wide again,
And he tossed his branching antlers high   75
As he headed the hunt down the Charlock glen,
As he raced down the echoing glen,
For five miles more, the stag, the stag,
For twenty miles, and five and five,
Not to be caught now, dead or alive,   80
The stag, the runnable stag.

Three hundred gentlemen, able to ride,
Three hundred horses as gallant and free,
Behind him escape on the evening tide,
Far out till he sank in the Severn Sea,   85
Till he sank in the depths of the sea—
The stag, the buoyant stag, the stag
That slept as last in a jewelled bed
Under the sheltering ocean spread,
The stag, the runnable stag.   90

85 **Severn Sea:** the Bristol Channel (southwestern England) into which the Severn River empties

A. E. Housman
(1859–1936)

At Oxford Housman studied classics and philosophy, but to everyone's surprise failed his final exams, it seems as a result of the turmoil he was suffering because of his suppressed affection for a fellow student. For over 10 years, while holding a job in the patent office, he continued to work at classical studies, building up such a reputation that he was appointed professor of Latin at University College and later at Cambridge. He published several rigorous editions of Roman poets and wrote many erudite and acerbic articles. In 1896 *A Shropshire Lad* was published; it brought him such fame that his *Last Poems*, 26 years later (1922), enjoyed record-breaking sales. A few months after his death a third volume, *More Poems*, was brought out by his brother.

From Far, from Eve and Morning

From far, from eve and morning
    And yon twelve-winded sky,
The stuff of life to knit me
    Blew hither: here am I.

1891–1893. *A Shropshire Lad,* 1896.

2 **twelve-winded:** Early drafts of the poem show that Housman wrote "four-winded" (and "four quarters" in line 11). In the final version he crossed *four* out in favor of the surprising *twelve.* Some ancient systems of counting or dividing, especially those based on circles or cycles, tend to have 12 divisions (the dozen, the clockface, the year, the zodiac, etc.). Medieval drawings of the zodiac sometimes show each of the 12 signs accompanied by a puffing face—its appropriate wind. The ancient "wind-rose" (cf. "compass-rose" as a name for the compass dial) showed 12 winds with their 12 Latin names.

Now—for a breath I tarry   5
    Nor yet disperse apart—
Take my hand quick and tell me,
    What have you in your heart.

Speak now, and I will answer;
    How shall I help you, say;   10
Ere to the wind's twelve quarters
    I take my endless way.

With Rue My Heart Is Laden

With rue my heart is laden
    For golden friends I had,
For many a rose-lipt maiden
    And many a lightfoot lad.

By brooks too broad for leaping
    The lightfoot boys are laid;
The rose-lipt girls are sleeping
    In fields where roses fade.

1893. Ibid.

To an Athlete Dying Young

The time you won your town the race
We chaired you through the market-place;
Man and boy stood cheering by,
And home we brought you shoulder-high.

To-day, the road all runners come,   5
Shoulder-high we bring you home,
And set you at your threshold down,
Townsman of a stiller town.

Smart lad, to slip betimes away
From fields where glory does not stay   10
And early though the laurel grows
It withers quicker than the rose.

Eyes the shady night has shut
Cannot see the record cut,
And silence sounds no worse than cheers   15
After earth has stopped the ears:

Now you will not swell the rout
Of lads that wore their honours out,
Runners whom renown outran
And the name died before the man.   20

1895. Ibid.

9 **betimes:** early, in good time   11 **laurel:** symbol of victory   12 **rose:** symbol of beauty   17 **rout:** crowd

So set, before its echoes fade,
The fleet foot on the sill of shade,
And hold to the low lintel up
The still-defended challenge-cup.

And round that early-laurelled head   25
Will flock to gaze the strengthless dead,
And find unwithered on its curls
The garland briefer than a girl's.

23 **lintel:** the horizontal piece of stone or timber over a door or window (here, over a tomb)

Along the Field as We Came By

Along the field as we came by
A year ago, my love and I,
The aspen over stile and stone
Was talking to itself alone.
"Oh who are these that kiss and pass?   5
A country lover and his lass;
Two lovers looking to be wed;
And time shall put them both to bed,
But she shall lie with earth above,
And he beside another love."   10

And sure enough beneath the tree
There walks another love with me,
And overhead the aspen heaves
Its rainy-sounding silver leaves;
And I spell nothing in their stir,   15
But now perhaps they speak to her,
And plain for her to understand
They talk about a time at hand
When I shall sleep with clover clad,
And she beside another lad.   20

1894–1895. Ibid.

3 **stile:** steps over a fence or wall   15 **spell:** make out, understand

Loveliest of Trees, the Cherry Now

Loveliest of trees, the cherry now
Is hung with bloom along the bough,
And stands about the woodland ride
Wearing white for Eastertide.

Now, of my threescore years and ten,   5
Twenty will not come again,
And take from seventy springs a score,
It only leaves me fifty more.

And since to look at things in bloom
Fifty springs are little room,   10

1895. Ibid.

3 **ride:** road for riding

About the woodlands I will go
To see the cherry hung with snow.

The Oracles

'Tis mute, the word they went to hear on high Dodona mountain
    When winds were in the oakenshaws and all the cauldrons tolled,
And mute's the midland navel-stone beside the singing fountain,
    And echoes list to silence now where gods told lies of old.

I took my question to the shrine that has not ceased from speaking,   5
    The heart within, that tells the truth and tells it twice as plain;
And from the cave of oracles I heard the priestess shrieking
    That she and I should surely die and never live again.

Oh priestess, what you cry is clear, and sound good sense I think it;
    But let the screaming echoes rest, and froth your mouth no more.   10
'Tis true there's better boose than brine, but he that drowns must drink it;
    And oh, my lass, the news is news that men have heard before.

The King with half the East at heel is marched from lands of morning;
    Their fighters drink the rivers up, their shafts benight the air.
And he that stands will die for nought, and home there's no returning.   15
    The Spartans on the sea-wet rock sat down and combed their hair.

---

c. 1904. *Last Poems,* 1922.

The ancient oracles were thought to be voices of the gods responding to human questions about personal or political matters. They might be compared to modern fortune-tellers—except that they had much more religious and even pseudoscientific validity. They were consulted on grave matters of national policy, and their frequently evasive answers were taken seriously and studiously interpreted.

1 **Dodona:** One of the most famous oracles was that of Jove at Dodona in the mountains of Epirus. Divine answers were interpreted from the rustlings of a sacred oak or the reverberating echoes of a bronze cauldron, or gong. 2 **oakenshaws:** oak woods (*shaws* means "woods") 3 **midland navel-stone:** At the most famous of the oracles, that of Apollo at Delphi, there was a navel-shaped stone thought to mark the center of the earth. Near it was the Castalian Fount, sacred to the Muses ("the singing fountain"). 6 **the heart:** Our own heart, unlike the lying oracles, tells the truth. 7 **priestess:** At Delphi the voice of the god was thought to be heard through the voice of a delirious young woman, the Pythia. There were also priestesses at Dodona. 13–15 The lines in italics represent the speech of an oracle telling the ancient Greeks that there was no use resisting the invasion of the Persian king Xerxes in 480 B.C. He had raised an enormous army; there was real concern about finding an adequate water supply for it. When it was said that their arrows were so many they would darken the sun, a brave Spartan replied: "Good news! we can fight in the shade." 16 Some 300 Spartans (as Herodotus tells the story in chapter VII of his *History*), with 700 allies and a few enforced hostages, chose to resist the Persian army at the narrow pass of Thermopylai, between the mountains and the sea—and resisted successfully until a traitor directed the Persians to a roundabout road. Before the battle, the Spartans showed their disdain for the enemy, and their cool courage, by doing gymnastic exercises and idly combing their long hair. The image is Housman's answer to his belief that much of life is made up of bad news: disdain it.

Francis Thompson
(1859–1907)

Thompson studied medicine but, with his mind set on literature, failed his examinations. For five years in London he struggled against poverty and the illness that drove him to opium. Friends helped Thompson through a long hospital convalescence and saw that his *Poems* were published. Though illness limited his productivity, he published two other books of poetry as well as critical and devotional prose.

In No Strange Land

The Kingdom of God is within you

O world invisible, we view thee,
O world intangible, we touch thee,
O world unknowable, we know thee,
Inapprehensible, we clutch thee!

Does the fish soar to find the ocean,   5
The eagle plunge to find the air—
That we ask of the stars in motion
If they have rumor of thee there?

Not where the wheeling systems darken,
And our benumbed conceiving soars!—   10
The drift of pinions, would we hearken,
Beats at our own clay-shuttered doors.

The angels keep their ancient places;—
Turn but a stone, and start a wing!
'Tis ye, 'tis your estrangèd faces,   15
That miss the many-splendored thing.

But (when so sad thou canst not sadder)
Cry;—and upon thy so sore loss
Shall shine the traffic of Jacob's ladder
Pitched between Heaven and Charing Cross.   20

Yea, in the night, my Soul, my daughter,
Cry,—clinging Heaven by the hems;
And lo, Christ walking on the water
Not of Gennesareth, but Thames!

By 1903. *Works*, ed. W. Meynell, 1913.

This poem was found among Thompson's papers after his death by his friend and editor, Wilfred
Meynell, who changed Thompson's title to "The Kingdom of God," under which it is still often print-
ed. For the title, cf. Ps. 137:4: "How shall we sing the LORD's song in a strange land?" The epigraph is
from Luke 17:21.

11 **pinions:** from the wings of angels   12 **clay-shuttered doors:** our physical senses   19 **Jacob's
ladder:** Cf. Jacob's dream: "And he dreamed, and behold a ladder set up on the earth, and the top of
it reached to heaven: and behold the angels of God ascending and descending on it" (Gen. 28:12).
20 **Charing Cross:** in the center of London   24 **Gennesareth:** the Sea of Galilee (cf. Matt. 14:25–26,
where Jesus is described walking on the water toward the frightened apostles). The Thames is of
course the river in London.

Rudyard Kipling
(1865–1936)

Kipling was born in India, raised partly in a foster home in England. In his late teens he
returned to India for several years as a journalist. His first book of poetry was published
when he was 20; his first book of stories the following year. Within a few years he was
among the most famous of living writers. In 1892 he and his American wife moved to
Vermont for five years. With at least 40 books to his credit, he was awarded the Nobel
Prize for literature in 1907.

Song of the Galley-Slaves

We pulled for you when the wind was against us and the sails were low.
  Will you never let us go?
We ate bread and onions when you took towns, or ran aboard quickly when
  you were beaten back by the foe.
The Captains walked up and down the deck in fair weather singing songs, but
  we were below.
We fainted with our chins on the oars and you did not see that we
  were idle, for we still swung to and fro.   5
  Will you never let us go?
The salt made the oar-handles like shark-skin; our knees were cut to the
  bone with salt-cracks; our hair was stuck to our foreheads; and our lips
  were cut to the gums, and you whipped us because we could not row.
  Will you never let us go?
But, in a little time, we shall run out of the port-holes as the water runs along
  the oar-blade, and though you tell the others to row after us you will
  never catch us till you catch the oar-thresh and tie up the winds in the bel-
  ly of the sail. Aho!
  Will you never let us go?   10

By 1891. "The Finest Story in the World," *Many Inventions,* 1893.

In his short story, "The Finest Story in the World," which Kipling published in July 1891 in *Contemporary Review,* there is a character who writes conventional poetry: "He rhymed 'dove' with 'love' and 'moon' with 'June,' and devoutly believed they had never been so rhymed before." He is apologetic when the above "pencil scrawl" is noticed; "Oh that's not poetry at all. It's some rot I wrote last night before I went to bed and it was too much bother to hunt for rhymes; so I made it a sort of blank verse instead." He meant *free verse* rather than *blank verse* (see the prosody section).

Harp Song of the Dane Women

What is a woman that you forsake her,
And the hearth-fire and the home-acre,
To go with the old grey Widow-maker?

She has no house to lay a guest in—
But one chill bed for all to rest in,   5
That the pale suns and the stray bergs nest in.

She has no strong white arms to fold you,
But the ten-times-fingering weed to hold you—
Out on the rocks where the tide has rolled you.

Yet, when the signs of summer thicken,   10
And the ice breaks, and the birch-buds quicken,
Yearly you turn from our side, and sicken—

Sicken again for the shouts and the slaughters.
You steal away to the lapping waters,
And look at your ship in her winter-quarters.   15

You forget our mirth, and talk at the tables,
The kine in the shed and the horse in the stables—
To pitch her sides and go over her cables.

Puck of Pook's Hill, 1906.

This poem is from a story about the times just after the Norman conquest of England (1066). The Widow-maker is the sea.

Then you drive out where the storm-clouds swallow,
And the sound of your oar-blades, falling hollow,   20
Is all we have left through the months to follow.

Ah, what is Woman that you forsake her,
And the hearth-fire and the home-acre,
To go with the old grey Widow-maker?

William Butler Yeats
(1865–1939)

Yeats—in the opinion of many the greatest twentieth-century poet—was born in a Dublin suburb of an Anglo-Irish Protestant family which soon after moved to London. Yeats went to school in England but returned during vacations to stay with his grandparents in northwestern Ireland. When he was 16 his family returned to Dublin; he studied at the School of Art there and began to write poetry. Back in London in his early twenties, he was active in literary circles and dreamed of creating a new Irish literature. His first book of poems (1889) led to a meeting with Maud Gonne, the exciting and beautiful agitator for Irish independence who became the chief inspiration of his poems for decades and the source of much suffering when she refused his love and in 1903 married (unhappily) an Irish soldier of fortune. In 1893 Yeats co-edited an edition of Blake, an influence which encouraged him in his lifelong study of esoteric and mystical writers and of spiritualism and magic. In 1899 he was active in founding what became the famous Abbey Theater; he wrote plays for it and for about seven years was its manager. In 1917, at the age of 52, he married Georgie Hyde-Lees, who shared his interest in the occult and had psychic gifts of her own. They had two children. From 1922 to 1928 Yeats was a senator of the Irish Free State; in 1923 he was awarded the Nobel Prize. Other biographical details are given in notes to individual poems.

The Lamentation of the Old Pensioner

Although I shelter from the rain
Under a broken tree
My chair was nearest to the fire
In every company
That talked of love or politics,   5
Ere Time transfigured me.

Though lads are making pikes again
For some conspiracy,
And crazy rascals rage their fill
At human tyranny,   10
My contemplations are of Time
That has transfigured me.

There's not a woman turns her face
Upon a broken tree,
And yet the beauties that I loved   15
Are in my memory;
I spit into the face of Time
That has transfigured me.

1890–1925. *The Rose*, 1893 (as "The Old Pensioner"). Revised—indeed rewritten—in 1925.

7 **pikes:** weapons consisting of a pointed steel head on a long wooden shaft—predecessors of the bayonet

Paudeen

Indignant at the fumbling wits, the obscure spite
Of our old Paudeen in his shop, I stumbled blind
Among the stones and thorn-trees, under morning light;
Until a curlew cried and in the luminous wind
A curlew answered; and suddenly thereupon I thought
That on the lonely height where all are in God's eye,
There cannot be, confusion of our sound forgot,
A single soul that lacks a sweet crystalline cry.

1913. *Poems Written in Discouragement*, 1913.

Paudeen is the typical Irish shopkeeper, of limited intelligence and limited cultural interests, who would have opposed (without quite knowing why) the artistic endeavors of Lady Gregory and her nephew. In his autobiographical reminiscences in "The Stirring of the Bones" Yeats describes a dream from which he woke to hear a voice saying, "The love of God is infinite for every human soul because every human soul is unique, no other can satisfy the same need in God."

4 **curlew:** a long-billed bird related to the woodcock

September 1913

What need you, being come to sense,
But fumble in a greasy till
And add the halfpence to the pence
And prayer to shivering prayer, until
You have dried the marrow from the bone?   5
For men were born to pray and save:
Romantic Ireland's dead and gone,
It's with O'Leary in the grave.

Yet they were of a different kind,
The names that stilled your childish play,   10
They have gone about the world like wind,
But little time had they to pray
For whom the hangman's rope was spun,
And what, God help us, could they save?
Romantic Ireland's dead and gone,   15
It's with O'Leary in the grave.

Was it for this the wild geese spread
The grey wing upon every tide;
For this that all that blood was shed,
For this Edward Fitzgerald died,   20
And Robert Emmet and Wolfe Tone,

1913. *Responsibilities*, 1914.

Sir Hugh Lane, the nephew of Yeats's friend Lady Gregory, had offered to give his valuable collection of French paintings (by Corot, Manet, Monet, Degas, Renoir, and others) to the city of Dublin provided it would build a suitable gallery for them. Yeats was angered not so much by the city's refusal to spend the money as by the publicity campaign that derided the paintings as the work of cranks and faddists.

1 **you:** the people of Ireland—especially the middle class, which Yeats sees as money-grubbing and hysterically religious 8 **O'Leary:** John O'Leary (1830–1907), Irish leader, imprisoned and exiled for a total of 20 years 17 **the wild geese:** Irishmen who served in the armies of France, Spain, and Austria, especially between 1690 and 1730 20 **Edward Fitzgerald:** Lord Edward Fitzgerald (1763–1798), romantic Irish leader who died of wounds suffered while being arrested 21 **Robert Emmet:** Born in 1778, Emmet was executed in 1803 after leading an unsuccessful revolt. **Wolfe Tone:** Theobald Wolfe Tone (1763–1798) was captured and condemned after leading a French force to Ireland. It is said he committed suicide in prison.

All that delirium of the brave?
Romantic Ireland's dead and gone,
It's with O'Leary in the grave.

Yet could we turn the years again,   25
And call those exiles as they were
In all their loneliness and pain,
You'd cry, 'Some woman's yellow hair
Has maddened every mother's son':
They weighed so lightly what they gave.   30
But let them be, they're dead and gone,
They're with O'Leary in the grave.

The Fisherman

Although I can see him still,
The freckled man who goes
To a grey place on a hill
In grey Connemara clothes
At dawn to cast his flies,   5
It's long since I began
To call up to the eyes
This wise and simple man.
All day I'd looked in the face
What I had hoped 'twould be   10
To write for my own race
And the reality;
The living men that I hate,
The dead man that I loved,
The craven man in his seat,   15
The insolent unreproved,
And no knave brought to book
Who has won a drunken cheer,
The witty man and his joke
Aimed at the commonest ear,   20
The clever man who cries
The catch-cries of the clown,
The beating down of the wise
And great Art beaten down.

Maybe a twelvemonth since   25
Suddenly I began,
In scorn of this audience,
Imagining a man,
And his sun-freckled face,
And grey Connemara cloth,   30
Climbing up to a place

1914. *The Wild Swans at Coole,* 1919.

1 **him:** This "wise and simple" outdoor man is the ideal reader Yeats imagines instead of the corrupt, vulgar, and cowardly audience of lines 15–24.   4 **Connemara clothes:** of homespun tweed from Connemara, in County Galway (western Ireland)   14 **dead man:** probably John Millington Synge (1871–1909), the Irish poet and dramatist whose *The Playboy of the Western World* (1907) caused rioting in the theater in Ireland (and in America) because it was thought to show the Irish character in an unflattering light   15 **craven man:** Yeats no doubt had individuals in mind in this line and those that follow, but their identities are neither certain nor essential to the tone of the poem.   17 **brought to book:** called to account for his actions   22 **catch-cries:** catchwords, catchy slogans repeated with little regard for their meaning   24 **great Art:** Cf. notes on "September 1913."

Where stone is dark under froth,
And the down-turn of his wrist
When the flies drop in the stream;
A man who does not exist,   35
A man who is but a dream;
And cried, "Before I am old
I shall have written him one
Poem maybe as cold
And passionate as the dawn."   40

Easter 1916

I have met them at close of day
Coming with vivid faces
From counter or desk among grey
Eighteenth-century houses.
I have passed with a nod of the head   5
Or polite meaningless words,
Or have lingered awhile and said
Polite meaningless words,
And thought before I had done
Of a mocking tale or a gibe   10
To please a companion
Around the fire at the club,
Being certain that they and I
But lived where motley is worn:
All changed, changed utterly: 15
A terrible beauty is born.

That woman's days were spent
In ignorant good-will,
Her nights in argument
Until her voice grew shrill.   20
What voice more sweet than hers
When, young and beautiful,
She rode to harriers?

1916. *Michael Robartes and the Dancer*, 1921.

This poem is a kind of *palinode* (a poem—or ode—which retracts the sentiments expressed in an earlier poem) to "September 1913," in which Yeats had denied the possibility of romantic heroism in the Ireland of that time. But in Easter week of 1916 the old courage—as he saw it—came to life when patriotic organizations in Dublin, numbering about 1500 men, took over the post office and other buildings and proclaimed the freedom and independence of Ireland. The insurgents, however, had small support from the people of Dublin, who regarded them, at first, as not much better than a destructive nuisance; their rifles were of little avail against British cannon; and they were soon greatly outnumbered by the trained British forces. After nearly a week of heroic but hopeless resistance (during which fires did millions of dollars worth of damage to the city), they were forced to surrender. Fifteen of the leaders were court-martialled and executed between May 3 and May 12. As the executions continued, the victims got more and more sympathy from the nation, whose earlier indifference and even mockery turned to pride in the courage of their martyred countrymen. Yet many of the Irish remained of two minds about the rebellion, as Yeats does in this poem: the heroism certainly had its beauty, but was the beauty "terrible" in that it was wasteful of life and politically unnecessary?

1 **them:** those who planned and took part in the rebellion   14 **motley:** clothes made of mixed colors; the costume of a fool   17 **that woman:** Constance Gore-Booth (1868–1927), whom Yeats had known as a beautiful girl famous for her daring as a horsewoman. Her interest in art had taken her to Paris, against the wishes of her aristocratic family; there she had met and married the Polish Count Casimir Markievicz. Returning to Ireland, she had become involved in anti-British activities. She was sentenced to death for her part in the rising, but the sentence was commuted.   23 **harriers:** a pack of hunting dogs; hunting parties

This man had kept a school
And rode our wingèd horse;   25
This other his helper and friend
Was coming into his force;
He might have won fame in the end,
So sensitive his nature seemed,
So daring and sweet his thought.   30
This other man I had dreamed
A drunken, vainglorious lout.
He had done most bitter wrong
To some who are near my heart,
Yet I number him in the song;   35
He, too, has resigned his part
In the casual comedy;
He, too, has been changed in his turn,
Transformed utterly:
A terrible beauty is born.   40

Hearts with one purpose alone
Through summer and winter seem
Enchanted to a stone
To trouble the living stream.
The horse that comes from the road,   45
The rider, the birds that range
From cloud to tumbling cloud,
Minute by minute they change;
A shadow of cloud on the stream
Changes minute by minute;   50
A horse-hoof slides on the brim,
And a horse plashes within it;
The long-legged moor-hens dive,
And hens to moor-cocks call;
Minute by minute they live: 55
The stone's in the midst of all.

Too long a sacrifice
Can make a stone of the heart.
O when may it suffice?
That is Heaven's part, our part   60
To murmur name upon name,
As a mother names her child
When sleep at last has come
On limbs that had run wild.
What is it but nightfall?   65
No, no, not night but death;
Was it needless death after all?

---

24 **this man:** Patrick Pearse (1879–1916), lawyer by training, had become a teacher in the boys' school he founded. He was known too as a poet in both English and Gaelic (the "wingèd horse" is Pegasus, the symbolic steed of poetic inspiration). Pearse commanded the insurgent forces in Dublin.   26 **this other:** Thomas MacDonagh (1878–1916), dramatist, poet, and critic, was on the faculty of University College, Dublin.   31 **this other man:** Major John MacBride (d. 1916) had made an unhappy marriage with Maud Gonne, Yeats's long-time love, in 1903; they had separated in 1905. MacBride, who had not been in on the plans for the rising, just happened to be in Dublin at the time, and willingly joined in against the British, whom he had fought against in Africa during the Boer War.   41–56 Yeats's uncertainty about the rightness and wisdom of the rising comes out in the imagery, if not directly in the statements, in this section: rigid devotion to any cause seems against the flow and fluency of nature, in which to live is to change. Were the heroes, he seems to wonder, only fanatics?   52 **plashes:** splashes   53–54 **moor-hens ... moor-cocks:** wading birds of the rail family—rather like small cranes

For England may keep faith
For all that is done and said.
We know their dream; enough   70
To know they dreamed and are dead;
And what if excess of love
Bewildered them till they died?
I write it out in a verse—
MacDonagh and MacBride   75
And Connolly and Pearse
Now and in time to be,
Wherever green is worn,
Are changed, changed utterly:
A terrible beauty is born.   80

68 **England may keep faith . . . :** Proposals for Home Rule for Ireland had been finding favor in England, but were postponed with the outbreak of World War I.   76 **Connolly:** James Connolly (1870–1916), a trade-union organizer and leader in the rebellion   78 **green:** symbolic of Ireland, the "Emerald Isle." A popular ballad is called "The Wearing of the Green."

The Cold Heaven

Suddenly I saw the cold and rook-delighting heaven
That seemed as though ice burned and was but the more ice,
And thereupon imagination and heart were driven
So wild that every casual thought of that and this
Vanished, and left but memories, that should be out of season   5
With the hot blood of youth, of love crossed long ago;
And I took all the blame out of all sense and reason,
Until I cried and trembled and rocked to and fro,
Riddled with light. Ah! when the ghost begins to quicken,
Confusion of the death-bed over, is it sent   10
Out naked on the roads, as the books say, and stricken
By the injustice of the skies for punishment?

The Green Helmet and Other Poems, 1912.

A bleakly brilliant winter sky reminds the poet, in a moment of piercing insight and self-accusation, of the troubles and errors of long ago—and especially of his long unhappy love.

1 **rook:** a European bird like the crow   11 **the books:** It is not clear exactly what books about the afterlife Yeats had in mind. Dante, the apocryphal book of Enoch, and others have been suggested.

The Magi

Now as at all times I can see in the mind's eye,
In their stiff, painted clothes, the pale unsatisfied ones
Appear and disappear in the blue depth of the sky
With all their ancient faces like rain-beaten stones,
And all their helms of silver hovering side by side,
And all their eyes still fixed, hoping to find once more,
Being by Calvary's turbulence unsatisfied,
The uncontrollable mystery on the bestial floor.

1913. *Responsibilities,* 1914.

See Additional Notes (p. 766).

The Second Coming

Turning and turning in the widening gyre
The falcon cannot hear the falconer;
Things fall apart; the centre cannot hold;
Mere anarchy is loosed upon the world,
The blood-dimmed tide is loosed, and everywhere   5
The ceremony of innocence is drowned;
The best lack all conviction, while the worst
Are full of passionate intensity.

Surely some revelation is at hand;
Surely the Second Coming is at hand.   10
The Second Coming! Hardly are those words out
When a vast image out of *Spiritus Mundi*
Troubles my sight: somewhere in sands of the desert
A shape with lion body and the head of a man,
A gaze blank and pitiless as the sun,   15
Is moving its slow thighs, while all about it
Reel shadows of the indignant desert birds.
The darkness drops again; but now I know
That twenty centuries of stony sleep
Were vexed to nightmare by a rocking cradle,   20
And what rough beast, its hour come round at last,
Slouches towards Bethlehem to be born?

1919. *Michael Robartes and the Dancer*, 1921.

See Additional Notes (p. 766).

Second Coming: In Matt. 24, Christ predicts "the coming of the Son of man" after a time of great tribulation, widespread warfare, and natural disasters. Yeats believed that about every 2000 years the trend of history reversed itself (cf. notes to "The Magi") and a new age began. As the birth of Christ began the 2000-year period now ending, so a new incarnation, that of the "rough beast" who is Christ's opposite, is due to appear as the twentieth century draws to a close.   **1 gyre:** spiral, vortex. Here the image is that of a falcon leaving the falconer's wrist and soaring upward in ever widening circles, which finally become so wide that the falconer's control is lost. (Some think the falcon is Christ; the falcon, man.) Yeats uses the image of the gyre to represent a historical cycle, which begins with a point of intensity (like that of an inverted cone) and as it develops spreads farther and farther from the center that gives it its character. Yeats could have said that our Christian era of 2000 years got less and less Christlike, until now it has almost reached an extreme of diffusion and will come to an end as the reverse process, symbolized by the "rough beast," is about to begin. (Though it is not referred to in this poem, Yeats also visualized a reversed cone interpenetrating the inverted one and symbolizing its opposite; when the first reaches its point of greatest diffusion, the inner one will (as it were—these are only images) be activated at its fine point and begin a downward spiral that reverses, unwinds, undoes the course of the first.

4-6 mere anarchy . . . : Yeats saw ample signs of the destructiveness of our age in the numerous wars and atrocities of the twentieth century—in what he called "the growing murderousness of the world."   **12 *Spiritus Mundi:*** "The Spirit of the World," which Yeats also called "Anima Mundi" (Soul of the World), is a kind of psychic pool of inherited images (like Jung's archetypal images) in which all human minds share and from which they can draw.   **14 a shape:** Many sources in art and literature have been suggested for the sphynxlike nightmare creature slowly stirring to life and preparing to take over the world.   **19 twenty centuries:** the historical cycle—through Babylon, Egypt, Greece, etc.—preceding the birth of Christ, the infant whose "rocking cradle" would bring cataclysmic changes to the world   **22 Bethlehem:** as the birthplace of Christ, especially appropriate (and ironic) for his successor's birthplace

A Prayer for My Daughter

Once more the storm is howling, and half hid
Under this cradle-hood and coverlid
My child sleeps on. There is no obstacle
But Gregory's wood and one bare hill
Whereby the haystack- and roof-levelling wind,   5
Bred on the Atlantic, can be stayed;
And for an hour I have walked and prayed
Because of the great gloom that is in my mind.

I have walked and prayed for this young child an hour
And heard the sea-wind scream upon the tower,   10
And under the arches of the bridge, and scream
In the elms above the flooded stream;
Imagining in excited reverie
That the future years had come,
Dancing to a frenzied drum,   15
Out of the murderous innocence of the sea.

May she be granted beauty and yet not
Beauty to make a stranger's eye distraught,
Or hers before a looking-glass, for such,
Being made beautiful overmuch,   20
Consider beauty a sufficient end,
Lose natural kindness and maybe
The heart-revealing intimacy
That chooses right, and never find a friend.

Helen being chosen found life flat and dull   25
And later had much trouble from a fool,
While that great Queen, that rose out of the spray,
Being fatherless could have her way
Yet chose a bandy-leggèd smith for man.
It's certain that fine women eat   30
A crazy salad with their meat
Whereby the Horn of Plenty is undone.

In courtesy I'd have her chiefly learned;
Hearts are not had as a gift but hearts are earned
By those that are not entirely beautiful;   35
Yet many, that have played the fool
For beauty's very self, has charm made wise,
And many a poor man that has roved,

1919. Ibid.

In 1917 Yeats married Georgie Hyde-Lees; the same year he bought an ancient ruined "castle"—a
square tower with attached cottages—at Ballylee, near Lady Gregory's estate. The tower, which for
Yeats became symbolic of the lonely search for wisdom, is the setting of the present poem. His daugh-
ter, Anne Butler Yeats, was born early in 1919.

25 **Helen:** Helen of Troy, whose great beauty brought her "trouble from a fool"—perhaps her hus-
band Menelaus, perhaps Paris, who took her off to Troy.   27 **Queen:** Aphrodite, goddess of love and
beauty, was born of the sea-foam. She married the crippled Hephaestus, god of fire and hence a
"smith"—the only ugly god.   32 **the Horn of Plenty:** a translation of *cornucopiæ* (Latin), the horn of
plenty, overflowing with whatever food or drink one wanted. In one version of the myth, Jupiter
broke it from the goat Amalthea, which had nursed him. Here it stands for abundance, prosperity,
etc.   36-40 probably a reference to Yeats's long unhappy love for the glamorous Maud Gonne and
his subsequent marriage to a woman who had "charm" and "kindness"

Loved and thought himself beloved,
From a glad kindness cannot take his eyes.   40

May she become a flourishing hidden tree
That all her thoughts may like the linnet be,
And have no business but dispensing round
Their magnanimities of sound,
Nor but in merriment begin a chase,   45
Nor but in merriment a quarrel.
O may she live like some green laurel
Rooted in one dear perpetual place.

My mind, because the minds that I have loved,
The sort of beauty that I have approved,   50
Prosper but little, has dried up of late,
Yet knows that to be choked with hate
May well be of all evil chances chief.
If there's no hatred in a mind
Assault and battery of the wind   55
Can never tear the linnet from the leaf.

An intellectual hatred is the worst,
So let her think opinions are accursed.
Have I not seen the loveliest woman born
Out of the mouth of Plenty's horn,   60
Because of her opinionated mind
Barter that horn and every good
By quiet natures understood
For an old bellows full of angry wind?

Considering that, all hatred driven hence,   65
The soul recovers radical innocence
And learns at last that it is self-delighting,
Self-appeasing, self-affrighting,
And that its own sweet will is Heaven's will;
She can, though every face should scowl   70
And every windy quarter howl
Or every bellows burst, be happy still.

And may her bridegroom bring her to a house
Where all's accustomed, ceremonious;
For arrogance and hatred are the wares   75
Peddled in the thoroughfares.
How but in custom and in ceremony
Are innocence and beauty born?
Ceremony's a name for the rich horn,
And custom for the spreading laurel tree.   80

42 linnet: an Old World songbird of the finch family   **59 loveliest woman born:** again, Maud
Gonne, who (Yeats believed) destroyed her loveliness by becoming a political agitator   **79 the rich
horn:** Cf. line 32.   **80 laurel tree:** Cf. line 47. The laurel is a symbol of triumph and also, as sacred to
Apollo, of poetry and the arts.

Leda and the Swan

A sudden blow: the great wings beating still
Above the staggering girl, her thighs caressed
By the dark webs, her nape caught in his bill,
He holds her helpless breast upon his breast.

How can those terrified vague fingers push   5
The feathered glory from her loosening thighs?
And how can body, laid in that white rush,
But feel the strange heart beating where it lies?

A shudder in the loins engenders there
The broken wall, the burning roof and tower   10
And Agamemnon dead.
                    Being so caught up,
So mastered by the brute blood of the air,
Did she put on his knowledge with his power
Before the indifferent beak could let her drop?

1923. *The Cat and the Moon and Certain Poems,* 1924.

Leda, wife of the King of Sparta, was the mother of Helen of Troy, Castor and Pollux, and Clytemnestra. Of the children, Helen (and possibly one of the brothers; versions vary) was born in an egg. Her father had been Zeus in the form of a swan—one of the many such disguises assumed by the wily Zeus when attracted by a beautiful mortal. In his scheme of historical periods, Yeats saw this union of heaven and earth, of bird and human being, as a sort of "annunciation" for the 2000-year period before the Christian era. He began the poem as a political one: he thought the times so barren and effete that only a new "birth from above" could redeem them. "My fancy began to play with Leda and the Swan for metaphor ... but as I wrote, bird and lady took such possession of the scene that all politics went out of it, and my friend [the editor who asked for the poem] tells me that 'his conservative readers would misunderstand the poem.'" (*The Cat and the Moon and Certain Poems,* 1924.)

10–11 **broken wall ... dead:** images of disaster evoking the Trojan War and its aftermath, all consequences of the conception and birth of Helen. Agamemnon, Helen's brother-in-law and commander of the Greek forces at Troy, was murdered by her sister Clytemnestra after the war.

Sailing to Byzantium

I

That is no country for old men. The young
In one another's arms, birds in the trees
—Those dying generations—at their song,
The salmon-falls, the mackerel-crowded seas,
Fish, flesh, or fowl, commend all summer long   5
Whatever is begotten, born, and dies.
Caught in that sensual music all neglect
Monuments of unageing intellect.

1926. *October Blast,* 1927. *The Tower,* 1928.

See Additional Notes (p. 766). In a talk prepared for a BBC broadcast in 1931, Yeats wrote: "Now I am trying to write about the state of my soul, for it is right for an old man to make his soul, and some of my thoughts upon that subject I have put into a poem called 'Sailing to Byzantium.' ... Byzantium was the center of European civilization and the source of its spiritual philosophy, so I symbolize the search for spiritual life by a journey to that city."

1 **that:** Ireland—though it might be anywhere   **old men. The young ... :** The juxtaposition *old-young* suggests the basic polarity of the poem: between youth caught in the sensual music of the lovely but corruptible body and its physical world, and old age which may rejoice in the vigor of an enduring soul nourished with thoughts of man's spiritual magnificence as seen in the monuments of art—a contrast brought home to Yeats in old age by his growing awareness of a body failing and a mind brilliant and alive as ever.

II

An aged man is but a paltry thing,
A tattered coat upon a stick, unless   10
Soul clap its hands and sing, and louder sing
For every tatter in its mortal dress,
Nor is there singing school but studying
Monuments of its own magnificence;
And therefore I have sailed the seas and come   15
To the holy city of Byzantium.

III

O sages standing in God's holy fire
As in the gold mosaic of a wall,
Come from the holy fire, perne in a gyre,
And be the singing-masters of my soul.   20
Consume my heart away; sick with desire
And fastened to a dying animal
It knows not what it is; and gather me
Into the artifice of eternity.

IV

Once out of nature I shall never take   25
My bodily form from any natural thing,
But such a form as Grecian goldsmiths make
Of hammered gold and gold enamelling
To keep a drowsy Emperor awake;
Or set upon a golden bough to sing   30
To lords and ladies of Byzantium
Of what is past, or passing, or to come.

11 **Soul clap its hands:** In his Introduction to *The Works of William Blake* (1893), Yeats tells how Blake, when his brother Robert died in 1787, "had seen his brother's spirit ascending clapping its hands for joy. . . ."   17 **sages:** wise saints   **God's holy fire:** perhaps the "refining fire" ("foco che li affina") in which souls are purified in Dante, *Purgatorio* XXVI. But since these sages seem beyond Purgatory, the fire may stand for the brilliance and intensity of God's love. *Fire* is suggested by the "gold mosaic" of the following line. Byzantine mosaics, which Yeats had seen at Ravenna in Italy and Palermo in Sicily, usually show the holy figures against a background of brilliant gold-leaf tiles, tilted askew to catch the light, so that they seem indeed bathed in golden fire.   19 **perne:** "When I was a child at Sligo I could see above my grandfather's trees a little column of smoke from 'the pern-mill,' and was told that 'pern' was another name for the spool, as I was accustomed to call it, on which thread was wound" [Yeats's note]. Here Yeats is using the word as a verb: to spin, to wind (like thread). *Pirn* is the common spelling.   **gyre:** Cf. the notes to "The Second Coming."   24 **the artifice of eternity:** eternity as God's great work of art.   27–29 **such a form . . . :** a product of art, of soul and intellect, which (compared with flesh) is enduring. The mode is only *such . . . as*—of course Yeats does not mean he would like to be some dinky jeweler's gimmick in the next world—or even a museum piece by Fabergé. What he wants is permanence, the timelessness of "what is past, or passing, or to come" instead of the transience of "whatever is begotten, born, and dies." "I have read somewhere that in the Emperor's palace at Byzantium was a tree made of gold and silver, and artificial birds that sang" [Yeats's note]. It has been suggested that he may be remembering his childhood reading of Hans Christian Andersen's "The Emperor's Nightingale," although the mechanical bird in that fairy tale is a poorer singer than a real bird.

Among School Children

I

I walk through the long schoolroom questioning;
A kind old nun in a white hood replies;

1926. *The Tower*, 1928.

In 1922 Yeats was chosen a senator of the Irish Free State. In 1926, as part of his official duties, he made a tour of inspection through a number of grammar schools. A school in Waterford based on the Montessori system, which stressed neatness, suggested the beginning of this poem. Back at home after the tour he jotted down a "topic for poem": "School children and the thought that life will waste

The children learn to cipher and to sing,
To study reading-books and history,
To cut and sew, be neat in everything   5
In the best modern way—the children's eyes
In momentary wonder stare upon
A sixty-year-old smiling public man.

II

I dream of a Ledaean body, bent
Above a sinking fire, a tale that she   10
Told of a harsh reproof, or trivial event
That changed some childish day to tragedy—
Told, and it seemed that our two natures blent
Into a sphere from youthful sympathy,
Or else, to alter Plato's parable,   15
Into the yolk and white of the one shell.

III

And thinking of that fit of grief or rage
I look upon one child or t'other there
And wonder if she stood so at that age—
For even daughters of the swan can share   20
Something of every paddler's heritage—
And had that colour upon cheek or hair,
And thereupon my heart is driven wild:
She stands before me as a living child.

IV

Her present image floats into the mind—   25
Did Quattrocento finger fashion it
Hollow of cheek as though it drank the wind
And took a mess of shadows for its meat?
And I though never of Ledaean kind
Had pretty plumage once—enough of that,   30
Better to smile on all that smile, and show
There is a comfortable kind of old scarecrow.

---

them—perhaps that no possible life can fulfill our dreams or even their teacher's hope. Bring in the old thought that life prepares for what never happens." But the poem developed further in the writing. In stanzas II and III it turns into a love poem (Yeats said of his later poems that, no matter what the topic, they turned into love poems). Then, as he thinks what happens to the bodies we love in this physical world (cf. "Sailing to Byzantium" and "The Tower"), he reflects on the nature of reality itself and on time and eternity. A routine schoolroom visit that projects him beyond outer space.

3 **cipher:** do arithmetic   9 **Ledaean:** like that of Helen, Leda's daughter, who as usual stands for Maud Gonne. The schoolroom and the schoolgirls remind him how she once told him about some unpleasant experience she had suffered in the schoolroom.   14 **a sphere:** a symbol of unity, of perfection or fullness of being   15 **Plato's parable:** In the *Symposium* (189-193) Aristophanes gives a comic account of the origin of love among men and women: once the two sexes were united in one body, which was round, had four arms and legs, and moved about rapidly by rolling. Since it was powerful and dangerous—like an army tank—the gods were worried about the threat it presented. So each was cut in two "as you might divide an egg with a hair." Each half was unhappy and has ever since been seeking its missing half—and such is the origin of love. If we continue to offend the gods, Aristophanes warns, they will again bisect us and we will hop around on one leg.   19 **she:** the woman he loved   20 **daughters of the swan:** girls so beautiful their parentage seems divine (cf. "Leda and the Swan")   21 **every paddler:** an ordinary duck   25 **her present image:** the way she looks now at the age of 60   26 **Quattrocento:** the 1400s in Italy, a century of great art, with such painters as da Vinci, Mantegna, Fra Lippo Lippi, Botticelli and such sculptors as Donatello, Verrocchio, and Desiderio da Settignano (An earlier version had "Da Vinci' finger.")   28 **mess:** serving, helping   29 **Ledaean:** Leda had also two handsome sons, Castor and Pollux.   30 **pretty plumage:** a head of raven-black hair

V

What youthful mother, a shape upon her lap
Honey of generation had betrayed,
And that must sleep, shriek, struggle to escape   35
As recollection or the drug decide,
Would think her son, did she but see that shape
With sixty or more winters on its head,
A compensation for the pang of his birth,
Or the uncertainty of his setting forth?   40

VI

Plato thought nature but a spume that plays
Upon a ghostly paradigm of things;
Solider Aristotle played the taws
Upon the bottom of a king of kings;
World-famous golden-thighed Pythagoras   45
Fingered upon a fiddle-stick or strings
What a star sang and careless Muses heard:
Old clothes upon old sticks to scare a bird.

VII

Both nuns and mothers worship images,
But those the candles light are not as those   50
That animate a mother's reveries,
But keep a marble or a bronze repose.
And yet they too break hearts—O Presences
That passion, piety or affection knows,
And that all heavenly glory symbolise—   55
O self-born mockers of man's enterprise;

VIII

Labour is blossoming or dancing where
The body is not bruised to pleasure soul,
Nor beauty born out of its own despair,
Nor blear-eyed wisdom out of midnight oil.   60
O chestnut-tree, great-rooted blossomer,
Are you the leaf, the blossom or the bole?
O body swayed to music, O brightening glance,
How can we know the dancer from the dance?

---

34 **honey of generation:** Yeats is adapting an image he found in the work of Porphyry, the Neo-Platonic philosopher of the third century A.D., who relates the sweetness of honey to the pleasure of generating. But in Yeats the honey is a drug that dulls the memory of our happy prenatal existence—without it we would never consent to be born into this world, but instead would "struggle to escape" (as babies seem to do).   41–42 **Plato:** (427?–347 B.C.) thought the natural world we see was only an imitation of the true reality, only a kind of froth (spume) on the spiritual framework (ghostly paradigm) of that reality.   43 **solider Aristotle:** "solider" because he (384–322 B.C.) took the physical world more seriously and based his investigations on it   **taws:** a schoolmaster's leather strap, for punishment (Aristotle was the tutor of the boy who was to become Alexander the Great.)   45 **Pythagoras:** Greek thinker of the sixth century B.C. who believed that all things were number, was interested in music, geometry, arithmetic, astronomy—and moral purity and perfection. From fingering on strings he discovered the ratios between length of string and the musical intervals—so that music too was number. Many legends grew up about him: that he had a golden bone in his hip or thigh, that he could hear the music of the spheres, etc.   48 **Old clothes . . . :** The line applies to Plato, Aristotle, Pythagoras, "even the greatest men," which (physically) are no better than scarecrows—said Yeats—by the time they become famous. He called the poem in part a "curse on old age."   49–64 See Additional Notes (p. 767).

A Last Confession

What lively lad most pleasured me
Of all that with me lay?
I answer that I gave my soul
And loved in misery,
But had great pleasure with a lad   5
That I loved bodily.

Flinging from his arms I laughed
To think his passion such
He fancied that I gave a soul
Did but our bodies touch,   10
And laughed upon his breast to think
Beast gave beast as much.

I gave what other women gave
That stepped out of their clothes,
But when this soul, its body off,   15
Naked to naked goes,
He it has found shall find therein
What none other knows,

And give his own and take his own
And rule in his own right;   20
And though it loved in misery
Close and cling so tight,
There's not a bird of day that dare
Extinguish that delight.

1926. *The Winding Stair*, 1929.

From a series called "A Woman Old and Young." The speaker is an old woman, looking back on a lifetime of amorous experience—and looking forward to the experience of eternity.

23 bird of day: as the song of the lark, "the herald of the morn," separates the lovers after their night together in *Romeo and Juliet*, III, v

Two Songs from a Play

I

I saw a staring virgin stand
Where holy Dionysus died,
And tear the heart out of his side,
And lay the heart upon her hand
And bear that beating heart away;   5

1926–1931. *Stories of Michael Robartes and His Friends*, 1931.

See Additional Notes (p. 767).

1–5 In Sir James Frazer's famous *The Golden Bough*, which Yeats knew, Dionysius, god of wine and revelry, is one of the fertility gods (like Adonis, Osiris, and others) whose death and rebirth symbolize the natural cycle of the seasons. In one version of the myth he is lured into the woods in the absence of his father, Zeus, and there torn limb from limb by the giant Titans. His sister Athene (the "staring virgin" of line 1) snatches his heart away and gives it to Zeus on his return; from it Dionysius is reborn with the help of a mortal mother. **5 beating heart:** the phrase (for Yeats at least) relates Dionysius to Christ. In "The Resurrection" a rational Greek calls the figure of the risen Christ, "a phantom . . . no flesh and blood." But when he touches it he cries out, "The heart of a phantom is beating!" (In his introduction to the play, Yeats mentions a psychical investigator who once touched a ghost and felt a beating heart.)

And then did all the Muses sing
Of Magnus Annus at the spring,
As though God's death were but a play.

Another Troy must rise and set,
Another lineage feed the crow,   10
Another Argo's painted prow
Drive to a flashier bauble yet.
The Roman Empire stood appalled:
It dropped the reigns of peace and war
When that fierce virgin and her Star   15
Out of the fabulous darkness called.

II

In pity for man's darkening thought
He walked that room and issued thence
In Galilean turbulence;
The Babylonian starlight brought   20
A fabulous, formless darkness in;
Odour of blood when Christ was slain
Made all Platonic tolerance vain
And vain all Doric discipline.

6 **all the Muses:** all kinds of poetry, song, and dance   7 **Magnus Annus:** the period, also called the Platonic year, in which the constellations swing around and return to their original positions. Estimates range from Plato's 36,000 years to the 26,000 favored by Yeats, who thought of it as divided into 12 cycles of about 2000 years. The Muses are celebrating eternal recurrence. **the spring:** It was thought earth was created at the vernal equinox. In *A Vision* Yeats mentions that Caesar was killed on March 15, and he calls March "the month of victims and saviors." He thought of the key figures of this poem as dying and restored to life in March.   8 **a play:** The death and rebirth of a godlike figure is a ritual event that happens again and again in the cycles of the Great Year. (The death of Dionysius actually became a play acted out at Cretan festivals.)   9–12 Cf. Shelley's "Chorus" from *Hellas* (p. 315) and the notes to it. The source for Shelley and Yeats is Vergil's Fourth Eclogue, with its prophecy of a new Golden Age:

> . . . The great sequence of the centuries begins anew;
> Now the Virgin returns. . . . there will be another Argo that carries
> Chosen heroes; there will be other wars,
> And great Achilles will again be sent to Troy. . . .

By "the Virgin" Vergil means Astraea, goddess of Justice, who left the world when the Golden Age ended but will return when Justice returns again.   10 **feed the crow:** as corpses   13 **appalled:** at the birth of Christ, who was to overturn much that the Empire stood for—and finally the Empire itself 15 **virgin and her star:** (1) Athene, with the pulsing heart of Dionysius in her hand; (2) Astraea (Justice) whose name means *starry* in Greek, and who was thought to have become (3) the constellation Virgo, depicted as holding the first-magnitude star Spica in her hand, sometimes depicted as a baby; (4) the Virgin Mary and Christ, the Star of Bethlehem, who most directly appalled the Empire. Vergil's "virgin" was sometimes interpreted as foreshadowing Mary.   16 **fabulous darkness:** Cf. note on line 21.   17–18 **in pity . . . He:** "He" is Christ. In "The Resurrection" it is said "Nobody before him had so pitied human misery." And in *A Vision* Yeats mentions that it was Christ's pity for man's lot that made Christianity.   18 **walked that room:** In the play, Christ appears and enters the upper room where "the Eleven" (the Apostles minus Judas) are gathered.   19 **Galilean turbulence:** perhaps a turbulence like that of the Sea of Galilee, on whose stormy waters the New Testament reports that Christ walked, or perhaps just a turbulence whose source was near Galilee. The "turbulence" (cf. *turbo: gyre* or *vortex*) is because Christ was to reverse the spirit of a whole historical cycle and initiate, not without violence from others, a new one—an era more passionate, irrational, and disruptive of established values than that of Platonic tolerance and Dorian discipline was.   20–21 **Babylonian starlight . . . darkness:** The scientific spirit of the Babylonians, with their interest in mathematics and astronomy, led, in Yeats system, inevitably to their opposite: the spirit of Christianity, which was miraculous rather than factual. Christianity was called "a fabulous formless darkness" by Proclus, the pagan Neo-Platonic philosopher of the fifth century A.D.   22–24 **odour of blood . . . :** The shocking physical reality of Christ's death made untenable the abstract generalities of Plato, who "thinks all things into unity" (*A Vision*) and the orderliness of the Dorians, those settlers of southeastern Greece, including the region of Sparta, who were thought to be more vigorous, sober, and controlled than the other Greeks.

Everything that man esteems   25
Endures a moment or a day.
Love's pleasure drives his love away,
The painter's brush consumes his dreams;
The herald's cry, the soldier's tread
Exhaust his glory and his might: 30
Whatever flames upon the night
Man's own resinous heart has fed.

31–32 It has been noticed that the last two lines do not seem to follow the theme of historical cycles, but introduce a new theory of causality into the poem.

Byzantium

The unpurged images of day recede;
The Emperor's drunken soldiery are abed;
Night resonance recedes, night-walkers' song
After great cathedral gong;
A starlit or a moonlit dome disdains   5
All that man is,
All mere complexities,
The fury and the mire of human veins.

Before me floats an image, man or shade,
Shade more than man, more image than a shade;   10
For Hades' bobbin bound in mummy-cloth
May unwind the winding path;
A mouth that has no moisture and no breath
Breathless mouths may summon;
I hail the superhuman;   15
I call it death-in-life and life-in-death.

Miracle, bird or golden handiwork,
More miracle than bird or handiwork,
Planted on the star-lit golden bough,
Can like the cocks of Hades crow,   20
Or, by the moon embittered, scorn aloud

1930. *Words for Music Perhaps*, 1932.

For what Byzantium meant to Yeats, cf. the notes to "Sailing to Byzantium." In "Pages from a Diary Written in Nineteen Hundred and Thirty," he wrote, as "subject for a poem": "Describe Byzantium as it is in the system towards the end of the first Christian millennium. A walking mummy. Flames at the street corners where the soul is purified, birds of hammered gold singing in the golden trees, [dolphins?] in the harbor, offering their backs to the wailing dead that they may carry them to Paradise."

1–8 The stanza juxtaposes images of gross physical reality with the spirituality of the dome—no doubt the great church of St. Sophia in Byzantium. 10 **more image . . . :** The "shade" of a man—the "walking mummy"—is seen in imagination. 11 **Hades' bobbin:** a *bobbin* is a kind of elongated spool on which threads are wound for weaving. "Hades' bobbin" is the shade of the dead person wrapped not only as a mummy is, but also swathed in the long reel of its experiences and actions during life—which must now be unwound, undone, like a film reversed, in the afterlife. Cf. the imagery of spirals in "The Second Coming." 13–14 We, in moments of excitement, exaltation (as "breathless mouths"), may establish contact with the dead. Or, if "mouth" is the subject: through ascetic discipline we may be able to contact the dead. 16 **death-in-life . . . :** Cf. Coleridge, *The Ancient Mariner*, line 193. 17 **bird or golden handiwork:** Cf. "Sailing to Byzantium," last stanza. 20 **cocks of Hades:** In Yeats's story "The Adoration of the Magi," a crowing cock declares itself to be "Hermes the Shepherd of the Dead," who runs errands for the gods; its crowing at that time signifies that a woman in a deep sleep "has been driven out of Time and has lain upon the bosom of Eternity." Here the cocks of Hades mean something like a call to or sign of rebirth. 21 **by the moon embittered:** The moon, always changing, is itself the symbol of change.

In glory of changeless metal
Common bird or petal
And all complexities of mire or blood.

At midnight on the Emperor's pavement flit   25
Flames that no faggot feeds, nor steel has lit,
Nor storm disturbs, flames begotten of flame,
Where blood-begotten spirits come
And all complexities of fury leave,
Dying into a dance,   30
An agony of trance,
An agony of flame that cannot singe a sleeve.

Astraddle on the dolphin's mire and blood,
Spirit after spirit! The smithies break the flood,
The golden smithies of the Emperor!   35
Marbles of the dancing floor
Break bitter furies of complexity,
Those images that yet
Fresh images beget,
That dolphin-torn, that gong-tormented sea.   40

25 **the Emperor's pavement:** suggested by a description Yeats read of "The Pavement" or marble floor of the Forum of Constantine at Constantinople (Byzantium)   26 **flames:** the purgatorial flames in which the souls of the dead are purified. Cf. Yeats's note on "subject for a poem."   32 **agony of flame...:** When Dante and Vergil have to pass through the purifying fire of Purgatory (*Purgatorio*, XXVII), Dante, terrified, is assured that though the flames are painful they cannot destroy (or "singe") anything. He is told to test them with the edge of his garment.   33 **the dolphin's mire and blood:** their physical or fleshly nature, which nevertheless enables them to transport spirits into the afterlife. Yeats got from his reading the notion that dolphins (emblems of the soul) transported the dead to their destination. A. N. Jeffares, in his *A Commentary on the Collected Poems of W. B. Yeats*, quotes a cancelled MS. passage of Yeats: ". . . in one poem [this one] I have pictured the ghosts swimming, mounted upon dolphins, through the sensual seas, that they may dance upon its [Byzantium's] pavements."   34 **The smithies:** the places where artisans in metal would work (perhaps in "God's holy fire"?). They, like the "marbles of the dancing floor," represent the spirit's control of the furious, complex, sensuous world of mortality.   40 **gong-tormented:** Recall line 4.

The Gyres

The gyres! the gyres! Old Rocky Face, look forth;
Things thought too long can be no longer thought,
For beauty dies of beauty, worth of worth,
And ancient lineaments are blotted out.
Irrational streams of blood are staining earth;   5
Empedocles has thrown all things about;

1936–1937. *New Poems*, 1938.

See Additional Notes (p. 767).

1 **the gyres:** Cf. especially "The Second Coming."   **Old Rocky Face:** Several candidates for this synecdoche ("a part for the whole") have been suggested: the Delphic oracle, Yeats himself, and others. The most likely is Ahasuerus in Shelley's poetic drama "Hellas," a character based on the medieval legend of the Wandering Jew, condemned to live until the Second Coming because he had mocked Christ on his way to Calvary. In "Hellas" the old man, who dwells in a "sea-cavern," knows "strange and secret and forgotten things"; his eye pierces "the present, and the past, and the to-come" (cf. the last line of "Sailing to Byzantium"); he has survived "cycles of generation and of ruin" and sees "the birth of this old world through all its cycles."   5 **irrational streams of blood:** The beginning of every new age is likely to seem irrational, as the coming of Christ did, and to involve violence.   6 **Empedocles:** the Greek philosopher (c. 490–430 B.C.) who thought all things were made of combinations of earth, air, fire, and water, and that Love combined them and Strife tore them apart by turns

Hector is dead and there's a light in Troy;
We that look on but laugh in tragic joy.

What matter though numb nightmare ride on top,
And blood and mire the sensitive body stain?   10
What matter? Heave no sigh, let no tear drop,
A greater, a more gracious time has gone;
For painted forms or boxes of make-up
In ancient tombs I sighed, but not again;
What matter? Out of cavern comes a voice,   15
And all it knows is that one word 'Rejoice!'

Conduct and work grow coarse, and coarse the soul,
What matter? Those that Rocky Face holds dear,
Lovers of horses and of women, shall,
From marble of a broken sepulchre,   20
Or dark betwixt the polecat and the owl,
Or any rich, dark nothing disinter
The workman, noble and saint, and all things run
On that unfashionable gyre again.

7 **Hector:** the greatest of the Trojan heroes, killed by Achilles   **a light:** fire (perhaps too the beauty of Helen)   8 **tragic joy:** The oxymoron (or apparent contradiction) is typical of Yeats's later thought. Sometimes lugubrious in youth, he came to believe, as he grew old, in laughing at the worst life could do, not only out of defiance but out of a conviction that the best would come again.   9 **numb nightmare:** the terrors of the Irish Civil War, especially the savage fighting between Irish and British forces in 1919–1920, and other atrocities of the century (cf. "The Second Coming")   13 **painted forms ... boxes:** relics of ancient civilizations (like those found in King Tut's tomb, for instance)   17 Modern civilization is shoddy and produces shoddy goods, compared with certain great civilizations of the past.   19 **lovers of horses and of women:** representatives of an aristocratic and chivalrous culture   20 **sepulchre:** possibly Christ's tomb, as standing for the beginning of Christianity   21 **dark ... owl:** a vaguely ominous image. A polecat is a kind of European weasel (not the American skunk) Yeats had referred to elsewhere as a symbol of savagery; at Coole he had seen weasels fighting. The owl [for us generally a symbol of wisdom] suggests also what is eerie; as an Egyptian hieroglyph it stood for death and night. Polecat and owl are both associated with desolate and lonely places. Here they are sinister nocturnal presences that are emblems of a civilization soon to be replaced by a better one in which the craftsman, the nobleman (or noble man), and the saint—at present out of fashion—will again be held in honor.

Under Ben Bulben

I

Swear by what the sages spoke
Round the Mareotic Lake
That the Witch of Atlas knew,
Spoke and set the cocks a-crow.

Swear by those horsemen, by those women   5
Complexion and form prove superhuman,

1938. *Last Poems*, 1939.

The poem was finished in September 1938. When Yeats died the following January, it was published in three Irish newspapers within a week. Ben Bulben is the mountain in Sligo. Cf. "The Tower," line 9.

2 **Mareotic Lake:** near Alexandria and the Mediterranean, a center of early Christian monasticism in Egypt   3 **the Witch of Atlas:** a symbol of the beauty of knowledge and the poetic imagination in Shelley's poem named after her; she liked to sail, in her magic boat, by "the Mareotid lakes" (LVIII)   4 **set ... a-crow:** woke up the world   5 **horsemen ... women ...:** Yeats's uncle George Pollexfen had a servant gifted with second sight who had visions of women "fine and dashing-looking, like the men one sees riding their horses in twos and threes on the slopes of the mountains with their swords

That pale, long-visaged company
That air in immortality
Completeness of their passions won;
Now they ride the wintry dawn   10
Where Ben Bulben sets the scene.

Here's the gist of what they mean.

II

Many times man lives and dies
Between his two eternities,
That of race and that of soul,   15
And ancient Ireland knew it all.
Whether man die in his bed
Or the rifle knocks him dead,
A brief parting from those dear
Is the worst man has to fear.   20
Though grave-diggers' toil is long,
Sharp their spades, their muscles strong,
They but thrust their buried men
Back in the human mind again.

III

You that Mitchel's prayer have heard,   25
'Send war in our time, O Lord!'
Know that when all words are said
And a man is fighting mad,
Something drops from eyes long blind,
He completes his partial mind,   30
For an instant stands at ease,
Laughs aloud, his heart at peace.
Even the wisest man grows tense
With some sort of violence
Before he can accomplish fate,   35
Know his work or choose his mate.

IV

Poet and sculptor, do the work,
Nor let the modish painter shirk
What his great forefathers did,
Bring the soul of man to God,   40
Make him fill the cradles right.

Measurement began our might:
Forms a stark Egyptian thought,

---

swinging. There is no such race living now, none so finely proportioned...." Yeats had another friend who saw "a procession of women in what seemed the costume of another age...." And he himself had visions, he said, of such "forms of this incredible beauty" ("The Trembling of the Veil," Book III, v). Such visions substantiated, for Yeats, his conviction that "many times man lives and dies." **14 two eternities:** In a letter to a friend Yeats called them "that of his family and that of his soul"—one might call the first what is inherited in the blood. **25 Mitchel:** John Mitchel (1815–1875), Irish leader whose imprisonment was the basis of his *Jail Journal*, from which Yeats is quoting. **30 completes his partial mind:** Yeats believed we can complete our personality by assuming the characteristics of our opposite—what we least are. So a timid man finds his completeness and "peace" in being warlike. **41 fill the cradles right:** have the right kind of children **42 measurement:** Yeats believed that passion expressed itself best in precision, as in the mathematical proportions of Egyptian and Greek sculpture, rather than in the imprecisions of the "vague Asiatic norm."

Forms that gentler Phidias wrought.
Michael Angelo left a proof   45
On the Sistine Chapel roof,
Where but half-awakened Adam
Can disturb globe-trotting Madam
Till her bowels are in heat,
Proof that there's a purpose set   50
Before the secret working mind:
Profane perfection of mankind.

Quattrocento put in paint
On backgrounds for a God or Saint
Gardens where a soul's at ease;   55
Where everything that meets the eye,
Flowers and grass and cloudless sky,
Resemble forms that are or seem
When sleepers wake and yet still dream,
And when it's vanished still declare,   60
With only bed and bedstead there,
That heavens had opened.
                                Gyres run on;
When that greater dream had gone
Calvert and Wilson, Blake and Claude,
Prepared a rest for the people of God,   65
Palmer's phrase, but after that
Confusion fell upon our thought.

                        V
Irish poets, learn your trade,
Sing whatever is well made,
Scorn the sort now growing up   70
All out of shape from toe to top,
Their unremembering hearts and heads
Base-born products of base beds.
Sing the peasantry, and then
Hard-riding country gentlemen,   75
The holiness of monks, and after
Porter-drinkers' randy laughter;
Sing the lords and ladies gay
That were beaten into the clay
Through seven heroic centuries;   80
Cast your mind on other days
That we in coming days may be
Still the indomitable Irishry.

---

44 Phidias: the Greek sculptor of the fifth century B.C.   **45 Michael Angelo:** the Florentine sculptor (1475–1564). His famous fresco on the ceiling of the Sistine Chapel in the Vatican in Rome took four years to paint. One detail shows the creation of Adam, whose figure, though done with "measurement" (technical precision), is sexually exciting.   **52 profane:** of this world   **53 Quattrocento:** the 1400s and the painters that flourished then in Italy. Cf. "Among School Children," line 26. **62 Gyres:** Cf. "The Gyres" and footnote references there.   **64 that greater dream:** that of Quattrocento art   **64 Calvert:** Edward Calvert (1799–1883), English visionary artist   **Wilson:** Richard Wilson, to whom Yeats is probably referring, was a British landscape painter (1714–1782)   **Blake:** William Blake, English poet and artist   **Claude:** Claude Lorrain (1600–1682), French painter of dreamily idealized romantic landscapes   **66 Palmer:** Samuel Palmer (1805–1881), visionary English painter, disciple of Blake; he spoke of how saints, sages [and artists] have enjoyed a glimpse of "the rest which remains to the people of God."   **77 Porter:** a kind of dark beer   **randy:** loud, earthy, coarse

VI

Under bare Ben Bulben's head
In Drumcliff churchyard Yeats is laid.   85
An ancestor was rector there
Long years ago, a church stands near,
By the road an ancient cross.
No marble, no conventional phrase;
On limestone quarried near the spot   90
By his command these words are cut:

> Cast a cold eye
> On life, on death.
> Horseman, pass by!

85 **Drumcliff churchyard:** In a letter Yeats described it as "a little remote country churchyard in Sligo where my great grandfather was the clergyman a hundred years ago. . . ." Drumcliff is a village under the slopes of Ben Bulben. The ancestor was the Rev. John Yeats (1774–1846), rector there for the last 40 years of his life. He was a friend of Robert Emmet (cf. "September 1913") and briefly imprisoned for suspected involvement in Emmet's rebellion.   92 **cold:** Cf. the last two lines of "The Fisherman." *Cold* for Yeats meant precise, controlled, unsentimental; even what is passionate can be *cold* in this sense.   94 **horseman:** T. R. Henn (*The Lonely Tower*, pp. 319 ff.) reminds us that for the Irish the word has richer connotations than for most of us: of respect, awe, strength, mystery, the supernatural, aristocracy, recklessness.

Ernest Dowson
(1867–1900)

Dowson, interested in Latin and French poetry, had written verse from boyhood. His short life was sordid and troubled; alcohol and tuberculosis brought it to an early end. For years he suffered too from his hopeless love for "Missie." Just 12 when he met her, she rejected him when she was 18 to marry the waiter in her parents' restaurant.

Vitae Summa Brevis Spem Nos Vetat Incohare Longam

They are not long, the weeping and the laughter,
    Love and desire and hate:
I think they have no portion in us after
      We pass the gate.

They are not long, the days of wine and roses:
    Out of a misty dream
Our path emerges for a while, then closes
      Within a dream.

Verses, 1896.

The title (Horace, *Odes*, I, 4) means: The brief span of life forbids us to entertain hopes reaching far into the future.

Non Sum Qualis Eram Bonae sub Regno Cynarae

Last night, ah, yesternight, betwixt her lips and mine
There fell thy shadow, Cynara! thy breath was shed
Upon my soul between the kisses and the wine;
And I was desolate and sick of an old passion,
    Yea, I was desolate and bowed my head: 5
I have been faithful to thee, Cynara! in my fashion.

1891. Ibid.

The title (Horace, *Odes*, IV, 1) means: I am not what I was when kind Cynara was my queen.

All night upon mine heart I felt her warm heart beat,
Night-long within mine arms in love and sleep she lay;
Surely the kisses of her bought red mouth were sweet;
But I was desolate and sick of an old passion,   10
    When I awoke and found the dawn was gray:
I have been faithful to thee, Cynara! in my fashion.

I have forgot much, Cynara! gone with the wind,
Flung roses, roses riotously with the throng,
Dancing, to put thy pale, lost lilies out of mind;   15
But I was desolate and sick of an old passion,
    Yea, all the time, because the dance was long:
I have been faithful to thee, Cynara! in my fashion.

I cried for madder music and for stronger wine,
But when the feast is finished and the lamps expire,   20
Then falls thy shadow, Cynara! the night is thine;
And I am desolate and sick of an old passion,
    Yea hungry for the lips of my desire:
I have been faithful to thee, Cynara! in my fashion.

Edgar Lee Masters
(1869–1950)

Born in Garnett, Kansas, Masters went to Knox College for a year, passed the bar examination in Chicago, and began to practice law there. He had published several volumes of plays by 1911, but his great success came with *The Spoon River Anthology* (1915). This was followed by many books of poetry, fiction, biography, and autobiography.

Daisy Fraser

Did you ever hear of Editor Whedon
Giving to the public treasury any of the money he received
For supporting candidates for office?
Or for writing up the canning factory
To get people to invest?   5
Or for suppressing the facts about the bank,
When it was rotten and ready to break?
Did you ever hear of the Circuit Judge
Helping anyone except the "Q" railroad,
Or the bankers? Or did Rev. Peet or Rev. Sibley   10
Give any part of their salary, earned by keeping still,
Or speaking out as the leaders wished them to do,
To the building of the water works?
But I—Daisy Fraser who always passed
Along the streets through rows of nods and smiles,   15
And coughs and words such as "there she goes,"
Never was taken before Justice Arnett
Without contributing ten dollars and costs
To the school fund of Spoon River!

1914. *Spoon River Anthology*, 1915.

The poems of Masters that follow are from his *Spoon River Anthology* (1915). Influenced by the *Greek Anthology* (a collection of ancient Greek poems, written over many centuries, in which the dead sometimes reflect on their lives), the *Spoon River Anthology* contains 215 short interrelated poems in which the citizens of a small Illinois town are imagined as speaking from beyond the grave.

Dora Williams

When Reuben Pantier ran away and threw me
I went to Springfield.   There I met a lush,
Whose father just deceased left him a fortune.
He married me when drunk.   My life was wretched.
A year passed and one day they found him dead.   5
That made me rich.   I moved on to Chicago.
After a time met Tyler Rountree, villain.
I moved on to New York.   A gray-haired magnate
Went mad about me—so another fortune.
He died one night right in my arms, you know.   10
(I saw his purple face for years thereafter.)
There was almost a scandal.   I moved on,
This time to Paris.   I was now a woman,
Insidious, subtle, versed in the world and rich.
My sweet apartment near the Champs Élysées   15
Became a center for all sorts of people,
Musicians, poets, dandies, artists, nobles,
Where we spoke French and German, Italian, English.
I wed Count Navigato, native of Genoa.
We went to Rome.   He poisoned me, I think.   20
Now in the Campo Santo overlooking
The sea where young Columbus dreamed new worlds,
See what they chiseled: *"Contessa Navigato
Implora eterna quiete."*

1914. Ibid.

15 **Champs Élysées:** "Elysian Fields"—the part of the underworld where, in classical mythology, the blessed lived after their death; here the beautiful parklike avenue in Paris   19 **Genoa:** city on the Mediterranean in northern Italy, probable birthplace and boyhood home of Columbus   21 **Campo Santo:** "Holy Field," Italian name for a cemetery   23–24 The Italian words mean "Countess Navigato implores eternal rest."

Lucinda Matlock

I went to the dances at Chandlerville,
And played snap-out at Winchester.
One time we changed partners,
Driving home in the moonlight of middle June,
And then I found Davis.   5
We were married and lived together for seventy years,
Enjoying, working, raising the twelve children,
Eight of whom we lost
Ere I had reached the age of sixty.
I spun, I wove, I kept the house, I nursed the sick,   10
I made the garden, and for holiday
Rambled over the fields where sang the larks,
And by Spoon River gathering many a shell,
And many a flower and medicinal weed—
Shouting to the wooded hills, singing to the green valleys.   15
At ninety-six I had lived enough, that is all,

1914. Ibid.

Lucinda Matlock was Masters's grandmother.

1–2 **Chandlerville ... Winchester:** small towns near Springfield, Illinois   2 **snap-out:** a party game like drop-the-handkerchief

And passed to a sweet repose.
What is this I hear of sorrow and weariness,
Anger, discontent and drooping hopes?
Degenerate sons and daughters,   20
Life is too strong for you—
It takes life to love Life.

Anne Rutledge

Out of me unworthy and unknown
The vibrations of deathless music;
"With malice toward none, with charity for all."
Out of me the forgiveness of millions toward millions,
And the beneficent face of a nation   5
Shining with justice and truth.
I am Anne Rutledge who sleep beneath these weeds,
Beloved in life of Abraham Lincoln,
Wedded to him, not through union,
But through separation.   10
Bloom forever, O Republic,
From the dust of my bosom!

1914. Ibid.

Ann (as it was spelled) Rutledge was a historical character, a resident of New Salem, Illinois, on the
Sangamon River. There the young Abraham Lincoln, in his early twenties, became fond of her and
was saddened by her death in 1835 at the age of 19. Evidence for the great romance the poem implies
is mostly imaginary.

3 **"With malice . . ."**: from Lincoln's Second Inaugural Address, March 4, 1865

Edwin Arlington Robinson
(1869–1935)

Robinson, a descendant of Anne Bradstreet, grew up in Gardiner, Maine, the scene of
some of his poems. He could afford only two years at Harvard and for years had to strug-
gle to support himself. In 1905 President Theodore Roosevelt, who saw and liked some of
his early poems, got him a job as clerk in the Customs House in New York. After 1911 he
spent his summers at the MacDowell Colony in New Hampshire, founded by the widow
of the composer Edward MacDowell as a haven for composers, artists, and writers. With-
in a decade, his fight against poverty and obscurity had been won; his third Pulitzer win-
ner, *Tristram* (1927), was even a best seller.

Richard Cory

Whenever Richard Cory went down town,
We people on the pavement looked at him:
He was a gentleman from sole to crown,
Clean favored, and imperially slim.

And he was always quietly arrayed,   5
And he was always human when he talked;
But still he fluttered pulses when he said,
"Good-morning," and he glittered when he walked.

1896–1897. *Children of the Night*, 1897.

4 **clean favored:** good-looking

And he was rich—yes, richer than a king—
And admirably schooled in every grace: 10
In fine, we thought that he was everything
To make us wish that we were in his place.

And so we worked, and waited for the light,
And went without the meat, and cursed the bread;
And Richard Cory, one calm summer night,   15
Went home and put a bullet through his head.

Eros Turannos

She fears him, and will always ask
    What fated her to choose him;
She meets in his engaging mask
    All reasons to refuse him;
But what she meets and what she fears   5
Are less than are the downward years,
Drawn slowly to the foamless weirs
    Of age, were she to lose him.

Between a blurred sagacity
    That once had power to sound him,   10
And Love, that will not let him be
    The Judas that she found him,
Her pride assuages her almost,
As if it were alone the cost.—
He sees that he will not be lost,   15
    And waits and looks around him.

A sense of ocean and old trees
    Envelops and allures him;
Tradition, touching all he sees,
    Beguiles and reassures him;   20
And all her doubts of what he says
Are dimmed with what she knows of days—
Till even prejudice delays
    And fades, and she secures him.

The falling leaf inaugurates   25
    The reign of her confusion;
The pounding wave reverberates
    The dirge of her illusion;
And home, where passion lived and died,
Becomes a place where she can hide,   30
While all the town and harbor side
    Vibrate with her seclusion.

1913. *The Man Against the Sky*, 1916.

The title of this tight-lipped poem about the complexities of an unhappy marriage, seen from what an observer guesses of the wife's point of view (and of the husband's in the third stanza), means "King Love" or "Love the Tyrant."

6 **the downward years:** the years of decline into old age   7 **foamless weirs:** quiet dammed-up pools, or the dams themselves   10 **sound:** fathom, understand   17–20 A feeling that things will go on as they are makes the man complacent.   22 **days:** the passage of time

We tell you, tapping on our brows,
    The story as it should be,—
As if the story of a house
    Were told, or ever could be;
We'll have no kindly veil between
Her visions and those we have seen,—
As if we guessed what hers have been,
    Or what they are or would be.

Meanwhile we do no harm; for they
    That with a god have striven,
Not hearing much of what we say,
    Take what the god has given;
Though like waves breaking it may be,
Or like a changed familiar tree,
Or like a stairway to the sea
    Where down the blind are driven.

42 a god: Eros, god of love

The Mill

The miller's wife had waited long,
    The tea was cold, the fire was dead;
And there might yet be nothing wrong
    In how he went and what he said:
"There are no millers any more,"
    Was all that she had heard him say;
And he had lingered at the door
    So long that it seemed yesterday.

Sick with a fear that had no form
    She knew that she was there at last;
And in the mill there was a warm
    And mealy fragrance of the past.
What else there was would only seem
    To say again what he had meant;
And what was hanging from a beam
    Would not have heeded where she went.

And if she thought it followed her,
    She may have reasoned in the dark
That one way of the few there were
    Would hide her and would leave no mark:
Black water, smooth above the weir
    Like starry velvet in the night,
Though ruffled once, would soon appear
    The same as ever to the sight.

1919. *The Three Taverns*, 1920.

"Stopping beside an abandoned mill in West Peterborough (New Hampshire), the poet thought of the hundreds of others in New England which had shared its fate when water ceased to be the chief motive power and when individual millers could no longer compete with the great companies" (Emery Neff, *Edwin Arlington Robinson*, Sloane, 1948, 197).

21 weir: dam

The Dark Hills

Dark hills at evening in the west,
Where sunset hovers like a sound
Of golden horns that sang to rest
Old bones of warriors under ground,
Far now from all the bannered ways
Where flash the legions of the sun,
You fade—as if the last of days
Were fading, and all wars were done.

Probably 1919. Ibid.

Mr. Flood's Party

Old Eben Flood, climbing alone one night
Over the hill between the town below
And the forsaken upland hermitage
That held as much as he should ever know
On earth again of home, paused warily.   5
The road was his with not a native near;
And Eben, having leisure, said aloud,
For no man else in Tilbury Town to hear:

"Well, Mr. Flood, we have the harvest moon
Again, and we may not have many more;   10
The bird is on the wing, the poet says,
And you and I have said it here before.
Drink to the bird." He raised up to the light
The jug that he had gone so far to fill,
And answered huskily: "Well, Mr. Flood,   15
Since you propose it, I believe I will."

Alone, as if enduring to the end
A valiant armor of scarred hopes outworn,
He stood there in the middle of the road
Like Roland's ghost winding a silent horn.   20
Below him, in the town among the trees,
Where friends of other days had honored him,
A phantom salutation of the dead
Rang thinly till old Eben's eyes were dim.

Then, as a mother lays her sleeping child   25
Down tenderly, fearing it may awake,
He set the jug down slowly at his feet
With trembling care, knowing that most things break;
And only when assured that on firm earth

1919–1920. *Avon's Harvest*, 1921.

8 **Tilbury Town:** Robinson's name for Gardiner, Maine, where he spent most of his boyhood and youth   9 **harvest moon:** the full moon nearest the September equinox   11 **the bird is on the wing:** Cf. *The Rubáiyát of Omar Khayyám*, VII.   20 **Roland:** in the medieval *Song of Roland*, Roland, in command of the rear guard of Charlemagne's army, is ambushed and greatly outnumbered in the pass of Roncevaux (Roncesvalles) in the Pyrenees. Out of courageous pride, he refuses to sound until too late the horn that would bring Charlemagne's army to his rescue.

It stood, as the uncertain lives of men 30
Assuredly did not, he paced away,
And with his hand extended paused again:

"Well, Mr. Flood, we have not met like this
In a long time; and many a change has come
To both of us, I fear, since last it was 35
We had a drop together. Welcome home!"
Convivially returning with himself,
Again he raised the jug up to the light;
And with an acquiescent quaver said:
"Well, Mr. Flood, if you insist, I might. 40

"Only a very little, Mr. Flood—
For auld lang syne. No more, sir; that will do."
So, for the time, apparently it did,
And Eben evidently thought so too;
For soon amid the silver loneliness 45
Of night he lifted up his voice and sang,
Secure, with only two moons listening,
Until the whole harmonious landscape rang—

"For auld lang syne." The weary throat gave out;
The last word wavered, and the song was done. 50
He raised again the jug regretfully
And shook his head, and was again alone.
There was not much that was ahead of him,
And there was nothing in the town below—
Where strangers would have shut the many doors 55
That many friends had opened long ago.

42 **auld lang syne:** (Scottish) literally, the "old long since," the good old days; from Robert Burns's
song beginning "Should auld acquaintance be forgot?"   47 **two moons:** Mr. Flood is now seeing
double.

The Sheaves

Where long the shadows of the wind had rolled,
Green wheat was yielding to the change assigned;
And as by some vast magic undivined
The world was turning slowly into gold.
Like nothing that was ever bought or sold 5
It waited there, the body and the mind;
And with a mighty meaning of a kind
That tells the more the more it is not told.

So in a land where all days are not fair,
Fair days went on till on another day 10
A thousand golden sheaves were lying there,
Shining and still, but not for long to stay—
As if a thousand girls with golden hair
Might rise from where they slept and go away.

Dionysius in Doubt, 1925.

Walter de la Mare
(1873–1956)

At 17, de la Mare went to work in the London office of the Anglo-American Oil Company, where he stayed for 20 years. On receiving a small annual grant from the government, he then resigned to give full time to writing. He published books for children, novels, plays, essays, anthologies, and over 20 books of poetry.

The Listeners

"Is there anybody there?" said the Traveller,
    Knocking on the moonlit door;
And his horse in the silence champed the grasses
    Of the forest's ferny floor:
And a bird flew up out of the turret,   5
    Above the Traveller's head:
And he smote upon the door again a second time;
    "Is there anybody there?" he said.
But no one descended to the Traveller;
    No head from the leaf-fringed sill   10
Leaned over and looked into his grey eyes,
    Where he stood perplexed and still.
But only a host of phantom listeners
    That dwelt in the lone house then
Stood listening in the quiet of the moonlight   15
    To that voice from the world of men:
Stood thronging the faint moonbeams on the dark stair,
    That goes down to the empty hall,
Hearkening in an air stirred and shaken
    By the lonely Traveller's call.   20
And he felt in his heart their strangeness,
    Their stillness answering his cry,
While his horse moved, cropping the dark turf,
    'Neath the starred and leafy sky;
For he suddenly smote on the door, even   25
    Louder, and lifted his head:—
"Tell them I came, and no one answered,
    That I kept my word," he said.
Never the least stir made the listeners,
    Though every word he spake   30
Fell echoing through the shadowiness of the still house
    From the one man left awake:
Ay, they heard his foot upon the stirrup,
    And the sound of iron on stone,
And how the silence surged softly backward,   35
    When the plunging hoofs were gone.

The Listeners and Other Poems, 1912.

Pooh!

Dainty Miss Apathy
Sat on a sofa,
Dangling her legs,

Bells and Grass, 1941.

And with nothing to do;
She looked at a drawing of   5
Old Queen Victoria,
At a rug from far Persia—
An exquisite blue;
At a bowl of bright tulips;
A needlework picture   10
Of doves caged in wicker
You could almost hear coo;
She looked at the switch
That evokes e-
Lectricity;   15
At the coals of an age
B.C. millions and two—
When the trees were like ferns
And the reptiles all flew;
She looked at the cat   20
Asleep on the hearthrug,
At the sky at the window,—
The clouds in it, too;
And a marvellous light
From the West burning through: 25
And the one silly word
In her desolate noddle
As she dangled her legs,
Having nothing to do,
Was not, as you'd guess,   30
Of dumbfoundered felicity,
But contained just four letters,
And these pronounced *POOH!*

In the Local Museum

They stood—rain pelting at window, shrouded sea—
Tenderly hand in hand, too happy to talk;
And there, its amorous eye intent on me,
Plautus impennis, the extinct Great Auk.

The Burning Glass and Other Poems, 1945.

4 ***Plautus impennis:*** scientific name for the great auk, an extinct large coastal bird incapable of flight. The Latin words mean "flatfoot wingless."

Robert Frost
(1874–1963)

Born in San Francisco, Frost returned to his family's native New England when he was 11. In high school, though his interests were baseball and football, he also published poems in the school magazine. For several years he worked at odd jobs: mill hand, reporter, teacher. He married at 22, taught for two years, returned to Harvard to prepare to be a high school Latin teacher. In his second year, with illness a factor, he left to buy a poultry farm. An indifferent farmer, he found six years of this enough; teaching was better. All this time he had been writing poetry, but in unpublished obscurity. In 1912, he sold his farm and with his wife and four children sailed for England, intending to devote full time to his writing. His first book was published there the next year, when Frost was nearly 40; a second book soon followed. The attention he received impressed American publishers; two of his books came out here soon after his return in 1915. No longer obscure, he settled down in New Hampshire and later in Vermont, but continued to teach much of the time: at the University of Michigan, at Amherst, at Harvard, at Dartmouth. In his last decade he travelled as good-will ambassador for the State Department to South America, Israel, Greece, and Russia.

Mending Wall

Something there is that doesn't love a wall,
That sends the frozen-ground-swell under it
And spills the upper boulders in the sun,
And makes gaps even two can pass abreast.
The work of hunters is another thing: 5
I have come after them and made repair
Where they have left not one stone on a stone,
But they would have the rabbit out of hiding,
To please the yelping dogs. The gaps I mean,
No one has seen them made or heard them made,   10
But at spring mending-time we find them there.
I let my neighbor know beyond the hill;
And on a day we meet to walk the line
And set the wall between us once again.
We keep the wall between us as we go.   15
To each the boulders that have fallen to each.
And some are loaves and some so nearly balls
We have to use a spell to make them balance:
"Stay where you are until our backs are turned!"
We wear our fingers rough with handling them.   20
Oh, just another kind of outdoor game,
One on a side. It comes to little more:
There where it is we do not need the wall:
He is all pine and I am apple orchard.
My apple trees will never get across   25
And eat the cones under his pines, I tell him.
He only says, "Good fences make good neighbors."
Spring is the mischief in me, and I wonder
If I could put a notion in his head:
"*Why* do they make good neighbors? Isn't it   30
Where there are cows? But here there are no cows.
Before I built a wall I'd ask to know
What I was walling in or walling out,
And to whom I was like to give offense.
Something there is that doesn't love a wall,   35
That wants it down." I could say "Elves" to him,
But it's not elves exactly, and I'd rather
He said it for himself. I see him there,
Bringing a stone grasped firmly by the top
In each hand, like an old-stone savage armed.   40
He moves in darkness as it seems to me,
Not of woods only and the shade of trees.
He will not go behind his father's saying,
And he likes having thought of it so well
He says again, "Good fences make good neighbors."   45

1912–1914. *North of Boston*, 1914.

Frost said he wrote "Mending Wall" in England when he was "very homesick for my old wall in New England."

40 **old-stone:** of the early Stone Age (the paleolithic), during which man developed stone tools and weapons—including the hand-ax, a stone sharpened at one end and grasped by the other

In Hardwood Groves

The same leaves over and over again!
They fall from giving shade above
To make one texture of faded brown
And fit the earth like a leather glove.

Before the leaves can mount again　　　　　　　　　　5
To fill the trees with another shade,
They must go down past things coming up.
They must go down into the dark decayed.

They *must* be pierced by flowers and put
Beneath the feet of dancing flowers.　　　　　　　　10
However it is in some other world
I know that this is the way in ours.

By 1926. *Collected Poems,* 1930.

The Road Not Taken

Two roads diverged in a yellow wood
And sorry I could not travel both
And be one traveler, long I stood
And looked down one as far as I could
To where it bent in the undergrowth;　　　　　　　　5

Then took the other, as just as fair,
And having perhaps the better claim,
Because it was grassy and wanted wear;
Though as for that the passing there
Had worn them really about the same,　　　　　　　10

And both that morning equally lay
In leaves no step had trodden black.
Oh, I kept the first for another day!
Yet knowing how way leads on to way,
I doubted if I should ever come back.　　　　　　　15

I shall be telling this with a sigh
Somewhere ages and ages hence:
Two roads diverged in a wood, and I—
I took the one less traveled by,
And that has made all the difference.　　　　　　　20

1914–1915. *Mountain Interval,* 1916.

Frost said that this poem was not about his own choice of a path in life, but only a way of making fun
of his friend, the English poet Edward Thomas, with whom he used to go on botanizing walks during
his stay in England (1912–1915). No matter how fine the walk, Thomas was likely to regret they had
not taken a different route. The poem can of course mean more to readers than Frost said he intended
it to mean.

An Old Man's Winter Night

All out-of-doors looked darkly in at him
Through the thin frost, almost in separate stars,

1906–1916. Ibid.

That gathers on the pane in empty rooms.
What kept his eyes from giving back the gaze
Was the lamp tilted near them in his hand.   5
What kept him from remembering what it was
That brought him to that creaking room was age.
He stood with barrels round him—at a loss.
And having scared the cellar under him
In clomping here, he scared it once again   10
In clomping off—and scared the outer night,
Which has its sounds, familiar, like the roar
Of trees and crack of branches, common things,
But nothing so like beating on a box.
A light he was to no one but himself   15
Where now he sat, concerned with he knew what,
A quiet light, and then not even that.
He consigned to the moon, such as she was,
So late-arising, to the broken moon,
As better than the sun in any case   20
For such a charge, his snow upon the roof,
His icicles along the wall to keep;
And slept. The log that shifted with a jolt
Once in the stove, disturbed him and he shifted,
And eased his heavy breathing, but still slept.   25
One aged man—one man—can't keep a house,
A farm, a countryside, or if he can,
It's thus he does it of a winter night.

The Hill Wife

LONELINESS

Her Word

One ought not to have to care
    So much as you and I
Care when the birds come round the house
    To seem to say good-by;

Or care so much when they come back   5
    With whatever it is they sing;
The truth being we are as much
    Too glad for the one thing

As we are too sad for the other here—
    With birds that fill their breasts   10
But with each other and themselves
    And their built or driven nests.

HOUSE FEAR

Always—I tell you this they learned—
Always at night when they returned
To the lonely house from far away,
To lamps unlighted and fire gone gray,
They learned to rattle the lock and key   5
To give whatever might chance to be

1905, 1906, 1913, 1916, 1913. *Mountain Interval*, 1916.

Warning and time to be off in flight:
And preferring the out- to the in-door night,
They learned to leave the house-door wide
Until they had lit the lamp inside.   10

THE SMILE

Her Word

I didn't like the way he went away.
That smile! It never came of being gay.
Still he smiled—did you see him?—I was sure!
Perhaps because we gave him only bread
And the wretch knew from that that we were poor.   5
Perhaps because he let us give instead
Of seizing from us as he might have seized.
Perhaps he mocked at us for being wed,
Or being very young (and he was pleased
To have a vision of us old and dead).   10
I wonder how far down the road he's got.
He's watching from the woods as like as not.

THE OFT-REPEATED DREAM

She had no saying dark enough
    For the dark pine that kept
Forever trying the window-latch
    Of the room where they slept.

The tireless but ineffectual hands   5
    That with every futile pass
Made the great tree seem as a little bird
    Before the mystery of glass!

It never had been inside the room,
    And only one of the two   10
Was afraid in an oft-repeated dream
    Of what the tree might do.

THE IMPULSE

It was too lonely for her there,
    And too wild,
And since there were but two of them,
    And no child,

And work was little in the house,   5
    She was free,
And followed where he furrowed field,
    Or felled tree.

She rested on a log and tossed
    The fresh chips,   10
With a song only to herself
    On her lips.

And once she went to break a bough
    Of black alder.
She strayed so far she scarcely heard   15
    When he called her—

And didn't answer—didn't speak—
    Or return.
She stood, and then she ran and hid
    In the fern.   20

He never found her, though he looked
    Everywhere,
And he asked at her mother's house
    Was she there.

Sudden and swift and light as that   25
    The ties gave,
And he learned of finalities
    Besides the grave.

"Out, Out—"

The buzz saw snarled and rattled in the yard
And made dust and dropped stove-length sticks of wood,
Sweet-scented stuff when the breeze drew across it.
And from there those that lifted eyes could count
Five mountain ranges one behind the other   5
Under the sunset far into Vermont.
And the saw snarled and rattled, snarled and rattled,
As it ran light, or had to bear a load.
And nothing happened: day was all but done.
Call it a day, I wish they might have said   10
To please the boy by giving him the half hour
That a boy counts so much when saved from work.
His sister stood beside them in her apron
To tell them "Supper". At the word, the saw,
As if to prove saws knew what supper meant,   15
Leaped out at the boy's hand, or seemed to leap—
He must have given the hand. However it was,
Neither refused the meeting. But the hand!
The boy's first outcry was a rueful laugh,
As he swung toward them holding up the hand   20
Half in appeal, but half as if to keep
The life from spilling. Then the boy saw all—
Since he was old enough to know, big boy
Doing a man's work, though a child at heart—
He saw all spoiled. "Don't let him cut my hand off—   25
The doctor, when he comes. Don't let him, sister!"
So. But the hand was gone already.
The doctor put him in the dark of ether.
He lay and puffed his lips out with his breath.
And then—the watcher at his pulse took fright.   30
No one believed. They listened at his heart.
Little—less—nothing!—and that ended it.
No more to build on there. And they, since they
Were not the one dead, turned to their affairs.

1910–1916. Ibid.

The title is from the speech of Macbeth when he learns his wife is dead: "Out, out, brief candle!/Life's but a walking shadow . . ." (*Macbeth*, V, v). Frost had known the 16-year-old boy the poem is about, and his family, from several summer visits to New Hampshire. See Additional Notes (p. 767).

Stopping by Woods on a Snowy Evening

Whose woods these are I think I know.
His house is in the village though;
He will not see me stopping here
To watch his woods fill up with snow.

My little horse must think it queer   5
To stop without a farmhouse near
Between the woods and frozen lake
The darkest evening of the year.

He gives his harness bells a shake
To ask if there is some mistake.   10
The only other sound's the sweep
Of easy wind and downy flake.

The woods are lovely, dark and deep,
But I have promises to keep,
And miles to go before I sleep,   15
And miles to go before I sleep.

1922. *New Hampshire*, 1923.

According to Frost's account, this poem about a winter evening was written at dawn in summer, after he had been working all night on another poem.

Once by the Pacific

The shattered water made a misty din.
Great waves looked over others coming in,
And thought of doing something to the shore
That water never did to land before.
The clouds were low and hairy in the skies,   5
Like locks blown forward in the gleam of eyes.
You could not tell, and yet it looked as if
The shore was lucky in being backed by cliff,
The cliff in being backed by continent;
It looked as if a night of dark intent   10
Was coming, and not only a night, an age.
Someone had better be prepared for rage.
There would be more than ocean-water broken
Before God's last *Put out the Light* was spoken.

By 1926. *West Running Brook*, 1928.

The poem grew out of a childhood memory: as a little boy Frost once lagged behind his family as they walked along the Pacific. Suddenly he found himself alone at dusk between the towering cliffs and the breakers, and in a panic ran after his parents.

14 *Put out the Light:* as God's "Let there be light" in Genesis began the drama of creation, so His "Put out the Light" might be imagined as concluding it. Some readers are also reminded of Othello's words as he enters to murder Desdemona: "Put out the light, and then put out the light" (V, ii).

Acquainted with the Night

I have been one acquainted with the night.
I have walked out in rain—and back in rain.
I have outwalked the furthest city light.

1927? Ibid.

I have looked down the saddest city lane.
I have passed by the watchman on his beat   5
And dropped my eyes, unwilling to explain.

I have stood still and stopped the sound of feet
When far away an interrupted cry
Came over houses from another street,

But not to call me back or say good-by;   10
And further still at an unearthly height,
One luminary clock against the sky

Proclaimed the time was neither wrong nor right.
I have been one acquainted with the night.

Neither Out Far nor In Deep

The people along the sand
All turn and look one way.
They turn their back on the land.
They look at the sea all day.

As long as it takes to pass   5
A ship keeps raising its hull;
The wetter ground like glass
Reflects a standing gull.

The land may vary more;
But wherever the truth may be—   10
The water comes ashore,
And the people look at the sea.

They cannot look out far.
They cannot look in deep.
But when was that ever a bar   15
To any watch they keep?

1932. *A Further Range,* 1936.

Provide, Provide

The witch that came (the withered hag)
To wash the steps with pail and rag,
Was once the beauty Abishag,

The picture pride of Hollywood.
Too many fall from great and good   5
For you to doubt the likelihood.

1934. Ibid.

The poem is said to have been written when humanitarians organized a strike of scrub-women. Frost, a rugged individualist, was suspicious of what looked to him like organized benevolence.

3 **Abishag:** the name of the "fair damsel" who was found to "cherish" and minister to King David when he was "old and stricken in years" (1 Kings 1:1–4).

Die early and avoid the fate.
Or if predestined to die late,
Make up your mind to die in state.

Make the whole stock exchange your own!   10
If need be occupy a throne,
Where nobody can call *you* crone.

Some have relied on what they knew;
Others on being simply true.
What worked for them might work for you.   15

No memory of having starred
Atones for later disregard,
Or keeps the end from being hard.

Better to go down dignified
With boughten friendship at your side   20
Than none at all. Provide, provide!

The Most of It

He thought he kept the universe alone;
For all the voice in answer he could wake
Was but the mocking echo of his own
From some tree-hidden cliff across the lake.
Some morning from the boulder-broken beach   5
He would cry out on life, that what it wants
Is not its own love back in copy speech,
But counter-love, original response.
And nothing ever came of what he cried
Unless it was the embodiment that crashed   10
In the cliff's talus on the other side,
And then in the far distant water splashed,
But after a time allowed for it to swim,
Instead of proving human when it neared
And someone else additional to him,   15
As a great buck it powerfully appeared,
Pushing the crumpled water up ahead,
And landed pouring like a waterfall,
And stumbled through the rocks with horny tread,
And forced the underbrush—and that was all.   20

---

c. 1929. *A Witness Tree*, 1942.

The title is abbreviated from the earlier "Making the Most of It." The poem is an answer to one written by a friend who seemed to expect something like human companionship from nature—an attitude that Frost thought sentimental.

11 **talus:** rocky debris at the base of a cliff

Never Again Would Birds' Song Be the Same

He would declare and could himself believe
That the birds there in all the garden round

1939–1942. Ibid.

From having heard the daylong voice of Eve
Had added to their own an oversound,
Her tone of meaning but without the words.   5
Admittedly an eloquence so soft
Could only have had an influence on birds
When call or laughter carried it aloft.
Be that as may be, she was in their song.
Moreover her voice upon their voices crossed   10
Had now persisted in the woods so long
That probably it never would be lost.
Never again would birds' song be the same.
And to do that to birds was why she came.

The Subverted Flower

She drew back; he was calm:
"It is this that had the power."
And he lashed his open palm
With the tender-headed flower.
He smiled for her to smile,   5
But she was either blind
Or willfully unkind.
He eyed her for a while
For a woman and a puzzle.
He flicked and flung the flower,   10
And another sort of smile
Caught up like finger tips
The corners of his lips
And cracked his ragged muzzle.
She was standing to the waist   15
In goldenrod and brake,
Her shining hair displaced.
He stretched her either arm
As if she made it ache
To clasp her—not to harm;   20
As if he could not spare
To touch her neck and hair.
"If this has come to us
And not to me alone—"
So she thought she heard him say;   25
Though with every word he spoke
His lips were sucked and blown
And the effort made him choke
Like a tiger at a bone.
She had to lean away.   30
She dared not stir a foot,
Lest movement should provoke
The demon of pursuit
That slumbers in a brute.
It was then her mother's call   35
From inside the garden wall
Made her steal a look of fear
To see if he could hear

1912–1942. Ibid.

See Additional Notes (p. 768).

16 **brake:** tall ferns   18 **He stretched her either arm:** He stretched out each of his arms toward her.

And would pounce to end it all
Before her mother came. 40
She looked and saw the shame:
A hand hung like a paw,
An arm worked like a saw
As if to be persuasive,
An ingratiating laugh 45
That cut the snout in half,
An eye become evasive.
A girl could only see
That a flower had marred a man,
But what she could not see 50
Was that the flower might be
Other than base and fetid:
That the flower had done but part,
And what the flower began
Her own too meager heart 55
Had terribly completed.
She looked and saw the worst.
And the dog or what it was,
Obeying bestial laws,
A coward save at night, 60
Turned from the place and ran.
She heard him stumble first
And use his hands in flight.
She heard him bark outright.
And oh, for one so young 65
The bitter words she spit
Like some tenacious bit
That will not leave the tongue.
She plucked her lips for it,
And still the horror clung. 70
Her mother wiped the foam
From her chin, picked up her comb
And drew her backward home.

Directive

Back out of all this now too much for us,
Back in a time made simple by the loss
Of detail, burned, dissolved, and broken off
Like graveyard marble sculpture in the weather,
There is a house that is no more a house 5
Upon a farm that is no more a farm
And in a town that is no more a town.
The road there, if you'll let a guide direct you
Who only has at heart your getting lost,
May seem as if it should have been a quarry— 10
Great monolithic knees the former town
Long since gave up pretense of keeping covered.

By 1946. *Steeple Bush*, 1947.

See Additional Notes (p. 768).

1 **back out of . . .** : before the confusions of life today, which can seem too complex for us to handle
9 **your getting lost:** Cf. Mark 8:35: "For whosoever will save his life shall lose it; but whosoever shall lose his life for my sake and the gospel's, the same shall save it."

And there's a story in a book about it:
Besides the wear of iron wagon wheels
The ledges show lines ruled southeast northwest,   15
The chisel work of an enormous Glacier
That braced his feet against the Arctic Pole.
You must not mind a certain coolness from him
Still said to haunt this side of Panther Mountain.
Nor need you mind the serial ordeal   20
Of being watched from forty cellar holes
As if by eye pairs out of forty firkins.
As for the woods' excitement over you
That sends light rustle rushes to their leaves,
Charge that to upstart inexperience.   25
Where were they all not twenty years ago?
They think too much of having shaded out
A few old pecker-fretted apple trees.
Make yourself up a cheering song of how
Someone's road home from work this once was,   30
Who may be just ahead of you on foot
Or creaking with a buggy load of grain.
The height of the adventure is the height
Of country where two village cultures faded
Into each other. Both of them are lost.   35
And if you're lost enough to find yourself
By now, pull in your ladder road behind you
And put a sign up CLOSED to all but me.
Then make yourself at home. The only field
Now left's no bigger than a harness gall.   40
First there's the children's house of make believe,
Some shattered dishes underneath a pine,
The playthings in the playhouse of the children.
Weep for what little things could make them glad.
Then for the house that is no more a house,   45
But only a belilaced cellar hole,
Now slowly closing like a dent in dough.
This was no playhouse but a house in earnest.
Your destination and your destiny's
A brook that was the water of the house,   50
Cold as a spring as yet so near its source,
Too lofty and original to rage.
(We know the valley streams that when aroused
Will leave their tatters hung on barb and thorn.)
I have kept hidden in the instep arch   55
Of an old cedar at the waterside
A broken drinking goblet like the Grail
Under a spell so the wrong ones can't find it,

---

13 **a story:** the story of the geological history of the area, and especially of the scraping of the glaciers during the ice age; most Adirondack lakes, where the glaciers gouged deepest, slant from northwest to southeast.   19 **Panther Mountain:** A nearly 4000-foot mountain in the Adirondacks in upper New York State, about 60 miles to the west of Frost's home near Ripton, Vermont.   20 **serial ordeal:** series of ordeals   21 **being watched:** by birds, animals—and as if by the spirits of those who once lived there   22 **forty firkins:** A firkin is a small barrel. Is forty suggested by the story of Ali Baba and the Forty Thieves, who hid in containers like leather firkins?   28 **pecker-fretted:** gouged by woodpeckers   36 **lost enough . . . :** Cf. note on line 9.   40 **harness gall:** the sore made by the chafing of a harness   46 **belilaced:** overgrown with lilacs   52 **original:** close to its origin—and also the usual meaning   57 **the Grail:** in medieval legend, the cup or chalice used by Christ at the Last Supper

So can't get saved, as Saint Mark says they mustn't.
(I stole the goblet from the children's playhouse.)   60
Here are your waters and your watering place.
Drink and be whole again beyond confusion.

59 St. Mark: Frost's friend Theodore Morrison has recalled (*The Atlantic Monthly,* July 1967) an eve-
ning of conversation, when Frost was present, that dealt with Mark 4:11–12: "Unto you [the apostles]
it is given to know the mystery of the kingdom of God: but unto them that are without, all these
things are done in parables: that seeing they may see, and not perceive; and hearing they may hear,
and not understand; lest at any time they should be converted, and their sins should be forgiven
them." A similar thought is found in Matt. 13. According to Frost, Christ almost said, "You can't be
saved unless you understand poetry. . . ." The parables have to be read symbolically, as much poetry
has to be, or it is true of the readers that "seeing they may see, and not perceive. . . ." In "Directive,"
Frost may mean that the "wrong ones" have not earned the visionary experience of his Grail by the
"serial ordeal" of the journey.   **61 your waters:** Some see here a reference to Revelation (Apocalypse)
7:14–17: ". . . the Lamb . . . shall lead them unto living fountains of waters. . . ." Frost warned however
that "the poet is not offering any general salvation—nor Christian salvation in particular." The key
lines of the poem, he said, are 51–52, and "the key word in the whole poem is source—whatever
source it is" (quoted in Theodore Morrison's article).

Carl Sandburg
(1878–1967)

Sandburg, son of a Swedish immigrant, was born in Galesburg, Illinois, where (after
serving in the Spanish-American War) he attended Lombard College. Secretary for two
years to the mayor of Milwaukee, he began in 1913 to do newspaper work in Chicago,
where some of his *Chicago Poems* soon appeared in the new magazine *Poetry.* Sandburg's
poems, democratic and Midwestern, were an immediate success. So were the readings
and lectures in which, accompanying himself on the guitar, he performed his own poems
and the folksongs he loved to collect.

The Shovel Man

    On the street
Slung on his shoulder is a handle half way across,
Tied in a big knot on the scoop of cast iron
Are the overalls faded from sun and rain in the ditches;
Spatter of dry clay sticking yellow on his left sleeve   5
        And a flimsy shirt open at the throat,
        I know him for a shovel man,
        A dago working for a dollar six bits a day
And a dark-eyed woman in the old country dreams of him for one of the
        world's ready men with a pair of fresh lips and a kiss better than all the
        wild grapes that ever grew in Tuscany.

Chicago Poems, 1916.

9 **Tuscany:** the region around Florence in Italy

Limited

I am riding on a limited express, one of the crack trains of the nation.
Hurtling across the prairie into blue haze and dark air go fifteen all-steel
        coaches holding a thousand people.
(All the coaches shall be scrap and rust and all the men and women laughing
        in the diners and sleepers shall pass to ashes.)
I ask a man in the smoker where he is going and he answers: "Omaha."

Ibid.

Cool Tombs

When Abraham Lincoln was shoveled into the tombs, he forgot the
    copperheads and the assassin . . . in the dust, in the cool tombs.

And Ulysses Grant lost all thought of con men and Wall Street, cash and
    collateral turned ashes . . . in the dust, in the cool tombs.

Pocahontas' body, lovely as a poplar, sweet as a red haw in November or
    a pawpaw in May, did she wonder? does she remember? . . . in the
    dust, in the cool tombs?

Take any streetful of people buying clothes and groceries, cheering a
    hero or throwing confetti and blowing tin horns . . . tell me if the
    lovers are losers . . . tell me if any get more than the lovers . . . in the
    dust . . . in the cool tombs.

By 1916. *Cornhuskers*, 1918.

1 **copperheads:** Northerners who sided with the South in the Civil War   2 **Ulysses Grant:** The Civil
War hero was president from 1869 to 1877, the "most unfortunate" president in our history. His ad-
ministration was plagued with financial scandals and Wall Street maneuverings not of his doing,
though to many he seemed involved.   3 **Pocahontas:** the Indian "princess," daughter of Chief Pow-
hatan, who was friendly to the English colonists who settled at Jamestown in 1607; she saved the life
of Captain John Smith, became a Christian, married John Rolfe, and died at the age of 22.   **red haw:**
hawthorn   **pawpaw:** an American tree with purple flowers

Edward Thomas
(1878–1917)

Thomas supported himself by miscellaneous kinds of writing, especially about rural na-
ture. His friendship with Robert Frost, just before World War I, turned him more and
more toward poetry. He was killed in action in Flanders.

Adlestrop

Yes. I remember Adlestrop—
The name, because one afternoon
Of heat the express-train drew up there
Unwontedly. It was late June.

The steam hissed. Someone cleared his throat.   5
No one left and no one came
On the bare platform. What I saw
Was Adlestrop—only the name

And willows, willow-herb, and grass,
And meadowsweet, and haycocks dry,   10
No whit less still and lonely fair
Than the high cloudlets in the sky.

1915. *Poems*, 1917.

Adlestrop is a little English town few of us will have heard of—that is partly the point of the poem.
The station, now closed, was about half a mile from the village, which is some 20 miles northwest of
Oxford.

4 **unwontedly:** as it did not usually do. A notebook entry mentions that the stop was only for a min-
ute, till a signal changed.   9 **willow-herb:** a plant with yellow flowers and willowlike leaves, yellow
loosestrife   10 **meadowsweet:** in England, a fragrant white meadow flower

And for that minute a blackbird sang
    Close by, and round him, mistier,
Farther and farther, all the birds   15
Of Oxfordshire and Gloucestershire.

16 **Oxfordshire and Gloucestershire:** adjoining counties, 50 or more miles across

Oliver St. John Gogarty
(1878–1957)

Born in Dublin, Gogarty was known there and at Oxford for his brilliant conversation, his poetry, his practical jokes, and his record as champion bicycle-racer. Later on he flew his own airplane. Coming from a family of physicians, he became an eminent ear, nose, and throat surgeon. Kidnapped and almost shot during the troubles between England and Ireland, he escaped by swimming a turbulent river in mid-winter. As life went on he gave more and more time to writing; by 1939 he had published three books of poetry and three of prose. Rejected by the R.A.F. at the beginning of World War II because of his age, he came to America for a lecture tour, and spent most of his remaining years here as lecturer and journalist.

Leda and the Swan

Though her Mother told her
    Not to go a-bathing,
Leda loved the river
    And she could not keep away:
Wading in its freshets   5
    When the noon was heavy;
Walking by the water
    At the close of day.

Where between its waterfalls,
    Underneath the beeches,   10
Gently flows a broader
    Hardly moving stream,
And the balanced trout lie
    In the quiet reaches;
Taking all her clothes off,   15
    Leda went to swim.

There was not a flag-leaf
    By the river's margin
That might be a shelter
    From a passer-by;   20
And a sudden whiteness
    In the quiet darkness,
Let alone the splashing,
    Was enough to catch an eye.

But the place was lonely,   25
    And her clothes were hidden;

By 1932. *Others to Adorn*, 1938.

For the myth, cf. Yeats's "Leda and the Swan" (p. 467).

17 **flag-leaf:** the *flag* is (1) a wild iris; (2) a cattail

Even cattle walking
    In the ford had gone away;
Every single farm-hand
    Sleeping after dinner,— 30
What's the use of talking?
    There was no one in the way.

In, without a stitch on,
    Peaty water yielded,
Till her head was lifted 35
    With its ropes of hair;
It was more surprising
    Than a lily gilded,
Just to see how golden
    Was her body there: 40

Lolling in the water,
    Lazily uplifting
Limbs that on the surface
    Whitened into snow;
Leaning on the water, 45
    Indolently drifting,
Hardly any faster
    Than the foamy bubbles go.

You would say to see her
    Swimming in the lonely 50
Pool, or after, dryer,
    Putting on her clothes:
"O but she is lovely,
    Not a soul to see her,
And how lovely only 55
    Leda's Mother knows!"

Under moving branches
    Leisurely she dresses,
And the leafy sunlight
    Made you wonder were 60
All its woven shadows
    But her golden tresses,
Or a smock of sunlight
    For her body bare.

When on earth great beauty 65
    Goes exempt from danger,
It will be endangered
    From a source on high:
When unearthly stillness
    Falls on leaves, the ranger, 70
In his wood-lore anxious,
    Gazes at the sky.

While her hair was drying,
    Came a gentle languor,
Whether from the bathing 75
    Or the breeze she didn't know.

34 **peaty:** rich with earthy sediment

Anyway she lay there,
    And her Mother's anger
(Worse if she had wet hair)
    Could not make her dress and go.   80

Whitest of all earthly
    Things, the white that's rarest,
Is the snow on mountains
    Standing in the sun;
Next the clouds above them,   85
    Then the down is fairest
On the breast and pinions
    Of a proudly sailing swan.

And she saw him sailing
    On the pool where lately   90
She had stretched unnoticed,
    As she thought, and swum;
And she never wondered
    Why, erect and stately,
Where no river weed was   95
    Such a bird had come.

What was it she called him:
    Goosey-goosey gander?
For she knew no better
    Way to call a swan;   100
And the bird responding
    Seemed to understand her,
For he left his sailing
    For the bank to waddle on.

Apple blossoms under   105
    Hills of Lacedaemon,
With the snow beyond them
    In the still blue air,
To the swan who hid them
    With his wings asunder,   110
Than the breasts of Leda,
    Were not lovelier!

Of the tales that daughters
    Tell their poor old mothers,
Which by all accounts are   115
    Often very odd;
Leda's was a story
    Stranger than all others.
What was there to say but:
    Glory be to God?   120

And she half-believed her,
    For she knew her daughter;
And she saw the swan-down
    Tangled in her hair.
Though she knew how deeply   125
    Runs the stillest water,

106 **Lacedaemon:** the region around Sparta in Greece

How could she protect her
    From the wingèd air?

Why is it effects are
    Greater than their causes?   130
Why should causes often
    Differ from effects?
Why should what is lovely
    Fill the world with harness?
And the most deceived be   135
    She who least suspects?

When the hyacinthine
    Eggs were in the basket,
Blue as at the whiteness
    Where a cloud begins;   140
Who would dream there lay there
    All that Trojan brightness;
Agamemnon murdered;
    And the mighty Twins?

134 **harness:** armor   137 **hyacinthine:** a rich blue   144 **the mighty Twins:** Castor and Pollux, sons
of Leda, accorded divine honors as sons of Zeus

Wallace Stevens
(1879–1955)

Born in Reading, Pennsylvania, Stevens went to Harvard, where he contributed poems
and stories to the college magazines; worked for a time as reporter in New York; went to
the New York Law School and practiced on his own for a few years. Even before college
he had decided that poetry was his real interest, but to write it his way he knew that fi-
nancial independence was desirable. In 1916 he joined the Hartford Accident and Indem-
nity Company; he was made a vice-president in 1934. Though interested in France and its
culture, he never went to Europe. Stevens's first book of poetry was published in 1923,
when he was over 40. In the last five years of his life, he was awarded the major prizes
available to American poets—amid general agreement that he was one of the best poets
of the century.

Sunday Morning

I

Complacencies of the peignoir, and late
Coffee and oranges in a sunny chair,
And the green freedom of a cockatoo
Upon a rug mingle to dissipate
The holy hush of ancient sacrifice.   5
She dreams a little, and she feels the dark
Encroachment of that old catastrophe,
As a calm darkens among water-lights.
The pungent oranges and bright, green wings
Seem things in some procession of the dead,   10
Winding across wide water, without sound.

1915. *Harmonium,* 1923.

See Additional Notes (p. 768).

5 **ancient sacrifice:** the spirit of the old religions; especially, it seems from the lines that follow, the
sacrifice of Calvary

The day is like wide water, without sound,
Stilled for the passing of her dreaming feet
Over the seas, to silent Palestine,
Dominion of the blood and sepulchre.   15

II

Why should she give her bounty to the dead?
What is divinity if it can come
Only in silent shadows and in dreams?
Shall she not find in comforts of the sun,
In pungent fruit and bright, green wings, or else   20
In any balm or beauty of the earth,
Things to be cherished like the thought of heaven?
Divinity must live within herself:
Passions of rain, or moods in falling snow;
Grievings in loneliness, or unsubdued   25
Elations when the forest blooms; gusty
Emotions on wet roads on autumn nights;
All pleasures and all pains, remembering
The bough of summer and the winter branch.
These are the measures destined for her soul.   30

III

Jove in the clouds had his inhuman birth.
No mother suckled him, no sweet land gave
Large-mannered motions to his mythy mind.
He moved among us, as a muttering king,
Magnificent, would move among his hinds,   35
Until our blood, commingling, virginal,
With heaven, brought such requital to desire
The very hinds discerned it, in a star.
Shall our blood fail? Or shall it come to be
The blood of paradise? And shall the earth   40
Seem all of paradise that we shall know?
The sky will be much friendlier then than now,
A part of labor and a part of pain,
And next in glory to enduring love,
Not this dividing and indifferent blue.   45

IV

She says, "I am content when wakened birds,
Before they fly, test the reality
Of misty fields, by their sweet questionings;
But when the birds are gone, and their warm fields
Return no more, where, then, is paradise?"   50
There is not any haunt of prophecy,
Nor any old chimera of the grave,
Neither the golden underground, nor isle
Melodious, where spirits gat them home,
Nor visionary south, nor cloudy palm   55
Remote on heaven's hill, that has endured
As April's green endures; or will endure
Like her remembrance of awakened birds,
Or her desire for June and evening, tipped
By the consummation of the swallow's wings.   60

---

35 **hinds:** farm servants, peasants; in line 38, the shepherds who saw the star of Bethlehem when
Christ was born   54 **gat them:** got them, betook themselves [archaic, as the context is]

V

She says, "But in contentment I still feel
The need of some imperishable bliss."
Death is the mother of beauty; hence from her,
Alone, shall come fulfilment to our dreams
And our desires. Although she strews the leaves   65
Of sure obliteration on our paths,
The path sick sorrow took, the many paths
Where triumph rang its brassy phrase, or love
Whispered a little out of tenderness,
She makes the willow shiver in the sun   70
For maidens who were wont to sit and gaze
Upon the grass, relinquished to their feet.
She causes boys to pile new plums and pears
On disregarded plate. The maidens taste
And stray impassioned in the littering leaves.   75

VI

Is there no change of death in paradise?
Does ripe fruit never fall? Or do the boughs
Hang always heavy in that perfect sky,
Unchanging, yet so like our perishing earth,
With rivers like our own that seek for seas   80
They never find, the same receding shores
That never touch with inarticulate pang?
Why set the pear upon those river-banks
Or spice the shores with odors of the plum?
Alas, that they should wear our colors there,   85
The silken weavings of our afternoons,
And pick the strings of our insipid lutes!
Death is the mother of beauty, mystical,
Within whose burning bosom we devise
Our earthly mothers waiting, sleeplessly.   90

VII

Supple and turbulent, a ring of men
Shall chant in orgy on a summer morn
Their boisterous devotion to the sun,
Not as a god, but as a god might be,
Naked among them, like a savage source.   95
Their chant shall be a chant of paradise,
Out of their blood, returning to the sky;
And in their chant shall enter, voice by voice,
The windy lake wherein their lord delights,
The trees, like serafin, and echoing hills,   100
That choir among themselves long afterward.
They shall know well the heavenly fellowship
Of men that perish and of summer morn.
And whence they came and whither they shall go
The dew upon their feet shall manifest.   105

---

70 **willow:** willows are traditionally associated with sorrow or loss in love   74 **on disregarded plate:** In a letter to Harriet Monroe (the founder of *Poetry*, where "Sunday Morning" was first printed), Stevens admitted the words were obscure. He explained: "Plate is used in the sense of so-called family plate. Disregarded refers to the disuse into which things fall that have been possessed for a long time. I mean, therefore, that death releases and renews. What the old have come to disregard, the young inherit and make use of. . . ."   100 **serafin:** seraphs, the six-winged angels that stand in the presence of God   105 **dew:** "Life is as fugitive as dew upon the feet of men dancing in dew. Men do not either come from any direction or disappear in any direction . . ." (Stevens, *Letters*, 250).

VIII

She hears, upon that water without sound,
A voice that cries, "The tomb in Palestine
Is not the porch of spirits lingering.
It is the grave of Jesus, where he lay."
We live in an old chaos of the sun,   110
Or old dependency of day and night,
Or island solitude, unsponsored, free,
Of that wide water, inescapable.
Deer walk upon our mountains, and the quail
Whistle about us their spontaneous cries;   115
Sweet berries ripen in the wilderness;
And, in the isolation of the sky,
At evening, casual flocks of pigeons make
Ambiguous undulations as they sink,
Downward to darkness, on extended wings.   120

The Snow Man

One must have a mind of winter
To regard the frost and the boughs
Of the pine-trees crusted with snow;

And have been cold a long time
To behold the junipers shagged with ice,   5
The spruces rough in the distant glitter

Of the January sun; and not to think
Of any misery in the sound of the wind,
In the sound of a few leaves,

Which is the sound of the land   10
Full of the same wind
That is blowing in the same bare place

For the listener, who listens in the snow,
And, nothing himself, beholds
Nothing that is not there and the nothing that is.   15

1921. Ibid.

See Additional Notes (p. 768).

The Emperor of Ice-Cream

Call the roller of big cigars,
The muscular one, and bid him whip
In kitchen cups concupiscent curds.
Let the wenches dawdle in such dress
As they are used to wear, and let the boys   5
Bring flowers in last month's newspapers.
Let be be finale of seem.
The only emperor is the emperor of ice-cream.

1922. Ibid.

See Additional Notes (p. 769).

Take from the dresser of deal,
Lacking the three glass knobs, that sheet   10
On which she embroidered fantails once
And spread it so as to cover her face.
If her horny feet protrude, they come
To show how cold she is, and dumb.
Let the lamp affix its beam.   15
The only emperor is the emperor of ice-cream.

9 **deal:** pine or fir boards   11 **fantails:** a kind of pigeons

The Idea of Order at Key West

She sang beyond the genius of the sea.
The water never formed to mind or voice,
Like a body wholly body, fluttering
Its empty sleeves; and yet its mimic motion
Made constant cry, caused constantly a cry,   5
That was not ours although we understood,
Inhuman, of the veritable ocean.

The sea was not a mask. No more was she.
The song and water were not medleyed sound
Even if what she sang was what she heard,   10
Since what she sang was uttered word by word.
It may be that in all her phrases stirred
The grinding water and the gasping wind;
But it was she and not the sea we heard.

For she was the maker of the song she sang.   15
The ever-hooded, tragic-gestured sea
Was merely a place by which she walked to sing.
Whose spirit is this? we said, because we knew
It was the spirit that we sought and knew
That we should ask this often as she sang.   20

If it was only the dark voice of the sea
That rose, or even colored by many waves;
If it was only the outer voice of sky
And cloud, of the sunken coral water-walled,
However clear, it would have been deep air,   25
The heaving speech of air, a summer sound
Repeated in a summer without end
And sound alone. But it was more than that,
More even than her voice, and ours, among
The meaningless plungings of water and the wind,   30
Theatrical distances, bronze shadows heaped
On high horizons, mountainous atmospheres
Of sky and sea.

1934. *Ideas of Order*, 1936.

See Additional Notes (p. 770).

Key West: the coral island in the Florida keys southwest of the southern tip of the state, a vacation spot especially attractive to artists and writers.

1 **beyond the genius:** surpassing the ability   2 **formed:** took on a form   8 **a mask:** a mere cover for something under it   16 **ever-hooded:** shrouded in mystery

It was her voice that made
The sky acutest at its vanishing.
She measured to the hour its solitude. 35
She was the single artificer of the world
In which she sang. And when she sang, the sea,
Whatever self it had, became the self
That was her song, for she was the maker. Then we,
As we beheld her striding there alone, 40
Knew that there never was a world for her
Except the one she sang and, singing, made.

Ramon Fernandez, tell me, if you know,
Why, when the singing ended and we turned
Toward the town, tell why the glassy lights, 45
The lights in the fishing boats at anchor there,
As the night descended, tilting in the air,
Mastered the night and portioned out the sea,
Fixing emblazoned zones and fiery poles,
Arranging, deepening, enchanting night. 50

Oh! Blessed rage for order, pale Ramon,
The maker's rage to order words of the sea,
Words of the fragrant portals, dimly-starred,
And of ourselves and of our origins,
In ghostlier demarcations, keener sounds. 55

33-34 See Additional Notes (p. 770). 35 **she measured . . .**: It is only a human interpretation that finds solitude in nature, which is impersonal (cf. "The Snow Man"). 36 **artificer:** craftsman, artisan, artistic creator [Stevens accented the first syllable when reading the poem]. 43 **Ramon Fernandez:** Stevens had read some of the work of the critic named Ramón Fernández (1894–1944), but said "the name was not intended to be anyone at all. I chose two everyday Spanish names." 53, 55 See Additional Notes (p. 770).

A Postcard from the Volcano

Children picking up our bones
Will never know that these were once
As quick as foxes on the hill;

And that in autumn, when the grapes
Made sharp air sharper by their smell 5
These had a being, breathing frost;

And least will guess that with our bones
We left much more, left what still is
The look of things, left what we felt

At what we saw. The spring clouds blow 10
Above the shuttered mansion-house,
Beyond our gate and the windy sky

Cries out a literate despair.
We knew for long the mansion's look
And what we said of it became 15

1936. Ibid.

See Additional Notes (p. 770).

13 **literate:** lucid, almost in words

A part of what it is . . . Children,
Still weaving budded aureoles,
Will speak our speech and never know,

Will say of the mansion that it seems
As if he that lived there left behind   20
A spirit storming in blank walls,

A dirty house in a gutted world,
A tatter of shadows peaked to white,
Smeared with the gold of the opulent sun.

17 **aureoles:** wreaths

The Man on the Dump

Day creeps down. The moon is creeping up.
The sun is a corbeil of flowers the moon Blanche
Places there, a bouquet. Ho-ho . . . The dump is full
Of images. Days pass like papers from a press.
The bouquets come here in the papers. So the sun,   5
And so the moon, both come, and the janitor's poems
Of every day, the wrapper on the can of pears,
The cat in the paper-bag, the corset, the box
From Esthonia: the tiger chest, for tea.

The freshness of night has been fresh a long time.   10
The freshness of morning, the blowing of day, one says
That it puffs as Cornelius Nepos reads, it puffs
More than, less than or it puffs like this or that.
The green smacks in the eye, the dew in the green
Smacks like fresh water in a can, like the sea   15
On a cocoanut—how many men have copied dew
For buttons, how many women have covered themselves
With dew, dew dresses, stones and chains of dew, heads
Of the floweriest flowers dewed with the dewiest dew.
One grows to hate these things except on the dump.   20

Now, in the time of spring (azaleas, trilliums,
Myrtle, viburnums, daffodils, blue phlox),

1938. *Parts of a World,* 1942.

See Additional Notes (p. 770).

2 **corbeil:** *Corbeille* (French) means *basket.* Stevens may mean that (he once said, "French and English constitute a single language"), though with the English spelling the word generally means a sculptured basket of fruit or flowers used as architectural decoration. In either case the word is rather arty, as he knows. **the moon Blanche:** the moon personified as a lady, punningly named "Blanche," which in French means "white" 3-4 **full/Of images:** It suggests such poeticisms as those of lines 1 and 2. 5 **bouquets . . . papers:** Cf. "The Emperor of Ice Cream," line 6. Here the old bouquets end up in the dump—as realities, not as images. 6 **the janitor's poems:** the objects he disposes of, like those named in the next few lines 12 **Cornelius Nepos:** the Roman biographer and historian (c. 99–c. 24 B.C.), friend of Cicero and Catullus. He wrote an anecdotal "On Illustrious Men" in at least 16 books, most of which is lost. As a writer he has not come in for much praise—so-so at best. He was easy but uneven ("more than, less than"). It is likely enough that Stevens mentions him only for the decorative value of his name. **reads:** as in "the book reads easily" 14 **the green:** spring vegetation, now dewy 16 **copied dew:** made shiny decorations—beads, jewels, sequins, and so on—that imitate natural ones 20 **these things:** such imitation gauds and gewgaws, only interesting when they turn up in the dump 21-22 **spring:** It suggests a renewal of vision, a "purifying change," as well as a renewal of vegetation. The plants named are spring-flowering ones.

Between that disgust and this, between the things
That are on the dump (azaleas and so on)
And those that will be (azaleas and so on),   25
One feels the purifying change. One rejects
The trash.

      That's the moment when the moon creeps up
To the bubbling of bassoons. That's the time
One looks at the elephant-colorings of tires.
Everything is shed; and the moon comes up as the moon   30
(All its images are in the dump) and you see
As a man (not like an image of a man),
You see the moon rise in the empty sky.

One sits and beats an old tin can, lard pail.
One beats and beats for that which one believes.   35
That's what one wants to get near. Could it after all
Be merely oneself, as superior as the ear
To a crow's voice? Did the nightingale torture the ear,
Pack the heart and scratch the mind? And does the ear
Solace itself in peevish birds? Is it peace,   40
Is it a philosopher's honeymoon, one finds
On the dump? Is it to sit among mattresses of the dead,
Bottles, pots, shoes and grass and murmur *aptest eve:*
Is it to hear the blatter of grackles and say
Invisible priest; is it to eject, to pull   45
The day to pieces and cry *stanza my stone?*
Where was it one first heard of the truth? The the.

28 **the bubbling of bassoons:** There are of course no real bassoons playing in the city dump. Stevens is using the figure of speech (and trick of mind) called *synesthesia,* which describes the data provided by one sense in terms of another (as when we say a necktie is loud, a musical note sour or blue, etc.). The rotundity, hue, look, and mood of the rising moon are translated into images of sound and seen— or heard—as bassoonlike.   29 **the elephant-colorings of tires:** one perceives freshly, imaginatively, in new similes   30 **as the moon:** and not as the fancy personification of a lady named Blanche   34 **beats an old tin can:** makes music (poetry) out of the ordinary, not on "Apollo's lyre" or anything of the sort   37 **merely oneself:** Is everything we think we perceive chiefly a creation of our own mind, which is superior to external reality, as the ear is more sophisticated than the crow's note which it perceives? But if we only imagine these realities, why not imagine nightingales instead of crows, which are "peevish birds"? And why not imagine some place more comfortable and pleasant than a dump to take our "philosopher's honeymoon" in? [But the fact is we do not only imagine these things, though our minds may improve on them, or at least try to.]   43 **aptest eve:** the kind of fancy poetic phrasing one might use for plain things   44 **blatter:** noisy chatter   45 ***invisible priest:*** a phrase one might use to poeticize or spiritualize the grackles, as romantic poets or sentimental nature-lovers might do (Stevens himself, in his *Adagia,* wrote: "The poet is the priest of the invisible.")   46 ***stanza my stone:*** an unnatural (and obscure!) "poetic" locution   47 **the the:** As the dictionary says, *the* is "used as a function word to indicate that a following noun . . . is definite and has been previously specified by context or by circumstance (put the cat out). . . ." The *the,* then, is the individual concrete thing, *the* dump, *the* sun, *the* can of pears, *the* cat, *the* corset. This is where truth is to be found—not in some abstraction or conventional notion about things in general.

The Sense of the Sleight-of-Hand Man

One's grand flights, one's Sunday baths,
One's tootings at the weddings of the soul
Occur as they occur. So bluish clouds
Occurred above the empty house and the leaves

1939. Ibid.

See Additional Notes (p. 770).

Of the rhododendrons rattled their gold,   5
As if someone lived there. Such floods of white
Came bursting from the clouds. So the wind
Threw its contorted strength around the sky.

Could you have said the bluejay suddenly
Would swoop to earth? It is a wheel, the rays   10
Around the sun. The wheel survives the myths.
The fire eye in the clouds survives the gods.
To think of a dove with an eye of grenadine
And pines that are cornets, so it occurs,
And a little island full of geese and stars: 15
It may be that the ignorant man, alone,
Has any chance to mate his life with life
That is the sensual, pearly spouse, the life
That is fluent in even the wintriest bronze.

13 **grenadine:** pomegranate-flavored syrup, or (as here) its color: orange-red   14 **cornets:** (1) the musical instrument, from the sound of wind in the pines; (2) anything cone-shaped (*cornet* is used in Britain for ice-cream cones)   15 **a little island . . . :** an example of the kind of fresh and surprising image that may occur to an imaginative person. The geese and stars are incongruous, yet strangely suggestive together, like a detail from a fairy tale.   16 **the ignorant man:** one whose fresh responses have not been rigidified by preconceptions, theories, paradigms, and so on. ("Ignorance is one of the sources of poetry" [Stevens, *Adagia*]). The ignorant man may "mate his life with life" because he is as unprogrammed, unscheduled, spontaneous as life itself.   18–19 **life/That is fluent . . . :** life that flows, is eloquent, in what seem chilly and rigid minerals (or in bronze statues)

The House Was Quiet and the World Was Calm

The house was quiet and the world was calm.
The reader became the book; and summer night

Was like the conscious being of the book.
The house was quiet and the world was calm.

The words were spoken as if there was no book,   5
Except that the reader leaned above the page,

Wanted to lean, wanted much most to be
The scholar to whom his book is true, to whom

The summer night is like a perfection of thought.
The house was quiet because it had to be.   10

The quiet was part of the meaning, part of the mind:
The access of perfection to the page.

And the world was calm. The truth in a calm world,
In which there is no other meaning, itself

Is calm, itself is summer and night, itself   15
Is the reader leaning late and reading there.

1946. *Transport to Summer*, 1947.

See Additional Notes (p. 770).

Large Red Man Reading

There were ghosts that returned to earth to hear his phrases,
As he sat there reading, aloud, the great blue tabulae.
They were those from the wilderness of stars that had expected more.

There were those that returned to hear him read from the poem of life,
Of the pans above the stove, the pots on the table, the tulips among them.   5
They were those that would have wept to step barefoot into reality.

That would have wept and been happy, have shivered in the frost
And cried out to feel it again, have run fingers over leaves
And against the most coiled thorn, have seized on what was ugly

And laughed, as he sat there reading, from out of the purple tabulae,   10
The outlines of being and its expressings, the syllables of its law:
Poesis, poesis, the literal characters, the vatic lines,

Which in those ears and in those thin, those spended hearts,
Took on color, took on shape and the size of things as they are
And spoke the feeling for them, which was what they had lacked.   15

1948. *The Auroras of Autumn,* 1950.

See Additional Notes (p. 770).

Red: suggests blood, ardor, vitality—the life the "man reading" has, as compared with the colorless ghosts   2 **blue tabulae:** *Tabulae* (Latin) are writing tablets, pages with writing on them. *Blue* for Stevens suggests the imagination. So the *blue tabulae* are pages of imaginative writing, or, as we find out later, poetry.   3 **had expected more:** in their afterlife   5 **pans ... pots:** poetry about ordinary things   10 **purple tabulae:** The blue of the imagination and the red of the reader's own vitality are now blended.   12 *Poesis:* (Latin, from the Greek *poiesis*) poetry, the art of poetry   **vatic:** prophetic, oracular (*Vates* is the Latin word for seer or prophet, or for the poet in his prophetic or oracular role.)

Final Soliloquy of the Interior Paramour

Light the first light of evening, as in a room
In which we rest and, for small reason, think
The world imagined is the ultimate good.

This is, therefore, the intensest rendezvous.
It is in that thought that we collect ourselves,   5
Out of all the indifferences, into one thing:

Within a single thing, a single shawl
Wrapped tightly round us, since we are poor, a warmth,
A light, a power, the miraculous influence.

Here, now, we forget each other and ourselves.   10
We feel the obscurity of an order, a whole,
A knowledge, that which arranged the rendezvous,

1951. *The Collected Poems,* 1955.

See Additional Notes (p. 770).

1 **first light:** the candle of line 15, which comes to symbolize the light of the imagination   2 **for small reason:** perhaps because we cannot be dogmatic about ultimates, "since we are poor" (in ability, knowledge, etc.)   4 **intensest rendezvous:** that between the "interior paramour" of the title and the world as imagined

Within its vital boundary, in the mind.
We say God and the imagination are one . . .
How high that highest candle lights the dark.   15

Out of this same light, out of the central mind,
We make a dwelling in the evening air,
In which being there together is enough.

14 **we say . . . :** Imagination is the supreme creative principle of our universe; "we say " it is God.
16 **same light:** the imagination   **the central mind:** man's composite consciousness, which provides a
kind of companionable shelter for all of us as the shadows darken

The Planet on the Table

Ariel was glad he had written his poems.
They were of a remembered time
Or of something seen that he liked.

Other makings of the sun
Were waste and welter   5
And the ripe shrub writhed.

His self and the sun were one
And his poems, although makings of his self,
Were no less makings of the sun.

It was not important that they survive.   10
What mattered was that they should bear
Some lineament or character,

Some affluence, if only half-perceived,
In the poverty of their words,
Of the planet of which they were part.   15

1953. Ibid.

The best-known of several Ariels in English poetry is the "airy spirit" in Shakespeare's *The Tempest*.
Here Ariel is a name for the poet.

The River of Rivers in Connecticut

There is a great river this side of Stygia,
Before one comes to the first black cataracts
And trees that lack the intelligence of trees.

In that river, far this side of Stygia,
The mere flowing of the water is a gayety,   5
Flashing and flashing in the sun. On its banks,

No shadow walks. The river is fateful,
Like the last one. But there is no ferryman.
He could not bend against its propelling force.

1953. Ibid.

1 **Stygia:** a made-up name for the region of the River Styx, which (in classical mythology) divided the
land of the living from that of the dead. The "great river" this side of it is the river of life, the river of
all things living.   3 **trees that lack the intelligence . . . :** that do not have the vital principle that de-
termines natural growth in this world   7 **fateful:** determining destiny   8 **the last one:** the Styx
no ferryman: as the Styx has, in Charon

It is not to be seen beneath the appearances   10
That tell of it. The steeple at Farmington
Stands glistening and Haddam shines and sways.

It is the third commonness with light and air,
A curriculum, a vigor, a local abstraction . . .
Call it, once more, a river, an unnamed flowing,   15

Space-filled, reflecting the seasons, the folk-lore
Of each of the senses; call it, again and again,
The river that flows nowhere, like a sea.

11 **Farmington:** a Connecticut town a few miles west of Hartford (where Stevens lived) 12 **Haddam:** a town on the Connecticut River, about 20 miles south of Hartford 13 **third commonness** . . . : As epigraph to his poem "Evening without Angels," Stevens quotes the Italian philosopher Mario Rossi: "the great interests of man: air and light, the joy of having a body, the voluptuousness of looking." 14 **curriculum:** a course of study—but also evoking the root meaning of what runs or flows, as in *current*

Not Ideas About the Thing but the Thing Itself

At the earliest ending of winter,
In March, a scrawny cry from outside
Seemed like a sound in his mind.

He knew that he heard it,
A bird's cry, at daylight or before,   5
In the early March wind.

The sun was rising at six,
No longer a battered panache above snow . . .
It would have been outside.

It was not from the vast ventriloquism   10
Of sleep's faded papier-mâché . . .
The sun was coming from outside.

That scrawny cry—It was
A chorister whose c preceded the choir.
It was part of the colossal sun,   15

Surrounded by its choral rings,
Still far away. It was like
A new knowledge of reality.

1954. Ibid.

8 **panache:** an ornamental plume, as on a helmet 11 **papier-mâché:** moulded paper—such as might be used to make imitative decorative objects 14 **whose c preceded** . . . : whose single musical note preceded the choir of birds to be heard when spring came 15 **sun:** the real world outside—reality

Vachel Lindsay
(1879–1931)

Lindsay, born in Springfield, Illinois, went to Hiram College in Ohio, left to study art in Chicago and New York, and for several summers wandered around the country reciting his poems in exchange for meals and a place to sleep. In 1913 *Poetry* published his poem on General William Booth, the founder of the Salvation Army. Lindsay soon became a celebrity as platform poet, giving performances of his poems that he called the "higher vaudeville." By the late twenties the novelty had worn off and he was less in demand. Failing health, discouragement, and financial troubles led to his suicide in Springfield.

I Heard Immanuel Singing

I heard Immanuel singing
Within his own good lands,
I saw him bend above his harp.
I watched his wandering hands
Lost amid the harp-strings;   5
Sweet, sweet I heard him play.
His wounds were altogether healed.
Old things had passed away.

All things were new, but music.
The blood of David ran   10
Within the Son of David,
Our God, the Son of Man.
He was ruddy like a shepherd.
His bold young face, how fair.
Apollo of the silver bow   15
Had not such flowing hair.

I saw Immanuel singing
On a tree-girdled hill.
The glad remembering branches
Dimly echoed still   20
The grand new song proclaiming
The Lamb that had been slain.
New-built, the Holy City
Gleamed in the murmuring plain.

The crowning hours were over.   25
The pageants all were past.
Within the many mansions
The hosts, grown still at last,
In homes of holy mystery
Slept long by crooning springs   30
Or waked to peaceful glory,
A universe of Kings.

1906. *The Tramp's Excuse*, 1909 (pamphlet). *The Congo and Other Poems*, 1914.

See Additional Notes (p. 770).

8 Old things had passed away: "The former things are passed away" (Rev. 21:4).   **9 All things were new** ...: "And I saw a new heaven and a new earth ..." (Rev. 21:1).   **10 The blood of David** ...: "I [Jesus] am the root and the offspring of David ..." (Rev. 22:16).   **12 the Son of Man:** "... I saw ... one like unto the Son of man ..." (Rev. 1:12–13).   **15 Apollo of the silver bow:** Apollo was god of music and archery, among other things. Homer mentions his silver bow at the beginning of the *Iliad* (I, 49).   **18 tree-girdled:** "and on either side of the river [of the water of life, flowing from the throne of God], was there the tree of life ..." (Rev. 22:1–2)   **hill:** in the Psalms, the Lord is described as being on his "holy hill"   **21 new song:** "And they sang a new song ..." (Rev. 5:9 and elsewhere). David in the Psalms speaks of singing a "new song."   **22 the Lamb that had been slain:** "and in the midst of the elders, stood a Lamb as it had been slain ..." (Rev. 5:6).   **23 Holy City:** "I John saw the holy city, new Jerusalem ..." (Rev. 21:2)   **30 springs:** "And he shewed me a pure river of water of life, clear as crystal ..." (Rev. 22:1).

He left his people happy.
He wandered free to sigh
Alone in lowly friendship   35
With the green grass and the sky.
He murmured ancient music
His red heart burned to sing
Because his perfect conquest
Had grown a weary thing.   40

No chant of gilded triumph—
His lonely song was made
Of Art's deliberate freedom;
Of minor chords arrayed
In soft and shadowy colors   45
That once were radiant flowers:—
The Rose of Sharon, bleeding
In Olive-shadowed bowers:—

And all the other roses
In the songs of East and West   50
Of love and war and worshipping,
And every shield and crest
Of thistle or of lotus
Or sacred lily wrought
In creeds and psalms and palaces   55
And temples of white thought:—

All these he sang, half-smiling
And weeping as he smiled,
Laughing, talking to his harp
As to a new-born child:—   60
As though the arts forgotten
But bloomed to prophecy
These careless, fearless harp-strings,
New-crying in the sky.

"When this his hour of sorrow   65
For flowers and Arts of men
Has passed in ghostly music,"
I asked my wild heart then—
What will he sing to-morrow,
What wonder, all his own   70
Alone, set free, rejoicing,
With a green hill for his throne?
What will he sing to-morrow
What wonder all his own
Alone, set free, rejoicing,   75
With a green hill for his throne?

---

34 to sigh: This is Immanuel's "hour of sorrow" (line 65) because, says Lindsay, "he sings a requiem for all the beauty destroyed by the Judgment Day"—he is sad for all the lost beauty of the world. **47 the Rose of Sharon:** "I am the Rose of Sharon" (Song of Sol. 2:1). Sharon is a coastal region in Israel. **48 Olive-shadowed bowers:** a reference to the Garden of Olives, Gethsemane, where Christ suffered an agony of thought before his death. In a notebook, Lindsay speculated on whether the experience was "the last act in the great character building" or "the seer's agony of loneliness, the gathering of resolution to make good at the trial." **49–56 other roses:** other achievements of human art and poetry outside of the Biblical tradition: Egypt, India, Greece, and the rest

William Carlos Williams
(1883–1963)

Williams was born in Rutherford, New Jersey; his father remained a British subject though in business in America, his mother was a Puerto Rican who had studied art in Paris. In his teens Williams went to school in Switzerland and Paris, returned to commute to a New York high school, then studied medicine at the University of Pennsylvania, where he met Ezra Pound. After three years of internship in New York and a year of study in Leipzig, Williams settled down as poet-pediatrician in Rutherford. He published close to 50 books of poetry, drama, essays, fiction, autobiography. *Paterson*, his ambitious epic named for the nearby New Jersey city, appeared in five parts (1946–1958). After a stroke in 1951, Williams gave up his medical practice; he continued to write busily in spite of other such attacks.

To Waken an Old Lady

Old age is
a flight of small
cheeping birds
skimming
bare trees   5
above a snow glaze.
Gaining and failing
they are buffetted
by a dark wind—
But what?   10
On harsh weedstalks
the flock has rested,
the snow
is covered with broken
seedhusks   15
and the wind tempered
by a shrill
piping of plenty.

By 1920. *Sour Grapes*, 1921.

The Widow's Lament in Springtime

Sorrow is my own yard
where the new grass
flames as it has flamed
often before but not
with the cold fire   5
that closes round me this year.
Thirtyfive years
I lived with my husband.
The plumtree is white today
with masses of flowers.   10
Masses of flowers
load the cherry branches
and color some bushes
yellow and some red
but the grief in my heart   15

Ibid.

is stronger than they
for though they were my joy
formerly, today I notice them
and turn away forgetting.
Today my son told me   20
that in the meadows,
at the edge of the heavy woods
in the distance, he saw
trees of white flowers.
I feel that I would like   25
to go there
and fall into those flowers
and sink into the marsh near them.

From **Spring and All**

I

By the road to the contagious hospital
under the surge of the blue
mottled clouds driven from the
northeast—a cold wind. Beyond, the
waste of broad, muddy fields   5
brown with dried weeds, standing and fallen

patches of standing water
the scattering of tall trees

All along the road the reddish
purplish, forked, upstanding, twiggy   10
stuff of bushes and small trees
with dead, brown leaves under them
leafless vines—

Lifeless in appearance, sluggish
dazed spring approaches—   15

They enter the new world naked,
cold, uncertain of all
save that they enter. All about them
the cold, familiar wind—

Now the grass, tomorrow   20
the stiff curl of wildcarrot leaf

One by one objects are defined—
It quickens: clarity, outline of leaf

But now the stark dignity of
entrance—Still, the profound change   25
has come upon them: rooted they
grip down and begin to awaken

Spring and All, 1923.

21 **wildcarrot:** The prettier name, which Williams uses elsewhere but may feel inappropriate to this stark poem, is Queen Anne's lace.

XXI

so much depends
upon

a red wheel
barrow

glazed with rain   5
water

beside the white
chickens

Ibid. (as "The Red Wheelbarrow").

We could think of this famous little snapshot-with-comment as another poem about "the the." The
spacing on the page slows and focuses our reading, so that our mind is made to dwell on the details.
The expressive use of space as a way of controlling tempo and meaning is sometimes called *spatial
scansion*.

Nantucket

Flowers through the window
lavender and yellow

changed by white curtains—
Smell of cleanliness—

Sunshine of late afternoon—   5
On the glass tray

a glass pitcher, the tumbler
turned down, by which

a key is lying—And the
immaculate white bed   10

Collected Poems 1921–1931, 1934.

Nantucket is a picturesque island (57 square miles in area) south of Cape Cod. Once a large whaling
port, it is now attractive to artists, tourists, vacationers.

The Dance

In Breughel's great picture, The Kermess,
the dancers go round, they go round and
around, the squeal and the blare and the
tweedle of bagpipes, a bugle and fiddles
tipping their bellies (round as the thick-   5
sided glasses whose wash they impound)
their hips and their bellies off balance
to turn them. Kicking and rolling about
the Fair Grounds, swinging their butts, those

By 1942. *The Wedge*, 1944.

1 **Breughel:** (generally spelled "Brueghel") Pieter Brueghel the Elder (c. 1525–1569), greatest of the
Flemish painters of his century. His "Kermess" ("Wedding Dance") is a lively depiction of swirling
figures.

shanks must be sound to bear up under such   10
rollicking measures, prance as they dance
in Breughel's great picture, the Kermess.

The Descent

The descent beckons
        as the ascent beckoned.
                Memory is a kind
of accomplishment,
        a sort of renewal   5
                even
an initiation, since the spaces it opens are new places
        inhabited by hordes
                heretofore unrealized,
of new kinds—   10
        since their movements
                are toward new objectives
(even though formerly they were abandoned).

No defeat is made up entirely of defeat—since
the world it opens is always a place   15
        formerly
                unsuspected. A
world lost,
        a world unsuspected,
                beckons to new places   20
and no whiteness (lost) is so white as the memory
of whiteness

With evening, love wakens
        though its shadows
                which are alive by reason   25
of the sun shining—
        grow sleepy now and drop away
                from desire

Love without shadows stirs now
        beginning to awaken   30
                as night
advances.

The descent
        made up of despairs
                and without accomplishment   35
realizes a new awakening:
        which is a reversal
of despair.
        For what we cannot accomplish, what
is denied to love,   40
        what we have lost in the anticipation—
                a descent follows,
endless and indestructible

By 1947. *Paterson*, Book Two, 1948. As a separate poem, "The Descent," *The Desert Music*, 1954.

The *descent* is from the prime of life into old age. For the rhythm of Williams's *variable foot*, see the prosody section.

The Orchestra

The precise counterpart
      of a cacophony of bird calls
            lifting the sun almighty
into his sphere: wood-winds
      clarinet and violins
            sound a prolonged A!   5
Ah! the sun, the sun! is about to rise
      and shed his beams
            as he has always done
upon us all,   10
      drudges and those
            who live at ease,
women and men,
      upon the old,
            upon children and the sick   15
who are about to die and are indeed
      dead in their beds,
            to whom his light
is forever lost. The cello
      raises his bass note
            manfully in the treble din: 20
Ah, ah and ah!
      together, unattuned
            seeking a common tone.
Love is that common tone   25
      shall raise his fiery head
            and sound his note.

The purpose of an orchestra
      is to organize those sounds
            and hold them
to an assembled order   .   30
      in spite of the
            "wrong note." Well, shall we
think or listen? Is there a sound addressed
      not wholly to the ear?   35
            We half close
our eyes. We do not
      hear it through our eyes.
            It is not
a flute note either, it is the relation   40
      of a flute note
            to a drum. I am wide
awake. The mind
      is listening. The ear
            is alerted. But the ear   45
in a half-reluctant mood
      stretches
              .   .   and yawns.

And so the banked violins
      in three tiers
            enliven the scene,   50

By 1952. *The Desert Music*, 1954.

pizzicato. For a short
      memory or to
           make the listener listen
the theme is repeated   55
      stressing a variant:
           it is a principle of music
to repeat the theme. Repeat
      and repeat again,
           as the pace mounts. The   60
theme is difficult   .
      but no more difficult
           than the facts to be
resolved. Repeat
      and repeat the theme   65
           and all it develops to be
until thought is dissolved
      in tears.
           Our dreams
have been assaulted   70
      by a memory that will not
           sleep. The
French horns
      interpose
        .   .   their voices: 75
I love you. My heart
      is innocent. And this
           the first day of the world!

Say to them:
"Man has survived hitherto because he was too ignorant   80
to know how to realize his wishes. Now that he can realize
them, he must either change them or perish."

Now is the time   .
      in spite of the "wrong note"
           I love you. My heart is   85
innocent.
      And this the first
           (and last) day of the world

The birds twitter now anew
      but a design   90
           surmounts their twittering.
It is a design of a man
      that makes them twitter.
           It is a design.

52 **pizzicato:** with strings plucked instead of being sounded by the bow

The Yellow Flower

What shall I say, because talk I must?
      That I have found a cure
           for the sick?

By 1953. Ibid.

I have found no cure
            for the sick   5
                        but this crooked flower
which only to look upon
            all men
                        are cured. This
is that flower   10
            for which all men
                        sing secretly their hymns
of praise. This
            is that sacred
                        flower!   15

Can this be so?
            A flower so crooked
                        and obscure? It is
a mustard flower,
            and not a mustard flower,   20
                        a single spray
topping the deformed stem
            of fleshy leaves
                        in this freezing weather
under glass.   25

An ungainly flower and
            an unnatural one,
                        in this climate; what
can be the reason
            that it has picked me out   30
                        to hold me, openmouthed,
rooted before this window
            in the cold,
                        my will
drained from me   35
            so that I have only eyes
                        for these yellow,
twisted petals   .   ?

That the sight,
            though strange to me,   40
                        must be a common one,
is clear: there are such flowers
            with such leaves
                        native to some climate
which they can call   45
            their own.

But why the torture
            and the escape through
                        the flower? It is
as if Michelangelo   50
            had conceived the subject

---

19 **mustard flower:** There are many varieties of the mustard flower in the United States. Typically, it is a tall weedlike plant with small pale-yellow flowers.   50–53 **Michelangelo ... *Slaves* ... :** The Florentine painter, sculptor, and architect Michelangelo Buonarroti (1475–1564) and his assistants left four unfinished marble statues called the "Captives" or the "Giants" or—as here—the "Slaves." Because unfinished, they seem to be struggling to free themselves from the stone in which they are half embedded.

                        of his *Slaves* from this
—or might have done so.
            And did he not make
                        the marble bloom? I   55
am sad
            as he was sad
                        in his heroic mood.
But also
            I have eyes   60
                        that are made to see and if
they see ruin for myself
            and all that I hold
                        dear, they see
also   65
            through the eyes
                        and through the lips
and tongue the power
            to free myself
                        and speak of it, as   70
Michelangelo through his hands
            had the same, if greater,
                        power.

Which leaves, to account for,
            the tortured bodies   75
                        of
the slaves themselves
            and
                        the tortured body of my flower
which is not a mustard flower at all   80
            but some unrecognized
                        and unearthly flower
for me to naturalize
            and accclimate
                        and choose it for my own.   85

D. H. Lawrence
(1885–1930)

Lawrence's father was a coal miner; his mother, who had been a teacher, encouraged the boy's artistic interests. After earning his teacher's certificate, he taught in a London suburb until 1912, when he fell in love with Frieda von Richthofen, the wife of his former French professor, and went off to Italy with her; after her divorce they were married. Unhappy with what he thought the constraints of our industrial world and in search of a place to lead a more natural life, Lawrence began the wanderings that took him from Italy to Germany to Ceylon to Australia to New Mexico to Mexico—and back to Europe, where he died in a tuberculosis sanatorium in southern France at the age of 44. Throughout his troubled life he wrote busily, producing over a dozen novels, works on literature, on psychology, and on travel, as well as several books of poetry.

Piano

Softly, in the dusk, a woman is singing to me;
Taking me back down the vista of years, till I see
A child sitting under the piano, in the boom of the tingling strings
And pressing the small, poised feet of a mother who smiles as she sings.

New Poems, 1918. A longer and very different early version (c. 1911) was left in MS.

In spite of myself, the insidious mastery of song   5
Betrays me back, till the heart of me weeps to belong
To the old Sunday evenings at home, with winter outside
And hymns in the cosy parlour, the tinkling piano our guide.

So now it is vain for the singer to burst into clamour
With the great black piano appassionato. The glamour   10
Of childish days is upon me, my manhood is cast
Down in the flood of remembrance, I weep like a child for the past.

10 **appassionato:** passionate, impassioned [Italian musical term]

Bat

At evening, sitting on this terrace,
When the sun from the west, beyond Pisa, beyond the mountains of Carrara
Departs, and the world is taken by surprise . . .

When the tired flower of Florence is in gloom beneath the glowing
Brown hills surrounding . . .   5
When under the arches of the Ponte Vecchio
A green light enters against stream, flush from the west,
Against the current of obscure Arno . . .

Look up, and you see things flying
Between the day and the night;   10
Swallows with spools of dark thread sewing the shadows together.
A circle swoop, and a quick parabola under the bridge arches
Where light pushes through;
A sudden turning upon itself of a thing in the air.
A dip to the water.   15

And you think:
"The swallows are flying so late!"

Swallows?

Dark air-life looping
Yet missing the pure loop . . .   20
A twitch, a twitter, an elastic shudder in flight
And serrated wings against the sky,
Like a glove, a black glove thrown up at the light,
And falling back.

Never swallows!   25
Bats!
The swallows are gone.

At a wavering instant the swallows give way to bats
By the Ponte Vecchio . . .
Changing guard.   30

1921. *Birds, Beasts and Flowers*, 1923.

The scene of the poem is Florence, famous for its artistic and cultural heritage, in Tuscany in north central Italy. To the west, near the sea, is Pisa, and above Pisa, on the coast, Carrara, famous for its white marble. The name *Florence* is related to words for "flower," hence the "tired flower" of line 4.

6 **Ponte Vecchio:** (ancient bridge) a picturesque bridge in Florence over the river Arno, rebuilt in 1345   22 **serrated:** with notched or saw-toothed edges

Bats, and an uneasy creeping in one's scalp
As the bats swoop overhead!
Flying madly.

Pipistrello!
Black piper on an infinitesimal pipe. 35
Little lumps that fly in air and have voices indefinite, wildly vindictive;

Wings like bits of umbrella.

Bats!

Creatures that hang themselves up like an old rag, to sleep;
And disgustingly upside down. 40
Hanging upside down like rows of disgusting old rags
And grinning in their sleep.
Bats!

In China the bat is symbol of happiness.

Not for me! 45

34 **pipistrello:** (Italian) bat. The word looks as if it might mean "little piper," but its derivation is different.

Bavarian Gentians

Not every man has gentians in his house
in Soft September, at slow, sad Michaelmas.

Bavarian gentians, big and dark, only dark
darkening the day-time, torch-like with the smoking blueness of Pluto's
    gloom,
ribbed and torch-like, with their blaze of darkness spread blue 5
down flattening into points, flattened under the sweep of white day
torch-flower of the blue-smoking darkness, Pluto's dark-blue daze,
black lamps from the halls of Dis, burning dark blue,
giving off darkness, blue darkness, as Demeter's pale lamps give off light,
lead me then, lead the way. 10

Reach me a gentian, give me a torch!
let me guide myself with the blue, forked torch of this flower
down the darker and darker stairs, where blue is darkened on blueness
even where Persephone goes, just now, from the frosted September
to the sightless realm where darkness is awake upon the dark 15
and Persephone herself is but a voice
or a darkness invisible enfolded in the deeper dark
of the arms Plutonic, and pierced with the passion of dense gloom,
among the splendour of torches of darkness, shedding darkness on the lost
    bride and her groom.

1929. *Last Poems*, Florence, 1932. Other versions were left in MS.

2 **Michaelmas:** September 29, the feast of St. Michael   4 **Pluto:** Greek god of the underworld. His Roman name was Dis (line 8)   9 **Demeter:** Greek goddess of grain and agriculture (Latin, Ceres, whence *cereal*, etc.)   14 **Persephone:** a spring goddess, daughter of Demeter. Because of her beauty she was carried off to the underworld by Pluto and became his queen. Though later released by Zeus, she still had to spend part of each year in the underworld, to which Lawrence now imagines her descending.

Middle of the World

This sea will never die, neither will it ever grow old
nor cease to be blue, nor in the dawn
cease to lift up its hills
and let the slim black ship of Dionysos come sailing in
with grape-vines up the mast, and dolphins leaping.   5

What do I care if the smoking ships
of the P. & O. and the Orient Line and all the other stinkers
cross like clock-work the Minoan distance!
They only cross, the distance never changes.

And now that the moon who gives men glistening bodies   10
is in her exaltation, and can look down on the sun
I see descending from the ships at dawn
slim naked men from Cnossos, smiling the archaic smile
of those that will without fail come back again,
and kindling little fires upon the shores   15
and crouching, and speaking the music of lost languages.

And the Minoan Gods, and the Gods of Tiryns
are heard softly laughing and chatting, as ever;
and Dionysos, young, and a stranger
leans listening on the gate, in all respect.   20

Ibid.

The Latin derivation of Mediterranean is from two words, *medius* and *terra*, that mean "middle of the world."

4 Dionysos: For the story of the magic ship of Dionysos, cf. Ezra Pound, "Canto II," lines 40 ff. The theme was often used in Greek art.   **7 P. & O.:** Like the Orient Line, the Peninsular & Oriental Company was a British steamship line in regular service through the Mediterranean.   **8 Minoan:** The Minoan civilization, named for the legendary King Minos, flourished on the island of Crete from about 3000 to 1100 B.C.   **13 Cnossos:** city in ancient Crete (also Knossos, Gnossos)   **the archaic smile:** the little curved smile like that on archaic Greek statues   **17 Tiryns:** pre-Homeric Greek city

Ezra Pound
(1885–1972)

Born in Hailey, Idaho, Pound grew up in a suburb of Philadelphia, where his father was an assayer at the Mint. Having decided to be a poet, Pound took an M.A. at the University of Pennsylvania in Romance literature. After teaching briefly at Wabash College, he went to Venice in 1908; there he published his first book of poems. For the next dozen years he was in London, where he held various editorial jobs, was secretary to Yeats, and became interested in Chinese. Disappointed in England, he left for Paris in 1920; four years later he moved to Rapallo, Italy, where he worked furiously on his *Cantos* and on writings about politics and economics, with which he was becoming increasingly involved. He always found time, however, to write generous letters of technical advice and exhortation to young writers who appealed to him for help. Through these letters, through his many reviews and essays and the example of his own poetry, and perhaps especially through his tireless energy and the force of his vivid personality, he exerted a powerful influence on the poets of his time—even on such giants as Yeats and Eliot. Eccentric on other topics, his mind rarely if ever lost its brilliant lucidity when dealing with poetry. When war broke out between the United States and Italy, Pound continued the pro-Italian, anti-American talks he had been making over Italian radio—they were now technically treasonable. In 1945 he was arrested. Taken to Washington and charged with treason, he escaped sentence when four psychiatrists found him unable to stand trial. The next 12 years he spent in a psychiatric hospital in Washington. There he continued his Chinese studies and worked at his *Cantos*, receiving visitors from all over the world. With the intercession of such distinguished men of letters as Archibald MacLeish and Robert Frost, he was released in 1958 and returned to Italy, where he died at the age of 87.

The Return

See, they return; ah, see the tentative
    Movements, and the slow feet,
    The trouble in the pace and the uncertain
    Wavering!

See, they return, one, and by one,   5
With fear, as half-awakened;
As if the snow should hesitate
And murmur in the wind,
            and half turn back;
These were the "Wing'd-with-Awe,"   10
    Inviolable.

Gods of the wingèd shoe!
With them the silver hounds,
          sniffing the trace of air!

Haie! Haie!   15
    These were the swift to harry;
These the keen-scented;
These were the souls of blood.

Slow on the leash,
         pallid the leash-men!   20

Ripostes, 1912.

On Pound and *free verse*, see the prosody section. Yeats, in 1914, thought this "the most beautiful poem that has been written in the free form, one of the few in which I find real organic rhythm"—he felt, that is, that the tentative and hesitant rhythms of the poem dramatized the irresolution and weakness of the ghostly figures.

1 **they:** the gods of line 12—probably the gods of the ancient world, who today have lost their vitality and are mere ghosts of themselves   10 **"Wing'd-with-Awe":** a compound epithet in the manner of the ancient Greek poets   15 **Haie!:** an exclamation probably modelled on the Greek αἴ or αλαί, which expressed grief or astonishment   18 **souls of blood:** full of vivacity and violence, as now they are bloodless. The ghosts in Homer's underworld can speak to Odysseus only after they have regained some strength by drinking animal blood.

Ité

Go, my songs, seek your praise from the young
        and from the intolerant,
Move among the lovers of perfection alone.
Seek ever to stand in the hard Sophoclean light
And take your wounds from it gladly.

By 1913. *Lustra*, 1916.

The Latin *Ité* is the imperative plural "Go."

3 **Sophoclean:** like that found in the dramas of Sophocles—firm, disciplined, severe

In a Station of the Metro

The apparition of these faces in the crowd;
Petals on a wet, black bough.

1911–1912. Ibid.

The Métro (Métropolitain) is the Paris subway. Pound (*Gaudier-Brzeska*, xi) tells how he got out of a subway train "and saw suddenly a beautiful face, and then another and another, and then a beautiful child's face, and then another beautiful woman, and I tried all that day to find words for what this had meant to me, and I could not find any words that seemed to me worthy, or as lovely as that sudden emotion. . . . I wrote a thirty-line poem, and destroyed it because it was what we call work 'of second intensity.' Six months later I made a poem half that length; a year later I made the following *hokku*-like sentence . . ." [and he quotes the poem as above]. A *hokku* or *haiku* is a Japanese poem whose three lines have 5, 7, and 5 syllables.

Alba

As cool as the pale wet leaves
                    of lily-of-the-valley
She lay beside me in the dawn.

1912–1913. Ibid.

Alba: (Provençal, *dawn*) a dawn-song or dawn-poem

The River-Merchant's Wife: A Letter

While my hair was still cut straight across my forehead
I played about the front gate, pulling flowers.
You came by on bamboo stilts, playing horse,
You walked about my seat, playing with blue plums.
And we went on living in the village of Chokan: 5
Two small people, without dislike or suspicion.

At fourteen I married My Lord you.
I never laughed, being bashful.
Lowering my head, I looked at the wall.
Called to, a thousand times, I never looked back.   10

At fifteen I stopped scowling,
I desired my dust to be mingled with yours
Forever and forever and forever.
Why should I climb the look out?

At sixteen you departed,   15
You went into far Ku-to-yen, by the river of swirling eddies,
And you have been gone five months.
The monkeys make sorrowful noise overhead.
You dragged your feet when you went out.
By the gate now, the moss is grown, the different mosses,   20

1914. *Cathay*, 1915.

In his version of this Chinese poem, based on the English notes of the scholar Ernest Fenollosa, Pound uses the Japanese place-names he found in those notes. Chokan (line 5) is the Chinese Ch'ang-kan, a port on the Yangtse River near what is now Nanking. Ku-to-Yen (Ch'ü-t'ang) (line 16) is a Yangtse gorge hundreds of miles to the west. The "river Kiang" (line 26) is a misunderstanding: *kiang* (Chinese *chiang*) means "river." Cho-fu-sa (Ch'ang-feng-sha: "Long Wind Sands") (last line) is itself a long way up the Yangtse. *Rihaku* is the Japanese name for the famous Chinese poet Li Po (eighth century).

Too deep to clear them away!
The leaves fall early this autumn, in wind.
The paired butterflies are already yellow with August
Over the grass in the West garden;
They hurt me. I grow older.   25
If you are coming down through the narrows of the river Kiang,
Please let me know beforehand,
And I will come out to meet you
                    As far as Cho-fu-Sa.

                                              By Rihaku

From **Hugh Selwyn Mauberley**

I

E. P. ODE POUR L'ELECTION DE SON SEPULCRE

For three years, out of key with his time,
He strove to resuscitate the dead art
Of poetry; to maintain "the sublime"
In the old sense. Wrong from the start—

No, hardly, but seeing he had been born   5
In a half savage country, out of date;
Bent resolutely on wringing lilies from the acorn;
Capaneus; trout for factitious bait;

'Ἴδμεν γάρ τοι πάνθ', ὅσ' ἐνὶ Τροίῃ
Caught in the unstopped ear;   10
Giving the rocks small lee-way
The chopped seas held him, therefore, that year.

His true Penelope was Flaubert,
He fished by obstinate isles;
Observed the elegance of Circe's hair   15
Rather than the mottoes on sun-dials.

Unaffected by "the march of events,"
He passed from men's memory in *l'an trentiesme*
De son eage; the case presents
No adjunct to the Muses' diadem.   20

1919. *Hugh Selwyn Mauberley*, 1920.

The poem is a farewell to London, where, Pound felt, his years of work to improve the state of poetry had been frustrated. This largely autobiographical ode for the choosing of his sepulcher (the death of his London hopes) takes its title from *Ode* IV, 5, of the French poet Pierre Ronsard (1524–1585).

I: 6 **half savage country:** Pound was born in Hailey, Idaho, in 1885.   7 **wringing . . . acorn:** The meaning (on the surface) is: doing the impossible, bringing loveliness out of what is ordinary.   8 **Capaneus:** as one of the Seven against Thebes, he defied the supreme power of Zeus. Dante (*Inferno*, XIV) shows him as still stubbornly rebellious.   **factitious:** artificial   9 The Greek quotation (from the song of the Sirens in the *Odyssey*, XII, 189) means: "For we know all the things which in Troy [the Greeks and Trojans suffered]." The speaker begins to see himself as an Odysseus-figure.   10 **unstopped:** Odysseus alone heard the Sirens; his men had their ears stopped up lest they be seduced by the music.   12 **chopped:** choppy   13 **Penelope:** here, goal or ideal. Penelope was the wife that Odysseus strove to reach during the ten years of wandering that followed the ten years' war at Troy.   **Flaubert:** Gustave Flaubert (1821–1880), the French novelist whose scrupulous technique, concern for the exact word, and contempt for received ideas Pound much admired   15–16 **elegance . . . mottoes:** the perilous attractions of an enchantress rather than prudent commonplaces   18–19 *l'an trentiesme . . . :* "the thirtieth year of his age," a variation of the first line of *Le Testament* of the French poet François Villon (1431–after 1462)   20 **adjunct:** significant addition

II

The age demanded an image
Of its accelerated grimace,
Something for the modern stage,
Not, at any rate, an Attic grace;

Not, not certainly, the obscure reveries   5
Of the inward gaze;
Better mendacities
Than the classics in paraphrase!

The "age demanded" chiefly a mould in plaster,
Made with no loss of time,   10
A prose kinema, not, not assuredly, alabaster
Or the "sculpture" of rhyme.

II: 4 **Attic:** of Attica, the region of ancient Greece in which Athens (home of the great Greek drama-
tists) was located   8 **the classics in paraphrase:** such as Pound's own *Homage to Sextus Propertius* (p.
533)   11 **kinema:** cinema—the Greek word means "movement," as of actors on a stage, or "moving
things"   **alabaster:** a fine translucent stone, generally white, from which vases, statues, etc. are
carved   12 **"sculpture":** because verse presumably takes more effort than a "prose kinema." Pound
liked the hardness and clarity of sculpture.

Envoi (1919)

Go, dumb-born book,
Tell her that sang me once that song of Lawes:
Hadst thou but song
As thou hast subjects known,
Then were there cause in thee that should condone   5
Even my faults that heavy upon me lie,
And build her glories their longevity.

Tell her that sheds
Such treasure in the air,
Recking naught else but that her graces give   10
Life to the moment,
I would bid them live
As roses might, in magic amber laid,
Red overwrought with orange and all made
One substance and one colour   15
Braving time.

Tell her that goes
With song upon her lips
But sings not out the song, nor knows
The maker of it, some other mouth,   20

1919. Ibid.

An *envoi* (or envoy) is generally the concluding section of a poem that sends it on its way, makes it an
envoy, or sort of ambassador, with a message, as this poem does.

2 **her:** Asked in 1959 who the girl of the poem was, Pound replied, "Your question is the kind of
damn-fool inquiry into what is nobody's damn business." [She was the French singer Raymonde
Collignon.]   **Lawes:** the composer Henry Lawes (1596–1662) set to music some of the poems of
Edmund Waller, whose "Go, Lovely Rose" (p. 131) is echoed in "Envoi (1919)."   3–4 if your (the
book's) poetic talent were as great as your subject, her beauty, is   7 **build . . . longevity:** make her
glory long lasting (as Elizabethan poets often promised to do—cf. the last line of Shakespeare's Son-
net 18)

May be as fair as hers,
Might, in new ages, gain her worshippers,
When our two dusts with Waller's shall be laid,
Siftings on siftings in oblivion,
Till change hath broken down   25
All things save Beauty alone.

21 **may be:** maybe

From Homage to Sextus Propertius

I

Shades of Callimachus, Coan ghosts of Philetas,
It is in your grove I would walk,
I who come first from the clear font
Bringing the Grecian orgies into Italy,
                                     and the dance into Italy.   5
Who hath taught you so subtle a measure,
                         in what hall have you heard it;
What foot beat out your time-bar,
                         what water has mellowed your whistles?

Out-weariers of Apollo will, as we know, continue their Martian
     generalities,   10
     We have kept our erasers in order.
A new-fangled chariot follows the flower-hung horses;
A young Muse with young loves clustered about her
                         ascends with me into the æther, . . .
And there is no high-road to the Muses.   15

Annalists will continue to record Roman reputations,
Celebrities from the Trans-Caucasus will belaud Roman celebrities
And expound the distentions of Empire,
But for something to read in normal circumstances?
For a few pages brought down from the forked hill unsullied?   20
I ask a wreath which will not crush my head.
                         And there is no hurry about it;
I shall have, doubtless, a boom after my funeral,
Seeing that long standing increases all things regardless of quality.

And who would have known the towers   25
                         pulled down by a deal-wood horse;
Or of Achilles withstaying waters by Simois,
Or of Hector spattering wheel-rims,
Or of Polydmantus, by Scamander, or Helenus and Deiphoibos?
Their door-yards would scarcely know them, or Paris.   30

1917. *Quia Pauper Amavi*, 1919.

Pound's "homage" here is a free translation or adaptation (frequently taking off on its own) of *Elegies*,
III, 1 and 2, of the Roman poet Propertius, who lived from about 50 to 15 B.C.

1 **Callímachus:** scholar-poet of the third century B.C. who, among the 800 volumes credited to him,
wrote a number of elegies **Philétas:** scholar-poet of the island of Cos, considered second to his
younger contemporary Callimachus as a writer of elegies 14 **æther:** upper air 15 **high-road:** easy
way 17 **Trans-Caucasus:** regions northwest of Turkey, in modern Russia 20 **the forked hill:** Par-
nassus, with its twin peaks, is sacred to the Muses. 25 **towers:** at Troy 26 **deal-wood:** made of
planks of fir or pine 27 **Simois:** a Trojan river (like Scamander, below) against which Achilles, the
Greek hero, fought 29 **Polydmantus:** Pound's spelling of Polydamas, who, like Hector, Helenus,
and Deiphobus [sic], was a Trojan leader 30 **Paris:** the lover of Helen of Troy

Small talk O Ilion, and O Troad

                          twice taken by Oetian gods,

If Homer had not stated your case!

And I also among the later nephews of this city

                          shall have my dog's day,   35

With no stone upon my contemptible sepulchre;

My vote coming from the temple of Phoebus in Lycia, at Patara,

And in the meantime my songs will travel,

And the devirginated young ladies will enjoy them

                     when they have got over the strangeness,   40

For Orpheus tamed the wild beasts—

                   and held up the Threician river;

And Cithaeron shook up the rocks by Thebes

                and danced them into a bulwark at his pleasure,

And you, O Polyphemus? Did harsh Galatea almost   45

Turn to your dripping horses, because of a tune, under Aetna?

We must look into the matter.

Bacchus and Apollo in favour of it,

There will be a crowd of young women doing homage to my palaver,

Though my house is not propped up by Taenarian columns from Laconia

         (associated with Neptune and Cerberus),   50

Though it is not stretched upon gilded beams;

My orchards do not lie level and wide

                  as the forests of Phaeacia,

                  the luxurious and Ionian,

Nor are my caverns stuffed stiff with a Marcian vintage,   55

My cellar does not date from Numa Pompilius,

Nor bristle with wine jars,

Nor is it equipped with a frigidaire patent;

Yet the companions of the Muses

              will keep their collective nose in my books,   60

And weary with historical data, they will turn to my dance tune.

Happy who are mentioned in my pamphlets,

        the songs shall be a fine tomb-stone over their beauty.

        But against this?

Neither expensive pyramids scraping the stars in their route,   65

Nor houses modelled upon that of Jove in East Elis,

Nor the monumental effigies of Mausolus,

           are a complete elucidation of death.

Flame burns, rain sinks into the cracks

And they all go to rack ruin beneath the thud of the years.   70

Stands genius a deathless adornment,

        a name not to be worn out with the years.

---

31 **Ilion, Troad:** Troy 32 **Oetian gods:** The god (not gods) of Mt. Oeta was Hercules, who died there. 37 **Lycia:** a province in what is now coastal Turkey (Patara is a town there.) 42 **Threician:** Thracian 43 **Cithaeron:** a mountain near Thebes 45 **Polyphemus:** a Cyclops in love with the sea-nymph Galatea 46 **Aetna:** Mt. Etna in Sicily 50 **Taenarian:** of black marble from Taenarum (near Sparta) in Laconia **Cerberus:** the three-headed dog guarding the underworld 53 **Phaeacia:** a fertile island, whose king, Alcinous, had a marvellous orchard described by Homer (*Odyssey*, VII) 54 **Ionian:** Ionia was Greek Asia Minor and the nearby islands. 55 **Marcian vintage:** Vintage from the Marcian aqueduct in Rome would have been water—which Pound changes into wine. 56 **Numa Pompilius:** the second king of Rome, who lived about 600 years before Propertius (who does not mention him here) 66 **that ... in East Elis:** the temple of Zeus at Olympia in Greece 67 **Mausolus:** His tomb, or "Mausoleum," was at Halicarnassus in Caria (Asia Minor).

From The Cantos

II

Hang it all, Robert Browning, there can be but the one "Sordello."
But Sordello, and my Sordello?
Lo Sordels si fo di Mantovana.
So-shu churned in the sea.
Seal sports in the spray-whited circles of cliff-wash,   5
Sleek head, daughter of Lir,
        eyes of Picasso
Under black fur-hood, lithe daughter of Ocean;
And the wave runs in the beach-groove:
"Eleanor, ἐλέναυς and ἐλέπτολις!"   10
        And poor old Homer blind, blind, as a bat,
Ear, ear for the sea-surge, murmur of old men's voices:
"Let her go back to the ships,
Back among Grecian faces, lest evil come on our own,
Evil and further evil, and a curse cursed on our children,   15
Moves, yes she moves like a goddess
And has the face of a god
        and the voice of Schoeney's daughters,
And doom goes with her in walking,
Let her go back to the ships,   20
        back among Grecian voices."
And by the beach-run, Tyro,
        Twisted arms of the sea-god,
Lithe sinews of water, gripping her, cross-hold,
And the blue-gray glass of the wave tents them,   25
Glare azure of water, cold-welter, close cover.
Quiet sun-tawny sand-stretch,
The gulls broad out their wings,
        nipping between the splay feathers;

1918–1919. *A Draft of XVI Cantos*, 1925.

See Additional Notes (p. 771).

2 **"Sordello":** the title of Browning's long poem of 1840, which gave one interpretation of the charac-
ter of Sordello, the thirteenth-century Italian troubadour who wrote in Provençal—an interpretation
which perhaps did not correspond with the character of the historical person or with Pound's inter-
pretation   3 **Lo Sordels . . . :** (Provençal) "Sordello was from Mantua"—the typical beginning of the
short biographies of the Provençal poets which accompany their work   4 **So-shu:** Pound said this
was the name of "a Chinese mythological figure," not further identified.   6 **Lir:** in Celtic mythology,
the father of Manannán mac Lir, god of the sea   7 **Picasso:** Pablo Picasso (1881–1973), the Spanish
artist, whom Pound thought of as having "eyes like a seal"   10 **"Eleanor . . .":** the Greek words, *he-
lēnaus* and *heléptolis*, which mean *destroyer of ships* and *destroyer of cities*, are two of the three words
with which the dramatist Aeschylus grimly puns on the name of Helen of Troy *(hele- = destroyer)* in
the *Agamemnon* (lines 688–689). His third word, *hêlandros*, which means *destroyer of men*, is further
punned into English here as *Eleanor*, almost surely Eleanor of Aquitaine (1122–1202), wife of Henry II
of England, mother of Richard the Lionhearted, and known to the Provençal poets.   11 **Homer
blind . . . :** Homer, as blind, was especially sensitive to sounds—to that of the sea, to that of the imag-
ined voices of the old men on the walls of Troy who, seeing how beautiful Helen is, say, "There is
nothing wrong in the Greeks and Trojans suffering so much, so long, for a woman like that, whose
beauty is terribly like that of the immortal gods. But, even such as she is, let her go back to the [Greek]
ships, so that, later, grief will not be in store for us and our children" *(Iliad,* III, 156–160).   18
Schoeney's daughters: Schoeneus was king of Boeotia in Greece and the father (some say) of the beau-
tiful warrior and athlete Atalanta. No other daughter is known. The phrase "Schoenyes daughters"
occurs in Arthur Golding's 1567 translation of Ovid's *Metamorphoses* (VIII, 428), a translation that
Pound thought "the most beautiful book in the language." The phrase has no basis in the Latin origi-
nal (VIII, 317).   22 **Tyro:** a girl ravished by Poseidon, god of the sea, who disguised himself as the
river-god she was in love with and threw up a great hanging wave as cover for his misconduct. The
story is told in *Odyssey,* 11, lines 235 ff.   29 **splay:** spread

Snipe come for their bath,   30
        bend out their wing-joints,
Spread wet wings to the sun-film,
And by Scios,
        to left of the Naxos passage,
Naviform rock overgrown,   35
        algæ cling to its edge,
There is a wine-red glow in the shallows,
        a tin flash in the sun-dazzle.

The ship landed in Scios,
        men wanting spring-water,   40
And by the rock-pool a young boy loggy with vine-must,
    "To Naxos? Yes, we'll take you to Naxos,
Cum' along lad." "Not that way!"
"Aye, that way is Naxos."
        And I said: "It's a straight ship."   45
And an ex-convict out of Italy
        knocked me into the fore-stays,
(He was wanted for manslaughter in Tuscany)
        And the whole twenty against me,
Mad for a little slave money.   50
        And they took her out of Scios
And off her course . . .
        And the boy came to, again, with the racket,
And looked out over the bows,
        and to eastward, and to the Naxos passage.   55
God-sleight then, god-sleight:
        Ship stock fast in sea-swirl,
Ivy upon the oars, King Pentheus,
        grapes with no seed but sea-foam,
Ivy in scupper-hole.   60
Aye, I, Acœtes, stood there,
        and the god stood by me,
Water cutting under the keel,
Sea-break from stern forrards,
        wake running off from the bow,   65
And where was gunwale, there now was vine-trunk,
And tenthril where cordage had been,
        grape-leaves on the rowlocks,
Heavy vine on the oarshafts,

30 **snipe:** slender-billed marsh birds   33 **Scios:** Chios, an island in the eastern Aegean Sea
34 **Naxos:** an island about 70 miles to the south of Chios   35 **naviform:** shaped like a ship—whose
metamorphosis is described in the account that follows   40–117 The story of the attempted kidnap-
ping of Dionysius, god of wine and Dionysiac revelry, is told in Book III of Ovid's *Metamorphoses*.
Pentheus, King of Thebes, is enraged at the spread of ritual revelry in honor of the god and resolves
to repress it. He seizes a certain Acoetes, now a devotee of Dionysius, who describes how, when he
was a ship's pilot, his crew found a handsome boy on the island of Chios. On the pretense that they
would take him to Naxos, his destination, the crew took him aboard, apparently with the intention of
selling him into slavery. Though Acoetes, sensing a divinity within the boy, protested, he was over-
powered by the crew. When Dionysius discovered the deception, miraculous events occurred: the
ship was overgrown with the vines and ivy sacred to him; the panthers, leopards, and other great cats
that attended him appeared out of nowhere; the evil crewmen were turned into fish and leapt into
the sea. Pound creates and realizes a scene which Ovid (and Golding) only outlines, as we can see
from the few lines of Golding (Additional Notes, p. 771).   41 **vine-must:** vine juice (wine)
47 **fore-stays:** ropes bracing the mast to the front of the ship   56 **god-sleight:** god-trick, god-magic;
miracle   58 **King Pentheus:** King of Thebes, to whom the story is being told (cf. note to lines 40–
117)   60 **scupper-hole:** opening on the side planking of a ship for water to drain off from the deck
64 **forrards:** forwards   67 **tenthril:** tendril (false archaism, as if it were an old spelling, like *nosethril*
for *nostril*)

And, out of nothing, a breathing,   70
      hot breath on my ankles,
Beasts like shadows in glass,
      a furred tail upon nothingness.
Lynx-purr, and heathery smell of beasts,
      where tar smell had been,   75
Sniff and pad-foot of beasts,
      eye-glitter out of black air.
The sky overshot, dry, with no tempest,
Sniff and pad-foot of beasts,
      fur brushing my knee-skin,   80
Rustle of airy sheaths,
      dry forms in the *æther*.
And the ship like a keel in ship-yard,
      slung like an ox in smith's sling,
Ribs stuck fast in the ways,   85
      grape-cluster over pin-rack,
      void air taking pelt.
Lifeless air become sinewed,
      feline leisure of panthers,
Leopards sniffing the grape shoots by scupper-hole,   90
Crouched panthers by fore-hatch,
And the sea blue-deep about us,
      green-ruddy in shadows,
And Lyæus: "From now, Acœtes, my altars,
Fearing no bondage,   95
      fearing no cat of the wood,
Safe with my lynxes,
      feeding grapes to my leopards,
Olibanum is my incense,
      the vines grow in my homage."   100

The back-swell now smooth in the rudder-chains,
Black snout of a porpoise
      where Lycabs had been,
Fish-scales on the oarsmen.
      And I worship.   105
I have seen what I have seen.
      When they brought the boy I said:
"He has a god in him,
      though I do not know which god."
And they kicked me into the fore-stays.   110
I have seen what I have seen:
      Medon's face like the face of a dory,
Arms shrunk into fins. And you, Pentheus,
Had as well listen to Tiresias, and to Cadmus,
      or your luck will go out of you.   115
Fish-scales over groin muscles,
      lynx-purr amid sea . . .
And of a later year,
      pale in the wine-red algæ,

---

82 **æther:** (Latin) air   94 **Lyæus:** the Deliverer, Dionysius   99 **olibanum:** an aromatic gum resin   103 **Lycabs:** one of the sailors, now turned into a porpoise   112 **Medon:** one of the sailors   **dory:** a European fish   114 **Tiresias:** the soothsayer who had warned Pentheus against dealing harshly with Dionysius   **Cadmus:** the founder of Thebes, whose daughter Semele was the human mother of Dionysius (and the aunt of Pentheus)

If you will lean over the rock,   120
        the coral face under wave-tinge,
Rose-paleness under water-shift,
        Ileuthyeria, fair Dafne of sea-bords,
The swimmer's arms turned to branches,
Who will say in what year,   125
        fleeing what band of tritons,
The smooth brows, seen, and half seen,
        now ivory stillness.

And So-shu churned in the sea, So-shu also,
        using the long moon for a churn-stick . . .   130
Lithe turning of water,
        sinews of Poseidon,
Black azure and hyaline,
        glass wave over Tyro,
Close cover, unstillness,   135
        bright welter of wave-cords,
Then quiet water,
        quiet in the buff sands,
Sea-fowl stretching wing-joints,
        splashing in rock-hollows and sand-hollows   140
In the wave-runs by the half-dune;
Glass-glint of wave in the tide-rips against sunlight,
        pallor of Hesperus,
Grey peak of the wave,
        wave, colour of grape's pulp,   145

Olive grey in the near,
        far, smoke grey of the rock-slide,
Salmon-pink wings of the fish-hawk
        cast grey shadows in water,
The tower like a one-eyed great goose   150
        cranes up out of the olive-grove,

And we have heard the fauns chiding Proteus
        in the smell of hay under the olive-trees,
And the frogs singing against the fauns
        in the half-light.   155
And . . .

123 **Ileuthyeria:** the name of a sea-nymph (Eleutheria?) in a myth which Pound invented: as Daphne was turned into a *laurel* to escape the pursuing Apollo, so Pound's sea-nymph was turned into *coral* to escape the pursuing tritons (sea-gods or mermen)   132 **Poseidon:** god of the sea (cf. the note on line 22)   133 **hyaline:** glassy   143 **Hesperus:** the evening star   152 **Proteus:** sea-god who had the power of changing his shape

From LXXXI

Has he tempered the viol's wood
To enforce   both the grave   and the acute?
Has he curved us the bowl of the lute?

1945. *The Pisan Cantos,* 1948.

In May 1945 Pound was put under arrest by the victorious American Army on the charge that his pro-Mussolini wartime broadcasts had been treasonable. He spent the next six months in the American Disciplinary Training Center near Pisa, at first in a wire and concrete "cage," later in a tent in the medical compound. Seeing his world in ruins, with few books at hand (the Bible, Confucius, a Chi-

Lawes and Jenkyns guard thy rest
Dolmetsch ever be thy guest   5 [104]
Hast 'ou fashioned so airy a mood
   To draw up leaf from the root?
Hast 'ou found   a cloud   so light
   As seemed neither mist nor shade?

      Then resolve me, tell me aright   10
      If Waller sang or Dowland played.

   Your eyen two wol sleye me sodenly
   I may the beauté of hem nat susteyne

And for 180 years almost nothing.

Ed ascoltando al leggier mormorio   15
      there came new subtlety of eyes into my tent,
whether of spirit or hypostasis,
      but what the blindfold hides
or at carneval
               nor any pair showed anger   20
      Saw but the eyes and stance between the eyes,
colour, diastasis,
      careless or unaware it had not the
   whole tent's room
nor was place for the full Ἐιδώς   25
interpass, penetrate
      casting but shade beyond the other lights
      sky's clear
      night's sea
      green of the mountain pool   30
      shone from the unmasked eyes in half-mask's space.
What thou lovest well remains,
                  the rest is dross
What thou lov'st well shall not be reft from thee
What thou lov'st well is thy true heritage   35

---

nese dictionary, a book of verse), but with his own rich memories to draw on, he wrote the eleven *Pisan Cantos* on a dispensary typewriter he was permitted to use at night. They include some of his finest and most moving poetry.

4 Lawes: Cf. note to "Envoi (1919)," p. 532.   **Jenkyns:** John Jenkins (1592–1678), English musician and composer   **5 Dolmetsch:** Arnold Dolmetsch (1858–1940), French-born musician, maker of clavichords, harpsichords, and other early instruments, did much to revive the music of earlier centuries.   **6–9** Patterned loosely on the third stanza, sometimes printed separately, of Ben Jonson's "Her Triumph" from "A Celebration of Charis . . ." (in *Works*, 1640, but in a play performed in 1616). The stanza reads:

   Have you seen but a bright lily grow
      Before rude hands have touched it?
   Have you marked but the fall of the snow
      Before the soil hath smutched it?

11 Waller: Cf. note to "Envoi (1919)," p. 532.   **Dowland:** John Dowland (1562–1626), English lutanist and composer, was among the most famous of his day.   **12–13** The first two lines of Chaucer's "Merciles Beautee" (c. 1390). Cf. p. 17.   **14 nothing:** nothing that successfully united words and music   **15 Ed . . . mormorio:** And listening to the soft murmuring (Italian). "Not a quote," said Pound. "Merely the author using handy language." (Or misusing it: *ascoltare* takes *il*, not *al*)   **16 new subtlety of eyes:** a memory, dream, or vision of beautiful eyes, masked, perhaps, as at the carnival in Venice (the spelling *carneval* in line 19 recalls the Italian form *carnevale*). The image suggests the presence of love or a loved person—an Aphrodite-figure.   **17 hypostasis:** substance, person   **22 diastasis:** separation (distance between the eyes)   **25 Ἐιδώς:** The Greek participle (eidōs) means "knowing."

Whose world, or mine or theirs
　　　　　　or is it of none?
First came the seen, then thus the palpable
　　　Elysium, though it were in the halls of hell,
What thou lovest well is thy true heritage　　　　　　　　　　40
What thou lov'st well shall not be reft from thee

The ant's a centaur in his dragon world.
Pull down thy vanity, it is not man
Made courage, or made order, or made grace,
　　　Pull down thy vanity, I say pull down.　　　　　　　45
Learn of the green world what can be thy place
In scaled invention or true artistry,
Pull down thy vanity,
　　　　　　　Paquin pull down!
The green casque has outdone your elegance.　　　　　　　50

"Master thyself, then others shall thee beare"
　　　Pull down thy vanity
Thou art a beaten dog beneath the hail,
A swollen magpie in a fitful sun,
Half black half white　　　　　　　　　　　　　　　　55
Nor knowst'ou wing from tail
Pull down thy vanity
　　　　　　How mean thy hates
Fostered in falsity,
　　　　　Pull down thy vanity,　　　　　　　　　　60
Rathe to destroy, niggard in charity,
Pull down thy vanity,
　　　　　I say pull down.

But to have done instead of not doing
　　　　　this is not vanity　　　　　　　　　　　　65
To have, with decency, knocked
That a Blunt should open
　　　To have gathered from the air a live tradition
or from a fine old eye the unconquered flame
This is not vanity.　　　　　　　　　　　　　　70
　　　Here error is all in the not done,
all in the diffidence that faltered . . .

39 **Elysium:** in ancient mythology, the happy abode of the souls of the virtuous dead—in the *Odyssey*, a plain at the end of the earth where life is effortless and untroubled　49 **Paquin:** Parisian dressmaker　50 **casque:** helmet, head covering　51 **"Master . . . beare":** the poet's remembrance, or misreading, or deliberate modification, of Henry Van Dyke's modernization of a line from Chaucer's "Truth"?—"Subdue thyself, and others thee shall hear" (for Chaucer's: "Daunte thyself that dauntest otheres deede")　61 **rathe:** hasty, eager　67 **Blunt:** Wilfred Scawen Blunt (1840–1922), English poet whose integrity Pound admired

Robinson Jeffers
(1887–1962)

Jeffers was born in Pittsburgh, where his father taught the Old Testament at a theological seminary. After early schooling in Switzerland and Germany, Jeffers studied at Occidental College (Los Angeles), the University of California, the University of Zurich, and at the School of Forestry at the University of Washington. Financially independent in 1912, thanks to a small legacy, he married and settled at Carmel on the California coast, where he built his own house out of the local stone. In 1924 he became immediately if controversially famous with *Tamar and Other Poems*; his adaptation of Euripides' *Medea* was a Broadway success in 1947.

The Purse-Seine

Our sardine fishermen work at night in the dark of the moon; daylight
      or moonlight
They could not tell where to spread the net, unable to see the
      phosphorescence of the shoals of fish.
They work northward from Monterey, coasting Santa Cruz; off New
      Year's Point or off Pigeon Point
The look-out man will see some lakes of milk-color light on the sea's
      night-purple; he points, and the helmsman
Turns the dark prow, the motor-boat circles the gleaming shoal and drifts
      out her seine-net. They close the circle   5
And purse the bottom of the net, then with great labor haul it in.

      I cannot tell you
How beautiful the scene is, and a little terrible, then, when the crowded
      fish
Know they are caught, and wildly beat from one wall to the other of their
      closing destiny the phosphorescent
Water to a pool of flame, each beautiful slender body sheeted with flame,
      like a live rocket   10
A comet's tail wake of clear yellow flame; while outside the narrowing
Floats and cordage of the net great sea-lions come up to watch, sighing in
      the dark; the vast walls of night
Stand erect to the stars.

      Lately I was looking from a night mountain-top
On a wide city, the colored splendor, galaxies of light: how could I help
      but recall the seine-net   15
Gathering the luminous fish? I cannot tell you how beautiful the city
      appeared, and a little terrible.
I thought, We have geared the machines and locked all together into
      interdependence; we have built the great cities; now
There is no escape. We have gathered vast populations incapable of free
      survival, insulated
From the strong earth, each person in himself helpless, on all dependent.
      The circle is closed, and the net
Is being hauled in. They hardly feel the cords drawing, yet they shine
      already. The inevitable mass-disasters   20
Will not come in our time nor in our children's, but we and our children
Must watch the net draw narrower, government take all powers—or
      revolution, and the new government
Take more than all, add to kept bodies kept souls—or anarchy, the mass-
      disasters.

        These things are Progress;

Such Councils You Gave to Me, 1937.

A purse-seine is a very large net which is pulled all around a school of fish and then closed at the bottom.

3 **Monterey:** The place-names are along the California coast south of San Francisco.

Do you marvel our verse is troubled or frowning, while it keeps its rea-
    son? Or it lets go, lets the mood flow   25
In the manner of the recent young men into mere hysteria, splintered
    gleams, cracked laughter. But they are quite wrong.
There is no reason for amazement: surely one always knew that cultures
    decay, and life's end is death.

Nova

That Nova was a moderate star like our good sun; it stored no doubt a
    little more than it spent
Of heat and energy until the increasing tension came to the trigger-point
Of a new chemistry; then what was already flaming found a new manner
    of flaming ten-thousandfold
More brightly for a brief time; what was a pin-point fleck on a sensitive
    plate at the great telescope's
Eye-piece now shouts down the steep night to the naked eye, a nine-day
    super-star.

                    It is likely our moderate   5
Father the sun will some time put off his nature for a similar glory. The
    earth would share it; these tall
Green trees would become a moment's torches and vanish, the oceans
    would explode into invisible steam,
The ships and the great whales fall through them like flaming meteors
    into the emptied abysm, the six mile
Hollows of the Pacific sea-bed might smoke for a moment. Then the
    earth would be like the pale proud moon,
Nothing but vitrified sand and rock would be left on earth. This is a
    probable death-passion   10
For the sun's planets; we have no knowledge to assure us it may not hap-
    pen at any moment of time.

Meanwhile the sun shines wisely and warm, trees flutter green in the
    wind, girls take their clothes off
To bathe in the cold ocean or to hunt love; they stand laughing in the
    white foam, they have beautiful
Shoulders and thighs, they are beautiful animals, all life is beautiful. We
    cannot be sure of life for one moment;
We can, by force and self-discipline, by many refusals and a few asser-
    tions, in the teeth of fortune assure ourselves   15
Freedom and integrity in life or integrity in death. And we know that the
    enormous invulnerable beauty of things
Is the face of God, to live gladly in its presence, and die without grief or
    fear knowing it survives us.

1935–1937. Ibid.

A Nova is an aging star which because of gravitational and nuclear tensions suddenly explodes, and
for a short while becomes thousands or even millions of times as bright as it was. Scientists think our
own sun may end as a Nova, though not for a few billion years. Progressive changes in the sun will
probably have vaporized the earth even before the final explosion.

Edwin Muir
(1887–1959)

When he was 14, Muir's family moved from a farm in the Orkney Islands (east of Scot-
land) to the industrial city of Glasgow. The change to urban poverty was disastrous;
within a short time both parents and two brothers had died. Muir educated himself
while holding a number of depressing jobs, one in a bone-processing factory. In 1919 he

married and moved to London, supporting himself as a journalist. Before World War II the Muirs travelled extensively on the continent, translating, among other works, the novels of Kafka. After the war he worked for the British Council in Edinburgh, Prague, and Rome.

The Horses

Barely a twelvemonth after
The seven days war that put the world to sleep,
Late in the evening the strange horses came.
By then we had made our covenant with silence,
But in the first few days it was so still   5
We listened to our breathing and were afraid.
On the second day
The radios failed; we turned the knobs; no answer.
On the third day a warship passed us, heading north,
Dead bodies piled on the deck. On the sixth day   10
A plane plunged over us into the sea. Thereafter
Nothing. The radios dumb;
And still they stand in corners of our kitchens,
And stand, perhaps, turned on, in a million rooms
All over the world. But now if they should speak,   15
If on a sudden they should speak again,
If on the stroke of noon a voice should speak,
We would not listen, we would not let it bring
That old bad world that swallowed its children quick
At one great gulp. We would not have it again.   20
Sometimes we think of the nations lying asleep,
Curled blindly in impenetrable sorrow,
And then the thought confounds us with its strangeness.

The tractors lie about our fields; at evening
They look like dank sea-monsters couched and waiting.   25
We leave them where they are and let them rust:
'They'll moulder away and be like other loam'.
We make our oxen drag our rusty ploughs,
Long laid aside. We have gone back
Far past our fathers' land.
                    And then, that evening   30
Late in the summer the strange horses came.
We heard a distant tapping on the road,
A deepening drumming; it stopped, went on again
And at the corner changed to hollow thunder.
We saw the heads   35
Like a wild wave charging and were afraid.
We had sold our horses in our fathers' time
To buy new tractors. Now they were strange to us
As fabulous steeds set on an ancient shield
Or illustrations in a book of knights.   40
We did not dare go near them. Yet they waited,
Stubborn and shy, as if they had been sent
By an old command to find our whereabouts
And that long-lost archaic companionship.
In the first moment we had never a thought   45
That they were creatures to be owned and used.
Among them were some half-a-dozen colts

1952–1955. *One Foot in Eden*, 1956.

Dropped in some wilderness of the broken world,
Yet new as if they had come from their own Eden.
Since then they have pulled our ploughs and borne our loads,   50
But that free servitude still can pierce our hearts.
Our life is changed; their coming our beginning.

Marianne Moore
(1887–1972)

Born in a suburb of St. Louis, Miss Moore moved with her family to Carlisle, Pennsylvania, when she was 7. At Bryn Mawr she was fascinated by science; on graduating she taught commercial subjects for several years at the Industrial Indian School in Carlisle—among her pupils was the famous athlete Jim Thorpe. In 1918 she moved to Greenwich Village in New York City. In 1921, without her knowledge, friends arranged for the publication in London of her first book; in 1925 she became editor of the *Dial*, one of the most distinguished literary magazines. When it ceased publication in 1929, she and her mother moved to the fifth-floor apartment in Brooklyn where they lived for most of the next 40 years. Her *Collected Poems* (1951) won all of the important awards. Interests of her later years included the *Fables* of the French poet La Fontaine (1621–1695), which she translated, and the Brooklyn Dodgers baseball team, which she celebrated in her poetry.

Poetry

I too, dislike it: there are things that are important beyond all this fiddle.
    Reading it, however, with a perfect contempt for it, one discovers that
            there is in
it after all, a place for the genuine.
        Hands that can grasp, eyes
        that can dilate, hair that can rise   5
            if it must, these things are important not because a

high sounding interpretation can be put upon them but because they are
    useful; when they become so derivative as to become unintelligible, the
    same thing may be said for all of us—that we
        do not admire what   10
        we cannot understand. The bat,
            holding on upside down or in quest of something to

eat, elephants pushing, a wild horse taking a roll, a tireless wolf under
    a tree, the immovable critic twinkling his skin like a horse that feels a
            flea, the base-
    ball fan, the statistician—case after case   15
        could be cited did
        one wish it; nor is it valid
            to discriminate against "business documents and

1919. *Poems*, 1921.

This is the text of the poem as it appeared in *Poems*, 1921 (Egoist Press, London). The poet is working in what became her characteristic form: See *syllabic verse* in the prosody section. In a later revision—the version generally printed—she omitted about 20 words, with the loss of a line in the third stanza. Lines 2 and 3 then no longer kept the original pattern; the other four lines did (allowing for the missing line). One guesses she came to prefer syntactical tightness to formal balance. The process of revision was carried on to excess in the *Complete Poems* of 1967: there the poem consists of the first three lines—and nothing more.

14 **twinkling:** later revised to "twitching"   18–19 **"business documents . . .":** "*Diary of Tolstoy*, p. 84: 'Where the boundary between prose and poetry lies, I shall never be able to understand. The question is raised in manuals of style, yet the answer to it lies beyond me. Poetry is verse: prose is not verse. Or else poetry is everything with the exception of business documents and school books'" [Marianne Moore's note].

school-books"; all these phenomena are important. One must make a
distinction
however: when dragged into prominence by half poets, the result is not
poetry,   20
nor till the autocrats among us can be
"literalists of
the imagination"—above
insolence and triviality and can present

for inspection, imaginary gardens with real toads in them, shall we have   25
it. In the meantime, if you demand on one hand, in defiance of their
opinion—
the raw material of poetry in
all its rawness and
that which is, on the other hand,
genuine then you are interested in poetry.   30

21 **autocrats:** those who have, or act as if they had, unlimited authority. Authoritarian poets, who lay
down laws for others? A later revision softened the word to "poets." 22–23 "'Literalists of the
imagination.' Yeats, *Ideas of Good and Evil* (A. H. Bullen, 1903), p. 182. 'The limitation of his view was
from the very intensity of his vision; he was a too literal realist of imagination, as others are of nature;
and because he believed that the figures seen by the mind's eye, when exalted by inspiration, were
"eternal existences," symbols of divine essences, he hated every grace of style that might obscure
their lineaments'" [Marianne Moore's note]. Yeats's remarks are from his "William Blake and His Il-
lustrations to the *Divine Comedy.*" 26 The line was later cut to "it. In the meantime, if you demand
on the one hand,".

A Grave

Man looking into the sea,
taking the view from those who have as much right to it as you have to it
yourself,
it is human nature to stand in the middle of a thing,
but you cannot stand in the middle of this;
the sea has nothing to give but a well excavated grave.   5
The firs stand in a procession, each with an emerald turkey foot at the
top,
reserved as their contours, saying nothing;
repression, however, is not the most obvious characteristic of the sea;
the sea is a collector, quick to return a rapacious look.
There are others besides you who have worn that look—   10
whose expression is no longer a protest; the fish no longer investigate
them
for their bones have not lasted:
men lower nets, unconscious of the fact that they are desecrating a
grave,
and row quickly away—the blades of the oars
moving together like the feet of water spiders as if there were no such
thing as death.   15
The wrinkles progress among themselves in a phalanx—beautiful under
networks of foam,
and fade breathlessly while the sea rustles in and out of the seaweed;
the birds swim through the air at top speed, emitting catcalls as
heretofore—
the tortoise shell scourges about the feet of the cliffs, in motion beneath
them;

By 1921. *Observations,* 1924.

and the ocean, under the pulsation of lighthouses and noise of bell
        buoys,   20
advances as usual, looking as if it were not that ocean in which dropped
        things are bound to sink—
in which if they turn and twist, it is neither with volition nor
        consciousness.

The Steeple-Jack

Dürer would have seen a reason for living
        in a town like this, with eight stranded whales
to look at; with the sweet sea air coming into your house
on a fine day, from water etched
        with waves as formal as the scales   5
on a fish.

One by one, in two's, in three's, the seagulls keep
        flying back and forth over the town clock,
or sailing around the lighthouse without moving their wings—
rising steadily with a slight   10
        quiver of the body—or flock
mewing where

a sea the purple of the peacock's neck is
        paled to greenish azure as Dürer changed
the pine green of the Tyrol to peacock blue and guinea   15
gray. You can see a twenty-five-
        pound lobster; and fishnets arranged
to dry. The

whirlwind fife-and-drum of the storm bends the salt
        marsh grass, disturbs stars in the sky and the   20
star on the steeple; it is a privilege to see so
much confusion. Disguised by what
        might seem austerity, the sea-
side flowers and

trees are favored by the fog so that you have   25
        the tropics at first hand: the trumpet-vine,
fox-glove, giant snap-dragon, a salpiglossis that has
spots and stripes; morning-glories, gourds,
        or moon-vines trained on fishing-twine
at the back   30

By 1932. *Selected Poems*, 1935.

The text is from *Selected Poems*, 1935. In *Complete Poems*, 1967, it is given as "Revised, 1961": one stanza is added, and there are a few unimportant verbal changes.

1 **Dürer:** Albrecht Dürer (1471–1528), the German painter and engraver. His interest in natural objects was so great that he once ventured into mosquito-infested swamps to see a whale that had been washed ashore; what he caught there was not a sight of the whale but malaria. Dürer, with his love for precise detail, would have liked the "etched" quality of the scene the poet describes.   15 **Tyrol:** an Alpine region in northern Italy and Austria   23 **austerity:** The revision of 1961 substituted "the opposite" (such changes are of interest when they throw light on the meaning of a passage).   27 **sal-piglossis:** The name means "trumpet-tongue," a plant native to Chile but grown elsewhere for its showy blossoms. Ocean currents encourage the growth of plants native to warmer climates. 30 After this line the 1961 revision inserts a new stanza which lists, with little detail, the names of nearly 20 common American plants.

door. There are no banyans, frangipani, nor
    jack-fruit trees; nor an exotic serpent
life. Ring lizard and snake-skin for the foot, or crocodile;
but here they've cats, not cobras, to
    keep down the rats. The diffident   35
little newt

with white pin-dots on black horizontal spaced
    out bands lives here; yet there is nothing that
ambition can buy or take away. The college student
named Ambrose sits on the hill-side   40
    with his not-native books and hat
and sees boats

at sea progress white and rigid as if in
    a groove. Liking an elegance of which
the source is not bravado, he knows by heart the antique   45
sugar-bowl-shaped summer-house of
    interlacing slats, and the pitch
of the church

spire, not true, from which a man in scarlet lets
    down a rope as a spider spins a thread;   50
he might be part of a novel, but on the sidewalk a
sign says C. J. Poole, Steeple Jack,
    in black and white; and one in red
and white says

Danger. The church portico has four fluted   55
    columns, each a single piece of stone, made
modester by white-wash. This would be a fit haven for
waifs, children, animals, prisoners,
    and presidents who have repaid
sin-driven   60

senators by not thinking about them. There
    are a schoolhouse, a post-office in a
store, fish-houses, hen-houses, a three-masted schooner on
the stocks. The hero, the student,
    the steeple-jack, each in his way,   65
is at home.

It could not be dangerous to be living
    in a town like this, of simple people,
who have a steeple-jack placing danger signs by the church
while he is gilding the solid-   70
    pointed star, which on a steeple
stands for hope.

31 **banyans:** picturesque East Indian trees whose branch-ends root to form secondary trunks **frangi-
pani:** a tropical American shrub or tree like the red jasmine, noted for its exotic fragrance 32 **jack-
fruit:** a tropical tree like the breadfruit 36 **newt:** little lizardlike salamander

The Pangolin

Another armored animal—scale
　　lapping scale with spruce-cone regularity until they
form the uninterrupted central
　　tail-row! This near artichoke with head and legs and grit-equipped
　　　　　　gizzard,
　　the night miniature artist engineer is,   5
　　　　yes, Leonardo da Vinci's replica—
　　　　　impressive animal and toiler of whom we seldom hear.
　　　　Armor seems extra. But for him,
　　　　　the closing ear-ridge—
　　　　　　or bare ear lacking even this small   10
　　　　　　eminence and similarly safe

contracting nose and eye apertures
　　impenetrably closable, are not; a true ant-eater,
not cockroach-eater, who endures
　　exhausting solitary trips through unfamiliar ground at night,   15
　　returning before sunrise; stepping in the moonlight,
　　　　on the moonlight peculiarly, that the outside
　　　　　edges of his hands may bear the weight and save the claws
　　for digging. Serpentined about
　　　　the tree, he draws   20
　　　　　away from danger unpugnaciously,
　　　　　with no sound but a harmless hiss; keeping

the fragile grace of the Thomas-
　　of-Leighton Buzzard Westminster Abbey wrought-iron vine, or
rolls himself into a ball that has   25
　　power to defy all effort to unroll it; strongly intailed, neat
　　head for core, on neck not breaking off, with curled-in feet.
　　　　Nevertheless he has sting-proof scales; and nest
　　　　　of rocks closed with earth from inside, which he can thus
　　　　　　darken.
　　　　Sun and moon and day and night and man and beast   30
　　　　　each with a splendor
　　　　　which man in all his vileness cannot
　　　　　set aside; each with an excellence!

"Fearful yet to be feared," the armored
　　ant-eater met by the driver-ant does not turn back, but   35
engulfs what he can, the flattened sword-
　　edged leafpoints on the tail and artichoke set leg- and body-plates
　　quivering violently when it retaliates

1935. *The Pangolin*, 1936.

In his introduction to the *Selected Poems* of Marianne Moore, T. S. Eliot has said that her work has "something like the fascination of a high-powered microscope." This is the fascination sympathetic readers might feel in the first five stanzas of her poem about this odd animal, so amply armored its against danger and so efficiently equipped to manage its own life. See Additional Notes (p. 771).

The pangólin (Malayan *peng-goling*, "the roller") is the scaly anteater of Africa and Asia.   9 " '**The closing ear-ridge**,' and certain other detail, from 'Pangolins' by Robert T. Hatt, *Natural History*, December 1935." [Marianne Moore's note. The correct date is December 1934.]   16–17 " '**Stepping . . . peculiarly**.' See Lyddeker's *Royal Natural History*" [Marianne Moore's note].   23–24 "**Thomas-of-Leighton Buzzard vine**: a fragment of ironwork in Westminster Abbey" [Marianne Moore's note]. What remains of Thomas of Leighton's thirteenth-century grille over Queen Eleanor's tomb—a grille called "the finest piece of blacksmithing in England"—is considerably more than a fragment.   34 "**Fearful . . . feared**": Caption of a photograph in the Hatt article   35 **driver-ant**: a kind of army ant, which moves in huge "armies"

and swarms on him. Compact like the furled fringed frill
　　on the hat-brim of Gargallo's hollow iron head of a   40
matador, he will drop and will
　　　then walk away
　　　　unhurt, although if unintruded on,
　　　　he cautiously works down the tree, helped

by his tail. The giant-pangolin-   45
　　tail, graceful tool, as prop or hand or broom or ax, tipped like
an elephant's trunk with special skin,
　　is not lost on this ant- and stone-swallowing uninjurable
　　artichoke which simpletons thought a living fable
　　　whom the stones had nourished, whereas ants had done   50
　　　　so. Pangolins are not aggressive animals; between
　　　dusk and day they have the not unchain-like machine-like
　　　　　form and frictionless creep of a thing
　　　　　made graceful by adversities, con-

versities. To explain grace requires   55
　　a curious hand. If that which is at all were not forever,
why would those who graced the spires
　　with animals and gathered there to rest, on cold luxurious
　　low stone seats—a monk and monk and monk—between the thus
　　　ingenious roof supports, have slaved to confuse   60
　　　　grace with a kindly manner, time in which to pay a debt,
　　　the cure for sins, a graceful use
　　　　　of what are yet
　　　　　approved stone mullions branching out across
　　　　　the perpendiculars? A sailboat   65

was the first machine. Pangolins, made
　　for moving quietly also, are models of exactness,
on four legs; on hind feet plantigrade,
　　with certain postures of a man. Beneath sun and moon, man slaving
　　to make his life more sweet, leaves half the flowers worth having,   70
　　　needing to choose wisely how to use his strength;
　　　　a paper-maker like the wasp; a tractor of foodstuffs,
　　　like the ant; spidering a length
　　　　　of web from bluffs
　　　　　above a stream; in fighting, mechanicked   75
　　　　　like the pangolin; capsizing in

disheartenment. Bedizened or stark
　　naked, man, the self, the being we call human, writing-
master to this world, griffons a dark
　　"Like does not like like that is obnoxious"; and writes error with four   80
　　r's. Among animals, *one* has a sense of humor.
　　　Humor saves a few steps, it saves years. Unignorant,

---

40 **Gargallo:** Pablo Gargallo (1881–1934), Spanish sculptor, one of the first of the twentieth century to work in iron. His "Picador" (1928) is in the Museum of Modern Art in New York.　61 **a kindly manner:** charitable behavior, courtesy　**time . . . :** for repentance, gratitude, etc.　64 **mullions:** vertical architectural members, as between panes of a window or for ornament on a wall　65–66 **"A sailboat was the first machine:** See F. L. Morse, *Power: Its Application from the 17th Dynasty to the 20th Century"* [Marianne Moore's note]. Here it represents graceful, precise, and quiet motion.　68 **plantigrade:** walking with sole and heel touching the ground　72 **tractor:** hauler　79 **griffons:** scrawls (French *griffoner*—from *griffe,* a claw)　80 **"Like does not like . . .":** Man is the only creature that finds his own like "obnoxious"—or that can make a pun.　**error with four / r's:** a sort of joke, like the spelling "THIMK." Only man makes up little jokes.

modest and unemotional, and all emotion,
he has everlasting vigor,
   power to grow,   85
      though there are few creatures who can make one
      breathe faster and make one erecter.

Not afraid of anything is he,
   and then goes cowering forth, tread paced to meet an obstacle
at every step. Consistent with the   90
   formula—warm blood, no gills, two pairs of hands and a few hairs—
            that
is a mammal; there he sits in his own habitat,
   serge-clad, strong-shod. The prey of fear, he, always
      curtailed, extinguished, thwarted by the dusk, work partly done,
   says to the alternating blaze,   95
      "Again the sun!
         anew each day; and new and new and new,
         that comes into and steadies my soul."

86 **few creatures who . . . :** few who are so scary, so startling   89 **tread paced:** his way of walking
shows that he anticipates trouble   93 **the prey of fear:** unlike the confident and prepared pangolin

A Carriage from Sweden

They say there is a sweeter air
   where it was made, than we have here;
   a Hamlet's castle atmosphere.
At all events there is in Brooklyn
something that makes me feel at home.   5

No one may see this put-away
   museum-piece, this country cart
   that inner happiness made art;
and yet, in this city of freckled
integrity it is a vein   10

of resined straightness from north-wind
   hardened Sweden's once-opposed-to-
   compromise archipelago
of rocks. Washington and Gustavus
Adolphus, forgive our decay.   15

1943. *Nevertheless,* 1944.

3 **Hamlet's castle:** around Hamlet's castle the air is "bitter cold" and "bites shrewdly." Perhaps Miss
Moore is thinking of Macbeth's castle (in Scotland) where "the air nimbly and sweetly recommends
itself / Unto our gentle senses" (I, iv).   9 **freckled:** spotty, not immaculate   12–13 **once-opposed-to-
/compromise:** Although Sweden took a strong stand against Germany in World War II, she did per-
mit German troops to cross her territory on certain trains. Such permission was cancelled in the late
summer of 1943, the year in which the poem was most probably written.   14–15 **Gustavus Adol-
phus:** Coming to the throne at the age of 17 in 1611, the great Swedish monarch and military leader
ruled until he was killed in battle in 1632. His reign marks one of the great epochs of Swedish history,
with significant reforms achieved in many branches of government and Sweden's prestige greatly en-
hanced abroad.

Seats, dashboard and sides of smooth gourd-
   rind texture, a flowered step, swan-
   dart brake, and swirling crustacean-
tailed equine amphibious creatures
that garnish the axletree! What   20

a fine thing! What unannoying
   romance! And how beautiful, she
   with the natural stoop of the
snowy egret, gray-eyed and straight-haired,
for whom it should come to the door—   25

of whom it reminds me. The split
   pine fair hair, steady gannet-clear
   eyes and the pine-needled-path deer-
swift step; that is Sweden, land of the
free and the soil for a spruce tree—   30

vertical though a seedling—all
   needles: from a green trunk, green shelf
   on shelf fanning out by itself.
The deft white-stockinged dance in thick-soled
shoes! Denmark's sanctuaried Jews!   35

The puzzle-jugs and hand-spun rugs,
   the root-legged kracken shaped like dogs,
   the hanging buttons and the frogs
that edge the Sunday jackets! Sweden,
you have a runner called the Deer, who   40

when he's won a race, likes to run
   more; you have the sun-right gable-
   ends due east and west, the table
spread as for a banquet; and the put-
in twin vest-pleats with a fish-fin   45

effect when you need none. Sweden,
   what makes the people dress that way
   and those who see you wish to stay?
The runner, not too tired to run more
at the end of the race? And that   50

cart, dolphin-graceful? A Dalén
   lighthouse, self-lit?—responsive and
   responsible. I understand;

24 **snowy egret:** a heron with beautiful curved neck 27 **gannet:** a sea-bird of wild coasts and open ocean, which dives from high air to seize its prey under water 35 **Denmark's ... Jews:** Denmark, unlike Sweden, was invaded by the Nazi armies in 1940; the "new order" they imposed meant that Jews were persecuted. Throughout the war Sweden was a refuge for victims of persecution in neighboring countries. 36 **puzzle-jugs:** jugs designed so that they are hard to drink from without dribbling 37 **kra[c]ken:** sea-monsters 38 **frogs:** ornamental braided loops for button and buttonhole 40 **the Deer:** Gunder Hägg, the Swedish runner who attributed the ease of his style to the springy pine-needled paths of his homeland, and who enjoyed running more than anything except playing his accordion, broke ten world records in the summer of 1942. 51 **Dalén:** In 1912 Nils Gustaf Dalén (1869–1937) won the Nobel Prize in physics for his contributions to coastal lighting. Among his inventions was a device that would start up an acetylene flame at twilight and extinguish it at dawn.

it's not pine-needle-paths that give spring
when they're run on, it's a Sweden 55

of moated white castles—the bed
  of white flowers densely grown in an S
  meaning Sweden and stalwartness,
skill, and a surface that says
Made in Sweden: carts are my trade. 60

John Crowe Ransom
(1888–1974)

Ransom was born in Pulaski, Tennessee, son of a Methodist minister. He graduated from Vanderbilt, spent three years as a Rhodes scholar at Oxford, where he studied chiefly classics and philosophy, taught Latin for a year in a prep school, during World War I served with the field artillery in France, then returned to Vanderbilt to teach English until 1937. From 1922 to 1925 he and younger colleagues—Tate, Warren, and others—published *The Fugitive*, in which much of his poetry appeared. Moving to Kenyon College in 1937 as professor of poetry, Ransom founded the influential *Kenyon Review*, which he edited until his retirement in 1959. As critic, Ransom was a founder of what came to be called the "new criticism": it encouraged close reading of the actual poem in itself rather than in the light of historical, social, or philosophical considerations.

Winter Remembered

Two evils, monstrous either one apart,
Possessed me, and were long and loath at going:
A cry of Absence, Absence, in the heart,
And in the wood the furious winter blowing.

Think not, when fire was bright upon my bricks, 5
And past the tight boards hardly a wind could enter,
I glowed like them, the simple burning sticks,
Far from my cause, my proper heat and center.

Better to walk forth in the murderous air
And wash my wound in the snows; that would be healing; 10
Because my heart would throb less painful there,
Being caked with cold, and past the smart of feeling.

And where I went, the hugest winter blast
Would have this body bowed, these eyeballs streaming,
And though I think this heart's blood froze not fast 15
It ran too small to spare one drop for dreaming.

Dear love, these fingers that had known your touch,
And tied our separate forces first together,
Were ten poor idiot fingers not worth much,
Ten frozen parsnips hanging in the weather. 20

1921–1924. *Chills and Fever*, 1924.

In the text as given in the *Selected Poems*, 1969, Ransom has made some changes that do not seem to be improvements: line 9, *frozen* for *murderous*; line 13, *murderous* for *hugest*.

Here Lies a Lady

Here lies a lady of beauty and high degree.
Of chills and fever she died, of fever and chills,
The delight of her husband, her aunt, an infant of three,
And of medicos marveling sweetly on her ills.

For either she burned, and her confident eyes would blaze,   5
And her fingers fly in a manner to puzzle their heads—
What was she making? Why, nothing; she sat in a maze
Of old scraps of laces, snipped into curious shreds—

Or this would pass, and the light of her fire decline
Till she lay discouraged and cold, like a stalk white and blown,   10
And would not open her eyes, to kisses, to wine;
The sixth of these states was her last; the cold settled down.

Sweet ladies, long may ye bloom, and toughly I hope ye may thole,
But was she not lucky? In flowers and lace and mourning
In love and great honor we bade God rest her soul   15
After six little spaces of chill, and six of burning.

Ibid.

The revised version of 1969 is, in the opinion of this editor, inferior.

13 **thole:** endure [obsolete]

Bells for John Whiteside's Daughter

There was such speed in her little body,
And such lightness in her footfall,
It is no wonder her brown study
Astonishes us all.

Her wars were bruited in our high window.   5
We looked among orchard trees and beyond
Where she took arms against her shadow,
Or harried unto the pond

The lazy geese, like a snow cloud
Dripping their snow on the green grass,   10
Tricking and stopping, sleepy and proud,
Who cried in goose, Alas,

For the tireless heart within the little
Lady with rod that made them rise
From their noon apple-dreams and scuttle   15
Goose-fashion under the skies!

But now go the bells, and we are ready,
In one house we are sternly stopped
To say we are vexed at her brown study,
Lying so primly propped.   20

Ibid.

3 **brown study:** state of reverie or daydreaming   5 **bruited:** sounded, heard because very noisy

The Equilibrists

Full of her long white arms and milky skin
He had a thousand times remembered sin.
Alone in the press of people traveled he,
Minding her jacinth, and myrrh, and ivory.

Mouth he remembered: the quaint orifice   5
From which came heat that flamed upon the kiss,
Till cold words came down spiral from the head.
Grey doves from the officious tower illsped.

Body: it was a white field ready for love,
On her body's field, with the gaunt tower above,   10
The lilies grew, beseeching him to take,
If he would pluck and wear them, bruise and break.

Eyes talking: Never mind the cruel words,
Embrace my flowers, but not embrace the swords.
But what they said, the doves came straightway flying   15
And unsaid: Honor, Honor, they came crying.

Importunate her doves. Too pure, too wise,
Clambering on his shoulder, saying, Arise,
Leave me now, and never let us meet,
Eternal distance now command thy feet.   20

Predicament indeed, which thus discovers
Honor among thieves, Honor between lovers.
O such a little word is Honor, they feel!
But the grey word is between them cold as steel.

At length I saw these lovers fully were come   25
Into their torture of equilibrium;
Dreadfully had forsworn each other, and yet
They were bound each to each, and they did not forget.

And rigid as two painful stars, and twirled
About the clustered night their prison world,   30
They burned with fierce love always to come near,
But honor beat them back and kept them clear.

Ah, the strict lovers, they are ruined now!
I cried in anger. But with puddled brow

By 1925, as "History of Two Simple Lovers." *Two Gentlemen in Bonds,* 1927.

The moral dilemma of two lovers whom physical attraction ("the beauty of their bodies" in an earlier version) draws together and "honor" holds apart is described. The reason—which could be the marriage of one or both—is never specified. They are "equilibrists," or tightrope walkers, because they have to walk a narrow line between their love and their sense of duty.

2 **remembered sin:** thought of her love, which could have led to sin   4 **jacinth . . . :** her physical charms. *Jacinth*= hyacinth, either the flower or the precious stone, which is blue or violet.   8 **tower:** Several of the images of the poem—tower, field, sword—are from the world of knighthood and romantic love.   29 **two painful stars:** The image is that of a "double star"—two stars orbiting each other at a fixed distance, drawn together by the gravitational pull (like their *love*), held apart by the centrifugal drive (like their *honor*).   34 **puddled:** troubled, confused

Devising for those gibbeted and brave   35
Came I descanting: Man, what would you have?

For spin your period out, and draw your breath,
A kinder saeculum begins with Death.
Would you ascend to Heaven and bodiless dwell?
Or take your bodies honorless to Hell?   40

In Heaven you have heard no marriage is,
No white flesh tinder to your lecheries,
Your male and female tissue sweetly shaped
Sublimed away, and furious blood escaped.

Great lovers lie in Hell, the stubborn ones   45
Infatuate of the flesh upon the bones;
Stuprate, they rend each other when they kiss,
The pieces kiss again, no end to this.

But still I watched them spinning, orbited nice.
Their flames were not more radiant than their ice.   50
I dug in the quiet earth and wrought the tomb
And made these lines to memorize their doom:—

Epitaph

Equilibrists lie here; stranger, tread light;
Close, but untouching in each other's sight;
Mouldered the lips and ashy the tall skull.   55
Let them lie perilous and beautiful.

35 **gibbeted:** as if fastened or exposed to ridicule on a scaffold 36 **descanting:** discoursing **what would you have?:** Such dilemmas are natural, even inevitable, in a world in which body and soul may be in conflict. 37 **period:** time of life 38 **saeculum:** age (Latin) 42 **no white flesh . . . :** no physical desire or physical love 44 **sublimed:** passed to a higher state, as (in physics) solids "sublime" when they pass from a solid state to a vaporous state 47 **stuprate:** Ransom seems to have made the word up from the Latin *stuprum*, which means "lewdness, debauchery." (Cf. Shakespeare, *Titus Andronicus*, IV, i, 85.) 49 **nice:** precisely

T. S. Eliot
(1888–1965)

Eliot was born in St. Louis and spent his boyhood summers at Eastern Point, on the ocean near Gloucester. After graduating from Harvard he studied at the Sorbonne in Paris; he then returned to Harvard for three years of graduate work in philosophy. A travelling fellowship took him to Germany and then to Oxford. On the way he met Ezra Pound in London; through Pound's influence "The Love Song of J. Alfred Prufrock" was published in *Poetry* in 1915. In 1917 he began to work in the foreign department of Lloyd's Bank—a position of responsibility that he held until 1925. (On his first marriage and the writing of *The Waste Land*, see the notes to that poem.) In 1922 Eliot began to edit *The Criterion*, one of the most important literary and cultural journals of the time; in 1925 he left Lloyd's to become an editor at, and later a director of, the publishing firm of Faber and Faber. Two years later he became a British subject and was confirmed in the Church of England. His first and most successful play, *Murder in the Cathedral*, was produced in 1935. In the years just before and during World War II he returned to poetry with *Four Quartets*, which many believe his finest work. After the war he wrote several more plays, among them *The Cocktail Party*. In 1948 he was awarded the British Order of Merit and the Nobel Prize for literature.

The Love Song of J. Alfred Prufrock

S'io credesse che mia risposta fosse
A persona che mai tornasse al mondo,
Questa fiamma staria senza più scosse.
Ma per ciò che giammai di questo fondo
Non tornò vivo alcun, s'i'odo il vero,
Senza tema d'infamia ti rispondo.

Let us go then, you and I,
When the evening is spread out against the sky
Like a patient etherised upon a table;
Let us go, through certain half-deserted streets,
The muttering retreats   5
Of restless nights in one-night cheap hotels
And sawdust restaurants with oyster-shells:
Streets that follow like a tedious argument
Of insidious intent
To lead you to an overwhelming question. . .   10
Oh, do not ask, "What is it?"
Let us go and make our visit.

      In the room the women come and go
Talking of Michelangelo.

      The yellow fog that rubs its back upon the window-panes,   15
The yellow smoke that rubs its muzzle on the window-panes
Licked its tongue into the corners of the evening,
Lingered upon the pools that stand in drains,
Let fall upon its back the soot that falls from chimneys,
Slipped by the terrace, made a sudden leap,   20
And seeing that it was a soft October night,
Curled once about the house, and fell asleep.

      And indeed there will be time
For the yellow smoke that slides along the street,
Rubbing its back upon the window-panes;   25
There will be time, there will be time
To prepare a face to meet the faces that you meet;
There will be time to murder and create,

1910–1911. *Prufrock and Other Observations*, 1917.

See Additional Notes (p. 771). The epigraph is from Dante's *Inferno*, XXVII, 61–66. The speaker, Guido da Montefeltro, condemned to hell as an evil counselor, is enclosed in a tongue-shaped flame which speaks for him. He says: "If I thought that my answer were to a person who would ever return to the world [and tell others], this flame would move no more [in speech]; but since from this depth no one ever returned alive, if what I hear is true, I'll answer without fear of disgrace." Prufrock feels he is in his own private hell; he would say nothing if he thought anyone would hear him and know his feelings.

1 **you and I:** Prufrock is urging on no one but himself. We can think of him as having a divided self, a split personality: that side of him which wants to act by daring and loving, and that other side which represses every such impulse.   3 **like a patient etherised:** This famous simile projects Prufrock's own state of mind on the evening, which he sees as pale, morbid, passive, insensible, incapable of action.   6–7 **one-night cheap hotels . . . oyster-shells:** The one-night hotels and seafood restaurants probably evoke for Prufrock a world of casual lovemaking by which he is both attracted and repelled.   13–14 **In the room . . . Michelangelo:** No serious talk about a great creative genius is likely to take place while the talkers "come and go" in an atmosphere of superficial artiness.   22 **fell asleep:** After its one "sudden leap," the cat (like the etherized patient) is an image of inactivity.   23–34 A famous section in Eccles. 3 says there is "a time to every purpose under the heaven," time for every kind of significant human activity. In "Prufrock" there is time for postponing, evading all such activity.

And time for all the works and days of hands
That lift and drop a question on your plate;   30
Time for you and time for me,
And time yet for a hundred indecisions,
And for a hundred visions and revisions,
Before the taking of a toast and tea.

    In the room the women come and go   35
Talking of Michelangelo.

    And indeed there will be time
To wonder, "Do I dare?" and, "Do I dare?"
Time to turn back and descend the stair,
With a bald spot in the middle of my hair—   40
[They will say: "How his hair is growing thin!"]
My morning coat, my collar mounting firmly to the chin,
My necktie rich and modest, but asserted by a simple pin—
[They will say: "But how his arms and legs are thin!"]
Do I dare   45
Disturb the universe?
In a minute there is time
For decisions and revisions which a minute will reverse.

    For I have known them all already, known them all:—
Have known the evenings, mornings, afternoons,   50
I have measured out my life with coffee spoons;
I know the voices dying with a dying fall
Beneath the music from a farther room.
    So how should I presume?

    And I have known the eyes already, known them all:—   55
The eyes that fix you in a formulated phrase,
And when I am formulated, sprawling on a pin,
When I am pinned and wriggling on the wall,
Then how should I begin
To spit out all the butt-ends of my days and ways?   60
    And how should I presume?

    And I have known the arms already, known them all—
Arms that are braceleted and white and bare
[But in the lamplight, downed with light brown hair!]
Is it perfume from a dress   65
That makes me so digress?
Arms that lie along a table, or wrap about a shawl.
    And should I then presume?
    And how should I begin?
          • • • • •

29 **works and days:** The *Works and Days* of the Greek poet Hesiod (eighth century B.C.?) stresses the need for doing the strenuous work of farming at the proper times.   30 **drop a question:** confront us with the need for an immediate response   33 **visions and revisions:** The first noun suggests what is lofty and noble; the second, what is petty, hesitant, tentative.   51 **I have measured out . . . :** The milestones in his life have been trivial social circumstances—nothing heroic. Coffee spoons are the very small spoons used with demitasse cups.   52 **a dying fall:** The phrase evokes the world of Shakespeare's romantic comedy, in which lovers do not suffer from the inhibitions that plague Prufrock. Cf. the opening of *Twelfth Night:* "If music be the food of love, play on;/ Give me excess of it . . . / That strain again! It had a dying fall. . . ." A dying fall is a cadence in music that seems to languish or fall away.   57 **sprawling on a pin:** The image is that of an insect specimen.   66 **digress:** It is so unlike Prufrock to be aroused by such physical appeals as perfume and bare arms that, even in his "love song," he considers the expression of his excitement a digression.   68 **presume:** dare to act, where perhaps action (he thinks) is uncalled for

Shall I say, I have gone at dusk through narrow streets   70
And watched the smoke that rises from the pipes
Of lonely men in shirt-sleeves, leaning out of windows? . . .

• • • • •

I should have been a pair of ragged claws
Scuttling across the floors of silent seas.

And the afternoon, the evening, sleeps so peacefully!   75
Smoothed by long fingers,
Asleep . . . tired . . . or it malingers,
Stretched on the floor, here beside you and me.
Should I, after tea and cakes and ices,
Have the strength to force the moment to its crisis?   80
But though I have wept and fasted, wept and prayed,
Though I have seen my head [grown slightly bald] brought in upon
          a platter,
I am no prophet—and here's no great matter;
I have seen the moment of my greatness flicker,
And I have seen the eternal Footman hold my coat, and snicker,   85
And in short, I was afraid.

And would it have been worth it, after all,
After the cups, the marmalade, the tea,
Among the porcelain, among some talk of you and me,
Would it have been worth while,   90
To have bitten off the matter with a smile,
To have squeezed the universe into a ball
To roll it toward some overwhelming question,
To say: "I am Lazarus, come from the dead,
Come back to tell you all, I shall tell you all"—   95
If one, settling a pillow by her head,
          Should say: "That is not what I meant at all.
          That is not it, at all."

And would it have been worth it, after all,
Would it have been worth while,   100
After the sunsets and the dooryards and the sprinkled streets,
After the novels, after the teacups, after the skirts that trail along the
          floor—
And this, and so much more?—
It is impossible to say just what I mean!

70 **Shall I say . . . :** Wondering how he might phrase his revelation to the lady, Prufrock imagines himself making a sentimental appeal to her pity, the prospect of which so embarrasses him that he cannot continue.   73 **a pair of ragged claws . . . :** far from the social world of the literary party and its problems. Claws are adapted to seize what they want, without "indecisions."   77 **malingers:** pretends illness, to avoid activity   80 **crisis:** the serious word is trivialized by *ices*, its foolish partner in rhyme   82 **my head . . . brought in upon a platter:** The reference is to St. John the Baptist, beheaded by order of Herod at the request of Salome, whose dancing had pleased the king. St. John's head was brought to the girl on a platter. As generally depicted in art, the severed head has magnificent locks. Prufrock, even imagining his own head in such a scene, cannot forget that he is "slightly bald"—a ridiculous hero.   85 **the eternal Footman:** The servant who is imagined snickering in derision as he helps Prufrock on with his coat here becomes a sort of cosmic figure who represents the attitude of Life, Fate, Death, the Universe itself toward the futile and insignificant figure Prufrock thinks he is.   87 **worth it . . . :** worth upsetting his neat, well-ordered life by making a daring move   89 **some talk of you and me:** Cf. "The Rubáiyát of Omar Khayyám," lines 111–112.   92 **squeezed . . . into a ball . . . :** Cf. Marvell, "To His Coy Mistress," lines 41–44: "Let us roll all our strength and all / Our sweetness up into one ball, / And tear our pleasures with rough strife/Through the iron gates of life. . . ." Hardly a Prufrockian attitude.   94 **"I am Lazarus . . . ":** the brother of Martha and Mary, raised from the dead by Jesus (John 11:1–44). Prufrock means that for him to change his ways now would be as drastic as if he had come from the dead. For him, except by miracle, impossible.

But as if a magic lantern threw the nerves in patterns on a screen: 105
Would it have been worth while
If one, settling a pillow or throwing off a shawl,
And turning toward the window, should say:
      "That is not it at all,
      That is not what I meant, at all."   110

                    • • • • •

No! I am not Prince Hamlet, nor was meant to be;
Am an attendant lord, one that will do
To swell a progress, start a scene or two,
Advise the prince; no doubt, an easy tool,
Deferential, glad to be of use,   115
Politic, cautious, and meticulous;
Full of high sentence, but a bit obtuse;
At times, indeed, almost ridiculous—
Almost, at times, the Fool.

      I grow old . . . I grow old . . .   120
I shall wear the bottoms of my trousers rolled.

      Shall I part my hair behind? Do I dare to eat a peach?
I shall wear white flannel trousers, and walk upon the beach.
I have heard the mermaids singing, each to each.

      I do not think that they will sing to me.   125

      I have seen them riding seaward on the waves
Combing the white hair of the waves blown back
When the wind blows the water white and black.

      We have lingered in the chambers of the sea
By sea-girls wreathed with seaweed red and brown   130
Till human voices wake us, and we drown.

111–119 The references are to characters in Elizabethan drama. Prufrock perceives he is no hero, like
Hamlet. He might play the role of the nameless actor called "First Lord," whose function is to fill in
during a procession ("progress"), or get a scene started by introductory comments. Or he might play
the role of a "tool villain," a minor villain used by a more important one. The character described in
lines 115–117 sounds like the wordy old Polonius in *Hamlet*. Several of Shakespeare's plays have a
character called "the fool"—who is often nobody's fool.   117 **full of high sentence:** the speech of the
"Clerk . . . of Oxenford" (Oxford scholar) in the Prologue to Chaucer's *Canterbury Tales* (line 306) is de-
scribed as "ful of hy sentence"—wise maxims.   121 **rolled:** turned up, with cuffs   131 **we drown:**
are submerged, overwhelmed by the actuality of life when summoned from the dream world of our
fantasies

Sweeney Among the Nightingales

ὤμοι, πέπληγμαι καιρίαν πληγὴν ἔσω.

Apeneck Sweeney spreads his knees
Letting his arms hang down to laugh,

1918. *Ara Vos Prec*, 1920. *Poems*, 1920.

See Additional Notes (p. 771). The epigraph in Greek is the cry of Agamemnon from offstage as he is
murdered by his wife in his bath. It means: "Alas for me! I have been struck a deadly blow in here!"—
line 1343 of the *Agamemnon* of Aeschylus (525–456 B.C.), the Athenian dramatist, a play in which Aga-
memnon is killed in part because of his adulterous love for Cassandra. Originally Eliot used another
epigraph from the anonymous Elizabethan "Reign of Edward the Third": "Why should I speak of the

The zebra stripes along his jaw
Swelling to maculate giraffe.

    The circles of the stormy moon   5
Slide westward toward the River Plate,
Death and the Raven drift above
And Sweeney guards the hornèd gate.

    Gloomy Orion and the Dog
Are veiled; and hushed the shrunken seas;   10
The person in the Spanish cape
Tries to sit on Sweeney's knees

    Slips and pulls the table cloth
Overturns a coffee-cup,
Reorganized upon the floor   15
She yawns and draws a stocking up;

    The silent man in mocha brown
Sprawls at the window-sill and gapes;
The waiter brings in oranges
Bananas figs and hothouse grapes;   20

    The silent vertebrate in brown
Contracts and concentrates, withdraws;
Rachel *née* Rabinovitch
Tears at the grapes with murderous paws;

    She and the lady in the cape   25
Are suspect, thought to be in league;
Therefore the man with heavy eyes
Declines the gambit, shows fatigue,

    Leaves the room and reappears
Outside the window, leaning in,   30
Branches of wistaria
Circumscribe a golden grin;

    The host with someone indistinct
Converses at the door apart,

---

nightingale? The nightingale sings of adulterous wrong?" (For the "adulterous wrong," cf. the notes on Swinburne's "Chorus" from *Atalanta in Calydon*). Both epigraphs, then, imply that the poem has to do with adultery and murder, though we are never shown either.

4 maculate: mottled, spotted—the opposite (as Sweeney is) of immaculate   **6 the River Plate:** the British name for the Río de la Plata, the estuary between Uruguay and Argentina on which Buenos Aires is located   **7 the Raven:** the southern constellation Corvus (the Crow)   **8 the hornèd gate:** In classical mythology, as related by Homer and Vergil, there are two gates through which dreams come: false dreams through a gate of ivory; true dreams through a gate of horn. If that is the allusion intended, it may mean that Sweeney has reason to be apprehensive about his disturbing dreams. But the Elizabethans frequently used "horns" as an allusion to a man who was unfaithful: Sweeney's dreams may relate to the adulterous desires because of which, or by means of which, his murder is contrived.   **9 Orion:** the brightest of our winter constellations is visible also in the southern hemisphere. "Gloomy" may refer to the fate of the mythological Orion, slain by Diana, or it may mean that the night is ominously clouded.   **the Dog:** either the constellation Canis Major or Sirius, the Dog Star, which it contains. They follow Orion across the sky.   **19–20** The lavish fruit imagery may suggest sexual indulgence.   **23 née:** born (French). Her maiden name was Rabinovitch.   **28 declines the gambit:** refuses an apparently advantageous offer (chess terminology)   **31 wistaria:** a flowering vine with lilac or purple blossoms   **32 golden grin:** a grin that shows his gold teeth

The nightingales are singing near 35
The Convent of the Sacred Heart,

And sang within the bloody wood
When Agamemnon cried aloud,
And let their liquid siftings fall
To stain the stiff dishonoured shroud. 40

35-37 **nightingales ... bloody wood:** There are no nightingales and no bloody wood in the play about Agamemnon quoted in the epigraph; he is murdered inside the house. See Additional Notes (p. 771). 36 **the Convent of the Sacred Heart:** perhaps an actual convent of Catholic nuns, or perhaps simply a name that contrasts with the violence of Agamemnon's murder—although imagery associated with "Sacred Heart" is itself bloody

Gerontion

> *Thou hast nor youth nor age*
> *But as it were an after dinner sleep*
> *Dreaming of both.*

Here I am, an old man in a dry month,
Being read to by a boy, waiting for rain.
I was neither at the hot gates
Nor fought in the warm rain
Nor knee deep in the salt marsh, heaving a cutlass, 5
Bitten by flies, fought.
My house is a decayed house,
And the jew squats on the window sill, the owner,
Spawned in some estaminet of Antwerp,
Blistered in Brussels, patched and peeled in London. 10
The goat coughs at night in the field overhead;
Rocks, moss, stonecrop, iron, merds.
The woman keeps the kitchen, makes tea,
Sneezes at evening, poking the peevish gutter.
        I an old man, 15
A dull head among windy spaces.

    Signs are taken for wonders. "We would see a sign!"
The word within a word, unable to speak a word,

1919. *Poems,* 1920.

See Additional Notes (p. 772). The epigraph is from Shakespeare, *Measure for Measure,* III, i, 34–36. The slightly misquoted lines are from a speech of the Duke meant to convince Claudio, who is sentenced to death, that he should not lament, since such life as we have in this world is "a thing that none but fools would keep."

1-2 Eliot's first two lines are derived from A. C. Benson's biography of Edward FitzGerald, the translator of the Rubáiyát: "Here he sits, in a dry month, old and blind, being read to by a country boy, longing for rain...." "Dry," here and in the last line of the poem, suggests what is devitalized, barren. The "rain," like the "warm rain" three lines below, is life-giving. 3 **the hot gates:** a translation of the Greek name *Thermopylai,* so called from its hot sulphur springs. This narrow pass by the sea was the site of heroic fighting in antiquity; cf. the last stanza of Housman's "The Oracles." Perhaps what the boy is reading is about ancient battles, or about more recent adventures in semi-tropical settings. 9 **estaminet:** bar, pub (French) **Antwerp:** a commercial town in Belgium, as is Brussels in the line below 11 **the goat:** Though often a symbol of intemperate sexuality, even the goat here is sick—like so much else in the world of the poem. 12 **stonecrop:** a mosslike plant that grows on rocky ground **merds:** obsolete word for excrement (French, *merde*) 14 **peevish gutter:** probably a stopped-up sink 16 **windy spaces:** Images of vacancy, vacuity, windiness are appropriate to Gerontion and his world. 17-19 The lines are from a sermon preached by Bishop Lancelot Andrewes (1555-1626) on Christmas Day, 1618: "Signs are taken for wonders. 'Master, we would fain see a sign,' that is, a miracle ... *Verbum infans,* the Word without a word; the eternal Word not able to speak a word ... a wonder sure ... and swaddled...." See Additional Notes (p. 772).

Swaddled with darkness. In the juvescence of the year
Came Christ the tiger   20

   In depraved May, dogwood and chestnut, flowering judas,
To be eaten, to be divided, to be drunk
Among whispers; by Mr. Silvero
With caressing hands, at Limoges
Who walked all night in the next room;   25

   By Hakagawa, bowing among the Titians;
By Madame de Tornquist, in the dark room
Shifting the candles; Fräulein von Kulp
Who turned in the hall, one hand on the door.
      Vacant shuttles   30
Weave the wind. I have no ghosts,
An old man in a draughty house
Under a windy knob.

   After such knowledge, what forgiveness? Think now
History has many cunning passages, contrived corridors   35
And issues, deceives with whispering ambitions,
Guides us by vanities. Think now
She gives when our attention is distracted
And what she gives, gives with such supple confusions
That the giving famishes the craving. Gives too late   40
What's not believed in, or if still believed,
In memory only, reconsidered passion. Gives too soon
Into weak hands, what's thought can be dispensed with
Till the refusal propagates a fear. Think
Neither fear nor courage saves us. Unnatural vices   45
Are fathered by our heroism. Virtues
Are forced upon us by our impudent crimes.
These tears are shaken from the wrath-bearing tree.

   The tiger springs in the new year. Us he devours. Think at last
We have not reached conclusion, when I   50
Stiffen in a rented house. Think at last
I have not made this show purposelessly
And it is not by any concitation

---

19 **juvescence:** apparently Eliot's alteration of *juvenescence* (youth; here, springtime)   20 **Christ the tiger:** Cf. Blake's "The Tyger" for its imagery of linked beauty and violence. See Additional Notes (p. 772).   21 **in depraved May . . . :** suggested by Henry Adams' description of the "delicate grace and passionate depravity that marked the Maryland May . . ." Adams mentions the same three trees as Eliot does. (*The Education of Henry Adams,* which Eliot reviewed about the time he was writing "Gerontion.") Legend has it that Judas hanged himself from the red-flowering tree now named for him.   22 **to be eaten . . . :** a reference to Christ in the eucharist   23–28 None of the individuals mentioned are identifiable. The first, Anglicized enough to be called "Mr.," has a name that, though vaguely Latin, is not Italian or Spanish or Portuguese. Perhaps he is at Limoges, in France, because he is interested in its famous china. His "caressing hands" are somewhat ominous; he has trouble sleeping. Hakagawa is also rootless, displaced: a Japanese, he is deferential among the paintings of Titian (1477–1576), an artist of the Venetian school. Madame de Tornquist seems to be conducting a séance. We see Fräulein von Kulp (does her name suggest the Latin *culpa*—sin or guilt?) in some kind of hesitant or indecisive action.   30–31 **shuttles / Weave the wind:** Cf. Job 7:6–7: "My days are swifter than a weaver's shuttle, and are spent without hope. O remember that my life is wind: mine eye shall no more see good."   33 **knob:** hill   34–48 See Additional Notes (p. 772).   48 **the wrath-bearing tree:** probably "the tree of knowledge of good and evil" of which Adam and Eve were forbidden to eat. Their disobedience led to their exile from the Garden of Eden, and to all the evils that have befallen man since (Gen. 2, 3). Blake's "A Poison Tree," which grew from wrath, has also been suggested—and the tree of Calvary.   53 **concitation:** urging

Of the backward devils.
I would meet you upon this honestly.   55
I that was near your heart was removed therefrom
To lose beauty in terror, terror in inquisition.
I have lost my passion: why should I need to keep it
Since what is kept must be adulterated?
I have lost my sight, smell, hearing, taste and touch: 60
How should I use them for your closer contact?

These with a thousand small deliberations
Protract the profit of their chilled delirium,
Excite the membrane, when the sense has cooled,
With pungent sauces, multiply variety   65
In a wilderness of mirrors. What will the spider do,
Suspend its operations, will the weevil
Delay? De Bailhache, Fresca, Mrs. Cammel, whirled
Beyond the circuit of the shuddering Bear
In fractured atoms. Gull against the wind, in the windy straits   70
Of Belle Isle, or running on the Horn,
White feathers in the snow, the Gulf claims,
And an old man driven by the Trades
To a sleepy corner.

Tenants of the house,
Thoughts of a dry brain in a dry season.   75

54 **backward:** (1) standing behind us with tempting suggestions; (2) perverse, twisted; (3) reluctant, hanging back, seldom appearing in our secular world   65–66 **multiply variety . . . :** a reminiscence of Ben Jonson's *The Alchemist*, II, ii, in which the voluptuary Sir Epicure Mammon imagines the fleshly pleasures he will have when rich. He plans to install mirrors in his bedroom to "multiply the figures, as I walk / Naked between my succubae [concubines]. . . ." Eliot quotes from the passage in his 1919 essay on Jonson.   66 **the spider:** See Eliot's note to "The Waste Land," line 408.   68 These three names, like the earlier ones, are made up to suggest individuals of different types and nationalities. 68–70 See Additional Notes (p. 772).   71 **Belle Isle:** an island at the mouth of the Straits of Belle Isle, which, in Newfoundland, run from the Atlantic to the Gulf of St. Lawrence   **Horn:** Cape Horn, at the southern end of South America   72 **Gulf:** probably the Gulf Stream, the ocean current in the north Atlantic which originates in the Gulf of Mexico   73 **Trades:** the trade winds, steady winds that blow toward the equator and the "doldrums," where ships are likely to be becalmed. "The Trades" also suggests that the speaker has been engaged in commercial activities.

The Waste Land

1922

*"Nam Sibyllam quidem Cumis ego ipse oculis meis vidi
in ampulla pendere, at cum illi pueri dicerent: Σίβυλλα
τί θέλεις; respondebat illa: ἀποθανεῖν θέλω."*

For Ezra Pound
il miglior fabbro.

1916–1922. *The Waste Land*, 1922.

See Additional Notes (p. 772). The Latin epigraph is from "Trimalchio's Dinner," from the picaresque novel by Petronius (first century A.D.). It means: "For I saw with my own eyes the Sibyl at Cumae hanging in a jar, and when the children said to her, 'Sibyl, what do you wish?,' she replied, 'I wish to die.' Her story (referred to in Frazer) is told by Ovid (*Metamorphoses*, XIV): Apollo tried to win her love by offering whatever she wanted. Showing him a handful of dust, she asked to live as many years as there were grains there. Forgetting to ask for lasting youth as well, she lived on to a fabulous age, but withered away as she did so, until she was little more than a voice in a jar in the temple of Apollo at Cumae (near Naples), teased by the children. Although in Petronius's satiric account the words are spoken by a vulgar and drunken braggart, and are of course a lie, it seems that they are to

I. The Burial of the Dead

April is the cruellest month, breeding
Lilacs out of the dead land, mixing
Memory and desire, stirring
Dull roots with spring rain.
Winter kept us warm, covering   5
Earth in forgetful snow, feeding
A little life with dried tubers.
Summer surprised us, coming over the Starnbergersee
With a shower of rain; we stopped in the colonnade,
And went on in sunlight, into the Hofgarten,   10
And drank coffee, and talked for an hour.
Bin gar keine Russin, stamm' aus Litauen, echt deutsch.
And when we were children, staying at the archduke's,
My cousin's, he took me out on a sled,
And I was frightened. He said, Marie,   15
Marie, hold on tight. And down we went.
In the mountains, there you feel free.
I read, much of the night, and go south in the winter.

    What are the roots that clutch, what branches grow
Out of this stony rubbish? Son of man,   20
You cannot say, or guess, for you know only
A heap of broken images, where the sun beats,
And the dead tree gives no shelter, the cricket no relief,
And the dry stone no sound of water. Only
There is shadow under this red rock,   25
(Come in under the shadow of this red rock),
And I will show you something different from either
Your shadow at morning striding behind you
Or your shadow at evening rising to meet you;
I will show you fear in a handful of dust.   30
        Frisch weht der Wind
        Der Heimat zu

---

be felt as solemnly portentous here. The dedication to Pound was earned by his work on the MS. In Dante's *Purgatorio,* XXVI, 117, the poet Guido Guinizelli, praised by Dante, points to the Provençal Arnaut Daniel as "miglior fabbro del parlar materno"—"a better craftsman of our mother tongue."

I. The Burial of the Dead: The title is from the Anglican services for the dead.   **1 April is the cruellest month:** the month when the world of nature is reborn is "cruellest" in reminding us that rebirth or renewal, whether literal or figurative, is more difficult for us than for the vegetable world. Pound had expressed a similar thought a few years earlier in *Cathay:* "The trees in my east-looking garden / are bursting out with new twigs, / They try to stir new affection . . . ." In the *Pervigilium Veneris,* the late Latin poem from which Eliot quotes later (cf. note on line 429), there is the same painful contrast between revival in man and nature.   **8 Starnbergersee:** a lake southwest of Munich, a city Eliot had visited in 1911   **10 Hofgarten:** "Royal Garden," a park in Munich   **12 Bin gar . . . :** The speaker is a woman who insists she is really German, yet whose roots are in Lithuania, and who has just been mistaken for a Russian. "I'm not Russian [feminine] at all; I come from Lithuania—real German." Something of a lost soul then? We feel symbolic overtones in her small talk, "mixing memory and desire," contrasting the excitement and exhilaration of childhood with her less natural adult life. (She reads when she should sleep; travels to escape the natural cycle of the seasons.)   **19 ff.** A more solemn voice, with Old Testament resonances, comments on the barren rubbish that makes up the lives of many.   **20** [The initials T.S.E. will indicate that this is one of Eliot's own original notes]: "Cf. Ezekiel II, i." [T.S.E.] Throughout the book of Ezekiel, the prophet is addressed by the Lord as "Son of man." In Ezek. 2, he is directed to carry his message to the children of Israel.   **22 broken images:** Cf. Ezek. 6:6: . . . and your idols may be broken and cease."   **23** "Cf. Ecclesiastes XII, v." [T.S.E.] The passage is about the evils of old age, when "the grasshopper [apparently Eliot's cricket] shall be a burden, and desire shall fail: because man goeth to his long home. . . ."   **24 water:** on the water symbolism throughout, see the note on *From Ritual to Romance* in Additional Notes.   **24–30** See Additional Notes (p. 774).   **31–34** "V. *Tristan und Isolde,* I, verses 5–8." [T.S.E.] The contrast in rhythm and tone evokes,

Mein Irisch Kind,
Wo weilest du?
"You gave me hyacinths first a year ago;   35
"They called me the hyacinth girl."
—Yet when we came back, late, from the Hyacinth garden,
Your arms full, and your hair wet, I could not
Speak, and my eyes failed, I was neither
Living nor dead, and I knew nothing,   40
Looking into the heart of light, the silence.
Oed' und leer das Meer.

Madame Sosostris, famous clairvoyante,
Had a bad cold, nevertheless
Is known to be the wisest woman in Europe,   45
With a wicked pack of cards. Here, said she,
Is your card, the drowned Phoenician Sailor,
(Those are pearls that were his eyes. Look!)
Here is Belladonna, the Lady of the Rocks,
The lady of situations.   50
Here is the man with three staves, and here the Wheel,
And here is the one-eyed merchant, and this card,
Which is blank, is something he carries on his back,
Which I am forbidden to see. I do not find
The Hanged Man. Fear death by water.   55
I see crowds of people, walking round in a ring.

from the opening of Wagner's opera (1859), the possibility of romantic love as an escape from the Waste Land. The words are sung by a young sailor on watch as Tristan is bringing the Irish princess Isolde to Cornwall as bride for King Mark. They mean: *"Fresh blows the wind / Toward our homeland: / My Irish child, / Where are you lingering?"* Tristan and Isolde themselves fall in love (though she marries King Mark); their passion is doomed to end in tragedy. Even in Wagner the song is ironic: it awakens Isolde, who takes it as an impertinence referring to herself. Later she hears it when thinking bitterly about Tristan.   35–41 See Additional Notes (p. 774).   42 Eliot's note refers us to *Tristan und Isolde*, III, 24. Tristan lies dying of a wound he permitted to be inflicted. Isolde has been summoned to heal him; they watch for her coming, but no sail is seen: *"Bleak and empty the sea."* Taken together, the two German quotations evoke the possibility of romantic love—and its failure. Just as the episode of the hyacinth girl does.   43 Madame Sosostris, the fortune-teller, can be seen as representing another delusive possibility of escape from the Waste Land: a pseudo-religion. Her name suggests Osiris, and possibly "so so." There is a pretended fortune-teller with the same name in Huxley's novel *Chrome Yellow* (1921), which Eliot had read.   46 **a wicked pack of cards:** wicked also in its colloquial sense ("He has a wicked backhand"). Her cards are the Tarot cards, used in fortune-telling, thought to go back to ancient Egyptian designs related to the rise of the Nile waters. They are discussed in Weston's book. The four suits—Cup, Lance, Sword, Dish—are sex symbols—life symbols—related to the Grail legend. See Additional Notes (p. 774).   47 **Phoenician Sailor:** The Phoenician Adonis was in a way a "sailor": an image of his head was cast into the sea and later recovered from the currents, to represent his death and resurrection. Such cults as those of Adonis were also carried westward by sailors, among others: Phoenician sailors, then, helped disseminate the fertility rituals.   48 **Those are pearls . . . :** from Ariel's song in Shakespeare's *The Tempest* (I, ii), where the theme of death (by drowning) and transfiguration is important. The song, which begins: "Full fathom five thy father lies; / Of his bones are coral made; / Those are pearls that were his eyes . . ." is about the change of a person thought drowned into "something rich and strange" (a phrase quoted by Weston).   49 **Belladonna:** The word means "beautiful lady" (Italian); it is the name of a poisonous plant (the deadly nightshade) which produces a cosmetic used to brighten the eyes. See Additional Notes (p. 775).   50 **situations:** the word suggests intrigue or maneuvering   51 **the Wheel:** a symbol of fortune, of the world of change, and, in the Hindu scriptures, "the terrible wheel of rebirth and death"   52 **one-eyed merchant:** Cf. "one-eyed jack" for a playing card with the figure in profile. There is a suggestion that those given to wordly concerns are lacking in vision. What he is carrying could be the mystery of the "mystery religions" (like those of Adonis, Attis, etc.) which Madame Sosostris, as merely superstitious, would be excluded from.   55 **the Hanged Man:** An actual card of the Tarot pack shows a man dangling by one ankle. Here he is one of the sacrificed gods Frazer writes about, and also the crucified Christ. Naturally she cannot see him.   **death by water:** One meaning is religious belief, as symbolized in baptism—the death of the old self.   56 **in a ring:** getting nowhere; circling meaninglessly on the wheel of existence. The souls in Dante's hell and purgatory, referred to below, also journey in circles.

Thank you. If you see dear Mrs. Equitone,
Tell her I bring the horoscope myself:
One must be so careful these days.

    Unreal City,   60
Under the brown fog of a winter dawn,
A crowd flowed over London Bridge, so many,
I had not thought death had undone so many.
Sighs, short and infrequent, were exhaled,
And each man fixed his eyes before his feet.   65
Flowed up the hill and down King William Street,
To where Saint Mary Woolnoth kept the hours
With a dead sound on the final stroke of nine.
There I saw one I knew, and stopped him, crying: "Stetson!
"You who were with me in the ships at Mylae!   70
"That corpse you planted last year in your garden,
"Has it begun to sprout? Will it bloom this year?
"Or has the sudden frost disturbed its bed?
"Oh keep the Dog far hence, that's friend to men,
"Or with his nails he'll dig it up again!   75
"You! hypocrite lecteur!—mon semblable,—mon frère!"

---

57 **Mrs. Equitone:** "Mrs. Neutral"—one who has no positive beliefs or convictions 59 **so careful:** One must be prudent, timid, take no chances, offend nobody (her activities may also be illegal). 60 "Cf. Baudelaire:

> 'Fourmillante cité, cité pleine de rêves,
> 'Où le spectre en plein jour raccroche le passant.'" [T.S.E.]

The lines, from "Les Sept Vieillards" ("The Seven Old Men") of Charles Baudelaire (1821–1867), mean: "Swarming city, city full of dreams, / Where the ghost in broad daylight accosts the passerby." Eliot thought Baudelaire important for bringing intensity to imagery of common life in a great modern city and for his sense of sin and redemption—important to *The Waste Land*. 62 **London Bridge:** the bridge across the Thames that leads into "the City," the financial and business section of London around the Bank of England, near where Eliot was working. 63 "Cf. Inferno III, 55–57:

> 'si lunga tratta
> di gente, ch'io non avrei mai creduto
> che morte tanta n'avesse disfatta.'" [T.S.E.]

The lines mean: "so long a line / Of people, that I would never have believed / That death had undone so many of them." See Additional Notes (p. 775). 64 "Cf. Inferno IV, 25–27:

> 'Quivi, secondo che per ascoltare,
> 'non avea pianto, ma' che di sospiri,
> 'che l'aura eterna facevan tremare'" [T.S.E.]

"Here, as far as I could tell by listening, / There was no lamentation, except for sighs, / Which caused the eternal air to tremble." See Additional Notes (p. 775). 66 **King William Street:** The crowds flowing over London Bridge into the City would find themselves on King William Street once they had crossed. It passes the Bank of England. 67 **St. Mary Woolnoth:** in King William Street. Of the chimes going dead on the final stroke, Eliot writes: "A phenomenon which I have often noticed." 70 **Mylae:** in 260 B.C., in the first Punic War, the Romans won a naval battle against the Carthaginians just off Messina, in northern Sicily. We might expect here a reference to a World War I battle; Eliot is saying that the same patterns recur in history: all wars are alike. 71 **That corpse you planted . . . :** In the ancient fertility rites, images of the god made of earth and corn were often buried. When they were disinterred later, the sprouting of the corn was taken as a favorable sign, signifying the resurrection of the god and the renewal of earth's fertility. 74–75 "Cf. the Dirge in Webster's *White Devil*." [T.S.E.] In that play (1612) of John Webster, Cornelia (V, iv) sings a lament for her son Marcello, killed by his brother Flaminio. In it she summons the robin, wren, and other friendly creatures to care for the grave. She concludes, "But keep the wolf far thence, that's foe to men, / For with his nails he'll dig them up again," See Additional Notes (p. 775). 76 "V. Baudelaire, Preface to *Fleurs du Mal*." [T.S.E.] The French words conclude "Au Lecteur" ("To the Reader"): "Hypocritical reader!—my fellow-man,—my brother!" The implication: we're all in this Waste Land together, admit it or not.

II. A Game of Chess

The Chair she sat in, like a burnished throne,
Glowed on the marble, where the glass
Held up by standards wrought with fruited vines
From which a golden Cupidon peeped out   80
(Another hid his eyes behind his wing)
Doubled the flames of sevenbranched candelabra
Reflecting light upon the table as
The glitter of her jewels rose to meet it,
From satin cases poured in rich profusion;   85
In vials of ivory and coloured glass
Unstoppered, lurked her strange synthetic perfumes,
Unguent, powdered, or liquid—troubled, confused
And drowned the sense in odours; stirred by the air
That freshened from the window, these ascended   90
In fattening the prolonged candle-flames,
Flung their smoke into the laquearia,
Stirring the pattern on the coffered ceiling.
Huge sea-wood fed with copper
Burned green and orange, framed by the coloured stone,   95
In which sad light a carvèd dolphin swam.
Above the antique mantel was displayed
As though a window gave upon the sylvan scene
The change of Philomel, by the barbarous king
So rudely forced; yet there the nightingale   100
Filled all the desert with inviolable voice
And still she cried, and still the world pursues,
"Jug Jug" to dirty ears.
And other withered stumps of time
Were told upon the walls; staring forms   105
Leaned out, leaning, hushing the room enclosed.
Footsteps shuffled on the stair.
Under the firelight, under the brush, her hair
Spread out in fiery points
Glowed into words, then would be savagely still.   110

        "My nerves are bad to-night. Yes, bad. Stay with me.
"Speak to me. Why do you never speak. Speak.
        "What are you thinking of? What thinking? What?
"I never know what you are thinking. Think."

        I think we are in rats' alley   115
Where the dead men lost their bones.

II. A Game of Chess: The title recalls two plays of Thomas Middleton (1570?–1627), *A Game at Chess* (1624), which Eliot called "that perfect piece of literary political art," and *Women Beware Women* (1621?), in which remarks made about a chess game onstage have double-meaning reference to a seduction carried on offstage. 77 "Cf. *Antony and Cleopatra*, II, ii, line 190." [T.S.E.] The blunt soldier Enobarbus is describing how glamorously Cleopatra first appeared to Antony: "The barge she sat in, / like a burnished throne, / Burned on the water . . . / on each side her / stood pretty dimpled boys, / like smiling Cupids / . . . From the barge / A strange invisible perfume hits the sense. . . ." See Additional Notes (p. 775). 80 **Cupidon:** Cupid 92 **laquearia:** the hollows between the crossbeams of a beamed ceiling. See Additional Notes (p. 775). 98 "Sylvan scene. V. Milton, *Paradise Lost*, IV, 140." [T.S.E.] The words are used of what Satan sees when he arrives outside the Garden of Eden—we are reminded that the presence of sin in the world is almost as old as the presence of man. 99 "V. Ovid, *Metamorphoses*, VI, Philomela." [T.S.E.] For the story of Philomela, see notes to Swinburne's "Chorus from *Atalanta in Calydon*" (p. 434). 100 "Cf. Part III, l. 204." [T.S.E.] 103 **Jug Jug:** onomatopoetic sounds for the song of the nightingale. To "dirty ears" they have an obscene meaning. 115 "Cf. Part III, l. 195." [T.S.E.] 116 See Additional Notes (p. 775).

"What is that noise?"
                    The wind under the door.
"What is that noise now? What is the wind doing?"
                    Nothing again nothing.   120
                              "Do
"You know nothing? Do you see nothing? Do you remember
"Nothing?"

        I remember
Those are pearls that were his eyes.   125
"Are you alive, or not? Is there nothing in your head?"
                              But

O O O O that Shakespeherian Rag—
It's so elegant
So intelligent   130
"What shall I do now? What shall I do?"
"I shall rush out as I am, and walk the street
"With my hair down, so. What shall we do to-morrow?
"What shall we ever do?"
                    The hot water at ten.   135
And if it rains, a closed car at four.
And we shall play a game of chess,
Pressing lidless eyes and waiting for a knock upon the door.

    When Lil's husband got demobbed, I said—
I didn't mince my words, I said to her myself,   140
HURRY UP PLEASE ITS TIME
Now Albert's coming back, make yourself a bit smart.
He'll want to know what you done with that money he gave you
To get yourself some teeth. He did, I was there.
You have them all out, Lil, and get a nice set,   145
He said, I swear, I can't bear to look at you.
And no more can't I, I said, and think of poor Albert,
He's been in the army four years, he wants a good time,
And if you don't give it him, there's others will, I said.
Oh is there, she said. Something o' that, I said.   150
Then I'll know who to thank, she said, and give me a straight look.
HURRY UP PLEASE ITS TIME
If you don't like it you can get on with it, I said.
Others can pick and choose if you can't.
But if Albert makes off, it won't be for lack of telling.   155
You ought to be ashamed, I said, to look so antique.

---

118 "Cf. Webster: 'Is the wind in that door still?'" [T.S.E.] (*The Devil's Law Case*, III, ii, 1. 162) The expression was idiomatic and meant "Is that the way things are?"   120–126 See Additional Notes (p. 775).   125 "Cf. Part I, 1. 37, 48." [T.S.E.] In an earlier version Eliot wrote (significantly): "I remember/ The hyacinth garden. Those are pearls that were his eyes, yes!" Cf. the hyacinth girl of line 36.   128 O O O O: The four "oh!"s and the extra syllable added to "Shakespearean" give the line an iambic lilt that imitates a ragtime dance tune; the two lines that follow imitate the silliness of a popular song lyric with its bad rhymes. Accused of being dull ("alive, or not?"), the speaker does a brief little song-and-dance.   131 "What shall I do now?": The woman suffers from a sense of boredom verging on hysteria. In the list of human vices which Baudelaire gives in the poem Eliot quotes in line 76, the one that is "most ugly, most evil, most filthy" is "l'Ennui"—boredom, which would swallow the world in one big yawn.   137 "Cf. the game of chess in Middleton's *Women Beware Women*." [T.S.E.]   139 ff. The scene of boredom and hysteria in a luxurious setting is paralleled now by some tacky chatter in a London pub—a scene reported to Eliot and his wife by their maid.   139 demobbed: demobilized. World War I ended in 1918.   141 HURRY UP PLEASE . . . : the bartender's loud announcement that the pub is about to close. Cf. the Biblical reminder that the time for good deeds is short: "the night cometh, when no man can work" (John 9:4).

(And her only thirty-one.)
I can't help it, she said, pulling a long face,
It's them pills I took, to bring it off, she said.
(She's had five already, and nearly died of young George.)   160
The chemist said it would be all right, but I've never been the same.
You are a proper fool, I said.
Well, if Albert won't leave you alone, there it is, I said,
What you get married for if you don't want children?
HURRY UP PLEASE ITS TIME   165
Well, that Sunday Albert was home, they had a hot gammon,
And they asked me in to dinner, to get the beauty of it hot—
HURRY UP PLEASE ITS TIME
HURRY UP PLEASE ITS TIME
Goonight Bill. Goonight Lou. Goonight May. Goonight.   170
Ta ta. Goonight. Goonight.
Good night, ladies, good night, sweet ladies, good night, good night.

III. The Fire Sermon

The river's tent is broken: the last fingers of leaf
Clutch and sink into the wet bank. The wind
Crosses the brown land, unheard. The nymphs are departed.   175
Sweet Thames, run softly, till I end my song.
The river bears no empty bottles, sandwich papers,
Silk handkerchiefs, cardboard boxes, cigarette ends
Or other testimony of summer nights. The nymphs are departed.
And their friends, the loitering heirs of city directors;   180
Departed, have left no addresses.
By the waters of Leman I sat down and wept . . .
Sweet Thames, run softly till I end my song,
Sweet Thames, run softly, for I speak not loud or long.
But at my back in a cold blast I hear   185
The rattle of the bones, and chuckle spread from ear to ear.
A rat crept softly through the vegetation
Dragging its slimy belly on the bank
While I was fishing in the dull canal
On a winter evening round behind the gashouse   190
Musing upon the king my brother's wreck
And on the king my father's death before him.
White bodies naked on the low damp ground
And bones cast in a little low dry garret,

---

159 **bring it off:** cause an abortion   161 **chemist:** druggist (British)   166 **gammon:** ham   172 **Good night, ladies . . . :** These words are spoken by Ophelia in *Hamlet* (IV, v). Driven out of her wits by her love for Hamlet and by his treatment of her, she drowns herself soon afterwards—has her own mournful "death by water."

III. The Fire Sermon: This section is named for Buddha's "Fire Sermon." Cf. note to line 308. 173 **the river's tent:** the foliage that in summer overarches the river—here the Thames in London. By now the leaves have fallen.   175 **nymphs:** somewhat ironically, the girls of summer who had been dating rich young men along the riverbank. Also, the more gracious ladies of another time, such as the "lovely daughters of the flood," which Spenser calls "nymphs" in the poem Eliot quotes from in the following line.   176 "V. Spenser, *Prothalamion.*" [T.S.E.] The poem was written by Edmund Spenser (cf. page 56) in 1596 to celebrate a double wedding—an event more meaningful than the casual amours of the modern nymphs. Spenser's poem describes how the daughters travelled by water for the ceremony; it describes the banks of the river as "painted all with variable flowers. . . ." In Eliot's poem, the banks are littered.   182 **the waters of Leman:** Lake Leman is the French name for Lake Geneva in Switzerland; Lausanne, where Eliot finished "The Waste Land," lies along it. See Additional Notes (p. 775).   185 **at my back . . . I hear . . . :** Cf. Marvell's "To His Coy Mistress," lines 21–22: "But at my back I always hear / Time's wingèd chariot hurrying near. . . ."   192 "Cf. *The Tempest*, I, ii." [T.S.E.] Ferdinand, Prince of Naples, is speaking about his father's supposed death by drowning: "Sitting on a bank, / Weeping again the King my father's wrack, / This music crept by me upon the waters . . ." (475–477).

Rattled by the rat's foot only, year to year.   195
But at my back from time to time I hear
The sound of horns and motors, which shall bring
Sweeney to Mrs. Porter in the spring.
O the moon shone bright on Mrs. Porter
And on her daughter   200
They wash their feet in soda water
Et O ces voix d'enfants, chantant dans la coupole!

    Twit twit twit
Jug jug jug jug jug jug
So rudely forc'd.   205
Tereu

    Unreal City
Under the brown fog of a winter noon
Mr. Eugenides, the Smyrna merchant
Unshaven, with a pocket full of currants   210
C.i.f. London: documents at sight,
Asked me in demotic French
To luncheon at the Cannon Street Hotel
Followed by a weekend at the Metropole.

    At the violet hour, when the eyes and back   215
Turn upward from the desk, when the human engine waits
Like a taxi throbbing waiting,
I Tiresias, though blind, throbbing between two lives,
Old man with wrinkled female breasts, can see
At the violet hour, the evening hour that strives   220
Homeward, and brings the sailor home from sea,

---

196 "Cf. Marvell, *To His Coy Mistress.*" [T.S.E.]   197 "Cf. Day, *Parliament of Bees:*

    'When of the sudden, listening, you shall hear,
    'A noise of horns and hunting, which shall bring
    'Actaeon to Diana in the spring,
    'Where all shall see her naked skin ...'" [T.S.E.]

See Additional Notes (p. 775).   199-201 "I do not know the origin of the ballad from which these lines are taken: it was reported to me from Sydney, Australia." [T.S.E.] It is said to have been popular with Australian soldiers in World War I. Eliot said later that "soda water" was not the bubbly kind, but baking soda in water.   202 "V. Verlaine, *Parsifal.*" [T.S.E.] He is quoting the last line of a sonnet by Paul Verlaine (1844–1896), suggested by Wagner's treatment of the Grail theme in *Parsifal* (1882). See Additional Notes (p. 775).   203-204 **Twit ... jug:** bird sounds, with possible double meanings   205 Cf. line 100. Here the spelling is archaized.   206 **Tereu:** a bird sound, but also a form of Tereus, the name of the ravisher of Philomela   207-208 **Unreal City ...:** Cf. lines 60-61.   209 **Eugenides:** Though the character sounds rather shoddy, the name means, ironically, well-born or noble.   **Smyrna:** a city in Asia Minor, the modern Izmir, in Turkey   210 "The currants were quoted at a price 'carriage and insurance free to London'; and the Bill of Lading etc. were to be handed to the buyer upon payment of the sight draft." [T.S.E.]   212 **demotic:** inelegant, vulgar (literally, of the people). Pound suggested the word instead of Eliot's *abominable.*   213 **Cannon Street Hotel:** a railroad hotel in Cannon Street, which ran into King William Street in the financial district   214 **Metropole:** a luxury hotel at Brighton, a popular seaside resort on the Channel south of London. "A weekend at Brighton" carries sexual implications (Southam). (Eliot denied that the passage had any such implications.)   215 **violet:** in color symbolism, violet can stand for nostalgia or memory (blood-red softened by dreamy blue). It also suggests mourning. See note to line 380.   218 "Tiresias, although a mere spectator and not indeed a 'character,' is yet the most important personage in the poem, uniting all the rest. Just as the one-eyed merchant, seller of currants, melts into the Phoenician Sailor, and the latter is not wholly distinct from Ferdinand Prince of Naples, so all the women are one woman, and the two sexes meet in Tiresias. What Tiresias *sees,* in fact, is the substance of the poem. The whole passage from Ovid is of great anthropological interest...." [T.S.E.] See Additional Notes (p. 775).   221 "This may not appear as exact as Sappho's lines, but I had in mind the 'longshore' or 'dory' fisherman, who returns at nightfall." [T.S.E.] He is referring to Sappho's two-line fragment (104a in D. Page's *Sappho and Alcaeus*) to Hesperus, the evening star, which may be translated: "Hesperus, bringing back all the bright dawn scattered, / You bring the sheep and the goat; you bring the child to its mother...." El-

The typist home at teatime, clears her breakfast, lights
Her stove, and lays out food in tins.
Out of the window perilously spread
Her drying combinations touched by the sun's last rays,   225
On the divan are piled (at night her bed)
Stockings, slippers, camisoles, and stays.
I Tiresias, old man with wrinkled dugs
Perceived the scene, and foretold the rest—
I too awaited the expected guest.   230
He, the young man carbuncular, arrives,
A small house agent's clerk, with one bold stare,
One of the low on whom assurance sits
As a silk hat on a Bradford millionaire.
The time is now propitious, as he guesses,   235
The meal is ended, she is bored and tired,
Endeavours to engage her in caresses
Which still are unreproved, if undesired.
Flushed and decided, he assaults at once;
Exploring hands encounter no defence;   240
His vanity requires no response,
And makes a welcome of indifference.
(And I Tiresias have foresuffered all
Enacted on this same divan or bed;
I who have sat by Thebes below the wall   245
And walked among the lowest of the dead.)
Bestows one final patronising kiss,
And gropes his way, finding the stairs unlit . . .

She turns and looks a moment in the glass,
Hardly aware of her departed lover;   250
Her brain allows one half-formed thought to pass:
"Well now that's done: and I'm glad it's over."
When lovely woman stoops to folly and
Paces about her room again, alone,
She smoothes her hair with automatic hand,   255
And puts a record on the gramophone.

"This music crept by me upon the waters"
And along the Strand, up Queen Victoria Street.
O City city, I can sometimes hear

---

iot seems to have in mind also the ending of R. L. Stevenson's famous "Requiem" (published in 1887): *"Home is the sailor, home from the sea, / And the hunter home from the hill."* The young Eliot spent his summers on Cape Ann, near Gloucester (Massachusetts), and had a first-hand knowledge of fishing and sailing. **224–225** See Additional Notes (p. 775). **227 camisoles:** undergraments **stays:** corsets **231 young man carbuncular:** the Miltonic word order (like "that old man eloquent") for purposes of irony. A carbuncle is a rubylike precious stone, or, as here, a purulent inflammation of the skin. **234 Bradford millionaire:** Bradford was an industrial town in northern England in which wartime fortunes were made by sales to the military. **243 I Tiresias . . . :** Tiresias, as both man and woman, had vicariously experienced all the sins against love. At Thebes he had been involved in the affairs of Oedipus, who had killed his father and married his mother (and so brought down a curse that had made a waste land of Thebes). In the *Odyssey* (XI), Homer had shown him among the dead, where Odysseus came to consult him. **248** See Additional Notes (p. 775). **253** "V. Goldsmith, the song in *The Vicar of Wakefield*." [T.S.E.] See page 234 of this anthology. In the world of Goldsmith's time, the seduced woman—perhaps only out of conventional morality—considers suicide; at least she feels something strongly enough to take drastic action. In Eliot's Waste Land world she feels almost nothing, and automatically puts on a phonograph record. **257** "V. *The Tempest*, as above" [T.S.E.] (line 192). The "music" may be the canned music of the gramophone, as above, or the more spontaneous, more natural music of the mandolin, as below. Or the two in contrast. **258 the Strand:** an important east-west street paralleling the Thames; continuing east, it becomes Cannon Street. **Queen Victoria Street:** a street that intersects with Cannon Street in the financial district (the "City")

Beside a public bar in Lower Thames Street,   260
The pleasant whining of a mandoline
And a clatter and a chatter from within
Where fishmen lounge at noon: where the walls
Of Magnus Martyr hold
Inexplicable splendour of Ionian white and gold.   265

    The river sweats
    Oil and tar
    The barges drift
    With the turning tide
    Red sails   270
    Wide
    To leeward, swing on the heavy spar.
    The barges wash
    Drifting logs
    Down Greenwich reach   275
    Past the Isle of Dogs.
        Weialala leia
        Wallala leialala

    Elizabeth and Leicester
    Beating oars   280
    The stern was formed
    A gilded shell
    Red and gold
    The brisk swell
    Rippled both shores   285
    Southwest wind
    Carried down stream
    The peal of bells
    White towers
        Weialala leia   290
        Wallala leialala

"Trams and dusty trees.
Highbury bore me. Richmond and Kew
Undid me. By Richmond I raised my knees
Supine on the floor of a narrow canoe."   295

260 **Lower Thames Street:** It runs eastward along the river from London Bridge to the Tower of London. Billingsgate Market, for centuries the chief London fish market, is located here. See Additional Notes (p. 776).   264 "The interior of St. Magnus Martyr is to my mind one of the finest among Wren's interiors. See *The Proposed Demolition of Nineteen City Churches*: (P. S. King & Son, Ltd.)." [T.S.E.] See Additional Notes (p. 776).   266 "The Song of the (three) Thames-daughters begins here. From line 292 to 306 inclusive they speak in turn. V. *Götterdämmerung*, III, i: the Rhine-daughters." [T.S.E.] See Additional Notes (p. 776).   266–276 See Additional Notes (p. 776).   275 Greenwich (pronounced "*grinnidge*") is a few miles downriver on the south bank. Queen Elizabeth was born at a palace there; she was entertaining Leicester (line 279) at Greenwich at the time of the river scene. 276 **the Isle of Dogs:** a tongue of land directly across the river from Greenwich   277 **Weialala leia . . . :** the Rhine-daughters sing such syllables, as part of their lament for the loss of the Rhinegold, at the beginning of Act III of *Götterdämmerung* (*The Twilight of the Gods*).   279 "V. Froude, *Elizabeth*, Vol. I, ch. iv, letter of De Quadra to Philip of Spain: 'In the afternoon we were in a barge, watching the games on the river. (The queen) was alone with Lord Robert and myself on the poop, when they began to talk nonsense, and went so far that Lord Robert at last said, as I was on the spot there was no reason why they should not be married if the queen pleased.'" [T.S.E.] See Additional Notes (p. 776).   289 **White towers:** probably the Tower of London, along the river   292–306 The songs of the three Thames-daughters, who correspond to Wagner's Rhine-daughters. These latter lament the lost beauty of their gold, but joyfully expect its return. The Thames-daughters spiritlessly recount the story of their own loss; they seem to have as little feeling about it as the typist did in her episode. 293 **Highbury:** A deleted line shows that Eliot thought of this North London suburb as typically mid-

"My feet are at Moorgate, and my heart
Under my feet. After the event
He wept. He promised 'a new start.'
I made no comment. What should I resent?"

"On Margate Sands.   300
I can connect
Nothing with nothing.
The broken fingernails of dirty hands.
My people humble people who expect
Nothing."   305
                            la la

To Carthage then I came

Burning burning burning burning
O Lord Thou pluckest me out
O Lord Thou pluckest   310

burning

IV. Death by Water

Phlebas the Phoenician, a fortnight dead,
Forgot the cry of gulls, and the deep sea swell
And the profit and loss.
                    A current under sea   315
Picked his bones in whispers. As he rose and fell
He passed the stages of his age and youth
Entering the whirlpool.
                    Gentile or Jew
O you who turn the wheel and look to windward,   320
Consider Phlebas, who was once handsome and tall as you.

---

dle class: "My father had a small business, somewhere in the city...." **Richmond and Kew:** These adjacent suburbs, favorite excursion spots, are on the river about ten miles west of London. "Cf. *Purgatorio*, V. 133:

> 'Ricorditi di me, che son la Pia;
> 'Siena mi fe', disfecemi Maremma.'" [T.S.E.]

"Remember me, who am called La Pia; / Siena made me, Maremma unmade me." What Eliot seems to care for here is the wordplay and sentence structure, not just the identity of the unhappily married (and perhaps murdered) lady who says she was born in Siena in central Italy and lost her life in the swampy Maremma nearby.   296 **Moorgate:** a northern continuation of King William Street in the City; it begins at the Bank of England.   300 **Margate Sands:** Margate is a vacation spot on the Thames estuary about 40 miles east of London. See Additional Notes (p. 776).   306 **la la:** a tired echo of the Rhine-daughters singing (line 391 and before). La-la also means "so-so," and is mildly derisive. 307 "V. St. Augustine's *Confessions*: 'to Carthage then I came, where a cauldron of unholy loves sang all about mine ears.' " [T.S.E.] The opening sentence of Book III. [Augustine's Latin has some untranslatable rhyming wordplay associating *Carthage* and *cauldron*: *Karthago* (Carthage)=*sartago* (cauldron).] Carthage was in Africa, just southwest of Sicily.   308 "The complete text of the Buddha's Fire Sermon (which corresponds in importance to the Sermon on the Mount) from which these words are taken, will be found translated in the late Henry Clarke Warren's *Buddhism in Translation* (Harvard Oriental Series). Mr. Warren was one of the great pioneers of Buddhist studies in the Occident." [T.S.E.] See Additional Notes (p. 776).   309 "From St. Augustine's *Confessions* again. [Book VI, 16; Book X, 34] The collocation of these two representatives of eastern and western asceticism, as the culmination of this part of the poem, is not an accident." [T.S.E.] Cf. Amon 4:11: "I have overthrown some of you, as God overthrew Sodom and Gomorrah, and ye were as a firebrand plucked out of the burning...." [The Lord is speaking to the people of Israel.] Cf. also Zech. 2:2.

IV. Death by Water This brief section invokes, without comment, several of the key images of the poem: the drowned Phoenician sailor, the warning about death by water, Mr. Eugenides with his "currants" (instead of the "currents" Phlebas knows), the Wheel of birth and death. See Additional Notes (p. 776).

V. What the Thunder Said

After the torchlight red on sweaty faces
After the frosty silence in the gardens
After the agony in stony places
The shouting and the crying   325
Prison and palace and reverberation
Of thunder of spring over distant mountains
He who was living is now dead
We who were living are now dying
With a little patience   330

  Here is no water but only rock
Rock and no water and the sandy road
The road winding above among the mountains
Which are mountains of rock without water
If there were water we should stop and drink   335
Amongst the rock one cannot stop or think
Sweat is dry and feet are in the sand
If there were only water amongst the rock
Dead mountain mouth of carious teeth that cannot spit
Here one can neither stand nor lie nor sit   340
There is not even silence in the mountains
But dry sterile thunder without rain
There is not even solitude in the mountains
But red sullen faces sneer and snarl
From doors of mudcracked houses   345
      If there were water
  And no rock
  If there were rock
  And also water
  And water   350
  A spring
  A pool among the rock
  If there were the sound of water only
  Not the cicada
  And dry grass singing   355
  But sound of water over a rock
  Where the hermit-thrush sings in the pine trees
  Drip drop drip drop drop drop drop
  But there is no water

  Who is the third who walks always beside you?   360
When I count, there are only you and I together

V. What the Thunder Said The title is explained by lines 400 ff. The idea of concluding, and resolving, the poem with "what the thunder said" occurred to Eliot at Lausanne during his illness. (He wrote later that certain kinds of illness are extremely favorable to both religious and artistic inspiration.) "In the first part of Part V three themes are employed: the journey to Emmaus, the approach to the Chapel Perilous (see Miss Weston's book) and the present decay of eastern Europe." [T.S.E.] See Additional Notes (p. 776).   322–328 The passage describes Christ's arrest after his agony in the Garden of Gethsemane, the clamorous mobs at his trial, and the earthquake ("reverberation of thunder") St. Matthew says occurred at his death and again when the angel of the Lord rolled back the stone from the door of the tomb.   331–366 The journey through waterless badlands invokes the water/desert symbolism that runs through the poem. It is like the knight's journey to the Perilous Castle, the disciples' journey to Emmaus.   339 **carious teeth:** decayed teeth (Cf. "Have them all out, Lil, and get a nice set," line 145.)   354 **cicada:** Cf. the cricket of line 23 and the grasshopper in the note to that line.   357 See Additional Notes (p. 776).   360 "The following lines were stimulated by the account of one of the Antarctic expeditions (I forget which, but I think one of Shackleton's): it was related that the party of explorers, at the extremity of their strength, had the constant delusion that there was *one more member* than could actually be counted." [T.S.E.] See Additional Notes (p. 776).

But when I look ahead up the white road
There is always another one walking beside you
Gliding wrapt in a brown mantle, hooded
I do not know whether a man or a woman   365
—But who is that on the other side of you?

What is that sound high in the air
Murmur of maternal lamentation
Who are those hooded hordes swarming
Over endless plains, stumbling in cracked earth   370
Ringed by the flat horizon only
What is the city over the mountains
Cracks and reforms and bursts in the violet air
Falling towers
Jerusalem Athens Alexandria   375
Vienna London
Unreal

A woman drew her long black hair out tight
And fiddled whisper music on those strings
And bats with baby faces in the violet light   380
Whistled, and beat their wings
And crawled head downward down a blackened wall
And upside down in air were towers
Tolling reminiscent bells, that kept the hours
And voices singing out of empty cisterns and exhausted wells.   385

In this decayed hole among the mountains
In the faint moonlight, the grass is singing
Over the tumbled graves, about the chapel
There is the empty chapel, only the wind's home.
It has no windows, and the door swings,   390
Dry bones can harm no one.
Only a cock stood on the rooftree
Co co rico co co rico
In a flash of lightning. Then a damp gust
Bringing rain   395

Ganga was sunken, and the limp leaves
Waited for rain, while the black clouds

365 **whether a man or a woman:** The inability to discriminate may suggest a state beyond that of the sexual troubles that plague the Waste Land.   367–377 "Cf. Hermann Hesse, *Blick ins Chaos....*" [T.S.E.] Eliot quotes a half dozen lines in German from Hesse's *A Glimpse into Chaos* (1920). They may be translated: "Already is half of Europe, already at least is half of Eastern Europe on the road to chaos; it goes drunken in spiritual delusion along the abyss and even sings, sings drunkenly and as if singing hymns the way Dmitri Karamazov did. The offended bourgeois laughs at these songs; the saint and seer hear them with tears." Hesse is thinking of the Russian revolution ("... endless plains ...") and other postwar troubles in Europe.   377 **Unreal:** Cf. "Unreal City" (line 60).   378–385 See Additional Notes (p. 777).   380 **violet light:** less pleasant here than the "violet hour" of line 215. During World War I street-lights were dimmed with blue paint; people looked cadaverous under them.   384 **bells, that kept the hours:** as the bells of St. Mary Woolnoth did, with their "dead sound" (line 67). A bell sometimes rang in the Chapel Perilous.   385 See Additional Notes (p. 777). 388 **graves:** In Grail legends, the Perilous Chapel is frequently associated with a Perilous Cemetery. 392 **a cock:** some see here a reference to the crowing of the cock that reminded Peter of his denial of Christ: "Before the cock crow, thou shalt deny me thrice" (Matt. 26:34). More likely the reference is to the cock as heralding the dawn of a new day, literally or figuratively; here, the dawn of a higher awareness, with the revelation of what the thunder has to say. See Additional Notes (p. 777). 393 **Co co rico co co rico:** the French form of what we in English render as *cock-a-doodle-do.* Perhaps the English has too many suggestions of barnyards and children's stories to seem right for the mystic import Eliot meant to give it; here it signals the flash of insight that brings on the life-giving rain. 396 **Ganga:** the Ganges, the great river of northeastern India

Gathered far distant, over Himavant.
The jungle crouched, humped in silence.
Then spoke the thunder   400
DA
Datta: what have we given?
My friend, blood shaking my heart
The awful daring of a moment's surrender
Which an age of prudence can never retract   405
By this, and this only, we have existed
Which is not to be found in our obituaries
Or in memories draped by the beneficent spider
Or under seals broken by the lean solicitor
In our empty rooms   410
DA
Dayadhvam: I have heard the key
Turn in the door once and turn once only
We think of the key, each in his prison
Thinking of the key, each confirms a prison   415
Only at nightfall, aethereal rumours
Revive for a moment a broken Coriolanus
DA
Damyata: The boat responded
Gaily, to the hand expert with sail and oar   420
The sea was calm, your heart would have responded
Gaily, when invited, beating obedient
To controlling hands

I sat upon the shore
Fishing, with the arid plain behind me   425

---

398 **Himavant:** a holy mountain in the Himalayas, which stretch 150 miles or so to the north of the
Ganges   402 "'Datta, dayadhvam, damyata' (Give, sympathise, control). The fable of the meaning of
the Thunder is found in the *Brihadaranyaka—Upanishad, 5, 1.* A translation is found in Deussen's *Sech-
zig Upanishads des Veda,* p. 489." [T.S.E.] See Additional Notes (p. 777).   402 **Datta:** give   404 **awful
daring . . . :** a sudden impulsive generosity (like Eliot's own decision to get married?), the conse-
quences of which will be lifelong   407 **not . . . in our obituaries:** not a matter of public record
408 "Cf. Webster, *The White Devil,* V, vi:

> '. . . they'll remarry
> Ere the worm pierce your winding-sheet, ere the spider
> Make a thin curtain for your epitaphs.'" [T.S.E.]

See Additional Notes (p. 777).   409 **solicitor:** attorney—perhaps here about to read a will
412 **Dayadhvam:** sympathize. "Cf. *Inferno,* XXXIII, 46:

> 'ed io sentii chiavar l'uscio di sotto
> all'orribile torre.'" [T.S.E.]

The quotation means: "and I heard [them] below locking the door of the horrible tower." See Addi-
tional Notes (p. 777).   417 **Coriolanus:** the hero of Shakespeare's tragedy of that name (c. 1607),
which Eliot called Shakespeare's "most assured artistic success." Coriolanus, shut up in his own self-
ish pride, is destroyed by it—but he is broken, in a more aetherial (heavenly) way, when he yields to
his mother's plea that he spare his native Rome, which had aroused his anger, and against which he is
marching. He knows that yielding will mean his own destruction: "But for your son . . ." he tells her,
/ "Most dangerously you have with him prevailed,/If not most mortal to him" (V, iii). Coriolanus can
represent, then, both the man confined in his self-destructive pride, and the man who escapes from it
by "the awful daring of a moment's surrender."   419 **Damyata:** control. The image, derived from
Eliot's youthful sailing experiences off Cape Ann, stands for the beauty of control, as shown in the ex-
pertly controlled sailboat. The "would have responded" implies that proper control over the heart has
not been exercised—as we have seen in many an incident in "The Waste Land."   425 "V. Weston:
From Ritual to Romance; chapter on the Fisher King." [T.S.E.] Weston contends that Fish and Fisher are
"Life symbols of immemorial antiquity. . . ." If the speaker here is upon the shore fishing, the sugges-
tion is that the Waste Land is on the way to regaining its vitality. And it is significant that now the
arid plain is *behind* the speaker, who has emerged, or is emerging, from the Waste Land, having
found, in the voice of the thunder, the true way out of its desolation.

Shall I at least set my lands in order?
London Bridge is falling down falling down falling down
Poi s'ascose nel foco che gli affina
Quando fiam uti chelidon—O swallow swallow
Le Prince d'Aquitaine à la tour abolie   430
These fragments I have shored against my ruins
Why then Ile fit you. Hieronymo's mad againe.
Datta. Dayadhvam. Damyata.
        Shantih shantih shantih

426 **set my lands in order:** An individual's first duty is to bring a right order into his own life. Cf. Isa.
23:1, the words of the prophet to the sick King Hezekiah: "Set thine house in order: for thou shalt die,
and not live. . . ." But the king's prayer to be spared is answered.   427 **London Bridge . . . :** Here the
nursery rhyme is not playful but ominous, and relates London to the "falling towers" (of line 374)
and other collapsing civilizations. The apparently innocent rhyme does go back to dark primitive be-
ginnings: Frazer's *The Golden Bough* tells of human beings sacrificed and buried in the foundations of
bridges as guardian spirits. See Additional Notes (p. 777).   428 "V. *Purgatorio,* XXVI, 148.

    "'Ara vos prec per aquella valor
    'que vos guida al som de l'escalina,
    'sovegna vos a temps de ma dolor.'
    Poi s'ascose nel foco che gli affina.'" [T.S.E.]

See Additional Notes (p. 777). 429 "V. *Pervigilium Veneris.* Cf. Philomela in Parts II and III." [T.S.E.] See
Additional Notes (p. 778).   **O swallow swallow:** A song in Tennyson's *The Princess* (1847) begins with
these words. It is a love song ("O tell her, brief is life but love is long. . . ."). See Additional Notes (p.
778).   430 "V. Gérard de Nerval, Sonnet *El Desdichado.*" [T.S.E.] See Additional Notes (p. 778).   431
Though the tower and the tradition of the poet-prince may lie in ruins, the fragments of their poetry
remain as support for others in their own troubles.   432 "V. Kyd's *Spanish Tragedy.*" [T.S.E.] Cf. earli-
er note on *The Spanish Tragedy.* Hieronymo says "Why then Ile fit you" when asked to supply an enter-
tainment for the king (V, v). "Fit you" means "supply you," "meet your requirements"—though he
may also have in mind fitting his enemies to roles in the play.   434 "Shantih. Repeated as here, a for-
mal ending to an Upanishad. 'The Peace which passeth understanding' is our equivalent to this
word." [T.S.E.] Although Eliot uses the Sanskrit word, he interprets it in Christian terms (from Phil.
4:7). Again he deliberately avoids using the familiar words, as if he hoped the strangeness and fresh-
ness of *Shantih* would make us take a closer look, startle us into awareness. And so the poem, which to
many readers—at least at first glance—itself "passeth understanding," concludes on the most positive
and reassuring of notes.

Journey of the Magi

'A cold coming we had of it,
Just the worst time of the year
For a journey, and such a long journey:
The ways deep and the weather sharp,
The very dead of winter.'   5
And the camels galled, sore-footed, refractory,
Lying down in the melting snow.
There were times we regretted
The summer palaces on slopes, the terraces,
And the silken girls bringing sherbet.   10
Then the camel men cursing and grumbling

Ariel Poems, no. 8 [1927].

Cf. Yeats, "The Magi." The account of the (traditionally three) Magi or wise men from the East who
followed the star of Bethlehem to the birthplace of Christ is told in Matt. 2. The first five lines of the
poem are from Bishop Lancelot Andrewes's Christmas sermon of 1622, which Eliot quotes in his 1926
essay on Andrewes: "It was no summer progress. A cold coming they had of it at this time of the year,
just the worst time of the year to take a journey, and especially a long journey in. The ways deep, the
weather sharp, the days short, the sun farthest off, *in solstitio brumali* [at the winter solstice, Dec. 22],
'the very dead of winter.'" Andrewes mentions details of the difficulty of the journey, but Eliot puts
them in contemporary terms: "wanting their liquor and women . . . charging high prices. . . ." In the
poem one of the wise men, now quite old, is looking back on the experience and wondering what
to make of it. See Additional Notes (p. 778).

And running away, and wanting their liquor and women,
And the night-fires going out, and the lack of shelters,
And the cities hostile and the towns unfriendly
And the villages dirty and charging high prices: 15
A hard time we had of it.
At the end we preferred to travel all night,
Sleeping in snatches,
With the voices singing in our ears, saying
That this was all folly.   20

    Then at dawn we came down to a temperate valley,
Wet, below the snow line, smelling of vegetation;
With a running stream and a water-mill beating the darkness,
And three trees on the low sky,
And an old white horse galloped away in the meadow.   25
Then we came to a tavern with vine-leaves over the lintel,
Six hands at an open door dicing for pieces of silver,
And feet kicking the empty wine-skins.
But there was no information, and so we continued
And arrived at evening, not a moment too soon   30
Finding the place; it was (you may say) satisfactory.

    All this was a long time ago, I remember,
And I would do it again, but set down
This set down
This: were we led all that way for   35
Birth or Death? There was a Birth, certainly,
We had evidence and no doubt. I had seen birth and death,
But had thought they were different; this Birth was
Hard and bitter agony for us, like Death, our death.
We returned to our places, these Kingdoms,   40
But no longer at ease here, in the old dispensation,
With an alien people clutching their gods.
I should be glad of another death.

23–28 See Additional Notes (p. 778).   29 **no information:** The phrase could imply that not even divine revelations are necessarily perceived as such.   33–34 **set down / This . . . :** The speaker seems to be relating his memories to someone who is recording them.   36 **Birth or Death:** The birth of a new order of being (as at the coming of Christ) is the death of the old order. Cf. Yeats, "Two Songs from a Play," "The Second Coming," and others. Conversion to a new belief is the death of the old. Once having seen the coming of Christ, the Magi were no longer happy in their "old dispensation" (old religious system)—though the speaker sounds as if he does not quite know what to make of the new one.

From **Four Quartets**

EAST COKER

I

In my beginning is my end. In succession
Houses rise and fall, crumble, are extended,
Are removed, destroyed, restored, or in their place
Is an open field, or a factory, or a by-pass.

1937–1940. *East Coker*, 1940.

"East Coker" is the second of the *Four Quartets*, which might be described as poetic meditations on the interrelated themes of time, change, age, history, suffering, love, religion, spirituality, redemption, and eternity. They have analogies with the quartet as a musical form: each is made up of five "movements," differing in spirit and rhythm, in which themes or statements are set against counterstate-

Old stone to new building, old timber to new fires,　　5
Old fires to ashes, and ashes to the earth
Which is already flesh, fur and faeces,
Bone of man and beast, cornstalk and leaf.
Houses live and die: there is a time for building
And a time for living and for generation　　10
And a time for the wind to break the loosened pane
And to shake the wainscot where the field-mouse trots
And to shake the tattered arras woven with a silent motto.

　　In my beginning is my end. Now the light falls
Across the open field, leaving the deep lane　　15
Shuttered with branches, dark in the afternoon,
Where you lean against a bank while a van passes,
And the deep lane insists on the direction
Into the village, in the electric heat
Hypnotised. In a warm haze the sultry light　　20
Is absorbed, not refracted, by grey stone.
The dahlias sleep in the empty silence.
Wait for the early owl.
　　　　　　In that open field
If you do not come too close, if you do not come too close,
On a Summer midnight, you can hear the music　　25
Of the weak pipe and the little drum
And see them dancing around the bonfire
The association of man and woman
In daunsinge, signifying matrimonie—
A dignified and commodious sacrament.　　30
Two and two, necessarye coniunction,
Holding eche other by the hand or the arm
Whiche betokeneth concorde. Round and round the fire
Leaping through the flames, or joined in circles,
Rustically solemn or in rustic laughter　　35
Lifting heavy feet in clumsy shoes,
Earth feet, loam feet, lifted in country mirth
Mirth of those long since under earth
Nourishing the corn. Keeping time,
Keeping the rhythm in their dancing　　40
As in their living in the living seasons
The time of the seasons and the constellations
The time of milking and the time of harvest
The time of the coupling of man and woman

---

ments, repeated and developed with variations, and brought to a resolution. Different kinds of speech, almost different voices (like the four instruments of the quartet) are heard reinforcing or resisting each other. See Additional Notes (p. 778). East Coker is a village in Somerset (in southwestern England) where the Eliot family had lived until an ancestor emigrated to New England in 1667. Eliot visited the village in 1937 and took photographs.

1 **In my beginning is my end:** *En ma fin est mon commencement* (In my end is my beginning) was the motto embroidered on the chair of state of Mary Queen of Scots during her captivity. The motto, which Eliot reverses but reestablishes at the end of the poem, may have meant that Mary (beheaded in 1587) felt she would begin to live at her death. As Eliot first gives the motto, it can mean that our death is implicit in our birth.　9–11 **a time . . . a time . . . :** Cf. "Prufrock," line 23 ff.; Eccles. 3. 12 **wainscot:** wooden panelling, especially on the lower part of a wall　13 **arras:** wall-hanging, tapestry (Many were made at Arras in France.) **silent motto:** The motto of the Eliot family was *Tace et fac* (*Be silent and act*.)　25–27 **you can hear . . . And see . . . :** in imagination　28–33 The lines are based on the beginning of Book I, chap. 21, of *The Book Named the Governor*, by Sir Thomas Elyot, the first English book (1531) about education. The archaic spelling suggests how ancient such rituals as dance and marriage are. See Additional Notes (p. 779).　30 **commodious:** beneficial, advantageous to humanity

And that of beasts. Feet rising and falling.   45
Eating and drinking. Dung and death.

    Dawn points, and another day
Prepares for heat and silence. Out at sea the dawn wind
Wrinkles and slides. I am here
Or there, or elsewhere. In my beginning.   50

II

What is the late November doing
With the disturbance of the spring
And creatures of the summer heat,
And snowdrops writhing under feet
And hollyhocks that aim too high   55
Red into grey and tumble down
Late roses filled with early snow?
Thunder rolled by the rolling stars
Simulates triumphal cars
Deployed in constellated wars   60
Scorpion fights against the Sun
Until the Sun and Moon go down
Comets weep and Leonids fly
Hunt the heavens and the plains
Whirled in a vortex that shall bring   65
The world to that destructive fire
Which burns before the ice-cap reigns.

    That was a way of putting it—not very satisfactory:
A periphrastic study in a worn-out poetical fashion,
Leaving one still with the intolerable wrestle   70
With words and meanings. The poetry does not matter.
It was not (to start again) what one had expected.
What was to be the value of the long looked forward to,
Long hoped for calm, the autumnal serenity
And the wisdom of age? Had they deceived us   75
Or deceived themselves, the quiet-voiced elders,
Bequeathing us merely a receipt for deceit?
The serenity only a deliberate hebetude,
The wisdom only the knowledge of dead secrets
Useless in the darkness into which they peered   80
Or from which they turned their eyes. There is, it seems to us,
At best, only a limited value
In the knowledge derived from experience.
The knowledge imposes a pattern, and falsifies,
For the pattern is new in every moment   85
And every moment is a new and shocking
Valuation of all we have been. We are only undeceived

---

47 **dawn points:** influenced by the French *le point du jour* (daybreak). The French verb *poindre* means "to dawn" (as well as "to point"). 51–67 The seasons, as they whirl and tumble by, portend the end of life and the destruction of the world. The poem is set in an unseasonably warm spell in November. 54 **snowdrops:** perhaps here the flower of that name 61 **Scorpion:** Scorpio is the sign of the zodiac that prevails from October 21 to November 21. It fights against the sun in that it marks the coming of the cold season. 63 **Leonids:** a shower of meteors that appears annually for about two days around November 17. It appears to radiate from the constellation Leo (the Lion). 66–67 **fire . . . ice-cap:** Cf. Robert Frost's "Fire and Ice": "Some say the world will end in fire, / Some say in ice. . . " Eliot envisages both; he sees the burnt out world as frozen over. 69 **periphrastic:** using periphrasis, roundabout language 78 **hebetude:** dullness

Of that which, deceiving, could no longer harm.
In the middle, not only in the middle of the way
But all the way, in a dark wood, in a bramble,   90
On the edge of a grimpen, where is no secure foothold,
And menaced by monsters, fancy lights,
Risking enchantment. Do not let me hear
Of the wisdom of old men, but rather of their folly,
Their fear of fear and frenzy, their fear of possession,   95
Of belonging to another, or to others, or to God.
The only wisdom we can hope to acquire
Is the wisdom of humility: humility is endless.

   The houses are all gone under the sea.

   The dancers are all gone under the hill.   100

III

O dark dark dark. They all go into the dark,
The vacant interstellar spaces, the vacant into the vacant,
The captains, merchant bankers, eminent men of letters,
The generous patrons of art, the statesmen and the rulers,
Distinguished civil servants, chairmen of many committees,   105
Industrial lords and petty contractors, all go into the dark,
And dark the Sun and Moon, and the Almanach de Gotha
And the Stock Exchange Gazette, the Directory of Directors,
And cold the sense and lost the motive of action.
And we all go with them, into the silent funeral,   110
Nobody's funeral, for there is no one to bury.
I said to my soul, be still, and let the dark come upon you
Which shall be the darkness of God.   As, in a theatre,
The lights are extinguished, for the scene to be changed
With a hollow rumble of wings, with a movement of darkness on
                    darkness,   115
And we know that the hills and the trees, the distant panorama
And the bold imposing façade are all being rolled away—
Or as, when an underground train, in the tube, stops too long
                    between stations
And the conversation rises and slowly fades into silence

89–90 **In the middle . . . in a dark wood:** Dante's *Divine Comedy* begins (in translation): "In the middle of the way of our life, I found myself in a dark wood. . . ." 91 **a grimpen:** Cf. A. Conan Doyle, "The Hound of the Baskervilles": " 'That is the great Grimpen Mire,' he said. 'A false step yonder means death to man or beast. Only yesterday I saw one of the ponies wander into it. He never came out. . . .'" Conan Doyle's "impassible Mire" was suggested by an actual bog in Dartmoor in southwestern England. 92 **fancy:** of fantasy—phantasmal, illusory 100 **under the hill:** Cf. (possibly) Blake's "Epilogue" to "The Gates of Paradise," "The lost traveller's dream under the hill"; and Tennyson's "Break, Break, Break"; "And the stately ships go on, / To their haven under the hill. . . ." 101 **O dark dark dark:** In Milton's "Samson Agonistes," line 80, the blinded Samson cries out, "O dark, dark, dark, amid the blaze of noon. . . ." 102 **vacant interstellar spaces:** Cf. "Samson Agonistes," line 89: "vacant interlunar cave." 107 **dark the Sun and Moon:** "Samson Agonistes," 86–87: "The Sun to me is dark / and silent as the Moon . . ." **Almanach de Gotha:** Originally published in French and German in the German city of Gotha (near Erfurt), it gave, in addition to statistical and historical information about the countries of the world, detailed genealogies of the royal and princely families of Europe. 108 **Stock Exchange Gazette:** an annual volume published in London whose title indicates its coverage **Directory of Directors:** a British annual which listed directors of the principal joint-stock companies of the United Kingdom 113 **the darkness of God:** In the works of the Spanish poet and mystic St. John of the Cross (1542–1591), the "dark night of the soul," the absence of even spiritual consolation, is a stage on the soul's journey toward knowledge of and union with God. 118 **an underground train, in the tube:** a subway train, called the "tube" in Britain

And you see behind every face the mental emptiness deepen   120
Leaving only the growing terror of nothing to think about;
Or when, under ether, the mind is conscious but conscious of nothing—
I said to my soul, be still, and wait without hope
For hope would be hope for the wrong thing; wait without love
For love would be love of the wrong thing; there is yet faith   125
But the faith and the love and the hope are all in the waiting.
Wait without thought, for you are not ready for thought:
So the darkness shall be the light, and the stillness the dancing.

   Whisper of running streams, and winter lightning.
The wild thyme unseen and the wild strawberry,   130
The laughter in the garden, echoed ecstasy
Not lost, but requiring, pointing to the agony
Of death and birth.
               You say I am repeating
Something I have said before. I shall say it again.
Shall I say it again? In order to arrive there,   135
To arrive where you are, to get from where you are not,
   You must go by a way wherein there is no ecstasy.
In order to arrive at what you do not know
   You must go by a way which is the way of ignorance.
In order to possess what you do not possess   140
   You must go by the way of dispossession.
In order to arrive at what you are not
   You must go through the way in which you are not.
And what you do not know is the only thing you know
And what you own is what you do not own   145
And where you are is where you are not.

           IV
The wounded surgeon plies the steel
That questions the distempered part;
Beneath the bleeding hands we feel
The sharp compassion of the healer's art   150
Resolving the enigma of the fever chart.

   Our only health is the disease
If we obey the dying nurse
Whose constant care is not to please
But to remind of our, and Adam's curse,   155
And that, to be restored, our sickness must grow worse.

   The whole earth is our hospital
Endowed by the ruined millionaire,
Wherein, if we do well, we shall
Die of the absolute paternal care   160
That will not leave us, but prevents us everywhere.

135–146 Based on St. John of the Cross, *The Ascent of Mount Carmel*, Book I, chapter xiii. See Addition-
al Notes (p. 779).   147–171 Helped by the poet's own comments, we know that in this allegorical lyr-
ic the "wounded surgeon" represents Christ, the "healer"; the "dying nurse" is the church in this
world; the "ruined millionaire" is fallen Adam, who once had grand estates.   152 **health ... disease
...** : We have to feel dis-ease with, be sick of, the things of this world in order to arrive at spiritual
health. St. John of the Cross also used the sickness-health image.   161 **prevents:** An older religious
meaning of the word, used of God's grace, was: *to go before* with spiritual guidance and help, to predis-
pose to repentance, faith, and good works. Cf. the Anglican *Book of Common Prayer:* "That thy grace
may always prevent and follow us." The usual meaning is also relevant: prevent from doing evil.

The chill ascends from feet to knees,
The fever sings in mental wires.
If to be warmed, then I must freeze
And quake in frigid purgatorial fires   165
Of which the flame is roses, and the smoke is briars.

The dripping blood our only drink,
The bloody flesh our only food:
In spite of which we like to think
That we are sound, substantial flesh and blood—   170
Again, in spite of that, we call this Friday good.

V

So here I am, in the middle way, having had twenty years—
Twenty years largely wasted, the years of *l'entre deux guerres*—
Trying to learn to use words, and every attempt
Is a wholly new start, and a different kind of failure   175
Because one has only learnt to get the better of words
For the thing one no longer has to say, or the way in which
One is no longer disposed to say it. And so each venture
Is a new beginning, a raid on the inarticulate
With shabby equipment always deteriorating   180
In the general mess of imprecision of feeling,
Undisciplined squads of emotion. And what there is to conquer
By strength and submission, has already been discovered
Once or twice, or several times, by men whom one cannot hope
To emulate—but there is no competition—   185
There is only the fight to recover what has been lost
And found and lost again and again: and now, under conditions
That seem unpropitious. But perhaps neither gain nor loss.
For us, there is only the trying. The rest is not our business.

Home is where one starts from. As we grow older   190
The world becomes stranger, the pattern more complicated
Of dead and living. Not the intense moment
Isolated, with no before and after,
But a lifetime burning in every moment
And not the lifetime of one man only   195
But of old stones that cannot be deciphered.
There is a time for the evening under starlight,
A time for the evening under lamplight
(The evening with the photograph album).
Love is most nearly itself   200
When here and now cease to matter.
Old men ought to be explorers
Here and there does not matter
We must be still and still moving
Into another intensity   205
For a further union, a deeper communion
Through the dark cold and the empty desolation,
The wave cry, the wind cry, the vast waters
Of the petrel and the porpoise.   In my end is my beginning.

167–169 **blood ... flesh:** the sacrament of the Eucharist 171 **call ... good:** call it Good Friday
172 **in the middle way:** Cf. line 89.   173 *l'entre deux guerres:* (French) between two wars, World
Wars I and II 202 **Old men ought to be explorers:** Cf. Tennyson's "Ulysses"—and also for the sea
imagery in the two poems.   209 **petrel:** a bird that keeps to the open sea

Conrad Aiken
(1889–1973)

Born in Savannah, Aiken was orphaned at 11 when his father, a distinguished physician, killed his wife and himself. Sent to live with relatives in New England, he became a friend of Eliot at Harvard. After college he divided his time between England and the United States until 1947, when he settled in Brewster, Massachusetts. A prolific writer all of his life, he produced many books of poetry, short stories, essays, an autobiography, and a play.

The Things

The house in Broad Street, red brick, with nine rooms
the weedgrown graveyard with its rows of tombs
the jail from which imprisoned faces grinned
at stiff palmettos flashing in the wind

the engine-house, with engines, and a tank   5
in which young alligators swam and stank,
the bell-tower, of red iron, where the bell
gonged of the fires in a tone from hell

magnolia trees with whitehot torch of bud
the yellow river between banks of mud   10
the tall striped lighthouse like a barber's pole
snake in the bog and locust in the hole

worn cigarette cards, of white battleships,
or flags, or chorus girls with scarlet lips,
jackstones of copper, peach tree in the yard   15
splashing ripe peaches on an earth baked hard

children beneath the arc-light in a romp
with Run sheep Run, and rice-birds in the swamp,
the organ-grinder's monkey, dancing bears,
okras in baskets, Psyche on the stairs—   20

and then the north star nearer, and the snow
silent between the now and long ago
time like a train that roared from place to place
new crowds, new faces, for a single face

no longer then the chinaberry tree   25
nor the dark mockingbird to sing his glee
nor prawns nor catfish; icicles instead
and Indian-pipes, and cider in the shed

arbutus under pinewoods in the spring
and death remembered as a tropic thing   30
with picture postcard angels to upraise it
and trumpet vines and hummingbirds to phrase it

The Coming Forth by Day of Osiris Jones, 1931.

1 **Broad Street:** Aiken spent his earliest years in Savannah. 18 **rice-birds:** several kinds of small birds found about rice-fields 20 **Psyche:** a statue of the mythological Psyche, who stands for the soul 21 **north star nearer:** Aiken moved to Massachusetts when about twelve. 27 **prawns:** shrimp or shrimplike seafood 28 **Indian-pipes:** a white waxy plant also called corpse-plant or ghost-flower

then wisdom come, and Shakspere's voice far off,
to be or not, upon the teacher's cough,
the latent heat of melting ice, the brief   35
hypotenuse from ecstasy to grief

amo amas, and then the *cras amet,*
the new-found eyes no slumber could forget,
Vivien, the affliction of the senses,
and conjugation of historic tenses   40

and Shakspere nearer come, and louder heard,
and the disparateness of flesh and word,
time growing swifter, and the pendulums
in shorter savage arcs that beat like drums—

hands held, relinquished, faces come and gone,   45
kissed and forgotten, and become but one,
old shoes worn out, and new ones bought, the gloves
soiled, and so lost in limbo, like the loves—

then Shakspere in the heart, the instant speech
parting the conscious terrors each from each—   50
wisdom's dishevelment, the purpose lamed,
and purposeless the footsteps eastward aimed

the bloodstream always slower, while the clock
followed the tired heart with louder knock,
fatigue upon the eye, the tardy springs   55
inviting to no longer longed-for things—

the birdsong nearer now than Shakspere's voice,
whispers of comfort—Death is near, rejoice!—
remember now the red house with nine rooms
the graveyard with its trumpetvines and tombs—   60

play jackstones now and let your jackstones be
the stars that make Orion's galaxy
so to deceive yourself until you move
into that house whose tenants do not love.

36 hypotenuse: here, the shortest line between   **37 amo amas:** *I love, you love;* part of a Latin les-
son   ***cras amet:*** *tomorrow let him love;* part of the refrain of the *Pervigilium Veneris* ("Tomorrow let him
love who was never in love before . . .") Cf. "The Waste Land," line 429.   **39 Vivien:** an enchantress
in Arthurian legends—any enchanting woman   **62 Orion:** the bright winter constellation imagined
as a hunter

Doctors' Row

Snow falls on the cars in Doctors' Row and hoods the headlights;
snow piles on the brownstone steps, the basement deadlights;
fills up the letters and names and brass degrees
on the bright brass plates, and the bright brass holes for keys.

Snow hides, as if on purpose, the rows of bells   5
which open the doors to separate cells and hells:

Brownstone Eclogues, 1942.

2 deadlights: windows not meant to open

to the waiting-rooms, where the famous prepare for headlines,
and humbler citizens for their humbler deadlines.

And in and out, and out and in, they go,
the lamentable devotees of Doctors' Row;   10
silent and circumspect—indeed, liturgical;
their cries and prayers prescribed, their penance surgical.

No one complains—no one presumes to shriek—
the walls are very thick, and the voices weak.
Or the cries are whisked away in noiseless cabs,   15
while nurse, in the alley, empties a pail of swabs.

Miserable street!—through which your sweetheart hurries,
lowers her chin, as the snow-cloud stings and flurries;
thinks of the flower-stall, by the church, where you
wait like a clock, for two, for half-past two;   20

thinks of the roses banked on the steps in snow,
of god in heaven, and the world above, below;
widens her vision beyond the storm, her sight
the infinite rings of an immense delight;

all to be lived and loved—O glorious All!   25
Eastward or westward, Plato's turning wall;
the sky's blue streets swept clean of silent birds
for an audience of gods, and superwords.

11 **liturgical:** as if at a solemn ritual   26 **Plato's turning wall:** probably a reference to the opening of
Book VII of Plato's *Republic*, where he likens the human condition to that of creatures living in a cave,
their eyes fixed on the wall before them. Behind them, where they cannot look, is a fire whose light
throws the shadows of moving figures on the wall—the creatures mistake these shadows for reality,
since they see nothing else. Or Aiken may simply be referring to the wall which the limitation of our
physical senses puts between us and the real world which lies beyond.

Edna St. Vincent Millay
(1892–1950)

Born in Rockland, Maine, and a graduate of Vassar, Millay was for some years a glamor-
ous figure around Greenwich Village in New York City—an early example of the liberat-
ed woman who wrote unashamedly of her amours. In 1923, after a breakdown, she mar-
ried the Dutch-Irish importer who spent much of the rest of his life caring for her,
mostly on their farm in upstate New York. The pressure of public events turned her more
and more toward propaganda-verse before and during World War II. Besides her many
books of poetry she wrote several plays, an opera libretto, and a book of prose sketches.

From **Fatal Interview**

VII

Night is my sister, and how deep in love,
How drowned in love and weedily washed ashore,
There to be fretted by the drag and shove
At the tide's edge, I lie—these things and more:
Whose arm alone between me and the sand,   5
Whose voice alone, whose pitiful breath brought near,

1929–1930. *Fatal Interview*, 1931.

Could thaw these nostrils and unlock this hand,
She could advise you, should you care to hear.
Small chance, however, in a storm so black,
A man will leave his friendly fire and snug   10
For a drowned woman's sake, and bring her back
To drip and scatter shells upon the rug.
No one but Night, with tears on her dark face,
Watches beside me in this windy place.

XXX

Love is not all; it is not meat nor drink
Nor slumber nor a roof against the rain,
Nor yet a floating spar to men that sink
And rise and sink and rise and sink again;
Love can not fill the thickened lung with breath,   5
Nor clean the blood, nor set the fractured bone;
Yet many a man is making friends with death
Even as I speak, for lack of love alone.
It well may be that in a difficult hour,
Pinned down by pain and moaning for release,   10
Or nagged by want past resolution's power,
I might be driven to sell your love for peace,
Or trade the memory of this night for food.
It well may be. I do not think I would.

Archibald MacLeish
(Born 1892)

MacLeish, born in Glencoe, a northern suburb of Chicago, has degrees from Yale and the Harvard Law School. In World War I he was an officer in the field artillery. After five years of lecturing on government at Harvard and working as an attorney, MacLeish went to France with his family to devote himself to poetry. On his return five years later, he began to hold a series of distinguished positions: editor of *Fortune*, Librarian at the Library of Congress, Director of the Office of Facts and Figures, Assistant Secretary of State, and Chairman of the American delegation to the London Conference at which UNESCO was founded. From 1949 to 1962 he was Boylston Professor of Rhetoric at Harvard. During his many years of public service, he found time for over a dozen books of poetry and many plays for screen, radio, and television.

Ars poetica

A poem should be palpable and mute
As a globed fruit,

Dumb
As old medallions to the thumb,

Silent as the sleeve-worn stone   5
Of casement ledges where the moss has grown—

A poem should be wordless
As the flight of birds.

Streets in the Moon, 1926.

The title means "The Art of Poetry," which, according to this poem, expresses itself in sensuous images rather than abstract statements; deals in imaginative truth, not mere fact; and has its perfection in the sum of all of its elements (phrasing, sound, rhythm, form, etc.) and not merely in its paraphrasable message.

• • •

A poem should be motionless in time
As the moon climbs,   10

Leaving, as the moon releases
Twig by twig the night-entangled trees,

Leaving, as the moon behind the winter leaves,
Memory by memory the mind—

A poem should be motionless in time   15
As the moon climbs.

• • •

A poem should be equal to:
Not true.

For all the history of grief
An empty doorway and a maple leaf.   20

For love
The leaning grasses and two lights above the sea—

A poem should not mean
But be.

Eleven

And summer mornings the mute child, rebellious,
Stupid, hating the words, the meanings, hating
The Think now, Think, the Oh but Think! would leave
On tiptoe the three chairs on the verandah
And crossing tree by tree the empty lawn   5
Push back the shed door and upon the sill
Stand pressing out the sunlight from his eyes
And enter and with outstretched fingers feel
The grindstone and behind it the bare wall
And turn and in the corner on the cool   10
Hard earth sit listening. And one by one,
Out of the dazzled shadow in the room,
The shapes would gather, the brown plowshare, spades,
Mattocks, the polished helves of picks, a scythe
Hung from the rafters, shovels, slender tines   15
Glinting across the curve of sickles—shapes
Older than men were, the wise tools, the iron
Friendly with earth. And sit there, quiet, breathing
The harsh dry smell of withered bulbs, the faint
Odor of dung, the silence. And outside   20
Beyond the half-shut door the blind leaves
And the corn moving. And at noon would come,
Up from the garden, his hard crooked hands
Gentle with earth, his knees still earth-stained, smelling

Ibid.

14 **mattocks:** digging tools—a pick and a hoelike blade on a shaft   **helves:** handles   15 **tines:** prongs

Of sun, of summer, the old gardener, like   25
A priest, like an interpreter, and bend
Over his baskets.
                  And they would not speak:
They would say nothing. And the child would sit there
Happy as though he had no name, as though
He had been no one: like a leaf, a stem,   30
Like a root growing—

You, Andrew Marvell

And here face down beneath the sun
And here upon earth's noonward height
To feel the always coming on
The always rising of the night:

To feel creep up the curving east   5
The earthy chill of dusk and slow
Upon those under lands the vast
And ever climbing shadow grow

And strange at Ecbatan the trees
Take leaf by leaf the evening strange   10
The flooding dark about their knees
The mountains over Persia change

And now at Kermanshah the gate
Dark empty and the withered grass
And through the twilight now the late   15
Few travelers in the westward pass

And Baghdad darken and the bridge
Across the silent river gone
And through Arabia the edge
Of evening widen and steal on   20

New Found Land, 1930.

For the title, cf. notes to "The Waste Land," line 185. In MacLeish's poem the pressure of onrushing time is felt in the image of the shadow of night creeping around the globe opposite the sun. Many of the place-names mentioned are associated with fallen empires. About his poem, MacLeish writes: "I spent the winter and spring of 1926 in Persia (as it was then called). . . . I was with a League of Nations Commission inquiring into the opium traffic in Persia. At that time travel was by rail, car and ship. We came home by car across the pass to Baghdad, thence across the desert to Palmyra by car, and on to Beirut where I heard my father, who was 88, was ill in Glencoe, Illinois, where I was born. The Commission sailed for Marseilles where I left them, going on across the Atlantic by ship to New York and by rail to Chicago. So my journey became, in retrospect, as continuous as the simple sentence of the poem which . . . is never finished. I saw my father and went to the edge of the bluff above Lake Michigan among the sunflowers and lay 'face down.'"

The sentence with which the poem opens ("And here . . . to feel . . .") is never finished. It is significant that there is no punctuation between lines 5 and 33.   9 **Ecbatan:** Ecbatana (the modern Hamadan in Iran) was the capital of the Empire of the Medes, which the Persians under Cyrus the Great took over in the sixth century B.C. Pound, who had mentioned Ecbatan in his early *Cantos*, "abused" MacLeish for his mention of a city Pound considered his private property. MacLeish's reply to his friend Ezra was that he, MacLeish, had actually *been* there. Had Pound? No more was said about the matter.   13 **Kermanshah:** a city in modern Iran about 100 miles to the west of Ecbatana   17 **Baghdad:** now the capital of Iraq, about 150 miles farther west, long a center of culture and trade between East and West. It was destroyed by the Mongols in the thirteenth century.   19 **Arabia,** though to the south of Baghdad, does stretch several hundred miles farther west.

And deepen on Palmyra's street
The wheel rut in the ruined stone
And Lebanon fade out and Crete
High through the clouds and overblown

And over Sicily the air   25
Still flashing with the landward gulls
And loom and slowly disappear
The sails above the shadowy hulls

And Spain go under and the shore
Of Africa the gilded sand   30
And evening vanish and no more
The low pale light across that land

Nor now the long light on the sea:

And here face downward in the sun
To feel how swift how secretly   35
The shadow of the night comes on . . .

21 **Palmyra:** about 300 miles to the west of Baghdad, an important city on the trade routes to Syria. Taken over by Rome, it was for a while capital of the Eastern empire. The ruins—temples, colonnaded streets, and so on—are impressive.   23 **Lebanon:** originally Phoenician territory, now a small nation on the Mediterranean about 150 miles west of Palmyra   **Crete:** this Mediterranean island south of Greece is some 500 miles to the west of Lebanon. To readers visualizing the geography the night is taking bigger and bigger steps as it advances: Sicily is about 500 miles farther, Spain a somewhat greater distance beyond Sicily. Night then leaps the Atlantic in a single line (33) and is on its way to Illinois.

Hugh MacDiarmid
(Christopher Murray Grieve)
(1892–1978)

Christopher Murray Grieve (who wrote as "Hugh MacDiarmid"), the greatest Scottish poet of modern times, was largely self-educated in his local library. Before and after World War I (in which he served with the medical corps in Greece, Italy, and France) he supported himself as a journalist. In 1933, with his wife and young son, he moved to one of the Shetland Islands, northeast of Scotland, where he spent ten years in isolation and poverty. During World War II he worked in Glasgow in a steel factory and then in a shipyard. After the war he settled in a small country town, assisted, after 1950, by a government pension. A staunch Scottish nationalist, he hoped to revive—or recreate—the Scots language as a form of literary expression. In middle life, however, his interest in scientific and political subjects often induced him to return to English as more useful. MacDiarmid has over 70 books of poetry and prose to his credit.

The Bonnie Broukit Bairn

Mars is braw in crammasy,
Venus in a green silk goun,
The auld mune shak's her gowden feathers,
Their starry talk's a wheen o' blethers,
Nane for thee a thochtie sparin',
Earth, thou bonnie broukit bairn!
—But greet, an' in your tears ye'll droun
The haill clanjamfrie!

Sangschaw, 1925.

1 **braw in crammasy:** handsome in crimson   2 **goun:** gown   3 **auld mune:** old moon   **gowden:** golden   4 **wheen o' blethers:** empty talk (literally, a few bladders)   5 **nane:** none   6 **thochtie:** little thought   6 **broukit bairn:** neglected child   7 **greet:** weep   8 **haill clanjamfrie:** whole shebang

Wheesht, Wheesht

Wheesht, wheesht, my foolish hert,
For weel ye ken
I widna ha'e ye stert
Auld ploys again.

It's guid to see her lie
Sae snod an' cool,
A' lust o' lovin' by—
Wheesht, wheesht, ye fule!

Penny Wheep, 1926.

1 **wheesht:** hush 2 **weel ye ken:** well you know 3 **widna ha'e:** would not have 4 **auld ploys:** old tricks 5 **guid:** good 6 **Sae snod:** so neat 7 **a':** all **by:** over, done 8 **fule:** fool

On the Ocean Floor

Now more and more on my concern with the lifted waves of genius
     gaining
I am aware of the lightless depths that beneath them lie;
And as one who hears their tiny shells incessantly raining
On the ocean floor as the foraminifera die.

Second Hymn to Lenin and Other Poems, 1935.

4 **foraminifera:** tiny shelled sea creatures about the size of a pinhead. Accumulations of their chalky remains form the White Cliffs of Dover and the chalk beds in Mississippi and Georgia.

Cattle Show

I shall go among red faces and virile voices,
See stylish sheep, with fine heads and well-wooled,
And great bulls mellow to the touch,
Brood mares of marvellous approach, and geldings
With sharp and flinty bones and silken hair.   5

And through th' enclosure draped in red and gold
I shall pass on to spheres more vivid yet
Where countesses' coque feathers gleam and glow
And, swathed in silks, the painted ladies are
Whose laughter plays like summer lightning there.   10

By 1922. *Stony Limits and Other Poems, 1934.*

8 **coque:** The French word means "shell," as of an egg or a nut. Could MacDiarmid have meant *coq*, a rooster, pheasant, or other game bird with showy feathers?

Crystals Like Blood

I remember how, long ago, I found
Crystals like blood in a broken stone.

I picked up a broken chunk of bed-rock

Poetry Scotland, no. 4, 1949. Collected Poems, 1967.

Cinnebar is mercuric sulphide (HgS), the generally red crystallized ore from which mercury is derived by such a process as MacDiarmid describes. A precise knowledge of science (cf. the foraminifera of "On the Ocean Floor") is one of the sources of his poetry.

And turned it this way and that,
It was heavier than one would have expected   5
From its size. One face was caked
With brown limestone. But the rest
Was a hard greenish-grey quartz-like stone
Faintly dappled with darker shadows,
And in this quartz ran veins and beads   10
Of bright magenta.

And I remember how later on I saw
How mercury is extracted from cinnebar
—The double ring of iron piledrivers
Like the multiple legs of a fantastically symmetrical spider   15
Rising and falling with monotonous precision,
Marching round in an endless circle
And pounding up and down with a tireless, thunderous force,
While, beyond, another conveyor drew the crumbled ore
From the bottom and raised it to an opening high   20
In the side of a gigantic grey-white kiln.

So I remember how mercury is got
When I contrast my living memory of you
And your dear body rotting here in the clay
—And feel once again released in me   25
The bright torrents of felicity, naturalness, and faith
My treadmill memory draws from you yet.

Wilfred Owen
(1893–1918)

Owen dropped out of the University of London for financial reasons; for a couple of years he worked as lay assistant to a minister, dealing with cases of sickness and poverty; in 1913 he began to teach English at the Berlitz school in Bordeaux. In 1916 he enlisted in the British army, in which he rose to be company commander; he was killed at the age of 25, just a week before the war ended.

Anthem for Doomed Youth

What passing-bells for these who die as cattle?
    Only the monstrous anger of the guns.
    Only the stuttering rifles' rapid rattle
Can patter out their hasty orisons.
No mockeries now for them; no prayers nor bells,   5
    Nor any voice of mourning save the choirs,—
The shrill, demented choirs of wailing shells;
    And bugles calling for them from sad shires.

What candles may be held to speed them all?
    Not in the hands of boys, but in their eyes   10
Shall shine the holy glimmers of good-byes.
    The pallor of girls' brows shall be their pall;
Their flowers the tenderness of patient minds,
And each slow dusk a drawing-down of blinds.

1917? *Poems*, 1920.

4 **orisons:** prayers   8 **shires:** counties   12 **pall:** cloth to drape a coffin

Arms and the Boy

Let the boy try along this bayonet-blade
How cold steel is, and keen with hunger of blood;
Blue with all malice, like a madman's flash;
And thinly drawn with famishing for flesh.

Lend him to stroke these blind, blunt bullet-heads 5
Which long to nuzzle in the hearts of lads,
Or give him cartridges of fine zinc teeth,
Sharp with the sharpness of grief and death.

For his teeth seem for laughing round an apple.
There lurk no claws behind his fingers supple; 10
And God will grow no talons at his heels,
Nor antlers through the thickness of his curls.

1918. Ibid.

The title is an ironic echo of the opening words of Vergil's *Aeneid*: "Arma virumque cano . . ." ("Arms and the man I sing . . .").

E. E. Cummings
(1894–1962)

Edward Estlin Cummings earned A.B. and M.A. degrees from Harvard, where his father, a Congregational minister, taught English and social ethics. As a child he started to paint; as a young man he also wrote poetry, concentrating on sonnets (long a favorite form) and elaborate stanza forms he found in the literature he was studying. During World War I he served with an ambulance corps in France. Through an administrative error he spent three months in a French prison camp; his description of that experience in *The Enormous Room* (1922) brought him to the attention of the public. For two years in the early twenties he lived in Paris, where he wrote and studied painting. In 1931 he visited Russia, registering his indignation at the lack of freedom there in his *Eimi* (I Am) in 1933. Cummings lived in New York most of the year, in New Hampshire in the summer—frugally supporting himself mostly on his returns from writing and painting. Besides a dozen books of poetry and his autobiographical prose, he wrote several plays.

a man who had fallen among thieves

a man who had fallen among thieves
lay by the roadside on his back
dressed in fifteenthrate ideas
wearing a round jeer for a hat

fate per a somewhat more than less 5
emancipated evening
had in return for consciousness
endowed him with a changeless grin

whereon a dozen staunch and leal
citizens did graze at pause 10

By 1923. *Is 5*, 1926.

Cf. Luke 10:30 ff., where, in response to the question "Who is my neighbour?" Christ answers with the parable of the good Samaritan: "A certain man went down from Jerusalem to Jericho, and fell among thieves, which stripped him of his raiment, and wounded him, and departed, leaving him half dead."

9 **leal:** loyal, true (archaic or Scottish, ironically suggesting the language of old ballads, etc.)

then fired by hypercivic zeal
sought newer pastures or because

swaddled with a frozen brook
of pinkest vomit out of eyes
which noticed nobody he looked   15
as if he did not care to rise

one hand did nothing on the vest
its wideflung friend clenched weakly dirt
while the mute trouserfly confessed
a button solemnly inert.   20

Brushing from whom the stiffened puke
i put him all into my arms
and staggered banged with terror through
a million billion trillion stars

18 **friend:** his other hand   20 **inert:** inactive—not buttoning, as buttons should

wherelings whenlings

wherelings whenlings
(daughters of ifbut offspring of hopefear
sons of unless and children of almost)
never shall guess the dimension of

him whose   5
each
foot likes the
here of this earth

whose both
eyes
love   10
this now of the sky

—endlings of isn't
shall never
begin
to begin to   15

imagine how(only are shall be were
dawn dark rain snow rain
-bow &

a   20
moon
's whis-
per
in sunset

or thrushes toward dusk among whippoorwills or   25
tree field rock hollyhock forest brook chickadee

50 Poems, 1940.

See Additional Notes (p. 779).

mountain. Mountain)
whycoloured worlds of because do

not stand against yes which is built by
forever & sunsmell   30
(sometimes a wonder
of wild roses

sometimes)
with north
over   35
the barn

anyone lived in a pretty how town

anyone lived in a pretty how town
(with up so floating many bells down)
spring summer autumn winter
he sang his didn't he danced his did.

Women and men(both little and small)   5
cared for anyone not at all
they sowed their isn't they reaped their same
sun moon stars rain

children guessed(but only a few
and down they forgot as up they grew   10
autumn winter spring summer)
that noone loved him more by more

when by now and tree by leaf
she laughed his joy she cried his grief
bird by snow and stir by still   15
anyone's any was all to her

someones married their everyones
laughed their cryings and did their dance
(sleep wake hope and then)they
said their nevers they slept their dream   20

stars rain sun moon
(and only the snow can begin to explain
how children are apt to forget to remember
with up so floating many bells down)

one day anyone died i guess   25
(and noone stooped to kiss his face)
busy folk buried them side by side
little by little and was by was

all by all and deep by deep
and more by more they dream their sleep   30
noone and anyone earth by april
wish by spirit and if by yes.

Ibid.
See Additional Notes (p. 779).

Women and men (both dong and ding)
summer autumn winter spring
reaped their sowing and went their came   35
sun moon stars rain

my father moved through dooms of love

my father moved through dooms of love
through sames of am through haves of give,
singing each morning out of each night
my father moved through depths of height

this motionless forgetful where   5
turned at his glance to shining here;
that if (so timid air is firm)
under his eyes would stir and squirm

newly as from unburied which
floats the first who, his april touch   10
drove sleeping selves to swarm their fates
woke dreamers to their ghostly roots

and should some why completely weep
my father's fingers brought her sleep:
vainly no smallest voice might cry   15
for he could feel the mountains grow.

Lifting the valleys of the sea
my father moved through griefs of joy;
praising a forehead called the moon
singing desire into begin   20

joy was his song and joy so pure
a heart of star by him could steer
and pure so now and now so yes
the wrists of twilight would rejoice

keen as midsummer's keen beyond   25
conceiving mind of sun will stand,
so strictly (over utmost him
so hugely) stood my father's dream

his flesh was flesh his blood was blood:
no hungry man but wished him food;   30
no cripple wouldn't creep one mile
uphill to only see him smile.

Scorning the pomp of must and shall
my father moved through dooms of feel;
his anger was as right as rain   35
his pity was as green as grain

septembering arms of year extend
less humbly wealth to foe and friend

Ibid.

See Additional Notes (p. 780).

than he to foolish and to wise
offered immeasurable is   40

proudly and (by octobering flame
beckoned) as earth will downward climb,
so naked for immortal work
his shoulders marched against the dark

his sorrow was as true as bread: 45
no liar looked him in the head;
if every friend became his foe
he'd laugh and build a world with snow.

My father moved through theys of we,
singing each new leaf out of each tree   50
(and every child was sure that spring
danced when she heard my father sing)

then let men kill which cannot share,
let blood and flesh be mud and mire,
scheming imagine, passion willed,   55
freedom a drug that's bought and sold

giving to steal and cruel kind,
a heart to fear, to doubt a mind,
to differ a disease of same,
conform the pinnacle of am   60

though dull were all we taste as bright,
bitter all utterly things sweet,
maggoty minus and dumb death
all we inherit, all bequeath

and nothing quite so least as truth   65
—i say though hate were why men breathe—
because my father lived his soul
love is the whole and more than all

being to timelessness as it's to time

being to timelessness as it's to time,
love did no more begin than love will end;
where nothing is to breathe to stroll to swim
love is the air the ocean and the land

(do lovers suffer?all divinities   5
proudly descending put on deathful flesh:
are lovers glad?only their smallest joy's
a universe emerging from a wish)

love is the voice under all silences,
the hope which has no opposite in fear;   10
the strength so strong mere force is feebleness:
the truth more first than sun more last than star

—do lovers love?why then to heaven with hell.
Whatever sages say and fools,all's well

By 1950. *95 Poems*, 1958.

(im)c-a-t(mo)

(im)c-a-t(mo)
b,i;l:e

FallleA
ps!fl
OattumblI   5

sh?dr
IftwhirlF
(Ul)(lY)
&&&

away wanders:exact   10
ly; as if
not
hing had,ever happ
ene

D   15

Χαῖρε, *Seventy-one Poems*, 1950.

This is a poem to be looked at; much of it cannot be pronounced. Cummings was a painter as well as a poet and sometimes liked to arrange letters on a page as a painter arranges colors—but always with something expressive in mind. This poem—or art object—is about a cat asleep on a shelf or a bed—something that he falls off of, awakes as he falls, turns his fall into a leap, lands on his feet, shakes himself, and walks casually away. Cummings arranges the first two lines the way he does so that he can embed the word *cat* (stretched out by hyphens, as the cat is stretched out) in its very immobility. If we saw the cat asleep, we might say, "The cat is immobile." But Cummings seems to feel that those words, and the order they are in, distorts what we perceive: we see the immobility as soon as we see the cat. So he puts the words together: the cat sleeps in its immobility. The rounded brackets at each end of the line give us the picture of a sleeping cat: one pair is the head, one the rounded haunch and curled tail.

In line 2, the punctuation between letters gets progressively stronger: , to ; to : As if he were braking the line to a stop to dramatize its immobility. When we follow this, the rest of the poem is easy to see.

Jean Toomer
(1894–1967)

Toomer, an important figure in the Harlem renaissance of the 1920s, was born in Washington, D.C., the grandson of a man who, during Reconstruction, had served briefly as Acting Governor of Louisiana. After studying at several universities, he became acting principal of a black rural school in Georgia; from the impressions gathered there he wrote the poems, stories, and sketches published as *Cane* (1923), which became an American classic. Much of his later work remained in manuscript after his death.

Reapers

Black reapers with the sound of steel on stones
Are sharpening scythes. I see them place the hones
In their hip-pockets as a thing that's done,
And start their silent swinging, one by one.

Cane, 1923.

Black horses drive a mower through the weeds,
And there, a field rat, startled, squealing bleeds,
His belly close to ground. I see the blade,
Blood-stained, continue cutting weeds and shade.

Robert Graves
(Born 1895)

Graves was born in London, the son of an Irish poet and songwriter. His great-uncle on his mother's side was the famous German historian Leopold von Ranke. By the time he was 13, Graves, influenced by Welsh poetry and translating Catullus, was doing "difficult technical experiments in prosody." After what we would call prep school he enlisted in the Royal Welsh Fusiliers as World War I broke out; during the four years of trench warfare that he survived, his first two books of poetry were published. After the war he returned to Oxford with his wife, meanwhile writing a book of poetry a year and helping take care of his several young children. After teaching in Cairo, he settled at Deyà on the Spanish island of Mallorca; except for wartime stays in England and various travels, he has been there ever since. Until 1939 he was associated with the American poet Laura Riding in various editorial and publishing ventures. From his youth on, Graves has supported himself by his writing, with well over 100 books to his credit, among them such popular successes as *I, Claudius*, on which a television series was based.

Sick Love

O Love, be fed with apples while you may,
And feel the sun and go in royal array,
A smiling innocent on the heavenly causeway,

Though in what listening horror for the cry
That soars in outer blackness dismally,   5
The dumb blind beast, the paranoiac fury:

Be warm, enjoy the season, lift your head,
Exquisite in the pulse of tainted blood,
That shivering glory not to be despised.

Take your delight in momentariness,   10
Walk between dark and dark—a shining space
With the grave's narrowness, though not its peace.

Poems, 1929, as "Between Dark and Dark." *Poems 1926–30*, 1931, as "O Love in Me." *Collected Poems*, 1938, as "Sick Love."

Theseus and Ariadne

High on his figured couch beyond the waves
He dreams, in dream recalling her set walk
Down paths of oyster-shell bordered with flowers,
Across the shadowy turf below the vines.
He sighs: 'Deep sunk in my erroneous past   5
She haunts the ruins and the ravaged lawns.'

The Golden Fleece, 1944.

On condition that he take her back to Athens and marry her, Ariadne had rescued Theseus from the Labyrinth at Crete after he killed the Minotaur. Theseus, however, abandoned Ariadne on a desert island after their escape. In the poem he somewhat smugly imagines how sad she now is. But in fact after he left her she was seen by the god Dionysius, who fell in love with her and made her "the queen to nobler company." She is happier now than she ever was with her deserter.

Yet still unharmed it stands, the regal house
Crooked with age and overtopped by pines
Where first he wearied of her constancy.
And with a surer foot she goes than when   10
Dread of his hate was thunder in the air,
When the pines agonized with flaws of wind
And flowers glared up at her with frantic eyes.
Of him, now all is done, she never dreams
But calls a living blessing down upon   15
What he supposes rubble and rank grass;
Playing the queen to nobler company.

Counting the Beats

You, love, and I,
(He whispers) you and I,
And if no more than only you and I
What care you or I?

Counting the beats,   5
Counting the slow heart beats,
The bleeding to death of time in slow heart beats,
Wakeful they lie.

Cloudless day,
Night, and a cloudless day,   10
Yet the huge storm will burst upon their heads one day
From a bitter sky.

Where shall we be,
(She whispers) where shall we be,
When death strikes home, O where then shall we be 15
Who were you and I?

Not there but here,
(He whispers) only here,
As we are, here, together, now and here,
Always you and I.   20

Counting the beats,
Counting the slow heart beats,
The bleeding to death of time in slow heart beats,
Wakeful they lie.

Poems and Satires, 1951.

Spoils

When all is over and you march for home,
The spoils of war are easily disposed of:
Standards, weapons of combat, helmets, drums
May decorate a staircase or a study,
While lesser gleanings of the battlefield—   5
Coins, watches, wedding-rings, gold teeth and such—
Are sold anonymously for solid cash.

Collected Poems, 1955.

The spoils of love present a different case,
When all is over and you march for home:
That lock of hair, these letters and the portrait   10
May not be publicly displayed; nor sold;
Nor burned; nor returned (the heart being obstinate)—
Yet never dare entrust them to a safe
For fear they burn a hole through two-foot steel.

Louise Bogan
(1897–1970)

Louise Bogan (she gave her name the usual pronunciation: *bôgan*) was born in Livermore Falls, Maine, of Irish descent; her grandfather had been a Portland sea captain. For a year she attended Boston University. Except for a year in Vienna and one in Santa Fe, she lived in New York City, where for 37 years she was poetry reviewer for *The New Yorker*. Her struggles to support herself and her daughter (by an early marriage) in the New York literary world are described in her selected letters, *What the Woman Lived* (1973), which also give vivid and witty accounts of her friendship with such literary figures as Theodore Roethke and Edmund Wilson.

Cassandra

To me, one silly task is like another.
I bare the shambling tricks of lust and pride.
This flesh will never give a child its mother,—
Song, like a wing, tears through my breast, my side,
And madness chooses out my voice again,
Again. I am the chosen no hand saves:
The shrieking heaven lifted over men,
Not the dumb earth, wherein they set their graves.

By 1926. *Dark Summer*, 1929.

Cassandra was the Trojan princess given the gift of prophecy by Apollo—but when she spurned his love he decreed that her prophecies would never be believed. Agamemnon brought her home from Troy; she was murdered when he was.

Old Countryside

Beyond the hour we counted rain that fell
On the slant shutter, all has come to proof.
The summer thunder, like a wooden bell,
Rang in the storm above the mansard roof,

And mirrors cast the cloudy day along   5
The attic floor; wind made the clapboards creak.
You braced against the wall to make it strong,
A shell against your cheek.

Long since, we pulled brown oak-leaves to the ground
In a winter of dry trees; we heard the cock   10
Shout its unplaceable cry, the axe's sound
Delay a moment after the axe's stroke.

Far back, we saw, in the stillest of the year,
The scrawled vine shudder, and the rose-branch show
Red to the thorns, and, sharp as sight can bear,   15
The thin hound's body arched against the snow.

Ibid.

Hart Crane
(1899–1932)

Harold Hart Crane was born in Garrettsville, Ohio, the son of a well-to-do candy manu-
facturer. His parents quarreled and finally separated. Crane, writing poetry by the time
he was 13, visited New York while still in high school and became acquainted there with
many prominent writers. For the next few years he was unemployed or worked at this or
that: wrote advertising, packed candy for his father, was briefly a riveter in a shipyard,
worked in a munitions factory. His friends in Cleveland included musicians and artists;
he read widely in poetry old and new and worked hard at his own. From 1923 to 1927 he
was in New York, where, though distracted by periods of drinking and homosexual ad-
ventures, he did some of his best work. In 1926 his first book, *White Buildings*, was pub-
lished; in that year he also completed two-thirds of his masterpiece, the long mythopoeic
poem or "symphony with an epic theme" on American history, in which Brooklyn
Bridge stood as a symbol for the triumph of engineering and the spiritual aspirations of
art. Though the disorders of personal life interfered, *The Bridge* was published in 1930.
Awarded a Guggenheim Fellowship, Crane went to Mexico, but, as his dissipations con-
tinued and his sense of failure grew, he got little work done. He died the next spring—
jumping into the Gulf of Mexico from the ship bringing him back to America.

Praise for an Urn

In Memoriam: Ernest Nelson

It was a kind and northern face
That mingled in such exile guise
The everlasting eyes of Pierrot
And, of Gargantua, the laughter.

His thoughts, delivered to me   5
From the white coverlet and pillow,
I see now, were inheritances—
Delicate riders of the storm.

The slant moon on the slanting hill
Once moved us toward presentiments   10
Of what the dead keep, living still,
And such assessments of the soul

As, perched in the crematory lobby,
The insistent clock commented on,
Touching as well upon our praise   15
Of glories proper to the time.

Still, having in mind gold hair,
I cannot see that broken brow
And miss the dry sound of bees
Stretching across a lucid space.   20

1922. *White Buildings*, 1926.

Ernest Nelson was a Norwegian immigrant whose talent for art and poetry were lost in his need to
earn a living as a lithographer. He had a fine library, which he made available to Crane, for whom he
was a "lasting influence." Nelson was struck by a car just before Christmas, 1921. Crane attended the
cremation services.

3 **Pierrot:** in French pantomime, a pathetic and melancholy clown.   4 **Gargantua:** a hearty giant
with a tremendous appetite in the novel (1534) named for him written by the French satirist François
Rabelais (c. 1494–c. 1553).

Scatter these well-meant idioms
Into the smoky spring that fills
The suburbs, where they will be lost.
They are no trophies of the sun.

At Melville's Tomb

Often beneath the wave, wide from this ledge
The dice of drowned men's bones he saw bequeath
An embassy. Their numbers as he watched,
Beat on the dusty shore and were obscured.

And wrecks passed without sound of bells,   5
The calyx of death's bounty giving back
A scattered chapter, livid hieroglyph,
The portent wound in corridors of shells.

Then in the circuit calm of one vast coil,
Its lashings charmed and malice reconciled,   10
Frosted eyes there were that lifted altars;
And silent answers crept across the stars.

Compass, quadrant and sextant contrive
No farther tides . . . High in the azure steeps
Monody shall not wake the mariner.   15
This fabulous shadow only the sea keeps.

1925–1926. Ibid.

Herman Melville (1819–1891), the author of *Moby-Dick*, is buried at Woodlawn Cemetery in New York City. Crane explained much of the poem in a letter he wrote to Harriet Monroe, the editor of *Poetry* (Chicago), which printed the poem in October 1926.

2 **dice:** the ground-up bones, which could be thought of as having an important message ("embassy") for mankind   6 **the calyx of death's bounty:** the vortex or whirlpool into which a ship sinks (*calyx* means "chalice" and is used of the cup of a flower). This calyx gives back loose wreckage from the ship, like hieroglyphs or mysterious characters which (like the dice of the bones) also have something to say. This may be the same message we hear when we put our ear to a seashell.   11 **frosted eyes . . . altars:** eyes lifted in reverence to the deity   13 **Compass, quadrant and sextant:** instruments for placing ourselves in and measuring the physical universe   15 **monody:** an ode or elegy for one voice. Cf. Milton's note at the beginning of "Lycidas."

From **Voyages**

II

And yet this great wink of eternity,
Of rimless floods, unfettered leewardings,
Samite sheeted and processioned where

1925. Ibid.

In 1924 Crane wrote his mother that he was "engaged in writing a series of six sea poems called 'Voyages' (they are also love poems). . . ." The two given here are the ones he later picked out as the best of the group. In the six, the sea, sometimes seen as a living body, is an ambivalent symbol for love, death, rebirth into eternity. The poems are constructed on a "logic of metaphor"; the intention of the imagery is sometimes easier to feel (like music) than to paraphrase.

1 **wink of eternity:** the sea, with its flashing light   2 **leewardings:** movements with the wind   3 **samite:** rich silk woven with silver or gold

Her undinal vast belly moonward bends,
Laughing the wrapt inflections of our love;   5

Take this Sea, whose diapason knells
On scrolls of silver snowy sentences,
The sceptred terror of whose sessions rends
As her demeanors motion well or ill,
All but the pieties of lovers' hands.   10

And onward, as bells off San Salvador
Salute the crocus lustres of the stars,
In these poinsettia meadows of her tides,—
Adagios of islands, O my Prodigal,
Complete the dark confessions her veins spell.   15

Mark how her turning shoulders wind the hours,
And hasten while her penniless rich palms
Pass superscription of bent foam and wave,—
Hasten, while they are true,—sleep, death, desire,
Close round one instant in one floating flower.   20

Bind us in time, O Seasons clear, and awe.
O minstrel galleons of Carib fire,
Bequeath us to no earthly shore until
Is answered in the vortex of our grave
The seal's wide spindrift gaze toward paradise.   25

4 **undinal:** like that of an *undine*, or water nymph, who by marrying a mortal and bearing him a child could be given a soul   **vast belly:** the pregnancy image suggests birth (or rebirth)   5 **wrapt:** suggests *rapt*   6 **diapason:** entire range of musical notes   10 **All but the pieties . . . :** the sea admits only lovers into her eternity   11 **San Salvador:** an island in the Bahamas; there is a legend of a sunken city there.   14 **adagios:** *Adagio* (Italian), used as a direction in music, means "slow." Crane said that "adagios of islands" was a more direct and creative statement than "coasting slowly through the islands." **Prodigal:** a wanderer, like the prodigal son; here the person to whom these love poems are addressed, who is often away on voyages   18 **superscription:** something written on or above; here, probably the foam-tipped waves as resembling lines of writing   22 **Carib:** Caribbean   23–25 Transcendent love, death, and eternity are suggested by the imagery that concludes the poem.   25 **spindrift:** blown seaspray

VI

Where icy and bright dungeons lift
Of swimmers their lost morning eyes,
And ocean rivers, churning, shift
Green borders under stranger skies,

Steadily as a shell secretes   5
Its beating leagues of monotone,
Or as many waters trough the sun's
Red kelson past the cape's wet stone;

1924–1925. Ibid.

"Voyages, II," a poem of happy love, was set in romantic southern waters, in "poinsettia meadows" "off San Salvador." "Voyages, VI," in which the lover is left "derelict and blinded" because of a separation or because of the lessening or loss of love, is set in wintrier seas. Belle Isle (line 25), associated with whiteness, is an island off the coast of Labrador. (Cf. "Gerontion," line 71.) Looking for some consolation—a "splintered garland" at least—the poet recalls that love endures in the "blithe and petalled word," "the imaged Word" of the poem—that is, in the sustaining imagination in which there are no betrayals or farewells.

8 **kelson:** timbers or plates inside a ship to add strength to the keel—here used loosely for the keel itself

O rivers mingling toward the sky
And harbor of the phoenix' breast—   10
My eyes pressed black against the prow,
—Thy derelict and blinded guest

Waiting, afire, what name, unspoke,
I cannot claim: let thy waves rear
More savage than the death of kings,   15
Some splintered garland for the seer.

Beyond siroccos harvesting
The solstice thunders, crept away,
Like a cliff swinging or a sail
Flung into April's inmost day—   20

Creation's blithe and petalled word
To the lounged goddess when she rose
Conceding dialogue with eyes
That smile unsearchable repose—

Still fervid covenant, Belle Isle,   25
—Unfolded floating dais before
Which rainbows twine continual hair—
Belle Isle, white echo of the oar!

The imaged Word, it is, that holds
Hushed willows anchored in its glow.   30
It is the unbetrayable reply
Whose accent no farewell can know.

10 **phoenix:** a beautiful bird that was periodically destroyed in fire and arose from its own ashes
17 **siroccos:** hot, oppressive winds   18 **solstice:** the point at which the sun is farthest north or far-
thest south, marking the beginning of summer or winter   22 **the lounged goddess:** perhaps Aphro-
dite, goddess of love, who was thought to arise from the sea; or perhaps Aurora, goddess of dawn
25 **covenant:** an agreement, promise

From The Bridge

Proem: To Brooklyn Bridge

How many dawns, chill from his rippling rest
The seagull's wings shall dip and pivot him,
Shedding white rings of tumult, building high
Over the chained bay waters Liberty—

Then, with inviolate curve, forsake our eyes   5
As apparitional as sails that cross
Some page of figures to be filed away;
—Till elevators drop us from our day . . .

I think of cinemas, panoramic sleights
With multitudes bent toward some flashing scene   10
Never disclosed, but hastened to again,
Foretold to other eyes on the same screen;

1926. *The Bridge*, 1930.

A "proem" is a prelude or introductory poem—here to Crane's long poem *The Bridge*.

And Thee, across the harbor, silver-paced
As though the sun took step of thee, yet left
Some motion ever unspent in thy stride,—   15
Implicitly thy freedom staying thee!

Out of some subway scuttle, cell or loft
A bedlamite speeds to thy parapets,
Tilting there momently, shrill shirt ballooning,
A jest falls from the speechless caravan.   20

Down Wall, from girder into street noon leaks,
A rip-tooth of the sky's acetylene;
All afternoon the cloud-flown derricks turn . . .
Thy cables breathe the North Atlantic still.

And obscure as that heaven of the Jews,   25
Thy guerdon . . . Accolade thou dost bestow
Of anonymity time cannot raise:
Vibrant reprieve and pardon thou dost show.

O harp and altar, of the fury fused,
(How could mere toil align thy choiring strings!)   30
Terrific threshold of the prophet's pledge,
Prayer of pariah, and the lover's cry,—

Again the traffic lights that skim thy swift
Unfractioned idiom, immaculate sigh of stars,
Beading thy path—condense eternity: 35
And we have seen night lifted in thine arms.

Under thy shadow by the piers I waited;
Only in darkness is thy shadow clear.
The City's fiery parcels all undone,
Already snow submerges an iron year . . .   40

O Sleepless as the river under thee,
Vaulting the sea, the prairies' dreaming sod,
Unto us lowliest sometime sweep, descend
And of the curveship lend a myth to God.

18 **bedlamite:** insane person, here bent on suicide   21 **Wall:** Wall Street, in the financial district
26 **guerdon:** reward   **Accolade:** ceremony or salute of praise or approval   32 **pariah:** outcast

Allen Tate
(1899–1979)

Tate was born in Winchester, Kentucky, a few weeks before the beginning of the twenti-
eth century—a circumstance he later mentioned with satisfaction. At Vanderbilt he was a
pupil of Ransom, a roommate of Warren. After three years in New York, two years
abroad on a Guggenheim Fellowship, and teaching posts at several colleges, Tate was
named consultant in poetry (1943–1944) at the Library of Congress. He was later an edi-
tor of the *Sewanee Review*. He taught at the University of Minnesota from 1951 until his
retirement in 1968, with leaves of absence to lecture in Rome, at Oxford, and elsewhere.
Besides his books of poetry, for which he received many awards, he wrote essays, a nov-
el, and biographies of Stonewall Jackson and Jefferson Davies.

The Mediterranean

Quem das finem, rex magne, dolorum?

Where we went in the boat was a long bay
A slingshot wide, walled in by towering stone—
Peaked margin of antiquity's delay,
And we went there out of time's monotone:

Where we went in the black hull no light moved   5
But a gull white-winged along the feckless wave,
The breeze, unseen but fierce as a body loved,
That boat drove onward like a willing slave:

Where we went in the small ship the seaweed
Parted and gave to us the murmuring shore,   10
And we made feast and in our secret need
Devoured the very plates Aeneas bore:

Where derelict you see through the low twilight
The green coast that you, thunder-tossed, would win,
Drop sail, and hastening to drink all night   15
Eat dish and bowl to take that sweet land in!

Where we feasted and caroused on the sandless
Pebbles, affecting our day of piracy,
What prophecy of eaten plates could landless
Wanderers fulfil by the ancient sea?   20

We for that time might taste the famous age
Eternal here yet hidden from our eyes
When lust of power undid its stuffless rage;
They, in a wineskin, bore earth's paradise.

Let us lie down once more by the breathing side   25
Of Ocean, where our live forefathers sleep
As if the Known Sea still were a month wide—
Atlantis howls but is no longer steep!

What country shall we conquer, what fair land
Unman our conquest and locate our blood?   30
We've cracked the hemispheres with careless hand!
Now, from the Gates of Hercules we flood

Westward, westward till the barbarous brine
Whelms us to the tired land where tasseling corn,
Fat beans, grapes sweeter than muscadine   35
Rot on the vine: in that land were we born.

1932. *The Mediterranean and Other Poems*, 1936.

The epigraph means "What end of sorrows do you give, great king?" It is from Vergil's *Aeneid*, I, 241, slightly changed. The poem was suggested by a lavish picnic on the French Riviera, held in just such a bay as Aeneas and his crew may have stopped in (VII, 107 ff.), when they consumed the tortilla-like cakes they had placed their food on, thereby fulfilling the prophecy that said they would find their home where hunger forced them to "eat their tables."

28 **Atlantis:** the legendary island west of Gibraltar thought to have been swallowed up by the sea   32 **the Gates of Hercules:** the straits between the Mediterranean and the Atlantic—Gibraltar   35 **muscadine:** a kind of grape

Sonnets at Christmas

(1934)

I

This is the day His hour of life draws near,
Let me get ready from head to foot for it
Most handily with eyes to pick the year
For small feed to reward a feathered wit.
Some men would see it an epiphany   5
At ease, at food and drink, others at chase
Yet I, stung lassitude, with ecstasy
Unspent argue the season's difficult case
So: Man, dull critter of enormous head,
What would he look at in the coiling sky?   10
But I must kneel again unto the Dead
While Christmas bells of paper white and red,
Figured with boys and girls spilt from a sled,
Ring out the silence I am nourished by.

II

Ah, Christ, I love you rings to the wild sky
And I must think a little of the past:
When I was ten I told a stinking lie
That got a black boy whipped; but now at last
The going years, caught in an accurate glow,   5
Reverse like balls englished upon green baize—
Let them return, let the round trumpets blow
The ancient crackle of the Christ's deep gaze.
Deafened and blind, with senses yet unfound,
Am I, untutored to the after-wit   10
Of knowledge, knowing a nightmare has no sound;
Therefore with idle hands and head I sit
In late December before the fire's daze
Punished by crimes of which I would be quit.

Ibid.

I: 5: **epiphany:** a sudden revelation or perception

Langston Hughes
(1902–1967)

Hughes, sometimes called the "poet laureate of Harlem," was born in Joplin, Missouri. He graduated from high school in Cleveland in 1921, the year in which his "The Negro Speaks of Rivers" was published. While visiting his father in Mexico he studied German and Spanish; after going to Columbia University for a year, he worked as a merchant seaman, visited Africa, lived for a time in Rome and Paris. While working as a busboy in a Washington hotel he let some of his poems be seen by Vachel Lindsay, who admired them and brought Hughes to the attention of the public. With the help of a benefactor Hughes went to Lincoln University in Pennsylvania; before graduating he published two books of poetry, both influenced by the rhythms of jazz and the blues, and by the free verse of Sandburg. Thirty-two of his books were in print when he died: they included poems, novels, short stories, plays, juveniles, autobiographies, and translations.

The Negro Speaks of Rivers

I've known rivers:
I've known rivers ancient as the world and older than the flow of human
    blood in human veins.

My soul has grown deep like the rivers.

I bathed in the Euphrates when dawns were young.
I built my hut near the Congo and it lulled me to sleep.   5
I looked upon the Nile and raised the pyramids above it.
I heard the singing of the Mississippi when Abe Lincoln went down to
    New Orleans, and I've seen its muddy bosom turn all golden in the
    sunset.

I've known rivers:
Ancient, dusky rivers.

My soul has grown deep like the rivers.   10

By 1921. *The Weary Blues,* 1926.

Dream Variations

To fling my arms wide
In some place of the sun,
To whirl and to dance
Till the white day is done.
Then rest at cool evening   5
Beneath a tall tree
While night comes on gently,
    Dark like me—
That is my dream!

To fling my arms wide   10
In the face of the sun,
Dance! Whirl! Whirl!
Till the quick day is done.
Rest at pale evening . . .
A tall, slim tree . . .   15
Night coming tenderly
    Black like me.

By 1924. Ibid.

Kenneth Fearing
(1902–1961)

Fearing was born in Chicago and graduated from the University of Wisconsin. Thereafter
he worked at several jobs: salesman, millhand, freelance writer, reporter. Besides his six
books of poetry, he wrote three novels of suspense, including *Dagger in the Mind* and *The
Big Clock,* which was made into a movie.

Love, 20c the First Quarter Mile

All right, I may have lied to you, and about you, and made a few
    pronouncements a bit too sweeping, perhaps, and possibly forgotten
    to tag the bases here or there,
And damned your extravagance, and maligned your tastes, and libeled
    your relatives, and slandered a few of your friends,
O.K.,
Nevertheless, come back.

Come home. I will agree to forget the statements that you issued so copi-
    ously to the neighbors and the press,   5
And you will forget that figment of your imagination, the blonde from
    Detroit;
I will agree that your lady friend who lives above us is not crazy, bats,
    nutty as they come, but on the contrary rather bright,
And you will concede that poor old Steinberg is neither a drunk, nor a
    swindler, but simply a guy, on the eccentric side, trying to get along.
(Are you listening, you bitch, and have you got this straight?)

Because I forgive you, yes, for everything,   10
I forgive you for being beautiful and generous and wise,
I forgive you, to put it simply, for being alive, and pardon you, in short,
    for being you.

Because tonight you are in my hair and eyes,
And every street light that our taxi passes shows me you again, still you,
    And because tonight all other nights are black, all other hours are cold
    and far away, and now, this minute, the stars are very near and
    bright.   15

Come back. We will have a celebration to end all celebrations.
We will invite the undertaker who lives beneath us, and a couple of the
    boys from the office, and some other friends,
And Steinberg, who is off the wagon, by the way, and that insane woman
    who lives upstairs, and a few reporters, if anything should break.

Collected Poems, 1940.

Ogden Nash
(1902–1971)

Born in Rye, New York, Nash left Harvard after a year. In New York he failed as a bond
salesman, did better in the advertising department at Doubleday, where he worked for
six years. Afterwards he joined the staff of *The New Yorker,* was associated with publish-
ing houses, and worked on scenarios in Hollywood. With S. J. Perelman he wrote a musi-
cal comedy, *One Touch of Venus.*

Very Like a Whale

One thing that literature would be greatly the better for
Would be a more restricted employment by authors of simile and meta-
    phor.

The Primrose Path, 1935.

Authors of all races, be they Greeks, Romans, Teutons or Celts,
Can't seem just to say that anything is the thing it is but have to go out of
    their way to say that it is like something else.   5
What does it mean when we are told
That the Assyrian came down like a wolf on the fold?
In the first place, George Gordon Byron had had enough experience
To know that it probably wasn't just one Assyrian, it was a lot of Assyr-
    ians.
However, as too many arguments are apt to induce apoplexy and thus
    hinder longevity,   10
We'll let it pass as one Assyrian for the sake of brevity.
Now then, this particular Assyrian, the one whose cohorts were gleam-
    ing in purple and gold,
Just what does the poet mean when he says he came down like a wolf on
    the fold?
In heaven and earth more than is dreamed of in our philosophy there are
    a great many things,
But I don't imagine that among them there is a wolf with purple and gold
    cohorts or purple and gold anythings.
No, no, Lord Byron, before I'll believe that this Assyrian was actually like
    a wolf I must have some kind of proof;   15
Did he run on all fours and did he have a hairy tail and a big red mouth
    and big white teeth and did he say Woof woof woof?
Frankly I think it very unlikely, and all you were entitled to say, at the
    very most,
Was that the Assyrian cohorts came down like a lot of Assyrian cohorts
    about to destroy the Hebrew host.
But that wasn't fancy enough for Lord Byron, oh dear me no, he had to
    invent a lot of figures of speech and then interpolate them.
With the result that whenever you mention Old Testament soldiers to
    people they say Oh yes, they're the ones that a lot of wolves dressed
    up in gold and purple ate them.   20
That's the kind of thing that's being done all the time by poets, from
    Homer to Tennyson;
They're always comparing ladies to lilies and veal to venison,
And they always say things like that the snow is a white blanket after a
    winter storm.
Oh it is, is it, all right then, you sleep under a six-inch blanket of snow
    and I'll sleep under a half-inch blanket of unpoetical blanket materi-
    al and we'll see which one keeps warm,   25
And after that maybe you'll begin to comprehend dimly
What I mean by too much metaphor and simile.

6 **the Assyrian:** Cf. Byron, "The Destruction of Sennacherib" (p. 294)   13 **In heaven and earth ...:**
Cf. *Hamlet*, I, v, 191–192: "There are more things in heaven and earth, Horatio, / Than are dreamt of in
your philosophy."

Stevie Smith
(1902–1971)

Florence Margaret Smith—nicknamed "Stevie" after a famous jockey because of her
small size—grew up in a London suburb; instead of going to a university she took a job
as secretary in a London publishing house, where she worked most of her life, resigning
early to take care of a bedridden aunt she loved. Tartly amusing at parties and in demand
at schools as a reader of her own poetry, she wrote three novels as well as nine books of
verse.

Not Waving but Drowning

Nobody heard him, the dead man,
But still he lay moaning:
I was much further out than you thought
And not waving but drowning.

Poor chap, he always loved larking   5
And now he's dead
It must have been too cold for him his heart gave way,
They said.

Oh, no no no, it was too cold always
(Still the dead one lay moaning)   10
I was much too far out all my life
And not waving but drowning.

———————————
Not Waving but Drowning, 1957.

The Frog Prince

I am a frog
I live under a spell
I live at the bottom
Of a green well

And here I must wait   5
Until a maiden places me
On her royal pillow
And kisses me
In her father's palace.

The story is familiar   10
Everybody knows it well
But do other enchanted people feel as nervous
As I do? The stories do not tell,

Ask if they will be happier
When the changes come   15
As already they are fairly happy
In a frog's doom?

I have been a frog now
For a hundred years
And in all this time   20
I have not shed many tears,

I am happy, I like the life,
Can swim for many a mile
(When I have hopped to the river)
And am for ever agile.   25

And the quietness,
Yes, I like to be quiet
I am habituated
To a quiet life,

———————————
The Frog Prince, 1966.

But always when I think these thoughts   30
As I sit in my well
Another thought comes to me and says:
It is part of the spell

To be happy
To work up contentment   35
To make much of being a frog
To fear disenchantment

Says, It will be *heavenly*
To be set free,
Cries, *Heavenly* the girl who disenchants   40
And the royal times, *heavenly,*
And I think it will be.

Come, then, royal girl and royal times,
Come quickly,
I can be happy until you come   45
But I cannot be heavenly,
Only disenchanted people
Can be heavenly.

Countee Cullen
(1903–1946)

Born in New York City, Cullen was raised there as the adopted son of a minister in Harlem. By the time he was 20 his poems had appeared in such magazines as *The Nation, Poetry,* and *Harper's. Color,* his first book, was published while he was still a student at New York University. After getting his M.A. at Harvard, he spent some months in France on a Guggenheim Fellowship. In the early 1930s he began teaching in the city high schools—a position he held for the rest of his life. Besides his several books of poetry he wrote a novel, a version of the *Medea* of Euripides, and compiled an anthology of black poetry; with his friend Arna Bontemps he collaborated on a Broadway musical. Cullen died in his early forties.

Simon the Cyrenian Speaks

He never spoke a word to me,
  And yet He called my name;
He never gave a sign to me,
  And yet I knew and came.

At first I said, "I will not bear   5
  His cross upon my back;
He only seeks to place it there
  Because my skin is black."

But He was dying for a dream,
  And He was very meek,   10
And in His eyes there shone a gleam
  Men journey far to seek.

Color, 1925.

As Christ was being led forth to crucifixion, "they found a man of Cyrene, Simon by name: him they compelled to bear his cross" (Matt. 27:32—cf. also Mark 15:21). Cyrene, a city in Africa on the Mediterranean, was the center of a Roman province at the time.

It was Himself my pity bought;
    I did for Christ alone
What all of Rome could not have wrought   15
    With bruise of lash or stone.

Brewster Ghiselin
(Born 1903)

Ghiselin, born in Webster Groves, Missouri, grew up in Missouri and in California. He has degrees from the University of California at Los Angeles and at Berkeley; he studied for a year at Oxford. Since 1929, except for two years at Berkeley, he has taught at the University of Utah, where he is now Professor Emeritus. Besides his four books of poetry he has published short stories and literary criticism, and edited *The Creative Process: A Symposium.*

Rattler, Alert

Slowly he sways that head that cannot hear,
Two-jeweled cone of horn the yellow of rust,
Pooled on the current of his listening fear.
His length is on the tympanum of earth,
And by his tendril tongue's tasting the air   5
He sips, perhaps, a secret of his race
Or feels for the known vibrations, heat, or trace
Of smoother satin than the hillwind's thrust
Through grass: the aspirate of my half-held breath,
The crushing of my weight upon the dust,   10
My foamless heart, the bloodleap at my wrist.

    1939–1941. *Against the Circle*, 1946.

Rattlesnakes "cannot hear," but sense the "known vibrations" of the earth beneath. Their darting tongue apprises them of the chemistry of what is around, and they are sensitive to heat—the blood-heat, for example, of prospective prey.

4 tympanum: "the eardrum, or any membrane or slab of substance resonating like a drumhead, yielding vibrations either audible or apparent to the sense of touch" [B.G.]   **5 tendril:** like a tendril (the delicate coiling appendage by which vines attach themselves)   **8 smoother satin:** "human skin, for example, lifting lightly against the air at each little leap of the pulse in the wrist" [B.G.]   **9 aspirate:** "an *h*-sound—as of the faint friction of breath expelled or indrawn" [B.G.]   **11 foamless:** "therefore smooth-flowing, quiet. Because air is excluded from the blood, where any bubble would cause a deadly clot, the lunging heart-stream flows without rustle of foam" [B.G.]

The Catch

The track of a broad rattler, dragged over dust at dawn, led us
Across the flats of morning under mesquite and paloverdes,
Path direct as hunger, up to a heaped grace of shade
Rodents had riddled into a hill of galleries. There it ended.

We dug into dust to take alive a lord of venom, whole   5
Rope and writhe as thick as a child's thigh, in halls of his Hell.

    1961–1964. *Country of the Minotaur*, 1970.

For an account of a similar capture, cf. John Clare's "Badger" (p. 316)

2 mesquite: "a spiny tree or shrub that forms thickets or grows solitary in the arid southwest" [B.G.]   **paloverde:** "a small desert tree, with light green bark, tiny pinnate leaves, and yellow flowers, also of the southwest" [B.G.]

But what we found, under a crust crumpling to knives of spades,
Was a path of fury: earth as light and loose as a harrow beds,
Smell of plowland cut and clawed, and darker down in the mound
A sprawling rag of dragon's pearly armor slubbered with mud.   10

The feasting grave trembled. It shook us. We heard the darkness grunt.
A snout full of snarls, of a hound or a hog, heaved the spade up and
        dug under.

But was stopped in its tunneling by the steel, as steel was stopped in
        its teeth. It turned
Quick, clawing and snapping up light, it charged and a choker rolled
        it at pole's end
A badger strap-throttled, flipping like a marlin, battling like a bull
        on a gaff   15
And snoring anger till over his bravery and scuffling the door of
        a cage clapped.

Burrowing bearclaws rattled in tin. He tasted wire all round.
He bucked, he bruised the ceiling, lunged at a beam and was eating
        oakwood.

But for that ravening he lived unfed and unslaked. His stench was
        immense,
His dung was the curved needle ribs of reptiles. He never slept—   20
Daylong, nightlong. His furious freedom resounded. At starlit dawn
Jaws and claws rasping and thudding thump of his thunder drummed
        once. Long

Silences rang for him, cage-eater greedy of snakes, abroad in the dawn.

8 **harrow:** a spiked farm implement that pulverizes the soil   10 **slubbered:** "daubed, smeared" [B.G.]   15 **marlin:** "a great deepsea game fish, noted for its fighting spirit and endurance when hooked and for its spectacular leaps out of water" [B.G.]   **gaff:** "a hook with a long handle, to snag and lift heavy fish from the water" [B.G.]   19 **ravening:** ravenous eating, gorging

Richard Eberhart
(Born 1904)

Born in Austin, Minnesota, Richard Ghormley Eberhart studied at the University of Minnesota; has degrees from Dartmouth and Cambridge; and did further work at Harvard. For a year he was tutor to the son of the King of Siam; for nine years master of English at St. Mark's School in Massachusetts. After four years in the navy, in which he rose to be lieutenant commander, he joined the Butcher Polish Company in Boston. Since 1952 he has been an honorary vice-president. He has taught at many universities, particularly, since 1956, at Dartmouth.

The Cancer Cells

Today I saw a picture of the cancer cells,
Sinister shapes with menacing attitudes.

1948. *Undercliff: Poems 1946–1953*, 1953.

Mr. Eberhart has described how his poem came to be written. While working for the Butcher Polish Company in the 1940s he was spending part of his time on the road. Tired at the end of one hot September day ("Fatigue," he says, "has something to do with creation") and finding himself "in such an unlikely place as Newark, N.J.," he was prompted by his sense of comedy to take a room at the Mili-

They had outgrown their test-tube and advanced,
Sinister shapes with menacing attitudes,
Into a world beyond, a virulent laughing gang.   5
They looked like art itself, like the artist's mind,
Powerful shaker, and the taker of new forms.
Some are revulsed to see these spiky shapes;
It is the world of the future too come to.
Nothing could be more vivid than their language,   10
Lethal, sparkling and irregular stars,
The murderous design of the universe,
The hectic dance of the passionate cancer cells.
O just phenomena to the calculating eye,
Originals of imagination. I flew   15
With them in a piled exuberance of time,
My own malignance in their racy, beautiful gestures
Quick and lean: and in their riot too
I saw the stance of the artist's make,
The fixed form in the massive fluxion.   20

I think Leonardo would have in his disinterest
Enjoyed them precisely with a sharp pencil.

---

tary Park Hotel—because he felt so unmilitary. "Before entering the elevator, wanting nothing so
much as to fall on the bed and rest a few hours, I bought a copy of *Life* magazine [the issue of Septem-
ber 27, 1948]. In the elevator I opened it to a two-page spread of cancer cells leaping out of test tubes.
This astonished and vitalized me with instant recognition: Beauty and Death perceived simultaneous-
ly. The cells were spiky-beautiful but could kill. . . . I entered the room and wrote the poem at once in
pencil on a used envelope. . . ." Whether or not it was subsequently reworked the poet does not re-
member.

21 **Leonardo:** Leonardo da Vinci (1452–1519), the Florentine painter, sculptor, architect, engineer
whose lively curiosity led him to draw many precise studies of things in nature

Cecil Day Lewis
(1904–1972)

Born in Ireland, Day Lewis was associated at Oxford with Auden and Spender. For five
years he worked in the Ministry of Information, London; he taught at several schools;
from 1954 until his death he was a director of a London publishing house. Besides sever-
al novels, many books of poetry, anthologies, and translations of Vergil, he published
over 20 detective novels under the name Nicholas Blake.

Two Songs

1

I've heard them lilting at loom and belting,
Lasses lilting before dawn of day:

A Time to Dance, 1935.

Both "songs" are ironic parallels to earlier poems. The first takes off from the Scottish dialect poem of
Jean Elliot (1727–1805), "The Flowers of the Forest" (about 1763), which begins: "I've heard them lilt-
in' at the ewe milkin', / Lasses a-liltin' before dawn o' day . . ." and has as its refrain "The flowers of
the forest are a' wede [all withered] away." Its theme is the loss of young men in war, as in the more
modern "Where Have All the Flowers Gone?" Day Lewis applies it to World War I ("lost in Flan-
ders"). The second song takes up the theme of Marlowe's "The Passionate Shepherd . . ." and Ralegh's
"The Nymph's Reply . . ." (p. 61) and applies it to the unemployment situation in England during the
Great Depression of the early 1930s.

1: 1 **loom and belting:** probably in textile mills, as contrasted with the "milkin'" of the Elliot poem.

But now they are silent, not gamesome and gallant—
The flowers of the town are rotting away.

There was laughter and loving in the lanes at evening;   5
Handsome were the boys then, and girls were gay.
But lost in Flanders by medalled commanders
The lads of the village are vanished away.

Cursed be the promise that takes our men from us—
All will be champion if you choose to obey: 10
They fight against hunger but still it is stronger—
The prime of our land grows cold as the clay.

The women are weary, once lilted so merry,
Waiting to marry for a year and a day:
From wooing and winning, from owning or earning   15
The flowers of the town are all turned away.

2

Come, live with me and be my love,
And we will all the pleasures prove
Of peace and plenty, bed and board,
That chance employment may afford.

I'll handle dainties on the docks   5
And thou shalt read of summer frocks:
At evening by the sour canals
We'll hope to hear some madrigals.

Care on thy maiden brow shall put
A wreath of wrinkles, and thy foot   10
Be shod with pain: not silken dress
But toil shall tire thy loveliness.

Hunger shall make thy modest zone
And cheat fond death of all but bone—
If these delights thy mind may move,   15
Then live with me and be my love.

2: 13 **zone:** girdle, waist

Robert Penn Warren
(Born 1905)

Born in Guthrie, Kentucky, Warren went to Vanderbilt with the intention of studying science. His meeting with Ransom, Tate, and others of the Fugitive group shifted his interest to literature. Besides taking degrees from Vanderbilt, the University of California at Berkeley, and Oxford (where he was a Rhodes scholar), he did additional graduate work at Yale. Warren has taught at Southwestern College (Memphis), Vanderbilt, Louisiana State, Minnesota, and, since 1950, at Yale. He has written nine novels (of which the best known is *All the King's Men*), plays, short stories, and many critical works; with Cleanth Brooks he wrote *Understanding Poetry*, one of the most influential textbooks of our time. Married to the novelist Eleanor Clark, he now lives in Connecticut.

Pursuit

The hunchback on the corner, with gum and shoelaces,
Has his own wisdom and pleasures, and may not be lured
To divulge them to you, for he has merely endured
Your appeal for his sympathy and your kind purchases;
And wears infirmity but as the general who turns   5
Apart, in his famous old greatcoat there on the hill
At dusk when the rapture and cannonade are still,
To muse withdrawn from the dead, from his gorgeous subalterns;
Or stares from the thicket of his familiar pain, like a fawn
That meets you a moment, wheels, in imperious innocence is gone.   10

Go to the clinic. Wait in the outer room
Where like an old possum the snag-nailed hand will hump
On its knee in murderous patience, and the pomp
Of pain swells like the Indies, or a plum.
And there you will stand, as on the Roman hill,   15
Stunned by each withdrawn gaze and severe shape,
The first barbarian victor stood to gape
At the sacrificial fathers, white-robed, still;
And even the feverish old Jew stares stern with authority
Till you feel like one who has come too late, or improperly clothed,
        to a party.   20

The doctor will take you now. He is burly and clean;
Listening, like lover or worshiper, bends at your heart.
He cannot make out just what it tries to impart,
So smiles; says you simply need a change of scene.
Of scene, of solace: therefore Florida,   25
Where Ponce de Leon clanked among the lilies,
Where white sails skit on blue and cavort like fillies,
And the shoulder gleams white in the moonlit corridor.
A change of love: if love is a groping Godward, though blind,
No matter what crevice, cranny, chink, bright in dark, the pale tentacle
        find.   30

In Florida consider the flamingo,
Its color passion but its neck a question.
Consider even that girl the other guests shun
On beach, at bar, in bed, for she may know
The secret you are seeking, after all;   35
Or the child you humbly sit by, excited and curly,
That screams on the shore at the sea's sunlit hurlyburly,
Till the mother calls its name, toward nightfall.
Till you sit alone: in the dire meridians, off Ireland, in fury
Of spume-tooth and dawnless sea-heave, salt rimes the lookout's devout
        eye.   40

Eleven Poems on the Same Theme, 1942.

8 gorgeous subalterns: the phrase "here carries a hint of a double meaning. It is literally the young
officers proud of their gaudy uniforms (in contrast to the general's 'famous old greatcoat'). But the
dead too are subalterns (dead, for one thing) and gorgeous with their decorations of blood as well as
(perhaps) their fine uniforms, too." [R.P.W.]   **26 Ponce de Leon:** the Spanish explorer (1460–1521)
who discovered Florida in 1513 while in search of the Fountain of Youth   **39 dire meridians:** Merid-
ians are the lines of longitude running north and south on a map. "These 'meridians' were especially
'dire' during World War II because of German submarines." [R.P.W.]   **40 spume-tooth:** the foam of
the breakers, keen as teeth   **rimes:** coats with frost or ice

Till you sit alone—which is the beginning of error—
Behind you the music and lights of the great hotel:
Solution, perhaps, is public, despair personal,
But history held to your breath clouds like a mirror.
There are many states, and towns in them, and faces,   45
But meanwhile, the little old lady in black, by the wall,
Admires all the dancers, and tells you how just last fall
Her husband died in Ohio, and damp mists her glasses;
She blinks and croaks, like a toad or a Norn, in the horrible light,
And rattles her crutch, which may put forth a small bloom, perhaps
   white.   50

49 Norn: in Scandinavian mythology, one of the three Fates (the goddesses who control the affairs
and fortunes of men)   **50 a small bloom:** a miraculous omen, as in myth or in fairy tale

Myth on Mediterranean Beach: Aphrodite as Logos

From left to right, she leads the eye
Across the blaze-brightness of sea and sky

That is the background of her transit.

Commanded thus, from left to right,
As by a line of print on that bright   5

Blankness, the eye will follow, but

There is no line, the eye follows only
That one word moving, it moves in lonely

And absolute arrogance across the blank

Page of the world, the word burns, she is   10
The word, all faces turn. Look!—this

Is what she is: old hunchback in bikini.

A contraption of angles and bulges, an old
Robot with pince-nez and hair dyed gold,

She heaves along beneath the hump.   15

The breasts hang down like saddle-bags,
To balance the hump the belly sags,

And under the belly-bulge, the flowers

Incarnations: Poems 1966–1968, 1968.

Aphrodite was the Greek goddess of love (the Roman Venus). *Logos* (Greek) means "word"; it came to
stand for the divine reason or wisdom immanent in nature and man, and later for Christ. Cf. John 1:1:
"In the beginning was the Word, and the Word was with God, and the Word was God...." The hid-
eous old lady of the poem is like a parody of Aphrodite; her presence and appearance tell us some-
thing about the nature of things. "She suggests what all the young and beautiful most ultimately
make terms with." [R.P.W.]

14 pince-nez: glasses clipped to the nose (French: pinch-nose)

Of the gee-string garland the private parts.
She grinds along by fits and starts   20

Beside the margin of the sea,

Past children and sand-castles and
The lovers strewn along the sand.

Her pince-nez glitter like contempt

For all delusion, and the French lad   25
Who exhibitionistically had

Been fondling the American college girl

Loses his interest. Ignoring him,
The hunchback stares at the horizon rim,

Then slowly, as compulsion grows,   30

She foots the first frail lace of foam
That is the threshold of her lost home,

And moved by memory in the blood,

Enters that vast indifferency
Of perfection that we call the sea.   35

How long, how long, she lingers there

She may not know, somnambulist
In that realm where no Time may subsist,

But in the end will again feel

The need to rise and re-enact   40
The miracle of the human fact.

She lifts her head, looks toward the shore.

She moves toward us, abstract and slow,
And watching, we feel the slow knowledge grow—

How from the breasts the sea recedes,   45

How the great-gashed navel's cup
Pours forth the ichor that had filled it up.

How the wavelets sink to seek, and seek,

Then languishing, sink to lave the knees,
And lower, to kiss the feet, as these   50

Find the firm ground where they must go.

47 **ichor:** the divine fluid thought to flow in the veins of the Greek gods, instead of mortal blood
49 **lave:** wash, flow around   51 **the firm ground:** "the earth of all doomed to mortality" [R.P.W.]

The last foam crisps about the feet.
She shivers, smiles. She stands complete

In Botticellian parody.

Bearing her luck upon her back,   55
She turns now to take the lifeward track,

And lover by lover, on she moves

Toward her own truth, and does not stop.
Each foot stumps flat with the big toe up,

But under the heel, the damp-packed sand,   ·   60

With that compression, like glory glows,
And glory attends her as she goes.

In rapture now she heaves along,

The pince-nez glitter at her eyes,
The flowers wreathe her moving thighs,   65

For she treads the track the blessèd know

To a shore far lonelier than this
Where waits her apotheosis.

She passes the lovers, one by one,

And passing, draws their dreams away,   70
And leaves them naked to the day.

52 **crisps:** curls, ripples   54 **Botticellian parody:** One of the most famous paintings of the Florentine artist Sandro Botticelli (1445–1510) is *The Birth of Venus* (c. 1485). It shows Venus (Aphrodite) as a beautiful young woman floating shoreward from the ocean on a great shell.   55 **her luck:** An old superstition associates good luck with the hump of the hunchback. "Her 'luck' here is to know from her infirmity the natural doom of all—somehow live through it." [R.P.W.]   68 **apotheosis:** deification, change from a human to a divine state

Stanley Kunitz
(Born 1905)

Born in Worcester, Massachusetts, Kunitz has A.B. and M.A. degrees from Harvard. From 1928 to 1943 he was editor of the *Wilson Library Bulletin;* he was co-editor of such essential reference works as *American Authors: 1600–1900* and *Twentieth Century Authors.* Since serving in the army from 1943 to 1945 he has taught at many colleges and universities, among them Bennington, The New School, the University of Washington, Brandeis, Yale, and, since 1967, at Columbia. Besides his several volumes of poetry, he has published critical essays and several books of translation from the Russian.

The War Against the Trees

The man who sold his lawn to standard oil
Joked with his neighbors come to watch the show

1957. *Selected Poems, 1928–1958*, 1958.

While the bulldozers, drunk with gasoline,
Tested the virtue of the soil
Under the branchy sky   5
By overthrowing first the privet-row.

Forsythia-forays and hydrangea-raids
Were but preliminaries to a war
Against the great-grandfathers of the town,
So freshly lopped and maimed.   10
They struck and struck again,
And with each elm a century went down.

All day the hireling engines charged the trees,
Subverting them by hacking underground
In grub-dominions, where dark summer's mole   15
Rampages through his halls,
Till a northern seizure shook
Those crowns, forcing the giants to their knees.

I saw the ghosts of children at their games
Racing beyond their childhood in the shade,   20
And while the green world turned its death-foxed page
And a red wagon wheeled,
I watched them disappear
Into the suburbs of their grievous age.

Ripped from the craters much too big for hearts   25
The club-roots bared their amputated coils,
Raw gorgons matted blind, whose pocks and scars
Cried Moon! on a corner lot
One witness-moment, caught
In the rear-view mirrors of the passing cars.   30

6 **privet:** an ornamental shrub often used for hedges   7 **forsythia:** an ornamental shrub with yellow flowers in spring   **hydrangea:** a flowering shrub much used in landscaping   9 **great-grandfathers:** ancient trees   14 **subverting:** overturning   15 **grub-dominions:** the home of grubs (worms, larvae, etc.)   17 **northern seizure:** grasp like that of the north wind   21 **foxed:** stained brown   27 **gorgons:** the snaky-haired sisters of Greek mythology whose gaze could turn the beholder to stone   28 **Cried Moon:** vividly suggested the surface of the moon

The Knot

I've tried to seal it in,
that cross-grained knot
on the opposite wall,
scored in the lintel of my door,
but it keeps bleeding through   5
into the world we share.
Mornings when I wake,
curled in my web,
I hear it come
with a rush of resin   10

1973. *The Poems of Stanley Kunitz 1928–1978,* 1979.

"A knot in a piece of lumber marks the place where a branch has been severed from the trunk of the tree. (This little note . . . may seem too obvious . . . but from my experience in reading the poem to urban audiences I doubt that it is.)" [S.K.]

out of the trauma
of its lopping-off.
Obstinate bud,
sticky with life,
mad for the rain again,   15
it racks itself with shoots
that crackle overhead,
dividing as they grow.
Let be! Let be!
I shake my wings   20
and fly into its boughs.

John Betjeman
(Born 1906)

Sir John Betjeman, who succeeded Day Lewis as poet laureate, was born in London, where his father, of Dutch descent, ran a firm of designers. In spite of his failing divinity studies at Oxford, church architecture has been a lifelong interest, as have old buildings, old villages, old railways—old anything, so long as it is English. Betjeman ("the Norman Rockwell of England") is England's most popular poet; his *Collected Poems* had sold, nearly a decade ago, a quarter of a million copies. Unlike most poets who achieve such popularity, Betjeman is also admired by many of the best poets.

A Subaltern's Love-Song

Miss J. Hunter Dunn, Miss J. Hunter Dunn,
Furnish'd and burnish'd by Aldershot sun,
What strenuous singles we played after tea,
We in the tournament—you against me!

Love-thirty, love-forty, oh! weakness of joy,   5
The speed of a swallow, the grace of a boy,
With carefullest carelessness, gaily you won,
I am weak from your loveliness, Joan Hunter Dunn.

Miss Joan Hunter Dunn, Miss Joan Hunter Dunn,
How mad I am, sad I am, glad that you won.   10
The warm-handled racket is back in its press,
But my shock-headed victor, she loves me no less.

Her father's euonymus shines as we walk,
And swing past the summer-house, buried in talk,
And cool the verandah that welcomes us in   15
To the six-o'clock news and a lime-juice and gin.

The scent of the conifers, sound of the bath,
The view from my bedroom of moss-dappled path,
As I struggle with double-end evening tie,
For we dance at the Golf Club, my victor and I.   20

New Bats in Old Belfries, 1945.

The subaltern is a British army officer below the rank of captain. Altershot (line 2), about 30 miles southwest of London, is famous as an army town, with the largest permanent military camp in the Commonwealth—so one might guess Joan is an "army brat."

12 **shock-headed:** with thick bushy hair, here probably dishevelled from the game   13 **euonymus:** a kind of shrub or small tree often used in landscaping   17 **conifers:** evergreens

On the floor of her bedroom lie blazer and shorts
And the cream-coloured walls are be-trophied with sports,
And westering, questioning settles the sun
On your low-leaded window, Miss Joan Hunter Dunn.

The Hillman is waiting, the light's in the hall,   25
The pictures of Egypt are bright on the wall,
My sweet, I am standing beside the oak stair
And there on the landing's the light on your hair.

By roads "not adopted", by woodlanded ways,
She drove to the club in the late summer haze,   30
Into nine-o'clock Camberley, heavy with bells
And mushroomy, pine-woody, evergreen smells.

Miss Joan Hunter Dunn, Miss Joan Hunter Dunn,
I can hear from the car-park the dance has begun.
Oh! full Surrey twilight! importunate band!   35
Oh! strongly adorable tennis-girl's hand!

Around us are Rovers and Austins afar,
Above us, the intimate roof of the car,
And here on my right is the girl of my choice,
With the tilt of her nose and the chime of her voice,   40

And the scent of her wrap, and the words never said,
And the ominous, ominous dancing ahead.
We sat in the car park till twenty to one
And now I'm engaged to Miss Joan Hunter Dunn.

25 **Hillman:** an English make of car (like the Rovers and Austins of line 37)   29 **"not adopted":** not maintained by local authorities; "travel at your own risk"   31 **Camberley:** a village about ten miles from Aldershot   35 **Surrey:** the county, just south of London, where these villages are

---

William Empson
(Born 1906)

Empson, educated at Cambridge, where his major was mathematics, published at 24 his famous critical work, *Seven Types of Ambiguity*. For many years he taught English literature in Japan and China and was Chinese editor for the BBC. For several summers he taught at Kenyon College.

Missing Dates

Slowly the poison the whole blood stream fills.
It is not the effort nor the failure tires.
The waste remains, the waste remains and kills.

It is not your system or clear sight that mills
Down small to the consequence a life requires;   5
Slowly the poison the whole blood stream fills.

Mid-1930s. *The Gathering Storm*, 1940.

The poem is a *villanelle*; see the prosody section.

They bled an old dog dry yet the exchange rills
Of young dog blood gave but a month's desires.
The waste remains, the waste remains and kills.

It is the Chinese tombs and the slag hills   10
Usurp the soil, and not the soil retires.
Slowly the poison the whole blood stream fills.

Not to have fire is to be a skin that shrills.
The complete fire is death. From partial fires
The waste remains, the waste remains and kills.   15

It is the poems you have lost, the ills
From missing dates, at which the heart expires.
Slowly the poison the whole blood stream fills.
The waste remains, the waste remains and kills.

7 **rills:** streams

W. H. Auden
(1907–1973)

Wystan Hugh Auden grew up in Birmingham (England); his physician father was a university professor. In prep school he majored in biology, planned to become a mining engineer, but at 15 decided to be a poet. The sciences, however, remained a lifelong interest. At college, Anglo-Saxon poetry and the work of Hopkins and Eliot attracted him. After five years as a schoolmaster and some months as writer with a film company, Auden made a three-month trip to Iceland (he claims Icelandic descent) with the poet Louis MacNeice; the following year he drove an ambulance for the anti-Franco forces in Spain. In youth sympathetic to Marx, he returned before long to the high Anglicanism of his youth. On a 1938 trip to China he crossed the United States; he returned here the following year and in 1946 became an American citizen. During his more than 30-year stay in this country he lived mostly in New York City, but taught at many universities. In 1957 Auden bought a farmhouse near Kirchstetten (Austria) for his annual European sojourns, previously spent near Naples. In 1972 he moved to Oxford; he died the following year in Austria. His bibliography lists over 50 books and chapbooks of poetry; 23 plays, opera librettos, and television programs; and nearly 50 anthologies, editions, translations, and books of essays.

Lullaby

Lay your sleeping head, my love,
Human on my faithless arm;
Time and fevers burn away
Individual beauty from
Thoughtful children, and the grave   5
Proves the child ephemeral:
But in my arms till break of day
Let the living creature lie,
Mortal, guilty, but to me
The entirely beautiful.   10

Soul and body have no bounds:
To lovers as they lie upon

1937. *Another Time,* 1940.

See Additional Notes (p. 780).

Her tolerant enchanted slope
In their ordinary swoon,
Grave the vision Venus sends   15
Of supernatural sympathy,
Universal love and hope;
While an abstract insight wakes
Among the glaciers and the rocks
The hermit's carnal ecstasy.   20

Certainty, fidelity
On the stroke of midnight pass
Like vibrations of a bell
And fashionable madmen raise
Their pedantic boring cry: 25
Every farthing of the cost,
All the dreaded cards foretell,
Shall be paid, but from this night
Not a whisper, not a thought,
Not a kiss nor look be lost.   30

Beauty, midnight, vision dies:
Let the winds of dawn that blow
Softly round your dreaming head
Such a day of welcome show
Eye and knocking heart may bless,   35
Find our mortal world enough;
Noons of dryness find you fed
By the involuntary powers,
Nights of insult let you pass
Watched by every human love.   40

Musée des Beaux Arts

About suffering they were never wrong,
The Old Masters: how well they understood
Its human position; how it takes place
While someone else is eating or opening a window or just walking
    dully along;
How, when the aged are reverently, passionately waiting   5
For the miraculous birth, there always must be
Children who did not specially want it to happen, skating
On a pond at the edge of the wood:
They never forgot
That even the dreadful martyrdom must run its course   10

1938. Ibid.

The title means museum of fine arts; we might say art gallery or art institute. The poem was suggested by paintings of Pieter Brueghel the Elder (cf. W. C. Williams's "The Dance," p. 520), which Auden saw in the Brussels museum, and in particular by the painting that shows the fall of Icarus. That incident is described in the eighth book of Ovid's *Metamorphoses*. Daedalus, the great inventor, was imprisoned with his son Icarus in the very labyrinth he had designed in Crete. Wishing to escape, he made a pair of wings for himself and one for his son, warning the young man not to fly too high because the heat of the sun could melt the waxy substance that held the feathers together. But Icarus, carried away by the exhilaration of the flight, did fly high, the wings did disintegrate, and he fell into the sea. Ovid had described how fishermen on the shore, shepherds leaning on their sheephooks, and plowmen at the plow had looked up in amazement at the flying figures. Brueghel gets all of these people into his painting, but not one is even glancing at Icarus as he plunges head first into the water—nothing is visible of the one who should be the central figure except a tiny pair of legs in one corner of the picture.

2 **Old Masters:** great painters of the past, especially of the Renaissance

Anyhow in a corner, some untidy spot
Where the dogs go on with their doggy life and the torturer's horse
Scratches its innocent behind on a tree.

In Brueghel's *Icarus*, for instance: how everything turns away
Quite leisurely from the disaster; the ploughman may   15
Have heard the splash, the forsaken cry,
But for him it was not an important failure; the sun shone
As it had to on the white legs disappearing into the green
Water; and the expensive delicate ship that must have seen
Something amazing, a boy falling out of the sky,   20
Had somewhere to get to and sailed calmly on.

In Memory of W. B. Yeats

(d. Jan. 1939)

I

He disappeared in the dead of winter:
The brooks were frozen, the airports almost deserted,
And snow disfigured the public statues;
The mercury sank in the mouth of the dying day.
What instruments we have agree   5
The day of his death was a dark cold day.

Far from his illness
The wolves ran on through the evergreen forests,
The peasant river was untempted by the fashionable quays;
By mourning tongues   10
The death of the poet was kept from his poems.

But for him it was his last afternoon as himself,
An afternoon of nurses and rumours;
The provinces of his body revolted,
The squares of his mind were empty,   15
Silence invaded the suburbs,
The current of his feeling failed; he became his admirers.

Now he is scattered among a hundred cities
And wholly given over to unfamiliar affections,
To find his happiness in another kind of wood   20
And be punished under a foreign code of conscience.
The words of a dead man
Are modified in the guts of the living.

But in the importance and noise of to-morrow
When the brokers are roaring like beasts on the floor of the Bourse,   25
And the poor have the sufferings to which they are fairly accustomed,
And each in the cell of himself is almost convinced of his freedom,
A few thousand will think of this day
As one thinks of a day when one did something slightly unusual.

1939. Ibid.

Yeats died on January 28.

8–9 wolves . . . evergreen . . . river . . . : The life of the world, wild and lusty, continued unaffected.
17 he became his admirers: He continued to exist only as his poetry was admired and cherished.
25 the Bourse: the stock exchange

What instruments we have agree   30
The day of his death was a dark cold day.

II

You were silly like us; your gift survived it all:
The parish of rich women, physical decay,
Yourself. Mad Ireland hurt you into poetry.
Now Ireland has her madness and her weather still,   35
For poetry makes nothing happen: it survives
In the valley of its making where executives
Would never want to tamper, flows on south
From ranches of isolation and the busy griefs,
Raw towns that we believe and die in; it survives,   40
A way of happening, a mouth.

III

Earth, receive an honoured guest:
William Yeats is laid to rest.
Let the Irish vessel lie
Emptied of its poetry.   45

Time that is intolerant
Of the brave and innocent,
And indifferent in a week
To a beautiful physique,

Worships language and forgives   50
Everyone by whom it lives;
Pardons cowardice, conceit,
Lays its honours at their feet.

Time that with this strange excuse
Pardoned Kipling and his views,   55
And will pardon Paul Claudel,
Pardons him for writing well.

In the nightmare of the dark
All the dogs of Europe bark,
And the living nations wait,   60
Each sequestered in its hate;

Intellectual disgrace
Stares from every human face,
And the seas of pity lie
Locked and frozen in each eye.   65

Follow, poet, follow right
To the bottom of the night,
With your unconstraining voice
Still persuade us to rejoice;

32 **silly:** probably a reference to Yeats's "system," as he described it in *A Vision*. Cf. footnotes to "The
Second Coming" (p. 564).   36 **poetry makes nothing happen:** has no effect on the affairs of execu-
tives, the Bourse, the problems of the poor, the world of politics, the course of history, etc.
46–57 These three stanzas were omitted when Auden published his *Collected Shorter Poems* (1966).
55 **Kipling:** Cf. p. 456. Auden probably found his views too imperialistic.   56 **Paul Claudel:** conserv-
ative Catholic French diplomat, poet, and dramatist (1868–1955)   58–59 **nightmare . . . bark:** World
War II broke out only months after the poem was written.

With the farming of a verse 70
Make a vineyard of the curse,
Sing of human unsuccess
In a rapture of distress;

In the deserts of the heart
Let the healing fountain start, 75
In the prison of his days
Teach the free man how to praise.

70 **farming:** careful tending, cultivation 71 **curse:** Cf. Gen. 3:17, the Lord to Adam after his sin:
"cursed is the ground for thy sake; in sorrow shalt thou eat of it all the days of thy life...."

In Memory of Sigmund Freud

(d. September 1939)

When there are so many we shall have to mourn,
When grief has been made so public, and exposed
        To the critique of a whole epoch
        The frailty of our conscience and anguish,

Of whom shall we speak? For every day they die 5
Among us, those who were doing us some good,
        And knew it was never enough but
        Hoped to improve a little by living.

Such was this doctor: still at eighty he wished
To think of our life, from whose unruliness 10
        So many plausible young futures
        With threats or flattery ask obedience.

But his wish was denied him; he closed his eyes
Upon that last picture common to us all,
        Of problems like relatives standing 15
        Puzzled and jealous about our dying.

For about him at the very end were still
Those he had studied, the nervous and the nights,
        And shades that still waited to enter
        The bright circle of his recognition 20

Turned elsewhere with their disappointment as he
Was taken away from his old interest
        To go back to the earth in London,
        An important Jew who died in exile.

Only Hate was happy, hoping to augment 25
His practice now, and his shabby clientele

1939. Ibid.

Freud, born in Freiberg in 1856, lived in Vienna until 1938, when Austria was annexed by Nazi Germany. At the age of 82 he went to London, where he died the following year. For Auden's use of *syllabics*, see the section on prosody.

1 **so many ... to mourn:** World War II had broken out in Europe in September 1939; the poem was
written the following November. 18 **the nights:** possibly a reference to Freud's *The Interpretation of
Dreams* (1900), which he considered his best book. Cf. lines 99 ff.

Who think they can be cured by killing
And covering the gardens with ashes.

They are still alive but in a world he changed
Simply by looking back with no false regrets;   30
    All that he did was to remember
    Like the old and be honest like children.

He wasn't clever at all: he merely told
The unhappy Present to recite the Past
    Like a poetry lesson till sooner   35
    Or later it faltered at the line where

Long ago the accusations had begun,
And suddenly knew by whom it had been judged,
    How rich life had been and how silly,
    And was life-forgiven and more humble,   40

Able to approach the future as a friend
Without a wardrobe of excuses, without
    A set mask of rectitude or an
    Embarrassing over-familiar gesture.

No wonder the ancient cultures of conceit   45
In his technique of unsettlement foresaw
    The fall of princes, the collapse of
    Their lucrative patterns of frustration.

If he succeeded, why, the Generalised Life
Would become impossible, the monolith   50
    Of State be broken and prevented
    The co-operation of avengers.

Of course they called on God: but he went his way,
Down among the Lost People like Dante, down
    To the stinking fosse where the injured   55
    Lead the ugly life of the rejected.

And showed us what evil is: not as we thought
Deeds that must be punished, but our lack of faith,
    Our dishonest mood of denial,
    The concupiscence of the oppressor.   60

And if something of the autocratic pose,
The paternal strictness he distrusted, still
    Clung to his utterance and features,
    It was a protective imitation

For one who lived among enemies so long: 65
If often he was wrong and at times absurd,
    To us he is no more a person
    Now but a whole climate of opinion

Under whom we conduct our differing lives:
Like weather he can only hinder or help,   70

---

50 **monolith:** single large stone, massive structure   54 **the Lost People:** Dante's "perduta gente" (*Inferno*, III, 3), the souls in hell   55 **fosse:** ditch   60 **concupiscence:** lust

The proud can still be proud but find it
A little harder, and the tyrant tries

To make him do but doesn't care for him much.
He quietly surrounds all our habits of growth;
    He extends, till the tired in even   75
    The remotest most miserable duchy

Have felt the change in their bones and are cheered,
And the child unlucky in his little State,
    Some hearth where freedom is excluded,
    A hive whose honey is fear and worry,   80

Feels calmer now and somehow assured of escape;
While as they lie in the grass of our neglect,
    So many long-forgotten objects
    Revealed by his undiscouraged shining

Are returned to us and made precious again;   85
Games we had thought we must drop as we grew up,
    Little noises we dared not laugh at,
    Faces we made when no one was looking.

But he wishes us more than this: to be free
Is often to be lonely; he would unite   90
    The unequal moieties fractured
    By our own well-meaning sense of justice,

Would restore to the larger the wit and will
The smaller possesses but can only use
    For arid disputes, would give back to   95
    The son the mother's richness of feeling.

But he would have us remember most of all
To be enthusiastic over the night
    Not only for the sense of wonder
    It alone has to offer, but also   100

Because it needs our love: for with sad eyes
Its delectable creatures look up and beg
    Us dumbly to ask them to follow;
    They are exiles who long for the future

That lies in our power. They too would rejoice   105
If allowed to serve enlightenment like him,
    Even to bear our cry of "Judas,"
    As he did and all must bear who serve it.

One rational voice is dumb: over a grave
The household of Impulse mourns one dearly loved.   110
    Sad is Eros, builder of cities,
    And weeping anarchic Aphrodite.

---

76 **duchy:** the territory of a duke or duchess 91 **moieties:** halves, divisions 109 **one rational
voice:** Freud's 110 **Impulse:** instinctive, natural behavior 111 **Eros:** in Greek mythology, the son
of Aphrodite, god of physical love, "builder of cities" in that he brings families and groups together
112 **Aphrodite:** Greek goddess of love and beauty, "anarchic" in that she goes her own natural way,
indifferent to prohibitions

In Praise of Limestone

If it form the one landscape that we the inconstant ones
    Are consistently homesick for, this is chiefly
Because it dissolves in water. Mark these rounded slopes
    With their surface fragrance of thyme and beneath
A secret system of caves and conduits; hear these springs   5
    That spurt out everywhere with a chuckle
Each filling a private pool for its fish and carving
    Its own little ravine whose cliffs entertain
The butterfly and the lizard; examine this region
    Of short distances and definite places: 10
What could be more like Mother or a fitter background
    For her son, for the nude young male who lounges
Against a rock displaying his dildo, never doubting
    That for all his faults he is loved, whose works are but
Extensions of his power to charm? From weathered outcrop   15
    To hill-top temple, from appearing waters to
Conspicuous fountains, from a wild to a formal vineyard,
    Are ingenious but short steps that a child's wish
To receive more attention than his brothers, whether
    By pleasing or teasing, can easily take.   20

Watch, then, the band of rivals as they climb up and down
    Their steep stone gennels in twos and threes, sometimes
Arm in arm, but never, thank God, in step; or engaged
    On the shady side of a square at midday in
Voluble discourse, knowing each other too well to think   25
    There are any important secrets, unable
To conceive a god whose temper-tantrums are moral
    And not to be pacified by a clever line
Or a good lay: for, accustomed to a stone that responds,
    They have never had to veil their faces in awe   30
Of a crater whose blazing fury could not be fixed;
    Adjusted to the local needs of valleys
Where everything can be touched or reached by walking,
    Their eyes have never looked into infinite space
Through the lattice-work of a nomad's comb; born lucky,   35
    Their legs have never encountered the fungi
And insects of the jungle, the monstrous forms and lives
    With which we have nothing, we like to hope, in common.
So, when one of them goes to the bad, the way his mind works
    Remains comprehensible: to become a pimp   40
Or deal in fake jewelry or ruin a fine tenor voice
    For effects that bring down the house could happen to all
But the best and the worse of us . . .

1948. *Nones,* 1952.

The poem gives us the requisite geological information: since limestone dissolves in rain water or ground water, landscapes based on it are sculptured by flowing water. They are soft, curvy, intimate, with cave systems and underground streams. Auden is thinking of Italy; he relates the character of the landscape to the character of the dwellers affected by it. The pleasure-loving natural man is comfortably at home in a limestone landscape, though it will not do for saints, Caesars, or adventurous voyagers.

22 **gennels:** channels, narrow passages   35 **comb:** One meaning is the crest or ridge of a roof.

That is why, I suppose,
The best and worst never stayed here long but sought
Immoderate soils where the beauty was not so external,   45
The light less public and the meaning of life
Something more than a mad camp. "Come!" cried the granite wastes,
"How evasive is your humor, how accidental
Your kindest kiss, how permanent is death." (Saints-to-be
Slipped away sighing.) "Come!" purred the clays and gravels,   50
"On our plains there is room for armies to drill; rivers
Wait to be tamed and slaves to construct you a tomb
In the grand manner: soft as the earth is mankind and both
Need to be altered." (Intendant Caesars rose and
Left, slamming the door.) But the really reckless were fetched   55
By an older colder voice, the oceanic whisper:
"I am the solitude that asks and promises nothing;
That is how I shall set you free. There is no love;
There are only the various envies, all of them sad."

They were right, my dear, all those voices were right   60
And still are; this land is not the sweet home that it looks,
Nor its peace the historical calm of a site
Where something was settled once and for all: A backward
And dilapidated province, connected
To the big busy world by a tunnel, with a certain   65
Seedy appeal, is that all it is now? Not quite:
It has a worldly duty which in spite of itself
It does not neglect, but calls into question
All the Great Powers assume; it disturbs our rights. The poet,
Admired for his earnest habit of calling   70
The sun the sun, his mind Puzzle, is made uneasy
By these solid statues which so obviously doubt
His antimythological myth; and these gamins,
Pursuing the scientist down the tiled colonnade
With such lively offers, rebuke his concern for Nature's   75
Remotest aspects: I, too, am reproached, for what
And how much you know. Not to lose time, not to get caught,
Not to be left behind, not, please! to resemble
The beasts who repeat themselves, or a thing like water
Or stone whose conduct can be predicted, these   80
Are our Common Prayer, whose greatest comfort is music
Which can be made anywhere, is invisible,
And does not smell. In so far as we have to look forward
To death as a fact, no doubt we are right: But if
Sins can be forgiven, if bodies rise from the dead,   85
These modifications of matter into
Innocent athletes and gesticulating fountains,
Made solely for pleasure, make a further point:
The blessed will not care what angle they are regarded from,
Having nothing to hide. Dear, I know nothing of   90
Either, but when I try to imagine a faultless love
Or the life to come, what I hear is the murmur
Of underground streams, what I see is a limestone landscape.

---

54 **intendant:** those intending to be   65 **tunnel:** railroad approaches to Italy are mostly by tunnel
through the Alps

The Shield of Achilles

    She looked over his shoulder
        For vines and olive trees,
    Marble well-governed cities
        And ships upon untamed seas,
    But there on the shining metal   5
        His hands had put instead
    An artificial wilderness
        And a sky like lead.

A plain without a feature, bare and brown,
   No blade of grass, no sign of neighbourhood,   10
Nothing to eat and nowhere to sit down,
   Yet, congregated on its blankness, stood
   An unintelligible multitude,
A million eyes, a million boots in line,
Without expression, waiting for a sign.   15

Out of the air a voice without a face
   Proved by statistics that some cause was just
In tones as dry and level as the place:
   No one was cheered and nothing was discussed;
   Column by column in a cloud of dust   20
They marched away enduring a belief
Whose logic brought them, somewhere else, to grief.

    She looked over his shoulder
        For ritual pieties,
    White flower-garlanded heifers,   25
        Libation and sacrifice,
    But there on the shining metal
        Where the altar should have been,
    She saw by his flickering forge-light
        Quite another scene.   30

Barbed wire enclosed an arbitrary spot
   Where bored officials lounged (one cracked a joke)
And sentries sweated for the day was hot:
   A crowd of ordinary decent folk
   Watched from without and neither moved nor spoke   35
As three pale figures were led forth and bound
To three posts driven upright in the ground.

The mass and majesty of this world, all
   That carries weight and always weighs the same
Lay in the hands of others; they were small   40

1952. *The Shield of Achilles,* 1955.

In Book XVIII of Homer's *Iliad,* the sea-goddess Thetis comes to Hephaestos, the crippled god of fire and blacksmiths, to ask him to make a new suit of armor for her son Achilles, then fighting at Troy. Hephaestos first makes him an ornately decorated shield, which does show many such scenes as Thetis looks for in Auden's poem. But, instead, here she finds only scenes of mass horror in a totalitarian state, with its torture and execution (lines 31–44), and its urban savagery (lines 53–59). But the poem is not simply a contrast between an idyllic past and a brutal present: the great Achilles too is "iron-hearted man-slaying," doomed to die young if he chooses to win fame at Troy rather than live ingloriously at home.

15 **a sign:** Cf. T. S. Eliot's "Gerontion," line 17, and note.   36 **three . . . figures:** Cf. the crucifixion of Christ.

And could not hope for help and no help came:
What their foes liked to do was done, their shame
Was all the worst could wish; they lost their pride
And died as men before their bodies died.

　　　She looked over his shoulder　　　　　　　　　45
　　　　　For athletes at their games,
　　　Men and women in a dance
　　　　　Moving their sweet limbs
　　　Quick, quick, to music,
　　　　　But there on the shining shield　　　　　50
　　　His hands had set no dancing-floor
　　　　　But a weed-choked field.

A ragged urchin, aimless and alone,
　　　Loitered about that vacancy, a bird
Flew up to safety from his well-aimed stone:　　　55
　　　That girls are raped, that two boys knife a third,
　　　Were axioms to him, who'd never heard
Of any world where promises were kept,
Or one could weep because another wept.

　　　The thin-lipped armourer,　　　　　　　　　60
　　　　　Hephaestos hobbled away,
　　　Thetis of the shining breasts
　　　　　Cried out in dismay
　　　At what the god had wrought
　　　　　To please her son, the strong　　　　　65
　　　Iron-hearted man-slaying Achilles
　　　　　Who would not live long.

Ode to Terminus

The High Priests of telescopes and cyclotrons
keep making pronouncements about happenings
　　　on scales too gigantic or dwarfish
　　　to be noticed by our native senses,

discoveries which, couched in the elegant　　　　　5
euphemisms of algebra, look innocent,
　　　harmless enough but, when translated
　　　into the vulgar anthropomorphic

tongue, will give no cause for hilarity
to gardeners or housewives: if galaxies　　　　　10
　　　bolt like panicking mobs, if mesons
　　　riot like fish in a feeding-frenzy,

it sounds too like Political History
to boost civil morale, too symbolic of

1968. *City Without Walls*, 1969.

Terminus, in the religion of ancient Rome, was the god of boundaries, of "definite/outlines" (lines 29–30).

1 **cyclotron:** a scientific apparatus for experiments with subatomic particles　8 **anthropomorphic:** conceiving things in human shape, human terms　10–11 **galaxies/bolt . . . :** a reference to theories of the expanding universe, according to which the galaxies are rushing farther and farther apart 11 **mesons:** strongly interacting nuclear particles

the crimes and strikes and demonstrations   15
we are supposed to gloat on at breakfast.

How trite, though, our fears beside the miracle
that we're here to shiver, that a Thingummy
    so addicted to lethal violence
    should have somehow secreted a placid   20

tump with exactly the right ingredients
to start and to cocker Life, that heavenly
    freak for whose manage we shall have to
    give account at the Judgement, our Middle-

Earth, where Sun-Father to all appearances   25
moves by day from orient to occident,
    and his light is felt as a friendly
    presence not a photonic bombardment,

where all visibles do have a definite
outline they stick to, and are undoubtedly   30
    at rest or in motion, where lovers
    recognize each other by their surface,

where to all species except the talkative
have been allotted the niche and diet that
    become them. This, whatever micro-   35
    biology may think, is the world we

really live in and that saves our sanity,
who know all too well how the most erudite
    mind behaves in the dark without a
    surround it is called on to interpret,   40

how, discarding rhythm, punctuation, metaphor,
it sinks into a driveling monologue,
    too literal to see a joke or
    distinguish a penis from a pencil.

Venus and Mars are powers too natural   45
to temper our outlandish extravagance:
    You alone, Terminus the Mentor,
    can teach us how to alter our gestures.

God of walls, doors and reticence, nemesis
overtakes the sacrilegious technocrat,   50
    but blessed is the City that thanks you
    for giving us games and grammar and metres.

---

18 **Thingummy:** (pronounced *thíng-a-me*), thingamajig, whatchamacallit   21 **tump:** mound of earth (such as may mark a prehistoric settlement)   22 **cocker:** pamper, indulge   24–25 **Middle-Earth:** a medieval term (*myddelerde*) for the world, as being between heaven and hell, or as being at the center of the universe. J. R. R. Tolkien, a medieval scholar, uses the term as a place-name in his Hobbit series.   25 **Sun-Father:** the sun as father, as in many mythologies   26 **orient to occident:** rising to setting, east to west   28 **photonic:** A photon is a quantum of electromagnetic energy, like those given off by the sun.   33 **the talkative:** the human species   45 **Venus and Mars:** the ancient divinities of love and war; here, the erotic and aggressive drives   50 **technocrat:** one who engineers society by scientific means

By whose grace, also, every gathering
of two or three in confident amity
    repeats the pentecostal marvel,   55
    as each in each finds his right translator.

In this world our colossal immodesty
has plundered and poisoned, it is possible
    You still might save us, who by now have
    learned this: that scientists, to be truthful,   60

must remind us to take all they say as a
tall story, that abhorred in the Heav'ns are all
    self-proclaimed poets who, to wow an
    audience, utter some resonant lie.

55 **the pentecostal marvel:** Acts 2 tells how the Holy Spirit descended on the apostles at Pentecost in the form of tongues of fire, so that they began to speak in languages not their own and were understood by all present, no matter what their native language was. 62 **Heav'ns:** Auden uses the apostrophe to show that we should count the word as one syllable, not two, in his 11-syllable lines.

A. D. Hope
(Born 1907)

Alec Derwent Hope, the leading Australian poet of our time, was born in New South Wales and was educated at Sydney University and at Oxford. Until his retirement in 1972 he was a professor of English at several Australian universities. Besides his eight books of poetry, he has written on Australian literature and on the nature of poetry.

The Brides

Down the assembly line they roll and pass
Complete at last, a miracle of design;
Their chromium fenders, the unbreakable glass,
The fashionable curve, the air-flow line.

Grease to the elbows Mum and Dad enthuse,   5
Pocket their spanners and survey the bride;
Murmur: "A sweet job! All she needs is juice!
Built for a life-time—sleek as a fish. Inside

"He will find every comfort: the full set
Of gadgets; knobs that answer to the touch   10
For light or music; a place for his cigarette;
Room for his knees; a honey of a clutch."

Now slowly through the show-room's flattering glare
See her wheeled in to love, console, obey,
Shining and silent! Parson with a prayer   15
Blesses the number-plate, she rolls away

1951. *The Wandering Islands,* 1955.

The upbringing of attractive girls who become brides is seen in terms of the production of smart new cars. "I had in mind glossy fashion magazines like *Vogue,* especially issues devoted to bridal finery, and the advertisements for expensive cars, in the same glossy magazines, in which an attractive girl is often pictured with the car." [A.D.H.]

6 **spanners:** (British) wrenches

To write her numerals in his book of life;
And now, at last, stands on the open road,
Triumphant, perfect, every inch a wife,
While the corks pop, the flash-light bulbs explode.   20

Her heavenly bowser-boy assumes his seat;
She prints the soft dust with her brand-new treads,
Swings towards the future, purring with a sweet
Concatenation of the poppet heads.

21 **bowser-boy:** "Bowser" is an Australian term for a pump at a filling station (named for the manufacturer).   24 **concatenation:** smooth working in sequence   **poppet heads:** (British) valves. *Poppet* has the advantage here of also meaning "doll, darling."

Imperial Adam

Imperial Adam, naked in the dew,
Felt his brown flanks and found the rib was gone.
Puzzled he turned and saw where, two and two,
The mighty spoor of Jahweh marked the lawn.

Then he remembered through mysterious sleep   5
The surgeon fingers probing at the bone,
The voice so far away, so rich and deep:
"It is not good for him to live alone."

Turning once more he found Man's counterpart
In tender parody breathing at his side.   10
He knew her at first sight, he knew by heart
Her allegory of sense unsatisfied.

The pawpaw drooped its golden breasts above
Less generous than the honey of her flesh;
The innocent sunlight showed the place of love;   15
The dew on its dark hairs winked crisp and fresh.

This plump gourd severed from his virile root,
She promised on the turf of Paradise
Delicious pulp of the forbidden fruit;
Sly as the snake she loosed her sinuous thighs,   20

And waking, smiled up at him from the grass;
Her breasts rose softly and he heard her sigh—
From all the beasts whose pleasant task it was
In Eden to increase and multiply

1951. *Australian Writers*, ed. T. I. Moore, 1953.

"This was sort of an after-birth at the end of delivering a term's lectures on the theology of *Paradise Lost*. But I also had in mind those splendid primitive paintings in so many American galleries of all the beasts gathering round the child and the lion lying down with the lambs etc." [A.D.H.]

1–2 Cf. Gen. 2:21–22: "And the Lord God caused a deep sleep to fall upon Adam, and he slept: and he took one of his ribs, and closed up the flesh instead thereof; and the rib, which the Lord God had taken from man, made he a woman...."   4 **spoor:** tracks   **Jahweh:** Yahweh (Hebrew), of which Jehovah is a mistaken reading   8 Cf. Gen. 2:18: "And the Lord God said, It is not good that the man should be alone; I will make him an help meet for him...."   13 **pawpaw:** here the tropical papaya, which has lush golden fruit—not the American pawpaw

Adam had learned the jolly deed of kind: 25
He took her in his arms and there and then,
Like the clean beasts, embracing from behind,
Began in joy to found the breed of men.

Then from the spurt of seed within her broke
Her terrible and triumphant female cry,   30
Split upward by the sexual lightning stroke.
It was the beasts now who stood watching by:

The gravid elephant, the calving hind,
The breeding bitch, the she-ape big with young
Were the first gentle midwives of mankind;   35
The teeming lioness rasped her with her tongue;

The proud vicuña nuzzled her as she slept
Lax on the grass; and Adam watching too
Saw how her dumb breasts at their ripening wept,
The great pod of her belly swelled and grew,   40

And saw its water break, and saw, in fear,
Its quaking muscles in the act of birth,
Between her legs a pigmy face appear,
And the first murderer lay upon the earth.

25 **kind:** nature, sex   33 **gravid:** pregnant   **hind:** deer   37 **vicuña:** a South American animal like the llama   44 **first murderer:** Cf. Gen. 4:1: "And Adam knew Eve his wife; and she conceived, and bare Cain...." And Gen. 4:8: "Cain rose up against Abel his brother, and slew him."

Louis MacNeice
(1907–1963)

MacNeice, born in Belfast in Northern Ireland, took his Oxford degree in philosophy and classics; for ten years he was a classics professor in English universities, later a visiting professor at Cornell and Sarah Lawrence. For 20 years a feature writer and producer for the BBC in London, he has many plays and other programs to his credit. Besides some 20 books of poetry, he wrote a screenplay (*The Conquest of Everest*, 1953), a novel, and a number of other volumes ranging from literary criticism to astrology.

The Sunlight on the Garden

The sunlight on the garden
Hardens and grows cold,
We cannot cage the minute
Within its nets of gold;
When all is told   5
We cannot beg for pardon.

Our freedom as free lances
Advances towards its end;
The earth compels, upon it
Sonnets and birds descend;   10

Poems, 1937.

7 **free lances:** A "free lance" was originally a knight or soldier available for hire.

And soon, my friend,
We shall have no time for dances.

The sky was good for flying
Defying the church bells
And every evil iron   15
Siren and what it tells:
The earth compels,
We are dying, Egypt, dying

And not expecting pardon,
Hardened in heart anew,   20
But glad to have sat under
Thunder and rain with you,
And grateful too
For sunlight on the garden.

18 Cf. Shakespeare's *Antony and Cleopatra*, IV, xv, Antony's words—almost his last—to the queen of
Egypt: "I am dying, Egypt, dying."

Theodore Roethke
(1908–1963)

Roethke (pronounced *rĕtt-key*) was born of German descent in Saginaw, Michigan, where
his father owned a large floral nursery. With a B.A. and an M.A. from the University of
Michigan, he did a year of further study at Harvard. He taught English, and sometimes
served as tennis coach, at Lafayette, Michigan State, Pennsylvania State, and Bennington
before going to the University of Washington in 1947, where, though troubled by peri-
ods of nervous illness, he was known as an inspiring teacher who influenced such
younger men as James Wright, David Wagoner, and Richard Hugo.

My Papa's Waltz

The whiskey on your breath
Could make a small boy dizzy;
But I hung on like death:
Such waltzing was not easy.

We romped until the pans   5
Slid from the kitchen shelf;
My mother's countenance
Could not unfrown itself.

The hand that held my wrist
Was battered on one knuckle;   10
At every step you missed
My right ear scraped a buckle.

You beat time on my head
With a palm caked hard by dirt,
Then waltzed me off to bed   15
Still clinging to your shirt.

By 1942. *The Lost Son and Other Poems*, 1948.

In an essay the poet wrote apparently while still in high school, he says: "Sometimes he dreamed
about Papa. Once it seemed Papa came in and danced around with him. John put his feet on top of Pa-
pa's, and they'd waltz. Hei-dee-dei-dei. Rump-tee-tump. Only babies expected dreams to come true"
(Allan Seager, *The Glass House*, McGraw-Hill, 1968, p. 24).

Where Knock Is Open Wide

1

A kitten can
Bite with his feet;
Papa and Mamma
Have more teeth.

Sit and play   5
Under the rocker
Until the cows
All have puppies.

His ears haven't time.
Sing me a sleep-song, please.   10
A real hurt is soft.

Once upon a tree
I came across a time,
It wasn't even as
A ghoulie in a dream.   15

There was a mooly man
Who had a rubber hat
And funnier than that,—
He kept it in a can.

What's the time, papa-seed?   20
Everything has been twice.
My father is a fish.

2

I sing a small sing,
My uncle's away,
He's gone for always,   25
I don't care either.

I know who's got him,
They'll jump on his belly,

1948–1949. *Praise to the End!*, 1951.

See Additional Notes (p. 780).

The title is line 462 of Christopher Smart's "A Song to David" (p. 232), itself based on Matt. 7:7. Even if we don't know this, it suggests beginnings, searchings, revelations. This section is about the young child's efforts to sort out the data of experience, to put them into the categories of the adult world. He is especially preoccupied with the mysteries of birth, death, sex, and guilt. No attempt is made in the notes that follow to account for every line; they are only a few clues as to how the poem might be read.

1–2 **kitten ... feet:** The young child, not at home with distinctions and discriminations, sees no difference between what adults call "bite" and what they call "scratch." Both hurt. But though the kitten can hurt, parents have power to hurt more. (Some think lines 3–4 a reference to the child's view of his parents' sex life.) 7–8 **until the cows ... puppies:** perhaps a memory of "until the cows come home"—a very long time. Though sex and birth are on the child's mind, he is confused about details. 9 **his ears haven't time:** The father has shut his ears to some request of the child (probably to sing him to sleep) with an "I don't have time." Such a hurt is "soft" compared to the kitten's bite or scratch, but goes deeper. 12–19 Perhaps a nonsense sleep-song the child sings to himself, scrambling his sentences, making up words; nonsense—but not without relevance to himself and his parents. 20 **papa-seed:** Roethke's father was a nurseryman, and as father a begetter himself. Cf. "fish" two lines below, and recall its symbolic role in "The Waste Land." 23–30 Roethke's uncle and father died (the first by suicide) within two months of each other when he was 14. He now projects

He won't be an angel,
I don't care either.   30

I know her noise.
Her neck has kittens.
I'll make a hole for her.
In the fire.

Winkie will yellow I sang.   35
Her eyes went kissing away
It was and it wasn't her there
I sang I sang all day.

3

I know it's an owl. He's making it darker.
Eat where you're at. I'm not a mouse.   40
Some stones are still warm.
I like soft paws.
Maybe I'm lost,
Or asleep.

A worm has a mouth.   45
Who keeps me last?
Fish me out.
Please.

God, give me a near. I hear flowers.
A ghost can't whistle.   50
I know! I know!
Hello happy hands.

4

We went by the river.
Water birds went ching. Went ching.
Stepped in wet. Over stones.   55
One, his nose had a frog,
But he slipped out.

I was sad for a fish.
Don't hit him on the boat, I said.
Look at him puff. He's trying to talk.   60
Papa threw him back.

Bullheads have whiskers.
And they bite.

He watered the roses.
His thumb had a rainbow.   65

these memories back to an earlier age. His "don't care" is the child's evasive defense mechanism.
31–34 The lines suggest a love-hate relationship with the mother.   39 The child is confused about
cause and effect when he hears an owl hoot as it gets dark. (Cf. Dylan Thomas, "Fern Hill," line 24, p.
674)   43–44 **lost, / Or asleep:** more confusion, this time between states of consciousness   49 **a near:**
with a pun on "an ear." Cf. the child's "Give me a napple."   **I hear flowers:** confusion between the
senses of smell and hearing. Very young children do not have neatly compartmentalized senses. (As a
deliberate literary device, rendering of the data of one sense in terms of another is called *synesthesia*,
as when we say, "That's a loud necktie" or "That music is cool.")   53–64 memories of going fishing,
when older, with the father who died   56 **his nose had a frog:** The bird—probably a heron—had a
frog in its beak.   62 **Bullheads:** a kind of catfish

The stems said, Thank you.
Dark came early.

That was before. I fell! I fell!
The worm has moved away.
My tears are tired.   70

Nowhere is out. I saw the cold.
Went to visit the wind. Where the birds die.
How high is have?
I'll be a bite. You be a wink.
Sing the snake to sleep.   75

5

Kisses come back,
I said to Papa;
He was all whitey bones
And skin like paper.

God's somewhere else,   80
I said to Mamma.
The evening came
A long long time.

I'm somebody else now.
Don't tell my hands.   85
Have I come to always? Not yet.
One father is enough.

Maybe God has a house.
But not here.

68 **before:** before the loss of the paradisal innocence of childhood, before the death of his father, and before the development of guilt feelings about sex, his attitude toward his parents, etc. 76 ff. The last section is about the death of his father, a sort of god-figure to the child, and its effect on him.

The Lost Son

1. The Flight

At Woodlawn I heard the dead cry:
I was lulled by the slamming of iron,
A slow drip over stones,
Toads brooding in wells.
All the leaves stuck out their tongues;   5
I shook the softening chalk of my bones,
Saying,
Snail, snail, glister me forward,
Bird, soft-sigh me home,
Worm, be with me.   10
This is my hard time.

1945–1946. *The Lost Son and Other Poems*, 1947.

See Additional Notes (p. 780).

1 **Woodlawn:** the cemetery where his father is buried 2 **slamming of iron:** perhaps of shovels, perhaps of the closing gates 6 **softening chalk:** as if his vigor were dissolving with the calcium in his bones 9 See Additional Notes.

Fished in an old wound,
The soft pond of repose;
Nothing nibbled my line,
Not even the minnows came.   15

Sat in an empty house
Watching shadows crawl,
Scratching.
There was one fly.

Voice, come out of the silence.   20
Say something.
Appear in the form of a spider
Or a moth beating the curtain.

Tell me:
Which is the way I take;   25
Out of what door do I go,
Where and to whom?

    Dark hollows said, lee to the wind,
    The moon said, back of an eel,
    The salt said, look by the sea,   30
    Your tears are not enough praise,
    You will find no comfort here,
    In the kingdom of bang and blab.

    Running lightly over spongy ground,
    Past the pasture of flat stones,   35
    The three elms,
    The sheep strewn on a field,
    Over a rickety bridge
    Toward the quick-water, wrinkling and rippling.

    Hunting along the river,   40
    Down among the rubbish, the bug-riddled foliage,
    By the muddy pond-edge, by the bog-holes,
    By the shrunken lake, hunting, in the heat of summer.

The shape of a rat?   45
        It's bigger than that.
        It's less than a leg
        And more than a nose,
        Just under the water
        It usually goes.

    Is it soft like a mouse?   50
    Can it wrinkle its nose?
    Could it come in the house
    On the tips of its toes?

12 **an old wound:** painful memories of the past, "that dark pond, the unconscious"   28–33 Nature, in its kingdom of bang and blab, gives him only childlike riddles for an answer, but they add up to "no comfort."   40–43 He goes deeper into the subconscious—but in imagery of a convincingly realistic world: real ooze.   44–61 What he finds in the pond or bog-hole, the fertile primeval ooze, is a greasy gliding otterlike shape, usually submerged, that we can guess stands for the fact of sex, which the poet feels underlay his frantic distractions. Though some readers have felt that the creature suggests a revulsion against sex, it seems more like an animal in a nursery rhyme, more mysterious than repulsive.

Take the skin of a cat
And the back of an eel,— 55
Then roll them in grease,—
That's the way it would feel.

It's sleek as an otter
With wide webby toes
Just under the water 60
It usually goes.

2. The Pit

Where do the roots go?
    Look down under the leaves.
Who put the moss there?
    These stones have been here too long. 65
Who stunned the dirt into noise?
    Ask the mole, he knows.
I feel the slime of a wet nest.
    Beware Mother Mildew.
Nibble again, fish nerves. 70

3. The Gibber

At the wood's mouth,
By the cave's door,
I listened to something
I had heard before.

Dogs of the groin 75
Barked and howled,
The sun was against me,
The moon would not have me.

The weeds whined,
The snakes cried, 80
The cows and briars
Said to me: Die.

What a small song. What slow clouds. What dark water.
Hath the rain a father? All the caves are ice. Only the snow's here.
I'm cold. I'm cold all over. Rub me in father and mother. 85
Fear was my father, Father Fear.
His look drained the stones.

        What gliding shape
        Beckoning through halls,
        Stood poised on the stair, 90
        Fell dreamily down?

2. The Pit: See Additional Notes (p. 781). 70 **nibble again:** In line 14 "nothing nibbled" when the speaker fished in the old wound; now he has a nibble of insight. **3. The Gibber:** See Additional Notes. 71–72 **mouth . . . door:** The images represent some kind of beginning or initiation, which "dogs of the groin" (line 75) specify as sexual 77–78 **The sun . . . The moon:** Since these are ancient and well-known symbols of male and female, they imply rejection by both parents—a rejection which, in the following stanza, all nature endorses. 84 **Hath the rain . . . ?:** Job 38:28, in which the Lord, answering Job out of the whirlwind, points out his impotence and ignorance by asking what part he played in producing the marvels of the universe. The same chapter asks, "Out of whose womb came the ice?" and "Hast thou entered into the treasures of the snow?" Recall also the "caves of ice" in Coleridge's "Kubla Khan," line 36. The Lord as father-image recalls the poet's dead father, and the awe in which the child held him. 88–99 This little lyric evokes the alluring phantom of love—or sex—and the wasteful autoeroticism it leads to. The "slither of eels" recalls the slimy swimmer of lines 44 ff.

From the mouths of jugs
Perched on many shelves,
I saw substance flowing
That cold morning.   95

Like a slither of eels
That watery cheek
As my own tongue kissed
My lips awake.

Is this the storm's heart? The ground is unstilling itself.   100
My veins are running nowhere. Do the bones cast out their fire?
Is the seed leaving the old bed? These buds are live as birds.
Where, where are the tears of the world?
Let the kisses resound, flat like a butcher's palm;
Let the gestures freeze; our doom is already decided.   105
All the windows are burning! What's left of my life?
I want the old rage, the lash of primordial milk!
Goodbye, goodbye, old stones, the time-order is going,
I have married my hands to perpetual agitation,
I run, I run to the whistle of money.   110

Money money money
Water water water

How cool the grass is.
Has the bird left?
The stalk still sways.   115
Has the worm a shadow?
What do the clouds say?

These sweeps of light undo me.
Look, look, the ditch is running white!
I've more veins than a tree!   120
Kiss me, ashes, I'm falling through a dark swirl.

4. The Return

The way to the boiler was dark,
Dark all the way,
Over slippery cinders
Through the long greenhouse.   125

The roses kept breathing in the dark.
They had many mouths to breathe with.
My knees made little winds underneath
Where the weeds slept.

There was always a single light   130
Swinging by the fire-pit,
Where the fireman pulled out roses,

---

100 ff. A sense of desolation and guilt follows the experience of the preceding song.   109–110 **agitation ... money:** As if to make up for the evil agitation of his hands, he turns to the adult world of money-making, but forsakes it (lines 112 ff.) for the more meaningful questioning of nature. 118 **sweeps of light:** moments of illumination. Throughout the poem, the progress is from darkness to light, though at the end of this section (line 121) he falls back into a "near-blackout."   **4. The Return.** The return is to the reassuring greenhouse of his childhood. See Additional Notes (p. 781). 132 **the fireman:** the man tending the fire

The big roses, the big bloody clinkers.

Once I stayed all night.
The light in the morning came slowly over the white   135
Snow.
There were many kinds of cool
Air.
Then came steam.

Pipe-knock.   140

Scurry of warm over small plants.
Ordnung! ordnung!
Papa is coming!

A fine haze moved off the leaves;
Frost melted on far panes;   145
The rose, the chrysanthemum turned toward the light.
Even the hushed forms, the bent yellowy weeds
Moved in a slow up-sway.

5. "It was beginning winter"

It was beginning winter,
An in-between time,   150
The landscape still partly brown:
The bones of weeds kept swinging in the wind,
Above the blue snow.

It was beginning winter,
The light moved slowly over the frozen field,   155
Over the dry seed-crowns,
The beautiful surviving bones
Swinging in the wind.

Light traveled over the wide field;
Stayed.   160
The weeds stopped swinging.
The mind moved, not alone,
Through the clear air, in the silence.

Was it light?
Was it light within?   165
Was it light within light?
Stillness becoming alive,
Yet still?

A lively understandable spirit
Once entertained you.   170
It will come again.
Be still.
Wait.

133 **clinkers:** the red-hot mass of fused cinders from the furnace   142 **Ordnung!:** Order! (German).
"By the *Ordnung! Ordnung!* I had also hoped to suggest the essentially Germanic character of the
'Papa,' the authority, whose Prussian love for order and discipline had been sublimated into a love
for, and a creating of the beautiful (the flowers). . . . The child, a kind of sentry guarding the flowers,
both lolling sleepily, guiltily; but jumping to attention at the *approach*" (*Letters*, p. 162).   **5. "It was
beginning winter."** See Additional Notes (p. 781).

Elegy for Jane

My Student, Thrown By a Horse

I remember the neckcurls, limp and damp as tendrils;
And her quick look, a sidelong pickerel smile;
And how, once startled into talk, the light syllables leaped for her,
And she balanced in the delight of her thought,
A wren, happy, tail into the wind,   5
Her song trembling the twigs and small branches.
The shade sang with her;
The leaves, their whispers turned to kissing;
And the mold sang in the bleached valleys under the rose.

Oh, when she was sad, she cast herself down into such a pure depth,   10
Even a father could not find her:
Scraping her cheek against straw;
Stirring the clearest water.

My sparrow, you are not here,
Waiting like a fern, making a spiny shadow.   15
The sides of wet stones cannot console me,
Nor the moss, wound with the last light.

If only I could nudge you from this sleep,
My maimed darling, my skittery pigeon.
Over this damp grave I speak the words of my love: 20
I, with no rights in this matter,
Neither father nor lover.

1949. *The Waking*, 1953.
17 "Definitely I mean the last light to imply sunset . . ." (*Letters*, 262).

The Waking

I wake to sleep, and take my waking slow.
I feel my fate in what I cannot fear.
I learn by going where I have to go.

We think by feeling. What is there to know?
I hear my being dance from ear to ear.   5
I wake to sleep, and take my waking slow.

Of those so close beside me, which are you?
God bless the Ground! I shall walk softly there,
And learn by going where I have to go.

1952. Ibid.
A *villanelle*; see the section on prosody.

1 "To wake here means to be awakened into full awareness: a paradox that this wakening does partake of the nature of an eternal wakening" (*Letters* 262). 3 Cf. the journeys of "The Lost Son." 4 **We think by feeling:** Cf. "Reason, that dreary shed . . ." ("I Cry, Love! Love!," line 14.) "This, in its essence, is a description of the metaphysical poet who thinks with his body: an idea for him can be as real as the smell of a flower or a blow on the head. And those so lucky as to bring their whole sensory equipment to bear on the process of thought grow faster, jump more frequently from one plateau to another more often." Roethke, "On 'Identity,'" in *On the Poet and His Craft*, edited by Ralph J. Mills, Jr., U. of Washington Press, 1965). 5 **I hear my being dance . . . :** "It means that the being of the speaker does its own internal dance within the mind, within the brain" (*Letters*, 262). But cf. "grin from ear to ear."

Light takes the Tree; but who can tell us how?   10
The lowly worm climbs up a winding stair;
I wake to sleep, and take my waking slow.

Great Nature has another thing to do
To you and me; so take the lively air,
And, lovely, learn by going where to go.   15

This shaking keeps me steady. I should know.
What falls away is always. And is near.
I wake to sleep, and take my waking slow.
I learn by going where I have to go.

16 **This shaking:** the changes of life: the "going," the "dance," the "walk," etc.   17 **always ... near:**
the movement of time, in which the near present flows always away

I Knew a Woman

I knew a woman, lovely in her bones,
When small birds sighed, she would sigh back at them;
Ah, when she moved, she moved more ways than one:
The shapes a bright container can contain!
Of her choice virtues only gods should speak,   5
Or English poets who grew up on Greek
(I'd have them sing in chorus, cheek to cheek).

How well her wishes went! She stroked my chin,
She taught me Turn, and Counter-turn, and Stand;
She taught me Touch, that undulant white skin;   10
I nibbled meekly from her proffered hand;
She was the sickle; I, poor I, the rake,
Coming behind her for her pretty sake
(But what prodigious mowing we did make).

Love likes a gander, and adores a goose: 15
Her full lips pursed, the errant note to seize;
She played it quick, she played it light and loose;
My eyes, they dazzled at her flowing knees;
Her several parts could keep a pure repose,
Or one hip quiver with a mobile nose   20
(She moved in circles, and those circles moved).

Let seed be grass, and grass turn into hay:
I'm martyr to a motion not my own;
What's freedom for? To know eternity.
I swear she cast a shadow white as stone.   25
But who would count eternity in days?
These old bones live to learn her wanton ways:
(I measure time by how a body sways).

By 1954. *Words for the Wind*, 1958.

If readers find amorous double-meanings in this playfully affectionate love poem, they are probably
not imagining them. Roethke was fond of puns.

9 **Turn ... :** The three capitalized words translate *strophe, antistrophe,* and *epode,* the parts of a classical
Greek ode, which correspond to dance patterns. They are so used in Ben Jonson's ode "To the Mem-
ory and Friendship of that Noble Pair Sir Lucius Cary and Sir H. Morison" (1630).   14 **mowing:** The
word follows from the sickle-and-rake image (in which *rake* has a double meaning), but Roethke prob-
ably knew *mow* (also a verb) was an obsolete Scottish word for *intercourse.*

In a Dark Time

In a dark time, the eye begins to see,
I meet my shadow in the deepening shade;
I hear my echo in the echoing wood—
A lord of nature weeping to a tree.
I live between the heron and the wren,   5
Beasts of the hill and serpents of the den.

What's madness but nobility of soul
At odds with circumstance? The day's on fire!
I know the purity of pure despair,
My shadow pinned against a sweating wall.   10
That place among the rocks—is it a cave,
Or winding path? The edge is what I have.

A steady storm of correspondences!
A night flowing with birds, a ragged moon,
And in broad day the midnight come again!   15
A man goes far to find out what he is—
Death of the self in a long, tearless night,
All natural shapes blazing unnatural light.

Dark, dark my light, and darker my desire.
My soul, like some heat-maddened summer fly,   20
Keeps buzzing at the sill. Which I is *I?*
A fallen man, I climb out of my fear.
The mind enters itself, and God the mind,
And one is One, free in the tearing wind.

1958. *The Far Field*, 1964.

The words of this poem are very simple, the thoughts they are meant to convey are not. The poem is about what we might call a "mystical experience" that brings one to the verge of madness—from which, however he recovers himself after a flash of mysterious illumination. Roethke, we remember, sometimes fell over that verge into actual derangement. See Additional Notes (p. 781).

Stephen Spender
(Born 1909)

Spender was born in London in 1909, the son of a writer; he was educated at Oxford. An editor of *Horizon* and *Encounter*, he has, during the course of a busy and varied career, made many visits to the United States and lectured and taught at many American universities. Since 1970 he has been professor of English literature at University College, London. He has written, edited, or translated over 75 books of poetry, plays, fiction, and criticism.

I Think Continually of Those Who Were Truly Great

I think continually of those who were truly great.
Who, from the womb, remembered the soul's history
Through corridors of light where the hours are suns,
Endless and singing. Whose lovely ambition
Was that their lips, still touched with fire,   5
Should tell of the Spirit, clothed from head to foot in song.
And who hoarded from the Spring branches
The desires falling across their bodies like blossoms.

1931–1932. *Poems*, 1934.

What is precious, is never to forget
The essential delight of the blood drawn from ageless springs   10
Breaking through rocks in worlds before our earth.
Never to deny its pleasure in the morning simple light
Nor its grave evening demand for love.
Never to allow gradually the traffic to smother
With noise and fog, the flowering of the Spirit.   15

Near the snow, near the sun, in the highest fields,
See how these names are fêted by the waving grass
And by the streamers of white cloud
And whispers of wind in the listening sky.
The names of those who in their lives fought for life,   20
Who wore at their hearts the fire's center.
Born of the sun, they travelled a short while toward the sun
And left the vivid air signed with their honour.

Robert Fitzgerald
(Born 1910)

Born in Geneva, New York, Fitzgerald grew up in Springfield, Illinois; his college work was done at Harvard and Cambridge. For two years he was a reporter for the *New York Herald-Tribune*; and for about ten years a staff writer for *Time*. During World War II he served for three years in the navy; for over ten years he lived with his family in Italy. He has taught at Sarah Lawrence, Princeton, and, since 1965, at Harvard, where he succeeded Archibald MacLeish as Boylston Professor of Rhetoric. In addition to writing four books of poetry, he has translated the *Iliad* and *Odyssey* and is now engaged in translating Vergil's *Aeneid*.

Cobb Would Have Caught It

In sunburnt parks where Sundays lie,
Or the wide wastes beyond the cities,
Teams in grey deploy through sunlight.

Talk it up, boys, a little practice.

Coming in stubby and fast, the baseman   5
Gathers a grounder in fat green grass,
Picks it stinging and clipped as wit
Into the leather: a swinging step
Wings it deadeye down to first.
Smack. Oh, attaboy, attyoldboy.   10

Catcher reverses his cap, pulls down
Sweaty casque, and squats in the dust:
Pitcher rubs new ball on his pants,
Chewing, puts a jet behind him;
Nods past batter, taking his time.   15
Batter settles, tugs at his cap:
A spinning ball: step and swing to it,

1941. *A Wreath for the Sea*, 1943.

Tyrus Raymond ("Ty") Cobb (1886–1961), known as a fierce competitor during his 22 years as an outfielder for the Detroit Tigers, may have been the greatest baseball player of all time. He holds many records: most times at bat, most hits, highest lifetime batting average (.367).

3 **deploy:** take their positions (chiefly military)   12 **casque:** helmet; here, the catcher's mask

Caught like a cheek before it ducks
By shivery hickory: socko, baby:
Cleats dig into dust. Outfielder,   20
On his way, looking over shoulder,
Makes it a triple. A long peg home.

Innings and afternoons. Fly lost in sunset.
Throwing arm gone bad. There's your old ball game.
Cool reek of the field. Reek of companions.   25

Elizabeth Bishop
(1911–1979)

Miss Bishop's own rephrasing of her biographical note reads as follows: "Born in Massa-
chusetts in 1911 but spent some childhood years with her Canadian grandparents in
Nova Scotia. Graduated from Vassar; lived in New York and Key West and later for 17
years in Brazil, translated a famous Brazilian diary and co-edited and helped translate a
volume of modern Brazilian poetry. . . . She has taught briefly at the University of Wash-
ington, at Harvard for seven years, and recently at New York University and MIT, one
term each." She died suddenly in Cambridge, Massachusetts.

The Fish

I caught a tremendous fish
and held him beside the boat
half out of water, with my hook
fast in a corner of his mouth.
He didn't fight.   5
He hadn't fought at all.
He hung a grunting weight,
battered and venerable
and homely. Here and there
his brown skin hung in strips   10
like ancient wallpaper,
and its pattern of darker brown
was like wallpaper:
shapes like full-blown roses
stained and lost through age.   15
He was speckled with barnacles,
fine rosettes of lime,
and infested
with tiny white sea-lice,

North and South, 1946.

In a letter of October 6, 1979, Elizabeth Bishop objected "rather violently" to the idea of having foot-
notes for her poems. While admitting that poems of earlier centuries might need them, she wrote:
"With one or two exceptions . . . I don't think there should be ANY footnotes—for me [my poems],
that is . . . the book is for college students, and I think anyone who gets as far as college should be able
to use a dictionary. . . . If a poem catches a student's interest at all, he or she should damned well be
able to look up an unfamiliar word in the dictionary. . . . 'Isinglass' is in the dictionary; so is 'gunnel';
so is 'thwart.' . . . All flower names can be looked up, certainly—some students even SEE flowers still
although I know only too well that TV has weakened the sense of reality so that very few students see
anything the way it is in real life. . . ." She concluded with: "If you can get any students to *reading* you
will have done a noble work." Her objections to the footnotes that would otherwise have been here
have been honored. But since she once said she was more pleased by a remark of Ernest Hemingway
than by any praise in the literary quarterlies, she would not mind our repeating it: shown "The Fish"
Hemingway said, "I wish I knew as much about it as she does." Miss Bishop said she "knew that un-
derneath Mr. H and I were really a lot alike."

and underneath two or three   20
rags of green weed hung down.
While his gills were breathing in
the terrible oxygen
—the frightening gills,
fresh and crisp with blood,   25
that can cut so badly—
I thought of the coarse white flesh
packed in like feathers,
the big bones and the little bones,
the dramatic reds and blacks   30
of his shiny entrails,
and the pink swim-bladder
like a big peony.
I looked into his eyes
which were far larger than mine   35
but shallower, and yellowed,
the irises backed and packed
with tarnished tinfoil
seen through the lenses
of old scratched isinglass.   40
They shifted a little, but not
to return my stare.
—It was more like the tipping
of an object toward the light.
I admired his sullen face.   45
the mechanism of his jaw,
and then I saw
that from his lower lip
—if you could call it a lip—
grim, wet, and weaponlike,   50
hung five old pieces of fish-line,
or four and a wire leader
with the swivel still attached,
with all their five big hooks
grown firmly in his mouth.   55
A green line, frayed at the end
where he broke it, two heavier lines,
and a fine black thread
still crimped from the strain and snap
when it broke and he got away.   60
Like medals with their ribbons
frayed and wavering,
a five-haired beard of wisdom
trailing from his aching jaw.
I stared and stared   65
and victory filled up
the little rented boat,
from the pool of bilge
where oil had spread a rainbow
around the rusted engine   70
to the bailer rusted orange,
the sun-cracked thwarts,
the oarlocks on their strings,
the gunnels—until everything
was rainbow, rainbow, rainbow!   75
And I let the fish go.

At the Fishhouses

Although it is a cold evening,
down by one of the fishhouses
an old man sits netting,
his net, in the gloaming almost invisible
a dark purple-brown, 5
and his shuttle worn and polished.
The air smells so strong of codfish
it makes one's nose run and one's eyes water.
The five fishhouses have steeply peaked roofs
and narrow, cleated gangplanks slant up 10
to storerooms in the gables
for the wheelbarrows to be pushed up and down on.
All is silver: the heavy surface of the sea,
swelling slowly as if considering spilling over,
is opaque, but the silver of the benches, 15
the lobster pots, and masts, scattered
among the wild jagged rocks,
is of an apparent translucence
like the small old buildings with an emerald moss
growing on their shoreward walls. 20
The big fish tubs are completely lined
with layers of beautiful herring scales
and the wheelbarrows are similarly plastered
with creamy iridescent coats of mail,
with small iridescent flies crawling on them. 25
Up on the little slope behind the houses,
set in the sparse bright sprinkle of grass,
is an ancient wooden capstan,
cracked, with two long bleached handles
and some melancholy stains, like dried blood, 30
where the ironwork has rusted.
The old man accepts a Lucky Strike.
He was a friend of my grandfather.
We talk of the decline in the population
and of codfish and herring 35
while he waits for a herring boat to come in.
There are sequins on his vest and on his thumb.
He has scraped the scales, the principal beauty,
from unnumbered fish with that black old knife,
the blade of which is almost worn away. 40

Down at the water's edge, at the place
where they haul up the boats, up the long ramp
descending into the water, thin silver
tree trunks are laid horizontally
across the gray stones, down and down 45
at intervals of four or five feet.

Cold dark deep and absolutely clear,
element bearable to no mortal,
to fish and to seals . . . One seal particularly
I have seen here evening after evening. 50
He was curious about me. He was interested in music;
like me a believer in total immersion,

By 1947. *Poems: North and South—A Cold Spring,* 1955.

so I used to sing him Baptist hymns.
I also sang "A Mighty Fortress Is Our God."
He stood up in the water and regarded me   55
steadily, moving his head a little.
Then he would disappear, then suddenly emerge
almost in the same spot, with a sort of shrug
as if it were against his better judgment.
Cold dark deep and absolutely clear,   60
the clear gray icy water . . . Back, behind us,
the dignified tall firs begin.
Bluish, associating with their shadows,
a million Christmas trees stand
waiting for Christmas. The water seems suspended   65
above the rounded gray and blue-gray stones.
I have seen it over and over, the same sea, the same,
slightly, indifferently swinging above the stones,
icily free above the stones,
above the stones and then the world.   70
If you should dip your hand in,
your wrist would ache immediately,
your bones would begin to ache and your hand would burn
as if the water were a transmutation of fire
that feeds on stones and burns with a dark gray flame.   75
If you tasted it, it would first taste bitter,
then briny, then surely burn your tongue.
It is like what we imagine knowledge to be:
dark, salt, clear, moving, utterly free,
drawn from the cold hard mouth   80
of the world, derived from the rocky breasts
forever, flowing and drawn, and since
our knowledge is historical, flowing, and flown.

Filling Station

Oh, but it is dirty!
—this little filling station,
oil-soaked, oil-permeated
to a disturbing, over-all
black translucency.   5
Be careful with that match!

Father wears a dirty,
oil-soaked monkey suit
that cuts him under the arms,
and several quick and saucy   10
and greasy sons assist him
(it's a family filling station),
all quite thoroughly dirty.

Do they live in the station?
It has a cement porch   15
behind the pumps, and on it
a set of crushed and grease-
impregnated wickerwork;
on the wicker sofa
a dirty dog, quite comfy.   20

_____
By 1955. *Questions of Travel*, 1965.

Some comic books provide
the only note of color—
of certain color. They lie
upon a big dim doily
draping a taboret   25
(part of the set), beside
a big hirsute begonia.

Why the extraneous plant?
Why the taboret?
Why, oh why, the doily?   30
(Embroidered in daisy stitch
with marguerites, I think,
and heavy with gray crochet.)

Somebody embroidered the doily.
Somebody waters the plant,   35
or oils it, maybe. Somebody
arranges the rows of cans
so that they softly say:
ESSO—SO—SO—SO
to high-strung automobiles.   40
Somebody loves us all.

39 **ESSO:** (S.O.) a name for Standard Oil, now replaced by Exxon in the United States. Looking along a line of cans marked ESSO, one might see only the SO SO SO on all but the first. "So-so-so was—or still is in some places—the phrase people use to calm and soothe nervous horses." [E.B.]

One Art

The art of losing isn't hard to master;
so many things seem filled with the intent
to be lost that their loss is no disaster.

Lose something every day. Accept the fluster
of lost door keys, the hour badly spent.   5
The art of losing isn't hard to master.

Then practice losing farther, losing faster:
places, and names, and where it was you meant
to travel. None of these will bring disaster.

I lost my mother's watch. And look! my last, or   10
next-to-last, of three loved houses went.
The art of losing isn't hard to master.

I lost two cities, lovely ones. And, vaster,
some realms I owned, two rivers, a continent.
I miss them, but it wasn't a disaster.   15

—Even losing you (the joking voice, a gesture
I love) I shan't have lied. It's evident
the art of losing's not too hard to master
though it may look like (*Write* it!) like disaster.

Geography III, 1976.

J. V. Cunningham
(Born 1911)

James Vincent Cunningham, born in Cumberland, Maryland, was educated at St. Mary's College (Kansas) and at Stanford, from which he has a Ph.D. He has taught at Stanford, the University of Chicago, and, since 1953, at Brandeis, though serving as visiting professor at Harvard, the University of Washington, and elsewhere. Besides his eight books of poetry, he has written several volumes of criticism.

From **A Century of Epigrams**

39. This is my curse. Pompous, I pray
    That you believe the things you say
    And that you live them, day by day.

53. On a cold night I came through the cold rain
    And false snow to the wind shrill on your pane
    With no hope and no anger and no fear.
    Who are you? and with whom do you sleep here?

54. And what is love? Misunderstanding, pain,
    Delusion, or retreat? It is in truth
    Like an old brandy after a long rain,
    Distinguished, and familiar, and aloof.

First, 1944; others, 1950. *The Collected Poems and Epigrams of J. V. Cunningham*, 1971.

Kenneth Patchen
(1911–1972)

Born in Niles, Ohio, the son of a steelworker, Patchen began to work in the mills when he was 17. For a year he attended the University of Wisconsin at Milwaukee as honor student and all-round athlete. During the Depression he worked at odd jobs; in his twenties he began to suffer from the spinal ailment that, after two operations, confined him to his bed, often in pain, for the last dozen years of his life. Even so he produced over 50 books of poetry, fiction, and drama, some of which he illustrated himself.

O All down within the Pretty Meadow

> *how many times, Death*
> *have you done it*

The Lovers

> *to just such golden ones*   5
> *as these*

Toss at Their Wondrous Play

O how many times, Death, have you done it
To just such golden ones as these

Pictures of Life and Death, 1946.

Robert Hayden
(1913–1980)

Born in Detroit, Hayden was educated at Wayne State and the University of Michigan. After some 20 years of teaching at Fiske University (Nashville), he returned to the University of Michigan as Professor of English. In 1976 he was appointed Consultant in Poetry at the Library of Congress. Besides his teaching, he was poetry editor of the Baha'i journal *World Order*.

Those Winter Sundays

Sundays too my father got up early
and put his clothes on in the blueblack cold,
then with cracked hands that ached
from labor in the weekday weather made
banked fires blaze. No one ever thanked him.   5

I'd wake and hear the cold splintering, breaking.
When the rooms were warm, he'd call,
and slowly I would rise and dress,
fearing the chronic angers of that house,

Speaking indifferently to him,   10
who had driven out the cold
and polished my good shoes as well.
What did I know, what did I know
of love's austere and lonely offices?

A Ballad of Remembrance, 1962.

O Daedalus, Fly Away Home

Drifting night in the Georgia pines,
coonskin drum and jubilee banjo.
    Pretty Malinda, dance with me.

Night is juba, night is conjo.
    Pretty Malinda, dance with me.   5

Night is an African juju man
weaving a wish and a weariness together
    to make two wings.

    O fly away home fly away

Do you remember Africa?   10

    O cleave the air fly away home

My gran, he flew back to Africa,
just spread his arms and
    flew away home.

By 1943. Ibid.

Daedalus: Cf. note on W. H. Auden's "Musée des Beaux Arts" (p. 626).   4 **juba:** a dance with hand clapping   **conjo:** magical objects used in rituals   6 **juju man:** man who knows use of magical objects

Drifting night in the windy pines;   15
night is a laughing, night is a longing.
    Pretty Malinda, come to me.

Night is a mourning juju man
weaving a wish and a weariness together
    to make two wings.   20

    O fly away home fly away

Karl Shapiro
(Born 1913)

Shapiro, born in Baltimore, was educated at the University of Virginia, Johns Hopkins,
and Pratt Library School. From 1941 to 1945 he was with the army in the South Pacific.
He has taught at Johns Hopkins, the University of Nebraska, the University of Illinois at
Chicago Circle, and, since 1968, at the University of California at Davis. From 1950 to
1956 he was editor of *Poetry* (Chicago); from 1956 to 1966, of *Prairie Schooner*. Besides
about a dozen books of poetry, he has written a play, a novel, and several books of criti-
cism.

A Cut Flower

I stand on slenderness all fresh and fair,
I feel root-firmness in the earth far down,
I catch in the wind and loose my scent for bees
That sack my throat for kisses and suck love.
What is the wind that brings thy body over?   5
Wind, I am beautiful and sick. I long
For rain that strikes and bites like cold and hurts.
Be angry, rain, for dew is kind to me
When I am cool from sleep and take my bath.

Who softens the sweet earth about my feet,   10
Touches my face so often and brings water?
Where does she go, taller than any sunflower
Over the grass like birds? Has she a root?
These are great animals that kneel to us,
Sent by the sun perhaps to help us grow.   15
I have seen death. The colors went away,
The petals grasped at nothing and curled tight.
Then the whole head fell off and left the sky.

She tended me and held me by my stalk.
Yesterday I was well, and then the gleam,   20
The thing sharper than frost cut me in half.
I fainted and was lifted high. I feel
Waist-deep in rain. My face is dry and drawn.
My beauty leaks into the glass like rain.
When first I opened to the sun I thought   25
My colors would be parched. Where are my bees?
Must I die now? Is this a part of life?

Person, Place, and Thing, 1942.

The Leg

Among the iodoform, in twilight-sleep,
What have I lost? he first inquires,
Peers in the middle distance where a pain,
Ghost of a nurse, hazily moves, and day,
Her blinding presence pressing in his eyes   5
And now his ears. They are handling him
With rubber hands. He wants to get up.

One day beside some flowers near his nose
He will be thinking, *When will I look at it?*
And pain, still in the middle distance, will reply,   10
At what? and he will know it's gone,
O where! and begin to tremble and cry.
He will begin to cry as a child cries
Whose puppy is mangled under a screaming wheel.

Later, as if deliberately, his fingers   15
Begin to explore the stump. He learns a shape
That is comfortable and tucked in like a sock.
This has a sense of humor, this can despise
The finest surgical limb, the dignity of limping,
The nonsense of wheel chairs. Now he smiles to the wall: 20
The amputation becomes an acquisition.

For the leg is wondering where he is (all is not lost)
And surely he has a duty to the leg;
He is its injury, the leg is his orphan,
He must cultivate the mind of the leg,   25
Pray for the part that is missing, pray for peace
In the image of man, pray, pray for its safety,
And after a little it will die quietly.

The body, what is it, Father, but a sign
To love the force that grows us, to give back   30
What in Thy palm is senselessness and mud?
Knead, knead the substance of our understanding
Which must be beautiful in flesh to walk,
That if Thou take me angrily in hand
And hurl me to the shark, I shall not die!   35

V-Letter and Other Poems, 1944.

1 **iodoform:** an antiseptic   **twilight-sleep:** a state produced by an injection of morphine and scopolo-
mine in which awareness and memory of pain is dulled or effaced

Elegy for a Dead Soldier

I

A white sheet on the tail-gate of a truck
Becomes an altar; two small candlesticks
Sputter at each side of the crucifix

V-Letter and Other Poems, 1944.

The soldier the poem was about was killed in the South Pacific during World War II.

Laid round with flowers brighter than the blood,
Red as the red of our apocalypse,   5
Hibiscus that a marching man will pluck
To stick into his rifle or his hat,
And great blue morning-glories pale as lips
That shall no longer taste or kiss or swear.
The wind begins a low magnificat,   10
The chaplain chats, the palmtrees swirl their hair,
The columns come together through the mud.

II
We too are ashes as we watch and hear
The psalm, the sorrow, and the simple praise
Of one whose promised thoughts of other days   15
Were such as ours, but now wholly destroyed,
The service record of his youth wiped out,
His dream dispersed by shot, must disappear.
What can we feel but wonder at a loss
That seems to point at nothing but the doubt   20
Which flirts our sense of luck into the ditch?
Reader of Paul who prays beside this fosse,
Shall we believe our eyes or legends rich
With glory and rebirth beyond the void?

III
For this comrade is dead, dead in the war,   25
A young man out of millions yet to live,
One cut away from all that war can give,
Freedom of self and peace to wander free.
Who mourns in all this sober multitude
Who did not feel the bite of it before   30
The bullet found its aim? This worthy flesh,
This boy laid in a coffin and reviewed—
Who has not wrapped himself in this same flag,
Heard the light fall of dirt, his wound still fresh,
Felt his eyes closed, and heard the distant brag   35
Of the last volley of humanity?

IV
By chance I saw him die, stretched on the ground,
A tattooed arm lifted to take the blood
Of someone else sealed in a tin. I stood
During the last delirium that stays   40
The intelligence a tiny moment more,
And then the strangulation, the last sound.
The end was sudden, like a foolish play,
A stupid fool slamming a foolish door,
The absurd catastrophe, half-prearranged,   45
And all the decisive things still left to say.
So we disbanded, angrier and unchanged,
Sick with the utter silence of dispraise.

---

5 apocalypse: a revelation, generally after such widespread destruction as that of a world war   **6 hibiscus:** a plant with showy flowers   **10 magnificat:** song or speech of praise (from the Latin version of Luke 1:46: "My soul *doth magnify* the Lord . . .")   **21 flirts:** flicks   **22 reader of Paul:** a Christian, who would know St. Paul's preachings on the immortality of the soul   **fosse:** ditch, grave

V

We ask for no statistics of the killed,
For nothing political impinges on   50
This single casualty, or all those gone,
Missing or healing, sinking or dispersed,
Hundreds of thousands counted, millions lost.
More than an accident and less than willed
Is every fall, and this one like the rest.   55
However others calculate the cost,
To us the final aggregate is *one*,
One with a name, one transferred to the blest;
And though another stoops and takes the gun,
We cannot add the second to the first.   60

VI

I would not speak for him who could not speak
Unless my fear were true: he was not wronged,
He knew to which decision he belonged
But let it choose itself. Ripe in instinct,
Neither the victim nor the volunteer,   65
He followed, and the leaders could not seek
Beyond the followers. Much of this he knew;
The journey was a detour that would steer
Into the Lincoln Highway of a land
Remorselessly improved, excited, new,   70
And that was what he wanted. He had planned
To earn and drive. He and the world had winked.

VII

No history deceived him, for he knew
Little of times and armies not his own;
He never felt that peace was but a loan,   75
Had never questioned the idea of gain.
Beyond the headlines once or twice he saw
The gathering of a power by the few
But could not tell their names; he cast his vote,
Distrusting all the elected but not law.   80
He laughed at socialism; *on mourrait*
Pour les industriels? He shed his coat
And not for brotherhood, but for his pay.
To him the red flag marked the sewer main.

VIII

Above all else he loathed the homily,   85
The slogan and the ad. He paid his bill,
But not for Congressmen at Bunker Hill.
Ideals were few and those there were not made
For conversation. He belonged to church
But never spoke of God. The Christmas tree,   90
The Easter egg, baptism, he observed,
Never denied the preacher on his perch,

---

69 **Lincoln Highway:** Interstate 80, the first transcontinental highway   81–82 *on mourrait pour les*
industriels?: (French) One would die for the factory owners? "I got [this] from an Anatole France nov-
el but can't remember which, or what character said it. Some socialist? Maybe *The Revolt of the An-*
gels?" [K.S.]   84 **the red flag:** the flag of communism or revolution   85 **homily:** sermon   87 **Bunk-**
er Hill: site of the famous Revolutionary War battle at Boston—in our time, the poem implies, a
favorite spot for patriotic speeches

And would not sign Resolved That or Whereas.
Softness he had and hours and nights reserved
For thinking, dressing, dancing to the jazz.   95
His laugh was real, his manners were homemade.

IX

Of all men poverty pursued him least;
He was ashamed of all the down and out,
Spurned the panhandler like an uneasy doubt,
And saw the unemployed as a vague mass   100
Incapable of hunger or revolt.
He hated other races, south or east,
And shoved them to the margin of his mind.
He could recall the justice of the Colt,
Take interest in a gang-war like a game.   105
His ancestry was somewhere far behind
And left him only his peculiar name.
Doors opened, and he recognized no class.

X

His children would have known a heritage,
Just or unjust, the richest in the world,   110
The quantum of all art and science curled
In the horn of plenty, bursting from the horn,
A people bathed in honey, Paris come,
Vienna transferred with the highest wage,
A World's Fair spread to Phoenix, Jacksonville,   115
Earth's capital, the new Byzantium,
Kingdom of man—who knows? Hollow or firm,
No man can ever prophesy until
Out of our death some undiscovered germ,
Whole toleration or pure peace is born.   120

XI

The time to mourn is short that best becomes
The military dead. We lift and fold the flag,
Lay bare the coffin with its written tag,
And march away. Behind, four others wait
To lift the box, the heaviest of loads.   125
The anesthetic afternoon benumbs,
Sickens our senses, forces back our talk.
We know that others on tomorrow's roads
Will fall, ourselves perhaps, the man beside,
Over the world the threatened, all who walk: 130
And could we mark the grave of him who died
We would write this beneath his name and date:

Epitaph

Underneath this wooden cross there lies
A Christian killed in battle. You who read,
Remember that this stranger died in pain;   135
And passing here, if you can lift your eyes
Upon a peace kept by a human creed,
Know that one soldier has not died in vain.

---

111 **quantum:** bulk   116 **Byzantium:** Cf. notes on Yeats's "Sailing to Byzantium" (p. 467).

Waiting in Front of the Columnar High School

Waiting in front of the columnar high school (the old ones look like
    banks, or rather insurance companies) I glance over the top of my
    book. The bells go off like slow burglar alarms; innumerable six-
    teeners saunter out. There's no running as in the lower schools,
    none of that helpless gaiety of the small. Here comes a surly defi-   5
    ance. As in a ritual, each lights a cigaret just at the boundary
    where the tabu ends. Each chews. The ones in cars rev up their
    motors and have bad complexions like gangsters. The sixteeners
    are all playing gangster.

The sea of subjectivity comes at you like a tidal wave, splashing the cuffs   10
    of middle-aged monuments. War is written on their unwritten
    faces. They try out wet dreams and wandering mind. They're rub-
    bing Aladdin's lamp in the locker room. They pray for moments
    of objectivity as drunkards pray for the one that puts you out.
    They've captured the telephone centers, the microphones, the   15
    magazine syndicates (they've left the movies to us). I wait behind
    the wheel and spy; it's enemy territory all right. My daughter
    comes, grows taller as she approaches. It's a moment of panic.

But once at night in the sweet and sour fall I dropped her off at the foot-
    ball game. The bowl of light lit up the creamy Corinthian col-   20
    umns. A cheer went up from the field so shrill, so young, like a
    thousand birds in a single cage, like a massacre of child-brides in
    a clearing, I felt ashamed and grave. The horror of their years
    stoned me to death.

The Bourgeois Poet, 1964.

Dudley Randall
(Born 1914)

Born in Washington, D.C., Randall was educated at Wayne State University and the Uni-
versity of Michigan. From 1943 to 1946 he was with the army signal corps. He has had
posts as librarian at several universities; since 1969 he has been librarian and poet-in-
residence at the University of Detroit. Besides writing his own poetry, he has, as founder
of the Broadside Press in Detroit, published many of the leading black poets.

Blackberry Sweet

Black girl black girl
lips as curved as cherries
full as grape bunches
sweet as blackberries

Black girl black girl   5
when you walk you are
magic as a rising bird
or a falling star

Black girl black girl
what's your spell to make   10
the heart in my breast
jump stop shake

1956; revised 1969. *The New Black Poetry*, ed. by Clarence Major, 1969.

William Stafford
(Born 1914)

Born in Hutchinson, Kansas, educated at the University of Kansas and the University of
Iowa, from which he has a Ph.D., Stafford has spent most of his adult life in Oregon,
where he now teaches at Lewis and Clark College in Portland. Besides several volumes of
poetry, he has written some critical essays and a book on his experiences as a conscien-
tious objector in World War II.

The Farm on the Great Plains

A telephone line goes cold;
birds tread it wherever it goes.
A farm back of a great plain
tugs an end of the line.

I call that farm every year,   5
ringing it, listening, still;
no one is home at the farm,
the line gives only a hum.

Some year I will ring the line
on a night at last the right one,   10
and with an eye tapered for braille
from the phone on the wall

I will see the tenant who waits—
the last one left at the place;
through the dark my braille eye   15
will lovingly touch his face.

"Hello, is Mother at home?"
No one is home today.
"But Father—he should be there."
No one—no one is here.   20

"But you—are you the one . . . ?"
Then the line will be gone
because both ends will be home:
no space, no birds, no farm.

My self will be the plain,   25
wise as winter is gray,
pure as cold posts go
pacing toward what I know.

1956. *West of Your City*, 1960.

Traveling Through the Dark

Traveling through the dark I found a deer
dead on the edge of the Wilson River road.
It is usually best to roll them into the canyon:
that road is narrow; to swerve might make more dead.

1956. *Traveling Through the Dark*, 1962.

2 **Wilson River:** a river in the Coast Range of northwestern Oregon

By glow of the tail-light I stumbled back of the car   5
and stood by the heap, a doe, a recent killing;
she had stiffened already, almost cold.
I dragged her off; she was large in the belly.

My fingers touching her side brought me the reason—
her side was warm; her fawn lay there waiting,   10
alive, still, never to be born.
Beside that mountain road I hesitated.

The car aimed ahead its lowered parking lights;
under the hood purred the steady engine.
I stood in the glare of the warm exhaust turning red;   15
around our group I could hear the wilderness listen.

I thought hard for us all—my only swerving—,
then pushed her over the edge into the river.

At the Un-National Monument Along the Canadian Border

This is the field where the battle did not happen,
where the unknown soldier did not die.
This is the field where grass joined hands,
where no monument stands,
and the only heroic thing is the sky.   5

Birds fly here without any sound,
unfolding their wings across the open.
No people killed—or were killed—on this ground
hallowed by neglect and an air so tame
that people celebrate it by forgetting its name.   10

1962. *Stories That Could Be True,* 1977.

The poem "came from my seeing a picture of the border between Montana and Alberta—there was nothing, just grass. But it is true, also, that there is a well-known 'Peace Arch' between Washington and British Columbia, and I guess I was partly relying on that 'un-national' feeling. I prefer the monument that isn't there, though." [W.S.]

Randall Jarrell
(1914–1965)

Jarrell, born in Nashville, spent most of his childhood in California. His major at Vanderbilt was in psychology; under the influence of Ransom and other Fugitives he switched to English. For two years he taught at Kenyon College (where Ransom had gone); then for three at the University of Texas (Austin). During World War II he served in Illinois and Arizona as a celestial navigation tower operator. Afterwards he taught at the University of North Carolina at Greensboro and was poetry editor and reviewer for several distinguished magazines. Besides his poetry, he wrote a novel, several books for children, and half a dozen volumes of translation and criticism.

The Death of the Ball Turret Gunner

From my mother's sleep I fell into the State,
And I hunched in its belly till my wet fur froze.
Six miles from earth, loosed from its dream of life,
I woke to black flak and the nightmare fighters.
When I died they washed me out of the turret with a hose.   5

1944. *Little Friend, Little Friend,* 1945.

"A ball turret was a plexiglass sphere set in the belly of a B-17 or B-24, and inhabited by two .50 cali-
ber machine-guns and one man, a short small man. When this gunner tracked with his machine-guns
a fighter attacking his bomber from below, he revolved with the turret; hunched upside-down in his
little sphere, he looked like the foetus in the womb. The fighters which attacked him were armed
with cannon firing explosive shells. The hose was a steam hose." [Jarrell]

4 **flak:** shells from antiaircraft guns

The Woman at the Washington Zoo

The saris go by me from the embassies.

Cloth from the moon. Cloth from another planet.
They look back at the leopard like the leopard.

And I. . . .
            this print of mine, that has kept its color
Alive through so many cleanings; this dull null   5
Navy I wear to work, and wear from work, and so
To my bed, so to my grave, with no
Complaints, no comment: neither from my chief,
The Deputy Chief Assistant, nor his chief—
Only I complain. . . . this serviceable   10
Body that no sunlight dyes, no hand suffuses
But, dome-shadowed, withering among columns,
Wavy beneath fountains—small, far-off, shining
In the eyes of animals, these beings trapped
As I am trapped but not, themselves, the trap,   15
Aging, but without knowledge of their age,
Kept safe here, knowing not of death, for death—
Oh, bars of my own body, open, open!

The world goes by my cage and never sees me.
And there come not to me, as come to these,   20
The wild beasts, sparrows pecking the llamas' grain,
Pigeons settling on the bears' bread, buzzards
Tearing the meat the flies have clouded. . . .
                                        Vulture,
When you come for the white rat that the foxes left,
Take off the red helmet of your head, the black   25
Wings that have shadowed me, and step to me as man:
The wild brother at whose feet the white wolves fawn,

1958. *The Woman at the Washington Zoo,* 1960.

1 **saris:** A sari is a gracefully draped garment worn by Hindu women. (The speaker in this poem, in
her "dull null navy" print, is a woman, an office-worker who feels trapped in her job, in her life. She
envies the leopardlike Hindu women, envies the animals themselves.)   23 **Vulture:** She addresses
the vulture, in its "red helmet," as if it were an enchanted prince from a fairy tale who could appear
to her as a man whose love could save her from the monotony of her life.

To whose hand of power the great lioness
Stalks, purring. . . .
>   You know what I was,
You see what I am: change me, change me!   30

Next Day

Moving from Cheer to Joy, from Joy to All,
I take a box
And add it to my wild rice, my Cornish game hens.
The slacked or shorted, basketed, identical
Food-gathering flocks   5
Are selves I overlook. Wisdom, said William James,

Is learning what to overlook. And I am wise
If that is wisdom.
Yet somehow, as I buy All from these shelves
And the boy takes it to my station wagon,   10
What I've become
Troubles me even if I shut my eyes.

When I was young and miserable and pretty
And poor, I'd wish
What all girls wish: to have a husband,   15
A house and children. Now that I'm old, my wish
Is womanish:
That the boy putting groceries in my car

See me. It bewilders me he doesn't see me.
For so many years   20
I was good enough to eat: the world looked at me
And its mouth watered. How often they have undressed me,
The eyes of strangers!
And, holding their flesh within my flesh, their vile

Imaginings within my imagining,   25
I too have taken
The chance of life. Now the boy pats my dog
And we start home. Now I am good.
The last mistaken,
Ecstatic, accidental bliss, the blind   30

Happiness that, bursting, leaves upon the palm
Some soap and water—
It was so long ago, back in some Gay
Twenties, Nineties, I don't know . . . Today I miss
My lovely daughter   35
Away at school, my sons away at school,

My husband away at work—I wish for them.
The dog, the maid,
And I go through the sure unvarying days

1964. *The Lost World*, 1965.

The title refers to "the funeral I went to yesterday" (lines 49–50).

1 **Cheer . . . Joy . . . All**: the well-known detergents, their names ironic in this cheerless poem
6 **William James**: the American psychologist and philosopher (1842–1910), brother of Henry James

At home in them. As I look at my life,   40
I am afraid
Only that it will change, as I am changing:

I am afraid, this morning, of my face.
It looks at me
From the rear-view mirror, with the eyes I hate,   45
The smile I hate. Its plain, lined look
Of gray discovery
Repeats to me: "You're old." That's all, I'm old.

And yet I'm afraid, as I was at the funeral
I went to yesterday.   50
My friend's cold made-up face, granite among its flowers,
Her undressed, operated-on, dressed body
Were my face and body.
As I think of her I hear her telling me

How young I seem; I *am* exceptional;   55
I think of all I have.
But really no one is exceptional,
No one has anything, I'm anybody,
I stand beside my grave
Confused with my life, that is commonplace and solitary.   ·60

John Berryman
(1914–1972)

Born as John Smith in McAlester, Oklahoma, Berryman (who took the name of his step-father) was the son of a banker whose suicide when the boy was 12 was a source of life-long trauma. As a child he moved about from his birthplace to Tampa to Gloucester to New York City; upon graduating from Columbia he went to Cambridge on a fellowship. Berryman taught at Wayne State, Princeton, Harvard, and elsewhere before moving, in 1955, to the University of Minnesota. Though hospitalized at times for his drinking and nervous collapses, he managed to do a tremendous amount of work in poetry and in several fields of scholarship. He had a dozen books of poetry published; he also wrote a novel, a scholarly biography, and a book of essays. Much work remained unpublished when he died by suicide in Minneapolis.

From **Berryman's Sonnets**

37

Sigh as it ends . . . I keep an eye on your
Amour with Scotch,—too *cher* to consummate;
Faster your disappearing beer than late-
ly mine; your naked passion for the floor;
Your hollow leg; your hanker for one more   5

1947. *Berryman's Sonnets*, 1967.

The poem is from a series of 115 sonnets that the poet wrote in the course of his summer-long love af-fair with an impetuous and beautiful young married woman who was passionately fond of classical music, but also—as the poet, no puritan himself, is worried to note—perhaps too fond of Scotch, beer, Daiquiris—or whatever.

1 **Sigh as it ends:** *It* is probably the piece of music which the girl, stretched out on the floor, is lost in.   2 **cher:** dear (French). The whole phrase seems to mean that her amour, instead of ever culminat-ing and perhaps concluding, is tenderly nursed on for years. *Cher* also means "expensive."

Dark as the Sundam Trench; how you dilate
Upon psychotics of this class, collate
Stages, and . . how long since you, well, *forbore.*

Ah, but the high fire sings on to be fed
Whipping our darkness by the lifting sea   10
A while, O darling drinking like a clock.
The tide comes on: spare, Time, from what you spread
Her story,—tilting a frozen Daiquiri,
Blonde, barefoot, beautiful,
        flat on the bare floor rivetted to Bach.   15

6 **the Sundam Trench:** a deep gorge in the ocean floor off Malaya in southeast Asia   6–7 **dilate . . . collate . . . :** The young woman (worried? defensive? feeling "I'm not *that* way!"?) is given to discussing and comparing alcoholics.   8 ***forbore:*** exercised self-restraint in abstaining (from anything desired)   12 **spread:** strew, scatter—as the tide spreads its wrack and wreckage   13 **Daiquiri:** a cocktail made of rum, lime juice, and sugar, often served frozen   14 The line is all the more passionate because it is an intrusion in the otherwise regular 14-line Petrarchan sonnet   15 **Bach:** The girl is listening to the purest and most "classic" of all composers, the German Johann Sebastian Bach (1685–1750).

From **The Dream Songs**

4

Filling her compact & delicious body
with chicken páprika, she glanced at me
twice.
Fainting with interest, I hungered back
and only the fact of her husband & four other people   5
kept me from springing on her

or falling at her little feet and crying
'You are the hottest one for years of night
Henry's dazed eyes
have enjoyed, Brilliance.' I advanced upon   10
(despairing) my spumoni.—Sir Bones: is stuffed,
de world, wif feeding girls.

—Black hair, complexion Latin, jewelled eyes
downcast . . . The slob beside her   feasts . . . What wonders is
she sitting on, over there?   15
The restaurant buzzes. She might as well be on Mars.
Where did it all go wrong? There ought to be a law against Henry.
—Mr. Bones: there is.

---

77 Dream Songs, 1964.

The Dream Songs is a long poem of 385 related "songs" dealing with the troubles, adventures, reminiscences, reflections, dreams, etc. of a character called "Henry" who is very much like Berryman himself—so that what they give us is glimpses into his emotional autobiography. Henry is sometimes addressed by a character in blackface called "Sir Bones" or "Mr. Bones," who gets his name from the "end man" in minstrel shows—the actor who engages in dialogue with the main speaker in the middle of the line. The poet uses many kinds of language (or "Henryspeak") in his songs, from the grandeurs of traditional poetry and of exotic and pedantic diction to coinages, slang, and baby-talk. The form of each poem, from which Berryman rarely departs, consists of three six-line stanzas, which rhyme in different ways. Besides the 385 poems of the edition that the poet thought of as definitive, hundreds of other "dream songs" were written and omitted. Some have been published posthumously; others are still appearing.

11–12 Mr. Bones is suggesting that Henry relax: there are lots of other attractive girls in the world. (One of the themes of the poems, especially prominent in the earlier ones, is that of lust.)

14

Life, friends, is boring. We must not say so.
After all, the sky flashes, the great sea yearns,
we ourselves flash and yearn,
and moreover my mother told me as a boy
(repeatedly) 'Ever to confess you're bored   5
means you have no

Inner Resources.' I conclude now I have no
inner resources, because I am heavy bored.
Peoples bore me,
literature bores me, especially great literature,   10
Henry bores me, with his plights & gripes
as bad as achilles,

who loves people and valiant art, which bores me.
And the tranquil hills, & gin, look like a drag
and somehow a dog   15
has taken itself & its tail considerably away
into mountains or sea or sky, leaving
behind: me, wag.

Ibid.

12 **achilles:** The Greek hero Achilles withdrew from participation in the battles of the Trojan War and sulked in his tent because he felt he had been insulted by Agamemnon.   15–18 The dog—something alive or vital in the landscape—has disappeared, tail and all, leaving only a "wag" behind. The word *wag* means "a wit or joker:" Henry is the abandoned wag.

29

There sat down, once, a thing on Henry's heart
só heavy, if he had a hundred years
& more, & weeping, sleepless, in all them time
Henry could not make good.
Starts again always in Henry's ears   5
the little cough somewhere, an odour, a chime.

And there is another thing he has in mind
like a grave Sienese face a thousand years
would fail to blur the still profiled reproach of. Ghastly,
with open eyes, he attends, blind.   10
All the bells say: too late. This is not for tears;
thinking.

But never did Henry, as he thought he did,
end anyone and hacks her body up
and hide the pieces, where they may be found.   15
He knows: he went over everyone, & nobody's missing.
Often he reckons, in the dawn, them up.
Nobody is ever missing.

Ibid.

Henry is tormented by, first, a terrible depression or memory (Berryman often refers to his father's suicide—he heard the shot fired, just outside his window, when he was 12), and, secondly, the possibility of doing something terrible himself, perhaps while drunk.

8 **a grave Sienese face:** such a face as the artists of Siena (in Italy) might have painted. Their art was prevailingly religious, so that the "face" could be that of Christ, his mother, or one of the saints.

219

So Long? Stevens

He lifted up, among the actuaries,
a grandee crow. Ah ha & he crowed good.
That funny money-man.
Mutter we all must as well as we can.
He mutter spiffy. He make wonder Henry's   5
wits, though, with a odd

... something ... something ... not there in his flourishing art.
O veteran of death, you will not mind
a counter-mutter.
What was it missing, then, at the man's heart   10
so that he does not wound? It is our kind
to wound, as well as utter

a fact of happy world. That metaphysics
he hefted up until we could not breathe
the physics. *On our side,*   15
monotonous (or ever-fresh)—it sticks
in Henry's throat to judge—brilliant, he seethe;
better than us; less wide.

His Toy, His Dream, His Rest, 1968.

A number of the *Dream Songs* are about writers recently dead: Faulkner, Hemingway, Frost, Roethke, Delmore Schwartz. This one is about Wallace Stevens, who was vice-president of one of the great insurance companies ("among the actuaries," or insurance men). Berryman praises him for the elegance of his style, for his *spiffy mutter*, and yet feels a lack, in his brilliant work, of something like the ability to pierce or shock us.

2 **grandee crow:** a noble crowing

Lauds

Let us rejoice on our cots, for His nocturnal miracles
antique outside the Local Group & within it
& within our hearts in it, and for quotidian miracles
parsecs-off yielding to the Hale reflector.

Oh He is potent in the corners. Men   5
with Him are potent: quasars we intuit,
and sequent to sufficient discipline
we perceive this glow keeping His winter out.

1970–1971. *Delusions, Etc.*, 1972.

Lauds: The word (which means "praises") is the liturgical term for prayers of praise that accompany matins (morning prayers).

2 **the Local Group:** the astronomer's term for the 18 or so galaxies closest to (and including) our own   3 **quotidian:** daily   4 **parsecs:** units of measurement for interstellar space (a parsec is about 19 trillion miles).   **the Hale reflector:** the 200-inch reflecting telescope at the Palomar Mountain Observatory in California. Since 1948 it has been the world's largest telescope (the Russians are completing a 236-inch one); its tremendous light-gathering capacity revealed many things about the universe not known before.   6 **quasars:** "quasi-stellar radio sources," very distant starlike objects that emit powerful radio waves   **intuit:** here, apprehend by something like guesswork from the evidence available. Berryman is saying that the universe is mysterious and marvellous, but so is the mind of man that can perceive it.   8 **glow:** "glowing stove" (MS.)

My marvellous black new brim-rolled felt is both stuffy & raffish.
I hit my summit with it, in firelight.   10
Maybe I only got a Yuletide tie
(increasing sixty) & some writing-paper

but ha (ha*ha*) I've bought myself a hat!
Plus-strokes from position zero! Its feathers sprout.
Thank you, Your Benevolence!   15
permissive, smiling on   our silliness You forged.

9–16 Berryman has been praising God for the wonders of the universe; he now praises the permissive
Benevolence that indulges our human silliness: such as the pleasure we take in a swanky new hat.
stuffy and raffish: conventional and showy at the same time

Dylan Thomas
(1914–1953)

Born in Swansea (Wales), where his father was an English teacher, Thomas dropped out
of school at 16 to become a reporter. Before he was 20 he had written a good deal of poet-
ry and published his first book. Always a scrupulous craftsman, he continued to work on
his poetry while supporting himself in London by freelance writing. After his marriage
in 1937 he moved to the little Welsh town of Laugharne (pronounced *larn*); during the
war he was back in London at work on film scripts. In 1950 he made the first of three tri-
umphant if rambunctious reading tours of the United States. Though troubled in his last
years by financial mismanagement, poor health, and spells of excessive drinking, he con-
tinued to write well and give brilliant readings. He died in New York a few days after his
thirty-ninth birthday. Besides his poetry, he wrote plays, screenplays, autobiographical
short stories, and sketches.

In My Craft or Sullen Art

In my craft or sullen art
Exercised in the still night
When only the moon rages
And the lovers lie abed
With all their griefs in their arms,   5
I labour by singing light
Not for ambition or bread
Or the strut and trade of charms
On the ivory stages
But for the common wages   10
Of their most secret heart.

Not for the proud man apart
From the raging moon I write
On these spindrift pages
Nor for the towering dead   15
With their nightingales and psalms
But for the lovers, their arms
Round the griefs of the ages,
Who pay no praise or wages
Nor heed my craft or art.   20

1945. *Deaths and Entrances*, 1946.

14 **spindrift:** seaspray, windblown seafoam

Fern Hill

Now as I was young and easy under the apple boughs
About the lilting house and happy as the grass was green,
    The night above the dingle starry,
        Time let me hail and climb
    Golden in the heydays of his eyes,   5
And honoured among wagons I was prince of the apple towns
And once below a time I lordly had the trees and leaves
        Trail with daisies and barley
    Down the rivers of the windfall light.

And as I was green and carefree, famous among the barns   10
About the happy yard and singing as the farm was home,
    In the sun that is young once only,
        Time let me play and be
    Golden in the mercy of his means,
And green and golden I was huntsman and herdsman, the calves   15
Sang to my horn, the foxes on the hills barked clear and cold,
        And the sabbath rang slowly
    In the pebbles of the holy streams.

All the sun long it was running, it was lovely, the hay
Fields high as the house, the tunes from the chimneys, it was air 20
    And playing, lovely and watery
        And fire green as grass.
    And nightly under the simple stars
As I rode to sleep the owls were bearing the farm away,
All the moon long I heard, blessed among stables, the nightjars   25
        Flying with the ricks, and the horses
            Flashing into the dark.

And then to awake, and the farm, like a wanderer white
With the dew, come back, the cock on his shoulder: it was all
    Shining, it was Adam and maiden,   30
        The sky gathered again
    And the sun grew round that very day.
So it must have been after the birth of the simple light
In the first, spinning place, the spellbound horses walking warm
        Out of the whinnying green stable   35
            On to the fields of praise.

And honoured among foxes and pheasants by the gay house
Under the new made clouds and happy as the heart was long,
    In the sun born over and over,
        I ran my heedless ways,   40
    My wishes raced through the house high hay
And nothing I cared, at my sky blue trades, that time allows

1945. *Deaths and Entrances*, 1946.

Fern Hill was the farm in Wales where Thomas spent many happy times as a child. It was occupied by an aunt and uncle, who were tenant farmers.

2 **happy as the grass . . . :** naturally and essentially happy. Cf. lines 11, 22, 38.   3 **dingle:** small wooded valley   5 **heydays:** times of greatest vigor, happiness, etc.   7 **once below a time:** a play on "once upon a time." The memory is deep in time, which swept over it.   10 **green:** used in its several senses in the poem: young, fresh, thriving, inexperienced. Green and gold (grass and sun) are the key colors.   24 Cf. Roethke, "Where Knock Is Open Wide," line 39 (p. 642).   25 **nightjars:** nocturnal birds, like the nighthawk or whippoorwill   26 **ricks:** hayricks   30 ff. **Adam and maiden . . . :** To the child, the world was as fresh as it must have been on the very first day, when newly created.

In all his tuneful turning so few and such morning songs
    Before the children green and golden
        Follow him out of grace,   45

Nothing I cared, in the lamb white days, that time would take me
Up to the swallow thronged loft by the shadow of my hand,
    In the moon that is always rising,
        Nor that riding to sleep
    I should hear him fly with the high fields   50
And wake to the farm forever fled from the childless land.
Oh as I was young and easy in the mercy of his means,
        Time held me green and dying
    Though I sang in my chains like the sea.

47 **swallow thronged loft:** The light-breasted swallows flitting in the gloom under the roof were to the child an image of ghostliness—of the other world.   54 **sang in my chains . . . :** was happily unaware of the limitations of mortality

Do Not Go Gentle into That Good Night

Do not go gentle into that good night,
Old age should burn and rave at close of day;
Rage, rage against the dying of the light.

Though wise men at their end know dark is right,
Because their words had forked no lightning they   5
Do not go gentle into that good night.

Good men, the last wave by, crying how bright
Their frail deeds might have danced in a green bay,
Rage, rage against the dying of the light.

Wild men who caught and sang the sun in flight,   10
And learn, too late, they grieved it on its way,
Do not go gentle into that good night.

Grave men, near death, who see with blinding sight
Blind eyes could blaze like meteors and be gay,
Rage, rage against the dying of the light.   15

And you, my father, there on the sad height,
Curse, bless, me now with your fierce tears, I pray.
Do not go gentle into that good night.
Rage, rage against the dying of the light.

1951. *Collected Poems,* 1952.

Thomas sent the poem in a letter to a friend with a P.S. that read: "The only person I can't show the little enclosed poem to is, of course, my father, who doesn't know he's dying." The father lived on for more than a year after the poem was written.

Robert Lowell
(1917–1977)

Lowell, whose grandfather was a younger brother of James Russell Lowell, was born in Boston; his father was a naval officer who after retirement became an unsuccessful businessman. Lowell left Harvard after two years to study with Ransom at Kenyon College. During World War II, after trying to enlist in the navy, he refused to be drafted on the grounds that the bombing of cities was immoral; he was sentenced to a year in a federal prison but released after five months. In 1946 he published *Lord Weary's Castle*, and in 1962 a book of translations which he called *Imitations*. Over the years he taught at several universities: Iowa, Boston University, The New School, and Harvard among them. During the last few years of his life, when he lived much of the time in England, he taught at Kent University (Canterbury). He died suddenly on a visit to New York.

The Quaker Graveyard in Nantucket

(For Warren Winslow, Dead at Sea)

Let man have dominion over the fishes of the sea
and the fowls of the air and the beasts and the
whole earth, and every creeping creature that mov-
eth upon the earth.

I

A brackish reach of shoal off Madaket,—
The sea was still breaking violently and night
Had steamed into our North Atlantic Fleet,
When the drowned sailor clutched the drag-net. Light
Flashed from his matted head and marble feet,   5
He grappled at the net
With the coiled, hurdling muscles of his thighs:
The corpse was bloodless, a botch of reds and whites,
Its open, staring eyes
Were lustreless dead-lights   10
Or cabin-windows on a stranded hulk
Heavy with sand. We weight the body, close
Its eyes and heave it seaward whence it came,
Where the heel-headed dogfish barks its nose
On Ahab's void and forehead; and the name   15
Is blocked in yellow chalk.
Sailors, who pitch this portent at the sea
Where dreadnoughts shall confess
Its hell-bent deity,
When you are powerless   20
To sand-bag this Atlantic bulwark, faced
By the earth-shaker, green, unwearied, chaste
In his steel scales: ask for no Orphean lute

Lord Weary's Castle, 1946.

Nantucket, the island south of Cape Cod, was settled by Quakers, who made it a center of the whaling industry. Warren Winslow was Lowell's cousin; the ship on which he was serving in World War II went down with all hands. In writing his elegy, Lowell seems to have had Milton's "Lycidas" in mind.

Let man have dominion . . . : Gen. 1:28. See Additional Notes (p. 782).

1 **Madaket:** (Maddaket) a harbor town on the western end of Nantucket   5 ff. **matted head . . . :** Like Eliot, Lowell reinforces his experiences with phrasing from favorite books. The description of the drowned sailor owes a good deal to a passage near the beginning of Thoreau's *Cape Cod* (published 1864), which describes a visit to the scene of a shipwreck: "I saw many marble feet and matted heads . . . one . . . body . . . quite bloodless,—merely red and white,—with wide-open and staring eyes, yet lustreless, dead-lights; or like the cabin windows of a stranded vessel, filled with sand. . . ." 10 **dead-lights:** heavy glass portholes   14 **dogfish:** a small shark   15 **Ahab:** Lowell also thinks of Captain Ahab, the vengeful and self-willed captain of the Pequod, which sailed from Nantucket in search of the White Whale in Melville's *Moby-Dick* (1851). Ahab was drowned when his ship was destroyed by the savage whale, a symbol of mysterious malignity.   18 **dreadnoughts:** battleships 21 **sand-bag:** protect with sand-bags. A bulwark is a defensive wall, or seawall.   22 **the earth-shaker:** the classical epithet for Neptune, god of the sea, used in Homer and elsewhere   23 **Orphean:** for Orpheus, see note on "Lycidas," line 58. Here the reference is to his power to bring back the dead by the magic of his music, as he did with his wife Eurydice (though he lost her at the last moment by looking back).

To pluck life back. The guns of the steeled fleet
Recoil and then repeat   25
The hoarse salute.

II

Whenever winds are moving and their breath
Heaves at the roped-in bulwarks of this pier,
The terns and sea-gulls tremble at your death
In these home waters. Sailor, can you hear   30
The Pequod's sea wings, beating landward, fall
Headlong and break on our Atlantic wall
Off 'Sconset, where the yawing S-boats splash
The bellbuoy, with ballooning spinnakers,
As the entangled, screeching mainsheet clears   35
The blocks: off Madaket, where lubbers lash
The heavy surf and throw their long lead squids
For blue-fish? Sea-gulls blink their heavy lids
Seaward. The winds' wings beat upon the stones,
Cousin, and scream for you and the claws rush   40
At the sea's throat and wring it in the slush
Of this old Quaker graveyard where the bones
Cry out in the long night for the hurt beast
Bobbing by Ahab's whaleboats in the East.

III

All you recovered from Poseidon died   45
With you, my cousin, and the harrowed brine
Is fruitless on the blue beard of the god,
Stretching beyond us to the castles in Spain,
Nantucket's westward haven. To Cape Cod
Guns, cradled on the tide,   50
Blast the eelgrass about a waterclock
Of bilge and backwash, roil the salt and sand
Lashing earth's scaffold, rock
Our warships in the hand
Of the great God, where time's contrition blues   55
Whatever it was these Quaker sailors lost
In the mad scramble of their lives. They died
When time was open-eyed,
Wooden and childish; only bones abide
There, in the nowhere, where their boats were tossed   60
Sky-high, where mariners had fabled news
Of IS, the whited monster. What it cost
Them is their secret. In the sperm-whale's slick
I see the Quakers drown and hear their cry:
'If God himself had not been on our side,   65

29 **terns:** small seagulls   31 **Pequod:** see note on line 15   33 **'Sconset:** Siasconset, on the eastern end
of Nantucket   **S-boats:** sailboats of the "S" class, sometimes described as "family-type"   34 **spinna-
kers:** large sails that fill like balloons when a ship is running before the wind   35 **mainsheet:** rope
that controls and secures the mainsail   36 **lubbers:** clumsy amateur sailors   37 **lead squids:** artificial
bait   38 **blue-fish:** an Atlantic fish prized for its flavor   43 **hurt beast:** the whale   45 **Poseidon:**
Neptune   46 **harrowed:** plowed, tormented by man   49 **westward:** a mistake for "eastward"?
51 **eelgrass:** an underwater plant with long narrow leaves   **waterclock:** a device for telling time by
the flow or dripping of water. Here, the sea, with its tidal changes, revolving currents, etc.   52 **roil:**
disturb, make muddy or dirty   53 **lashing:** making firm, binding   55 **the great God:** Poseidon, in
whose hand they are—but also the God of the Bible, punishing man for his offenses against nature
58–59 **open-eyed:** naïve   60 **tossed:** by storms or attacking whales   62 **IS:** perhaps this means exis-
tence, what *is*, especially in its violent aspect. (As in Exod. 3:14 God calls Himself "I AM.") Moby-Dick
is sinister partly because of his very whiteness.   65 **'If God himself . . .':** The self-righteous cry of the
Quakers is ironic in that they *are* drowning: God is not taking their side against the Atlantic.

If God himself had not been on our side,
When the Atlantic rose against us, why,
Then it had swallowed us up quick.'

IV

This is the end of the whaleroad and the whale
Who spewed Nantucket bones on the thrashed swell   70
And stirred the troubled waters to whirlpools
To send the Pequod packing off to hell:
This is the end of them, three-quarters fools,
Snatching at straws to sail
Seaward and seaward on the turntail whale,   75
Spouting out blood and water as it rolls,
Sick as a dog to these Atlantic shoals:
Clamavimus, O depths. Let the sea-gulls wail

For water, for the deep where the high tide
Mutters to its hurt self, mutters and ebbs.   80
Waves wallow in their wash, go out and out,
Leave only the death-rattle of the crabs,
The beach increasing, its enormous snout
Sucking the ocean's side.
This is the end of running on the waves;   85
We are poured out like water. Who will dance
The mast-lashed master of Leviathans
Up from this field of Quakers in their unstoned graves?

V

When the whale's viscera go and the roll
Of its corruption overruns this world   90
Beyond tree-swept Nantucket and Wood's Hole
And Martha's Vineyard, Sailor, will your sword
Whistle and fall and sink into the fat?
In the great ash-pit of Jehoshaphat
The bones cry for the blood of the white whale,   95
The fat flukes arch and whack about its ears,
The death-lance churns into the sanctuary, tears
The gun-blue swingle, heaving like a flail,
And hacks the coiling life out: it works and drags
And rips the sperm-whale's midriff into rags,   100
Gobbets of blubber spill to wind and weather,
Sailor, and gulls go round the stoven timbers
Where the morning stars sing out together

---

78 *Clamavimus*: (Latin) We have cried out. Cf. Ps. 130: "Out of the depths have I cried unto thee, O
LORD. . . ." 86–88 **dance . . . up**: bring, as with dancing motions, from the dead 87 **mast-lashed**:
roped to the mast, as for security in a storm. Here, it applies to any of the dead whaling captains in the
cemetery. **Leviathans**: giant sea-creatures mentioned several times in the Bible; here, taken as
whales. At the beginning of *Moby-Dick* Melville quotes many passages about "Leviathan." 88 **un-
stoned**: without headstones 91 **tree-swept**: swept free of trees **Wood's Hole**: on the southwest tip
of Cape Cod, now a center of oceanographic studies 92 **Martha's Vineyard**: the island to the west of
Nantucket **will your sword . . . ?**: Are you guilty, as the whalers were? 94 **ash-pit of Jehoshaphat**:
"The valley of judgment. The world, according to some prophets and scientists, will end in fire"
(Lowell's note, quoted in K. Friar and J. M. Brinnin, *Modern Poetry*). Cf. Joel 3:12: "Let the heathen be
wakened, and come up to the valley of Jehoshaphat: for there will I sit to judge all the heathen round
about." 95 **white whale**: here apparently an innocent victim of man's cruelty rather than (as in
Moby-Dick) a symbol of the malign forces of nature 96 ff. images of the violent brutality attending
the death of a whale **flukes**: the lobes of a whale's tail 97 **sanctuary**: of the whale's life: his vi-
tals 98 **swingle**: the swinging part of a flail 102 **stoven timbers**: of the boat crushed by the
whale's attack 103 **the morning stars . . .**: Cf. Job 38:6–7: the Lord to Job: "who laid the cornerstone
thereof [of the earth]; when the morning stars sang together, and all the sons of God shouted for joy?"

And thunder shakes the white surf and dismembers
The red flag hammered in the mast-head. Hide, 105
Our steel, Jonas Messias, in Thy side.

VI
Our Lady of Walsingham

There once the penitents took off their shoes
And then walked barefoot the remaining mile;
And the small trees, a stream and hedgerows file
Slowly along the munching English lane, 110
Like cows to the old shrine, until you lose
Track of your dragging pain.
The stream flows down under the druid tree,
Shiloah's whirlpools gurgle and make glad
The castle of God. Sailor, you were glad 115
And whistled Sion by that stream. But see:

Our Lady, too small for canopy,
Sits near the altar. There's no comeliness
At all or charm in that expressionless
Face with its heavy eyelids. As before, 120
This face, for centuries a memory,
Non est species, neque decor,
Expressionless, expresses God: it goes
Past castled Sion. She knows what God knows,
Not Calvary's Cross nor crib at Bethlehem 125
Now, and the world shall come to Walsingham.

VII

The empty winds are creaking and the oak
Splatters and splatters on the cenotaph,
The boughs are trembling and a gaff
Bobs on the untimely stroke 130
Of the greased wash exploding on a shoal-bell
In the old mouth of the Atlantic. It's well;
Atlantic, you are fouled with the blue sailors,
Sea-monsters, upward angel, downward fish:
Unmarried and corroding, spare of flesh, 135
Mart once of supercilious, wing'd clippers,
Atlantic, where your bell-trap guts its spoil
You could cut the brackish winds with a knife

---

105 **the red flag:** The last thing we see of the Pequod, on the last page of *Moby-Dick*, is the red flag of Ahab nailed to the last few inches of the mast as the ship, stove in by Moby-Dick, goes under. 106 **Jonas Messias:** see Additional Notes to Part V (p. 782). Jesus and Jonas are associated in Matt. 12:39-41. **Part VI:** Lowell has pointed out that this section "is an adaptation of several paragraphs from E. I. Watkins's *Catholic Art and Culture*." These describe the shrine that is there today. Lowell follows Watkins about as closely as he followed Thoreau near the beginning of the poem, but at more length. He adds the cows, the "dragging pain," and the "druid tree." 113 **druid tree:** the Druids were ancient Celtic priests 114 **Shiloah:** Cf. Milton, *Paradise Lost,* I, 11-12: "Siloa's brook that flowed / Fast by the oracle of God." It came from a spring near Mount Sion or Zion, a central hill in Jerusalem which came to stand for the city itself. 122 ***Non est species . . . :*** (Latin) translated just above: "There's no comeliness . . . or charm." In Isa. 53:2, a similar phrase is used of a servant of the Lord, sometimes taken as foreshadowing the Messiah. Here, as often, it is applied to Mary. 124 **what God knows:** a knowledge beyond generation and decay, the "crib" and "Cross" of this life 128 **cenotaph:** an empty tomb, like that in honor of the drowned sailor whose body was never found 129 **gaff:** hook or spear for taking fish 131 **shoal-bell:** bell warning ships of shallow water 134 **sea-monsters:** Cf. Milton, *Paradise Lost,* I, 462-463: "Dagon his name, sea monster, upward man / And downward fish. . . ." Here the line refers to the mixed nature of man, part good, part evil. 136 **clippers:** the splendid and speedy clipper-ships of the nineteenth century 137 **bell-trap:** a bell-shaped trap for fish

Here in Nantucket, and cast up the time
When the Lord God formed man from the sea's slime   140
And breathed into his face the breath of life,
And blue-lung'd combers lumbered to the kill.
The Lord survives the rainbow of His will.

139 **cast up:** calculate—or perhaps cast ashore traces of   143 **rainbow:** After the flood God promised Noah not to destroy mankind again. "I do set my bow in the cloud, and it shall be for a token of a covenant between me and the earth" (Gen. 9:13).

After the Surprising Conversions

September twenty-second, Sir: today
I answer. In the latter part of May,
Hard on our Lord's Ascension, it began
To be more sensible. A gentleman
Of more than common understanding, strict   5
In morals, pious in behavior, kicked
Against our goad. A man of some renown,
An useful, honored person in the town,
He came of melancholy parents; prone
To secret spells, for years they kept alone—   10
His uncle, I believe, was killed of it:
Good people, but of too much or little wit.
I preached one Sabbath on a text from Kings;
He showed concernment for his soul. Some things
In his experience were hopeful. He   15
Would sit and watch the wind knocking a tree
And praise this countryside our Lord has made.
Once when a poor man's heifer died, he laid
A shilling on the doorsill; though a thirst
For loving shook him like a snake, he durst   20
Not entertain much hope of his estate
In heaven. Once we saw him sitting late
Behind his attic window by a light
That guttered on his Bible; through that night
He meditated terror, and he seemed   25
Beyond advice or reason, for he dreamed
That he was called to trumpet Judgment Day
To Concord. In the latter part of May
He cut his throat. And though the coroner
Judged him delirious, soon a noisome stir   30
Palsied our village. At Jehovah's nod
Satan seemed more let loose amongst us: God
Abandoned us to Satan, and he pressed
Us hard, until we thought we could not rest
Till we had done with life. Content was gone.   35

Ibid.

In a note with the poem when it was first published, Lowell said, "I hope the source ... will be recognized." That source is the account by Jonathan Edwards, the American preacher and theologian (1703–1758), of a wave of religious revivalism in Massachusetts that reached its peak in March and April of 1735. First written as a letter dated November 6, 1736, it was called "A Faithful Narrative of the Surprising Work of God in the Conversion of Many Hundred Souls in Northampton and the Neighboring Towns and Villages...." Supplementary material was published as "A Narrative of Surprising Conversions." See Additional Notes (p. 782).

3 **Lord's Ascension:** The Feast of the Ascension is 40 days after Easter   13 **Kings:** 1 Kings and 2 Kings are among the historical books of the Old Testament.   28 **Concord:** a town about 15 miles northwest of Boston

All the good work was quashed. We were undone.
The breath of God had carried out a planned
And sensible withdrawal from this land;
The multitude, once unconcerned with doubt,
Once neither callous, curious nor devout,   40
Jumped at broad noon, as though some peddler groaned
At it in its familiar twang: "My friend,
Cut your own throat. Cut your own throat. Now! Now!"
September twenty-second, Sir, the bough
Cracks with the unpicked apples, and at dawn   45
The small-mouth bass breaks water, gorged with spawn.

Skunk Hour

(For Elizabeth Bishop)

Nautilus Island's hermit
heiress still lives through winter in her Spartan cottage;
her sheep still graze above the sea.
Her son's a bishop. Her farmer
is first selectman in our village,   5
she's in her dotage.

Thirsting for
the hierarchic privacy
of Queen Victoria's century,
she buys up all   10
the eyesores facing her shore,
and lets them fall.

The season's ill—
we've lost our summer millionaire,
who seemed to leap from an L. L. Bean   15
catalogue. His nine-knot yawl
was auctioned off to lobstermen.
A red fox stain covers Blue Hill.

And now our fairy
decorator brightens his shop for fall;   20
his fishnet's filled with orange cork,
orange, his cobbler's bench and awl;

1957. *Life Studies*, 1959.

The scene is around Castine, Maine, on Penobscot Bay. Lowell summarized his intentions in a symposium on the poem in *The Contemporary Poet as Artist and Critic*, Little, Brown, 1964: "The first four stanzas are meant to give a dawdling more or less amiable picture of a declining Maine sea town. . . . Sterility howls through the scenery, but I try to give a tone of tolerance, humor, and randomness to the sad prospect. . . . Then all comes alive in stanzas V and VI. This is the dark night. I hoped my readers would remember John of the Cross's poem. My night is not gracious, but secular, puritan, and agnostical. . . . Somewhere in my mind was a passage from Sartre or Camus about reaching some point of final darkness where the one free act is suicide. Out of this comes the march and affirmation, an ambiguous one, of my skunks in the last two stanzas. The skunks are both quixotic and barbarously absurd, hence the tone of amusement and defiance."

5 **first selectman:** senior elected town official (New England)   9 **Queen Victoria's century:** Victoria was queen from 1837 to 1901.   15 **L. L. Bean:** a store and mail order house in Freeport, Maine, specializing in sportswear and camping equipment   16 **nine-knot yawl:** a large sailboat capable of going 9 nautical miles an hour   18 **red fox stain:** "the rusty reddish color of autumn on . . . a Maine mountain near where we were living" [Lowell]   22 **cobbler's bench:** a workbench once actually used by cobblers; now, chiefly a decorator's item

there is no money in his work,
he'd rather marry.

One dark night,   25
my Tudor Ford climbed the hill's skull;
I watched for love-cars. Lights turned down,
they lay together, hull to hull,
where the graveyard shelves on the town. . . .
My mind's not right.   30

A car radio bleats,
"Love, O careless Love . . ." I hear
my ill-spirit sob in each blood cell,
as if my hand were at its throat. . . .
I myself am hell;   35
nobody's here—

only skunks, that search
in the moonlight for a bite to eat.
They march on their soles up Main Street:
white stripes, moonstruck eyes' red fire   40
under the chalk-dry and spar spire
of the Trinitarian Church.

I stand on top
of our back steps and breathe the rich air—
a mother skunk with her column of kittens swills the garbage pail.   45
She jabs her wedge-head in the cup
of sour cream, drops her ostrich tail,
and will not scare.

25 **one dark night:** The work of the Spanish poet St. John of the Cross (1542–1591) which Lowell
hopes we remember is generally called in English "The Dark Night" from its first line: "En una noche
oscura." It is about divine love, but wholly in terms and images of human love.   26 **Tudor:** "two-
door," the manufacturer's name for a two-door model   **hill's skull:** the suggestion is Calvary, which
means "skull" in Latin *(calvaria)*   32 **"Love, O careless Love . . .":** the well-known folksong, which
touches on seduction, murder, and suicide   35 **I myself am hell:** Cf. Milton's *Paradise Lost*, IV, 75,
where Satan says: "Which way I fly is hell; my self am hell."   42 **Trinitarian:** believing in the Trin-
ity—as opposed to Unitarian, at least in theory. By naming the church, Lowell may be suggesting
fruitless theological squabbles.

For the Union Dead

> *"Relinquunt Omnia Servare Rem Publicam."*

The old South Boston Aquarium stands
in a Sahara of snow now. Its broken windows are boarded.
The bronze weathervane cod has lost half its scales.
The airy tanks are dry.

Life Studies, 1960. *For the Union Dead*, 1964.

The poem was first published in 1960 as "Colonel Shaw and the Massachusetts 54th." Robert Gould
Shaw (1837–1863) was commander of the first all-black regiment in the Union army during the Civil
War. He was killed leading the attack on Fort Wagner, South Carolina. A bronze memorial, in high re-
lief, showing Shaw on horseback with his troops, was made by Augustus Saint-Gaudens (1848–1907),
the Irish-born American sculptor. Dedicated in 1897, it faces the State House on Boston Commons. It
bears the inscription "Omnia relinquit servare rempublicam" ("He gave up everything to preserve
the republic"), which Lowell's Latin changes to "They gave up . . . ."

1 **old . . . Aquarium:** The aquarium Lowell had known as a child was now closed. The poem was writ-
ten during a time of reconstruction in downtown Boston.

Once my nose crawled like a snail on the glass;   5
my hand tingled
to burst the bubbles
drifting from the noses of the cowed, compliant fish.

My hand draws back. I often sigh still
for the dark downward and vegetating kingdom   10
of the fish and reptile. One morning last March,
I pressed against the new barbed and galvanized

fence on the Boston Common. Behind their cage,
yellow dinosaur steamshovels were grunting
as they cropped up tons of mush and grass   15
to gouge their underworld garage.

Parking spaces luxuriate like civic
sandpiles in the heart of Boston.
A girdle of orange, Puritan-pumpkin colored girders
braces the tingling Statehouse,   20

shaking over the excavations, as it faces Colonel Shaw
and his bell-cheeked Negro infantry
on St. Gauden's shaking Civil War relief,
propped by a plank splint against the garage's earthquake.

Two months after marching through Boston,   25
half the regiment was dead;
at the dedication,
William James could almost hear the bronze Negroes breathe.

Their monument sticks like a fishbone
in the city's throat.   30
Its Colonel is as lean
as a compass-needle.

He has an angry wrenlike vigilance,
a greyhound's gentle tautness;
he seems to wince at pleasure,   35
and suffocate for privacy.

He is out of bounds now. He rejoices in man's lovely,
peculiar power to choose life and die—
when he leads his black soldiers to death,
he cannot bend his back.   40

On a thousand small town New England greens,
the old white churches hold their air
of sparse, sincere rebellion; frayed flags
quilt the graveyards of the Grand Army of the Republic.

The stone statues of the abstract Union Soldier   45
grow slimmer and younger each year—
wasp-waisted, they doze over muskets
and muse through their sideburns . . .

---

28 **William James:** (1842–1910) American psychologist and philosopher   29 **sticks like a fishbone:**
is a continual rebuke in times of racial discrimination   44 **Grand Army . . . :** Union veterans

Shaw's father wanted no monument
except the ditch,   50
where his son's body was thrown
and lost with his "niggers."

The ditch is nearer.
There are no statues for the last war here;
on Boylston Street, a commercial photograph   55
shows Hiroshima boiling

over a Mosler Safe, the "Rock of Ages"
that survived the blast. Space is nearer.
When I crouch to my television set,
the drained faces of Negro school-children rise like balloons.   60

Colonel Shaw
is riding on his bubble,
he waits
for the blessèd break.

The Aquarium is gone. Everywhere,   65
giant finned cars nose forward like fish;
a savage servility
slides by on grease.

54 **the last war:** World War II   55 **Boylston Street:** a main Boston street that passes the Common
56 **Hiroshima:** the Japanese city destroyed by the first atom bomb in 1945   57 **"Rock of Ages":** The
religious phrase is here put to commercial uses—as is the destruction of Hiroshima.   60 **drained
faces . . . :** in news reports of integration disorders   65–68 See Additional Notes (p. 782)

Gwendolyn Brooks
(Born 1917)

After a month spent in Topeka, her birthplace, Gwendolyn Brooks has been a life-long
resident of Chicago, where she attended Wilson Junior College. She has taught at several
local colleges and universities, as well as in New York and Wisconsin. Since 1968 she has
been poet laureate of Illinois. Besides her dozen books of poetry, she has written a novel,
Maud Martha, an autobiography, *Report from Part One*, and edited anthologies.

The Rites for Cousin Vit

Carried her unprotesting out the door.
Kicked back the casket-stand. But it can't hold her,
That stuff and satin aiming to enfold her,
The lid's contrition nor the bolts before.
Oh oh. Too much. Too much. Even now, surmise,   5
She rises in the sunshine. There she goes,
Back to the bars she knew and the repose
In love-rooms and the things in people's eyes.
Too vital and too squeaking. Must emerge.
Even now she does the snake-hips with a hiss,   10
Slops the bad wine across her shantung, talks
Of pregnancy, guitars and bridgework, walks
In parks or alleys, comes haply on the verge
Of happiness, haply hysterics. Is.

c. 1947. *Annie Allen*, 1949.

11 **shantung:** A fabric named for the Chinese province of Shantung. Made from the silk of the wild
silkworm, it has an attractively irregular weave, like raw silk.   13 **haply:** by chance, perhaps

The Bean Eaters

They eat beans mostly, this old yellow pair.
Dinner is a casual affair.
Plain chipware on a plain and creaking wood,
Tin flatware.

Two who are Mostly Good.   5
Two who have lived their day,
But keep on putting on their clothes
And putting things away.

And remembering . . .
Remembering, with twinklings and twinges,   10
As they lean over the beans in their rented back room
    that is full of beads and receipts and dolls and cloths,
    tobacco crumbs, vases and fringes.

c. 1958. *The Bean Eaters*, 1960.

We Real Cool

The Pool Players.
Seven at the Golden Shovel.

We real cool. We
Left school. We

Lurk late. We
Strike straight. We

Sing sin. We   5
Thin gin. We

Jazz June. We
Die soon.

c. 1957–1958. Ibid.

In her autobiographical *Report from Part One*, the poet tells us that her pool players "have no preten-
sions to any glamor. They are supposedly dropouts, or at least they're in the poolroom when they
should be possibly in school. . . ." The poem is set out the way it is because "These are people who are
essentially saying, 'Kilroy is here. We *are*.' But they're a little uncertain of the strength of their identi-
ty. The 'We'—you're supposed to stop after the 'We' and think about *validity*; of course, there's no way
for you to tell whether it should be said softly or not, I suppose, but I say it rather softly because I
want to represent their basic uncertainty, which they don't bother to question every day, of course."

Margaret Avison
(Born 1918)

Born in Galt, Ontario, Miss Avison spent her childhood in Western Canada. Most of her
adult life has been spent in Toronto; she has a B.A. from the university there. Her first
book of poetry (1960) won her the Governor-General's Award; since then she has pub-
lished two other books and become known as one of the best Canadian poets. Her jobs
have included inner-city social work and secretarial work in the Canadian office of a
Southeast Asia mission.

Hiatus

The weedy light through the uncurtained glass
Finds foreign space where the piano was,
And mournful airs from the propped-open door
Follow forlorn shreds of excelsior.
Though the towel droops with sad significance   5
All else is gone; one last reviewing glance,
One last misplacing, finding of the key,
And the last steps echo, and fade, and die.
    Then wanderer, with a hundred things to see to,
Scores of decisions waiting on your veto,   10
Or worse, being made at random till you come
So weeks will pass before you feel at home,
Mover unmoved, how can you choose this hour
To prowl at large around a hardware store?
When you have purchased the superfluous wrench   15
You wander still, and watch the late sun drench
The fruit-stalls, pavements, shoppers, cars, as though
All were invisible and safe but you.
    But in your mind's ear now resounds the din
Of friends who've come to help you settle in,   20
And your thoughts fumble, as you start the car,
On whether somebody marked the barrel where the glasses are.

1948–1950. *Winter Sun*, 1960.

Water and Worship: An Open-Air Service
on the Gatineau River

On the pathway mica glints.
Sun from the ripple-faceted water
shines,   angled,   to gray cliffs and the blue sky:
    from up here the boat-braided river is
    wind-riffled, fishes' meadows.   5
                But at
        eye-level, on the dock, the water looks deep,
             cold,   black,   cedar-sharp.
        The water is self-gulping under
        clefts and pier posts.   10

We listen.
your all-creating stillness,   shining Lord,
trembles on our unknowing
             yearning
                    yielding lives: 15
    currents within us course
    as from released snow, rock-
    sluiced, slow welling from
             unexpected hidden springs,
    waters still acid,   20

1966. *Sunblue*, 1978.

The Gatineau is a river that flows from the north down toward Hull in Quebec Province (Canada).

metallic with old wrecks—
        but Love draws near,
        cut-glass glory, shattering everything else in
        the one hope known: 25

        (how are You so
        at home with what we know?)
The waters lap.
Rocks contain and wait
in the strong sun.   30
        "Joyful, joyful, we adore Thee. . . ."

31 **"Joyful, joyful . . .":** the title of a hymn, "words by Henry Van Dyke (1852–1933), sung to an Edward Hodges arrangement of Beethoven's 'Hymn to Joy.'" [M.A.]

A Lament

A gizzard and some ruby inner parts
glisten here on the path where wind has parted
the fall field's silken ashblonde.

I fumble in our fault
("earth felt the wound," said Milton).   5
Cobwebs of hair glued
to cheekbone, among
gnat eddies and silences,
I clamber on through papery leaves and slick
leathering leaves between   10
the stifling meadows.

Eyeblink past blue,   the far
suns herd their flocks.

Crumbling comes,
voracious, mild as loam—   15
but not restoring. Death has us glassed in
for all the fine airflow and the
auburn and wickerwork beauty of this valley.

Somewhere a hawk swings, stronger,
or a weasel's eyes brighten.   20

The viscera still shine
with sun, by weed and silver riverflow.

1964. Ibid.

5 **"earth felt the wound":** The reference is to the passage in *Paradise Lost* in which the sin of Eve in eating the forbidden fruit brings evil into the world:

> . . . her rash hand in evil hour
> Forth reaching to the fruit, she plucked, she ate:
> Earth felt the wound, and Nature from her seat
> Sighing through all her works gave signs of woe,
> That all was lost . . . (IX, 780–784).

William Meredith
(Born 1919)

Born in New York City, Meredith, a Princeton graduate, served with the army air force and for several years was a naval aviator. He has taught at Princeton, the University of Hawaii, and since 1955 at Connecticut College. In 1955–1956 he was opera critic for *The Hudson Review*. Besides his half-dozen books of poetry he has written a play, edited collections of poetry, and translated *Alcools* from the French of Apollinaire.

Thoughts on One's Head

(In Plaster, with a Bronze Wash)

A person is very self-conscious about his head.
It makes one nervous just to know it is cast
In enduring materials, and that when the real one is dead
The cast one, if nobody drops it or melts it down, will last.

We pay more attention to the front end, where the face is,   5
Than to the interesting and involute interior:
The Fissure of Rolando and such queer places
Are parks for the passions and fears and mild hysteria.

The things that go on there! Erotic movies are shown
To anyone not accompanied by an adult.   10
The marquee out front maintains a superior tone:
Documentaries on Sharks, and The Japanese Tea Cult.

The fronts of some heads are extravagantly pretty.
These are the females. Men sometimes blow their tops
About them, launch triremes, sack a whole city.   15
The female head is mounted on rococo props.

Judgment is in the head somewhere; it keeps sums
Of pleasure and pain and gives belated warning.
This is the first place everybody comes
With bills, complaints, writs, summons, in the morning.   20

This particular head, to my certain knowledge
Has been taught to read and write, make love and money,
Operate cars and airplanes, teach in a college,
And tell involved jokes, some few extremely funny.

It was further taught to know and to eschew   25
Error and sin, which it does erratically.
This is the place the soul calls home just now.
One dislikes it of course: it is the seat of Me.

By 1955. *The Open Sea*, 1958.

6 **involute:** curled, coiled, complicated   7 **the Fissure of Rolando:** a crevice that marks an important division between lobes of the brain   15 **triremes:** ancient warships having three banks of oars 16 **rococo:** a style of architecture or decoration marked by fanciful curved spatial forms and much ornament

May Swenson
(Born 1919)

May Swenson, born in Logan, Utah, and educated at Utah State University, worked as a reporter for a year in Salt Lake City and for some years was an editor at the publishing house New Directions in New York. She has been teacher and poet-in-residence at several universities, including Purdue, Bryn Mawr, and North Carolina at Greensboro. Besides eight books of poetry, she has written short stories, a play, and books for children and done translations of the Swedish poet Tomas Tranströmer.

Cat & the Weather

Cat takes a look at the weather:
snow;
puts a paw on the sill;
his perch is piled, is a pillow.

Shape of his pad appears: 5
will it dig? No,
not like sand,
like his fur almost.

But licked, not liked:
too cold.   10
Insects are flying, fainting down.
He'll try

to bat one against the pane.
They have no body and no buzz,
and now his feet are wet;   15
it's a puzzle.

Shakes each leg,
then shakes his skin
to get the white flies off;
looks for his tail,   20

tells it to come on in
by the radiator.
World's turned queer
somehow: all white,

no smell. Well, here   25
inside it's still familiar.
He'll go to sleep until
it puts itself right.

1961. *To Mix with Time*, 1963.

The Watch

When I
took my
watch to the watchfixer I
felt privileged but also pained to watch the operation. He
had long fingernails and a voluntary squint. He   5
fixed a magnifying cup over his
squint eye. He
undressed my
watch. I
watched him   10
split her
in three layers and lay her
middle—a quivering viscera—in a circle on a little plinth. He
shoved shirtsleeves up and leaned like an ogre over my
naked watch. With critical pincers he   15
poked and stirred. He
lifted out little private things with a magnet too tiny for me
to watch almost. "Watch out!" I
almost said. His
eye watched, enlarged, the secrets of my   20
watch, and I
watched anxiously. Because what if he
touched her
ticker too rough, and she
gave up the ghost out of pure fright? Or put her   25
things back backwards so she'd
run backwards after this? Or he
might lose a minuscule part, connected to her
exquisite heart, and mix her
up, instead of fix her.   30
And all the time,
all the time-
pieces on the walls, on the shelves, told the time,
told the time
in swishes and ticks,   35
swishes and ticks,
and seemed to be gloating, as they watched and told. I
felt faint, I
was about to lose my
breath—my   40
ticker going lickety-split—when watchfixer clipped her
three slices together with a gleam and two flicks of his
tools like chopsticks. He
spat out his
eye, lifted her   45
high, gave her
a twist, set her
hands right, and laid her
little face, quite as usual, in its place on my
wrist.   50

1963. *Half Sun Half Sleep,* 1967.

13 **plinth:** the block at the bottom of a column; here, a tiny raised base

HOW EVERYTHING HAPPENS (Based on a Study of the Wave)

```
                                        happen.
                                     to
                                  up
                          stacking
                          is
                  something
When nothing is happening

When it happens
                something
                      pulls
                          back
                          not
                             to
                               happen.

When                              has happened.
        pulling back        stacking up
                  happens

        has happened                        stacks up.
When it              something          nothing
                  pulls back while

Then nothing is happening.

                                  happens.
                               and
                        forward
                  pushes
              up
          stacks
      something
Then
```

1967. *Iconographs,* 1970.

Howard Nemerov
(Born 1920)

Born in New York City, a Harvard graduate, in World War II a flyer with the Royal Canadian Air Force and the U.S. Air Force, Nemerov has taught at Hamilton, Bennington, Brandeis, and, since 1969, at Washington University in St. Louis. From 1946 to 1951 he was an associate editor of the literary magazine *Furioso*. He has written novels, short stories, and critical essays, as well as a dozen books of poetry.

Brainstorm

The house was shaken by a rising wind
That rattled window and door. He sat alone

Mirrors and Windows, 1958.

In an upstairs room and heard these things: a blind
Ran up with a bang, a door slammed, a groan
Came from some hidden joist, and a leaky tap,   5
At any silence of the wind, walked like
A blind man through the house. Timber and sap
Revolt, he thought, from washer, baulk and spike.
Bent to his book, continued unafraid
Until the crows came down from their loud flight   10
To walk along the rooftree overhead.
Their horny feet, so near but out of sight,
Scratched on the slate; when they were blown away
He heard their wings beat till they came again,
While the wind rose, and the house seemed to sway,   15
And window panes began to blind with rain.
The house was talking, not to him, he thought,
But to the crows; the crows were talking back
In their black voices. The secret might be out:
Houses are only trees stretched on the rack.   20
And once the crows knew, all nature would know.
Fur, leaf and feather would invade the form,
Nail rust with rain and shingle warp with snow,
Vine tear the wall, till any straw-borne storm
Could rip both roof and rooftree off and show   25
Naked to nature what they had kept warm.

He came to feel the crows walk on his head
As if he were the house, their crooked feet
Scratched, through the hair, his scalp. He might be dead,
It seemed, and all the noises underneath   30
Be but the cooling of the sinews, veins,
Juices, and sodden sacks suddenly let go;
While in his ruins of wiring, his burst mains,
The rainy wind had been set free to blow
Until the green uprising and mob rule   35
That ran the world had taken over him,
Split him like seed, and set him in the school
Where any crutch can learn to be a limb.

Inside his head he heard the stormy crows.

8 **baulk:** beam, rafter   11 **rooftree:** ridgepole, the horizontal timber along the ridge of the roof

Santa Claus

Somewhere on his travels the strange Child
Picked up with this overstuffed confidence man,
Affection's inverted thief, who climbs at night
Down chimneys, into dreams, with this world's goods.
Bringing all the benevolence of money,   5
He teaches the innocent to want, thus keeps
Our fat world rolling. His prescribed costume,
White flannel beard, red belly of cotton waste,
Conceals the thinness of essential hunger,
An appetite that feeds on satisfaction;   10

The Next Room of the Dream, 1962.

1 **the strange Child:** the Christ Child

Or, pregnant with possessions, he brings forth
Vanity and the void. His name itself
Is corrupted, and even Saint Nicholas, in his turn,
Gives off a faint and reminiscent stench,
The merest soupçon, of brimstone and the pit.   15

Now, at the season when the Child is born
To suffer for the world, suffer the world,
His bloated Other, jovial satellite
And sycophant, makes his appearance also
In a glitter of goodies, in a rock candy glare.   20
Played at the better stores by bums, for money,
This annual savior of the economy
Speaks in the parables of the dollar sign:
Suffer the little children to come to Him.

At Easter, he's anonymous again,   25
Just one of the crowd lunching on Calvary.

12–13 **name...is corrupted...**: Santa Claus is a "corrupt" form of Saint Nicholas (through the Dutch *Sinterklass*), the fourth-century bishop in Asia Minor who was a patron of children. But "Nick," or especially "Old Nick," is also a name for the devil.   15 **soupçon:** (French, "suspicion") little bit, trace, hint   **brimstone:** sulphur   24 **"Suffer the little children..."**: Mark 10:14: "Jesus... said unto them, Suffer the little children to come unto me... for of such is the kingdom of God."

Learning by Doing

They're taking down a tree at the front door,
The power saw is snarling at some nerves,
Whining at others. Now and then it grunts,
And sawdust falls like snow or a drift of seeds.

Rotten, they tell us, at the fork, and one   5
Big wind would bring it down. So what they do
They do, as usual, to do us good.
Whatever cannot carry its own weight
Has got to go, and so on; you expect
To hear them talking next about survival   10
And the values of a free society.
For in the explanations people give
On these occasions there is generally some
Mean-spirited moral point, and everyone
Privately wonders if his neighbors plan   15
To saw him up before he falls on them.

Maybe a hundred years in sun and shower
Dismantled in a morning and let down
Out of itself a finger at a time
And then an arm, and so down to the trunk,   20
Until there's nothing left to hold on to
Or snub the splintery holding rope around,
And where those big green divagations were
So loftily with shadows interleaved
The absent-minded blue rains in on us.   25
Now that they've got it sectioned on the ground

The Blue Swallows, 1967.

23 **divagations:** divergings, branchings

It looks as though somebody made a plain
Error in diagnosis, for the wood
Looks sweet and sound throughout. You couldn't know,
Of course, until you took it down. That's what   30
Experts are for, and these experts stand round
The giant pieces of tree as though expecting
An instruction booklet from the factory
Before they try to put it back together.

Anyhow, there it isn't, on the ground.   35
Next come the tractor and the crowbar crew
To extirpate what's left and fill the grave.
Maybe tomorrow grass seed will be sown.
There's some mean-spirited moral point in that
As well: you learn to bury your mistakes,   40
Though for a while at dusk the darkening air
Will be with many shadows interleaved,
And pierced with a bewilderment of birds.

Richard Wilbur
(Born 1921)

The son of an artist, Wilbur was born in New York City; he has degrees from Amherst and Harvard. From 1943 to 1945 he was with the U.S. army in Italy and France. He has taught at Harvard, Wellesley, Wesleyan, and, since 1977, at Smith. Besides writing some ten books of poetry, he has translated four plays of Molière (often presented) and the *Andromaque* of Racine, done an adaptation of Voltaire's *Candide*, written books for children, and edited collections of the poetry of Poe, Keats, and others.

A Voice from Under the Table

> *To Robert and Jane Brooks*

How shall the wine be drunk, or the woman known?
I take this world for better or for worse,
But seeing rose carafes conceive the sun
My thirst conceives a fierier universe:
And then I toast the birds in the burning trees   5
That chant their holy lucid drunkenness;
I swallowed all the phosphorus of the seas
Before I fell into this low distress.

You upright people all remember how
Love drove you first to the woods, and there you heard   10
The loose-mouthed wind complaining *Thou* and *Thou;*
My gawky limbs were shuddered by the word.
Most of it since was nothing but charades
To spell that hankering out and make an end,
But the softest hands against my shoulder-blades   15
Only increased the crying of the wind.

1953. *Things of This World*, 1956.

This meditation on idealism and reality is delivered by a man lying drunk under the table.

3 **conceive the sun:** seem to flame up as the sunlight strikes them. "I suppose I was influenced by the resemblance of some carafes to bellies or wombs." [R.W.]   7 **phosphorus:** The line "is meant to express by exaggeration the speaker's insatiable thirst, enlarging the fire-in-fluid idea begun in line 3 by an evocation of oceans, which of course are often full of phosphorescence." [R.W.]

For this the goddess rose from the midland sea
And stood above the famous wine-dark wave,
To ease our drouth with clearer mystery
And be a South to all our flights of love.   20
And down by the selfsame water I have seen
A blazing girl with skin like polished stone
Splashing until a far-out breast of green
Arose and with a rose contagion shone.

"A myrtle-shoot in hand, she danced; her hair   25
Cast on her back and shoulders a moving shade."
Was it some hovering light that showed her fair?
Was it of chafing dark that light was made?
Perhaps it was Archilochus' fantasy,
Or that his saying sublimed the thing he said.   30
All true enough; and true as well that she
Was beautiful, and danced, and is now dead.

Helen was no such high discarnate thought
As men in dry symposia pursue,
But was as bitterly fugitive, not to be caught   35
By what men's arms in love or fight could do.
Groan in your cell; rape Troy with sword and flame;
The end of thirst exceeds experience.
A devil told me it was all the same
Whether to fail by spirit or by sense.   40

God keep me a damned fool, nor charitably
Receive me into his shapely resignations.
I am a sort of martyr, as you see,
A horizontal monument to patience.
The calves of waitresses parade about   45
My helpless head upon this sodden floor.
Well, I am down again, but not yet out.
O sweet frustrations, I shall be back for more.

17 **the goddess:** Aphrodite, goddess of love, born of the sea **midland:** Cf. D. H. Lawrence, "Middle
of the World." 18 **the famous wine-dark wave:** *Wine-dark* is often used to translate *oinops*, a word
Homer used of the sea: it means "having the appearance (or color) of wine." 25–26 The two lines
translate a three-line fragment of the early Greek poet Archilochos (eighth or seventh century B.C.),
which survives only because a Greek grammarian quoted it to illustrate the use of a word. Literally,
the Greek lines mean: "Holding a sprig of myrtle and a lovely rose, she rejoiced; and her hair covered
her shoulders and back with its shadow." 33 **Helen:** Helen of Troy **discarnate:** fleshless, disembo-
died 34 **dry symposia:** the Greek meaning of *symposion* is "drinking-party." Hence the irony of
"dry." "Of course I was thinking, to some extent, of Plato's *Symposium* and its subject, though that oc-
casion was not dry and has never seemed dry to me." [R.W.] [The "subject" was the nature of love.]
44 **monument to patience:** Cf. Shakespeare, *Twelfth Night*, II, iv, 129–130: "She sat like patience on a
monument,/Smiling at grief. . . ."

Love Calls Us to the Things of This World

The eyes open to a cry of pulleys,
And spirited from sleep, the astounded soul
Hangs for a moment bodiless and simple
As false dawn.

1954–1955. Ibid.

The title, Wilbur has told us, comes from St. Augustine's commentary on the Psalms. Half awakened
by the sound of the pulleys that control the clotheslines, and drowsily seeing the flapping white
shapes on the line, the speaker in the poem imagines they are angels.

Outside the open window
The morning air is all awash with angels.   5

Some are in bed-sheets, some are in blouses,
Some are in smocks: but truly there they are.
Now they are rising together in calm swells
Of halcyon feeling, filling whatever they wear
With the deep joy of their impersonal breathing;   10

Now they are flying in place, conveying
The terrible speed of their omnipresence, moving
And staying like white water; and now of a sudden
They swoon down into so rapt a quiet
That nobody seems to be there.
                       The soul shrinks   15

From all that it is about to remember,
From the punctual rape of every blessèd day,
And cries,
        "Oh, let there be nothing on earth but laundry,
Nothing but rosy hands in the rising steam
And clear dances done in the sight of heaven."   20

Yet, as the sun acknowledges
With a warm look the world's hunks and colors,
The soul descends once more in bitter love
To accept the waking body, saying now
In a changed voice as the man yawns and rises,   25

"Bring them down from their ruddy gallows;
Let there be clean linen for the backs of thieves;
Let lovers go fresh and sweet to be undone,
And the heaviest nuns walk in a pure floating
Of dark habits,
            keeping their difficult balance."   30

---

9 **halcyon:** peaceful, happy (The halcyon was a bird thought to breed on the sea; *halcyon days* were those calm enough for the bird to do so.)   13 **white water:** frothing water, as in rapids or waterfalls   17 **punctual rape:** desecration that is immediate, right on time   26 **ruddy:** (1) reddened by the sunrise; (2) damned (British: a kind of cussword, like "bloody")   30 **habits:** the religious garments nuns wear (or used to wear), and also the usual meaning

Junk

    Huru Welandes
              worc ne geswiceð
    monna ænigum
              ðara ðe Mimming can
    heardne gehealdan.

                WALDERE

1961. *Advice to a Prophet*, 1961.

The epigraph, taken from a fragmentary Anglo-Saxon poem [called "Waldere"], concerns the legendary smith Wayland, and may roughly be translated: "Truly, Wayland's handiwork—the sword Mimming which he made—will never fail any man who knows how to use it bravely." [Wilbur's note]

For the rhythm, see *strong-stress rhythm* in the prosody section.

An axe angles
        from my neighbor's ashcan;
It is hell's handiwork,
        the wood not hickory,
The flow of the grain
        not faithfully followed.
The shivered shaft
        rises from a shellheap
Of plastic playthings,
        paper plates,   5
And the sheer shards
        of shattered tumblers
That were not annealed
        for the time needful.
At the same curbside,
        a cast-off cabinet
Of wavily-warped
        unseasoned wood
Waits to be trundled
        in the trash-man's truck.   10
Haul them off! Hide them!
        The heart winces
For junk and gimcrack,
        for jerrybuilt things
And the men who make them
        for a little money,
Bartering pride
        like the bought boxer
Who pulls his punches,
        or the paid-off jockey   15
Who in the home stretch
        holds in his horse.
Yet the things themselves
        in thoughtless honor
Have kept composure,
        like captives who would not
Talk under torture.
        Tossed from a tailgate
Where the dump displays
        its random dolmens,   20
Its black barrows
        and blazing valleys,
They shall waste in the weather
        and toward what they were.
The sun shall glory
        in the glitter of glass-chips,
Foreseeing the salvage
        of the prisoned sand,
And the blistering paint
        peel off in patches,   25
That the good grain
        be discovered again.
Then burnt, bulldozed,
        they shall all be buried

---

20 **dolmens:** prehistoric tombs or monuments consisting of a stone slab laid across upright stones
21 **barrows:** heaps of earth or rocks marking an ancient grave

To the depth of diamonds,
                    in the making dark
Where halt Hephaestus
              keeps his hammer
And Wayland's work
          is worn away.   30

29 **Hephaestus:** Cf. the notes to Auden's "The Shield of Achilles."

A Grasshopper

But for a brief
Moment, a poised minute,
He paused on the chicory-leaf;
Yet within it

The sprung perch   5
Had time to absorb the shock,
Narrow its pitch and lurch,
Cease to rock.

A quiet spread
Over the neighbor ground;   10
No flower swayed its head
For yards around;

The wind shrank
Away with a swallowed hiss;
Caught in a widening, blank   15
Parenthesis,

Cry upon cry
Faltered and faded out;
Everything seemed to die.
Oh, without doubt   20

Peace like a plague
Had gone to the world's verge,
But that an aimless, vague
Grasshopper-urge

Leapt him aloft,   25
Giving the leaf a kick,
Starting the grasses' soft
Chafe and tick,

So that the sleeping
Crickets resumed their chimes,   30
And all things wakened, keeping
Their several times.

1959. Ibid.

"It's rather obvious that it's a poem about conceptions of peace or blessedness." [R.W.]

23 **aimless:** "I *think* that one reason for the word is that grasshoppers, when they jump, are not too sure where they are going to land. I've always admired good broken-field running . . . do you think the Pittsburgh Steelers would do better still if they could find an innately random running back?" [R.W.]

In gay release
The whole field did what it did,
Peaceful now that its peace   35
Lay busily hid.

Mona Van Duyn
(Born 1921)

Born in Waterloo, Iowa, Mona Van Duyn (pronounced *dine*) received degrees from the
University of Northern Iowa and the University of Iowa; she has taught at the University
of Iowa, the University of Louisville, and Washington University. A founder (with her
husband, Jarvis Thurston) of *Perspective: A Quarterly of Literature*, she was its co-editor
from 1947 to 1967.

Footnotes to "The Autobiography of Bertrand Russell"

II

> *"Her objections to [marrying] him are the following:*
> *(a) He sleeps with 7 dogs on his bed. She couldn't*
> *sleep a wink in such circumstances. (b) . . ."*

This seems, in a world where love must take its chances,
undue distaste for the first of its circumstances.

What in so snug a sleeper could be more rare
than to sense in so snuggling a crowd something lacking there?

And it seems that the lady lacks sensitivity   5
to how brilliant her hymeneal reception might be:

First, on the heated bed he'd push aside
seven drowsing dogs to insert one blushing bride,

and surely all other nuptial welcome pales
before a sweet thrashing given her by seven tails!   10

Fourteen ears attuned to their master's voice
would attend the orisons of their master's choice

in bitches, and should some Donne-reading flea propose
a speedy union, he'd suffer twenty-eight paws.

Garlanded, guarded, graced with panting devotion,   15
the human pair would partake of wedded emotion,

she with unwinking eyes on the dogs, and he
jostling dogs with his old impunity

To See, To Take, 1971.

"Bertrand Russell, British mathematician and philosopher of science [1872–1970], revealed in his
Autobiography a vivid and unrepressed emotional life, and in doing so wrote many unintentionally
humorous passages." [M.V.]

12 orisons: prayers   **13** John Donne has a poem with the title "The Flea," in which the blood of the
lovers mingles when a flea bites both.

until, under his lips, her eyelids would close
and the dear beast of the heart come to discompose   20

the bed whereon seven pairs of canine eyes
would gaze at each other with a wild surmise.

22 Cf. John Keats, "On First Looking into Chapman's Homer," line 13 (p. 320).

Philip Larkin
(Born 1922)

Larkin, born in Coventry, England, has B.A. and M.A. degrees from Oxford. Since 1955,
he has been librarian at the University of Hull, in Yorkshire. For ten years he was jazz
feature writer for the London *Daily Telegraph*. Besides his several books of poetry, which
have won many awards in Britain, he has written two novels and a critical book on jazz
and edited *The Oxford Book of Twentieth Century Verse*.

Lines on a Young Lady's Photograph Album

At last you yielded up the album, which,
Once open, sent me distracted. All your ages
Matt and glossy on the thick black pages!
Too much confectionery, too rich:
I choke on such nutritious images.   5

My swivel eye hungers from pose to pose—
In pigtails, clutching a reluctant cat;
Or furred yourself, a sweet girl-graduate;
Or lifting a heavy-headed rose
Beneath a trellis, or in a trilby hat   10

(Faintly disturbing, that, in several ways)—
From every side you strike at my control,
Not least through these disquieting chaps who loll
At ease about your earlier days:
Not quite your class, I'd say, dear, on the whole.   15

But o, photography! as no art is,
Faithful and disappointing! that records
Dull days as dull, and hold-it smiles as frauds,
And will not censor blemishes
Like washing lines, and Hall's-Distemper boards,   20

But shows the cat as disinclined, and shades
A chin as doubled when it is, what grace
Your candor thus confers upon her face!
How overwhelmingly persuades
That this is a real girl in a real place,   25

The Less Deceived, 1955.

3 **matt**: not glossy   10 **trilby hat**: a rather mannish hat with brim and indented crown, so called be-
cause worn in the dramatization of George Du Maurier's novel *Trilby* (1894), the story of an artist's
model in Paris who becomes a famous singer under the influence of the hypnotist Svengali, but loses
her voice and dies soon after he dies   20 **washing lines**: clotheslines   **Hall's-Distemper boards**:
billboards advertising patent medicines

In every sense empirically true!
Or is it just *the past?* Those flowers, that gate,
These misty parks and motors, lacerate
Simply by being over; you
Contract my heart by looking out of date.   30

Yes, true; but in the end, surely, we cry
Not only at exclusion, but because
It leaves us free to cry. We know *what was*
Won't call on us to justify
Our grief, however hard we yowl across   35

The gap from eye to page. So I am left
To mourn (without a chance of consequence)
You, balanced on a bike against a fence;
To wonder if you'd spot the theft
Of this one of you bathing; to condense,   40

In short, a past that no one now can share,
No matter whose your future; calm and dry,
It holds you like a heaven, and you lie
Unvariably lovely there,
Smaller and clearer as the years go by.   45

At Grass

The eye can hardly pick them out
From the cold shade they shelter in,
Till wind distresses tail and mane;
Then one crops grass, and moves about
—The other seeming to look on—   5
And stands anonymous again.

Yet fifteen years ago, perhaps
Two dozen distances sufficed
To fable them: faint afternoons
Of Cups and Stakes and Handicaps,   10
Whereby their names were artificed
To inlay faded, classic Junes—

Silks at the start: against the sky
Numbers and parasols: outside,
Squadrons of empty cars, and heat,   15
And littered grass: then the long cry
Hanging unhushed till it subside
To stop-press columns on the street.

Do memories plague their ears like flies?
They shake their heads. Dusk brims the shadows.   20

XX *Poems,* 1951.

The title means "in retirement." The "them" of line 1 refers to race horses once famous.

9 **fable:** make fabulous or legendary   18 **stop-press:** news (of the races) sensational enough to "stop the presses"

Summer by summer all stole away,
The starting-gates, the crowds and cries—
All but the unmolesting meadows.
Almanacked, their names live; they

Have slipped their names, and stand at ease,   25
Or gallop for what must be joy,
And not a fieldglass sees them home,
Or curious stop-watch prophesies:
Only the groom, and the groom's boy,
With bridles in the evening come.   30

29 **groom:** man in charge of caring for the horses

The Explosion

On the day of the explosion
Shadows pointed towards the pithead:
In the sun the slagheap slept.

Down the lane came men in pitboots
Coughing oath-edged talk and pipe-smoke,   5
Shouldering off the freshened silence.

One chased after rabbits; lost them;
Came back with a nest of lark's eggs;
Showed them; lodged them in the grasses.

So they passed in beards and moleskins,   10
Fathers, brothers, nicknames, laughter,
Through the tall gates standing open.

At noon, there came a tremor; cows
Stopped chewing for a second; sun,
Scarfed as in a heat-haze, dimmed.   15

The dead go on before us, they
Are sitting in God's house in comfort,
We shall see them face to face—

Plain as lettering in the chapels
It was said, and for a second   20
Wives saw men of the explosion

Larger than in life they managed—
Gold as on a coin, or walking
Somehow from the sun towards them,

One showing the eggs unbroken.   25

By 1972. *High Windows,* 1974.

2 **pithead:** the top of a mine-shaft   10 **moleskins:** clothes made of tough cotton cloth

Anthony Hecht
(Born 1923)

Anthony Hecht was born in New York City, and has degrees from Bard and Columbia; during World War II he was with the U.S. Army. He has taught at Kenyon, Iowa, Smith, Bard, and, since 1967, at the University of Rochester. Besides his several books of poetry he has translated (with Helen Bacon) the *Seven Against Thebes* of Aeschylus and coedited (with John Hollander) a collection of comic double dactyls, *Jiggery-Pokery.*

The End of the Weekend

A dying firelight slides along the quirt
Of the cast-iron cowboy where he leans
Against my father's books. The lariat
Whirls into darkness. My girl, in skin-tight jeans,
Fingers a page of Captain Marryat,   5
Inviting insolent shadows to her shirt.

We rise together to the second floor.
Outside, across the lake, an endless wind
Whips at the headstones of the dead and wails
In the trees for all who have and have not sinned.   10
She rubs against me and I feel her nails.
Although we are alone, I lock the door.

The eventual shapes of all our formless prayers,
This dark, this cabin of loose imaginings,
Wind, lake, lip, everything awaits   15
The slow unloosening of her underthings.
And then the noise. Something is dropped. It grates
Against the attic beams.
                    I climb the stairs,

Armed with a belt.
                    A long magnesium strip
Of moonlight from the dormer cuts a path   20
Among the shattered skeletons of mice.
A great black presence beats its wings in wrath.
Above the boneyard burn its golden eyes.
Some small grey fur is pulsing in its grip.

By 1959. *The Hard Hours*, 1967.

1 **quirt:** riding whip   5 **Captain Marryat:** Frederick Marryat (1792–1848), English naval officer and novelist who wrote tales of adventure at sea   20 **dormer:** a gable window

"More Light! More Light!"

For Heinrich Blücher and Hannah Arendt

Composed in the Tower before his execution
These moving verses, and being brought at that time
Painfully to the stake, submitted, declaring thus:
"I implore my God to witness that I have made no crime."

Nor was he forsaken of courage, but the death was horrible,   5
The sack of gunpowder failing to ignite.
His legs were blistered sticks on which the black sap
Bubbled and burst as he howled for the Kindly Light.

And that was but one, and by no means one of the worst;
Permitted at least his pitiful dignity;   10
And such as were by, made prayers in the name of Christ,
That shall judge all men, for his soul's tranquillity.

We move now to outside a German wood.
Three men are there commanded to dig a hole
In which the two Jews are ordered to lie down   15
And be buried alive by the third, who is a Pole.

Not light from the shrine at Weimar beyond the hill
Nor light from heaven appeared. But he did refuse.
A Luger settled back deeply in its glove.
He was ordered to change places with the Jews.   20

Much casual death had drained away their souls.
The thick dirt mounted toward the quivering chin.
When only the head was exposed the order came
To dig him out again and to get back in.

No light, no light in the blue Polish eye.   25
When he finished a riding boot packed down the earth.
The Luger hovered lightly in its glove.
He was shot in the belly and in three hours bled to death.

By 1961. Ibid.

"More light!..." were reportedly the last words of the great German poet Goethe as he lay dying. Though perhaps only a request to open the shutters, they have usually been taken in a symbolic sense.

1–8 The incident is a conflation, or composite, of such martyrdoms as those of the English Protestants Latimer and Ridley (burned to death in 1555) or of the many others whose death was described in John Foxe's *Book of Martyrs* (English version, 1663). The last words of Latimer (then age 75) were: "Be of good comfort, Master Ridley, and play the man: we shall this day light such a candle by God's grace in England as I trust shall never be put out." 1 **the Tower:** the Tower of London, where important prisoners were confined 2 **these moving verses:** Cf. Tichborne's "Elegy," "Written with his own hand in the Tower before his execution" (p. 72), and Ralegh's "Even Such Is Time" (p. 64). 6 **the sack of gunpowder:** sometimes attached to those burned at the stake to mercifully hasten their death 8 **the Kindly Light:** "Lead, Kindly Light," a hymn composed (1833) by John Henry Newman—later Cardinal Newman 13–32 "The incident is based on one described in *The Theory and Practice of Hell*, a book on the Nazi concentration camps written by Eugen Kogon, a survivor of such camps (English translation, 1966)." [A.H.] The setting is at Buchenwald, one of the most notorious of the extermination centers, just to the north of Weimar, where the trains were unloaded for the camp. Goethe spent most of his life at Weimar; the Goethe National Museum there (cf. the "shrine" of line 17) occupies a house he once lived in. 19 **Luger:** brand name of a German automatic pistol

No prayers or incense rose up in those hours
Which grew to be years, and every day came mute   30
Ghosts from the ovens, sifting through crisp air,
And settled upon his eyes in a black soot.

31 **ovens:** Bodies of the Nazi victims were burned in the camp body-disposal plant, which had a capacity of 400 bodies per ten-hour day.

The Feast of Stephen

I

The coltish horseplay of the locker room,
Moist with the steam of the tiled shower stalls,
With shameless blends of civet, musk and sweat,
Loud with the cap-gun snapping of wet towels
Under the steel-ribbed cages of bare bulbs,   5
In some such setting of thick basement pipes
And janitorial realities
Boys for the first time frankly eye each other,
Inspect each others' bodies at close range,
And what they see is not so much another   10
As a strange, possible version of themselves,
And all the sparring dance, adrenal life,
Tense, jubilant nimbleness, is but a vague,
Busy, unfocused ballet of self-love.

II

If the heart has its reasons, perhaps the body   15
Has its own lumbering sort of carnal spirit,
Felt in the tingling bruises of collision,
And known to captains as *esprit de corps.*
What is this brisk fraternity of timing,
Pivot and lobbing arc, or indirection,   20
Mens sana in men's sauna, in the flush
Of health and toilets, private and corporal glee,
These fleet caroms, *pliés* and genuflections
Before the salmon-leap, the leaping fountain
All sheathed in glistening light, flexed and alert?   25
From the vast echo-chamber of the gym,

By 1976. *Millions of Strange Shadows,* 1977.

The feast-day of St. Stephen, the first Christian martyr, is celebrated on December 26. His story is told in Acts 6 and 7. One of the first seven deacons, he was stoned to death because of his zeal for the Christian cause. Part I, summed up in its first line, describes the athleticism, the "adrenal life," of young men. Part II continues the theme with its focus on drilling, teamwork. Its last line leads into III, concerned with the brutal uses to which the beauty and strength of the body can be put, as shown in the career of the art-loving German officer or the "punks" who use violence to defend their "turf," a violence which may lead to such lynchings as that of St. Stephen, stoned to death "in the terrible name of rectitude," as described in IV.

3 **civet:** a substance with musky odor found near the sexual organs of the civet cat and used in the manufacture of perfume. *Musk* is a similar substance found in a species of male deer.   12 **adrenal life:** The adrenal glands produce various hormones stimulating physical activity.   18 ***esprit de corps:*** (French) team spirit, pride in the group one belongs to. It also "quite literally means 'the spirit of the body,' in which the word 'body' denotes a corporate entity of several individuals. The section also has puns on *flush, private,* and *corporal.*" [A.H.]   21 ***mens sana:*** a healthy mind (Latin)—generally completed with *in corpore sano:* in a healthy body. Here completed with a pun.   23 **caroms:** reboundings, as after physical contact   ***pliés:*** bendings of the knee (French, ballet term)

Among the scumbled shouts and shrill of whistles,
The bounced basketball sound of a leather whip.

III

Think of those barren places where men gather
To act in the terrible name of rectitude,   30
Of acned shame, punk's pride, muscle or turf,
The bully's thin superiority.
Think of the *Sturm-Abteilungs Kommandant*
Who loves Beethoven and collects Degas,
Or the blond boys in jeans whose narrowed eyes   35
Are focussed by some hard and smothered lust,
Who lounge in a studied mimicry of ease,
Flick their live butts into the standing weeds,
And comb their hair in the mirror of cracked windows
Of an abandoned warehouse where they keep   40
In darkened readiness for their occasion
The rope, the chains, handcuffs and gasoline.

IV

Out in the rippled heat of a neighbor's field,
In the kilowatts of noon, they've got one cornered.
The bugs are jumping, and the burly youths   45
Strip to the waist for the hot work ahead.
They go to arm themselves at the dry-stone wall,
Having flung down their wet and salty garments
At the feet of a young man whose name is Saul.
He watches sharply these superbly tanned   50
Figures with a swimmer's chest and shoulders,
A miler's thighs, with their self-conscious grace,
And in between their sleek, converging bodies,
Brilliantly oiled and burnished by the sun,
He catches a brief glimpse of bloodied hair   55
And hears an unintelligible prayer.

27 **scumbled:** blurred, confused   33 ***Sturm-Abteilungs Kommandant:*** Commander of Storm Troops
(German)   34 **Degas:** Edgar Degas (1834–1917), French artist   47 **dry-stone wall:** a wall of stones
put together without mortar   49 **Saul:** the name of St. Paul before his conversion, when he was a
persecutor of the Christians. Cf. Acts 7:58 ff.: "and the witnesses laid down their clothes at a young
man's feet, whose name was Saul. . . . And Saul was consenting unto his death. . . ."   56 **unintelligi-
ble prayer:** when dying, Stephen prayed: "Lord, lay not this sin to their charge" (Acts 7:60).

James Dickey
(Born 1923)

Born in Atlanta in 1923, Dickey obtained degrees from Clemson (where he was a star
halfback) and Vanderbilt (where he was on the track team). He was a night fighter pilot
with the air force in World War II and in the Korean War, with over 100 missions to his
credit. After the war he was for some years an advertising executive in New York and At-
lanta. He has taught as poet-in-residence at several universities, among them Rice, Reed,
and, since 1969, the University of South Carolina. Besides his several books of poetry, he
has written criticism, translations, and the novel *Deliverance,* for which he also wrote the
screenplay.

Cherrylog Road

Off Highway 106
At Cherrylog Road I entered
The '34 Ford without wheels,
Smothered in kudzu,
With a seat pulled out to run   5
Corn whiskey down from the hills,

And then from the other side
Crept into an Essex
With a rumble seat of red leather
And then out again, aboard   10
A blue Chevrolet, releasing
The rust from its other color,

Reared up on three building blocks.
None had the same body heat;
I changed with them inward, toward   15
The weedy heart of the junkyard,
For I knew that Doris Holbrook
Would escape from her father at noon

And would come from the farm
To seek parts owned by the sun   20
Among the abandoned chassis,
Sitting in each in turn
As I did, leaning forward
As in a wild stock-car race

In the parking lot of the dead.   25
Time after time, I climbed in
And out the other side, like
An envoy or movie star
Met at the station by crickets.
A radiator cap raised its head,   30

Become a real toad or a kingsnake
As I neared the hub of the yard,
Passing through many states,
Many lives, to reach
Some grandmother's long Pierce-Arrow   35
Sending platters of blindness forth

From its nickel hubcaps
And spilling its tender upholstery
On sleepy roaches,
The glass panel in between   40
Lady and colored driver
Not all the way broken out,

1960. *Helmets*, 1964.

See Additional Notes (p. 782).

4 kudzu: a vine used for forage and erosion control, now widespread and growing wild in parts of the South   **31 kingsnake:** a brightly colored, nonpoisonous, rodent-eating snake

The back-seat phone
Still on its hook.
I got in as though to exclaim,   45
"Let us go to the orphan asylum,
John; I have some old toys
For children who say their prayers."

I popped with sweat as I thought
I heard Doris Holbrook scrape   50
Like a mouse in the southern-state sun
That was eating the paint in blisters
From a hundred car tops and hoods.
She was tapping like code,

Loosening the screws,   55
Carrying off headlights,
Sparkplugs, bumpers,
Cracked mirrors and gear-knobs,
Getting ready, already,
To go back with something to show   60

Other than her lips' new trembling
I would hold to me soon, soon,
Where I sat in the ripped back seat
Talking over the interphone,
Praying for Doris Holbrook   65
To come from her father's farm

And to get back there
With no trace of me on her face
To be seen by her red-haired father
Who would change, in the squalling barn,   70
Her back's pale skin with a strop,
Then lay for me

In a bootlegger's roasting car
With a string-triggered 12-gauge shotgun
To blast the breath from the air.   75
Not cut by the jagged windshields,
Through the acres of wrecks she came
With a wrench in her hand,

Through dust where the blacksnake dies
Of boredom, and the beetle knows   80
The compost has no more life.
Someone outside would have seen
The oldest car's door inexplicably
Close from within:

I held her and held her and held her,   85
Convoyed at terrific speed
By the stalled, dreaming traffic around us,
So the blacksnake, stiff
With inaction, curved back
Into life, and hunted the mouse   90

79 **blacksnake:** a harmless dark-colored snake

With deadly overexcitement,
The beetles reclaimed their field
As we clung, glued together,
With the hooks of the seat springs
Working through to catch us red-handed   95
Amidst the gray breathless batting

That burst from the seat at our backs.
We left by separate doors
Into the changed, other bodies
Of cars, she down Cherrylog Road   100
And I to my motorcycle
Parked like the soul of the junkyard

Restored, a bicycle fleshed
With power, and tore off
Up Highway 106, continually   105
Drunk on the wind in my mouth,
Wringing the handlebar for speed,
Wild to be wreckage forever.

96 **batting:** stuffing, padding

Pursuit from Under

Often, in these blue meadows,
I hear what passes for the bark of seals

And on August week ends the cold of a personal ice age
Comes up through my bare feet
Which are trying to walk like a boy's again   5
So that nothing on earth can have changed
On the ground where I was raised.

The dark grass here is like
The pads of mukluks going on and on

Because I once burned kerosene to read   10
Myself near the North Pole
In the journal of Arctic explorers
Found, years after death, preserved
In a tent, part of whose canvas they had eaten

Before the last entry.   15
All over my father's land

The seal holes sigh like an organ,
And one entry carries more terror
Than the blank page that signified death
In 1912, on the icecap.   20
It says that, under the ice,
The killer whale darts and distorts,
Cut down by the flawing glass

1963. *Buckdancer's Choice*, 1965.

9 **mukluks:** sealskin or reindeer-skin boots worn by Eskimos

To a weasel's shadow,
And when, through his ceiling, he sees   25
Anything darker than snow
He falls away
To gather more and more force

From the iron depths of cold water,
His shadow dwindling   30

Almost to nothing at all, then charges
Straight up, looms up at the ice and smashes
Into it with his forehead
To splinter the roof, to isolate seal or man
On a drifting piece of the floe   35

Which he can overturn.
If you run, he will follow you

Under the frozen pane,
Turning as you do, zigzagging,
And at the most uncertain of your ground   40
Will shatter through, and lean,
And breathe frankly in your face

An enormous breath smelling of fish.
With the stale lungs staining your air

You know the unsaid recognition   45
Of which the explorers died:
They had been given an image
Of how the downed dead pursue us.
They knew, as they starved to death,

That not only in the snow   50
But in the family field

The small shadow moves,
And under bare feet in the summer:
That somewhere the turf will heave,
And the outraged breath of the dead,   55
So long held, will form

Unbreathably around the living.
The cows low oddly here

As I pass, a small bidden shape
Going with me, trembling like foxfire   60
Under my heels and their hooves.
I shall write this by kerosene,
Pitch a tent in the pasture, and starve.

60 **foxfire:** an eerie phosphorescent glow, as from decaying wood

Alan Dugan
(Born 1923)

Dugan was born in Brooklyn, educated at Olivet College (Michigan) and Mexico City College. During World War II he was with the air force. Besides teaching at Connecticut College, Sarah Lawrence, and the University of Colorado, he has made frequent visits to other colleges.

Funeral Oration for a Mouse

This, Lord, was an anxious brother and
a living diagram of fear: full of health himself,
    he brought diseases like a gift
to give his hosts. Masked in a cat's moustache
but sounding like a bird, he was a ghost   5
    of lesser noises and a kitchen pest
for whom some ladies stand on chairs. So,
Lord, accept our felt though minor guilt
    for an ignoble foe and ancient sin:
        the murder of a guest   10
who shared our board: just once he ate
    too slowly, dying in our trap
from necessary hunger and a broken back.

Humors of love aside, the mousetrap was our own
    opinion of the mouse, but for the mouse   15
    it was the tree of knowledge with
    its consequential fruit, the true cross
and the gate of hell. Even to approach
    it makes him like or better than
its maker: his courage as a spoiler never once   20
impressed us, but to go out cautiously at night,
    into the dining room;—what bravery, what
    hunger! Younger by far, in dying he
was older than us all: his mobile tail and nose
spasmed in the pinch of our annoyance. Why,   25
then, at that snapping sound, did we, victorious,
    begin to laugh without delight?

Our stomachs, deep in an analysis
    of their own stolen baits
(and asking, "Lord, Host, to whom are we the pests?"),   30
    contracted and demanded a retreat
from our machine and its effect of death,
    as if the mouse's fingers, skinnier
than hairpins and as breakable as cheese,
    could grasp our grasping lives, and in   35
their drowning movement pull us under too,
into the common death beyond the mousetrap.

1945–1946. *Poems*, 1961.

16 the tree of knowledge . . . : Cf. Gen. 2:16–17: "And the Lord God commanded the man, saying, Of every tree of the garden thou mayest freely eat: but of the tree of the knowledge of good and evil, thou shalt not eat of it: for in the day that thou eatest thereof thou shalt surely die."

W. D. Snodgrass
(Born 1926)

Born in Wilkinsburg, Pennsylvania, Snodgrass earned three degrees from the University of Iowa. After service with the navy, he taught at several colleges, including Cornell, Wayne State, Syracuse, and Delaware. Besides his poetry, he has written criticism and translated (with Lore Segal) the *Gallows Songs* of the German poet Morgenstern. A trained musician, Snodgrass has translated many songs from the Provençal, Hungarian, and other languages to fit the original music.

April Inventory

The green catalpa tree has turned
All white; the cherry blooms once more.
In one whole year I haven't learned
A blessed thing they pay you for.
The blossoms snow down in my hair;   5
The trees and I will soon be bare.

The trees have more than I to spare.
The sleek, expensive girls I teach,
Younger and pinker every year,
Bloom gradually out of reach.   10
The pear tree lets its petals drop
Like dandruff on a tabletop.

The girls have grown so young by now
I have to nudge myself to stare.
This year they smile and mind me how   15
My teeth are falling with my hair.
In thirty years I may not get
Younger, shrewder, or out of debt.

The tenth time, just a year ago,
I made myself a little list   20
Of all the things I'd ought to know,
Then told my parents, analyst,
And everyone who's trusted me
I'd be substantial, presently.

I haven't read one book about   25
A book or memorized one plot.
Or found a mind I did not doubt.
I learned one date. And then forgot.
And one by one the solid scholars
Get the degrees, the jobs, the dollars.   30

And smile above their starchy collars.
I taught my classes Whitehead's notions;
One lovely girl, a song of Mahler's.
Lacking a source-book or promotions,
I showed one child the colors of   35
A luna moth and how to love.

Heart's Needle, 1960.

32 **Whitehead:** Alfred North Whitehead (1861–1947), the English mathematician and philosopher
33 **Mahler:** Gustav Mahler (1860–1911), Austrian composer   36 **luna moth:** a large North American moth with pale-green wings with crescent markings

I taught myself to name my name,
To bark back, loosen love and crying;
To ease my woman so she came,
To ease an old man who was dying.   40
I have not learned how often I
Can win, can love, but choose to die.

I have not learned there is a lie
Love shall be blonder, slimmer, younger;
That my equivocating eye   45
Loves only by my body's hunger;
That I have forces, true to feel,
Or that the lovely world is real.

While scholars speak authority
And wear their ulcers on their sleeves,   50
My eyes in spectacles shall see
These trees procure and spend their leaves.
There is a value underneath
The gold and silver in my teeth.

Though trees turn bare and girls turn wives,   55
We shall afford our costly seasons;
There is a gentleness survives
That will outspeak and has its reasons.
There is a loveliness exists,
Preserves us, not for specialists.   60

A. R. Ammons
(Born 1926)

Born in Whiteville, North Carolina, Ammons majored in the sciences at Wake Forest University and in English at the University of California at Berkeley. From 1944 to 1946 he was with the U.S. navy. After a period as principal of an elementary school, he worked for ten years as executive vice-president of a New Jersey firm that manufactured biological glassware. Since 1964 he has taught at Cornell. He has written ten or more books of poetry.

Mechanism

Honor a going thing, goldfinch, corporation, tree,
        morality: any working order,
    animate or inanimate: it

has managed directed balance,
        the incoming and outgoing energies are working right,   5
    some energy left to the mechanism,

1959. *Expressions of Sea Level,* 1964.

Looking at a goldfinch (a small black and yellow bird), A. R. Ammons, whose majors in college were pre-med, biology, chemistry, and general science, sees something quite different from what a romantic poet might have seen. He might exclaim, with Shelley, "Bird thou never wert," but in a different sense, and with deeper knowledge than a nineteenth-century poet could have had of the chemical and biological processes whose "billion operations" make the bird a "going thing," admirable as any successful process—biological, financial, moral—is admirable.

some ash, enough energy held
    to maintain the order in repair,
    assure further consumption of entropy,

expending energy to strengthen order: 10
    honor the persisting reactor,
    the container of change, the moderator: the yellow

bird flashes black wing-bars
    in the new-leaving wild cherry bushes by the bay,
    startles the hawk with beauty,   15

flitting to a branch where
    flash vanishes into stillness,
    hawk addled by the sudden loss of sight:

honor the chemistries, platelets, hemoglobin kinetics,
    the light-sensitive iris, the enzymic intricacies   20
    of control,

the gastric transformations, seed
    dissolved to acrid liquors, synthesized into
    chirp, vitreous humor, knowledge,

blood compulsion, instinct: honor the   25
    unique genes,
    molecules that reproduce themselves, divide into

sets, the nucleic grain transmitted
    in slow change through ages of rising and falling form,
    some cells set aside for the special work, mind   30

or perception rising into orders of courtship,
    territorial rights, mind rising
    from the physical chemistries

to guarantee that genes will be exchanged, male
    and female met, the satisfactions cloaking a deeper   35
    racial satisfaction:

heat kept by a feathered skin:
    the living alembic, body heat maintained (bunsen
    burner under the flask)

---

9 **entropy:** the measure of unavailable or declining energy in a closed and changing system, such as a goldfinch—or the universe   14 **new-leaving:** producing new leaves   18 **addled:** confused, baffled   19 **platelets:** disks of protoplasm in the blood that promote clotting   **hemoglobin kinetics:** the laws of motion or change that govern the red blood corpuscles, which carry oxygen to the tissues and remove carbon dioxide   20 **iris:** the colored diaphragm of the eye, which expands or contracts to allow more or less light to enter   **enzymic:** pertaining to an enzyme, a substance that facilitates chemical reactions in the body   22 **gastric:** pertaining to the stomach and the digestive processes   24 **chirp:** birdsong   **vitreous humor:** the transparent semiliquid substance in the eyeball   26 **genes:** the biological units that carry hereditary characteristics and determine species   28 **nucleic grain:** The nucleic acids are complex organic acids found in all living cells and essential to life.   31–32 **orders of courtship,** / **territorial rights:** aspects of bird behavior   38 **alembic:** a flask or container formerly used (as in alchemy) for heating, distilling, etc.   38–39 **bunsen** / **burner:** a small gas burner much used in laboratories

so the chemistries can proceed, reaction rates   40
      interdependent, self-adjusting, with optimum
    efficiency—the vessel firm, the flame

staying: isolated, contained reactions! the precise and
      necessary worked out of random, reproducible,
    the handiwork redeemed from chance, while the   45

goldfinch, unconscious of the billion operations
      that stay its form, flashes, chirping (not a
    great songster) in the bay cherry bushes wild of leaf.

47 **stay:** stabilize, steady, preserve

The Constant

When leaving the primrose, bayberry dunes, seaward
I discovered the universe this morning,
      I was in no
mood
for wonder,   5
    the naked mass of so much miracle
already beyond the vision
of my grasp:

along a rise of beach, a hundred feet from the surf,
a row of clam shells   10
    four to ten feet wide
    lay sinuous as far as sight:

in one shell—though in the abundance
      there were others like it—upturned,
four or five inches across the wing,   15
a lake
three to four inches long and two inches wide,
all dimensions rounded,
    indescribable in curve:

and on the lake a turning galaxy, a film of sand,   20
co-ordinated, nearly circular (no real perfections),
    an inch in diameter, turning:
turning:
counterclockwise, the wind hardly perceptible from 11 o'clock
    with noon at sea: 25
    the galaxy rotating,
    but also,
at a distance from the shell lip,
revolving
round and round the shell: 30

1962. *Northfield Poems*, 1966.

1 **bayberry:** a shrub common on the eastern coast   2 **the universe:** as figured or represented in the
"galaxy" of sand rotating in the clam shell (line 20)

        a gull's toe could spill the universe:
two more hours of sun could dry it up:
a higher wind could rock it out:

the tide will rise, engulf it, wash it loose:
utterly: 35

the terns, their
        young somewhere hidden in clumps of grass or weed,
were diving *sshik sshik* at me,
                then pealing upward for another round and dive:

I have had too much of this inexhaustible miracle: 40
miracle, this massive, drab constant of experience.

36 **terns:** seabirds like gulls, but smaller

Life in the Boondocks

Untouched grandeur in the hinterlands:
large-lobed ladies laughing in brook
water, a clear, scrubbed ruddiness lofted

to cones and conifers: frost blurs
the morning elk there and squirrels   5
chitter with the dawn, numb seed: clarity,

the eagle dips into scary nothingness,
off a bluff over canyon heights: trout
plunder their way up, thrashing the shallows

white: ladies come out in the gold-true sun   10
and loll easy as white boulders
in the immediate radiance by wind-chilling

streams: I have been there so
often, so often and held the women, squeezed,
tickled, nuzzled their rose-paint luxury: 15

so many afternoons listened to the rocky
drone of bees over spring-water weed-bloom,
snow-water violets, and distant moss turf.

1969. *Uplands*, 1970.

boondocks: rural areas, the "sticks," the backwoods (from the Tagalog [Philippine] *bundok*, moun-
tain—orginally World War II slang)   2 **large-lobed:** a gentler and more playful way of saying big-
breasted   4 **cones and conifers:** the surrounding evergreens   6 **chitter:** twitter, chirp, chatter

Cut the Grass

The wonderful workings of the world: wonderful,
wonderful: I'm surprised half the time:
ground up fine, I puff if a pebble stirs:

1969. *Briefings*, 1971.

I'm nervous: my morality's intricate: if
a squash blossom dies, I feel withered as a stained   5
zucchini and blame my nature: and

when grassblades flop to the little red-ant
queens burring around trying to get aloft, I blame
my not keeping the grass short, stubble

firm: well, I learn a lot of useless stuff, meant   10
to be ignored: like when the sun sinking in the
west glares a plane invisible, I think how much

revelation concealment necessitates: and then I
think of the ocean, multiple to a blinding
oneness and realize that only total expression   15

expresses hiding: I'll have to say everything
to take on the roundness and withdrawal of the deep dark:
less than total is a bucketful of radiant toys.

8 **burring:** bustling, fumbling, hurrying, etc.   12 **glares ... invisible:** makes invisible in the glare
14-15 **multiple ... oneness:** its countless sparkles making a single vast dazzle   18 **radiant toys:** bril-
liant details only—not a unified totality

James Merrill
(Born 1926)

Merrill, born in New York City, served for a year in the U.S. army before graduating
from Amherst in 1947. He has travelled widely; in recent years has lived much of the
time in Greece. He has written plays and novels as well as his dozen or more books of
poetry.

The Broken Home

Crossing the street,
I saw the parents and the child
At their window, gleaming like fruit
With evening's mild gold leaf.

In a room on the floor below,   5
Sunless, cooler—a brimming
Saucer of wax, marbly and dim—
I have lit what's left of my life.

I have thrown out yesterday's milk
And opened a book of maxims.   10
The flame quickens. The word stirs.

1962. *Nights and Days*, 1967.

This sequence of seven sonnets, which takes minor liberties with the form, is about events and feel-
ings connected with the 1938 divorce of the poet's parents when he was 12 and about its effect on
him, as he looks back on it now from the age of 36.

1-4 Going to his rented room, the speaker noticed a happy family scene on the floor above.   7 **sau-
cer of wax:** The candle, with its "flame," "word," "tongue of fire," is like the life of poetry he has cho-
sen, and which he hopes is as "real" as the life of domestic happiness above.

Tell me, tongue of fire,
That you and I are as real
At least as the people upstairs.

My father, who had flown in World War I,   15
Might have continued to invest his life
In cloud banks well above Wall Street and wife.
But the race was run below, and the point was to win.

Too late now, I make out in his blue gaze
(Through the smoked glass of being thirty-six)   20
The soul eclipsed by twin black pupils, sex
And business; time was money in those days.

Each thirteenth year he married. When he died
There were already several chilled wives
In sable orbit—rings, cars, permanent waves.   25
We'd felt him warming up for a green bride.

He could afford it. He was "in his prime"
At three score ten. But money was not time.

When my parents were younger this was a popular act:
A veiled woman would leap from an electric, wine-dark car   30
To the steps of no matter what—the Senate or the Ritz Bar—
And bodily, at newsreel speed, attack

No matter whom—Al Smith or José María Sert
Or Clemenceau—veins standing out on her throat
As she yelled *War mongerer! Pig! Give us the vote!*,   35
And would have to be hauled away in her hobble skirt.

What had the man done? Oh, made history.
Her business (he had implied) was giving birth,
Tending the house, mending the socks.

Always that same old story—   40
Father Time and Mother Earth,
A marriage on the rocks.

One afternoon, red, satyr-thighed
Michael, the Irish setter, head

15 **my father:** Merrill's father, born in 1885, was a highly successful investment banker, member of
the Stock Exchange, founder of companies, etc. He was married three times; the poem suggests a
fourth marriage was in the offing when he died in 1956 at the age of 70.   29–36 Demonstrations for
women's rights were especially passionate in the years before and during World War I. The Nine-
teenth Amendment of 1920 gave women the right to vote. The man–woman conflict, "that same old
story," has a bearing on the divorce.   30 **electric . . . car:** Elegant battery-powered automobiles were
fashionable in the twenties.   31 **Ritz Bar:** *the* Ritz Bar is in Paris   33 **Al Smith:** Alfred E. Smith
(1873–1944), New York political leader, was three times governor of the state (1919–1928) and candi-
date for president, against Herbert Hoover, in 1928.   **José María Sert:** Spanish painter (1876–1945),
famous especially for his murals. Some are in the RCA Building and the Waldorf-Astoria in New
York.   34 **Clemenceau:** Georges Clemenceau (1841–1929), French statesman and wartime leader; pre-
mier 1906–1909, 1917–1920.   35 **War mongerer:** The correct form is *warmonger.* [Modern as the word
sounds, it was used by Edmund Spenser in 1590.]   36 **hobble skirt:** a long skirt, narrow below the
knees so that walking was difficult, especially popular 1910–1914   43 **satyr-thighed:** with shaggy
upper legs, like those depicted on the goat-footed satyrs of mythology

Passionately lowered, led   45
The child I was to a shut door. Inside,

Blinds beat sun from the bed.
The green-gold room throbbed like a bruise.
Under a sheet, clad in taboos
Lay whom we sought, her hair undone, outspread,   50

And of a blackness found, if ever now, in old
Engravings where the acid bit.
I must have needed to touch it
Or the whiteness—was she dead?
Her eyes flew open, startled strange and cold.   55
The dog slumped to the floor. She reached for me. I fled.

Tonight they have stepped out onto the gravel.
The party is over. It's the fall
Of 1931. They love each other still.

She: Charlie, I can't stand the pace.   60
He: Come on, honey—why, you'll bury us all!

A lead soldier guards my windowsill:
Khaki rifle, uniform, and face.
Something in me grows heavy, silvery, pliable.

How intensely people used to feel!   65
Like metal poured at the close of a proletarian novel,
Refined and glowing from the crucible,
I see those two hearts, I'm afraid,
Still. Cool here in the graveyard of good and evil,
They are even so to be honored and obeyed.   70

. . . Obeyed, at least, inversely. Thus
I rarely buy a newspaper, or vote.
To do so, I have learned, is to invite
The tread of a stone guest within my house.

Shooting this rusted bolt, though, against him,   75
I trust I am no less time's child than some
Who on the heath impersonate Poor Tom
Or on the barricades risk life and limb.

---

50 **whom we sought:** the child's mother   58 **the party is over:** an actual party—but with possible symbolic overtones relating to the marriage of 1926 (and—possibly?—to the mood of the country when the carefree party-loving twenties ended in the Great Depression)   66 **a proletarian novel:** a novel about the sufferings and difficulties of the working class—steel-workers, for example   67 **crucible:** the hollow at the bottom of an ore furnace, where the molten metal collects   71 **Obeyed . . . inversely:** by doing the exact opposite of what they would have wanted   73-74 **to invite . . . stone guest:** as Don Giovanni, in Mozart's opera of that name, invites the stone statue of the commander whom he has killed to come to dinner. The statue comes, with heavy footsteps, seizes Don Giovanni in a stone handclasp, and drags him off to hell.   75 **Shooting this . . . bolt:** fastening the door with a bolt   76 **time's child:** "Cf. line 41 for principal meaning. Same business in line 84." [J.M.]   77 **heath . . . Poor Tom:** in Shakespeare's *King Lear* (III, iv) the suffering old king finds himself in a storm in desolate open country ("the heath"). His son Edgar chooses to share his sufferings by disguising himself as a "Bedlam beggar" (cf. "Loving Mad Tom," p. 110), who says, among other things, "Obey thy parents."   78 **on the barricades:** by taking an active part in revolutionary activities

Nor do I try to keep a garden, only
An avocado in a glass of water—   80
Roots pallid, gemmed with air. And later,

When the small gilt leaves have grown
Fleshy and green, I let them die, yes, yes,
And start another. I am earth's no less.

A child, a red dog roam the corridors,   85
Still, of the broken home. No sound. The brilliant
Rag runners halt before wide-open doors.
My old room! Its wallpaper—cream, medallioned
With pink and brown—brings back the first nightmares,
Long summer colds, and Emma, sepia-faced,   90
Perspiring over broth carried upstairs
Aswim with golden fats I could not taste.

The real house became a boarding-school.
Under the ballroom ceiling's allegory
Someone at last may actually be allowed   95
To learn something; or, from my window, cool
With the unstiflement of the entire story,
Watch a red setter stretch and sink in cloud.

87 **Rag runners:** long narrow rugs, as in a hall, woven of colorful strips of cloth   90 **Emma:** the
child's nurse   94 **allegory:** allegorical paintings, as of figures from mythology   98 **red setter:** The
Irish setter of lines 44 and 85 here suggests a pun for imagery of the setting sun.

Robert Creeley
(Born 1926)

Born in Arlington, Massachusetts, Creeley attended Harvard for three years, and has de-
grees from Black Mountain College and the University of New Mexico. In 1944–1945 he
was with the American field service in India and Burma. He taught in Guatemala for two
years, at Black Mountain College, and, since 1966, at SUNY at Buffalo. For two years he
directed the Divers Press in Mallorca; he has been editor of the *Black Mountain Review* and
associated with other literary magazines.

A Wicker Basket

Comes the time when it's later
and onto your table the headwaiter
puts the bill, and very soon after
rings out the sound of lively laughter—

Picking up change, hands like a walrus,   5
and a face like a barndoor's,
and a head without an apparent size,
nothing but two eyes—

So that's you, man,
or me. I make it as I can,   10
I pick up, I go
faster than they know—

1956. *A Form of Women*, 1959.

Out the door, the street like a night,
any night, and no one in sight,
but then, well, there she is,   15
old friend Liz—

And she opens the door of her cadillac,
I step in back,
and we're gone.
She turns me on—   20

There are very huge stars, man, in the sky,
and from somewhere very far off someone hands me a slice of apple pie,
with a gob of white, white ice cream on top of it,
and I eat it—

Slowly. And while certainly   25
they are laughing at me, and all around me is racket
of these cats not making it, I make it

in my wicker basket.

The Act of Love

> *For Bobbie*

Whatever constitutes
the act of love,
save physical

encounter, you are
dear to me,   5
not value as

with banks—
but a meaning self-
sufficient, dry

at times as sand,   10
or else the trees,
dripping with

rain. How shall
one, this so-
called person,   15

say it? He
loves, his mind
is occupied, his

hands move .
writing words   20
which come

into his head.
Now here,
the day surrounds

1970. *St. Martin's*, 1971.

this man
and woman
sitting a small

distance apart.
Love will not
solve it—but

draws closer,
always, makes
the moisture of their

mouths and bodies
actively
engage. If I

wanted
a dirty picture,
would it always

be of a
woman straddled?
Yes

and no, these
are true opposites,
a you and me

of non-
sense,
for our love.

Now, one
says, the wind
lifts, the sky

is very blue, the
water just
beyond me makes

its lovely sounds.
How *dear*
you are

to me, how love-
ly all your
body *is*, how

all these
senses do
commingle, so

that in your very
arms I still
can think of you.

Allen Ginsberg
(Born 1926)

Ginsberg was born in Newark in 1926, the son of the poet Louis Ginsberg. After graduating from Columbia he worked at various jobs: in a ribbon factory, on an AFL newspaper, as a market researcher. In the 1950s he was prominently associated with the Beat movement and the San Francisco Renaissance. He has travelled widely and participated in many peace demonstrations. Ginsberg has written plays, journals, and essays as well as some two dozen books or chapbooks of poetry.

A Supermarket in California

What thoughts I have of you tonight, Walt Whitman, for I walked down the sidestreets under the trees with a headache self-conscious looking at the full moon.

In my hungry fatigue, and shopping for images, I went into the neon fruit supermarket, dreaming of your enumerations!

What peaches and what penumbras! Whole families shopping at night! Aisles full of husbands! Wives in the avocados, babies in the tomatoes!—and you, Garcia Lorca, what were you doing down by the watermelons?

I saw you, Walt Whitman, childless, lonely old grubber, poking among the meats in the refrigerator and eyeing the grocery boys.

I heard you asking questions of each: Who killed the pork chops? What price bananas? Are you my Angel?   5

I wandered in and out of the brilliant stacks of cans following you, and followed in my imagination by the store detective.

We strode down the open corridors together in our solitary fancy tasting artichokes, possessing every frozen delicacy, and never passing the cashier.

Where are we going, Walt Whitman? The doors close in an hour. Which way does your beard point tonight?

(I touch your book and dream of our odyssey in the supermarket and feel absurd.)

Will we walk all night through solitary streets? The trees add shade to shade, lights out in the houses, we'll both be lonely.   10

Will we stroll dreaming of the lost America of love past blue automobiles in driveways, home to our silent cottage?

Ah, dear father, graybeard, lonely old courage-teacher, what America did you have when Charon quit poling his ferry and you got out on a smoking bank and stood watching the boat disappear on the black waters of Lethe?

Berkeley 1955

Howl, 1956.

1 **Walt Whitman:** the American poet (1819–1892) whose technique—long lines in free rhythm, accumulation of details, and so on—were an influence on Ginsberg.   3 **Garcia Lorca:** Federico García Lorca (1899–1936), Spanish poet and dramatist. "See his *Ode to Walt Whitman*." [A.G.]   9 **odyssey:** an adventurous journey or quest, like that of Odysseus (as related by Homer) in his ten years of wandering after the Trojan War   12 **Charon:** in classical mythology, the ferryman who carried the dead across a river generally called the Styx. Lethe is another underworld river whose waters caused forgetfulness in the drinker.

Cafe in Warsaw

These spectres resting on plastic stools
leather-gloved spectres flitting thru the coffeehouse one hour
spectre girls with scarred faces, black stockings thin eyebrows
spectre boys blond hair combed neat over the skull little chin beards
new spectres talking intensely crowded together over black shiny tables
     late afternoon   5
the sad soprano of history chanting thru a hi-fidelity loudspeaker
—perspective walls & windows 18th century down New World Avenue
     to Sigmund III column'd
sword upraised watching over Polish youth 3 centuries—
O Polish spectres what've you suffered since Chopin wept into his ro-
     mantic piano
old buildings rubbled down, gaiety of all night parties under the air
     bombs,   10
first screams of the vanishing ghetto—Workmen step thru prewar pink-
     blue bedroom walls demolishing sunny ruins—
Now spectres gather to kiss hands, girls kiss lip to lip, red witchhair from
     Paris
& fine gold watches—to sit by the yellow wall with a large brown brief-
     case—
to smoke three cigarettes with thin black ties and nod heads over a new
     movie—
Spectres Christ and your bodies be with you for this hour while you're
     young   15
in postwar heaven stained with the sweat of Communism, your loves and
     your white smooth cheekskin soft in the glance of each other's eye.
O spectres how beautiful your calm shaven faces, your pale lipstick
     scarves, your delicate heels,
how beautiful your absent gaze, legs crossed alone at table with long eye-
     lashes,
how beautiful your patient love together sitting reading the art jour-
     nals—
how beautiful your entrance thru the velvet-curtained door, laughing
     into the overcrowded room,   20
how you wait in your hats, measure the faces, and turn and depart for an
     hour,
or meditate at the bar, waiting for the slow waitress to prepare red hot
     tea, minute by minute
standing still as hours ring in churchbells, as years pass and you will re-
     main in Novy Swiat,
how beautiful you press your lips together, sigh forth smoke from your
     mouth, rub your hands
or lean together laughing to notice this wild haired madman who sits
     weeping among you a stranger.   25

1965. *Planet News*, 1968.

In 1970 Ginsberg wrote that he had travelled "half year Cuba Russia Poland Czechoslovakia culminating May Day 1965 election as King of May (Kral Majales) by 100,000 Prague citizens."

7 **New World Avenue:** the continuation of Cracow Boulevard, the oldest north-south thoroughfare in Warsaw, lined with Neoclassic houses of the eighteenth and early nineteenth centuries. **Sigmund III:** Sigismund III, the half-Swedish king of Poland from 1587 to 1632, was widely unpopular with his subjects and, though his armies won some victories in their many wars, on the whole more a source of trouble than triumph to Poland.   9 **Chopin:** Frédéric François Chopin (1810–1849), Polish pianist and composer, of French ancestry   10 **old buildings . . . :** Over 80 percent of Warsaw was destroyed by German armies in World War II.   23 **Novy Swiat:** Nowy Świat (Polish), "New World," the name of the street mentioned in line 6

David Wagoner
(Born 1926)

Wagoner, born in Massillon, Ohio, grew up in Whiting, Indiana. He has degrees from Pennsylvania State University and Indiana University, has taught at De Pauw, Penn State, and, since 1954, at the University of Washington, where he has been editor of *Poetry Northwest*. Wagoner has written ten novels and a play as well as his eleven books of poetry.

Meeting a Bear

If you haven't made noise enough to warn him, singing, shouting,
Or thumping sticks against trees as you walk in the woods,
Giving him time to vanish
(As he wants to) quietly sideways through the nearest thicket,
You may wind up standing face to face with a bear.   5
Your near future,
Even your distant future, may depend on how he feels
Looking at you, on what he makes of you
And your upright posture
Which, in his world, like a down-swayed head and humped shoulders,   10
Is a standing offer to fight for territory
And a mate to go with it.
Gaping and staring directly are as risky as running:
To try for dominance or moral authority
Is an empty gesture,   15
And taking to your heels is an invitation to a dance
Which, from your point of view, will be no circus.
He won't enjoy your smell
Or anything else about you, including your ancestors
Or the shape of your snout. If the feeling's mutual,   20
It's still out of balance:
He doesn't *care* what you think or calculate; your disapproval
Leaves him as cold as the opinions of salmon.
He may feel free
To act out all his own displeasures with a vengeance: 25
You would do well to try your meekest behavior,
Standing still
As long as you're not mauled or hugged, your eyes downcast.
But if you must make a stir, do everything sidelong,
Gently and naturally,   30
Vaguely oblique. Withdraw without turning and start saying
Softly, monotonously, whatever comes to mind
Without special pleading:
Nothing hurt or reproachful to appeal to his better feelings.
He has none, only a harder life than yours.   35
There's no use singing
National anthems or battle hymns or alma maters
Or any other charming or beastly music.
Use only the dullest,
Blandest, most colorless, undemonstrative speech you can think of.   40

1975. *Travelling Light,* 1976.

"The advice in 'Meeting a Bear' and 'Walking in a Swamp' is sound wilderness behavior instruction on one level." [D.W.]

37 **alma maters:** school or college songs. *Alma mater* (Latin): means "fostering mother."

Bears, for good reason, find it embarrassing
Or at least disarming
And will forget their claws and cover their eyeteeth as an answer.
Meanwhile, move off, yielding the forest floor
As carefully as your honor.   45

Walking in a Swamp

When you first feel the ground under your feet
Going soft and uncertain,
It's best to start running as fast as you can slog
Even though falling
Forward on your knees and lunging like a cripple.   5
You may escape completely
Being bogged down in those few scampering seconds.
But if you're caught standing
In deep mud, unable to walk or stagger,
It's time to reconsider   10
Your favorite postures, textures, and means of moving,
Coming to even terms
With the kind of dirt that won't take no for an answer.
You must lie down now,
Like it or not: if you're in it up to your thighs,   15
Be seated gently,
Lie back, open your arms, and dream of floating
In a sweet backwater.
Slowly your sunken feet will rise together,
And you may slither   20
Spread-ottered casually backwards out of trouble.
If you stay vertical
And, worse, imagine you're in a fearful struggle,
Trying to swivel
One stuck leg at a time, keeping your body   25
Above it all,
Immaculate, you'll sink in even deeper,
Becoming an object lesson
For those who wallow after you through the mire,
In which case you should know   30
For near-future reference: muck is one part water,
One part what-have-you,
Including yourself, now in it over your head,
As upright as ever.

1975. Ibid.

John Ashbery
(Born 1927)

Born in Rochester, New York, Ashbery went to Harvard, where he was an editor of the *Advocate*, to Columbia, and to New York University. For four years he was a copywriter for New York publishers; for ten years he lived in France as art critic for the *New York Herald Tribune* and as correspondent for *Art News*, whose executive editor he became on his return to New York in 1965. He is now teaching at Brooklyn College. He has written plays, a novel (with James Schuyler), and translated from the French, as well as publishing about a dozen books of poetry.

The Instruction Manual

As I sit looking out of a window of the building
I wish I did not have to write the instruction manual on the uses of a
      new metal.
I look down into the street and see people, each walking with an
      inner peace,
And envy them—they are so far away from me!
Not one of them has to worry about getting out this manual on schedule.   5
And, as my way is, I begin to dream, resting my elbows on the desk and
      leaning out of the window a little,
Of dim Guadalajara! City of rose-colored flowers!
City I wanted most to see, and most did not see, in Mexico!
But I fancy I see, under the press of having to write the instruction
      manual,
Your public square, city, with its elaborate little bandstand!   10
The band is playing *Scheherazade* by Rimsky-Korsakov.
Around stand the flower girls, handing out rose- and lemon-colored
      flowers,
Each attractive in her rose-and-blue striped dress (Oh! such shades of
      rose and blue),
And nearby is the little white booth where women in green serve you
      green and yellow fruit.
The couples are parading; everyone is in a holiday mood.   15
First, leading the parade, is a dapper fellow
Clothed in deep blue. On his head sits a white hat
And he wears a mustache, which has been trimmed for the occasion.
His dear one, his wife, is young and pretty; her shawl is rose,
      pink and white.
Her slippers are patent leather, in the American fashion,   20
And she carries a fan, for she is modest, and does not want the crowd to
      see her face too often.
But everybody is so busy with his wife or loved one
I doubt they would notice the mustachioed man's wife.
Here come the boys! They are skipping and throwing little things on the
      sidewalk
Which is made of gray tile. One of them, a little older, has a toothpick in
      his teeth.   25
He is silenter than the rest, and affects not to notice the pretty young
      girls in white.
But his friends notice them, and shout their jeers at the laughing girls.
Yet soon all this will cease, with the deepening of their years,
And love bring each to the parade grounds for another reason.
But I have lost sight of the young fellow with the toothpick.   30
Wait—there he is—on the other side of the bandstand,
Secluded from his friends, in earnest talk with a young girl
Of fourteen or fifteen. I try to hear what they are saying
But it seems they are just mumbling something—shy words of love,
      probably.

Some Trees, 1956.

See Additional Notes (p. 783).

4 so far away . . . : The daydreamer enters more deeply into the minds of the creatures he imagines
than into the minds of the real people on the street.   **7 dim:** dim only until he begins to dream about
it   **11 Rimsky-Korsakov:** Russian composer (1844–1908). "Scheherazade" is one of his most popular
orchestral pieces.

She is slightly taller than he, and looks quietly down into his sincere
    eyes.   35
She is wearing white. The breeze ruffles her long fine black hair against
    her olive cheek.
Obviously she is in love. The boy, the young boy with the toothpick, he
    is in love too;
His eyes show it. Turning from this couple,
I see there is an intermission in the concert.
The paraders are resting and sipping drinks through straws   40
(The drinks are dispensed from a large glass crock by a lady in dark blue),
And the musicians mingle among them, in their creamy white uniforms,
    and talk
About the weather, perhaps, or how their kids are doing at school.

Let us take this opportunity to tiptoe into one of the side streets.
Here you may see one of those white houses with green trim   45
That are so popular here. Look—I told you!
It is cool and dim inside, but the patio is sunny.
An old woman in gray sits there, fanning herself with a palm leaf fan.
She welcomes us to her patio, and offers us a cooling drink.
"My son is in Mexico City," she says. "He would welcome you too   50
If he were here. But his job is with a bank there.
Look, here is a photograph of him."
And a dark-skinned lad with pearly teeth grins out at us from the worn
    leather frame.
We thank her for her hospitality, for it is getting late
And we must catch a view of the city, before we leave, from a good
    high place.   55
That church tower will do—the faded pink one, there against the fierce
    blue of the sky. Slowly we enter.
The caretaker, an old man dressed in brown and gray, asks us how long
    we have been in the city, and how we like it here.
His daughter is scrubbing the steps—she nods to us as we pass into
    the tower.
Soon we have reached the top, and the whole network of the city extends
    before us.
There is the rich quarter, with its houses of pink and white, and its
    crumbling, leafy terraces.   60
There is the poorer quarter, its homes a deep blue.
There is the market, where men are selling hats and swatting flies
And there is the public library, painted several shades of pale green
    and beige.
Look! There is the square we just came from, with the promenaders.
There are fewer of them, now that the heat of the day has increased,   65
But the young boy and girl still lurk in the shadows of the bandstand.
And there is the home of the little old lady—
She is still sitting in the patio, fanning herself.
How limited, but how complete withal, has been our experience of
    Guadalajara!
We have seen young love, married love, and the love of an aged mother
    for her son.   70
We have heard the music, tasted the drinks, and looked at colored
    houses.

69 **withal:** nevertheless

What more is there to do, except stay? And that we cannot do.
And as a last breeze freshens the top of the weathered old tower, I
    turn my gaze
Back to the instruction manual which has made me dream of Guadalajara.

73 **freshens the top:** "I was somewhat struck by my use of the word 'freshens' . . . Of course, a breeze
can freshen, but it usually doesn't freshen something as it is made to do here. The normal way of say-
ing it would be: 'the breeze freshens, and the weathered old tower feels cool as a result.' Why did I
sneak in this slight contraction which most people wouldn't notice [?] I have no idea, but it might be
justified by the fact that the poem is ending here, the tape is running out and perhaps skipping a
word or two." [J.A.]

Mixed Feelings

A pleasant smell of frying sausages
Attacks the sense, along with an old, mostly invisible
Photograph of what seems to be girls lounging around
An old fighter bomber, circa 1942 vintage.
How to explain to these girls, if indeed that's what they are,   5
These Ruths, Lindas, Pats and Sheilas
About the vast change that's taken place
In the fabric of our society, altering the texture
Of all things in it? And yet
They somehow look as if they knew, except   10
That it's so hard to see them, it's hard to figure out
Exactly what kind of expressions they're wearing.
What are your hobbies, girls? Aw nerts,
One of them might say, this guy's too much for me.
Let's go on and out, somewhere   15
Through the canyons of the garment center
To a small café and have a cup of coffee.
I am not offended that these creatures (that's the word)
Of my imagination seem to hold me in such light esteem,
Pay so little heed to me. It's part of a complicated   20
Flirtation routine, anyhow, no doubt. But this talk of
The garment center? Surely that's California sunlight
Belaboring them and the old crate on which they
Have draped themselves, fading its Donald Duck insignia
To the extreme point of legibility.   25
Maybe they were lying but more likely their
Tiny intelligences cannot retain much information.
Not even one fact, perhaps. That's why
They think they're in New York. I like the way
They look and act and feel. I wonder   30
How they got that way, but am not going to
Waste any more time thinking about them.
I have already forgotten them

Self-Portrait in a Convex Mirror, 1975.

See Additional Notes (p. 783).

15–17 Here the speaker's imagination works away from the "Aw nerts" kind of diction to clichés of
another sort, in which the New York streets are seen as "canyons" and there is the "small café," often
European, of fiction and popular song. 16 **garment center:** The "garment district" in Manhattan,
south of 42nd Street and mostly between Seventh Avenue and Broadway, is the center of the clothing
industry in New York. 18 **creatures (that's the word):** They are literally creatures, creations, of his
fantasy.

Until some day in the not too distant future
When we meet possibly in the lounge of a modern airport,   35
They looking as astonishingly young and fresh as when this
   picture was made
But full of contradictory ideas, stupid ones as well as
Worthwhile ones, but all flooding the surface of our minds
As we babble about the sky and the weather and the forests of change.

As One Put Drunk into the Packet-Boat

I tried each thing, only some were immortal and free.
Elsewhere we are as sitting in a place where sunlight
Filters down, a little at a time,
Waiting for someone to come. Harsh words are spoken,
As the sun yellows the green of the maple tree. . . .   5

So this was all, but obscurely
I felt the stirrings of new breath in the pages
Which all winter long had smelled like an old catalogue.
New sentences were starting up. But the summer
Was well along, not yet past the mid-point   10
But full and dark with the promise of that fullness,
That time when one can no longer wander away
And even the least attentive fall silent
To watch the thing that is prepared to happen.

A look of glass stops you   15
And you walk on shaken: was I the perceived?
Did they notice me, this time, as I am,
Or is it postponed again? The children
Still at their games, clouds that arise with a swift
Impatience in the afternoon sky, then dissipate   20
As limpid, dense twilight comes.
Only in that tooting of a horn
Down there, for a moment, I thought
The great, formal affair was beginning, orchestrated,
Its colors concentrated in a glance, a ballade   25
That takes in the whole world, now, but lightly,
Still lightly, but with wide authority and tact.

The prevalence of those gray flakes falling?
They are sun motes. You have slept in the sun

Ibid.

The title is from the beginning of Andrew Marvell's poem "Tom May's Death," which opens:

> As one put drunk into the packet-boat,
> Tom May was hurried hence and did not know't.
> But was amazed on the Elysian side,
> And with an eye uncertain, gazing wide,
> Could not determine in what place he was.

Tom May was a minor poet and man of letters who died in 1650. A packet-boat was originally intend-ed to carry packets of official and diplomatic letters. The relevance of the title to the poem is that we too, like Tom May or a drunk carried aboard a ship, do not really know where we are going. See Additional Notes (p. 783).

Longer than the sphinx, and are none the wiser for it.   30
Come in. And I thought a shadow fell across the door
But it was only her come to ask once more
If I was coming in, and not to hurry in case I wasn't.

The night sheen takes over. A moon of cistercian pallor
Has climbed to the center of heaven, installed,   35
Finally involved with the business of darkness.
And a sigh heaves from all the small things on earth.
The books, the papers, the old garters and union-suit buttons
Kept in a white cardboard box somewhere, and all the lower
Versions of cities flattened under the equalizing night.   40
The summer demands and takes away too much,
But night, the reserved, the reticent, gives more than it takes.

W. S. Merwin
(Born 1927)

Born in New York, where his father was a Presbyterian minister, Merwin grew up in
New Jersey and Pennsylvania. He has a B.A. from Princeton. In 1949 he went to France
as a tutor and until the 1970s spent much of his time in Europe. More recently he has
lived in New York, Mexico, and Hawaii. He made a living for some years by translating
from Romance languages, and since 1954 he has been assisted at intervals by grants and
fellowships. His published works include nine books of poetry, two of prose, and numer-
ous translations; he has also written for radio and the theater.

Separation

Your absence has gone through me
Like thread through a needle.
Everything I do is stitched with its color.

The Moving Target, 1963.

Things

Possessor
At the approach of winter we are there.
Better than friends, in your sorrows we take no pleasure,
We have none of our own and no memory but yours.
We are the anchor of your future.   5
Patient as a border of beggars, each hand holding out its whole treasure,

We will be all the points on your compass.
We will give you interest on yourself as you deposit yourself with us.
Be a gentleman: you acquired us when you needed us,
We do what we can to please, we have some beauty, we are helpless,   10
Depend on us.

Ibid.

Letter

By the time you read this

it is dark on the next page

the mourners sleep there
feeling their feet in the tide

before me in the dusk an animal rose and vanished   5
your name

you have been with me also in the descent
the winter
you remember
how many things come to one name   10
hoping to be fed

it changes but the name for it
is still the same
I tell you it is still the same

hungry birds in the junipers   15
all night
snow

all night

by the time you read this

the address of the last house   20
that we will sleep in together on earth
will have been paid as a price
dialled on a telephone
worn as identification
passed on speedometers in unmarked places   25
multiplied by machines
divided divided
undistracted
standing guard over us all the time
over past future   30
present
faceless angel

The Carrier of Ladders, 1970.

This poem, like many of Merwin's later poems, "does not at first appear to be set in the actual world around us, the one we accept as real. On the other hand, if we recognize a truth of some kind, emotional or visual, in the imagery, we are invited by that recognition to question what we have taken for granted about the reality of the everyday world. In what sense could it be true to say 'It is dark on the next page' and what could such a recognition be saying about the experience the poem is speaking for, and about experience as a whole? Is this different from ordinary metaphor?" [W.S.M.] We might be tempted to call the poem *surrealist*, but Merwin objects: "I'm particularly averse to the label 'surrealist,' for a number of reasons, including the fact that I think it's often misapplied to my own writing." Perhaps we can say that we have to accept the data of the poem as if they were details given in a dream, without asking common-sense questions about them such as "How can it be dark on the next page?" The meaning of such a poem is not to be found in a logical argument, but in the associations and suggestions that cluster around the images and phrases. Or that lurk in the white spaces between them—even in "real life" we speak of the necessity of "reading between the lines."

whom each rain washes nearer to himself

but I tell you
by the time you read this   35
wherever

I tell you

James Wright
(1927–1980)

Born in Martin's Ferry, Ohio, Wright graduated from Kenyon College, studied at the
University of Vienna, had a Ph.D. from the University of Washington. He travelled
widely in Europe and Japan, where he served with the U.S. army. He taught at the Uni-
versity of Minnesota and at Hunter College. Besides translating poetry from the German
and Spanish, he published seven books of his own poetry.

Lying in a Hammock at William Duffy's Farm in Pine Island, Minnesota

Over my head, I see the bronze butterfly,
Asleep on the black trunk,
Blowing like a leaf in green shadow.
Down the ravine behind the empty house,
The cowbells follow one another   5
Into the distances of the afternoon.
To my right,
In a field of sunlight between two pines,
The droppings of last year's horses
Blaze up into golden stones.   10
I lean back, as the evening darkens and comes on.
A chicken hawk floats over, looking for home.
I have wasted my life.

The Branch Will Not Break, 1963.

Speak

To speak in a flat voice
Is all that I can do.
I have gone every place
Asking for you.
Wondering where to turn   5
And how the search would end
And the last streetlight spin
Above me blind.

Then I returned rebuffed
And saw under the sun   10

Shall We Gather at the River, 1968.

9–12 **I returned . . . the battle won:** Cf. Eccles. 9:11: "I returned, and saw under the sun, that the race
is not to the swift, nor the battle to the strong, neither yet bread to the wise, nor yet riches to men of
understanding, nor yet favor to men of skill; but time and chance happeneth to them all."

The race not to the swift
Nor the battle won.
Liston dives in the tank,
Lord, in Lewiston, Maine,
And Ernie Doty's drunk   15
In hell again.

And Jenny, oh my Jenny
Whom I love, rhyme be damned,
Has broken her spare beauty
In a whorehouse old.   20
She left her new baby
In a bus-station can,
And sprightly danced away
Through Jacksontown.

Which is a place I know,   25
One where I got picked up
A few shrunk years ago
By a good cop.
Believe it, Lord, or not.
Don't ask me who he was.   30
I speak of flat defeat
In a flat voice.

I have gone forward with
Some, a few lonely some.
They have fallen to death.   35
I die with them.
Lord, I have loved Thy cursed,
The beauty of Thy house:
Come down. Come down. Why dost
Thou hide thy face?   40

13 **Liston:** In May 1965, at Lewistown, Maine, the heavyweight boxer "Sonny" Liston was K.O.'d by Cassius Clay (Mohammed Ali) in the first round of one of the shortest title fights on record—giving rise to the suspicion that Liston, who was the favorite, had "taken a dive" (lost on purpose).   15 **Ernie Doty:** "a distant family friend who was executed for rape and murder. I had written about him in an earlier poem called 'At the Executed Murderer's Grave.'" [J.W.]   18 **rhyme be damned:** Though every line of the poem rhymes with another line, most of the rhymes are not perfect rhymes (*do-you; sun-won,* etc.) but the kind of off-rhymes favored by many modern poets (*voice-place; end-blind; damned-old,* etc.)—a kind of rhyme especially expressive in this "flat voice" poem with its "rhyme be damned" urgency.   37–38 **Lord, I have loved . . . Thy house:** Cf. Ps. 26:8: "LORD, I have loved the habitation of thy house. . . ." *The Jerusalem Bible,* a Catholic version published in 1966, points out that the Hebrew means "the beauty of your house." In Ps. 26 and elsewhere, David (less charitable than our poet?) points out that he has not loved or associated with "Thy cursed": "I have hated the congregation of evildoers; and will not sit with the wicked" (26:5).   39–40 **Why dost/ Thou hide thy face?:** "Hide not thy face far from me . . ." (Ps. 27:9).

To a Blossoming Pear Tree

Beautiful natural blossoms,
Pure delicate body,
You stand without trembling.
Little mist of fallen starlight,

To a Blossoming Pear Tree, 1977.

Perfect, beyond my reach,   5
How I envy you.
For if you could only listen,
I would tell you something,
Something human.

An old man   10
Appeared to me once
In the unendurable snow.
He had a singe of white
Beard on his face.
He paused on a street in Minneapolis   15
And stroked my face.
Give it to me, he begged.
I'll pay you anything.

I flinched. Both terrified,
We slunk away,   20
Each in his own way dodging
The cruel darts of the cold.

Beautiful natural blossoms,
How could you possibly
Worry or bother or care   25
About the ashamed, hopeless
Old man? He was so near death
He was willing to take
Any love he could get,
Even at the risk   30
Of some mocking policeman
Or some cute young wiseacre
Smashing his dentures,
Perhaps leading him on
To a dark place and there   35
Kicking him in his dead groin
Just for the fun of it.

Young tree, unburdened
By anything but your beautiful natural blossoms
And dew, the dark   40
Blood in my body drags me
Down with my brother.

Donald Hall
(Born 1928)

Born in New Haven, Hall has degrees from Harvard and Oxford. After teaching at the
University of Michigan from 1957 to 1975, he returned to the New Hampshire farm that
had belonged to his great-grandfather to give full time to his writing. Besides his several
books of poetry, he has written critical works, reminiscences, and textbooks and has edit-
ed collections of poetry.

Names of Horses

All winter your brute shoulders strained against collars, padding
and steerhide over the ash hames, to haul
sledges of cordwood for drying through spring and summer,
for the Glenwood stove next winter, and for the simmering range.

In April you pulled cartloads of manure to spread on the fields,   5
dark manure of Holsteins, and knobs of your own clustered with oats.
All summer you mowed the grass in meadow and hayfield, the
            mowing machine
clacketing beside you, while the sun walked high in the morning;

and after noon's heat, you pulled a clawed rake through the same acres,
gathering stacks, and dragged the wagon from stack to stack,   10
and the built hayrack back, up hill to the chaffy barn,
three loads of hay a day from standing grass in the morning.

Sundays you trotted the two miles to church with the light load
of a leather quarter top buggy, and grazed in the sound of hymns.
Generation on generation, your neck rubbed the windowsill   15
of the stall, smoothing the wood as the sea smooths glass.

When you were old and lame, when your shoulders hurt bending to graze,
one October the man who fed you and kept you, and harnessed you
            every morning,
led you through corn stubble to sandy ground above Eagle Pond,
and dug a hole beside you where you stood shuddering in your skin,   20

and lay the shotgun's muzzle in the boneless hollow behind your ear,
and fired the slug into your brain, and felled you into your grave,
shoveling sand to cover you, setting goldenrod upright above you,
where by next summer a dent in the ground made your monument.

For a hundred and fifty years, in the pasture of dead horses,   25
roots of pine trees pushed through the pale curves of your ribs,
yellow blossoms flourished above you in autumn, and in winter
frost heaved your bones in the ground—old toilers, soil makers:

O Roger, Mackerel, Riley, Ned, Nellie, Chester, Lady Ghost.

1975–1976. *Kicking the Leaves*, 1978.

2 **ash hames:** the ashwood frame inside of the horse collar, to which the traces (straps) are attached
3 **cordwood:** firewood stacked or sold in cords (stacks equal to 4x4x8 ft.)   4 **Glenwood:** the name of
the maker   6 **Holsteins:** large black and white dairy cows   8 **clacketing:** making a clackety sound
11 **chaffy:** full of chaff, the dusty remains of hulls, seed-coverings, bits of straw, etc.   14 **quarter top:**
having a top with "quarters," or panels, generally of leather, extending part-way down

Thom Gunn
(Born 1929)

Born in Gravesend (Kent) in England, Thom (for Thomson) Gunn served in the British
army from 1948 to 1950. With a degree from Cambridge, he came to America, studied for
several years at Stanford, and taught at the University of California at Berkeley from 1958

to 1966. Since then he has been a freelance writer in San Francisco. Besides publishing several books of his own poetry, he has edited selections of the poetry of Fulke Greville and Ben Jonson.

On the Move

The blue jay scuffling in the bushes follows
Some hidden purpose, and the gust of birds
That spurts across the field, the wheeling swallows,
Has nested in the trees and undergrowth.
Seeking their instinct, or their poise, or both,   5
One moves with an uncertain violence
Under the dust thrown by a baffled sense
Or the dull thunder of approximate words.

On motorcycles, up the road, they come:
Small, black, as flies hanging in heat, the Boys,   10
Until the distance throws them forth, their hum
Bulges to thunder held by calf and thigh.
In goggles, donned impersonality,
In gleaming jackets trophied with the dust,
They strap in doubt—by hiding it, robust—   15
And almost hear a meaning in their noise.

Exact conclusion of their hardiness
Has no shape yet, but from known whereabouts
They ride, direction where the tires press.
They scare a flight of birds across the field: 20
Much that is natural, to the will must yield.
Men manufacture both machine and soul,
And use what they imperfectly control
To dare a future from the taken routes.

It is a part solution, after all.   25
One is not necessarily discord
On earth; or damned because, half animal,
One lacks direct instinct, because one wakes
Afloat on movement that divides and breaks.
One joins the movement in a valueless world,   30
Choosing it, till, both hurler and the hurled,
One moves as well, always toward, toward.

A minute holds them, who have come to go:
The self-defined, astride the created will
They burst away; the towns they travel through   35
Are home for neither bird nor holiness,
For birds and saints complete their purposes.
At worst, one is in motion; and at best,
Reaching no absolute, in which to rest,
One is always nearer by not keeping still.   40

California

1954–1955. *The Sense of Movement*, 1957.

32 **toward:** "I wrote this poem in my first year in the U.S. and pronounced the word 'toward' as two syllables [*to-wårred*, not *tord*], in the English style." [T.G.]

Moly

Nightmare of beasthood, snorting, how to wake.
I woke. What beasthood skin she made me take?

Leathery toad that ruts for days on end,
Or cringing dribbling dog, man's servile friend,

Or cat that prettily pounces on its meat,   5
Tortures it hours, then does not care to eat:

Parrot, moth, shark, wolf, crocodile, ass, flea.
What germs, what jostling mobs there were in me.

  These seem like bristles, and the hide is tough.
No claw or web here: each foot ends in hoof.   10

Into what bulk has method disappeared?
Like ham, streaked. I am gross—grey, gross, flap-eared.

The pale-lashed eyes my only human feature.
My teeth tear, tear. I am the snouted creature

That bites through anything, root, wire, or can.   15
If I was not afraid I'd eat a man.

Oh a man's flesh already is in mine.
Hand and foot poised for risk. Buried in swine.

  I root and root, you think that it is greed,
It is, but I seek out a plant I need.   20

Direct me, gods, whose changes are all holy,
To where it flickers deep in grass, the moly:

Cool flesh of magic in each leaf and shoot,
From milky flower to the black forked root.

From this fat dungeon I could rise to skin   25
And human title, putting pig within.

I push my big grey wet snout through the green,
Dreaming the flower I have never seen.

Moly, 1971.

In Book X of Homer's *Odyssey*, Odysseus describes how his crew has been turned into swine by the magic of the enchantress Circe. On his way to help them, Odysseus meets the god Hermes, who gives him a magic plant called Moly, milk white with black root, which will protect him against Circe's spells. "This poem is supposed to be spoken by one of his seamen unfortunate enough to have been transformed into a pig some minutes before the poem begins." [T.G.]

Gary Snyder
(Born 1930)

Born in San Francisco, Snyder studied anthropology and literature at Reed College and Japanese and Chinese at Berkeley, working between times in the woods and mountains. From 1956 to 1968 he lived mostly in Japan, studying Zen Buddhism. He now lives in California and is active in ecological and environmental movements. Over a dozen books of his poetry have been published.

Mid-August at Sourdough Mountain Lookout

Down valley a smoke haze
Three days heat, after five days rain
Pitch glows on the fir-cones
Across rocks and meadows
Swarms of new flies.   5

I cannot remember things I once read
A few friends, but they are in cities.
Drinking cold snow-water from a tin cup
Looking down for miles
Through high still air.   10

1953. *Riprap*, 1959.

In 1953 Snyder was a forest-fire lookout on Sourdough Mountain in northwestern Washington.

An Autumn Morning in Shokoku-Ji

Last night watching the Pleiades,
Breath smoking in the moonlight,
Bitter memory like vomit
Choked my throat.
I unrolled a sleeping bag   5
On mats on the porch
Under thick autumn stars.
In dream you appeared
(Three times in nine years)
Wild, cold, and accusing.   10
I woke shamed and angry:
The pointless wars of the heart.
Almost dawn. Venus and Jupiter.
The first time I have
Ever seen them close.   15

1959. *The Back Country*, 1968.

Shokoku-ji is a temple complex in northern Kyoto in Japan where Snyder was for some time a student of Zen during his ten or so years in that country.

1 **Pleiades:** a star cluster in the constellation Taurus; six (some say seven) are visible to the naked eye   13 **Venus and Jupiter:** the planets, with Venus here the morning star. "It was a literal closeness of the two planets—the reader may read symbolic content in if he likes." [G.S.]

The Dead by the Side of the Road

How did a great Red-tailed Hawk
    come to lie—all stiff and dry—
        on the shoulder of
            Interstate 5?

Her wings for dance fans   5

Zac skinned a skunk with a crushed head
    washed the pelt in gas; it hangs,
        tanned, in his tent

1972. *Turtle Island*, 1974

4 **Interstate 5:** the main highway running parallel to the coast through Washington, Oregon, and California

Fawn stew on Hallowe'en
   hit by a truck on highway forty-nine   10
     offer cornmeal by the mouth;
        skin it out.

Log trucks run on fossil fuel

I never saw a Ringtail til I found one in the road:
   case-skinned it with the toenails   15
     footpads, nose, and whiskers on;
        it soaks in salt and water
        sulphuric acid pickle;

she will be a pouch for magic tools.

The Doe was apparently shot   20
   lengthwise and through the side—
     shoulder and out the flank
        belly full of blood

Can save the other shoulder maybe,
   if she didn't lie too long—
                                25
Pray to their spirits. Ask them to bless us:
   our ancient sisters' trails
     the roads were laid across and kill them:
        night-shining eyes

The dead by the side of the road.   30

---

10 **highway forty-nine:** a lesser highway running north to south along the Sierras, not far from the poet's home   13 **Log trucks . . . :** For Snyder, the logging industry (and the use of fossil fuel) represents destruction of the environment.   14 **Ringtail:** the cacomistle, a raccoonlike animal "of California and the Southwest. ***Bassariscus astutus, Procyon*** (Raccoon) family." [G.S.]   26 **Pray to their spirits:** Snyder believes that a communion exists—or should exist—between all living things, including not only man but plants and animals.

Prayer for the Great Family

Gratitude to Mother Earth, sailing through night and day—
   and to her soil: rich, rare, and sweet
     in our minds so be it.

Gratitude to Plants, the sun-facing light-changing leaf
   and fine root-hairs; standing still through wind   5
   and rain; their dance is in the flowing spiral grain
     in our minds so be it.

Gratitude to Air, bearing the soaring Swift and the silent
   Owl at dawn. Breath of our song
   clear spirit breeze
     in our minds so be it.   10

1970. Ibid.

4 **light-changing:** (1) changing in the light; (2) utilizing the energy of light to synthesize the chemical compounds it needs for life (in the process of photosynthesis)   8 **Swift:** a bird that resembles the swallow

Gratitude to Wild Beings, our brothers, teaching secrets,
    freedoms, and ways; who share with us their milk;
    self-complete, brave, and aware
        in our minds so be it.   15

Gratitude to Water: clouds, lakes, rivers, glaciers;
    holding or releasing; streaming through all
    our bodies salty seas
        in our minds so be it.

Gratitude to the Sun: blinding pulsing light through   20
    trunks of trees, through mists, warming caves where
    bears and snakes sleep—he who wakes us—
        in our minds so be it.

Gratitude to the Great Sky
    who holds billions of stars—and goes yet beyond that—   25
    beyond all powers, and thoughts
    and yet is within us—
    Grandfather Space.
    The Mind is his Wife.

        so be it.   30

                after a Mohawk prayer

Ted Hughes
(Born 1930)

Born in Yorkshire (England), Hughes served for two years with the Royal Air Force as wireless operator in an isolated post before completing his work at Cambridge. In 1956 he married the American poet Sylvia Plath; for two years they lived in the United States. He has worked as a rose gardener, night watchman, and reader for a British film company. Besides his many books of poetry he has also written plays, some for radio and television.

Pike

Pike, three inches long, perfect
Pike in all parts, green tigering the gold.
Killers from the egg: the malevolent aged grin.
They dance on the surface among the flies.

Or move, stunned by their own grandeur,   5
Over a bed of emerald, silhouette
Of submarine delicacy and horror.
A hundred feet long in their world.

In ponds, under the heat-struck lily pads—
Gloom of their stillness: 10
Logged on last year's black leaves, watching upwards.
Or hung in an amber cavern of weeds

Lupercal, 1960.

Pike: a large strong-jawed freshwater game fish noted for the suddenness and savagery of its attack on other fish (or even small animals) that come near the place where it lurks, motionless, among the waterplants. "It grows to a great size: specimens up to six feet long have been recorded." [T.H.]

The jaws' hooked clamp and fangs
Not to be changed at this date;
A life subdued to its instrument;   15
The gills kneading quietly, and the pectorals.

Three we kept behind glass,
Jungled in weed: three inches, four,
And four and a half: fed fry to them—
Suddenly there were two. Finally one.   20

With a sag belly and the grin it was born with.
And indeed they spare nobody.
Two, six pounds each, over two feet long,
High and dry and dead in the willow-herb—

One jammed past its gills down the other's gullet: 25
The outside eye stared: as a vice locks—
The same iron in this eye
Though its film shrank in death.

A pond I fished, fifty yards across,
Whose lilies and muscular tench   30
Had outlasted every visible stone
Of the monastery that planted them—

Stilled legendary depth:
It was as deep as England. It held
Pike too immense to stir, so immense and old   35
That past nightfall I dared not cast

But silently cast and fished
With the hair frozen on my head
For what might move, for what eye might move.
The still splashes on the dark pond,   40

Owls hushing the floating woods
Frail on my ear against the dream
Darkness beneath night's darkness had freed,
That rose slowly towards me, watching.

16 **pectorals:** fins that correspond to the forepaws of animals   24 **willow-herb:** loose-strife, a yel-low- or purple-flowered plant that grows in marshy ground   25 **one jammed . . . :** The teeth of pike point backward, so that objects which enter the jaws cannot leave them.   30 **tench:** a European fresh-water fish of the carp family   34 **deep as England:** "The pond was in limestone, and fed by an under-water hole that went down a great depth into the natural water-reservoirs in the limestone deep un-derground." [T.H.]

Hawk Roosting

I sit in the top of the wood, my eyes closed.
Inaction, no falsifying dream
Between my hooked head and hooked feet:
Or in sleep rehearse perfect kills and eat.

Ibid.

Although the hawk into whose consciousness we enter has been seen by some as a "fascist" and "the symbol of some horrible totalitarian genocidal dictator," Hughes has said that what he had in mind was that "in this hawk Nature is thinking. Simply Nature."

The convenience of the high trees!   5
The air's buoyancy and the sun's ray
Are of advantage to me;
And the earth's face upward for my inspection.

My feet are locked upon the rough bark.
It took the whole of Creation   10
To produce my foot, my each feather:
Now I hold Creation in my foot

Or fly up, and revolve it all slowly—
I kill where I please because it is all mine.
There is no sophistry in my body: 15
My manners are tearing off heads—

The allotment of death.
For the one path of my flight is direct
Through the bones of the living.
No arguments assert my right: 20

The sun is behind me.
Nothing has changed since I began.
My eye has permitted no change.
I am going to keep things like this.

Skylarks

I
The lark begins to go up
Like a warning
As if the globe were uneasy—

Barrel-chested for heights,
Like an Indian of the high Andes,   5

A whippet head, barbed like a hunting arrow,

But leaden
With muscle
For the struggle
Against   10
Earth's centre.

And leaden
For ballast
In the rocketing storms of the breath.

Wodwo, 1967.

Whereas Shelley's ethereal bird in "To a Skylark" (p. 312) is an "unbodied joy" that "shadow of an-
noyance / Never came near . . . ," Hughes sees his "barrel-chested" singer in all of its tortured physi-
cality as it fights gravity, "wings almost torn off backwards," and turns heaven into a "madhouse" of
"squealing and gibbering and cursing . . ."—a creature agonized, delirious—and yet triumphant
against terrible odds. The version of the poem printed here is as given in *Wodwo* (1967). In *Selected Po-
ems* (1972), two sections were added which stress the bird's agony and its role as sacrificial victim.
Some feel that the weighty additions—perhaps made to prevent the poem's being read as a mere de-
scriptive nature poem—violate the unity and spirit of the poem.

5 **the high Andes:** mountains in South America   6 **whippet:** a small swift dog like a greyhound

Leaden   15
Like a bullet
To supplant
Life from its centre.

II

Crueller than owl or eagle

A towered bird, shot through the crested head   20
With the command, Not die

But climb

Climb

Sing

Obedient as to death a dead thing.   25

III

I suppose you just gape and let your gaspings
Rip in and out through your voicebox
                              O lark

And sing inwards as well as outwards
Like a breaker of ocean milling the shingle   30
                              O lark

O song, incomprehensibly both ways—
Joy! Help! Joy! Help!
                    O lark

IV

My idleness curdles   35
Seeing the lark labour near its cloud
Scrambling
In a nightmare difficulty
Up through the nothing

Its feathers thrash, its heart must be drumming like a motor,   40
As if it were too late, too late

Dithering in ether
Its song whirls faster and faster
And the sun whirls
The lark is evaporating   45
Till my eye's gossamer snaps
                    and my hearing floats back widely to earth

After which the sky lies blank open
Without wings, and the earth is a folded clod.

Only the sun goes silently and endlessly on with the lark's song.   50

30 **shingle**: accumulations of loose stones and pebbles on the seashore   42 **dithering**: acting in a
confused or excited way   46 **gossamer**: fine cobweb—here a thread imagined as connecting the eye
with what it sees

V

All the dreary Sunday morning
Heaven is a madhouse
With the voices and frenzies of the larks,

Squealing and gibbering and cursing

Heads flung back, as I see them, 55
Wings almost torn off backwards—far up

Like sacrifices set floating
The cruel earth's offerings

The mad earth's missionaries.

VI

Like those flailing flames 60
That lift from the fling of a bonfire
Claws dangling full of what they feed on

The larks carry their tongues to the last atom
Battering and battering their last sparks out at the limit—
So it's a relief, a cool breeze 65
When they've had enough, when they're burned out
And the sun's sucked them empty
And the earth gives them the O.K.

And they relax, drifting with changed notes

Dip and float, not quite sure if they may 70
Then they are sure and they stoop

And maybe the whole agony was for this

The plummeting dead drop

With long cutting screams buckling like razors

But just before they plunge into the earth 75

They flare and glide off low over grass, then up
To land on a wall-top, crest up,

Weightless,
Paid-up,
Alert, 80

Conscience perfect.

---

74 buckling like razors: folding in their wings to drop faster—like a straight razor closing. "Your idea of the cut-throat razor closing is novel to me—though in fact I see it fits the actual down-glide of the bird quite richly and exactly. But what I had in mind (inadequately suggested by my words, I admit) was the thin blade of a safety razor—buckling as it buckles in your fingers when you try to cut through something tough. I imagined, grotesquely enough, but to me expressively—the screams buckling in this way as they cut through the gristly throat of the bird—i.e. screams that were self-immolatory, as the worshippers of Cybele, in their frenzy, slashed themselves, or as the ecstasy-dancers in that order of Sufis re-dedicate their bodies to God with self-slashings and self-stabbings. The actual inflection of these descending screams suggests thin cutting steel buckling as it cuts, and the ecstatic abandon suggests self-immolation to a god." [T.H.]

Geoffrey Hill
(Born 1932)

Born in Bromsgrove, Worcestershire (England), Hill has an Oxford degree. He is now on the English faculty of the University of Leeds in West Yorkshire. A careful and intense writer, he has published four highly acclaimed books of poetry in the last 20 years.

Genesis

I

Against the burly air I strode,
Where the tight ocean heaves its load,
Crying the miracles of God.

And first I brought the sea to bear
Upon the dead weight of the land;   5
And the waves flourished at my prayer,
The rivers spawned their sand.

And where the streams were salt and full
The tough pig-headed salmon strove,
Curbing the ebb and the tide's pull,   10
To reach the steady hills above.

II

The second day I stood and saw
The osprey plunge with triggered claw,
Feathering blood along the shore,
To lay the living sinew bare.   15

And the third day I cried: 'Beware
The soft-voiced owl, the ferret's smile,
The hawk's deliberate stoop in air,
Cold eyes, and bodies hooped in steel,
Forever bent upon the kill.'   20

III

And I renounced, on the fourth day,
This fierce and unregenerate clay,

Building as a huge myth for man
The watery Leviathan,

And made the glove-winged albatross   25
Scour the ashes of the sea
Where Capricorn and Zero cross,

For the Unfallen, 1959.

13 **osprey:** a large fish-eating hawk   17 **ferret:** a weasellike animal sometimes trained to hunt rodents   18 **stoop:** swift descent to seize its prey   III The "I" of the poem turns from the cruelty of real animals to creatures of mythology or legend: Leviathan, a sea-monster mentioned in the Old Testament; the albatross which, though real, became a focus of legend and superstition; and the phoenix, a bird which, according to fable, was consumed in fire every 500 years and reborn from its own ashes.   27 **Capricorn and Zero:** if taken literally, and not simply as a bit of mystic geography, the Tropic of Capricorn and 0 degrees longitude would cross in the South Atlantic. The "wandering albatross," the most legendary and spectacular of its species, does frequent the southern oceans and may range as far north as the Tropic of Capricorn.

A brooding immortality—
Such as the charmed phoenix has
In the unwithering tree.   30

IV

The phoenix burns as cold as frost;
And, like a legendary ghost,
The phantom-bird goes wild and lost,
Upon a pointless ocean tossed.

So, the fifth day, I turned again   35
To flesh and blood and the blood's pain.

V

On the sixth day, as I rode
In haste about the works of God,
With spurs I plucked the horse's blood.

By blood we live, the hot, the cold,   40
To ravage and redeem the world:
There is no bloodless myth will hold.

And by Christ's blood are men made free
Though in close shrouds their bodies lie
Under the rough pelt of the sea;   45

Though Earth has rolled beneath her weight
The bones that cannot bear the light.

IV But since these legends are lacking in reality, are "cold," "lost," "pointless," the "I" returns to the world of flesh and blood, which, as we see in V, entails an acceptance of suffering (and of redemption).

From **Mercian Hymns**

I

King of the perennial holly-groves, the riven sandstone: overlord of the M5: architect of the historic rampart and ditch, the citadel at Tamworth, the summer hermitage in Holy Cross: guardian of the Welsh Bridge and the Iron Bridge: contractor to the desirable new estates: salt-

---

Mercian Hymns, 1971.

See Additional Notes (p. 784).

I: 1 **holly-groves:** Holly, if permitted to grow, becomes a large tree with beautiful wood prized by furniture makers. Holiday superstitions also cluster around it, as we might guess from its use at Christmas today. Forests and groves were often royal preserves.   **riven sandstone:** Cut sandstone was much used for building.   1-2 **the M5:** a modern north-south highway (through Offa's country) in western England   2 **rampart and ditch:** The famous Offa's Dike, of which impressive sections remain, was constructed to protect Mercia from the Welsh tribes to the west.   2-3 **Tamworth:** a town in Staffordshire where Offa built a palace with entrenchments   3 **Holy Cross:** the site of an ancient religious settlement near Pershore in Worcestershire   3-4 **Welsh Bridge . . . Iron Bridge:** The Welsh Bridge crosses the Severn at Shrewsbury, near Wales; the Iron Bridge, about ten miles down river at the town named for it, was the first all-iron bridge (1779).   4-5 **saltmaster:** Salt, essential in those days for preserving fish and meat, was an important commodity. The king owned many of the "saltpans"—basins along the ocean in which seawater was evaporated to leave the salt.

master: money-changer: commissioner for oaths: martyrologist: the   5
friend of Charlemagne.

'I liked that,' said Offa, 'sing it again.'

III

On the morning of the crowning we chorused our remission from school.
It was like Easter: hankies and gift-mugs approved by his foreign gaze,
the village-lintels curlered with paper flags.

We gaped at the car-park of 'The Stag's Head' where a bonfire of beer-
crates and holly-boughs whistled above the tar. And the chef stood   5
there, a king in his new-risen hat, sealing his brisk largesse with 'any
mustard?'

VI

The princes of Mercia were badger and raven. Thrall to their freedom, I
dug and hoarded. Orchards fruited above cleíts. I drank from honey-
combs of chill sandstone.

'A boy at odds in the house, lonely among brothers.' But I, who had
none, fostered a strangeness; gave myself to unattainable toys.   5

Candles of gnarled resin, apple-branches, the tacky mistletoe. 'Look' they
said and again 'look.' But I ran slowly; the landscape flowed away, back
to its source.

In the schoolyard, in the cloakrooms, the children boasted their scars of
dried snot; wrists and knees garnished with impetigo.   10

VII

Gasholders, russet among fields. Milldams, marlpools that lay unstirring.
Eel-swarms. Coagulations of frogs: once, with branches and half-bricks,
he battered a ditchful; then sidled away from the stillness and silence.

Ceolred was his friend and remained so, even after the day of the lost
fighter: a biplane, already obsolete and irreplaceable, two inches of   5
heavy snub silver. Ceolred let it spin through a hole in the classroom-
floorboards, softly, into the rat-droppings and coins.

---

5 **money-changer:** Offa established a new form of currency and issued handsome coins with his
name and portrait. In 1979 a silver penny of Offa's time was sold at a London auction for $22,000.
martyrologist: one who studies or writes about the lives of martyrs. Offa was a patron of learning.
6 **Charlemagne:** Born in 742, Charlemagne was ruler of the Frankish kingdom (most of western Eu-
rope) from 768 until his death in 814, and emperor of the West from 800 on.

III: The *Mercian Hymns* move freely through time, the poet imagining himself now in one century,
now in another. (As if on a sci-fi time machine.) In III, the crowning of Offa is described as if it took
place today, with a giant bonfire in the parking lot of a hotel and a "chef" passing out hot dogs.
3 **lintels:** the beams or slabs over a doorway   6 **largesse:** generosity, hand-outs

VI: 1 **Thrall to their freedom:** doing slavishly or imitatively what badger and raven did naturally
and freely (thrall=slave, subject)   4 **'A boy . . .':** Dissatisfied with what was around him, the boy—
perhaps the poet, or any boy—gave himself over to dreams of the past.   9 **In the schoolyard . . . :**
Compared with the figures of history, our own schoolmates seem scabbed and dirty—or the image
may mean that figures of the past would be scruffy too, if we could see them as they were. *Impetigo* is
an ugly and contagious skin disease.

VII: 1 **Gasholders:** tanks for storing gas   **milldams:** dams to hold back the water that powers a wa-
termill   **marlpools:** pools in marl (clay soil)   2 **Coagulations of frogs:** Cf. Seamus Heaney, "Death
of a Naturalist" (p. 755)   6–11 Another anachronism—the incident, the loss of the toy airplane, is
modern; the name of the careless and sniggering friend, Ceolred, is that of an earlier king of Mercia
(he ruled 709–716), described as a "dissolute youth" whom one of his contemporaries saw, in a vision,

After school he lured Ceolred, who was sniggering with fright, down to
the old quarries, and flayed him. Then, leaving Ceolred, he journeyed
for hours, calm and alone, in his private derelict sandlorry named   10
Albion.

X

He adored the desk, its brown-oak inlaid with ebony, assorted prize
pens, the seals of gold and base metal into which he had sunk his
name.

It was there that he drew upon grievances from the people; attended to
signatures and retributions; forgave the death-howls of his rival. And   5
there he exchanged gifts with the Muse of History.

What should a man make of remorse, that it might profit his soul? Tell
me. Tell everything to Mother, darling, and God bless.

He swayed in sunlight, in mild dreams. He tested the little pears. He
smeared catmint on his palm for his cat Smut to lick. He wept, attempt-   10
ing to master *ancilla* and *servus*.

XI

Coins handsome as Nero's; of good substance and weight. *Offa Rex* reso-
nant in silver, and the names of his moneyers. They struck with ac-
countable tact. They could alter the king's face.

Exactness of design was to deter imitation; mutilation if that failed. Ex-
emplary metal, ripe for commerce. Value from a sparse people, scrapers   5
of salt-pans and byres.

Swathed bodies in the long ditch; one eye upstaring. It is safe to presume,
here, the king's anger. He reigned forty years. Seasons touched and re-
touched the soil.

Heathland, new-made watermeadow. Charlock, marsh-marigold. Crepi-   10
tant oak forest where the boar furrowed black mould, his snout inti-
mate with worms and leaves.

XIV

Dismissing reports and men, he put pressure on the wax, blistered it to a
crest. He threatened malefactors with ash from his noon cigar.

---

as already in hell.   10 **flayed:** took the skin off, punished   11 **sandlorry:** sand-truck   12 *Albion:*
an old or poetic name for England, also, the brand name of a British truck

X: The consciousness of the eighth-century king, with his grievances and retributions, flows into
that of the twentieth-century schoolboy, trying to learn the declensions (grammatical forms) of the
Latin words *ancilla* (maid-servant) and *servus* (male servant)

XI: 1 **Nero:** born A.D. 37; Roman emperor 54–68; his coins were of that series of Roman portraits con-
sidered artistically outstanding.   *Offa Rex:* King Offa, or Offa the King   4 **mutilation:** coun-
terfeiters could be punished by the loss of a hand   6 **salt-pans:** See note on I, 6.   **byres:** cow barns
10 **Heathland:** open uncultivated country   **watermeadow:** meadow flooded when the streams were
high   **Charlock:** wild mustard   **marsh-marigold:** cowslip, a swamp herb of the buttercup family
10–11 **Crepitant:** crackling

XIV: 1 **put pressure ... blistered ...:** as he did when closing a letter or attesting a document with
sealing wax, and then pressing his seal or signet into it   2 **threatened ... cigar:** as if he were a mod-
ern cigar-smoking tycoon instead of an eighth-century ruler

When the sky cleared above Malvern, he lingered in his orchard; by the
quiet hammer-pond. Trout-fry simmered there, translucent, as though
forming the water's underskin. He had a care for natural minutiae.   5
What his gaze touched was his tenderness. Woodlice sat pellet-like in
the cracked bark and a snail sugared its new stone.

At dinner, he relished the mockery of drinking his family's health. He
did this whenever it suited him, which was not often.

XXII

We ran across the meadow scabbed with cow-dung, past the crab-apple
trees and camouflaged nissen hut. It was curfew-time for our war-
band.

At home the curtains were drawn. The wireless boomed its commands. I
loved the battle-anthems and the gregarious news.   5

Then, in the earthy shelter, warmed by a blue-glassed storm-lantern, I
huddled with stories of dragon-tailed airships and warriors who took
wing immortal as phantoms.

XXV

Brooding on the eightieth letter of *Fors Clavigera,* I speak this in memory
of my grandmother, whose childhood and prime womanhood were
spent in the nailer's darg.

The nailshop stood back of the cottage, by the fold. It reeked stale miner-
al sweat. Sparks had furred its low roof. In dawn-light the troughed   5
water floated a damson-bloom of dust—

not to be shaken by posthumous clamour. It is one thing to celebrate the
'quick forge,' another to cradle a face hare-lipped by the searing wire.

Brooding on the eightieth letter of *Fors Clavigera,* I speak this in memory
of my grandmother, whose childhood and prime womanhood were   10
spent in the nailer's darg.

---

3 **Malvern:** a range of hills in western England   4 **hammer-pond:** a pond in which water is stored to
power a small forge with a hammer   6 **Woodlice:** small insects that live under bark   7 **sugared:**
Snails leave fine whitish trails where they move.

XXII The poem is about boys playing soldier during World War II—much as boys in Offa's day might
have done.   2 **nissen hut:** A prefab like a quonset hut, named after Peter Nissen, the British engineer
who designed it   6 **a blue-glassed storm-lantern:** a lantern with the flame shielded from wind and
rain by glass which is blue so as not to be conspicuous in wartime

XXV: 1 *Fors Clavigera:* a collection of letters (1871–1884) to the workmen and laborers of Great Brit-
ain, written by John Ruskin (1819–1900). They deal with social injustice and the poverty and misery
of the working class—with the problems of a society, Ruskin said, in which one out of a thousand was
well off. In the eightieth letter, Ruskin describes how the mayor of Birmingham showed him two
women in their cottage, working from seven in the morning to seven at night, earning a poor living
at a little forge at which they snip and hammer red-hot iron rods into railroad nails. "Darg" is a short-
ened form of daywork, a day's work.   4 **fold:** a pen for sheep   5 **damson-bloom:** a film or dustiness
like that on a plum   7–8 **the 'quick forge':** Cf. Shakespeare, *Henry V,* V, chorus, 23. "The phrase re-
quires acknowledgement but the source has no bearing on the poem." [G. H.]   8 **hare-lipped:** with
lip burned through. Hill corrects himself in a note: hand-made nails were made from rods, not wires.

XXIX

'Not strangeness, but strange likeness. Obstinate, outclassed forefathers, I
  too concede, I am your staggeringly-gifted child.'

So, murmurous, he withdrew from them. Gran lit the gas, his dice
  whirred in the ludo-cup, he entered into the last dream of Offa the
  King.

XXIX: 1 **strangeness:** Cf. VI, 6.   4 **ludo-cup:** cup to hold the dice in a game of ludo, an old-fashioned
game (like Parcheesi) played with dice and counters on a special board

From **The Pentecost Castle**

1
They slew by night
upon the road
Medina's pride
Olmedo's flower

shadows warned him   5
not to go
not to go
along that road

weep for your lord
Medina's pride   10
Olmedo's flower
there in the road

2
Down in the orchard
I met my death
under the briar rose
I lie slain

I was going   5
to gather flowers
my love waited
among the trees

down in the orchard
I met my death   10
under the briar rose
I lie slain

Tenebrae, 1979.

See Additional Notes (p. 784).

1 Almost a literal translation—though with graceful changes of phrase and rhythm—of a lyric from
El Caballero de Olmedo, one of the most famous plays of the Spanish dramatist and poet Lope de Vega
(1562-1613). The first four lines are from an old song popular in Lope's day; he seems to have added
the rest. Medina and Olmedo are towns 13 miles apart and about 100 miles north of Madrid. In the
play, the gallant and noble Don Alonso, "the knight of Olmedo," in love with Doña Inés of Medina, is
murdered by a jealous rival (whose life he has saved in the bullring) as he is riding home to Olmedo
by night, in spite of his own forebodings and the warnings of an apparition, or *Sombra*, which is the
ghost of himself, and in spite of hearing the song, here translated, sung in prophetic warning by an
old peasant. The dramatist seems to have felt that the gallant knight, who lost his life for love, was a
kind of Christ figure.

8

And you my spent heart's treasure
my yet unspent desire
measurer past all measure
cold paradox of fire

as seeker so forsaken   5
consentingly denied
your solitude a token
the sentries at your side

fulfilment to my sorrow
indulgence of your prey   10
the sparrowhawk the sparrow
the nothing that you say

13

Splendidly-shining darkness
proud citadel of meekness
likening us our unlikeness
majesty of our distress

emptiness ever thronging   5
untenable belonging
how long until this longing
end in unending song

and soul for soul discover
no strangeness to dissever   10
and lover keep with lover
a moment and for ever

15

I shall go down
to the lovers' well
and wash this wound
that will not heal

beloved soul   5
what shall you see
nothing at all
yet eye to eye

depths of non-being
perhaps too clear   10
my desire dying
as I desire

Sylvia Plath
(1932–1963)

Born in Boston, Sylvia Plath received her degree in English from Smith College; while
there she spent one summer as guest editor at *Mademoiselle*. For two years she was a Ful-
bright scholar at Cambridge. In 1956 she married Ted Hughes; they had a daughter and a
son. In 1957–1958 she taught at Smith; in 1959 she moved to England. She died by suicide

in 1963 at the age of 30. Besides her several books of poetry she wrote short stories, a play, and an autobiographical novel about a prize-winning college writer who has a nervous collapse and attempts suicide.

Blackberrying

Nobody in the lane, and nothing, nothing but blackberries,
Blackberries on either side, though on the right mainly,
A blackberry alley, going down in hooks, and a sea
Somewhere at the end of it, heaving. Blackberries
Big as the ball of my thumb, and dumb as eyes   5
Ebon in the hedges, fat
With blue-red juices. These they squander on my fingers.
I had not asked for such a blood sisterhood; they must love me.
They accommodate themselves to my milkbottle, flattening their sides.

Overhead go the choughs in black, cacophonous flocks—   10
Bits of burnt paper wheeling in a blown sky.
Theirs is the only voice, protesting, protesting.
I do not think the sea will appear at all.
The high, green meadows are glowing, as if lit from within.
I come to one bush of berries so ripe it is a bush of flies,   15
Hanging their blue-green bellies and their wing panes in a Chinese screen.
The honey-feast of the berries has stunned them; they believe in heaven.
One more hook, and the berries and bushes end.

The only thing to come now is the sea.
From between two hills a sudden wind funnels at me,   20
Slapping its phantom laundry in my face.
These hills are too green and sweet to have tasted salt.
I follow the sheep path between them. A last hook brings me
To the hills' northern face, and the face is orange rock
That looks out on nothing, nothing but a great space   25
Of white and pewter lights, and a din like silversmiths
Beating and beating at an intractable metal.

1960–1962. *Crossing the Water*, 1971.

10 **choughs:** (pronounced *chuffs*) a European bird like the crow   **cacophonous:** (from the Greek: bad-sounding) harsh-sounding, raucous   27 **intractable:** unmanageable, stubborn, resistant

Mirror

I am silver and exact. I have no preconceptions.
Whatever I see I swallow immediately
Just as it is, unmisted by love or dislike.
I am not cruel, only truthful—
The eye of a little god, four-cornered.   5
Most of the time I meditate on the opposite wall.
It is pink, with speckles. I have looked at it so long
I think it is a part of my heart. But it flickers.
Faces and darkness separate us over and over.

Now I am a lake. A woman bends over me,   10
Searching my reaches for what she really is.
Then she turns to those liars, the candles or the moon.
I see her back, and reflect it faithfully.

1960–1962. Ibid.

She rewards me with tears and an agitation of hands.
I am important to her. She comes and goes.   15
Each morning it is her face that replaces the darkness.
In me she has drowned a young girl, and in me an old woman
Rises toward her day after day, like a terrible fish.

Tulips

The tulips are too excitable, it is winter here.
Look how white everything is, how quiet, how snowed-in.
I am learning peacefulness, lying by myself quietly
As the light lies on these white walls, this bed, these hands.
I am nobody; I have nothing to do with explosions.   5
I have given my name and my day-clothes up to the nurses
And my history to the anaesthetist and my body to surgeons.

They have propped my head between the pillow and the sheet-cuff
Like an eye between two white lids that will not shut.
Stupid pupil, it has to take everything in.   10
The nurses pass and pass, they are no trouble,
They pass the way gulls pass inland in their white caps,
Doing things with their hands, one just the same as another,
So it is impossible to tell how many there are.

My body is a pebble to them, they tend it as water   15
Tends to the pebbles it must run over, smoothing them gently.
They bring me numbness in their bright needles, they bring me sleep.
Now I have lost myself I am sick of baggage—
My patent leather overnight case like a black pillbox,
My husband and child smiling out of the family photo;   20
Their smiles catch onto my skin, little smiling hooks.

I have let things slip, a thirty-year-old cargo boat
Stubbornly hanging on to my name and address.
They have swabbed me clear of my loving associations.
Scared and bare on the green plastic-pillowed trolley   25
I watched my tea-set, my bureaus of linen, my books
Sink out of sight, and the water went over my head.
I am a nun now, I have never been so pure.

I didn't want any flowers, I only wanted
To lie with my hands turned up and be utterly empty.   30
How free it is, you have no idea how free—
The peacefulness is so big it dazes you,
And it asks nothing, a name tag, a few trinkets.
It is what the dead close on, finally; I imagine them
Shutting their mouths on it, like a Communion tablet.   35

The tulips are too red in the first place, they hurt me.
Even through the gift paper I could hear them breathe
Lightly, through their white swaddlings, like an awful baby.
Their redness talks to my wound, it corresponds.
They are subtle: they seem to float, though they weigh me down,   40
Upsetting me with their sudden tongues and their colour,
A dozen red lead sinkers round my neck.

1961. *Ariel*, 1965.

Nobody watched me before, now I am watched.
The tulips turn to me, and the window behind me
Where once a day the light slowly widens and slowly thins,   45
And I see myself, flat, ridiculous, a cut-paper shadow
Between the eye of the sun and the eyes of the tulips,
And I have no face, I have wanted to efface myself.
The vivid tulips eat my oxygen.

Before they came the air was calm enough,   50
Coming and going, breath by breath, without any fuss.
Then the tulips filled it up like a loud noise.
Now the air snags and eddies round them the way a river
Snags and eddies round a sunken rust-red engine.
They concentrate my attention, that was happy   55
Playing and resting without committing itself.

The walls, also, seem to be warming themselves.
The tulips should be behind bars like dangerous animals;
They are opening like the mouth of some great African cat,
And I am aware of my heart: it opens and closes   60
Its bowl of red blooms out of sheer love of me.
The water I taste is warm and salt, like the sea,
And comes from a country far away as health.

Seamus Heaney
(Born 1939)

Born in County Derry in Ireland, Seamus Heaney (pronounced *sháy-mus hée-nee*, not *háy-nee*) was educated at St. Columb's College there and at Queen's University in Belfast, where he has taught since 1966. More recently he has been a visiting professor at Harvard and the University of California at Berkeley.

Death of a Naturalist

All year the flax-dam festered in the heart
Of the townland; green and heavy headed
Flax had rotted there, weighted down by huge sods.
Daily it sweltered in the punishing sun.
Bubbles gargled delicately, bluebottles   5
Wove a strong gauze of sound around the smell.
There were dragon-flies, spotted butterflies,
But best of all was the warm thick slobber
Of frogspawn that grew like clotted water
In the shade of the banks. Here, every spring   10
I would fill jampotfuls of the jellied
Specks to range on window-sills at home,
On shelves at school, and wait and watch until
The fattening dots burst into nimble-
Swimming tadpoles. Miss Walls would tell us how   15
The daddy frog was called a bullfrog

Death of a Naturalist, 1966.

1 **flax-dam:** In the process of making linen from the long stems of the flax plant, the stalks are "retted," partially rotted by soaking in water to loosen the fibers. The flax-dams retain the water in the kind of pond Heaney describes.   5 **bluebottles:** flies with iridescent blue bodies   9 **frogspawn:** gelatinous masses of fertilized frog eggs that float in the water or cluster around the stems of water plants. The tadpoles or pollywogs hatch from the eggs in a week or so.

And how he croaked and how the mammy frog
Laid hundreds of little eggs and this was
Frogspawn. You could tell the weather by frogs too
For they were yellow in the sun and brown   20
In rain.

       Then one hot day when fields were rank
With cowdung in the grass the angry frogs
Invaded the flax-dam; I ducked through hedges
To a coarse croaking that I had not heard
Before. The air was thick with a bass chorus.   25
Right down the dam gross-bellied frogs were cocked
On sods; their loose necks pulsed like sails. Some hopped:
The slap and plop were obscene threats. Some sat
Poised like mud grenades, their blunt heads farting.
I sickened, turned, and ran. The great slime kings   30
Were gathered there for vengeance and I knew
That if I dipped my hand the spawn would clutch it.

The Barn

Threshed corn lay piled like grit of ivory
Or solid as cement in two-lugged sacks.
The musty dark hoarded an armoury
Of farmyard implements, harness, plough-socks.

The floor was mouse-grey, smooth, chilly concrete.   5
There were no windows, just two narrow shafts
Of gilded motes, crossing, from air-holes slit
High in each gable. The one door meant no draughts

All summer when the zinc burned like an oven.
A scythe's edge, a clean spade, a pitch-fork's prongs: 10
Slowly bright objects formed when you went in.
Then you felt cobwebs clogging up your lungs

And scuttled fast into the sunlit yard.
And into nights when bats were on the wing
Over the rafters of sleep, where bright eyes stared   15
From piles of grain in corners, fierce, unblinking.

The dark gulfed like a roof-space. I was chaff
To be pecked up when birds shot through the air-slits.
I lay face-down to shun the fear above.
The two-lugged sacks moved in like great blind rats.   20

Ibid.

2 **two-lugged:** with two "lugs" or ears at the top where the corners are gathered and tied   4 **plough-socks:** ploughshares (the parts of a plow that cut through the sod)   7 **motes:** specks of dust etc.
9 **zinc:** of the roof, sides   15 **bright eyes:** of the rats   17 **chaff:** Cf. Donald Hall, "Names of Horses,"
line 11.

Margaret Atwood
(Born 1939)

Margaret Atwood, born in Ottawa, has degrees from the University of Toronto and Radcliffe. She won the Governor General's Award for her first book of poetry—at 27, the youngest poet ever to do so. She has taught in universities in Vancouver and Montreal, has published four novels, seven books of poetry, and a "thematic guide" to Canadian literature. She lives on a farm in Ontario.

You Take My Hand And

You take my hand and
I'm suddenly in a bad movie,
it goes on and on and
why am I fascinated

We waltz in slow motion   5
through an air stale with aphorisms
we meet behind endless potted palms
you climb through the wrong windows

Other people are leaving
but I always stay till the end   10
I paid my money, I
want to see what happens.

In chance bathtubs I have to
peel you off me
in the form of smoke and melted   15
celluloid

      Have to face it I'm
finally an addict,
the smell of popcorn and worn plush
lingers for weeks   20

Power Politics, 1971.

At First I Was Given Centuries

At first I was given centuries
to wait in caves, in leather
tents, knowing you would never come back

Then it speeded up: only
several years between   5
the day you jangled off
into the mountains, and the day (it was
spring again) I rose from the embroidery
frame at the messenger's entrance.

That happened twice, or was it   10
more; and there was once, not so

Ibid.

long ago, you failed,
and came back in a wheelchair
with a moustache and a sunburn
and were insufferable.   15

Time before last though, I remember
I had a good eight months between
running alongside the train, skirts hitched, handing
you violets in at the window
and opening the letter; I watched   20
your snapshot fade for twenty years.

And last time (I drove to the airport
still dressed in my factory
overalls, the wrench
I had forgotten sticking out of the back   25
pocket; there you were,
zippered and helmeted, it was zero
hour, you said Be
Brave) it was at least three weeks before
I got the telegram and could start regretting.   30

But recently, the bad evenings
there are only seconds
between the warning on the radio and the
explosion; my hands
don't reach you   35

and on quieter nights
you jump up from
your chair without even touching your dinner
and I can scarcely kiss you goodbye
before you run out into the street and they shoot   40

Siren Song

This is the one song everyone
would like to learn: the song
that is irresistible:

the song that forces men
to leap overboard in squadrons   5
even though they see the beached skulls

the song nobody knows
because anyone who has heard it
is dead, and the others can't remember.

Shall I tell you the secret   10
and if I do, will you get me
out of this bird suit?

I don't enjoy it here
squatting on this island
looking picturesque and mythical   15

You Are Happy, 1974.

Cf. Samuel Daniel, "Ulysses and the Siren" (p. 75).

with these two feathery maniacs,
I don't enjoy singing
this trio, fatal and valuable.

I will tell the secret to you,
to you, only to you.   20
Come closer. This song

is a cry for help: Help me!
Only you, only you can,
you are unique

at last. Alas   25
it is a boring song
but it works every time.

Epilogue

In our galaxy of poets, there are swirls within swirls of creative activity. No doubt there are other galaxies that time will discover. There is hardly a campus, hardly a suburb or village, that does not have its Local Group. Everywhere the spirit of poetry continues to regenerate, as ebulliently as ever. Like the DNA molecule, which passes on the genetic code of our humanity from generation to generation (spiraling round itself like a mystic gyre of Yeats), it projects the past into the future. What it reproduces is itself—but with a difference. Although "there is no new thing under the sun," yet in living creatures, as in living poems, the turning spiral shows always a new aspect of the ancient truth.

Our anthology opened with an anonymous poem of nearly 800 years ago on the themes of love, separation, death. Now it comes to a close with a poem on similar themes and nearly as anonymous, presented here to stand for all those being written by the young in whose vision poetry proliferates. It is "nearly as anonymous" because the poet is not yet a presence in our literary world. This is his first published poem.

By one of the coincidences the Muses love, his poem takes its form from the DNA model which is the emblem of our Epilogue. A young man, writing a young woman, notices that their names have in common the runic letters that hold the key to life. That is the way of poets: they seize on something in the sound of words that echoes, as by magic, something in experience. The DNA that links two lovers' names (like the initialed hearts we carve in treebark) gives the poem a form that pulses, that expands and narrows, like the double helix of the molecule, bringing with it much from the past. We find in it parallels with poems of other centuries. In these graphic stanzas we recognize a game centuries old; we saw a famous example in George Herbert's "Easter-Wings." Yet here it is played with up-to-date equipment; before our time no one knew about the secret structure of that molecule. Nor did anyone know as we do the world of Orlando (Florida), of Duke and NYU, of peach brandy and alpha waves, of the right brain, of Bryant Park and the lions in front of the New York Public Library. The poet's timeless themes are youth and joy and love and death, yet everywhere he confers on them—as Shakespeare says the poet must—"a local habitation and a name."

Andy-Diana DNA Letter

ANDREW WEIMAN

Dear
Diana,
Hi! and a
white note probably
unlike any you've *evuh*
eyed before. Doodling inertia,
good-bye. This took considerable
time, but it's worth it, for say, a banana.
Yep! a ripe munchy monkey's fruit & a smooch intricately
entwined around my lips would be absolute nirvana.
How's psychology in provincial Philadelphia?
Lie down, yawn to stir up alpha waves
and use the right brain's retina
to visualize a ballerina
lithely *en pointe*
among these lines,
staccato & undying,
amid the bells & fierce fire
of a tintinnabulating typewriter
—sparks & syncopation, rhythm & rhyme—
The parable of the Phoenix! Everything dies & rises
again, the wanderers strain through long night's
passage, weary as a flicker of light (flame!)
on water, but together they fight (flame!)
against the soft slow silent
inevitable steady slide
asleep til sunrise &
petals & ignite
alive! On
arrival in
Orlando,
Florida, untanned
& disordered, I meandered
through the airport amid thousands
of visitors: some rushing, some stranded
for simply hours with no apparent explanation,
short people with lean, lanky, vociferous demands,
torn sneakers, fur coats, t-shirts, Panama hats & bandanas,
quarreling parents, caged pets, & carefree children hugging panda
or pooh bears, or hidden beneath Mickey Mouse hats from the fantasy
world of Disney, smiles & tears, the wheezy propaganda
of a preacher denouncing vice, smelly sandals,
snoring fat men & gabby wives, and I
saw that the colorful banter of
foreign accents seems bland &
boring when a chewy pecan
corn pone lazily expands,
"Shor is grand!"
Oranges,

                    yes, but also
                tangerines,
            cantaloupes, watermelons,
        mangos, & other exotic flavors
            tantalize the tongue & olfactory
        glands so much so that trees & orchards
    lay ransacked in neat net bags of nasty Northern
    vandalism and are replaced by an obese synthetic forest
of outlandish paisleys & plaids reflecting New York's
standards of fastidious & impeccable tastelessness in form
and in style unsurpassed on the globe for its garish adoration
of vanity (South 1, North 0). Under the eye of the preacher
haranguing on hell (South, North—even), I put a quarter
in a dandy zodiac machine of the future & fortune.
He ranted, I smiled and said, "I'm Scorpio, how
'bout you, Grandpa?"   "Damn the orbits
    of planets and horoscopes!"
        the old man snorted.
            Andrew Lawrence
                Weiman or
                    "Happy,"
                either
                name will do,
            my aim stays true
        nicknamed or just Andrew.
    Came home to rest from the university
        game: lectures, exams, readings of ridiculous
            claims by soporific professors striving for elusive
                fame, and in the face of it, higher tuition
                    payments. What nerve! The tune's
                        the same at big NYU in
                    shameless New
                        York City
                    or at rustic, tame
                    Duke. There, inflamed
                newly by love, I exclaimed
            pure joy—Once!—when this dame's
        dewsoft kisses turned to the bite of a lamia's
    shrewdness. Despite the tender chamber's
wounds one tries to keep on gamely—
        blue, dejected, blameful,
            brooding aimlessly on
                Adieus & Amens,
                    the used-
                        to-be
                    tuxedo of triumph
                shucked when rudely dumb-
            struck by the stark rumbling
        ineluctability of death, unhandsome
            destruction of skin used to summer
                ruckuses, the joys of a sexy jumble, and
                    accustomed to the coming
                        instruction of lissom
                            plucky women.

55

60

65

70

75

80

85

90

95

100

Death!

Hmm. It sucks,

it's crummy. The knuckle

and thumb motionless, the singing miracles

dumb, eyes fingered shut, and the body tucked

numb in the coffin. Enough! No reluctance,

no more grumbling. Let the steadily struck

drum stutter. I'll fashion of success

a humble hearted structure

with some luck.

Or so

I hope.

Hey

Diana!

Why can't

sky, streams & land

suffice as the elegant

life woven in a fabric of annual

revival? A place where deer, plants,

mice, leaf falls, water & spring are candidates

for messiahs, & gentle as dawn we become cognizant of

a miry beginning, not the sudden solemn entrance from a

titan's hand (And God Created The etc.), intolerant of acute

Why?s & founded on devout, religious & necessary commandments &

sacrifice. Agreeing the sun's a savior & with similar fanaticism

I propose an ancient alternative. Here's the game plan:

Recline on the grass & sip some cheap peach brandy

as the bright hot sun paddlewheels grandly

across the sky in hazy Bryant Park,

improve bucolic romance,

ride the shaggy urban

lions exultantly, then

devise a human,

vibrant,

sanguine

answer to dissatisfy

many or most non-Gentiles

& Christians. Perhaps a wisely

animated world of whistling vitality,

incessant motion, & grinning feistiness,

predominantly full-tilt, 3% mellow, & at times

frantic, where All Good Things Count, electrifying

or blank, & especially the darkly decadent, ribald

and naked acts. The goal isn't a strict, simplified

understanding of this & that nonsense, but a precise

unununderstanding of things—to take the frightening

chance of peering behind snug dusty disguises,

embrace dissonance, strip stout pride's

extravagance, learn to laugh & smile

with glances more blind

than narrowly sighted,

and then finally,

to dance & cry,

thank life,

and die.

Love,

Andy

Born in Orlando, Florida, in 1956, **Andrew Weiman** wrote his "epistolary poem" while a student in clinical psychology at New York University in 1980.

12 alpha waves: the electrical pulsations, about 10 per second, set up in the brain when in a state of relaxation. They are related to, and stimulate, visual imagination.   **13 right brain:** the right cortex (hemisphere) of the brain is the source of intuitive, artistic, visual activity. The left cortex is logical and articulate.   **15 en pointe:** toe-dancing (literally, *on tiptoe*)   **19 tintinnabulating:** ringing, like the sound of bells   **21 the Phoenix:** the mythology of the Phoenix, which "dies and rises" from its own ashes, has been referred to by many earlier poets—among them John Donne in "The Canonization," lines 23–26 ("we die and rise the same") (p. 98).   **41 world of Disney:** Walt Disney World is about 15 miles to the southwest of Orlando   **87 lamia:** in folklore, an alluring vampire, half woman, half snake   **98 ineluctability:** inescapability, inevitability   **106–109** This straight look at the physical horrors of death is more in the medieval mode than the modern one, recalling as it does thirteenth-century lyrics on "the signs of death." The best known begins:

> When my eyes are misted . . .
> And my nose like ice,
> And my tongue all twisted,
> And my cheeks are sagging,
> And my lips are blackened . . .

119 ff. Although we may not all share the poet's advocacy of earthly happiness as the be-all and end-all of existence (any more than we may not share his preferences in liquor), we recognize that his view is, as he says, "an ancient alternative" we have met with in other poets, though rarely put with such exuberance. Mr. Weiman's "game plan: Recline on the grass and sip some cheap peach brandy . . ." is essentially Omar Khayyám's

> A Book of Verses underneath the Bough,
> A Jug of Wine, a Loaf of Bread—and Thou
>   Beside me singing in the Wilderness—
> Oh, Wilderness were Paradise enow!

As for the book of verses, he is writing his own. The loaf of bread—or maybe a cheeseburger or pizza—will no doubt be along. The lovely earlier lines about "sky, streams & land . . . deer, plants, mice, leaf falls . . ." will remind us of such lines of Wallace Stevens as those near the end of "Sunday Morning," a poem concerned with the same philosophic problem Mr. Weiman is coping with:

> Deer walk upon our mountains, and the quail
> Whistle about us their spontaneous cries;
> Sweet berries ripen in the wilderness . . .

Weiman's "agreeing the sun's a savior" may even recall Stevens's devotees, who

> chant in orgy on a summer morn
> Their boisterous devotion to the sun,
> Not as a god, but as a god might be . . .

His thought is parallel with that of earlier poets; not derivative from it. The point of such observations as we are making is to show his poem as a combination of tradition and innovation.   **126 titan:** one of the early giant gods of Greek mythology   **And God Created The:** Few readers will be scientifically alert enough to catch the allusion: the capital letters A...G...C...T... stand for adenine, guanine, cytosine, and thymine, the chemical bases that bind together, like rungs, DNA's double helix. Cf. the corresponding capitals in line 145. Though the reference is a source of private pleasure and structural reassurance to the poet, an understanding of it is fortunately not necessary to our reading of the poem.   **132 Bryant Park:** a park behind the New York Public Library   **135 lions:** famous statues in front of the Library   **144 3%:** just a little

Probably many readers will not have been aware, and will now be surprised to learn, that the poem has a more complex and ingenious structure than at first it seems to have. As we have said, Mr. Weiman has taken the form of his poem from Nature itself, from the intertwined double helix (spiral) of the long DNA molecule, which we now know transmits the genetic code from generation to generation. His poem is "wound about a lean phonemic double helix" to suggest on a flat surface the three-dimensional structure of the molecule. His "phonemic double helix" is the strand of sound that bonds together the outside edges of the expanding and contracting sections. Long *i*-sounds run down the left-hand edge at the beginning (*Diana, Hi, white, unlike, eyed,* etc.); at line 15 they cross over to the right-hand edge (*lines, undying, fire,* etc.) A- or *na*-sounds run down the right-hand edge (*Diana, and a, probably, evuh,* etc.). They also cross to the opposite side at line 15 (*among, staccato, amid,* etc.). The whole section is enclosed in something like a figure 8 made of two strands of sound. The same mechanism (with different sounds) is found in the three following sections, with the last section returning to the original sounds. Though the poet has set himself some rigorous hurdles, he takes them with apparent ease: the poem reads so easily and colloquially we could miss the difficulties he has overcome. As he says at the beginning, it "took considerable/time." And considerable care—but nothing like the care Nature herself, working within limits much narrower than a millionth of an inch, takes to preserve the integrity of her far more complicated DNA molecule—if she is careless about the tiniest detail, a child may be born without limbs or eyes.

James Scully
Marcia Masters
Norman Rosten   Paul Petrie   Gary Soto   Ruth Whitman   Van Brock
Gjertrude Schnackenberg   Lawson Fusao Inada   Gray Burr   Gregory Orr   June Jordan
Elder Olson   Ann Deagon   Lewis Turco   William Sylvester   Karen Snow   Judith Leet
Anne Winters   George MacBride   Henry Carlile   Lawrence Kearney
Edward Hirsch   John Glassco   William H. Matchett   Ellen Gilchrist
Mary Baron   Hilda Morley   Miller Williams   Arthur Gregor
Dan Gerber   Alicia Ostriker   Etheridge Knight   Philip Lamantia   James Bertolino
John Engels   Gerald Barrax   Henry Braun   Carol Muske   Turner Cassity
Samuel Hazo   Frederick Bock   Philip Dacey   Ben Belitt   David Walker
Ron Padgett David Young   Carl Dennis   James Reiss   George Barlow
Barbara Guest   Lynne Lawner   Harvey Shapiro   Stephen Sandy   Richmond Lattimore
Jascha Kessler   R. P. Dickey   Lucille Clifton Earle Birney   Rosalie Moore
William Everson   Robert Pinsky
Marcia Southwick   Robert Bly   Stanley Kunitz   Philip Levine   John Wain
Stanley Kiesel
John Morgan   Maura Stanton   Tess Gallagher   Karl Shapiro   William Empson
Kathleen Fraser   Richard Howard David Slavitt   Donald Hall   Peter Porter
Carol Bergé   Lisel Mueller   John Ciardi   Thom Gunn   John Peck   Frances Hoekstra
William Mills
Julia Alvarez   Marvin Bell   Robert Creeley   Dave Smith   Al Young   Maxine Kumin
Margaret Kent   Margaret Avison   Donald Davie   Jane Shore   Robert Duncan
Ralph Pomeroy
Steve Orlen   Louise Glück   Peter Klappert William Jay Smith
Linda Pastan   Louis Simpson   Dan Jaffe   Laurence Lieberman Kingsley Amis
Constance Carrier   Adrienne Rich   George Barker   Lawrence Raab
James Broughton   William Dickey Harry Mathews Alice Walker   John Montague
William Matthews   Hollis Summers
Jeanne Murray Walker   Cid Corman   Faye Kicknosway   George Oppen   Anne Stanford
Robert B. Shaw   William Heyen   Robert Francis   Richard Shelton   A. G. Sobin Edward Brash
Irving Feldman   Conrad Hilberry   Robert Huff
Brewster Ghiselin   James Dickey   J. V. Cunningham   Paul Breslin
William Stafford   Roberta Spear   Reed Whittemore
Russell Edson
Alan Dugan   Anthony Hecht   John Betjeman   Donald Justice   Judson Jerome
Margaret Atwood   Josephine Miles   Florence Elon
Jerome Mazzaro
Eleanor Ross Taylor   Norman Dubie   Stephen Dunn   Jack Micheline
Charles Simic   Denise Levertov   Philip Whalen   Christopher Bursk
Robert Wallace   Marilyn Hacker Charles Wright   David Wevill   Madeline DeFrees
Paris Leary   Leonard Nathan   Leonie Adams   Daryl Hine   Nikki Giovanni
Edwin Brock   Wendell Berry   W. S. Graham   Gerald Stern   Philip Schultz
Gibbons Ruark
Michael Hamburger Mary Barnard   Robert Pack   Kenneth Rexroth   Bea Howa
Sidney Goldfarb   Dan Masterson   J. Laughlin   Peter Viereck
Karen Swenson   Edward Dorn
Anne Waldman   David Ignatow   Gary Snyder
Roberta Bienvenu   John N. Morris   Richard Eberhart   A. R. Ammons
Jane Mayhall
Frederick Seidel Elizabeth Spires   Carolyn Kizer   Stephen Spender   W. S. Merwin
Virginia Terris
Isabella Gardner   Ralph Mills   Stanley Plumly   Laura Riding Jackson   Helen Chasin
Primus St. John   Horace Gregory   John Logan
Kenneth Rosen   John Hollander   Derek Walcott
Clarence Major   Ernest Sandeen   Vern Rutsala
Katha Pollitt   Carolyn Forché   Philip Booth   Thomas Lux   Alan Feldman
Ned O'Gorman   Margaret Walker   Sandra McPherson
Laura Jensen   Michael McClure   Barbara Howes
Víctor Hernández Cruz James Schuyler   Bin Ramke   Naomi Lazard   Robin Skelton
Bink Noll   Stanley Burnshaw   Raymond Patterson   James Atlas   George Garrett   Robert Chatain
Jay Wright John Wieners James J. McAlley   Willis Barnstone   Judith Hemschemeyer   R. H. W. Dillard
Calvin Forbes   Jared Carter   Bruce Guernsey   Tom Johnson   Diane Ackerman
Thomas Disch   Diane dr Prima   David Meltzer   Cynthia Macdonald   Anselm Hollo
Evan Zimroth   John Matthias   Bruce Berlind   Conrad Kent Rivers Dave Etter   Paul Monette
Rochelle Ratner   A. J. M. Smith   Ronald Gross.   Rachel Hadas   James Cameron
Janet Winters   Robert Mazzocco Robert Sward   Harold Norse
Sonia Sanchez   Greg Pape   Fred Chappell   David Madden   Ronald Koertge
Kenneth Hanson   Joseph Bruchac   Elizabeth Libbey   Rosellen Brown
Leon Stokesbury   James Whitehead   Ruth Hershberger   John Unterecker
Mary Kinzie   Stephen Berg   Thomas Whitbread   Susan Fromberg Schaeffer

GALAXY OF CONTEMPORARY POETS

les Martin · Andrew Glaze · Michael Dennis Browne

Charles Guenther · Tom Clark · Ruell Denney · Sandra Gilbert · Belle Randall · Michael Anania

John Stone · Eve Merriam · Jon Silkin · Fanny Howe · Robert Peterson · Olga Broumas

Charles Gullans · Robert Kelly · Louis Coxe · Edwin Honig · Philip Larkin · Roy Fisher · Ross Talarico

Myra Sklarew · Lawrence Ferlinghetti · Michael Mott · Daniel Hoffman · Ted Hughes · Grace Schulman

Phyllis Thompson · Dannie Abse · Dudley Randall · Calvin Hernton

Annie Dillard · Ted Kooser · Charles Olson · Felix Stefanile

Erica Jong · Kathleen Spivack · Judith Minty · Ira Sadoff · Kenneth Koch · Dennis Schmitz · Wendy Salinger

Paul Hoover · Larry Levis · Reg Saner · Mac Hammond · Robert Bagg · John Fandel

Diana Ó Hehir · Barry Spacks · Eve Triem · Peter Schjeldahl · Bob Kaufman · Carole Oles · C. K. Williams

Michael Ryan · Kenneth Irby · Edward Field · Carol Frost · Donald Junkins

Leslie Ullman · Tom Parkinson

Larry Woiwode · Gloria Oden · Thomas Kinsella · James Seay · Joel Oppenheimer

Paul Zweig · John Bennett · Gerard Malanga

eth Bentley · Paul Smyth · Gwendolyn Brooks · Barbara Kirkpatrick · Stuart Dybek · James McMichael

Larry Neal · Dick Allen · Robert Penn Warren · Dara Wier · John Woods · John Thompson

Michael Benedikt · Robert Stock · Henry Taylor

Robert Watson · Richard Wilbur · William Meredith · Colette Inez · Paul Zimmer

Galway Kinnell · Allen Ginsberg · David Ray · John Ridland

David Wagoner · Vassar Miller · Jim Hall · Michael Heffernan

Joseph Langland · Charles Bukowski · H. R. Hays · Chris Feder · Nathaniel Tarn

uce Bennett · Stephen Dobyns · Ai · James Tate · Bern Porter · M. L. Rosenthal

David McAleavey · Patricia Goedicke · William Virgil Davis

T. Alan Broughton · Gilbert Sorrentino · Edmund Keeley · Richard Moore · Theodore Enslin

Michael Ondaatje · Pamela White Hadas · Catherine Petroski

John Tagliabue · Ishmael Reed · Debora Greger

Allen Grossman · Henry Petroski · Howard Moss · Ntozake Shange

Audre Lorde · David Bottoms · Constance Urdang · William Pitt Root

D. J. Enright · Diana Der Hovanessian · Ki Davis · Clayton Eshleman · James Welch · Heather McHugh

William Packard · James Schevill · Kelly Cherry

David St. John · Don L. Lee · Edgar Bowers · John Ashbery · Alberta Turner

Christopher Middleton · Nancy Willard

Alvin Feinman · Julia Randall · Mark McCloskey · Josephine Jacobsen · James Baker Hall

Robert Dana · Jane Cooper

Diane Niatum · Robert Graves · Paul Carroll

John Balaban · Margaret Danner · Richard Hugo

Jonathan Aaron · Frank Bidart · Hugh Seidman · W. D. Snodgrass · R. G. Vliet

Hayden Carruth · Charles Tomlinson · Geoffrey Grigson · Diane Wakoski · David Bromwich

Philip Appleman · Rosemary Daniell · Ian Hamilton Finlay · D. M. Thomas · William Hunt

Thomas McGrath · James Applewhite · Albert Goldbarth · Peter Redgrove · Judith Johnson Sherwin

Brendan Galvin · Kenward Elmslie · Ron Loewinsohn · Siv Cedering Fox

Ted Joans · Imamu Amiri Baraka · Mary Shumway · Peter Michelson · Edward Lueders

Warren Carrier · John Williams · Richard Brautigan · Ted Berrigan

John Malcolm Brinnin · Mark Perlberg · Ronald Johnson · Jerome Rothenberg · Sarah Appleton

Mark Rudman · Theodore Weiss · Herbert Scott · Everett Hoagland · Verandah Porche · William Bronk · Gregory Corso

Robert Hass · Archibald MacLeish · Philip Legler · Gary Margolis

Peter Davison · May Sarton · Harold Witt

Robley Wilson · X. J. Kennedy · Peter Levi · Bill Knott · Gary Gildner · Radcliffe Squires

Carl Rakosi · Stephen Stepanchev · Helen Adam · Mary Swander

R. S. Thomas · Jean Valentine · Robert Morgan · Dennis Saleh

glas Crase · Judith Kröll · Paul Engle · Rod Taylor

Adrien Stoutenburg · F. D. Reeve · Maya Angelou · David Shapiro · John Fuller · Greg Kuzma

Timothy Steele · Joyce Carol Oates · Peter Everwine · Mona Van Duyn · Dabney Stuart

Peter Wild · George Starbuck · Sterling Brown · Geoffrey Hill · Jim Harrison

Ann Darr · Jonathan Williams · Richard Frost

David Lehman · Roger Weingarten · James Merrill · Howard Nemerov · David Wilk

Al Poulin · Phyllis Janowitz · Owen Dodson · May Swenson · Seamus Heaney · James Hearst

Robert Mezey · Frederick Morgan · Mark Strand · Lucien Stryk · Daniel Halpern

Laurel Blossom · Marge Piercy · George Keithley

Richard Emil Braun · Michael Harper · Sonia Raiziss

Henri Coulette · Sandra Hochman · Celia Gilbert · J. D. Reed

Jack Hirschman · Janet Beeler · Gary Miranda · A. D. Hope · Bill Zavatsky

Lorrie Goldensohn · Barton Sutter

Ai Lee · J. D. McClatchy · Judith Moffett · Alfred Corn · Keith Waldrop

Marya Zaturenska · Robert Fitzgerald · Ronald Perry · Guy Owen · Mari Evans · Peter Meinke

David Steingass · Caroline Knox · Alan Williamson · Ruth Stone

James Crenner · Jane Kenyon

Leslie Silko · Pauline Hanson

Mekeel McBride · Ellen Bryant Voigt · Andrew Weiman · Martha Friedberg · A. K. Ramanujan

ADDITIONAL NOTES

Blake/The Tiger (p. 241)

This poem makes sense if we think of it as about a beast at once beautiful and savage. But it makes more sense if we think of it as about everything tigerlike or tigerish in existence: the violence of which nature is capable, the fiery passions within our souls, the wrath of Jehovah or the Son that T. S. Eliot called "Christ the tiger." Existence, Blake believed, is made up of such contraries as those we call good and evil: the lamb and the tiger. Every sentence in the poem is a question: what can we do but ask questions of an ultimate reality? The central question is in line 20. Did the same God make lamb and tiger? Can they exist in the same universe? The fact is that they do.

Blake/The Sun-Flower (p. 242)

We may think of the sun-flower as any soul longing for the end of time and the beginning of eternity, in which the sexual frustrations of this life (lines 5–6) will find their happy solution. The west, for Blake, signified liberation, the beginning of a new life as the sun of this life sets.

Blake/The Sick Rose (p. 243)

When Cowper wrote a poem to his pet hare, he had a real hare, Tiny, in mind. When he wrote about the poplar trees that were levelled, he had a real grove in mind. But in "The Sick Rose" and the two poems that follow it, Blake has more in mind than a real rose, a real tiger, a real sun-flower. Of course he knew the real things; he might even have come straight from a zoo when he wrote the tiger poem. But he is more concerned with what these things stand for or represent in the great scheme of the universe. They are symbols of something greater than themselves, symbols of passions or qualities or general truths that Blake finds in experience. Critics disagree on what exactly each such symbol stands for, and indeed it would not be like Blake to want a single label pinned on each. His own ideas shifted. "May God us keep," he wrote, "from a single vision and Newton's sleep!" His symbols, however, are natural, not arbitrary: nearly everyone would agree that a rose is beautiful and therefore associated with love; nearly everyone would agree that a tiger is beautiful, though its beauty is of a kind that could be deadly to us.

We are safe in assuming that the rose, in its bed of vivid joy, is a symbol of natural human love. The worm, associated with secrecy, storm, darkness, is something that can destroy love: some restraint, inhibition, hypocrisy, perversion because of which love is sick instead of healthy. If we should think that the poem is about nothing more than gardening and the need for pesticides, Blake's illustration (meant to be seen with the poem) with its despairing human figures, should make us think again. And if we know anything about his life and thought, we know that he believed one of the great evils of our fallen world is the way its restrictions can frustrate our natural inclination to love.

Wordsworth/Resolution and Independence (p. 253)

Coleridge thought this poem "especially characteristic of the author. There is scarce a defect or excellence in his writings of which it would not present a specimen. But it would be unjust not to repeat that this defect is only occasional" (Biog. Lit. XXII). Wordsworth's modern biographer thinks it "perhaps the poem in which we see more of Wordsworth than in any other single poem: here are many of his most characteristic moods and states of soul; joy and despondency; trance and vision; here too are stanzas and lines almost as 'homely' in style as some of the Lyrical Ballads, side by side with tones of deepest passion" (Mary Moorman, William Wordsworth: The Early Years, p. 538).

Wordsworth/Ode: Intimations of Immortality ... (p. 257)

The intimations of our immortality given in childhood are chiefly two: the vividness and splendor with which a child perceives the world; and the child's feeling that his life will go on forever. In the "Ode," Wordsworth laments the loss of these glorious feelings as we age, but is consoled by the fact that the very memory of them shows they were real—and that something of them, after all, remains through life.

Shelley/Ode to the West Wind (p. 310)

A comment which Shelley made in a letter to Thomas Love Peacock is helpful with such poems as this. "I always seek in what I see the manifestation of something beyond the present and tangible object." Here "the present and tangible object" was the west wind blowing up a storm one October day in Florence, actually clearing away dead vegetation, lodging the seeds for their spring rebirth, heralding the autumnal rains that ensured fertility. The "something beyond" in which Shelley was even more interested was a vitalizing and revolutionary force in the universe to sweep away what was old and dead and nurture what was fresh and alive.

Shelley/To a Skylark (*p. 312*)

With this poem even more than the preceding one, it helps to remember that Shelley is less interested in "the present and tangible object" (the bird) than in "the manifestation of something beyond" (the "blithe spirit" of instinctive joy in existence and the spontaneous expression of that joy). It is only because of this that he can address what seems to be a bird with the assertion that "Bird thou never wert" and go on to credit the bird with "sweet thoughts" and fidelity in love.

Emerson/Brahma (*p. 341*)

This poem comes out of Emerson's reading of the Hindu scriptures, especially the *Bhagavad-Gita* and the *Upanishads*. In the Hindu trinity, Brahma is the creative aspect of the supreme godhead. The other two aspects are Vishnu the Preserver and Siva the Dissolver (or, the Destroyer, though Siva destroys to recreate). The poem, however, is not about Brahma but about Brahman, the supreme God of the Hindu religion, the ultimate reality, the primal energy which produces and sustains everything in the universe. In a sense, everything there is, *is* Brahman—since there is nothing else from which it could derive its being. As the *Chandogya Upanishad* has it: "Thus out of himself he projected the universe; and having projected out of himself the universe, he entered into every being. All that is has its self in him alone."

1 **red slayer:** In the *Katha Upanishad*, the warrior Arjuna is reluctant to take part in a battle in which kinsmen of his will be killed—perhaps by him. He is told by Krishna, an incarnation of Brahman, that the apparent slaying is an illusion: in Brahman nothing dies. "Some say this Atman [the Brahman within each of us] / Is slain, and others / Call It the slayer: / They know nothing." And in the *Katha Upanishad* Emerson found: "If the slayer think that he slays, if the slain think that he is slain, neither of them knows the truth. The Self [Brahman] slays not, nor is he slain." Some annotators say the slayer is Vishnu. (Many American readers have seen a hostile redskin in the line.) 5–8 In Brahman are resolved all the oppositions that make up life on earth: "pleasure and pain, gain and loss, victory and defeat, are all one and the same . . ." (*Bhagavad-Gita*, II). 8 The enlightened man "regard[s] happiness and suffering as one. . . . He pays no attention to praise or blame. His behavior is the same when he is honored and when he is insulted" (*Bhagavad-Gita*, XIV). 12 **Brahmin:** a member of the Hindu priestly caste 13 **the strong gods:** In the Hindu religion there are many orders of lesser gods (like the orders of angels in Western religions) who aspire to union with the Brahman. 14 **the sacred Seven:** wise men, famous in Hindu religious history ("Forth from my thought / Came the seven Sages," *Bhagavad-Gita*, X) 15 **meek lover:** the true yogi (aspirant to perfection) is "gentle and modest" 16 **turn thy back** . . . : to desire heaven because it is a state of happiness, is like any other form of pleasure-seeking, impure and selfish. *Bhagavad-Gita*, II, speaks of those who "are full of worldly desires, and hungry for the reward of heaven." We should desire the Brahman for itself alone, not for any gain we might receive.

Dickinson/I Heard a Fly Buzz—When I Died (*p. 422*)

The significance of the fly, which appears just as some majestic revelation is expected, remains mysterious. Some suggested interpretations: (1) the fly represents the petty irritabilities that make up our living (and dying); (2) the fly, breeder of maggots, is a reminder of the nastiness and corruption of the grave; (3) the fly is a last dear homely sound from the pleasant world of the living; (4) the fly, with its "uncertain—stumbling Buzz" represents our own futile and ignorant efforts to understand the meaning of life and death. Whatever exactly the fly means, it is made interesting enough for us to puzzle over its presence.

Dickinson/I Started Early—Took My Dog (*p. 424*)

This poem seems to tell a simple story, or to be a simple fable. But, in poetry as elsewhere, still waters run deep. One authority calls the poem "downright horrifying" in the way it shows a little girl molested by a savage "he" bent on corrupting her purity. Happier interpretations are possible; what is interesting is that the poem is open to interpretation—it means more that it seems to mean.

My Life Had Stood—a Loaded Gun (*p. 425*)

Lines 21–24: There is no agreement as to what these paradoxical but exciting lines mean. Guns generally outlast their owners. Perhaps the meaning is: the owner, or loved one, *must* live longer than the lover because the lover's life, without someone to love, has no meaning. (Such a *must* expresses only a strong hope or desire: "It *must* snow; I want to go skiing!" The last two lines could mean that love can do everything for another, but nothing for itself. Perhaps too much can be made of the fact that a gun can destroy: here its purpose is to protect.

Hopkins/The Windhover (*p. 446*)

Lines 9–14 have been explained often and in various ways. Here is a simple suggestion that readers may prefer to develop further (or dispense with): In the skill and daring of the bird many brilliant physical qualities mesh together (*buckle*); the moral brilliance of Hopkins's chevalier (Christ, the knight to whom the poem is dedicated) must then be far more glorious. Mere dull duty (*sheer plod*) can make beauty like that of a gleaming ploughshare; the mere dull embers of a life devoted to such duty may have a brilliant interior glory, like that which shows when bleak ashes crumble or are gashed, as if wounded. (Such a summary over-simplifies a rich complex of images.)

Yeats/The Magi (*p. 463*)

The Magi are the three wise men from the East who came with gifts to pay homage to the infant Christ. Yeats's note on another poem, "The Dolls," describes how he "looked up one day into the blue of the sky, and suddenly imagined, as if lost in the blue of the sky, stiff figures in procession. I remembered that they were the habitual image suggested by blue sky, and looking for a second fable called them 'The Magi.'" To a reader who comes to the poem with no special preparation except humanity, the images will probably suggest that the stiff—rather stuffy—hierarchical solemnity of the Magi is shocked to find at the end of their quest not a great king but a real baby born in a stable among animals, a baby destined to come to a disgraceful and "turbulent" end on Calvary. They expected something nicer, and will go off looking for another embodiment of their ideal. The poem can then lead to reflections on the real and the ideal, on the way in which our preconceptions and formulations may not measure up to what we actually find in reality. But those who come to the poem with a knowledge of the symbolic system which Yeats later evolved find a good deal more in it. Yeats published an account of his system in *A Vision* in 1925. Almost immediately he began revising this account, which he called "inaccurate, obscure, incomplete" in the light of later reading; his "corrected" version was published in 1937. In his system, which attempted to find patterns in human personality, history, and culture, he sees reality (as so many other thinkers have done) as made up of conflicts and reconciliations between opposed tendencies—like the Yin and Yang of Oriental thought. In history these opposites show themselves in the interplay between an objective (or outward-looking) world of reason, science, practical action, and a subjective (or inward-looking) world of instinct and emotion, of artistic creation, of imagination and reverie. In "The Magi" the polarities might be called the rational and the miraculous. Yeats further believed that the interplay between opposites divided history into great cycles of about 2000 years each. Each cycle begins with one of the two tendencies on the upsurge, the other in decline. In "The Magi," the wise men represent the old world of reason and theory giving way to the new world of miracle, as represented by the birth of Christ. The mysterious and turbulent new Christian world is quite "uncontrollable" by reason, which is stiff, painted, pale, and ancient. Yeats himself explained the poem in this way when he wrote, in *A Vision*, "the old realisation of an objective moral law is changed into a subconscious turbulent instinct. The world of rigid custom and law is broken up by 'the uncontrollable mystery upon [sic] the bestial floor.'"

Yeats/The Second Coming (*p. 464*)

Like "The Magi," this is a poem which will make sufficient sense without reference to Yeats's elaborate "system" as described in *A Vision*. It says that the world is worsening in our time and that some mysterious force visualized as a sphinxlike monster will appear as the embodiment or symbol of the terrifying new spirit. But the focus of the poem is sharpened if one is familiar with the framework described in *A Vision* (cf. the notes to "The Magi"). Based on Yeats's readings in literature, mythology, philosophy, history, mysticism, alchemy, astrology, and so on, the work for *A Vision* began in earnest when Yeats discovered, a few days after his marriage in 1917, that his wife had an aptitude for automatic writing—writing apparently not controlled by the mind but by some external telepathic or spiritualistic agency. The ghostly "instructors" said they had come to give Yeats "metaphors for poetry." From later spiritualistic communications over the years (they filled 50 copybooks) and from dreams and psychic phenomena such as strange sounds and odors, Yeats evolved his symbolic system, based on a distinction between "the perfection that is from a man's combat with himself and that which is from a combat with circumstances" (cf. notes to "The Magi" on the "inward-looking" and "outward-looking" mind). From this "simple distinction" was built up an elaborate classification of human types, national characteristics, historic periods, and so forth, often supported by geometric symbols. Some would call this mysticism, and some mere mumbo-jumbo. However that may be, the work excited Yeats to some of his best writing. In regard to whether he actually believed in his "circuits of sun and moon," he wrote, after declaring some "plainly symbolical": "I can but answer that if sometimes, overwhelmed by miracle as all men must be when in the midst of it, I have taken such periods literally, my reason soon recovered. . . ."

Yeats/Sailing to Byzantium (*p. 467*)

At the end of the third century A.D., for military and administrative reasons, the capital of the Roman Empire was shifted to the east. On the site of the ancient Greek city of Byzantium on the Bosphorus (the strait, in modern Turkey, which divides Europe from Asia), a grand new city was built on the model of Rome and dedicated as Constantinople by the Emperor Constantine in 330 A.D. (It is now Istanbul.) Rome itself fell to "the barbarians" in 476, but the Christianized Byzantine Empire was to last for over a thousand years. The early Empire reached its peak of splendor under the Emperor Justinian, who reigned from 527 to 565, and his wife, the beautiful ex-actress Theodora. Justinian built, among other great works, the church of Hagia Sophia; this and other projects attracted to Constantinople many of the best artists and artisans of the time. For Yeats, Byzantium stands for a culture in which spirituality, especially as expressed in art, was triumphant. In *A Vision* he wrote: "I think if I could be given a month of Antiquity and leave to spend it where I chose, I would spend it in Byzantium a little before Justinian opened St. Sophia. . . . I think I could find in some little wine-shop some philosophical worker in mosaic who could answer all my questions, the supernatural descending nearer to him than to Plotinus [the Roman Neoplatonic philosopher of the third century A.D.] . . . maybe never before or since in recorded history, religious, aesthetic and practical life were one . . . architect and artificers . . . spoke to the multitude and the few alike. . . ."

Yeats/Among School Children (*p. 468*)

49-64 The poem turns from a world in which intellectual grandeur can be linked with physical decrepitude to symbols of an ideal world: the mother's idealization of her child, the nun's idealization of an image lit by holy candles. The nun's image—like the emperor's golden bird in "Sailing to Byzantium"—may keep its repose for 60 years—whereas the child will be changed for the worse. Though only marble or bronze, the image—or rather what it stands for—can arouse as much passion as a child we love. It would seem that "Presences" refers to what the images symbolize, since a child cannot be called "self-born"—though perhaps both the idealized baby and the ideal image refer us to the world of "heavenly glory." Whatever exactly the references may be, the love we have for children and for religious images points to another order of reality beyond this corruptible world—so far beyond that it mocks all of our endeavors.   57-64 Yeats is not so much making statements as presenting images which suggest meanings. There is no single official interpretation to be given these images; the power of an image is in its being able to suggest different and sometimes even contradictory meanings—just as things in life do (fire is warmth and love, it is also destruction and death; water is life and baptism, it is also drowning). Therefore paraphrases of such stanzas as this are likely to be incomplete or, for individual readers, mistaken. Tentatively, we may suggest the stanza means something like this (though readers are welcome to other interpretations): Unity of being is not to be achieved in this world, in which we always choose one value at the expense of another: we deny the demands of our pleasure-loving body if we wish spiritual perfection; we are never more beautiful than when we overcome suffering and tragic loss (the empty doll faces of cosmetic models are hardly human); we accumulate great knowledge only by getting bleary-eyed by reading late at night, while others are having fun. The greatest thinkers and artists become old, feeble, and ugly—perhaps even senile. Such is the world we live in. (With this stanza, cf. the third stanza of Keats's "Ode to a Nightingale.") But *if* we could indulge both body and soul at once, be beautiful and also wise and happy, have the wisdom of the very old and yet the bodies of the young—*if* we could do this, then our "labour" would be fruitful and joyous, like a kind of blossoming or a kind of dancing. The poem concludes with two images of perfect unity: the blossoming chestnut, which is not its leaf, nor its blossom, nor its trunk, but all three at once; and the dancer who (while dancing) cannot be separated from the dance she is dancing. The two are one. This is a kind of unity we may hope to find in "heavenly glory." The poem—like many of Yeats's—concludes with a question, not a statement.

Yeats/Two Songs from a Play (*p. 471*)

Yeats's short play, "The Resurrection," which is about Christ's appearance to the apostles after the resurrection, opens with the first two of these stanzas; it closes with the last two. The first three stanzas were written in 1926, the last probably in 1930–1931, when the play was written. The poems are based on Yeats's belief in recurring historical cycles of about 2000 years (cf. notes to "The Magi" and "The Second Coming"). They see a parallel between the legendary suffering, death, and resurrection of Dionysius and of Christ, who each initiated a new historical cycle. The language and imagery are vivid and passionate and in themselves may satisfy some readers; but the thought is difficult, depending as it does on allusions to Yeats's reading and to the symbolic system he developed.

Yeats/The Gyres (*p. 474*)

The poem deals with the historical cycles: how one civilization is destroyed and another—its opposite—succeeds, itself to give place in time to one like the one it supplanted, in a pattern of eternal recurrence (until, at last, time ends). Cf. the notes on "The Magi," "The Second Coming," "Two Songs from a Play," and "Leda and the Swan." What is new here is the exultation Yeats feels in the mighty spectacle.

Frost/"Out, Out—" (*p. 492*)

Edward Connery Lathem, Frost's editor, has discovered a newspaper account of the accident, which happened at the end of March 1910. Differences between the poem and the newspaper account are interesting for what they tell us about the nature of poetry, showing what the poet adds and what he omits. It reads: "Raymond Tracy Fitzgerald, one of the twin sons of Michael G. and Margaret Fitzgerald of Bethlehem, died at his home Thursday afternoon, March 24, as the result of an accident by which one of his hands was badly hurt in a sawing machine. The young man was assisting in sawing up some wood in his own dooryard with a sawing machine and accidentally hit the loose pulley, causing the saw to descend upon his hand, cutting and lacerating it badly. Raymond was taken into the house and a physician was immediately summoned, but he died very suddenly from the effects of the shock, which produced heart failure . . ." (in Lawrance Thompson, *Robert Frost: The Early Years*, Holt, Rinehart and Winston, 1966, p. 567).

Frost/The Subverted Flower (*p. 496*)

Though a draft existed as early as 1912, according to Frost, this poem was not published until 30 years later, after the death of Frost's wife. The incident, in which a girl is shocked and repelled by some physical expression of the boy's love for her, is thought to refer to a misunderstanding that occurred during Frost's courtship of his future wife. The "subverted flower" stands for an innocent natural force corrupted by the girl's "too meager heart"—all as seen, of course, from the young man's point of view.

Frost/Directive (*p. 497*)

The poem could be describing a real trip to the site of what was once a farmhouse (with a children's playhouse near it) on a farm the woods have now nearly overgrown, near two villages now deserted. Such places exist in New England; the geology and landscape of the poem are convincingly real. And yet some details—the riddling guide, the now travelled road that can be pulled up like the ladder to a tree-house, the legendary Grail, the ritual drinking close to a source—suggest that the journey is also symbolic and has to do with escaping the confusions of modern life and getting back to one's source, one's roots, to whatever one feels is deepest and truest in one's soul; perhaps to a world of the imagination, or the simplicities of childhood, or the security of a personally felt religion—to anything preserved from the contamination of our workaday anxieties.

Stevens/Sunday Morning (*p. 504*)

I: The woman (who is "anybody," said Stevens) is enjoying the self-satisfied leisurely happiness of being still in a dressing-gown (peignoir) late one Sunday morning. Her thoughts turn to the church service she is not at, and to the question of an afterlife. The poem is a dialogue between her feeling that there may be or should be a life after death, and a voice—perhaps from within her own soul, perhaps from the poet—that tells her, reassuringly, that life in this world, with all of its beauty and excitement, is enough.

II: The physical realities of our native earth and of our passionate life here is all we are destined for.

III: The god of the Greeks and Romans did not share in our humanity, but remained remote. Christ, however, had a human mother. Cannot we continue this religious development and further humanize our belief, in the realization that earth is our real home?

IV: The woman admits her contentment with earth when its pleasures are at hand—but when they disappear? The answer given is that even so the satisfactions of earth, though in memory or in anticipation, are more real to us than such legendary beliefs as are alluded to in lines 51–56.

V: The woman still longs for a happiness that will never end. The answer given her is that it is our very mortality which gives life its beauty—mournful or tragic as it may sometimes be.

VI: An existence in which nothing changed would not be as beautiful as our ever-changing earth is.

VII: The stanza imagines and advocates a natural religion that celebrates the happiness of earth and human companionship.

VIII: We live in a physical universe whose grandeur, loveliness, and richness (it is implied) should be enough for us, without hope of a further life. Even the mysterious evening of death is to be accepted as a part of that natural beauty.

Stevens/The Snow Man (*p. 507*)

Wallace Stevens is thought of as a "difficult" poet. In any university library one could find at least a dozen books about him—hundreds and hundreds of pages explaining what he means by his poems. Stevens's own explanations, which he sometimes gives in his letters, are likely to be simpler than those of the critics. Of "The Snow Man" he writes: "I shall explain [it] as an example of the necessity of identifying oneself with reality in order to understand and enjoy it." To expand that a little: if we are going to appreciate winter for what it is, really savor the essence of winter as we stand (for example) in a snowy field listening to the winter wind and looking at the winter landscape, what we have to do is let ourselves enter into the spirit of winter, let ourselves *become* winter, become a sort of snow man or "snow person" as we might say of someone really fond of winter and winter sports. To do this, we have to forget our own preconceptions of what winter is (bleakness, misery—or their opposite), we have to stop personifying things as if they were human, have to stop projecting our own feelings and prejudices onto the landscape and become receptive to what *it* is.

But in reading Stevens and other poets—particularly, it may be, modern poets—it is important to remember that a poem is not simply a message, not simply a way of telling us something. A poem is a kind of art object, a beautiful or (better) an expressive thing made out of images and words and sounds and rhythms and shapes—just as a statue is an expressive object made out of clay or wood or stone, or a picture an expressive object made out of watercolors or oils or acrylic, on paper or canvas or wood. In these, we take pleasure in the way the colors and shapes are handled as well as in what they may be representing—or nonrepresenting. So in a good poem: we take pleasure in the images and the words and the other elements in addition to the pleasure we take in what they are saying. In "The

Snow Man," there is a pleasure in surrendering ourselves to the movement of the one long clear supple sentence, its easy rhythms paced by their arrangement on the page, in trim units of three. There is a pleasure in seeing how the sentence works out and ends neatly where it ends, in a line which has the reassurance of the most familiar line in English poetry (the solemnly named iambic pentameter), here enlivened with its two anapestic (∪ ∪ −) substitutions. The poem has form; there is a human mind here organizing the chaos of phenomena. (If we type the poem out as prose, we can see what a clear and fluent sentence it is: sinewy English.) There is a pleasure in the sound of the words: the sustained music of high, clear vowels in *mind-pine-time-ice*, of quick middle ones in *in-distant-glitter*, of low ones in *snow-cold-behold*; the texturey play of consonants in *must-frost-crusted, sound-land-wind*. Continuity of sound is stressed in the repetition of such key words as *sound, same, nothing*. There is a pleasure in the words which we feel are apt without being over-pretty: *crusted, shagged, rough, glitter*; and also in the very purity and plainness of most of the vocabulary. The words of the poem *taste* right for what they are saying. There is a pleasure, like that we get from fine photographs, in the starkness of the winter imagery: the burdened pines and junipers and spruces—not just vague "trees"—that glitter in the winter sun. And in with all these pleasures, the poet is telling us something important: that we are fully alive only when we are open to sympathy for what else is in the universe. Poems, an earlier note reminded us, rarely have official meanings. Possible meanings are suggested for this and other poems, but only as a way of getting readers started on their own interpretations—based, of course, on the facts of the poem.

8 **misery:** To think that there is misery in the scene is to project our own feelings on the landscape, which is itself innocent of such feelings.   14 **nothing himself:** because he is trying to set aside his own selfness in order to empathize with that of winter. Instead of imposing his own personality on it, his own prejudices, personifications, and so forth, he is trying to be receptive to what *it* is.   15 **nothing that is not there:** He does not imagine qualities (such as "misery") not really there.   **the nothing that is:** the purity of the thing itself, which owes *nothing* to our interpretation of it; perhaps too that quality in the winter landscape which we might interpret, in human terms, as negation, absence, emptiness. Compared with those of other seasons, certain winter landscapes might be said to be empty. To call this quality "the nothing" is to remove it from a human order of the emotions to a scientific one of mathematics or physics. (Some would probably feel that Stevens is contradicting himself by reading a "nothing" into the winter landscape. What is really there, a physicist might say, is a fiery dance of impassioned electrons, in controlled patterns of a complexity and power the human mind cannot begin to imagine.) For a very different poem suggested by a winter landscape, cf. Yeats's "The Cold Heaven."

Stevens/The Emperor of Ice-Cream (*p. 507*)

This poem has been found puzzling by many readers. Stevens himself had a good deal to say about it. Ten years after it was written, he selected it as his favorite among his poems, because, he said, "it wears a deliberately commonplace costume, and yet seems to me to contain something of the essential gaudiness of poetry...." He said too that he could not remember the circumstances under which it was written, but that it "represented what was in his mind at the moment, with the least possible manipulation." Perhaps we should not worry too much about what it "means"; Stevens himself insisted, "After all, the point of that poem is not its meaning." The situation he shows us is very clear: we are in a house in which a woman has just died; we are given a graphic glimpse of the corpse, not yet in its coffin, amid realistic details of the woman's past. At the same time, out in the kitchen, preparations are being made for the feeding of guests at the wake. A husky man, very much alive, is whipping up an ice-cream mix—which might seem trivial and out of place under the circumstances. Life is going on much as usual: young ladies are lolling about; the florists' boys are delivering flowers wrapped in the customary old newspapers. Instead of asking what we are supposed to make of such a poem, we might ask what we are supposed to make of such a situation in real life. It would probably give us pause, give us something to think about, this juxtaposition of the corpse with its calloused feet showing and the finger-lickin' ice-cream being whomped up in the kitchen. That may be the point of the poem: something to think about. Do poems have to be clearer than life itself is?

3 **in kitchen cups concupiscent curds:** The five catchy *k*-sounds make the line quite a mouthful: they physicalize the imagined experience of slurping ice-cream. "Concupiscent" (which has sexy suggestions, with the *cupi-* of Cupid right in the middle) means physically desirous or desirable: arousing a gluttonous lust. "Curds" are any coagulated dairy product. In speaking of a French translation of the poem, Stevens said that French words that literally mean "libidinous milks" were closer to what he had in mind than words which meant "delectable creams." The words express, he said, "the concupiscence of life, but, by contrast with the things in relation to the poem, they express or accentuate life's destitution, and it is this that gives them something more than cheap lustre." (Cf. Frost, "Directive," line 44: "Weep for what little things could make them glad.") It is ironic that ice-cream should matter in the house of death—yet it does matter.   7 **let be be finale of seem:** In 1939, Stevens explained that "the true sense [of the line] is, let being become the conclusion or denouement of appearing to be: in short, ice-cream is an absolute good. The poem is obviously not about ice-cream but about being distinguished from seeming to be." In other words, no matter what *seems* in the house (seems wrong, seems shocking, seems funny, etc.), what is, is. Such little pleasures as ice-cream help life go on; holding such sway over life, they are its "only emperor."   15 The line means something like: there is no evading this reality.

Stevens/The Idea of Order at Key West (*p. 508*)

Notes toward an interpretation: in the poem, two voices are heard, that of the sea, and that of a girl singing beside it. The first is inhuman, mindless, meaningless. The second is human, mindful, meaningful; its words interpret what the sea might be imagined as saying. It gives form to the formless, order to the disorderly. The human mind, that is, through its art, gives order and significance to a universe that has neither. Just as, when we look at the stars, we see patterns, constellations, so when we look at the lights of fishing boats in the harbor we see geometric patterns they impose on the night. Our human "rage for order" demands that we organize the chaos of experience. Stevens said that in the poem "life has ceased to be a matter of chance. It may be that every man introduces his own order into the life about him. . . . These are tentative ideas for the purposes of poetry. . . ." (The poet, that is, is not stating an idea so much as using one in order to help him write a poem, in which "words and sounds" are what matter. Not explanations. "I have the greatest dislike for explanations," said Stevens, in a letter in which he discusses this poem.)

33–34 **It was her voice . . . its vanishing:** If *its* refers back to the nearest noun (*sky*), this means that the fading of the light at evening is most poignant because of the way her song gives it meaning; if *its* refers back to the subject (*voice*), then this means that a poignant absence is felt in nature when her song is at an end.   53 **the fragrant portals:** perhaps whatever, in sea, sky, and so forth, attracts us to look beyond it   55 **ghostlier:** more abstract, more spiritual, because in our mind, not in the physical world

Stevens/Postcard from the Volcano (*p. 509*)

The title means something like: news from the beyond, from a place of destruction and extinction. The news is that the influence of the dead somehow pervades the places they were associated with and contributed to the legend of, but their influence will be perceived only vaguely by the living.

Stevens/The Man on the Dump (*p. 510*)

Recall, from the notes to "The Idea of Order at Key West," that Stevens said he had "the greatest dislike for explanations" and that "words and sounds" are what matter in poetry. We have every right, then, to be leery of any discussion of a poem which gives us only a paraphrase of its thought. What we should do is look at the "the" of a poem (cf. the last line of this one), at the concrete reality of its words and sounds and images, and see what they suggest. The notes given here have to do with such suggestions; there is no reason readers should feel bound by them. The city dump, Stevens seems to be saying, is a good place to contemplate the concrete reality of things, their "the," free of their conventional associations, and of the poetic halos they might have under nicer circumstances. The dump is real enough, but it is also symbolic of the junking of old images, old ways of thought, old conventions, so that we can see reality afresh, as the poet sees the objects in the dump in the dewy light of springtime.

Stevens/The Sense of the Sleight-of-Hand Man (*p. 511*)

Here the "sleight-of-hand man" (one who performs clever tricks of magic) is Nature, the world, reality, which gives us pleasant or exhilarating moments when it will. Some things just seem to happen—arrangements of clouds over a landscape, one's "tooting" (rejoicing, celebrating) at some spiritual event. In the same way, some thoughts just seem to occur to us—the myths and metaphors that strike us for things in nature: the sun, the eye of a dove, pine trees.

Stevens/The House Was Quiet and the World Was Calm (*p. 512*)

The poem expresses a feeling of the unity of existence: a reader, his book, the quiet house, a summer night, the world itself—all seem for once in harmony, the being of each enriching the being of the others.

Stevens/Large Red Man Reading (*p. 513*)

The dead would willingly return to this life, even to its pain, if they could hear poetry express for them its interpretation of reality so that the words came alive in their hearts.

Stevens/Final Soliloquy of the Interior Paramour (*p. 513*)

The paramour is the "lover" (of reality) within each of us. The title suggests that these are its last words, its final considered judgment, on its imaginative relationship to reality.

Lindsay/I Heard Immanuel Singing (*p. 516*)

Lindsay tells us that the poem originated in a dream of Christ as Shepherd singing on a hill. Unlike "Kubla Khan," it was not completed in the dream; Lindsay awoke with the first three stanzas half-formed in his mind. This is his poem of a Second Coming; unlike Yeats, he sees it brought in by no rough beast, but by the Lamb of God, who introduces the new Golden Age of the Millennium, or thousand years of peace and happiness in the New Jerusalem, as described in Revelation, from which much of the imagery comes. The name Immanuel (for Christ) derives from Isa. 7:14: "Behold, a virgin shall conceive, and bear a son, and shall call his name Immanuel." This was taken (in Matt. 1:23, for example) as prophetic of the birth of Christ. Lindsay said his poem "shows the Master, with his work done, singing to free his heart in heaven." He indicated that stanzas 1, 5, and 9 were to be sung very softly, to the well-known tune "Last night I lay a-sleeping,/There came a dream so fair,/I stood in Old Jerusalem. . . ." The other stanzas were to be read "very softly, but in spirited response." Lindsay wrote such directions for several of his poems, which he intended as performances—examples of what he called the "Higher Vaudeville."

Pound/The Cantos (*p. 535*)

For over half a century Pound worked at his famous *Cantos*, into which he packed—or sometimes diffused—details from his widely scattered reading and the memories of his eventful life. A difficulty for most readers is that he seems to assume they have all done the same reading as he and shared the same experiences, so that he can draw on either as freely as if he were talking to himself. His itinerary through time and space is not clear; he could still admit, after writing 11 cantos, "I hope, heaven help me, to bring them into some sort of design and architecture later." In general the poem intends to show a progress from an underworld or inferno through a purgatory to a paradise of light—though the progress is by no means as clearly marked as in Dante, the number of whose 100 cantos (in the *Divine Comedy*) Pound seems to have originally aimed at—though his poem spilled over into many more than that, and was finally abandoned rather than completed. What we see in them when the story line emerges is a kind of Odyssean voyage, with extensive documentation, through Pound's reading of human history, with long stopovers in and frequent returns to ancient Greece, medieval Provence, Renaissance Italy, China over the centuries, the America of Jefferson and the Adamses, the Italy of Mussolini, or whatever areas and periods happened to engage Pound's lively and crotchety mind. His vision of the battle between good and evil in the world tended to focus on economics; he saw bad banking practice and what he considered the unnatural breeding of money from money as responsible for the ills of the world, all the way from mass-produced art and bad architecture to social injustice, corrupt government, and the horrors of war.

40–117

> The ship stood still amid the sea as in a dusty dock . . .
> But ivy troubled so their oars that forth they could not row;
> And both with berries and with leaves their sails did overgrow.
> And he himself with clustered grapes about his temples round,
> Did shake a javelin in his hand that round about was bound
> With leaves of vines; and at his feet there seemèd for to couch,
> Of tigers, lynx, and panthers, shapes most ugly for to touch . . .
> Golding's *Ovid* (III, 838–847)

Moore/The Pangolin (*p. 548*)

So *graceful* in coping—the idea of grace leads, in the sixth stanza, to a brief meditation on spiritual grace that has the eternal in view—the grace not only of a good life but the grace of good church architecture. Grace moral and aesthetic, such as man alone among the animals may hope for. The last three stanzas consider, with amusement, pity, and dismay, the nature of man, who, less well armored for his life than the pangolin and sharing the same knacks that many lower creatures do, is a paradox of strength and weakness, dependent for courage on the daily sunrise, the daily bread of grace.

Eliot/The Love Song of J. Alfred Prufrock (*p. 556*)

For a working hypothesis, which individual readers may prefer to correct or complete from their own interpretations, let us say that J. Alfred Prufrock, whose name is appropriate to his character, is an over-sensitive, self-conscious, timid, inhibited person of literary tastes (he likes to quote). He feels that life is passing him by and that he is growing old. Eliot said that he thought of Prufrock as in part about 40 and in part his own age. On his way to an evening party at which—perhaps unfortunately for him—nothing stronger than tea will be served, he sees a possible escape from his lonely repressions if he can bring himself to a declaration to a woman he knows will be there. But unable to face the embarrassment of the rejection he thinks likely, together with the social derision it may entail, he fails to make his declaration, and has recourse instead to Walter Mitty-ish dreams of mermaids, which he settles for instead of risking the hazards of intimacy with a real woman. His failure saddens him; because of the acuteness of his suffering he is a tragicomic figure rather than merely a ridiculous one. His "love song," of course, will never be sung to anyone.

Eliot/Sweeney Among the Nightingales (*p. 559*)

Eliot is reported to have said that all he consciously set out to create in this poem was "a sense of foreboding." If that is so, precise identification of setting and characters would seem unnecessary—a certain vagueness is even desirable in a poem whose purpose is to be scary. We are apparently in South America, since the River Plate is mentioned; and yet neither nightingales nor wistaria are native to South America. The setting seems to be in a sinister tavern or "dive" in a warm climate; exactly what the characters are up to is not clear, but it seems that some sort of plot is thickening, aimed most probably at "Apeneck" Sweeney, who is likely enough drowsy with drink and may have become involved with one of the women in the room. The character Sweeney, a coarsely physical type who is Prufrock's opposite and who appears in other Eliot poems, may have been based on a Boston Irish boxing instructor Eliot had while at Harvard and on a Boston bartender he knew. It may be relevant that the word "nightingale" is an English slang term for "prostitute."

35-37   Eliot here (as he admitted) is borrowing imagery from another Greek tragedy, the *Oedipus at Colonus* of Sophocles (495-406 B.C.). In that play, Oedipus, old and blind, takes refuge in the grove of the Furies (the avenging spirits) near Colonus, which is celebrated for its nightingales. It is not actually bloody, though the work of the Furies themselves might be.

Eliot/Gerontion (*p. 561*)

Gerontion (*gher-ôn-tee-on*) is the Greek word for a little old man. Here the speaker, looking back on his past, is old and emotionally shrivelled, quite possibly the kind of man Prufrock might turn into: one who feels he has never really lived, never made a meaningful commitment to life and love, never whole-heartedly embraced any vital belief. He is not alone in his failure, which seems to be shared by others he mentions. He seems, in fact, representative of the failure of a whole culture, or of fallen man himself throughout his paradoxical history, in which the chances of a more abundant life and of such salvation as Christ came to offer have been rejected. The speaker's physical failure, his need for artificial stimulants and "pungent sauces" to arouse sensation represent a deeper spiritual failure that results in something like numb despair.

Eliot had been doing intensive reading in the Elizabethan and Jacobean dramatists; the diction and rhythms of his poem vividly and deliberately recall their works, which he frequently alludes to in order to give a sense of the contemporaneity of all human experience. The large number of quotations and allusions make "Gerontion" one of the most laborious of his poems to annotate. Only the most significant threads in the texture of allusion are indicated in the notes.

17-19   In Matt. 12 the unbelieving scribes and Pharisees, having witnessed miracles performed by Christ, still cry out for "a sign." *Verbum infans* means "the word that cannot speak" or "the infant word"; the etymological meaning of *infans* (*infant*) is "not speaking." The play on *word* in Andrewes's sermon is suggested by John 1: "In the beginning was the Word, and the Word was with God, and the Word was God." Eliot quotes from the Christmas sermon in his 1926 essay on Lancelot Andrewes. 20 ff.   Christ the tiger is the Christ who came to bring "not peace but a sword," to shock the pre-Christian world out of its apathy with the "odor of blood" which Yeats mentions in "Two Songs from a Play." In the lines that follow he is associated with the fertile exuberance of the springtime, depraved in that it was the time of the betrayal and death of Christ, in that its powerful physicality can lead to pagan excesses—and perhaps always depraved, even in its innocence, to puritanical eyes.   34-48   This section sees "history," the record of man's progress in the world with only worldly means and ends, as a series of deceptions, disappointments, frustrations: our minds are seldom or never in harmony with what life gives.   35   **contrived corridors:** Some think this a reference to the " Polish Corridor" contrived by the Treaty of Versailles (June 1919); it took a strip of land from Germany and gave it to Poland. Much resentment was aroused by this provision of the treaty.   68-70   **whirled . . . atoms:** Eliot tells us that these lines were suggested by George Chapman's play *Bussy D'Ambois* (pub. 1607), V, iv, 103-105:

> fly where men feel
> The burning axletree; and those that suffer
> Beneath the chariot of the snowy Bear . . .

It was thought that sinful souls were whirled off into space when they died. The Bear is the Great Bear, or Big Dipper, whose circuit is its revolution around the Pole Star. In *Measure for Measure*, III, i (cf. the note on the epigraph), Claudio imagines the souls of the dead as

> imprisoned in the viewless winds
> And blown with restless violence round about
> The pendant world. . . .

Eliot/The Waste Land (*p. 563*)

We have seen many good poems that require no footnotes at all, make no reference to what is outside of the ordinary experience of life. Others require quite a few notes to introduce us to the personal world of the poet and permit us to share in the poet's experiences. Probably no poem in this anthology is more in need of such notes, and of a few introductory paragraphs, than "The Waste Land." Critics have admitted it is the most "controversial" poem of the century; the same critics hasten to add that it is the most "influential." The obscurity we may find in it at first is typical of the "obscurity" of much modern poetry—of much good poetry, in fact, of any age. (In Charles S. Singleton's edition of Dante's *The Divine Comedy* the volumes given to the notes are much longer than the volumes given to the text they annotate.) Formidable as our footnotes look, most of them deal with such interesting human concerns as sex and religion; an hour or so spent on them is not much to pay for an understanding of a literary work fascinating in itself—and with it an understanding of the why's and wherefore's of much of the poetry to follow. The poet and critic Allen Tate said that when he first read "The Waste Land" he did not understand a word of it, but knew that it was a great poem. Our footnotes explain what some lines mean, but not why the poem is "great." That is indeed something many of us can feel without the notes: it lies in the brilliance with which Eliot uses images, words, sounds, rhythms—all of those elements which make something rich and strange out of the dead bones of statement.

It can be read as a satiric criticism of the postwar scene in England as Eliot saw it just before 1922, as well as of the American scene he knew in his youth. Some have read it as a poem about the collapse of political systems; others, as spiritual autobiography. Eliot himself played down any grand intentions. He said the poem was not expressing social criticism, but came out of his own troubles: "only the relief of a personal and wholly insignificant grouse against life; it is just a piece of rhythmical grumbling." When certain admiring critics said he had expressed the "disillusionment of a generation," he called their opinion "nonsense."

It is easier to approach the poem with sympathy if we remember how desperate Eliot's personal situation was during the years just before he wrote the poem. He himself feared he had been brought to the verge of a breakdown. After Harvard he had gone to England and, in 1915, after years of shyness and inhibition, made what was no doubt the most impulsive decision of his life: he married the "terrifying, haunted" Englishwoman he had met only two months before. The marriage proved almost immediately a disaster: not only were there basic incompatibilities, but his wife's almost constant illness involved him in anxieties about her and about their household finances. For years he was overworked, first as a schoolteacher whose evenings were spent in lecturing or writing reviews, then for several years as a valued employee in Lloyd's Bank in London, where his knowledge of languages qualified him to deal with problems of foreign exchange. Though he faced his domestic problems with courage and energy, he wrote that the year 1916 was "the most awful nightmare of anxiety that the mind of man could conceive. . . ." Perhaps worst for him was the fact that his fatiguing days, with evenings of extra work, left little time for his own writing—though he already had in mind parts of a long poem. His own health was sometimes in "a very shaky state," as he admitted; in 1921 he was ordered by his doctor to take a three-month rest, away from everyone. In late October he went to Margate (cf. line 300) for three weeks and there worked at "The Waste Land"; in mid-November he went to Lausanne, Switzerland, to consult a "specialist in psychological troubles," and there completed his manuscript. A few weeks later he showed what he had written to Ezra Pound in Paris. Pound, always a severe critic, thought the poem would be strengthened if about half were omitted. Eliot accepted most of Pound's deletions. The biographical data are relevant because they show how Eliot was expressing his own anxieties, confusions, and torments, trying to find meanings and solutions—trying, in short, to put his own house in order (line 426).

Many readers have been put off by the way Eliot quotes from other writers. Actually not much more than one-tenth of the poem relies on quotations. But these can be important: often key ideas are expressed by such allusions. If a writer had deliberately sat down to compose such a poem, with much shuffling through dictionaries of quotations and world masterpieces, the result might well have been intolerable—merely a sort of patchwork or literary word-game. But this is not the way the poem came about. Sections of it—generally autobiographical—accumulated in Eliot's mind over many years. Meanwhile he was reading widely in several literatures; he went to the trouble of studying Sanskrit at Harvard to read the Hindu scriptures in the original. Every now and then, perhaps only a few times a year, a line or passage would strike him as so meaningful to his own experience that he would treasure it forever. It became a very real part of his experience; things we read may exert quite as powerful an influence as things we experience physically. Eliot likes to refer to such influences. Such references also recall the context of the original: a quotation from Dante can establish, as he said, "a relationship between the medieval inferno and modern life." He may feel that something has happened to him for which the prophet Isaiah had long ago found the perfect image, or for which Shakespeare had found the perfect words.

Most of his allusions are to works a reasonably educated person might be expected to know: the Bible, Shakespeare, Dante. He had read intensively in Elizabethan and Jacobean drama. He was familiar with such French poets as Baudelaire, de Nerval, and Verlaine. He knew Wagnerian opera. He refers to such figures from mythology as Tiresias and Philomela. He may pick up hints from Joseph Conrad's *The Heart of Darkness*, from a recent work about antarctic exploration, from a bawdy army song of World War I. Eastern religions were at times more appealing to him than the somewhat cold Unitarianism of his childhood; he said that while writing "The Waste Land" he almost became a Buddhist.

We can feel the effect of many of his allusions without knowing their source or being able to identify them. The echo of Dante in lines 62–63 makes the passage more meaningful if we recognize it, as Eliot hopes we will—but the lines are already meaningful without that recognition. As for the foreign languages—there are less than a dozen lines of them within the body of the poem itself. Hardly a major stumbling block—at least until the end of the poem, when Eliot hopes they will send us reeling into a new awareness. He knew he was gambling in using the technique he did—in using, for example, Hindu religious phrases instead of the standard English ones, which he felt had become, for many of us, insincere formulas repeated out of custom. His gamble seems to have paid off. At first derided by many and understood by few, "The Waste Land" is now seen as one of the most influential poems in the language. So well known are parts of it that even sports writers may be heard quoting its famous opening, "April is the cruellest month" (the writer of these notes heard it used three times within a month in the spring of 1979 by baseball reporters covering the training camps).

When the poem was first published in magazines in England and America, no explanatory notes were appended. But when prepared for book publication, it was found to be "inconveniently short," so Eliot provided a few pages of notes. Originally they were meant to identify his quotations, to protect him from such critics as would assert he was not quoting but plagiarizing. Later Eliot tended to make light of the notes as "bogus scholarship"; he came to regret "having sent so many enquirers off on a wild goose chase after Tarot cards and the Holy Grail."

Eliot printed his notes at the end of the poem; here they are identified as his by his initials. His introductory note tells us that

> Not only the title, but the plan and a good deal of the incidental symbolism of the poem were suggested by Miss Jessie L. Weston's book on the Grail legend: *From Ritual to Romance* (Cambridge). Indeed, so deeply am I indebted, Miss Weston's book will elucidate the difficulties of the poem much better than my notes can do; and I recommend it (apart from the great interest of the book itself) to any who think such elucidation of the poem worth the trouble. To another work of anthropology I am indebted in general, one which has influenced our generation profoundly; I mean *The Golden Bough*; I have used especially the two volumes *Adonis, Attis, Osiris.* Anyone who is acquainted with these works will immediately recognise in the poem certain references to vegetation ceremonies.

Miss Weston had written a dozen or so books on the Holy Grail before *From Ritual to Romance* (1920). What is relevant to "The Waste Land" can be summarized as follows.

The legend of the quest for the Holy Grail (supposedly the chalice Christ used at the Last Supper) has no basis in Christian legend or in folklore, but derives from ancient pagan nature cults (or "mystery" cults) whose purpose was to encourage the fertility of the earth. Their rituals represented the death and resurrection of a vegetation god whose career symbolized the recurrence of withering and rebirth in the seasons. Versions of the Grail legend differ, but typically they concern a Waste Land in which crops and animal life have failed because of the drying up of the waters. The desolation of the land is related to the sickness or disability of the aged ruler, often referred to as the Fisher King. Fish are an ancient symbol of the fecundity of life; the king's castle, significantly, is near the water. The object of the Grail quest is to restore the fertility of the land by restoring the vigor of the ailing king. This can be done by the hero, the knight of the Grail, provided he asks the meaning of the Grail vision of Cup and Bleeding Lance; his inquiry will heal the king, release the waters, restore the land to its vitality. The Grail quest, like ancient nature cults, is a quest for the source of life.

Sir James Frazer's *The Golden Bough,* first published in two volumes in 1908, later expanded to twelve volumes and a supplement, is a study in magic and religion which traces many institutions and folk customs back to the primitive concepts from which they developed. Adonis, Attis, and Osiris were vegetation gods (fertility figures)—the first was Phoenician, the second Phrygian, the third Egyptian—whose death and resurrection were taken to represent the seasonal decay and revival of nature.

(Anyone annotating "The Waste Land" today will be indebted to numerous earlier researchers. Three of the most helpful books for students are Grover Smith, *T. S. Eliot's Poetry and Plays*; B.C. Southam, *A Guide to the Selected Poems of T. S. Eliot*; and Lyndall Gordon, *Eliot's Early Years*.)

The poem comes out of Eliot's experiences; in a sense he is always the speaker. He does, however, have a number of characters or personae who, speaking for him, seem to speak on their own; voices fade in and out of his lines, nor is it always clear whose voices they are. See his note on line 218. Unless the poet is projecting his voice into one of his personages, it seems fair to assume, as here, that we hear the poet's own voice—as he chooses to show himself in this poem.

24–30 These lines are adaptations of Eliot's earlier poem "The Death of St. Narcissus," written about eight years before. The cool shadow under the rock recalls the refuge the desert fathers found when they turned their backs on society for the loneliness and austerity of their hermitages. Cf. also Isa. 32:2, "as the shadow of a great rock in a weary land. . . ." The earlier version of lines 27–29 is helpful here: "And I will show you something different from either/ Your shadow sprawling over the sand at daybreak, or/ Your shadow leaping behind the fire against the red rock. . . ." The images imply idleness or revelry, with "shadow" itself suggesting the unreal or illusory character of worldly activity. In the early poem what was to be shown was the martyr's "bloody cloth and limbs," as representing a higher reality than the nervous shadow did. In "The Waste Land" the Christian symbolism (as often) is dropped, to be replaced by "fear in a handful of dust," perhaps a reference to the Sibyl's desiccated existence. It recalls also "for dust thou art, and unto dust shalt thou return" (Gen. 3:19). The phrase "a handful of dust" has been found in a Meditation of John Donne.   35–41 **"You gave me hyacinths . . .":** someone's memory of a romantic episode that came to nothing because the man who gave the flowers to his "hyacinth girl" was inadequate to the experience, numbed as he was by the overwhelming possibility of love. His failure is like Prufrock's, though he comes so close to a fulfillment that he is dazzled by it. The name of the flowers recalls Hyacinth of Greek mythology: the young man loved by Apollo and killed accidentally by his discus. From his blood grew the flower named after him. Hyacinth—like Adonis, Attis, Osiris—is one of the vegetation figures discussed by Frazer. 46 To try to discover exactly how the Tarot cards are used in "The Waste Land" is what Eliot called "a wild goose chase." His own note on line 46 indicates he handled the symbolism pretty much as he wanted to, for the purposes of his poem:

> I am not familiar with the exact constitution of the Tarot pack of cards, from which I have obviously departed to suit my own convenience. The Hanged Man, a member of the traditional pack, fits my purpose in two ways: because he is associated in my mind with the Hanged God of Frazer, and because I associate him with the hooded figure in the passage of the disciples to Emmaus in Part V. The Phoenician Sailor and the Merchant appear later; also the "crowds of people," and Death by Water is executed in Part IV. The Man with Three Staves (an authentic member of the Tarot pack) I associate, quite arbitrarily, with the Fisher King himself.

49 A source has also been found in Walter Pater's *The Renaissance* (1873), in his description of the Mona Lisa: "She is older than the rocks among which she sits . . . she has been dead many times . . . and been a diver in deep seas . . . and trafficked with Eastern merchants. . . ."   **63** What is significant is not just the number, but the part of his Inferno in which Dante put them: among the "trimmers," the safety-loving timid people who always went along with the crowd and were afraid of taking a positive or unpopular stand on anything. For such people, Dante has only contempt, believing as he does that the exercise of free will is one of the glories of mankind. In Dante, such characters are not even admitted to Hell itself, since their presence would give the damned souls something to feel complacent about—they, the damned, at least had the courage to make a choice. Eliot believes that many in our time are only "trimmers," afraid to choose.   **64** Dante is speaking of the first circle of his Inferno, in which he found souls guiltless of sin, but unfortunately born before the time of Christ, so that they did not have the benefit of baptism—death by water. Their only punishment is loss of the vision of God. Of this passage and the preceding one Eliot wrote: "I gave the references in my notes, in order to make the reader who recognized the allusion, know that I meant him to recognize it, and to know that he would have missed the point if he did not recognize it."   **74–75** Several suggestions have been made as to why Eliot changed the wolf to the dog. Sirius, the Dog Star, arose about the time the Nile overflowed. As the star of the summer (the "dog days"), it could be harmful to sprouting grain. In the Old Testament, the dog is unclean, an eater of corpses (Southam). Cf. also the last note to Part IV, on the "big dog."   **77** Other details in the scene are suggested by Iachimo's description of Imogen's bedchamber in Shakespeare's *Cymbeline* (II, iv): the tapestry there showed Cleopatra meeting Antony on the river; there were two winking Cupids. Iachimo had earlier noticed that she had been reading "The tale of Tereus. Here the leaf's turned down/Where Philomel gave up" (II, ii).   **92** The word recalls another opulent setting; Eliot's note refers us to Vergil's *Aeneid*, I, 726, a description of the setting of Dido's banquet for Aeneas, whose subsequent desertion leads to her suicide. Eliot's note quotes two lines that mean: "Lamps hang ablaze from the gilded laquearia, and torches conquer the darkness with their flames."   **116 lost their bones:** Perhaps a reminiscence of the chapter of Ezek. referred to in line 22. The sentence after the one quoted in the note is "And I will lay the dead carcases of the children of Israel before their idols; and I will scatter your bones round about your altars." Cf. also the note to line 48: "of his bones are coral made. . . ."   **120–126 Nothing . . . :** In using "nothing" six times in reply to the woman's "What are you thinking of?" Eliot may be recalling Webster's *The White Devil*, V, vi, 202 ff. Lodovico asks: "What dost think on?" and Flaminio replies: "Nothing; of nothing . . . /To prate were idle, I remember nothing./There's nothing of so infinite vexation/ As man's own thoughts. . . ."   **182** *Leman* is also an old English word for "sweetheart" or "mistress"—relevant to the theme of "unholy loves" that runs through this section. The line also echoes Ps. 137: "By the rivers of Babylon, there we sat down, yea, we wept, when he remembered Zion." Eliot may have remembered, from Byron's *Hebrew Melodies*: "We sate down and wept by the waters/Of Babel, and thought of the day/When . . . ye, oh her desolate daughters!/Were scattered all weeping away. . . ."   **197** John Day's rarely read dramatic allegory seems to have been published in 1607. For coming upon the naked Diana bathing, Actaeon, though innocent of evil intent, was punished by being turned into a stag who was pursued and killed by his own dogs. Eliot here turns him into Sweeney (cf. introductory notes to "Sweeney Among the Nightingales").   **202** The sonnet was published in *La Revue Wagenrienne* in January 1886, with a quotation from Tennyson's "The Holy Grail": "Sir Percivale/Whom Arthur and his knighthood called The Pure. . . ." Percival was the original Grail hero, a role later taken over by Galahad. Verlaine's poem tells how Parsifal had overcome the temptations he felt for pleasant young girls and also for a mature, exciting woman, how he had been given the holy Lance (associated with the Grail), and how he had cured the wounded king. The last three lines could be translated: "In a golden robe he adores, as glory and symbol, The pure vessel where the real Blood was shining./And, O these voices of children singing in the dome!" The line Eliot quotes is not as innocent as it seems. The pure Parsifal, at his holiest moment, is distracted by boys singing in church. In Wagner's opera, light streams from the dome in a great vaulted hall, and later are heard "Knabenstimmen (auf der Kuppel)"—"the voices of boys from the dome." The bisexual Verlaine, who had had affairs with boys, said the sonnet was autobiographical. The reference fits in, then, with the other "unholy loves" that Eliot sees as having put a curse on his Waste Land.   **218** Eliot then quotes 19 lines from Ovid (*Metamorphoses*, III, 320 ff.) which can be paraphrased as follows: Jove once jokingly told his wife Juno that women get more pleasure out of sex than men do. When she denied it, they decided to ask the opinion of the prophet Tiresias, the expert in love, since he had experienced it both as man and as woman. Once in the woods he had seen two large snakes mating, and had impiously struck them with a stick. For this offense he was turned into a woman for seven years, at which time he again saw the snakes entwined. "If hitting you is so effective in bringing about a sex change," he said, "I'll try hitting you again." He did so, and regained his former male appearance and abilities. Being made the arbiter of the playful debate, he sided with Jove. Juno, more irritated than she should have been over such a matter, punished Tiresias with blindness. Jove, unable to undo what another divinity had done, gave Tiresias in compensation the gift of prophecy. What the blind prophet *sees*, says Eliot's note, "is the substance of the poem." We could hardly get a clearer clue to its meaning. What Tiresias sees is the degradation of love, its defeat by selfishness and apathy—by sex without affection or care for the other person—and almost without interest. What ought to be one of the most vital of experiences has gone dead for the people involved.   **224–225** We may wonder if a contrast is intended between these lines and Keats's "Charmed magic casements opening on the foam/Of perilous seas . . ." ("Ode to a Nightingale," lines 69–70).   **248** Here Pound made an instructive deletion, removing as "probably over the mark" the two crude lines that would have completed the rhymes of the quatrain. They were: "And at the corner where the stable is, / Delays only to urinate, and spit."

260 The "fishmen" are perhaps from the fishmarket, but more likely are fishermen from a wharf Eliot used to wander toward during his lunch hour at Lloyd's Bank. The fish, fertile and surrounded by the life-giving waters, is an ancient symbol of vitality; the fishermen seem happier and more alive than other inhabitants of the Waste Land.   264 Sir Christopher Wren (1632–1723), scientist and architect, who designed, after the Great Fire of 1666 had ravaged much of the city, over 50 churches to replace those destroyed. Among them was St. Magnus the Martyr (1676–1705) at London Bridge in the Billingsgate area. In Eliot's time a fish-harvest festival was held there annually. The interior, with its Ionian columns, is prevailingly white and gold.   266 In the four music dramas (operas) that make up Wagner's *The Ring of the Nibelungen* (1848–1874), the three Rhine-daughters are the possessors and guardians of a marvellous golden treasure, the Rhinegold, which is stolen. The operas are the story of the misfortunes that overtake the unrighteous possessors—for a curse, as well as great power, goes with the treasure. In "The Waste Land" three London girls, the "Thames-daughters," have been seduced, robbed of their treasure—and the curse of that violation seems to hang over the region.   266–276 The description of the river owes some details to the opening of Joseph Conrad's short novel, *The Heart of Darkness* (1902). With the modern river's "oil and tar," cf. Spenser's "silver-streaming Thames"; with its seduced Thames-daughters, cf. Spenser's "lovely daughters of the flood."   279 The letter, on p. 243 of volume I of the Everyman edition of J. A. Froude's *The Reign of Elizabeth*, is dated June 30, 1561. Elizabeth had become queen in 1558 at the age of 25. Her favorite then was Sir Robert Dudley, a few years later made Earl of Leicester; in 1559 the Spanish ambassador had reported, "He is in such favor that people say she visits him in his chamber day and night" (Froude, vol. 1, p. 60). Elizabeth seems to have been infatuated with Dudley, whom the ambassador called "the worst young fellow I ever encountered. He is heartless, spiritless, treacherous, and false" (Froude, p. 143). It looked to many as if the queen planned to marry Dudley, but there was one difficulty: he was already married. The difficulty was resolved when his wife fell downstairs—or was pushed—and broke her neck, less than a year before the queen and Dudley are shown disporting themselves on the river and jesting about getting married. The letter Eliot quotes was written by the Spanish ambassador Alvarez de Quadra, who, as Bishop of Aquila, might have performed the ceremony. Though the queen remained friends with Dudley for many years, she did not marry him—her cool head probably told her that the scandal would have been hard to live down. Lines 284–285 could refer to the gossip that indeed rippled not only England but all Europe. The scene on the barge (cf. Cleopatra's barge, note to line 77) shows a love which is frivolous and barren, so that the queen and her noble lover are somehow paralleled with the three seduced London girls and their seducers.   300 "It has nine miles of unbroken sands and every attraction for the thousands of visitors who flock there every summer...." Among the thousands in the fall of 1921 was Eliot, who stayed there for a month when told by his doctor he badly needed a rest. While there he worked on "The Waste Land," which he finished in Lausanne a couple of weeks later.   308 Buddha's brief sermon says that the senses, the images they give us, and the ideas and feelings that arise from these images are all "on fire ... with the fire of passion ... with the fire of hatred, with the fire of infatuation; with birth, old age, death, sorrow, lamentation, misery, grief, and despair are they on fire." Hence the good man conceives an aversion for things of the senses and all they give rise to in the mind (such as the "unholy loves" of this part of the poem); in this way he becomes divested of passion and free from the attachments of this world. (Some readers will feel that the sins of the typist and the Thames-daughters are too tepid to be called "burning.") IV. It translates, with minor changes, the last seven lines of "Dans Le Restaurant," which Eliot had written in French a few years before. What precedes the translated lines is an incident described by a scruffy waiter who tells how he had been frightened away from his own hyacinth girl by a big dog. V. The journey to Emmaus is described in Luke 24:13–31: on the day that Christ's resurrection was reported, two disciples were walking to the village of Emmaus, about seven miles from Jerusalem. As they were discussing the recent events, Christ fell in with them but was not recognized. He talked to them about how the Old Testament prophecies had foretold all that had just happened. Later, when he blessed the food at the dinner he shared with them, they suddenly recognized him—and he vanished from their sight. They went back to report that "The Lord is risen indeed." Weston's book has a chapter on "The Perilous Chapel." On his quest for the Grail, the hero often meets with an eerie adventure in a deserted chapel—an experience involving the corpse of a knight, a mysterious giant hand, a ghostly apparition: something that shows the hero in contact with the supernatural. The theme of the decay of eastern Europe is referred to in Eliot's note on lines 367–377.   357 "This is *Turdus aonalaschkae pallasii*, the hermit-thrush which I have heard in Quebec Province. Chapman says (*Handbook of Birds of Eastern North America*) 'it is most at home in secluded woodland and thickety retreats.... Its notes are not remarkable for variety or volume, but in purity and sweetness of tone and exquisite modulation they are unequalled.' Its 'water-dripping song' is justly celebrated." [T.S.E.] The purity and sweetness of the "water-dripping song" contrast with the bloody mythology and "Jug Jug" of the nightingale (lines 99–103). Cf. the hermit-thrush in Whitman's "When Lilacs Last in the Dooryard Bloomed," lines 18 ff.   360 The reference has more meaning (especially when seen together with the journey to Emmaus) if we know that for the antarctic explorers the mysterious *"one more member"* was Providence. The story is told in Sir Ernest Shackleton's *South*, 1920, in the last paragraph of chap. 10 (Macmillan, 1962, p. 211). "When I look back at those days I have no doubt that Providence guided us, not only across the snow fields, but across the storm-white sea that separated Elephant Island from our landing-place on South Georgia. I know that during that long and racking march of thirty-six hours over the unnamed mountains and glaciers of South Georgia it seemed to me often that we were four, not three. I said nothing to my companions on the point, but afterwards Worsley said to me, 'Boss, I had a curious feeling on the march that there was another person with us.' Crean confessed to the same idea. One feels 'the dearth of human words, the roughness of mortal speech' in trying to describe things intangible, but a record of our journeys would be incomplete without a refer-

ence to a subject very near to our hearts." 378–385 Eliot said that some of the hallucinatory imagery—related to the eerie visions in the Chapel Perilous—were suggested by the fantastic paintings of the Dutch artist Hieronymus Bosch (c. 1450–1516). The grotesque torments in Bosch's vision of hell often make use of musical instruments. The upside-down bats with baby faces may suggest perversions of normal fertility. 385 **cisterns ... wells:** both should be sources of life-giving water. Here they are dried up. Southam quotes Jer. 2:13: "For my people have committed two evils; they have forsaken me the fountain of living waters, and hewed them out cisterns, broken cisterns, that can hold no water." 392 It was also the belief that the crowing of the cock was a signal for night-wandering ghosts and spirits to return to their confines in the other world. In *Hamlet*, I, i, the ghost of Hamlet's father disappears when the cock crows. With the ghosts gone from the haunted chapel, "dry bones can harm no one." 402 Of the 108 extant *Upanishads* (Hindu sacred scriptures), the one Eliot quotes from is recognized as among the most significant. In it we are told how three classes of beings—the gods, the daemons (who are not necessarily malign, like our devils), and the human beings—all came to Prajapati, the lord of creation, to learn from him. When they asked for enlightenment, he answered only with a thunderous DAAA. Each group took it to stand for a different Sanskrit word beginning with that syllable. The gods thought it meant *Damyata*, be self-controlled. The daemons thought it stood for *Dayadhvam*, be compassionate. Men thought it meant *Datta*, give, or be charitable. Prajapati agreed with each group; each had indeed understood his meaning. "The storm cloud thunders: Da! Da! Da!—Be self-controlled! Be compassionate! Be charitable!" This advice—to be unselfish and loving—is the water that could restore life to the Waste Land. Everywhere there we have seen selfishness, particularly in what should be love relationships, as the cause of evil. The advice the Creator gives is common to all the great religions; Eliot could have put it in Biblical terms. An earlier rejected passage did say plainly "I am the resurrection, and the life" (John 11:25). Perhaps fearing that such phrasing had lost its impact through over-familiarity, he prefers to leave his message to the thunder that "rumbles obscure Sanskrit words" (Gordon). 408 Eliot may have in mind here not only the imagery, but also the context of Webster's passage. The cynical Flaminio is speaking about women: "O men/That lie upon your deathbeds, and are haunted/With howling wives, ne'er trust them! they'll remarry. . . ." Taken that way, the reference suggests that we exist by our own impulsive generosity even though it leads to our betrayal. 412 The speaker is Count Ugolino of Pisa, whom political enemies had left locked in a tower with his four children (or so Dante thought) to die of starvation. Here the image of fatal isolation fits the unsympathetic person, locked selfishly within his own personality. Eliot adds a quotation from the philosopher F. H. Bradley, on whom he wrote his accepted thesis for the Harvard Ph.D. he did not return to take:

> My external sensations are no less private to myself than are my thoughts or my feelings. In either case my experience falls within my own circle, a circle closed on the outside; and, with all its elements alike, every sphere is opaque to the others which surround it. . . . In brief, regarded as an existence which appears in a soul, the whole world for each is peculiar and private to that soul [*Appearance and Reality*, p. 346].

428 ff. Before we look at the strange conclusion of "The Waste Land"—a conclusion that no doubt many have considered gibberish—we might do well to review the progress of the poem. What Eliot has been showing us is a world made desolate, in which there is little hope for meaningful life. Something like a curse has been laid on this world because of the selfishness of its inhabitants—and particularly that selfishness as revealed in what ought to be the most sensitive and sympathetic of relationships: the expression of sexual love. In Part II we saw unhappiness within marriage, on high and low levels of society; in Part III we saw the loveless sex life of the typist and her bumptious friend, the apathy of the seduced Thames-daughters, the dalliance and infatuation, mixed with self-interest, at the court of Elizabeth. In Part V we are finally told, through the voice of Hindu wisdom in the sound of the thunder, the way out of the desolation: the practice of generosity, sympathy, self-control. These can free the waters, renew the earth.

This is where we now find ourselves in the poem. If Eliot had simply *said* such things as are summarized above, we would have not a poem but a sermon. And a sermon made up of platitudes at that; it would have said no more than what the great religions of man have preached again and again. But Eliot has done more than tell us things; he has shown us things: fear, for example, in a handful of dust. Broken images. Hyacinths, playing cards, crowds on London Bridge, a dressing-table with its perfumes, gossipy talk in a pub, littered riverbanks, a tacky merchant with his pocket full of currants, a girl's underwear hung out to dry, surrealist visions of a woman using her own long hair as violin strings, thunder clouds in India. Things, things, things. Generally without comment—and hence the famous "obscurity" of the poem. It is up to us to interpret not his words, which are simple, but his images—which are simple too, but we are less used to reading images than to reading words.

Eliot has himself anticipated the objections we might make to the difficulties of the final section of his poem. We say it is fragmentary—he refers to it as "these fragments." We say it looks insane—and he admits that too: "Hieronymo's mad againe." The phrase comes from what was perhaps the most popular and influential of all Elizabethan plays, Thomas Kyd's tragedy of about 1586. The 1616 title-page reads: THE SPANISH TRAGEDY: or, *Hieronimo is mad againe*. The play is about how Hieronymo, Marshal of Spain, half out of his mind with grief over the murder of his son Horatio, determines to get revenge. Asked to provide an evening's entertainment at court, he puts on a play he says he wrote long before, casting the killers of his son (who are unaware of his intentions) in leading roles. In the course of the play they are actually killed on stage, while the audience believes they are seeing only the pretended murders of the drama. In Hieronymo's odd play, the speeches of each of the main characters are said to have been written in different languages, "to breed the more variety," as Hieronymo explains: one speaks Latin, one Greek, one Italian, one French. Eliot himself now uses three of these languages within three lines (428–430). Mad as he seems to be, Eliot is telling us, there is method in his madness.

Why use quotations at all? For years Eliot himself had read widely in the languages he quotes and had committed long passages to memory. There is no affectation in his recalling here lines that had been in his mind for years, etched deeper and deeper by experiences of his own that seemed to confirm their validity. Now that he has learned something from the thunder, lines that reinforce what is said occur to him from several literatures—almost as if, at this moment of grace, the Biblical gift of tongues had been conferred on him. The quotations give a sort of universal sanction, from many times and places, to his own individual insights and experiences. He has treasured such fragments; "shored" them (used them as props or supports) against his breakdown. They have been, to change the image, something to hold on to in the chaos of life. Now he shares them with us.   428 The speaker of the first three lines (which are not in Italian but Provençal—Dante too quoted other languages) is Arnaut Daniel, the twelfth-century poet who spent much of his time at the court of Richard the Lionhearted. For those who think only modern poetry is "obscure," it is interesting to recall that Daniel wrote in the deliberately obscure style known as *trobar clus* (closed poetry). The lines mean: " 'Now I pray you, by that power / That guides you to the top of the stairway, / Remember, while the time is ripe, my pain.' Then he hid himself in the fire that purifies them." After asking for their prayers, he dives back into the penitential fire of Purgatory that purifies the souls defiled by that other "burning" of lust in this life. The relevance of the quotation is that penance, purification, is part of the escape from the Waste Land we make for ourselves.   429 "The Vigil of Venus," in honor of the Roman goddess of love and fertility, is a late Latin poem written between the second and fifth centuries A.D. It celebrates the coming of spring, as the time of love and lovers—but, like "The Waste Land," it finds there is cruelty in April. For some reason spring, which has come to the world of Nature, has not come to the heart of the poet. The lines from which Eliot quotes are: "Illa cantat, nos tacemus: quando ver venit meum? / *Quando fiam uti chelidon* ut tacere desinam? ("She [Philomela] sings, we are silent; when does my spring come?/ *When will I be like the swallow,* so that I can stop being silent?") The Latin poet follows the version of the myth in which Philomela becomes a swallow, not a nightingale. Swinburne's "Itylus" (1866), about another version of the nightingale myth, opens with: "Swallow, my sister, O sister swallow, / How can thine heart be full of the spring . . . ?"   430 Gérard Labrunie (1808–1855) wrote poems and short stories under the pseudonym Gérard de Nerval. A romantic, he lived mostly a vagabond existence. Often on the verge of insanity after a mental breakdown in 1841, he ended his life (a hanged man) in 1855. Hallucinatory and delirious as his subjects often are, his writing is for the most part beautifully clear. Gautier described his work as "Madness writing its memoirs—but as if Reason were dictating." "El Desdichado" is from *Les Chimères* (1854), a series of 12 sonnets. Its title (which means "the ill-fated" or "the unlucky," but is generally translated as "the disinherited") is said to be taken from the motto of the disguised champion in Scott's *Ivanhoe* (1819). The first two lines of the sonnet mean: "I am the man of gloom, the widower, the unconsoled,/The Prince of Aquitaine, he of the ruined tower. . . ." Aquitaine (the name meant "the land of waters") is the old name for southwestern France, a region associated with the Provençal poets of the southeast; one of the first of the Provençal troubadours was a duke of Aquitaine. Since even the name passed out of use in the Middle Ages, the speaker is indeed disinherited of his legacy. "Ruined tower" suggests the devastation of the land. One of the Tarot cards shows a tower struck by lightning. The allusion, then, is relevant in many ways.

Eliot/Journey of the Magi (*p. 577*)

10 the silken girls bringing sherbet: In the *Anabasis* of St.-John Perse (1887–1975), the French poet and diplomat who was awarded the Nobel prize in 1960, there are similar memories: "our scented girls clad in a breath of silk webs . . . For so long the ice sang in our glasses. . . ." Eliot was translating the French poem about the time he was writing "Journey of the Magi."   23–28 The imagery alludes to the passion and death of Christ: the three crosses of Calvary, the soldiers casting dice at the foot of the cross for Christ's garments, the betrayal for pieces of silver. Christ as Conquerer appears on a white horse in Rev. 6 and 9. Since so many of Eliot's images seem drawn from his reading, it is interesting to see what he has to say about this passage, in the concluding lecture of the series he gave at Harvard in 1932–1933, published as *The Use of Poetry and the Use of Criticism:* "And of course only a part of an author's imagery comes from his reading. It comes from the whole of his sensitive life since early childhood. Why, for all of us, out of all that we have heard, seen, felt, in a lifetime, do certain images recur, charged with emotion, rather than others? The song of one bird, the leap of one fish, at a particular place and time, the scent of one flower, an old woman on a German mountain path, six ruffians seen through an open window playing cards at night at a small French railway junction where there was a water-mill: such memories may have symbolic value, but of what we cannot tell, for they come to represent the depths of feeling into which we cannot peer" (p. 148).

Eliot/East Coker (*p. 578*)

The *Quartets* are often compared with the last quartets of Beethoven, whose late work Eliot had praised in 1933 as striving to get beyond music, as Eliot himself said he had worked to get beyond poetry. Eliot himself is reported to have said that he was "paying attention" chiefly to the quartets, numbers 2–6, of the Hungarian composer Béla Bartók (1881–1945). The five sections of Eliot's quartets correspond from poem to poem: the first part has some description of the place for which the quartet is named and meditations suggested by it; the second has a formal lyric in rhyme followed by a more colloquial commentary; the third tends to be about some kind of journey or movement; the fourth is a short stanzaic lyric (as in "The Waste Land"); the fifth works toward a conclusion or resolution of the themes.

28–33 The words that caught Eliot's eye are: "the associatinge of man and woman in daunsing . . . was not begonne without a speciall consideration, as well as for the necessarye coniunction of those two persones, as for the intimation of sondry vertues, which be by them represented. And for as moche as by the association of a man and a woman in daunsinge may be signified matrimonie, I coulde in declarynge the dignitie and commoditie of that sacrament make intiere volumes . . . In euery daunse of a most auncient custome, there daunseth to gether a man and a woman, holding eche other by the hande or the arme, whiche betokeneth concorde. . . ." Sir Thomas Elyot had something more courtly in mind than Eliot's peasant folkdance in the woods at midnight. **Commodious:** beneficial, advantageous to humanity 135–146 St. John, who also drew a design of the route of the ascent, is describing the ascent of the Mountain of Perfection that leads through the darkness to union with Gòd. As translated by E. Allison Peers (*The Complete Works of St. John of the Cross*, The Newman Press, Westminster, Maryland, 1933) the lines that Eliot adapts read:

> In order to arrive at that wherein thou hast no pleasure,
> Thou must go by a way wherein thou hast no pleasure.
> In order to arrive at that which thou knowest not,
> Thou must go by a way that thou knowest not.
> In order to arrive at that which thou possessest not,
> Thou must go by a way that thou possessest not.
> In order to arrive at that which thou art not,
> Thou must go through that which thou art not.

The original Spanish is simpler and more colloquial:

> Para venir a lo que no gustas,
> Has de ir por donde no gustas. . . .

Cummings/wherelings whenlings (*p. 594*)

Some of the poems of Cummings that follow look odd and difficult at first glance. They become simple if we understand that he is taking two liberties with language. First, he uses words as if parts of speech did not exist: he uses nouns as verbs or conjunctions as nouns or—anything as anything. We all do this to some extent: when a baseball player hits a "homer" we easily say he "homered." We say a situation is "iffy," or that someone is a "has been," or that the rich and poor are the "haves and have nots." English permits great freedom in this respect; Cummings makes full use of that freedom. In line 1, "wherelings and whenlings" are people always worried about *where* and *when* instead of just living and doing. They are children of "ifbut"—all *ifs* and *buts* instead of acting with conviction. They won't do things *unless*; they only do them *almost*. The genuine human being, on the other hand, likes the *here* and *now* of life. He likes *is* instead of *isn't*: *yes* instead of *no*. These examples show us the second apparently odd thing Cummings does with language: he reduces it to the simplest words possible. An affirmative person is a *yes*. Worlds of worry and speculation become *whycolored* worlds. The result is a very simple vocabulary.

Cummings/anyone lived in a pretty how town (*p. 595*)

This poem shows a typical person (called "anyone") in a typical town who makes a typical marriage with a person (called "noone" or no one) whom others might think a nobody; she sympathizes with him through the joys and sorrows of life; they die, and begin to live, the poet suspects, life after death. They live their ordinary life against a background of the wonders of the earth: the seasons, the moon and stars, the beauty of birdsong and snowfall, etc. The thought, when paraphrased, is as ordinary as can be: life is a marvellous mixture of joy and sorrow. What makes this cliché so totally fresh is the language in which Cummings describes it—as nobody ever had before, and yet (once we are used to his language) with vigor and clarity. The rhymes and lilting stanzas are among the oldest of such patterns in English—and yet they too are freshened by the novelty and brightness of the language. Only a few additional notes to start us out:

1 **a pretty how town:** an average town. Any question one might ask about its "how?" would be answered by a "pretty." "How lively is it?" "Oh, pretty lively." "How much fun do you have?" "Pretty much." "How's the weather there?" "Pretty good—or sometimes pretty bad!" 2 Bells symbolize many of the important events of life, because actually associated with them: Christmas bells, wedding bells, funeral bells, bells when wars end, etc. 4 **he sang his didn't:** What he couldn't actually do or have, he sang about. (Think how many folksongs are about someone or something far away or long ago—something we yearn for.) **he danced his did:** Dancing is an expression of positive joy right now—as when children dance for joy. 5 **both little and small:** because all human beings, as subject to their mortality, are equally small; no one rises above the human condition 15 **bird by snow and stir by still:** summer and winter, day and night. With this as pattern, one should be able to follow the other "—— by ——" phrases. Part of the fun of a poem like this is figuring it out. Given his assumptions about language, we can see that Cummings is perfectly consistent in his use of it.

Cummings/my father moved through dooms of love (*p. 596*)

By now we are probably familiar enough with Cummings's language to follow him on our own. We realize that Cummings is telling us that his father (who was a minister) was a man so kind and charitable, even when it cost him pain and sacrifice, that he lived as if under a "doom" or sentence to love others. His "am"s were all "same"—or, as we might put it ourselves, his nature was consistent. His dearest possession, his "have," was his ability to "give" to others. The rather vague unfocused "where" of this world was actualized by his presence into a vivid "here," so that even people hardly alive, hardly better than things, under his influence became really human: he could turn a *which* into a *who*. If a woman came to him who was only a "why" ("*Why* did my child die?" "*Why* do I have to be sick?"), he consoled her. And so on, through the discoveries and delights of the language. If occasionally there is something we cannot understand, well, that happens even when we are talking with our friends.

Auden/Lullaby (*p. 625*)

11 **have no bounds:** do not exclude each other, are not opposed. The rest of the stanza is saying that physical love can lead to "supernatural sympathy"; the "abstract" vision of the hermit can lead to an ecstatic state in some way like that of the lover. The poem sees love as imperiled by many things, but concludes with a blessing for the beloved "sleeping head" that combines spiritual and physical protection ("the involuntary powers" and "every human love").

Roethke/Where Knock Is Open Wide (*p. 641*)

In this group of poems, Roethke is making voyages of exploration into the interior of the self, sometimes going back to the earliest prelogical or even prenatal impressions of the infant, sometimes going to fish, as he said, "in that dark pond, the unconscious, or dive in, with or without pants on, to come up festooned with dead cats, weeds, tin cans, and other fascinating debris. . . . " Such poems require a different sort of annotation from that of "The Waste Land" (which Roethke often has in mind, and to which he is writing his own kind of answer). Whereas Eliot's lines may require the kind of clarification we can get from books, Roethke's require only that we look deep into ourselves and recall what it was like to be two years old, or ten years old, or an adolescent. The poet assures us that "you will have no trouble if you approach these poems as a child would, naïvely, with your whole being awake, your faculties loose and alert. . . . Listen to them, for they are written to be heard, with the themes often coming alternately, as in music, and usually a partial resolution at the end. . . . Each poem . . . is a stage in a kind of struggle out of the slime; part of a slow spiritual progress; an effort to be born, and later, to become something more. . . ." (These quotations are from the "Open Letter" with which Roethke prefaced some of these poems in 1950 in John Ciardi's anthology *Mid-Century American Poets*.)

A few other quotations help us to read the poems. "I believe that to go forward as a spiritual man it is necessary first to go back. Any history of the psyche (or allegorical journey) is bound to be a succession of experiences, similar yet dissimilar. There is a perpetual slipping back, then a going-forward; but there is *some* 'progress.' . . . Some of these pieces, then, begin in the mire; as if man is no more than a shape writhing from the old rock. This may be due, in part, to the Michigan from which I come. Sometimes one gets the feeling that not even the animals have been there before; but the marsh, the mire, the Void, is always there, immediate and terrifying. It is a splendid place for schooling the spirit. It is America. None the less, in spite of all the muck and welter, the dark, the *dreck* of these poems, I count myself among the happy poets. 'I proclaim, once more, a condition of joy!' says the very last piece. . . . " It may seem odd to say that poems that "begin in the mire" are really a search for spiritual illumination and perfection, but that is the direction in which the poet is working. "Except for the saint, everything else is dog, fish, minnow, bird, etc., and the euphoric ride resolves itself into a death-wish. Equationally, the poem can be represented: onanism [masturbation] equals death, and even the early testament moralists can march out happily." Odd as the method may look to us, Roethke insists these are "traditional poems," influenced by folk literature (especially Mother Goose), Elizabethan and Jacobean drama, the Bible, Blake and Traherne, and Dürer. "Much of the action is implied or, particularly in the case of erotic experience, rendered obliquely. . . . Rhythmically, it's the spring and rush of the child I'm after. . . . " This kind of poem "must be able to telescope image and symbol, if necessary, without relying on the obvious connectives: to speak in a kind of psychic shorthand when his protagonist is under great stress. . . . The clues will be scattered richly—as life scatters them; the symbols will mean what they usually mean—and something more. . . . " The first of these poems, he says, "is written entirely from the viewpoint of a very small child: all interior drama; no comment; no interpretation. To keep the rhythms, the language 'right,' i.e. consistent with what a child would say or at least to create the 'as if' of the child's world, was very difficult technically . . . there is no cutesy prattle; it is not a suite in goo-goo." "Everything in the mind of the kid," as he put it informally in a letter.

Roethke/The Lost Son (*p. 643*)

This poem represents a later stage of the poet's self-exploration, the mental and spiritual struggle he went through when he felt himself a "lost son" after the death of his father, which also intensified feelings of guilt he may have toward the father-guilt arising from archetypal son-father envy and the substitute sexual activity he devised for himself. The poet had agonizing powers of self-scrutiny: "His history, as he saw it, was one of losses, betrayals, shame, many fears, and guilt. To immerse himself in these, to force them into images or to contemplate them until they became images that he, hence others, could accept, and to find a suitable diction for them was not only taxing but may have been dangerous." In him it was dangerous, as the several nervous breakdowns he suffered testify. Believing that going forward involves going back, in this poem Roethke again investigates experiences of his earlier years. We are aided in understanding the poem by the brief explanations he gives in the "Open Letter" referred to before. " 'The Flight' is just what it says it is: a terrified running away—with alternate periods of hallucinatory waiting (the voices, etc.); the protagonist so geared-up, so over-alive that he is hunting, like a primitive, for some animistic suggestion, some clue to existence from the sub-human. These he sees and yet does not see: they are almost tail-flicks, from another world, seen out of the corner of the eye. In a sense he goes in and out of rationality; he hangs in the balance between the human and the animal."

9 snail: Cf. what Roethke said in his 1963 talk "On 'Identity' ": "If the dead can come to our aid in a quest for identity, so can the living—and I mean *all* living things, including the subhuman. This is not so much a naïve as a primitive attitude: animistic, maybe.... Everything that lives is holy: I call upon these holy forms of life.... St. Thomas [Aquinas] says, 'God is above all things by the excellence of His nature; nevertheless, He is in all things as causing the being of all things.' Therefore, in calling upon the snail, I am calling, in a sense, upon God.... For there is a God, and He's here, immediate, accessible. I don't hold with those thinkers that believe in this time He is farther away—that in the Middle Ages, for instance, He was closer. He is equally accessible now, not only in works of art or in the glories of a particular religious service, or in the light, the aftermath that follows the dark night of the soul, but in the lowest forms of life, He moves and has His being. Nobody has killed off the snails...." 2. *The Pit.* " 'The Pit' is a slowed-down section; a period of physical and psychic exhaustion. And other obsessions begin to appear (symbolized by mole, nest, fish)." [Roethke] The title of the section and the phrase "ask the mole" indicate that Roethke is referring us (as Eliot might do) to a literary parallel, the "Motto" William Blake put at the beginning of his early *The Book of Thel* (1789): "Does the Eagle know what is in the pit? / Or wilt thou go ask the Mole: / Can Wisdom be put in a silver rod? / Or love in a golden bowl?" The mole, who lives embedded in "the slime of a wet nest" where life begins, would have more experience of this fundamental reality than the soaring eagle, who is above it all. Mildew is a sort of primitive slimy life form. "Beware Mother Mildew" is not too far from Eliot's "Fear death by water." 3. *The Gibber.* "These obsessions begin to take hold; again there is a frenetic activity, then a lapsing back into almost a crooning serenity ('What a small song,' etc.). The line, 'Hath the rain a father?' is from Job—the only quotation in the piece. (A third of a line, notice—not a third of a poem.) The next rising agitation is rendered in terms of balked sexual experience, with an accompanying 'rant,' almost in the manner of the Elizabethans, and a subsequent near-blackout." [Roethke] **Gibber:** gibberish. 4. *The Return.* "a return to a memory of childhood that comes back almost as in a dream, after the agitation and exhaustion of the earlier actions. The experience, again, is at once literal and symbolical. The 'roses' are still breathing in the dark; and the fireman can pull them out, even from the fire. After the dark night, the morning brings with it the suggestion of a renewing light: a coming of 'Papa.' Buried in the text are many little ambiguities, not all of which are absolutely essential to the central meaning of the poem. For instance, the 'pipe-knock.' With the coming of steam, the pipes begin knocking violently, in a greenhouse. But 'Papa,' or the florist, as he approached, often would knock the pipe he was smoking on the sides of the benches, or on the pipes. Then, with the coming of steam and 'papa'—the papa on earth and heaven are blended—there is the sense of motion in the greenhouse, my symbol for the whole of life, a womb, a heaven-on-earth." [Roethke] 5. *"It was beginning winter."* "In the final untitled section, the illumination, the coming of light suggested at the end of the last passage occurs again, this time to the nearly-grown man. But the illumination is still only partly apprehended; he is still 'waiting.' "

Roethke/In a Dark Time (*p. 650*)

In a symposium devoted to this poem, three distinguished poets wrote over 20 pages of explanation. Roethke then wrote over four pages of response. He describes it as "a drive toward God: an effort to break through the barrier of rational experience ... to break from the bondage of the self, from the barriers of the 'real' world, to come as close to God as possible." To greatly abridge what Roethke calls his "clumsy paraphrase": *Stanza I*: in darkness, the soul confronts its other self; it shares its sorrow with a simple living tree. The heron was "a solitary bird that nested in the corner of my father's preserve"; it symbolizes purity, wisdom, toughness. The wren was "a happy, courageous, lecherous little bird that always nested in our back yard." He feels sympathy, kinship now with one, now with another of the creatures. *Stanza II*: " 'Madness' is a sociological term ... what is madness in the Northwest is normal conduct in Italy, and a hero's privilege in western Ireland." The mind is on fire—with revelation. "As a child, I was always a passionate cave—and path—watcher, curious as to where things led. The cave and the winding path are older than history. And the edge—the terrible abyss—equally old." *Stanza III*: the correspondences are analogies in the world we see—birds, moon, and so on—to things in the invisible, the divine world. "The time sense is lost; the natural self dies in the blaze of the supernatural." *Stanza IV*: "And perhaps *should* die, say the next lines.... Am I this many-eyed, mad, filthy thing [the fly], or am I human?... The moment before Nothingness, before near-annihilation, the moment of supreme disgust is the worst: when change comes it is either total loss of consciousness—symbolic or literal death—*or* a quick break into another state, not necessarily serene, but frequently a bright blaze of consciousness that translates itself into action.... I return to the human task of climbing out of the pits of fear.... The mind has been outside itself, beyond itself, and now returns home to the domain of love...." Very complicated thoughts are behind the simple words of the last two lines. To oversimplify: the mind returns to itself, with God present in it; one feels united with the all—but is still subject to the "tearing wind," the violence of the natural world. Roethke intends an ambiguity in "tearing": the wind is destructive, but also pitying, shedding tears (cf. the "tearless" of line 17). (The "symposium" is in *The Contemporary Poet as Artist and Critic*, ed. by Anthony Ostroff; Little, Brown, 1964.)

Lowell/The Quaker Graveyard in Nantucket (*p. 676*)

I. The imagined discovery of the dead sailor's body and its burial at sea.

II. As in a classical elegy, nature is imagined in sympathy with and lamenting for the dead sailor.

III. A parallel between the war, with its destructive savagery, and the whaling of the Quakers, whose "mad scramble" for profits at the expense of nature cost them their lives—and perhaps their souls.

IV. Summed up in its first line.

V. A vision of spreading corruption caused by such human misconduct as the killing and butchery of the whales. It ends with a prayer to Jesus (buried and resurrected as Jonah was in the whale) to take on and atone for man's sins.

VI. An answer to the evil shown in earlier sections may be found in such penitential devotion as that symbolized by the ancient shrine of the Virgin at Walsingham (cf. Sir Walter Ralegh, "As You Came from the Holy Land," line 2, p. 61).

VII. Though nature is disordered and destructive, and man subject to evil impulses, the Lord endures and preserves the covenant he made with Noah after the flood.

Lowell/After the Surprising Conversions (*p. 680*)

The phraseology of "A Faithful Narrative . . ." provided Lowell with about one-third of his text, taken either verbatim or with slight changes, as a single paragraph will show: "In the latter part of May, it began to be very sensible [apparent] that the Spirit of God was gradually withdrawing from us, and after this time Satan seemed to be more let loose, and raged in a dreadful manner. The first instance wherein it appeared, was a person putting an end to his own life by cutting his throat. He was a gentleman of more than common understanding, of strict morals, religious in his behavior, and a useful and honorable person in the town; but was of a family that are exceedingly prone to the disease of melancholy, and his mother was killed with it. He had, from the beginning of this extraordinary time, been exceedingly concerned about the state of his soul, and there were some things in his experience that appeared very hopeful; but he durst entertain no hope concerning his own good estate. Towards the latter part of his time, he grew much discouraged, and melancholy grew amain upon him, till he was wholly overpowered by it, and was in a great measure past a capacity of receiving advice, or being reasoned with to any purpose. . . . He was kept awake at nights, meditating terror, so that he had scarce any sleep at all for a long time together; and it was observed at last, that he was scarcely well capable of managing his ordinary business, and was judged delirious by the coroner's inquest. The news of this extraordinarily affected the minds of people here, and struck them as it were with astonishment. After this, multitudes in this and other towns seemed to have it strongly suggested to them, and pressed upon them, to do as this person had done. And many who seemed under no melancholy, some pious persons, who had no special darkness or doubts about the goodness of their state—nor were under any special trouble or concern or mind about anything spiritual or temporal—had it urged upon them as if somebody had spoke to them, Cut your own throat, now is a good opportunity. Now! Now!" It was Edwards's own uncle who committed suicide.

Lowell/For the Union Dead (*p. 682*)

65–68 The poem has been showing, among other things, how *life*, heroic, spiritual, natural (the fish), is being taken over by the rigidity of machines (the "giant finned cars"), which are at once brutal and slavish. It sees racial injustice as a crucial instance of such rigidity.

Dickey/Cherrylog Road (*p. 707*)

In *James Dickey: Self-Interviews* (ed. B. and J. Reiss, Doubleday, 1970), the poet has this to say: " 'Cherrylog Road' is a much-anthologized piece. I think it's sort of funny and innocent. It seems to me to have a Huckleberry Finn quality about it, even though it deals with motorcycles and junk yards. What I attempted to show by means of a boy and girl having a sexual rendezvous in an old junk yard full of bootleggers' cars and wrecked stock cars was that magical moment when you realize that this year you can do a lot of things you couldn't do last year. You know, last year you were riding around on a bicycle, and this year you've got a big, powerful motorcycle.

"Junk yards are oddly surrealistic. Growth is heavy in the South. If junked automobiles are left in a lot, it's going to look like a jungle in a few months, especially in summertime. Kudzu vines will be growing through the cars; and snakes, turtles, roaches, mice, toads—everything you can think of— will be living there. It is a strange place for human love; where man's castoff goods and nature meet. And I suppose the factual experience is changed somewhat simply by virtue of writing about it in one way rather than another. I don't think Cherrylog Road was the name of the road. It's a place name I picked up on a fishing trip I took one time, but it seemed like a good name. I realize it doesn't matter whether the incidents in a poem are true, but people might be interested to know that in this case they really are."

Ashbery/The Instruction Manual (*p. 726*)

John Ashbery is celebrated for being a "difficult" poet, but there is no difficulty in this early poem. A man bored by a routine writing assignment lets his mind drift away into daydreams of a Mexican city which in reality he has never seen. But he has browsed through enough travel brochures and popular novels, seen enough posters and sentimental movies to know what a south-of-the-border town is supposed to be. Such a poem could be as prosaic as the writing assignment itself, but here it is saved by something strange, droll, and charming in the language of the long lines, reminiscent of Whitman in their rhythm and their accumulation of catalogue detail. The very notion that there could be an instruction manual "on the uses of a new metal," though deadpanned here, is a fanciful one. In the highly colored but cliché description of the unseen town, the language is continually making fun of itself, parodying sometimes the glamor of travel ads, sometimes the romantic corniness of movies and soap opera. Sometimes it is deliberately highflown: the "dapper fellow" in line 16 is not "dressed" but "clothed" in blue; he is not just "the man with a mustache" but "the mustachioed man." The town itself is romanticized; we are never shown its seamy side. Even the homes of the poor are a picturesque "deep blue"; nothing more sordid occurs than the swatting of flies. A musical comedy town, as seen through the dreamer's rose-colored glasses. "Rose" indeed seems to be his favorite color in this poem, with its some 25 color references (mostly pretty). (But no references to smell; not even the flowers have fragrance.) By the middle of the poem the imagined scene takes on a kind of surreality when we, the readers, find ourselves also within it: "Let us take this opportunity to tiptoe into one of the side streets" (line 44); "Slowly we enter . . ." (line 56). Solemn readers, not content with enjoying an exercise in fantasy, might say that this is a poem about levels of reality and the power of the imagination.

Ashbery/Mixed Feelings (*p. 729*)

Again, as in the preceding poem, the speaker's mind shifts from what is present to his senses into a world of fantasy, this time moved by a faded photo of what seem to be girls posing around a World War II fighter-bomber. In his imagination they take on more and more reality, are given names perhaps typical of the forties, speak in the slang of the period, and are fancied as dismissing the speaker as too stuffy for them. As they, like most people, have contradictory ideas, so he has mixed feelings about them: he gets back at them for their imagined brush-off by crediting them with "tiny intelligences" that cannot tell California from New York (part of his own "flirtation routine"?). Yet he likes the way "they look and act and feel" and imagines coming on them—real girls "astonishingly young and fresh"—in the lounge of a modern airport, though they began as nothing more than vague blurs or smudges on a mostly invisible photo. Not explicitly about much of anything, the poem can be seen as hinting at a meditation on youth and sex and love and war and time and change and, if we care to go so far, on "the meaning of life" itself, though it comes to no conclusion.

Ashbery/As One Put Drunk into the Packet-Boat (*p. 730*)

This is the kind of poem, typical of much of Ashbery's work, which many readers would find difficult. Comparisons with modern art and modern music may be of help here (Ashbery has an expert's knowledge of both). His poetry is sometimes explained by comparing it to abstract art, which may arrange (or not arrange) colors, masses, and shapes so that, while interesting in themselves, they refer to nothing in the natural world. His work has been viewed as similar: viewed as giving us words, phrases, and sentences interesting in themselves but seeming to have no message or meaning, seeming to add up to nothing beyond themselves. It has also been compared to music: when we listen to a piece of music we may be aware that a mood, an attitude, is being developed, but we do not continually ask, "What does the music mean?" We can also read some poetry that way: letting the words, images, sounds suggest moods and themes though they present no argument and have no logical structure. Ashbery has indeed been influenced by music and musical theory, perhaps most notably by the contemporary American composer John Cage (born 1912), who holds that all sounds (and indeed all things) are related, whether the composer (or artist or poet) brings out the relationship or not. Everything in the universe goes with everything else, and therefore, he might say, it is arbitrary and unnatural for an artist to impose his own rigid form on things.

In a poem written on such principles, there would be no reason why one sentence should logically be hooked to another, or why we should demand what the relationship is. Any more than we ordinarily demand to know what it is in nature, by wondering what landscapes *mean* or by asking questions like "Why is that green tree by that blue lake?" It just *is*. Some might say that of an Ashbery poem: it just *is*. Never mind why. Enjoy the sounds, the words, the images. If a poem seems unarranged, so does our stream of consciousness and association; if we really stared into our minds for a while we would be surprised at how disorderly and random they are, with thought changing into thought for no apparent reason, or being interrupted by other thoughts, or by the sound of a car passing, or by an overheard remark, or by a feeling that the chair we are sitting on is uncomfortable. Instead of forcing into formation a process of thought or feeling, Ashbery may admit into his poem whatever seems to cross his mind at the time he is writing it, so that some of his poems, instead of having a subject, become their own subject. They seem to be about themselves.

Such an account is true as far as it goes, but it is by no means the whole truth. The poet is not merely following random motions of the mind—if he were we would have a kind of flux or chaos instead of the traditional syntax of these beautifully controlled sentences. He is obviously giving a shape to the shapelessness of consciousness, though perhaps not as obvious a shape as we are used to in much poetry of the past. But—because words do have "meaning" in a sense in which colors and tones do not—he has not gone nearly so far in expunging reference to external reality as the abstract artist or composer of aleatory (chance-determined) music has done. That he would agree his poems have a substructure would seem to be indicated by his occasional willingness to give line-by-line explications of them. Suppose we try something like that, on our own, with this poem. Like all other such explorations in this book, this one is only suggestive and tentative—in no sense official.

1–5 Human activity is limited, not infinite. We experience reality only a little at a time, and it is never all that we wish it to be—something, someone, is missing. There is a lack of harmony in our relationships; as time goes by it destroys all that it begets (as it yellows the green of the maple tree). 6–14 And yet sometimes we feel, as the seasons change, that something rich and meaningful is about to happen; that possibility rivets our attention. 15–27 Though we may be self-conscious, unsure of ourselves, and even guilty (as if we had caught sight of ourselves in a mirror or pane of glass, or perhaps been fixed by the glassy stare of another), the processes of nature go on undisturbed, again giving us the sense that it is readying itself, or us, for some wonderful change, signalled perhaps by the arrival of a car, or by a single glance full of meaning. 25 **ballade:** (1) a verse form with recurring rhymes and a refrain; (2) a musical composition, generally romantic or narrative, especially for the piano. 28–33 Long as man has been in the world, he does not really understand the nature of things. We know only, like dust in sunlight, the little events of our day—someone appearing, for instance, to ask if we are coming into the house. 34–42 Amid the fretfulness of trivial detail and the bustle of living, the purity of a moonlit night may suggest something like quiet solace and consolation. (The Cistercians, or "White Monks," were an order of Benedictine monks who chose to follow the strictest form of their rule; there were also Cistercian nuns. Both wore white.) If these are indeed the ideas of the poem, we can see that there is nothing particularly new or revolutionary in them; thinking men in all ages have shared them. Good poems rarely present new ideas—the basic human experiences remain very much the same. What this poem does is what all good poems do: it presents the ancient truths or uncertainties of our existence in terms that startle and delight us because never used in exactly that way before.

Hill/*From* **Mercian Hymns** (*p. 747*)

Geoffrey Hill's sequence of prose poems called "Mercian Hymns" might seem "modern" or "experimental" in that they go even beyond free verse in their independence of meter. But—like much that seems new because it has been long forgotten—the poems return to an ancient tradition. We have seen (p. ooo) Richard Rolle's prose lyric of the fourteenth century. But long before that a number of Christian hymns, influenced by the Psalms, were so free-flowing we have to call them prose poems. The most famous is the "Te Deum" of the fourth century, which is sung up to the present time. Hill acknowledges the influence of such poems, and the even more immediate influence of the half a dozen "Mercian Hymns" of the eighth and ninth centuries printed in Sweet's *Anglo-Saxon Reader*, which gave him his title. Hill's poems, "difficult" at first sight, become easy to follow if we keep in mind the words with which they conclude: "he entered into the last dream of Offa the King." The poems are the dreamings, the day-dreamings, of an English schoolboy at the time of World War II. The boy's reading has acquainted him with the achievements of Offa, greatest of the English kings before Alfred. He imagines himself into Offa's time and even into Offa's consciousness, mingling incidents and feelings from his own schooldays with those of Offa's life, or seeing events of Offa's time as if they were happening in the forties, or today. Hill's own note on his 30 short poems begins: "The historical King Offa reigned over Mercia (and the greater part of England south of the Humber) in the years A.D. 757–796. During early medieval times he was already becoming a creature of legend. The Offa who figures in this sequence might perhaps most usefully be regarded as the presiding genius of the West Midlands, his dominion enduring from the middle of the eighth century until the middle of the twentieth (and possibly beyond)." We could think of the ancient kingdom of Mercia, which included most of England directly east of Wales, as the heartland of England; Offa is its consciousness. Some of his titles and accomplishments are recited in the first of the hymns, and then Offa himself chimes in, amusingly, in modern English.

Hill/*From* **The Pentecost Castle** (*p. 751*)

As epigraphs for his sequence of 15 love poems, Hill gives two quotations: "It is terrible to desire and not possess, and terrible to possess and not desire" (W. B. Yeats); and "What we love in other human beings is the hoped-for satisfaction of our desire. We do not love their desire. If what we loved in them was their desire, then we should love them as ourself" (Simone Weil). The sequence was influenced by Spanish poems of the fifteenth and sixteenth centuries—particularly, Hill tells us, by some of the poems in J. M. Cohen's *The Penguin Book of Spanish Verse* (1956). His little lyrics suggest a tragic story of a lover killed for love. The great Spanish poet St. John of the Cross (1542–1591), an influence on these poems, had the habit of interpreting human love poems and even popular songs *a lo divino*—in a divine way, so that human love, with its pain and ecstasy, became a symbol for divine love. So in Hill's sequence: the lover's death for love stands for the saint's dying to all things but the love of God. Mystical writers are fond of paradox; perhaps the basic one is that life is a kind of death until they die to gain the fuller life of love. In these poems we get such paradoxes as "measurer past all measure," "consentingly denied," "splendidly-shining darkness."

Index to Prosody

PROSODY
Tools of the Trade

I

RHYTHM

We cannot think about rhythm without thinking *in* it: the activity of the mind itself is stream on stream of brainwaves. Our life in the world depends on the many rhythms of which we are composed; if we put our thumb to our wrist we feel the pulsing of a rhythm whose failure would bring within minutes unconsciousness and death. For months before we were born, we were aware of little except the surging of our mother's heart and the arterial seas around us; probably from this earliest environment comes the feeling of reassurance and elation that rhythms often bring in later life.

The physical universe too is a system of rhythms, from the tiny clockwork of the atom to the spiraling of galaxies our lives are too brief to calendar. In between the tiny and the vast, waves break in rhythm on the shore, trees in their freer rhythms sway with the wind, day follows night and night the day, while season follows season. Color comes to the eye as rhythmic waves of light; speech comes to the ear as waves of sound. All things, said ancient Pythagoras, are number; we could just as well say all natural things are rhythm.

But what is rhythm? When "Fats" Waller, the famous jazz pianist, was asked that question he replied, "Man, if you got to ask, you just ain't got it." Most of us are happy to live with rhythm without asking what it is. Even people who cannot carry a tune can tap their feet and clap their hands in time to the music. When dancing, they accommodate their whole body to its tempo. In athletes, we see rhythm as a source of not only grace but power: the swimmer, the speed skater, the boxer all do more efficiently what they do in rhythm. We know too how powerfully rhythm can affect our emotions, can seize and hold our interest to the exclusion of other objects. There are many it can hypnotize.

Earlier men and women were stirred and delighted with rhythms that modern human beings are out of touch with. Among these is the rhythm of poetry, which today needs a kind of explanation. In the world of movies and television, where much is for the eye alone, and where whole programs can go by with only a few grunts or gags or chuckles from the shadowy actors, speech does not have the importance it had in earlier centuries. In Shakespeare's theater, on a bare stage in the glare of afternoon, the dramatist had to do with gorgeous words what today we do with gorgeous color. When Romeo tells Juliet he has to leave her after their night of love, words serve for lighting and stage scenery:

> Look, love, what envious streaks
> Do lace the severing clouds in yonder East.
> Night's candles are burnt out, and jocund day
> Stands tiptoe on the misty mountain top.

All this is unnecessary in films or on the modern stage; we need no description of what our eyes are seeing. The Elizabethans had to pay more attention to speech and to its rhythms; in the playhouses they thrilled to Shakespeare and his fellows; in their churches and their homes, where family reading was both edification and entertainment, they were stirred by the rhythms of the Bible. Visitors to London would ask where the popular preachers were to be heard; they savored language and its cadences in a way few do today. What once came naturally has to be explained.

In anything we feel as rhythm, there is a regular recurrence of something: the drumstick hits the drum, heart muscles contract and send the blood-flood rushing, the telephone poles go by the car as we drive. We have recurrence when something occurs and occurs and occurs with regularity—becomes so regular we can predict it. So that rhythm is an alternation: of sound and silence, of contraction and relaxation, of pole and no-pole. In the rhythm of waves, we have an alternation of crest and trough; in the rhythm of swaying trees, an alternation of back and forth.

II

SYLLABLE-STRESS

The first rhythmical system we will look at is called **syllable-stress;** it is based on *both* syllable-count and on the placing of accents (also called *stresses*). In our music the basis of rhythm is the sequence of notes with their beat; in our poetry, it is the sequence of syllables with their accent. Most of us have a working knowledge of what a syllable is; we see how dictionaries divide words into syllables to help us with pronunciation: *dic . tion . ar . y, syl . la . ble, pro . nun . ci . a . tion.* Such examples show a syllable as consisting of a vowel sound, usually with consonants before or after or around it. It may be a whole word, as *mom* or *pop,* or it may be part of a word, as in *ther . mom . e . ter, pop . u . lar.* As music is a series of notes, our speech is a series of syllables: *Four . score . and . sev . en . years . a . go . our . fa . thers . . .*

A series of undifferentiated units, however, will not give us a rhythm, any more than an unvarying hum will, or a perfectly flat lake surface. For rhythm we need waves, an up and down of something, crests and troughs, an alternation of *two*—and then we have a rhythm. Such an alternation is not only possible but inevitable in English because we pronounce some syllables with more energy than others—some have more weight, more mass, more charge, more stress, more of the kind of prominence we call *accent.* Alternations of accent and lack of accent make up the waves that give our speech its rhythm. No one speaking natural English pronounces a series of syllables so that each is given the same amount of energy. If we use little circles to represent the relative amount of energy that goes into each syllable, we might show the beginning of Lincoln's speech in this way:

    O   O   o Oo O oOo Oo
Four score and seven years ago, our fathers . . .

If we heard the line read with exactly the same amount of emphasis on each syllable, like this,

    O   O   O OO   O OO   O OO
Four score and seven years ago, our fathers . . .

we might suspect that this was not a human being talking, but perhaps a robot wired for sound in a science-fiction movie. Real voices are not fixed at a dead level.

When a syllable is pronounced with more energy than those around it, by being made just a little longer, a little louder, a little higher, we say it has an *accent.* Speakers will not agree on exactly how much accent should be given each syllable. Some might say, "FOUR score and SEV. en . . ." Others might say, "Four SCORE and SEV. en . . ." Both *four* and *score* have more accent than the *and* which follows them; they might be equally accented, or one might be given more accent than the other. Enough syllables in English, however, are definitely accented or unaccented for rhythms to be established. No one would reasonably give *and* an accent, or could possibly pronounce *SEV. en* as *se . VENN* or *FA . thers* as *fa . THURRS*. With most syllables, especially in longer words, little or no choice is possible: we agree where the accent goes.

Not all accented syllables have exactly the same degree of accent, any more than all ocean waves are of exactly the same height. Waves can differ in height and still be waves. A typical sequence of waves would probably look not so much like this

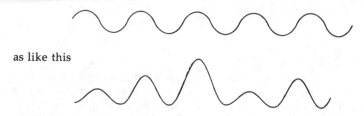

as like this

And so with accents: there is no official energy level at which a syllable changes from unaccented to accented. Some scholars say there are four degrees of accent, but there are no doubt many "degrees" in between those four, if we were sensitive enough to distinguish them. Accent is like loudness; it increases imperceptibly, not stairstep fashion like the notes on a piano. In speech we no doubt use many different intensities of accent, but, fortunately for students of prosody, poets take into account only *two* intensities; out of these two the rhythms of poetry are made. We could call the two *more* and *less*. If a syllable has more accent than the syllables with it, it counts as accented; if it has less, it counts as unaccented. No good English poet has ever devised a rhythmical system using more than the two intensities (accented, unaccented); two alone can make all the waves needed for a rhythm, as crests and troughs by themselves make a pattern of waves.

The amount of energy we expend to differentiate an accented syllable from an unaccented one is of course trivial; not even the very ill are too weak to accent their syllables. Yet we are so sensitive to the sounds of speech that when an accent is misplaced the difference can seem enormous—just as the tiniest piece of sand in the eye can. In the word *understanding*, the first and third syllables have the accent:

un der stand ing

Suppose we try to remove the accents from where they belong and put them on the second and fourth syllables:

$$\circ \, O \, \circ \, O$$
un der stand ing

This sounds like a piece of bad German:

un dúrsten Díng

If we heard the sounds *un dursten Ding* we might well have trouble recognizing a common word, and only because the accents are misplaced. If we can hear the difference between *únderstánding* and *un dúrsten Díng* we are well on our way to únderstánding the technicalities of versification.

If one spoke a line whose syllabic energies could be represented as follows

then one's speech-flow would be coming in waves

and one would be speaking in a rhythm.

Sometimes, without being aware of it, we do speak such rhythmical lines (from now on, since only the *more* and *less* matter, and not the degree of difference, suppose we confine ourselves to circles of two sizes):

o O o O o O o O o O
I'd like to buy another denim shirt.

o Oo O o O o OoO
That color's really nice with corduroy.

o O o O o O o Oo O
It's bound to rain by Tuesday afternoon.

o O o O o O o O o O
By Tuesday, heck! It's bound to rain tonight.

o O o O o O o O o O
You mean we talk in poems? How absurd!

These lines, though not exalted, are rhythmically as regular as anything in Shakespeare. But most of the things we say do not come out in so regular a rhythm:

O o o OO o O O o O o O O o
Help me to pick up a new shirt while here, I guess denim.

o Ooo Oooo O Oo o Oo O
That color is actually quite pretty in corduroy.

oo O oo O O o oo Oo O
It'll probably rain Tuesday in the afternoon.

These last three do not have a rhythmic alternation of more and less; the energy circles do not make a pattern. If a poet, meaning to write in a regular rhythm, wanted to make use of one of these lines, the poet would have to tinker with it and tune up the mechanism of accents until it worked in sync. This is not hard to do, especially for a writer who has worked so long with words and rhythms that their handling has become second nature.

Our language itself, like so many forces in nature, likes to come in waves of sound. English has thousands of accent-heavy monosyllables like *boy, girl, day, night, love, hate, sea, hill.* Often they are preceded by an article (practically always unaccented): *a boy, the girl.* When this occurs we have a o-O unit. Infinitives of monosyllabic verbs have the same pattern: *to love, to play, to dream.* o-O phrases are common: *at home, by night, in turn, for fun.* Sequences of o-O units will come in our speech whether we like it or not.

Single words also tend to come as rhythmical units. Most two-syllable words (except perhaps for such compound ones as *pint-size, car-door,* etc.) are either o-O (*adore, excite*) or O-o (*happy, broken*). If we look at three-syllable words, the usual patterns are o-O-o (*decrepit, unhappy*) or O-o-O with one of the large O's stronger than the other (*flabbergast, discontent*). Longer words almost always pick up a little rhythmic lilt or singsong, as we notice paging through a dictionary—they distribute the o's and O's so that accents do not clash or jar together, but tend to alternate. (Since we are concerned only with the more and less of syllables, we disregard here the fact that two accented syllables in a word will have different intensities, will constitute *primary* and *secondary* accents. The first accented syllable in *dictionary,* for example, is stronger than the second.)

dictionary ○ o ○ o

annunciation o ○ o ○ o

anthropology ○ o ○ o o

barometric ○ o ○ o

biochemistry ○ o ○ o o

cardiovascular ○ o o ○ o o

characteristic ○ o o ○ o

demolition ○ o ○ o

depreciation o ○ o ○ o

effervescent ○ o ○ o

embryological ○ o o ○ o o

filibuster ○ o ○ o

fragmentation ○ o ○ o

flexibility ○ o ○ o o

In the set elements of English, the long words whose "sayability" (○ o ○ o o) has been tested by millions of mouths over the centuries, there is a strong tendency to alternate accented and unaccented syllables; that is, to get a wavelike rhythm and the ease and fluency that go with it.

Alternations of low-energy syllables and high-energy syllables are not unnatural, then; the language seems to move most easily when it moves in waves of energy. A poet consciously working in o-○ units of rhythm is not doing violence to the language; that poet is working to achieve a more powerful undulatory movement than the one already present.

THE MODEL LINE: METER AND RHYTHM

Suppose then the poet achieves a perfectly regular line in its commonest (five-unit, or *pentameter*) length:

o ○ o ○ o ○ o ○ o ○

But now we might as well drop our big-circle little-circle graphics and start using the traditional system, which indicates accented (high-energy) syllables with a firm straight line (−), unaccented (low-energy) syllables with a little droop (∪), and separates the units by a bar (|).

∪−|∪−|∪−|∪−|∪−

The unit (here ∪−) whose repetition makes up a pattern is called a **foot**; someone keeping time with tapping foot would bring it down once for each such unit, five times to the line. This particular foot, called **iambic,** is the one we would probably decide on if we were trying to make up the simplest possible combination of English syllables which would give us a unit of rhythm. Units of one, or two of the *same* kind, would not give us a wavelike rhythm; we need two syllables of different kinds—one accented, one unaccented; one a crest, one a trough. Most people would prefer to put the strong syllable last. Psychologically, it is more interesting to work up to a peak of energy than to decline from it. The nature of English also encourages putting the stronger last: *the day, the night, the end.* Equally important is the fact that there is no physical rhythm more deeply embedded in our consciousness—and our subconscious—than the *Ka-BOOM, ka-BOOM* of the double-action heart, a rhythm resounding in the depths of our being some 100,000 times a day from before the dawn of consciousness. Ancient Greek medical writers suggested that this is why the iambic rhythm is, as Aristotle observed, the most conversational of the rhythms—an observation as true of modern English as of ancient Greek. A sequence of five iambic feet—five probably because the breath can manage that number without haste or strain—has become the commonest line of English poetry. In the *Oxford Anthology of English Poetry* about two-thirds of the poems are in **iambic pentameter**—and that does not represent the hundreds of thousands of lines of it in dramatic literature.

We might think of it, to illustrate our point, as the model line. Not "model" in the sense of "ideal," but only in the sense of "basic pattern," which the poet is not so much interested in conforming to as in creatively varying—as Shakespeare varies it when he begins Sonnet 116 with

$$– \;\cup\; | \; – \;\cup\; | \;\cup\; \; – \; | \;\cup\; \cup\; | \; – \;\;\; –$$
Let me not to the mar riage of true minds . . .

which no speaker of English would accent

Let ME not TO the MARriage OF true MINDS . . .

The rhythm of Shakespeare's actual line is not that of the model line.

Model line: $\cup\; – \;|\;\cup\; – \;|\;\cup\; – \;|\;\cup\; – \;|\;\cup\; –$

Actual line: $– \;\cup\; | \; – \;\cup\; | \;\cup\; \; – \; | \;\cup\; \cup\; | \; – \; –$

He does not, however, reject his model line for a different model. He remolds it nearer to his heart's desire, as Omar Khayyám urges us to do with any imperfect scheme of things. The line keeps its fiveness; it uses feet that are serviceable substitutes for the iambics of the model. How this comes about is what we have to look at next.

We might think of the model line as the metronome-line. It does exactly what the metronome does for a musician: rigidly marks the basic meter or measure, which a good musician will not slavishly follow but will interpret in a personal way. The same piece of music, though fixed on the page, will not sound the same when played by two talented performers. The poet and the poet's reader have no ticking metronome beside them; the metronome-line exists only in the head of the poet or reader; by it he or she measures each actual line written or heard. The poet is pleased not so much by the correspondence between model and actual as by the exciting tingles of difference as they interact in a kind of stereo fashion. The model line gives the **meter** (iambic pentameter in this case); what the poet does with it is **rhythm.** Meter and rhythm are quite different; the difference is all-important if we are to understand the nature of rhythm in English.

Another analogy with music is helpful here. In bands we have what is called the "rhythm section." Consisting of such instruments as the drums and the bass viol, the rhythm section maintains the rhythm by beating it out regularly and emphatically. Meanwhile the other instruments—saxophones, clarinets, piano, and the rest—have freedom to take off on their own and engage in inventive variations compatible with the basic rhythm. Our model line of regular pentameter has the same function as the rhythm section of a band, though it is heard only in our head.

The line of Shakespeare quoted above, which has only one iambic foot out of five, is exceptional; Shakespeare rarely departs that far from the meter, and only a very strong conviction (*"Let* me *not* . . ."*) permits him to do so here. The model line exerts a kind of magnetic tug on the actual line, with a strong syllable in the model more often than not attracting a strong syllable in its place, and a weak syllable attracting a weak one. *More often than not*—or else we would not recognize the presence of the model at all, and the sense of interplay between the two would be lost. Our *more often than not* still leaves a good deal of play; the gusto, verve, and expressiveness of good English verse is in the interplay between model line and actual line.

One principle that Shakespeare and others hold to in working with the model is never to break the five-foot structure. They encourage mutations in one or more of the five feet, but they do not drop a foot or add a foot. Though the examples that follow are mostly from Shakespeare, they represent standard practice and could easily be paralleled from the work of twentieth-century poets who use this line, as many do.

The mutations (variations) possible within the individual foot of the actual iambic line are of four kinds.

1. A foot which has no accented syllable, as in

<pre>
    | | | ∪ ∪|
Let me not to the mar riage of true minds . . .
</pre>
(Sonnet 116)

or as (twice) in the fourth line of the same poem:

<pre>
    | ∪ ∪| |∪ ∪|
Or bends with the remov er to remove . . .
</pre>

In such feet we may imagine we hear an accent because the model line has one—so that our mind supplies what is not actually there. Such a foot (∪∪) is called **pyrrhic;** in reading verse we can easily take one of these in our stride, but not two in a row. With two adjacent supports missing, the meter collapses. Since unaccented syllables are slimmer and move faster than the more weighty accented ones, the presence of pyrrhics accelerates a line.

2. A foot which has two weighty (accented) syllables, as in

<pre>
    | | | | −   −
Let me not to the mar riage of true minds . . .
</pre>

or as in line 9 of the same poem:

<pre>
     | −   − |
Love's not time's fool, though rosy lips and cheeks . . .
</pre>

which some would even pronounce "Love's not time's fool. . . ." In this foot (− −), called a **spondee,** the two syllables, though both heavy, need not have exactly the same degree of stress—perhaps no two adjoining syllables ever have. Some would stress *true* in *true minds;* some Platonic souls would stress *minds.* So with *time's fool,* in which our personal interpretation would determine which syllable gets the heavier accent. But all four of these words have accentual mass compared with the run of words in the line. Since spondees are strong supports, we can have two or more together, though natural English is not likely to produce a series of level syllables. Since a spondee packs as much energy as possible into a single foot, it can reinforce ideas of muchness, gravity, slowness, etc.

<pre>
     | −   − | −   − | | −   −
And with old woes new wail my dear time's waste . . .
</pre>
(Sonnet 30)

<pre>
     | −   − |
Not mine own fears, nor the prophetic soul
</pre>

<pre>
   | −   −
Of the wide world . . .
</pre>
(107)

3. A foot in which the accents are reversed, as in:

<pre>
 −   ∪ | −   ∪|
Let me not to the marriage of true minds
</pre>

<pre>
   | −   ∪|
Admit impediments. Love is not love . . .
</pre>

This reversed foot (− ∪), called a **trochee,** is so common at the beginning of a line, or after a strong pause within it, that it is hardly felt as a variation:

<pre>
   | −   ∪|
To be or not to be, that is the question:
</pre>

$$- \cup |$$
Whether 'tis nobler in the mind to suffer . . .

Elsewhere, since it goes against the gait of the meter, it can be felt as doing violence to it. It can be expressive with words that are themselves violent, defiant, emphatic, challenging, as in

When I have seen the hungry ocean gain
Advantage on the kingdom of the shore,

$$| - \cup |$$
And the firm soil win of the watery main . . .   (64)

$$| - \cup |$$
For precious friends hid in death's dateless night . . .   (30)

$$| - \cup |$$
My mistress, when she walks, treads on the ground . . .   (130)

Two trochees in a row are especially emphatic, as in

$$- \cup | - \cup |$$
Let me not to the marriage of true minds . . .

The use of two consecutive reversed feet was called **counterpoint** by Gerard Manley Hopkins, who used the musical term because we are hearing two rhythms at once, or what we have been describing as interplay between the model line and the actual line. Examples of counterpoint in Hopkins's "God's Grandeur" (p. 445) are:

$$\cup \quad - \ | \cup \quad - \quad | - \quad \cup | - \quad \cup | \cup \quad -$$
The world is charged with the grandeur of God . . .

$$- \cup | - \cup \ | \cup \quad - \ | \cup \quad - \ | \cup \quad -$$
Gener ations have trod, have trod, have trod . . .

4. A foot in which a second unaccented syllable is added to the one normally there:

$$| \cup \cup \ - \ |$$
I sigh the lack of man y a thing I sought . . .   (30)

O how shall summer's honey breath hold out

$$| \cup \cup \ -$$
Against the wreckful siege of bat tering days . . .   (65)

$$| \cup \cup \ - \ |$$
Is perjured, mur derous, blood y, full of blame . . .   (129)

In these examples one of the unaccented syllables is so light it could be suppressed in pronunciation: *batt'ring, murd'rous*. This trisyllabic foot ($\cup \cup -$), called **anapest,** tends to speed up a line, since two syllables are pronounced in what is normally the time for one.

These are the four variations frequently substituted for the basic foot in iambic rhythms. It is common also to find an unaccented eleventh (or even twelfth) syllable after the last accented one:

$$| \cup$$
To be or not to be, that is the quest ion:

$$| \cup$$
Whether 'tis nobler in the mind to suf fer

$$| \cup$$
The slings and arrows of outrageous for tune . . .

Not every variation combines with every other one. With many weak syllables in a row, the structure of rhythm collapses. The skill and expressiveness of a poet's personal style can be seen in the art with which the variations are used.

Besides having these options, a poet can bring variety into what might seem a monotonous meter by the way in which the line-endings are handled; sometimes the poet will prefer **end-stopped lines,** with punctuation generally serving as the stop sign, as in:

> Shall I compare thee to a summer's day?
> Thou art more lovely and more temperate.
> Rough winds do shake the darling buds of May,
> And summer's lease hath all too short a date. (18)

Or at other times the poet may prefer **run-on lines,** in which sense and syntax leap to the next line without a pause, as in

> That time of year thou mayst in me behold
> When yellow leaves, or none, or few, do hang
> Upon those boughs which shake against the cold . . . (73)

The use of run-on lines is called **enjambment,** from the French *enjamber,* which means "to straddle" or "to encroach on."

The poet can also break the sameness of the meter and give it a change of pace by shifting the position of the one or more internal pauses which a line, read naturally, is likely to have. Such pauses (each called a **caesura,** which means a *cut*) are often marked in the scansion by a double bar (‖). (By **scansion** we mean the process of representing graphically the pattern of accents in a line, as we have been doing.) We can see examples of the shifting caesura and of end-stopped and run-on lines in the first verse paragraph—a single sentence—of Milton's *Paradise Lost.* The number after each line indicates the syllable after which the caesura falls, sometimes in midfoot.

Of man's first disobedience, ‖ and the fruit	7
Of that forbidden tree, ‖ whose mortal taste	6
Brought death into the world, ‖ and all our woe,	6
With loss of Eden, ‖ till one greater Man	5
Restore us, ‖ and regain the blissful seat,	3
Sing, heav'nly muse, ‖ that on the secret top	4
Of Oreb, ‖ or of Sinai, ‖ didst inspire	3,7
That shepherd, ‖ who first taught the chosen seed,	3
In the beginning ‖ how the heav'ns and earth	5
Rose out of chaos: ‖ or if Sion hill	5
Delight thee more, ‖ and Siloa's brook that flowed	4
Fast by the oracle of God, ‖ I thence	8
Invoke thy aid ‖ to my adventrous song,	4
That with no middle flight ‖ intends to soar	6
Above th'Aonian mount, ‖ while it pursues	6
Things unattempted yet ‖ in prose or rhyme. . . .	6

And iambic pentameter in our time? Some poets, and among them the best, continue to use it in a way that would have been recognized as familiar by Shakespeare and probably even by Chaucer; it has no more changed than the heartbeat has. Yeats in "Sailing to Byzantium" (p. 467); Frost in "Directive" (p. 497); Stevens in "Sunday Morning" (p. 504); Cummings in a sonnet like "being to timelessness as it's to time" (p. 598); Crane in "Proem: To Brooklyn Bridge" (p. 605); Roethke in "I Knew a Woman . . ." (p. 649)—these and others handle the model line as poets had long handled it. They make it new, however, by using it with a kind of language it had not been used with before: twentieth-century English as spoken in Ireland or America; and by using it to express a personality—their own—it had not expressed before.

Other poets keep it in the back of their mind, a ghostly presence by which they are teased and stimulated. Casual readers, misled by the varying line-length, could miss the fact that at least half the lines in Eliot's "The Waste Land" are iambic pentameter, no more free in its options than that of the Jacobean poets Eliot was reading at the time:

Madame Sosostris, famous clairvoyante . . .

A crowd flowed over London Bridge, so many,
I had not thought death had undone so many . . .

"What are you thinking of? What thinking? What?
I never know what you are thinking. Think. . . ."

U   – |U – | U U – | U   U   – |U U – | U
He'll want to know what you done with that mon ey he gave you
To get yourself some teeth. He did, I was there . . .

– –|– – | U – |U – |U –
C.i. f. Lon don: doc uments at sight . . .

I made no comment. What should I resent?

U   – | U –| U   – |U – | U –|U
These frag ments I have shored against my ru ins . . .

In Robert Penn Warren's "Pursuit" (p. 618) we can clearly hear the five-beat structure of the lines, relaxed often into a mixed measure of iambs and anapests, with two extra unaccented syllables at the ends of some lines, and with only a couple of uncommon feet that look odd in the scansion but are easily absorbed into the flow of the rhythm. The last two lines of each stanza are regular enough but longer. Caesuras, generally obvious, are not marked. Not all readers will hear every accent exactly as marked here; scansion is not an exact science, and personal interpretation affects it. But though we may differ about details, the over-all rhythm should be clear.

U   – | U   U| U – | U U   – | U   – |U U
The hunch back on the cor ner, with gum and shoe laces,

U U |–   – | U   U   – | U   U   – | U U –
Has his own wis dom and plea sures, and may not be lured

U U – | U U – | U –| U   – |U U –
To divulge them to you, for he has mere ly endured

U U –| U U   – |U U| U   U   – | – U |U
Your appeal for his sym pathy and your kind purchas es;

U   – |U – |U U –|U U – | U   U   –
And wears infirm ity but as the gen (e)ral who turns

U – |U U – | U U   – | U   – | U U –
Apart, in his fam ous old great coat there on the hill

U – | U   U – |U U   – | U – |U –
At dusk when the rap ture and can nonade are still,

U   – | U – | U U – | U U – | U   U –|U
To muse withdrawn from the dead, from his gor geous subal terns . . .

The rhythm here has so many anapestic (U U –) variations that it might be thought of as mixed iambic-anapestic, or what is called *logaoedic*—a term to be discussed later under *anapests*.

William Stafford's "Traveling Through the Dark" (p. 665) illustrates the contemporary handling of iambic pentameter. It begins regularly enough:

<pre>
 – ∪ | ∪   – | ∪ – | ∪ – | ∪ –
Travel ing through the dark I found a deer
</pre>

<pre>
  – ∪ | ∪   – | ∪ ∪ – | ∪   – | ∪   –
dead on the edge of the Wil son Riv er road . . .
</pre>

Line 7 begins with two reversed feet and ends with a spondee, just as Shakespeare's "Let me not to the marriage of true minds" does. As the feeling of the poem intensifies, strain between the model line and the actual one is evident: line 10 shows a rare reversal of the last foot; line 11 is defective (as meter)—the emotion has wrenched the rhythm from the expected one. One of the advantages of having a model line in mind is that one can abruptly and expressively break from it; whereas if no regular rhythm is expected, there can be no surprise. Another expressive reversal is felt in the next-to-last line:

<pre>
      | – ∪ | | | |
I thought hard for us all—my on ly swerv ing—
</pre>

Sometimes the model line (or any other basic rhythm) fades in and out of a poem, now strongly present, now heard only in snatches, now imperceptible. We can tell it is in the writer's mind, which, however, allows only so much of it into the poem as the rhythms permit. Sometimes its integrity is camouflaged by line breaks. Such a description would hold for much of the work of A. R. Ammons. If we listen to his "The Constant" (p. 715), with our model line in mind, we find that his rhythms coincide often with the meter in our head:

<pre>
      | | | |
the nak ed mass of so much mir acle
</pre>

<pre>
∪ – | ∪ ∪ – | ∪   – | ∪   ∪ | ∪   –
alread y beyond the vis ion / of my grasp . . .
</pre>

<pre>
      | | | |
Along a rise of beach, a hun dred feet . . .
</pre>

<pre>
      | | | |
a row of clam shells / four to ten feet wide . . .
</pre>

<pre>
      | | | |
three to four in ches long and two inch es wide . . .
</pre>

<pre>
      | | | |
and on the lake a turn ing gal axy . . .
</pre>

<pre>
      | | | |
co-ord inat ed, near ly cir cular . . .
</pre>

<pre>
      | | | | |
with noon at sea: / the gal axy rotat ing . . .
</pre>

And so on to the logaoedic conclusion:

<pre>
      | | | | | ∪ ∪
I have had too much of this in exhaust ible mir acle:
</pre>

<pre>
      | | | | | ∪ ∪
miracle, this mas sive drab con stant of exper ience.
</pre>

We are surprised when we first notice how many poems that look "new" are respacings on the page of an ancient cadence. The beginning of Robert Creeley's "The Act of Love" (p. 721) could be written like this, in iambic pentameters so regular we need mark only the variations, which are the usual ones:

Whatev er con stitutes the act of love,

save phy sical encount er, you are *dear*

to me, not val ue as with banks— [∪ −]

but a mean ing self- suffic ient, dry at times

as sand, or else the trees, dripping with rain.

How shall one, this so-called person say it?

He loves, his mind is oc cupied, his hands

move writ ing words which come into his head . . .

Some readers might think this unfair, and hold that any poem, no matter how free, could be domesticated in this way. But it could not. Creeley's mind is really running in a rhythm, one so common we could almost call it a folk rhythm, which his line-breaks disguise, but which can be heard. On the page he gives the poem an additional rhythm, also orderly, of short lines arranged in threes, with the line breaks pacing the cadence and often stressing important words.

A poem we could not rehandle in this way is Gary Snyder's "Mid-August at Sourdough Mountain Lookout" (p. 739), which has a really different cadence—no less rhythmical, but different. A traditional rhythm is more apparent, but far from insistent, in his "Prayer for the Great Family" (p. 740):

Gratitude to Moth er Earth, sailing through night

and day— / and to her soil: rich, rare, and sweet . . .

Gratitude to Air, bearing the soar ing Swift /

and the sil ent Owl at dawn. Breath of our song . . .

Gratitude to Wat er: clouds, lakes, riv ers, glac iers . . .

Grandfath er Space. The Mind is his Wife. *so be it.*

Though often throbbing under casual modern dress, the old heartbeat rhythm is alive and well and thriving in some of our best contemporary poets. Not, however, in all; there are other rhythms available.

LINE-LENGTH

So far we have been illustrating principles of meter and rhythm as found in iambic pentameter and its variations. The same principles would hold in the other line-lengths, which are still referred to by the old Greek names. Examples in the lists below are iambic. But the names apply to lines in any rhythm.

monómeter: lines of one foot. Not at all common; Herrick's "Upon His Departure Hence" is an example:

> Thus I
> Pass by,
> And die;
> As one
> Unknown
> And gone;
> I'm made
> A shade,
> And laid
> I'th grave,
> There have
> My cave.
> Where tell
> I dwell,
> *Farewell.*

dímeter: lines of two feet, as in John Skelton's "Upon a Dead Man's Head" (p. 35).

trímeter: lines of three feet, as in "A God and Yet a Man" (p. 28), Ralegh's "The Lie" (p. 63), Yeats's "The Fisherman" (p. 460), and many other poems.

tetrámeter: Lines of four feet. Faster moving than pentameter, it is the next most common line. Many examples, among them: "I Wende to Dede" (p. 26), Donne's "The Ecstasy" (p. 100), Marvell's "On His Coy Mistress" (p. 163), E. E. Cummings's "my father moved through dooms of love" (p. 596), Philip Larkin's "At Grass" (p. 701).

pentámeter: Lines of five feet. Many examples in every period since Chaucer.

hexámeter: Slower moving lines of six feet, sometimes called *alexandrines*, probably after a medieval French poem about Alexander the Great. Examples: Beaumont's "Aspatia's Song" (p. 113), Dowson's "Non Sum Qualis Eram . . ." (p. 478), Yeats's "The Cold Heaven," and "The Magi" (p. 463).

heptámeter: Lines of seven feet, often called *fourteeners* from the number of syllables. Examples: Byron's "Stanzas for Music" (p. 295), Housman's "The Oracles" (p. 455). When lines are this long they tend to break up, for easier breathing, into the four-beat and three-beat lines of the **ballad stanza**, as in "Sir Patrick Spens" (p. 37):

> 1   2   3   4   5   6   7
> The king sat in Dumferline town, / Drinking the blood-red wine . . .

octámeter: Lines of eight feet, possible but not common. The lines of Browning's "A Toccata of Galuppi's" (p. 372) are eight-foot lines, but the feet are trochaic ($-\cup$) rather than iambic, with the last unaccented syllable omitted.

Line-length sometimes remains the same throughout a poem, sometimes is varied in accordance with a fixed pattern or at random.

TROCHEE, ANAPEST, DACTYL

Our discussion of rhythm, up to now, has been confined to one meter alone, that of the iambic foot. But there are three other basic ways of shaping the energy-flow of syllables into waves of rhythm.

The other two-syllable foot (for neither the pyrrhic foot [∪∪] nor the spondaic foot [– –] could give us a sustained rhythm) is the **trochee** (– ∪), the opposite of the iamb, with the more energetic syllable coming first. Since the energy lessens or subsides within the foot, it is known as a **falling rhythm,** as the iamb is known as a **rising rhythm.** There are far fewer trochaic poems than iambic, presumably because the rhythm fits less naturally the rhythm of spoken English. Sir Philip Sidney was the first to employ trochees with conspicuous success, as in his "Only Joy . . ." (p. 70). Other trochaic poems are Samuel Johnson's "A Short Song of Congratulation" (p. 223); Browning's "A Toccata of Galuppi" (p. 372); Gogarty's "Leda and the Swan" (p. 501); and Larkin's "The Explosion" (p. 702). Larkin's poem is in trochaic tetrameter, the rhythm of Longfellow's "Hiawatha"; the singsong of the short line can become tedious when used at length. The long lines of Poe's "The Raven," as mentioned before, are trochaic; they illustrate other features of meter: here Poe's feet tend to bond together in units of two and are therefore called **dipodic feet** (which means *having two feet*):

> While I nodded, | nearly napping, | suddenly there | came a tapping . . .

Lines 2, 4, 5, and the short last line of Poe's stanza omit the final unaccented syllable and are therefore called **catalectic,** which means "leave off, cut short":

> – ∪| – ∪∪| – ∪ |– ∪∪|– ∪ |∪ ∪ | – ∪ | –   [∪]
> Over many a quaint and curious volume of for gotten lore . . .

> – ∪| – ∪ | – ∪ | – [∪]
> Only this and nothing more.

Feet can also be composed of three syllables. The most frequently used of these is a rising foot akin to the iamb; it has the pattern ∪ ∪ – and is called **anapest.** We would not be likely to see ocean waves in nature which would have an anapestic pattern, at least for long:

As a speech rhythm, too, sustained anapests are somewhat artificial. We might accidentally say something which would have an anapestic swing:

> ∪ ∪ – |∪ ∪ – |∪ ∪ – |∪ ∪ –
> I arrived at my unc le's in plen ty of time

but we would not be likely to keep it up very long—unless we had deliberately set out to get a jingly effect:

> When I asked for a nickel, he gave me a dime.

The anapestic rhythm can have the vigorous physical movement that goes with strenuous subjects, as in Byron's "The Destruction of Sennacherib" (p. 294) or in Davidson's "A Runnable Stag" (p. 450). But it need not have; see Blake's "The Sick Rose" (p. 243) and "Ah, Sun-Flower!" (p. 242). Other anapestic poems are Jordan's "The Careless Gallant" (p. 150); Watts's "The Sluggard" (p. 197); Cowper's "The Poplar Field" (p. 236); and Betjeman's "A Subaltern's Love Song" (p. 623). The meter becomes more interesting when using such variations as – –, – ∪ –, ∪ – –, as in Blake:

> – – | – ∪ – |∪∪ –
> Ah Sun- flower, wear y of time,

U – | U U – | U U –
Who count est the steps of the Sun,

– U – | U U – | – U –
Seeking af ter that sweet golden clime

U   U – | U U   – | U   U –
Where the trav eler's jour ney is done . . .

Or as in Byron:

U   U – | –   –   – | U U – | – U –
When the blue wave rolls night ly on deep Galilee . . .

U   U – | U U – | U –   – | U U   –
And the eyes of the sleep ers waxed dead ly and chill,

U   U   – | U   –   – | U U – | U   –   –
And their hearts but once heaved— and for ev er grew still . . .

Sometimes so many iambs, spondees, and mutant triple feet are substitut-
ed for the anapests that we have a mixed rhythm called **logaoedic** (which
means prose-song) from its metrical freedom. Logaoedics can be very musical,
as in Swinburne's "Chorus" (p. 434):

U   U   – | U – | U U – | U – | U
When the hounds of spring are on win ter's tra ces,

U – | U U – | U – | U U –
The moth er of months in mead ow or plain

– | U – | U U – | U – | U
Fills the shad ows and wind y plac es

U – | U – | U – | U U   –
With lisp of leaves and rip ple of rain;

U   U – | –   – | U – – | U –
And the brown bright night ingale am orous

U – | U – | U – | U –
Is half assuaged for It ylus,

U   U – | U   – | U   U – | U   – | U
For the Thra cian ships and the for eign fac es

U   – | U – | U U – | U   –
The tongue less vig il and all the pain.

However we represent it in our symbols, the rhythm of the lines is prevail-
ingly iambic-anapestic, or logaoedic, as is Davenant's "Wake All the Dead" (p.
133) and Hardy's "Neutral Tones" (p. 438). An interesting example of the great-
er freedom with which a twentieth-century poet handles such a rhythm is Wal-
lace Stevens's "Large Red Man Reading" (p. 513).

The other three-syllable foot (–∪∪) is called the **dactyl,** from the Greek
word for *finger* (a finger has a long bone and two short ones). A falling rhythm
akin to the trochaic, dactyls are less common in English than the rising ana-
pests. Examples: Beddoes's "Dream-Pedlary" (p. 342); Hardy's "The Voice" (p.
442); and de la Mare's "Pooh!" (p. 486). In all of these poems, we find variant
feet parallel to those found with anapests.

Besides the four kinds of feet we have listed (in addition to the variant
pyrrhic and spondee), others, such as the ∪∪––, or –∪∪– of Greek and Latin
verse, are theoretically possible in English but rarely found.

III

STRONG-STRESS RHYTHM

Up to now we have been talking about a single metrical system—that which takes into account both accented and unaccented syllables and establishes a ratio between them of one-to-one or one-to-two. Both the accented syllables and the unaccented syllables matter; one gives us the crest and one the trough of the waves of rhythm. The system was established by Chaucer about 600 years ago; it apparently was derived from his reading of Italian and French poetry, though a basis for his iambic rhythms has been found too in the native English background.

For centuries before Chaucer a different metrical line had prevailed, the Old English alliterative line, as used in "Beowulf" and other Anglo-Saxon poems and later in such Middle English poems as "Sir Gawain and the Green Knight," written in Chaucer's own lifetime. In the older system, rhythm is determined by the stressed syllables alone, with the unstressed falling as they will.

To oversimplify a matter of some refinement, the **strong-stress** line consists of two half-lines with a distinct pause between; each half-line has two strongly stressed syllables and whatever number of unstressed they happen to bring with them. Three of the four stresses are made even more emphatic by **alliteration:** they begin with the same consonant sound, or with a vowel sound not necessarily the same. (Generally the repetition of a vowel sound is called **assonance.**) Chaucer's triumph was so complete that the older line passed out of use or went underground for centuries, to surface now and then with modifications and to be revived in our own century by Pound, Auden, Wilbur, and others.

In his poem "Junk" (p. 696), Wilbur makes use of the older rhythm, associated as it is with a heroic age of well-made weapons, implements, and furnishings, to lament the shoddy products of our own time, but to honor them too for the elemental goodness of matter. He indicates the half-line division typographically, by dropping the second half-line below the first. If we print the first dozen or so lines in half-lines, as below, we can see that each half has two strong syllables and a random occurrence of weak ones, which may come before, after, or around the strong ones. We can see how three of the four strong syllables in each line alliterate: in the first line, AXE/ANG/ASH; in the second, HELL'S/HAND/HICK. We can see too that syllable count does not matter: the number and placing of the unaccented syllables varies from line to line. This freedom means that many arrangements of stressed and unstressed are possible; in the first 12 half-lines there are 11 different such arrangements.

an	AXE		ANG les
from my	NEIGH bor's		ASH can
it is	HELL'S		HAND iwork
the	WOOD	not	HICK ory
the	FLOW	of the	GRAIN
not	FAITH fully		FOL lowed
the	SHIV ered		SHAFT
	RIS es	from a	SHELL heap
of	PLAS tic		PLAY things
	PA per		PLATES
and the	SHEER		SHARDS
of	SHAT tered		TUM blers
that were	NOT		anNEALED
for the	TIME		NEED ful

This rhythm, which has two big thumps in each half of the line, is quite different in effect from the five more measured *ka-booms* of iambic pentameter.

Wilbur's poem resurrects an obsolete rhythm. The earliest example of it in our anthology is not very early: the fifteenth-century "Swarte-Smeked Smithes," in which the final vowels that were possibly pronounced are not dotted, as they had been in Chaucer's text and elsewhere, because here, pronounced or not, they are of no account to the rhythm. What had happened to the strong-stress rhythm was that even before 1400 writers had been influenced by the regular cadences of Provençal poetry and the Latin hymns of the church. From these sources the brusque Old English line had learned its manners, picked up a lilt, and lost much of its alliteration. The unaccented syllables were no longer quite ignored, but related proportionally to the accented syllables. The very earliest poem we have, dating from about 1200, already has an iambic base:

| | |

Theh thet hi can wittes fule-wis

| | |

of world les bliss e nabbe ic nout . . .

The older rhythm is given an iambic (or logaoedic) lilt also in the four-beat lines of "Ubi Sunt Qui Ante Nos Fuerunt?" (p. 4):

> Whére beth théy   bifóren us wéren
> Hoúndes ládden   and hávekes béren . . .

Lines 3 and 6 of these stanzas is a three-beat line. With this lilt it turns up through the centuries, as in Hardy's "Neutral Tones" (p. 438), and, in our own time, in Ransom's "Bells for John Whiteside's Daughter" (p. 553):

> There was SUCH SPEED   in her LIT tle BOD y
> And SUCH LIGHT ness   in her FOOT FALL
> It is NO WON der   her BROWN STUD y
> As TON ishes US ALL

The fourth line shifts from four to three beats, like the short lines in "Where Beth They. . . ." We hear the same four-beat rhythm in Cummings's "anyone lived in a pretty how town" (p. 595):

> ANY one LIVED   in a PRET ty how TOWN
> With UP so FLOAT ing   MAN y bells DOWN . . .

This would seem to be the prevailing rhythm, although there are individual lines that individuals might read differently.

The interest in stress as more important than syllable ratio had appeared now and then over the centuries. Coleridge thought his "Christabel" (1797–1800) was "founded on a new principle: namely, that of counting in each line the accents, not the syllables." More complicated, and still influential, is the **sprung rhythm** which Gerard Manley Hopkins theorized about and practiced in the 1870s and 1880s in some (but not all) of his poems.

An account of sprung rhythm could be very long and very technical; only enough will be said about it here to enable readers to feel in Hopkins's poems the rhythms he meant to embody there. In his sprung rhythm, Hopkins counted only the accented syllables, but went even further than the Old English system in his disregard for the syllables that were unaccented or that he chose to consider so. In his system, he thought it "a great convenience" to consider the accent as coming first in its foot, as it does in music. For him, then, a foot could consist of a single accented syllable, a trochee ($-\cup$), a dactyl ($-\cup\cup$), or a **first paeon** ($-\cup\cup\cup$); combinations of these made up his "mixed or 'logaoedic' " lines. In addition, he allowed for what he called "hangers" or "outrides," groups of up to three slack (unaccented) syllables which he simply omitted from his metric count. Since there was no way of knowing when an "outride" occurred, or often where an accent was intended (some depended on his highly personal reading of a line), he marked his manuscripts with the equivalent of musical symbols to assist the reader. By *sprung* Hopkins meant *abrupt*; he used the word because his system sometimes brought two accents abruptly together. It might be thought of as sprung too because unstressed syllables were sometimes forced out of the line, as if sprung out, by the pressure of accents around them.

In "Spring and Fall" (p. 448), for example, the second line is perfectly regular trochaic tetrameter:

$$- \cup | - \cup | - \cup | - \cup$$
Over Golden grove un leaving . . .

But in other lines some such words as those bracketed below have been sprung out of the line. Normally the omitted words would buffer the strongly stressed syllables, but when they are omitted, Hopkins said, "the stresses come together and so the rhythm is sprung."

> Márgarét, [and] áre you gríeving . . .
> Leáves, [so] líke the things of man, you . . .
> Áh! [and] ás the heart grows older . . .
> Sórrow's spríngs [,they] áre the same . . .
> (What) heart [had] heard of, ghost [had] guessed . . .
> (It) ís the blight [that] man was born for . . .

With such missing syllables inserted, the poem is heard as regular trochaic tetrameter, especially when we remember that Hopkins permitted lines to be "rove over": that is, when a line seems short (catalectic), the missing syllable is found at the beginning of the next line (line 7 seems to lack a last syllable, which we find in the "Though" of the next line). "What" and "It," in parentheses in the examples above, are "rove over" from the preceding lines.

Hopkins gets a similar effect of abruptness with what he calls "sprung leadings": dropping the unaccented first syllable of a line, as in "Spring" (p. 446):

$$[\cup] - | \cup \cup | - - | \cup - | \cup \qquad -$$
Noth ing is so beau tiful as spring . . .

Such lines in Chaucer, who also used "sprung leadings," are referred to as "headless."

Since the poems of Hopkins that are in sprung rhythm cannot be read with the rhythms he intended unless we follow the rhythmic notations in his manuscripts, these are given below. Unless otherwise indicated, they are as given in *The Poems of Gerard Manley Hopkins*, 4th ed., edited by W. H. Gardner and N. H. MacKenzie, Oxford University Press, 1967.

"The Windhover" (p. 446): "Falling paeonic rhythm, sprung and outriding." *Falling paeonic rhythm* means we can expect to find feet that are $- \cup \cup \cup$; *outriding* means we can expect to find groups of syllables disregarded in the rhythm count—but what these are we might not know except for the poet's manuscript notations. The first line is regular, though "rove over" into "dom of." The next three lines are to be read as follows:

$$\cup \; \cup | - \; \cup \; | - \; \cup \; \cup \; \cup | - \qquad \cup \; | - \cup \; \cup \; \cup | - \cup$$
dom of daylight's dauphin, dapple- dawn-drawn Falcon, in his riding

$$\cup \; \cup | - \quad \cup \cup \cup | - \cup | \quad - \quad \cup \quad \cup \cup | - \quad \cup | - \cup$$
Of the rolling level under neath him steady air, and striding

– ∪ ∪ ∪| – ∪∪ ∪| – ∪∪| – ∪ | –
High there, how he rung upon the rein of a wimpling wing

We do not count "dom of" or "Of the" as feet, since they are "rove over" from the line above. In line 7, "wind" seems to be a monosyllabic foot. The Oxford editors suggest that the accents in line 10 are

– ‾ – ‾ –
Buckle! AND the fire that breaks from thee then, a billion . . .

with "AND" having "extrametrical emphasis."

"Pied Beauty" (p. 447): "Curtal Sonnet: sprung paeonic rhythm." A **curtal sonnet** is one whose proportions resemble those of the 14-line sonnet, "namely 6+4 instead of 8+6, with however a half-line tailpiece (so that the equation is rather $\frac{12}{2} + \frac{9}{2} = \frac{21}{2} = 10\frac{1}{2}$." We might think the rhythm of the poem is

–∪ ∪ ∪| – ∪| – ∪ | –
Glory be to God for dappled things . . .

But since it is a sort of sonnet, with five-beat lines, it has to be

–∪|– ∪| – ∪ | – ∪ | –
Glory be to God for dappled things

With our ear listening for paeons ("cōloŭr aš ă") and monosyllabic feet, we can follow the rhythm easily enough.

"Felix Randal" (p. 447): "Sonnet; sprung and outriding rhythm; six-foot lines." The sonnet is easier to read in rhythm if we notice that the lines of six feet (rather than the usual five) tend to fall into half-lines each having three accents:

– ∪| – ∪ ∪| – ∪ ∪ ∪ ∪‖ – ∪ ∪| – ∪ ∪| – ∪
Felix Randal, the farrier, O is he dead then? my duty all ended . . .

The long third foot adds an extrametrical unaccented syllable (or two) to the first paeon. Presumably one hurries through this foot in the reading.

In line 8, the accents Hopkins intended are:

Téndered to him. Áh well, God rést him áll road éver he offénded!

In line 9, "to" and "too" both have accents. Line 13 begins:

"When thóu't the rándom grim fórge . . ."

Historically, the strong-stress rhythm began as a four-beat line, but we have seen it diversified with three-beat lines as early as the medieval "Ubi Sunt. . . ." Hopkins had used his strong-stress sprung rhythm in lines of five and six feet. We feel the strong-stress principle in any rhythm in which the beat comes from strongly stressed syllables however spaced rather than from a regular alternation of stressed and unstressed syllables.

Elizabeth Bishop's "The Fish" (p. 652) has lines that range, in no order, from four to nine syllables. Clearly then her rhythm is not based on any regular alternation. But the lines do have a pattern of three strong syllables, which we can be sure of in all but about half a dozen lines. A few times she seems to make use of rather weak secondary accents, like those heard faintly on the last syllable of *venerable* and *wavering*. If we arrange the strong syllables of each line in columns, the three-beat form is quite clear.

```
    i  CAUGHT     a tre  MEN dous              FISH
  and  HELD     him be  SIDE           the    BOAT
       HALF    out of  WA ter      with my    HOOK
       FAST     in a  COR ner      of his    MOUTH
       HE            DID n't               FIGHT
   he  HAD n't      FOUGHT           at     ALL
   he  HUNG       a  GRUNT ing             WEIGHT . . .
```

In some half dozen lines the three beats are not heard clearly. Perhaps the poet permits herself a few two-beat lines. Or perhaps the three-beat tempo that prevails makes us treat as emphatic some syllables we might otherwise take too lightly: "Hé dídn't fíght . . . ," "Was líke wáll páper . . . ," "And thén Í sáw . . ." (or "And then Í sáw . . .").

A similar three-beat strong-stress rhythm can be felt in most of the lines of James Dickey's "Cherrylog Road" (p. 707):

```
off HIGH way   ONE o SIX
at CHER rylog   ROAD i ENT ered . . .
```

IV

SYLLABIC VERSE

The rhythmical systems we have reviewed so far recognize that there are two kinds of syllables: high-energy (accented) syllables and low-energy (unaccented) ones. Rhythms are made out of waves of more and less. This is possible in English because the energy levels really do show a noticeable difference. Other languages allot their energy much more evenly. In French, which is not strongly accented, the standard verse line is the alexandrine, thought of as a line of twelve syllables rather than as a pattern of alternations. In Japanese, in which there is little stress accent, verse lines can be measured by number of syllables alone, so that it is natural for the Japanese to write **haiku**, their 17-syllable poems in which the three lines have 5, 7, and 5 syllables.

In the last half-century or so, a number of poets writing in English have been measuring their lines by syllable count alone, with no regard for accent—except of course the regard even a good prose writer would have in order to avoid tongue-twisting combinations. Though there were earlier attempts at **syllabics**, as it is called, Marianne Moore was its first distinguished practitioner. The original version of her "Poetry" (p. 544), dated 1919, shows what became her characteristic form. Her stanzas look alike on the page; they are far more alike than they look. The correspondence is mathematically exact between corresponding lines of the stanzas: the first line of each has 19 syllables; the second, 22; the third, 11; the fourth, 5; the fifth, 8; the sixth, 13. There are no exceptions. We might think all the poet had to do was write prose, then chop it into pieces after the nineteenth syllable, the forty-first syllable, and so on. But if she had done that, some lines would have ended in the middle of a word that had more than one syllable. This never happens—except with the word *baseball*, which is really two words combined. In most of her poems (though not in "A Grave") Miss Moore uses a system of syllabic count; when irregularities are found, it is likely to be because she later revised a version originally exact.

The system in itself allows no opportunity for effects of interplay or counterpoint, though a writer may establish accentual over-rhythms or interesting prose rhythms. Since there is little rhythmical expectation in syllable count, there is little rhythmical surprise. Looking at such poetry on the page, readers no doubt feel a pleasant sense of form and control, though they are not likely to apprehend its source with any precision. Though we can all learn, rather easily, to follow five-beat accentual lines, none of us, just by listening, can tell a 19-syllable line from a 22-syllable one. Accent can affect meaning and convey emotion; syllable-count cannot. Syllabic rhythms, therefore, are of more value to the writer than the reader in that they give a reassuring framework within which to work and the certainty of knowing what formal obligations come next; they make the poet look more carefully at words—and syllables!—than otherwise; they prevent one from just putting down, without regard for limit, anything that floats up, trash or treasure, from the uncritical subconscious. Syllabic discipline—though it may leave the reader unaffected—makes the writer a more scrupulous writer.

Many contemporary poets have found it satisfactory. Auden's "In Memory of Sigmund Freud" (p. 629) has 4-line stanzas in which the first two lines have 11 syllables, the third 9 syllables, and the fourth 10 syllables. Out of its more than 100 lines, four or five seem irregular by a syllable; some apparent irregularities are resolved by pronunciations like *obed-yence* and *mis-ra-ble*. The difference between syllabic and accentual rhythms can be felt if we try to read his 10-syllable lines as iambic pentameter. Very few fit; avoiding the familiar cadence cannot have been easy. Auden's "Ode to Terminus" (p. 635), written 30 years later, has the same syllable count; it is off the mark by perhaps two syllables out of over 600.

Dylan Thomas, in his "Fern Hill" (p. 674), has a more complicated syllabic pattern. The first 7 lines of his 9-line stanzas have the following number of syllables: 14, 14, 9, 6, 9, 14, 14. The last two lines are either 7,9 or 9,6. The 14-syllable lines twice seem too long by a syllable; one of these can be normalized if we elide "the apple" into "th'apple." Many recent poets have preferred simpler syllabic structures to those used by Moore, Auden, and Thomas. In particular they favor short-line poems with five or seven syllables to the line.

V

BLANK VERSE

So far we have been investigating the micro-units of rhythm: the syllables and their organization (by alternating energies or simply by number) into the larger units we call lines. But lines cannot flow on forever; as waves of water confine themselves to pools, ponds, lakes, lagoons, etc., so waves of rhythm confine themselves to the various enclosures we can now enumerate.

The commonest and most serviceable all-purpose framework is **blank verse**, as unrhymed iambic pentameter is called. (Blank verse is not at all the same as free verse, which we will come to later.) Used in the thousands of lines of Elizabethan and Jacobean drama, in *Paradise Lost*, and many other poems, blank verse is closer to actual speech than any other metrically based rhythm; we have already shown the many ways in which it can be diversified. It first appears prominently in our anthology in Wordsworth's "Tintern Abbey" (p. 248), the selections from "The Prelude" (p. 264), and Coleridge's "conversation poem" "Frost at Midnight" (p. 286). The great Victorians made frequent use of it, as Tennyson does in "Ulysses" (p. 356) and "Tithonus" (p. 357), and as Browning does in "The Bishop Orders His Tomb . . ." (p. 369) and often elsewhere. It continues a favorite form of many twentieth-century poets; examples include Yeats's "The Second Coming" (p. 464); Frost's "Mending Wall" (p. 488); and Stevens's "The Man on the Dump" (p. 510). Stevens, while using unrhymed iambic pentameter, likes to give a further idea of order by organizing it into stanzalike divisions (frequently given numbers) of the same length, as in the 15-line verse paragraphs of "Sunday Morning" (p. 504) or in such three-line units as those in "Final Soliloquy of the Interior Paramour" (p. 513). Except for a few scattered end-rhymes, "The Idea of Order at Key West" (p. 508) is in blank verse.

RHYME AND RHYMING STANZA FORMS

Most of the forms we are now going to discuss are earmarked—marked for the ear—by a structure of **rhyme**, which is found in the poems and folksongs of nearly all cultures in all centuries, in languages as different as Chinese, Provençal, Persian, and Swahili. Psychologically, rhyme satisfies an expectation, completes a circle by bringing us back to where we started. In rhyming verse, we wait for the rhyme as we wait for the other shoe to drop. When it comes, it can mark a break or conclusion: Shakespeare often ends scenes in blank verse with two lines that rhyme—they are as conclusive as a curtain falling.

We have rhyme whenever two words, often in parallel or emphatic positions, are identical in their last accented vowel-sound and whatever follows it, but have some difference just before that accented sound: *bright/light, ohm/home, candy/dandy, liquor/quicker, delightfully/frightfully, dieter/rioter, Zenobia/phobia, odium/podium, dopiness/soapiness, cozily/Rosalie, intellectual/henpecked you all* (Byron), *interpolate them/purple ate them* (Ogden Nash). When rhyme is on an accented syllable with no syllable after it, it is called **masculine rhyme**; when on an accented syllable followed by an unaccented one, **feminine rhyme**. The terms are not discriminatory; they come from the fact that, in French, words often add an *e* (heard as a weak syllable in versification) to the feminine form: *blanc/blanche, noir/noire*. Alterations of masculine and feminine rhymes are pleasant, as in "The Gypsy Laddie" (p. 44), Gay's "'Twas When the Seas Were Roaring" (p. 199), and the first and third stanzas of Roethke's "My Papa's Waltz" (p. 640).

End-rhyme is the common type: rhyme at the end of lines. **Internal rhyme** occurs within the line, as in

Once upon a midnight dreary, while I pondered, weak and weary . . .

or as in the fifth line of each stanza in Clough's "Natura Naturans" (p. 381):

As rose to rose that by it blows . . .

When lines are end-stopped, the rhyme is heard clearly, since it has a brief silence in which to reverberate. In run-on lines it is less conspicuous, as in Browning's "My Last Duchess" (p. 367). In line 2 we read "call" so quickly that we hardly notice it rhymes with "wall" above it. Robert Lowell's "After the Surprising Conversions" (p. 680) shows a similar use of rhyme. When the lines of a poem are of uneven length, the rhymes far apart, rhyme can also be muted, subdued, as it is in Auden's "Musée des Beaux Arts" (p. 626). In few poets is the presence of rhyme so well camouflaged as in some of the poems of Marianne Moore. Few readers of "A Carriage from Sweden" (p. 550) will notice that in the first line of each stanza the third syllable (in one line the fourth) rhymes with the last one: *there/air, may/away*, and so on, or that in the last line of each stanza the first and last syllables rhyme: *some-/home, in-/vein, A-/decay*.

Among the poets who have used rhyme in an individual way is John Skelton, for whom **Skeltonic** verse has been named. In "Upon a Dead Man's Head" (p. 35) the "tumbling verse," whose two-beat lines are mainly in couplets, scrambles on through as many additional rhymes as Skelton can think of or find a use for: beginning with line 18 there are seven rhymes on *el*. May Swenson does something similar in "The Watch" (p. 690), though she repeats entire words instead of rhyming syllables.

The *some-/home* and *in-vein* rhyme of Marianne Moore is an example of *imperfect rhyme*. (The perfect rhyme, or *full rhyme*, for *some* is *hum*, not *home*; for *in* is *vin*, not *vein*.) Called also **off-rhyme**, slant rhyme, oblique rhyme, half rhyme, near rhyme, it differs from perfect rhyme in changing the vowel sound (or the concluding consonants) that perfect rhyme demands. Emily Dickinson, though in her earliest poems she rhymes perfectly, came to prefer the little dissonance of off-rhyme, which she uses so frequently it becomes a characteristic. In "I Dreaded That First Robin So" (p. 422), there is only one perfect rhyme: *see/me*. The others are all off-rhymes: *gown/own, plumes/drums,* etc. She also considered all vowels as rhyming with one another: *now/though, by/me, away/ me*. In some of her poems, the rhymes will seem very far off to an ear used to traditional rhyming: *refined/ashamed, heel/pearl, ring/sun, death/earth*. She could have found a precedent for off-rhyme in earlier poets; Emerson, for example, has quite a bit of it in his "Ode" (p. 338): *horse/purse, chattel/saddle, woods/solitudes*. Twentieth-century poets feel free to employ it at will. Yeats makes an increasing use of it; in "Under Ben Bulben" (p. 475) we hear such rhymes as *spoke/lake, knew/a-crow, won/dawn*. In Cummings's "being to timelessness as it's to time" (p. 597), all the lines end with off-rhymes except for the last two; many poets still prefer to end a poem with the conclusiveness of full rhyme. In "Speak" (p. 733), James Wright calls attention to his self-consciously expressive use of off-rhyme.

Rhyme, involving expectations that can be teased and frustrated, can also be comic, as it often is in Byron's "Don Juan" (p. 296) and in the poems of Ogden Nash in our century (p. 610).

If we end-rhyme two adjoining lines of iambic pentameter, we get the commonest form of **couplet**. First used consistently by Chaucer, it has never been long out of favor. In Jonson's "On My First Son" (p. 105), "To Heaven" (p. 106), and other poems, it tends to be more of a self-contained unit than in Chaucer, in whose work the narrative sense runs on from couplet to couplet, with no particular inclination to pause at the end of every two lines. The tendency shown in Jonson is stronger in Herrick, in whose "The Argument of His Book" (p. 116) we find that a sentence ends with every two lines. The couplet reached its tightest and trimmest form in the "closed," or self-contained, couplets of Pope, in which the inner dynamics of sense and syntax often balanced half-line against half-line or line against line, as we easily see in the first eight lines of "An Essay on Criticism" (p. 200). The couplet, as used by Dryden and Pope, is called the **heroic couplet,** from its employment in translations of the heroic poems of antiquity, such as Chapman's *Odyssey* (c. 1614), Dryden's *Aeneid* (1697), and Pope's *Iliad* and *Odyssey* (1715–1720; 1725–1726). We find such couplets in the work of the first two American poets in this anthology, Anne Bradstreet (p. 149) and Edward Taylor ("Preface," p. 187). Less in vogue in the nineteenth century, they still occur in Clare's "Badger" (p. 316) and—more freely—in J. R. Lowell's "Tempora Mutantur" (p. 385). Though it is a little rigid for modern taste, twentieth-century poets return to it now and then without embarrassment. Examples: Frost's "Once by the Pacific" (p. 493); Margaret Avison's "Hiatus" (p. 686—modernized by off-rhyme and given a concluding fourteener); and Thom Gunn's "Moly" (p. 738—in which the couplets are spaced separately as units). Although the Chaucerian and heroic couplets are in iambic pentameter, couplets can be of other lengths and in other meters. In our selection we have quite a few poems in tetrameter couplets, among them Marvell's "To His Coy Mistress" (p. 163).

As meters are represented by the symbols of scansion, rhyme schemes are represented by letters, with a different letter for each sound. Rhyming couplets would be *aabbccdd* and so on. The simplest way to bind lines in units of three (each unit called a **tercet**) is to rhyme them *aaa, bbb*, etc., as in Herrick's "Upon Julia's Clothes" (p. 120), Kipling's "Harp Song of the Dane Women" (p. 457), or Frost's "Provide, Provide" (p. 494).

a
b
a
b
c
b
c
d
c
etc.

A three-line unit with a more illustrious history is **terza rima** ("rhyme in threes"), in which the middle line of each tercet becomes the first and third line of the following one, as in the scheme to the left, until the passage or poem concludes with a couplet. The forward momentum of the linked tercets is put to powerful use in Dante's *Divine Comedy.* We have examples in Shelley's "Ode to the West Wind" (p. 310) and Frost's "Acquainted with the Night" (p. 493).

The unit of four lines, called a **quatrain,** is the commonest stanza-form in English. (**Stanza,** the name for one of the generally identical sections of a poem, is an Italian word which means *room, compartment, place to stop.*) Our oldest form is probably the medieval **carol,** originally associated with dancing in a circle. Stanzas in a carol have three rhyming tetrameter lines and a fourth line that rhymes with a two-line **refrain** (a phrase, line, or group of lines repeated at regular intervals). "Another Year" (p. 27) is an example of a carol. Originally the carol had no necessary association with Christmas, although quite a few Christmas songs were carols.

When in iambic pentameter and rhyming *abab,* the quatrain is called a **heroic stanza,** as in Gray's "Elegy . . . " (p. 224) or in Rochester's "The Disabled Debauchee" (p. 191), in which the "heroic" form is used ironically. Another iambic pentameter quatrain is the **Omar Khayyám stanza,** which Fitzgerald uses (p. 394); with an *x* to indicate an unrhymed line, the scheme is *aaxa,* although an occasional stanza is found in monorhyme *(aaaa),* like that in Rossetti's four-beat "The Woodspurge" (p. 416).

The commonest quatrain in English is the **ballad stanza,** in which the old fourteener breaks down into lines of four and three beats rhyming *xaxa* or *abab.* Early examples: "Western Wind" (p. 30); "Sir Patrick Spens" (p. 37); and most, but not all, of the ballads in quatrains that follow. Throughout the course of English poetry this has remained one of the most popular of stanza forms. Representative examples: Cowper's "Epitaph on a Hare" (p. 234); Burns's "A Red, Red Rose" (p. 247); Wordsworth's "She Dwelt Among the Untrodden Ways" (p. 251); Landor's "Rose Aylmer" (p. 290); Emily Bronte's "Song" (p. 379); Emily Dickinson's "I Dreaded that First Robin, So" (p. 422—and most of the other Dickinson poems in our selection—it was by far her favorite form); Hardy's "The Oxen" (p. 444); and Frost's "Her Word" (in "The Hill Wife," p. 490). Hardy in "Drummer Hodge" (p. 438) adds two additional lines to give us *ababab;* Yeats adds two lines in "A Last Confession" to give *xaxaxa.* Several poets have run two ballad stanzas together to give *ababcdcd,* as in Daniel's "Ulysses and the Siren" (p. 75) and Hardy's "The Darkening Thrush" (p. 439).

The ballad stanza is often used in hymns; it is the **Common Meter** or C.M. of the hymnbooks. When the first line is shortened to a trimeter to match lines 2 and 4, it is known as **Short Meter** or S.M. Examples of S.M. are : Gascoigne's "And If I Did, What Then?" (p. 53); Dickinson's "The Bustle in a House" (p. 427); and Hardy's "I Look into My Glass" (p. 438) and "The Man He Killed" (p. 441). "Loving Mad Tom" (p. 110) is written in stanzas of doubled S.M. When lines 2 and 4 of C.M. are lengthened to tetrameters, we have the **Long Meter** or L.M. of the hymnbooks. Examples: "Thomas Rymer" (p. 39); "Waly, Waly" (p. 43); and Hardy, "Channel Firing" (p. 443). Yeats uses L.M. doubled *(ababcdcd)* in "September 1913" (p. 459).

Another quatrain in tetrameters is called the **"In Memoriam" stanza** from its use in Tennyson's poem (p. 360). The rhyme-scheme is *abba.* Five-line stanzas do not commonly have a name. Often they are made up by adding an *a* or *b* rhyme to an *abab* quatrain.

Among six-line stanzas, a quatrain followed by a couplet *(ababcc)* in iambic pentameter is called the **Venus and Adonis stanza,** from Shakespeare's use of it in his poem of that name. We have seen many examples, among them: "Tichborne's Elegy" (p. 72), Munday's "I Serve a Mistress" (p. 74), and "Thule, the Period of Cosmography" (p. 94). Robert Burns gave his name to the **Burns stanza,** used in "To a Mouse" (p. 246); it rhymes *aaabab,* with the *a*-lines tetrameter and the *b*-lines dimeter. For his "Dream Songs" (p. 670), John Berryman devised what we might call the "Berryman stanza"; each of the "songs" has typically three six-line stanzas, with lines 1, 2, 4, and 5 iambic pentameter, lines 3 and 6 shorter, with various combinations of rhyme. In our selection, "So Long? Stevens," represents the norm; the others are freer than most in departing from it. Lowell's "Skunk Hour" (p. 681) also has six-line stanzas in which the line-length varies; rhyme is used, but unpredictably, though in four of the seven stanzas the first and last lines rhyme.

Of seven-line stanzas, the best known is **rhyme royal,** thought to be so called because used by King James I of Scotland in his "The Kingis Quair" ("The King's Book," 1423–1424). The rhyme scheme: *ababbcc*—the Venus and Adonis stanza with a third *b* inserted. We see an example in the "Hyd, Absolon" (p. 17) of Chaucer, who also used it in his long *Troilus and Criseyde.* Other early examples are Skelton's "My Darling Dear, My Daisy Flower" (p. 36) and Wyatt's "They Flee from Me . . ." (p. 48). Nearly 300 years later we find Wordsworth retrieving it for his "Resolution and Independence" (p. 253) with the novelty of a final alexandrine (p. 798). Auden uses it, rather ironically, to describe the world of our century in the longer-line stanzas of "The Shield of Achilles" (p. 634), a poem interesting also as showing how two different stanza forms within the same poem can dramatize two kinds of material, two emotional states, etc.

We have seen some examples of eight-line stanzas which are made up of two four-line units. Many other eight-line combinations are possible. One of the best known derives from the Italian poets; the Italian name **ottava rima** (rhyme in eights) is still used for its *abababcc* rhyme scheme. The final couplet permits a witty twist after the linked rhyming of the first six lines; Byron found the form, with its narrative and satiric possibilities, congenial for his "Don Juan" (p. 296). Yeats used it for some of his greatest poems, including such philosophical lyrics as "Sailing to Byzantium" (p. 467) and "Among School Children" (p. 468).

The only nine-line stanza which has a name is the **Spenserian stanza,** which Spenser devised for his "The Faerie Queene" (1589–1596): *ababbcbcc,* eight iambic pentameter lines with a concluding alexandrine. (If Spenser had known Dunbar's "Done Is a Battell . . .," p. 31, he could simply have added an alexandrine to it.) Keats uses the Spenserian stanza in "The Eve of St. Agnes" (p. 327); Byron and Shelley were also fond of it. A number of twentieth-century poets have enjoyed keeping it alive.

RECOMBINANT STANZA FORMS

Beyond nine lines, there are no fixed stanza forms, but poets are free to range among the possibilities, innovating as their fancy chooses. Generally the poet does not so much create as reassemble out of the modules already described: couplets, tercets, and quatrains rhyming *abab* or *abba.* With various line-lengths available, poets have an endless supply of new stanza forms at their disposal. Here are a few examples of how older verse forms can be recycled.

Shirley's "The Glories of Our Blood and State" (p. 131): Shirley has taken the Venus and Adonis stanza, contracted its lines to tetrameter, added two short rhyming lines between quatrain and couplet—and come up with a new look in stanza forms.

Traherne's "Wonder" (p. 183): the poet begins with what sounds like a ballad stanza, but surprises us by writing a third line which is not the expected tetrameter rhyming (if at all) with line 1, but a pentameter rhyming with line 2! He closes the off-balance *abba* with a tetrameter. He then writes another pentameter, but follows it this time not with a tetrameter, as just before, but with a trimeter. Then he completes his *abab* with another trimeter and a dimeter. Surprise after surprise, achieved by varying the line-length of familiar elements.

Arnold's "The Scholar Gypsy" (p. 407): to build up his ten-line stanza, Arnold has taken a heroic quatrain and enclosed it in *a* rhymes, which are five lines apart: *abcbca*. The second *a* is a trimeter; every other line a pentameter. He concludes the stanza with another quatrain, this time with the *abba* pattern instead of the *abab* one. So the ten-line stanza is made up of two quatrains of different kinds, with an off-balance couplet enclosing one of them.

Yeats's "Prayer for my Daughter" (p. 465): the stanza is made up of two mutant quatrains—the first begins as the heroic *abab* but curtails the fourth line by a foot. The second quatrain has the *abba* module, but its two middle lines are short.

Roethke's "I Knew a Woman . . ." (p. 649): a mutant rhyme royal, with *ababccc* instead of *ababbcc*.

Few recombinant stanza forms are as elaborate as the one Spenser devised for his "Prothalamion" (p. 56). In his 18-line stanza, in pentameters and trimeters, with often three or more rhymes on the same sound, we find units of *abab*, *abba*, and couplets.

NON-STANZAIC RHYMING

Instead of writing in matched stanzas, a poet may prefer a continuity that moves, without stanza or sections, from beginning to end of the poem, a continuity assured by continuous rhyming, but in no foreseeable pattern. Milton's "Lycidas" (p. 141) is a classic of this nature. All of the lines except about ten are mortared in by end-rhyme, although some of the rhymes, extending over many lines, may escape our notice. Basically the line is iambic pentameter, varied by about a dozen trimeters, nearly all in the first half of the poem—as intensity mounts, the trimeters are phased out. We cannot be sure in advance where the rhymes will come, but when they do come we see they often initiate, sustain, or complete a familiar figure: there are many *abab*'s and *abba*'s, many couplets. Generally uncommitted to definite patterns, the poem closes with the formality of eight lines in ottava rima: *abababcc*. If we had been listening closely, we would have heard another ottava rima in lines 124–131.

The orchestration of "Lycidas" is unusually rich; poems that employ more modestly a similar procedure are Marvell's "On a Drop of Dew" (p. 161) and Coleridge's "Kubla Khan" (p. 288). In Coleridge's poem the tetrameters and pentameters occur in blocks instead of being distributed. A skillful miniature of the method is Patmore's "Magna Est Veritas" (p. 414), with its line of from two to five feet rhyming *ababccdede*. Arnold's "Dover Beach" (p. 406) is similar in procedure, but with freer patterns of rhyming and more amplitude.

THE ODE

With poems as elaborately structured as "Lycidas" and "Prothalamion," we come close to the kind of poem called an **ode**, which might be defined as a lyric poem (a poem, that is, expressing strong personal emotion) about exalted persons, or momentous events or occasions, or lofty themes, in an elaborately ceremonious manner. One type of English ode—the **Pindaric ode**—was thought of as deriving from the style of the Greek poet Pindar (522–442 B.C.); it was irregular, spontaneous, impulsive in the variety of its unpatterned stanzas, with line-length of several sorts and intricate rhyme in no set pattern. The other type, the **Horatian ode,** thought of as deriving from the practice of the Roman poet

Horace (65–8 B.C.), was likely to be more reasoned, less enraptured, and in relatively simple identical stanzas.

An example of the Pindaric type is Dryden's "A Song for St. Cecilia's Day" (p. 180), with its seven sections, no two alike, and its "Grand Chorus." Line-length and meter vary to fit the spirit of each section and to imitate the kind of music described; rhyming is intricate, with alternations of masculine and feminine rhymes; in the second section, nine lines rhyme on only two sounds.

The most celebrated of English Pindaric odes is Wordsworth's "Ode: Intimations of Immortality . . ." (p. 257). Of the 11 sections, no two have the same pattern; they range from 8 to 39 iambic lines, from dimeter to hexameter. The structuring of the rhyme makes use of the same modules as we have seen in "Lycidas" and other poems: the first section, for example, has an *abab(a)* unit and one of *abba*.

Although the emotional nature of the romantic odes of Shelley to the west wind (p. 310) and of Keats to the nightingale, to melancholy, to autumn, and on the Grecian urn (pp. 322 ff.) allies them to the Pindaric model, the regularity of their stanzaic pattern comes closer to the Horatian ideal. Shelley's poem, as we have noticed, is in terza rima. The stanzaic pattern of the four odes by Keats is not only identical within each poem, but very similar among all four: three have 10-line stanzas, one an 11-line stanza, all stanzas beginning with the very same 7-line arrangement: *ababcde*. In two of the odes, the *cde* is repeated, to conclude the stanza. In another, it is varied—by not much—to *dce*. In the fourth an eleventh line is added: *dcce*. The ten-line stanzas are like a sonnet half English, half Italian (see sonnet, below) with an omitted quatrain. Keats apparently had almost none of the Pindaric love of variety.

Closer to the Roman model is Marvell's "An Horatian Ode upon Cromwell's Return from Ireland" (p. 167), in which the stanzas even have something of the look of the four-line Alcaic strophes (stanzas) in which many of Horace's odes were written. Marvell's rhythm is not Horace's (of which we will say something below); for the complicated Latin meters he substitutes rhyming tetrameter and trimeter couplets. Collins has a similar stanza form in his "Ode to Evening" (p. 228), but with pentameter instead of tetrameter and no rhyme. Milton had used the same form in translating Horace's Pyrrha ode (I, v).

Many English poets have attempted to transpose the rhythms of Greek and Latin poetry into English. The difficulty is that classical poetry and English poetry have quite different metrical bases: the first is paced by length of syllable, not by accent; the second by accent, not length of syllable. Isaac Watts's "The Day of Judgement" (p. 198) describes itself as "An Ode Attempted in English Sapphics." The **Sapphic stanza,** used by the Greek poet Sappho (about 600 B.C.) and by the Latin poets Catullus and Horace five centuries later, consists of three lines with this metrical pattern:

$$- \;\cup \,| \;- \;\; - \;\; | \; - \;\| \;\cup \;\;\; \cup \,|-\cup| \;- \;\; \cup$$
When the fierce north wind   with his airy forces . . .

and one line with this one:

$$- \;\; \cup \;\cup \,| \;- \;\;\; \cup$$
Rushing a main down . . .

In English, the long (–) and short (∪) syllables have to be turned into accented and unaccented ones. Watts has caught the rhythm perfectly in his first line: the strong syllables fall just where they should when we read the line naturally. All of his short lines are correctly done. Many of the longer lines, however, do not fit the classical pattern. If we look at line 2 against its model line we see:

$$- \; \cup \, | - \; - | - \| \cup \, \cup | - \; \cup \, | - \cup$$
Rears up the Bal tic to a foaming fury . . .

But there is no way we can pretend that "the" deserves an accent or could be considered long. Nor could we say *Bál-tíc* today. There is a similar "the" in line 9, and throughout the poem quite a few weak, unaccented syllables that have to be aggrandized to fit the Sapphic pattern. But Watts admits that his metrical scheme is "attempted"—better to just read the poem without insisting on exactitude. In his "Lines Written During a Period of Insanity" (p. 235), Cowper also attempted English Sapphics—with similar results. Most readers will not think of metrical correctness in reading this powerful poem.

FIXED-FORM POEMS

We have now contemplated the various shapes which stanzas can take, and the way in which stanzaic elements can be integrated into a poem that (like "Lycidas") has a continuity not broken into stanzaic segments. There are also prescribed patterns (like the regulations that govern a game) not just for stanzas but for whole poems. The ones to be found in this anthology include the **roundel**, the **sonnet**, the **sestina**, and the **villanelle**. All except perhaps the first are alive in the practice of some of the best contemporary poets.

A	A
B1	B
B2	b
a	a
b	b
A	b
B1	A
	B
a	a
b	b
b	b
A	a
B1	A
B2	B

The **roundel,** as Chaucer calls it, is a short poem of from 8 to 14 lines in which the first line or lines recur as a refrain in the middle and at the end. With capital letters to indicate lines repeated in the refrain, Chaucer's rhyme-scheme (as in "Now Welcom, Somer," p. 16, and "Merciles Beautée," p. 17) is indicated in the first column to the left. It is not clear from Chaucer's manuscripts exactly how many lines are to be repeated. The form used by Charles d'Orléans (p. 27) is a little different, as indicated in the second column. A simple early form was AB aA ab AB, revived by Robert Bridges as the *triolet* and much used for light verse toward the end of the nineteenth century.

The **sonnet** derives its name from the Italian *sonetto,* which means a "little sound." In its original sense, the word might be used of any short poem: Donne's *Songs and Sonnets* contains no sonnet in the accepted sense of the word. Originating in Italy in the thirteenth century, the sonnet spread, in the following centuries, throughout Europe and even beyond. It assumed several forms.

The **Italian** (or Petrarchan) **sonnet,** as written by Dante (1265–1321) and Petrarch (1304–1374), is made up of an *octave* (eight-line unit) and a *sestet* (six-line unit) with the octave rhyming always as at the left and the sestet rhyming as indicated or in other ways that do not end with a couplet.

a
b
b
a
a
b
b
a

c c
d d
e c
c d
d c
e d

Examples of the classic Italian scheme in English iambic pentameter (the standard sonnet line) can be seen in Milton's "On the Late Massacre in Piedmont" (p. 145) and "On His Blindness" (p. 146); in Wordsworth's "The World Is Too Much with Us" (p. 253) and "Composed upon Westminster Bridge" (p. 256) (but not in his "Surprised by Joy . . . ," p. 262, which has the easier *abbaacca,* as often in Wordsworth); in Hunt's "The Fish, the Man, and the Spirit" (p. 292); in Keats's "On First Looking into Chapman's Homer" (p. 320); in Robinson's "The Sheaves" (p. 485); and in Berryman's "Sigh as It Ends . . ." (p. 669), with a parenthetical line between the thirteenth and fourteenth. Many of the earlier English writers of Italian sonnets found a final couplet desirable, as in Wyatt's "Whoso List to Hunt" (p. 48); Sidney's "With How Sad Steps . . ." (p. 69), and the two sonnets of his that follow it; and Donne's three "Holy Sonnets" (p. 103).

Since there are far more vowel sounds in English than in Italian (in which *a*, for example, is always pronounced *ah*, whereas we pronounce it in three or four ways), and hence fewer words to each sound, it is harder to find rhyming words in English than in Italian. The Italian sonnet demands four rhymes on its *a* and *b* sounds; English writers developed a form of the sonnet that allowed words to rhyme only in pairs. Known as the **English** (or Elizabethan or Shakespearean) **sonnet,** it has a rhyme scheme made up of three quatrains and a concluding couplet, as indicated at the left. Surrey was the first to use it; see his "Set Me Whereas the Sun . . ." (p. 50). We find it in all of Shakespeare's sonnets (p. 80 ff.). Other examples: Keats's "When I Have Fears . . ." (p. 320) and "Bright Star! . . ." (p. 322); the sonnets of Jones Very (p. 320 ff.); Frost's "Never Again Would Birds' Song . . ." (p. 376); and, with off-rhyme, in "being to timelessness . . ." (p. 598) of E. E. Cummings, who reckoned the sonnet among his favorite forms.

(rhyme scheme at left: a b a b c d c d e f e f g g)

The **Spenserian sonnet,** which, with its rhyme-linked quatrains, resembles the Spenserian stanza, was invented by Spenser. The rhyme scheme is to the left; the three sonnets from *Amoretti* (p. 55) are examples. Twelve lines of terza rima followed by a couplet are called a terza rima sonnet; the 14-line sections of Shelley's "Ode to the West Wind" (p. 310) might be thought of as sonnets.

(rhyme scheme at left: a b a b b c b c c d c d e e)

Poets have always felt free to take liberties with the sonnet, while abiding by its essential structure. Sidney's "Loving in Truth . . ." (p. 69) is a sonnet in alexandrines, in the French fashion. Hopkins's "Felix Randal, the Farrier . . ." (p. 447) is also in six-beat lines—and "sprung" ones at that. There and elsewhere Hopkins prefers the stricter Italian form. He also wrote what he called "Curtal Sonnets," described in our treatment of *sprung rhythm.* Meredith was another poet who, in his *Modern Love* (p. 415), changed the proportions of the sonnet; joining four of the Italian *abba* units, each with its own rhyme, he produced 16-line "sonnets." His later "Lucifer in Starlight" (p. 416) preserves the regular Italian form.

The four sonnets of Tuckerman (p. 405), all beginning with the Italian *abba,* take off on their own for the rest of the 14 lines. Many other sonnets— some among the most celebrated—have broken with the traditional rhyme schemes. A few examples: Shelley's "Ozymandias" (p. 310); Yeats's "Leda and the Swan" (p. 467); Tate's "Sonnets at Christmas" (p. 608); and Gwendolyn Brooks's "The Rites for Cousin Vit" (p. 684). It seems that the sonnet, though appearing so rigid, is not yet, after all these centuries, a totally closed form.

Of even more ancient lineage than the sonnet is the **sestina** (which means something like "poem in sixes"), invented by a Provençal poet in the twelfth century. Instead of repeating sounds, as in rhyming forms, it repeats entire words. Though a favorite of quite a few modern poets, no modern sestinas happen to be represented here. We do have, however, a *double sestina* from Elizabethan days, Sidney's "Ye Goatherd Gods" (p. 67), which has 12 stanzas instead of the usual 6. In a sestina, the six words that end the lines in the first stanza also end the lines in the second, in a different order; in the third, in a yet different order; and so on through the poem. They are shifted in accordance with a definite formula. If we number the end-words of the first stanza from 1 to 6, then their order becomes, in the second stanza, 6, 1, 5, 2, 4, 3—the last word of the first stanza, that is, becomes the first of the second, the first of the first stanza becomes the second of the second, the next-to-last becomes the third, and so on. The diagram shows the path we follow to get the arrangement of the words for the second stanza. We

```
A1
b
A2
a
b
A1
a
b
A2
a
b
A1
a
b
A2
a
b
A1
A2
```

follow the same process with the words of the second stanza to get the words for the third, and so on through the poem, which concludes with a three-line *envoi* (or envoy), a kind of summary or finale which uses all six words in their original order, three of them in mid-line.

A 19-line poem on only two rhymes, the **villanelle,** originally Italian, was transplanted to France in the sixteenth century and became a favorite light-verse vehicle in England in the nineteenth. Like the roundel, it repeats entire lines, in accordance with the pattern at the left. (The capital letters mean that the whole line is repeated.) Frivolous as its past has been, the villanelle has been taken seriously by some of the best twentieth-century poets, who have used it with earnestness and passion. Examples: Empson's "Missing Dates" (p. 624); Roethke's "The Waking" (p. 648); Elizabeth Bishop's "One Art" (p. 656); and Dylan Thomas's "Do Not Go Gentle into That Good Night" (p. 675).

VI

FREE VERSE

Some would be inclined to characterize **free verse** — in tones of dislike, satisfaction, or defiance—as "none of the above." Though the term is a relative one—how free is *free?*—free verse has liberated itself from what its practitioners would regard as the restraints, shackles, and strait-jackets of rhyme, fixed form, prescribed line-length, and regular meter—precisely those elements which a number of other poets would regard as the bone and muscle of poetry.

Nearly every good poet has felt that he or she, and not the verse form, was the master. Richard Rolle's fourteenth-century "Ghostly Gladness" (p. 16) is as free as modern free verse; as written, it is actually what we would call a prose poem. In "The Collar" (p. 128), written in the 1630s, Herbert proclaims that his "lines and life are free," and his poem, with its irregularities of line-length and rhyme, is working toward free verse. In "Jubilate Agno" (p. 229), written about 1760, Christopher Smart may be seen as anticipating Whitman in naturalizing the long lines (called *versets*) of such poetic books of the Old Testament as the Psalms. Swift had also written verse in long free lines, mostly with comic intent.

Any verse that seems to discard the accepted measures will seem like free verse to a reader who accepts those measures as proper for poetry. The prevalence of free verse in our time makes it seem new; to some conventional readers of poetry it may seem more novel, and more lawless, than in fact it is. For those who have grown up accustomed to it, it needs neither explanation nor defense; free verse is the accepted measure for many writers of poetry today. Some of our best poets, it is true, have had little or no interest in it, among them Yeats, Frost, Robinson, Hart Crane, Marianne Moore, Stevens (in most poems), Auden, and Elizabeth Bishop. But still much excellent work has been done in it.

Quite a few different kinds of writing have been swept together into the bins of free verse. Perhaps we could simplify its nature by looking at the practice of four poets—not in chronological order, but in the degree of their departure from traditional procedure.

1. **T. S. Eliot.** Some poetry which is called free verse carries the already

accepted freedoms a step beyond what had been allowed before. Eliot's "The Love Song of J. Alfred Prufrock" (p. 556) is an example. To those who read it in *Poetry* in 1915—those whose ears were still attuned to the rhythms of Tennyson—young Eliot's poem probably seemed free verse. The lines were not the same length, for one thing. Milton, of course, had varied his line-length in "Lycidas," but not often, and all he did was shift from five feet into three. An eight-beat line in "Lycidas"?—unthinkable. Arnold in "Dover Beach" (p. 406) had shown more variety, with his many four-beat lines and even a two-beat line. But he allowed nothing longer than pentameter. Eliot freely uses hexameters, as in

> Shall I párt my háir behínd? Do I dáre to éat a péach?

He has a dozen or so of the rarer fourteeners:

> My morning coat, my collar mounting firmly to my chin . . .

He even has a few of the very rare eight-beat lines:

> My necktie rich and modest but asserted by a simple pin . . .

Occasionally there is a line whose rhythm takes us by surprise:

> After the novels, after the teacups, after the skirts that trail along the floor . . .

or

> I grow old . . . I grow old . . .

But mostly what we have in "Prufrock" is the familiar iambic with its familiar reversals and variations in lines of differing length. The basic meter—heard in about 70 of the 121 lines—is iambic pentameter, no more free than that of Shakespeare's later plays or of many Jacobean dramatists:

> I should have been a pair of ragged claws
> Scuttling across the floors of silent seas . . .

The poem is a combination, then, of tradition and innovation, taking greater liberties than had previously been taken. Much "free verse" is of this sort. Another example would be Roethke's "Where Knock Is Open Wide" (p. 641), which certainly has a new look. But the unexpected rhythms are often the old rhythms of nursery rhymes, recovered and recycled:

> A kitten can
> Bite with his feet;
> Papa and mama
> Have more teeth . . .
>
> Once upon a tree
> I came across a time,
> It wasn't even as
> A ghoulie in a dream . . .

   2. **Walt Whitman.** If we backtrack about half a century before Eliot, we find that Whitman had made a more daring break with the traditional meters of English poetry—but not with the natural rhythms of the language, nor with those rhythms as reinforced by stylistic devices in the poetic books of the Old Testament. Whitman's line-lengths vary much more than Eliot's were to vary, and he is more free from a single basic meter, so that it is with something like a

sense of release and exhilaration that we launch forth on these powerful waves of rhythm. But waves they certainly are, as we feel in the first eight lines of "When Lilacs Last in the Dooryard Bloom'd" (p. 394).

    ∪ |– ∪|– ∪ ∪|– – ∪ | –
When lilacs last in the dooryard bloom'd,

    ∪ ∪| – –|– ∪| – ∪ ∪|– ∪ |– ∪ ∪|–
And the great star early droop'd in the western sky in the night,

    ∪| – ∪ |– ∪ | – ∪ |–∪ ∪|– ∪ | –
I mourn'd, and yet shall mourn with ever-re turning spring.

    – ∪ ∪|– ∪ | – |–∪∪| – ∪|– ∪ | –
Ever-re turning spring, trinity sure to me you bring,

    – ∪| – ∪ ∪|– ∪ ∪ | – ∪ |– ∪ ∪| –
Lilac blooming per ennial and drooping star in the west,

    ∪ – |∪ – |∪ –
And thought of him I love.

    –| – ∪ ∪| – ∪ |– ∪ | –
O powerful western fallen star!

    –| – ∪| – –| – ∪| – ∪| –
O shades of night—O moody, tearful night!

The way the feet are divided here shows this as a predominantly falling rhythm. Without changing a single accent, we could diagram it as rising:

    ∪ –|∪ – |∪ ∪ – | ∪ –
When lil acs last in the door yard bloom'd,

    ∪ ∪ – | – –|∪ – |∪ ∪ – | ∪ –|∪ ∪ –
And the great star ear ly droop'd in the west ern sky in the night,

    ∪ – | ∪ –|∪ – | ∪ –|∪ ∪ –| ∪ –
I mourn'd, and yet shall mourn with ev er-return ing spring.

Some might prefer to hear it that way; and though we might feel they are wrong, it could be hard to prove them so. What it comes down to is: in looking at a series of waves, do we see them primarily as troughs rising into crests, or as crests subsiding into troughs? Whether we are, in this case, troughers or cresters, the waves remain the same, and are really there. Perhaps the only reason to divide such verse into feet at all is to make graphic the fact that there are indeed repeated units.

Each of the lines, by itself, is easily classifiable as a combination we have seen before. The prevailing rhythm is logaoedic: trochees, dactyls, spondees, reversed iambs, several monosyllabic feet, and maybe a first paeon (– ∪ ∪ ∪)

    – ∪ ∪ ∪   – ∪ ∪
in "ennial and" (line 5), unless one pronounces it "ennyal and."

This is typical of Whitman's rhythm, though he sometimes has more monosyllable feet and more paeons. He has simply put old units to new and eloquent use. Many of his lines are tetrameters, pentameters, or especially hexameters; some range freely beyond these limits and become so long they have no name.

Whitman also freely modulates from rhythm to rhythm as the poem progresses. We can find runs of all the metrical feet we have discussed, but more often we have logaoedic combinations. Occasionally there may be two or three syllables that seem to break the rhythm, syllables not easy to fit into a pattern of scansion. It may help to think of these as like grace-notes in music—or perhaps even more like the "hangers" or "outrides" that Hopkins allows into his sprung rhythm.

Some might prefer not to represent Whitman's rhythms with the symbols of traditional scansion. All that matters is that in his rhythms the strong accentual surges do come at regular intervals—not at tidy metronomic intervals, and not always at the same pace, but as waves themselves come on a night of veering winds, sometimes piling, sometimes spilling over, but always waves. As the Anglo-Saxon poets emphasized their strongly physical rhythms by alliteration, so Whitman emphasizes the beginnings and endings of his cadences by parallel syntax, as in sections 2, 6, and 8 of "When Lilacs Last. . . ."

Whitman has had many descendants, Carl Sandburg and Allen Ginsberg among them. Probably too such poets as Jeffers and Fearing; in any poet who today writes long loping lines we may suspect a Whitmanian influence.

3. **Ezra Pound.** Probably no twentieth-century poet had a finer ear for rhythmical effects than Pound. Even among the few poems in our selection there is a good deal of variety. One of Pound's beliefs was that a poem deserved its individual form, a form that exactly expressed *that* poem's urgencies, rather than a form it had inherited from other poems. One of the best examples of his "organic" rhythms is "The Return" (p. 529). We can tell from the very appearance of the poem on the page that it is free verse; the parts do not even look alike. No two of the first dozen lines have an identical rhythm. The first few lines have an organic rhythm in that the "tentative/Movements" of the returning wraiths are dramatized by the tentative movement of the verse itself, with the change from rising to falling rhythm in the first line and the instability of the many unaccented syllables in the paeons: "The trouble in the pace and the uncertain. . . ." The hesitancy continues in the fifth line. When, near the end of the poem, the lines describe the strength the wraiths once had, the rhythm strengthens briefly:

$$\text{—} \quad \text{U} \quad \text{—} \quad \text{—} \quad \text{U}$$
These the keen-scented;

$$\text{—} \quad \text{U} \quad \text{U} \quad \text{—} \quad \text{U} \quad \text{—}$$
These were the souls of blood . . . .

In the last two lines, Pound can surprise us again with a rhythmic figure he had not used before:

$$\text{— U U —}$$
$$\text{— U U — U}$$

Even the two-line "In a Station of the Metro" (p. 530) shows something about the nature of free verse. If a poet working strictly in traditional forms had written

$$\text{U} \quad \text{—} \mid \text{U} \text{—} \mid \text{U} \quad \text{U} \mid \quad \text{—} \quad \text{—} \mid \text{U} \quad \text{U} \mid \text{U} \quad \text{—}$$
The ap pari tion of these fa ces in the crowd

that poet would have felt obligated to close the poem with something like

Wet petals on a bough beneath the rainy cloud.

But the free-verse poet, having written one line that has a discernible pattern, feels no obligation to repeat it: the poet is free to do whatever feels right. Provided, of course, the poet gets away with it; there may be no rules about free verse, but there are penalties for failing.

"Alba" (p. 530) starts with a long, languorous line of iambic pentameter:

$$\cup \ - \ |\cup \ \cup \ -| \ - \ \ - \ \|\cup \ -| \ \cup \ \ \cup \ - \ | \ \cup$$
As cool as the pale wet leaves of lil y-of-the-val ley . . .

and concludes with a very different iambic tetrameter.

"The River-Merchant's Wife: A Letter" (p. 530) opens with two iambic pentameters, but from then on we are not sure what the rhythm of the individual lines will be.

In the first poem from *Hugh Selwyn Mauberley* (p. 531), we find a different kind of freedom. Pound takes as his model a form of the hymnbook quatrain, its rigidity emphasized by an *abab* rhyme scheme in which there is never an off-rhyme, even when rhyming on Greek, French, and Old French words. Yet over this rigid framework he drapes a very free texture of rhythm, the lines ranging from pentameter to trimeter, sometimes fluent and sometimes crabbed—a "chopped seas" rhythm.

The beginning of "Envoi" (p. 532) echoes, but not exactly, the stanza form used by Waller in "Go, Lovely Rose" (p. 131). Thereafter Pound takes off on his own, letting his line-length range from dimeter to pentameter throughout stanzas of unequal length, which are, however, strongly iambic.

The selection from *Homage to Sextus Propertius* (p. 533) is more richly logaoedic than the other Pound poems we have seen, with echoes of the classical hexameter in some of its divided lines:

> What foot beat out your time-bar,
> what water has mellowed your whistles?

The next line would have the same rhythm, except for its outriding "as we know." But Pound does not stay with this rhythm; his line-lengths vary, yet keep moving ahead musically on alternations of double and triple feet.

We can see from these examples what Pound meant when he said, as early as 1912, that the ideal "as regarding rhythm" was to "compose in the sequence of the musical phrase, not in the sequence of a metronome." His poems are often made up of musical phrases—sometimes, but not necessarily, in the cadence of phrases preceding or following. He is working, that is, with regard to larger rhythmic units than the foot. We can almost say that he is taking combinations of feet as his rhythmic unit.

The musical phrase is not itself timed by a metronome, but of course the bars or measures that make it up are. And so Pound's unmetronomic phrases are made up of metronomic feet, of fresh combinations of the old familiar units in existence since Chaucer and before.

His concern for the musical phrase is reinforced by his concern for the image; at times we feel that the rhythm of his phrases is imagistically determined—the unit is not so many feet long, but one image long. If we look at Canto II (p. 535), from about line 25 on, it is noticeable how many of the short lines (often three-beat strong-stress) are imagistic details.

> Heavy vine on the oarshafts,
> And, out of nothing, a breathing,
> hot breath on my ankles,
> Beasts like shadows in glass,
> a furred tail upon nothingness.
> Lynx-purr, a heathery smell of beasts . . .

Image generates rhythm. But even in the *Cantos* Pound can still become tranced in one of the traditional cadences he knows so well. In Canto LXXXI (p. 538), from about line 32 on (one of the emotional high points of the *Cantos*), he falls into iambic pentameter, with hardly an unexpected ripple in the traditional rhythm, for about 20 lines. Pound as technician is indeed "making it new," but with a scholar's knowledge and a poet's love for the centuries-old "it," the physically based rhythm which he refurbishes to cherish and preserve.

4. **William Carlos Williams.** A poet who has had a strong influence on a generation of younger poets and been a more available mentor than the spectacular Pound is William Carlos Williams. If we examine the poems of his we have in the anthology we find something new to us; for in the world of free verse there are many mansions—and not a few hovels, as everywhere else. Dr. Williams, in one of the mansions, deserves our admiring attention. In his earliest work we are not likely to hear any metronomes a-ticking. And yet "To Waken an Old Lady" (p. 518) and "The Widow's Lament in Springtime" (p. 518) are not completely free. The first is bound in all but two or three lines to something like two-beat strong-stress; the second has lines of two or three beats but not more. The first poem from *Spring and All* (p. 519) is more characteristic in its freedom; we can try to read it as strong-stress or as variations on a meter, but with neither attempt can we be comfortable: it does not fit either. If we try to mark strong and weak accents in the first half dozen lines, with our units determined by the words or by sense divisions, we get something like this:

> ∪ ∪ – ∪ ∪ ∪ – ∪ – ∪ ∪
> By the road to the contagious hospital

> – ∪ ∪ – ∪ ∪ –
> under the surge of the blue

> – ∪ – – ∪ ∪ ∪
> mottled clouds driven from the

> – – ∪ – – ∪ – ∪
> northeast—a cold wind. Beyond, the

> – ∪ – – ∪ –
> waste of broad, muddy fields

> – ∪ – – – ∪ ∪ – ∪
> brown with dried weeds, standing and fallen . . . .

Here, no noticeable runs of any metric unit except the "waste of broad, muddy fields/brown with dried. . . ." Otherwise feet do not go together in the accustomed ways, as in logaoedics. Perhaps we should not call them feet at all, since they do not seem to be beating time. We might as well throw away our metronome, and see what else the words have to offer. (A good deal, we will probably decide.) Now we know where we are: this is free verse—with which Williams himself later expressed dissatisfaction.

In "Nantucket" (p. 520), the first two lines seem to be starting out with a cadence:

> – ∪| – ∪| – ∪
> Flowers through the window

> – ∪| – ∪| – ∪
> laven der and yellow

But the poet does not care to sustain it:

> – ∪ –| – ∪
> changed by white curtains—

> – ∪| – ∪ ∪
> Smell of cleanliness—

> – ∪ ∪| – ∪ ∪ –
> Sunshine of late afternoon—

> ∪ ∪ – –
> On the glass tray . . .

The following poem, "The Dance" (p. 520), is exceptional in the work of Dr. Williams: describing a very physical peasant dance, it has a strong physical rhythm, in triple time, with runs of anapests and dactyls. With "The Descent" (p. 521) and the two poems that follow it, we are back with a rhythm that Williams made most characteristically his own. Williams particularly liked this poem because he realized later that in it he "had hit upon a device" he was to name the **variable foot**—characteristic of much of his later work, which was composed in units of three, or "triads." In his theory, which grew out of his dissatisfaction with free verse and out of his contemplation of Einsteinian relativity, he concluded that the rhythm of poetry too should have a kind of relativity: be based on a foot, but on a foot that varied: "Thus the verse becomes not free at all but just simply variable, as all things in life properly are." Each line in the poem is considered a foot and is to count as a single beat: though line 6 has two syllables and the line below it 17, they are considered metrically equivalent; even from Williams's reading of the poem one cannot tell why they are so. Readers have had a good deal of trouble knowing what Williams meant by his "variable foot"—but perhaps all that matters is that it helped him write some of his best poems. Rhythms move more fluently here than in the earlier free verse; there are sometimes runs of familiar feet, as in the last seven lines of "The Yellow Flower," in which the regular iambics are rippled only twice by anapests.

The free-verse theories and achievements of Pound and Williams had an influence on the **projective verse** of Charles Olson: poems are to project themselves forward into an "open field" instead of into the enclosures of a fixed form. This seems a new visualization of and a new term for what others had long been doing. As a key to breathing, length of pauses, progression, regression, and so on, Olson thought that the precise spacing the typewriter insists on was an important tool to utilize. Cummings of course had done this before him, but with more pictorial effect.

Such **prose poems** as those of Karl Shapiro (p. 664) are poems—in their concentration, their use of sound and imagery, even in their rhythms—presented on the page as if they were prose paragraphs. The rhythms, old or new, can still be heard; this poem, for instance, both opens and closes with an iambic pentameter:

Waiting in front of the columnar high school . . .

The horror of their years stoned me to death.

What is in between could just as well be written out in lines of rhythmical free verse—if the poet had not preferred the free-wheeling look of prose presentation.

The *Mercian Hymns* of Geoffrey Hill (pp. 747 ff.) might also seem to be prose poems, but the presentation on the page suggests that the poet thinks of them as made up of very long lines. For the derivation of his rhythms, see the note with the poems.

ACKNOWLEDGMENTS

(Continued from p. iv)

JOHN BERRYMAN: Sonnet 37 from *Berryman's Sonnets*, by John Berryman. Copyright © 1952, 1967 by John Berryman. Dream Songs 4, 14, 29, 219 from *The Dream Songs*, by John Berryman. Copyright © 1959, 1962, 1963, 1964, 1965, 1966, 1967, 1968, 1969 by John Berryman. "Lauds" from *Delusions, Etc.*, by John Berryman. Copyright © 1969, 1971 by John Berryman. Copyright © 1972 by the Estate of John Berryman. Reprinted with the permission of Farrar, Straus & Giroux, Inc.

JOHN BETJEMAN: "A Subaltern's Love-Song" from *Collected Poems*. Reprinted by permission of the author, John Murray (Publishers) Ltd, and Houghton Mifflin Co.

ELIZABETH BISHOP: "The Fish," "At the Fishhouses," and "The Filling Station" from *The Complete Poems*, by Elizabeth Bishop. Copyright © 1940, 1947, 1955, 1969 by Elizabeth Bishop. Copyright renewed © 1974 by Elizabeth Bishop. "One Art" from *Geography III*, by Elizabeth Bishop. Copyright © 1976 by Elizabeth Bishop. These poems appeared originally in *The New Yorker*. Reprinted with the permission of Farrar, Straus & Giroux, Inc.

WILLIAM BLAKE: "Mock on, Mock on, Voltaire, Rousseau" and "And Did Those Feet in Ancient Time" from *The Writings of William Blake*, edited by Geoffrey Keynes (Random House).

LOUISE BOGAN: "Cassandra" and "Old Countryside" from *The Blue Estuaries*, by Louise Bogan. Copyright © 1924, 1929, 1968 by Louise Bogan. Copyright renewed © 1964 by Louise Bogan. Reprinted with the permission of Farrar, Straus and Giroux, Inc.

MARK ALEXANDER BOYD: "Venus and Cupid" from *The Oxford Book of Verse* (Oxford University Press).

ROBERT BRIDGES: "The Evening Darkens Over" from *The Poetical Works of Robert Bridges*. Reprinted by permission of Oxford University Press.

GWENDOLYN BROOKS: "The Rites for Cousin Vit." Copyright 1949 by Gwendolyn Brooks Blakely. "The Bean Eaters" and "We Real Cool: The Pool Players. Seven at the Golden Shovel." Copyright 1959 by Gwendolyn Brooks. All from *The World of Gwendolyn Brooks*, by Gwendolyn Brooks. Reprinted by permission of Harper & Row, Publishers, Inc. Excerpt from *Report from Part One* reprinted by permission of Broadside Press.

GEOFFREY CHAUCER: Excerpt from "The Pardoner's Tale," from *The Works of Geoffrey Chaucer*, second edition, edited by F. N. Robinson. Copyright ©, 1957 by F. N. Robinson. Copyright 1933 by Houghton Mifflin.

A. H. CLOUGH: "The Latest Decalogue" and "Come Home, Come Home" from *Poems*, ed. by H. F. Lowry, A. L. P. Norrington, and F. L. Mulhauser (Oxford University Press).

HART CRANE: "Praise for an Urn," "At Melville's Tomb," "Voyages, II and VI," and "Proem: To Brooklyn Bridge." Selections are reprinted from *The Complete Poems and Selected Letters and Prose of Hart Crane*, by permission of Liveright Publishing Corporation. Copyright 1933, © 1958, 1966 by Liveright Publishing Corporation.

ROBERT CREELEY: "The Act of Love" from *St. Martin's* (Black Sparrow, 1971) and *A Day Book* (Scribner's, 1972). Reprinted by permission of the author. "A Wicker Basket" used by permission of Charles Scribner's Sons from *For Love*, by Robert Creeley. Copyright © 1962 Robert Creeley.

COUNTEE CULLEN: "Simon the Cyrenian Speaks" from *On These I Stand*, by Countee Cullen. Copyright 1925 by Harper & Row, Publishers, Inc.; renewed 1953 by Ida M. Cullen. Reprinted by permission of Harper & Row, Publishers, Inc.

E. E. CUMMINGS: "(im)c-a-t(mo)," copyright 1949 by E. E. Cummings. Reprinted from his volume *Complete Poems 1913-1962* by permission of Harcourt Brace Jovanovich, Inc. "wherelings whenlings," "anyone lived in a pretty how town," and "my father moved through dooms of love," copyright 1940 by E. E. Cummings, copyright 1968 by Marion Morehouse Cummings. Reprinted from *Complete Poems 1913-1962*, by E. E. Cummings by permission of Harcourt Brace Jovanovich, Inc. "being to timelessness as it's to time," copyright 1950 by E. E. Cummings. Reprinted from his volume *Complete Poems 1913-1962* by permission of Harcourt Brace Jovanovich, Inc. "a man who had fallen among thieves" is reprinted from *IS 5*, poems by E. E. Cummings, with the permission of Liveright Publishing Corporation. Copyright 1926 by Horace Liveright. Copyright renewed 1953 by E. E. Cummings.

J. V. CUNNINGHAM: From "A Century of Epigrams" from *The Collected Poems and Epigrams of J. V. Cunningham*. Reprinted by permission of Ohio University Press.

JOHN DAVIDSON: "A Runnable Stag," from *A Selection of His Poems*. Reprinted by permission of Hutchinson Publishing Group Limited.

C. DAY LEWIS: "Two Songs" from *Selected Poems*, by C. Day Lewis. Copyright 1935 by C. D. Lewis. Reprinted by permission of Harper & Row, Publishers, Inc., the Executors of the Estate of C. Day Lewis, Jonathan Cape Ltd and Hogarth Press.

WALTER DE LA MARE: "The Listeners," "Pooh!," and "In the Local Museum." Reprinted by permission of the Literary Trustees of Walter de la Mare and The Society of Authors as their representative.

JAMES DICKEY: "Cherrylog Road" and "Pursuit from Under." Copyright © 1963, 1964 by James Dickey. Reprinted from *Poems 1957-1967* by permission of Wesleyan University Press. "Cherrylog

Road" first appeared in *The New Yorker*. Excerpts on "Cherrylog Road" from *Self-Interviews*, by James Dickey, edited by B. and J. Reiss. Copyright © 1970 by James Dickey. Reprinted by permission of Doubleday & Company, Inc.

EMILY DICKINSON: Poems 258, 93, 187, 824, 754, 465, 348, 1078, 401, 986, 479, 712, and 520. Reprinted by permission of the publishers and the Trustees of Amherst College from *The Poems of Emily Dickinson*, edited by Thomas H. Johnson, Cambridge, Mass.: The Belknap Press of Harvard University Press, Copyright © 1951, 1955, 1979 by the President and Fellows of Harvard College. Poems 341, 747, 479, and 754. From *The Complete Poems of Emily Dickinson*, edited by Thomas H. Johnson. Copyright 1929 by Martha Dickinson Bianchi. Copyright © 1957, 1960 by Mary L. Hampson. By permission of Little, Brown and Company.

ALAN DUGAN: "Funeral Oration for a Mouse." © Alan Dugan. Reprinted by permission of the author.

RICHARD EBERHART: "The Cancer Cells" from *Collected Poems 1930–1976*, by Richard Eberhart. Copyright © 1960, 1976 by Richard Eberhart. Reprinted by permission of Oxford University Press, Inc. and Chatto & Windus Ltd.

T. S. ELIOT: "The Love Song of J. Alfred Prufrock," "Sweeney Among the Nightingales," "Gerontion," "The Waste Land," "Journey of the Magi," and "East Coker" from *Collected Poems 1909–1962*, by T. S. Eliot, copyright, 1936, by Harcourt Brace Jovanovich, Inc.; copyright © 1943, 1963, 1964, by T. S. Eliot; copyright 1971 by Esme Valerie Eliot. Reprinted by permission of Harcourt Brace Jovanovich, Inc. and Faber and Faber Ltd.

WILLIAM EMPSON: "Missing Dates" from *Collected Poems of William Empson*, copyright 1949, 1977 by William Empson. Reprinted by permission of Harcourt Brace Jovanovich, Inc. and Chatto & Windus Ltd.

KENNETH FEARING: "Love, 20c the First Quarter Mile" from *New and Selected Poems*. Published by Indiana University Press, 1956. Reprinted by permission of Russell & Volkening, Inc.

ROBERT FITZGERALD: "Cobb Would Have Caught It." Robert Fitzgerald, *Spring Shade (Poems 1931–1970)*. Copyright 1943 by Robert Fitzgerald. Reprinted by permission of New Directions.

ROBERT FROST: "In Hardwood Groves," "The Road Not Taken," "An Old Man's Winter Night," "The Hill Wife," "Out, Out—," "Stopping by Woods on a Snowy Evening," "Once by the Pacific," "Acquainted with the Night," "Neither Out Far nor In Deep," "Provide, Provide," "The Most of It," "Never Again Would Birds' Song Be the Same," "The Subverted Flower," "Directive," and "Mending Wall" from *The Poetry of Robert Frost*, edited by Edward Connery Lathem. Copyright 1916, 1923, 1928, 1930, 1934, 1939, 1947, © 1969 by Holt, Rinehart and Winston. Copyright 1936, 1942, 1944, 1951, © 1956, 1958, 1962 by Robert Frost. Copyright © 1964, 1967, 1970, 1975 by Lesley Frost Ballantine. Reprinted by permission of Holt, Rinehart and Winston, Publishers.

BREWSTER GHISELIN: "Rattler Alert." © 1942, renewed 1974, Brewster Ghiselin. "The Catch" © 1965, Brewster Ghiselin. Both reprinted by permission of Brewster Ghiselin and the University of Utah Press.

ALLEN GINSBERG: "A Supermarket in California." Copyright © 1956, 1959 by Allen Ginsberg. "A Cafe in Warsaw." Copyright © 1968 by Allen Ginsberg. Both reprinted by permission of City Lights Books.

OLIVER ST. JOHN GOGARTY: Permission to use poem "Leda and the Swan" from the *Collected Poems of Oliver St. John Gogarty* is granted by The Devin-Adair Co., Old Greenwich, Conn. 06870. Copyright © 1954 by Oliver St. John Gogarty.

ROBERT GRAVES: "Theseus and Ariadne" from *Collected Poems*, by Robert Graves. Copyright © 1944 by Robert Graves. Reprinted by permission of the author and Curtis Brown, Ltd. "Counting the Beats" and "Spoils." Copyright © 1955 by Robert Graves and © 1964 by Robert Graves. "Sick Love." Copyright © 1938 by Robert Graves. All reprinted by permission of Curtis Brown, Ltd.

THOM GUNN: "Moly" from *Moly and My Sad Captains*, by Thom Gunn. Copyright © 1961, 1971, 1973 by Thom Gunn. Reprinted by permission of Farrar, Straus and Giroux, Inc. and Faber and Faber Ltd. "On the Move" from *The Sense of Movement*, by Thom Gunn. Reprinted by permission of Faber and Faber Ltd.

DONALD HALL: "Names of Horses." Reprinted by permission of the author.

THOMAS HARDY: All poems from *Collected Poems of Thomas Hardy* (New York: Macmillan, 1953).

ROBERT HAYDEN: "Those Winter Sundays" and "O Daedalus, Fly Away Home." Selections are reprinted from *Angle of Ascent, New and Selected Poems*, by Robert Hayden, by permission of Liveright Publishing Corporation. Copyright © 1975, 1972, 1970, 1966 by Robert Hayden.

SEAMUS HEANEY: "The Barn" and "Death of a Naturalist" reprinted from *Death of a Naturalist*, by Seamus Heaney by permission of Faber and Faber Ltd.

ANTHONY HECHT: "The End of the Weekend" (Copyright © 1959 by Anthony E. Hecht), "More Light! More Light!" (Copyright © 1961 by Anthony E. Hecht) from *The Hard Hours* and "The Feast of Stephen" (Copyright © 1977 by Anthony E. Hecht) from *Millions of Strange Shadows* are reprinted by permission of Atheneum Publishers. "More Light! More Light!" originally appeared in *The Nation*.

GEOFFREY HILL: "The Pentecost Castle": 1, 2, 8, 13, 15. From *Tenebrae*, by Geoffrey Hill. Copyright © 1978 by Geoffrey Hill. "Genesis" and "Mercian Hymns": I, III, VI, VII, X, XI, XIV, XXII, XXV, XXIX. From *Somewhere Is Such a Kingdom*, by Geoffrey Hill. Copyright © 1975 by Geoffrey Hill. All reprinted by permission of Houghton Mifflin Company and Andre Deutsch Limited.

A. D. HOPE: "The Brides" and "Imperial Adam" from *Collected Poems: 1930–1965*, by A. D. Hope. Copyright © 1960, 1962 by A. D. Hope. Reprinted by permission of Viking Penguin Inc.

GERARD MANLEY HOPKINS: All from *Poems* (Oxford University Press).

A. E. HOUSMAN: "From far, from eve and morning," "With rue my heart is laden," "Along the field as we came by," "Loveliest of trees, the cherry now," and "To an Athlete Dying Young" from "A Shropshire Lad"—Authorised Edition—from *The Collected Poems of A. E. Housman*. Copyright

1939, 1940, © 1965 by Holt, Rinehart and Winston. Copyright © 1967, 1968 by Robert E. Symons. "The Oracles" from *The Collected Poems of A. E. Housman.* Copyright 1922 by Holt, Rinehart and Winston. Copyright 1950 by Barclays Bank Ltd. All reprinted by permission of Holt, Rinehart and Winston, Publishers and The Society of Authors as the literary representative of the Estate of A. E. Housman, and Jonathan Cape Ltd., publishers of A. E. Housman's *Collected Poems.*

LANGSTON HUGHES: "Dream Variations" and "The Negro Speaks of Rivers." Copyright 1926 by Alfred A. Knopf, Inc. and renewed 1954 by Langston Hughes. Reprinted from *Selected Poems of Langston Hughes,* by Langston Hughes, by permission of Alfred A. Knopf, Inc.

TED HUGHES: "Pike" and "Hawk Roosting" from *Lupercal.* Copyright © 1959 by Ted Hughes. "Skylarks" from *Wodwo.* Copyright © 1967 by Ted Hughes. All from *Selected Poems,* by Ted Hughes. Reprinted by permission of Harper & Row, Publishers, Inc. and Faber and Faber Ltd.

RANDALL JARRELL: "Next Day." Reprinted with permission of Macmillan Publishing Co., Inc. from *The Lost World,* by Randall Jarrell. Copyright © Randall Jarrell 1963, 1965. Originally appeared in *The New Yorker.* "The Woman at the Washington Zoo." From *The Woman at the Washington Zoo,* by Randall Jarrell. Copyright © 1960 by Randall Jarrell. Used by permission of Atheneum Publishers. "The Death of the Ball Turret Gunner" from *The Complete Poems,* by Randall Jarrell. Copyright © 1945, 1969 by Mrs. Randall Jarrell. Copyright renewed © 1972 by Mrs. Randall Jarrell. Reprinted with the permission of Farrar, Straus and Giroux, Inc.

ROBINSON JEFFERS: "Nova" and "The Purse-Seine." Copyright 1937 and renewed 1965 by Donnan Jeffers and Garth Jeffers. Reprinted from *The Selected Poetry of Robinson Jeffers,* by Robinson Jeffers, by permission of Random House, Inc.

RUDYARD KIPLING: "Song of the Galley-Slaves" from *Many Inventions* and "Harp Song of the Dane Women" from *Puck of Pook's Hill,* all by Rudyard Kipling. Reprinted by permission of Doubleday & Company, Inc.

STANLEY KUNITZ: "The War Against the Trees." Copyright © 1958 by Stanley Kunitz. "The Knot." Copyright © 1979 by Stanley Kunitz. From *The Poems of Stanley Kunitz 1928–1978,* by Stanley Kunitz. Reprinted by permission of Little, Brown and Co. in association with the Atlantic Monthly Press.

PHILIP LARKIN: "The Explosion" from *High Windows,* by Philip Larkin. Copyright © 1974 by Philip Larkin. Reprinted by permission of Farrar, Straus and Giroux, Inc. and Faber and Faber Ltd. "At Grass" and "Lines on a Young Lady's Photograph Album" are reprinted from *The Less Deceived* by permission of The Marvell Press, England.

D. H. LAWRENCE: "Piano," "Bat," "Bavarian Gentians," and "Middle of the World" from *The Complete Poems of D. H. Lawrence.* Copyright © 1964, 1971 by Angelo Ravagli and C. M. Weekley, Executors of the Estate of Frieda Lawrence Ravagli. Reprinted by permission of Viking Penguin Inc.

VACHEL LINDSAY: "I Heard Immanuel Singing" reprinted with permission of Macmillan Publishing Co., Inc., from *Collected Poems,* by Vachel Lindsay. Copyright 1914 by Macmillan Publishing Co., Inc., renewed 1942 by Elizabeth C. Lindsay.

ROBERT LOWELL: "Skunk Hour" from *Life Studies,* by Robert Lowell. Copyright © 1956, 1959 by Robert Lowell. "For the Union Dead" from *For the Union Dead,* by Robert Lowell. Copyright © 1960, 1964 by Robert Lowell. Reprinted with the permission of Farrar, Straus and Giroux, Inc. "The Quaker Graveyard in Nantucket" and "After the Surprising Conversions" from *Lord Weary's Castle,* copyright 1946, 1974, by Robert Lowell. Reprinted by permission of Harcourt Brace Jovanovich, Inc.

HUGH MacDIARMID: "Crystals Like Blood," "On the Ocean Floor," "The Bonnie Broukit Bairn," "Wheesht, Wheesht," and "Cattle Show." Reprinted with permission of Macmillan Publishing Co., Inc. from *Collected Poems,* by Hugh MacDiarmid. © Christopher Murray Grieve 1948, 1962.

ARCHIBALD MacLEISH: "Ars poetica," "Eleven," and "You, Andrew Marvell." From *New and Collected Poems, 1917–1976,* by Archibald MacLeish. Copyright © 1976 by Archibald MacLeish. Reprinted by permission of Houghton Mifflin Company.

LOUIS MacNEICE: "The Sunlight on the Garden" from *The Collected Poems of Louis MacNeice.* Reprinted by permission of Faber and Faber Ltd.

EDGAR LEE MASTERS: "Daisy Fraser," "Dora Williams," "Anne Rutledge," and "Lucinda Matlock," from the *Spoon River Anthology* (Macmillan). Reprinted by permission of Ellen C. Masters.

WILLIAM MEREDITH: "Thoughts on One's Head." From *Earth Walk; New and Selected Poems,* by William Meredith. Copyright © 1955 by William Meredith. Reprinted by permission of Alfred A. Knopf, Inc. Originally published in *The New Yorker.*

JAMES MERRILL: "The Broken Home" by James Merrill from *Nights and Days* is reprinted by permission of Atheneum Publishers. Copyright © 1965 by James Merrill. This poem originally appeared in *The New Yorker.*

W. S. MERWIN: "Separation" (Copyright © 1962 by W. S. Merwin), "Things" (Copyright © 1962 by W. S. Merwin) from *The Moving Target* and "Letter" (Copyright © 1970 by W. S. Merwin) from *The Carrier of Ladders* are reprinted by permission of Atheneum Publishers. "Things" and "Letter" originally appeared in *The New Yorker.*

EDNA ST. VINCENT MILLAY: "Night is my sister . . ." and "Love is not all . . ." from *Collected Poems* (Harper & Row). Copyright 1931, 1958 by Edna St. Vincent Millay and Norma Millay Ellis.

MARIANNE MOORE: "Poetry" and "A Grave" copyright 1935 by Marianne Moore, renewed 1963 by Marianne Moore and T. S. Eliot. "The Pangolin" copyright 1941 by Marianne Moore, renewed 1969 by Marianne Moore. "A Carriage from Sweden" copyright 1944 by Marianne Moore, renewed 1972 by Marianne Moore. "The Steeple-Jack" copyright 1951 by Marianne Moore. All reprinted with permission of Macmillan Publishing Co., Inc. from *Collected Poems,* by Marianne Moore.

EDWIN MUIR: "The Horses" from *Collected Poems,* by Edwin Muir. Copyright © 1960 by Willa Muir. Reprinted by permission of Oxford University Press, Inc. and Faber and Faber Ltd.

OGDEN NASH: "Very Like a Whale" from *Verses from 1929 On,* by Ogden Nash. Copyright 1934 by Ogden Nash. By permission of Little, Brown and Company.

HOWARD NEMEROV: "Brainstorm," "Santa Claus," and "Learning by Doing" from *The Collected Poems of Howard Nemerov* (The University of Chicago Press, 1977). Reprinted by permission of the author.

WILFRED OWEN: "Anthem for Doomed Youth" and "Arms and the Boy." *The Collected Poems of Wilfred Owen,* edited by C. Day Lewis. Copyright © Chatto & Windus, Ltd. 1946, 1963. Reprinted by permission of New Directions, the Owen Estate, and Chatto & Windus Ltd.

KENNETH PATCHEN: "O All down within the Pretty Meadow." Kenneth Patchen, *Collected Poems.* Copyright 1946 by Kenneth Patchen. Reprinted by permission of New Directions.

SYLVIA PLATH: "Tulips" from *Ariel* by Sylvia Plath. Copyright © 1962 by Ted Hughes. "Blackberrying." Copyright © 1962 by Ted Hughes. "Mirror." Copyright © 1963 by Ted Hughes. Both from *Crossing the Water,* by Sylvia Plath. "Tulips" and "Mirror" originally appeared in *The New Yorker.* *Ariel,* by Sylvia Plath published by Faber and Faber London, copyright © Ted Hughes 1965. Reprinted by permission of Harper & Row, Publishers, Inc. and Olwyn Hughes.

EZRA POUND: "The Return," "Ité," "In a Station of the Metro," "Alba," "The River-Merchant's Wife: A Letter," from "Hugh Selwyn Mauberly," and from "Homage to Sextus Propertius." Ezra Pound, *Personae.* Copyright 1926 by Ezra Pound. From "The Cantos." Ezra Pound, *The Cantos.* Copyright 1934, 1937, 1948 by Ezra Pound. All reprinted by permission of New Directions.

DUDLEY RANDALL: "Blackberry Sweet." Reprinted by permission of the author.

JOHN CROWE RANSOM: "Bells for John Whiteside's Daughter," "Here Lies a Lady," and "Winter Remembered." Copyright 1924 by Alfred A. Knopf, Inc. and renewed 1952 by John Crowe Ransom. "The Equilibrists." Copyright 1927 by Alfred A. Knopf, Inc. and renewed 1955 by John Crowe Ransom. Reprinted from *Selected Poems,* Third Edition, Revised and Enlarged, by John Crowe Ransom, by permission of Alfred A. Knopf, Inc.

EDWIN ARLINGTON ROBINSON: "Eros Turannos" copyright 1916 by Edwin Arlington Robinson, renewed 1944 by Ruth Nivison. "The Mill" and "The Dark Hills" copyright 1920 by Edwin Arlington Robinson, renewed 1948 by Ruth Nivison. "Mr. Flood's Party" copyright 1921 by Edwin Arlington Robinson, renewed 1949 by Ruth Nivison. "The Sheaves" copyright 1925 by Edwin Arlington Robinson, renewed 1953 by Ruth Nivison and Barbara R. Holt. All reprinted with permission of Macmillan Publishing Co., Inc. from *Collected Poems,* by Edwin Arlington Robinson. "Richard Cory" from *The Children of the Night,* by Edwin Arlington Robinson is reprinted by permission of Charles Scribner's Sons and is fully protected by copyright.

THEODORE ROETHKE: "My Papa's Waltz" copyright 1942 by Hearst Magazines, Inc. "The Lost Son" copyright 1947 by Theodore Roethke. "The Waking" copyright 1953 by Theodore Roethke. "I Knew a Woman" copyright 1954 by Theodore Roethke. "In a Dark Time" copyright © 1960 by Beatrice Roethke, Administratrix of the Estate of Theodore Roethke. "Where Knock Is Open Wide" and "Elegy for Jane" copyright 1950 by Theodore Roethke. All from *The Collected Poems of Theodore Roethke.* Reprinted by permission of Doubleday & Company, Inc. Excerpt from "Open Letter" in *Mid-Century American Poets.* Copyright 1950 by John Ciardi.

CARL SANDBURG: "The Shovel Man" and "Limited" from *Chicago Poems,* by Carl Sandburg; copyright 1916 by Holt, Rinehart and Winston, Inc.; copyright 1944 by Carl Sandburg. Reprinted by permission of Harcourt Brace Jovanovich, Inc. "Cool Tombs" from *Cornhuskers,* by Carl Sandburg; copyright 1918 by Holt, Rinehart and Winston, Inc.; copyright 1946 by Carl Sandburg. Reprinted by permission of Harcourt Brace Jovanovich, Inc.

KARL SHAPIRO: "A Cut Flower." Copyright 1942 and renewed 1970 by Karl Shapiro. "Elegy for a Dead Soldier" and "The Leg." Copyright 1944 by Karl Shapiro. "Waiting in front of the columnar high school." Copyright © 1962 by Karl Shapiro. Reprinted from *Selected Poems,* by Karl Shapiro, by permission of Random House, Inc.

CHRISTOPHER SMART: From "Jubilate Agno" from *Jubilate Agno,* by Christopher Smart. Edited by W. H. Bond (Rupert Hart-Davis Ltd.). Reprinted by permission of W. H. Bond.

STEVIE SMITH: "Not Waving but Drowning." Stevie Smith, *Selected Poems.* Copyright © 1964 by Stevie Smith. Reprinted by permission of New Directions and James MacGibbon, Executor for Stevie Smith. "The Frog Prince" from *The Collected Poems of Stevie Smith.* Copyright © James MacGibbon, 1975. Reprinted by permission of Oxford University Press, Inc., Allen Lane, and James MacGibbon, Executor for Stevie Smith.

W. D. SNODGRASS: "April Inventory." Copyright © 1957 by W. D. Snodgrass. Reprinted by *Heart's Needle,* by W. D. Snodgrass, by permission of Alfred A. Knopf, Inc.

GARY SNYDER: "The Dead by the Side of the Road" and "Prayer for the Great Family." Gary Snyder, *Turtle Island.* Copyright © 1974 by Gary Snyder. "An Autumn Morning in Shokoku-ji" from "Four Poems for Robin." Gary Snyder, *The Back Country.* Copyright © 1968 by Gary Snyder. Reprinted by permission of New Directions. "Mid-August at Sourdough Mountain Lookout." © Gary Snyder 1969. Reprinted by permission of the author.

STEPHEN SPENDER: "I think continually of those who were truly great." Copyright 1934 and renewed 1962 by Stephen Spender. Reprinted from *Selected Poems,* by Stephen Spender, by permission of Random House, Inc. Reprinted from *Collected Poems,* by Stephen Spender, by permission of Faber and Faber Ltd.

WILLIAM STAFFORD: "Traveling Through the Dark" and "The Farm on the Great Plains." Copyright © 1960 by William Stafford. "At the Un-National Monument Along the Canadian Border." Copyright © 1964 by William Stafford. All from *Stories That Could Be True,* by William Stafford. Reprinted by permission of Harper & Row, Publishers, Inc.

WALLACE STEVENS: "The River of Rivers in Connecticut," "The Planet on the Table," "Not Ideas About the Thing but the Thing Itself." Copyright © 1954 by Wallace Stevens. "The Idea of Order at Key West" and "A Postcard from the Volcano." Copyright 1936 by Wallace Stevens and renewed 1964 by Holly Stevens. "The Emperor of Ice-Cream," "The Snow Man," and "Sunday Morning." Copyright 1923 and renewed 1951 by Wallace Stevens. "The Man on the Dump" and "The Sense of the Sleight-of-Hand Man." Copyright 1942 by Wallace Stevens and renewed 1970 by Holly Stevens. "The House Was Quiet and the World Was Calm." Copyright 1947 by Wallace Stevens. "Large Red Man Reading." Copyright 1950 by Wallace Stevens. "Final Soliloquy of the Interior Paramour." Copyright 1951 by Wallace Stevens. Reprinted from *Collected Poems of Wallace Stevens*, by Wallace Stevens, by permission of Alfred A. Knopf, Inc.

MAY SWENSON: "Cat & the Weather." Copyright © 1963 by May Swenson. "The Watch." Copyright © 1967 by May Swenson. "How Everything Happens (Based on a Study of the Wave)." Copyright © 1969 by May Swenson; first appeared in *The Southern Review*. All from *New and Selected Things Taking Place*, by May Swenson. Reprinted by permission of Little, Brown and Company in association with the Atlantic Monthly Press.

ALLEN TATE: "The Mediterranean" and "Sonnets at Christmas," from *Collected Poems 1919-1976*, by Allen Tate. Copyright © 1952, 1953, 1970, 1977 by Allen Tate. Copyright 1931, 1932, 1937, 1948 by Charles Scribner's Sons. Copyright renewed © 1959, 1965 by Allen Tate. Reprinted with the permission of Farrar, Straus and Giroux, Inc.

EDWARD TAYLOR: "The Preface" to "God's Determinations," "While the Ark Was Building," and "The Sun of Righteousness" modernized from *The Poems of Edward Taylor*. Edited by D. E. Stanford (1960). Reprinted by permission of Yale University Press.

DYLAN THOMAS: "In My Craft or Sullen Art," "Fern Hill," and "Do Not Go Gentle Into That Good Night." Dylan Thomas, *The Poems of Dylan Thomas*. Copyright 1939, 1946 by New Directions Publishing Corporation. Copyright 1952 by Dylan Thomas. Reprinted by permission of New Directions, the Trustees for the Copyrights of the late Dylan Thomas, and J. M. Dent & Sons Ltd.

EDWARD THOMAS: "Adlestrop" from *Collected Poems*, by Edward Thomas. Reprinted by permission of Faber & Faber Ltd. and Myfanwy Thomas.

FRANCIS THOMPSON: "In No Strange Land." Published by Ernest Benn Ltd.

JEAN TOOMER: "Reapers" is reprinted from *Cane*, by Jean Toomer, by permission of Liveright Publishing Corporation. Copyright 1923 by Boni & Liveright. Copyright renewed 1951 by Jean Toomer.

THOMAS TRAHERNE: "Wonder" and "Shadows in the Water" from *Centuries, Poems, and Thanksgivings*, ed. by H. M. Margoliouth (Oxford University Press).

MONA VAN DUYN: "Footnotes to the Autobiography of Bertrand Russell, II" from *To See, To Take*, by Mona Van Duyn is reprinted by permission of Atheneum Publishers. Copyright © 1969 by Mona Van Duyn.

DAVID WAGONER: "Meeting a Bear" and "Walking in a Swamp" from *Travelling Light* copyright © 1976 by David Wagoner. Reprinted by permission of The Graywolf Press.

ROBERT PENN WARREN: "Myth on Mediterranean Beach: Aphrodite as Logos." Copyright © 1967 by Robert Penn Warren. Reprinted from *Incarnation: Poems 1966-1968*, by Robert Penn Warren, by permission of Random House, Inc. "Pursuit." Copyright 1942 by Robert Penn Warren. From *Selected Poems 1923-1975*, by Robert Penn Warren. Reprinted by permission of Random House, Inc.

ANDREW WEIMAN: "Andy-Diana DNA Letter," copyright 1980 by the Modern Poetry Association. Reprinted by permission of the editor of *Poetry*.

RICHARD WILBUR: "Love Calls Us to the Things of This World" and "A Voice from Under the Table" from *Things of This World*, © 1956, by Richard Wilbur. Reprinted by permission of Harcourt Brace Jovanovich, Inc. "Junk" © 1961 by Richard Wilbur. Reprinted from his volume *Advice to a Prophet and Other Poems* by permission of Harcourt Brace Jovanovich, Inc. "A Grasshopper" © 1959 by Richard Wilbur. Reprinted from his volume *Advice to a Prophet and Other Poems* by permission of Harcourt Brace Jovanovich, Inc. First published in *The New Yorker*.

WILLIAM CARLOS WILLIAMS: "To Waken an Old Lady," "The Widow's Lament in Springtime," "Spring and All, I, XXI" and "Nantucket." William Carlos Williams, *Collected Earlier Poems*. Copyright 1938 by New Directions Publishing Corporation. "The Descent" from *Pictures from Brueghel and Other Poems*. Copyright 1948 by William Carlos Williams. "The Orchestra" and "The Yellow Flower" from *Pictures from Brueghel and Other Poems*. Copyright 1954 by William Carlos Williams. "The Dance." William Carlos Williams, *Collected Later Poems*. Copyright 1944 by William Carlos Williams. All reprinted by permission of New Directions.

JAMES WRIGHT: "Lying in a Hammock at William Duffy's Farm in Pine Island, Minnesota," and "Speak." Copyright 1961, 1968 by James Wright. Reprinted from *Collected Poems* by permission of Wesleyan University Press. "Speak" first appeared in *The New Yorker*. "To a Blossoming Pear Tree" from *To a Blossoming Pear Tree*, by James Wright. Copyright © 1975, 1977 by James Wright. Reprinted with the permission of Farrar, Straus and Giroux, Inc.

WILLIAM BUTLER YEATS: "The Lamentation of the Old Pensioner" copyright 1906 by Macmillan Publishing Co., Inc., renewed 1934 by W. B. Yeats. "The Cold Heaven" copyright 1912 by Macmillan Publishing Co., Inc., renewed 1940 by Bertha Georgie Yeats. "September 1913," "Paudeen," and "The Magi" copyright 1916 by Macmillan Publishing Co., Inc., renewed 1944 by Bertha Georgie Yeats. "The Fisherman" copyright 1919 by Macmillan Publishing Co., Inc., renewed 1947 by Bertha Georgie Yeats. "Easter 1916," "The Second Coming," and "A Prayer for My Daughter" copyright 1924 by Macmillan Publishing Co., Inc., renewed 1952 by Bertha Georgie Yeats. "Sailing to Byzantium," "Two Songs from a Play," "Leda and the Swan," and "Among School Children" copyright 1928 by Macmillan Publishing Co., Inc., renewed 1956 by Georgie Yeats. "A Last Confession" and "Byzantium" copyright 1933 by Macmillan Publishing Co., Inc., renewed 1961 by Bertha Georgie Yeats. "The Gyres" and "Under Ben Bulben" copyright 1940 by Georgie Yeats, renewed 1968 by Bertha Georgie Yeats, Michael Butler Yeats and Anne Yeats. All reprinted from *Collected Poems*, by William Butler Yeats by permission of Macmillan Publishing Co., Inc., Michael and Anne Yeats, and Macmillan London Limited.

INDEX

Entries in boldface are poet names; entries in italics are poem titles; and entries in roman are poem first lines.